TESTIMONY

TAKEN BY

THE JOINT SELECT COMMITTEE

TO INQUIRE INTO

THE CONDITION OF AFFAIRS

IN

THE LATE INSURRECTIONARY STATES.

MISSISSIPPI.

VOLUME II.

WASHINGTON:
GOVERNMENT PRINTING OFFICE.
1872.

THE KU-KLUX CONSPIRACY.

This report consists of thirteen volumes.

Volume I contains the report of the committee and the views of the minority.

Volume II contains the testimony taken by the committee in relation to North Carolina, and the report of the trials in the United States circuit court held at Raleigh, North Carolina.

Volumes III, IV, and V contain testimony taken by the committee in relation to South Carolina, and the report of the trials in the United States circuit court held at Columbia, South Carolina. Index to the three volumes is contained in volume III.

Volumes VI and VII contain testimony taken by the committee in relation to Georgia. Index is contained in volume VI.

Volumes VIII, IX, and X contain testimony taken by the committee in relation to Alabama. Index is contained in volume VIII.

Volumes XI and XII contain testimony taken by the committee in relation to Mississippi. Index is contained in volume XI.

Volume XIII contains miscellaneous testimony taken by the committee, testimony in relation to Florida, and miscellaneous documents.

CONDITION OF AFFAIRS IN THE SOUTHERN STATES.

MISSISSIPPI—Continued.

MACON, MISSISSIPPI, *November* 8, 1871.

HAMPTON A. RICE sworn and examined.

The CHAIRMAN. As this witness is called by the minority, General Blair will please conduct his examination.

By Mr. BLAIR:

Question. Please state your residence and occupation or profession?

Answer. I reside in Bigby Valley, in this county. I am a planter by avocation. I have been acting as a magistrate and justice of the peace for the Bigby Valley beat.

Question. Was this matter with reference to the assault upon Bridges, and the arrest and commitment of a negro to his charge, examined before you?

Answer. Yes, sir.

Question. I want you to state to the committee clearly and distinctly all the evidence or the purport of the evidence taken before you in that matter.

Answer. This man Sam Nevelle, that was the name of the negro, was brought before me by C. W. Moore and Jim Moore, a colored man, charged with stealing a horse, the property of Mr. Moore, and I issued a warrant for Sam Nevelle, as required by our statute, and proceeded to investigate the case. After asking the usual question as to whether he was guilty or not, he replied that he took the mare. I then asked him if he desired to make a voluntary confession of the matter, and he stated that he acknowledged taking the mare. He went on to explain, giving his reason for taking it; that he was going to some friend or kinsman, I do not remember which it was, and that he was going to ride the mare up there. I then examined James Moore, and he stated to me that he had caught the man on the mare, and that he was then going west. He brought him back on the mare to my house.

Question. Did you commit him on that evidence?

Answer. Yes, sir; I issued a mittimus, directed to Mr. Bridges, who had been acting as a special deputy. I had no regularly commissioned officer there, and I deputized him as a special constable to convey him to jail. I suppose it was about 4 o'clock in the evening, or half-past 4. Mr. Bridges lived about a mile and a half north of my house. He not being present, I mentioned to Mr. Moore and this man Jim that I would have to send the boy out there by them to Mr. Bridges, with the mittimus, and they started off with him. That is all I knew about it until next morning. The next morning Mr. Bridges came up to my house very early and reported that this boy had got away. I asked him the question then as to how he got away, and he stated to me that they had put him in an out-house which had been a school-house, some twenty or twenty-five steps from the house he was living in; that he had locked a chain around his neck, and locked the chain around one of the studding of the school-house. The door was broken down, and the windows were out; it was an old school-house; the window-sash were out.

Question. Broken down when he was put in?

Answer. Yes, sir; and most if not all of the sash were out. I asked him then if he saw any marks or traces of any parties having been there, and he said that he had not; that he had gone out once or twice during the night; that he went out at 10, I think, or about 10, and the man was still there; and another gentlemen, a Mr. Charles Scott, who was living with him, went out a little while afterwards; and Mr. Bridges went out again between that and 12 o'clock; and about 1 o'clock, he supposed, that Mr. Scott went out there and found that the boy was gone. The chain was there; I do not remember whether he said the locks were there or not; he said the chain was there, but there was no person in the house at all.

Question. Did he say that he heard any person there, or had reason to believe that the man was taken out by any other persons, or had got away?

Answer. I asked him if he heard, or if he saw any traces of any persons having been there, or heard any noise. I recollect that I asked him that. I asked him if he heard his dog bark. He said he did not. He made the remark to me, "If any person took him away it was some person who acted very quietly or I would have heard them." He was on the lookout for the prisoner, lest he should get away.

Question. State what further transpired in reference to this matter.

Answer. He asked me what he should do about it. I told him to go to work and start some runners out, and try to find out what had become of this man; that he had probably made his escape; that some person had assisted him in making his escape, and that he had better make all the inquiries that he could; that he had accepted the prisoner, and of course I looked to him to make every effort he could to rescue him.

Question. To capture him?

Answer. Yes, sir; to capture him; and he stated that he would do so, and started off. I understand that he made a good deal of inquiry for several days afterwards, but could hear nothing of him. Shortly after that—a very few days after that—the father of this boy came to my house. I was not at home. He came back again the next day, and asked me if I knew anything about him, and wanted to learn about him. He said he understood the Ku-Klux had got him.

By Mr. BUCKLEY:

Question. This was the father of the boy who was taken as a prisoner and disappeared?

Answer. Yes, sir. I stated to him about what Mr. Bridges had stated to me in regard to him, and asked him if he had heard anything of him. He said no; he had heard nothing of him at all. I asked him if he had heard of any Ku-Klux having been there and taken him out, and he said no; only that some people had told him that the Ku-Klux were in the neighborhood in Alabama. He said he had understood that there was a good many over there; that he was gone; but if he had gotten away he would have come to his house. I then sent him off—or he went away. In a few days after that he came back again, and I think his son-in-law was with him at that time. He came back again, and asked me to have Mr. Bridges arrested; that he was satisfied that Bridges knew about this boy getting away. I told him, very well. I said, "I shall require you to make an affidavit that you have good reason to believe that Mr. Bridges is implicated in his escape." He asked me if I was going to swear him. I told him certainly I was. He went on then and stated his reason—that he had heard some people say that there was Ku-Klux around there. I told him he was running some risk in making such an affidavit against a party; that he had better inquire more into it. He declined making the affidavit, and went off. I saw or heard no more of him for several days afterwards; I think it was on the Sunday following. This was on Monday or Tuesday, at the trial, that we investigated the case; and on the Sunday following there was preaching down at the valley, at the church close to Mr. Bridges's house—in sight of it. This is all hearsay now that I am stating in regard to that affair on Sunday.

By Mr. BLAIR:

Question. Did you derive it from information that you think reliable?

Answer. I derived it from information on oath.

Question. Well, give it to us.

Answer. On Sunday there were four or five went over to Mr. Bridges's house and demanded of him——

Question. Four or five negroes?

Answer. Yes, sir. Went from the church over to the house and told him they wanted him to tell what had become of that man; that they knew he knew something about it. Mr. Bridges stated to them that he did not know anything about it; that the first he knew of it was when he went out that night, and he was gone; or when Mr. Scott went out that he was gone. A man by the name of Tom Barnett and Bob Lash, and another one, I do not remember his name, but Tom Barnett then made some threats about the Ku-Klux, saying that this thing of killing people and taking them away had to be stopped, and that the people thought he (Bridges) knew what had become of Sam Nevelle, and that he had to tell what had become of him.

By Mr. BUCKLEY:

Question. Was Sam Nevelle the prisoner?

Answer. Yes, sir; he was the prisoner. Bridges replied to him that he had better go slow. I think that was the exact language—that he had better go slow; that he had told him that he knew nothing about it. These men then told him they had been going slow too long already; and there were several other harsh things mentioned which I have forgotten now, but it had grown to its highest. Several of the negroes came up there, rather as peace-makers, I suppose, and they all went off. That matter was quieted then until the next day or Tuesday, I do not remember which, now—no, that night, Sunday night; in the night this man Bridges—or his wife—stated in her testimony before me—and so did Bridges in his statement—that about 12 o'clock, he supposed it was, his dog commenced barking very vigorously, and he went out, or stepped to the door, and when he opened the door he saw several men out in front of the house, and he then ran to the other door—ran back. He did not discover any persons on the other side, and he ran back and got his gun and started out without his clothes on. After he crossed the fence—there is a little fence between the school-house and the house in which he resided, I suppose ten steps from the house and about the same distance from the school-house—just after he crossed the fence he discovered that there was a line of men around the house, and he then started in a different direction—in an angling direction—from what he was going then, and saw some objects which he supposed were some cattle that were lying around there at night. He said that when he got up within a few steps of them they hollooed to him, "Halt," and he fired his gun at them, and turned back, and ran around the corner of the school-house, and just as he passed the corner of the school-house some fifteen or twenty, or probably thirty, guns fired almost simultaneously. He then ran out. The swamp was very near there, and he ran out to the swamp, and they fired a few scattering shots after he had passed the rear of the school-house. He went from there over to a neighbor's house, some miles off, and secured some clothing to put on, and went across the river into Alabama. The next day—Monday or Tuesday, I do not remember now which it was—there was a company of negroes went to Bigby Valley, and collected as they went along, going down in search of this boy. They had heard the news of a negro being found drowned in the river, and that he was buried down somewhere near the Alabama line. They went there, and as they went along they gathered up one and another, until there were some twenty or twenty-five in the company. They all had guns. They went down to the river, or near there, and stated as they went along, to different individuals, who testified before me, that they were going to hunt the dead body of Sam Neville; that they were satisfied, from what they had heard, that he was killed, and buried on the banks of the Bigby river, and they were going to search for him. They went down there, but found no body. They dispersed, and came back, and the next day Mr. Bridges came to Macon. I do not know that he came to Macon, but some parties came to Macon and made an affidavit before Justice Ames here, of the facts that I have just spoken of, and he issued a warrant for several of them that had gone there on Sunday. The deputy sheriff, Mr. Lucas, came to me the next day, and stated that he had heard of several other parties that were engaged in the assault on Mr. Bridges's house on Sunday night, for all of whom I issued warrants, and as many as could be caught were arrested and brought before me.

Question. How many were arrested?

Answer. I think there were twelve that were arrested for the assault on Sunday night. There were some thirty that were arrested for unlawful assembly, on Monday or Tuesday, whatever it was; I forget the day. It was either Monday or Tuesday after the Sunday. I issued a warrant for some thirty or forty, I do not remember exactly how many, but some twenty-odd, were committed to jail in default of bond or bail, twelve of whom true bills were found against at the last sitting of the grand jury. Those engaged in the unlawful assembly, I understand, were all released; that is, there was nothing found against them by the grand jury.

By the CHAIRMAN:

Question. What did these indictments charge them with?

Answer. With assault with intent to kill, I think.

Question. How many are in jail now connected with that affair?

Answer. I think they are all out of jail. There are twelve; there are indictments pending against twelve, and I think they are all out of jail.

Question. The rest were all discharged?

Answer. Yes, sir.

By Mr. BUCKLEY:

Question. Do you know what their bail was fixed at?

Answer. No, sir. I fixed the bail of those who made the assault at $500. Those who were in the unlawful assembly at $200, and two or three were fixed at $250, I think.

By Mr. BLAIR:

Question. Now what was the testimony, if there was any before you, going to identify the body that was found in Bigby River as the body of Sam Nevelle?

Answer. There never was any direct testimony in regard to that before me. That case was tried before Judge Orr, on a writ of *habeas corpus*, some few weeks since, where Bridges was arrested.

Question. What is the evidence, if you know it or have heard it?

Answer. Well, sir, I do not know that I can give a very perfect statement of the evidence. I will state this: at the time of the investigation of this case that I have just alluded to, the body of this man had not been found that was drowned in the river. The body that I alluded to that they were going in search of on that day, turned out to be all a mere rumor. There was nothing of it. There was no body of any person ever found at that time. But about a week after that a party of negroes, some ten or twelve in number, came to me for me to issue a writ of inquest, and summon a jury to sit upon the body of this man that was found hanging in some willows in the Bigby River. I issued the writ, and directed it to a special deputy constable, but when he went in search of the body he discovered that it was in the State of Alabama. I then sent a copy of the writ, and also wrote, to Mr. Parker, who is acting magistrate in Alabama, at Memphis——

By Mr. BUCKLEY:

Question. In what county?

Answer. That is in Pickens County. Mr. Justice Parker summoned a jury, so I was told, and the inquest was held upon that body. I have it from pretty good authority that Doctor Morehead, from Pickensville, Alabama, was there, and saw that body, and he stated in his affidavit which he made before the magistrate, or mayor, in Pickens County, that there was a body of a man found there, but it looked as though it had been dead some three months; that his teeth had fallen out, or were held so loosely that he pulled some of them out with his fingers.

Question. At what time of the year was this?

Answer. It was about the 20th of June that these parties made the attack upon Bridges's house.

Question. Do you think it probable that a body could have remained three months, at this season of the year, in the river, without decomposition?

Answer. I do not know enough about it to have a correct opinion. I would not suppose it could.

By Mr. BLAIR:

Question. Was Doctor Morehead a practicing physician?

Answer. Yes, sir.

Question. Do you suppose his judgment in regard to the matter would be better, probably, than yours, or any other person who was not a professional?

Answer. Yes, sir; better than mine.

By the CHAIRMAN:

Question. Did you hear this from Doctor Morehead?

Answer. No, sir; I got it. I have seen his affidavit and read it, and that was about the substance of it. I have heard several other parties speak about Doctor Morehead's statement in regard to it. It was substantially the same.

By Mr. BLAIR:

Question. You, yourself, never saw the body?

Answer. No, sir; I never saw the body.

Question. Did you ever hear that the body was recognized by any one as the body of Sam Nevelle?

Answer. Yes, sir; I heard that the father of this man when he went down there before the body was taken out of the river, stated that that was his son; that he knew it by his shirt.

Question. Was the body disfigured, as you understood, in any way except by decomposition?

Answer. No, sir. The flesh had fallen from the bones almost entirely, except around the abdomen. That was Doctor Morehead's statement in his affidavit, which I have read.

Question. Do you suppose that even at that season of the year, in a week's time, a body would have decomposed to that extent in the water?

Answer. Well, I do not know, sir. I could not say, never having had any experience at all. I could not give much idea how long it would take for the body of a person to decompose; my judgment would only be based on the judgment of others.

Question. Did you give any credit to the statement of Doctor Morehead in that respect?

Answer. Yes, sir; I know him to be a very reliable man. He is so considered in the community in which he lives.

Question. From all that came before you in the way of evidence and otherwise, was it your impression that this man was foully dealt with?

Answer. I never thought he was, sir, from the circumstances.

Question. You thought he had made his escape?

Answer. I thought he had made his escape. I always thought he was assisted in making his escape by some parties.

Question. And the fact that he has not been seen or heard of since is no evidence in your mind that he has been foully dealt with, as he had sufficient motive to keep out of the way, for fear of being punished for the stealing of the horse?

Answer. Yes, sir. I made a statement in his presence and Mr. Moore's, (this man I have mentioned, when they came to carry him down to this school-house,) which I learned afterward had considerable effect upon him. It was this: I told them to be very particular; that if he was guilty it was a penitentiary offense. They then proposed that they tie him, which they did. They tied his hands behind him and carried him down there tied.

Question. Did you learn that he had been very securely fastened in the school-house?

Answer. Yes, sir; he was locked around his neck or one leg and the other end chained around the studding; it is a frame house.

Question. There was no violence done to the studding?

Answer. No, sir.

Question. You think from that that he must have been released by some one?

Answer. That is my reason for thinking he must have been released. There was no evidence before me which showed any violence at all, and the evidence was that the locks were not injured.

By Mr. BUCKLEY:

Question. Ordinary padlocks through the links of the chain?

Answer. Yes, sir. I never saw the locks myself.

By Mr. BLAIR:

Question. Was the evidence that they must have been unlocked?

Answer. There was no evidence in regard to that. The only evidence was that the locks were not injured at all; that they were not broken or mashed at all.

Question. Was it in evidence that it was possible for him to have released himself without assistance?

Answer. No, sir; I do not remember that there was any evidence in regard to that; if there was I do not remember it now.

Question. Is there evidence that he has ever been seen anywhere since?

Answer. None, only hearsay evidence.

Question. Who does that hearsay come from?

Answer. I have understood from the deputy sheriff here, Mr. Lucas, that Mr. Robert O. Ware, of this county, had either seen him, or seen some person that did see him, near West Point a few days after this occurrence at Bigby Valley.

Question. West Point, in Alabama?

Answer. No, sir; in this State.

Question. Where is West Point situated?

Answer. It is about fifteen miles west of Columbus. It is on the Mobile and Ohio Railroad.

Question. Mr. Ware told that to the deputy sheriff of this county?

Answer. The deputy sheriff told me that Mr. Ware had said so.

Question. Is that all that there is in connection with this affair that you desire to state to the committee?

Answer. I believe I have stated, sir, about all that I know, of my own knowledge, and about all that was stated before me in evidence; all I remember of now.

Question. You are not confined to what was stated before you in evidence, but any other reliable information in regard to this matter you are at libery to state.

Answer. There has been some controversy in regard to the clothing that this boy, Sam, had on. The pieces of clothing which were exhibited before the grand jury in this county for my inspection did not correspond with my recollection of the clothing that this man had on at the time of his commitment or at the time he was tried before me.

Question. The clothing exhibited before the grand jury was taken from the body of the man found in the river?

Answer. Yes, sir. It was a blue checked cloth, what we term cotton stripe. My recollection of the shirt of this boy is, that it was a very dirty white Osnaburgh shirt. His coat, I think, had been a colored coat of some kind, but had faded until it was almost white. It was a dirty white and a long-tailed coat; I remember that distinctly, and that was the main reason I doubted that this boy that was found in the river was the same one that was tried before me.

Question. What sort of a coat was on the boy found in the river?

Answer. It was said to have been a jacket and roundabout and a cotton check shirt.

Question. Does your recollection of his clothing correspond with that of Mr. Moore, who took him down to Bridges's house?

Answer. I do not know, sir. I do not know what Mr. Moore's recollection of it is.

Question. Have you ever asked either Mr. Moore, or the negro that was with Mr. Moore, what they recollected about it?

Answer. No, sir. I recollect that Mr. Moore asked me one day if I recollected whether he had on a long coat or a short one, and I told him my recollection was that it was a long coat, and he remarked that was his recollection of it. That is all that I ever said to him, or Mr. Moore ever said to me, with regard to it. Now, I learned from Mr. Fitzgerald, who lives near Pickensville, in this State, that Dr. Morehead told him that his hat was in the waistband of his pants. I have heard that from several parties, but not from anybody who had seen him.

Question. The hat with the body found in the river was in the waistband of the pants?

Answer. Yes, sir; I have heard that from several parties, but never directly from any person who had seen it. It is the general understanding, I believe, in my section of country, that there was a boy drowned that had fallen off of the steamboat Bertha, some time about the 1st of June, or in the first part of June.

Question. You speak of the fact of the hat being found under the belt of the body. Do you recollect anything of the hat worn by Nevelle when he was before you?

Answer. No, sir; I do not remember.

Question. Did he have any hat?

Answer. Yes, sir; he had a hat; I think it was an old hat; but I could not state positively now whether it was a white hat or a brown hat; I am very well satisfied that it was not a black hat.

Question. Was it a black hat that was found on the body?

Answer. I do not know; I never heard what kind of a hat it was that was found on the body. I have understood from parties in Pickensville that there was a hat in the waistband of his pants.

By the CHAIRMAN:

Question. Do the friends of Nevelle still believe that he was murdered?

Answer. Well, sir, I have heard nothing in regard to it recently; they did believe it very strongly and, I suppose, still believe it; I have heard nothing to the contrary. I think the matter seems to have quieted down very much.

Question. With the exception of this information you derived from the deputy sheriff, you have not heard any rumor of his being alive, have you?

Answer. No, sir.

Question. And the deputy sheriff got his information from Mr. Ware, and Mr. Ware got his information from somebody else?

Answer. I do not know how that was. The deputy sheriff had derived his information from Mr. Ware.

Question. Has that rumor been circulated through that neighborhood where the friends of Neville live, that he has been seen at West Point?

Answer. I suppose it has; I heard it.

Question. If it were true that he was there, is it not probable that his friends would have discovered him before this time?

Answer. I expect they would, sir.

Question. I understand that this point at which he should have been seen was upon the Mobile and Ohio Railroad?

Answer. Yes, sir.

Question. And only fifteen or twenty miles distant?

Answer. From Columbus it is fifteen or twenty miles. It is thirty to thirty-five miles to where he lives.

Question. Where is the constable, Bridges, now?

Answer. I do not know, sir.

Question. Has he left that part of the country?

Answer. He was under arrest. He was arrested in Columbus.

Question. On what charge?

Answer. On this charge.

Question. Letting this man escape?

Answer. Yes, sir.

Question. On the charge of being privy to the murder of this boy?

Answer. I think he was arrested on the charge of letting the prisoner escape.

Question. Has he made his escape himself?

Answer. No, sir. He was tried on a writ of *habeas corpus*, before Judge Orr, some weeks since, and permitted to give bail for his appearance at this court of this county.

Question. Did he give bail?

Answer. I think so, sir; I have understood so, sir.

Question. He has not come back to your neighborhood?

Answer. No, sir; he was very much alarmed after that.

Question. Judge Orr, after hearing the evidence on a writ of *habeas corpus*, determined that the case was so far made out as to require him to give bail?

Answer. I understood that he required him to give bail in the sum of three hundred dollars to appear at this court, to answer any charge that might be made against him. There was no special charge against him, I understood.

Question. If there was no special charge against him at the time of the trial on the writ of *habeas corpus*, what power had Judge Orr to hold him at all?

Answer. Well, sir, he was arrested there by a colored magistrate in Columbus, without any affidavit being made, on the mere suggestion of Ben Clay, and was put in jail, without the privilege of bond, and he was then taken before Judge Orr on a writ of *habeas corpus*. I was there at the examination of the witnesses. I was called in as a witness myself, and I heard this man, Ben Clay, whose name was signed to the affidavit, swear before the court there that he never authorized his name to be put there; that he did not swear that Bridges had let this man get away; that he merely mentioned in the presence of the justice of the peace—Harrison was his name—as Bridges passed through town, "There goes the man that let this man Sam Nevelle get away."

Question. If there was no charge made by a responsible man, in writing, against Bridges, what power had Judge Orr to bind him to appear at court?

Question. Well, sir, I do not know. It was thought by the counsel of the accused that he had no power to do it. That was one point that was raised in the examination.

Question. Is not Judge Orr a very good lawyer and a very correct judge?

Answer. He is said to be, and I suppose he is.

Question. The probability, then, would be that he never would have directed him to be committed, on failure to give bond for his appearance here at court, without a written accusation?

Answer. Well, I do not know, sir.

Question. I understood you to say that you talked with Bridges in relation to the circumstance of the confinement of this boy and his escape, and you asked him, among other things, what signs there were about the house of parties having rescued this boy?

Answer. Well, sir, I asked him on the morning he came there to me.

Question. What account did he give of that?

Answer. Well, sir, when I asked him if there were any traces of any parties having been there, he said he could not discover any; that the chain was there, and that he heard nothing. I asked him about his dog—if he made any unusual barking that night. He said no; that the first he knew of it was he had gone out about ten o'clock; that Mr. Scott went out after that, and he went out a second time, and that the third time, or the second time, that Mr. Scott went out, which was about twelve or one o'clock, Scott came back and told him the boy was gone.

Question. I remember what you said in relation to that, but what I wish to ask you is whether he made diligent search about the school-house, to discover traces of men or foot-prints of horses, and whether he made any discovery of that kind?

Answer. I do not think he stated anything about that. I asked him the question I mentioned; I asked him whether he saw any traces. Our conference did not last but a few minutes.

Question. Was any investigation made about them; nothing in relation to these foot-prints or horse-tracks about the house within a day or two after the disappearance of the boy; had nobody the curiosity to go there and examine?

Answer. None that I know of, sir; I heard of none.

Question. Was he of opinion that the boy could not have got away without aid?

Answer. That seemed to be his impression.

Question. Whether he was rescued by friendly or unfriendly hands, therefore, could not be known?

Answer. No, sir. The inference I drew from what he said was that some of the boy's friends had gone there and released him. That was my first impression in regard to it from what he stated to me the next morning.

Question. But if the boy's friends had released him, how would you account for the great ferment among the negroes of the community, including the boy's relatives and friends, and the anxious efforts, amounting, it seems, to unlawful assemblies and riots, that they made to discover his whereabouts, or what had become of him? How do you account for that on the theory that the boy had been rescued by his own friends?

Answer. Well, sir, that is the only evidence that has ever been brought to my mind.

Question. Are you not thoroughly persuaded that the negroes thought that the boy had been foully dealt with? Can you account for their conduct upon any other theory?

Answer. Well, there is only one other that could be suggested that I know of, and that would be that they must make some demonstration in order to prevent the civil authorities from making extra efforts to capture.

Question. Do you not think that a very far-fetched theory, and very unreasonable?

Answer. Well, it never has impressed me as strongly as the other, and, as I stated a while ago, that was the strongest evidence to my mind.

Question. That they thought he was murdered?

Answer. That they thought he was murdered. There was no other evidence, in fact, that would lead to that conclusion.

Question. Have you ever heard that the mother of that boy, upon the discovery of this dead body in the willows, identified the clothing as that of her son?

Answer. Yes, sir; I have heard that she said that was his shirt; that was the kind of a shirt that he had on when he left; and that is one reason why I never gave much credit to what she said about it, from the fact of my recollection of the shirt he had on when he came before me.

Question. You never conversed with her yourself upon that subject?

Answer. No, sir; I never have seen her. I have only heard what she said.

By Mr. RICE:

Question. You say that Bridges thought he would have been likely to have heard parties if they came there to rescue this prisoner?

Answer. Yes, sir. I asked him this: If he had seen any traces of any person having been there. I asked him if he saw any next morning when he came down to me. He said that he had not. I then asked him if his dogs had made no noise. He said not; that it was done very quietly.

Question. Would not they have been as likely to have heard the friends of the boy if they had come to his rescue as to have heard others that wanted to commit violence upon him?

Answer. Well, sir, I do not know. It would depend entirely upon the manner of procedure in the matter.

Question. How do you consider the fact that the locks were not injured as being an evidence that the friends of the boy released him, or that he was released by some one having access to the key?

Answer. Well, sir, that has always been a mystery to me, because I would have as much right to believe the one as the other.

Question. You would have as much right to suppose that those who had no access to to the key had released him, as those who did have access to it?

Answer. That might be different. At the same time, in the case of an ordinary padlock, a great many keys might fit the same lock. I never saw the locks; I do not know what kind of locks they were.

Question. How many days after the rescue was it that the body was found in the river?

Answer. I think it was about ten days. I do not remember exactly. It was not far from ten days—somewhere from a week to ten days.

By the CHAIRMAN:

Question. And some five miles below?

Answer. Yes, sir.

By Mr. RICE:

Question. You have given a statement upon the authority of the deputy sheriff. Do you regard that statement as reliable, and do you believe that this boy was seen here at West Point.

Answer. Well, sir, I do not. Of course it is not positive evidence.

Question. Have you given credence to it in your own mind?

Answer. Well, I can't say that I have, sir.

By the CHAIRMAN:

Question. The constable in locking him up retained the key?

Answer. Yes, sir, I think he did.

Question. What became of that key?

Answer. I do not know, sir.

Question. Did the constable ever give any account of it?

Answer. None before me.

By Mr. BLAIR:

Question. Did you have Scott before you?

Answer. Yes, sir.

Question. What account did he give of it?

Answer. He gave substantially the same statement that Bridges gave to me of it.

Question. Were there any servants about the house—any negroes?

Answer. Well, sir, I do not know whether there were or not. I never have learned in regard to that.

Question. Did you have Mrs. Bridges before you.

Answer. Yes, sir.

Question. What account did she give of the matter?

Answer. Well, she stated that about 11 or 12 Mr. Bridges thought he heard the dog bark, and they stepped to the door. Do you mean of the prisoner getting away?

Mr. BLAIR. Yes.

The WITNESS. She said nothing, except that she knew that Mr. Bridges had gotten up once or twice, probably, and gone out there, and she heard Mr. Scott, who was sleeping in an adjoining room, go out once.

By Mr. RICE:

Question. Did Scott and Bridges profess to have kept awake all the time; to have got up at intervals?

Answer. At intervals.

Question. When they happened to wake up?

Answer. I suppose so.

By the CHAIRMAN:

Question. What reason did Bridges assign for locking this boy up at some distance in his house—in the school-house—which would cause him and Scott to break their rest very often in the night in order to see if he was still there, when he could with ease have confined the man in his own house?

Answer. I do not remember that he ever gave any reasons. The case of Bridges never was investigated before me; that is, he never was arrested by me.

Question. Are there not some white people up there as well as colored people who think that Mr. Bridges is connected with the disappearance of that boy?

Answer. I do not know of any, sir.

Question. Of his being spirited away?

Answer. Of course it is a mystery that has created a good deal of anxiety and excitement on the part of the whole community, and there have been speculative ideas advanced by a great many in regard to it.

By Mr. BUCKLEY:

Question. Does Mr. Ware, who gave this information to the deputy sheriff, live in that section of the State?

Answer. No, sir; he lives about eight miles this side of there. He has a brother, I think, who resides in West Point, or a connection of his in some way. I understood from the deputy sheriff that he was up there, and that he knew this boy.

By Mr. BLAIR:

Question. In reference to the stress that has been laid upon this man Neville never having been heard of since, had he not a sufficient motive to keep the fact of his escape concealed in the fact that there was positive proof that he had stolen this horse, and that he was liable to be sent to the penitentiary, which was known to him, and which would have induced him, after having made his escape, to have induced such of his friends as aided him in making that escape to conceal his whereabouts, even his existence?

Answer. Yes, sir; I should think it would.

By the CHAIRMAN:

Question. If that were so, and he were hiding, do you think he would select a prominent point on the Mobile and Ohio Railroad to secrete himself from observation?

Answer. I do not think any intelligent man would.

By Mr. RICE:

Question. Why did not the deputy sheriff send for him if he heard he was there?

Answer. I think there were inquiries made for him.

Question. They could not find him?

Answer. No, sir; he has never been found. When this old man—his father—came to my house he seemed to be very solicitous about him, and I told him he was guilty of an offense that would put him in the penitentiary if he ever came back or was caught. I recollect mentioning to him that I did not think he need suffer any uneasiness, because if the man had made his escape he knew enough about the laws of the county to know that it would never do for him to stay about where he would be seen, which statement seemed to reconcile his father—in fact, I did not see any more of him then until several days afterward.

By Mr. BUCKLEY:

Question. Was the key to this padlock found the next morning there?

Answer. No, sir; I think not. My information was that the lock which was around his neck was unlocked, and that the chain and lock were left in the house.

Question. Did you ever hear it stated that there was a note found there about that school-house after this boy was taken out?

Answer. Yes, sir; I heard that.

Question. Have you ever heard what the contents of that note were?

Answer. No, sir; I made an effort to get the note, but I could not find any person who had ever seen it.

Question. Still you heard such a note was found?

Answer. I think there was a note there.

By the CHAIRMAN:

Question. Did you hear that it was signed "K. K. K."?

Answer. Yes, sir; I suppose I did.

By Mr. BLAIR:

Question. Who told you that there was such a note there?

Answer. I heard it from freedmen; one was Bob Lash—no, Circe Manning stated that Bob Lash said there was a note there.

Question. Could Bob Lash read?

Answer. No, sir; and Bob Lash stated in his testimony before me that the reason why he went up to the house that day was that he had heard that there was a note there, and he went up to see what it was; and I asked him the question if he could read, and he said no; and I asked him if he had seen the note, and he said he had not. He said that there was paper scattered about there, and that his reason for going up there was not to join in the tumult that was at Mr. Bridges's house, but to see what that paper was.

Question. What did Bridges say to you about the note, if anything?

Answer. Yes, sir; he said that there was nothing in the note there that he knew anything about.

Question. What did Scott say?

Answer. I never asked Scott. I never heard that Scott said anything about it.

By the CHAIRMAN:

Question. Is Scott there in the country yet?

Answer. Yes, sir; he was there a few days ago.

By Mr. BUCKLEY:

Question. What day was it that Sam had his trial before you?

Answer. I think it was Monday.

Question. What day of the month?

Answer. It was the Monday before the Sunday that this affray took place, and that was about the 20th or 21st, I think.

Question. It was about the 20th that these negroes came up to Bridges's house?

Answer. Yes, sir; that was on the Monday before that Sunday.

Question. Were steamboats running up the Bigbee River at that time?

Answer. I think that the last boat that was up the Bigbee River was on the 16th of June.

Question. So that if the boy had fallen from that boat and been drowned in the river it could not have been the one whose body was found?

Answer. I do not know, sir; it was three months. It was very possible that it might, if he had been drowned three months. I do not know at what time it was that this boy fell off the boat.

By the CHAIRMAN:

Question. Do you know that in point of fact he did fall off and was drowned?

Answer. I do not know that he was, of my own knowledge. I have heard persons state that he was.

By Mr. RICE:

Question. How many rooms are there in Bridges's house?

Answer. Only two, I think.

Question. Does the kitchen adjoin?

Answer. No, sir; I think not. I do not remember. I think it was a frame house with an open passage. There was one room.

Question. Used as a kitchen?

Answer. Yes, sir; I think Mr. Scott staid in one room, and Bridges and his family in the other.

By the CHAIRMAN:

Question. Any house adjoining?

Answer. None except the school-house, which is twenty steps off. It was a house which was built for a school teacher. The school-house is near there. It belonged to the sixteenth section school fund of this county.

By Mr. BUCKLEY:

Question. I understood you to say that about ten days elapsed between the time that Sam. Neville was taken out of the school-house and the time that the body was found in the Bigbee River?

Answer. A week or ten days; I do not remember exactly; I cannot state to a day. I think that it was about a week that a party of negroes—ten or twelve in number—came to me and told me of this negro being found in the river.

By the CHAIRMAN:

Question. Must it not have been more than that, because you first saw the boy at the examination Monday, and it was the Sunday following the attack was made on Bridges; so it must have been more than a week?

Answer. I suppose probably it was. It was ten days, I reckon.

MACON, MISSISSIPPI, *November* 8, 1871.

EDMUND L. CARPENTER sworn and examined.

The CHAIRMAN. This witness is called by the minority, and I will ask General Blair to conduct his examination.

By Mr. BLAIR:

Question. Please give your residence and business, or profession?

Answer. Brooksville, Noxubee County, Mississippi. I am a farmer and planter.

Question. Do you know a negro by the name of Sam. Coger?

Answer. Yes, sir; I know a colored man by the name of Sam. Coger.

Question. Where does he live?

Answer. He lives in Noxubee County, about a mile and a half from Brooksville.

Question. Is he living now?

Answer. He is, or was a day or two ago.

Question. Did you see him?

Answer. I did.

Question. It has been in testimony before us here, and at Washington, that this negro was killed?

Answer. It is not the case, sir, unless he has been killed within the last two or three days.

Question. Do you know anything about the killing of a man named Dick Malone.

Answer. I know nothing of the killing of him. I saw him after he was dead, sir.

Question. What do you know, from reliable information, about his death?

Answer. I cannot state, sir, that I know anything about the killing. I was acting as justice of the peace in that district, and was sent for by the gentleman who was living on the place to go up there and have an inquest held over the body. I proceeded as soon as I got the information, and had an inquest. I summoned three colored men and three white men, a lawful jury, and made all the investigation I could of the matter.

Question. What was brought out as to the mode, manner, and cause of his killing.

Answer. There was a statement given in there by all the witnesses I could get of colored people; they were all negroes who gave testimony in reference to the case, except one white witness, the gentleman running the place. They said some persons were seen there around the yard, on their horses, inquiring for another negro. I forget his full name now. Lowry is his name; but I forget his given name.

By Mr. RICE:

Question. Isham Lowry?

Answer. Yes, sir; Isham Lowry. They wanted to see Isham Lowry; and they found out, I don't know how, where his house was, and went to the door and knocked and got entrance. I don't know whether they broke the door open or not; I don't remember whether they broke it open, or whether it was open; but they got in, and commenced whipping the negro Isham, and slapping him about over the face; and they knocked him some, and inquired for another negro on the place, but not Dick, and they told them he wasn't there, or in that house, or something of the sort, and they went out, and started off, and Dick, hearing the disturbance around the premises, got up and came out of his house, and told some of the balance of the people on the place that he intended to see who these men were. As the company rode off, he followed them up. I suppose it was nearly a quarter of a mile, or three or four hundred yards from his house, where he was killed. I never learned what passed between the parties, except that as he started off, he said, "I think I know who you are, and I intend to know better about it." He just followed them down the hill; down a little trail that took off from the cabins into the field. The people stated that after these men had been gone a few minutes, they heard a gun, or pistol, or something fired; and after awhile they commenced searching round, and everybody had disappeared, and they finally found Dick's body, but they didn't suppose the party was after Dick at all; and stated that they believed that if Dick had remained in his house he never would have been hurt; that it was the other parties that they were after, and Dick wasn't inquired for.

By Mr. BLAIR:

Question. The supposition was that he was killed because he pursued these people to ascertain who they were?

Answer. That was the supposition of all who testified in the matter, white and black. Mr. Baldwin, a reliable gentleman, and minister of the Gospel, too, living on the place, stated that Dick was a good, peaceable, quiet man, and that he had no idea that the parties were in search of Dick at all; and that he didn't believe he would have been hurt if he had staid in his house.

Question. Who was the man they had whipped?

Answer. Isham Lowry.

Question. What did they whip him for?

Answer. I don't know. He said he didn't know. I learned from some other source, however, that the supposition was then that there had been some hogs stolen in the neighborhood a day or two before that, and they rather accused Isham; and that the other man they were inquiring for was in the crime. Whether that was reliable or not, I don't know; I am not able to state. It was just rumor; I don't tell it as a fact.

Question. Was it ever ascertained who any of these parties were?

Answer. No, sir; not as I know of. I never heard one defined at all.

Question. Dick Malone said he knew them?

Answer. Yes, sir.

Question. Did he tell anybody who they were?

Answer. He never did. He told those two men, or some parties, "I know you, and I will find you out better before you leave here." Then he followed them off.

Question. Did he say that in a way to be heard by them?

Answer. I don't know whether they heard that or not. That was the testimony of some of the witnesses before the jury.

Question. Were those parties in disguise?

Answer. They didn't know whether they were or not. They said they didn't recognize their features. They had something over their faces, they said. They believed their horses were covered up, or had something on them; but I didn't hear whether they stated that the persons themselves were in disguise at all or not.

Question. Did Mr. Baldwin see them?

Answer. He just saw them riding about around his lot. He didn't come out. I asked him why he didn't come out. He said he didn't know they were after him, and he thought he had better attend to his own business, and concluded that he would not have anything to do with them.

Question. What did he say in reference to the disguises?

Answer. He said the horses, seen from the distance he was at, appeared to have something over them.

Question. But the men did not?

Answer. The men did not, as he knew of. He didn't know whether they were white men or black ones, but their horses seemed to be covered with something.

Question. What did the negroes say about their being white or black?

Answer. They said the same thing Mr. Baldwin did. The one named Isham, that got whipped, said the two that came into his house were white men; that is, he took them to be white men; they looked like white men to him; they had heavy whiskers; he said he didn't recognize them.

Question. Was that the only means by which he knew them to be white men—their whiskers.

Answer. Yes, sir. He said they didn't give him time to get much light in his house. He knocked up a light, and they commenced knocking him about or slapping him in the face, and with the fist. He was alarmed. He knew he hadn't done anything. They found out who he was, and inquired for another party.

Question. They didn't whip him with anything but their hands?

Answer. No; I suppose not. There was a bruise—a right smart bruise—over one of his eyes; it looked like it might have been made by a man's knuckles, or something of that sort; and he was cut in other places over the eyes, on the forehead. I examined him, as well as the man who was killed. He was slapped about with the fist, or hand, or something. There didn't seem to be any marks of any violence about him of any other sort.

By the CHAIRMAN:

Question. Where is this Sam. Coger you speak of living now

Answer. He is living with a man named Nuckles, about a mile and a half south of where I am living.

Question. On Nuckles's plantation?

Answer. Yes, sir.

Question. How long has he been living there?

Answer. Ever since the 1st of January.

Question. Where did he live before that?

Answer. He had lived with Widow Coger, just in sight of where he now lives, last year—at least that is my recollection; I am satisfied he did.

Question. What aged man is he?

Answer. I suppose he is thirty years old.
Question. Has he a family?
Answer. I do not know whether he has or not.
Question. Have you ever heard of his being whipped?
Answer. I never have.
Question. Never to your knowledge has he been interfered with by the Ku-Klux, or any one?
Answer. Never except that shooting, you know.
Question. What shooting?
Answer. He was shot at.
Question. Sam. Coger?
Answer. Yes, sir,
Question. When?
Answer. That was, I reckon, in May.
Question. May last?
Answer. Yes, sir;
Question. Just detail to the committee the circumstances of this being shot at.
Answer. Well, the report came to Brooksville that Sam. Coger was killed, and a short time after that report came, it was reported to me, as a magistrate there, I suppose, that Sam. Coger was still living, and could identify the parties that had shot him. I got on my horse as quick as I could get him, and rode right straight over there, and went in to see him, and found him alive and pretty talkative. He answered every question I asked him. I inquired of him if he knew who had done it. He said he didn't. Said I, "Sam, it was told me you could identify the parties, and that is my business here to see you. I understood you got shot, and knew who did it, and I came to see if you could identify the parties." He says, "I couldn't; I don't know who it was any more than you do, not a bit." Said I, "Sam, what is the matter; what sort of a scrape have you been in that has brought this upon you?" He says, "I don't know, Mr. Carpenter, unless it is for a little scrape that I have been accused of, stealing meat. Missis Sally Coger, a widow living in sight, has had her smoke-house broken open, and meat taken, and accused me of taking it, and she has been searching and inquiring around, and come to me about it and attacked me with it, and they say I gave Miss Sally some impertinent language. I didn't aim to do it. If that isn't the cause of it, I don't know what is." That is about his statement to me. My impression at the time, from the statement he gave, and from what I knew, was this: Mrs. Coger complained to me of her meat being stolen. She came to me and swore out a search-warrant, and had a search made, but found no meat. What I knew of the circumstances, and the statement Sam. made, led me to believe that it was some people—friends of Mrs. Coger, and who felt, I suppose, interest in her protection—who did this thing.
Question. That shot him?
Answer. Yes, sir; that is my impression.
Question. Where was he when shot?
Answer. He was in his house. He said two persons came and knocked at the door, and he would not open it; they kicked it down, or picked up a chunk, or something, and beat it down, and came in, and asked him if he was Sam. Coger. He wouldn't give his name, and never gave it. He refused to give his name. They took it for granted, I suppose, that he was the party, and shot at him.
Question. How many shots were fired at him?
Answer. Two.
Question. With pistols?
Answer. Yes, sir.
Question. How was he wounded?
Answer. One took effect somewhere about the face, passing across the mouth somewhere, I don't remember exactly where. The other one was in the side, just a glancing shot; a flesh wound in the edge of his side.
Question. They obviously intended to kill him, then, from the direction of the shots?
Answer. I have no doubt the intention was to kill him.
Question. Was he laid up long with the wounds?
Answer. No, sir; some two or three weeks.
Question. The first report that came to town was that he was killed?
Answer. Yes, sir; it was reported to me directly after that he was alive, and I knew it was my duty to see into the matter, and proceeded forthwith.
Question. Has it ever been discovered who his assailants were?
Answer. No, sir; never. He didn't know, and I don't know that anybody does.
Question. But from the fact of this trouble about the meat, the supposition was that some friends of that lady had done it?
Answer. That was the supposition.
Question. This is the only Sam. Coger you know of?
Answer. Yes, sir; the only one in the country I know of.

Question. Did you question him as to whether the men were disguised that came to his house?

Answer. I do not remember that I did, sir.

Question. From the fact that he could not identify them, you inferred that they had some disguise on?

Answer. It might have been men he wasn't acquainted with; I don't know about that.

Question. Nobody has ever been taken up for shooting him?

Answer. No, sir.

Question. He still lives on the same place?

Answer. Yes, sir; working with the same man, and is in as good health as he ever was; I saw him three or four days ago, and conversed with him; he was only down two or three weeks.

Question. Was Isham Lowry knocked down?

Answer. No, sir; not that I know of. He didn't state to me that he was; he said they slapped him, and knocked him about over the head, and they had cut his face and scarred it; he didn't know what he was doing, he said.

Question. What was their motive in treating him so roughly, if they were not after him?

Answer. He said they were inquiring of him for another party. Any question you see proper to put to me, I will answer it if I know anything about it; I have nothing to conceal.

Question. What is your information as to the number of men that killed Dick Malone?

Answer. From the account of Mr. Baldwin, and the observation he had of them, I suppose they may have been a dozen; perhaps ten or twelve, from what he said about the horses and the bulk of them.

Question. What motive would they have for disguising their horses, if they did not disguise their faces and persons?

Answer. That is a question I couldn't answer, from the fact that I know nothing about that sort of parties. I suppose their horses might have been known easier than men; men are very hard to distinguish at night, most of them in our country wearing their big face-whiskers and long mustaches.

Question. At what hour of night was that?

Answer. About 10 o'clock, was the statement of the witness.

Question. Had the people gone to bed?

Answer. No, sir; they had not. Some of them may have gone to bed.

Question. Why did Baldwin say he was afraid to go out?

Answer. I didn't ask him that question there, sir; he said that there were several came, and he didn't suppose that he had any business with them, and therefore he didn't feel like going to them.

Question. Did he suppose them to be Ku-Klux?

Answer. He said he didn't know anything about them. No, sir; I didn't infer that he did, from what he said and the way he talked to me.

Question. When men have been visited by Ku-Klux, or by men in disguise, at night, are they not a little cautious and reluctant about giving information, for fear they may be visited again?

Answer. Did you mean the parties they visit?

Question. I ask you where men are visited by the Ku-Klux, are they not cautious and reluctant about giving any testimony in relation to the parties who have visited them, for fear of their return?

Answer. I suppose not, sir.

Question. You suppose there is no fear operating on their minds?

Answer. I would not think there was; from what I have seen and heard, I would not suppose there were any fears.

Question. From what you have heard of the Ku-Klux Klan you think they would not have any disposition to visit punishment upon any man who attempted to discover who they were, and bring them to justice?

Answer. I can only speak of myself. If they were to visit me and do me a wrong, and leave life, I should be very apt to report them, if I could know how to do it.

Question. Have you never heard that any of this community of men were afraid to complain against these Ku-Klux, for fear of being whipped or killed?

Answer. I never have, sir.

Question. You think these Ku-Klux, then, have not created any alarm in the community?

Answer. I do not think they have, sir, any. There has been some talk—some rumor; but a man can hear anything he wants to hear, now, in this day and time, it seems. So far as this Ku-Klux organization is concerned, I could not say that I believe conscientiously that there is any in the country.

Question. What do you mean by Ku-Klux Klan?

Answer. I don't know; I suppose it is a disguised body of men that enter into an organization to do mischief, or something of that sort.

Question. You believe that there are disguised men in this community who have repeatedly done mischief in the night-time; do you not?

Answer. If there is, I don't know it, and never heard of it, sir; that is, to know it to be a fact, or ever to have heard of its being a fact.

Question. You have never heard, from first to last, in this community, that there were any disguised men prowling around in the night-time inflicting mischief?

Answer. No; not disguised men. This Dick Malone case—I stated to you the testimony there was that their horses looked like they might have had something over them.

Question. Is that the only case you have ever heard of where disguises were used?

Answer. Well, there were parties interfered with out west of where I live, out of my district; some of the boys taken out—a white man taken out in the night; whether they were disguised or not I don't know; I never understood.

Question. Some white men were taken out in the night?

Answer. Yes, sir.

Question. What was done with them?

Answer. I don't know. They were just threatened, I suppose. I don't know that any violence was used at all.

Question. What threats were made?

Answer. I suppose they were parties living with some colored women.

Question. In what neighborhood was that?

Answer. One was Jackson, another was Cosby. It is out west of Brooksville neighborhood.

Question. Some four white men, were they not?

Answer. Three or four.

Question. Did you understand that they were taken out?

Answer. Just taken out and talked to, and told what would be done to them if they didn't quit the way they were living.

Question. What was told would be done?

Answer. I didn't hear the particulars.

Question. Did you hear whether that was by disguised men?

Answer. No, sir.

Question. How large a body of men was it?

Answer. I never understood the number.

Question. It must have been more than four?

Answer. I never heard the number. It must have been, I suppose.

Question. Did you understand that on the same night these men whipped some colored women?

Answer. Yes, sir; just a rumor that there was one whipped; only one.

Question. Did you not hear that these white men were all of them sleeping with colored women?

Answer. No, sir; only one.

Question. Which one?

Answer. Jackson.

Question. Why did they take out four, if only one was sleeping with a colored woman?

Answer. The balance may have done the like before, for what I know.

Question. Did you understand that they had done the like before?

Answer. It was the general impression. They had no white wives, you know; were living that way with colored women.

Question. Was that the understanding?

Answer. It was the general impression through the neighborhood that that was the way in which they were living.

Question. And these gentlemen, who took them out, whether Ku-Klux or not, just sermonized a little with them?

Answer. That was all, according to my understanding.

Question. Administered a little moral suasion?

Answer. Yes, sir; used no violence.

Question. Talked ethics to them?

Answer. Yes, sir; I suppose so.

Question. The testimony before this committee is, that there were three or four colored women whipped by this same party on that night.

Answer. I never heard of but one. I heard of one who said she was whipped, that lived entirely out of my district, in a portion of the country I have no business in, and therefore I didn't try to investigate it at all, nor bother with it.

Question. Did you understand that this discipline broke up the little arrangement that was subsisting between those white men and colored women?

Answer. I understand it did with some of them; with some of them it didn't.

Question. Did you understand that those who continued in the error of their ways were visited again?

Answer. I never heard that they were visited any more, sir.

Question. Did you ever hear of one Peter Gregory, who was killed at or near Mushulaville?

Answer. I never heard; if I have, it has escaped my memory.

Question. Did you ever hear of Solomon Triplett being shot?

Answer. No, sir.

Question. Did you ever hear of Alexander Hughes being whipped?

Answer. No, sir, I never did.

Question. Did you ever hear of Lydia Anderson being whipped on the Richards's place?

Answer. No, sir.

Question. Did you ever hear of Betsey Lucas being whipped?

Answer. Yes, sir.

Question. Who did you understand she was whipped by?

Answer. By this same party. She was one of the women who was living with one of these white men; I don't know who it was.

Question. Was that on the May's place?

Answer. No, sir; it was on Jackson's place.

Question. Did you ever hear or know of negroes being run off from May's place?

Answer. Yes, sir. I heard of there being some negroes settled in the woods, on some land belonging to Mr. May.

Question. Did you ever hear of Bully Jack being killed?

Answer. Yes, sir.

Question. Did you hear that he was killed by the Ku-Klux?

Answer. No, sir; I don't know anything about it whatever; it's away down in the lower part of the county.

Question. Who did you hear killed him?

Answer. I never heard anybody suspected; never heard any more than that he was killed; that is all.

Question. Did you understand that these women were whipped and white men preached to on the same night that Sam Coger was shot?

Answer. No, sir, it was not the same night, or at least I don't think it was.

Question. Did you hear of any women being whipped on the same night Coger was shot?

Answer. I did not.

Question. Do you know Bill Coleman, a negro?

Answer. No, sir.

Question. Did you ever hear of his being whipped?

Answer. No, sir; I don't know that I ever heard of him before.

Question. Did you ever hear of Johnson Kitt being killed?

Answer. No, sir. Where did that happen—in what part of the county?

Mr. BLAIR. That was in Winston County.

The WITNESS. I reckon it was; I never heard of it here.

By the CHAIRMAN:

Question. In what part of the county do you live?

Answer. At Brooksville, in the north end of the county.

Question. You are very well acquainted over the country generally?

Answer. No, sir. I have been a planter all my life, and have always tried to attend to my own business, and let other people alone. My personal acquaintance is not extensive.

Question. Do you live near the Alabama line?

Answer. No, sir; twelve or fifteen miles from it.

Question. What county is opposite to you?

Answer. Pickens.

Question. Did you ever hear of any disturbance over there?

Answer. Nothing more than this Bridges case you have been investigating, I suppose.

Question. You never heard of any Ku-Klux disturbances over there?

Answer. No, sir; I have heard of rumors flying through the country, but nothing reliable that I could tell.

Question. You never gave any credit to these rumors about Ku-Klux?

Answer. I never did.

Question. You do not believe that there is any such organization as the Ku-Klux?

Answer. If there is, I have no knowledge of it.

Question. You do not believe there is?

Answer. I don't believe there is, if I was to swear. From what I know, I do not believe there is.

Question. Do you believe there ever was?

Answer. There may have been; I wouldn't swear positively that there had not been.

Question. What makes you think there has been such an organization?

Answer. Just from these little depredations. I don't know what you would term a Ku-Klux organization.

Question. What "little depredations?"

Answer. That one you have been interrogating me about of Sam Coker, and that of Dick Malone, &c. I don't think a man just in cold blood, with his right mind about him, would go in the hour of night and interfere with a man that way.

Question. Still they did interfere with Coger, and they did interfere with Dick Malone?

Answer. Yes, sir.

Question. So the thing is possible for bad men to do these things under cover of night?

Answer. Yes, sir.

Question. It would not be any worse to do it under cover of masks or disguises?

Answer. I suppose not.

Question. Then it is not improbable that bad men disguised themselves to commit felonious acts and keep from detection?

Answer. I think so.

Question. Then you think it is highly reasonable that men should commit depredations at night, disguising themselves to avoid detection?

Answer. Yes, sir.

Question. Then you think these reports, to that extent, have had foundation?

Answer. I think so.

Question. Do you think they have all stopped?

Answer. I think so.

Question. How long since Sam Coger was shot at?

Answer. In May, I think.

Question. Do you think they all stopped suddenly with that case of Sam Coker?

Answer. I have never heard of anything since.

Question. When was Dick Malone killed?

Answer. Some time before that, early.

Question. Is what induces you to think they have stopped their outrages because you have not heard of anything since?

Answer. A man will judge from circumstances. I hear no rumors of the sort.

Question. You never have seen any people in disguise yourself?

Answer. I never have.

Question. Have you ever talked with anybody that had?

Answer. I saw one man ride through the streets of Brooksville; I don't know whether it was a man or woman. It happened in the latter part of the winter or fore part of last spring. There was a kind of anticipated riot expected there between the negroes and whites. The negroes did mask themselves, or assembled there altogether by the hundred, but it was stopped without any great damage being done.

Question. You saw the negroes mask themselves?

Answer. No, sir; they collected there, and I reckon it was a week or ten days after that passed off, that I was standing on the sidewalk one night, and saw something on a horse pass through the streets. It looked like it might have had a sheet, or something laid over it. I didn't attack it or ask what it was. It just went on from there. It said nothing, and I said nothing. That was the last I saw of it.

Question. Was there a sheet over the horse?

Answer. Yes, sir; a something around him or over.

Question. Was there anything over his face?

Answer. Not that I could tell.

Question. Had he a hat on?

Answer. Yes, sir.

Question. Did not the people call him a Ku-Klux?

Answer. No, sir; there was only me and one or two others saw it. We didn't call it anything. It just passed on. It is the only disguised animal, man or beast, I have ever seen.

Question. He was a solitary horseman enjoying a moonlight ride?

Answer. I don't know what you might call him; he was moving along.

Question. You did not know whence he came or whither he went?

Answer. No, sir; that is so.

Question. Did you ever talk with anybody who had seen or professed to have seen any of those disguised men?

Answer. I never did, sir.

Question. You stay at home, I suppose, and attend to your own business, and do not go abroad much?

Answer. That is it; I stay at home and let other people alone.

By Mr. Rice:

Question. When did the news come to Brooksville that Sam Coger was killed?

Answer. The next morning early. It came that night, before morning. The doctor was sent for immediately. He went forthwith when he was sent for.

MACON, MISSISSIPPI, *November* 8, 1871.

ELISHA DISMUKES sworn and examined.

The CHAIRMAN. As this witness is called by the minority, General Blair will please examine him.

By Mr. BLAIR:

Question. Please state your residence and occupation.

Answer. I am a resident of Macon; by profession a lawyer.

Question. Do you know Mr. Allgood?

Answer. I do, sir.

Question. Was he in the confederate army?

Answer. He was, sir.

Question. Has he ever had his disabilities removed?

Answer. Not that I know of.

Question. Has he ever taken the iron-clad oath?

Answer. He has.

Question. How often?

Answer. Three times, to my knowledge.

Question. What was the iron-clad oath?

Answer. I cannot repeat it, sir.

Question. State the sum of it; the substance of it.

Answer. I can give you the way that I have read it repeatedly. It is the iron-clad oath that he has neither aided in the war nor afforded, as I understand it, any assistance or comfort to those who did.

Question. Was he a volunteer in the army?

Answer. He was a volunteer; I saw him volunteer.

Question. Not a conscript?

Answer. Not a conscript, sir.

Question. What was his occupation before the war?

Answer. A negro-trader, for years.

Question. The lieutenant governor of this State, Colonel Powers, was before this committee this morning, and gave an account of a visit to his place in Kemper County by a number of persons, one of whom was killed. He stated that they were disguised, and had come with a view of killing a negro, he supposed. His testimony is: "A body of men came to my plantation in Kemper County; took a man with the apparent intention of murdering him. They fired into the manager's sleeping-room on the place; burst in the room. One of their own men was shot and killed, and they left without any further violence. They were mounted and disguised; left two of their disguises. George Evans was the name of the young man killed." I wish you to state to the committee whether you ever heard Lieutenant Governor Powers give an account of that case.

Answer. I have, sir.

Question. State the account he gave and the circumstances, and where he told you.

Answer. It was in this town, in the sheriff's office, in this court-house. Lieutenant Governor Powers was at Jackson at the time of that occurrence. He came home, coming by his plantation, which is south of this place. After visiting his plantation he came to town. I called his attention to the matter, and asked him what had occurred. He said there had been a set of drunken, rowdy fellows there in that neighborhood; drunken men that had gone there for that purpose, and in their melee they had shot one another; that is, they had shot one of their own crowd and left; that there was no harm done; and I asked if they were Ku-Klux. He said if they were he did not know it; that they were drunken men. He said that they were young men of the community that were drinking, and went there on an expedition of that kind for fun and humor.

Question. Did you ask him whether they were disguised?

Answer. I did not.

Question. Did he say?

Answer. I do not think he said that they were disguised, or anything else, but that they were just a set of drinking men in the neighborhood, and that they knew who they were.

Question. Did he say they were young men?

Answer. Yes, sir; he said that drinking men, young men, had got on a general bender.

Question. His statement about it here was, that they were disguised, and took a negro out with the evident intent of murdering him.

Answer. My understanding was that they did not take anybody out, because there was nobody murdered; nobody killed but one, the young man. One young man was killed in the company, and that ended the affair, and the young man was carried off by their company. This young man who was killed was one of their own company.

Question. That is his statement here, too, that a young man of their company was killed, after they had fired into the manager's house.

Answer. I never heard of that before.

Question. What did he state to you about that? Did he state that they had fired into the house before this man was killed?

Answer. I never heard of it before; if they did, he never told me any such thing, and that is not my understanding of the matter.

Question. You say Governor Powers had been on the place?

Answer. No, sir; Governor Powers was in the city of Jackson when this occurrence took place, and he was telegraphed to come home—that there was a disturbance on his plantation, in the edge of Kemper, and he came home; and coming from Jackson he came by there, and then came home here, and after he arrived here I sought this information from him, because we all had an anxiety to know what had occurred there and to learn from him. I thought I would get the exact manner in which the thing occurred; therefore I called upon him and asked him, and he told me it was a set of rowdy drunken young men who had got on a spree, and had gone down there for some purpose, he didn't know what; that they were shooting among themselves in some way, and one of their men got shot and killed. I asked him distinctly, were they Ku-Klux? "No," said he, "it wasn't Ku-Klux in my opinion at all; it was simply a set of men that were drunk, and that owed him no harm, nor anybody else that he knew," and we passed it over just as one of these occurrences which transpire in life.

Question. Do you know anything about a man being killed at Craker's?

Answer. Which Craker's?

Question. The name is Craker.

Answer. Yes, sir; it is Peter Craker.

Question. What were the circumstances under which he was killed?

Answer. I only know the circumstances from the testimony of witnesses brought before me.

By the CHAIRMAN:

Question. Brought before you as a justice of the peace?

Answer. No, sir, brought before me in the prosecution of the coroner's inquest.

Question. Were you the coroner?

Answer. No, sir; I was prosecuting attorney on the part of the State. They were brought before me in that capacity. I heard the witnesses and took down the testimony. All their testimony is a matter of record in the county to-day. That is all I know in relation to it.

By Mr. BLAIR:

Question. State the purport of the testimony.

Answer. The purport of the testimony is this: About half an hour before day, on a certain morning, which morning I cannot now recollect, but it was some two or three months ago, three men and a boy came up to this freedman's house just as he walked out in his lot, and gathered him and carried him off. He was carried about three-quarters of a mile, or may be a mile from the place where he was first, and hung and shot. His body was taken down and carried about three hundred yards from the place of his hanging, and then buried in the bottom of a creek; that was done on a Saturday morning. On the Wednesday following he was found by the sheriff of Noxubee County, with his *posse.* I think it was Wednesday; it may have been Tuesday his grave was found. He was disinterred and taken up, and a coroner's inquest held over him. Upon that inquest, or inquiry by the coroner no one could give any account why he was killed. The inquest sat some three or four days, and no one could give any reason. He was said by all the witnesses to have been an orderly, quiet, peaceable citizen. On the third day of the inquiry, there were some witnesses brought before the court, of whom I asked the question, if they knew of any reason why this man was killed. They, at that inquiry, hesitated. The court informed them that they must give an answer to my question. The witness stated that it was on this account; that there was a young lady, whose name I will not call, who was on undue terms of intimacy with two Mr. Richards—a Mr. Richards, a neighbor, living in the vicinity—and that this boy, a day or two before this killing took place, had caught them in the forest cohabiting, and that he was killed because of his detecting them in order to prevent exposure. As soon as that fact was developed before the court, I caused the coroner, on the part of the State, to issue a warrant for the arrest of these men. The sheriff was sent immediately, and these two men had fled the country. These two men's name was Richards; they were brothers. One brother was the man who had been accused, whom the witness stated had been cohabiting with this lady, and a brother-in-law of Mr. Montgomery. I had a warrant issued for the arrest of all three of them. They were identified as being the parties who took the negro away from the house. When the sheriff with his warrant repaired to that neighborhood, they were gone, and they have not been heard of since, that I know of.

Question. This violence, then, to the negro, arose entirely out of the fact you have stated?

Answer. Entirely so, sir. We had before that jury the entire neighborhood, both white and black. I suppose maybe thirty or forty persons were brought before them; none of them knew of any cause until this account came up.

Question. Was this testimony confirmed by the statements of others?

Answer. It was; it was confirmed by others in this way. They stated that there had been an undue intimacy between that woman and certain other men for years previous, but had been concealed.

Question. How long have you lived in this county, Mr. Dismukes?

Answer. I have lived here since 1834.

Question. Are you pretty well acquainted with this and adjoining counties?

Answer. I am, sir.

Question. Do you practice in them?

Answer. I practice in all the adjoining counties.

Question. What is the present condition of this and adjoining counties, as far as concerns the observance and execution of law, and the maintenance of peace and quiet?

Answer. My opinion is, sir, that there is a disposition on the part of the community at large to observe law and order everywhere. There are, however, disturbances. There are bad men in all communities who violate law, but the general disposition here is to law and order, and the great anxiety of the people is that we shall have peace and quietude in our community.

Question. Have you known of any disposition or any instance of an attempt to intimidate the negroes in this or any of the adjoining counties?

Answer. None whatever, by any man, but, on the contrary, the reverse.

Question. Is there any disposition to interfere with their right to vote?

Answer. None on earth; only as I have been informed to-day at the recent election; I do not know this of my own knowledge, but if I am permitted to state it, I will state it.

Question. If you have any information that you rely upon, state it.

Answer. I never have known before that there was a disposition of the kind evinced. On yesterday, at a very important precinct in the county east of this, men with clubs in their hands required others, before they should go to the polls, to show their tickets, to show who they were voting for, and if they did not vote the ticket that they wanted them to, they would make them go back and get others.

Question. What men were these?

Answer. Their names I cannot call. Mr. ———, I cannot think of his name, informed me not two hours ago, that at Cliftonville there were a set of men who required a certain ticket to be voted, and that if the voters did not vote it, they should not vote at all. Dr. Clay informed me of that to-day. I do not know of myself that it is so. He said that they made them show their tickets before they could vote.

Question. Who were the men that required this?

Answer. It was done by two freedmen; I think Mr. Jeffreys and Mr. Lewis stated the fact emphatically. I may be mistaken in the name.

Question. Were those black men?

Answer. Black men.

Question. That had clubs in their hands?

Answer. Yes, sir; and when black men approached the box, if they did not have a certain ticket, they would not let them vote without it. There was an arrangement made by the managers of the election that only so many should enter in a file, and pass to the ballot-box by ropes stretched up, and two men were placed there to keep them off; two freedmen were placed there, and as they came up, they made the freedman show his ticket, and if he was not going to vote their ticket, they made him go back and get another one; a ticket with a peculiar mark upon it; some device at the head of the ticket. That is the only interference in election I think I have ever known in the county of Noxubee.

Question. There has been testimony before this committee, that of the lieutenant governor to-day, that in Winston County the negroes were intimidated and driven from the polls.

Answer. I never have heard of such a thing.

Question. He did not say driven from the polls; he said they were so intimidated that they would not go out to public meetings.

Answer. I cannot think such a thing as that occurred. I know the people of Winston well. I cannot think any such thing occurred. I never heard such a thing before. I am astonished that any gentleman would make that remark.

Question. Are there many negroes in that county?

Answer. Not a great many. It is a poor county in lands. It is not a country where a negro population has been congregated hitherto.

Question. Not enough to make it any object to drive them from the polls?

Answer. None in the world, because the whites outnumber them largely.

By the CHAIRMAN:

Question. Do the whites all vote the democratic ticket in Winston County?

Answer. No, sir.

Question. Then a part of the whites there vote with the negroes?

Answer. They do, and here also.

Question. Which party has the majority in Winston County?

Answer. I cannot say, for I do not remember now how they stand; my impression is that the democratic party, or the white party, you may call it what you please, have the majority. I am not certain on that point.

Question. Are they pretty nearly balanced?

Answer. Well, I think the whites have the majority.

Question. At all events, so nearly balanced that political or moral suasion is employed, I suppose, to produce a majority at the election?

Answer. I suppose so, sir.

Question. You know nothing about the use of these clubs at Cliftonville yourself?

Answer. No, sir; I did not see them.

Question. Did you understand that those two men were policemen?

Answer. Policemen that were appointed to stand and only let in men. It seems that there were, as I understand it, ropes stretched up, and they were only to let in men as they would mount to the polls.

Question. You had policemen here at the door, did you not?

Answer. Yes, sir.

Question. And they all had clubs?

Answer. Not a one.

Question. Did you not see the short policemen's clubs?

Answer. O, yes; the policemen always have them.

Question. They were about the polls yesterday?

Answer. Yes, sir.

Question. If it was competent for a policeman, at any time, to carry a club, it would be competent for a policeman at an election to keep a club?

Answer. Most assuredly.

Question. You say you are acquainted in Winston County. Have you ever heard of any colored school-houses or churches being burned there?

Answer. I have, but I cannot locate them. I have heard of several being burned; several houses and churches, and gin-houses, and private residences.

Question. I was asking only as to the colored churches and schools. You need not argue, but simply answer my questions. General Blair will call out all those things which you seem desirous of putting on record.

Answer. Not at all.

Mr. BLAIR. The Senator does not want to hear that.

WITNESS. I supposed his question comprehended all the burning?

By the CHAIRMAN:

Question I want a response to my questions, and General Blair will attend fully to the other side.

Answer. I will do it promptly, colonel.

Question. Have you heard of school-houses or churches being burned?

Answer. I have heard of a church being burned.

Question. How many school-houses have you heard of as having been burned?

Answer. I have heard of two.

Question. Have you heard of any colored school-houses being broken up?

Answer. Not that I know of.

Question. Have you ever heard of colored teachers being warned off in Winston County?

Answer. Not one.

Question. Have you in this county?

Answer. No, sir.

Question. Have you heard of Peter Cooper's school being broken up?

Answer. No, sir; never.

Question. Did you hear of Robbin Coleman being whipped in Winston County?

Answer. Never.

Question. Did you hear of a man named Gladney being whipped?

Answer. Never.

Question. Did you ever hear of a man named McMillan being shot at?

Answer. No, sir.

Question. Or a man named Nathan Cannon being whipped?

Answer. No, sir; never.

Question. Of a man named Allen Bird being killed in jail in Winston County?

Answer. Yes, sir.

Question. State the particulars.

Answer. I do not know any particulars about it. My understanding is that he was killed in jail. I am not certain about the name; it may be that name; I cannot call names. I have understood that there was a man in the jail in Louisville, in Winston County, and that a set of men went there, demanded the keys of the jailer, and did kill him in the jail. That is all I know about it.

Question. When did that occur?

Answer. Some time this year, I think, sir; I paid little attention to it. That was one of the occurrences that pass before us.

Question. Did you understand whether they were disguised men?

Answer. I did not, sir.

Question. Did you hear of Mordecai Mitchell being whipped?

Answer. I did not, sir. Now, colonel, I may have heard of all these whippings you allude to, but if so, they have passed out of my mind.

Question. Is Webster in Winston County?

Answer. It is, sir.

Question. Did you ever hear of a colored man being killed at Webster, or about there?

Answer. Yes, sir; I think I did, but the circumstances under which he was killed I cannot recollect. It is a very peculiar neighborhood; the neighborhood of Webster is peculiar.

Question. In what respect?

Answer. Well, they are men that manage their own affairs.

Question. They do not resort to such small affairs as the courts to settle their difficulties; is that your idea?

Answer. No. They are willing to do it when the courts can afford them relief, but when the courts cannot, they afford themselves relief.

Question. What grievances have they in that community that the courts are not competent to grapple with?

Answer. None that I know of, sir.

Question. What are the peculiar grievances at Webster that the courts are not competent to adjust?

Answer. I do not know of any, personally.

Question. What was said about the grievances that demanded redress by the Ku-Klux?

Answer. I do not know of anything.

Question. Did you understand why this man was killed?

Answer. I did not.

Question. You spoke about a peculiar state of things existing there; explain what you meant?

Answer. There is a peculiar state of things existing there. There was a number of men at Webster, and in that region, who were opposed to this late war. They were men that conducted themselves during the war in a manner that attracted attention. They would not go to the war, and they had to be made to go.

Question. They were conscripted?

Answer. Yes, sir.

Question. They did not like it. Is that the only peculiarity?

Answer. The only peculiarity.

Question. That conduct, then, did not meet much favor?

Answer. Not much, sir, with the good people of the country; it does not meet with any favor from the good people of the country yet.

Question. The good people of the country think everybody that was able ought to have turned out and gone to the war?

Answer. Certainly they do, sir.

Question. And that man is under the ban of public displeasure who was able to go to the war and refused to go until he was conscripted?

Answer. He would be with me, sir.

Question. Did you go yourself?

Answer. No, sir; I did not. I did not go to the field; I was in another position.

Question. Why are you so intolerant with those who staid at home like yourself?

Answer. I am not intolerant with them. I think every man ought to have done his duty to his country.

Question. I understood you to say that such men were out of favor with you, who, being able to go to the war, refused to go until they were conscripted.

Answer. That is true; because they should have done their duty if they remained in the country. A man should obey the laws of his country; as I am now in favor of every man's doing his duty toward his country as it stands.

Question. Then you thought it was every man's duty to fight against his Government?

Answer. No, sir.

Question. Against the Government of the United States?

Answer. Then the Government had seceded and gone away from it, and they were here and could not do otherwise

Question. And therefore it was their duty, willingly or unwillingly, to fight against the Government of the United States?

Answer. I was opposed to the war, worked against it, fought against it, from the beginning to its end.

Question. Why did you not make your way North, then, and join the Federal Army?

Answer. Because I could not. All my interest was here; I had my family here to protect. That is the reason I did not do it.

Question. What position did you hold in the army?

Answer. I held the position of a quartermaster, in the quartermaster's department, but was opposed to the war from beginning to the end.

Question. Did you make your sentiments known?

Answer. I did before the war opened.

Question. But after the war commenced?

Answer. After the war commenced, I joined in with it, because my destiny was there.

Question. You did not go into it with any heart at all?

Answer. I went into it because of the circumstances which surrounded me; my family, my property, my all was here.

Question. But I still understand you to blame all these men who refused to volunteer?

Answer. I blame all those men who were in favor of war, who advocated the war, urged it, pressed it upon me, and then refused to go to it. That class of men I blame.

Question. Was that the case with the men about Webster?

Answer. I think so.

Question. You think they were active in bringing on the war, and then skulked?

Answer. And then skulked. Now you have my idea.

Question. You have heard of a good many outrages in Winston County inflicted upon colored people?

Answer. Yes, sir; but it has passed before me; I paid little attention to it.

Question. I am not asking for your feelings.

Answer. I paid no attention to it; that gives you a reason why I cannot recollect.

Question. But you have a general knowledge that there have been, from first to last, a good many disturbances there?

Answer. Certainly there have been.

Question. How is it as to this county in which you live, Noxubee?

Answer. There never has been any in this county, to my knowledge; in this county we have had no disturbances, except one at Brooksville; it was some time last year, I cannot state exactly the time.

Question. What case do you refer to; who was killed?

Answer. No one was killed. I refer to a riot at Brooksville. I then lived at my plantation two or three miles from Brooksville. A young gentleman by the name of Farmer had an altercation with a freedman in the town of Brooksville.

Question. We have had a full account of that; I will not trouble you to repeat it.

Answer. That is the only disturbance I know of that has ever occurred between the black and white races in Noxubee County.

Question. Did you ever hear of the case of Solomon Triplett, who was shot in Winston County?

Answer. I cannot recollect it. I do not recollect names. I have heard of several men; I cannot recollect the names nor the circumstances under which they were killed.

Question. Have you heard of the case of Dick Malone.

Answer. Yes, sir; that was in this county.

Question. You have heard of the case of Bully Jack?

Answer. Yes, sir; I have.

Question. Both those men were killed?

Answer. So it was stated before the courts. In both cases there were trials here, in which I participated, either in the defense or prosecution.

Question. Have you heard of the case of Isham Lowry, who was whipped?

Answer. Where?

Question. In Noxubee County.

Answer. I have not, that I can recollect now.

By Mr. BLAIR:

Question. It was on the same plantation on which Dick Malone was shot, and on the same night.

Answer. I do not know anything of that. I did not hear of that. I know when Dick Malone was shot; nobody was whipped that night, according to the testimony before the court. I attended the trial in that case.

By the CHAIRMAN:

Question. Have you heard of Bill Coleman being whipped in Winston County?

Answer. No, sir; I do not recollect it.

Question. Have you heard of Johnson Kitt being killed?

Answer. Where?

Question. That was in Winston County.
Answer. I could not tell you.
Question. I believe I have asked you about Sol Triplett, and you have not heard of that?
Answer. No, sir; I have heard of several being killed there, but I do not know their names.
Question. Have you heard of any colored women being taken out and whipped for living in a state of fornication with white men?
Answer. I have.
Question. Did you hear that the white men were whipped too?
Answer. Yes, sir.
Question. That justice was impartially administered to both?
Answer. Impartially administered to both; impartially.
Question. How many have you understood there were, sir?
Answer. I have understood that there were two cases of that kind in this county. I understand that there was a white man whipped for living in fornication and adultery with a negro woman, now in town here, and a man named Jackson. I have heard of that; I don't know whether it is true or not.
Question. Have you heard of the case of Mr. Wissler, who was murdered here in town a week since?
Answer. I was in Selma, Alabama, at the time of his murder. I have heard of it since I came here, which was when you did.
Question. Have you heard of a boy who had been committed by Squire Rice, and who was put in charge of a deputy constable by the name of Bridges, and then disappeared very mysteriously?
Answer. I have.
Question. In view of all these facts, do you say that the laws are well administered here, and adequate protection given to life and person?
Answer. I do, sir.
Question. Have you ever known that any man has been brought to justice for any of these murders?
Answer. Which murders; those in Winston County?
Question. Yes, sir; or for any that occurred in this county?
Answer. Yes, sir; I have known them to be investigated before the grand juries of the country, and the grand juries have brought in no bills of indictment that I know of.
Question. The point I wish distinctly to make is, whether any man, disguised or otherwise, has been punished for any of the various whippings or murders of colored people in this, or Winston County?
Answer. Yes, sir; I know of two men. In 1866, the latter part of 1866, or in 1867, there were two men brought before the court-martial here for whipping an old negro man up near Brooksville, and they plead guilty to the fact and were fined heavily. That was in the latter part of 1866, or in 1867.
Question. Have you heard of any punishment inflicted since that time upon persons guilty of outrages upon colored people?
Answer. Frequently, sir; it is done in the courts of the country—every court that passes.
Question. Give the committee an instance.
Answer. I could not do it without the records.
Question. I mean where outrage has been inflicted, under cover of night, by bodies of men.
Answer. O, no.
Question. My question refers to parties banded together.
Answer. Nothing of that, sir; because it has never occurred in the county, that I know of. There has never been such a thing brought before the courts, that I know of.
Question. You never have heard of a case in which outrage was inflicted upon negroes by bands of men in the night-time?
Answer. No, sir; there has never been such a thing punished in this county, that I know of.
Question. Do you mean that such punishment has escaped your recollection?
Answer. No, sir; but there has been no such case brought before the courts of the county, that I recollect of. There may have been, but if it has, it has escaped my recollection.
Question. Do you mean to be understood as saying that, if outrages of the kind I have described have occurred, they have not been brought into the courts?
Answer. They have not, as far as I recollect.
Question. Then, of course, they are not punished?
Answer. Not punished, of course. I know of none at present.
Question. You were notified before you came before this committee this afternoon of what Lieutenant Governor Powers testified here?
Answer. Yes, sir.

Question. Who told you?
Answer. I read it from the minutes of the meeting.
Mr. BLAIR. I told him.

By the CHAIRMAN:

Question. They were furnished to you?
Answer. Yes, sir; they were furnished to me.
Question. How long after this affair, which occurred in Kemper County, on the plantation of Lieutenant Governor Powers, was it before you had this conversation with him?
Answer. Let me see. Governor Powers was in Jackson at the time of the occurrence; he was telegraphed, and, I think, as he told me, he came home immediately, and came to the point of Scooba, on the railroad, and went out to his plantation, and returned here as quickly as he could go there. It was but a few days afterward when I had the conversation with Governor Powers, and he told me this was a drunken set of men that went there just on a general bust.
Question. Was he then speaking of this affair on his plantation in Kemper?
Answer. He was, because I asked him the question direct.
Question. Did you say he said nothing in that conversation about their taking out a colored man?
Answer. I did not.
Question. From his house?
Answer. No, sir; I know the great idea was—my inquiry led to this—to ascertain whether it was an organized band of Ku-Klux that did it.
Question. Your mind was fixed upon that?
Answer. My mind was fixed upon it. I was interrogating him upon that point, and his idea then conveyed to me was, that it was not, but it was a set of drunken men in the neighborhood.
Question. Did you note all the particulars of this conversation at the time?
Answer. No; I did not. That was the main point I wanted to inquire of.
Question. You will not undertake to give all the details of his conversation now?
Answer. No, sir; not a bit, only that that was the impression created in my mind, that it was a set of drunken men on a riot or row, who went down for some purpose, I don't know what, but that there was no harm done by them.
Question. May he not have said that there was a colored man taken out of his house?
Answer. He may have said it.
Question. Did he say anything about this party firing on his superintendent?
Answer. He did not that I recollect. If he had, I think it would have struck my mind so that I would have noted it. I don't think he did.
Question. Did he tell you how large a party of young men were there?
Answer. He did not; he said a party of young men.
Question. Did he say in the night-time?
Answer. He said in the night-time, as he was informed.
Question. How large a party?
Answer. He did not say; I do not understand at present what the number was; it was a party of young men.
Question. Did you get the impression that there were a dozen or fifteen?
Answer. I would have supposed ten or twelve; that was my idea; I am confident that he mentioned no number.
Question. Did he tell you the name of the young man shot?
Answer. He did, but the name I cannot recollect now. I know it; he was from the high country. I think the name was Adams, or Edwards.
Question. Was it George Evans?
Answer. Evans; perhaps it was.
Question. Did you understand that this party left any disguises there that were picked up?
Answer. None on earth, until I read it in Colonel Powers's testimony to-day; I never heard of it before.
Question. Was George Evans a respectable young man?
Answer. So he was reported to me.
Question. Did he belong to a respectable family?
Answer. An honorable and respectable family, I believe.
Question. Was there a public burial?
Answer. I do not know, sir.
Question. Did you know of any effort to cover up this affair on the part of his family or friends?
Answer. I did not; none whatever.
Question. Was the matter of general notoriety that George Evans was killed?
Answer. George Evans was killed; it was of general notoriety; the papers, I think, had it.

Question. What kind of fun, or frolic, was it supposed that these lot of youngsters were bent on that night?

Answer. I do not know.

Question. You have talked about a "bender;" what species of bender?

Answer. They just simply had a little too much whisky aboard.

Question. Did they have any pistols aboard, too?

Answer. I do not know; I was not there.

Question. Did you hear that they were armed?

Answer. I heard that they were shooting, and they could not shoot without pistols or guns.

Question. How much shooting did you understand there was?

Answer. I do not remember now.

Question. Did you understand that there was more than one shot fired?

Answer. Yes, sir; several shots, I suppose.

Question. Why should these gentlemen, on an innocent frolic, or bender, shoot pistols?

Answer. I do not know, but it is a common occurrence with them.

Question. Why should they have selected this plantation as the scene of their bender?

Answer. I do not know.

Question. It was some distance from their homes?

Answer. I do not know where their homes were.

Question. It was some distance from George Evans's home?

Answer. I do not know where he lived. I know there are some Evanses live in that part of the county.

Question. What induces you to believe that they were a set of innocent young men on a frolic?

Answer. I have no belief on the subject, only what Governor Powers stated to me; his opinion is mine.

Question. Did this thing make a stir in the community; did you never hear from anybody else about it?

Answer. Never. It was on Lieutenant Governor Powers's plantation; he wanted an investigation made, and came and told me it was all an innocent affair.

Question. Innocent?

Answer. When I say innocent, I do not mean that word in its strictest sense. I mean it was an affair got up by a set of young men that were on a drunken frolic, but my impression is that there was no intention to do anything wrong, only as drunken men will do, if you have ever seen them.

Question. Why should they have gone loaded with both pistols and whisky, if on an innocent errand?

Answer. Do not understand me as saying "on an innocent errand." I meant an innocent errand compared to what is supposed to be the object of Ku-Kluxing.

Question. You simply want to impress the committee with the idea that they were not on a Ku-Klux excursion?

Answer. Not a Ku-Klux excursion, according to Colonel Powers.

Question. What is a genuine Ku-Klux excursion, according to your idea?

Answer. My idea would be—I do not know anything about it; I never saw one. I never met up with one that I know of.

Question. Nobody in this country has ever seen one, but still I want your idea?

Answer. My idea is this: a Ku-Klux excursion would be where, if they had an opposition to you or me, or any man living here, they would come and take us out, and either whip us or kill us, or do something else that is pretty brash, or make us leave the country if they did not wish us in it.

Question. Would they come disguised?

Answer. I reckon they would, if they went on that errand.

Question. That would be human nature?

Answer. Well, candidly, I think it would, colonel.

Question. You have heard of such fellows about the country?

Answer. I have heard, and so have you; we have all heard it; the papers have teemed with it for three or four years.

Question. What is your belief on that subject?

Answer. Honestly, my belief is that there is not a Ku-Klux organization in Mississippi.

Question. Do you think there ever has been one?

Answer. I do not know; if there has, it has never come under my observation. I have been a man that has mixed with the world a good deal, and seen a good deal.

Question. What is your opinion on the subject?

Answer. About Ku-Klux?

Question. Yes, sir.

Answer. I have no opinion. I do not think the thing has existed here. Now, there are organizations, I have no question.

Question. You believe the Loyal League existed here?

Answer. I do; I think they brought up the other.

Question. You think the Loyal League brought up the Ku-Klux League?

Answer. Yes, sir; if there be such a thing.

Question. If there be such a thing as a Loyal League, you think there may be such a thing as a Ku-Klux-Klan?

Answer. I know one thing: there was such a thing existing as an organized body, and they called themselves Loyal Leaguers.

Question. Were you ever in their council-chamber?

Answer. Never on earth.

Question. Did you ever see their parades?

Answer. Never. I have seen them muster here with banners and badges, and parade the streets.

Question. Did you ever hear their oath or obligation?

Answer. I have read it, but I could not tell what it is.

Question. Are you now speaking of the Loyal Leaguers?

Answer. Yes, sir.

Question. Did you understand that they contemplated violence or mischief?

Answer. From the oath, my idea was, and from what I have seen and heard, that it was an eternal, everlasting opposition to white men and the white race; that, in other words, the bottom rail had got on top, and they were going to keep it there.

Question. The opposition to the white race was to be both eternal and everlasting?

Answer. Yes, sir.

Question. That would last a good while?

Answer. Yes, sir; there is an abundance of meaning in "everlasting."

Question. Did you ever hear that this Ku-Klux Klan was got up to put these Loyal Leaguers down?

Answer. Of course, if there was any such thing, that was the object. It was to counterbalance, not to put them down; it was to meet them at their own game.

Question. What were they to do with them?

Answer. Just whatever was necessary in order to put them down, to stop that, to prevent hatred, to prevent a disposition on the part of one race against the other, to prevent opposition on the part of one race to the other.

Question. And likewise to promote the success of the democratic party?

Answer. No, sir; not exactly.

Question. Was it to promote the success of the radical party?

Answer. No, sir; it was to promote justice and right.

Question. And peace and good order?

Answer. Peace and good order among men, when the laws could not take hold of it.

Question. Then in the interest of peace and good order they were to whip, kill, and murder, were they?

Answer. Just as far as the others went, they were to prevent any innovation on peace and good order by the opposite party.

Question. When the Loyal Leaguers stopped they would stop?

Answer. Of course, when that thing was at an end there was no use for the Ku-Klux.

Question. Suppose the Loyal Leagues did not kill, were the Ku-Klux to kill?

Answer. I don't know; I suppose not; I don't know what their purposes and mark were; I am not a Ku-Klux; I don't believe in the order; I do not believe in anything of the sort; I am a peace and order man.

Question. You never saw nor read the obligation of the Ku-Klux?

Answer. Yes, sir; I have read in the newspapers what all of us have seen; I have seen divers and sundry things published about them; I do not know whether they were true or not.

Question. I understood you to state that one of their obligations was to oppose the designs of the radical party?

Answer. No, sir; to oppose the designs of the Loyal Leaguers, who had sworn vengeance and eternal hatred to the white man and his race, and to put themselves above the white man.

Question. Do you think any Loyal Leaguers were sworn to do that?

Answer. I do not know; I couldn't tell you. I told you I did not know, and how can I tell you what I said I do not know? You asked me a while ago what I supposed might be the object of these parties going out to Governor Powers's plantation. It might have been that they wanted to go there to get with the women.

Question. The colored women?

Answer. Yes, sir; it might have been that.

Question. Did you ever hear that stated as one of their objects?

Answer. No, sir, never; but you asked me my opinion.

Question. That is a surmise of your own?

Answer. Yes, sir; a surmise of my own. They might have been on such an excursion.

Question. Is that your opinion?

Answer. It might have been on that; I couldn't form an opinion; but it might have been.

Question. It is possible that they were after the colored women, and wanted to get at that overseer and whip him?

Answer. It might have been that, too.

Question. Did you understand that the overseer had shot at the men?

Answer. No, sir; Colonel Powers did not tell me that. All my information was from him.

Question. You understood that the young men had fired into each other?

Answer. No, sir; the idea was that it was an accidental shot; that some pistol or gun had gone off accidentally, and killed a young man accidentally. That is the way I know Colonel Powers stated it to me.

By Mr. BUCKLEY:

Question. Was Governor Powers under oath when he gave you this information?

Answer. No, sir; not at all; he was speaking as a citizen and acquaintance of mine, sir, telling me this. I asked him the question for information. I felt interested in the matter. It disturbed me when I heard it, and I called on Governor Powers when he came. He was a friend and acquaintance of mine, and he told me these facts.

By the CHAIRMAN:

Question. How long a time did he occupy in his statement to you?

Answer. It was just like a conversation that you and I might have, sitting down in my office.

Question. Five minutes?

Answer. Five or ten minutes, or maybe half an hour.

MACON, MISSISSIPPI, *November* 8, 1871.

MICHAEL A. METTS sworn and examined.

The CHAIRMAN. As this witness is called at the request of the minority, General Blair will please examine him.

By Mr. BLAIR:

Question. Please state your residence.

Answer. I live at Louisville, in Winston County.

Question. What is your occupation?

Answer. I am engaged principally in the mercantile business at the present time. I am also engaged in farming.

Question. You have been sheriff of that county?

Answer. Yes, sir; for a number of years.

Question. How long?

Answer. Since 1860, except a short interval of about fourteen months during that time.

Question. We had before us a negro boy, named William Coleman, the other day, who testified that he was the owner of a tract of three or four hundred acres of land there; that he had hogs, sheep, and a mule; that he had paid for this property, except a mule; that his brother was hired out to pay for that mule. Do you know anything about such a boy as William Coleman?

Answer. Yes, sir; I knew him there.

Question. Was he the owner of any land?

Answer. No, sir; he never owned a foot of land in his life.

Question. Did he own hogs and sheep?

Answer. I think it is likely he had a few hogs.

Question. Any sheep?

Answer. Not that I know of.

Question. Any mule?

Answer. There was a very indifferent mule on the place. I don't think he had paid for it.

Question. He stated that he also had a filly.

Answer. I don't think he had any filly, sir.

Question. He said that the Ku-Klux came to his house, and shot through the house; that he looked through a hole and saw the Ku-Klux. Did you hear anything about his having been visited, and shot at, and beaten by the Ku-Klux?

Answer. Yes, sir; I heard of a party in disguise having gone to his house and whipped him, and, as an officer, I went to see him the day or the second day afterward; it was, at least, a short time afterward; and I had a conversation with William Coleman myself. He evidently had been whipped, but he told me that there was no shooting; I questioned him very closely in regard to it; he said that there was no shooting; that they demanded entrance to his house; that he opened the door; that they would have broken his door down; and he opened it and came out, and they took him out to the road; he showed me where they took him, some forty or fifty yards, to a public road, and they whipped him there in that road.

Question. He says he was whipped because he was a radical and the owner of land.

Answer. Well, sir, he never owned any land, sir. As to his politics, I don't know what they are.

Question. What was he whipped for?

Answer. The general opinion in the neighborhood was, that he was whipped for stealing hogs.

Question. Was it known by whom he was whipped?

Answer. No, sir; it never was known there. He intimated to me that he knew two of the men—one a black man and the other a white man. He said that those two were all that he knew; that he didn't know but two that came.

Question. What was the white man's name?

Answer. He didn't tell me; I urged him to tell me that I might apply to the proper authorities to have the men arrested and tried for the offense. He would not do it.

Question. He gave the name of Coleman A. Carlisle?

Answer. Yes, sir; I know that man.

Question. What sort of a man is he?

Answer. A very quiet, clever, good citizen, living about fifteen miles from where William Coleman lived.

Question. He named Jim Boyd Hughes?

Answer. Jim Boyd Hughes is a black man, about two miles and a half from me in Louisville.

Question. Theodore Ellis?

Answer. I know Theodore Ellis; he lives about a mile from Coleman's house.

Question. Murray Ellis?

Answer. He lives in the neighborhood.

Question. Bog. Ellis?

Answer. He is a brother.

Question. Francis Ellis?

Answer. Another brother.

Question. He identified or named all these men before the committee?

Answer. He told me he only knew two—one a black man, and one a white man. I urged him strongly to tell me who they were; I thought it for the best interests of the country to have him do so, and to have the matter investigated before the court.

Question. And he would not tell?

Answer. No, sir; he would not.

Question. What reason did he give for not telling?

Answer. He just said he didn't want to tell me, and wouldn't tell; my idea was that he was not fully persuaded in his mind that he knew, and would not swear it.

Question. You say Hughes lives at Louisville?

Answer. Yes, sir.

Question. You say the impression is that Bill Coleman was whipped for stealing hogs?

Answer. Yes, sir; the general impression is that he was whipped for stealing hogs. On the west side of him is a very large neighborhood of colored persons, perhaps twenty families, who have bought land and are living there, conducting themselves very well; they are really doing very well; they accused him of stealing hogs, and the presumption was at the time that it was them. The white neighborhood on the east side of him also accused him of stealing hogs, and some thought it was done by these men on the east side of him; but that was altogether an opinion as to who did it.

Question. This man Hughes you know to be a negro?

Answer. Yes, sir; I know him very well; I saw him this morning, sir.

Question. Does Coleman Carlisle live in that neighborhood?

Answer. He lives fourteen or fifteen miles from there.

Question. Did you ever hear him say anything about this affair?

Answer. Nothing at all.

Question. Do you believe he was in this scrape in any way?

Answer. I have no idea that he knows anything about it. I could not see any reason why he should have done so; he is a long way off.

Question. In all probability the depredations were not committed on him?

Answer. No, sir; it could not have been so, because this man Coleman A. Carlisle lives on the extreme eastern side of the county, some fifteen miles from where Bill Coleman lived.

Question. He says that he knew them all, and that they lived right in his neighborhood. You say that Carlisle does not live in his neighborhood?

Answer. He does not. My acquaintance is thorough in that county. I know every man that has been in the county in a long time; every white man.

Question. Do you know anything about the whipping of Mordecai Mitchell?

Answer. Yes, sir.

Question. What was he whipped for, and by whom?

Answer. As to who did it is a question I never have been able to learn. I saw Mitchell the morning after he was whipped, and conversed with him.

Question. What did he say was the reason they whipped him?

Answer. He said they only asked him about a negro named Jim Hudson. The presumption was that he knew where Jim Hudson was, and the party that whipped him wanted him to disclose that fact.

Question. And whipped him for refusing to do it.

Answer. Yes, sir; they whipped him only fifteen or twenty licks. He told me himself it didn't hurt him. The object, he thought, was to scare him.

Question. Were they disguised?

Answer. He said they were.

Question. Do you know Robin Coleman?

Answer. Yes, sir.

Question. Was he whipped?

Answer. Yes, sir; he was said to have been. I conversed with Mr. Perkins, on whose plantation he lived, the next day, and investigated the thing.

Question. What did Perkins say he was whipped for?

Answer. He said he didn't know. He said he had no fault to find with him; that he was a very clever negro, and good worker.

Question. Were the men disguised.

Answer. Yes, sir.

Question. Do you know George Gladney?

Answer. Yes, sir.

Question. Was he whipped?

Answer. He was said to have been.

Question. By whom?

Answer. I don't know.

Question. Do you know a man by the name of Sam. McMillen?

Answer. Yes, sir.

Question. Did you ever hear of his being visited?

Answer. No, sir; George Gladney lived near him; they were working together this year.

Question. It is testified that McMillen shot at a party, and they shot at him.

Answer. I never heard of that before. I conversed with Mr. Perkins and Mr. David McMillen, a white man, with whom Sam. McMillen was working cultivating land.

Question. Did you ever hear of a negro being whipped for buying land there?

Answer. No, sir.

Question. Did a great many of them own land?

Answer. A great many; I have now a contract for selling a tract of land for fifteen hundred dollars to two freedmen; we encourage it.

Question. Do you know a black man named Nathan Cannon?

Answer. I did know him; he is not there now.

Question. Was he whipped last year?

Answer. Said to have been.

Question. What for?

Answer. I was not sheriff at that time; Mr. Hudson filled the office, and investigated that case, and I don't know much about it. My impression, my understanding, was that it was for some remarks he had made at a school that he was teaching; he was teaching a school at that time, and he gave some advice to his scholars in regard to their conduct that it was not thought proper for him to give; that is a mere rumor.

Question. Did you understand what that advice was?

Answer. The advice, or the substance of it, was, that they ought to conduct themselves in such a way as to throw themselves altogether on an equality with the white race, in every respect.

Question. Did you hear of the death of Sol. Triplett?

Answer. Yes, sir.

Question. Do you know anything about it; did you investigate it?

Answer. I did, sir; I went to the place where he lived the day after he died; I saw his wife, and conversed with her both publicly and privately; I visited her when I had company with me; and as I thought perhaps she might have objection to talking when others were along with me, I went back and had a private interview with her.

Question. Who did she say did it?

Answer. She said she did not know.

Question. What cause did she give?

Answer. She didn't know any cause; she was perfectly surprised at the act, and was at a loss to assign any reason for it at all. He seems to have been a negro of very good character in the neighborhood, and there was nothing that I could find alleged against him.

Question. It is stated by one witness here that he was killed by Jack Triplett's son; that he had had a quarrel with Jack Triplett with reference to some meat, and the man says Sol. Triplett's wife told him that she had sent the meat back to Jack Triplett's father; and that he was angry, and said he would get even with him.

Answer. I know Mr. Triplett and I know his son; they live in the neighborhood in which Sol. Triplett was killed; I urged upon Sol.'s wife the necessity of telling me, as an officer, if she knew who did it; and she told me emphatically she did not know.

By the CHAIRMAN:

Question. You say that Mrs. Triplett told you that?

Answer. No, sir; Sol. Triplett's wife.

By Mr. BLAIR:

Question. Do you know a man by the name of Bird, who was killed in jail?

Answer. Yes, sir.

Question. What was he killed for?

Answer. He was committed to jail for an attempt to commit a rape upon a white lady in the neighborhood of Louisville—a Miss Taylor—upon an indictment by the grand jury.

Question. Did you hear anything of Peter Cooper, who says he was keeping a colored school there, and was driven away?

Answer. Yes, sir; I knew Peter Cooper there; at the same time he was teaching a little school there; and a party of men visited our town, and the same party that whipped Mordecai Mitchell visited Peter Cooper that night, and he left there; they didn't find him; they didn't see him at all.

Question. They did not whip Peter?

Answer. No, sir; they never saw him.

Question. Did they take his money?

Answer. I understand they found his trunk. A negro man he was operating with told me they found his trunk, and just threw it on the fire.

Question. Threw his trunk on the fire?

Answer. Yes, sir. If they took his money, I don't know it. The opinion of the negro women was that the money got burned up.

Question. Do you know of any interference with the negroes voting there?

Answer. None in the world. I know emphatically, of my own knowledge, that they vote without any interference whatever, and vote as they please. They did it at the election yesterday, and do it upon all occasions. They have done it ever since the right of suffrage has been extended to them.

Question. There is a large number of white people who vote the radical ticket there?

Answer. Yes, sir; a good many.

Question. Did you ever hear that the colored people were so much alarmed at these Ku-Klux that they staid out of their houses at night and slept in the woods?

Answer. I have heard of a few instances of that kind; general. I think, on the plantation at Mr. Perkins's, last spring, they did that thing for perhaps a week; some of his hands did it. That is four miles above Louisville, on Mr. Reese Perkins's plantation.

Question. This boy stated that Mose Bird knocked this Jim Boyd Hughes with a rock, and that Mose was killed. Did you ever hear of Mose Bird being killed?

Answer. No, sir. Mose Bird absconded from three different indictments that are now pending against him. The last I heard of him he was in the southwest corner of the county; and he went from there, and his family say they don't know where he went.

Question. He is not supposed to be dead?

Answer. No, sir; he has simply run away.

Question. Did you hear of his knocking this Hughes with a brick?

Answer. Yes, sir; he was indicted for it.

Question. Hughes is also a colored man?

Answer. Yes, sir. What ran Mose Bird off was a *capias* was sent for him for stealing something in this town.

Question. Do you know a black man named Jesse Thomas, who was killed up there?

Answer. Jesse Thompson; I knew him once very well.

Question. Was he killed?

Answer. Yes, sir.

Question. By whom?

Answer. It is unknown. That happened several years ago, perhaps in 1865; I think in the latter part of that year, or the first part of 1866.

Question. Peter Cooper says he was killed for voting the republican ticket.

Answer. That is a great mistake.

Question. There was no radical party in the county then?

Answer. I don't think there was. I think he was killed before the right of suffrage was extended to colored men.

Question. Were the men that killed Allen Bird in jail disguised?

Answer. Yes, sir; so the jailer reported. That is his evidence before the jury of inquest.

Question. There is a great deal of testimony here upon the subject of burning school-houses; and one witness, the lieutenant governor of the State, stated on oath to-day that every colored school-house in the county was burned.

Answer. That is a mistake, sir.

By Mr. RICE:

Question. But one?

Answer. The history of the burning of school-houses in the county is this: there have been six burned up. I gave that matter considerable attention. The first one burned was in the southeast corner of the county. A school was being taught there by a man named Avery, who was very objectionable to the people as a teacher. The next house burned was a vacant house, and no school was being held in it at all.

By Mr. BUCKLEY:

Question. Had there been a school in it?

Answer. No, sir; not for some time.

Question. It had been used for a school-house?

Answer. Yes, sir, in time; it was regarded as a school-house, and also a place for preaching, but there was no school there at that time. Both of these were white school-houses. The next house burned was in the northwest corner of the county. I went up there and investigated that case immediately afterward, and saw some of the most prominent citizens. Three were burned in the northwest corner of the county; two were colored, and one white, taught by a very excellent young lady in the neighborhood, a daughter of one of our most prominent citizens. The first negro school-house burned was burned on Sunday, in open daylight.

By Mr. BLAIR:

Question. Who was it burned by?

Answer. No one knew for certain. The presumption in the neighborhood, from the best information I could get, was that it was done by one of the students, a colored boy, who had been dismissed from school by the teacher.

By the CHAIRMAN:

Question. Was that the one taught by Avery?

Answer. No, sir.

Question. It was one of those three schools in the northwest corner of the county?

Answer. Yes, sir. The first one burned there was thought to have been burned by a colored boy, who had been dismissed from the school, who took objections to having been dismissed. Whether this occurred or not I do not know. It is only an opinion.

By Mr. BLAIR:

Question. Is there great opposition to schools in that county?

Answer. There was, general, considerable opposition to the free-school law as it existed last spring when the subject first opened, and when they went first into operation there.

Question. What was the objection—the taxes?

Answer. Yes, sir; the objection originated from the idea that the taxes to support them would be so burdensome that the people could not stand them; that idea existed with most persons, and it seemed to be a general impression that if they could get shut of school-house, they would get shut of taxes.

Question. You say there are a good many white radicals up there?

Answer. Yes, sir.

Question. Do they, as well as the democrats, object to school-houses?

Answer. The same opinion seemed universal in regard to the taxes.

Question. Was there any action taken by the citizens in regard to it?

Answer. Yes, sir; and there has has not been a house burned since the 6th of April last, or about that time; we then called a meeting of citizens to express our regrets at such things occurring in the county. It was generally attended from every section of the county. The citizens condemned that course in public, and expressed their regret at it, and we have not had a school-house interrupted yet, nor a school in the county.

Question. Are there many schools in operation there now?

Answer. Not at this time; the fund has become exhausted; there are perhaps half a dozen going on in the county now, I do not know the exact number; but several in certain localities where they could not have schools last spring have preferred waiting until fall; they teach four or five months; the schools are going on now where they could not get a school last spring. There seems no opposition at all now by anybody.

Question. In reference to voting, you already have spoken, have you not, as to whether there was any intimidation?

Answer. Yes, sir; there is none in the world; I have never seen any. I have been a constant attendant on those occasions—often a candidate myself, and I have never seen the time nor place in Winston County but what any man, white or black, could vote as he pleased without intimidation from anybody.

Question. Governor Powers stated in his testimony to-day, that when he was up there the negroes did not turn out to his meeting, and he concluded from that that they were deterred by violence or threats of violence?

Answer. Governor Powers has been in our county this fall.

Question. I do not know whether he said it was this fall, but that he had been there.

Answer. We have not a great many there, but I have seen them there as many as could get into our court-house, often.

Question. You were there when Governor Powers spoke?

Answer. Yes, sir.

Question. Were many negroes there together?

Answer. A good many, but not such a crowd as I have seen there. I suppose Governor Powers got that idea from the fact that he was accustomed to seeing them by the thousands, and we have not got a great many there. I will give an instance. They had an appointment for the secretary of state to speak there, and there was a large number of negroes in town came out to hear him.

Question. This fall?

Answer. Not more than ten days ago; that was a Mr. Lynch; he failed to come, but my opponent and myself occupied the time; there was a large number of colored men out.

Question. That is all I desire to ask.

Answer. I wish to state this as a suggestion: while we have had a good many of these depredations in our county, it is true, yet we have not had any since the meeting of citizens I referred to last spring; everything has been very quiet since that time. As to the killing of Allen Bird in jail, as a public officer I gave the matter very strict attention, and I became convinced that no man was ever interfered with in the county in consequence of this political opinion.

By the CHAIRMAN:

Question. What murders, other than those you have named, have been committed in Winston County since the surrender?

Answer. Well, I don't know that I can mention them all.

Question. You have mentioned the cases of Jesse Thompson, Allen Bird, and Sol Triplett.

Answer. Yes, sir; that is three.

Question. And those are the only cases of killing you have mentioned, I believe.

Answer. Well, there was a negro man killed his wife there in the county since the surrender, that is one case; I think there was a negro killed in the county immediately after the surrender, named Nelson Yarborough.

Question. What are the circumstances of his killing?

Answer. I don't know; no one ever knew anything about it.

Question. Was he said to have been killed by a body of men?

Answer. O, no, sir; the case was investigated by the military authorities while they were there; it was soon after the surrender, sir. I do not remember any others, sir, now.

Question. Are there any other cases of negro whipping than those you have referred to? You have given the cases of William Coleman, Mordecai Mitchell, Reuben Coleman, George Gladney, and Nathan Cannon; and I believe that is all.

Answer. There are no others that I recollect of. I think I heard of one whipped in the southeastern corner of the county, but I do not remember his name; it was a small circumstance I judge.

Question. Did you understand whether it was done by a band of men in disguise?

Answer. No, sir; I did not understand that.

Question. When did it occur?

Answer. It has been within the last twelve months.

Question. Was he a colored man?

Answer. Yes, sir.

Question. Are there any other cases you have heard of?

Answer. No, sir; I don't remember any now. I think you have all that I know anything about.

By Mr. BLAIR:

Question. I see a man named George Worth, a colored preacher, was killed in Winston?

Answer. There is no such man there.

Question. It is in Lydia Anderson's testimony; perhaps the name is Murf.

Answer. He was killed in Winston County.

By the CHAIRMAN:

Question. When?

Answer. It has been about eighteen months ago; it was a short time after the whipping of Nathan Cannon.

Question. Do you know the particulars of his murder?

Answer. No, sir; I know he was killed. I was not the sheriff of the county at the time. He was working with a gentleman named McQuinn. I learned that the reason of his death was this: it was a short time after the whipping of this Nathan Cannon. He held a meeting. I didn't know him as a preacher; but he was at a meeting—a large negro meeting—a short time after that, and he called upon all the colored men present to volunteer and go up with him, and they would hang some white men that he suspected of having done it.

Question. What is your knowledge of his having made such a proposition as that?

Answer. My knowledge was derived from other parties; I did not hear him say that.

Question. Was that the imputed offense for which he was killed?

Answer. That is what I heard, sir; that he was trying to breed up an insurrection, and that he had some of these men. This I know, that he did assemble a considerable crowd, and the sheriff, a man named Hudson, went down and broke up this arrangement, sir.

Question. How long after this was it that he was killed?

Answer. After he made that threat?

Question. Yes.

Answer. Until the assembling of that crowd?

Question. Yes.

Answer. It was not very long, sir; I don't remember the time.

Question. Did I understand you to say he was a preacher?

Answer. I did not know him as a preacher. He was at a meeting.

Question. Do you know anything about his character?

Answer. No, sir; I don't know but little about him.

Question. Was he said to have been visited by men in disguise?

Answer. I do not know. He was killed about dusk, coming from the field. This Mr. McQuinn, the man he was working with, told me that.

Question. Did you understand whether more than one man was concerned in the killing?

Answer. I never knew; I did not understand that anybody else was along; I believe the tracks indicated some two or three.

Question. Were there any horse-tracks?

Answer. No, sir; it was in a field; there were no horse-tracks there.

Question. Any sign of horses in the neighborhood that the men had ridden?

Answer. Not as I know of.

Question. Was there an inquest held?

Answer. Yes, sir; I think a justice of the peace held an inquest. There was an inquest held.

Question. Nothing was ever discovered?

Answer. No, sir.

By Mr. BLAIR:

Question. Was McQuinn arrested in connection with that or any other transaction?

Answer. He has been arrested and taken to Jackson; I don't know whether it was in connection with this case of Murf's or not. They never found anything against him, I learn; never sustained anything against him. He was arrested and committed to jail for several days, in Jackson.

Question. Who was he arrested by?

Answer. The deputy United States marshal, sir.

By the CHAIRMAN:

Question. Did you understand what Peter Cooper's offense was, beyond the fact of his being a teacher of a colored school?

Answer. No, sir.

Question. It is supposed that this outrage was committed upon him and his property because of the fact that he was a teacher?

Answer. No, sir; I don't think it was. There have been colored schools taught there in the neighborhood, and in town, several of them.

Question. What was supposed to be the cause of that outrage?

Answer. I never heard any cause. He was a man wholly incompetent to teach school, as to that.

Question. Was he a man of good character?

Answer. Yes, sir; I never heard anything particular alleged against him.

Question. You may state the particulars of the murder of Allen Bird, who, you say, was committed to jail on the charge of an attempt to commit a rape upon a white woman. Were you sheriff at that time?

Answer. Yes, sir.

Question. Give the committee the particulars of that case.

Answer. Well, sir, he was arrested a few days before that. Our circuit court was in session at the time the offense was said to have been committed. He was arrested, and the grand jury investigated the case, and found an indictment against him. The court adjourned without trying him, and left him in my possession as a prisoner, and I did not have any promise of any one interfering with him; I did not anticipate anything of the kind. I was not at home when he was killed. I will give my jailer's statement before the inquest. It was that he was visited in the night-time, between twelve and one o'clock, by a party of disguised men. Twelve of them came to the jail, and four of them remained down-stairs. They had taken the keys from him by force, and they unlocked the doors and went up; this man was confined in a cage, and they had a good deal of difficulty in getting the cage open. The jailer refused to give the key up, but did finally. He gave them the wrong keys at the start, thinking he would get out from that fact to, perhaps, give the alarm and prevent the murder of Bird. But they got the keys from his wife; they scared her; and they finally got the cage unlocked; but the jailer got a chance about that time—they had taken him along upstairs with them; the prisoners were up above—he ran down, and the party below hallooed to him, "Halt!" and he supposes that the party above thought there was some one approaching, that they hallooed "Halt!" and they shot the negro in the jail.

Question. They did not succeed in entering his cell?

Answer. Yes, sir; they had the cage door open, and the jailer's opinion was that they designed taking him out.

Question. And that they were frustrated in the attempt by the apparent approach of some one?

Answer. Yes, sir.

Question. Your information is that there were about twelve men?

Answer. Twelve came inside of the house.

Question. Was there a party outside still?

Answer. There were some of the party outside; I don't know how many.

Question. Did the party come on horseback?

Answer. Yes, sir; they all came upon horseback, and those outside held the horses.

Question. Did he describe the manner in which the men were disguised?

Answer. He said they had something on their faces. He could not tell who they were.

Question. Any gowns or frocks on?

Answer. He said they had something over the faces, and a kind of wrapper round the bodies, and were all in white except one, and he was in a black wrapper.

Question. Was he the leader?

Answer. No; he said he did not seem to be; he never had anything to say.

Question. Did he say any one seemed to be captain?

Answer. He said one did the talking entirely. What talking was done was by one man.

Question. Did he notice whether the horses were disguised?

Answer. If he did he never told me. I recollect his telling me that they got off very easily. He said he didn't know how the horses could travel so easily, unless they had their feet muffled; but that, I think, was a mere idea of his.

Question. This was at what time of the year?

Answer. Our circuit court met the second or third Monday in July; it was the week after that.

Question. About the 1st of August?

Answer. It was the latter part of July, I think, sir.

Question. Of the present year?

Answer. Yes, sir; 1871.

Question. Were the horses' tracks followed?

Answer. Yes, sir; they all went out one way.

Question. Did he give the alarm that night?

Answer. Yes, sir; immediately.

Question. Was any pursuit made before morning?

Answer. No, sir; I was not at home; I was off twelve miles from home; they sent me word next day; I did not go home until evening.

Question. Had any pursuit been made in the mean time by the citizens?

Answer. Yes, sir; they followed the tracks a mile or two out, but they scattered; the weather was dry, and it was a public highway, and it was difficult to tell one track from another.

Question. You say there were appearances of their having scattered?

Answer. Yes, sir; that was the understanding.

Question. And dropped off one by one on some by-road?

Answer. Yes, sir; I suppose so.

Question. After your return, did you make any pursuit?

Answer. No, sir; I didn't make any further pursuit; I regarded it as unnecessary. I could not follow a track that went just along the public road of travel where everybody was coming to town. When I got home the traveling had been going on all day.

Question. The nights at that time were short, were they not?

Answer. Yes, sir; it was July.

Question. Daylight would come about four o'clock?

Answer. Yes, sir; it would break about four o'clock.

Question. The presumption is, then, that these men would get to cover before daylight?

Answer. Yes, sir.

Question. And from the time they executed this man until daylight how much time would elapse?

Answer. It was a short time to midnight that they were there; that would be four or five hours. A man might ride twenty miles in that time.

Question. Before daylight?

Answer. Yes, sir.

Question. Hardly, if they moved at such a slow rate, and made so little noise, as when they left town?

Answer. He said they made very little noise in going out of town; went off on a walk.

Question. Were they seen that night, coming or going, by any people on the highway?

Answer. No, sir; no one saw them at the town; there was a negro named Abram Yarborough, I understood, saw them. He didn't tell me so; but I understood he said he did see them when they left, or when they came in, I don't know which; I think it was when they left.

Question. Did they leave by the same road by which they came in?

Answer. Yes, sir.

Question. A public highway?

Answer. Yes, sir.

Question. On which dwellings are situated?

Answer. There are very few dwellings on that road; our town is a very small village; there is one dwelling on it, about a mile and a half from town; then there is no other residence on the road for six or eight miles.

Question. Did you question the man living nearest to town—about a mile and a half?

Answer. Yes, sir; he knew nothing about it.

Question. Had he dogs?

Answer. Yes, sir.

Question. Did they bark?

Answer. He heard no noise; he knew nothing about it.

Question. Did you extend your investigations to the families along beyond—five or six miles out?

Answer. Yes, sir; we made a general inquiry, but could never ascertain anything about it; where they went to, or which way, except that their tracks went out to the road.

Question. Is that jail situated in the heart of the town?

Answer. Yes, sir; pretty much so; it is on the court-house square—the public square; there are dwellings on both sides of it.

Question. At what distance from the jail?

Answer. The nearest dwellings are about eighty or ninety yards, or perhaps a hundred.

Question. What is the population of Louisville?

Answer. I really disremember.

Question. Four or five hundred?

Answer. Yes, sir; about that.

Question. Did the jailer or his wife make any outcries?

Answer. They would not let them, at the time; they did as soon as they could.

Question. After the party had gone?

Answer. Yes, sir.

Question. Did they arouse the neighbors then?

Answer. Yes, sir; they raced up and down immediately.

Question. Did you understand that any one went out in the direction the party had left until daylight?

Answer. No, sir; I don't think they did.

Question. Were there any neighbors, except the negroes you mentioned, who heard the approach of this party?

Answer. No, sir.

Question. The town was buried in sleep at the time?

Answer. Yes, sir; it was about midnight.

Question. The jailer lived in the jail?

Answer. Yes, sir; in the first story; he had a small family.

Question. Any children grown up?
Answer. No, sir; he had a brother living with him, about grown.
Question. Was he at home?
Answer. Yes, sir.
Question. Was any constraint put upon him?
Answer. Yes, sir; he was kept closely watched all the time they were in there.
Question. Were the party all armed?
Answer. All armed.
Question. Did they state the cause of their business to the jailer or his wife?
Answer. O, no, sir; they just demanded the keys; they went up; there were two or three colored men in the jail; this same Allen Bird had a brother confined there for larceny, and there was another negro there for larceny; and they went up and looked at them. There are two departments or rooms above in the jail. They went up and looked at all of them that were there.
Question. Was any one in the same cell with Allen Bird?
Answer. No, sir.
Question. In what part of the county did Allen Bird live at the time he was arrested?
Answer. Right in town. It is about a mile from the court-house.
Question. Was the offense said to have been perpetrated in the neighborhood?
Answer. About four miles from town.
Question. Where this young lady lived?
Answer. Yes, sir. Let me correct that. His mother lives about a mile from the court-house, but he was working about five or six miles from town this year, and this young lady lived on the road between his mother's and where he was at work.
Question. Was that on the road that this disguised party came?
Answer. No, sir.
Question. A different road?
Answer. Yes, sir; they went the public road; this was a more private way.
Question. Where was this assault on Miss Taylor said to have been made—at her father's house?
Answer. Yes, sir; she was going from her father's to school. She was attending school.
Question. What is that neighborhood called in which this offense is said to have been committed?
Answer. I know of no particular name for it, sir. The church she was attending is called "Poplar Flat Church."
Question. Is that a populous, thickly settled neighborhood?
Answer. Not very; it is a very hilly, broken country.
Question. You say this party did not come from that direction?
Answer. No, sir; that direction is north from the town, where this attack on this young lady was made; it is a little west of north, and they went out in a direction rather northeast, on the public road.
Question. Would that road lead them into the neighborhood where this young lady lived attending school?
Answer. No, sir; unless they took a country road.
Question. They could have ridden out by a cross-road?
Answer. O, yes, sir.
Question. At what distance from the main road?
Answer. They could have got out on the main road at a distance of three miles.
Question. Was there any nearer road to this neighborhood?
Answer. Yes, sir; they could have come a direct road from that neighborhood to town.
Question. Did you ever institute an investigation in the neighborhood where this offense was alleged to have been committed, to discover who were implicated?
Answer. No, sir; not in that particular neighborhood. I should not have well known how to have made that, or what way to have found it out.
Question. Your own theory, I suppose, is that they were the friends of this girl who headed this enterprise?
Answer. That would be the conclusion of almost any individual—that it was by the intimate friends of this young lady. It would have been the general feeling, that such an act as that, of such an aggravated character, would meet condign punishment at once.
Question. What is your own opinion as to whether that body of men belonged to Winston County, or came from beyond the county line?
Answer. I could not tell you.
Question. Have you any theory upon the subject?
Answer. No, sir; I have not. The opinion of the jailer was, that the major part of them were from away from the county, but I could not see how he could ever know that, or anything about it.
Question. Did he recognize any one of them?

Answer. No, sir.

Question. Neither by voice, size, or any other means?

Answer. No, sir.

Question. So it remains a profound mystery to this day who the murderers were?

Answer. Yes, sir.

Question. Did your grand jury investigate the matter?

Answer. The grand jury has not met since that time. In all these other cases I have mentioned, I am satisfied from the witnesses that the grand jury had subpœnaed, and the location of those witnesses, that they thoroughly investigated them, as much as they possibly could, in every instance that I have spoken of.

Question. I will come to that directly. I will take up the case of Sol Triplett. I believe you did not state, in answer to General Blair, whether the men who killed him were disguised or not. What is your opinion upon that point?

Answer. I think, may be, his wife told me they were.

Question. Did she tell you how many were concerned in the murder?

Answer. No, sir; she said there were several of them, though. She and another woman were outside the door when she heard them coming, and she heard several coming, but she did not know how many.

Question. Did they approach on horseback?

Answer. No, sir; they were on foot.

Question. Were there any signs of horses in the neighborhood?

Answer. I think she said there were.

Question. At what hour in the night did she say the visit was made?

Answer. It was in the early part of the night. She had gone to bed, I think she told me, sir.

Question. Did they enter the house, take him out, and murder him?

Answer. No, sir; they shot him through a crack. She said they ordered him to open the door, and he came to the door; he had laid down; he got up and went to the door; he kept his gun just above the door; he reached up and got his gun down, and held it in his right hand, and stood at the door, with his left hand against the door, and the party that shot him shot him through a crack in the back part of the house.

By Mr. BUCKLEY:

Question. Did you ever hear that the horses were tied at some distance from the house where this man Triplett was killed?

Answer. No, sir.

Question. Did you ever hear that there was a hat found next morning?

Answer. Yes, sir; I saw the hat. I left it with a man named Parks. His wife gave me the hat.

Question. Ambrose Parks?

Answer. Yes, sir.

Question. Was it known to whom this hat belonged?

Answer. No, sir; nobody knew; the negro woman did not know; Parks did not know.

Question. Did you ever hear it suggested that that hat belonged to a man named McElhany?

Answer. No, sir; never before.

Question. Did you ever hear that McElhany the next day bought a hat at the old man Jack Triplett's store?

Answer. No, sir. I was at Triplett's making inquiry, as well as almost every other house in the neighborhood, a very short time after that, as quick as I could attend to it.

Question. Did you ever hear that this man Triplett was connected with any secret organization there?

Answer. Which Triplett?

Question. Jack Triplett.

Answer. Perhaps it would be necessary for you to tell me what secret organization you refer to.

Question. The Ku-Klux organization, as it is represented.

Answer. I have heard that thing suggested, that perhaps he did, but then, at the same time, it was only a mere suggestion. I have heard other men suggested. I never received it in any light that I could place any confidence in the thing at all, or that it would amount to anything reliable.

Question. Are you acquainted with his character in that community?

Answer. Yes, sir; I know him well.

Question. Will you state his character?

Answer. He is a man of excellent character; he is an energetic and enterprising man, and I have known him intimately for years, and have always looked upon him as a very high-toned gentleman.

Question. Did you ever hear that he was a rash, violent man?

Answer. He was regarded as rather a tight master in the days of slavery. He was a good worker. He is a man that likes to see a good deal of work done.

By the CHAIRMAN:

Question. How far was this from Jack Triplett's that Sol Triplett was killed?
Answer. About two miles.
Question. What effort was made to discover who the murderers were?
Answer. I went to the neighborhood and visited all the neighbors, as I told you. It is twelve or fourteen miles from our town. It was some days before I got up there. They did not send me any word. I went to the neighborhood, around generally, to almost every individual, black and white, and I could get no facts from any one that would lead to who did it at all. Now, I conversed with one gentleman named Barnhill, who lives on the opposite side of where Mr. Triplett lived. He said men passed his house that night.
Question. On foot?
Answer. On horseback. He did not know who they were.
Question. How large was the party?
Answer. Three, he said.
Question. Were they disguised?
Answer. He didn't say they were; it was dark, though. I don't know as he could have told from where he was standing. I don't know whether he said they were disguised or not.
Question. Did Sol. Triplett's wife say they were disguised?
Answer. She thought they were.
Question. When did that occur?
Answer. I think it was in January last, or February.
Question. You spoke of the case of Nathan Cannon, whipped last year, as it was supposed, for remarks he had made at a school he was teaching. I believe you did not say whether the party that whipped him were disguised or not?
Answer. I know but little about that case. I was not sheriff of the county at that time, and never investigated it.
Question. Did you ever understand whether the party which whipped him was disguised or not?
Answer. If I did, I do not remember it now.
Question. Has he left the county?
Answer. He is employed in preaching down here about Meridian now; he is not in the county now.
Question. Did he leave soon afterward?
Answer. No, sir; he staid some little time; I do not remember how long now.
Question. Did you understand whether the whipping was a severe one?
Answer. Yes, sir; I understand he was right severely whipped, sir.
Question. Have you any information as to the number of men who were concerned in it?
Answer. No, sir; I have not.
Question. Did they go to his house and take him out?
Answer. I understood so.
Question. In the night-time.
Answer. Yes, sir.
Question. I think you said you never heard the particulars of the whipping of George Gladney?
Answer. No, sir; I never heard much of the particulars of that.
Question. Did you hear that he was taken from his house in the night-time, and whipped?
Answer. Yes, sir; it was in the night-time. I do not know who it was. I understood that from some one, I don't know who, but some one told me it was in the night, though.
Question. Did you understand that the men who whipped him were in disguises?
Answer. I think they were.
Question. About how long since did that occur?
Answer. It occurred last spring, some time in March; I presume it was last March.
Question. You spoke also of the case of Robin Coleman, on Perkins's place. You said that the men who whipped him were reported to be disguised. When did that occur?
Answer. At the same time; they lived close together; at the same time they whipped Gladney.
Question. On the same night?
Answer. Yes, sir.
Question. Did you hear the particulars of Robin Coleman's case; how many were concerned in whipping him?
Answer. I think Mr. Perkins told me that Robin's family and Robin said there were but three or four or five; I will not state the number definitely, but not a great many.

Question. Did you understand that the party visited his house at night, after he had retired to rest?

Answer. Yes, sir; it was in the night; I don't know whether he had gone to bed or not.

Question. Did they take him out and whip him?

Answer. Yes, sir; so Mr. Perkins stated to me.

Question. I think you stated that Mordecai Mitchell was whipped also by men in disguise, but not very severely—fifteen or twenty lashes.

Answer. Yes, sir.

Question. You supposed the party were not after him, but Jim Hudson?

Answer. Yes, sir.

Question. What was their motive for whipping Mitchell; in disappointment for not finding Hudson, and a disposition to gratify their appetite?

Answer. I think they wanted to find Hudson, and thought Mitchell knew where he was.

Question. Do any other instances of whipping or killing occur to you now?

Answer. No, sir; I do not remember any other. I think I have related every one.

Question. Now let me inquire whether any of the parties implicated in these whippings or murders have ever been detected and brought to justice?

Answer. No, sir; there has never been a man arrested as a Ku-Klux in any of these cases. We never could identify them. There has been but one man arrested in the county as a Ku-Klux. We did have one man arrested as being in disguise.

Question. Was he implicated in any of these outrages you have described?

Answer. No, sir; in neither case.

Question. Have you ever seen any men disguised after the manner of Ku-Klux?

Answer. No, sir.

Question. Have you ever talked with parties who had seen them in disguise?

Answer. Yes, sir. Mitchell, for instance.

Question. Have you talked with other parties who have seen them parading through the country?

Answer. I have talked with this man Coleman they whipped, and I have talked with this woman, Sol Triplett's wife.

Question. Are they the only parties who have ever told you that they have seen these parties of disguised men?

Answer. I think I have, sir. I have heard one or two men say they had seen them on a night in passing—that they saw them in the southeast part of the county; but I don't remember the men's names who told me.

Question. Is there any particular locality in your county where it is supposed that this organization exists?

Answer. There have been more depredations on the eastern side or southeastern corner of the county than anywhere else. I have never heard of disguised men in the northwestern portion of the county; and in the section where these school-houses were burned, in the northwestern part, no man, white or black, ever saw a disguised man in it.

Question. Most of these outrages have been committed on the eastern line of Winston, bordering on this county—Noxubee?

Answer. Yes, sir.

Question. Is it supposed that this county contributes a quota of the men concerned in these midnight adventures?

Answer. As to that, I could not tell you whether they did or not.

Question. Has public opinion fixed upon any men in Winston County as being implicated in these affairs?

Answer. No, sir.

Question. These transactions run through some two or three years?

Answer. No, sir. About the whole of these depredations I have referred to by men in disguise, or most of them, occurred last February and March. I never heard of a disguised man in the county until then, at no time.

Question. Until the spring of this present year?

Answer. No, sir.

Question. You never heard of any body of men disguised riding through the county until this last spring?

Answer. No, sir, I never did; not in that county. I have read of them in other places. I never heard of one in that county until then. Last February or March was about the time of all the mischief I have spoken of.

Question. Did I understand you to say there was a public meeting of the citizens?

Answer. Yes, sir; we held a public meeting last April, condemning such a thing.

Question. At the court-house at Louisville?

Answer. Yes, sir.

Question. How largely was it attended?

Answer. Very largely. The court-house was full; and there was a general expression of sentiment condemning these things.

Question. You say resolutions were adopted?

Answer. Yes, sir.

Question. Have you a copy of them?

Answer. No, sir.

Question. Could you repeat the language of the resolutions?

Answer. No, sir; not to do it correctly. It condemned these depredations, and the burning of our school-houses, and called on the citizens or people, wherever they might be, to abstain from any such thing.

Question. Was there any pledge on the part of those participating in that meeting to use their utmost efforts to bring the guilty parties to justice?

Answer. I do not remember about that particular, sir; the genenal feeling was that it was in opposition to such conduct. I could not say whether there was any pledge on the part of them to assist in bringing them to justice, but I am satisfied that that was the feeling of the people—that they desired all such men punished, whoever they might be.

Question. Do you say there have been no cases of outrage by disguised men since that time?

Answer. Only one—the killing of this man Bird in jail. Everything has been quiet.

Question. That act would seem to indicate that the organization still lived, even after the denunciation of these resolutions?

Answer. It would show that there was a party of men there at that time.

Question. What evidence have you that this band of men may not rally on some similar enterprise at any time hereafter, if that expression on the part of the good people of the county did not restrain them from taking forcible poossession of the jail and murdering a prisoner in cold blood; what evidence have you that organization may not break out in fresh outrages at any time?

Answer. The only evidence we have is the general deportment and conduct of the people; they are very quiet; there have been no outrages of any kind committed for a series of months, at least.

Question. They were very quiet before this visitation of the jail?

Answer. Yes, sir.

Question. Nobody was anticipating that?

Answer. No, sir. I suppose the character of the offense had a good deal to do with it.

Question. Do you mean to say that, bad as the offense was, anybody pretended to justify this mode of executing justice?

Answer. No, sir; no one justifies the killing of a prisoner by any means in the jail; but I mean this: that that man was deemed guilty of an offense of a character that is looked upon with more abhorrence than almost any other offense that we think can be committed by a white man or black man.

Question. Was there any difficulty in convicting a prisoner found guilty of such an offense, in your courts?

Answer. No, sir. We could convict him.

Question. You had a secure jail, had you not?

Answer. Yes, sir.

Question. You had no apprehension that he would make his escape?

Answer. He could not have done it, sir, I think, without assistance.

Question. The evidence, in your opinion, was sufficient to have sustained the charge?

Answer. I do not know anything about that; it was, in the opinion of the grand jury. They found the bill. I never heard the evidence.

Question. They found a bill for assault, with intent to commit rape?

Answer. Yes, sir.

Question. The presumption is that the same evidence would have satisfied the traverse jury?

Answer Yes, sir.

Question. There is no reason that you know of why anybody should have interfered with the sentence of the law in punishing Bird?

Answer. No, sir. I think he would have been there at court, ready to have been tried. It was my intention to have kept him there.

Question. How do you know that William Coleman had not bargained for a piece of land?

Answer. Well, sir, I know he was living out on the road there. I have heard the gentleman, Mr. Foster, speak about it, and say that he had never sold him any land.

Question. Was he living upon Mr. Foster's land?

Answer. Yes, sir.

Question. Did he have a lease?

Answer. Mr. Foster pays the taxes on the land.

Question. Did Coleman have a lease of the land?

Answer. No, sir; I never heard any talk of it if he did.

Question. By what title was he holding possession?

Answer. He was just living out on it. Mr. Foster, I suppose, gave him possession—permission to go there.

Question. How long had he been there?

Answer. He had lived there a while and moved off. Then Mr. Foster let him go back again. I think Mr. Foster told him to go on the land, and pay him for some of the improvements.

Question. Do you know anything about the contract between him and Mr. Foster?

Answer. I do not think there was any contract at all, so far as purchase was concerned.

Question. What means have you of knowing it?

Answer. I know the parties; I know Doctor Foster intimately well.

Question. Did you ever converse with William Coleman about his title?

Answer. I heard him, when he said he was going off, speak about his hogs and all, and he didn't tell me anything about his land; he said nothing about leaving his land; he didn't speak of owning any land at all; he said he had a little crop. These parties that whipped him told him to stay there; I told him so myself.

Question. To stay there and make his crop?

Answer. Yes, sir. He didn't have much of a crop. He had about six or eight acres cleared on the place.

Question. Had he cleared it himself?

Answer. Yes, sir; I think he cleared it himself, with another freedman, a year or so before that.

Question. Under what contract?

Answer. I think Foster was to give him so much for making improvements on the place.

Question. Did you ever hear Dr. Foster say that he had not sold him any land?

Answer. The title of the land is in Dr. Foster.

Question. Did you ever hear him say so?

Answer. No, sir; I know the title is of record.

Question. He might have a written contract or bond?

Answer. But I know the character of Dr. Foster too well to believe he would have made a trade of that kind.

Question. Would he not sell a piece of land to a negro?

Answer. Yes, sir, he would. He sold a thousand acres to freedmen near there, but a very good set of freedmen—very different from this man; and they were men who would pay him; but I know he knew Coleman never would pay him.

Question. You say you know Coleman did not own any sheep?

Answer. No, sir; I don't know whether he owned any sheep or not.

Question. There is no doubt but that he was whipped?

Answer. Yes, sir; he was whipped.

Question. I understand you to say there were six school-houses in all that were burned?

Answer. Yes, sir.

Question. When did that occur?

Answer. All occurred near the same time; I think they occurred from near the 1st of February to the 1st part of April.

Question. Within a space of two or three months?

Answer. Yes, sir.

Question. You suppose that part of them were burned in consequence of this opposition to schools?

Answer. Well, sir, there was a feeling of opposition to the schools, originating from the idea that the tax would be so burdensome that the people could not pay it. There was a feeling, whether originating from that idea or not I do not know; but that was rather my opinion. Now, Avery was suspected, really, of burning his own school-house. Some of his own neighbors suspected him. One of them published a card to the effect that Avery burned his school-house to keep from teaching school; and if he could make it appear that other parties did it, he would get his pay anyhow.

Question. Was he a colored man?

Answer. No, sir; a white man.

Question. Was that a colored school?

Answer. Yes, sir. He was getting fine pay—$100 per month; and he would get his pay anyhow; and some thought that he burned it.

Question. Is not that a far-fetched theory, in your opinion?

Answer. Well, sir, I could not see why a man would do it; but I say a man named Hooker published a card in the newspaper, and Avery didn't deny it.

Question. Is it not a more reasonable supposition that it grew out of the opposition to public schools?

Answer. My opinion is, that house was burned from the fact that the neighborhood had had a great opposition to having him stuck upon them as a teacher. He was evidently a worthless man, and the neighborhood knew it; and he had been accused of some bad conduct in the school before, towards a young lady, and they did not wish him there; they thought that it was bad policy to have him among their children; and I think his school-house was burned up in opposition to the man that was teaching it.

Question. So the burning of that school-house resulted from opposition to the teacher, rather than the system?

Answer. Yes, sir; that was my actual opinion; and then he got another school-house. While I am on that I will mention it. He got another one in the neighborhood, close by, that had been occupied as a dwelling by a man. It was a small house. That was burned up also. Those are two of the six that were burned up at the same place.

Question. That theory is utterly inconsistent with the theory that Avery himself burned the school-houses?

Answer. Yes, sir.

Question. Which is the better theory?

Answer. I think the better theory is that it was burned from opposition to Avery as a teacher. That was my opinion about it.

Question. Do I understand you to say that the white republicans of your county are opposed to common-schools?

Answer. I could not make any difference; they were as much opposed to the tax. It was not the idea of being opposed to the common-schools. That idea is supported by all men of all parties. The feeling among the people is general, irrespective of parties. Partyism never had anything to do with this thing, in my mind. I never could see any point it did have; but the system of the public schools would bring such a tax on the people that they could not pay it. There was that feeling in the county. Whether the burning of the school-houses arose from that feeling I do not know.

Question. When the idea was first broached of admitting the negro children to go to school at the public expense, did it not meet with strong opposition from the democratic party in Winston County?

Answer. Yes, sir; and others, too. All hands were opposed to it.

By Mr. RICE:

Question. How did the colored men in Winston County vote at this election?

Answer. Most of them voted the republican ticket; many of them voted, I could not tell how. I could only tell from the general feeling, and passing through the county, and seeing them out yesterday.

Question. Did they turn out pretty generally?

Answer. They pretty generally turned out, and we had a very quiet day of it.

By the CHAIRMAN:

Question. Which party succeeded in that county?

Answer. The democratic party succeeded.

Question. By what majority?

Answer. We didn't learn. We succeeded, I say; I suppose we did rather, but the returns had not come in when I left town this morning.

Question. Is there an increase of former majorities?

Answer. The vote had not come in when I left town.

Question. I did not know but you had learned the vote at some of the precincts.

Answer. I did not. What was your question?

Question. My question was, whether there was an increase on the democratic vote.

Answer. We have had no question that tested that thing, except in 1869. It was a considerable increase over that vote.

Question. That would imply that the increase must have proceeded mainly from colored voters?

Answer. No, sir; it is in part, perhaps, owing to that; but there was an extreme feeling of opposition, even among the democratic party, to the Dent ticket, in the last election. The Dent ticket was very unpopular in our county at the last general election, and about half of the democratic party did not vote at that election.

By Mr. RICE:

Question. Is your school tax here collected as a State tax, or is it by counties?

Answer. It is collected by counties; the county board of supervisors levy so much.

Question. Is the school tax levied by the counties?

Answer. Yes, sir, it varies; in some counties it is higher than in others.

Question. Was the school superintendent interfered with there in regard to his papers?

Answer. Not at all; he has never been molested. I saw him yesterday; he has never been interfered with. There were some school papers burned that belonged to the original sixteenth section fund, before they ever reached him—one or two townships; that was supposed to have been done by parties interested that had notes falling due.

Question. Money due from citizens for the sixteenth-section land.
Answer. Yes, sir; the original sixteenth-section land.
Question. These papers were taken and burned?
Answer. Yes, sir; some of them. In one place I know, one of the original trustees, though, held a list of all the papers. These papers were measurably rendered worthless anyway.

By Mr. BUCKLEY:

Question. Did you ever hear of a white woman named Tripley Ann Tacket, who was driven from Winston County by a band of men?
Answer. Yes, sir; I heard something of her case. I never see her. She was living near where Sol. Triplett lived. I never heard of her by so much name as that before. She was called Tacket, simply. I reckon it is the same woman.
Question. Do you know the circumstances?
Answer. No, sir; she was regarded as a mighty sorry character; that is all I ever knew about her.

By Mr. RICE:

Question. There was a woman named Johnson Keitt killed in that county?
Answer. No, sir, there was not a man named Johnson killed there that I know of.
Question. Johnson Keitt?
Answer. There was one or two men. One of them was a man named Peter Cunningham, and Johnson Keitt arrested them for attempting to assassinate the United States marshal, and I understood that one of these men was killed, but I understood it was Cunningham. That was just on the line between this county and Noxubee. They were indicted for the murder, or attempt to assassinate the marshal.

By Mr. BLAIR:

Question. What was the name of this marshal?
Answer. Parks; he was taking the census. He was shot at on the eastern side of Winston County. I was with him myself; he was shot in the arm, and the proof was sufficient to have those two characters bound over to the grand jury to find an indictment, but the indictment never was sustained.

By Mr. RICE:

Question. You understand one of them was afterward killed?
Answer. Yes, sir; one of them was killed afterward.
Question. Under what circumstances?
Answer. I do not know.

By the CHAIRMAN:

Question. Did you ever hear the name of Jerry Brown?
Answer. No, sir; I don't know Jerry Brown.

MACON, MISSISSIPPI, *November* 8, 1871.

ROBERT G. RIVES sworn and examined.

The CHAIRMAN. As this witness has been called by the minority, General Blair will please conduct his examination.

By Mr. BLAIR:

Question. Please give your residence and profession.
Answer. I reside in Louisville, Winston County, Mississippi. I am a lawyer by profession.
Question. How long have you resided in Winston County?
Answer. I have resided in Louisville, sir, since December, 1865.
Question. Practicing law in that county?
Answer. Yes, sir, since that time. I practiced law there before, but did not live there. I practiced there before the war.
Question. What is the condition of your county in respect to the maintenance of order, obedience to law, and the execution of law.
Answer. There have been some violations of law there. There has never been, to my knowledge, or according to the best of my information, any resistance to the authority of the law since I have been living there. No officer has ever failed to arrest any man there for want of force. No resistance has ever been offered to any officer since I have been there, according to my best information.
Question. Are the people generally quiet and peaceable?

Answer. They are, sir.

Question. Do you know a negro boy by the name of William Coleman?

Answer. I do.

Question. He reported in his testimony before this committee that he was shot at, and severely whipped, and driven away from that county, where he owned land, and hogs, sheep, and a mule, and a filly, and perhaps other property.

Answer. William Coleman, sir, to the best of my information, never owned any land in Winston County; never lived on any land under any contract of purchase. He lived within two miles and a half of Louisville, upon a piece of land owned, I understand, by Dr. Edward Foster. He never owned, as far as my information extends, any mule at all. As to whether he ever owned any other stock I do not know anything about that. He might or he might not have owned other stock. He had in his possession at one time a mule. That mule belonged to me. He had it for the purpose of making a crop. I let him have it to make a crop. He expected to buy that mule. There was a contract between us by the terms of which he was to purchase the mule at the end of the year, provided a brother of his, who worked awhile, and himself, succeeded in paying by the work of his brother or by his crop, but he was specially cautioned, by the justice who attested the contract, that he had no right whatever to dispose of the mule any more than he had to come into my lot and take any mule. Shortly after I let him have the mule a negro from Oktibbeha County, whose name I do not remember, informed me that Coleman was wishing to trade the mule to him that he understood I had some right to. He desired to know whether it was so or not. I told him the mule was mine, and not Coleman's. I went to see Coleman immediately about it. He denied ever having offered to trade the mule at all. The negro who had given me the information then called for another negro from the same county—Oktibbeha—and proved by him that Coleman did seek to trade him the mule; that Coleman had told him that he had paid the cash for the mule. Whereupon I went before the justice of the peace and asked him what should be done in the premises; that I could not trust that man to keep that mule any longer. He told me I would be very right in taking my mule; that he never had paid one cent on the mule. His brother had remained with me a short time, and I paid him up for the time. He never paid a cent on the mule. I only took the mule because it would not be safe for me to let him have the mule any longer. That is the only mule I know of his having been in possession of in Winston County. I know he could not have been in possession of stock to any considerable extent, for I have passed his place frequently and never saw any stock there at all. I was informed by several gentlemen who knew him that I was very fortunate indeed in getting my mule back; and I assure you had I heard as much as I did afterward I never would have allowed him to have had anything to do with anything that belonged to me. He was regarded there as utterly unreliable and unworthy of trust in any way.

Question. What is his character for truth and veracity?

Answer. I cannot say that I ever heard his character for truth and veracity particularly discussed. I heard him spoken of as being a very trifling, unreliable, lazy vagrant—a very trifling fellow—utterly unworthy of trust.

Question. Did you ever hear of his being whipped?

Answer. I heard of his being whipped. I never heard of his being shot at.

Question. Did you ever talk with him after he was said to have been whipped?

Answer. No, sir; not upon that subject.

Question. He says he was shot at and whipped, and that he knew the parties who did it. That their names were Coleman P. Carlysle, Jim Boyd Hughes, Peter Ellis, Henry Ellis, Bog Ellis, and Francis Ellis. Do you know any of these parties?

Answer. I know Coleman P. Carlyle and Jim Boyd Hughes. The Ellises I may have seen, but I do not remember them now.

Question. Does Coleman P. Carlyle live in the neighborhood?

Answer. I do not know exactly where Coleman P. Carlyle lives. I have seen the man. He does not live, though, in my immediate neighborhood. I know he lives some distance from Louisville.

Question. What is his character?

Answer. As far as I have ever heard him spoken of he is a very steady, quiet, law-abiding man. I have never heard anything to the contrary. I never heard his character much discussed.

Question. Do you know Jim Boyd Hughes?

Answer. Yes, sir; he is a black man living in Louisville.

Question. Is he a man of good character?

Answer. Well, sir, his character is pretty—— I do not know much about it. I have heard him spoken of frequently. He works—that is one thing I know about him—he works about town. Some regard him as truthful; others do not.

Question. Would you suspect Coleman P. Carlyle of associating, in an affair of this kind, with Jim Boyd Hughes?

Answer. I never should.

Question. Is Carlyle a man of character?

Answer. I think he is. My acquaintance with him is not extensive, but as far as it goes he is a man of good character. I never heard anything to the contrary.

Question. Is he a turbulent man?

Answer. I never heard it.

Question. A sober man?

Answer. I never heard of his being drunk.

By the CHAIRMAN:

Question. A planter?

Answer. He is a planter, according to my information. I am not thoroughly acquainted with him.

Question. Owning a farm in his own right?

Answer. I am not acquainted with the fact.

Question. A temperate man?

Answer. I never heard of his being intoxicated in my life.

By Mr. BLAIR:

Question. Do you think he is a man who would associate himself with Jim Boyd Hughes in an affair of that kind?

Answer. I should think not. I should never suspect Carlyle, from the acquaintance I had, of being guilty of any violation of law whatever; nothing of the kind; at any rate nothing outrageous.

Question. Do you know George Walker, a colored man, who lives near Carlyle?

Answer. No, sir.

Question. Do you know Ware McMorris, who lives at Mr. Cole's?

Answer. No, sir.

Question. Did you hear anything about this whipping of this man Coleman?

Answer. Yes, sir; I heard he was whipped; and whipped for stealing hogs. It was very questionable. There seemed to be some difference of opinion among those who spoke to me in reference to it, as to who whipped him—whether they were negroes or white people. There was quite a number of families of negroes who were living upon land under contract of purchase—upon which they make purchases from Dr. Foster. He lived near these negroes. On the other side of him were settlements of white men. These negroes had stock and hogs, and these white people also had, and Coleman had the reputation of taking the hogs from both sides. He helped himself whenever he got ready. Some thought the negroes whipped him, and some thought the white people did it. The majority I have heard speak of it think that the negroes did it. There is no diversity of opinion among them as to the cause of it. It was for stealing hogs.

Question. They all agree upon that point?

Answer. All that I heard from agree upon that point, that he was whipped for stealing hogs.

By Mr. BUCKLEY:

Question. Do you not think they whipped him in partnership?

Answer. I would not be surprised if several took a hand in it.

By the CHAIRMAN:

Question. Was the party said to be disguised?

Answer. I do not know as to that.

Question. What is your understanding?

Answer. I am under the impression that they were disguised. That was my information.

By Mr. BLAIR:

Question. Nobody told you he had been shot at?

Answer. I never heard of it.

Question. Was he very seriously hurt in this whipping?

Answer. I never heard of his being seriously hurt. I understood he was thrashed some and had left.

Question. He said his head was cut all to pieces by blows on his head.

Answer. I saw him not long after he left there. I was over here, and saw him near the house of a widow lady, a particular friend of mine, Mrs. Greer. I saw him in conversation with what I supposed to be her servants, and she being a friend of mine, I took it upon myself to warn her against employing such a fellow, telling her that his character was very bad; but I did not discover any marks of injuries upon him at that time.

By the CHAIRMAN:

Question. How long was this after the whipping?

Answer. I do not remember. It was not a great while after the whipping.

Question. Was it within two or three weeks?

Answer. I suppose so; I saw no marks of violence upon him.

Question. Did you examine his head?

Answer. No, sir; I passed close to him on the street.

Question. You did not examine his skin?

Answer. No, sir; he was not stripped. I saw him, and knew the boy.

By Mr. BLAIR:

Question. He said he was whipped because he was a radical and worked his own land.

Answer. I can only give the information I had. I know a number of negroes there had been working their own land and are not whipped. Some of them voted the radical ticket; as far as my information extends they have never been disturbed. They own lands and work them, and vote the radical ticket, and have done so every time they have had a chance to vote.

Question. He never owned any land?

Answer. Never.

Question. He could not have been whipped then on that account?

Answer. No, sir.

By Mr. RICE:

Question. From the description, he did not vote the radical ticket.

Answer. I think he did.

By Mr. BLAIR:

Question. You would not believe him on oath?

Answer. No, sir.

Question. Even if he stated he voted the radidal ticket?

Answer. I would believe from his character, but not from his statement.

Question. Did you hear of Mordecai Mitchell who was whipped?

Answer. Yes, sir; about two miles from Louisville.

Question. Was he whipped?

Answer. I heard of a slight whipping he got—a few licks. I never heard of his being seriously whipped. My information was that a party of disguised men went to his house in search of one James Hudson, who I know myself to have been a very turbulent and bad nego, and a disturber of the peace—a turbulent man. This party of disguised men went, as I understood, to the house of a Mordecai Mitchell in search of Jim Hudson. Mordecai denied his being about, and they took him out and whipped him a few licks. I never understood that the whipping was very serious.

Question. Do you know anything of Robin Coleman being whipped?

Answer. I do not know him.

Question. George Gladney?

Answer. I am not sure that I know him—not by that name. I know many of these negroes.

Question. Did you ever hear of either of them having been whipped?

Answer. I cannot say that I did. Sometimes I would hear these rumors, but cannot remember them.

Question. Sam McMillan is said to have been shot at by the Ku-Klux, and it is said that he shot at them?

Answer. I know one Sam McMillan, a white man, living within four or five miles of Louisville. I do not know a black man of that name. I never heard of a McMillan of my acquaintance being shot at by anybody.

Question. Did you ever hear of the other McMillan?

Answer. No, sir; if I should state my opinion about it, I would say that no negro has ever been whipped there for being a radical or owning land, for I have known numbers of them that are radicals, and vote the radical ticket, and who own land too, and they pass peaceably among their white neighbors.

Question. And have never been disturbed?

Answer. Never, at all.

Question. Do you know Nathan Cannon?

Answer. No, sir; I do not think I do. I may know some of these negroes, but I do not remember them.

Question. Did you hear of the killing of a man named Sol Triplett?

Answer. I think I did, sir; but I never heard any of the circumstances; if I did I do not remember them.

Question. Did you hear of the killing of a man named Sol Triplett?

Answer. Yes, sir; I heard the circumstances of that. He was killed, I think, sir, in the jail of Winston County. That was my information. When I went to my office on the morning of the killing, I understood he had been killed.

Question. What was he in jail for?

Answer. He was in jail under indictment for an attempt to commit a rape upon a white girl.

Question. Was it a very bad case?

Answer. A very bad case indeed, sir, if he was the guilty party, as I suppose he was. The grand jury, at least, thought so, after a patient investigation of several days. I think they were engaged two or three days in the investigation.

Question. Did you hear anything of the testimony?

Answer. I heard nothing of the testimony before the grand jury.

Question. Did you hear anything of the testimony in any other way; did you hear any of the parties who testified, speak of the matter?

Answer. No, sir; none of the witnesses. I heard other persons who conversed with them. I did not converse with the witnesses.

Question. What were the facts in regard to it?

Answer. The facts, as far as I heard them, were, that this young lady was, with her little brother, passing along a path, when she was overtaken by a negro, supposed to have been Allen Bird, who seized her, handled her very roughly indeed, and attempted to commit a rape, unquestionably. There is no question that some negro attempted to commit a rape upon her person, and the only question in the mind of any one was whether it was Allen Bird or not; but the grand jury seemed to have come to the conclusion that it was Allen Bird. It was a most aggravated case of attempt at rape against some one. Whether Allen was the guilty party or not I can't say. The grand jury thought he was.

Question. Did the girl recognize Allen?

Answer. I suppose she did after he was caused to put on the clothes he took off when he was arrested. He was arrested and brought with several other black men before her to see if she could identify the one who had committed the deed. When he was arrested he put on a different hat and different clothes. The parties who had arrested him permitted him to change his clothes, and she did not at that time recognize him. Afterward, he was caused to put on the same clothes, as I understood, he had on when he was arrested, and then the test was submitted again, with others, and she identified him. That was my understanding. I do not know what passed before the grand jury, of course; I could not know.

Question. Did her brother recognize him also?

Answer. I do not know whether he did or not at that time. He did not at the first; her little brother was not able to point out the negroes at that time—at the time the other negroes all came in the clothes in which they were arrested, except Allen. Allen had changed his clothes after he was arrested. He changed his hat and put on a very wide-brimmed hat.

Question. Did you ever hear of a man named Peter Cooper being run away from there for keeping school?

Answer. I know a man named Peter Cooper, who pretended to teach the school there. He was a very ignorant man indeed; not capable of teaching even the rudiments of an education. That I know from conversation with him myself. The same men who got after Mordecai Mitchell went to the house—or are said to have gone to the house —he boarded at, and called for him and probably destroyed some of his property. He did not have but very little. I know Peter did not leave there for some time afterward. He remained there for some time after that. There was no other demonstration that I heard of after that, or between that time and the time he left. He remained for a considerable length of time after the only Ku-Klux demonstration that could have caused him to leave, for it was the only one at all until the killing of Bird. I wish to state this by way of explanation of a part of the testimony which I gave in at the outset. I was asked in reference to the disposition of the people there as to law and order, or something of the kind. I stated I believed that they were well disposed. When I say that I do not mean to say that there have not been disturbances. There were disturbances, and men in disguise, according to my information, have committed some disturbances there. As soon as it was asserted that there were men doing that, there was a county meeting called at our county-seat, participated in by a large portion of the best citizens of the county, to express their sentiments with reference to such conduct, after which I heard of no more demonstrations of that kind at all until the killing of Allen Bird. That was the only demonstration of the kind I heard of afterward. I think the great majority of the people are disposed to be law-abiding, peaceable people, and to frown down any violation of the law.

Question. Did you ever hear of a man who lived with old man Croker, in Winston County, a colored man?

Answer. I do not remember.

Question. A colored man killed in Winston County, who lived with old man Croker. In the night two men came; the dogs barked, and the old man went out and never came back. He was found hanging to the limb of a tree soon after supper.

Answer. I do not remember, sir, of that occurrence at all.

Question. Is there such a man living in the county as Croker?

Answer. There are two or three there of that name.

Question. An old man?

Answer. There is an old man—Isaac Croker.

Question. Did you hear of a circumstance of that kind in the county?

Answer. No, sir. The only case I ever heard of a man being found hanging to a tree was one where I do not think he was living with Croker. That was several years ago The negro was said to have behaved very rudely, and committed a rape. He was only prevented by interference from committing a rape on a white woman. He was hung to a tree in a swamp. No one knew how that was done, whether by men disguised or not. I never heard of this Croker case.

Question. The man you spoke of did not live with Croker?

Answer. I do not know with whom he lived.

By the CHAIRMAN:

Question. Do you refer to George Murphy who lived with McQueen?

Answer. I believe that was the case. I am not sure that it was George Murphy. It was several years ago.

Question. Did you hear of the case of George Murphy, killed about eighteen months ago, who lived with McQueen? It occurred a short time after the whipping of Cannon. He was a man who it was said had excited the negroes, and proposed to hang certain white men?

Answer. I think I did hear of that, sir.

Question. At all events, that was the pretext for the killing?

Answer. No, sir; I do not know whether it was or not. If I am not mistaken in the man, it was. There seems to be a different opinion there who killed him. He had been a leading witness—a prosecuting witness—in a case. He had taken a very active part in the prosecution of a negro, Henry Hanner, who had killed his wife; I think George Murphy had been very active in the prosecution of the negro and in his arrest, and it was very doubtful whether the friends of Henry Hanner had killed him. Henry Hanner was hung, by sentence of the court, for killing his wife, and it was very questionable whether George Murphy—I think this witness was George—was killed by the friends of Hanner, or by those white men who spoke in the manner you referred to.

Question. That occurred about eighteen months ago?

Answer. Yes, sir.

Question. Did you hear of the killing of a colored man by the name of Nelson Yarborough?

Answer. I heard of the killing of Nelson Yarborough; I think that occurred before I went to Louisville, while there was a Federal garrison at Louisville, soon after the surrender.

Question. Did you hear of the killing of Jesse Thompson, a colored man?

Answer. I do not remember that I did.

Question. Have you stated all the cases of murder that occur to you as having taken place in Winston County?

Answer. I do not remember, sir; I cannot say. There was a white man killed there not long since; not a great while since; I do not know whether it would be considered murder or justifiable homicide. He was killed by his father-in-law in a difficulty. A man named Cherry was killed by a Mr. Buford.

Question. Have you heard of negroes being killed by bands of men in disguise?

Answer. I remember of two or three instances; I do not remember any others except those instances of which I have spoken.

Question. You have never heard of Robin Coleman, George Gladney, Samuel McMillen, and Nathan Cannon?

Answer. I may have heard of them, but I do not remember now.

Question. You have heard of the burning of sundry school-houses?

Answer. Yes, sir; I do not know anything about it. I heard of the burning of some school-houses, and that caused the meeting I spoke of.

Question. That meeting does not seem to have produced much moral effect upon these men who move around in disguise after night, because I understand you to say that after that meeting occurred the murder of Allen Bird in jail.

Answer. I think that occurred after that meeting, but I think that is the only occurrence of which I have any knowledge since that meeting.

Question. That was a very flagrant case, where a good many men in disguise overawed the jailer and his wife and effected an entrance into the jail, and shot him in cold blood.

Answer. Yes, sir; I suppose it was. I do not know any other case now; I do not know any case that has come under my observation in which the perpetrator of the crime of rape has been permitted to go under less punishment than death. Our laws do not inflict capital punishment for even the rape itself.

Question. Do you mean to say that your people inflict the death-penalty irrespective of law?

Answer. I do not remember any time before the war or since that I have ever known of a negro who committed a rape upon a white woman who was suffered to live afterwards.

Question. I did not understand you to say that Allen Bird committed a rape on this woman?

Answer. No, sir; I do not suppose he did. But the grand jury thought that he attempted to commit the rape and was only prevented by the timely interference of one or two white men who ran to her rescue.

Question. Was that transaction approved by your community?

Answer. No, sir; I think not.

Question. Was it denounced by the community?

Answer. There was no public meeting on the occasion that I know of.

Question. Did the community express regret?

Answer. A great many did express regret.

Question. They thought, possibly, the man was innocent?

Answer. I never heard any expression of regret on that account; I heard many express regret that he had not been allowed to come before the court and have his trial and let the law take its course.

Question. It seems that the girl herself was in doubt as to who made the attempt, and that it required the second appearance of the negro in a different dress before she could identify him.

Answer. No, sir; it required the appearance of the negro before her in the same dress, and not in a different dress.

Question. But a different dress from that in which he was first brought before her?

Answer. Yes, sir; in a different dress from that which he had taken upon his arrest.

Question. There is a possibility that the girl may have been mistaken as to the person who made the assault upon her virtue, is there not?

Answer. I cannot tell what the testimony was before the grand jury, whether enough to exclude the possibility or not, but it was sufficient to satisfy the grand jury that he was the guilty man. But I cannot tell what that testimony was. I will state this: that a call was made, and some gentlemen proposed to have a public meeting for the purpose of denouncing the act. A gentleman proposed it to me. I had taken a very active part in the former meeting. I stated to him that I would take no part in any other public meeting at all; that we had had a public meeting there, and those who had been disposed to act in that way had seemed disposed to listen to us until numbers of men, who were well known to be innocent—as well known as we could know any one—of any violation of the enforcement law, had been dragged up to Oxford to be tried before the Federal court there. I stated that if the Government was disposed to take that course, I, for one, was disposed to let the Government take its own course with criminals, and I should not seek to exercise any influence one way or the other. I should not favor any such demonstrations, or take any part to put them down, unless required to do so.

Question. Is it a fact that the arrests of several men, supposed to be connected with these outrages, have been made in Winston County?

Answer. There have been several arrests made of men that I suppose were for that purpose. I do not know for what purpose they were taken. Some were carried to Oxford, and some to Jackson.

Question. How many arrests were made in your county under the enforcement act?

Answer. I do not know.

Question. A dozen, or fifteen?

Answer. I presume so. I do not know the number.

Question. Were bills of indictment found against them?

Answer. I do not know. I presume so, or they would not have been arrested.

Question. You understood that they were charged under the act passed by Congress in April last?

Answer. Yes, sir. I do not remember now the date of the passage of the law.

Question. With the exception of the arrests made by the Federal court, have you known of any arrests made by the State courts of any parties charged with the commission of these outrages?

Answer. I know of one arrest. There was a man arrested in our town who was charged with having appeared with a mask, in disguise, and demanded entrance into the house of a negro woman at 1 o'clock at night, making a great fuss—sufficient noise to wake up another party who lived three hundred yards off. The negro woman very promptly, next morning, made a complaint. The man was arrested and brought before a justice of the peace. I prosecuted him myself. It was a violation of our statute law upon that subject.

Question. Was he a white man?

Answer. He was a mulatto.

Question. Was he disguised?

Answer. The negro woman swore he was so completely disguised that she never would have detected him but for his voice, which he sought to disguise, but could not.

Question. Was he punished?

Answer. He was not punished, except that he was held to bail; in default of that was put in jail to answer at the next term of the circuit court. At the next term of the circuit court the grand jury failed to find any bill, and he was discharged by Judge Orr.

Question. My question related especially to white men. Are there any white men connected, or supposed to be connected, with these bands of disguised men prowling through the country and committing these outrages, who have ever, to your knowledge, been arrested and brought to trial in Winston County?

Answer. I know of none, sir. I know of no man who is suspected by the community of being connected with any of these things. I have no doubt of the fact that disguised bodies of men have inflicted outrages in Winston County upon divers parties. I have no doubt of that, but where these men come from I have no idea. I have no idea now of any man; I would not know now who, if I were required to point out a man that I suspected myself; I would not know who to suspect as being guilty of any of these offenses.

Question. It seems that the Federal grand jury has been more fortunate than your county grand juries in ferreting out the offenders?

Answer. I think, sir, that that is owing to the fact that some parties have made themselves very busy to get up indictments they could not sustain.

Question. That remains to be tried?

Answer. I think some of them have been discharged already, if I am not mistaken; I may be mistaken.

Question. But the fact remains that your State courts have proved entirely inadequate to discover and punish the perpetrators of these offenses, which you have referred to, committed by bands of men in disguise?

Answer. The State courts, sir, have never lacked the power of enforcing any law of the State.

Question. Perhaps there has been a lack of public sentiment in aiding the grand juries to detect the men.

Answer. I cannot say as to that; I think not. I think the public sentiment of Winston County is decidedly against anything like these Ku-Klux outrages or anything like outrages by disguised bands.

Question. It is barely possible that some of these Ku-Klux or their friends or sympathizers have found their way on your grand juries?

Answer. I cannot tell about that. I have no idea who is a Ku-Klux; I never saw but one, and that one was a mulatto.

Question. You have heard of them?

Answer. I have heard of men being in disguise, but I never heard of any particular man; I never have heard of any one suspected; I never have heard any particular individual charged or suspected of belonging to the organization or being engaged in these things.

Question. It seems to imply a lack of detective ability in your community that they are not discovered, does it not?

Answer. I do not know; that is a matter of opinion merely; I cannot say as to that. I wish to state this: that if there be one idea that has prevailed to a greater extent than any other with those who have committed outrages there, that is, in the way of driving off negroes, it has been the agrarian idea, "We do our own work, and our families have to do their own work, and you must do it too; we are not going to let you have servants." That has prevailed in one portion of the county. Those who have suffered most from these disturbances have not been the class of men who are generally supposed to have suffered from Ku-Klux demonstrations; but those who have suffered most, pecuniarily, at least, have been very substantial democrats.

Question. The men who have suffered scourgings and lost their lives have generally been negroes, have they not?

Answer. Well, sir, I have never heard that any suffered by scourging or loss of life on account of being negroes. I have heard of some suffering scourging or loss of life, and have heard of some white men suffering loss of life and pretty severe beatings on account of bad talk.

Question. Have you heard of white men in your community being Ku-Kluxed—visited and outraged by bands of men in disguise?

Answer. I have heard of white men being visited there and made to leave the county.

Question. By a band of men in disguise?

Answer. Yes, sir.

Question. When did that occur?

Answer. Not a great while ago.

Question. It was a white man?

Answer. Yes, sir.

Question. Give us the particulars of that case.

Answer. I do not know that I can tell the particulars of it; I only know this: that he was a man, according to the best of my information, who was a very substantial democratic planter, who lived in the eastern part of the county, and some one, I do not know for what purpose, concluded that he had to leave there, and they made him leave.

Question. How many men did you understand visited him?

Answer. I do not remember that I heard the number.

Question. Did you understand that he was whipped?

Answer. No, sir; he was not; he was warned.

Question. What coercion was brought to bear?

Answer. He was warned to leave.

Question. By this band?

Answer. Yes, sir.

Question. And he left?

Answer. Yes, sir.

Question. Left in fear?

Answer. Yes, sir; that is my information.

Question. Did you learn his offense?

Answer. I did not.

Question. Had he taken an active part against the Ku-Klux?

Answer. No, sir; I think not; I never heard of his taking a part against the Ku-Klux. I, myself, took as active a part against the Ku-Klux in our county as any man in the State could do, so far as talking was concerned.

Question. What part did you take?

Answer. I took the part of denouncing that course on all public occasions when it was mentioned.

Question. What course?

Answer. Appearing in masks or disguised for any purposes.

Question. You regarded it as such a public evil as ought to be——

Answer. As ought to be discountenanced and frowned down by all right-minded men.

Question. Yet you did not think it necessary to take the stump and denounce it?

Answer. No, sir; I did not take the stump at all; I spoke, I believe, once or twice in Louisville, merely; in one or two public meetings; I think, during two public meetings.

Question. Had these acts been so numerous as to make it necessary to call public attention to the fact?

Answer. They had been as I have recited, and I thought one or two even ought to be discountenanced.

Question. Did you denounce them as the Ku-Klux organization?

Answer. I did not denounce them as organizations at all, for I had no reason to suspect an organization at all.

Question. Did you denounce them as combinations of bad men?

Answer. I denounced the manner in which their purposes were accomplished. I did not denounce them as any regular organization, for I did not believe there was any regular organization, and do not believe so now.

Question. You denounced these combinations of men, for whatever purpose, who, in point of fact, inflicted these outrages upon person and property?

Answer. I denounced the infliction of outrages upon person and property by men masked and in disguise; not by an organization, for I did not believe there was any organization, and I do not believe so now. As far as my information extends I do not believe there has been any such organization at all. I believe when any man, white or black, by his conduct renders himself odious, some classes of men, some kind of men would adopt that course.

Question. In every case of outrage there was an actual organization in point of fact, was there not? As, for example, in the killing of Bird, thirty or forty men could not have come together by accident. It must have been by preconcert, arrangement and combination and organization to commit that specific deed?

Answer. There might have been an organization in that sense. They may have understood and agreed that some one should be their leader in that instance.

Question. Is it not quite possible that the same body of men who killed Bird, killed these other men who have been mentioned, and inflicted these whippings?

Answer. I have no idea that the same body of men who killed Bird made that man leave the county, that I spoke of.

Question. What other evidence have you that they were distinct organizations improvised for the occasion?

Answer. The only evidence I have of it is this: that these persons against whom wrongs are perpetrated in that way were of entirely different characters.

Question. Different characters? How could you know they were different characters when they disguised and screened their persons?

Answer. I say the men on whom the acts were committed, not the men who committed them. But the men upon whom the outrages were committed were of different character entirely, and not the same order of men. For instance, that man I spoke of just now.

Question. That planter?

Answer. Yes, sir. In the first place, this negro school-teacher I spoke of was a negro pretending to teach a school. He was a very ignorant fellow, not capable of teaching school at all. I suppose that the men who made him leave were a band of men determined that such fellows as he was should not be the recipients of the taxes they paid, under the pretence of teaching school. I do not suppose that class of men were actuated by the same motive when they went to this old planter that I spoke of and made him leave the county. I supposed, for that reason, that these were two different bands of men.

Question. Is it not quite possible that the combination of men who inflicted murder upon Bird and others could have inflicted elsewhere other outrages upon negroes and white men?

Answer. They might have done so, but I noticed that some injuries were inflicted upon negroes, and some upon white men. The white men were made to leave, which was an injury. Some were upon radicals, and some upon democrats. I never heard of the same band of men going again.

Question. May they not have been portions of the same band?

Answer. They may have been.

Question. Do you regard this raid on the negro in the jail as having been made in the interest of law and order?

Answer. I do not. I think it was very improper, and I believe it was the public opinion of Winston County that it was wrong.

Question. At the same time public opinion decrees that any man who commits a rape or attempts it should die.

Answer. That has been the universal opinion of the Southern people since my recollection. Not the man who attempts a rape, but the man who commits the rape; and the law, I think, has not come up to public opinion. I think that it does not inflict capital punishment upon the crime of rape.

Question. Public sentiment, then, would not demand that a person who had simply attempted a rape should be punished with death?

Answer. I do not think it would.

Question. You think, then, that those who lynched Bird went beyond the requirements of public opinion?

Answer. I am inclined to think they did, sir. I am not sure about that. I heard different expressions of opinion. Some thought they did right.

By Mr. BLAIR:

Question. What is the theory about those men that made that planter, as you say, leave the county; who were they?

Answer. I do not know who they were.

Question. Who, in your judgment, were they, and what was the motive of their doing it?

Answer. From my best information I formed this opinion: that they wanted to get his lands and cultivate them. He was owning lands there in the county of Winston—good lands, and I suppose they wanted to get his lands, or something of that sort. He lived in that part of the county where this agrarian spirit I spoke of seemed to prevail, and it had been frequently said that "such and such men have servants to do their work, and we have to do ours, and there shan't be any servants here."

By the CHAIRMAN:

Question. Was there not public sentiment enough in that community to protect that man from this outrage?

Answer. I think there was public sentiment enough to protect him if he had not been timorous.

By Mr. BLAIR:

Question. It was not supposed that it was done by democrats?

Answer. Of course not. He was a democrat, and, according to my information, has never voted other than a democratic ticket.

Question. Was it supposed that his being a democrat had anything to do with his being driven off?

Answer. I do not think it was. My information is that the political opinion of a man has never caused him to be punished in any way in Winston County. They have never been punished, democrats or radicals, in Winston County.

By the CHAIRMAN:

Question. Do you affiliate with the democratic party?

Answer. I do.

Question. Were you in the war?

Answer. Yes, sir.

Question. What rank did you hold in the confederate army?

Answer. I was a private in the First Regiment of Mississippi Cavalry.

Question. All through the war?

Answer. I volunteered in 1861, but I was a married man at the time, and a couple of brothers who were, at the time, single men, and they insisted that the exigencies of the country did not demand all the family, and that I should stay at home, as I was the only married one. I therefore remained at home until after the fall of Fort Pillow. I volunteered then, and joined the company made up by my brother, afterward organized in the First Mississippi Cavalry, commanded by Colonel Pinson. I was with him until May, 1863. In May, 1863, I was discharged from the service for physical disability. In the fall or winter, I think, in the latter part of 1863, I again joined his regiment, and continued in it until after the fight with General Kilpatrick—raid, as we call it—on the 28th of August—some time in the latter part of August—out in Georgia, at Lovejoy. I was very much heated in running through a creek there in pursuit of the general's troops—waded through until nearly waist-deep—and the next morning I was scarcely able to move at all. I was then sent home on a certificate of physical disability, with a recommedation to the department having charge of that matter to have me appointed auditor of public accounts for my congressional district, and I came home. Another man received the appointment, however; but the surgeon of my regiment and the medical board certified to my physical disability, and I never entered the service any more after August, 1864.

COLUMBUS, MISSISSIPPI, *November* 9, 1871.

JOSEPH F. GALLOWAY sworn and examined.

By the CHAIRMAN:

Question. State your place of residence and occupation.

Answer. My home goes by the name of Mary's Academy, up here near Caledonia.

By Mr. BLAIR:

Question. Are you a teacher there?

Answer. Yes, sir.

By the CHAIRMAN:

Question. How long have you lived in Lowndes County?

Answer. I have lived here since the fall of 1867. I lived in this town, though, the last part of 1867 and the first part of 1868. Since July, 1868, I have lived close to where I live now.

Question. What has been your occupation since you have lived in this county?

Answer. I have been teaching and preaching.

Question. Have you ever been molested in pursuing your avocation as a teacher?

Answer. Yes, sir; on the 29th of March last, I think, a band of, I suppose, about a hundred Ku-Klux came to my house.

Question. Were you, at the time, teaching the Mary's academy, near Caledonia?

Answer. Yes, sir. They called on me to give me orders to stop teaching.

Question. Did they call in the day-time or in the night?

Answer. It was a little after 12 o'clock at night, sir.

Question. Were they disguised?

Answer. Yes, sir.

Question. Were they on horseback?

Answer. They were; some of them on horseback and some on the ground. The horses were there, though, sir, and in disguise, too, most of them.

Question. Did you notice whether they were armed?

Answer. No, sir; I did not see any arms at that time.

Question. Did they have a leader?

Answer. Yes, sir; they had a chief spokesman. I think they called him captain.

Question. Did any one beside him address you?

Answer. When they first came to the house there were a good many voices hallooing and calling for Galloway.

Question. Were you in bed at the time?

Answer. Yes, sir; and asleep when they came. I did not know anything of it until they were running around the house. My wife shook me and said the Ku-Klux had come, and I woke up and heard them running around the house.

Question. Did they effect a forcible entrance into your house.

Answer. No, sir; they just rapped to the door, and told me to come to the door, and I did. I went to the door and talked to them.

Question. What occurred after you opened the door and met them?

Answer. I just opened the door a little and looked so I could see them. They were very lordly in their demand that I should come to them. They seemed like they were angry, and determined that I should step right in the door. When I stepped in the door they told me they had come to tell me not to teach the school any more. They asked me if I would do so, but I would not tell them whether I would or not. They went on then to say that if I did not, I believe they said, "We are not going to let the tax be collected," and they said if I taught I would have to lose it. Then they said if I did not stop teaching—that they did not want to call on me again, but if they did call on me again, they would give me two hundred lashes on my naked back, and they all said, "Woe unto that back of yours." I believe those were the words.

Question. Was that all.

Answer. Yes, sir. They were just going off when they said that. There were some shook their heads and horns at me, and acted like cows.

Question. Did what?

Answer. They had horns, and they shook their horns at me when I was in the door. They were just leaving, though, when they said, "Woe unto that back of yours."

Question. You may describe their disguises as near as you can.

Answer. They had on long gowns or robes—they looked more like gowns of some kind than anything else. Their masks were pieces of cloth, as well as I could tell, sewed to the seam of the coat on the shoulder, and brought over the head and fastened under the chin. I could see some parts of their faces. The first time they came to my house some of them had horns fastened to the top of the mask.

Question. Top of the head?

Answer. Yes, sir.

Question. Had they any beards?

Answer. Some of them had long beards about this long, [eighteen inches,] and some were black and some were white.

Question. The beards were black and white?

Answer. Yes, sir.

Question. Who did they say they were, and where did they say they came from?

Answer. Well, when they got outside of the yard they looked back and asked if I knew any of these gentlemen, and my wife says, "Are you gentlemen?" as though she did not think that people could be gentlemen that would act in that way, and then they muttered something, I could not tell what, and said they had come from Manassas Gap to see that the poor widows are not imposed upon. They also said that the rebels were not going to let the taxes be paid. From the two things you would infer that they were rebels killed at Manassas. They said they were risen from the dead, and that they were rebels, too. They said I did not have to tell if I knew any one, bnt if I knew it I had to know it to myself.

Question. Did they threaten any punishment if you told on them?

Answer. No, sir. My wife was having them in derision, so they did not have time to say anything more to me.

Question. Did you recognize any of them?

Answer. I thought, sir, that I did. I felt confident that I knew one voice when they hallooed at the door, but I do not know. I thought it was Robert Stevenson; but since then I have learned—that is, I have heard—that John Stevenson was in the crowd, and the Stevensons all talk so much alike that I would not be willing to say it was Robert.

Question. Is that a thickly settled neighborhood where the academy is situated?

Answer. No, sir; not very. Those men did not come from that immediate neighborhood.

Question. How do you know?

Answer. I know them too well. They may have come from above me and around me. I am rather at the outside of the neighborhood. When they were shaking their horns at me, I thought because of the movements—I could not tell any other way only from the movements—that one of them must be Henry Anderson. I went to school with him, and he moved very peculiar, and I thought it was him, though I did not believe he would be caught in such a place as that. I heard a few days after that he was seen going to Caledonia, where the Ku-Klux met, a few hours after night, the night they came to my house.

Question. How far is this village of Caledonia from the school?

Answer. It is two miles, I suppose, sir; may be a little more. He was seen just above my house, going to Caledonia. He was also seen just a while before night in Caledonia.

Question. Is it your opinion that he was one of the gang or crowd?

Answer. Yes, sir. I will state that they went from my house to the house of a man named Wat Kendricks.
Question. Did they do any mischief at Kendricks's?
Answer. What they went there for was this: a man named McLaughlin had lived in the house Kendricks had moved to, and he had got Kendricks to go there, The house belonged to some orphan children—the nephews of Ben and Henry Anderson. The Andersons were determined that Kendricks should not live there, and wanted the house for some other parties, and they went there to get Kendricks to leave.

By Mr. BLAIR:

Question Belonged to Henry Anderson?
Answer. To the nephews of Henry Anderson and Benjamin Anderson, and they were determined that the Kendricks should not stay in the house.

By the CHAIRMAN:

Question. You say they warned Kendrick that night to leave?
Answer. Yes, sir.
Question. Did they make any threats of what they would do if he did not leave?
Answer. I believe they did, but I cannot say what the threats were. They told him he had to leave, and by such a time.
Question. Did he leave?
Answer. Yes, sir; he did get out. As soon as this Ku-Klux law was passed he went back to the house, and he has not been disturbed since, I think.
Question. That was on the same night you were visited?
Answer. Yes, sir.
Question. On the 29th of March last?
Answer. They went from Kendricks's to my brother-in-law's, Eli Tapley.
Question. How far does Tapley live from you?
Answer. About half a mile.
Question. How far does Kendricks live from you?
Answer. A mile, I suppose, or more.
Question. Did they go to Kendricks's first?
Answer. They went by my brother-in-law's, and then they came back to Kendricks's.
Question. What did they do there?
Answer. They did not do anything there, except whistle, and whoop, and go on around the house a while, trying to scare him, I suppose.
Question. Did they give him any warning?
Answer. No, sir. They had ordered him some days before to go. Some parties had told him if he did not quit sticking up tracts they would visit him—Ku-Klux him.
Question. Religious tracts?
Answer. Masonic tracts and religious tracts, too.
Question. What did they order him to do?
Answer. They ordered him to stop posting them up by the road-side.
Question. Or they would do what?
Answer. That they would Ku-Klux him. That is what they said they would do. They went from there to Squire Webb's.
Question. How far does he live from you?
Answer. A mile and a half; perhaps more. He was a teacher. But before they went there they first called on a man named Elsie Mintur, and told him not to send his children to my sister-in-law to school any more. I was teaching freedmen's school and she was teaching white school.
Question. Did you and your sister-in-law teach in the same building?
Answer. No, sir; she taught at Ridgeway Academy, this side of there.
Question. Did they call her up out of her bed?
Answer. No, sir; they told me to tell her, and told this man to tell her. They told me to tell her to stop teaching; and they did not want her to teach at all. And they told Mintur not to send his children there.
Question. Was she boarding at your house?
Answer. No, sir; she was living at home.
Question. You may come back to Squire Webb and state what they said or did to him.
Answer. They just told him to stop teaching school. That is all I ever heard.
Question. Was he teaching a white or colored school?
Answer. A white school.
Question. Did your sister-in-law, or Webb, or yourself, quit teaching?
Answer. I stopped a few days. My sister-in-law never stopped any.
Question. Did you stop in consequence of this warning?
Answer. Yes, sir.
Question. Did Webb stop?
Answer. No, sir; he did not care. He went to the school and told them they would

have to be responsible for the pay, and the parents said they would be responsible if the taxes were not collected, and he taught on.

By Mr. BLAIR:

Question. What did he do?

Answer. He told the parents of the children that they would have to be responsible for the pay if the tax was not collected; that they would have to pay him for teaching the school, and they said that they would do it.

Question. Who; Webb?

Answer. Yes, sir.

By the CHAIRMAN:

Question. The object seemed to be in all these cases to break up the school?

Answer. Yes, sir; that was the intent. That was what they said. They called on Mr. Myers and Miss Booth before they came to my house on the same night.

Question. Did they deliver similar messages to them?

Answer. Yes, sir. They were teaching white schools and never stopped a day. They kept right on. The parents said that they would see that they were paid. They called on another gentleman—a man, I cannot call him a gentleman—after they left Webb's, and told him he had to stop drinking and take care of his wife.

Question. What was the name of the man they called on that they said must stop drinking and attend to his wife?

Answer. Jim Kohn.

Question. Was he a German?

Answer. No, sir.

Question. Was any violence inflicted by these men upon any of these persons?

Answer. No, sir.

Question. Was their property interfered with in any way?

Answer. No, sir. Somebody has disturbed my property since that, but I do not know whether they did it or not.

Question. Did you ever before that time receive any Ku-Klux letter, or have you since that time received any?

Answer. I received a Ku-Klux message.

Question. Tell us about the message.

Answer. They sent word to me I had to stop teaching.

Question. Was that before you were visited?

Answer. Yes, sir.

Question. Who brought that?

Answer. A colored woman brought it. I do not know how she got it. She sent it by her children, that were coming to school to me, that I would have to stop teaching.

Question. Did you see the colored woman and ascertain from her who told her?

Answer. No, sir. She said, I understood, that a child told her—a little boy.

Question. So you could not trace it up to any responsible source?

Answer. No, sir. Since that I received a letter written by Leonard Stewart.

Question. Who is Leonard Stewart?

Answer. He is a man that lives in Monroe County. They went to visit a man teaching over in Monroe County, and when they were there they gave Leonard orders and told him I did not have to preach in Monroe County any more.

By Mr. BLAIR:

Question. Was Stewart in Monroe County?

Answer. Yes, sir; just across from Kellick's Ferry.

By the CHAIRMAN:

Question. What Christian denomination do you belong to?

Answer. Congregational.

By Mr. BLAIR:

Question. Leonard Stewart wrote to you that they said this?

Answer. Yes, sir; the statement that the Ku-Klux made.

By the CHAIRMAN:

Question. Did he say that the Ku-Klux had directed him to send that message?

Answer. Yes, sir.

Question. Have you seen Stewart since?

Answer. Yes, sir; I saw him the next day after I got the letter—I think Thursday or Friday—and the Ku-Klux called on me the next night after I got it—no; they called on me Friday night, and I saw Stewart the next day.

Question. Did he inform you who communicated that message to him?

Answer. He said it was the Ku-Klux; that he did not know who they were.

Question. That it was a band of Ku-Klux visited his house, and directed him to send that message?

Answer. They visited Brown, the teacher, who was boarding at his house, and while they were there they told him to send this message to me.

Question. Was Brown the teacher of a colored school?

Answer. Yes, sir.

Question. Did they warn him to quit teaching?

Answer. Yes, sir.

Question. What part of Monroe County is that in?

Answer. It is in the southern part of Monroe County.

Question. That part which joins upon Lowndes?

Answer. Yes, sir; where the man taught was about three miles from the edge of the county line; where Stewart taught, too.

Question. Did Brown quit teaching?

Answer. Yes, sir. He has never taught any more.

Question. Have you talked with Brown upon this subject?

Answer. Yes, sir.

Question. Please repeat what he stated to you in relation to the visit he received from the Ku-Klux, and what they said to him, and what violence, if any, they offered or threatened.

Answer. They never offered any violence at all. He said they treated him very gentlemanly.

Question. Did he say they threatened any punishment in case he continued to teach?

Answer. I do not remember that they did threaten any violence at all. They told him positively that he had to stop, and that they did not want to call on him again; that he had to stop immediately, and not teach any more; and they also, after that, gave him orders, and told him not to come back and live with the Feemsters—they are my wife's people. He was an orphan boy, and we got him and educated him, and he will stay with us.

By Mr. BLAIR:

Question. They did not want him to live with whom?

Answer. They did not want him to go and live with the Feemsters.

Question. You say that is a family related to your wife?

Answer. Yes, sir.

By the CHAIRMAN:

Question. Does that finish the catalogue of teacher warnings?

Answer. Well, there was a lady, a Miss Booth, that taught over there close to Mr. Brown's, that they visited after that.

Question. Did she teach in Monroe County?

Answer. Yes, sir.

Question. A colored or white school?

Answer. She was teaching a white school.

By Mr. BLAIR:

Question. Did you say she was visited?

Answer. Yes, sir; they called her up one night and had her come out to the gate, and gave her instruction not to teach any more; they said she might teach pay school, where the parents paid for themselves.

By the CHAIRMAN:

Question. Did she quit teaching?

Answer. No, sir. The parents told her to teach on; that they would pay it, and she kept on.

Question. Have any of these teachers been interfered with since these visits that you know of?

Answer. There has not any one received a second visit but myself, to my knowledge.

Question. When did you receive a second visit?

Answer. I think it was the 19th of April.

Question. You may state the particulars.

Answer. Would it be lawful for me to state a few things I heard beforehand—the reasons why I expected them to visit me?

Question. Yes, sir.

Answer. I was preaching in Monroe, and I was very much interested that they should have a Sabbath-school, and told the colored children if they would keep on they would soon be before the white children, and I saw some parties of the white people were trying to get them to have a Sabbath-school and told them if they would I would encourage them and take them cards and tracts and papers. They taught a few days, and tried to get them to receive the cards and papers and tracts, but when I saw there was no hope of having a Sabbath-school, and that the white children could not read, I told the colored children that they would soon be before the white children if they kept on, and I encouraged them to keep on, and they made a great deal of capital there about that, and said I was teaching the colored children things they ought not to be taught. It was rumored around by some one (I do not know who) that I was drilling the colored people all around; that I had been seen twenty miles below Columbus here, drilling them to make war upon the Ku-Klux, or some such things as that.

Question. Was there any foundation for that charge?

Answer. No, sir; I never drilled a day in my life; I do not know anything about military drill.

Question. The charge, then, was without foundation?

Answer. Yes, sir.

Question. Go on.

Answer. They also said that I had been preaching false doctrine. I had heard that they said they were coming to the church to make the colored people—the members of the church, and all that were there—swear that I did teach false doctrine. When they came to my house, after that I had heard of these things, and more too—it is not necessary to state all—I let them halloo and whoop and go on and knock around the house. I thought I would not say anything to them. Then I concluded I would go to the door. They said if I would please come to the door they would not hurt a hair of my head; they wanted to talk to me. I went to the door then and opened it and talked over all these things. They said they had come to tell me to stop preaching over there, for they had preachers enough in Monroe County without me; that I was living there, and I had to stop. They asked me if I would do it. I would not answer any questions at all. I had said all I wished to say, and then I just answered in the words of the apostle, that whether it would be right to hearken unto men more than unto God judge ye. Then one of them seemed to think that I had said I would quit, and another seemed to think I had said I would not quit, but they went off without any further explanation. They went on then, and said that if I did not stop I would have to bear the consequences, and my wife replied that we would; that I was willing to bear any consequences that came from doing right. They said they had disposed of one man in one way and another in another way; that they had not received any orders in regard to me and they did not know what they would do with me, but when they did get the orders they would carry them out. They said they would not tell me what they would do with me then.

Question. Who did they say they received their orders from?

Answer. They did not say, sir. I have forgotten the exact words, but I got the idea that they had some chief man that they received the orders from. I do not remember the words.

Question. Did they say anything about a grand cyclops?

Answer. No, sir. The chief spokesman called one of their number the "captain of the gun-boat."

Question. Were they disguised in the same way on the second visit?

Answer. No, sir; altogether different.

Question. Were they disguised at all?

Answer. Yes, sir.

Question. What was the form of their disguise?

Answer. They were dressed in white, similar to the overall clothes of carpenters and such like wear up North, and had what looked like these tight sacks the ladies wear, trimmed in black, that are white. They had some kind of white caps, and they were trimmed with white, with horns. Some of them had horns I suppose this long, [illustrating,] two feet long—curled horns like sheep's horns—tied on.

Question. The whole character of the disguise, I understand, was unlike that of the former body that visited you?

Answer. Yes, sir. The chief spokesman, though, was dressed in white. He had white overalls and a white sack.

Question. Were they on horseback also?

Answer. Yes, sir.

Question. In what number did they come?

Answer. There were seven stood at the door and one held the horses. They said the rest of the party were out at the road, about one hundred and fifty or two hundred yards from the house.

Question. How many were there in all?

Answer. Eight in all. There were seven by the door and one held the horses. The balance of their company was at the road.

Question. Did you verify the statement next morning by examining the horses' tracks?

Answer. Yes, sir; there were a great many tracks in the road next morning.

Question. So you were of opinion that they were simply a detachment from a larger body?

Answer. Yes, sir. They said they were a detachment, and they said if I did not answer the questions they would call the rest of the company up.

Question. Did they say anything in relation to your teaching school in this second visit?

Answer. They said they did not have any objection to that. They hadn't any objection to colored people being instructed the last time they came; but I thought that was so the whole time, that they just wanted to pick up with me for something else.

Question. Did they tell you where they came from?

Answer. Yes, sir; they said they came from "Alabam."

Question. How far were you from the Alabama line?

Answer. About seven or eight miles; but they never went to Alabama.

Question. What county in Alabama is opposite Caledonia?

Answer. I think it is about opposite the line of Fayette County and Marion County, in Alabama.

Question. They are opposite to that portion of Monroe County, Mississippi?

Answer. Yes, sir; Monroe County is opposite to Marion and Fayette County, Alabama. I think the Marion line is not far above that point.

Question. Had you then, or have you now, any means of determining whether the men who visited you the second time were the same persons who visited you the first time?

Answer. No, sir. The first time I did not have any idea who the chief spokesman was. I think there was a Stevenson voice there, and I think Henry Anderson. I do not know exactly where John Stevenson lives, but since they heard of this investigating committee he has gone off. They got him and took him to Aberdeen, and he has left since that.

By Mr. BLAIR:

Question. Who do you speak of?

Answer. John Stevenson. I heard a colored man say a while ago that he saw him lying out; but the last rumor is he has gone to Texas. Some other parties they have tried to get up there have gone away.

By the CHAIRMAN:

Question. Some that the marshal tried to get?

Answer. Yes, sir.

Question. On warrants from the district court?

Answer. Yes, sir. Henry Anderson lived about a mile from there. These men I could not name positively, but from the voices and from the size of the men, especially of the chief spokesman, I should say it was Stewart.

Question. You are speaking now of the second visit?

Answer. Yes, sir.

By Mr. BLAIR:

Question. Who was the chief?

Answer. Leonard Stewart. If it was not him it was as near him, and his exact figure, as could be, in my judgment, in size, height, and everything.

By the CHAIRMAN:

Question. This Leonard Stewart was the same one who wrote you the letter at the instance of the Ku-Klux?

Answer. Yes, sir; and the visit was the next day, I think, or the next night, after I got that letter.

Question. Have you discontinued preaching in Monroe County in consequence of that notice?

Answer. No, sir. The next day after they came I went to see him to know whether they wanted me to stop or not.

Question. To see Stewart?

Answer. Yes, sir; I preached on his land. He gave permission, and said I could have preaching there as long as it seemed to do any good.

Question. What did he say after that visit?

Answer. He advised me not to preach there any more. He said he was afraid that these Ku-Klux would get hold of me and would kill me. He did not say that in so many words, but that was the idea. He said they had killed men, and he gave an instance of one man that they had killed, who was found dead, that had made threats against the Ku-Klux. I told him I was willing, if he would show me where I had done wrong, to stop. I told him if he would show me that the preaching in that church did not do good I would stop. He did not do that, nor did not try. He simply advised several times not to go on. I told him that would be succumbing to Ku-Klux orders, and I never intended to do it. I told him if they continued to do this way I had to report; that I was commissioned by the American Missionary Society to teach and preach, and I had to make my report, and if they went to interfere with me I would make it and tell how things were, and I had the promise that I should be protected and should preach there if I had to have a standing guard, and I intended to do it.

Question. What did he say to that?

Answer. He said he would not like to have any soldiers there. I told him I did not wish any either if the people would behave and let me alone, but I intended to have my rights.

Question. Have you continued to preach?

Answer. Yes, sir; I preach there every week now. I used to preach once in two weeks.

Question. Do they molest you?

Answer. No, sir; they do not do anything openly.

Question. Explain what you said a while ago about stimulating competition among the children by making presents of tracts and cards. What kind of cards were they?

Answer. They were missionary society tracts—nothing more than just common religious tracts and cards.

Question. What kind of cards?

Answer. They were little picture cards with verses on them.

Question. Not playing-cards?

Answer. O, no, sir. If they had been that kind I do not suppose they would have disturbed them at all.

Question. Do you know of any other, or have you heard of any other, Ku-Klux visitations in the northeastern part of this county, or in Monroe?

Answer. Yes, sir. While we are talking about these visitations and molestations, I will state that one man that visited my church, and two members of his family——

Question. What was his name?

Answer. Albert Hardy; he was visited.

Question. When was he visited?

Answer. He was visited, I think, a short time before they visited me the last time.

Question. That would be shortly before the 1st of April?

Answer. It would be shortly before the 19th of April.

Question. You may state the particulars as you learned them from him or other reliable sources.

Answer. They went to his house and surrounded the house.

Question. Who do you mean by "they?"

Answer. The Ku-Klux.

Question. In the night-time?

Answer. Yes, sir; after night. I do not know at what hour it was, but it was evidently considerably in the night. They had gone to bed.

Question. Did you understand in what numbers?

Answer. No, sir.

Question. What did they do?

Answer. They kicked around the house and guarded the doors until they got him out, and then they run at him with their pistols cocked and their guns, and stuck them against his breast, and made him stand out in the yard until they examined his house, and told him he must never go to my church again. I think they told him if he did he would be in hell before long, and he was a wicked man. He said he was afraid he would get in hell before long if the gun should happen to go off. He would be there then, for they were punching him in his breast and all over his body. That stopped him from going to my church for several months, and he cannot go to church to-day or any time now. He is rather afraid to go.

Question. Did you get this information directly from Hardy?

Answer. Yes, sir; from him and other parties, too.

Question. You say they went through his house?

Answer. They went in his house and looked under the bed and on the bed.

Question. What were they looking for?

Answer. They were looking for the deacon of the church.

Question Who was he?

Answer. James Stewart.

Question. Was he there that night?

Answer. No, sir; he had got word a few days before that they were coming to his house for some purpose. I never heard him say what they were going to do. I think he was afraid to say. He had run away and gone to Tennessee, to Memphis. They were looking for him, and also giving orders for people not to attend my church.

Question. What umbrage did they take to your church? Was it to the doctrines?

Answer. No, sir; I preached to the colored people and I taught them.

Question. Was this Hardy a colored man?

Answer. Yes, sir.

Question. And Stewart also, the deacon?

Answer. Yes, sir.
Question. Then this was a colored church that had the trouble?
Answer. Yes, sir.
Question. I did not know from what you said but what their objection was that you were teaching false doctrines?
Answer. That was only a pretense. I tried to get them to appoint a day, when they came to my house, and we would investigate the whole matter. I told them I would be anxious, would come with them any day, to prove that I had not done any such thing, or any of these things they accused me of—any day except Sunday; I would not come Sunday for I would not feel it proper to follow out such lies on Sunday, but any other day I would came. They said they did their work in the night. This was all a pretense to get hold of me.
Question. Your opinion is that their real objection was against the establishment of a colored church there, and against your preaching?
Answer. Yes, sir; and then they said I had so much influence with the colored people, and that I was a white man outside and black inside—that is, that I was a republican.
Question. Did they say you were a republican?
Answer. No; they did not say I was a republican. They asked me whether I was, and I told them I was.
Question. Did they ask you about your politics?
Answer. Yes, sir; about my politics, and I told them I was a republican.
Question. What did they reply to that?
Answer. They said after that that I was white outside and black inside.
Question. Did they charge you with preaching politics to the colored people?
Answer. Yes, sir; they said they wanted me to stop, because I had so much influence over the colored people.
Question. In point of fact, did you ever preach politics to the colored people when they were assembled together in church capacity?
Answer. I never preached a political sermon in my life. Indeed, there are few men have as little to do with politics as I do.
Question. Was it true that you had a good deal of influence over the colored people?
Answer. Yes, sir.
Question. They had confidence in you?
Answer. Yes, sir.
Question. Confidence in you as an educational teacher and a religious teacher?
Answer. Yes, sir. They seemed to think that whatever I said was so. They had perfect confidence that if they came to me for any purpose that I would give them justice and tell them what was right as well as I could.
Question. Did they seem to think that you influenced the political sentiments and the political action of the colored people when they came to vote?
Answer. Yes, sir.
Question. Did they say or imply that in their language?
Answer. I drew that inference from their saying I had a great influence over the colored people; that they did not want me over there.
Question. You say that, in point of fact, you have taken very little part in politics?
Answer. I have taken no part at all, unless it was some one asking me my opinion.
Question. You did not make it your business to instruct the negroes how to vote?
Answer. No, sir; if the negroes asked me about it, or asked me what I thought, I would tell them. There have been some questions asked me about the Ku-Klux, too. I suppose that rather aroused them. You ask me what I had taught the colored people. Some men have been threatened—they had threatened to visit them, and after sermon one day, when I was getting on my horse, or about to get on my horse, they came to me and asked me if there was any way to get rid of the Ku-Klux, and I told them yes.
Question. Who asked that question?
Answer. A colored man—a member of the church. They asked if there was not some way to get rid of these Ku-Klux.
Question. What was your reply?
Answer. I told them that there was. They then asked me if shooting them would make them stop. I told them it would frighten them very much if they would be shot into. A colored man then says, "Will you go with me," or "go with us, if we shoot them?" I said, "No." They wanted to know why. I told him I did not think it was our business to go and shoot them. They wanted to know, or rather he did—there were a good many men around to hear it—he wanted to know what would be the course. I told them to get along as well as they could, and the United States would take it in hand before long and give them their rights; that they would have to look to the Government; that we could not be the Government ourselves and take the Government into our own hands.
Question. You never counseled armed resistance?
Answer. No, sir; on the contrary, I discountenanced it all the time, unless they thought there was an absolute necessity for it to save their lives. This colored man

got angry when I told him we would have to wait on the Government of the United States to defend us and take care of us. He said they had waited on the Government a good while now, and were getting killed and whipped and abused all around, and they thought they would have to take it into their own hands. He said he would die any day before he would submit to it.

Question. Did the Ku-Klux, in either of these visits, charge you with making war upon their order, or counseling the negroes to arm themselves?

Answer. Yes, sir. They said I had advised the negroes to shoot them. I told them the whole truth of it was, if I had not stood between them and the negroes, they would have got killed.

Question. Did that seem to satisfy them?

Answer. No, sir; they were not very well satisfied unless I would tell them I would stop preaching. I told them I would give them security, and I would insure them that no member of my church would hurt them without my knowledge, or, if it came to my knowledge, they would not do it with my consent. I had always advised them not to interfere with them.

Question. Did they state the objection to preaching to the colored people?

Answer. They did not care, they said, for my preaching to the colored people, but not to preach to the white people. I said I had invited them to come and hear me, and I could not preach to them if they did not come.

Question. They claimed that you discriminated—preaching to the colored and not to the white people?

Answer. Yes, sir; but in fact, when the white people came in, we offered them the chief seats, and they would not have them, and of course I could not do anything more than invite them in.

Question. Do you know any other instance of Ku-Klux outrages? The last you spoke of was a case of Albert Hardy.

Answer. Jim Hicks lives in this county, about six miles from here; and he and his wife have both been whipped.

Question. In what direction from here?

Answer. They live up on the military road, in about a northeastern direction from here, about six miles or a little more from here.

Question. When were they whipped?

Answer. They were whipped, I suppose, a month before they came to my house the first time, sir.

Question. That would be a month before the 29th of March?

Answer. Yes, sir. I am not certain about the time, but it was before they came to my house.

Question. You may state the particulars as you learned them from Hicks, his wife, or other reliable sources.

Answer. I know very few of the particulars. The way it started was, Hicks was living with a man who is in town to-day, whose name is Durden. They had some falling out about the crop—the crop was nearly made—the night before, and they got into a difficulty about it somehow, and some words passed, and Durden shot at him; and they undertook then to run him off, but he did not want to go. A few days after the fuss the Ku-Klux went there, but he found out that they were coming and slipped off into the woods. They went in, and his wife talked with them. They went to the bed where she was, and she talked with them. They told her he did not have to come back any more into that neighborhood, and he had to leave immediately, and he did. As soon as he could, he left, and came down to where he lives now. He said the Ku-Klux might come on now; he had enough to back him. That is the report I heard to that effect, at any rate. They got hold of this, and went down there, and got him, and were whipping him; and his wife hollered and took on so that they hit her, I think, about fifty licks to make her stop.

Question. How far was this from the neighborhood in which they removed from Durden's plantation?

Answer. I suppose it was some six or seven miles. I do not know exactly where he lives, but I think it was about that far, sir.

Question. About how long was this after they had left Durden's?

Answer. That first difficulty was in the fall, and this was some time in the winter.

Question. In February?

Answer. Yes, sir; I suppose so. I am not certain that it was in February, but it was some time before they came to my house and called on me. I think it was, perhaps, a month before that.

Question. That would be in February or March, then, probably?

Answer. Yes, sir.

Question. Were Hicks and his wife colored people?

Answer. Yes, sir.

Question. Was he whipped severely?

Answer. Yes, sir; he was badly whipped.

Question. Did you ever talk with him?

Answer. No, sir.

Question. You got this information from other sources?

Answer. Yes, sir.

Question. Did you understand how large the crowd was that whipped him?

Answer. I understood that there were twenty or thirty went there to his house.

Question Were they disguised men?

Answer. Yes, sir; they were all disguised.

Question. Did they tell him what they were whipping him for?

Answer. I never heard whether they did or not. It seems that I did hear that they said something about what he had said.

Question. Against the Ku-Klux?

Answer. Yes, sir.

Question. That was in this county?

Answer. Yes, sir. And then the night they visited my house—the last time I talked with them—they whipped a man by the name of George Irion.

Question. Was that in this county?

Answer. Yes, sir; between here and my house, somewhere.

Question. That was along in the latter part of April?

Answer. Yes, sir; the 19th of April, I think.

Question. Was he a colored man?

Answer. Yes, sir.

Question. What were the circumstances of his whipping? What was the cause or pretext of their whipping him?

Answer. That he was keeping a white woman.

Question. Was that true, in point of fact?

Answer. Yes, sir.

Question. Was he a mulatto or full-blooded negro?

Answer. I do not know, sir.

Question. Go on with your statement?

Answer. I think the same week that they whipped Irion they whipped, I think, three colored women about Caledonia. I am not certain who they were. One of them was Montgomery's wife. I do not know who the others were. They whipped them, I think, because of some difficulty they had in the family teaching them to keep the peace.

Question. How many were concerned in their whipping?

Answer. I do not know; I never heard. One of them they whipped because they said she was lazy and did not work well. I do not know what they whipped the third one for. Then there was a colored man by the name of Murphy, about this same time, that they whipped.

Question. Do you recollect his first name?

Answer. I think they called him Ned Murphy. I am not certain. He lives with Ed Hutchinson.

Question. In what part of the county?

Answer. About two miles and a half from where I do. I do not know exactly where he lives.

Question. When was he whipped?

Answer. He was whipped about the time these last people were whipped. I do not know the time exactly.

Question. Was it this year?

Answer. Yes, sir; some time in April.

Question. You may give the particulars?

Answer. They said they whipped him because he did not keep stove-wood in the kitchen. He said that Ed Hutchinson, the man he was living with, was the man whipping, and he hallooed "O, Massa Ed," all the time they were whipping him. He asked Ed Hutchinson's mother if it was not Ed, how the people knew there was not stove-wood in the kitchen, and that fires were not made at the right time. She told him it was some parties that came from hell and got the grease and greased their stove and found there wasn't any wood in the kitchen.

Question. That is what the mother of Ed Hutchinson is reported to have said to Murphy?

Answer. Yes, sir.

Question. How many were said to have been concerned in Murphy's whipping?

Answer. I do not know; I never heard of any but three or four. I heard of three or four names that they said were there. Ed Hutchinson, John Stevenson, and Daniel Stevenson.

Question. Do you recollect any other case?

Answer. Bob Wells, a colored man that lives up about me, was whipped; but I do not know what time it was. He lives about four or five, or perhaps six miles above where I do.

Question. Did you understand how many men were concerned in whipping him?

Answer. He told me about it. He said the hill was covered with ghostly looking folks, and did not seem to know how many there were. He seemed to have an idea that there were a great many there.

Question. Did he say they were disguised?

Answer. Yes, sir.

Question. Did he know for what he was whipped?

Answer. Yes, sir; he told me for what they said they whipped him, but I have forgotten it. It was some of his business affairs.

Question. Was that in the present year?

Answer. It was last winter some time; I do not know exactly what time. It was this summer that was told me about it. I went up to his house to preach, and he told me about it then.

Question. Do any other cases occur to you?

Answer. There are other cases but I do not remember their names now. There have been a great many whipped around there. I do not pretend to keep them all.

Question. You say it was a frequent occurrence?

Answer. Yes, sir; there was a while that it was every night somebody was whipped, or visited, or something. They were riding, and they never stopped it either until after they sent and took me to Oxford to appear before the grand jury. When I came back they had stopped riding.

Question. What time did you go to Oxford?

Answer. I think it was the last of June, or first of July. It was about the last of June.

Question. You appeared before the grand jury?

Answer. Yes, sir.

Question. At Oxford, in the district court?

Answer. Yes, sir.

Question. Have you known or heard of any outrages since that time, up in that part of the country?

Answer. No, sir. I have heard of threats sometimes, but I have not heard of any one being molested.

Question. Were indictments found against any parties in the district court?

Answer. Well, they have taken Warren Gardner, and Jim Herron, and John Stevenson. They took them to Oxford. They took Stevenson to Aberdeen and he got away.

Question. The other two were taken to Oxford?

Answer. Yes, sir; They are under bail to appear at court next month.

Question. Did you understand what the charge was against them?

Answer. It was for having a part in this Ku-Klux matter. I do not know what the evidence is; I suppose I know, too; they whipped Joe Turner very badly, and I suppose they took them up on that.

Question. Tell us about Joe Turner's case?

Answer. He was working with John Stevenson, and they had some falling out; he left John and would not work with him, and went up to Caledonia to his brother or brother-in-law's—I think it is his brother-in-law—and they worked around after him a good while, trying to get him, to come upon him when he did not have any arms. One night he went down to his brother in-law's and left his pistol off. Not long after he went to bed they came upon him and caught him, and whipped him. They whipped him badly.

Question. These ghostly fellows are afraid of arms, are they?

Answer. Yes, sir; very much so. They whipped him; I do not know as they told him what they whipped him for; but some parties had told the ferryman that they were going to whip him before that, and they went up to Caledonia and left. They found that he had his arms that night and went back, and told them that it would not do any good to whip him, so they let him off. But when they found he did not have any arms they whipped him. I have heard that they whipped him for leaving Stevenson.

Question. Did you understand how many men were concerned in whipping him?

Answer. No, sir.

Question. And the arrests, you speak of now, were for the whipping of Joe Turner?

Answer. Yes, sir; I think that is it; I do not know. I understood that John Stevenson, and I think Daniel Stevenson, and John Kidd were concerned in it. I know that when they arrested Warren Gardner they tried to get Kidd.

By Mr. Blair:

Question. What Kidd is that?

Answer. John Kidd; and John Stevenson is also gone; that is he is not seen.

By the Chairman:

Question. This action in the United States court has created a great panic among the Ku-Klux?

Answer. Yes, sir; they are very much alarmed about it. Is it right for me to state anything I know since I came back?

Question. Certainly.

Answer. Directly after I came back I heard a great many parties that lived in Caledonia had run away and got into the woods. One—the bar-keeper there; I cannot think of his name now——

By Mr. BLAIR:

Question. You say you found a great many had left town and gone to the woods?

Answer. Yes, sir; they had. When I came back they left. I know that man's name as well as my own, but I cannot think of it; anyhow, he is the only bar-keeper there in Caledonia—it is Tom Barrentine. He run away about a mile, I suppose, back of my house, east of my house in the pine thicket, and a colored man found him after he had been out about a week. He was very bad off; sick. The colored man tried to get him to come home, but he would not come. The colored man was afraid he would die. He said, "Let me go; I can find the way home." He said, "I will take you." He said, "No; if I die, I will die; I don't want to go to Caledonia." That is what the colored man reported.

By the CHAIRMAN:

Question. Was he a man implicated in these Ku-Klux operations?

Answer. I do not know anything about it, only I suspected him from a horse-track that was in the road every morning that the Ku-Klux rode. I did not know the horse, but the colored people said they knew it was Tom Barrentine's horse. When I came back he run away, and Jim Herron also run away. He is bound over to appear, and these Stevenson boys, Daniel and John; Andy Ager and Daniel Mayfield, too, and Ager is gone; he run away not long ago, and Daniel Mayfield lives up there now; he has got back. I never thought about Tom Barrentine being in it, until he ran away, but he seemed to want to keep away so he could not be arrested.

Question. You have hitherto spoken only of whippings, of people being warned to leave and quit teaching school or preaching, or something of the sort. Do you know or have you heard of any person being murdered by these bands of disguised men?

Answer. Well, sir, I spoke to you about the man Stewart spoke of being killed over in his county. He said he was killed, and then he modified it and said he was found dead.

By Mr. BLAIR:

Question. Who reported that?

Answer. Stewart reported when he was at my house, that a man had been killed over there.

By the CHAIRMAN:

Question. Do you know or have you heard of any other case?

Answer. Well, sir, there was a man, I suppose, that was found dead in the same manner; nearly the same time.

Question. Do you recollect his name?

Answer. His name was Perkins. I have forgotten if I ever knew his given name. He was found dead about two miles, I think, from my house.

Question. When was that?

Answer. I am not certain, but I think he was buried either the 27th or 28th of March, and the parson, Wood, gave out that there would be a meeting of the lodge that night if it did not rain.

Question. What lodge; the masonic lodge?

Answer. Yes, sir; Woodlawn. That if it did rain there would not be any until next night; and it did rain that night, and the next night they went there. I do not know whether they went there the evening they came to my house or not.

Question. Who came to your house?

Answer. The Ku-Klux came to my house. They said there would be a meeting of the lodge. Some colored man told me they had come to the lodge that night, and they saw the horses' tracks coming from the lodge. There is a lodge and a school-house close together; they did not know whether they went to the lodge or the school-house. They saw the horses tracks coming from toward the lodge until they met those coming from Caledonia. There were two companies of Ku-Klux.

Question. What were the marks found upon Perkins's body; had he been shot or hung, or how had he come by his death?

Answer. There were not any marks. His wife said that he got up and went out two or three times in the night, and was found dead next day.

Question. Where?

Answer. In bed. What made me suspicion it was the colored people, they were all such friends of mine; they said that this man was a Ku-Klux; these colored men; I do not know how they knew. That was the rumor about among the colored people that he was a Ku-Klux.

Question. That he was Ku-Kluxed, or was a Ku-Klux?

Answer. That he was a Ku-Klux; and immediately after his death they met and came to my house, and it was said to be a meeting of the lodge, but I never thought it was.

By Mr. BLAIR:

Question. His wife said he had gotten up and gone out that night two or three times, and the colored people thought he was a Ku-Klux?

Answer. Yes, sir.

By the CHAIRMAN:

Question. How was he supposed to have come to his death?

Answer. He was found dead in the way these other parties were found, and he was a friend of mine, and I thought and the colored people thought, too, that he was opposed to them coming to my house, and perhaps they were afraid he would tell on them if he did come to my house. That is my supposition.

Question. Your supposition is, that he was killed by the Ku-Klux?

Answer. Yes, sir; I thought perhaps he was poisoned.

Question. Did you ever talk with his wife about it?

Answer. No, sir.

By Mr. BLAIR:

Question. You say you thought he was poisoned?

Answer. Yes, sir; he was dead next morning, and nothing was the matter with him the night before.

By the CHAIRMAN:

Question. He was a well and hearty man the night before?

Answer. Yes sir.

Question. He was a friend of yours?

Answer. Yes, sir.

Question. Did the circumstances of his death create much talk?

Answer. No, sir. The colored people talked about it. I never heard any talk among the white folks about it, except among my friends.

Question. Was Perkins a white man?

Answer. No, sir; a colored man. I do not suppose there could be any way got to prove that he was killed.

Question. Your notion is, that he was a member of the order, and the order fell out with him because he was not faithful to them?

Answer. Yes, sir. I rather think he could not bear the idea of them persecuting me and stopping the colored school; and I think, and the colored people seem to have expressed the same idea, that they were afraid he would tell who did it if they did it.

Question. Was it supposed that he, a colored man, was a member of this Ku-Klux band?

Answer. Yes, sir.

Question. So the band was not supposed to be composed exclusively of white men?

Answer. No, sir.

Question. Do you think of any other case?

Answer. No, sir.

COLUMBUS, MISSISSIPPI, *November* 9, 1871.

HIRAM W. LEWIS sworn and examined.

By the CHAIRMAN:

Question. Where is your residence and what is your occupation or official position?

Answer. I live at Crawford, in Lowndes County. I have a plantation there which I have been running for some time.

Question. Are you the sheriff elect of this county?

Answer. I believe so; the returns are not fully made up yet, but the indications are that I am sheriff elect.

Question. How long have you lived in this county?

Answer. I have lived here constantly for about three years and a half.

Question. Where did you live before coming here?

Answer. I lived in Ohio.

Question. Does your acquaintance extend into Noxubee and Winston counties?

Answer. Well, sir, I have a limited acquaintance in those counties.

Question. Are you pretty well acquainted throughout those counties?

Answer. Throughout the western portion of the county I am pretty well acquainted; but not a great deal in the eastern border—this side of the river.

Question. State to the committee whether you have any knowledge or information in relation to outrages committed upon colored men in this county.

Answer. I have no personal knowledge of anything of the kind. Nothing has ever come under my immediate observation of that kind that I can tell of. All that I know is from report. Some of them were very near me—in one case especially it was within four miles of me.

Question. What case was that?

Answer. That was in the edge of Noxubee County, on the Malone place. It was the killing of a colored man named Dick Malone.

Question. That case was testified to very fully by the witnesses in Noxubee County, while we were at Macon, and I will not trouble you to repeat the particulars of it. Have you heard of any other outrage?

Answer. I have heard of a number of outrages on this side of the river, last spring, in the matter of threatening teachers of colored schools, a young man named Farmer and also a Mr. Leake.

Question. What was Farmer's case?

Answer. The report that came to me at that time was that they had gone to his house, a body of masked men at night—a small number.

By Mr. BLAIR:

Question. You say they came to his house?

Answer. They came to the place where he was living. I think he was living in the school-house, or near it.

Question. Who came to his house?

Answer. A number of masked men, it was reported.

By the CHAIRMAN:

Question. When was that?

Answer. That was some time in the spring; I think perhaps in April or May. I should say April.

Question. What did you understand that they did?

Answer. I understood that they warned him to discontinue his school, and to leave the country.

Question. Was he teaching a white or colored school?

Answer. A colored school.

Question. Was he a colored man?

Answer. No, sir; he was a white man.

Question. Did he obey the warning?

Answer. I understand he discontinued his school and left the country. At all events I have not heard of him, by inquiring, for a number of months.

Question. Can you tell of any other case?

Answer. Mr. Leake was teaching, also, in that vicinity, out on this side of the river. I understood they came to his house, which is one end of the school-house—the same building—a number of them masked, at night, and warned him to discontinue his school.

Question. Was he teaching a colored or a white school?

Answer. A colored school.

Question. Did he discontinue his school?

Answer. No, sir; he did not. I believe he taught out the full term for which he was engaged. I so understood.

Question. Did you hear whether he was subsequently visited?

Answer. I never have heard that he was.

Question. Has any other case come to your knowledge?

Answer. Not so directly. There have been cases in Monroe County. There was a case here a short time ago—I have heard it from general report—it was not a case of a school-house, however. That was a case in which a colored man had been tried before a magistrate, charged with the murder of a white man; and, I believe, committed to the circuit court at Aberdeen. He was put in charge of a constable and two men, to be taken to Aberdeen. They had gone perhaps a mile or two from the place where the colored man was tried, when they——

By Mr. BLAIR:

Question. In charge of an officer?

Answer. Yes, sir; in charge of an officer. They reported that a masked body of men attacked them and killed the negro.

By the CHAIRMAN:

Question. Was this said to have been in the day-time or night?

Answer. I understood it was in the evening. What I mean by the evening is the early part of the night, or late after sundown. The negro was found next day with a piece of rope around his neck, and a sapling near by, where he had apparently been hung. I think one end of the rope was tied around the sapling, or one end of the piece, and that several balls were put through him, or into him—some half-dozen balls.

Question. Do you recollect the negro's name?

Answer. No, sir; I do not recall the name now.

Question. This occurred in Monroe County?

Answer. Yes, sir; these men were arrested, and I think have probably been carried before the district court; the officer and the men who were in charge of the prisoner conveying him to Aberdeen were arrested and probably bound over.

Question. Were they arrested on process from the United States court?

Answer. Yes, sir; I think they were; at all events they were carried as far as Corinth by Colonel Rose, or his command of soldiers at Aberdeen.

Question. When did this occur?

Answer. That occurred probably four weeks ago; it was about four weeks; it might have been five weeks ago.

Question. Did you learn in what part of Monroe County this happened?

Answer. No, sir; I do not know exactly; I got the impression that it was twelve or fifteen miles from Aberdeen, towards the Alabama line, perhaps in a northeasterly direction; not due east; that is the impression I got.

Question. Have you heard of any other cases in Monroe County?

Answer. No, sir; I heard of the burning of some buildings in Winston that were used for school purposes—a number of them.

Question. As the committee have inquired into that matter at Macon we will not trouble you to give the particulars of these burnings. Have you heard of any other interference with schools in this county besides the cases of Farmer and Leake?

Answer. Well, Mr. Phillips came to Crawford last spring, to teach a colored school, from Columbus here—hired by the county superintendent—and he had been there but a few days when he was accosted by a crowd of ten or twelve men, in the day-time near town, not in disguise, who were evidently full of liquor, and they threatened him considerably.

Question. Did the threats have relation to the teaching of that school?

Answer. Yes, sir; they told him that he must stop teaching school; that if he did not he would see trouble; that they had no use for any of his sort. Mr. Phillips was a very fine Christian gentleman as I ever met.

Question. Did he go on with his school or discontinue it?

Answer. He taught his school to the full end of his term.

Question. Was he interrupted?

Answer. He was not.

Question. Do you know of any secret organization of men in this county, banded together for any unlawful purpose?

Answer. No, sir; I cannot say that I have positive knowledge of any such.

Question. Have you any information upon the subject?

Answer. I have no reliable information. There is a society formerly called the "Native Sons of the South," but what their object is I cannot say. They wear glazed caps and a medal; perhaps it was for campaign purposes; I do not know; it is reported that they took an oath, and that they took an oath to drive out carpet-baggers beyond the borders of the State.

Question. What other badge besides a glazed cap do they wear?

Answer. They wear a brass medal with a mirror on one side, and "Native Sons" is printed on the other, or stamped on it, rather; it is also printed on their caps.

Question. Do they have any parades or processions?

Answer. Yes, sir.

Question. Have you seen them?

Answer. Yes, sir; I saw one procession that came to a barbecue, given at Crawford—given some six weeks ago.

Question. How long has that organization existed?

Answer. I should think the first I heard of it was probably two months ago, or perhaps two months and a half.

Question. You say the society is said to be oath-bound?

Answer. Yes, sir; it is so reported. A colored man that claims to have belonged to it has given to me a part of the ceremony, as he said. That is all the information I have on the subject positively. He gave me a portion of the ceremony, which, he said, was correct.

Question. You say he told you he belonged to that society?

Answer. He told me that he did.

Question. How does he vote?

Answer. I cannot say, sir.

Question. What did he tell you was the obligation the members took?

Answer. I have a copy of it; I had it printed in the paper—the last week's paper in this town—the Columbus Press. I could produce a copy of it in five minutes.

Question. What, if anything, do you know of the Ku-Klux organization in this part of Mississippi?

Answer. Well, sir, I never saw a man in disguise in this part of the country that I know of; I never have heard anything of the kind; all I know is from the reports of colored men, who report them as having appeared and made demonstrations against them in their houses; that is all that I know. Then there is this case of Dick Malone, down near me there, which is the only case near me that I have heard of.

Question. What do the negroes say in relation to the operations of this order?

Answer. They seem to be greatly intimidated. After that affair occurred down there they were exceedingly intimidated throughout all my part of the country.

Question. You refer to the Dick Malone affair?

Answer. Yes, sir.

Question. Is it your understanding that a good many colored men have, from time to time, been whipped by men in disguise?

Answer. I do not think there have ever been more than six or eight cases in this county of that kind. They have been on this side of the river. I was away at Jackson during the whole session of the legislature and was not home. I heard reports, but paid no particular attention to them at the time; reports came from different parts of the State so thick and fast that I paid no particular attention to any special report of that kind.

Question. When did these six or eight cases, that you refer to, occur?

Answer. A number of them occurred in the same night of the Dick Malone affair. It was near the county line, and they rode over several plantations, and I think a number, or at least a portion of them, were in this county, on this side of the line. The other cases, if there were any, were on that side of the river. I have no positive knowledge of any of them. It is only an impression that I have.

Question. So far as you have studied the subject, and examined the particulars of the various outrages committed, or said to have been committed, by disguised men, what seems to be the general purpose of the organization?

Answer. Well, sir, the purpose, so far as I have observed or studied it at all, seems to be to put down the republican party.

Question. You may give to the committee your reasons for believing this to be its purpose.

Answer. I never have heard in this country of an outrage perpetrated upon any person who was not either a republican or acting under that party as an officer, or in some manner carrying out republican measures.

Question. Heretofore, what cognizance have the State courts taken of this class of outrages? How successful have they been in discovering the offenders and bringing them to justice?

Answer. I never have heard of a single instance in which they have been brought to justice or punishment in any manner for any of these crimes.

Question. What is the practical difficulty, if any, in bringing these men to justice?

Answer. I should suppose that the principal difficulty was in getting a jury that would convict.

Question. Is it supposed that this organization has its friends and sympathizers, who find their way upon the juries?

Answer. It is so supposed, and that the witnesses in these cases are afraid to testify to the facts that they know, for fear of coming under the vengeance of the men against whom they testify, or of the organization. They believe it to be a compact organization, and that if they testify against one member of it they will arouse the anger of the whole organization.

Question. Is that the feeling on the subject, of the negroes generally?

Answer. It seems to be so.

Question. Have you any reason to believe that this organization has sought to control the vote of the negroes?

Answer. I do not know that it has, except by the general intimidation which would be brought to bear by making these attacks upon them.

Question. Has it, so far as your knowledge extends, had that effect upon any considerable number of colored voters?

Answer. I do not think it has in this county, during the past election, had any at all. I think our county organization, or rather our organizations throughout the county here have been so perfect that they have not been able to intimidate.

Question. How has it been in former elections in this State?

Answer. I think that there was probably something of the kind in 1868. I am satisfied that a great many were intimidated. Our vote was not as large as it has been since, and our majority was a great deal smaller in 1868. I think there was a great deal of intimidation during that election.

Question. What has been the course of the democratic press in this State in relation to this Ku-Klux organization, as to denouncing it?

Answer. They do not seem to recognize it as a fact that there is any such organization, as far as I have been able to read them. They scout the idea that there is any such organization in the country.

Question. How do they speak of the outrages themselves; do they attempt to throw discredit on the fact that they exist?

Answer. Yes, sir; I think they do.

Question. Do they seek to palliate or excuse them?

Answer. In some instances. For example, in the case of the man who was killed in the Winston County jail, who was accused of a very heinous crime; they were disposed to deal with the heinousness of the crime, instead of saying anything about these men who came there and killed him. They seemed to hold up the crime of the man rather than to say anything about the crime of the men who went there and killed him, and the inference would be that they thought the crime was sufficient to warrant the people in going there and taking him out and killing him. Also, in the case of this man in Monroe County, they seemed to cover up the crime that was committed in killing him by calling attention to the fact that he had killed a white man, perhaps an innocent white man, without provocation. They seemed to carry that idea. I never have known any of the papers in this vicinity to come out openly and denounce these acts, as I think a fair-minded man and a law-abiding citizen should denounce them

Question. You say they persist in denying the existence of any such secret organization?

Answer. Yes, sir; so far as I have heard they do deny the existence of any such organization.

Question. Have you seen anything in the platform of the party, county, district, or State, in denunciation of these Ku-Klux outrages?

Answer. No, sir; I have not.

Question. Has the democratic party, in any of its political meetings, passed any resolutions of denunciation, that you have noticed?

Answer. I do not remember any. I have now the paper of which I spoke, and this I submit to you now is what was handed to a friend of mine, Mr. Bliss, who is in town The rest of the article appears as editorial, but this was the original matter which was handed to us as part of the original ceremony of the Native Sons of the South.

The CHAIRMAN. You may read it.

The WITNESS. The oath is as follows:

"I do solemnly swear, in the presence of Almighty God and this band of faithful brethren, that I will never reveal or make known, except when authorized so to do by proper authority, any of the secrets, signs, passwords, grips, or other obligations, so help me God, and keep me steadfast therein.'

"Ques. 'Who will protect the rights of all men?'

"Res. 'The Native Sons of the South.'

"Ques. 'Whom do we in this most solemn hour swear vengeance against?'

"Res. 'The carpet-bagger, and all who affiliate with him.'

"Ques. 'What is to be done with the carpet-baggers and their friends?'

"Res. 'They are to be driven from the borders of the State.'

"Ques. 'Who is to accomplish this most noble work?'

"Res. 'The Native Sons of the South.'"

Question. Who do you understand are classified as carpet-baggers in this State?

Answer. Well, sir, I understand that all men who have come here since the war, especially from the North, and are known as republicans.

Question. Are they classified as carpet-baggers who came from the North to engage in farming, or business pursuits, without making themselves especially active in politics, provided they are republicans?

Answer. Well, sir, if a man announces his political principles so that it is generally known that he is a republican, he will at times be classified as a carpet-bagger. I think if he had no other business or occupation whatever, besides being a planter or man of other business, he would not be generally denounced. I think a man who comes here and pays no attention to politics whatever, if he votes, and does not let it be known how he votes, the mere suspicion that he was a republican would perhaps not call down any denunciation upon him.

Question. Suppose, without being a candidate for any position himself, he takes an active part in political canvasses, and seeks to promote the success of the republican party; is he classed as a carpet-bagger, and denounced as such?

Answer. He is, most assuredly, if he takes an active part in the canvass, whether he is a candidate or not.

Question. What is the feeling toward white republicans who come here from the Northern States?

Answer. Exceedingly bitter.

Question. What effect does this feeling have upon immigration to this part of the State?

Answer. I think it is a check upon immigration, amounting almost, perhaps, to stopping the immigration at the present time.

Question. What is the sentiment of the democratic whites in this county, in relation to the education of the colored children by the common-school tax?

Answer. Well, sir, I think that all of the substantial citizens of the county, the men of intelligence and wealth—at least I think the majority of them—at the present time, are in favor of schools; at least they do not oppose the system, and that is becoming more so, I think, every day. Last spring, at the time the tax was being collected, when it was levied by the board of supervisors, there was great opposition to it, and I think a majority of the white people of all classes were opposed to the system to such an extent that the board of supervisors, under the pressure of public opinion, repealed the school tax entirely; but a number of the schools have gone on, and the people see the children are becoming educated, and are beginning to believe in them, and making up their minds that perhaps it is the best thing for the country not to interrupt the schools. At the present time, I think the school system would have the moral support of a great many, if not the majority, of the substantial, intelligent citizens of Lowndes.

Question. Have you at this time any other school fund except that arising from the sale of the sixteenth section, known as the congressional township fund?

Answer. We have the poll-tax, which goes to that fund. We have the fines that are imposed in the county, and all the licenses from sale of liquors, and some other licenses perhaps, that go into the State fund, and each county draws its proportion from that general fund.

By Mr. BUCKLEY:

Question. Do you not receive a share of what is called the "Chickasaw fund?"

Answer. Yes, sir; we receive a portion of it in this county.

By the CHAIRMAN:

Question. How long do these revenues combined run the schools; what portion of the year?

Answer. I do not know. I suppose they would not run the schools more than two months, at the outside, taking the county at large. In some townships we have the "Chickasaw fund," and perhaps the sixteenth section fund in some townships, which, being applied to districts, would run the schools longer than in others; but throwing it all into a general county fund it would probably not run the schools more than a month and a half.

Question. Then your common schools are maintained mainly by subscriptions?

Answer. Yes, sir; mainly by taxes upon the people at large—upon the property through the county.

Question. The supervisors refused to levy it?

Answer. Yes, sir; they did. They refused to levy it, and the teachers went on. The teachers are without their pay. They have their warrants in their pockets, and the members of the board of supervisors have levied another tax, or some school tax, to be collected between the present time and the first of December, which, if paid up, will go to pay up the warrants, and run the schools a portion of the next year.

Question. Did you understand that the opposition to schools extended to the white as well as the black schools, last spring?

Answer. I do not know, indeed. I think the opposition arose from the fact that the black children were being taught. I think if we had had only a white system, to educate white children, there would have been no opposition. There have been instances where they have interfered with white schools, I understand, in Winston County. I understood that there was one instance of that kind.

Question. Have you known of any colored churches being burned in this county?

Answer. No, sir; I do not remember any.

By Mr. BUCKLEY:

Question. Were you present, a short time ago, at a public meeting held at Artesia?

Answer. Yes, sir; I was.

Question. At the time of the recent disturbance there?

Answer. Yes, sir; I was present there at the time a young man was killed.

Question. Were you one of the speakers on that occasion?

Answer. Yes, sir.

Question. Will you please state to the committee what occurred there?

Answer. We had held a meeting about four miles from Artesia that day, at Prairie Hill. We had a quiet, orderly meeting, and when the meeting was adjourned a number of the leading colored men, presidents of clubs, that lived in that direction, proposed that they should march in procession together as far as Artesia. They requested that I should accompany them, and I did so, and marched in procession to Artesia. It was about or nearly sundown—perhaps quite so—when we reached Artesia. We passed through the town in an orderly procession, the colored men giving cheers for leading men of the party—local candidates—but disturbing no one by way of insult or anything of the kind; simply waving their hats and cheering for leading men of the party in the county. They got to the south end of town. I was riding in my buggy in the center of the procession, and I saw there was a crowd of white people in the town—perhaps a hundred or so—and the question occurred to me at once how it would be best to disperse the clubs in an orderly and peaceable way, and avoid any collision that might take place in case they staid about town and whisky should get among them and among the white people, as it might do; and I drove my buggy out of the procession to the center of the common, and called upon the leaders of the different clubs to gather their men around to have a formal dismissal. They did so. They gathered around on the common on the south end of the town, and I got up and spoke perhaps five minutes, not longer, congratulating them upon their large turnout, and the prospects of the party, announcing another meeting to take place the following week, and sat down, and told Mr. Bliss, who was with me, to get up and speak three or five minutes, and to close by telling all the clubs to disperse in a quiet, orderly manner to their several homes. Mr. Bliss had just got upon his feet, and had not spoken more than a sentence, when a voice was heard probably eight or ten feet from the buggy, directly on the left-hand side of my buggy, saying, "Are you a white man?" I looked instantly, and saw that it was a white man standing there in the midst of the crowd—in fact the only white man that was within several rods of the buggy. I hunched Mr. Bliss, and told him to pay no attention whatever to his remarks, and he did not seem disposed to do so anyhow, but kept right on without appearing to notice the man at all. In perhaps a minute and a half or two minutes I heard the report of a pistol in that direction. I looked instantly, and saw the man running—this same man who had asked the question. Whether he shot or not I could not say. I saw the man running, and I saw at the instant that nobody was hurt or shot, and called out as loud as I could to let him go and come back, but there was great excitement and confusion, and the colored men took after him. One colored man standing in the buggy called as loud as he could to catch him. He called three or four times to catch him. The man ran until he got out some four or five rods, and instantly all at once there were five of six shots fired in rapid succession. I should think they were all pistol-shots from the sound, but I could not see any man that shot—could not see who shot. A number of colored men said to me that he fired when he got out that far, and found he could not escape from them; that he began to fire at them, and that he fired the first shot after he began to run. He dropped instantly and was dead. A number of colored men came to me that night at Crawford, and told me they saw him when he pulled his pistol and fired. They said he drew it from his inner breast-pocket, and fired quickly at Mr. Bliss or myself in the buggy, and instantly dropped his head and ran through the crowd with his pistol in his hand. I did not see him when he fired. The first I heard was the report of the pistol, and when I looked he was running. It was a pistol-shot, I am satisfied, but I could not swear that he fired it. I only know that from the testimony of those who said they saw him.

Question. This white man was killed was he?

Answer. Yes, sir; he was killed on the spot.

By the CHAIRMAN:

Question. Was he under the influence of liquor?

Answer. I think he was. After he asked the question, I looked toward him, and met his eye once or twice, and one or two of the freedmen were talking to him—not in an angry or loud manner. I could not hear what they said, although it was as close as, say, eight or ten feet, and I spoke to them quietly, and said, "Boys, don't say anything more; he don't mean any harm," or something of that kind; but I caught his eye at that time, and his face, and I thought then that he had been drinking, and was considerably in liquor, although he stood erect. I should say he was under the influence of liquor from his countenance.

By Mr. BUCKLEY:

Question. After this did you have any conversation with the colored men who stood about him, and who held conversation with him?

Answer. I did. I had a conversation with some that night. We immediately went to Crawford that night. The crowd dispersed at once, and I conversed with some of them, and the next morning—Sunday morning early—I came back to attend the inquest, and I talked with other colored men when I got near Artesia. They gave me the same account that those did with whom I conversed at Crawford the night before, and they were men who I am certain had no correspondence with these other colored men.

Question. Was this white man living at Artesia?

Answer. No, sir. It is reported that his home was at Enterprise, Mississippi.

By the CHAIRMAN:

Question. What was his occupation?

Answer. An account in the Mobile Register is the only thing I have to go upon. It is said he had, at that time, contracted for the building of some culverts, or something or other on the railroad, but his former occupation had been that of a druggist, or clerking perhaps in a drug store at Mobile.

By Mr. BUCKLEY:

Question. Do you know what took place subsequently at the coroner's inquest?

Answer. I went out immediately when I found he was killed. I left the buggy and went directly out there. Some two or three white citizens came into the crowd, and they did not seem to know him. He could not be identified for five or ten minutes. He was finally identified by a young man that came in, and he was taken to the hotel. The justice of the peace of that district was there, and I advised him to hold an inquest. There was a great deal of excitement, and one of the citizens came to me and urged me very much to disperse the colored men. He said that he was afraid that there might be a collision or something of the kind, and they did not seem disposed to go until Mr. Bliss and myself went. They said they were afraid we would be killed, or something of the kind, and they did not seem disposed to go. I at once got into my buggy and told them all they must disperse, and I drove out myself and they all went; they evacuated the town, every man of them, nearly every colored man in town. It seems that they immediately telegraphed to Columbus here, for two lawyers to come down there, and Mr. Weed, Mr. Mathews, and Mr. Lowe, at least those three, came down in obedience to that dispatch, and they were to bring a force with them. The first dispatch was that a mob of infuriated blacks had already killed one man and they wanted them to come down with a force. Upon that a great many of the young men of the town assembled at the depot with their guns; but just before the train started they got another dispatch that everything was quiet, and those lawyers went on and some half dozen young men with their guns also. They got there at about nine o'clock.

Question. At night?

Answer. Yes, sir; at night, that night. This young man was killed about dark. It seems that they urged the justice of the peace to hold an inquest, which he did, by putting on two of these young men and four of the citizens about Artesia, and besides that they put on six colored men. They put on men, a portion of whom I believe—I understood so, at least—were identified with the Native Sons, or at least were working against the interests of our party there—the whole six; they thus formed a jury of twelve men. The statute provides for a jury of six.

By Mr. BLAIR:

Question. Six colored men?

Answer. Yes, sir; six democratic colored men were put on.

Question. Who else?

Answer. Six white men. They summoned some eight or nine witnesses. All of them, I believe, were white citizens of the town, except two who were colored men, and they held an inquest that night. The verdict was rendered, I understood, about 1 o'clock. The sheriff came down with it, and they immediately dispatched him——

By Mr. BUCKLEY:

Question. Came down with whom?

Answer. The deputy sheriff came down with those men, and they, immediately on arriving there, dispatched him on the down-train for myself and Mr. Bliss to attend the inquest, which was to be held next morning. He came down with his summons, and we went back next morning and found it was all over, and the verdict was rendered at 1 o'clock that night.

Question. What time was the summons served?

Answer. The summons was served on us next morning. The deputy sheriff went down and remained in the hotel in Crawford all night, and came out about 6 o'clock and summoned us to go to Artesia and attend the inquest. We went and found that the verdict was rendered, and the next night the sheriff came down and arrested myself and Mr. Bliss, and produced his writ, which had a copy of the verdict of the coroner's jury upon it. The verdict rendered was that the deceased had come to his death at the hands of a band of armed rioters under the control of myself and Mr. Bliss and another gentleman named Rose, who was a bystander and had nothing to do with the meeting, and that we were guilty of the charge of murder. Thereupon, the judge issued a warrant for our arrest or ordered the sheriff to arrest us.

By Mr. BLAIR:

Question. The verdict was that the man had come to his death at the hands of whom?

Answer. Of a band of armed rioters, under the control of Lewis and Bliss and Rose, and I think it named also Levi Jones, or Bean—he goes by that name principally; he is called by both names. Mr. Rose was a bystander. He was a friend of mine who had come to visit me that day and attended the meeting with me. When that affair occurred he was standing at the side of the buggy, having nothing to say to any one. He had nothing to say in the whole transaction that I know of. The next morning he went up and took charge of his mail-train; he is United States mail-agent on the Mobile and Ohio Railroad, and has two days off at West Point every week. It was during that vacation that he was down there. He went up and took charge of his mail Sunday night at West Point, and when he got to Artesia the sheriff with his *posse* came to him to arrest him, and he was obliged to leave his mail-matter in his car. He locked it up. They did not allow him sufficient time to carry his registered letters to the postmaster. Thus he was obliged to either carry them with him, or leave them, and he left them with the station-agent. They brought him to Columbus and put him in jail that night. The mail-car went through to Mobile without any person in charge.

By Mr. BUCKLEY:

Question. How many parties were arrested in all?

Answer. We were arrested on Monday morning and came on up with the sheriff. We gave him the names of a number of witnesses that we told him we would like to have subpœnaed. The grand jury ordered a number subpœnaed also, but it seems from all——

Question. Was the grand jury in session at the time?

Answer. It was. By some means or other the sheriff arrrested sixty-four men, among them all the witnesses who names he had obtained. He arrested and brought in sixty-four of them on Monday night and put them jail. Judge Orr was sent for immediately, and about 10 or 12 o'clock they were released. A number of these are still in jail. There were also arrests made at Crawford of a number the following day. My overseer on my plantation was arrested by twelve men with double-barreled shotguns, on a charge of resisting an arrest. It seems that they had gone to get one of our witnesses, a colored man living on my place, and said they had a warrant for him. The deputy sheriff, Green, said he had a warrant for his arrest. My overseer told the colored man that if he was in his place he would not go without the man should read his warrant to him or produce it, but the man insisted that the colored man should go, and he did go. In about an hour there were twelve armed men came to my house. My wife was there, and this Dutchman that I have overseeing came there. They were about surrounding the house when he appeared from his room, and they leveled their guns at him, and told him that he was their prisoner, charged with undertaking to resist an officer, or with resisting an officer. He asked them for their warrant, but they would not produce it. They took him to Crawford, put him under guard in the depot all night, brought him to Columbus next morning under guard, compelling him to pay his own fare, and as soon as he got here the sheriff himself discharged him, saying that he had no warrant for his arrest.

Question. Is it a fact that a number of parties were arrested without warrants?

Answer. Yes, sir. There seemed to have been probably as many as fifty arrests without warrants; that, at least, was my understanding. I was confined up at the mayor's office in this city, but I understood that there was no warrant for the arrest of any of them except myself, Mr. Bliss, and Mr. Rose and Bean. It is true that the verdict ot the coroner's inquest said that the rioters were under the control of Lewis, Bliss, and divers others, and it might be that the sheriff construed that into a warrant for the arrest of all parties who were present. That, I think, is the only warrant he had for arresting these witnesses.

Question. Is it true that persons were arrested living in another county and outside of the jurisdiction of the sheriff?

Answer. I understood that there was quite a number arrested from Oktibbeha County.

By the CHAIRMAN:

Question. Beyond the county line?

Answer. Yes, sir; I understood that there was.

By Mr. BUCKLEY:

Question. That county joins this?

Answer. Yes, sir.

Question. Is there anything further you wish to state in this case?

Answer. No, sir; I believe not.

By Mr. BLAIR:

Question. You have stated that you were informed by the negroes on the ground that this man Lee fired his pistol first?

Answer. I was so informed upon the spot. A colored man who hallooed, "Catch him! catch him!" at the time he ran, informed me immediately after the man was killed.

He called me to one side and informed me that the ball of the man's pistol just grazed his head; that he heard it whistle close to his ear. He was sitting in the buggy at the time, in front of myself. I was sitting on the seat, and he sat with his back against the dash-board.

Question. In the buggy?

Answer. Yes, sir; a sort of spring wagon.

Question. In the same buggy with yourself?

Answer. Yes, sir; he was sitting in the front of the buggy.

Question. What is his name?

Answer. Stanton Cromwell.

Question. What other negroes told you that they saw the man fire?

Answer. Robert Thomson.

Question. When did he tell you?

Answer. After I returned home that night I called him on the street and inquired of him; I knew that he was standing by the side of the man at the time the man asked the first question. I knew that Robert Thomson was standing close to him; I had seen him there; I asked him if he saw anything of the occurrence, and if he saw the man's pistol, or knew anything about it; to tell me all he did know about it if he knew anything, and to tell me nothing but what he did know. I knew there would be a great many reports, and that in all such cases there is always a great difference of opinion among different men who would see the same thing, white as well as black. I asked him to tell me what he saw of it, or how it was; that I was looking in another direction the moment it was fired. He told me he saw the man pull the pistol from his coat pocket; that he was watching him all the time, or standing close to him after he spoke the word; that he was standing close to him. He said the man had his hand under his coat when he first asked the question, and that he therefore kept his eye upon him, and that he saw the man when he pulled his pistol and fired.

Question. Did any other negro give you that information?

Answer. There was a woman standing in a wagon.

Question. What was her name?

Answer. She is the wife of John Brown—I think that is his name—of Artesia. She was off a few rods. In fact, there are a number that I have never seen that I have heard of. I talked with but this one that night. Yes, there were one or two there, too; one named Washington Jennings, who is on my place, that I talked to next morning.

Question. What did he tell you?

Answer. He said he saw the man pull that pistol and fire.

By Mr. BUCKLEY:

Question. What did this woman tell you?

Answer. I did not see her; I saw only her husband next morning as I was going to Artesia; he told me she saw the man fire the pistol, but I never have seen the woman. There are a number of others that I have heard of; I have heard their names spoken. There are, I suppose, ten or twelve that I have heard of who say that they saw the man fire; but I was confined; I was not allowed to see any of them, and I did not see any of them that night except those two that I spoke of. After I was confined here I had no opportunity to see any of them. I heard of a number that had seen the man fire.

Question. Did any white people present see it?

The WITNESS. See the man shoot?

Mr. BUCKLEY. Yes.

The WITNESS. No, sir, I believe not. There were no white persons within six or eight rods that I know of; I did not see any myself. There was a dense crown of probably a thousand or twelve hundred circled about the buggy, but no white person within five or six rods except this man.

Question. Where was Mr. Bliss?

Answer. He was in the buggy. He was looking toward the crowd that had collected in front of us, or rather toward the right of the buggy, while the man stood off to his left, square to the left, on the side. He was not looking in that direction; he saw the smoke of the pistol as he turned quickly after hearing the report; then he saw the smoke of the pistol.

By the CHAIRMAN:

Question. Do I understand you to say that they saw the pistol-shot fired?

Answer. Yes, sir; they saw the first shot fired—the beginning of the disturbance.

By Mr. BLAIR:

Question. Mr. Bliss was addressing the crowd?

Answer. Yes, sir.

Question. I understood you to say in your examination-in-chief that Mr. Bliss had his eye on him; that he had already addressed a remark to Mr. Bliss, and Mr. Bliss was looking at him.

Answer. I made no such statement.

Question. What statement did you make, then, sir?

Answer. I stated that the man first asked the question; that I told Mr. Bliss to pay no attention to it, which he did not, but kept on addressing the crowd, without appearing to notice the man who made the remark, and in fact was not looking in the direction when the shot was fired, but was looking straight ahead or a little to the right of the horse, which stood in the buggy, while the man stood square to the left of the buggy or wagon.

Question. What was the testimony before the coroner's jury?

Answer. I never saw the testimony, and I could not say.

Question. Did you hear what it was?

Answer. No, sir; I read the Columbus Index here, but I do not know whether that claimed to give the testimony of those men or not. They claimed to give what those men said who were summoned as witnesses, but I do not believe that these men gave in such testimony as was presented as the testimony given before the jury of inquest. My impression is that they simply gave this as the statement of men who claimed to have been on the ground at the time.

Question. There were white men on the ground?

Answer. Yes, sir; within eight or ten rods there were a good many—that is, off at two stores, ten or fifteen rods, were quite a number, and in the outskirts of the crowd, six or eight rods away, there were perhaps, one, two or three.

Question. And they did testify before the grand jury?

Answer. I do not know, sir, how they testified there.

Question. They did testify before the jury of inquest?

Answer. My impression is that they did.

Question. You have seen statements of their testimony?

Answer. No, sir; I have not. I say I have seen in the Columbus Index what claimed to be statements that they made, but whether they were made under oath, or whether they claimed that they were made before the jury of inquest, I do not remember. My impression is that the Index gave them simply as the statement of these men.

Question. What were the statements?

Answer. I do not remember. The statement of Doctor Brothers, or what it was claimed that Doctor Brothers said, was, that he saw a gun in the hands of a freedman, when he heard the shot, or just before, elevated at an angle of 40°, and that he saw the smoke issuing from the mouth of the gun. Doctor Brothers made certain statements to me while the man lay dead. I do not know whether you wish these statements or not. Doctor Brothers was the first man I saw when I ran out to where the man was lying.

Question. What did he state to you?

Answer. The first statement of Doctor Brothers was, "I don't believe the man meant to shoot anybody. I believe he was shot accidentally. I saw the smoke issuing from the mouth of his pistol. His pistol was pointed upward, as though it was an accidental shot." That was the statement he made on the ground at the instant when I ran out there and the man lay dead.

By the CHAIRMAN:

Question. He was speaking of Lee, the man who was killed?

Answer. Yes, sir; another gentleman who came in there also made the same statement, that he thought it was an accidental shot.

By Mr. BLAIR:

Question. That he saw the smoke issue from the mouth of his pistol?

Answer. Yes, sir,

Question. Who was present when he made that statement to you?

Answer. I think Mr. Bliss was present; a number of colored men were present. There was a good deal of excitement, and another young man was present, a white man, whose name I do not remember, who also said that he thought the man fired accidentally; that he saw the smoke issuing upward.

Question. Who was that?

Answer. The white man that stood upon the ground. He was a young man. I do not know his name. He came in there and said that he saw the smoke issuing upward, as though it came from the mouth of his pistol, and that he believed the shot was accidental; that he fired accidentally; that he did not mean to shoot anybody.

Question. Did you see any other testimony that purported to be delivered before the inquest?

Answer. I saw the testimony there. I saw the statement that certain men had made statements in regard to the character of the man; that they thought he was a quiet, inoffensive, industrious man, and all that sort of thing. I understood that certain men had made these statements; whether they made them to the jury of inquest or not, I do not know.

Question. Were there not other witnesses before the jury whose statements have appeared to the effect that it was a gun that was fired and not a pistol, and not in the hands of this man?

Answer. I have heard of only one man who made that statement.

Question. Who was that?

Answer. That was Doctor Brothers, but whether he made it before the jury or not, I am not able to say.

Question. You do not know the name of the young man who was present when this occurred?

Answer. No, sir; I was not acquainted with him, and I do not think I have ever met him since; at least, if I did, I did not know his name.

Question. Did Bliss ever make any statement about this?

Answer. No, sir; not any sworn statement—not that I know of.

Question. Have all the parties who were charged with this act who were arrested been discharged?

Answer. I heard an hour or so ago that there were a number in jail yet. If they have been discharged, they have been discharged within an hour or two. The grand jury was to adjourn this afternoon, and if it adjourned without finding a bill, I suppose they are discharged. I do not know how that may be.

Question. Have the sheriff and his deputies been arrested?

Answer. Yes, sir; the sheriff and one of his deputies and three other persons who were summoned, I believe, as a *posse*.

Question. You say they have been arrested?

Answer. Yes, sir.

Question. What for?

Answer. For interrupting the United States mail. The affidavit of the party upon whose affidavit the arrest was made, states that it was in violation of the postal laws of the United States, and also of the enforcement act, interfering with the postal agent and throwing him into prison.

By the CHAIRMAN:

Question. I understand that there was no written accusation against Rose by name at all?

Answer. Yes, sir; his name appeared in the verdict of the jury of inquest. It went on to state that he was present, aiding and abetting, I think it said.

By Mr. BLAIR:

Question. And it was for his arrest?

Answer. Yes, sir; for his arrest while in the discharge of his duties, in charge of his mail-car.

Question. Where were they taken when they were arrested?

Answer. Mr. Rose was brought to Columbus and put in jail.

Question. I mean where were the sheriff and his deputy and his *posse* taken?

Answer. I understood they left yesterday morning with the United States marshal for Oxford.

Question. On what process were they arrested?

Answer. A warrant issued by the United States commissioner at Holly Springs.

Question. I understand you to say that the sheriff had a warrant in his hands to arrest parties named and implicated by the verdict of the coroner's inquest?

Answer. He had a warrant for the arrest of myself and Mr. Bliss, I believe, and he had the verdict of the coroner's inquest, and I think upon the back of it was indorsed an order from the judge to arrest the within-named parties. I think that is the way of it.

Question. I do not of course refer to the parties implicated by the finding of the jury of inquest.

Answer. I do not remember how it read; I know it covered my case and that of Mr. Bliss; but whether it meant all the parties named or not I am unable to say. I was satisfied at the time that it covered my case, and did not look any further.

By the CHAIRMAN:

Question. Were more than four persons named in the finding of the jury of inquest?

Answer. No, sir; I think not—myself, Mr. Bliss, Mr. Rose, and Levi Jones.

By Mr. BLAIR:

Question. Mr. Rose was named?

Answer. He was named as blank Rose. They arrested also, I believe, a Rose in Oktibbeha County, a freedman, who was not at the meeting that day.

Question. And for arresting Rose under this process, they have since, all of them, been arrested and carried to Oxford?

Answer. Yes, sir; they arrested Rose without a warrant; I do not know whether that was brought in the affidavit or not. The deputy of the sheriff with his *posse* arrested him. I do not know whether the sheriff was there present or not.

Question. Was not the sheriff also dismissed from office by the governor?

Answer. The governor removed the sheriff some days ago—previous to this.

Question. Previous to this prosecution?

Answer. No, sir; previous to the arrest of these parties; previous to the arrest of the sheriff himself and his deputies, I mean.

Question. His dismissal was by reason or on account of his action in this case?

Answer. I think not entirely. There was sufficient ground, the party thought, for his removal before this transaction occurred.

Question. What party thought?

Answer. The republican party. He had acted as a republican, and he was taking very strong ground in the campaign against the interests of the party, and there was sufficient ground, we thought, in the action for his removal.

Question. Do you pretend to say that he was removed by reason of any of these grounds and not for the action he took in this case?

Answer. I think, sir, that all of the actions put together combined to make up a cause sufficient in the governor's mind to remove him.

Question. Do you not know the fact to be that he was at once telegraphed in reference to this matter, and, when it was explained, that the removal was made?

Answer. No, sir; I do not.

Question. You have no reason to believe that?

Answer. No, sir; I have reason to believe that was not the case.

Question. What is the reason you have to believe that was not the case?

Answer. A paper was gotten up in Columbus, signed by the executive committee and other influential republicans in the State, asking that he be removed, and I think upon that request he was removed.

Question. When was that paper gotten up?

Answer. That was gotten up some three or four days before his removal.

Question. Prior to his action in this case?

Answer. No, sir; after his action in this case.

Question. You say it was subsequent to his action in this case of which you have been speaking?

Answer. Yes, sir.

Question. What grounds of removal did it set out? Did it set out his connection with this case?

Answer. It set out his connection with this case, and I think also his connection with the republican party—his action in opposition to the interests of the party. In other cases he has acted not in the interests of peace, as in making an attack upon one of our candidates. He has laid himself, of course, liable to be removed in that matter. He attacked one of our candidates when he was making a speech, and took him by the hair of the head and jerked him about. We thought that was sufficient ground to ask for his removal at that time, taken in connection with other acts he had done tending to promote disorder and break the peace. That was some time prior to this affair.

Question. In your own opinion, did his action in this case justify his removal?

Answer. Well, sir, I think it would have justified his removal, with nothing less.

Question. Did the party here make that statement to the governor?

Answer. No, sir; I think not. I do not think that the petition signed by the executive committee set forth the particulars of this case. If it did, it did not place the grounds of removal entirely upon that, I am satisfied.

Question. It laid no stress on this case?

Answer. It might have laid stress upon it. I think it used the words "in making arrests without warrant," but I do not know. I do not pretend to be able to quote the language of the paper. I never read it but once, and then very hastily, and I do not pretend to remember it. I know there was talk of getting up such a paper before this affair at Artesia occurred.

Question. Did you sign it?

Answer. No, sir; I did not.

Question. Was it gotten up at your instigation?

Answer. It was not, although I certainly was in favor of its being gotten up. But I was not the mover in the matter at all.

Question. You took no steps in getting it up?

Answer. None in the least, sir.

Question. Neither by advice or any other way?

Answer. If any person spoke to me in regard to the advisability of it, I most certainly expressed my opinion as being in favor of it.

Question. Did they ask you?

Answer. I do not remember whether they did ask me or not. I know before this affair occurred I had been in favor of it, although I did not urge it, and had not been the mover; and the republicans did not get up the paper then; they were very busy.

When this affair occurred parties were going down to Jackson, and they got up the paper, unknown to me until after it was drawn up and partially signed, and they continued getting signers to sign it down to Jackson. I had nothing to say about getting it up. It was got up outside, at least, when I did not know anything about it.

By the CHAIRMAN:

Question. What did you say about the deputy sheriff and his *posse* arresting Rose without a warrant?

Answer. Mr. Rose asked the deputy sheriff if he had a warrant. His reply was that he did not need any; that he was the deputy sheriff.

Question. Did he produce none upon the occasion?

Answer. He did not.

Question. Do you know whether he had a warrant in his possession at the time?

Answer. I do not know.

Question. And Rose's Christian name was not inserted in the warrant?

Answer. No, sir.

Question. Was it blank Rose?

Answer. Yes, sir.

Question. There were two Roses in the county?

Answer. Yes, sir; I think three. My impression is that there was another Rose that they got after or arrested, out in another direction. That is my impression. I would not swear to it, but I heard that a Rose in Oktibbeha County was arrested.

By Mr. BLAIR:

Question. But not in this county?

Answer. I understood that there was also another, in the direction of Mayhew or Tippah, that was arrested, or they proposed to arrest him, or something of the kind, but I am not positive about it. I have the impression that there were three Roses that they got after. Colonel Meek, the leading lawyer, said he supposed it was a freedman all the time. He was attending the inquest. He stated that to me afterward.

By the CHAIRMAN:

Question. Was this a regular deputy sheriff, or one appointed by the sheriff for that particular occasion?

Answer. He is a jailer out here, and, I think, a regular deputy.

Question. Did Rose know him as a deputy, or was he acquainted with him at all?

Answer. No, sir; he did not know him at all.

By Mr. BLAIR:

Question. You stated, in your direct examination, that a number of colored men came to you and stated that they saw him pull a pistol and fire?

Answer. Yes, sir.

Question. And that was immediately after the occurrence?

Answer. Well, there were two at my place, after I got there that night, that made that statement, one of them that night and the other next morning.

Question. You do not mean to say, then, that it was done immediately after the occurrence, but a short time afterward?

Answer. I do not remember the name of any one, but my impression is that several of them said they saw his pistol right on the ground. I spoke of one having said he heard the ball whistle, but I do not think he said he saw the pistol. My impression is that a number told me on the spot that they saw him pull his pistol and fire. I do not remember the names. There was great excitement, and everybody was talking.

Question. Did you go up to the body immediately?

Answer. Yes, sir; as soon as I learned that he was killed.

Question. Was any pistol found on him?

Answer. No, sir. I did not see any. His hand lay out open.

Question. Did you see any pistol on the ground, that had fallen from his hand?

Answer. I did not.

Question. Did you go up to him before many persons came about him?

Answer. Well, sir, it was, I suppose, a minute and a half or two minutes after the firing before I got there. I did not go until I heard he was killed. I heard the firing, and there was a great surging about, and Mr. Rose as soon as the firing ceased run out there, and came back, and told me the man was killed. That was probably a minute or a minute and a half after the firing ceased. I then went out immediately and saw him lying there.

Question. Did anybody say they saw a pistol lying by him or in his hand?

Answer. No, sir; no person made the statement that they saw any after he fell. I never heard of it.

Question. No one ever saw it after he fell?

Answer. Not that I know of; I have not conversed with any of the witnesses, as I told you, except these few that I saw that night, two or three, and the next morning I was arrested then.

Question. You were looking at him when he fell?

Answer, I was not; I did not see him any other time after I saw him start to run. He only ran a few steps until I lost sight of him as the crowd surged about. I next heard the firing and lost sight of the man. It was growing dusk then; it was almost dusk at the time.

By the CHAIRMAN:

Question. Have you ever heard a pistol was picked up on the ground, supposed to be the one he held?

Answer. Yes, sir.

By Mr. BLAIR:

Question. By whom?

Answer. I heard a gentleman from Starkville here the other day, named Sanders, the chancery clerk over there, say that a colored man—I have forgotten his name now; it was reported that he had a pistol, that he had found it, but I do not remember his name now. It was some colored man in Oktibbeha County. It was so reported in that county at that time.

Question. Who did you see standing over his body when you went up?

Answer. Dr. Brothers is the only man that I can remember was there. Mr. Bliss followed me up immediately. It was but a few minutes until the others came in.

Question. Dr. Brothers and Mr. Bliss were the only white men standing there near the body when you went up that you knew?

Answer. No, sir; there was another white man, a young gentleman. I do not know his name.

Question. Do you know who was the first white man that reached the place where his body lay after he was shot?

Answer. No, sir; there were a number of colored men about there, but I do not remember many of them. I do not know the names, and would not know their countenances.

Question. Did you hear that the colored men ran up and jumped upon him?

Answer. I have heard that that statement was made by some of the citizens of Artesia.

Question. As he lay there?

Answer. Yes, sir.

Question. When he fell?

Answer. I have heard that that statement was made. I do not know that I have seen it in print.

Question. Have you heard that he was cut down with a saber?

Answer. Yes, sir; I have heard that he was cut to pieces with a saber. I have read it in a paper somewhere; I think, perhaps, in the Jackson Clarion. It was some democratic paper, but I do not know what paper. It stated that he was cut to pieces with a saber or with sabers.

Question. I ask you, have you heard any one who was there say he was struck with a saber or cut down with a saber?

Answer. I never have heard any such statement from anybody who saw him.

Question. Who was there on the ground and saw him?

Answer. No, sir.

Question. How many balls were in him; how many wounds did he receive?

Answer. As he lay on the ground, I could not see any marks of violence whatever; none at all. He lay there with his hat off, upon his back, flat. I saw no marks of violence whatever, and I did not know where he had been hit; but as soon as he was picked up I saw a very small stain of blood on the ground, which made me believe it was in the side or back—probably in the right side. It was in his side or back; I think in his right side, just under that portion of the back, [illustrating.] As they took him up I stood square behind him, or a little to the right, and the little stain of blood seemed to be directly under that, although he had been shot in the side, or rather the corner of the body, if the body had been square.

Question. You do not know how many bullets were received?

Answer. No, sir.

Question. Have you ever heard?

Answer. I have heard that there was but one; but I do not know.

Question. You heard that several persons fired at him?

Answer. I heard five or six shots, but whether fired by himself or others I do not know.

Question. Was the crowd of negroes generally armed?

Answer. I think not. I think there was perhaps one man out of eight or ten that had a pistol.

Question. How many had guns?

Answer. Probably half a dozen on the ground had guns. I do not think there were more than that; at least I did not see them.

By the CHAIRMAN:

Question. Did you see any saber-cuts on his body?

Answer. I did not.

Question. Did you see any evidence upon his person as if he had been stamped when he fell?

Answer. No, sir. His clothes did not look as though there had been anything of the kind. He lay there, and his clothes seemed to be as little ruffled—his shirt, vest, and all—as though he had just fallen down without any violence. I saw no marks of anything of the kind.

By Mr. BLAIR:

Question. Did he fall upon his face or back?

Answer. He was lying flat upon his back when I came to him.

Question. You did not see him fall?

Answer. I did not.

Question. Were you sitting in the buggy when all this occurred?

Answer. I was.

Question. In that position you had the advantage of seeing over the crowd?

Answer. At the time the shot was fired I was talking to this man, Stanton Cromwell, that I have spoken of, who sat with his back against the dash-board of the buggy, or spring-wagon. He pretended to have something very important to communicate; and in order not to disturb the meeting, he asked me to listen, and was whispering, and I had my head inclined forward, so that it was really behind Mr. Bliss. Mr. Bliss's body was between my face and this man.

Question. Stanton Cromwell was talking to you?

Answer. Yes, sir; whispering to me.

Question. How then could he have seen any pistol in the hands of this man?

Answer. I never heard that he said he saw a pistol. He claims that the ball grazed his head; that he heard it whistle by his ear; and that he saw the smoke coming from where the man stood. That is what he told us at the time. He was very anxious to communicate something, and called me aside instantly, and, in a very excited manner, he said he saw the smoke, and that the ball whistled by his ear, and grazed his head.

Question. His ear must have been pretty close to yours?

Answer. Yes, sir.

Question. Did you hear any ball whistle?

Answer. No, sir; I did not.

Question. Did you look instantly in the direction of the shot?

Answer. I jumped to my feet instantly, and saw the man running. I instantly gave a glance about, and saw that nobody was hurt; and I believed the man would probably get into trouble. I saw the men running after him excitedly, and while I was calling to them to let him go, Stanton Cromwell jumped up beside me in a very excited manner, and cried out, "Catch him! Catch him! Damn him, catch him!" That was the language of Cromwell, while I was calling to them, with all my might, to let him go, and come back and hear the speaking.

Question. Did you see the smoke?

Answer. I did not. My first glance was to see if anybody was hurt. I jumped to my feet when I heard the report, and instantly glanced about to see whether anybody was hit, but I saw that nobody was hit. I did not know whether it had been fired accidentally, or who fired it. I was satisfied that it was a pistol-shot, from the report.

Question. If he had fired the pistol, you do not believe that the smoke could have disappeared before your eye glanced in that direction?

Answer. I do not know whether I would have noticed the smoke or not. I do not know whether I would. My first thought was that somebody was killed. I looked about instantly to see who it was, and by that time he had got, perhaps, two or three rods away. I followed him as long as I could with my eye, until the crowd surging about obstructed my view. It was probably not over half a minute from the time of the shot first fired until these five or six shots were fired, and then the thing was all over.

Question. How far had he got from the crowd when he fell?

Answer. He had only got in the outskirts of the crowd—not further than probably six rods from the buggy.

Question. How far was he then from the opposite side of the street?

Answer. There was no street there. On the other side of the buggy was the railroad-track, but the street, or the beginning of the stores, was north of us.

Question. Did he make in that direction?

Answer. He was making toward the stores.

Question. How far had he got in that direction?

Answer. He was probably half way from the buggy to the stores.

Question. When he was shot down?

Answer. Yes, sir. He did not run directly to the stores at first, but he turned almost at a right angle—at least that was the way the crowd ran after the firing—so that after he turned this angle there was a straight opening from where we stood to the stores; that is, the ground was level. He first ran almost directly toward the stores, westward, and then turned in a direction more nearly parallel with the course of the street, or the front of the stores; and after he turned this angle the firing occurred.

By the CHAIRMAN:

Question. Was this meeting on the west side of the railroad?

Answer. Yes, sir; and southeast of the stores. The stores are in line at some distance from the railroad depot, and parallel with the railroad, which runs north and south, the line of stores standing probably fifteen or twenty rods from the railroad-track, westward, and extending north and south parallel with the railroad. The depot is on the east side of this street or common.

By Mr. BLAIR:

Question. Can you draw a diagram of it?

Answer. Yes, sir; I will try to. There is an open common about fifteen rods wide west of the railroad-track, which runs north and south. Then on the west side of this common, and parallel with the railroad-track, stands a line of stores. The highway runs through the middle of this common. We were between it and the stores. The intervening space is open common. Near the south end of this common, and a little nearer to the stores than to the railroad, is where I stood in the center of the crowd and spoke, while the crowd was gathered around me. Lee stood within eight or ten feet of me, on the west side of the buggy, and he started out, first, almost directly westward, toward the line of the stores, but after getting perhaps half way across the distance between the buggy and the stores, and reaching the outskirts of the crowd, he turned more to the northward, and there he was shot, and fell.

Question. How far was he from the stores when he fell?

Answer. I should think he was about eight rods from the nearest store.

Question. Were there any white persons standing in front of these stores at the time he fell?

Answer. Yes, sir. Not exactly in front of the stores there, but in front of the stores further northward. The nearest store is a small concern, and probably the persons were standing a little further north. When we passed down in procession from the north there were a number of white men standing there. That was fifteen minutes before the firing occurred.

Question. Were there any standing there at the time he fell?

Answer. I think there were. While I was speaking, I remember there were quite a number there; some colored and some white.

Question. Any that you recognized?

Answer. No, sir. I do not think I could have recognized them at that distance.

Question. Where was Dr. Brothers?

Answer. I do not know. I think that Mr. Bliss stated to me that he was on the common at a point northwest of the buggy, and about eight rods from the buggy. I think Mr. Bliss stated to me that he saw him there while he was speaking.

Question. You say there were white and colored men in the village who belonged to the Native Sons of the South?

Answer. I understood that there were.

Question. Did you understand that they gathered there that day?

Answer. No, sir; not that they were gathered there.

Question. You had no idea of it when you marched in with your body of men?

Answer. No, sir.

Question. You had no idea of making a demonstration by way of intimidating the colored Native Sons of the South?

Answer. No, sir. I had an idea, which I can give you if you desire it.

Question. I should like to have the idea.

Answer. Our idea was this: There had been a demonstration two days previous, headed by Dr. Landrum, the man that got up the Native Sons. They had had a barbecue there, and he had marched through town with his eighty colored men, making a demonstration, cheering, and in his speech he had denounced Mr. Bliss and myself and others of the party, using very bitter and inflammatory language. These colored people, when they first proposed marching over there, said they wanted to let the people know that Dr. Landrum and his crowd were unequal in point of numbers with us, and they thought it would have the effect, when these few colored men there saw how large a crowd there was of us, and how many republicans there were in comparison to their handful, that they probably would disband the thing and have no more to do with the Native Sons. That was the argument that was used at Prairie Hill before starting, and there was nothing more hostile than that. I did not say a word.

Question. You say Dr. Landrum denounced you in very bitter terms?

Answer. I understood so, and Mr. Bliss, also.

[The witness makes the following diagram, illustrative of the answer given:]

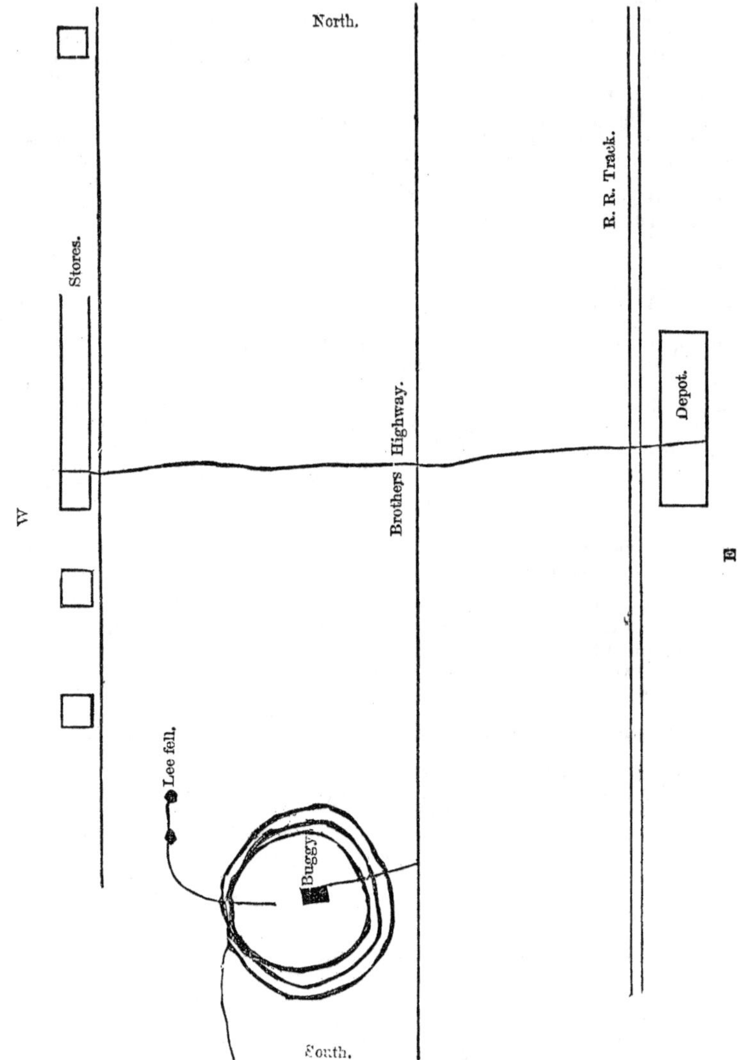

Question. What did he say about you?

Answer. I understood he said something about making me swallow hot lead, or other things of the kind, and something very similar to what I had heard before. I was not there, but I understood that he made such a one as he had been making all over the county, and such a one as he made in my hearing shortly before.

Question. He is a very inflammatory man, is he?

Answer. Well, he is on paper.

Question. The juries under the Federal courts are composed of citizens of this State, as well as the juries of the State courts?

Answer. I suppose so.

Question. Taken from the same body of men as the juries in the State courts?

Answer. I do not know as to that; I never have seen any of them. I do not know who they do summon on these juries.

Question. What I mean to ask is this: is there the same class of citizens on both juries—citizens of this State?

Answer. I suppose they are. I do not know anything about it. I never have had any acquaintance with juries in the Federal courts. I never attended one.

Question. Why should the witnesses be afraid to testify before the one jury any more than the other?

Answer. They seem to believe that if they go away from home they are safer. If the Federal court were sitting in this county I doubt whether it would be any different from testifying before a State court in this county. But if there is a change of venue, I think it tends to relieve them of that dread and intimidation.

By the CHAIRMAN:

Question. Is there not a higher degree of safety felt in the administration of criminal justice in the Federal court from the fact that men belonging to the Ku-Klux Klan cannot be drafted upon the juries, as the oath which the jurors there take would forbid or preclude a person belonging to a secret oath-bound organization from becoming a juror?

Answer. Yes, sir; I should suppose there would be if that fact was generally known. I have never become conversant enough with the Ku-Klux act to know anything of its workings. In fact, I did not know that the oath was different. I have not studied it at all.

Question. Is there also a confidence felt that the General Government will protect those witnesses in obeying its process or subpœna better than your State courts will?

Answer. Certainly there is. They believe that when they go into the Federal courts, they have the Federal Government to stand at their back and protect them in their rights, and that if there is any danger they will receive protection.

COLUMBUS, MISSISSIPPI, *November* 9, 1871.

WOODSON H. KENNON, JR., sworn and examined.

By the CHAIRMAN:

Question. State your place of residence.

Answer. I live now in this town, Columbus, Lowndes County, Mississippi.

Question. What is your occupation?

Answer. I am in the warehouse business. I do not know what you would call it exactly—with Mr. H. S. Merritt, of this place—the fire-proof warehouse business.

Question. Were you in the confederate service, and did you lose an arm in that service?

Answer. I was. I lost an arm at Harrisburgh, North Mississippi, July 14, 1864.

Question. Are you a native of the South?

Answer. Yes, sir.

Question. You may state whether you were engaged at any time in teaching a public school in this county, near Caledonia, in connection with your step-mother?

Answer. Yes, sir; I was engaged as an assistant teacher in a public school, public white school. I taught about two and a half miles northeast of Caledonia for two months. I commenced about the 1st of February, and taught about two month.

Question. You may state whether your father was an infirm old mans?

Answer. Yes, sir; he was.

Question. Your step-mother was an elderly lady?

Answer. Yes, sir; she is about forty.

Question. And you were engaged in teaching in connection with her?

Answer. Yes, sir.

Question. Now, you may state whether you were interfered with or molested while you were engaged in teaching this white school; and, if so, upon what occasion, and by whom, and for what cause.

Answer. Well, sir, I do not know the exact date, but it could be got from the school reports from Mr. Bishop, so that I could tell the exact date when I was interrupted, but I cannot tell exactly now.

Question. Was it this last spring?

Answer. Yes, sir; we commenced about the 1st of February. I think I commenced there the first or second Monday in February, and taught two months, lacking three days. The three days were the three last days in the week. On Tuesday night of either the last week in March or the first week in April—I cannot be positively certain about that—there was a small body of disguised men who came to my father's house, very late in the night, and called me out to the gate. I went out, and they asked me my name, and if I was not teaching a public school. I told them I was; that I and my step-mother were engaged in teaching a public school. They told me that that school must be discontinued; that the tax would be resisted, and would not be paid; that I would get nothing for my services, and I must, therefore, quit teaching. I remarked to them that I was a disabled man. I had lost my arm in the service of my country; that I had spilt as much blood as any of them for this country; that I had nothing to do with creating the public-school system, one way or another; that it was a State institution; that I was teaching that school, because I was thereby making my living; that I had no other means right then of doing so, and that I would rather not stop. They seemed to be very determined, and told me they had notified other teachers, and that they could not look over me; that I must not teach any longer.

Question. Did you make any promise to them to discontinue your school?

Answer. Well, sir, I believe I told them I did not suppose I would teach any more, that I did not think I would. They did not threaten me with anything at all. They did not tell me that they would hang me, or kill me, or anything of that sort. They just told me positively that I must quit teaching, and of course I did not pretend to resist a body of disguised men whom I did not know, when I had no way of finding them out.

Question. They could see that you were a disabled man and had lost your right arm, could they not?

Answer. Yes, sir; I suppose they could. I was in my shirt sleeves. I just slipped on my boots when I went out. I did not dress.

Question. Did you tell them that you had been in the confederate service?

Answer. I did.

Question. Did they seem to know you? Did any one speak to you in such terms as to imply that they knew anything about you?

Answer. No, sir; they asked me my name, or they asked if my name was Kennon. I believe that was about the first thing they said to me.

Question. Did any one of them seem to be a leader or the captain of the company, taking the lead?

Answer. There was one who was spokesman. None of the rest of the party spoke much. There was only one man who spoke to me at all; he did all the talking. I do not know that he had any command of them any further than that there was a spokesman that did all the talking.

Question. Were they mounted or dismounted during the time of this parley?

Answer. They were mounted.

Question. Were their horses disguised?

Answer. No, sir. I think that party were riding mules.

Question. Were the mules disguised?

Answer. No, sir.

Question. Were the bodies of the men as well as their faces disguised?

Answer. Yes, sir.

Question. You think there were not more than ten or twelve in the company?

Answer. No, sir; I have forgotten exactly. There were either six or nine or sixteen; I believe there were nine. I have not thought about the thing really until Mr. Whitfield told me that I would be expected to come before you gentlemen. That was the first time I had thought of it for some time. I made pretty much such a statement to him the day after it occurred. I came down to inform Mr. Bishop, and he was in Mr. Bishop's office, and my step-mother and myself said we did not think we could teach any more.

Question. Was anything said to your step-mother?

Answer. No, sir.

Question. Did they direct you to convey to her any message, or was the prohibition simply directed against your teaching the school?

Answer. Well, I think it was intended for both of us. I reckon so. They did not give me any message for her at all. What they said they said to me, and did not leave any message for her.

Question. You lived with your father and your step-mother?

Answer. Yes, sir; until the last week of this September. Since that I have been living in this town.

Question. Did you continue your school after that?

Answer. No, sir; I did not teach any more after that. I was engaged planting, and my father being infirm, and not able to see to his little planting interests there, I remained at home that winter in order to look after it, and I got the school for my step-mother. She has had a great deal of experience in school-teaching. She has taught a great deal. She taught it one month, and the school was so very large that she could not do the children justice without an assistant teacher, and it being more pleasant for her to have me as an assistant teacher in the school than a stranger, I made application and got the position.

Question. Did your step-mother discontinue her school?

Answer. No, sir; she taught on to the end of the session. These men told me that the school must not be continued unless we held the patrons responsible for the pay. My step-mother notified all the patrons of the school that she would teach on and hold them responsible for the balance of the tuition if the public fund did not pay.

Question. Did the patrons consent to that?

Answer. Yes, sir.

Question. So, under those circumstances, she continued the school?

Answer. Yes, sir; and taught out the session.

Question. And no further objection was made to her teaching?

Answer. No, sir.

Question. Did you hear of other schools where the teachers were visited by bodies of disguised men and warned?

Answer. Yes, sir; about the same time I heard that other teachers were also visited.

Question. Have you known or heard of any scourgings or whippings inflicted by bodies of men in disguise?

Answer. I do not know of any, sir, of my own knowledge. I have heard reports of that sort in the country, but I could not swear to anything of that sort. I never saw anybody whipped.

Question. All that you know is simply from information?

Answer. Yes, sir; simply from rumor.

Question. You have heard of such cases repeatedly?

Answer. I have heard of white men and negroes being whipped up in that country for stealing.

Question. By disguised men?

Answer. Yes, sir; they say they were disguised. That is a rumor.

By Mr. Blair:

Question. What did you say they were whipped for?

Answer. Stealing. I have had men to tell me that they heard that such a negro or such a white man had been whipped for stealing at such a time, but I never saw it. I do not know that I know of a case. I know I never heard any persons who have told me that they saw disguised men whipping any man, but I have had men to tell me that they have heard that such a man was whipped at such a time by what they called Ku-Klux.

Question. Where did you say you were living?

Answer. I live now, sir, in this town.

Question. But at the time of this occurrence?

Answer. At the time I was teaching this school I lived two miles northeast of Caledonia, in this county. The school was taught about two and a half miles northeast of Caledonia.

Question. The only objection that these parties had to the school, I understand, was on account of the tax?

Answer. Yes, sir; that was the only objection they made. They told me the tax would be resisted and not paid, and I would not receive anything for my services, and I must therefore not teach any more.

Question. No threats at all were used?

Answer. No, sir; they did not threaten me with anything in the world.

Question. Was not that rather a matter of kindness to you, to let you know that they did intend to resist the tax and that you would get nothing?

Answer. I reckon they thought so. They told me they were doing it as an act of kindness.

Question. That they did not want you to spend your time without compensation?

Answer. Yes, sir; they told me they did not think I ought to teach for nothing, and I would not be paid, and on that account I must not teach any longer.

Question. You did not understand them to convey any threat beyond this, that they intended to resist that tax and not pay it?

Answer. Yes, sir; I did not understand them to make any threat at all. That was the reason they gave me for warning or compelling me to quit teaching. They did not threaten me with anything. They did not say what they would do if I taught on, or anything of that sort. They did not make any threats at all. They did not try to frighten me I do not think. They did not say anything to frighten me.

Question. They did not give you to understand that they would visit you again and injure you personally, or in your property in any way, did they?

Answer. No, sir; they did not.

Question. They did not use threatening language of any kind, saying it would be better for you, except in the sense that you would not get your pay?

Answer. No, sir; they did not use any.

By the Chairman:

Question. Were you acting at that time with the democratic or conservative party?

Answer. Well, sir, I was not acting with either party. I was at home, and was not engaged in anything political.

Question. I refer to your voting?

Answer. Well, sir, I consider that I am a democrat. I have never voted in any other way.

Question. Was that fact generally known throughout the neighborhood?

Answer. Yes, sir; I reckon there is not a man in Lowndes County but what knows that I am a democrat. I have never pretended to be anything else. I have never voted in any other way except that.

Question. If these men in disguise lived in that part of the country, then they probably knew what your politics were?

Answer. I could not tell anything about that. I pledge you my honor I did not know them, and I had no idea where they lived. I do not know where they came from. I was asleep when they came up to the gate. I only could tell you in what direction they went away. I do not know from what direction they came up to the house. I have no idea on earth where they came from.

Question. Did you make any efforts afterward to discover who they were?

Answer. No, sir.

Question. Had you heard at the time of such a thing as the Ku-Klux Klan?

Answer. Yes, sir; I had heard of the existence of such a thing before they came to my house. I had heard that there were some in Tennessee a long time ago.

Question. Did you notice the character of their disguise?

Answer. It was principally white, sir. There was some color about the face. The cheeks were painted red, but from the face down it was all white.

Question. Was there any artificial beard?

Answer. Yes, sir.

Question. Hanging down pretty low?

Answer. Well, I do not know that it was any longer than ordinarily. Some of them, I noticed, pretended to have beards, but nothing extraordinarily long.

Question. Were there any horns on their heads?

Answer. No, sir.

Question. Did you hear a whistle?

Answer. No, sir.

By Mr. BLAIR:

Question. You told them you had no employment; that you had shed your blood for the country; did they understand you from that remark, or did you intend them to understand, that you had been wounded in the confederate service?

Answer. Yes, sir; that was it.

Question. That was the idea you intended to convey?

Answer. Yes, sir.

Question. That you had been wounded in the confederate service?

Answer. Yes, sir; that was the idea.

Question. And they understood it so, you think?

Answer. Yes, sir.

Question. You showed them that you had been mutilated; that you had lost your arm?

Answer. Yes, sir.

By the CHAIRMAN:

Question. It was generally known through that part of the country where you lived that you had been in the confederate service, and lost your arm?

Answer. Yes, sir; that fact is well known to every man in this county. I was elected probate clerk soon after the surrender, and served for three years, and nearly every white man in the county knows me; if he does not know me personally he knows me when he sees me.

By Mr. BUCKLEY:

Question. Do you not think that those persons who called upon you that night knew you?

Answer. I have no reason to think that they did. They did not seem to recognize me, or do anything by which I could tell that they knew me.

By the CHAIRMAN:

Question. What interest could they have in the taxation of Lowndes County unless they were citizens of that county, and would share the burden of raising these taxes to support the common schools?

Answer. Well, sir, I do not know; I do not know anything about that.

Question. Would you not infer from the fact that they wanted this school system discontinued, because of the oppressive taxation which would follow if it were kept up, that they were interested in that question?

Answer. No, sir; I will tell you why: I live near the line. It is only half a mile to the line of Monroe County. It is not very far to the line of Monroe County, Mississippi. Then going over to the right it is not very far to the line of Sanford County, Alabama.

Question. If they were citizens of Alabama, or citizens of Monroe County, Mississippi, what possible interest could they have in the county taxation of Lowndes County?

Answer. I do not know, sir. I do not know what interest they had in it. They may have been citizens of Lowndes County, for all I know. I do not know where they lived or came from.

COLUMBUS, MISSISSIPPI, *November* 10, 1871.

JEHU A. ORR sworn and examined.

By the CHAIRMAN:

Question. Please to state your place of residence, and the official position you hold.

Answer. Judge of the seventh judicial district of Mississippi. I reside in Columbus, Mississippi.

Question. What counties are embraced in that judicial district?

Answer. Lowndes, Oktibbeha, Winston, and Noxubee.

Question. For what period of time have you held the position of circuit judge?

Answer. Since the 10th of May, 1870.

Question. What, if any, position did you hold before that time?

Answer. For what period?

Question. I had an impression that you had been circuit judge for a good many years?

Answer. No, sir.

Question. The committee wish to inquire into the condition of this part of Mississippi, so far as regards the execution of the laws and the safety of the lives and property of the citizens. Please give the committee any information you have on that subject, derived from your personal knowledge or from sources you deem reliable.

Answer. Outside of criminal offenses growing out of political causes, the criminal laws have been well and faithfully executed in my district since I have been presiding as judge. I believe there are fewer violations of law outside of the offenses referred to in my district since I have been presiding than there were before the war.

Question. You speak of criminal cases growing out of political causes; you may state to the committee what class of cases you have reference to—what class of disturbances.

Answer. Murders, assassinations, intimidations; perhaps that would cover the whole ground.

Question. Any whippings by combinations of men which you have reason to believe grew out of political causes?

Answer. I am personally cognizant of not one act of violence or murder.

Question. You may give the committee any instances of murders, assassinations, and intimidations which you have any knowledge or information of.

Answer. The most tangible information which I have of acts of violence occurred during the sessions of my court at this place, at the last term or term before. I shall have to reflect a moment to locate the terms. Our terms are very often; we have three terms a year here. I am almost constantly holding a court somewhere in the district.

Question. You may say at a recent term of the court.

Answer. I cannot undertake to locate whether it was at the last term or term before. It was brought to my knowledge that a freedman had been severely whipped, and that a school-teacher had been notified to leave his school—to close it up, and leave the neighborhood. The grand jury were in session. At the organization of the grand jury, at the opening of the term, I had given an elaborate charge, in obedience to a Mississippi statute, against masked men and marauders. I recalled the grand jury, and repeated the charge on the particular offense which had been brought to my knowledge. I notified them that they had compulsory process at their command, by which they could summon before them every citizen in the State; and that the interests of society and their own oaths as jurors demanded a thorough investigation of the case which had just occurred; and while investigating that case, two other acts of violence occurred within the town, the city of Columbus. These were upon two men who had been tried and acquitted under a charge of robbery. One of the parties was clearly guilty of the charge. His guilt was so apparent that when the jury returned the verdict into court, for the first time in the history of my judicial administration, I discharged the jury, and ordered the sheriff to summon another. On the following night, I learned that they were taken out and severely chastised by men in disguise. That information having been communicated to me on the next morning, I recalled the grand jury, and very earnestly charged them upon that offense, reminding them of their great powers to require testimony and witnesses. The grand jury finally returned, or rather the grand jury made their final report, in which they represented to the court that it was impossible for them to make any discoveries as to the perpetrators of either of the offenses. In the county of Winston, it was brought to my knowledge that certain school-houses, where free schools were taught, had been burned. With a more than ordinarily intelligent grand jury, they were specially charged to inquire as to these offenses. After a week's deliberation they reported that they were unable to make any discoveries. In the county of Oktibbeha, I was informed that a negro had been murdered while on his way from the place of commitment by the committing court to the jail. I gave that case in special charge to the grand jury, and the report of that jury was that they were not able to make any discoveries. In the county of Noxubee, I was informed that a negro man was missing under suspicious circumstances. He had been placed in the charge of an officer, committed for horse-stealing, having confessed his guilt to the committing court. On the night of his committal to the constable he disappeared. I gave the case in charge to the grand-jury of Noxubee. No bill was returned against any of the parties for the escape of the prisoner, and according to the information received by the grand jury, they were not able to make any discoveries as to the cause of the absence or the absconding of the prisoner.

By Mr. BLAIR:

Question. That was the Bridges case?

Answer. Yes, sir. A few weeks since the constable Bridges was arrested in this town, on the affidavit of a colored man, by the order of a colored justice, and committed to jail for murder. A writ of *habeas corpus* was applied for to me, and I granted it. He was brought before me. After several days' investigation, it was made very clearly to appear, to my satisfaction, that the officer had been guilty of gross negligence; but, after examining a number of witnesses, I have no definite opinion as to whether the missing prisoner is dead or alive. A body has been found in the Tombigbee River, caught in a willow tree. The body had been removed, and was visited by the father of the missing prisoner. It was taken up on the willow. The body had been deposited there during high water, and one leg but caught in the fork of a willow tree, and when the water fell it was left suspended up in the willow tree, and was discovered lying in that position, with one leg caught in the limb. The body was removed, and visited by the father of the missing prisoner. The father testified before me that it was his son. He exhibited some clothing, and identified the clothing as a part of the clothing worn by his son when he left home. That occurred three or four, not more than four, weeks from the time his son was missing. A physician who made an examination of the body described its condition to the court, and three or four other physicians were called as experts, and, according to the testimony of the four physicians examined, it was utterly impossible, or, rather, physically impossible, that the body examined could have been the body of the missing prisoner. The body found in the river, as described by the physician who examined it, had reached that state of putrefaction, as was shown by all the physicians who were examined, to have been beyond that possible for the missing prisoner to have reached in that length of time. Each one of the physicians testified that it was impossible for the decay shown to have existed with the body examined; that that putrefaction, that decay, could not have reached the point which it did reach in a less period than four months. The hair and skin had all disappeared from the head; the skull was hollow, the brain having disappeared through some—I am not able to give you the medical terms—the skull was hollow; the brain was gone; it was not there; the flesh of the body had all fallen from the bones, except where it was held by the clothing, which prevented it from falling; in other words, the body was a skeleton, except where the clothing held the putrefied mass together. It would require more direct interrogatories, gentlemen, to draw out anything else you may desire that is within my knowledge.

By the CHAIRMAN:

Question. Returning to Winston County, did you ever have any information of a colored man of the name of Solomon Triplett having been killed by men in disguise, in the night-time?

Answer Yes, sir; but the information I received of the killing of Triplett is too vague and indefinite for me to reply to that interrogatory further than to say that I have heard a rumor of the killing of such a man as Triplett.

Question. Did you hear of the case of Allen Bird, a colored man committed to jail by a magistrate on a charge of attempting to commit rape on a white female?

Answer. Yes, sir.

Question. And of his being taken out of jail, or, rather, having been killed in jail, by a body of disguised men?

Answer. Yes, sir; I have heard of that case, and will bring the attention of the grand jury, on next Monday, to that matter.

Question. That was a recent occurrence?

Answer. Yes, sir. He was indicted, and I knew, from the sheriff and from the district attorney, something of the testimony before the grand jury, and something of the case, before I adjourned the last term of my court in Winston. That has occurred since I left there, and I propose to make that the subject of special investigation by my grand jury before the next term of the court, to meet there on Monday.

Question. Did you hear of the killing, in that county, of a freedman by the name of George Murf, who lived with one McQueen, and who had been charged with using inflammatory language to the negroes? He was said to have been killed about eighteen months since.

Answer. Well, sir, if I have ever heard of it, I have no such recollection of it now as to give you any information on the subject.

Question. Have you heard of the killing in that county of a negro by the name of Nelson Yarborough?

Answer. I have heard of acts of violence and lawlessness in Winston, but I could not undertake to give names, for two reasons: first, my memory of names is exceedingly treacherous; and next, my information, except in one or two cases enumerated, has been of so indefinite a character as not to be made the subject of testimony in any tribunal.

Question. There is another colored man of the name of Jessy Thompson, alleged to have been killed by unknown parties some years since; as far back, probably, as 1866. Have you any recollection of that case?

Answer. I have not.

Question. It has been stated to the committee that several colored men of that county have been whipped by men in disguise, and in the night-time. I will call your attention to some names furnished to the committee, and ask you to state whether you have any recollection of having heard of these cases. Mordecai Mitchell is one of the men that was whipped, but not very severely—fifteen or twenty lashes—at the time the disguised men were after one Jim Hudson. Do you remember of hearing of that case?

Answer. No, sir.

Question. Robin Coleman is another. He was whipped in March last by a body of disguised men.

Answer. I have no recellection of that.

Question. And on the same night George Gladney was whipped. Do you remember of hearing of his case?

Answer. No, sir.

Question. Nathan Cannon was another case. He was whipped last year for remarks he made in a school he was teaching, said to be inflammatory.

Answer. I never heard of it.

Question. Did you hear of the case of one Peter Cooper, a teacher of a colored school, who was said to have been visited, and his trunk containing his money burned up?

Answer. I never heard of it.

Question. Have you heard generally that colored men have been whipped by disguised men in Winston County; without reference to names or particular circumstances, have you heard it as a fact?

Answer. No, sir; I have not heard in the shape in which you put the question that it has been done; perhaps I misunderstand the question.

Question. The question is whether you have heard the general fact that colored men in Winston County have been visited at their cabins at night by disguised parties, taken out and severely whipped for one cause or another?

Answer. I have heard of some cases; but to use the term general, I could not say that. I have heard of some cases, but I do not recollect the name of the gentleman who is my informant. He is a citizen of Winston County, living in the eastern part of the county; and he detailed to me a number of acts of violence. Who the parties were, I could not make the subject of testimony. Your question compels me to answer that I have heard such things; but I have no such definite information of them as to give you any satisfaction; nor could I to-day furnish you with the name of the old gentleman who made the communication to me.

Question. Were the acts of violence, of which you heard, committed by disguised men?

Answer. Such is my understanding; invariably by disguised men.

Question. And in the night-time generally?

Answer. Yes, generally in the night time. Indeed I do not remember now any act of violence that has ever come to my knowledge which was perpetrated in the day-time.

Question. In your testimony respecting Winston County, you spoke of your information that certain school-houses had been burned, and that you had given that matter in charge to the grand jury. What is your information as to the number of school-houses burned in the county, and how recently was it done?

Answer. My information was that, up to the July term of the court in Winston there had been seven—my recollection is seven.

Question. Were all of them colored schools or white and colored indiscriminately?

Answer. We have no white and colored mixed-schools, you know, in the State.

Question. I understand that.

Answer. I understand that some of them were colored and some white. There is with many persons very decided opposition to the free-school system, on two grounds: first, of educating the negroes; and second, of taxing the people for public schools at all. There are two grounds of opposition, and I have no doubt but what the destruction of school-houses in Winston resulted from both causes—opposition to negro education, and opposition to taxation for public schools.

Question. How general, in your opinion, is the opposition in that county to the education of colored children, or to the establishment of colored schools?

Answer. I cannot answer that question more directly than to express an opinion that if the white voters of the county were called upon to express a voluntary and free opinion, that the system would not be adopted—that the system could not be carried by a free election.

Question. I understand you to say that Noxubee County, of which Macon is the county-seat, is embraced in your judicial circuit?

Answer. Yes, sir; it is one of the counties.

Question. Are you pretty well acquainted with the condition of affairs in that county?

Answer. Only such as I obtained from my official position, from having visited the county and held four terms of the court there. Neither one of these counties were within the range of my personal acquaintance. Without putting that down, unless you desire it, here I would simply make the explanation: I have been living at Columbus only some five years. My practice has never extended, when I have been at the bar, either west or south. I was a stranger, both to Noxubee, Winston, and Oktibbeha, when I was placed upon the bench. My field of practice has been nearly all in Chickasaw, and in that direction. I am an old citizen of Chickasaw, having lived there since 1843; but in these three counties I had never been in the habit of practicing; never attended as a practicing lawyer; and when I went there I was almost an entire stranger to the citizens of the three counties. I have derived no information, except what would be furnished to me in my official position in the three visits I have made there.

Question. In your general statement you have referred to no case in Noxubee County supposed to be a case of violence, except that of the negro man who was missing, under suspicious circumstances?

Answer. There was another case which I did not remember—the case of a negro man who was shot off of his team whilst driving.

Question. Do you remember his name?

Answer. No, sir.

Question. You may state the particulars as far as you are informed.

Answer. I know nothing in the world of the case except the information, and that was nothing more than reports that he was passing home with a load of corn, and his employer was lying down in the wagon asleep, and he was driving along on the road, and was shot by some unknown person who was on the side of the road, and killed dead, and the party made his escape.

Question. Was this in the night-time?

Answer. I said I had never heard of any case, except this, occurring in the night. My recollection is that that was about dusk. Perhaps not exactly in the night, but late in the afternoon or early in the evening.

Question Did you ever hear the case of Dick Malone, a colored man.

Answer. Yes, sir; I recollect that case since you have called my attention to it. I have heard of that from the Rev. John Baldwin. I spent the night with Rev. John Baldwin, at Webster, in Winston County, the latter part of July of this year. He was living on the place at the time of the death of Malone.

Question. What account did he give you of it?

Answer. [Pausing.]

Question. I will not tax your memory if you do not readily recall the particulars, inasmuch as the committee have taken some testimony in relation to his killing. That was near the line, between Noxubee and Lowndes, was it not?

Answer. Yes, sir.

Question. It is reported to the committee that he was supposed to have been killed because of certain threats that he had made to give the Ku-Klux a warm reception in case they visited him. Do you remember of having any information upon that point?

Answer. Yes, sir; my recollection from Mr. Baldwin is that the idea that he (Baldwin) had of the killing was that he identified some parties. I will not be certain, however.

By Mr. BLAIR:

Question. Was he reported to have followed the party up?

Answer. No, sir; he was killed very near the quarters, according to my understanding. I only have the statement in a casual conversation as a guest. I was staying all night with Baldwin, and in the course of the conversation he referred to it and made the statement. I am not definite as to the details—the particulars which Baldwin communicated to me. I have an idea, however, that Baldwin's suggestion was that they had killed him because he had identified some of them, and had threatened to expose them. I will not state that I am even certain as to that point.

Question. The testimony was, judge, that the party was there and whipped some man on the place, and that Dick Malone followed up the party, telling them that he knew some of them, and that he meant to find out all about them, and followed them some distance from his cabin, and was shot.

Answer. Well, the distance was not great, because Mr. Baldwin went and saw him, and my recollection is that it was not two hundred yards from Baldwin's house, where he was killed. If he followed it was a very short distance. My recollection is that he was killed within two hundred yards of Mr. Baldwin's residence.

By the CHAIRMAN:

Question. Baldwin had the lease of that plantation?

Answer. Yes, sir; he was living there.

Question. Did you hear of the case of Bully Jack, a negro man who was killed near Shuqulak in June or July, 1870?

Answer. Yes, sir; I heard of it. I would not have referred to it, though, if you had not called my attention to the name of the place. There is an indictment pending against James Murdock for his murder. Murdock made his escape. He was a colored man, and he lived about two miles from Shuqulak, on the Louisville road.

Question. Did you hear it stated as the belief that he was killed on account of having testified before the grand jury at Macon?

Answer. No, sir; the version that was given me of that killing was that Murdock wanted to make him with him; that they had had a misunderstanding, and that Murdock was a drinking, reckless man, and went to his house and killed him at his house. The impression is on my mind that that is the information I received of that killing.

Question. Did you hear that he was visited by some men, and requested to come out on a pretext that something was wrong with a wagon or a wheel had come off, or something, and that he was induced to go up the road?

Answer. No, sir; I did not hear of that.

Question. And that his wife heard a scuffling and the shooting?

Answer. No, sir. The information I received was that he was killed in his house; that there was another man with him out at the gate within twenty or thirty steps of the house, and that Murdock shot inside of the man's house and killed him in the presence of his wife. That is my information of it. I know that there is an indictment now pending, and a reward has been offered for his arrest. He made his escape immediately.

Question. Did you hear of the killing, in Winston County, of a colored man named Johnson Keitt, some time in the spring of 1871. I cannot give you the particulars of his killing further than that.

Answer. If you can aid my memory in reference to the place, the time, or something that would enable me to recall it, I might perhaps be able to answer the question. As it is, I have no recollection of it.

Question. Did you hear of a colored man being killed by a party of men near Brooksville, about the middle of June last, in Noxubee County?

Answer. May I ask his name?

Question. I do not know his name. The witness who mentioned him did not know his name.

Answer. No, sir; I have no recollection of it.

Question. Do you remember of hearing of the case of Samuel Coker, a colored man, who was shot in Noxubee County, but, I believe, recovered from his wounds?

Answer. There has been, and there is now, I think, an indictment pending in Noxubee County for some such offense as that, but I had not identified the case by the name.

Question. It is reported to the committee that several cases have occurred in Noxubee County, where colored men, and, in some instances, colored women, have been taken out and whipped by disguised men. Do you remember of hearing of any such cases, or have you any information as to the existence in that county of such outrages?

Answer. No such information as to throw any light upon your investigation.

Question. Do you remember of hearing of a case where some three or four white men, one a widower, and the others bachelors, were said to be living in cohabitation with colored women, and the colored women and, perhaps, the white men, were taken out by a body of men in disguises and whipped and told to go and sin no more?

Answer. No, sir; not without the questions are more specific, or my attention is more specifically directed to it; it is possible I have heard of some such case, but I do not now recall it.

Question. You spoke of a case occurring in Oktibbeha County, where a negro had been murdered on his way to jail; you may give the particulars in that case, so far as your memory serves you.

Answer. I can only state the rumor; I know nothing of it myself. Do you desire me to state what I have heard?

Question. As you have heard it.

Answer. Two young men—white men—were said to have been starting out on a masking expedition; one of them was shot from a tree or some kind of ambush. Suspicion rested upon a negro man; he was arrested, and by the committing officer committed to jail; he was placed in charge of the officer an hour or two before dark, to be conveyed to the jail at Starkville, some twelve, fourteen, or sixteen miles off. Starkville is the county-seat of Oktibbeha. On the route a dense swamp had to be passed through, and night intervened before they reached the swamp. The account that the guard gave of it was that a large number of masked persons presented themselves in the road ahead of them, and presented their weapons, and demanded the prisoner, and that they retired, leaving the prisoner in their hands; he ran off some fifty or sixty yards, and by the time he was caught he was riddled with bullets.

Question. When is that said to have occurred?

Answer. Last winter—the latter part of this last winter, or early in the spring; I will say during the last winter. I gave that case in special charge to the grand jury.

Question. They reported no bill against any person?

Answer. No, sir; no bill.

Question. Have you known of any case where a person charged as having been connected with any of these outrages, committed in the night-time by bodies of men in disguise, has been discovered and brought to justice? Has there been any such case within your judicial experience?

Answer. None in my district. I understand that Judge Davis plumes that feather, as having caught the Ku-Klux up in his district, but there have been more caught in my district.

Question. Where is the difficulty in discovering them, judge? Take the case you last spoke of, occurring in Oktibbeha County, where a large number of disguised persons met an officer having charge of a prisoner, took him and riddled him with bullets. If vigorous, determined effort had been made by the citizens of that neighborhood to discover the offenders, is it probable that they would have failed in discovering one or more?

Answer. The difficulty of detection, in my judgment, arises mainly from the terror which is inspired, not only in the minds of witnesses, but of citizens who would otherwise have an inclination to pursue them—not knowing what to strike, who to strike, and how big a force they had to strike, and the rebound which was to follow their striking.

Question. Is that the reason, in your opinion, why the law has been paralyzed in its efforts to detect these men, and bring them to justice?

Answer. I think that is mainly the reason; not entirely.

Question. What is the condition of public sentiment in relation to these outrages? Have you known of any combined expression of opinion by the good citizens of the country, assembled in meetings?

Answer. Not in meetings. I have, at every term of the court since I have been on the bench, delivered an elaborate charge against what was believed to be the existence of that organization in this country. I have argued it as a question of law, as a question of policy, and a question of interest to our people; and I have never yet met in the circuit an individual who defended the organization. On the contrary, so far as I have heard an expression of opinion from the best citizens of the country, it is an expression of condemnation. It has been a very common and usual thing, after the charges have been delivered, in my social intercourse with the people, for the matter to be a subject of conversation.

Question. If those men belonged to that organization, or were friendly to it, or sympathized with it, is it likely, knowing your official position, and your views in relation to such outrages, that they would give expression to any other sentiment than that of condemnation?

Answer. No, sir; I have no idea that they would, because if they belonged to that, their conduct would at once mark duplicity in their conversation and in their demeanor; and I should be ready to believe that they would suppress or misrepresent, if they belonged to the order.

Question. Your grand juries are composed of twelve or fifteen?

Answer. Twenty, usually.

Question. Does your law require the concurrence of all the members of the grand jury to the finding of a bill?

Answer. Twelve.

Question. Out of twenty?

Answer. Yes, sir.

Question. If there were nine, then, upon a jury who sympathized with this organization or its objects, or who had friends mixed up with the organization, they could defeat the finding of any bill?

Answer. Yes, sir.

Question. And if there was a single man upon a traverse jury, he could defeat a verdict against a member of the organization?

Answer. Yes, sir.

Question. Have you any reason to believe that persons who are cognizant of these outrages are deterred from going before the grand jury and making known their grievances, or the outrages within their knowledge, from an apprehension that they might become objects of vengeance on the part of this organization?

Answer. Did that question seek for facts, or an expression of opinion?

Question. An opinion.

Answer. My opinion is that if there is such an organization in this country, with our grand juries, composed as they are, that not one freedman in a thousand could be induced to go before a mixed grand jury where he would recognize different shades of color and politics, and detail any outrage that might be committed.

Question. Have you any information or belief as to the existence at this time, or in the past, of a secret, oath-bound organization, which has committed these various outrages that I have referred to?

Answer. I have no definite knowledge, and never have had. I have my opinion that there has been such an organization throughout the South.

Question. What is your opinion as to the purposes or objects of that organization?

Answer. It is mere conjecture.

Question. I am asking simply for your opinion.

Answer. I can merely conjecture the design of the order. I believe it to be twofold: first, to control the politics of the South; and next, the feeling which has in a great measure taken possession of many of the old citizens—the slave-holding citizens, the men of the South, who have been raised up under the institution of slavery, and particularly in localities where the colored population is largely in the ascendent—in their social and business relations of life they have felt some kind of necessity for their own protection, feeling that they were not the favored parties either of the State or Federal Government. I think that it has arisen in a great degree from that feeling of a want of protection, a want of confidence in the vindication of right and in the enforcement of contracts, and of the protection of property.

Question. Do you know, or have you heard, of any attempts of employers to control the action or will of their laborers, as to voting, by threats of discharge or other oppressive means?

Answer. No, sir, I do not; I have not.

Question. I am asking now in relation to the whole country over which your jurisdiction extends.

Answer. I have no such knowledge.

Question. Do you think that all persons have an opportunity to vote freely without restraint or fear?

Answer. In the last election in this county I have an undoubted opinion that they have had a free expression.

Question. Have you observed in the verdicts, which your own juries have rendered, any discrimination made at any time on account of color or political opinion? I am asking for your opinion, of course.

Answer. My opinion is that there have been occasionally some convictions of colored men for larceny when the same testimony would not have convicted white men.

Question. In no other offenses?

Answer. Several colored men have been tried before me for murder, and in cases involving life I have not discovered any difference in the verdicts of juries, as between whites and colored.

By Mr. BUCKLEY:

Question. In what consists the inability of the courts to reach these offenses of which you have made mention in the former part of your examination?

Answer. First, the want of specific information on the part of the witnesses as to the individuals perpetrating the offenses.

Question. And that grows out of the fact, does it, to some extent, that persons are deterred from going before grand juries and making their complaints?

Answer. It is a little back of that. In my answer I expressed the opinion that citizens and witnesses who would be inclined to ferret out the offenders were deterred by fear from obtaining such information as would be necessary to base a prosecution upon.

Question. Do you think that the Federal courts have superior advantages over the State courts in ferreting out that particular class of offenses?

Answer. No, sir, I do not. My belief is that the difference between the State courts and the Federal courts on that question is that the Federal courts have at their control agencies that the State courts have not.

Question. What, in your opinion, is the feeling of the people of this section toward the General Government?

Answer. That would require a pretty lengthy answer, if you desire me to make an answer at length.

Question. As reference has been made directly to that point, we would like to know very much your opinion in regard to it. We are seeking to get at the bottom of these troubles, and to know how to remedy them.

Answer. My impression is that the great majority, white and colored, are what is termed loyal to the Federal Government; that they have no idea of resorting to force to resist the laws of the United States. I have never heard of a Federal officer in Mississippi being interfered with in the discharge of his duties, while acting either in a military or a civil capacity as a civil officer of a court. I believe that the southern people—the people of this section—entertain no such idea as rebellion to the lawful authority of the United States. I do not think that one democrat in five hundred in the State of Mississippi has any love for the Federal Government. I think that if the national democratic party were in power, the democrats of Mississippi would be as loyal to the Government of the United States as they ever were.

Question. Why should any portion of the community here feel that they are outside of the protection of the Federal Government?

Answer. They feel that the Government is in reality the republican party.

Question. Do I infer from that that a portion of the community here have no confidence in Federal office-holders, or that Federal office-holders or repulican office-holders will enforce the law?

Answer. It goes deeper than that; they believe that the settled policy of the republican party is a line of policy that is not intended to look specially to their interest; that there may be some diversity of interest between themselves and the elements which are first with the republicans, the national republicans, in the community here. I may say further, that as a general thing there is a want of respect on the part of the people to office-holders generally of the present day in Mississippi, both State and Federal. I must be permitted, however, to qualify that remark as far as I am individually concerned. I have no cause of complaint against the people of this country on the score of respect. I have received the assurance from very many of the most uncompromising democrats of their cordial support and co-operation with me in a rigid enforcement of the laws, and I am sure that I have in many instances received it.

Question. In some localities, judge, the pretext is assigned for these outrages committed by disguised men that the judiciary is partial and incompetent; is such a charge true of the judiciary of your State?

Answer. I am not, of course, the proper party to answer as to the competency.

Question. Do you hear complaints of that kind?

Answer. As to the partiality the charge is utterly groundless. The criminal laws have been enforced in my district with a rigor and determination. The idea I desire to convey is, that the laws have been enforced with a rigor, to the utmost extent that the law would permit, with a due regard to humanity. I have never received a petition or a remonstrance for administering too mild a punishment. I have repeatedly received petitions for the diminution of penalties. I have no cause of complaint against the finding of my juries in the district, from the time I have been on the bench, except in one solitary instance, and for that I discharged the jury.

Question. If that be the case, judge, why should any class of persons in this judicial district seek to take the law into their own hands to punish offenses?

Answer. No such reason exists in fact.

Question. And yet such outrages are committed, are they not, by combinations of men invading the homes of citizens, whipping and scourging them?

Answer. The juries of my district generally, mixed with white and colored, have more generally convicted than juries in criminal cases before the war were in the habit in this country of convicting.

Question. Have you ever known persons who had been visited by these bands of disguised men charged with crimes which could not have been reached and punished by the civil tribunals of the country? In many cases we find that persons have been whipped or scourged on the charge of killing stock, or some other pretext of that kind.

Answer. Yes, sir; I have heard of one instance where, according to the common law which exists in the public mind and heart of the white men of this country, the laws of the State were not adequate to reach the offense, and that was the case of this colored man who was whipped eight or ten miles from this place, the same instance to which I referred. I stated that the offense alleged against him was his boasting of his having had criminal intercourse with a respectable white woman in the neighborhood. According to the unwritten common law of the white man of the South there is no provision in the Mississippi code that is adequate to meet that offense.

By Mr. BLAIR:

Question. What case was that, judge?

Answer. That was the case in which I charged the grand jury specially—a colored man was taken out and whipped.

Question. The case of Hicks?

Answer. I do not remember his name. I do not remember names. There are names of members of the bar in my district I do not pretend to remember. I don't remember whether it was Hicks or not.

By the CHAIRMAN:

Question. If it were true in point of fact there would be the liability for the offense of fornication or adultery, would there not; and if it were not true he would be liable in damages for slander, would he not?

Answer. If it were true in point of fact he would not be punished for adultery under the decisions of the supreme court of this State, following those of Indiana and Illinois, that it required more acts than one to make out a case of adultery.

Question. It would not be in the case of open and notorious adultery?

Answer. Yes, sir; under our decision it must be an act of open and notorious adultery to justify a conviction.

By Mr. BLAIR:

Question. Where the party should be living with the woman as man and wife?

Answer. Yes, sir; as man and wife. An action of slander would be wholly useless if it were false. If the statement of the colored man had been false an action of slander would be useless, for the reason that the exemption laws would secure the property which may have been owned by the defendant.

By the CHAIRMAN:

Question. Do your exemption laws extend to judgment for torts?

Answer. Yes, sir.

Question. Equally to judgments for contracts?

Answer. Yes, sir; there is no distinction.

Question. Such a charge, however, would meet with no credit on the part of the community would it? The charge preferred by the negro that he had cohabited with a respectable white woman?

Answer. I do not think such a charge would have met with any credit from the respectable people of the country. Mr. Buckley, will you repeat your question?

By Mr. BUCKLEY:

Question. I will repeat my question. Have any of the offenses alleged against the victims of these outrages, as a pretext for their commission by these disguised men, been such as the ordinary civil tribunals would not reach?

Answer. I have heard of no other case except the one referred to. One of the most common causes of complaint by the whites against the colored is their disposition to steal; and the juries in my district, both white and colored, have been very prompt in convicting of these offenses.

By the CHAIRMAN:

Question. Is there, as a general rule, any difficulty in convicting and punishing colored men where they have been guilty of offenses?

Answer. None in the world.

Question. Is there in your community or judicial district, in your opinion, any lack of detective ability to discover and bring to justice the perpetrators of violence in case a white man of respectability in the community were taken from his house at night by a body of twenty-five or thirty masked and disguised men, and whipped or killed?

Answer. Yes, sir; I cannot say that there is any greater lack in that power in this than in any other county not of older settlement than this is; but it has been the source of inconvenience, and the source of charges by me to my officers, who, under the statute of Mississippi, are required to hear the charges of the judges, the constables, and the justices of the peace, the magistrates, and all other county officers; all county officers under our statutes are conservators of the peace. There is a general want, and a general failing on the part of the conservators and officers, not only now, but during the whole past history of Mississippi since I have known it, in bringing that energy, and tact, and management to the detection of crime which exists in the older States.

Question. When a white man of respectability and position has been murdered under circumstances of secrecy, where difficulty is apprehended in discovering the murderers, has it not been common to offer rewards in order to stimulate the cupidity of people in bringing the offenders to justice?

Answer. Yes, sir.

Question. Have you ever known such rewards offered where a colored man has been whipped or murdered?

Answer. I have not, except by the governor. It is the governor's constant habit to offer rewards in all those cases brought to his knowledge.

Question. These gentlemen who parade at night, masked and disguised, are understood to disappear or take off their ghostly costumes with the crowing of the cock in the morning, are they not?

Answer. I suppose that that is their custom. I have no such information of that as to be able to tell exactly the mode and manner either of their assembling or dispersing.

Question. You have never heard of their raiding in daylight when the sun was up?

Answer. Never. I have never heard of their being visible in the day-time, either singly or in companies.

Question. Would not the presumption, therefore, be that they could not have come from any considerable distance to the locality where they inflict the punishment? Would not that be the nature of the supposition.

Answer. If I were called upon as a judge to give that charge I would say that would be an inference for the jury to draw.

Question. You are the jury here.

Answer. That is a natural inference.

Question. Where then should be the practical difficulty, if they rode in a body, riding past men's houses who have good watch-dogs that bark,, and they stop in places to refresh their horses, where should be the practical difficulty if fresh, earnest pursuit were made upon their tracks in finding one or more of them?

Answer. The difficulty is just so strong as is the love of life against the fear of death. If there was a company immediately at hand of equal numbers, there are very many men in this county that would not hesitate to make pursuit. But they come unexpectedly. They pass by the house of a citizen when he is alone, and so far from having an idea of pursuing them, his mind is so confused with terror and alarm that he has no idea of making any pursuit. He is sufficiently relieved when he has understood that he is not the object of their search or vengeance.

Question. These men wear masks, and they wear costumes which have been fashioned and made up either by their wives or daughters, or by tailors, I suppose, and the materials have been purchased at some store, and there should be no practical difficulty in ascertaining where the materials were bought, or who made them up, if earnest effort were made.

Answer. Yes, sir, I believe, and simply because they have not been detected—I base that belief upon the fact that their management is so perfect, and their system so well devised, that with the secrecy on their part, and the circumspection, and with the terror inspired in the minds of other persons, who would undertake to seek them out or expose them; with the two causes it would be an exceedingly difficult matter, either by tracing them from the purchase of the goods or the manufacture of them, the making up of the materials, their signals for assembling, the disguises of their horses, or the times and manner of their dispersion. I have an idea that it is composed of men who have been thoroughly drilled in military camps.

Question. Of course, the families that the different members belong to must be cognizant of their absence and of the absence of the horses that they ride; the horses themselves would show next day signs of fatigue if the ride was a long one, would they not?

Answer. Unquestionably; but the father, mother, and sisters of any man who had been united to such an organization as that would feel that they outraged humanity to divulge or take any steps for the exposure of those who had been the perpetrators.

Question. Their neighbors, however, might know the same facts?

Answer. Yes, sir; but let it be borne in mind that the same terror is in the mind of the neighbor to prevent divulging that there would be to prevent pursuing them if he saw them collecting.

Question. The real trouble lies right there, does it not, judge, that the people who do know of these offenses are not disposed to make that knowledge known?

Answer. I think so. I think that is the main cause, the main source of the trouble.

By Mr. BLAIR:

Question. You spoke of certain crimes that were not punished adequately by the laws of the State, according to the public opinion of the people of the State. I will ask you if the crime of rape, and especially the crime of rape by a negro upon a white woman, is not one of the crimes which the public sentiment of this State considers is inadequately punished by the statute?

Answer. Rape is punished by the statute by imprisonment for life in the penitentiary.

Question. And the attempt at rape?

Answer. There is a discretion vested in the court as to the form of imprisonment where there is an attempt; that is my recollection of the statute.

Question. Does the public sentiment of the State hold that either of these punishments is sufficient for the crime of rape, or attempt at rape, committed by a black man upon a white woman?

Answer. It is not deemed an adequate punishment by the white people of this country.

Question. It is not so regarded?

Answer. It is not regarded as an adequate punishment.

Question. Is it not a common crime?

Answer. Not within my district.

Question. Was not Allen Bird killed in jail in Winston County for an attempt at rape?

Answer. For a charge of attempting.

Question. He was indicted for it?

Answer. He was indicted for it.

Question. And he was in jail under an indictment?

Answer. Yes, sir.

Question. You spoke of a case where a negro was punished with whipping for having boasted of his intercourse with a respectable white woman. Did you refer to the case to which you alluded in the opening of your testimony, where, during the session of your court in this place, it was brought to your knowledge that a freedman had been severely whipped and a school-teacher notified to leave?

Answer. Yes, sir; that was the case.

Question. That was the case of the negro Hicks, was it not?

Answer. I forget his name.

Question. You also spoke of a case which occurred during the session of the court, and in regard to which you charged the grand jury, the case of a respectable man having been robbed here in the city by two parties, strangers here, and the jury failed to convict them, one of whom you believed to have been guilty, and they were taken out and whipped by the people of this town; what were the facts attending that robbery, or attempt at robbery?

Answer. Mr. Tyler, an enterprising northern citizen, settled in this place eighteen months ago. He was the building contractor for the erection of a $10,000 residence in this place. He had completed the contract. Two men from Chicago had been in his employment. They supposed that he had money. One of them was at the time in the employment of a livery-stable keeper in this place, Colonel Marshall Cady. The other was, perhaps, out of employment. They evidently formed a conspiracy, by which one of them was to take a note in, after tea, to Mr. Tyler, requesting him to come at once to the Gilmore hotel. The names of the two men, I think, were Reynolds, the other Stinson. Stinson delivered the note, and it was badly written—not signed. It arrested the attention of Tyler. He invited him to come into his house; invited Stinson, the messenger. The manner of Stinson excited Tyler's suspicions the more, and he at once declined going, and told him he would come in the morning; and Stinson retired. The next morning—he knew that Stinson was in the employment of Colonel Cady—he took the note to Cady. Cady called John, took him into the office with Mr. Tyler, and spoke pretty roughly to him; wanted to know why he had carried that note to Mr. Tyler. He made a clean breast of it, and divulged the whole conspiracy; that Reynolds, his co-conspirator, was out in the dark, and that whenever Tyler came out they were either to knock him down with brass knuckles, or to club him with some other instrument. I recollect that the brass knuckles were used in the evidence as one of the instruments they had provided to knock him down with and rob him. Immediately both of them were arrested and conveyed to the mayor's office. They were then called upon by the mayor to make any statement, if they desired to do so. And they were charged by the mayor, at the request of counsel who was then representing them, not to make any statement or confession unless it was purely voluntary on their part; that whatever statement they made before the committing court would be used as evidence against them in the trial before the circuit court. A discussion on that question arose in the presence of the two prisoners. They had the benefit of that discussion, in which it was impressed upon them by counsel that they were not to make any confession unless they chose to do so; and when the argument of counsel closed, the mayor, as he testified, charged them that they would make no statement or confession unless it was done voluntarily and freely; that whatever they said would be used against them in the trial in the circuit court. The same party who made the confession when there was alleged duress over him at the livery-stable, renewed the confession in full to the mayor. The other, Reynolds, remained silent. The same party, Stinson, made a third confession to the jailer, or captain of police—Captain Donnelly, I believe it was. The confession was substantially the same as made on these three different occasions; and whatever the duress may have been on the first, there was clearly none on the second and third occasions—several days intervening, and the parties by the mayor notified in the most formal manner that they could state or not state what they desired; that it would be used against them. That testimony went to the jury. There were seven colored men and five white men on the jury. The jury retired and returned a verdict of not guilty against both of them. These men were subsequently, after their release, whipped.

Question. You say you yourself disapproved of the verdict in a very marked manner?

Answer. I discharged the jury in open court.

Question. Did you make any remark at the time you discharged them as to the result of discharging them?

Answer. No, sir.

Question. You intended to manifest your disapprobation?

Answer. It was intended, and so received and understood by them and by the community, as a rebuke. It was in the midst of the term, and they were discharged, and the sheriff ordered to summon another jury for 9 o'clock the next morning. It was after dark when they returned their verdict into court.

Question. The subsequent whipping of these two men, you think, arose not from any previous organization, but was to prevent and punish their escape from justice, as it was deemed by the community?

Answer. I so understood it. The public morals of this town were shocked by the offense, and then by the action of the jury. It was a class of offense that was very rare in this country. It is the second case of the kind, I believe, that I have ever seen on a criminal docket in Mississippi. The people of this town were very much startled when it was announced that there was a scheme for robbing a man, calling him out of his house, and garroting him on the street.

Question. Tyler was a northern man, and a recent comer into the place, against whom this conspiracy was made?

Answer. Yes, sir.

Question. And the evidence was that the force they intended to use was such as might have led to his killing?

Answer. Yes, sir.

Question. Under that state of circumstances, the people, with one mind, resented it?

Answer. Yes, sir.

Question. And such was the public opinion that you think no indictment could be found against them?

Answer. No, sir. I believe an indictment would have been found against the parties who whipped them if it could have been ascertained who those parties were.

By the CHAIRMAN:

Question. How large was the body of men implicated in the whipping of these two men?

Answer. I heard some thirty or forty.

Question. Disguised, were they?

Answer. Yes, sir.

By Mr. BLAIR:

Question. In the case of the negro man whose body was found drowned in the Bigbee River, supposed to have been the prisoner committed to the hands of Bridges, the officer, I understand you to say that the surgeon who saw the body, Dr. Morehead, belonged to Pickens County?

Answer. He was from Pickensville. I do not remember his name.

Question. He testified that the body was in such a state of putrefaction and decay that it must necessarily have been deceased some three or four months?

Answer. Yes, sir.

Question. And from his statement of his condition, other surgeons and physicians of this city, three or four in number, I believe, testified, as experts, that the condition Dr. Morehead described the body to be in would necessarily have required that the body should have been dead three or four months?

Answer. Yes, sir; four months.

Question. This testimony was totally inconsistent with the idea that it was the body of the prisoner committed to the hands of Bridges, and who escaped, or was taken from his custody?

Answer. Yes, sir.

Question. Did you believe that testimony?

Answer. The physician's testimony?

Question. Yes, sir.

Answer. Unquestionably I did.

Question. Were you not then convinced that whatever might have happened to the prisoner committed to the hands of Bridges, this body could not have been the body of that man?

Answer. I so announced it in my decision in disposing of Bridges's writ of *habeas corpus.*

Question. You disposed of Bridges on the ground that there was no testimony showing that he had been in any way accessory to the killing of the prisoner, if he had been killed?

Answer. Yes, sir.

Question. And you held him simply on the ground that he was guilty of negligence n permitting the escape?

Answer. Yes, sir.

Question. The testimony of the negro's father that the clothing was part of the clothing worn by his son, you did not consider by any means as strong as that of the surgeon's?

Answer. No, sir; not by any means as strong as the surgeon's, for the further reason that his testimony, in my judicial opinion, was entirely broken down on cross-examination.

Question. Besides that, the raiment of this negro was the common raiment of the negroes of the country, and he might have had precisely the same character of raiment without leading necessarily to the inference that he was the same man?

Answer. Yes, sir. In reference to the breaking down on cross-examination, the old man testified that he went to the grave where he was buried and dug down and caught hold of his head and hair, and that it all came off; slipped off; that then he dug around and got hold of a part of his shirt—his shirt-collar—and pulled it out from under his neck. On cross-examination the piece of clothing which he exhibited as the piece which he said came from around his neck, when it was stretched out was seen to be too short to encircle the neck, and the question was propounded to him, "Will that go around your neck? How large was your son?" "A grown man." "Now," says the counsel, "didn't you get this off of his wrist? Was it not his wrist that you got this off of?" Says he, "O, yes; it was off of his wrist." But in his examination-in-chief he had been examined in reference to how much of the body was exhumed, and he had testified that neither of his hands were exhumed, but only his head and one of his feet; that the balance of his body, arms, hands, and everything, were covered; and in the cross-examination, when it was discovered that the piece of goods that he represented to have come from the neck was too short to have encircled the neck, he retreated from that statement and said that he got it from the wrist—the left or right wrist—and he manifested confusion when he discovered the discrepancy in his testimony. That, coupled with the testimony of the surgeons, brought me to the conclusion which I stated in my previous examination, that I now have no definite opinion as to whether the prisoner who was missing from Bridges is dead or alive.

Question. But you have a very decided opinion that that body was not the body of the prisoner?

Answer. Yes, sir; my mind is very clear upon that proposition.

By the CHAIRMAN:

Question. Was the mother of this missing man before the court?

Answer. No, sir; and I am not informed that she ever saw the body. On the contrary, I think she did not.

By Mr. BLAIR:

Question. In the case that occurred in Oktibbeha County, you stated that two young white men were shot from ambush?

Answer. One of the two.

Question. Were they attempting anything against the negro man who was arrested and committed to jail?

Answer. I am not informed.

Question. Was the fact made clear in any way, as far as you have information, that he did actually shoot and kill one of these men?

Answer. It was, as I understood, believed by the friends of the young man that he is the party who killed him.

Question. He was committed upon a preliminary examination for the crime?

Answer. Yes, sir.

Question. And supposed to have been killed by the parties friendly to the man who was killed?

Answer. I cannot say that.

Question. The killing of this man was supposed to have been the exciting cause of his killing?

Answer. Yes, sir.

Question. Now, judge, you have spoken in reference to all these questions; you have stated that there is no difficulty in administering justice except in cases of a political character; do you pretend to say that there was anything political in the killing of that man?

Answer. As a matter of fact, I do not; as a matter of opinion, I believe that he was killed by parties—if he was killed at all—and I have no definite knowledge about it. I believe that he was killed, but the committee will understand that I have, in giving a history of the affair, only pretended to give the rumor.

Question. I understand that.

Answer. I believe that if the other features of the rumor are true that the parties who killed him were parties in the interest of a political organization.

Question. Here is a killing of this young man outright that stands in the foreground as the cause of this killing, and by what sort of argument can you convert it into a killing on account of politics?

Answer. Because the number of parties who came upon the officer conducting him to Starkville jail seemed to have been well organized, well drilled, with masks and disguises. The arrangements were too extensive to have been improvised for the occasion. There were too many of them; they were too well disguised; too well disciplined; too well armed.

By Mr. Rice:

Question. In other words you think it was the Ku-Klux that did it?

Answer. I do. I say I think they were Ku-Klux. I would prefer not to say that. I would prefer to say they were men in disguise, and that those men were in the interest of a political organization.

By Mr. Blair:

Question. Well, sir, suppose that a man were killed in your town to-day, and it were known that he were killed by ten republicans, and that the man happened to be a democrat, and had been guilty of a rape upon the wife of one of those republicans, and he should be killed whilst being conveyed to jail; would you say that was political; suppose it was the Loyal League that killed him?

Answer. I should use the term political in the same sense there that I did in reference to the offense just referred to in Oktibbeha County. I should regard that as an offense which had resulted from political feeling. In view of the mere fact that ten republicans had killed a democrat, no matter what the cause was, I should say that the killing had occurred because either of their personal or political association growing out of their politics. I do not mean to say that the killing from the rape was a political offense; but the combination of these persons, who finally did do the killing, was a combination which I should suspect grew out of their association as Leaguers together or as republicans together.

Question. The man would resort naturally to those with whom he was in friendship?

Answer. Yes, sir.

Question. To help him or assist him in this case?

Answer. Yes, sir.

Question. And if he was a Leaguer—a republican—he would naturally resort to those who were his friends, and those with whom he associated?

Answer. Yes, sir; that is the idea I intended to convey.

Question. But do you suppose it would be any part of the motive that he was a democrat? Do you not suppose in that case the man would address his friends in this way, "Here is a man who has committed this outrage upon my wife, and I want your assistance to punish the crime?"

Answer. Certainly.

Question. Would he say he was a democrat?

Answer. Certainly not. Certainly the instigating cause would be the outrage that had been committed.

By the Chairman:

Question. In the case under consideration in Oktibbeha County, I understand that the person killed was in a measure identified with this organization, and was shot while he was masked and disguised by this negro. Am I right in that?

Answer. I am not certain that he was actually in disguise at the time. I am not certain that my informant went to that extent; but they were on the eve or in the act of starting on an expedition of the maskers.

Question. Would it not be natural to suppose that the men who belonged to that organization, if there was such an organization, took this matter in hand and killed the negro because of the fact that he had killed one of their number?

Answer. It occurs to me that that is a natural inference.

By Mr. Blair:

Question. In the case which occurred here in your own town, where men having been tried for an attempt to commit a robbery, perhaps to kill a northern man who had been here some eighteen months, was it supposed those were all northern men that combined?

Answer. I have no idea that they were all northern men.

Question. Is it supposed they they were all men of his particular politics?

Answer. I do not know what his politics are; I have never heard.

Question. Is it supposed that those men did it for any political cause—that wore masks; they combined for the occasion—is it supposed that any one scintilla of politics had anything to do with the thrashing of these two men who attempted to rob Mr. Tyler?

Answer. I have previously stated that, in my judgment, it resulted from an outraged public sentiment in regard to the crime which Stinson and Reynolds had committed, and the unblushing conduct of the jury in discharging those men without punishment.

Question. That I wanted to bring out clearly. Is not the other case—the one in Oktibbeha County, I think—although not in every particular parallel to the case here, somewhat similar; and is not the crime—the killing of this young man by a negro from ambush—the moving cause, according to your information, for the killing of the negro?

Answer. The prime cause; I have no doubt of that.

Question. And is it supposed that in any sense politics had anything to do with it?

Answer. The killing of the young man was the prime cause; but the agents who were resorted to to punish the outrage were agents and political allies, in my belief.

Question. You have no information as that?

Answer. I have not.

Question. You have no knowledge as to that?

Answer. I have not.

Question. You simply assume that because they wore disguises and were banded together that some political cause intermingled with their action?

Answer. My opinion is as stated, without having any definite knowledge as to the existence of that organization either in that county or elsewhere, that it was such an organization and that the objects and purposes of the organization were as I have heretofore stated.

Question. Political? The objects of the organization were as you have heretofore stated, you say. I ask how; political?

Answer. Yes, sir; I gave a twofold answer to that question—political, and growing out of the associations.

Question. And protective of the interests of certain parties in the State?

Answer. Political; and for further answer to that I refer to the statement which I have given as to what my conceptions were of the plans and purposes of the organization.

Question. I wanted in this way to get at a clear understanding of what you consider the political part of this organization. Do you conceive that in the other cases, for instance, the killing of Allen Bird by a party of men in disguise in the jail, charged with the crime of rape, and indicted for it, that there was any politics in that?

Answer. I think the prime cause of the killing of the man charged with rape at Louisville, in Winston County, whose name I do not remember, was the outraged sentiment of the white people at the idea of a negro undertaking to commit rape upon a white woman. I believe, however, in that case, that the same resort was had to agents who had their political affinities and alliances.

Question. The great body of the white people in both of these counties, I believe, are democrats?

Answer. Yes, sir.

Question. It would be necessary to resort to the white people of the country to find people among whom the sentiment would revolt against this crime to the extent of which you speak?

Answer. Yes, sir; in those counties it would.

Question. And I apprehend that the sentiments of the negroes throughout the land would not be so startled at the heinousness of an attempt to commit rape on a white woman as would the minds of the whites. The whipping of this man who boasted of his intimacy or illicit intercourse with a white woman, in order to have banded together any party of men to resent that in the way in which it was resented, it would be necessary to appeal to the white men?

Answer. Yes, sir.

Question. There would be intermingled in all of these matters a sentiment of race rather than of politics?

Answer. Yes, sir; rather of races than of politics. A great deal more of races than of politics.

Question. In all the matters to which you have referred, no reference has yet been made to a very flagrant case at Artesia, in which we have been given to understand that a white man was shot to death by a crowd of black people. That case, I think, has come before you in some of its aspects?

Answer. Yes, sir; it is now before me.

Question. If there is no impropriety in your doing so, I would like you to make a statement to the committee of the occurrences as you know them from testimony and from information.

Answer. I presume there is no impropriety in giving a statement as requested, although our statute prohibits the revelation of any testimony which has been taken before a grand jury until after the expiration of six months from the time of its having been given. Without undertaking, therefore, to state distinctly the testimony of the witnesses before the grand jury, or even to state that my information is drawn from the testimony before the grand jury, I will state what I believe to be the history of the affair. There had been a public meeting on Thursday, October 19, 1871, at Prairie Hill, which was addressed by Dr. Landrum. The effect of that meeting was to create what I supposed to be a corresponding amount of excitement and passion on the part of the republicans. That meeting was followed by another republican meeting at the same place on Saturday.

By Mr. RICE:

Question. Was that a republican meeting on Thursday?

Answer. No, sir; it was a democratic meeting.

Question. You said, "another republican meeting."

Answer. I will say another meeting on Saturday. There was a great deal of feeling and excitement as indicated at both meetings; pretty hard blows by speakers struck on both sides. On Saturday evening a large company of negroes, with Mr. Lewis and Mr. Bliss, who had made speeches at Prairie Hill, left in the direction of Crawfordsville, in Oktibbeha County, where large numbers of them resided, announcing their purpose to go to or by Artesia. The procession moved into town boisterously, halted on the commons. A short speech had been delivered by Lewis; Bliss was speaking; a white man by the name of Lee interrupted him, asking if he was a white man. I believe that a gun, in the hands of a colored man, which was being handled by him—in view of what was going on between the white man and the colored, who replied to him when he asked Bliss the question if he was a white man—from the awkward manner in which he handled his gun, it was discharged accidentally. I do not think that it was discharged at any person. That startled the crowd, and there was a calm for a moment—almost a breathless calm for a moment—and then a panic. "Who was that white man? Damn him; kill him; go for him." A general stampede and uproar in the crowd ensued. Lee was overtaken, and in a very short time slain by sabers—two saber cuts and three gunshot wounds. I do not think Lee was armed. I do not think he shot. I think he interrupted the meeting. I think that, in consequence of the interruption, this awkward freedman allowed his gun to be discharged, and that produced the panic which resulted in his death.

Question. Were any of the parties arrested upon your warrant for this killing?

Answer. Yes, sir.

Question. Did your warrant specify any particular names, or simply the names included in the verdict of the coroner's jury?

Answer. It did both. I heard nothing of the riot until Sunday morning. I was sent for, as was district attorney Mr. Muldrow, who had spent the night with me, by Colonel Meek, who informed us that the justice of the peace, from Artesia, desired to see us on urgent business. We came to the office of Lee & Evans, where we met Elmore, the justice of the peace, who had acted as coroner, and some eight or ten gentlemen. A moment or two afterward the sheriff came in. We were then apprised of the object which we had been sent for. The question was addressed to me, "What should be done." The justice of the peace asked for instructions. We have two statutes; they submitted to me the inquest of the jury; there had been a jury of twelve persons, which was unnecessary—a jury of six is the lawful jury for holding an inquest under our statute. The verdict of the jury was that six persons, naming them, were guilty of the murder of Hugh Lee, and added, "others, whose names to the jurors are unknown." Of the two statutes, the first to which I refer requires the coroner holding the inquest, if the jury should say that the deceased was murdered, and the party who murdered him is not in custody, to immediately issue his warrant for the arrest of the party named by the jury, and take him before some justice of the peace, there to be dealt with according to law. The only jurisdiction which the statute confers upon the justice of the peace, would be either to take the bail, or to commit without bail the guilty party to await such action as might be taken against him by the grand jury of the county. The grand jury in this county was then in session, and was likely to be for several days. The other statute to which I referred is the statute which authorizes the arrest of persons committing felony. It authorizes any officer or private person to make arrests without warrant where a felony has been committed, the officer verily believing and suspecting that the person proposed to be arrested was the person perpetrating the offense. The only thing necessary for an officer to do, when a felony had been committed under that statute, was to notify the party of the causes of his arrest; and no liability criminally or civilly is to be attached to the officer making the arrest under such circumstances.

By Mr. BLAIR:

Question. Without warrant?

Answer. Without warrant. Upon consultation with the district attorney, he and I concluded that rather than to have a two, three, or four days', or a week's trial, at Artesia, before a justice of the peace, with the public mind as irritated and excited as it was, and when that had been gone through with the only points which could be accomplished by the trial would be a reference to the very tribunal that was then in session, and would be in session when the examination had been gone through with, that for the preservation of the public peace, for the economy of time and of expense, both as to the officers and as to the State, that it was infinitely better to direct the officers to proceed under the second statute, and bring the parties immediately before the grand jury, whose action would be much more definite and final than the action of a justice of the peace. In that view of the case I did instruct the sheriff to arrest the six parties named. The impression made on my mind at the time I made the order was, that the two first parties, Bliss and Lewis, were the only white persons mentioned. My impression was that all four of the other parties mentioned in the verdict of the jury were colored persons; but I have since been informed that one of them was a young man by the name of Rose, who was a United States mail-agent, and that he was arrested while in the discharge of his duty as a mail-agent. I did not know it at the time; but it would not have made any difference in my order if I had. I would have ordered his arrest, I do not care in what service he had been. It was a murder, which was reported by the jury of inquest to have been committed, and I am not aware that any service exempts a felon when such a representation as that has been made as to his having been guilty of a felony. Still, I was not aware of it, and had no knowledge of his even being a white man at the time I ordered the arrest. The question was then asked, what should be done with those others referred to. I read the statute to the sheriff. I had it in my hand at the time and told him clearly that he had the same authority, and it was not only his authority but his duty to arrest any other parties not named in the verdict of the jury of inquest, under the statute which I had read to him, whenever he ascertained that they had committed a felony, or whenever he knew that a felony had been committed, and had good reason to suspect and believe that a particular party proposed to be arrested was one of the guilty parties.

Question. It was not necessary that he should have been on the ground and in view of the commission of the felony?

Answer. Not at all. There is another clause of the same statute which provides for that. It gives him the authority when a felony has been committed in his presence; then there is this subsequent clause, which authorizes any officer or private person, when a felony has been committed, without warrant to make the arrest, he verily believing and suspecting that the party proposed to be arrested was the party committing the offense; and the statute relieves him from any criminal or civil liability if he acted in good faith upon information which gave him the right, not in a mere visionary, foolish way, but a definite, tangible belief—any facts which produce on his mind the belief that these are the parties guilty of the felony.

By the CHAIRMAN:

Question. Does not the statute require that there must be probable cause?

Answer. No, sir.

Question. So that there is nothing to limit the discretion of the sheriff or the private person where a felony in point of fact has been committed, except their own suspicions or surmises?

Answer. My construction of that statute, or the limitation of it, is this: that the sheriff in making the arrest is criminally or civilly liable, unless he shows such a state of facts to have been in existence, and to have been brought to his knowledge, to his mind, as to create in the mind of a reasonable creature the opinion which the statute required him to have—to verily believe and suspect that the party had been guilty of a felony. I think that is the limitation, and the only limitation, in that statute—that it would be incumbent upon him to show he had reason for that belief; that it is not competent for him to say, "I entertained this opinion and suspected him," without showing such a state of facts as gave him the right to suspect.

Question. In other words, he must show in his justification that there was a probable cause for implicating the persons arrested in the felony?

Answer. Well, "probable cause" is a technical term, and expresses rather more than our statute was intended to.

By Mr. BLAIR:

Question. You think they would have used the word itself if they had wanted it or meant it?

Answer. Yes, sir; I think that expression is too strong.

Question. The sheriff, under your direction, did arrest Lewis, Bliss, Rose, and the others named in the verdict of the coroner's jury, and went on to arrest even other persons. What action was had with reference to these arrests made by the sheriff; was he subsequently arrested himself for acting under your orders?

Answer. I have endeavored to avoid, because so far I have conceived that the ends of public justice required it at my hands—I have endeavored to avoid making such a statement as would involve parties in trouble, because I believe that they acted at the time in good faith. The truth is, however, that my orders were greatly transcended. The instructions were given Sunday morning. The sheriff went with his party, and on Monday evening I was notified by the mayor here that he had received a dispatch from the chief of police here, Captain Donnelly, requesting a police force to be at the depot; that he had some fifty or sixty prisoners. Later in the evening, about 8 o'clock, I received a note from the sheriff requesting my immediate presence in town. I reside one mile from the town. I came in immediately, and was at once notified that the cause thereof was, that a very large number of persons had been arrested; not only those who were suspected of having killed Lee, but the witnesses who were present; that they, too, had been arrested, and that some sixty or seventy were confined in the jail. There were very serious demonstrations. The sheriff informed me what he had done. I immediately informed him that he had misconstrued my instructions; that I never intended them to be construed so broadly as to authorize the arrest of every person who happened to be at Artesia on Saturday, and I instructed him then, immediately to get his assistants who were with him in making the arrests, and I explained to him exactly the construction of that statute which I have undertaken to explain to you, gentlemen—that it would be incumbent upon him when he was called upon for making the arrest of A., to show that the only thing he would have to show, to save himself from criminal or civil liability, was a state of facts which convinced him, as a reasonable man, that A. had been guilty of the felony; and to do that that he would be called upon to give his informant and state that he had heard that A. was there; that A. did certain things, and what acts A. did do. He must be able to say, "I received that information from a credible person, and I acted upon information that A. had committed certain acts; that he had done certain things toward the commission of this felony;" and I told him to get his officers and take up the list, and unless he could point out against each one what he had heard that particular one had been doing, and give the names of witnesses who had communicated to him what the parties had done, or the supposed acts they had done, to release them. They went to work at once, and reformed their list, and discharged all of the sixty-five or seventy, except eleven, that night. The examination has been proceeding; the examination is going on yet before the grand jury. On last Thursday or Friday the grand jury made two counter reports to the court, eight republicans, as I understand them to be, asking for the discharge of Lewis Bliss and Levi Bean and others, without mentioning who the others were. I considered the "others" to mean all who were in jail. Seven of the grand jury, who, I think, are all democrats, remonstrated against the release.

By Mr. BLAIR:

Question. Of any of them?

Answer. Of any of them, as I construed it; each report referring me to the testimony of fifty-six witnesses who had been examined before them—a voluminous mass of testimony. I received the testimony and adjourned the court, notifying them that it would be impossible for me to make any response to either of their reports before 9 o'clock the next morning. I read the testimony very carefully. I devoted that afternoon and most of that night to the examination of the testimony and its classification. The next morning, when the grand jury returned to the room, I was in the act of announcing the conclusion at which I had arrived, when the foreman interrupted me, and stated that they desired to change their reports, to make an alteration in the report; that the majority who had requested the discharge desired to erase or proposed to erase the two words "and others" in the report. That would make the majority report simply request the release of Lewis, Bliss, and Bean on the one side, and the counter report remonstrate against the release of Lewis, Bliss, and Bean. I instructed them to retire and consider their reports. I had their reports returned to them. They did so, and in a few minutes returned with the reports changed as had been intimated by the foreman. One additional point in the report the next morning was a statement on the part of the foreman that there were other witnesses whose testimony they desired, and whose testimony they were informed would throw material light on the examination. With that statement in the report of the minority, my instructions to them were to retire to their room; that they should have whatever compulsory process it was necessary for them to have to obtain the witnesses; that the court would be in session for several days, and all facilities which the court could afford them would be afforded to compel the attendance of absent witnesses or witness not then before them. They deliberated on Friday and Saturday, and on Monday the minority still insisted upon the discharge of these three individuals.

Question. The majority?

Answer. It started the majority; but two of the grand jurors became sick and were absent temporarily. That made that which was the majority report at the commencement the minority report at the close.

By the CHAIRMAN:

Question. They have not withdrawn their names from the majority report?

Answer. No, sir.

Question. They had not dissented from that?

Answer. No, sir.

Question. It was still the majority report?

Answer. It was still as far as the names were concerned. Their names are still on the paper, and I have never been informed that they desired to withdraw their names from it.

By Mr. BLAIR:

Question. Further evidence had been taken, though, after they had been sick and had retired from the city?

Answer. It turned out to be only a temporary absence, and the two sick jurors on Wednesday returned to their places in the jury-room; and no report had been made, except their coming into court, as I have apprised you. Those who continued to act simply erased the two words "and others" from the report, and came back into court, and returned the report in the absence of the two sick jurors. The next morning the two sick ones came back, and, I suppose, they have been with the grand jury ever since. I am not aware that they have been absent from it. They still insisted upon the discharge of Lewis and Bliss. I examined the testimony and classified it, and on Monday I furnished to the district attorney, in the presence of the grand jury, a statement showing the names of six parties who, I thought, ought to be indicted, and referring to the testimony in detail—six colored men. I saw no testimony implicating either Bliss or Lewis, and I ordered their discharge. They were discharged on Monday under my orders.

By the CHAIRMAN:

Question. What was done with Rose?

Answer. Rose had been discharged four days before, at the request of the grand jury.

Question. And Bean?

Answer. When I furnished to the district attorney the statement on the day I discharged Lewis and Bliss, I discharged four or five other colored men who were in jail, Bean among the number.

Question. What is the number actually held now, judge, on that charge?

Answer. Three or four are in custody in jail, in this place.

By Mr. BLAIR:

Question. Was there any arrest of the sheriff and his deputy, and his *posse*, or any part of them, for arresting this mail-agent, whose name was included in your warrant?

Answer. I have seen the sheriff this morning. He has returned.

Question. From where?

Answer. From Oxford.

Question. What has he been doing there?

Answer. From the United States court, where he was recently arrested and carried before Judge Hill, of the United States court.

Question. For what?

Answer. The warrant for his arrest specified a violation of the enforcement act of 1870. The affidavit was not exhibited; it, (the warrant) went on to recite, "that whereas H. G. Rose, having made affidavit that the said Dowsing, sheriff," and mentioning others of his party, "are guilty of having violated the enforcement act of 1870; this, therefore, to command you." It was issued by a United States commissioner, and made returnable to Judge Hill, the judge of the district court of the United States, at Oxford. They were arrested on Saturday night.

Question. That is not the Ku-Klux law, is it—the enforcement act.

Answer. I understand it to be. They called it the enforcement law, and I understood it to be the Ku-Klux law.

Question. I wanted to know whether it was under that act or not?

Answer. I understood it to be the same act. He informs me this morning that when the charges were exhibited to him, it was for the arrest of Rose, the mail-agent, while in the discharge of his duties, and before he had finished or ended his trip.

Question. I suppose that the other parties who were arrested upon this affidavit of Rose were arrested on the same charge?

Answer. I do not know. There was nothing in the warrant which was exhibited to me except the charge of having violated the provisions of the enforcement act of 1870. Dowsing waived a preliminary examination, as did the other parties who were arrested at the same time that he was, and they gave their bond for their appearance at the December term of the Federal court—United States court at Oxford. If Dowsing and his *posse* had been arrested for arresting Rose, and his name is the name of the young man who was in the verdict of that jury of inquest, whatever responsibility attached to it belongs to me, although I did not know that he was a United States mail-agent.

Question. You ought to have been taken up, then, under the enforcement act, or Ku-Klux act.

Answer. It was my act. I gave specific orders to the sheriff to arrest these parties whose names were mentioned in the verdict of the jury of inquest.

By the CHAIRMAN:

Question. I wish to inquire at this point whether, under your statute, that verdict of the coroner's jury was not an absolute nullity—whether there is any such jury known to the law as a jury of twelve men in a coroner's inquest?

Answer. The statute requires six.

Question. In your judgment, was that verdict a nullity, or otherwise?

Answer. I do not think it was a nullity.

By Mr. BLAIR:

Question. Even if it was a nullity, your warrant naming those parties was an ample protection to the sheriff, and required him to make the arrest?

Answer. I do not think it was a nullity in this; if you mean to say that it was not legally composed—that, as a jury of inquest, speaking with technical accuracy, it was not the thing defined by the statute, then I agree with you.

By the CHAIRMAN:

Question. I mean, then, had the coroner, under the law, any power to summon a body of twelve men and hold that inquest?

Answer. No, sir; he had not.

Question. Then what legal effect had the finding of a jury of twelve, unauthorized by law, beyond a mere expression of opinion by twelve citizens not empaneled by the coroner?

Answer. The committee will discover in the explanation which I have made of the two statutes, that my direction to the sheriff was not based upon the first clause of the law to which I have referred, which provides that, when a jury of inquest have reported a murder as having been committed, then the duty of the coroner is to issue his warrant for the arrest of the parties mentioned as the murderers in the verdict of the jury of inquest. The committee will recollect that I acted under the second statute. I applied the verdict of a jury of inquest to the second statute, as the affidavit of twelve men made before a competent officer, that these six men had committed murder, and so far as the jury of inquest was concerned, I abandoned that altogether. I did not pursue the statute; I did not give direction to the sheriff under that statute which would treat it as the inquest of a jury.

Question. Was it an affidavit?

Answer. It was an affidavit signed and sworn to by twelve men.

Question. Not in the form, certainly, of an affidavit?

Answer. Not in the form of an affidavit, but in the form of a report of a jury of inquest.

Question. But you treat it substantially as an affidavit of twelve men?

Answer. Yes, sir, as an affidavit of twelve men; that is the legal effect, at all events, to an officer whom I feel it incumbent upon him to exercise any degree of vigor in the enforcement of the criminal law, and the arrest of criminals. I accept that as sufficiently definite information to act upon, to give a verbal order to the sheriff of my county to make the arrests.

By Mr. BLAIR:

Question. And your warrant?

Answer. Not warrant. I never issued any warrant.

Question. Your instructions to the sheriff?

Answer. My instructions were only verbal to the sheriff.

Question. Your instructions made it his duty to arrest these parties under the statute?

Answer. Not under that statute. There is another statute, however, which makes the sheriff liable if he does not discharge his duty in making arrests. There is still a different statute which makes it specially the duty of the sheriff to be vigilant, and industrious, and energetic, and prompt, in the arrest of all parties who have violated the laws.

By the CHAIRMAN:

Question. The sheriff, then, I understand, had no warrant at all from you or the coroner?

Answer. No, sir; nothing from me.

Question. He had nothing but the finding of the jury?

Answer. He had nothing from me but my instructions as to his duty.

Question. Was this verdict an affidavit? Isn't your understanding that an affidavit written out, and sworn to after being written out and subscribed by the party?

Answer. Yes, sir.

Question. Was this ever sworn to after being subscribed by the jury; or was there simply a general oath administered by the coroner before they entered upon this inquiry how this man came to his death?

Answer. I take it from the statement in the verdict that it was the ordinary oath taken by a jury preceding the investigation.

Question. Do you hold that that verdict was, in a legal sense, an affidavit such as would have authorized the coroner to have issued a warrant?

Answer. It was, in my judgment, such a verdict as would have authorized the coroner to have issued his warrant for the arrest of the parties named in the verdict. In my judgment it is not technically an affidavit; but, in my judgment, it was sufficient, as furnishing definite information that a crime had been committed, and that these parties committed it.

By Mr. BLAIR:

Question. That is all that is required by the statute to authorize the sheriff to arrest?

Answer. Yes, sir.

Question. In the arrest of this man Rose, was there anything in the fact that he was an employé of the Government of the United States that exempted him from arrest?

Answer. If there is any such exemption, I am profoundly ignorant of it.

By the CHAIRMAN:

Question. Was Rose's Christian name mentioned?

Answer. No, sir; his Christian name was not mentioned. It was blank Rose.

By Mr. BLAIR:

Question. It referred to him?

Answer. It gave his name, and referred to the man who, I understand, was arrested.

The CHAIRMAN. There are different Roses in the county; at least one other Rose?

Answer. There may be.

Question. Referring to the circumstances of the killing of Lee, have you heard the statements, under oath, made by either Bliss, Lewis, Bean, or Rose? Do you know what their evidence is upon the point whether Lee drew and discharged a pistol?

Answer. I can state negatively, without incurring what I would conceive to be a violation of official duty, that Lewis, Bliss, and Bean have not been before the grand jury, or I have never heard any testimony from them. I know that there was an effort made yesterday to obtain Bean as a witness, but I don't know that he has been before the grand jury.

Question. Was Rose before the grand jury?

Answer. Yes, sir; Rose has been before the grand jury, and I have read his testimony. In my preceding statement there I have endeavored to avoid stating that my information is the testimony of witnesses. I may have committed myself in making the statement, but it was my intention to avoid that if I could.

Question. You stated, I believe, that when the two reports came in from the grand jury, you took took the evidence home with you, and examined it that evening and the next morning?

Answer. Yes, sir.

Question. I suppose that was the evidence given to the grand jury and taken down by them?

Answer. Yes, sir; but I have not—if I did, it was inadvertently. I did not mean to state any part of the testimony in that; I only stated that I had taken the testimony and read it, and my conclusion or opinion.

By Mr. BLAIR:

Question. But not any part of the testimony?

Answer. No, sir.

By the CHAIRMAN:

Question. Is there any testimony which has come to your knowledge going to show that Lee had a pistol upon his person at the time that he interrupted the speaker?

Answer. Without stating where the conflict has arisen, I will state that it has come to my knowledge that on that particular point there is a very great conflict of opinion.

Question. That is what I wanted to get at; that there is upon that very point a great conflict of opinion.

Answer. Yes, sir.

Question. Is there not one theory that he drew a pistol, and in the act of retreating discharged that pistol in the direction of the stand?

Answer. That is the theory of many persons.

Question. And is it not likewise a theory on the part of some persons that a pistol was found upon the ground afterward, supposed to be the pistol he discharged?

Answer. I have not heard of that.

Question. And is there not also a theory that he was not cut by a saber at all—simply perforated with bullets?

Answer. I have not heard of that.

Question. Where, according to your information, was the saber wound inflicted?

Answer. On the head—on the top of the head. And my information as to that wound was, that it would have been a mortal one.

By Mr. BLAIR:

Question. Is it your information that this body of negroes were armed?

Answer. Not as a body. There were six or seven hundred negroes there.

Question. Generally speaking, were they all armed?

Answer. O, no; comparatively very few of them; there were a few of them that were armed.

Question. With guns?

Answer. Yes, sir; with guns.

Question. And pistols?

Answer. It is further in evidence that there was a carpet-bag of pistols and some guns in a wagon, a few guns and some pistols in a carpet-sack, and then a few of the party had their guns; but the great bulk of the crowd, as I understand it, were unarmed.

Question. Some of them had sabers?

Answer. Yes, sir; some of them had sabers, some army rifles, some shot-guns.

Question. You say they returned and passed through Artesia from a meeting elsewhere; was it your information that they went there with any design to intimidate other parties?

Answer. It is not so demonstrated; no such idea as that is demonstrated.

Question. Demonstrated?

Answer. Developed. I have not heard that idea developed from any reliable source.

By the CHAIRMAN:

Question. Is there any evidence going to show that they went there with an expectation of meeting a body of men and committing violence?

Answer. No, sir; none that I have ever heard.

COLUMBUS, MISSISSIPPI, *November* 10, 1871.

ROBERT GLEED (colored) sworn and examined.

By the CHAIRMAN:

Question. Please state where you live.

Answer. I live here in Columbus.

Question. What official position do you hold at this time?

Answer. Senator from the eighteenth senatorial district.

Question. How long have you lived in this State?

Answer. I have been here since 1855.

Question. Are you pretty well acquainted with the people of this county?

Answer. Yes, sir.

Question. When were you elected State senator?

Answer. In 1869.

Question. Do you know or have you heard of any outrages of any character committed upon colored people by bands of men disguised?

Answer. I cannot say I know of my own personal knowledge. I have heard of a good many outrages being committed on colored people.

Question. Have you ever received any Ku-Klux notices yourself?

Answer. Yes, sir; I have.

Question. When and what was the character of the notices?

Answer. I forget the exact date, about this time last year. The character of the notice was that my behavior would not be long tolerated as it was; that I had to change my course, or they would visit me on the first bloody moon.

Question. How was it signed?

Answer. It was signed by the Ku-Klux Klan, three Q's.

Question. Three K's?

Answer. I mean three K's was the signature.

Question. Have you ever received more than the one letter?

Answer. No, sir.

Question. Have you ever seen disguised men?

Answer. No, sir; I have never seen any.

Question. You say you have been informed of several outrages committed. You may take them up without further question, one by one, and give the names of the persons outraged, and when and where the occurrences took place?

Answer. There was a man in the lower part of this county, I forget his first name, by the name of Mason, that was killed by persons in disguise, about ten miles from here; that was the name he went by when he was killed; don't know what his master's was prior. Some people go by two or three names; some people call them by the master's name; and very often they assume their own name. His name was Mason when he was killed.

Question. How long ago was this?

Answer. That was last fall.

Question. Was he a colored man?

Answer. Yes, sir.

Question. Did you understand how large the party was that visited him?

Answer. The persons told me there were about fifty in the gang that killed him.

Question. Did they tell him what they were killing him for?

Answer. I think not, sir; they came to his house in the night, and called him up and he refused to come out, and, I think, fired on them at the time, and they shot him through the cracks of his house; and some other parties were there and would have fired on them, but there was so many of them, and there was only one or two guns on the plantation, and they would not attempt any resistance.

Question. What plantation?

Answer. It was on young Halbert's, about nine miles from here.

Question. What is the next case?

Answer. There was a man killed below here about sixteen or eighteen miles, by the name of Dick Malone.

Question. By persons in disguise?

Answer. They say they were disguised.

Question. That was in Noxubee County?

Answer. Yes, sir; it's the adjoining county bordering on this county.

Question. We have heard the particulars of Malone's death, and you need not pause upon that.

Answer. Well, there was another man that was whipped very severely up above here. I don't know that I know his name, but he was whipped almost to death. He can be had here now; he has been before the grand jury; he lives a few miles above here; I have seen him.

Question. When was he whipped?

Answer. That was along about June or July of this year, while he was making his crop, because he said he came very near losing his crop from the whipping.

Question. You do not remember his name?

Answer. No, sir.

Question. What plantation was he on?

Answer. I don't remember the place. I can ascertain his name and the name of the plantation. There was a man by the name of Joshua Hustin; he says he knew the parties; he is on the grand jury now; he lives in this county, down at Crawfordsville. However, he said that the parties that visited him were not in disguise in the face; they were disguised otherwise, but their faces were not covered up.

Question. Go on with the list.

Answer. I don't know that I know of any other cases.

Question. Have you heard of any other cases of colored people being whipped?

Answer. Yes, sir; I have heard of others being whipped, several others, but I cannot think of the places and times. Out here last spring, prior to that, a man was taken out; he was whipped very severely; that was about May, I think.

Question. Do you remember his name?

Answer. No, sir; I can get both the names, though. They lived here near town; they came to town at the time and had considerable trouble about it.

Question. You had?

Answer. No, sir; the grand jury was then in session, and we tried to get him to report the names of the persons to the grand jury, but he said for fear of personal violence he would not do it, and we could not force him to do it. He said about fifty visited him, and he knew a good many of them that whipped him.

Question. Fifty?

Answer. Yes, sir; others said the same thing who saw them pass along the road that night.

Question. How many cases in all do you suppose you have heard of colored men being whipped by men in disguise in this county?

Answer. I don't think I know of or have heard of more than about six in this county. There was a colored woman taken out up here on Buttahatchie, on Mr. Herring's plantation; I don't know her name.

Question. She was taken out and whipped?

Answer. Yes, sir.

Question. By disguised men?

Answer. Yes, sir; by persons in disguise; that is, they said they were in disguise.

Question. How long ago was this?

Answer. This was along about July, I think, sir.

Question. What was she whipped for?

Answer. They said she and Mrs. Herring a few days prior to the whipping had had some words, and it was supposed they whipped her on that account. There has been two cases taken out, white men; they were taken out in this town and whipped.

Question. The committee has heard of those—the men that were tried for attempting to rob Mr. Tyler?

Answer. Yes, sir.

Question. The committee have been informed of that case; you need not pause upon that. Have you known of any schools being interrupted in this county?

Answer. The schools in the northern portion, northeastern portion, and northwestern portion of the county have been broken up, and in some places you could not establish schools at all on account of these parties. You could not get teachers to teach them. All the schools in the first district, that is, north of this place, have been broken up, excepting one that was in a thickly colored population or neighborhood; but all the others were broken up that I had knowledge of up there, and some they could not establish on that account. They could not get anybody to teach them up there, for fear of their lives, either white or colored.

Question. Have you heard of a man by the name of Jacob Hicks, and his wife, living about six miles from there in a northeast direction, being whipped early last spring?

Answer. That is the man I spoke of, not his wife, but himself.

Question. The man I refer to was living with Mr. Durden.

Answer. I don't know that I know who he was living with, but he was living between five and six miles from town.

Question. Is that the man you referred to in your evidence?

Answer. Yes, sir.

Question. Have you heard of the case of George Iron, who was whipped in this county about the 19th of April—a colored man?

Answer. No, sir. The legislature met on the 1st of January, and, up to the 1st of May, I was at home very little. There was considerable excitement here concerning the whipping, and one thing and another. I was not here.

Question. Have you heard of a colored woman, who lived near Caledonia, being whipped?

Answer. Yes; the woman, I presume, I have told you of, on Mr. Herring's place.

Question. Have you heard of Ned Murphy, a colored man, living at Ed Hutchinson's, having been whipped?

The WITNESS. How far is that from town?

Mr. RICE. In the neighborhood of Caledonia.

Answer. No, sir; I don't think I have. At what time?

The CHAIRMAN. It was last April.

Answer. No, sir; I have heard of a great many cases, passing back and forth, but I could not remember the time; and then there was a great deal of excitement about that time. Very little of the time from January to the 1st of May, I was not at home; a great deal of the time I was not at home at all between the 1st of January and the 13th of May.

Question. Have you heard of the case of Joe Turner, who worked with John Stevenson?

Answer. No, sir, I have not heard of his case that I know of, by that name, as I told you there are some parties that I don't know the names of; he probably may be one of those.

Question. Do you know the condition of things in any of the adjoining counties, as to the existence of any Ku-Klux disturbances?

Answer. Well, last spring, from March until about the 1st of July, there was a great deal of disturbance, and it was really difficult in the northern portion of this county, and the eastern portion of Monroe County, to get the people to remain at home at all; they were leaving home altogether, and squads moving off to Louisiana; from Monroe County whole families moved from the neighborhood on the east side of the river, and went away from there on account of the murdering of several parties there. Monroe is bordering on Lowndes County, and there was a great deal of excitement in the northern portion of this county, and in Monroe County.

Question. Growing out of these outrages committed upon the colored people?

Answer. Yes, sir; they were raiding about there, so the people say, every night pretty nearly, and whipping and threatening some, and they killed several men; that is, they took them off, and they have never been heard of since; but there has been a great deal more done in Monroe County than in this county. There was a time, along during all the month of April, and a good deal the month of May, that the people in the northern portion of this county were taken to moving out of it. They could not be protected. Men were raiding about in squads of fifty or sixty a night.

Question. What were they doing?

Answer. They were threatening teachers; taking out some people and whipping them, ordering others to go away, and such like things.

Question. Do you know, or have you heard of any of these Ku-Klux being arrested and brought to justice and punished?

Answer. Not one in this county.

Question. What is the trouble in bringing them to justice?

Answer. The trouble seems to be that there is sufficient influence in their favor—enough men in the organization, in the first place, to get on the different departments of the judiciary, on the grand jury, and on the petit jury, one place and another—to keep any bill from being brought; and first they terrify parties so they are afraid to report them, and if they should be reported, they get in such positions that there can be no bill found against them. Now, as to this man who was whipped up here, there was about twenty men, I reckon, came in with him, and several of us got around him and told him that he must go and report; that he should do it. He said he knew the parties; he told us he knew the parties; we got some two or three white men, and tried to get him to go with us and report them before the grand jury, and have them arrested, and we could not force him to do it; he said they would kill him; he would not hazard his life in that way; and we could not make him do it. That is the first thing. They are afraid on account of bodily injury to report a case, and if these parties are reported, they seem to have enough sympathy in the community not to be brought to justice. In this community there has been a great disposition since the passage of what is called the Ku-Klux bill to deny such an organization; but prior to the passage of that bill there was not a child of eight years that would not threaten us in the streets, and all over this county, with these midnight assassins.

Question. When was that bill passed?

Answer. I forget the exact time of its passage; but it was some time in the first of June, I think; about the time of the adjournment of the legislature. I think it was about the last of May or first of June.

Question. Of this year?

Answer. Yes, sir; along about that time. I know it was after the adjournment of the legislature, from the fact that, prior to the adjournment of the legislature, they passed a resolution memorializing the President to send protection to us in this State, and it was after the passage of that resolution that the bill was passed. I know we instructed the delegates from this State, the members of Congress and Senators, to vote for the then pending bill—what was called, I believe, the Ku-Klux bill.

Question. Was that bill supported by the democrats in your legislature?

Answer. They opposed it wilh all their souls; so much so, that one conservative said the object of the resolution then pending was to get up sensation; and that if we wanted sensation, that he would kill a goat and smear his blood on the streets of Jackson, and we could get up sensation on that; that was a conservative senator from La Fayette County. Every representative at that time—I charged upon them myself individually, as senator from this district, that every democrat in the Congress of the United States opposed it, and every member in every legislature, or at least in the legislature of Mississippi, opposed it; and we supposed they must be accessory to the crime for our oppression and all these assassinations, from the simple fact that if they wanted justice administered, they would not oppose a law suppressing this violence. They, however, denied it; but I told them their acts corresponded with the acts of the assassins; that while they were going about murdering our people, they opposed laws bringing them to justice.

Question. I suppose the great body of the white people in this region are democrats?

Answer. Yes, sir; nearly all of them are democrats.

Question. What earnest effort has been made by the democratic party of this county to put a stop to these outrages; have they even denounced them in any of their resolutions at their democratic conventions or meetings?

Answer. No, sir; the nearest we ever had any denunciation of Ku-Klux in this county was last fall, when they killed this man, Mr. Mason, down in the lower part of this county. We had a meeting at the court-house, at least I called the people together, and told them we must do something; that we could not stand quietly by and see our people murdered, and that we would not do it; and we must do something. We met at the court-house, and denounced the assassins in the bitterest terms we knew how, and in that meeting a man by the name of Doctor Landrum, of this county, also denounced them, and said he would give his assistance to bring them to justice. That is the nearest that we have ever had any expression.

Question. Who was this meeting called by?

Answer. By the colored people themselves.

Question. Was it attended largely by democrats?

Answer. Very few were there.

By Mr. BLAIR:

Question. Whose killing was that?

Answer. It was after the killing of Mason; we had a meeting. Soon after he was killed we called a meeting to devise what must be done, and to ask the white people to assist us in bringing those parties to justice; that if we were to be murdered up in this way, we were to call upon the Government for protection, or to protect ourselves; we could not stand quietly by and be murdered in cold blood by midnight assassins who went about in disguise; after we had performed a day's labor and laid down to rest, to have assassins come in; and that if we could not put an end to it, we all proposed to do as one man, at one time; that was about the sentiment of the meeting.

By the CHAIRMAN:

Question. Do you think the passage of the Ku-Klux bill by the Mississippi legislature has had a good effect?

Answer. I think if it had not been for the passage of that bill that by this time the reign of terror would have been such that we could not have raised any crop, and there would have been no peace through the eastern portion of Mississippi at least. That seems to be the case. I know prior to the passage of the bill there was a perfect reign of terror through this county and adjoining counties, and since its passage and temporary enforcement some of these parties have been arrested, and there has been a great change in this community.

Question. Have there been some arrests by the Federal court or by the United States commissioner that have had the effect of creating consternation among the Ku-Klux?

Answer. I think it has had a beneficial effect, the arresting of the supposed perpetrators of crime in the northern portion of this county and the southern portion of Monroe.

Question. You say they joined up here at a place called Buttahatchie?

Answer. There is where a great many outrages have been committed.

Question. State what, from your best information, seems to be the purpose of these outrages, if there was any general purpose?

Answer. Well, sir, we have thought from their organization and from other indications we have had, that the organization, that is, the purposes of the organization, have been to remand the colored men of the country to as near a position of servitude as possible, and to destroy the republican party if possible; it has been, in other words, political. We believe it had two objects, one was political, and the other was to hold the black man in subjection to the white man, and to have white supremacy in the South; that has been the tendency; and then we have evidence of it from the parties who have sworn and bound themselves together under oaths, that is, in clubs, to do all they can from year to year, and from month to month, as long as they live, to establish white supremacy in Mississippi, and the disfranchisement of the black man.

Question. Do you refer to the organization known as the "Native Sons of the South," now?

Answer. No, sir; prior to that organization.

Question. Do you think one of the objects of this Ku-Klux organization in its various visits has been to break down the growing spirit of independence in the black man?

Answer. Yes, sir; and to establish white supremacy in the South, and to destroy the republican party. I do believe these are its main objects, for no democrat has ever yet been injured by that party.

Question. I was about inquiring whether you knew of any case where democrats have been visited by these Ku-Klux and punished?

Answer. Not one; I have never heard of an instance of a white one or black one, not a white democrat nor a black traitor—we don't consider a black democrat, we simply call them traitors—I have not heard of a white democrat or black traitor being punished by these parties in disguise. I will tell you, for illustration of what I have said: We had, in 1868, an election, and the constitution was defeated; we had a contest over that, a very heated contest. There were two men put in prison then; that is, they had kept a man at their house that had stolen—who was with them dodging out from having perpetrated some crime, I think stealing horses—and after everything got quiet, he went away from the colored men's house and stole one of their mules, and they went on in pursuit of him; they were two republicans, both of them; and they got him; the man was named Perk Blewitt who stole the mule, and they put him in jail here; he staid several days, and these men came in pursuit of him, and they put them in jail. I came into town from the country, and they told me about it. The men went down this way to carry them to Macon jail. I asked the colored men why they submitted to allow these men to go down here with chains to the jail, when they ought to have gone by railroad to Macon. However, that was Saturday; Sunday morning the men who came here with chains were back, and we inquired why they were here. and they said the men got away from them. On Monday morning we commenced inquiring how it was they brought the chains back, and we heard that they made them wade the creek down here; we told them it was wrong to make them wade the creek when they had not committed any crime, and were here in pursuit of their property. They had to be responsible. These men were afterwards found dead, and the two republicans were found dead, and this colored democrat (what we call traitors) he turned up alive; he is now living to-day, unless he died in the last few days in New Orleans. These men that took them off were strong democrats, and the two republicans were killed, and this man was turned loose, and we could not account for it in any other way except that they were killed because they were republicans; because these men had lost the property; they were in pursuit of it; they were put in jail; the two men were killed when they had committed no crime, excepting to take back their property; and this man that had committed a crime, stealing from them, was turned loose.

Question. When did this occur?

Answer. This occurred in 1868, directly after the election; one of the parties escaped, and the other was taken under custody.

Question. Was any notice taken of this affair by the courts?

Answer. No, sir, not by the courts; the military here arrested one man; the other man ran off, and after awhile the other one got away and ran off; and he is to-day in town, and has never been molested to this day. The military arrested one and the other escaped. I am speaking now of the white men who took them away; one of them ran away, and the other is here to-day; at least, he was here last Tuesday. That has been, it seems to me, a striking evidence that the object of the whole thing is to destroy the republicans; in fact, some of the papers openly defend the killing of leading colored men, and the allowing of the quiet, inoffensive or least offensive ones to leave; that is the open advocacy of the papers, and to some extent it has been carried out.

By Mr. RICE:

Question. Do the colored people of this county, in the country part of it, feel at liberty to stand up for their rights as against a white, as boldly as a white man does for his rights?

Answer. O, no, sir, they can't, nor could not be expected to do so, from their lately being emancipated.

Question Are they regarded as insolent if they do stand up for their rights?

Answer. Yes, sir; by the white people.

Question. Is it regarded as an offense to be what they call insolent?

Answer. Yes, sir; that is regarded as an offense to stand up for our constitutional and equal rights, as equal to other people, that is, white people.

Question. How do the colored people of this county usually vote when left free?

Answer. In this county they have always voted straight republican, whether free or not; we have always gone straight forward.

Question. How many democratic colored men are there in the county, according to your judgment?

Answer. I suppose not more than fifty or sixty outspoken in the whole county.

Question. What is the voting strength of the colored people?

Answer. I forget the exact strength.

Question. About what?

Answer. I think it is now about 4,500 and some odd; 4,600 and odd.

Question. There are only fifty or sixty that claim to be democratic?

Answer. Yes, sir; down in the worst neighborhood we know of—Landrum's—where the organization of the "Native Sons of the South" is, there are five, I think, there; he said he had sixty, but there were five, they said, voted; the others didn't.

Question. The balance voted the republican ticket?

Answer. Yes, sir; about sixty promised to vote, but five voted it, I believe.

Question. Are the colored people that are hired out, or that have been employed by different white people of the country, ordered around somewhat similar to what they were in slave times?

Answer. Not much of it in this community.

Question. In the country?

Answer. In portions of the county they are—up in the eastern portion of the county and the northern part. I will give you a little illustration of the condition of the county. On last January 1—we have an organization here called the "Union Aid Society;" that is a benevolent organization—we celebrate the emancipation proclamation every January and have a general good time; last January we were to meet at the court-house, and I was over there to see about some other matters in having the meeting, and there were two men from up in the neighborhood of Caledonia, and two, or three, or four white men around them; I went in there, and asked them what they were doing there. They told me that these men had charged them or accused them of stealing $50. I asked them were they guilty; they said they were not. I asked them why they remained there. They said these men said they must stay there. I said, "Are these men officers?" "No, they are not." I asked, "Have they a warrant for your arrest?" "No, they have not." I said, "If they have no warrant for your arrest, you may go where you please, and let them seek you." They started away, and these men tried to prohibit them from going; after awhile they went on away; they got out a warrant for their arrest but did not find them; they went on about other matters; they did not have any more to do with them; they told me these men had taken them down in the woods and had made them say that they would live with them next year, and took them down there, and after they got them down there threatened to hang them if they did not consent to stay this year; they did not want to, but told them they would stay; but they went back to the house, and got up before day, and made a fire in the house, and ran off here, and they caught them after they came to town, and charged them with stealing $50, but told them if they would go back they would not put them in jail; if they did not, they would. The father of these same two white men met these colored men, here in town, in the summer, and told them he would pay them the $50; that they had not stolen it; that he did not know anything about it at all; that he would pay them what he owed them for last year's services. That will give you a little inkling of what the people have to undergo. These are fact justs as they occurred without any putting on to them, without anything added or taken away. A good deal of that exists in that portion of the county; the other side, or bordering on Alabama, until recently, though, we had a little threatening of the Ku-Klux in the corner in 1868; they stuck up signs in 1868 by the Ku-Klux organization, but after that we had no threatening until last fall, that I know of. From that time on until after the passage of the Ku-Klux bill and its enforcement, there was scarcely any peace in this county for colored people. In every portion of it they were harrassed until after these arrests were made on Buttahatchie.

By Mr. BLAIR:

Question. What newspapers are those that you spoke of that have been advocating the killing of the leading colored men?

Answer. The one I have reference to was a paper published in Eutaw, Alabama. I forget the name of it. The paper there says in plain words—I can get you a copy if you want it—that such men as Whitfield, Lewis, Bliss, and Gleed should not be allowed to breathe the free air. That is the Index over across the way there. I think I can find a copy of it around at the store. You can find it on file. I think I saved the copy.

Question. Do you mean that they meant the leaders of the colored men—not the leading colored men?

Answer. No, sir. I was not speaking then of that. I was saying that this paper in Alabama said in plain words—so many words: "We must kill or drive away the leading negroes, or the intelligent negroes, and only let the humble and the submissive remain among us."

Question. Was that the Eutaw Whig?

Answer. No, sir; I do not think it was the Whig. I forget the name of it. That was in 1868. I was down there canvassing in favor of the railroad, and read the paper and saved the copy. I kept it a long time—until I wore it out. That particular piece I have read often.

Question. Can you read?

Answer. Yes, sir.

Question. Have you read it yourself?

Answer. Yes, sir, I read it myself.

Question. You don't know the paper, though?

Answer. I forget the name of the paper. It was at Eutaw, Alabama, where the paper was printed.

Question. A democratic paper?

Answer. Yes, sir. It was taken from the Tuscaloosa Monitor, I believe the name is.

Question. The article was taken from the Tuscaloosa Monitor?

Answer. Yes, sir. I know it was a Tuscaloosa paper, and I think it was the Monitor. I know that was the language. I spoke of it often, and spoke of it in private—the idea of a party being built up on the principle of advocating the open slaughter of human beings to carry out a principle. I have told men about it in private conversation, and told them about it on the stump. My understanding was that I was sworn to state what I knew to the best of my ability, knowledge, and information. What I state here I will say on the public squares, if there's five hundred thousand people standing there.

Question. You have not got that paper with you?

Answer. Which, sir?

Question. The one you alluded to as using the language you referred to?

Answer. In reference to the killing of the leading negroes?

Question. Yes.

Answer. No, sir; had it a long time, but wore it out. I carried it in my pocket—that was in 1868. I used it for a long while, but neglected to have any copies of it printed, and wore it out; but if you can find the numbers along about September, 1868, or get the parties there to get them, you will get the language in so many words. I have traveled all through there advocating the railroad, the Memphis and Selma Railroad; that is why I came in possession of it and noticed it particularly. I was on the plantation owned by Charley Hays. I traveled from here down to Charley Hays's place in advocacy of the tax for the Memphis and Selma Railroad. Why I took such particular notice of it was, it was startling to me; the advocacy of such a principle and act, and it was well carried out, I think, around about Tuscaloosa, and in Tuscaloosa County, and in Pickens County. You will find but three colored men who at the time would dare openly speak of republican principles, except in the districts where a great many colored people lived, in Pickens County, in the northern portion of it, and Tuscaloosa County. Since then it has been a great deal worse. I have seen people there that have been mangled in every w ıy, it seemed to me, that people could be.

Question. You say you call the colored people that vote the democratic ticket, traitors?

Answer. We do.

Question. What else do you call them?

Answer. Well, we call them enemies to our people.

Question. You are pretty much down on them?

Answer. We are, in toto.

Question. They are very bad men, are they not?

Answer. We consider them so. We would not consider them so if the democratic party accepted the situation, and were willing to accord to the black man the right to vote and to hold office, or the right in common with other citizens; then we would think they had a right to acquiesce with that party; but we don't believe they have a right to acquiesce with a party who refuse to recognize their right to participate in public affairs; that is why we brand them as traitors.

Question. They have not a right to do as they please, like the rest of you?

Answer. We have a right, under the law, but the democratic party declares, as far as I learn, that these rights were given to us by fraud and violence, and were unconstitutional and void; and, we think, if the republicans have violated the Constitution guaranteeing to us these rights, it is traitorous in these men to acquiesce with a party who says we have no rights in the community in common with other citizens that they should enjoy.

Question. Still, they have a right to do that?

Answer. I know they have the right, but it does not look reasonable to me that they should exercise that right to the benefit of these parties who say they don't have it constitutionally.

Question. If they can't do as they please, they have no rights, have they?

Answer. They have the right to do it just like Benedict Arnold had a right to trade off the army like he did; but that does not make it justice and equity because he did.

Question. They have no better right than Benedict Arnold had?

Answer. I think not—not a bit.

Question. You think they ought to be punished for it, like Benedict Arnold?

Answer. They should, in the estimation of other people, until the democratic party recognizes our rights, then we cease all opposition to them.

Question. Do you ever do anything with these men?

Answer. We do not other than ostracise them.

Question. These men that are such traitors, do you ever do anything to them?

Answer. Not in the way of bodily punishment or violence; we ostracise them; we won't associate with them, nor treat them with that respect and courtesy that we do other men. Other than that we have nothing more to do with them.

Question. You don't associate with them?

Answer. No, sir; we don't associate with them.

Question. You never heard of any of them being whipped?

Answer. No, sir; not for that principle, I have not.

Question. Not for that principle?

Answer. I have heard of men getting into fusses with them and whipping them, but not for being democrats; I never heard of that in this county, anywhere.

Question. What do they whip them for?

Answer. They get into fusses like other men; and sometimes the other man gets the better of them.

Question. What?

Answer. They get into difficulties like other men, and sometimes they get the better of them.

Question. You don't make difficulties with them on purpose, do you?

Answer. I do not know as they do. They sometimes get into conversation with them, and they are generally pretty high, because they feel that they are sustained by the white community, and sometimes they say a good many things we cannot bear from them, and we treat them just as we would any other men that would say things that we cannot endure—individually and collectively.

Question. You don't whip them for being democrats, but only because they say they are democrats?

Answer. No, sir. We sometimes argue with them, and they give us unbecoming language, and of course we don't propose to submit to it any more than any other party.

Question. They are impudent to you?

Answer. Sometimes they are.

Question. You don't like impudence from these fellows?

Answer. It is not like what you might call impudence, but when they insult us we don't take it. What I thought you meant by the question was, whether we banded together to take advantage of them and whip them; we don't do that. If I get into a difficulty with one I tell him what I think of him. If he insults me I will hurt him for it, or slap his jaws, or do anything else to him, and if he can whip me it's all right; but three or four of us don't band ourselves together; that is what I thought you had reference to.

Question. Did you ever hear of twenty or thirty negroes running a negro man into a store here in this town, for voting the democratic ticket?

Answer. No, sir; they ran one into a store in this town for going into a republican meeting and insulting the meeting, and they called upon him to keep order, and he did not do it, and they put him out of the house, and some of them, injudiciously, I think—for we do not approve of it—ran him down into what is called Blair's corner, into a store, but if any other man had imposed on our meeting, we would have put him out likewise.

Question. And run him down?

Answer. No, sir; I do not say we did it. I say that was injudicious; we did not approve of such an act, nor do I.

Question. The men that ran him down approved of it, didn't they?

Answer. They may have done it as individuals; they are individually responsible, but they did not injure him. We do not approve of acts of violence.

Question. Did any of you do anything to prevent its being done?

Answer. Yes, sir.

Question. What?

Answer. It was only through the influence of the colored people that they did not injure him.

Question. I think it was through the influence of some white men that protected him.

Answer. O, no; they could not have protected him against the men there, had it not been for the influence of the colored men, for I suppose there was a thousand or fifteen hundred men in town, and I do not suppose over two or three hundred white men; I don't suppose more than forty or fifty there, and they could not have protected him against that number. I remember the case.

Question. There were a thousand negroes after him, were they?

Answer. No, sir; I said there was that many in town, not after him; there was only a very few after him, so far as I learned, at the time he went down there; however, I was in the court-house.

Question. Don't you think the white men could have protected him against these few?

Answer. If they had been determined to have had him anyhow, I do not know that they could have done so, from the number there, and the assistance they would have wanted had a difficulty occurred.

Question. They could have got assistance, however, if they had needed it?

Answer. Of course, if they had got into a general difficulty they would doubtless have had assistance.

Question. Now, if those twenty or thirty colored men, intent upon whipping that colored man, had been resisted by——

Answer. I say we assisted to resist them ourselves.

Question. I say if they had been resisted, and had continued in their effort to whip him, would the other colored men have assisted them?

Answer. In violation of law? No, sir; I do not think they would have done it. I speak for myself, I would not have done it.

Question. Was it not violence for them to run after him for the purpose of whipping him?

Answer. I know that was wrong.

Question. That was in violation of law?

Answer. Yes, sir.

Question. He was protected by a few white men?

Answer. Yes; and by colored men, I remember, at the same time and place that these parties——

Question. Were you there?

Answer. I was not at the corner; I was at the court-house.

Question. You did not go down to the corner?

Answer. No, sir; I was there afterward; I told them if they did such things we ourselves would assist in putting them down; that we were for enforcing the law.

Question. I asked you if you knew of any violence by colored men against colored democrats, and you denied it.

Answer. I said I did not know of any, that is, I did not remember any; I did not remember that case at the time; that is the only case that ever has occurred here, to my memory, since I have been here, and that was not on account of his sentiments, but he came into the court-house when we were having a meeting; I believe it was about —I forget the exact purpose of the meeting now—but it was a republican meeting, a nominating convention, and he had been affiliating with the democrats in the county, and we told him, when he spoke, he had no lot or part in that matter; to desist and sit down and behave himself, and he did not do it, but continued to meddle with the business of the meeting, which he had no right to do. Some said, "Put him out." I opposed that, but they put him out. After they put him out, they got into a difficulty, and in the difficulty he received the worst of it; and they got after him and ran him down to Blair's corner; but it was colored men who interfered and kept them back from interfering; it was not white men, because there was no white men who, from the time he started, interfered in his behalf, until he got down to the corner; but it was a colored man. Christmas Lipscomb told me so himself that he did it afterward.

Question. That is not the case I referred to; I refer to the case where a Mr. Humphreys protected him.

Answer. That is the same case, and the same time; the case of Abraham Blake in 1868; I have been here all the time.

Question. Did not Humphreys protect him?

Answer. I do not know who did at the corner; a good many were there; Mr. Bell was then sheriff, and some others were there. Mr. Bell told me he told the men that if any man shot a pistol or attempted to get into the door, white or black, he would shoot him, and that is what he told me afterward; I was not down at the corner at the time.

Question. This man Hicks you talk of, was he whipped for boasting of his intimacy with a white woman?

Answer. That was the charge. He says, however, that it was not true. I don't know, sir; he told me it was not so; that was charged against him. I don't know that it was Hicks, but I suppose it was Hicks; it was the man that was whipped about six miles from here. I do not think it was from his intimacy with her; I think it was for saying something about a white woman, not about his intimacy with her, but from his saying something about her.

Question. You spoke of a man who took two republicans—two men arrested two republican negroes and a democratic negro; the democratic colored man turned up alive in New Orleans; the men who took them were democrats; this occurred in 1868; both of these parties by the military?

Answer. Yes, sir.

Question. One of them escaped?

Answer. No, sir; one of them was arrested and the other escaped afterward.

Question. What were the names of those men?

Answer. One was named McCawley; he lives here now; the other was Cook.

Question. What was McCawley's first name?

Answer. I forget his first name, but he is named McCawley.

Question. What has become of Cook?

Answer. He escaped; they did not arrest him. I heard he went to Texas. McCawley is here.

Question. What did you say about Blewitt?

Answer. The man that was chained with those other two men that were turned loose was named Perk Blewitt.

Question. Was he killed?

Answer. No, sir; the democratic black man that was turned loose was named Perk Blewitt.

Question. Where is Perk?

Answer. They say he is living now in New Orleans, and sometimes in Mobile. The military arrested his father at the time for conveying information to him, and they would have caught him but for his father, and they arrested his father for conveying information and keeping him out of the way.

Question. The military arrested Perk's father?

Answer. Yes, sir.

Question. What did the military do with the man they arrested?

Answer. He got loose, they said; he got away from them and went to Texas, and staid there a long while, and last spring he came back here again. He was one of the foremost men. He said, when I came back from Jackson he was going to dig my grave in my front yard; that is what the people told me; I did not hear him say so.

I knew he was very active when I came back; he took a very active part in the matter when I came back. They told me at Jackson that he said to some white men there; that is, in their presence; a man at West Point and others told me about it.

Question. You say that warning you got was signed by three Q's?

Answer. With three K's—Ku-Klux Klan.

Question. You say they did not tell Mason why they killed him?

Answer. No, sir; not that I heard. I do not think they told him at all, for they just killed him up, and the firing commenced and they killed him.

Question. That was on Halbert's place?

Answer. Yes, sir, Halbert's.

Question. What was it said they killed him for?

Answer. I do not know; the colored people say—that is, they told me afterward—that he was a leading man among them down there, and had been in some difficulty with them, and was pretty thrifty in getting along with them, and having a general political information, and they suppose that was why. He had a difficulty with a man in the neighborhood, but was of general good character otherwise; they could not account for his being killed, except on account of his being a leading republican among them, and a thrifty workingman.

Question. What difficulty did he get into?

Answer. I did not learn the particulars of the difficulty, but he had some words with some one, I think—with some merchant, I think—in reference to a settlement, a few days, or a day or two before, or the same day of his death.

Question. What was the name of the merchant?

Answer. I do not know his name.

Question. Did you ever know it?

Answer. No, sir; I can give you the name of a man who knows his name—knows all about the circumstances of the case, Ralph Brownlee; he lives there in the neighborhood, and knows all about it, I guess, for he was right there, and one of the parties living on his place, and came here and testified and said he knew some of the men, and one of the parties would have shot at them had he not been prevented by some older man on the place. He was a youngster.

Question. That is, Ralph Brownlee?

Answer. Yes, sir; he is living there in the neighborhood, and he has got a boy with him who was right at the place, who was there, and would have shot them had he not been prevented by some one older, and was afraid of endangering the life of his mother, who was on the place, if they could not have got him.

COLUMBUS, MISSISSIPPI, *November* 10, 1871.

JAMES SYKES sworn and examined.

The CHAIRMAN. As this witness is called at the instance of the minority, General Blair will please open the examination.

By Mr. BLAIR:

Question. Please to state your residence and occupation.

Answer. Columbus, Mississippi. I have been a planter all my life, but I very recently sold all the planting interest I had—at least, I rented it out to the negroes. I am really engaged in no occupation. I am a planter, I will say, and it has been my occupation all my life, until the last few months.

Question. Are you familiar, Mr. Sykes, with the school-system that was established in this county, and the measures taken in regard to it by the citizens here?

Answer. In answer to that, gentlemen, I will say I paid but very little attention to this thing, and do generally in regard to taxation. I generally pay what taxes are imposed on me. I have heard a great deal, but, really, so far as my own knowledge extended, I paid but very little attention to the doings of our legislature. The tax was generally complained of as being very burdensome at the time; but time rolled on, and the sheriff advertised and notified the people that they must come forward and pay it. I, in common with many others, went forward and paid mine. In paying it I noticed that the school-tax was an enormous one, and I remarked to him that, if he had charged other people the same way, or if my tax was correct, that I was confident that the people of Lowndes County could not pay it. I knew their situation pretty well, and I was confident they could not pay it. He said they were all alike, and they had paid up a large portion of it. That led me to inquire. I went then to the books and examined. I knew prior to that time the subdivison of the county into school-districts. I went particularly to inquire into the district in which most of my property had been taxed—the plantation I held—and that was the first time that I was aroused to the importance of looking into this matter. I found that they had taxed it there; it is a very small sub-district, not necessarily requiring more than two schools, one white and one colored, both of which were in operation and had been for some time. One of them was on my place—the colored school, in a house that was built prior to the war for a negro church. They came to me, the school commissioners, you might call them, I suppose, not came to me either, but wrote to me; I received a letter from them which I might have brought with me; I received a letter from them requesting me, and not a very modest request at that, that they must have it, (it was mine;) demanding that they must have the house for school purposes. I really at that time did not know whether they had the authority to take a man's house or not, and I answered the note very abruptly, and said that I had given that house to the negroes. It belonged to the negroes on the plantation for a church and church purposes. If they, the negroes, chose to have a school there, I had no objection. I had known something of Mr. Bishop, the county superintendent, before that time, for he had been teaching school here some years. While I knew some of his acts, I heard of a great many more. I remarked in that note that Mr. Bishop could not superintend that school—could not have anything to do with it; that if it was a necessity that he must do it, they must get some other house; that his conduct had been such that I did not approve of it, and I did not want him around there at all; but anything the negroes chose to do with the house, they could do it. I presume Mr. Henry Whitfield has the note now. I was provoked with the demand, and perhaps answered abruptly. I saw him a day or two afterward, and told him I really did not know that I could give him that house; that I had told the negroes to use it; that they might have it as a church prior to the war; that they had a regular sabbath-school there; that I had built it there for that purpose, and if they chose to have a school there, I had no objection, but again remarked to him, "Mr. Bishop can't go down there; his conduct has been such that I don't want him on the place at all." I went down there, and in examining the records of the court, I found that they had charged, I think it was $150 or $170 for rent of the school-house; they had assessed $75 for a stove; they had $50 for repairing the school-house. Now, I will not be exact, but I will come within a few dollars of it—and perhaps $75 or thereabouts for wood fuel, and then there were various other items, I don't know about. That much I do know about. I knew they were not paying a dime for the house, and I did not believe they had a stove there, for there was a stove in it before, that had been there—not a very good one—but I had not heard of their putting another in. In fact, I seldom went down there. A negro superintended the plantation; he had done so since the war, and I had paid him a salary since the war—a boy that formerly belonged to me. I paid him $500 a year to superintend the place. He did it very well. I only went down to the plantation two or three times a year. It is ten or twelve miles down in the country. Seeing these items, and more coming on in the aggregate in that sub-school district where it was not necessary, nor did they pretend to have but two schools, they had $3,800 charged——

Question. Assessed as taxes?

Answer. Assessed as taxes for that sub-district—it occurred to me that that was enormous, and if that thing run through the county in that way, I was confident the people would not pay it, and so told the sheriff at the time. I said, "I will pay my own, but you will find you will not collect the tax; the people are not able, they have not got the money, and cannot do it." I took my horse, however, in a day or two, and rode down there. The house is on my place, not more than a quarter of a mile from the cabins, the negro quarter. I had my horse fed, and walked up there and found a yellow boy there teaching school. It was about dinner-time, play-time for the children. I asked him if he was teaching the school. He said he was. I asked him several other questions, where he was from, perhaps. He said he was from somewhere in Michigan, I think; I don't remember where, somewhere northwest. I asked him what he was getting, "What do they pay you here or agree to pay you?" "Fifty dollars a month," he said. Says I, "How many months have they engaged you for?" He said, "They engaged me for four or five," or probably five, certainly four. Says I, "You have a large school; have you no assistants?" I think he told me some eighty odd children. He said, "Yes," he had two or three assistants. "What do you pay them?" I asked. "Nothing," he said. He pointed out to me two or three—one or two girls and boys; he said they were scholars, but still assisted him in carrying on the school—heard the lessons of the others. I walked in the house; this was near the house. I said, "Let us go in the house, I want to see the inside." I said, "You have no stove here; that is the same old stove you found here." He said "Yes, and it was a very indifferent one too." I said, "Where are all those fine seats they have charged? They have seven to ten dollars charged here for seats; here are only the common benches." I don't know whether they were even plank; I am not certain whether they were not logs split open; they were very rough benches. One of the desks I saw charged in the assessment and apparatus; I said "They have charged us for school apparatus; what have you in that way?" "Nothing," he said. "Don't you contemplate or have not you the promise of some?" He said, "No." I made all the inquiries about that, and found that there was not one solitary thing that was charged there that they had any right to charge, none whatever. I charged nothing for the house; I did not think of charging anything. I did not charge anything for the wood they consumed. The school-house was in the woods; I did not think of charging anything for it. I found that not one solitary item they had down there could be found. It was not there; I came back home.

Question. Did you visit the other school?

Answer. Before I came home I wrote a note to Mr. Hairston; I sent a boy to Mr. Hairston; I did not write a note; I tried to get a piece of paper, but sent a sensible boy, and I told him to see Mr. Hairston and ask him to write to me everything connected with his school, the rent of the house, and everything in fact pertaining to it, which he did, and it was a similar case to mine. It was a house he had built for the education of his own children prior to the war. He is a man who had a great many children; most of them girls I believe. He had built a very good house near his dwelling, and had had a school there for several years. He wrote to me that he had charged nothing in the world for it, or any such thing, and wound up by saying that about $14 was the amount. It did not exceed $20 I know—somewhere in the tens; that was the sum and substance of every dollar that the county was charged for except the teacher, and she received $75 a month.

Question. Then the whole actual expense, as I understand you, was the $50 a month to the colored boy who kept the school on your place?

Answer. And fourteen or fifteen dollars in addition; that included the whole expense.

Question. And for that the school district——

Answer. Was assessed $3,800 on their books, as their books will show.

Question. This was for four months?

Answer. The boy said he was employed four months, but that they expected to continue the school five months. It was then I came home, and saw that we were being taxed here in a way we should not stand; and, at my instance, we called a meeting of the citizens.

Question. The total expense—to get back to the other thing—would be $250 for the boy for five months and $375, making altogether about $660?

Answer. Yes, sir.

Question. With $20 of additional expense on the other school, would make $680 as the total?

Answer. Yes, sir.

Question. The total sum for which the sub-district was charged was what?

Answer. Thirty-eight hundred dollars.

Question. Go on.

Answer. As I say, I returned from there, and spoke to several about town here. At my instance, we called the citizens together. In the mean time several of them had gone to the records and found that was a pretty general thing. The extravagance was outrageous. They declared they could not stand it, and appointed a committee—but perhaps you could better understand it, if you have not seen it, by the report. Here are the proceedings, not only what I wrote, but the county meeting called by the citizens, after two weeks' notice. They wanted everybody to come that was interested in the condition of the county. It is rather a long document, [producing Columbus, Mississippi, Index, June 1, 1871, containing report of the investigating committee, which will be found at the end of this witness's testimony.]

Question. We want it.

Answer. It not only appertains to the school fund, but that opened the eyes of the citizens to a great many other things. They appointed, in connection with myself, six or seven of the best book-keepers they could get, and for two weeks we examined their books. Here is the report of that committee, both of the school funds and everything else, and that report would explain the thing, perhaps, better than I could. There is my own name.

Mr. BLAIR. There has been a great deal said about this school business, and I want this report of the investigating committee to go into the record. It is time that we understand this school system, and the other systems here. It is a very long report.

The WITNESS. Yes, sir; we were directed to examine into everything.

Mr. BLAIR. You had better read it to the committee.

The WITNESS. It is very lengthy, and it will take some time.

Mr. BLAIR. There has been a great deal of testimony taken in relation to this matter, and a great deal of calumny thrown on the people of this county and adjoining counties in relation to it. Since it has been opened, I want it fully understood.

The WITNESS. I will read it. This is the Columbus Index, 1st of June, 1871.

The CHAIRMAN. I desire to examine that paper before cross-examining upon it.

Mr. BLAIR. The reading of it may be omitted now; the cross-examination can be afterward had.

The WITNESS. I was going to remark, you will find, not included in this report, a sum that was received from licenses in the State of Mississippi, but we did not put that in here. Mr. Stallings, the clerk, informed us—we asked him if he had been advised from Jackson what amount of that sum Lowndes County would receive—he said he had been corresponding with the authorities at Jackson, and they had told him about $20,000; that twenty thousand would be about the portion of Lowndes County. That is not in the report.

Question. (By Mr. BLAIR.) You say this meeting was attended by the people pretty generally?

Answer. Throughout the county; the court-house was pretty well filled up.

Question. This report was read, and what action was had by the meeting?

Answer. You will see there what action was taken; the report tells itself.

Question. So the report itself is the action of the meeting?

Answer. Yes, sir; they adopted the report, and I don't know that anything was particularly done with it; because, prior to that meeting, a first meeting was held, as I told you, after I returned from my plantation. At the first meeting of the citizens of the town, the next evening, they appointed a committee to wait on the supervisors. The board of supervisors were then in session and were going to adjourn the next day. They appointed a committee consisting of three or four—I was on that committee myself, I know—to go and to examine this thing, and to try to get them to reduce this tax, as it was too burdensome; the people could not stand it; and we were instructed to say we would not stand it. We did not tell them so; we made no threats. We went and showed them—several gentlemen went with them—and we tried to show them the utter uselessness of attempting to collect such a tax, and the extravagance of the thing; that it was unexpected and uncalled for. One of them got up and moved that they rescind the whole business for the present, and instruct the sheriff to return that portion of the tax which had been collected. I asked the sheriff—I had paid mine—and I think he told me he had collected about a third of it. Any how, the board of supervisors instructed him to return to those from whom he had collected it the school-tax; that they would rely on the $20,000 they would get from the State. There was nothing further to do; they did that; and the money was refunded to those who had paid it. They had then advised the teachers. Well, there was a great deal of fuss made about it; they said we were opposed to it. The citizens assured them that we were not opposed to the schools. We assured them we were not acting from any such motives, but to protect ourselves from this exorbitant and unnecessary tax to keep up these schools. I was offered here in the town of Columbus, by the then editor of the radical paper here, to take the schools if we would give him the $20,000; he said he had been familiar with the schools in Illinois; he was educated at one, and he knew all about them, and to give him the $20,000 coming from the State of Mississippi, and that he would take the schools by contract and would have as good schools as we ever had in Lowndes County. He would take the contract himself and run the schools. Well, he was a man who had written weekly in his paper in favor of the party that was putting this tax on us. I told them what he said he would do it for, $20,000.

Question. From your statement of the sum of $3,800 assessed against your beat, there was only $660 of that actually to be expended?

Answer. That was all, sir, that was expended. After that, now, when I came back again, I was ridiculing the idea to some of them—the board was then in session—I told them the condition of the house; says I, "The idea of my charging you $150 for that house!" They did make an appropriation to repair that house, which was never received, and it has never been done; they had appointed me to do it; I never made any application for it, because the whole thing was done; that was every dime, every solitary dime, except $50, which was an after-consideration, an appropriation of $50, after I returned and told them the condition of the house.

Question. Under whose management or superintendence were those charges made, and by whom was the money to have been expended?

Answer. That report will clearly show; there is the law and everything of the sort, and you will see from that report by whom it was to have been expended; you will not see who did it. The board of supervisors, of course, was a board in unison with the State government and had been appointed by them, appointed by Governor Alcorn.

Question. I meant to ask whether this money passed through Mr. Bishop's hands; whether he made those charges and the disbursements which were to meet them.

Answer. There is a very small paragraph that will explain that better than I could. I will answer that in these words: "The committee find that the board of school directors have confided very large discretionary powers to the county superintendent—that is Mr. Bishop—authorizing him to do this, that, and the other, requesting him to visit Saint Louis, to buy school furniture, and inspect the position of public schools, requesting him to appoint Mr. H. B. Whitfield to collect sixteenth-section funds, for which collection he allows Mr. Whitfield five per cent. for collection." He had no business whatever to do that—"authorizing him to make contracts with teachers, to assign them to their stations, and allow such pay as he thinks proper; in fact, the whole burden of their duties seem to have been thrown upon the superintendent's willing hands. In fact, the board appear to have substantially given him *carte blanche* in the dischaige of his duties. In addition to the large amount, $3,600, allowed him to pay for school-furniture and freight, his expenses to and from Saint Louis, and to and from Jackson, where he went at the suggestion of the board on school business, there was also allowed him the amount of Chickasaw school-fund in hands of board of supervisors to pay for school furniture at West Point, amounting to $695. The history of this money is curious; it was turned over to and received by the board, by Mr. Spears, when he left office in July, 1869. The law requires this fund to be used exclusively for school purposes, and does not authorize the board of supervisors to receive and pay out any money whatever," &c. There is about the powers they had, and they confided everything to Mr. Bishop; he was managing everything.

Question. Was the tax in the other beats or school districts about the same as in yours?

Answer. Just about; the others who lived in them, who had examined them, said they were; I did not examine any others.

Question. Were the schools that were established in them similar to the one in your beat?

Answer. Some of them were very dissimilar to mine. At one place they purchased a house for $7,000—I don't know but $7,500, and another $6,500. The records of the court will show the whole of them.

Question. Did they complete those purchases?

Answer. Yes, sir; and had them paid for.

Question. We have testimony here, before the committee, that a number of these schools were stopped.

Answer. All of them, I believe, pretty much, or the larger portion of them, by the intervention of the inhabitants, or a portion of them, of the different school districts.

Question. Tell us what you know about them.

Answer. I only know this, that the school commissioners told me—I think I heard one, or two, or three—I know I did one, who told me that they immediately, or soon after the action of this board, and advised the teachers that they could not pay them, and they, at the end of a certain time—I could not say how long, but perhaps three months, (they were employed for four months)—at the end of a certain time which was in the future, they must stop their schools, unless some further provision was made; that they had gone so far in debt that it would take the whole amount of money to liquidate their indebtedness, and they would have to go without being paid, and if they continued the schools it would be at their own risk, and not to look to them for pay; which I understood some of them, both colored and white, did.

Question. Did you ever hear of persons in disguise going to these different schools, or other persons, and notifying the teachers that the tax would not be paid, and they would not be paid their salaries.

Answer. I don't know that I ever did, except in one instance, and that was very much condemned, I know, very much; it was by a party of young men up here in the north-eastern portion of the county, near Caledonia. There was a lady and her step-son teaching school there; she as principal and her step-son as assistant. They heard of our action down here, and I understand before that they had gone there; they were very poor people; it is a poor part of the county; they said they could not pay; and they complained perhaps more in that part of the county; they said they could not pay it; it would break them up and ruin them all. I did hear of their going to Mr. Woodson Kennon and telling him so. I think they were in disguise—going that night in disguise, and telling him that he must abandon that school.

Question. And that he must look, if he continued it, to the scholars and patrons?

Answer. That he must look to somebody else; that they could not pay the tax.

Question. Did you ever hear of their going to Joseph Galloway?

Answer. I do not know that I ever did.

Question. Do you know him?

Answer. No, I do not know him.

Question. He lives near Caledonia, and testified here.

Answer. I am not very much acquainted up in that portion of the county. I have been in the county down here thirty years, but out in that country I am as little acquainted as almost any man in it.

Question. Did you understand that these notices were generally given in that way?

Answer. No, sir; they were given, as they told me after this action, to all of them; they said that they had gone in debt for a great deal of furniture, &c., and they could not pay them. We regarded it as perfect folly—all of it. I don't suppose any man in town had been educated in such seats, and with such desks, &c., as they had bought. They had contracted for these houses; and they told me they had expended the amount of money they would probably receive from the State. The teachers were advised that they could not pay them if they continued beyond a certain point which was in the future. I do not know how long; they proposed one month or two months, but it was in the future, and to continue to that time, and then to quit, or they would not be responsible for their pay; and they did, a good many of them, quit, I know; at least I have heard it; and I have heard that some did not quit; some of them continued; the people told them to go on; white and colored would tell them to go on, and I believe some of the schools are in existence, now going on.

Question. Being paid by the persons who send their children to them?

Answer. Yes, sir; to school. I have heard since—really I have not interrested my self very much in the matter since—I heard the other day a gentleman discussing it, and some of those who levied the present tax said they had levied enough now, and it would be collected. I think everybody is satisfied with the present tax. I have heard no complaint about it. I think I heard one of the school commissioners say they would be more economical. They were conscious of the folly of the way they had commenced these schools, and he said they thought they would refund this money; that the present tax, which is to be collected before the 1st of January, would be sufficient to carry on the schools, and perhaps, I think he told me, to reimburse those who had continued on and those who had paid out their money for the education of the children. I reckon he had reference to the neighbors alone. I did not ask him what school it was. I know one Mr. Woodson Kennon; his mother has been continuing that school since. I heard that she was. She used to live here, and I knew her. I made inquiry, and I learned she was still teaching the school, but whether she is looking to the parents or county, I do not know. She has had the school, I think, since. I know very little about the operations since that time, or soon after that meeting. The county paper was at a low discount, and they were paid in county warrants. They thought they would not be paid; people would not stand the tax; and I heard one man here offer to take 25 cents, I believe, for his. Some of them told him it was folly; that they would all be paid; and they will be paid, I suppose, every one of them.

Question. I understand you, the entire opposition to this system was the extravagance and the fraud?

Answer. Well, sir, it was the fraud more than the extravagance, but it was both. I do not suppose it would have been noticed but for that extravagance. I doubt whether it would have been; but just at the time when they were paying, the sum was so great that it opened the eyes of the people. They were going ahead, and paid a portion of it. I heard no complaints. I believe I was the first one that made a complaint. When I saw mine, I knew the whole would raise a large amount, and I could not see what they were doing with it. I knew they were not paying it out down here.

Question. Was there any hostility to the schools in themselves—that is, to the teaching of the colored or white children?

Answer. Not one particle that I ever heard, sir; I never heard it from the lips of any man. I did hear one solitary man, perhaps, who, speaking of the system, said he did not believe it was right for one man to educate the children of another. He did not speak of colored or white. He had no children himself, and loved money. He said he did not believe in any such law to compel one man to educate the children of another; that every man should educate his own children. I believe that is the only complaint I ever heard of it in my life. No, sir, I am confident of that fact, that there was no opposition to the system at all, and that it would have been carried out had it not been for their extravagance.

Question. And these palpable frauds in pretending to incur expense which was not incurred?

Answer. Yes, sir.

Mr. Blair. That is all I desire to ask the witness. If the chairman desires time to examine the report, he can be recalled.

The Chairman. I will ask a few general questions this evening without going into the details of that report.

Question. (By the Chairman.) When was your common-school system inaugurated; when did the law pass establishing your present system of common schools?

Answer. At the last session of our legislature.

Question. That was adjourned when?

Answer. I hardly know when they were adjourned; but they were there a long time:

By Mr. Blair:

Question. All last winter and spring?

Answer. They staid there. We complained a great deal of their extravagance, running the people in debt with staying so long.

By the Chairman:

Question. The school system was established some time during that session?

Answer. Yes, sir. I do not know the date.

Question. Are you familiar with the school law?

Answer. I am not. I never read it in my life, except when this report was made.

Question. Have you a common-school fund; is there a general common-school fund?

Answer. Yes, sir.

Question. That is loaned out and the interest applied, year by year, to the education of the children?

Answer. Well, we have what is called the Chickasaw fund that was appropriated to common schools.

Question. What is the amount of that fund?

Answer. Well, sir, I do not know. I think this report tells; I am not certain—no, it does not; it only tells the portion of this county. I do not know what that fund is, sir.

Question. Is the interest on that fund distributed annually to the different counties?

Answer. It should be. I do not know how it goes; that is the object of the fund.

Question. Do you know the amount of the principal of that fund?

Answer. I do not.

Question. What is the proportion to which Lowndes County is entitled by reason of the number of its children?

The WITNESS. Do you mean in the Chickasaw school fund?

The CHAIRMAN. Yes, sir.

Answer. I do not know; I only know Lowndes County is entitled to a certain portion. A portion of the Chickasaw school-lands lay in the bounds of Lowndes County, near West Point. Lowndes County, I understand; but I do not know about it myself. I never interested myself in it, except as that report shows.

Question. You spoke of $20,000 as due from the State to this county; will you please explain on what account that is due?

Answer. I will first state that when I spoke of $20,000, I did not do it on my own knowledge. This committee I spoke of applied to the clerk of the court to know—he was one of the school commissioners also, I think; I am not certain of that, however—to know if he knew what portion of a certain fund would go to Lowndes County; and he remarked he had been corresponding at Jackson to know what amount, and he was told that about $20,000 would be the amount.

Question. That would be the proportion of this county?

Answer. Yes, sir. That fund is from various licenses in this State; for all liquor licenses, and others I could not enumerate, poll-tax, and, perhaps, fifty or one hundred different items that make up that sum; all the poll-tax and liquor licenses, and from various other sources.

Question. Are these collected by the State, and paid into the State treasury, and then distributed in the different counties according to the number of their children?

Answer. I understand that is the *modus operandi.*

Question. Then this $20,000 would be the proportion which Lowndes County was entitled to of the taxes levied and collected by the State for common-school purposes?

Answer. Yes, sir.

Question. The next step in my inquiry is, what powers the law gives the local authorities to assess a school tax on property of citizens of the county beyond this that is received from the State?

Answer. A special act of the legislature gave them that authority.

Question. A special act applying to Lowndes County alone?

Answer. No; every county in the State.

Question. To what body in your county is that power communicated by the legislature?

Answer. It is in the hands of the board of supervisors, I think, sir; I may not be certain of that, but I am pretty confident it is. They have a board of school commissioners and a board of county supervisors, and I think the school commissioners have been done away with.

Question. And the board of supervisors have power to lay school tax?

Answer. Yes, sir; at least they have no authority to do it, except by sanction of the board of supervisors.

Question. You understand the levying of the school tax of the county is by the board of supervisors?

Answer. Yes, sir; it goes through them if it is not directly by them.

Question. What are the functions of the school commissioners? You speak of that as a distinct agency?

Answer. Well, it was to establish these schools in different parts of the counties wherever it was necessary; I don't know whether it was specified—that wherever a certain number of scholars could be collected in a certain district they were to establish schools, build the houses, employ teachers, and do everything of that sort. They made their estimates, and they had to be sanctioned by the board of supervisors; and when they did it then they levied the tax to collect that amount. The board of supervisors levied the tax to collect that amount.

Question. You spoke of a school superintendent; what are his functions?

Answer. We have have one school superintendent for the State, who is elected by the people; and then they have one superintendent in each county of the State. He manages the affairs of the county. Well, I do not know what his powers are, I do not pretend to know; it seems that he did everything in our county.

Question. I wish you to draw a line between his powers and the powers of the school commissioners and the board of supervisors, so that we will understand precisely what powers the school superintendent has.

Answer. I think I can tell you from this report. I do not know that I know myself, for I paid but little attention to it at the time. There are men here who could tell you everything of that sort in a much more intelligible manner, and perhaps more correctly, than I could. The report says:

"SECTION XXV of the law organizing the school system of the State directs that the county treasurer shall receive and pay out all school funds and makequarterly report to board of school directors, who shall examine and approve same, if correct.

"The committee do not find any part of this law complied with except that the treasurer has received some school funds.

SECTION XXIV directs that the board of supervisors shall issue warrants for the pay of the county superintendent, upon his report, approved by the board of school directors, contained in a field-book of operations. This we could not find nor hear anything of, but did find that warrants were issued for his pay, amounting, up to April 3, 1871, to $685.

"SECTION 1 of amendments to above law directs that the board of school directors to succeed the section board of trustees, and therefore to receive all moneys due from sixteenth section funds.

"SECTION 2 of same directs that the county superintendent, by and with consent of the school board, shall demand and receive all moneys due it, and to bring suit and employ competent legal counsel, and to turn over all collections to the county treasurer, as directed by the general school law; and this law directs—

"SECTION XLIII.—That any officer authorized to receive moneys of the school fund shall pay it over to the county treasurer immediately, and on failure to do so, makes it the duty of the school board to proceed at law against him, and the court is authorized to award judgment and damages same as against a defaulting sheriff."

Question. That is all you know about his powers?

Answer. Yes, sir.

Question. Did you draught that report yourself and have that school law before you?

Answer. Yes, sir.

Question. Did you embrace there a description of all the powers of the superintendent?

Answer. Yes, sir; we intended to.

Question. Has he not supervision of the schools and the mode in which they are carried on in the different school districts of the county?

Answer. I understand that is his special business to superintend, the different schools of the county. He is appointed by the State superintendent for that purpose.

Question. What you read seemed to imply that his chief duty was in relation to collecting the funds for the running of the common schools—seeing to their collection, and payment to the county treasurer. That was the import of what you read. You say now you understand he has the general supervision of the schools in the different districts throughout the country?

Answer. Yes, sir; that is my understanding.

Question. Does he provide the different school-houses with furniture?

Answer. No, sir; that is not his business.

Question. Does he prescribe what books shall be used or taught in the schools?

Answer. I presume not, sir.

Question. Does he have anything to do with the establishment or building of school-houses?

Answer. Not apart from the county supervisors. The board of school commissioners have that.

Question. Then he has no power in that matter at all?

Answer. Nothing, sir; it is just to superintend the schools, I understand.

Question. Has he any power relative to the employment or dismissal of teachers?

Answer. He is given that power by this board.

Question. Has he by the law?

Answer. No, sir; I think he has none whatever.

Question. Has he any power to examine teachers, with a view to their qualifications?

Answer. Not without the consent of this board of school commissioners.

Question. Is the power given by the law to the board? Does the law allow them to delegate it to the superintendent?

Answer. I am no lawyer, and do not pretend to know now all these legal questions. You ask me whether it is the law. I never read a law-book in my life. I don't pretend to know it. My occupation in life has been one that did not call me into court-houses.

Question. I understood you to say you draughted that report, and had the school law before you?

Answer. Yes, sir.

Question. I suppose you were advised as to the different agencies and their respective powers?

Answer. I might have read from it. I think you will find my answers to these questions correct; but I don't pretend to say I do it with full knowledge of the fact before me.

Question. In the levying of taxes for the building of school-houses and the running of schools in the different districts throughout the county, is there a uniform tax laid, so much upon each hundred dollars, throughout the county, for that purpose, creating a general fund?

Answer. No, sir. It is levied in this way in each district: The county is divided off into districts and sub-districts; each district is taxed to pay for its own school, not the entire county. For instance, a district in the southern portion of the county may be taxed $5,000 to build school-houses and carry on schools; another, in the northern part of the county, may be taxed double that amount, because there may be more children and it may require a larger sum of money to carry on that school than it does in the southern part. The people of that district pay their tax themselves; the whole county does not pay it.

Question. So that each district is taxed for the purpose of building its own school-houses, furnishing them, and carrying them on?

Answer. I understand that to be the law, sir.

Question. What power establishes the school districts? I mean what power divides the county up into districts?

Answer. The board of school commissioners.

Question. How many school districts were established by your board in Lowndes County?

Answer. I really don't know, but I think about seven districts.

Question. Then do I understand you that sub-districts are formed by the same board?

Answer. They are all in sub-districts; the county is a district, and is divided into sub-districts.

Question. I misunderstood you. I supposed from your examination that when you referred to a sub-district you spoke of a general school-district being sub-divided?

Answer. No, sir; a school district embraces a county, over which a general superintendent is appointed. He is appointed by the superintendent of the State.

Question. Then you have seven school-districts in Lowndes County?

Answer. I think there are seven.

Question. Lowndes County has a population of about thirty-one thousand, has it not?

Answer. I really don't know the population of the county.

Question. I speak of the census of '70?

Answer. It is very probable; I do not remember.

Question. I see your recent map states that the white population, according to the census of 1870, was seven thousand eight hundred and forty and your black population twenty-three thousand and twenty-two, which would make pretty near thirty-one thousand. Do you know what the enumeration of your school children is?

Answer. I do not.

Question. What are the ages of pupils entitled to the benefits of your common-school system; I mean within what ages must they be?

Answer. I have heard that they must be five or six, up to eighteen or twenty, or twenty-one. I do not say positively that is so; but my opinion is that it is between either five or six, and from that to twenty-one; and all I know about that is from looking over this school-law. We ascertained that some attending this school were thirty, forty, and fifty, and one of them it was said was sixty, and we told Mr. Bishop he was going beyond the law, because the law said it should not be after twenty-one. I recollect it was five or six to twenty-one. We got witnesses to the fact that a great many were going from forty to fifty years old.

Question. What is the number of your school-district?

The WITNESS. Do you mean this district here?

The CHAIRMAN. I mean the district in which you were assessed and paid the taxes.

Answer. Well, sir, I paid very little attention to that, too, and I don't know whether I could answer that. It was a school-district; I cannot tell; I do not remember. I can answer that question, though, at any time, because I have the document laid aside somewhere that I took from the records. I can answer it by going to the court-house.

Question. You don't know either the population or the number of school children in that district?

Answer. I do not.

Question: Do you know what the appraisement of the property subject to school taxation in that district amounted to, out of which, or from which, this sum was to be collected?

Answer. I do not know that I am able to answer that question even. I don't think

I am. All of that I have looked at and seen, but I do not remember now, not expecting to be called on. I do not know but the aggregate is in that report; probably it is.

Question. What was your own tax—your school-tax?

Answer. If I mistake not, I had a little farm there, which I told you I paid little attention to, run by a negro ever since the war—never has been any white man on it until this year. It was a small concern, so small that I did not conceive it advisable for me to be spending time there; I had other places to attend to; I think it some seventy or eighty dollars school-tax.

Question. How large was that farm?

Answer. Only about five hundred and twenty-one or five hundred and thirty-one acres.

Question. Was it a cotton-farm?

Answer. Yes, sir.

Question. What was it appraised at for the purpose of tax?

Answer. I do not remember that; but I presume about $10 an acre. That is only guess-work though. I know we generally put it in at about or in that neighborhood—$10 an acre.

Question. And there were five hundred and thirty acres?

Answer. Five hundred and thirty-one, I believe.

Question. That would have made the place worth $5,310, according to that?

Answer. O, well, other things were taxed—everything, I think, was taxed—mules, and everything else. There was not a wagon or harness not taxed.

Question. Was that a fair valuation for your place there?

Answer. I can answer that better by stating that there are on that place five hundred acres of broken land. I had a white man there since the war. He told me there were sixteen hands that would make about eighty bags of cotton. I went down there two weeks ago and rented out the entire concern; the plantation and fifteen good mules, and three or four wagons—everything necessary to carry on a farm—corn-fodder, and everything; and I rented the whole out for $1,200. I offered it for a thousand to a white man, and no white man would give it. I rented it to the negroes on the place. If that will suit you, that is an answer.

Question. It is an argumentative answer. I asked for your opinion of the cash value of the estate.

Answer. I don't know how I could arrive at the cash value of the property better than what it brings; that is, what I rented it to them at for five years.

Question. What would you sell it for?

Answer. I could not sell it at all; it belongs to my grand-children. I do not own a place in Lowndes County, except the lot I live on. I had two large plantations.

Question. What is its fair valuation?

Answer. I presume what it was assessed at at the time would be a fair valuation.

Question. Now, then, we have the value of the land, $5,310; what was the value of the personal property on it?

Answer. I have no idea without looking at the tax-book.

Question. You were complaining to the board that the taxes are excessive, and you thought and you spoke of an appeal to your fellow-citizens.

Answer. Yes, sir.

Question. I desire to inquire into the foundation of your grievances by asking how much property you had on which this tax was levied.

Answer. Well, sir, if you will give me until to-morrow I will give the figures verbatim. I will give you the per cent. I was taxed at the time on my property and I will give you all the figures. I do not remember these things.

Question. I supposed you knew the value of the personal property.

Answer. No, sir. I think the best way of ascertaining the value is what a man will take for it; and I have leased each field to the negroes for five years.

Question. If you cannot state the value, state what the articles were at the time.

Answer. There were about sixteen mules, and, I will say, four wagons; and I could not tell you now all the little things on the place to save my life. They were all the implements necessary to carry on a plantation of that size.

Question. Massing the personal property altogether, was it worth $3,000?

Answer. Yes, sir; the mules were worth that; they cost me that nearly.

Question. Was it $5,000, do you think?

Answer. No; I do not.

Question. Somewhere between $3,000 and $5,000?

Answer. Yes, sir; I suppose so.

Question. I will go back a step further.

The WITNESS. In addition to that I would like you to recall me to-morrow and let me give you a statement. We were complaining of taxation generally. We were taxed here $150,000 for a railroad in the county. The county was taxed, and the town of Columbus pays more than one-half of the entire tax of the county. We were taxed in the town of Columbus $100,000, apart from the $150,000 for the railroad, and this was done by a vote of the county, including the blacks, who, without a solitary exception, not one, I don't suppose there was one voted against it. We are taxed here to keep up public schools. Our lots are taxed. I want to show you the entire taxation that we were burdened with at the time. We objected to this unnecessary burden.

Question. Then I will not allude to that again this evening, but give you the opportunity of making the examination you desire; but I will go back a step and inquire the condition of your common-school system before the war—you of course were familiar with it—and I will ask you to state, when the war commenced, how many school-houses, outside of Columbus, you had in the county of Lowndes.

Answer. Well, sir, you can get that information from persons who know more about it than I do. I only know the particular region in which I lived. I tell you I have lived here thirty years, and have gone to my plantation and back. Throughout the State there was a sixteenth section in every township for public schools; a great many of them had been sold; houses had been erected on them, and they having been sold, and houses taken down. At the beginning of the war, I do not know of one, or but one, solitary public school-house, outside of Columbus, in my knowledge.

Question. In the whole county of Lowndes?

Answer. Yes, sir.

Question. Was that a log school-house?

Answer. Yes, sir.

Question. Do you know of any other than that one school that was maintained outside of the city of Columbus before the war—I mean common-schools?

Answer. O, yes; they mostly had schools in the neighborhood. They were maintained from the funds arising from this sixteenth section.

Question. How many congressional townships had you in this county of Lowndes—do you remember?

Answer. No, sir; I do not.

Question. To state that in other terms, how many sections, called the sixteenth section, had you in this county?

Answer. I do not know that I could count them up exactly. There is the town of Columbus is on one of them. I really don't know, but at a mere guess—and it would be entirely guess-work—I should suppose some six or eight sections—sixteenth sections.

Question Do you know as a general rule?

Answer. I want to state distinctly, I do not know; it is mere guess-work. I know one in my neighborhood, and one out there is two, and Columbus is three, and one down below here is four. I do not know of but four of my own knowledge, but I presume there must be others. Now, the town of Columbus is in the center, and they run north and south, and there must be one up north here, but I do not know it of my own knowledge.

Question. Do you know, as a general rule, what these school sections sold for?

Answer. They sold very high.

Question. They were sold many years ago, in early times?

Answer. Yes, sir.

Question. On an average, what did they bring?

Answer. I suppose twenty to thirty dollars an acre; that is, where it was good; some of them were of no account. It was given to the State by an act of Congress; and the sixteenth section sometimes was land of not much account.

Question. Averaging the good and the bad?

Answer. It might not average twenty or thirty dollars. The one down in my neighborhood averaged more than twenty to thirty.

Question. That was good land?

Answer. That was very fine land.

Question. Were they sold for part down and balance on time?

Answer. I think there was none down. I do not know of the sales, or of but two. I do not think any money was paid down. I think they took bond and security and 10 per cent. on the money.

Question. Have these school sections to this day all been paid up?

Answer. I don't suppose half of them have.

Question. The purchasers pay year by year?

Answer. Yes, sir. Some of them broke all to pieces; and the security broke all to pieces, like the balance; so that it is a loss to the State.

Question. So that there has been an absolute loss on the part of that fund?

Answer. Yes; pretty much an entire loss. The war came on and broke up everybody—broke up the securities, the principal land security, and there was nothing left. The lands have been sold and resold; perhaps half a dozen individuals had owned them since the time they were sold up to the commencement of the war, and, as they sold, dividing them.

Question. But, of course, no title was ever made until the purchase was made good?

Answer. The title was made.

Question. And no bond?

Answer. No, sir.

Question. So that when the bondsmen failed the whole was lost. When they sold the sixteenth-section lands, did they not take a mortgage?

Answer. No, sir; they had security and a bond.

Question. And the security failed, and the bond proved good for nothing?

Answer. Yes, sir. I think in my section it was paid in confederate money during the war; but some have not been paid at all.

Question. Then there is not much of this fund remaining in this county?

Answer. Very little, I reckon.

Question. So that, if your children are educated at all, they cannot look to the pro ceeds of that fund?

Answer. No, sir.

Question. But must look to the general fund provided by the school-law?

Answer. Yes, sir; or educate themselves.

Question. You state that, previous to the war, you know of but one school-house, and that a log one, built on the sixteenth section?

Answer. Yes, sir.

Question. What mode was provided for the education, then, of the children or inhabitants?

Answer. Let me correct that a little. While we were not building on the sixteenth section, in every neighborhood, pretty near, there was a school-house supported by the proceeds of the sixteenth section. The sixteenth section had passed into other hands, and the persons living in the country entitled to the proceeds had erected a house, perhaps, in a distant locality, and were carrying on public schools from the proceeds of the ground thus sold them, in almost every case. I scarcely know an exception to that rule; but there was none on the sixteenth section; that had passed from the hands of the State to other persons, and had been sold and resold, up to the time of the war. They had erected houses, not on the sixteenth section, but in more suitable localities, and were supporting these schools from the sales of the sixteenth section.

Question. Now, how many schools in a township would the income from the sale of the sixteenth section carry on?

Answer. That would depend entirely upon the quality of the land—the amount it sold for; some were very poor and did not sell for much. It would depend entirely upon the amount the land sold for.

Question. In point of fact, was there a school-house in each congressional town before the war?

Answer. Yes, sir; many of them.

By Mr. RICE:

Question. Public school-houses; take a congressional township, I mean, six miles square?

Answer. Why, there was one in every—I will not state the distance, for I don't know that my knowledge of this county will enable me to—township; that is, six miles square, and running north and south. I will commence on the west end of the county: down in my neighborhood there was one school-house; coming up farther, right opposite this town, there is another sixteenth section, and there was a school-house; that is the one I have reference to now, that is there now; and while I don't know of a sixteenth section farther north in the county, I presume there is one; I presume there are three running on north in the county. These two are only about five miles apart at the farthest.

By the CHAIRMAN:

Question. About what is the length of the county north and south?

Answer. I do not know that I can answer that exactly; I would not state, for I do not know.

Question. Do you remember the number of square miles in your county?

Answer. No, sir; I do not; it is a small county, though—quite a small county.

Question. How long each year did the income from the sixteenth section run your schools?

Answer. So far as my recollection goes, it was generally kept up during the year.

By Mr. BLAIR:

Question. Six hundred and one square miles is the area?

The WITNESS. Well, now, in our muddy country, in the prairie, the schools were discontinued in the winter, for it was too muddy; but I don't know that it was for want of funds.

By the CHAIRMAN:

Question. Did I understand you to say that the income from the sale of the sixteenth section in each town would keep your common schools running during the year?

Answer. No, sir; I told you some of them had no income scarcely at all. They were sold and the lands were almost worthless.

Question. Then they would not run a school at all.

Answer. No, they did sell for something; I didn't say they had no school at all.

Question. There then would be an entire town without any funds to run a school; the inhabitants were without any school provided the sixteenth section turned out to be worthless?

Answer. You don't mean a township; there is more than one sixteenth section in a township.

Question. In a congressional township more than one sixteenth section?

Answer. Yes, sir.

Question. There is only one.

Answer. I don't know what you mean by a congressional township.

Question. I mean thirty-six sections.

Answer. O, yes, sir; if you ask me how many sixteenth sections there are in Lowndes County, I don't know now.

Question. If it happened that the sixteenth section was worthless. then it would result, under the old system, that the inhabitants of that township would have no means provided by law for the education of their children?

Answer. Yes, sir; if it was entirely worthless they would not. I know of no other provision.

By Mr. BLAIR:

Question. The Chickasaw fund?

Answer. Yes, sir; there was the Chickasaw fund?

By the CHAIRMAN:

Question. Do you know the condition of the various school-sections in your county; that is to say, how many of them were indifferent and how many of them were first-rate?

Answer. I do not know; I can only give you on the west side of the river here. I have no knowledge of the sixteenth sections on the east side of the river. In the region where my plantation was it was a fine section. There was one out here west was a very good section, selling for not less than $25 an acre, I suppose. Whether there is one farther north I do not know, but I presume there is. Here is a sixteenth section upon which this town of Columbus is. There was a fund here bringing in three or four thousand dollars a year.

Question. What was the interest that fund yielded?

Answer. It was three or four thousand dollars.

Question. Was that the principal?

Answer. No, sir; the interest. The income amounted to that.

By Mr. BLAIR:

Question. The town itself is built on the sixteenth section.

Answer. Yes, sir; and let me state to you—perhaps you will not care to hear it—but none of us own our property here. This building is on merely leased property; it is built on a sixteenth section; they leased it for ninety-nine years, renewable forever. Every man pays here a certain amount on his property for school purposes.

By the CHAIRMAN:

Question. Year by year?

Answer. Year by year. It is not what you might term in law real estate; it is built on the sixteenth section, by those who leased it for ninety-nine years, renewable forever. A portion of the town is not on the sixteenth section. The town embraces more than the sixteenth section.

Question. You spoke a moment since of the Chickasaw fund; you may explain that—what amount year by year the county of Lowndes is entitled to on account of its children.

Answer. I don't know that I can tell you. You can be informed about that.

By Mr. BLAIR:

Question. Is it contained in your report?

Answer. I believe so. I know you will find it in the records of the court.

By the CHAIRMAN:

Question. I understood you to say the school commissioners had purchased two houses in view of the tax they had levied—one at seventy-five hundred?

Answer. I think so.

Question. And another at six?

Answer. Five or six.

Question. These were existing—built or constructed?

Answer. Yes, sir; and sold to the county by the owners. We doubt whether they were worth it.

Question. Were they frame-buildings?

Answer. I never saw one of them. One of them is at Crawfordsville, on the railroad; the other at West Point.

Question. Besides these two houses, outside of Columbus, is there any other than log school-houses in the county?

Answer. Yes, sir.

Question. Where?

Answer. It is upon what is called the Hamilton road, between here and Aberdeen.

Question. What kind of a house?

Answer. It was originally built for a store, I think. It is a large frame building. The county paid seven, or eight, or nine hundred dollars.

Question. Is that the only exception before this late purchase?

Answer. Well, sir, I am not familiar with the county—particularly in matters of that sort—and I do not know. There are men who can tell you all about that thing. I really don't know. I have been a home person—remained at home.

Question. I should not have asked you these questions, but General Blair has brought you in as a witness to testify generally in relation to the enormity of this school tax, and I thought these questions necessary to put to you.

Answer. Yes, sir. If it had been the school tax, as I said, alone, and the ordinary expenses of our State government, I don't suppose one solitary citizen of Lowndes County would ever have complained. We would have paid it, while it might have been large; but we were burdened here with every imaginable kind of tax, and the aggregate of that tax is such that we, at least I, did not believe the people could pay it; and I complained of it because it was a degree of extravagance I thought the people should not have gone to.

Question. As you have made a new statement, it compels me to ask you a few questions in relation to that, leaving out the question of municipal taxes levied in Columbus. Will you tell this committee the aggregate of all the taxes levied—I mean to say the rate per $100 of all the taxes levied?

Answer. It would amount to more than two and a half. As I remarked just now, if you will give me until to-morrow I will figure it up and tell you.

Question. You are not able to answer now?

Answer. I am not.

Question. You don't know whether it amounts to a dollar and a half on a hundred, or two and a half?

Answer. I am sure it amounts to more than that.

Question. Outside of Columbus?

Answer. I mean the entire tax now—railroad tax and everything. Our tax here, municipal tax or mere household tax, does not amount to very much. The raising of three or four thousand dollars, divided among the people of Columbus, is a very small amount.

The CHAIRMAN. If you prefer informing yourself more fully before answering these questions, I will not press you further at this time.

By Mr. RICE:

Question. You said the school-house at Crawfordsville cost how much?

Answer. Six thousand dollars, I believe.

Question. How large a place is Crawfordsville?

Answer. Really, I don't know; but I don't suppose they have more than one hundred and fifty or two hundred inhabitants.

Question. Do you mean the township or the town?

Answer. I mean the town; I don't know the township.

Question. How large is West Point?

Answer. That is a much larger place. I don't know what they claim.

Question. Seven or eight hundred?

Answer. I suppose so.

Question. You spoke of your tax in your township. Did the board of commissioners report the items of expenditure that amounted up to $3,800?

Answer. Yes, sir; every solitary item.

Question. Can you tell what those items were?

Answer. I can to-morrow, if you want them.

Question. We want them. You can't give them now?

Answer. No, sir; I have not got them.

COLUMBUS, MISSISSIPPI, *November* 11, 1871.

JAMES SYKES recalled.

By the CHAIRMAN:

Question. This report, which was presented to a meeting of the citizens of this county, I notice is printed in the Columbus Index, issued on the 1st of June, 1871. I will ask you to state whether you have ever examined the circular or report made by J. N. Bishop, county superintendent of education, and president of the board of school directors, dated the 7th of June, 1871? [See page 453.]

Answer. I do not know that I have particularly, but it was handed to me to-day to bring here. I told him I did not know I should have any use for it. My attention was called to it, and it was handed to me. I would like, before you proceed with this investigation—you asked me several questions yesterday that I really did not know—never informed myself in regard to them—and I would like to answer those questions before you proceed with this investigation. I put them down here. I did not look for anything; I really did not know; I gave my opinion. One thing I do want you to do. You asked me for my authority in regard to the assessment of the several sub-districts in this county by a board of school commissioners. I told you it was a matter of record, and my knowledge of it was obtained from the records. I told you I would bring that record. You said you wanted to see it. I told you I would bring it this morning. I applied to Mr. Stallings, the clerk of the circuit court, for that record. He is the proper custodian of the record. He told me he did not have it. I asked him if he knew where it was. I said, "This is the proper office for it to be kept." He said he didn't, but he supposed it was in the office of the county clerk. I called to see him, and I told him what Mr. Stallings had said. He said it was not there, and had not been there. I said, "Gentlemen, have you lost your public records in a matter of such importance?" He said he did not know; it did not belong to his court at all. He referred me to Mr. Whitfield, the mayor of the town, who is one of the principal men in the whole matter. I went to him and told him what had occurred; that one of the records was gone; that I wished to show from the record the statement I made here yesterday of what they had assessed in my district, and I wanted to look at other districts, too. I wanted that record to show that I had stated correctly when I said they had assessed in my district thirty-eight hundred, but collected not more than six or seven hundred, and that was the first thing that ever caused me to look into this matter. The first was—the very first item was the rent of a house, which I knew was not so—my own house—for which I did not contemplate their paying any rent; and then the fuel, which I knew was not so—$75; there was no fuel but my own on the land. I took it for granted if the very commencement of the record was false the whole of it might be so. It proved to be so throughout the $3,800. There was not to be collected in that district but four times $75 and four times $50, and about fourteen or fifteen dollars at Mr. Hairston's school.

Question. You are speaking of the record of the board of supervisors?

Answer. No, sir; the board of school commissioners; there are two boards.

Question. Is there any such office known to the law here; do you not refer to the board of school directors?

Answer. Well, school directors.

Question. Who was the custodian of the record?

Answer. Mr. Stallings, clerk of the circuit court.

Question. Does the law make him the depositary of that record?

Answer. I will get the law. I thought you might ask me that. He was custodian of that anyhow. I went to Mr. Whitfield. He said he thought Mr. Bishop had it; that he had warned Mr. Bishop to take care of it. I told him I had searched around enough for a public record. I saw Mr. Bishop again during the day, this morning, and asked him. He said he knew nothing about it. So much as to the record and my statement. If it is necessary to prove my statement, I will prove it by a hundred men—the most respectable men in the town—if the record cannot be found.

Question. Has the board of school directors any power to make a levy at all; have they the power to do anything except make an estimate?

Answer. Yes, sir; that is it, and the board of supervisors make the allowance.

Question. The supervisors make the actual levy?

Answer. Yes, sir.

Question. Have you examined the record of the board of supervisors, to ascertain the sum levied by them for school purposes?

Answer. I did not. I understood there was a great deal of complaint made. This was long anterior to finding that they rescinded the matter; there was a great deal of complaint, and they reduced. I have the amount here—can give the figures, [consulting a paper.] The first assessment, as I stated here, brought an amount of about ninety or ninety-five thousand dollars in this county for school purposes. Such complaint was made then that the board of school directors or commissioners, or directors, as you call them, reduced that to about one-half—I think about one-half—making perhaps about $45,000. The superintendent of education, and president of the board of school directors, in his report or circular of June 7, 1871, says as follows:

"In accordance with section 31 the board of school directors asked the board of supervisors to levy a tax of $21,000 upon the taxable property in each sub-district to pay for the cost of school-sites, construction and rental of suitable school-buildings, for contingent expenses, and the deficit in the teachers' fund."

Question. Now, do you know that the board of supervisors have made a levy for a greater sum than this $21,000?

Answer. No, I do not.

Mr. BLAIR. That was in each sub-district?

The CHAIRMAN. No, for the entire county.

The WITNESS. I think that is about right, because they expected to get $20,000 from the State, making forty-two thousand in all. There was some other, I recollect, making about forty-five thousand in all. There was that twenty-one thousand, and what they would get from the State, they said, would be a sufficiency to carry on the schools of the county.

By the CHAIRMAN:

Question. You stated yesterday that there were only seven sub-districts; are there not fourteen in this county?

Answer. No, sir; I did not tell you that; I told you I did not know the number of them. I told you I did not know; I know of seven; how many more I do not know.

Question. Do you not now know there are fourteen?

Answer. I do not; I presume that is right, though; there may be fourteen; they were scattered all over the county—some little schools and some large ones. I do not remember the number of districts, and told you yesterday I did not know the number of them.

Question. Again, do you not know that the number of children between the ages of six and twenty-one years enumerated in this county amounts to eight thousand and ten.

Answer. I do not.

Question. In other words, that there are nineteen hundred and two white children and six thousand one hundred and eight colored children?

Answer. I do not know anything about it.

Question. Have you ever taken any pains to inform yourself whether that is the correct number?

Answer. I have not; none at all.

Question. Did you say you had examined the circular or report of the county superintendent?

Answer. My attention was called to it yesterday. I told him I did not suppose I would have any use for it.

Question. Do you know the number of children, white and colored, that have attended the common schools in this county?

Answer. I do not.

Question. Do you not know that all of the funds belonging to what is called the "congressional township fund" were lost during the war, except about the sum of twelve or fifteen thousand dollars, which remained in solvent notes, which were held by the trustees of the schools under the former common-school system?

Answer. I made a little memorandum of that from a bank officer, who told me he had the money in his bank. I stated to you yesterday that I considered the sixteenth-section fund all gone; that they had, in the common ruin, been lost, and I knew no better until I asked the question yesterday if anybody knew. I made a memorandum of what he told me. The fund arising from the sale of the sixteenth section had been lost, I told you. I learned, however, that much of it has been paid recently, and still further payments secured; that is not lost.

Question. How much do you find has been saved?

Answer. Captain Benoit told me about three thousand of it was paid the other day on a section. I did not suppose he would ever get a dollar on it.

Question. What did you learn was the total amount saved?

Answer. I did not inquire. I understand from a lawyer that he has brought suit in another case of a sixteenth section, in which he has secured, perhaps, the entire payment.

Question. You spoke yesterday of the portion to which this county would be entitled of the Chauncey school fund; must that not all be expended in that portion of the county which is west of the Tombigbee and north of Tibbyhah Creek?

Answer. Yes, sir; I do not know; I do not state that of my own knowledge, but I have so understood it.

Question. Does the income from that fund amount to more than $600 a year.?

Answer. It has been very much underestimated, if it does not.

Question. The superintendent says that the proportion to which this county is entitled is $298 semi-annually.

Answer. That is less than I had supposed.

Question. Do you know that the school board have bought three school-houses, at a cost of $6,600?

Answer. If I had that record, I could show you what they paid for every one in the county. If you will make the proper officer produce that record, you will have before you what each school-house in this county cost; what they paid down; what they say they gave for it. I do not know; that is their own document. I cannot obtain it from any of them. I stated yesterday that I knew of one that perhaps cost seventy-five hundred. I did not know I was exactly correct. I knew I was in the neighborhood of it; another cost sixty-five hundred. I know those school-houses belonged to the teachers who sold them, and that they continued the schools, and I know I heard men in whom I have as much confidence as any man living, who lived in the towns of Crawfordsville and West Point, say they would leave it to all West Point that an honest man would say that one they got $6,500 for that it would sell at auction, nor could they find a man in that region to give fifteen hundred for it. The man that taught the school sold the house. He owned the house. I only speak of these things to let you know what produced the general dissatisfaction here among the people in regard to taxation. I have no idea to-day you could get a thousand dollars for it.

By Mr. BLAIR:

Question. How was it with the one in Crawford?

Answer. That is the one I have reference to, and the one at West Point is about the same; and the county superintendent and board say to the people, "You have nothing to do with it. This particular district pays for its own school." That is true; I am not taxed to pay for the one in Crawford or West Point. They say the people there petitioned for it. We took the pains to inquire, and found that nobody petitioned but a few individuals interested in the matter, and that the citizens, the tax-payers, who had this tax to pay, did not petition. It is unnecessary to say what occurred. I heard one of them tell one of these men, "You know that you tell" (with an oath) "a lie—every one of them; that you have forced this thing on us."

Question. Do you know how many school-houses the board of directors determined it was necessary should be secured for the education of these eight thousand and ten children?

Answer. I again appeal to you to produce that book, and it will show.

Question. I ask you the number of school-houses.

Answer. I do not know.

Question. The superintendent says, June 7, 1871, "To this date there has been needed forty-six houses, for school purposes. Of this number, twenty-six have been furnished free, fourteen have been rented, or repaired, at the expense of the county, and six have been erected, or purchased."

Answer. That may all be true; I do not know anything about it.

Question. The superintendent states, also, that the board has contracted for the following sums:

Amount for erection and purchase of buildings for white schools	$7,408
Amount for rent or repairs of buildings for white schools	563
Amount for erection and purchase of buildings for colored schools	1,040
Amount for rent of buildings for colored schools	226
Total	9,237

Are you prepared to —— the statement?

Answer. I am not; not at all. I know nothing in the world about that.

Question. According to this statement you will see that the total amount charged for rent, or repairs of buildings for white children, is $563, and the total amount of rent for buildings for colored schools is only $226, for the entire county.

Answer. I do not know about that.

By Mr. BLAIR:

Question. Two hundred and fifty dollars of that was charged in the case you speak of?

Answer. Was charged, and not a dime was paid.

By the CHAIRMAN:

Question. What book did you see that charged on?

Answer. On a public record kept by the board of school directors, as you call them, as they are bound to keep, too, under the law, I believe.

Question. Charged as paid?

Answer. No, sir; I say they had assessed this amount to be collected from these various points—that the people complained of it, and said they could not and would not stand it; and they then reduced it about one-half. It made an aggregate of about ninety or ninety-five thousand dollars for Lowndes County.

By Mr. RICE:

Question. The assessment amounted to that?

Answer. Yes, sir; with the amount they would derive from the State funds and these other taxes.

By the CHAIRMAN:

Question. You have said already that the amount of assessment for the whole county was only twenty-one thousand?

Answer. I say they reduced it and made it forty-five thousand, and twenty-one thousand they expected to get from Jackson; the Chickasaw school-fund making up to forty-five thousand.

By Mr. RICE:

Question. That reduction was before that meeting?

Answer. Yes, sir; it was before that immediately, or the same time.

By Mr. BLAIR:

Question. But the original assessment was ninety thousand?

Answer. Yes, sir; and there is where the original complaint began. You asked me about the sixteenth sections. I told you there were seven, I believed; there are fourteen; I went to the map and looked. Then the tax, the license, and poll-tax, as I learned, in the State, amounts to $700,000. I asked a man who was competent to inform me, if Lowndes County would get $20,000, and he said he did not know; he knew the aggregate, and supposed that Lowndes County would get at least twenty thousand, that being the proportion of the county.

By the CHAIRMAN:

Question. This report shows that the original land records show that there were sixteen whole sections and three fractional parts of sections reserved for school purposes in Lowndes County?

Answer. The map of Lowndes county does not show it, the map at the court-house; I called there this morning. I went there with a man that understands land better than I do, who is in the office. He said there were fourteen and two fractions, making sixteen; you may call them sixteen; one of them extended over into Monroe County, and the other into Oktibbeha County.

Question. Have you ascertained yet in which sub-district you live?

Answer. I have not, for the want of that book.

Question. So you do not know the number of your sub-district yet?

Answer. I do not.

Question. Do you know the limits of that sub-district?

Answer. I do not know; I can tell where we have understood they come.

Question. How do you know but two schools have been established in the sub-district?

Answer. I know two have.

Question. How do you know only two have.

Answer. Because I am right there; I know there have not been more than two; I know they did start a day or two at Mrs. Fountain's; a negro commenced there.

Question. If you do not know the limits how do you know that?

Answer. I will state that McGower's swamp bounds it on the south; I do not know exactly where it runs; but I know about where it runs, but I don't know how I could describe it to you for the want of this book which has been removed; I say it here, and I have said it elsewhere, they had no right to destroy that book; it was a public record of Lowndes County, as much so as any record in that court.

Question. How do you know it is destroyed?

Answer. I do not know that it is; they ought to produce it when called for.

Question. I understand you it is the record of the board of supervisors you are talking about.

Answer. No, sir.

Question. It is the record in which the tax is levied?

Answer. No, sir.

Question. What is the record you refer to?

Answer. I refer to a record made by the board of school directors.

Question. Was it the estimate that they made?

Answer. Yes, sir; and of the moneys they paid out, and everything all scattered through it; and the taxable property in each sub-district is in that book; the aggregate amount of the taxable property in each sub-district is in that book; and various other items of importance.

By Mr. BLAIR:

Question. They have made away with it?

Answer. I do not know what has become of it; they seemed to have very great indifference to give it to me; I finally went and told them I was requested to bring it before this committee; I told them I had made a statement here, and I demanded it in the name of this committee; I cannot find it.

By the CHAIRMAN:

Question. Do you know what the real estate of Lowndes County is valued at for taxable purposes?

Answer. I do not; but I could come very near it from one circumstance; it was complained here a great deal that the town paid most of the taxes, and on examining we find that the taxable property of the town is between three and four millions, and we pay about one-half, or little over half of the county; so that it would be six or about that; I do not state that as definite at all.

Question. The taxable property outside of the city of Columbus is about double that in it?

Answer. No, sir; it is about the same; there is very little difference.

Question. That would make the taxable property, real and personal, of Lowndes County, outside of Columbus, between three and four millions?

Answer. Yes, sir; I suppose so. It is guess-work—not entirely guess-work either, for I have heard it computed. I know the taxable property of the town is between three and four millions, and we pay perhaps a little more than one-half the taxes of the county.

By Mr. BLAIR:

Question. Three or four millions taxable in the town, or in the town and county?

Answer. In the town. I do not know that it is real estate, but taxable property in the town of Columbus. In other words, the town of Columbus pays about one-half of the taxes derived from the county of Lowndes.

By the CHAIRMAN:

Question. Were not the school-houses that were purchased by the board of directors devoted exclusively to the education of white children?

Answer. I do not know.

Question. Have any houses been purchased for the education of colored children?

Answer. I do not know that, sir. I presume there have been. On reflection, I think I know one that was purchased up here.

Question. For colored children?

Answer. It was.

Question. Where was that?

Answer. I will not state it, because I stated the other day in this case where the man had been directed to stop his school that it was a colored school. I learned to-day that it was a white school. I did not feel interested in it, and I did not know about it.

Question. The superintendent states that, "acting upon the petitions of different citizens, and by their repeated personal requests, the board purchased three school-buildings of a high order, payments to be made this year, amounting in all to $6,600." Do you know that statement to be true or untrue?

Answer. No, sir; I do not know whether it is true or untrue.

Question. He further states, in regard to school-furniture, that "no furniture was purchased except for first-class white schools." You testified yesterday in regard to expensive purchases made at Saint Louis.

Answer. Of expensive furniture, I did.

Question. He states that "it was necessary to purchase seats, desks, &c., for these schools; and the board, after investigation, found it cheaper to purchase furniture that would be permanent, than to have them made up of an inferior quality;" and then he states that "the following is a true statement of the cost of these articles;" first——

The WITNESS. Recollect one thing, he was charged in this public meeting——

The CHAIRMAN. Let me finish.

"Furniture for white schools	$1,678 70
Furniture for colored schools	none.
Maps, reading-charts, geographical charts, globes, blackboards, &c., furnished white schools	805 90
Maps, reading-charts, blackboards, &c., furnished colored schools	300 00
Total for furniture, maps, &c	2,784 60"

Now, are you prepared to say that is a prodigal expenditure of public money for furniture, maps, charts, blackboards, &c.?

Answer. I am not. I do not know anything about the cost of maps, whether it was extravagant or not. I only say that it is an extravagance for a man to give double what another will agree to furnish them for.

Question. Do you know that this furniture could have been bought cheaper in this market?

Answer. I do not know that there is any such made in the market.

Question. Do you know that these charts, globes, &c., could have been purchased here at all?

Answer. No, sir, I do not. I suppose they would have had to have gone to some other market.

Question. Then, are you prepared to condemn the purchase of these articles that I have just enumerated, all of which are essential to the education of children; are you prepared to condemn them as unwise or extravagant?

Answer. I will say this: if we were a prosperous people, and had anything to pay out of; if we could support things that would to others seem necessary, I would not object. What I call extravagant now, I would not have regarded as extravagant ten years ago at all, not at all. I would not regard a millionaire, who paid five per cent. tax on his property as bearing anything compared to what a poor laboring man, who had his wife and children, bore in paying one-half of one per cent. The millionaire could pay his five per cent. easier than the poor man could pay one-half of one per cent. on his property. Therefore I look upon it as extravagant.

Question. Do you regard this provision as extravagant, when you consider that the enumeration of your children entitled to the benefits of a common-school education was eight thousand and ten in number, and when, according to your own showing, the taxable wealth of the county outside of Columbus is between three and four millions? Do you regard the expenditure of $2,784.60 to afford those necessary facilities for the education of the children as extravagant?

Answer. Well, sir, if the figures be true, it would look like it was not. I am not prepared to say that those figures are true. Mr. Bishop was called in then to make his report. He said he wanted to explain, and did explain, and it was just about such as that.

Question. Has not this report been before the public ever since the 7th of June last?

Answer. Well, sir, the public had very little to do with public matters here.

Question. Was it not a circular published and distributed?

Answer. I do not know that it was. I suppose so.

Question. Have you ever heard the facts and figures in the circular successfully challenged?

Answer. I have heard them challenged to-day, but I do not know whether successfully or not. I do not know what you mean by successfully, and I do not know whether they were challenged successfully or not.

Question. He states in this report that "the total number of teachers in the county is fifty-six, forty-seven white teachers and nine colored teachers; number of white schools thirty-one, of colored schools twenty-five." Are you prepared to say that that is too large a number of teachers for the number of children enumerated in this county?

Answer. I am not; but I am prepared to say in regard to it, and I will get you facts and figures, and good evidence, that these teachers were employed at double what they could have been employed for.

Question. I am coming to that directly. I ask you now whether that number of teachers is too large for the number of children to be educated?

Answer. I should think not, sir.

Question. Now he states that the—

Aggregate of salaries contracted for teachers in white schools is	$14,190
Aggregate of salaries contracted for teachers in colored schools	6,200
Number of schools yet to open, in accordance with the school laws, to enable the county to receive the *pro rata* share of the State school-fund, about 7.	
Probable salary for teachers of these seven schools	1,120
Total	21,510

Are you prepared to say that that amount of money is an extravagant expenditure for that number of teachers?

Answer. I would say not; but I would say in addition, that is not all the money; that is only the direct tax levied by the county, or assessed here by the county directors, and ordered to be collected by the county supervisors from the people of the county, in addition to twenty thousand dollars they expected to get from the State of Mississippi as her due of the seven hundred thousand collected from the people for this purpose; a portion of the Chickasaw fund they expected, and three or four thousand from the town of Columbus, making in all about forty-five thousand dollars. That was the amount, as Mr. Bishop well knows, and the board knew they were to derive, to carry on the schools this year. When they asked for the twenty-one thousand they said that would do, and they were asked the question, "Why did you assess then about sixty thousand dollars on the people?" Well, it was something novel; we did not know. We found they were going it too high, too strong, and they reduced it to twenty-one thousand; and that in addition to the amount from licenses and other taxes, which they said would be twenty thousand—that was their own estimate—twenty thousand from Jackson, and then the Chickasaw fund, and three or four thousand from the town of Columbus.

Question. My question is distinct, and I wish it answered, whether $21,510 is too large a sum, in your judgment, to be expended in the payment of the whole corps of teachers throughout the county, exclusive of Columbus, for the white and colored schools for a school-year of five months?

Answer. Well, I hardly know how to answer that question. I will answer it again in this way: I do know that the editor of the paper here, who was in unison with the party in power, who was denouncing us for all these things, agreed in the presence of the people of Columbus that, having a full knowledge of the public schools, having been educated in Illinois in one, that he would take the contract, he would furnish good schools and houses throughout Lowndes County, and he would do it for twenty thousand dollars.

Question. Build and purchase school-houses and all, and furnish them?

Answer. He said he would take the contract and do it all. I don't suppose he would purchase seven-thousand-dollar school-houses.

Question. And purchase fuel?

Answer. They did not purchase fuel; there is not a solitary school in the county, that I have any idea, pays it; not one.

Question. Have you any idea that forty-six schools could be established here, and necessary provision for the education of the children, the furniture obtained, and teachers employed and paid, and the schools to continue for five months in the year for twenty thousand dollars a year?

Answer. They were employed only four months; at least that man told me distinctly that he was employed only four months.

Question. My proposition is five months; I go by this report.

Answer. I will say this, sir, from my knowledge of what was going on. I will give you a case here in town: Mr. Pope had a negro girl he was paying eight dollars a month, and she was very well satisfied; and they gave her sixty dollars to teach a school, when she would gladly have done so for fifteen or twenty; and I can give you a plenty of such cases.

Question. What would be a fair sum, in your judgment, to be paying to teachers competent to teach the various grades of school, white and colored? What sum per month would be, in your judgment, an adequate salary, considering now that there are thirty-one white schools and twenty-five colored schools?

Answer. I make no difference between the whites and blacks. A great many poor white people would teach school here now for half their teachers received, and would be glad to get it.

Question. Give us your estimate of how much a competent teacher ought to be paid per month; the teachers have to board themselves.

Answer. He ought to be paid more in some localities than in others.

Question. Average it.

Answer. Where people are unable to pay and have nothing to pay with, he ought to receive less compensation than where they are able. The first year I went to school I paid the teacher $5 a year. Ten dollars was the highest ever paid at that time. I went to school in the country. Ten dollars was regarded as perfectly extravagant, and that, too, teaching from sunrise to sunset.

Question. You evade the question.

Answer. I cannot answer the question. You ask me whether it was a large one or a small one. I think it depended on the circumstances entirely; the circumstances of the teachers employed and of the people who employed them, whether it would be a large salary. It would not have been a large salary in bygone times, but we can now get teachers out of employment, almost begging bread, for much less than is paid. We have a school down here of a high grade, as good a school as perhaps you will find in the southern country. Young ladies there are as competent as you can find anywhere in the world. They have a hundred and odd young ladies from different parts of the State and other States at that school, and these young ladies did not get any more than the negro woman of this county does who was taken from a cook-house there.

Question. Do you think that is just?

Answer. No, I think it is very unjust. I think it is very unjust that an incompetent person should get what a competent person ought to get. I do not think it equal. I think the qualifications of the parties ought to be taken into consideration.

Question. I want your opinion. I will put the question in a different form. What ought to be the compensation per month of a teacher competent to teach the highest branches taught in the common schools?

Answer. Well, sir, I will answer that by giving you what our teachers got here in our high schools. I know what they got. Fifty dollars a month to teach ten months, a good many of them.

Question. The teachers in your high schools?

Answer. It is the highest we have got.

Question. The highest you have in the city of Columbus?

Answer. No, sir; perhaps there are two ladies in that school that get $700 for ten months. That is the highest in the school. That is the maximum of any teacher in that school; $700 for ten months.

Question. That would be $70 per month?

Answer. Yes, sir. Some get $50, some $60.

Question. Is it worth more or less to teach in the country than in Columbus?

Answer. It is worth a great deal less.

Question. If it is worth $70 in Columbus what is it worth in the country per month?

Answer. I should suppose the expense would not be one-half what it would be in town.

Question. What is board worth in the country in respectable families?

Answer. I have no idea.

Question. It is worth $3 a day in Columbus, is it not?

Answer. No, sir, I reckon not, unless in some hotel. I reckon you can get board here for $25 or $30 a month.

Question. What would it be per month in the country?

Answer. I have no idea. I don't know anybody that boards in the country, and have never heard. I don't suppose it would be anything like as much.

Question. We want information on that point.

Answer. Your information on that point would be about like my own; you know that in all countries where men travel and live, board is higher in the town than in the country, and it is in about the same ratio in the country to the town here that it is in your country. You can go in a private family in the country and board a great deal cheaper than in a hotel. I have no data by which I could form an idea of what it would be in the country. I know nobody boarding in the country.

Question. If you cannot answer what would be the expense of a teacher per month for board, room, light, fuel, &c., how can you express an opinion what compensation a competent teacher should receive per month?

Answer. I will answer in this way, as I did yesterday: I think everything is worth what it will bring, as I told you about a tract of land. My property that I own in this sub-district, whatever it will bring in the market, that is what it is worth. Whatever a teacher will bring in the market, that is what he is worth. If he can be had for $15, for $20, or $30, he is presumed to be worth that much. If I can get one for $20 and you choose to get a good one for $50, and mine is as good as yours is, I think you have made a bad bargain. I do not know whether they can afford to teach for that or not, but if I can get them to teach for that, if they are willing to do it, I suppose they do not consider their services worth but that; it is all they can get; it is what the country gives.

Question. Is it your opinion that competent teachers could be obtained in the country and find themselves, to teach for less than $50 a month?

Answer. Well, sir, if the teachers employed by this board are competent—I do not say they are—I say they could be got for one-half of that; plenty of them.

Question. For $25 a month?

Answer. Yes, sir; just as many as you want.

Question. Of that $25 per month, how much would be consumed in their personal necessary expenses—board, washing, &c.

Answer. I have no idea, sir. Some, perhaps, would not consume more than a few dollars and others would run in debt. I have no idea what would be the cost of their sustenance.

Question. Have you any idea they could be boarded for less than three or four dollars a week?

Answer. By their own color they could.

Question. I spoke of white teachers?

Answer. I didn't know you were confining yourself to whites. I should suppose they could be boarded in the country for less than $3 a week.

Question. Two and a half?

Answer. I should think they could, within two and a half.

Question. That would be $10 a month for board. Does that include washing?

Answer. I recken so, n the country, for they generally do it in the country.

Question. That would leave $15 a month for services as teacher; do you think that an adequate compensation for teachers of white schools.

Answer. I do not know whether I am prepared to say I think it an adequate compensation or not. Men do not get adequately paid for what they do, frequently. I do not know whether they could live on it. I could not say. It might be regarded by some as a small pittance—a mere nothing. Others might think it a good salary, and they could save two or three calico dresses to go and teach school in.

Question. What would it probably cost for a teacher to cloth himself or herself?

Answer. That would depend entirely upon her taste and extravagance. Some men and women will dress on the tenth part of others.

Question. Don't you think the whole of the $25 a month would be consumed in board and clothing?

Answer. With some it would, and others would save half or two-thirds of it.

Question. Two-thirds?

Answer. Yes, sir; I have met with plenty in my life who would do it.

Question. Your opinion is that the children of the present day ought to be educated in the manner of their fathers?

Answer. I think they should be educated according to the means of the people.

Question. In log school-houses?

Answer. Yes, sir; in this country we have only log school-houses.

Question. Would you send your children to a log school-house?

Answer. I have no children. I have grandchildren. You ask me the question. I will answer it. Why, my grandson went to school in a house. I asked the carpenter what it cost; he says, "I will put up forty of them at ten dollars." He went to that school-house in this town. I sent him to that school-house that cost not more than $10.

Question. Is that school-house standing in Columbus now?

Answer. I presume it is.

Question. Is a common school taught in it?

Answer. There was. I am not certain whether it was taken down or not.

Question. How does that compare with your stables?

Answer. Nothing like so good. I have a much more costly stable.

Question. Then your children are educated in a building inferior to your stables; is that your policy?

Answer. Whether it is my policy or not, it is a house good enough, and I, in common with others, sent to this school. I say those who sent to this school were able to have had a better house. It was of plank put up and down. I do not know whether it is standing now or not.

Question. Was there any floor to it?

Answer. Yes, sir.

By Mr. BLAIR:

Question. You said that you sent your child to that school-house and were taxed for a $6,000 house.

Answer. Yes, sir; not for $6,000. I did not pay that tax because I did not live in the town; but I am paying my portion of a tax of three or four thousand for a fine building down here where the negro school is. I do not know how much they paid for it now. If you ask me how much this large negro school-building cost, where there are five hundred children, I cannot tell. There is a building these negroes go to for which, I presume, I pay. My own is a stable compared to that where my grandchildren went. It is worse than a stable—it is a back-house compared to it.

By the CHAIRMAN:

Question. The colored children need the same facilities for education white children do.

Answer. Yes, sir; I do not object to it. My objection is to any degree of extravagance, and that was the complaint in this whole taxation. It was not because negroes went to school; it was not because we did not want to educate the negroes; it was the extravagance and our utter inability to meet the taxes.

Question. Did not this board of directors act strictly in pursuance of law, and don't the thirty-first section of the school law require "that the board of school-directors shall, as soon as practicable, submit a report to the board of county supervisors, containing an estimate of the cost of school-sites, construction and rental of such number of school buildings as may be necessary to afford school facilities for each and every sub-school district in the county or city, and that they should also make an estimate of the necessary contingent expenses, such as repairs upon school-buildings, improvement of school-grounds, fuel, necessary school-apparatus, and any deficit in the teachers' fund which may arise?"

Answer. All of which they are bound to do.

Question. Very well; the laws required the board to make that estimate?

Answer. Yes, sir.

Question. Does not the very next section of the law require that it should be the duty of the county board of supervisors thereupon to levy a tax on the taxable property of each district sufficient to defray such estimated costs and expenditure for the district?

Answer. That is so.

Question. Then neither the school-board nor the board of supervisors exceeded their powers?

Answer. I say they did—both of them.

Question. Was it not imperative on the board of supervisors to levy the tax whenever the estimate was made?

Answer. I suppose it was imperative; but they ought not to have done a thing which they knew was burdensome.

Question. I notice in this law there is a limitation on their power; that not more than ten mills should be levied for school purposes or five mills for the teachers' fund. Did they exceed that limit in the estimates or levy?

Answer. I do not pretend to know.

Question. If they do not exceed the limits, they are within the law.

Answer. I do not deny but what they are within the law. I do not say they were not within the law.

Question. If there was a solitary expenditure for an improper purpose, were not the proceedings of the board of directors and the superintendent always open to the public—accessible to the public—so that they could be brought to justice if there was any corrupt use of money?

Answer. I have never known it to be so until now. It seems so now.

Question. Do you know that the sums you mentioned in your testimony yesterday have ever been paid? Do you know that there has been paid one hundred and fifty or one hundred and seventy dollars for the rent of school-houses in your sub-district?

Answer. I do not know what in the world has been done there.

Question. Do you know that $75 has been paid for a stove?

Answer. I do not know one solitary thing of what has been paid.

Question. Do you know that $50 has been paid for repairs of school-house?

Answer. I do not.

Question. Or $75 for wood?

Answer. I do not. I do not know what has been paid. I never inquired. I did not state that it had been paid. I stated that they had assessed it, and that first called our attention to the fact that they had made an assessment or estimate of what it would take to run that school. I told you that they afterward reduced that about one-half.

Question. Was the board of supervisors induced, by the action of this public meeting, to rescind the tax levied?

Answer. Not at all; they did it before the meeting took place.

Question. Do you mean to say no tax was levied and collected this year?

Answer. O, no.

Question. For common-school purposes?

Answer. None.

Question. There has been none collected?

Answer. None, sir.

Question. You say that this tax was repealed before this public meeting was held?

Answer. Yes, sir; I do.

Question. This public meeting was held in May?

Answer. The date of the paper will show, I think; it was about the 1st of June.

Question. This report is made on the 7th of June, after the public meeting, and says, in direct terms, that $21,000 was levied by the board of supervisors and the larger part of it collected by the sheriff?

Answer. There was no larger part of it, I don't suppose. I knew a portion of it had been collected, but I did not suppose the larger portion of it had. I paid mine.

By Mr. BLAIR:

Question. It was refunded?

Answer. Yes, sir; and when that board of directors told them they could run these schools successfully throughout the county for $21,000, and then, in addition to that, said, "We will get $20,000 from the State, and still get from the Chickasaw fund and others, making in all"—my recollection is, and my recollection corresponds with everybody else's I have had conversation with—"about $45,000"—that was the amount they would have, independent of this $21,000, to run the schools, and $20,000 from Jackson—that was their own estimate. I do not know that they have yet received it from Jackson; but they estimated that they would receive, of this $700,000 paid to the State, about $20,000; and we were advised by Mr. Stallings, the clerk, who said that he had corresponded with Jackson, and they were advised that that would be the amount for Lowndes County. With that, and the other funds arising from the sixteenth section and other sources, they could run the schools for that; and the board of supervisors rescinded this tax of $21,000. "If you can run it for that, do it," they said.

By the CHAIRMAN:

Question. Has not that tax been levied again?

Answer. Yes, sir; and levied on us now double. They had gone on in what we supposed to be their extravagance.

Question. What became of the board of supervisors that repealed that tax? Are they still in office?

Answer. No, sir; we change them here every few months.

Question. There is a new board?

Answer. Yes, sir.

Question. The new board has directed a new levy?

Answer. Yes, sir; for the following year—the coming year. We are paying two taxes this year, State and county, and everything else. We are paying State and county taxes both, twice. We have paid one State and county tax, and have to pay it again between now and the 1st of January. It is all over the State so. The legislature altered it; for what purpose, I do not know. Their motives were impugned; it was said they wanted it because they wanted to get hold of the distribution of it. We have been paying taxes in the spring, which suited us better. Our cotton was got out then, and we had the money; but this legislature said they would change it, and they have changed it now to the 1st of December, so that it forces us to pay two taxes this year. We have already paid one tax. It extends to every ramification of government, and everything is changed to pay the double tax this year before the 1st of January.

Question. Before the war the tax on real estate was very light, was it not?

Answer. It was all light, compared to what it is now.

Question. It was about one mill?

Answer. Yes, sir; it was very small.

Question. And you built no school-houses in the county except those that were built out of the sale of the sixteenth section?

Answer. No, sir; no public school-houses.

Question. You had, however, under your former system, your special taxes, had you not? Particular professions and occupations were taxed; lawyers, physicians, barbers, &c.?

Answer. I think not; bar-rooms were taxed, maybe.

Question. Barbers, I said?

Answer. I don't think they were taxed. There was nothing of the sort, I think; no special taxes. I presume licensed liquor-shops were taxed, but not as to professions.

Question. Are they now?

Answer. Yes, sir; my pocket-knife is taxed.

Question. By your State government?

Answer. Yes, sir; and by my county government and by my school government.

Question. Specific tax is it? Under what head?

Answer. In the first place, the State taxes it—my knife.

Question. Upon pocket-knives?

Answer. Yes, sir; everything, even to my spectacles, that I wear before my eyes.

Question. Are they enumerated?

Answer. The law says every species of property of every character whatever.

Question. Is not that right?

Answer. That is my knife. [Exhibiting pocket-knife.]

Question. Is it not right every man should be taxed according to the property he owns?

Answer. I think so.

Question. Why do you single out your knife as a subject of grievance?

Answer. I do not single it. I show that to show that everything is taxed?

Question. Was it not always so?

Answer. No, sir.

Question. In the good old slavery times, was not personal property taxed?

Answer. Yes, sir; but not specifically.

Question. You do not mean to say that your pocket-knife and spectacles are specifically taxed?

Answer. Nothing is specially enumerated.

Question. Was not all personal property taxed before the war?

Answer. It was specific; certain specific property was taxed before the war.

Question. What articles were taxed before the war?

Answer. There were very few.

Question. Tell the committee what they were.

Answer. I can only go so far as I am individually concerned. I will take my plantation: I have been a farmer all my life; my mules were not taxed; my farm utensils were not taxed; I had no specific tax, prior to the war, so far as I was individually concerned.

Question. Suppose you raised two or three hundred bales of cotton, were they taxed?

Answer. No, sir.

Question. Neither your mules nor farm implements?

Answer. No, sir.

Question. Nor the products of your soil?

Answer. No, sir.

Question. And only one-tenth of one per cent. on your lands?

Answer. I don't know that. I know the tax was light on lands.

Question. From what other source were your revenues derived?

Answer. I have no idea—various other resources of the State, as it is now. There is $700,000, I am told, to-day. I do not know the amount from various licenses. I do not know the amount myself. I made a memorandum to-day of the various sources of revenue to Mississippi that goes into this school fund.

Question. Are you speaking of the present system?

Answer. Yes, sir.

Question. I am speaking of the old system.

Answer. In the old system I presume billiard-saloons, and liquor-shops, and many other things were taxed that I had nothing to do with.

Question. But the planter, most able to pay, was taxed next thing to nothing.

Answer. No, sir; taxed as much as anybody else.

Question. How could that be if all his cotton, mules, and farm implements, and everything else were not taxed, and his cotton plantation only taxed one-tenth of one per cent.?

Answer. That one-tenth of one per cent. was when the profit was a great deal more than the whole of it is now.

Question. The real trouble now is that the planter has to pay according to what he is actually worth.

Answer. No, sir; the real trouble is the planter is not able to pay anything. I have tried it a few years, and I have rented it to the negroes and told them to take it for five years. I begged the white people of the county to take it for five years for $1,000 a year. I tried it last fall; I could not make anything at it, and I just got out of it, and about a month ago the negroes took it at $1,200 a year.

Question. That yields you about ten per cent. on what it is worth?

Answer. I suppose so.

By Mr. BLAIR:

Question. That is, if they can pay?

Answer. Yes, sir.

By the CHAIRMAN:

Question. You have not your rent secured?

Answer. No, sir; I have not a dime to secure it.

Question. If your rent is paid you get more than ten per cent. on the value of your property?

Answer. Estimating it at what I rented it for, I suppose it is ten per cent. on the value of the five hundred and thirty-one odd acres—say thirty-five.

Question. If your rent is paid according to contract, don't you get upon the valuation you have placed upon your plantation and all the personal property connected with it, more than twelve per cent. interest?

Answer. If it is paid I suppose I will get about ten per cent. interest.

Question. Is not that a good income upon fixed property?

Answer. Yes, sir; I think it is. It is not fixed, though, unfortunately. It is very unstable.

Question. According to your present system of taxation, Mr. Sykes, I understand that every man pays now according to what he owns?

Answer. Yes, sir; that is so.

Question. Do you find any fault with that principle of taxation?

Answer. Not a bit.

Question. Is it just?

Answer. I think it just. It is right.

Question. You promised yesterday to give me the rate of taxation that you paid upon your property—to combine all the taxes.

Answer. It was late when I left here yesterday evening, and looking for that book this morning, and being ordered here at 9 o'clock, and my tax receipts being scattered around town in different vaults, I had not time. I asked two or three gentlemen to give the taxation to me. "Take your tax receipts," I said, "and tell me what you are taxed." And one man says he is taxed—he is a clever man, Mr. Mitchell, a first-rate accountant—he says he is taxed three per cent.

Question. He lives in Columbus?

Answer. Yes, sir.

Question. I asked for the tax outside of Columbus.

Answer. It don't matter about that; it is the same.

Question. You have your municipal tax here, and I don't want it mixed up with the State, county, and school tax. It is frequently as much as all the rest combined. I want to know what is the rate of taxation outside of the city limits.

Answer. It is not less than two and a half per cent. outside of Columbus.

Question. Will you figure it up and tell us how you make it out two and a half per cent.?

Answer. I don't say it myself. I got others to do it. There is one. [Producing a memorandum.] One was handed me where he had each item specified; but I have lost that. I have never made any estimate of what it was; but it is not under two and a half per cent.

Question. I want you to figure it up. We are inquisitive gentlemen and ask for particulars.

Answer. Yes, and the impression is that you are prepared for these things. But I made no estimate, really, of these things. Here is a paper handed me by a man who made an estimate this morning. I asked him what per cent. he was paying. He has nothing in Columbus. "State tax, one-half of one per cent.; county, two-thirds of State;" then the "paupers" is one-third of the State tax, and the "railroad" one-half of the State tax.

Question. You can't figure out two and one-half on that. It makes it one and a quarter. Then one and a quarter is the rate of taxation outside of Columbus?

Answer. I suppose so; for he has no property in town.

Question. That settles the rate of taxation in Lowndes County?

Answer. No; I do not say that. It was just one man handed me this paper, and said he made an estimate of his tax; and I know he owns no property in Columbus. I don't know that he has got it right or all the entries on. He handed it to me. I do not know that is correct.

Question. Is he a reliable gentleman?

Answer. Yes, sir; as much so as any in this town.

Question. You applied to him as a business gentleman and asked him the question?

Answer. Yes, sir; I asked him what per cent. his tax was.

Question. Do you know anybody else outside of Columbus that pays a higher rate than one and a fourth?

Answer. I don't know whether they pay either that or more. I do not know what any man pays, outside or inside of Columbus.

Question. Do you know any man chargeable, outside of Columbus, for all purposes, with more than one and a quarter per cent.?

Answer. If you ask me if I know any man charged more than that, I answer I don't know, because I don't know whether he is charged more or less. I don't know anything about it.

Question. Then, outside of Columbus, a man who owns $100 of property is charged $1 25 for all purposes.

Answer. I don't know. You ask me whether that is so. I tell you I don't know. I only have the statement a man handed me here. And here is one a gentleman in town handed me makes it upward of three per cent.

Question. That does not afford us any light, because we are inquiring for those out of town.

By Mr. BLAIR:

Question. Does that, at one and a quarter, include the school tax?

Answer. No, sir.

Question. Therefore it does not include everything?

Answer. No, sir; it don't mention it. I called it over.

Question. Therefore it does not fix the tax our chairman is asking for.

Answer. No, sir.

By the CHAIRMAN:

Question. He properly made that out on the theory that the school tax was repealed and not re-enacted.

Answer. It is re-enacted, and we are called on now to pay it. Men are forcing cotton into the market to pay it.

Question. Have you had the curiosity to look into your books and ascertain the total assessments for every purpose in Lowndes County, to know what they amount to?

Answer. No, sir; but they amount to a good deal more than the people can pay.

Question. The treasurer's books would show that?

Answer. Yes, sir.

Question. The aggregate of all levied is considerably less than one hundred thousand for Lowndes County?

Answer. I cannot answer such a question without looking at the books to see. I am not familiar with it, and I am not prepared to answer it.

Question. I understood you to say yesterday you are a planter?

Answer. Yes, sir; that has been my occupation for a living.

Question. I believe you stated that you were a native of one of the Southern States; was it North Carolina?

Answer. Virginia. I did not state that, as I recollect.

Question. Were your in the South during the war?

Answer. I was, sir; in the State of Mississippi.

Question. Did you take any part in the war?

Answer. Well, sir, perhaps I did, to some extent.

Question. You know, and I do not.

Answer. I will tell you my position, now you have come to that. I am going to tell you everything connected with it. I have been politically through life, up to the time of the war, what is called an "old-line whig." Democracy I detested. I had been a whig all my life. I was totally opposed to this war, totally opposed to it. I had many difficulties, made many enemies here in the town of Columbus, urging the folly of going to war as we were. During the war I still spoke as I had and have here. I would not have spoken here perhaps half the words I have if I had known all this thing was being put down. I am one that always speak my opinion, and will do it if it is the last act of my life. I will tell what I think. During the war I still condemned it; I said we would be whipped all the time, inevitably be whipped, and that it would be the downfall of slavery; and when the first gun was fired, I recollect, I was down at the corner here when the news came of the first firing begun at Charleston, and I said, "Gentlemen, free your slaves; sell them, if you can; give them away, for that is an end of slavery." For this sentiment I was denounced here. I did not care for the denunciation; it was my honest conviction. I don't care for denunciation when that is at stake. I received letters through this post-office frequently, asking me to leave here and go North; that my sentiments were not such as were conducive to our interests here. They were anonymous; I do not know who from. Things went on, our country was invaded, and then I would have given the last dollar I had on earth to have whipped the North—the last dollar and life itself. I would have given everything.

Question. To have whipped the North?

Answer. Yes, sir.

Question. That is, to have whipped the Government of the United States?

Answer. Yes, sir. When I speak of the North, of course I speak of the Government of the United States. I did not want to be whipped. Since the war I have hated radicalism worse than I ever hated democracy. I hate them both to-day; but I would go for the devil himself before I would for radicalism, the present form of government; the rule and ruin, the devastation, putting negroes up at the polls that are no more fit to vote——it makes me completely outdone with the old Government. I often wish it was sunk.

Question. Do you go with the democrats now?

Answer. I don't go any way now.

Question. You vote?

Answer. Yes, sir; and I will vote against every radical that ever offers himself for office where I am.

Question. You go with the democracy?

Answer. Yes, sir; I go with what is called the democracy. I have no love for democracy, any more than I have for radicalism, not a bit; but such has been the action of the Government since the close of the war—I do not blame northern men. We were whipped, badly whipped, and I do not blame them for whipping us; it was what I would have done myself if I had been with them. I had no feeling against the northern people myself, nor had the southern people generally. If they had gone on and let us alone, we would have freed the negroes. We would never have attempted to enslave them again.

Question. You don't object to the Government for freeing negroes or to the republican party for that?

Answer. Not a bit.

Question. Do you object to the republican party giving them civil rights?

Answer. Yes, sir.

Question. Power to make contracts?

Answer. No; I do not. I do object to giving them the franchise.

Question. You don't object to their being invested with power to sue and testify in the courts?

Answer. Not a bit; it is very right.

Question. But you do object to the right of voting being conferred upon them?

Answer. Yes, sir; I am opposed to it, and I have ever been opposed to many white men voting. Before the war I did not think that many of them were fit to vote. The democracy would crowd up, and they did not know what they were voting for.

Question. Now that the negroes are made voters by law, are you opposed to their education?

Answer. Not a bit.

Question. You think they should be educated?

Answer. Yes, sir.

Question. You are willing to pay your fair share of taxes to educate them?

Answer. Yes, sir, perfectly willing, and I believe I speak for the people of Lowndes County. You will find some men different.

Question. But you would be in favor of taking away the right to vote.

Answer. Yes, sir.

Question. Would the democrats here generally?

Answer. Yes, sir; I think they would; that is, to a certain extent. I don't think they would take it entirely away; some negroes are capable of voting, and some have sense enough, and where they have education to justify voting, or where property to be protected would justify it, I think they ought to vote.

Question. Were you a slaveholder?

Answer. Yes, sir.

Question. How many slaves had you?

Answer. I had about one hundred and forty or one hundred and fifty.

Question. Valued, I suppose, at eight or ten hundred dollars apiece?

Answer. Yes, sir; I was offered a thousand dollars before the war for them, plantation and all.

Question. The general sentiment of the democratic party here now is opposed to negro suffrage.

Answer. No, sir, I do not say to negro suffrage; but to their unlimited suffrage. I have talked with pretty near all the democrats in the town and county. I have heard no objection to the negro who is capable of voting. If his education is sufficient they are willing for him to vote. If his property is sufficient to justify his voting to protect his property, they are willing.

Question. Your proposition would exclude the white man from voting also unless he had property and educational qualifications.

Answer. Yes, sir; I would do that if I had the power.

Question. Is that the sentiment of your democratic friends here?

Answer. I don't know what their sentiment is.

Question. Do they think with you on that subject?

Answer. They have done it in times past. I know in the State of Virginia negroes were allowed to vote who had property and in North Carolina too, for I lived near the line of North Carolina. No man was allowed to vote there in my day unless he owned a certain quantity of real estate in the county, and my judgment has ever been that suffrage has been too unlimited.

By Mr. RICE:

Question. The board of directors that levied this tax about which this public meeting was held, you say have gone out of office?

Answer. I do not know that any of them are in office. I think they have all gone out of office. I think the board of supervisors has been changed twice.

Question. Who was the chairman of the board.

Answer. B. G. Hendrick.

Question. What was his politics?

Answer. He was a whig; he acts with the radical party.

Question. With what party did the other four supervisors act?

Answer. I reckon every one acted with the radical party. I am not certain, but I don't think there was a solitary exception. Hendrick acts with the radical party. He has been appointed by Governor Alcorn sheriff. He is in unison with it.

Question. How about the other four?

Answer. I think they do, too. I don't know any exception.

Question. Do you know who they were?

Answer. I know most of them. If there was an exception it was a member from the southeast part of the county. I forget his name. I am not certain whether he was a radical or not.

Question. Name those who were radicals.

Answer. I think if there was a solitary exception he was the man.

Question. Name such of them as were radicals.

Answer. I really do not know that I can name all the board of supervisors. One was named Smith—Smith and Hendricks. I cannot think of the names. If I meet them in the street, I can call their names; but I cannot think of them now.

Question. Speaking of the tax in your school district, you say there was rent, fuel, and repairs charged there that never had been furnished or done?

Answer. Yes, sir.

Question. No rent had been charged and no repairs had been done?

Answer. No, sir; no fuel, no stove, and various other items—not one thing.

Question. Are you not aware that was not an estimate of what had been done, but an estimate of what should be done?

Answer. As I remarked just now, that was the original estimate as made by this board, and when the people became acquainted with the estimate and learned it, they complained and said it was too much; that they could not stand any such estimates, and they then reduced that estimate to about one-half.

Question. It did not purport to be money they had expended, but purported to be an estimate of what they would require to carry on the schools?

Answer. Yes, sir; that was it exactly; what they would expend.

Question. So that the fact that there was no stove there was no evidence that they were charging for it, and was no evidence of fraud?

Answer. The only evidence of that was that they were collecting the money. They were collecting the money to buy a stove with.

Question. They could not buy it until they collected the money?

Answer. Yes, sir; they bought the house and everything without money.

Question. They did not buy one there?

Answer. There is no telling what they did buy. As I said just now, it was a difficult matter to tell how much they had spent.

Question. On this estimate if the money was collected and any of these things that were estimated, such as fuel, rent, or repairs, cost less than the estimate, would not the money be left on hand there?

Answer. We did not suppose it would. That was my supposition. When money is once collected they don't keep it on hand in Mississippi, in Lowndes County.

Question. Would not the report show how much they expended for each item. Would not they have an account with vouchers for expenses?

Answer. We found that they had not done what the law required in many instances, for the county superintendent was instructed, when he collected money, (and he was authorized to collect money,) to put it immediately, says the law, into the hands of the county treasurer; but when that examination was made, we found he had collected money and that he had not deposited it with the treasurer. The county treasurer said he had never seen it—he had never deposited it there. Some two or three thousand dollars were in his hands. Whether he has ever paid it to this day, I do not know. That report states it. I have never inquired whether he has paid it over; he certainly had not then, and the law required him to go immediately and pay it in the county treasury, and from there it was to be drawn out under the warrant of the county supervisors. Instead of that he collected and appropriated it to other—I will not say appropriated, but he collected it, and there is no evidence at all—in fact, the county treasurer says he did not pay it into the treasury as directed.

Question. How long had he collected it?

Answer. Some time.

Question. From what source did he get it?

Answer. Perhaps that report will tell you. I do not remember.

By the CHAIRMAN:

Question. Do not all your school taxes have to be paid into the treasury?

Answer. Yes, sir.

Question. Who collects them?

Answer. The county superintendent.

Question. No, he collects from the old board of school trustees what is left in their hands; but he has no power to collect the tax.

Answer. No, sir; that is collected by the sheriff.

Question. He gives a bond and ample security?

Answer. Yes, sir.

Question. He pays it into the county treasury?

Answer. Yes, sir. There was nothing of that, sir; but Mr. Bishop, the county superintendent, had collected money, as he will acknowledge to-day.

Question. That was on those old township notes?

Answer. I do not pretend to say what it was on; but he had collected, and some two or three thousand had never been paid into the treasury. I do not know what the law permits him to collect from.

Question. Allow me to call your attention to his report, page 454, of Mississippi testimony, and read what he says on this very point:

"The board of school directors, in accordance with law, authorized the county superintendent, with the assistance of legal counsel, to collect the above funds, in order that they might be safely invested as required by the constitution and laws.

To this date, there has been received at this office	$5,982 63
Which has been disposed of as follows:	
Turned over to county treasurer, vouchers on file	4,640 57

Commission retained by attorney for collecting vouchers on file	$142 06
Paid by order of the board of school directors, and at their own responsibility, for school-house purposes, vouchers on file	1,200 00
Total..	5,982 63"

Are you prepared to controvert that statement?

Answer. Yes, sir; I am prepared to say that is not so. If that is the 7th of June, I say Mr. Bishop, at that time, had not paid the money over—the 7th day of June. Hold on ——

By Mr. RICE:

Question. Your report is published in the Columbus Index of the 1st of June?

Answer. I will take that back if that is the 1st of June, and Mr. Bishop's report is the 7th; I will take it back.

By Mr. BLAIR:

Question. But at the time of your report he had not?

Answer. He had not.

Question. How long had he had it in his hands?

Answer. I wish I knew the exact time; but it had been some time; I know there was great complaint of it.

By the CHAIRMAN:

Question. This school system was never put in force until this year?

Answer. No, sir; they commenced it, I think, in January.

By Mr. RICE:

Question. Do you know that he had got it from the sheriff, who collected it prior to the time he made his report?

Answer. I think that report of our committee tells where he got it from. Mr. Bishop was present when it was done and listened to the reading of this. I think this tells here, if I am not mistaken. [Examining his own report.] He received that money from the sixteenth-section fund: "With the laws in view, directing his course, the county superintendent has received $5,969 from sixteenth-section funds, according to his statements, made by him from his books, at various times, since the 1st of October, 1870, and up to May 15, 1871, had paid into the treasury only $2,628, leaving a balance in his hands to account for of $3,341, when it was his express duty to have paid over the entire amount, immediately on collection, to the treasurer again, while, as above expressed, the law authorizes only one person, the county treasurer, to pay out moneys of the school fund. The superintendent has paid out, by his statement, $1,800; some by order of the board of school directors and some without such order, including $332.30 to H. B. Whitfield (a school director) for collection fees," &c.; all of which was without law.

Question. You say the railroad tax here was voted for almost unanimously by the colored voters of the county?

Answer. Yes, sir; pretty much so.

Question. Didn't the white voters also vote for it?

Answer. What few voted did; but most generally they did not vote at all.

Question. The white people of the county were for it, were they not?

Answer. I doubt that very much.

Question. Why did they not vote against it then?

Answer. There was no use; they flocked here by the thousand. Why did not many white people vote the other day? Because it was unnecessary; it would do no good.

Question. It was nearly a unanimous vote for it?

Answer. I believe the votes given were almost entirely for it; very few voted against it. I think, probably, a majority of the white people of the county were against it; but those who voted were almost a unit. Those opposed to it did not vote at all.

Question. Taking the whole case, do you know of any money that has been corruptly or fraudulently expended by the officers of this county?

Answer. Having no dealings in any way with the officers or offices—for I attend to my own business—I do not know that I could say I do know of any. You ask me if I know of any; I do not; I have no knowledge of any.

By the CHAIRMAN:

Question. I want to mass together certain statistics before you leave the stand. I see that the census of 1870 puts down the population, white and colored, of Lowndes County at 30,862; I see that your map states that the area of the county is six hundred and one square miles; you have stated that the valuation of property in the city of Columbus for the purposes of taxation is between three and four millions of dollars?

Answer. Yes, sir; upwards of three.

Question. You have given the opinion that the property, real and personal, in Lowndes County, outside of the city of Columbus, is about an equal amount?

Answer. That opinion is based on the general opinion of the community.

Question. That would make, then, the total valuation of property, personal and real, in Lowndes County, including the city of Columbus, somewhere between six and eight millions of dollars?

Answer. Yes, sir; I will put it at six millions.

Question. Now the question which, in this connection, I desire to ask you is, how many cotton bales were raised in Lowndes County last year; what was the cotton product?

Answer. As simple a thing as that is, I have never refreshed my memory with it, though it could be ascertained in a minute here. All the offices here show what was the amount received. Those are matters I did not refresh my memory with. I could go out here and in ten minutes bring you a statement of every bale of cotton brought here last year.

Question. Is this a good cotton county?

Answer. Yes, sir, pretty fair.

Question. The land is of more than the average quality?

The WITNESS. Of the State generally?

The CHAIRMAN. Yes, sir.

Answer. Take the State generally, this is not as good as some other lands in the State.

Question. Not as good as the Mississippi bottoms?

Answer. No, sir.

Question. It is as good as the average of the State?

Answer. Yes, sir; it is good for an average of the State.

Question. It is as good as the counties along the State line of Alabama?

Answer. I do not know but that the counties of Green and along there are better than Lowndes.

Question. If you can't remember the number of bales, can you give the product in dollars?

Answer. I will say between twenty and thirty thousand bales; that is as near as I can give it.

Question. And they were worth $80 a bale last year?

Answer. No, sir, not that much; mine brought twelve and a half cents. Say sixty to sixty-five dollars a bale last year.

Question. It is worth $80 a bale now?

Answer. Yes, sir; good cotton is to-day worth about $80 a bale, at sixteen cents, for a bale of five hundred pounds.

Question. Is the product this year equal to that of last year?

Answer. No, sir; not so large.

Question. What proportion of your tillable land is put in corn? I want to learn from you about the division of crops. How much cotton and how much corn was raised?

Answer. Well, now, you include the county east and west of the river, and, mark you, east of the river is a poor, sandy country, and a great deal of corn is planted there. Take the whole county, I should say nearly one-half is put in corn.

Question. Your corn, on an average here, is worth about how much per bushel, year by year?

The WITNESS. How many years back will you go?

The CHAIRMAN. Two or three years back.

Answer. A dollar and upward. We didn't have half enough of it, and it took half the cotton to get the corn we wanted from Illinois and Kentucky.

By Mr. BLAIR:

Question. And Missouri?

Answer. Yes, sir.

By the CHAIRMAN:

Question. How much corn to an acre do you raise?

Answer. I cannot tell. I have seen acres that did not bring a quart. I have seen them make nothing. I have seen negroes plant, but not have the first nubbin.

Question. I am speaking of it as an average.

Answer. As an average it must be very small. It would be very small.

Question. Twenty or twenty-five bushels to the acre?

Answer. No, sir; nothing like that. Twenty-five bushels or twenty bushels would supply the demand for corn here, and we have generally imported, I should say, nearly half of our corn; one-third, at least, on the west side of the river.

Question. What other crops besides corn and cotton do you raise?

Answer. Very little of anything else.

Question. About what proportion of your county is in cultivation? I see you have considerable wood-lands.

Answer. I think about three-quarters; a great many would say not so much as that. When I say in cultivation I mean it is planted; but many times the negro does not make anything; the negro makes nothing sometimes.

By Mr. BLAIR:

Question. In reference to these school matters, you complained of great extravagance, considering the condition of the country, and you also complained of fraudulent misapplication of the funds?

Answer. We feared it and complained of it; and in that particular instance we found that the money had not gone according to law.

Question. Did you not have a conversation with this superintendent of schools? Did you not arrange and consent to the use of your school-building; and did he not well know that there was no rent to be charged?

Answer. He did know it; no doubt of it.

Question. Then his estimate or charge was fraudulent?

Answer. I should call it fraud; I should call that fraud, where a man states a thing he knows is not so.

Question. In respect to the other school-house in your own school-district, was there any arrangement made to pay rent for it?

Answer. Not one particle, as I am advised by a letter from the gentleman in whose yard the house is located, and it belongs to him.

Question. Then was not the estimate in respect to that school-house fraudulent and false?

Answer. Well, sir, it certainly was a false representation to say they were going to pay for things that they had no idea of, and knew and were told they had nothing to pay for.

Question. In respect to the wood, the fuel that was used at your school-house, for which there was an estimate made, was it not well known and understood that there was to be no charge made for the use of the fuel?

Answer. They certainly could not have understood that there would be any charge made for that fuel.

Question. That was also false and fraudulent?

Answer. It was.

Question. And in respect to the other matters, the repairs, none had been made?

Answer. Not a bit.

Question. And none were contemplated?

Answer. None in the world. Let me stop you right there. You say none were contemplated; they were not. I came home from there, and remarked one day to the board, "If you are going to continue your school down yonder you must spend about $50 on that house; it leaks, and it needs about two or three hundred feet of plank there to make it comfortable." They forthwith—for they were in session at the time—or, anyhow, I was advised the next day that they had made the appropriation of $50 for the repairs of that house, and had appointed me to attend to it and have it done. This was after the appropriation of $50 had previously been made; rent, one hundred and fifty; repairs, fifty; they told me that they had made an appropriation of $50 to repair it, and wanted me to do it; I did not do it; the lumber was high.

Question. These things all being within your own knowledge, that there was no rent charged in either of these cases and no rent to be paid—this estimate which pretended that there was a rent to be paid and the other matters to which I have referred being within your own knowledge, and you knowing that there was no such amount to be paid for fuel and other matters—was not that conclusive to your mind that it was a fraudulent attempt?

Answer. There can be no other conclusion to any rational being.

By Mr. RICE:

Question. Do you know the date of that estimate?

Answer. I do not.

Question. Do you know they knew, at the time that estimate was made, that neither you nor this other man were going to charge rent for the houses?

Answer. Yes, sir; they did know that I was not.

Question. If you do not know the date of the estimate, how do you know they knew that when the estimate was made?

Answer. I know they knew it before any school was established; they came to me and asked me, and I told them.

Question. Did they not make the estimate before they established the school?

Answer. I do not know; I do not pretend to know that.

By Mr. BLAIR:

Question. You saw the estimate that was made in the office where it properly belongs?

Answer. I did.

Question. Did you see that estimate before or after you had the conversation with the superintendent of schools in referencce to the use of your school-house?

Answer. Long, long after. It was in January I spoke to him, and this was in the month of June—by the last of May if not the 1st of June.

Question. That estimate spoke of other transactions, of other school-houses bought; had this school-house been bought prior to the conversation had with you in reference to this matter in January?

The WITNESS. Do you mean school-houses in the same, or other districts?

Mr. BLAIR. In other districts which are estimated in this report?

Answer. Well, sir, that assessment and that report in record in the court was there long before they knew about—it was there long before the tax commenced to be paid, and not until the people commenced to pay their taxes did they know that estimate had been reduced; but the complaint of the people caused them to reduce it about one-half. That estimate was reduced—for instance, that $150 house, that $50 repairs, $75 wood-bill, and the $75 stove, and various other items, making $3,800—was reduced about one-half.

By Mr. RICE:

Question. Before the collection commenced?

Answer. Yes, sir; before the collection commenced—just about one-half; and the people were going on paying that estimate of one-half. I went and paid mine. Many had paid it, and it was still what we thought very burdensome. We thought they had received too much money. We did not know what they would do with it unless they spent it foolishly—the way they were doing.

By Mr. BLAIR:

Question. Our chairman asked you what was taxed in the good old times of slavery; do you suppose he meant to eulogize those times, or merely to have a fling at you and your people?

Answer. Heaven knows! we have been flung at enough. If he wants to fling any more at us, I pity the man that could have the heart to do it. I can only pity him. If being ruled by negroes, mobbed by them, killed by them, and everything of the sort—but I do not want to talk about that.

By the CHAIRMAN:

Question. I wish to ask one further question, and that is this: If those estimates had been collected just as you saw them upon the book of the board of directors, $3,800 first, and $1,900 after the reduction, would not the money have all remained in the treasury, subject to future use, unless in point of fact the rent had been paid to you and to your neighbor, and unless those repairs had been made upon the school-houses, and this $75 had been expended for wood—would not the money have all remained in the treasury?

Answer. I answer—you ask me what I think would have been done in future—I answer, most emphatically, I do not believe one solitary dollar would have ever been paid; that is my opinion; that those that collected it and had it in hand would have used it for their own benefit.

By Mr. RICE:

Question. It could not have been got out of the hands of the county treasurer without an order from the board?

Answer. It was all paid to his hands. The report shows he did not——

By the CHAIRMAN:

Question. I will ask whether every dollar levied by the board was not required to be paid into the county treasury?

Answer. It was, every dollar.

Question. Then, if those estimates had been collected, would not they have been paid, in pursuance of law, by the sheriff, into the county treasury?

Answer. The sheriff did not collect all of them by a good deal.

Question. If the tax had not been repealed, if the sheriff had proceeded to collect all the taxes assessed, including those estimates, was not he bound by the law to pay the money collected into the treasury?

Answer. He was. The law compelled Mr. Bishop to do it, but he did not do it.

Question. I will come to that directly. Then, could the county treasurer have paid out this money except upon an appropriation made by the board of directors?

Answer. The county treasurer complained to the citizens that he could not get the money out of his hands into the treasury.

Question. I am speaking of the taxes levied.

Answer. That was tax-money received by the superintendent for school purposes.

Question. I am coming to that directly. I am speaking now of the taxes levied by the board of supervisors. Had any officer power to collect them, except the sheriff?

Answer. None, but——

Question. Had any other officer the right? Must not he, by the law, pay it into the county treasury?

Answer. But I will say no, even to that question. I don't know whether he was. I don't know what the law was. I know he was bound to do certain things. You have the law before you. I don't know whether he was or not. I will not state a thing that I don't know to be so. I know there were certain moneys he was authorized to collect.

Question. Now, was the county superintendent authorized by the board of school directors to collect any other funds whatever, except those that were in the hands of the old school trustees?

Answer. Probably not. Probably that was the law.

Question. Did any other moneys come into his hands, as superintendent of the schools, except those that he was thus authorized by the board of school directors to collect?

Answer. I don't know that. I don't know whether any other came to his hands or not.

The report referred to by the foregoing witness, James Sykes, as published in the Columbus, Mississippi, Index, June 1, 1871, is as follows:

REPORT OF THE INVESTIGATING COMMITTEE.

The meeting was called to order by the chairman at 11 o'clock, pursuant to adjournment. Mr. George E. Redwood, secretary of the committee, then made the following report:

Indebtedness, assessment, and amount not collected.

The total indebtedness of the county could only be approximated. To insure exactness in ascertaining it and reducing to precise figures would require more time and labor than the committee could give to the subject. Our investigation began at the point where the grand jury was supposed to have left off in 1869, and taking their results as correct. We would have been greatly assisted in this matter if the board of supervisors had complied with the law in making, at the end of last year, a detailed report of the receipts and expenditures, and a statement of the financial condition of the county. This they failed to do. The grand jury referred to gave the following figures:

County warrants outstanding	$35,887 85	
Pauper warrants outstanding	10,146 79	
Jury tickets (estimated)	5,000 00	
		$51,034 64

There have since then been issued, (1st February, 1869, to 13th May, 1871:)

County warrants	$21,383, 01	
Pauper warrants	7,303 13	
		28,686 14
Total		79,720 78

Of this amount the following have been taken up and canceled:

County warrants	$45,098 02	
Pauper warrants	9,536 95	
		54,634 97
Leaving outstanding		25,085 81

Of this amount probably $5,000 consists of warrants and jury tickets that have been made out but have not been, and perhaps will never be, called for and used against the county, so that we think we are safe in estimating the indebtedness of the county for all purposes as not exceeding $25,000, and we do not think there are over $20,000 outstanding valid warrants.

As to assessments to meet the county debts, we could not learn from the members of the board, or its clerk, that taxes were assessed upon any recognized plan or principle —further than that of following precedents established by previous boards, and levying a round amount of tax without knowing whether it would raise more or less money than was required for county purposes; in fact, we could not ascertain upon what basis of needed supply assessments were made, and it would seem that no examination or inquiry was made with a view to ascertain the necessities of the county in order to levy a suitable tax to provide for them, but a per centum tax, supposed to be *large enough*, levied blindly. The result is that, to meet general county purposes, requiring annually not over $15,000, a tax is levied that, by the assessor's books, will bring in over $30,000. The requirements for pauper purposes, as evidenced by the warrant-book, (which shows the warrants issued for current expenses,) do not reach $3,000 a year; yet the tax of 33⅓ per cent. on our State tax shows an assessment for that purpose of over $10,000; so with the other county expenses, the warrants issued for other than pauper purposes have not exceeded, annually, since the 1st of January, 1869, $9,000, yet the tax levied, 66⅔ per cent., on State tax, shows an assessment of over $20,000. In this connection your committee would respectfully suggest that as the poor-house reports show an average of not over fifteen persons during the year, that it is an absurdity to suppose that the requirements of this service should take up one-third of the present income of the county, and that it is an outrage on the community that ought at once to be abated.

The committee have compiled from the records the following tabulation of assessments, collections, and insolvencies for the taxes of the years 1868–'69:

Assessment for 1868: county tax, 100 per cent. on State, $23,674; pauper tax, 50 per cent. on State, $11,837; total $35,511—50 per cent. more than allowed by law. Amount collected: county tax, $13,286; pauper tax, $6,630; total, $19,916. Insolvencies: county tax, $10,388; pauper tax, $5,207; total, $15,595. Cotton tax collected, 5,341; cotton tax collected for 1866, $4,140; insolvent tax for 1867, $2,405; total, $31,802.

Assessment for 1869: county tax, $20,995; pauper tax, $10,498; total, $31,493. Collections: county tax, $13,176; pauper tax, $6,587; total, $19,763. Insolvencies: county tax, $7,819; pauper tax, $3,911; total, $11,730. There is no record or report from Sheriff Kline of his collections of taxes on cotton; but, as near as can be estimated from various official resources, it amounted to $9,638; making the total collections for 1868–'69, $61,203. This amount was disposed of as follows: In cancellation of county warrants, $45,098; of pauper warrants, $9,536; total, $54,635. Leaving a balance to be accounted for of $6,568. This was probably disposed of in paying sheriff's and treasurer's commissions, judges' salary, and some small items, as coroner's warrants, &c.

In the above calculation the amounts collected and paid out on account of Hill's bridge and railroad tax are not included.

The result shows a county tax collected in two years of about $60,000, while the average issue annually of warrants does not exceed $12,000, ($24,000 in two years,) and the amount canceled was $54,500 in the same time; thus showing a rapid reduction of amount outstanding, and leading to the opinion that there cannot be outstanding at present an excessive amount; and it may be that nearly the entire balance will be used in the payment of the taxes for 1870.

POLL-TAX.

The committee deem it proper to invite the attention of the community and the appropriate officers of the law to the matter of poll-taxes. In 1869 the number of polls assessed was 4,266, and the board of police have indorsed on their minutes that after a careful examination they did approve the assessor's report in all things; so, also, they did with the assessor's report for last year, 1870, which shows the number of polls assessed 3,832, over 400 less than the preceding year. If we take the votes of the county, which exceeded 6,000 in 1867, as a basis to estimate the number who are liable for poll-tax, there should be at least 5,000 polls taxed, paying $10,000 tax annually. It would seem, therefore, that the poll-tax has not been fully assessed, and that a careful examination of these assessments on the part of the board of police, as the law requires, would have resulted in a much larger assessment. Besides this, it would follow that many of those who were not assessed for poll-tax escaped assessment, also, for property tax, and if a full assessment had been made a much larger amount would have been assessed and a larger collection made, and thus the treasury would be in a better condition than at present. In this connection the committee would state that their investigations disclose a great deal of indifference and laxity on the part of officials generally in the administration and execution of the law and of the duties imposed upon them—and for which they are paid.

HILL'S BRIDGE.

In regard to the tax levied to pay warrants issued to Green T. Hill for Hill's bridge, the amount issued originally, September, 1866, was for $10,000. The judgment calls for this amount, with interest at 8 per cent. from that time. In 1869 a special tax was levied to raise the amount of 50 per cent. on the State tax. This, if all collected, would have brought in, from other sources than cotton, $10,498, and the cotton would have swelled it (25 cents per bale) at least $2,500, making in all $12,998. The amount collected, however, and reported by Sheriff Kline, is (as per report of Swearingen, treasurer) $7,750; by Sheriff Dowsing, $1,090, making in all $8,840. The amount reported to have been paid over to Mr. Harrison, attorney for Hill, by treasurer Swearingen, is

$8,841, leaving still due on this account $1,159; and the accrued balance of interest which would swell the actual balance due to between $3,000 and $4,000.

NOTE.—While Mr. Swearingen's report gives $7,750 as amount received from Sheriff Kline for special tax collections, the amount set down in the books is, in one entry, $8,389, and afterward there is an entry of $1,051, making, apparently, this amount collected $9,440. (See report on treasury.) This one matter will give an idea of the confusion existing in the official records.

MEMPHIS AND SELMA RAILROAD BONDS.

This important subject has occupied the grave attention of the committee. The ordinance passed by the board of supervisors in July, 1869, was to the effect that the bonds of the county, to the amount of $150,000, should be issued to the president of the road "on and after the 1st day of November, 1869, in payment for the amount of capital stock, in such sums and at such times as the same may be wanted and needed, to survey, grade, construct, and equip said railroad from the State line to Columbus, and thence through said county." It would appear from this clearly that the bonds were not to be issued all at once, but only as the work progressed, and when the road was about completed through the county, then only the last bonds were to issue; just as is done with private parties subscribing to stock, who pay from time to time a portion of such subscription, until the last payment is needed to complete the work. These bonds, however, were all issued, as we learn, at the same time, and before the work had made any progress. Meanwhile our people, through this act of the board of supervisors, are being taxed for $20,000 in 1869, and $15,000 in 1870, to meet the entire $12,000 interest on these bonds, when there should not, it appears to us, have been more than half of them issued—that is, instead of paying $15,000 tax for railroad purposes, we should be paying not over $6,000. The committee are of the opinion that this matter demands from our people such action as will lead to a legal investigation and opinion as to whether the bonds so issued may not be partially annulled, until the completion of the railroad through the county, thus saving us a large amount of tax in the interim. The committee inquired for a copy of the bonds given to the railroad, but, strange to say, no copy of so important a document was on record on the supervisor's books.

SCHOOL MATTERS.

In regard to the public schools, the committee find that warrants have been issued by the school board for $21,500, and by the board of supervisors, for pay to members of that board and to county superintendent, of about $2,000 more, making a total expenditure for educational purposes of, say $23,500. Of this amount—

Warrants were issued to teachers, about	$10,600
For school furniture, freight, and expenses	3,600
For school sites, buildings, &c	6,500
Expenses, &c	600
Total	21,300

The committee find that the board of school directors have confided very large discretionary powers to the county superintendent, authorizing him to do this, that, and the other; requesting him to visit Saint Louis, to buy school furniture and inspect the position of public schools; requesting him to appoint Mr. H. B. Whitfield to collect sixteenth-section funds, (for which collection he allows Mr. Whitfield five per cent. for collection;) authorizing him to make contracts with teachers, to assign them to their stations, and allow such pay as he thinks proper; in fact, the whole burden of their duties seem to have been thrown upon the superintendent's willing hands. In fact, the board appear to have substantially given him *carte blanche* in the discharge of his duties. In addition to the large amount ($3,600) allowed him to pay for school furniture and freight, his expenses to and from Saint Louis and to and from Jackson, where he went at the suggestion of the board, on school business, there was also allowed him the amount of Chickasaw school fund in the hands of the board of supervisors to pay for school furniture at West Point, amounting to $695. The history of this money is curious. It was turned over to and received by the board, by Mr. Spiers, when he left office, in July, 1869. The law requires this fund to be used exclusively for school purposes, and does not authorize the board of supervisors to receive and pay out any money whatever; and yet after receiving this money, the president of the board paid out over $400 of it for county and pauper purposes, for which there are vouchers, leaving a balance of $225, which the committee have not been able to find any account of. Though the receiving of this money was not strictly legal, yet there were circumstances at the time which seemed to justify it; but the using of it being entirely illegal, the board ought to account for it, as it was disbursed by the then president thereof. The county superintendent has been directed by the board of school directors to take proper steps to recover the funds.

The question of the school-tax having been dismissed by the action of the board of supervisors, the committee did not proceed further into the examination of it. The county superintendent informed us that he would shortly issue a report giving details of the state of the schools, number of teachers employed, salaries, &c. Our examination resulted in finding that there were about sixty teachers employed, at salaries ranging from $150 to $25 per month, but the largest number were paid from $65 to $85 per month. The superintendent could not inform us how many scholars were in attendance at the various schools of the county, and the committee were somewhat astonished to find that, though he employed a book-keeper, yet no statistics as to school matters in the county could be given us, except that in the city of Columbus there were nine teachers employed, 520 scholars in attendance, 120 white and 400 colored. The committee regret not being able to give more information in regard to school matters, but trust that the superintendent's forthcoming report will cover the whole subject.

The community having intimated a desire to have the subject of finances, as intrusted to the county superintendent, fully examined, the committee looked scrupulously into that subject, and make report as follows:

Section 25.—The law organizing the school system of the State directs, in section 25, that the county treasurer shall receive and pay out all school funds and make quarterly reports to the board of school directors, who shall examine and approve the same, if correct. The committee do not find any part of this law complied with, except that the treasurer has received *some* school funds.

Section 24 directs that the board of supervisors shall issue warrants for the pay of the county superintendent upon his report, approved by the board of school directors, contained in a field-book of operations. This we could not find nor hear anything of, but did find that warrants were issued for his pay, amounting, up to April 3, 1871, to $685.

Section 1 of amendments to above law, directs that the board of school directors to succeed to section boards of trustees, and therefore to receive all moneys due from sixteenth-section funds.

Section 2 of same directs that the county superintendent, by and with consent of the school board, shall demand and receive all moneys due it, and to bring suit and employ competent legal counsel, and to turn over all collections to the county treasurer, as directed by the general school law, and this law directs—

Section 43, that any officer authorized to receive moneys of school fund, shall pay it over to the county treasurer immediately, and, on failure to do so, makes it the duty of the school board to proceed at law against him, and the court is authorized to award judgment and damages the same as against a defaulting sheriff.

With these laws in view, directing his course, the county superintendent has received $5,969 from sixteenth-section funds, according to his statements, made by him from his books, at various times since the 1st of October, 1870, and up to May 15, 1871, had paid into the treasary only $2,628, leaving a balance in his hands, to account for, of $3,341, when it was his express duty to have paid over the entire amount, immediately on collection, to the treasurer. Again, while, as above expressed, the law authorizes only one person, the county treasurer, to pay out moneys of the school fund, the superintendent has paid out, by his statement, $1,800, some by order of the board of school directors and some without such order, including $332.30 to H. B. Whitfield, (a school director,) for collection fees and legal services. The board of school directors also ordered a warrant to issue to H. B. Whitfield, for legal services, of $50. A portion of this money, some $1,200, has also been used to make part payment on the school-house at Crawford, which Mr. Bishop, superintendent, was directed by the board to pay to Mr. Turner, the seller of the house, (though collected in another school section,) expecting to pay it out of moneys to be collected by the school-tax. As that has been rescinded, the question is, how are the board and the superintendent to escape the legal difficulties now surrounding them in this matter?

After allowing for payments made by the superintendent, he acknowledged to a balance on hand, due the treasury, of $1,500. This statement concludes the results of our examination into school matters.

COUNTY TREASURY.

The affairs of the county treasury have given the committee more trouble and are more embarrassing to report upon than those of any other department. Mr. Swearingen, the present treasurer, entered into office about the 1st of August, 1869, and took charge of an empty treasury.

Section 29.—The law directs the treasurer to report to every regular meeting of the board of police, (or supervisors,) and these reports to be recorded by the clerk of the board of supervisors, in a book kept exclusively for that purpose. These reports are to be carefully examined, compared with the vouchers, approved by the board, and a copy posted, within five days after recorded, at court-house door. On examination, the committee found only one report recorded in the treasurer's docket, though another paper was produced, stated to be a treasurer's report, which contained a short, condensed statement of receipts and expenditures. Of this further on.

Section 31 requires that every settlement made by the board with the treasurer, or his reports, his accounts and books, shall be examined and compared, by the board, with the register of warrants issued. The committee had no means of verifying whether this was done or not, but are of the opinion the careful examination required, and the comparison of warrants with the register was omitted, because any examination into the books of the treasurer would show such glaring inconsistency, when compared with the reports, as could not fail to have been noticed. In fact, the "memorandum" books offered by the treasurer for the examination of the treasury were not such as the law evidently intended should be kept by him, and would be too much honored in being called "treasurer's books." This whole business, the regular inspection of the treasury department, evidently intended and provided for by the law, seems to be entirely slurred over and neglected, and the committee have been forced to the conclusion that the financial condition of the county and the treasury are in a state of complete chaos, and it will be the work of months to bring it to an intelligible and reliable condition. The treasurer's books should verify the sheriff's report as to his payment into the treasury, and of course these books should tally with the treasurer's reports. Yet, while we find that the board of supervisors have entered on their minutes their approval of Treasurer Swearingen's first report, and, by consequence, that they have compared it with his "books," we find, on reference to his books, that it is impossible to make the report and the books agree.

The report is as follows:

TREASURER SWEARINGEN'S FIRST REPORT.

Receipts from Sheriff Kline:		
City taxes collected	$23,548 05	
Poor taxes collected	11,774 02	
Special taxes collected	7,450 60	
Railroad taxes collected	10,155 05	
		$53,229 72
Expenditures:		
County purposes	27,653 06	
Poor purposes	5,812 41	
Special bridge purposes	7,783 40	
Railroad purposes	10,099 30	
Commissions of sheriff	2,120 98	
		53,469 15
Excess of expenditures due treasurer		241 43

TREASURER'S BOOKS.

The treasurer's memorandum shows his affairs in such confusion that we do not suppose he claims to understand them himself, and, as near as we could make out, his receipts and expenditures are as follows:

Cash receipts—Sheriff Kline:		
County tax	$1,756 39	
Pauper tax	7,591 00	
Special tax	8,389 67	
Other sources	228 50	
		$17,965 56
County warrants:		
Kline	21,791 66	
Cashed	3,003 18	
		24,794 84
Pauper warrants:		
Kline	4,183 02	
Cashed	1,991 20	
		6,174 22

DISPOSITION OF CASH.

		$17,965 56
Commissions to Sheriff Kline	$1,373 12	
Commissions to Treasurer Swearingen	1,319 95	
Salary to Judge Van Hook	2,090 00	
County warrants to G. B. Hendrick	400 00	
County warrants to Treasurer Swearingen	762 00	
County warrants on account Jamison's bridge	592 86	
County warrants sundry purposes	1,248 32	
Pauper warrants to B. G. Hendrick	1,601 60	
Pauper warrants, sundry parties	389 60	
Hill's Bridge	7,783 48	
		17,560 93
Balance due county		404 63

WARRANT ACCOUNT.

Total warrants received in Treasury:

Pauper	$6,174 22
County	24,794 84
Total	30,969 06

Disposed of:

Amount turned over to and canceled by board of supervisors, as per report:

Pauper	$5,812 41
County	27,653 06
Total	33,465 47

Thus there were more warrants turned over and canceled than, by the treasurer's books, were received into the treasury.

Of pauper warrants:

Amount received by him	$6,174 22
Amount canceled	5,812 41
Balance, not canceled, on hand	361 81

County warrants:

Amount received	$24,794 84
Amount canceled	27,653 06
Balance, (more canceled than received)	2,858 22

There are other entries of amounts received, in the treasurer's books, but it was impossible to know whether or not they were included in the large amounts reported to have been received from Sheriff Kline. Mr. Allen, who kept the books for Mr. Swearingen, stated, however, that they were received *after* the larger entries were made. They are entered on a different page from the larger entries. If this is correct, then the book will show as follows:

Cash received as above	$17,965 56
Cash received since	2,200 00
	20,165 56
Cash paid out	17,560 93
Balance cash due county	2,604 63
Pauper warrants received as above	6,174 22
Pauper warrants received since	2,853 81
	9,028 03
Canceled	5,812 41
Balance due county	3,215 62

Amount cash and pauper warrants due county	$5,820 25
Amount county warrants due treasurer	2,858 22
Balance due county	2,962 03

TREASURER SWEARINGEN'S REPORT.

It will be noted that in his report Treasurer Swearingen acknowledges having received from Sheriff Kline for pauper tax the amount of $11,774.02, and that all the warrants for payment on that account are $5,812.41, leaving balance due treasury, $5,961.61.

The question arises what disposition was made of this amount? It was not expended, though it was collected for pauper purposes and should be on hand, if not spent; and, if spent for other than pauper purposes, it was a misapplication of funds, and makes the treasurer liable to be proceeded against at law. Well, the evident facts are, as the books show—

The pauper tax collected and received by Treasurer Swearingen	$11,774 02
Of which was in warrants	4,183 02
Balance in cash	7,591 00
Of which was paid out for pauper warrants	1,991 20
Leaving an actual cash balance of	5,559 80
Usable only for pauper purposes, and it was applied partly—	
To pay Judge Van Hook	2,090 00
To pay Sheriff Kline	2,120 98
To pay Treasurer Swearingen	1,319 95
Total	5,530 93

The committee do not claim that these figures are, all of them, correct exponents of the facts, but only that they correctly represent the treasurer's report and the treasurer's books. As before stated, it was found impossible to make the two coincide and agree. Had the treasurer made regular reports to the board of supervisors, as required by law, and had the supervisors examined his reports and books, as required by law, carefully, the present confusion in treasury matters might have been avoided, and the board of supervisors could have made, at the end of the fiscal year 1870, that useful and important statement which the law directed, showing the receipts and expenditures for the year, and the indebtedness and financial condition of the county.

ESTIMATE FOR BASIS OF TAXATION.

As heretofore taxes seem to have been levied without regard to any intelligible principle, and the maximum of tax allowed by law always imposed upon the people, the committee have deemed it well to lay before the meeting an estimate they have made, to show the amounts probably needed to provide current annual county expenses. In arriving at this, they considered that the amount of warrants issued annually would serve as the most reliable and practical guide; and, on investigation, find amount, in dollars, of warrants issued from 1869 to 1871—two years and four months—was in round numbers, $28,000.

The average amount per year, therefore, was	$12,000
Of which the actual average issue for pauper purposes is	2,600
Leaving for county purposes	9,400
Adding to this 33⅓ per cent., for expense of collection and for allowance for taxes that would not probably be collected, we get, as the needs of the county, annually	$16,000

The simple problem, then, is what percentage on the State tax will be necessary to raise this amount?

The State tax or property for this year is	$31,000
If a thorough assessment were made it would be at least	$34,000

Fifty per cent. on this amount would bring a county income of $17,000, more than sufficient for the liberal estimate of necessities.

The present tax is 100 per cent	$31,000

Fifty per cent. on State tax, divided into 35 for county purposes	$10,850
And 15 for pauper purposes	4,650
Would afford an income of	15,500

upon the basis of the present assessment.

The committee are of opinion that with proper economy this amount will more than pay all the current expenses of the county annually, and thus enable the board of supervisors to reduce the present tax 50 per cent., or one-half; and they respectfully suggest to the meeting a careful consideration of this subject and appropriate action to secure the practical benefits to accrue from the adoption of the committee's suggestion.

The committee beg to suggest, also, that the custom has been among collectors of revenue and treasurers to pay themselves their commissions, and they think this custom is not founded in law, and is a baleful one. They are of opinion that the law requires that reports of such officers shall first be submitted to the board of supervisors, and that all moneys received be promptly and *in toto* handed in to the treasurer, and acknowledged and receipted for by him, and, when these reports are examined and approved, that then warrants for their commissions be issued by the board of supervisors. In this way an exact account of county finances can be kept, and county officials be placed on an equality with tax-payers in receiving payment from the county. But as the custom now is, while the sheriff and treasurer pay themselves in cash, the creditor of the county, for equally valuable consideration given, to say the least, is paid by warrants, which at present and for the past years have been at a discount.

The committee take pleasure in acknowledging the courtesy and cheerful alacrity generally shown by the county officers in giving information and assistance in the progress of their investigations, and this acknowledgment they feel especially due to Mr. Stallings, Mr. Richard, and Mr. Diffenduffer.

All of which is respectfully submitted.

JAMES SYKES,
R. E. MOORE,
H. S. MERRITT,
H. W. IBBOTTSON,
SAMUEL HESSLEIN,
GEO. E. REDWOOD,
Committee.

The report was unanimously received and the most sincere thanks of the meeting returned to the committee for the very able and thorough report, which caused them so much labor and the people so much profit.

JAS. SYKES, *Chairman.*

W. D. HUMPHRIES, *Secretary.*

ANALYSES OF POOR-HOUSE FOR 1871.

Brazier, superintendent, and medical services	$332 00
Sundry parties, medical services	78 00
Coffins and burials	134 50
Medicines	124 00
Board and clothing	138 00
Provisions	226 00
Repairs, poor-house	91 00
West Point	900 00
Total	2,023 50

COLUMBUS, MISSISSIPPI, *November* 11, 1871.

JOSEPH TURNER (colored) sworn and examined.

By the CHAIRMAN:

Question. Where do you live?

Answer. I live here in town.

Question. State to the committee whether you have ever been visited and whipped by the Ku-Klux in this county.

Answer. Yes, sir; I have.

Question. Was it near Caledonia?

Answer. Yes, sir.

Question. How long ago was it?

Answer. It has been, as nigh as I can remember, three weeks before the court sat in Oxford in the summer.

Question. Were you at your house at the time?

Answer. No, sir; at my sister's house.

Question. What time in the night did they visit you?

Answer. About 11 o'clock.

Question. Were you in bed?

Answer. No, sir.

Question. State the circumstances, and how many men were concerned.

Answer. There was ten men that came in the yard; and there was, as nigh as I could get at it, it looked like the crowd was twenty; they did not come in; they stopped down in the lane in the road. When they first came in I was sitting down; the door was standing open; I saw them before they got to the house, but I was not afeard; I knew very well that they were going to ride that night; I was at Mr. Gardner's store that evening.

Question. In Caledonia?

Answer. Yes, sir.

By Mr. BLAIR:

Question. Whose store?

Answer. Mr. Warren Gardner's. I was there at the store before night. I started down to my sister's, and another sister of mine came from the other side of the river, out of Monroe County, about four miles from Caledonia; she came with her husband, and I waited there until they got ready to go; she was going down to stay all night, and I waited until she got ready to go; that was about 10 o'clock at night before they came away from the store. The men kept gathering in two or three at a time until there was twenty or thirty men in there; some of them I didn't know. In about three-quarters of an hour after I got down there, up they all rode; they heard me say where I was going to. I never thought, at the time, they were going to interrupt me. They heard me say where I was going to, and right on the back of it they came right down after me.

Question. You say they were at the store?

Answer. Yes, sir; they were all at the store.

By the CHAIRMAN:

Question. Who questioned you where you were going that night?

Answer. Tom Barrentine. I was in his grocery-store.

Question. Were those people that collected in the store disguised or not?

Answer. No, sir; they were not disguised at that time.

By Mr. RICE:

Question. Were they when they came to the house?

Answer. Yes, sir; they were.

By the CHAIRMAN:

Question. How long after you got to your sister's before they came?

Answer. About three-quarters of an hour, as nigh as I can get at it.

Question. What did they do?

Answer. They came up there; I saw them coming before they got to the house, and I said, "Here comes the Ku-Klux," and everybody sat still in the house. I thought they were going on by, there was so many of them; the front part of them went on by, but there was ten men got down off of the horses and hitched the horses at the fence, and they came up and asked for Joe Turner. I said, "He is here." They said, "Tell him to come out; we want to talk to him." I would not come out. Two men came in, and caught me by the waistband of my pants on each side and took me out. Both of them had a pistol in his hand, and one before me with a pistol; and they carried me up the road, and another one spoke sitting on a horse; and they brought me down the road like they were going to the bottom. They took me about a hundred yards, to a little pine bush by the roadside, and there they whipped me.

Question. How many whipped you?

Answer. Only one.

Question. How many licks?

Answer. He gave me fifty licks with a concern—a half switch and half stick—and they struck me five licks with a stick—two licks on each arm. To keep the licks off, I put up my arms, and they killed my arms dead, and they struck me one over the head. It was six weeks before I could grab anything in my hand.

Question. What did they say they whipped you for?

Answer. They said they heard I was carrying a pistol to shoot the Ku-Klux with. I had one, but it was not that long, [illustrating;] a little pocket-pistol. I only paid seventy-five cents for it. I could not hit a man across this house. I did not have it at the house with me; it was at the shop.

Question. Was that all they alleged?

Answer. Yes, sir.

Question. They searched you?

Answer. Yes, sir; but I did not have it.

Question. You had the belt around you?

Answer. Yes, sir. He pulled the belt off of me.

Question. Were those men disguised?

Answer. Yes, sir.

Question. Did they come from the direction of Caledonia?

Answer. Yes, sir.

Question. How far did your sister live from Caledonia?

Answer. About one mile from Caledonia, near Louis Booth's mill, about three-quarters from the river.

Question. Were their horses disguised?

Answer. The horses were half covered, back to the saddle; the head and neck were covered.

Question. What kind of disguise did the men have on?

Answer. White, with horns on their heads, and then they had belts around them—leather belts, and pistols stuck down outside, and most every one had a stick about a foot and a half long, with a string in it to the wrist.

Question. Did you hear any of the Ku-Klux whistle?

Answer. Yes, sir; they were whistling when they came there, making all kinds of fuss—some hollering like owls, some whippoorwills, and some talked talk I could not understand. They talked while they were getting me out of the house in broken language; and after they got outside, where they whipped me, they all got in a row, and asked me did I know any of them.

Question. Did they talk in natural voices?

Answer. They talked in natural voices after they got me out of the house. They asked me if I knew any of them. I knew them, but I did not dare own it for fear they would kill me.

Question. You say when they were trying to get you out of the house they disguised their voices?

Answer. Yes, sir; they talked like they were Irishmen, or something—talked broken language.

Question. Did you know any of the men by their voices or size?

Answer. Yes, sir; some of the men I worked with; I knew them by their horses and by their voices.

Question. Were they some of the same men you had seen at the store that night?

Answer. Yes, sir; they were some of the same men; and the man that done the whipping, he as good as said that he intended to do it. I worked with him three months in the year. I was not making anything. I was only getting $10 a month and feeding my family, and I could not make anything; and I told him I could not make anything and I quit; and he told me when I went away from his house that if I left there I had better go farther than Columbus. I told him I would go to Columbus, where I moved from. He told me I had better go farther than Columbus; I had better go clear out of his reach.

Question. Had you been working on his plantation?

Answer. Yes; better than three months.

Question. What is his name?

Answer. John Stinson.

Question. What other men did you recognize?

Answer. There was John Stinson, Will Stinson, (his brother,) Jess Stinson—he was old man Andy Stinson's son—and then there was one Gardner; he is a merchant there; and there was Laney Williams; there was John Kidd and his son John; and there was Fullen Wiler and Jasper Webb.

Question. Had you seen all these men up in town that evening?

Answer. Yes, sir; and they were all there that night. They came in when it was between 8 and 9 o'clock; and they kept coming in until I went away.

Question. Your opinion is that they were among the crowd that whipped you?

Answer. Yes, sir; I knew these men by their horses. They were boys I had been with a great deal before the surrender. I refuged down here before the surrender, and had been with them. They lived right there in the neighborhood.

Question. Were they sons of farmers in that part of the country?

Answer. Yes, sir.

Question. Are they decent, respectable young men?

Answer. I suppose they are; but it did not seem so from the way they were Ku-Kluxing me.

Question. They passed for respectable young men?

Answer. Yes, sir; they passed for respectable men; all good livers they were there.

Question. Where did they go after whipping you?

Answer. They went on down to old man Hugh Ager—Andy Ager, he was there too.

Question. What did they do there?

Answer. They went down there after Henry Troop.

Question. Was Henry Troop a colored man?

Answer. Yes, sir. What they went after him was, he had a fish-trap in the river down there, and McLean—I think he caught McLean on his fish-trap. He spoke to him about it, and he gave him some insulting words about being on his trap; and that was what he was gone on for, because he had insulted Mr. McLean about being on his fish-trap. They went after him that night, but didn't get him; he left.

Question. Had he had notice?

Answer. No, sir; but it happened he was gone from home.

Question. Did they ever catch him afterward?

Answer. No, sir.

Question. Did he leave that neighborhood?

Answer. No, sir; he went down to Mrs. Shelby's that night, and on Sunday he came to town and staid a week or so; and when they found out he had reported, or some party had reported, they all quieted down, and he went back home. They all dried up.

Question. Did you hear of their going to any other house that night?

Answer. Yes, sir; two houses.

Question. What houses?

Answer. They went to White's and whipped Albert Murphy; and they went to Edward Hutchinson's and whipped Dick Halliday. They whipped another at Hutchinson's. They did not whip him exactly at Hutchinson's; but they whipped a fellow named Ed Murphy at his mother's house, down there at Bankheads. They whipped her son there one night. He lived with Ed Hutchinson; but he went to his mother's house that night; and they whipped him because he did not keep stove-wood cut. They told him they called by Mrs. Hutchinson's to supper, and there was not any stove-wood there. They told him that.

Question. That made four colored men whipped that night.

Answer. Yes, sir.

Question. Including you?

Answer. Yes, sir. Now, when they whipped Dick Halliday they made him run naked, and made him get down and pray, and then they made him take sacrament with them; they had bread in their pockets, and they made him eat bread.

Question. What was the reason of that?

Answer. I don't know, sir.

Question. Was he a preacher?

Answer. No, sir; he was just a young strip of a fellow. He is a man grown—about twenty-one or two years old.

Question. Was he severely whipped?

Answer. Yes, sir; right bad. And they whipped another woman down there somewhere. I don't know where the place was. They whipped her down below there mighty bad. They whipped her and the old man both. I don't know the names.

Question. What did they whip the colored woman for?

Answer. Because she let the children cry too much at night. They said they could not sleep in the grave-yard, and had to come out and whip her for letting her children cry at night so much.

Question. They claimed to be spirits from the other world?

Answer. Yes, sir.

Question. What time in the morning did they get through with their whipping?

Answer. I do not know what time they got through. It was late in the night, I know, before they got through. I never saw them out any more. For myself, I never laid down the whole night; I could not lay. When I would lay down it felt like my arms would all burst off of me. I walked about all night in the yard or in the house. I could not sit, I was in such misery. They like to have broken both my arms.

Question. Did you continue to stay there?

Answer. No, sir. I came down to Columbus here and went to Aberdeen on the train, and came back through the country over there, but did not stay but a day. I came in the evening and went back next day, and on the next day I went to Oxford.

Question. To attend court there?

Answer. Yes, sir.

Question. Did you go before the grand jury?

Answer. Yes, sir.

Question. Did you tell the grand jury substantially the same tale you have told this committee?

Answer. Yes, sir. Just the men I knew I reported.

Question. Have these men been arrested, any of them?

Answer. Yes, sir; some of them has; some it was supposed ran off. I have not been up there; but I heard they had run off; some that they did not get ran off before they got their hands on them; some gave bonds; they have not all gone yet; some gave bond and then run off; but there is another man I like to have forgot; the same party that whipped me whipped him; they whipped him before they did me.

Question. Who was that?

Answer. Jim Hicks. He lives ten miles from this town. I saw him election day—last Tuesday.

Question. Was he whipped the same night?

Answer. No, sir; he was whipped before I was whipped. I don't exactly know what night he was whipped, but he was whipped this year.

Question. By the Ku-Klux?

Answer. Yes, sir; I was talking with him, and he was telling me about who was there, and the same men—several more men were there—or if they were there they did not come in, or I did not know them; but the most of the men that whipped him were the same men that whipped me.

Question. Do you know of any other colored people being whipped in this county?

Answer. Yes; they whipped another man—Jim Verner.

Question. When was that done?

Answer. That was done before they whipped me.

Question. Is he a colored man?

Answer. Yes, sir.

Question. Whipped by the Ku-Klux?

Answer. Yes, sir; he was whipped by the Ku-Klux?

Question. Have you known of any colored people being murdered by the Ku-Klux?

Answer. No, sir; not in this county. I know of some being murdered in Monroe County.

Question. Are you acquainted in Monroe County?

Answer. Yes, sir; I am acquainted right smart in Monroe. I used to live over there since the surrender. I was acquainted with both the men that were killed in Monroe.

Question. What were their names?

Answer. Jack Dupree and Aleck Page.

Question. When was Jack Dupree killed?

Answer. He was killed the first of this year.

Question. State to the committee the particulars of the killing of Dupree.

Answer. Jack Dupree—he lived about, I reckon it is eighteen or nineteen miles from here, on Widow Robert's land; or, if it is not on Widow Robert's, its near there, on Addison Robert's place. I suppose they went there after him; he would not come out, or at least they beat him mightily before they could get him out. His wife has two young children. They took him out and carried him out as far as the bridge; they carried him farther than the bridge, and there they found his drawers on the bridge. They carried him on farther, I suppose, out toward Ross's Mill, and they killed him in there somewhere, in some of those old fields. Nobody has ever found him at all.

Question. Did you understand that this was done by disguised men?

Answer. Yes, sir; they have witnesses; there is men followed them and know who did it. Let me see how many witnesses there is. Wash Willis, or Wash Halliday, is one, and Tob Roberts, and Henry Allen, and Jehu Wolf, and Pet Roberts, and Pete Atkins; that is all I know.

Question. Are those the men charged with being implicated in the murder or are they witnesses who know of that transaction?

Answer. These are witnesses. They were all at Oxford at the same time, and we came away together. There was three black men that were Ku-Klux with them.

Question. They were with the white men?

Answer. Yes, sir; and they still hold out that they were Ku-Klux. Jehu Wolf—it is supposed he was one too, but he turned State's evidence, and told on the whole crowd, so they told me, and they did not imprison him while he was there at all.

Question. How did these colored men come to be concerned in the murder of a colored man?

Answer. I suppose they were there; they were disguised and were Ku-Kluxing with the white men.

Question. What was Jack Dupree killed for?

Answer. I don't know, sir, what he was killed for; yes, I suppose he had cursed Austin Willis, I believe through the year some time; in passing the road, I suppose he stopped and was talking with him and cursed him. That was all they had against him that anybody could get any idea of.

Question. Was he a man of family?

Answer. Yes, sir.

Question. They went to his house in the night-time and took him out?

Answer. Yes, sir. Aleck Page—they found him where he was killed.

Question. Tell the committee the particulars of the killing of Page.

Answer. Aleck Page was killed. He was taken off from home and was hanged; and then they cut his throat after hanging him and buried him by the side of an old log, in an old field, at the edge of the field where the bushes had grown up. It has been a good many years since it has been cultivated. They killed him and covered him up in leaves; and Jehu was there, so it is supposed; it was proved on him he was there.

Question. Was Page killed the same night Dupree was killed?

Answer. Yes, sir; the same night.

Question. Was Page a man of family?

Answer. Yes, sir; he had a wife and two children.

Question. Was he at home when taken out?

Answer. Yes, sir; they took him out from home.

Question. Was it supposed he was killed by the same band of men who killed Dupree?

Answer. Yes, sir; the witness says Jehu was there and helping to Ku-Klux; and they saw him and knew him; and if he hadn't been there he couldn't have gone right to the man and found him. He was the only man that could go right to him and find him.

Question. And he was the one who turned State's evidence?

Answer. Yes, sir. He went and found the man where he was killed at; and if he had not been there he could not have gone so straight to him.

Question. When did this happen?

Answer. I could not tell you exactly what night.

Question. Was it this year or last year?

Answer. This year. It was shortly after Christmas.

Question. Did Jehu take the Ku-Klux to the men, or the people hunting the body to the body?

Answer. He took the men hunting the body to the body.

Question. Has anybody been arrested?

Answer. Yes, sir; they have been arrested and got bond and came back home.

Question. They were arrested upon a warrant that issued from the United States court at Oxford?

Answer. Yes, sir; they were arrested. I saw them all there—all the fellers when I was there at Oxford.

Question. Have they had their trial yet?

Answer. No, sir; none of them have had their trial.

Question. Have any of the men in Monroe Country concerned in these murders run off?

Answer. No, sir; not that I have heard. I have not been over in Monroe County. It has been two months since I was there.

Question. Have you heard of any other Ku-Klux murders in that county?

Answer. No, sir.

Question. Have you heard of any colored men being whipped in that county?

Answer. Yes, sir; I heard of two being whipped in that county: Simon Dunning and Aleck Willis.

Question. Were Dunning and Willis whipped by the Ku-Klux?

Answer. Yes, sir.

Question. When did that happen?

Answer. That happened this summer, a while before court began at Oxford. Willis and Dunning both were at Oxford.

Question. Has anybody been arrested for whipping them?

Answer. Yes, sir; the same men that whipped them killed Dupree and Aleck Page.

Question. Supposed to be the same band of men?

Answer. Yes, sir. As I said to you, I don't know whether anybody ran away out of Monroe County; I did hear week before last that Mike Forsbee—he was a colored Ku-Klux—I heard he ran away; he ran away, I suppose. Jefferson Willis—he has not run away; he is at home. He was another colored Ku-Klux. Burrell Willis—he was a brother of his; he is at home.

By Mr. BLAIR:

Question. Have not they run away?

Answer. No, sir; if they have I have not heard of it. They kept them in jail all the time they were at Oxford until they got bond and came home. I saw Jeff. here in June about three weeks ago on a wagon, loading it up; about two weeks ago I was at Oxford, and I reckon I will have to go back there again.

By the CHAIRMAN:

Question. As a witness?

Answer. Yes, sir.

Question. Do you remember any other whipping in Monroe County?

Answer. No, sir; that is all I remember. There was another man that was killed down on Muddy Creek, but I don't know his name. And there is Henry Hatch; he was another colored Ku-Klux. He turned State's evidence when he found they were being taken up and arrested. He said they killed one man down on Muddy Creek. He said he shot one of the guns that killed the man on Muddy Creek; but he said, "I did not shoot the man." He said Andy Crosby was the captain, and they shot at the wave of a handkerchief; seven men shot, and he shot one gun—a single-barreled shot-gun; but he said he did not hit the man. He did not want to shoot the man; and when the word was given to fire he turned off his gun and shot. He was a witness. He was a Ku-Klux himself. He did not tell the man's name.

By Mr. BLAIR:

Question. Who did he say was the captain?

Answer. Andy Crosby.

By the CHAIRMAN:

Question. How many colored men have been identified as concerned in the Ku-Klux band in Monroe County?

Answer. There is five; that is all I know.

Question. How many white men were concerned?

Answer. Some twenty of them; there may be more than that; they have not got them all yet. There are twenty-odd that they already had when they were at Oxford.

By Mr. BLAIR:

Question. You say that Tom Barrentine was one of those disguised men that whipped you?

Answer. No, sir; he asked me where was I going to that night, and I told him where I was going to stay at.

Question. What did they whip you for?

Answer. What they told me they whipped me for was they said they heard I was toting a pistol to shoot them or the Ku-Klux with. That is all they told me anything about it. There is another thing, after they went away from the house—after they whipped me and went away from the house—they turned around and came back again and called me out. I went to the fence; and the court was to commence here on the next Monday, in Columbus; this was Saturday night. They told me and Allen Harefoot that they did not want it to ever get out of the family about their whipping me that night, and if it did get out of the family they said, "Wo be unto you." And Mr. Gardner—on Sunday evening I was going back down home—met me; he was coming from his house to the store or his room, and he stopped me and squat down, and was whittling with his knife, on the ground. He had a stick in his hand, and began to talk with me. I asked him when he was talking whether his wagon was going to town to-morrow, and he said, "Yes," his wagon was going; but he said he would have about a thousand pounds of flour to fetch down here, and he did not reckon I could go on his wagon. Then he asked me what was I going to town for. I told him, "There is a law somewhere in the country, at some of these places, for beating black people, and I am going to town to report them that beat me." He says, "Have you any idea who beat you?" and I says, "Yes, I have an idea who beat me." Says he, "Let me tell you, if I was you, I would not go to town to report. It would make it just worse on you. If you go to town and report them they will be after you again." I says, "Let them be after me; they can't hurt me any worse than they have if they kill me, and I would rather they should kill me." He says, "People say I belong to this Ku-Kluxing; but," he says, "there is nothing of it;" but I noticed at the same time he was there, because I saw him with my two eyes; but I never told him I saw him there, because I did not dare to do it.

Question. He told you he belonged to it?

Answer. He told me the people said he belonged to it, but he said there was nothing of it, and told me if he was me he would not report it, because it would just make it worse on me.

Question. What Gardner was that told you he belonged to it?

Answer. Warren Gardner; the merchant there, in Caledonia.

Question. Did you say you recognized him that night?

Answer. Yes, sir; I did. There is a brother-in-law of mine there. He has been a man that has been all the time mighty well thought of there among the white people; they would always tell him more. He came to me several times and told me. He told me one time: "If I was you"—he married my sister—"If I was you, I would not stay here, Joe. I heard whispering around that the Ku-Klux were going to get after you."

Question. Who told you that?

Answer. Allen Harefoot, a brother-in-law of mine. He said they were going to get after me. He said he heard it whispered around; but still he never would tell me who whispered it to him. I told him, "No, I shall not go away." That was after I left John Stinson's, the man I was working with I was telling you awhile ago. I told him "No, I was not going nowhere myself." Nobody never came after me in a long time after that until I done give them up. I had no idea they were ever going to bother me; and, therefore, I believe, as earnest as I ever did believe anything, that he knows something about them, and knew who they were too; because that Saturday night they came there and whipped me. I told him that night I was coming down to his house, and he promised to meet me in Caledonia that night, and he failed to do it; and I went down to his house. He knew I was going to his house, because he promised to meet me in Caledonia, and failed to do it.

Question. What McLean was that who you say was caught at a man's fish-trap?

Answer. It is just McLean; I don't know his given name. I just know him when I see him. I am noways acquainted with him.

Question. Was he in the crowd?

Answer. If he was I did not recognize him; there was a great many more there that did not stop, that did not come in at all; they went on down and did not stop at the house; they stopped way down the lane. I saw them all standing in the road. After they got me out and got me in the trees, they hollered about from one to the other; hunted for a rope, like they wanted to tie me; but they did not tie me.

Question. They went to White's then, did they?

Answer. Yes, sir; they went to Ager's in the first place.

Question. And then to White's?

Answer. Yes, sir.

Question. And whipped Albert Murphy?

Answer. Yes, sir.

Question. What for?

Answer. I do not know. I believe it was because he belonged to a club; they had a club-meeting, and I think he was captain of the club. That was why they whipped him.

Question. What club did he belong to?

Answer. I do not know, sir, what club it was. It was the Loyal League or something or other; I do not remember; I did not belong to it myself.

Question. They whipped Dick Halliday at Ed. Hutchinson's?

Answer. Yes, sir.

Question. What did they whip him for?

Answer. Because he left Andy Stinson's. They made him go back there. He went back, too; he went back next morning.

Question. You say they made him eat bread?

Answer. Yes, sir; they made him take the sacrament with them; they made him eat bread; they made him pray first and after they made him pray they made him eat bread.

Question. What did they whip Jim Hicks for?

Answer. I do not know what they whipped him for.

Question. Didn't he tell you what he was whipped for?

Answer. No, sir.

Question. Didn't he tell you it was because he had bragged about sleeping with a white woman?

Answer. I never heard whether it was about a white woman or not.

Question. You never heard anything about that?

Answer. No, sir. I just know they whipped him. He says they whipped him, but he never told me what they whipped him for; he never said anything to me about it.

Question. Did you tell him what they whipped you for?

Answer. Yes, sir; I told him what they said they whipped me for. My belief is they whipped me because I did not stay at John Stinson's—because I quit there.

Question. What did they say they whipped you for?

Answer. That's what they said—that they heard I said I was toting a pistol for them; but I don't believe they heard it; I never told anybody so. The pistol I had wouldn't shoot.

Question. Was it not rather singular that when you were telling him what you were whipped for that Hicks did not tell you what he was whipped for?

Answer. No, sir; in fact, I did not ask him what they whipped him for. He did not tell me what they whipped him about.

Question. Were there any colored Ku-Klux among the men that whipped you?

Answer. No, sir; if there was they did not come into the yard.

Question. You know Jack Dupree?

Answer. Yes, sir; I knew him.

Question. What was it said they killed him for?

Question. I suppose nobody knows what they killed him for; but they supposed they killed him because he was cursing Aust. Willis; at least, he insulted him in passing the road.

Question. What did he say to Austin Willis?

Answer. I don't know what he said to him. I was not there myself. There are men, though, that do know what he said. It is supposed that was what they killed him for.

Question. That is the supposed reason?

Answer. Yes, sir.

Question. What did they kill Aleck Page for?

Answer. I don't know what they killed him about.

Question. You spoke of two men that were whipped—Simon Dunning and Aleck Willis; did you hear what they were whipped for?

Answer. I never heard what Aleck was whipped for. I heard what Sim. was whipped for.

Question. What?

Answer. He was living with Bob May and quit.

Question. He was whipped for quitting Bob May?

Answer. Yes, sir.

Question. You don't know what Aleck was whipped for?

Answer. Aleck was whipped because he sued a white man there for some money he was owing to him. His name was Bill Kneeland; I think it was Bill. He used to be a tax collector. I am almost confident that that is the name. It was Kneeland, and I think the name was Bill. He sued him for some money. That's what he was whipped for.

Question. Was Bill Kneeland recognized among those that whipped him?

Answer. Yes, sir; they had him at Oxford.

By the CHAIRMAN:

Question. Had you heard of the Ku-Klux in the country before these outrages that you have described as occurring in this and Monroe Counties?

Answer. No, sir; I did not know that there was any Ku-Klux over there in Monroe County until I heard of their killing these two men.

Question. Had you heard of the Ku-Klux in this county before you were whipped?

Answer. Yes, sir; before they killed these two men.

Question. How long before that had you heard of them here?

Answer. That was last year—first of the year.

Question. Had they done any mischief last year?

Answer. No, sir; they had not done any mischief around in my hearing.

COLUMBUS, MISSISSIPPI, *November* 11, 1871.

Miss SARAH A. ALLEN sworn and examined.

By the CHAIRMAN:

Question. Please state your place of residence and occupation to the committee.

Answer. Geneseo, Henry County, Illinois. I have no occupation at home. I am teaching here.

Question. State whether you have been engaged in the business of teaching in this county.

Answer. In this county I have been teaching a few weeks.

Question. In what part of the county?

Answer. In this place.

Question. Were you engaged as a teacher of a school outside of Columbus at any time?

Answer. If you refer to my teaching school last spring, I taught in Monroe County. I was teaching at Cotton Gin Port, twelve miles northeast of Aberdeen.

Question. Were you teaching a white or colored school?

Answer. A colored school.

Question. You may state to the committee whether you were interrupted by any persons in your business.

Answer. I taught six weeks, until I think the 18th of March, when I was told to leave; warned to leave, between 1 and 2 o'clock at night by about fifty men, I think; they were disguised; there were but two that came into my room.

By Mr. BLAIR:

Question. Do you say they came into your room?

Answer. Between 1 and 2 o'clock at night I was wakened by a great noise around on the outside of the house. They told me to get up. I went to the window and asked them what they wanted. They said they wanted me to get a light and dress; that they wanted to talk to me; that they would not harm me. I said, "Very well," I would be ready in a few moments. I admitted them. The captain said, "If you will take a seat the lieutenant shall come in the room and the rest shall stay out." The lieutenant came in with a pistol in his hand. He sat down opposite the fire-place. The captain sat in the center of the room. There were eight or ten men stood inside the door, and the porch was full.

Question. What did they say to you?

Answer. They asked me my name and occupation, and where I came from, and what I was doing, and who I boarded with, and what my wages were. We talked about an hour on politics, mostly against Colonel Huggins and his whipping. He had been whipped about one week before that. They asked me if I had heard of it and what I thought of it; and also asked if I had heard that other teachers had been sent away, and what I intended to do. I told them it was a very short notice, and I did not know. They said they never gave a warning but once; that I was to understand it so. I told them I did. They said I should leave—I believe the lieutenant told me I should leave—Monday morning. That was Saturday evening, or Saturday night. The captain said he thought that would be rather hard; he would give me till Thursday morning to leave; that probably some one of them would be around. I told them they need not trouble themselves to come around; I would go if I said I would, if it was possible to get away; the roads were very bad. I did not get away until the next Tuesday.

By the CHAIRMAN:

Question. Tuesday following the Saturday night you were visited?

Answer. Yes, sir.

Question. Was there any threat made of what would be the consequence of your continuing to teach school?

Answer. No, sir.

Question. Further than the remark that they never gave a second notice?

Answer. Yes, sir; that was all.

Question. What did you infer from that?

Answer. Well, I supposed that they would, if I should stay and continue, take harsher means.

Question. That was your impression?

Answer. Yes, sir.

Question. Did you discontinue your school in consequence of this warning?

Answer. Yes, I did.

Question. After you had been teaching about six weeks?

Answer. I taught just six weeks.

Question. For how long a term had you been engaged as a teacher?

Answer. Four months.

Question. What wages were you receiving per month?

Answer. Seventy-five dollars.

Question. Did they say what their motive was for breaking up your school?

Answer. Yes. They did not want radicals there in the South; did not want northern people teaching there; they thought the colored people could educate themselves if they needed any education; they advised me to go home again.

Question. They knew you were a northern woman?

Answer. Yes, sir; they asked me where I came from and when I came down, and if some one, some radical in the North, had not sent me down.

Question. You think the number in all, outside and inside, was as much as fifty?

Answer. I concluded so. The colored people that were in the other part of the house thought the number was much higher; but I suppose, of course, they exaggerated. From the appearance of the place they made the next morning I judged that to be about the number.

Question. Did they come mounted?

Answer. Yes, sir; they were all mounted, but I heard no noise when they came up.

Question. Did you notice whether their horses were disguised?

Answer. I did not see them; the colored people said they were.

Question. The men were all disguised that you saw?

Answer. Yes, sir.

Question. Can you give the committee a description of the disguises they wore?

Answer. They were long white robes, a loose mask covered the face, trimmed with scarlet stripes. The lieutenant and captain had long horns on their head, projecting over the forehead; a sort of device in front—some sort of figure in front, and scarlet stripes.

Question. Did you recognize any one of the number?

Answer. I did not.

Question. Did they tell you where they came from?

Answer. They said when they first came they had a long way to go, and were in a hurry. They wished me to dress quickly. I supposed they came from Alabama. It was about twelve miles from the border, and they went that way and came from that way.

Question. You were opposite to Pickens County, Alabama, were you?

Answer. I do not know the name of the county opposite.

Mr. RICE. Marion County is opposite that point.

By the CHAIRMAN:

Question. Did they say they had come from Alabama?

Answer. They did not.

Question. That was an inference you drew?

Answer. That was all. I did not think they were men I had ever seen, or that lived in the place, for they were large, tall men; larger men than any in the place I had seen. It was a very small place, and I had seen nearly all that lived there.

Question. What was the name of the place?

Answer. Cotton Gin it is usually called.

Question. Do you know any other school-teachers who were visited the same night by disguised men?

Answer. No, sir; I do not.

Question. You have not heard of any other visitation in that part of the country except there?

Answer. There was a teacher left Smithville the week before I did.

Question. A female teacher?

Answer. Yes, sir.

Question. Was she said to be warned off?

Answer. She heard they were coming there, and the man she was boarding with, who was one of the school directors, thought it was best for her to leave.

Question. Was she a northern woman?

Answer. Yes, sir.

Question. Have you heard of any other schools in Monroe County broken up by the same means?

Answer. Yes, sir; nearly all the schools in Monroe County were broken up in that term, with the exception of some in the larger places.

Question. Did these men have anything to say about the heavy taxation to support the common schools?

Answer. Yes, sir; that was their principal subject of conversation. The captain talked, as I said, about an hour about the heavy taxation, and against Colonel Huggins's conduct, and politics generally.

Question. Colonel Huggins had been whipped at that time?

Answer. Yes, sir. They finally asked me what time it was. I told them I did not know. One of the men stepped up and said it was seventeen minutes past two. I supposed they would talk a while longer. I said it was a very unseasonable hour of the night, and I preferred they would not remain, and after a few minutes longer they left. They threatened the colored woman that lived in the house pretty severely; they used strong language to her after they left my room.

Question. What threats did they use towards her?

Answer. That radicals should be cleaned out of the country if they died, every man. They treated me gentlemanly and quietly, but when they went away I concluded that they were savages—demons.

By Mr. BLAIR:

Question. They did not threaten you, I understand?

Answer. They yelled like Comanche Indians.

By the CHAIRMAN:

Question. When they went away?

Answer. Yes, sir.

Question. They did not remove their disguises or masks while they were talking to you?

Answer. Not at all. They even had on gloves. I thought they could just as well have sent me a letter, as they had done to the other teachers of the county, as to come in that way.

Question. Did they inquire what your political sentiments were?

Answer. No, sir; they did not.

Question. Did they say it was their intention to get rid of northern people, or simply northern people with radical sentiments?

Answer. They said radicals.

Question. Did they say what cause of complaint they had against radicals?

Answer. The heavy taxes—school-tax—was their principal subject.

By Mr. BLAIR:

Question. Did they say they were not able to pay the taxes, they were so enormous?

Answer. They didn't say anything about that.

Question. Did they say they did not intend to pay them?

Answer. I do not remember.

Question. Did they advise you to leave because you would not be paid?

Answer. No; they advised me to leave because I was a white person teaching a colored school.

COLUMBUS, MISSISSIPPI, *November* 18, 1871.

Captain THOMAS E. ROSE sworn and examined.

By the CHAIRMAN:

Question. State your name and rank.

Answer. Thomas E. Rose; captain in the Sixteenth Infantry.

Question. In what portion of the Department of the South have you been assigned to duty?

Answer. I have been assigned for duty since the 29th of March at the post of Aberdeen, Mississippi.

Question. What opportunities or means have you had of informing yourself as to the condition of the different parts of Mississippi as to peace, order, and the execution of the laws?

Answer. I have been in command of the post of Aberdeen most of the time since I was there; the chief part of what I know is from the reports of the citizens; in fact, that is all that I know.

Question. If there have been disturbances of the peace by men banded together, which have been reported to you, or otherwise came to your knowledge, you may furnish the committee with a statement of the case, and their particulars as far as you are able to do so?

Answer. All that I know of these matters has been from reports of citizens, as I have said.

Question. If you deem those reports reliable you may state any other facts brought to your notice?

Answer. Two days after I arrived at the post of Aberdeen I was informed that a black man by the name of Aleck Page was killed across the river. A few days after that there was a report came to me that a man in the Forks was killed. I think they said his name was Thomas Hornberger.

By Mr. BLAIR:

Question. Was he a negro?

Answer. Yes, sir. On Thursday afternoon, about the middle of May, I cannot remember the date exactly, there was a man came to me by the name of Dawkins, a black man, who told me that the night before a party of men had assaulted his house; he said that they came up to his house; that they had masks on, and told him that they were from hell. He said that he was very fearful that they would come to his place on that night. He seemed very earnest about it, and I sent a detachment, and also took another detachment and went myself into that region of country. We were out all that night; there was no disturbance took place. He told me that they would certainly be there on that night, or Saturday night; he expected the same party, but as they did not come on Thursday night, and it rained on Saturday night, I did not send out the detachment, nor did I go myself. The next morning was inspection, and I did not like to go out with muskets in the rain, and then appear with them right away on inspection. I thought it probable there was no occasion for going out; but on Monday, or, probably, Tuesday morning, this party came to me and told me that a man by the name of Wamble was killed on that night.

By Mr. RICE:

Question. On Saturday night?

Answer. Yes, sir; on Saturday night.

By the CHAIRMAN:

Question. Was he the colored man who came to you and desired your protection?

Answer. No; but he lived in that neighborhood. Since that time there has been no disturbance reported to me of any kind, until about four weeks ago, some time in the last of October; I cannot tell the exact date without referring to my morning report. The sheriff then called on me to send out a detachment to assist him in arresting some parties that had murdered a man up in the same locality, within a short distance of where Wamble was killed. I went with a detachment and assisted him in arresting three men charged with the murder of the man.

Question. What man had been murdered?

Answer. I don't remember his name.

Question. Was he a colored man?

Answer. He was a black man; yes, sir; I do not remember what his name was. I passed the place where he was murdered, and went within a short distance of his body. I did not know at the time that it was there I arrested two parties. Although I was within a short distance of where the murder occurred, I was obliged to take another direction, in order to arrest another man. Two lived close to the place, and another lived in another direction. I was in a hurry to try and get the parties. Those are all the disturbances that have been reported to me that I now remember. There have been a good many rumors, but those are all that have been substantiated by the coroner's inquests that I now remember.

Question. Have you heard of any cases of colored men being taken out and whipped?

Answer. Yes, sir; there are a great many of these, but I cannot recollect the circumstances. They were reported to me after the deeds were done, but I do not remember very much about them.

Question. Have all those outrages occurred in Monroe County?

Answer. In Monroe County.

Question. And since what date?

Answer. Since the 29th March.

Question. I will take up the first case you mentioned, that of Alexander Page, a colored man. You may state the circumstances under which he was killed, as you learned them.

Answer. Well, I don't think I could give them; I do not remember very much about the circumstances; there was a great deal said about it.

Question. Do you recollect whether he was killed by a band of men in disguise?

Answer. He was killed by a band of men in disguise.

Question. Now, the case of Thomas Hernberger, in the Forks; please state the circumstances.

Answer. He was killed by a band of men in disguise.

By Mr. RICE:

Question. Taken out of his house?

Answer. Yes, sir; he was taken out of his house.

Question. Was that similar to the former case; was he taken out of his house?

Answer. Yes, sir; in all these cases, except the last.

By the CHAIRMAN:

Question. You speak of the case of Dawkins, which occurred about the middle of May; was Dawkins killed?

Answer. No, sir; he gave me the information.

Question. Did you understand that Wamble was killed by a body of men in disguise?

Answer. By a band of men in disguise. I inferred that it was the same band of men that Dawkins told me would be there that night. I should not have remembered the circumstances if it had not been that it actually occurred as he had predicted; that is the reason I remember about Dawkins making the report.

Question. You spoke of a colored man having been killed in the same neighborhood where Wamble lived; do you recollect his name?

Answer. That is the last case.

Question. Yes, sir; please give us his name?

Answer. I do not believe that his name was given to me.

Question. Did you understand that he was killed by a body of men disguised?

Answer. We arrested the parties that were charged with the murder. Upon passing the place where the murder occurred I noticed that there had been a scuffling; I noticed horse-tracks in the road. We passed a by-path in the woods by a short road to the house of these men; I saw it and ran up, and was going to call the attention of the sheriff to it, but he pointed ahead, and said there is the house where the men are; so we galloped ahead, and went up and arrested these men. Upon arresting one of these named Lagronne, he inquired if we were going to arrest Clint Marshall. The sheriff asked him why he asked him that question; he said he did not know; he supposed he would. I then immediately rode right to the next house where the other man was; his name was also Lagronne; they were brothers. Upon arresting him he asked, "Is that man killed." He was answered, "Yes." "Well," said he, "There must be something supernatural about that; we had charge of that man, but he was taken out of our hands, and what they did with him I do not know. There was a body of men in disguise took him from us."

Question. Who told you that?

Answer. The prisoner, the second Lagronne we arrested. We were after Clint Marshall, but we had not yet arrested him. We did arrest him afterwards, in a short time—half an hour—and they all said that this man was taken out of their hands; that they were deputized by a magistrate, before whom he had a trial for killing a white man; and these prisoners all stated that he was taken out of their hands by a band of men in disguise, and they did not know who they were.

Question. Did you understand from them that the prisoner had been rescued from their possession after night?

Answer. After night; yes, sir. They told me it was by moon-light, about an hour or an hour and a half after dark.

Question. Where did they say they were taking this colored man to?

Answer. To Aberdeen.

Question. To commit him to jail?

Answer. Yes, sir; they told me there were about twelve men that took him from them.

Question. Are those all the cases of which you are able to give the particulars to the committee?

Answer. Yes, sir. I cannot give any particulars further.

Question. You say a good many whippings have been reported to you, but you made no memorandum of them?

Answer. No, sir; I did not charge my memory with them at all.

Question. As a general thing, what has been the disposition of the community in which these outrages you have detailed were committed, to bring the perpetrators to justice and prevent their recurrence?

Answer. I have not heard of any cases in which any attempts of the kind were made at all; I have heard of no attempts to arrest them. Nobody seemed to know who they were. They all say the parties were entirely unknown who committed the offenses; that they were masked, and the parties upon whom these deeds were committed did not know who they were, on account of their being masked.

Question. When you have arrested men to whom have you turned them over?

Answer. We never arrested, ourselves; we go along with the civil authorities, and simply protect them in making arrests. The sheriff retained these three men in custody for a short time, and then turned them over to me. I placed them under guard and kept them until they were demanded by the deputy United States marshal. They were taken then to Corinth, I think; I do not know about that.

Question. Have you any information of the existence in Monroe County, or elsewhere, at present or in the past, of a secret combination of men organized and banded together, to redress what were supposed to be evils or grievances in the community?

Answer. Nothing only from what I would infer from what I have stated.

Question. Have you any information of disturbances of a like character outside of Monroe County?

Answer. I cannot say positively; there were so many reports came to me and I did not take any memorandum, and they are now so far off, in point of time, that I could not substantiate them by ascertaining the facts clearly and definitely.

Question. Were you at any time on service, in this State, previous to March last?

Answer. Yes, sir; I served from April 7, 1869, until the 15th March, 1870, in this State.

Question. In what part of the State?

Answer. I was at Jackson the 25th of April, 1870; I was at Jackson from the 7th of April, 1869, until the 15th of March, 1870, when I went to Vicksburgh and served there until the 25th of April, 1870, when I went to Kentucky, and served there until I came here on the 29th of March last, as I have stated.

Question. During this period, while you were on duty in the State of Mississippi, previous to your present service, did any disturbance of a like character to this you have described come to your knowledge?

Answer. Yes, sir; it was about the middle of April, 1869, I was ordered by General Ames, who then commanded the fourth military district, to proceed to Panola, Mississippi, and investigate the murder of a colored man—I cannot remember his name now, but it was Tom something—and also the whipping of some. I went to Grenada, Mississippi, where a man was confined, by the name of Tubbs, a white man, and examined him, and he told me that he belonged to an organization; that he was with a party that committed some of these depredations, or committed depredations, and were guilty of these acts, though not of the murder, and he stated the raids they made; he gave an account of the raids they made and those accounts were also corroborated by the testimony of these other parties, and I had no doubt of the truth of his statement.

Question. You may repeat them to the committee as briefly as you can.

Answer. It is long ago; my report is somewhere, and could be obtained; it ought to to be extant, though I do no know where it would be.

Question. As far as you can recall his statement at this distant period of time, you may repeat it to the committee.

Answer. The principal raid that I remember his giving an account of was upon a man by the name of Woods, a white man who lived in Panola County. They attacked his house and fired into it and endeavored to kill him, but he resisted, and they were obliged to retire without killing him. Then there was the taking out of some others there, about which he told me—I cannot remember, though, it was so very long ago. I took down the testimony and sent it in with my report to General Ames.

Question. What did he tell you about this organization that he belonged to; what did he say it's name was, and how extensive it was, and for what purpose it existed?

Answer. I do not remember now what he said they themselves styled the organization. He told me the names of the officers, one of which they called the grand cyclops, and another the cyclops, or something of that kind. He said that the chief part of what he knew of the organization was just that small company that he belonged to, which was in Panola County.

Question. How extensive did he say that was?

Answer. I think he told me there were about 150 of them, but I cannot remember now; I know it was very considerable; it was a pretty large body, I thought, for one county.

Question. Did he speak of a general organization in the State, of which this was a part?

Answer. I don't remember that.

Question. What did he say was the purpose of the order?

Answer. He told me that the object was to destroy the influence of the radicals and negroes; it was to frighten them off, and if they could not frighten them off, to kill them; that is, the white radicals, and this man Woods in particular, that they were determined to get rid of him. I do not remember all that he did say, but it was a good deal; I took it all down; I suppose that if the records of the fourth military district could be found, you could get the report, which would show all the testimony.

Question. Would that report be in the War Department?

Answer. I do not know where it would be.

Question. You made your report to General Ames, the military governor?

Answer. Yes, sir, and that is the last I have seen of it. It contains his testimony as written down.

Question. Does it contain an enumeration of all the outrages reported to you?

Answer. Yes, sir; it contained a great deal more than I can now remember.

Question. Were there many cases of outrages reported to you?

Answer. Yes, sir, a great many. I was sent on to investigate several; that was one, and another was here at West Point, in which a man named Cunningham was taken away. He was captured there and the man was never heard of afterward. I was sent to different parts of the State to try to find out. They would report that this man was seen here and there, but he never has been, in fact, seen since that time, as far as I have heard. His name was Cunningham. He was captured by a party of about sixty of them; that was in another part of the State. That band had their headquarters at Big Spring, only about twenty or thirty miles from this place; it is about fifteen miles from West Point; West Point is about fifteen miles from here. That is also one case of which I made a regular report. These are the two principal cases I recollect. There were some others, but I do not remember particularly about them.

Question. Has punishment been inflicted in any case you have enumerated, upon any of the persons concerned in any of these murders or whippings?

Answer. I have never heard of a single case in which it was; it may have been; I do not know.

Question. Have you known or been informed who constituted the band, combination, or association in Monroe County?

Answer. No, sir.

Question. Have you known or been informed whether the members of that band took an oath, or obligation, or entered into an agreement with one another, to be enforced by penalties?

Answer. Do you mean in Monroe County?

Question. Yes, sir.

Answer. Not in Monroe County. I do not know anything of the kind in Monroe County, except the facts I have stated in my testimony. This Tubbs told me the names of all connected with it; not only the officers, but also the number of the members of the organization. That was in 1869, but I do not remember them now. That report of which I speak will show the names.

Question. Did he tell you that the members took an oath, or obligation, or entered into an agreement with one another, to be enforced by penalties?

Answer. Yes, he did, and I think he gave me the substance of the oath at that time. I took it down, I think, but I will not be positive. I know he told me they took an oath, and I think he gave me the substance of the oath. He was not a very intelligent man, and, of course, could not give exactly the oath. I took it down, and I think it is in writing in that report, but I do not remember now what the nature of the oath was, except about that matter of driving out these white radicals, and I do not know that that was in the oath.

By Mr. Blair:

Question. You say you do not remember the circumstances of the killing of Aleck Page?

Answer. No; I do not remember anything more than that he was reported to have been killed. I have an indistinct recollection, but nothing that I would be willing to testify to, because I did not pay sufficient attention to that. There was a great deal said about the man being killed that I did not charge my memory with.

Question. Do you recollect the circumstances of Thomas Hornberger's killing?

Answer. I do not remember anything more than that he was reported to have been killed by a band of men in disguise, the same as Page.

Question. You say you arrested the man who killed Wamble, or a man who had Wamble in charge when he was killed?

Answer. Not Wamble; they had this man who had been recently killed in their charge, and whose name I do not remember; in fact, I do not believe that I learned his name; I do not think that it was told to me; I think I would have remembered it if they had told me, because the occurrence was quite recent.

Question. You arrested the two Lagronnes and Marshall?

Answer. Yes, sir.

Question. They, I understand you, had the man in charge at the time he was taken from their hands and killed?

Answer. Yes, sir; the man was last seen in their hands, and I suppose that was the reason they were charged with the murder.

Question. They had him under a warrant?

Answer. They were deputized by a magistrate to take him to Aberdeen, Mississippi, and they never brought him to Aberdeen, Mississippi, but the man was found at a short distance from the house of these Lagronnes, and they, upon their arrest, said that he was taken from them when they were on their road to Aberdeen with him. This was the statement of the prisoners.

Question. They were deputized by a magistrate?

Answer. By a magistrate.

Question. The negro himself was under arrest?

Answer. Under arrest.

Question. On a charge of murder?

Answer. Yes, sir.

Question. Do you recollect the circumstances of the murder with which he was charged?

Answer. Yes; I think they said this man that was murdered was out in a field, and he heard a shot fired, and went over into his field, and saw this man carrying a hog on his shoulder, and hollered at him. The man started to run, threw down the hog, and turned around and fired his gun and killed the old man. That is what the black man was charged with; and then this man was taken to Camargo, and there tried, and committed to Aberdeen, and placed in charge of these three men, the Lagronnes and Marshall. They started with him to Aberdeen, and did not bring him to Aberdeen, nor go to Aberdeen themselves, but the man was found dead a short distance from their house, whereupon a warrant was issued for the arrest of the Lagronnes and Marshall, and I went out to assist in making their arrest, and, upon their arrest, they made the statement I have told you.

By the CHAIRMAN:

Question. Was it supposed that these three men, the Lagronnes and Marshall, were privy to the murder of this colored man?

Answer. They were charged with the murder.

By Mr. BLAIR:

Question. Was there any evidence of it, except the finding of the body?

Answer. I do not know what the evidence was.

Question. Was there any ground to suspect their statement of facts?

Answer. I thought so myself, from the fact, as I told you, that I observed the horse-tracks in the road where the scuffle had taken place, although I did not see the body myself, but one of the jury of the inquest pointed to it, and I could tell that it was right there where I saw this scuffle. They told me there were twelve men, and that they were mounted, and by the number of horse-tracks I saw in the road, and the marks of scuffling there, I doubted their statement as to there having been twelve men or twelve horses, for there were not that many horse-tracks in the road.

Question. Have these men been tried?

Answer. Yes, sir; these men were taken by the deputy United States marshal out of my hands. The sheriff turned them over to me for safe keeping, and the United States marshal demanded them and took them away. I suppose they were tried.

Question. It must have been a preliminary examination of the men?

Answer. That is all; there was no preliminary examination, that I knew anything about.

Question. Was there any inquest?

Answer. There was a coroner's inquest.

Question. Do you know what the result of that was?

Answer. No, sir; I do not.

Question. You do not know by what process you held those men?

Answer. I held them only under an order from the sheriff.

Question. And you surrendered them?

Answer. I surrendered them as soon as they were demanded by the marshal; they were placed in my custody; the sheriff sent an order, or rather a request, to me to hold them in custody until he should demand them. It was on Saturday that he sent the prisoners up to me, and on Monday morning he sent another order to turn them over to the United States marshal, which I did.

Question. Then you know of no other authority except that of the sheriff for holding them; you had no other?

Answer. No, sir; I had no other. I do not know why he did it. As soon as we returned I proceeded with my detachment to camp, left them with him at the mayor's office, and, on going to camp, I went down to my quarters, and then when I went up to camp I found the three prisoners there.

By Mr. RICE:

Question. Did the Lagronnes or Marshall give any reason why they did not go on to Aberdeen and report the fact that these men had been taken out of their hands?

Answer. Yes, sir; they said that the party that took the men from them would not allow them to go on that night to Aberdeen, but compelled them to return to their homes.

By the CHAIRMAN:

Question. Does the white population of Monroe County evince an earnest disposition to aid in stopping these outrages, and to assist the officers of the law to discover the perpetrators?

Answer. I do not know whether they do or not. They all seem to say that they do not know anything about them; that there is nobody who knows anything about who commit these outrages; that it is impossible to find out anything about them. That is the way they talk. They say they do not know who commits them, and it is impossible to do anything toward arresting on that account.

Question. I will put the question in another form. It has been testified before the committee that all these disturbances of the peace could be prevented, or promptly redressed, but for the alleged inefficiency of the republican officers, such as sheriffs, constables, and judges, and that whole communities are peaceable and law-abiding in spite of the maladministration of the laws. The committee request your opinion as to whether any deficiency in the execution of the laws arises from any indisposition on the part of the community to aid the officers in the performance of their duties?

Answer. Well, it would be merely an opinion.

Question. That is just what the committee want.

Answer. That opinion, too, is formed more on generalities than on specific facts that I could just bring to my memory; my opinion is that the people do not use the proper energy, that they do not take the same interest, or as much interest as they ought to, in trying to repress these disturbances; but, as I said, that is a mere opinion, and formed from general observation; I cannot state any facts or instances where they have absolutely refused to assist the officers, or where they have actually thrust anything in the way of the officers of the law; I do not remember any such instance, yet I have formed that opinion.

Question. Do they seem ready to communicate any information that they have tending to lead to the discovery of the perpetrators of these outrages?

Answer. No information was ever given by them to me; all the information I have ever received was from black men.

COLUMBUS, MISSISSIPPI, *November* 13, 1871.

JAMES W. LEE sworn and examined.

By the CHAIRMAN:

Question. You may state your place of residence and official position.

Answer. I am mayor of Aberdeen, Mississippi.

Question. How long have you held that office?

Answer. I have held it since the 1st of April last.

Question. What office, if any, did you hold in the State of Mississippi previous to that?

Answer. Nothing, except selectman in the city of Aberdeen.

Question. How long have you lived in that city?

Answer. Since 1865.

Question. That place is the county-seat, I understand, of Monroe County?

Answer. The county-seat of Monroe County, Mississippi.

Question. You may state to the committee any instances of outrage which have come to your knowledge, or of which you have been informed from reliable sources, which have occurred in Monroe County since your residence there—more particularly those which have been inflicted by bodies of men in disguise, and at night.

Answer. The first thing I know of any importance was the taking out of three men from Athens jail about a year ago.

By Mr. BLAIR:

Question. Where is Athens?
Answer. In Monroe County. The jail is not at the court-house. Three men were taken out.

By the CHAIRMAN:

Question. Under what circumstances?
Answer. They had been committed by a magistrate for some offense, either in default of bail or without bail, I do not know which.
Question. Were they colored men?
Answer. Yes, sir; Saunders Flint and his two sons. Saunders Flint made his escape; the other two were said to have been killed.
Question. You may give the particulars of their rescue from the sheriff or jailer, and their assassination, as you have been informed of the facts.
Answer. The information I received was that the key was taken from the jailer; that they were taken out by a body of disguised men, and that two were killed. That is all I know of it.
Question. Did you understand how large the party was that took them out?
Answer. I think about twenty or twenty-five.
Question. Was this in the night-time?
Answer. It was so reported.
Question. Were their bodies ever found?
Answer. I think they were. Of that I am not positive.
Question. This was about a year since?
Answer. Yes, sir.
Question. Has the matter ever been investigated and this perpetrator of the outrage discovered?
Answer. Some parties were arrested on the charge and were brought before a jury of twelve men and acquitted, following soon after the perpetration of the act.

By Mr. RICE:

Question. Tried before the circuit court?
Answer. Yes, sir.

By the CHAIRMAN:

Question. Were you present at the trial?
Answer. I was in the city of Aberdeen, but did not attend the sitting of the court.

By Mr. RICE:

Question. Were they indicted previous to their trial?
Answer. I suppose a true bill was found. At any rate, there was an investigation of the matter before a jury, and they were acquitted.

By the CHAIRMAN:

Question. You may proceed to the next case.
Answer. I left the State and was gone for something over two months. I returned from Texas about the middle of March.
Question. March last?
Answer. Yes, sir; 1871. Everything was quiet at the time I left throughout the county, so far as I know, which was the 1st of January. When I came back there were some cases reported. There was the killing of one Jack Dupree, on the east side of the Tombigbee River, in Monroe County.
Question. You may state the particulars of that case.
Answer. I know nothing more than he was said to have been taken out by a body of disguised men, and I think his body was never found.
Question. Taken from his house, did you understand?
Answer. Yes, sir.
Question. Did you understand by how large a body of men?
Answer. I did not.
Question. Were they said to have been disguised?
Answer. They were said to have been disguised.
Question. Was his body ever found?
Answer. I think not.
Question. Does the river flow by Aberdeen?
Answer. Yes, sir; immediately by Aberdeen. Soon after that one Aleck Page was taken from his house by a body of disguised men, and soon after found dead.
Question. Was he shot or hanged?
Answer. I do not know. The next was on the west side of the river, north of Aber-

deen about fifteen or eighteen miles. It was the killing of a colored man known as Hernberger.

Question. Give the particulars of that case, as you learned them.

Answer. I only learned that he was taken out by a body of disguised men and killed. The next, I think in May, was the killing of one Abe Wamble, near the same place.

Question. Killed near the same place that Hernberger was?

Answer. Yes, sir; from near the same place, and under pretty much the same circumstances. The next was on or about the 8th of October; one Dock Hendricks was arrested on a charge of murder, was tried before a magistrate, and committed without bail. The guard in whose custody he was placed started to Aberdeen, to deliver him to the authorities, about night, or at night. The next morning his body was found only a short distance from where the other two, Wamble and Hernberger, had been killed. A writ was issued by me for the arrest of three men, the guards, and executed by the sheriff, and Captain Rose, of the United States Army, on the same.

Question. The three men who constituted the guard?

Answer. Yes, sir. They were to have been tried before me on a charge of murder, but before the investigation came off they were taken out of my hands by the United States court.

By Mr. BLAIR:

Question. You had never given them any preliminary examination?

Answer. No, sir. They were taken out of my hands before that. The day was set, but they were taken by a writ issued by the United States commissioner, I think, at Corinth, and hence there was no investigation before me.

By the CHAIRMAN:

Question. Do you know whether a true bill has been found against them?

Answer. No, sir; the grand jury has not been in session. This occurred in October, about a month ago.

By Mr. BLAIR:

Question. At Corinth?

Answer. Yes, sir; the writ was issued at Corinth. The next and only case I know since then was, one man was reported to have been taken out just over the Lee County line, by the name of Hutchinson, I think.

By the CHAIRMAN:

Question. What was done with him?

Answer. I have never heard of the matter since. He is still missing, as I understand.

Question. You say he was reported to have been taken out. What do you mean; that he was taken from his house by a body of disguised men?

Answer. Yes, sir; taken from his house about a week ago from last Friday night. A party applied for a writ to arrest certain parties for the offense, but it was in another county, and I could not issue the writ. That is all I know of killing.

Question. The cases you have hitherto mentioned are cases of murder. Do you know of any cases where men have been whipped by disguised men, or have you been informed of such cases?

Answer. Yes, sir; I have heard of a great many, but I am not prepared to give names except in one or two cases. Just about the time I returned from Texas, Mr. Huggins, who was United States assessor of internal revenue, also school commissioner for the county, was whipped, in the neighborhood of one George Ross's.

Question. That was in Monroe County, was it?

Answer. Yes, sir; and he was ordered to leave the county and State instanter.

Question. You need not go into the particulars of that case, as the general committee have taken evidence upon it.

Answer. That is all I know of it.

Question. Does any other case of whipping occur to you?

Answer. Not in which I can give names. I have heard of others, but I am not prepared to give the names.

Question. Can you give any particulars?

Answer. No, sir; not further than I am satisfied, and I know, in fact, that some few colored men have been taken out and whipped. I know of no other white men.

Question. What has been the disposition of the white citizens of Monroe County to sustain the officers in ferreting out these crimes to which you have referred, and aid in bringing the perpetrators to justice?

Answer. Very few of the citizens have taken any interest in ferreting out the perpetrators of these crimes.

Question. Do you think that any deficiency in the execution of the laws against these lawless men arises from an indisposition, on the part of the white community, to aid the officers in the performance of their duties?

Answer. There has been nothing like resistance to the officers enforcing the laws in the county, that I know of.

Question. Has there been an earnest disposition to aid them, so far as you have observed?

Answer. I cannot say that there has.

Question. Have you any information that you deem reliable that there now exists, or has at any time existed, in the community in which you live, any combination or organization of men, with signs and pass-words by which they recognize each other, formed for any of the following purposes:

First. To drive from the country objectionable persons;

Second. To harass or molest persons odious for any cause;

Third. To punish negroes suspected of theft or other crimes;

Fourth. To influence negroes in voting or abstaining from voting;

Fifth. To procure the success of the conservative or democratic party;

Sixth. To obtain for the conservative or democratic party the political control of the State and the possession of the offices?

Answer. I am satisfied that there has been an organization in the county, for what purpose I have no means of knowing.

Question. Do you think that organization has its signs and pass-words by which the members recognize each other?

Answer. I have no means of knowing that.

Question. You have thought on that subject a good deal, I suppose, and, in common with other good men, you have deplored these outrages, and sought for the cause. Does it not appear that when these men ride they have a common purpose; that is, that they know where they are going, and what they are going to accomplish?

Answer. I am satisfied that they do in all cases.

Question. Could such purpose be formed, except upon consultation, and would not that consultation necessarily bring all the men together at one place—some point agreed on?

Answer. Necessarily, I think.

Question. And then, again, if the purpose were an unlawful one, such, as if accomplished, would subject to punishment those concerned, would there not follow agreements and oaths to stand by each other, and punish those who betrayed their secrets?

Answer. I think so.

Question. In thus protecting their secrets, would not the member, if called as a witness, be strongly tempted to evade the truth, and would not that temptation be increased in just the proportion of the hazards he would incur in case the truth were known?

Answer. I think so.

Question. Would there not, then, in your opinion, be a double motive to prevaricate, first, in order to save themselves from the vengeance of their associates, and next, to protect themselves from punishment for being implicated in the outrage inflicted?

Answer. I think so.

Question. And would not the motive, in your opinion, become overruling, if the offense committed, in which they were implicated, were punishable by death or imprisonment for a long term in the penitentiary?

Answer. I think they would shelter their organization just as far as they could.

Question. Would not a similar motive operate upon the parents, brothers, and sisters of the member of the family charged with being a Ku-Klux, and implicated in outrages, and in a less degree operate upon remoter relatives and friends, rendering the discovery of the truth from any such persons difficult?

Answer. Yes, sir; I think the sympathy would render it so.

Question. In like manner would not the presence of a Ku-Klux, or the relative or friend of one upon the jury, render it impracticable to find an indictment, and in case of trial upon an indictment found, render a conviction impossible, or at least improbable?

Answer. I think it would have some influence over it at least.

Question. One other question in this same connection I wish to ask you. Would not men wholly unconnected with the order, and not sympathizing with its crimes, be reluctant, from motives of safety and personal interest to give information tending to implicate a member, from fear of drawing down the vengeance of the order or some of its members?

Answer. I think they would not put themselves to any trouble to inform on them, to give information leading to their conviction.

Question. Suppose a public meeting were held, which all friends of law, peace, and order were invited to attend, and a resolution to make war on the organization and break it up were adopted, would not that step compel all men to take sides and show who sympathized with it, and were, therefore, to be watched?

Answer. I think so.

Question. Now, have you known any such meeting called, or any such expression of opinion, on the part of the citizens of Monroe County?

Answer. About the middle of March there was a meeting in Aberdeen, of the citizens of Aberdeen, and they were opposed to this thing, but could do nothing in the matter

Question. How did they express their opposition?

Answer. I believe they passed resolutions in opposition to this thing. I was chairman of the meeting.

Question. How large a meeting was it?

Answer. It was a small meeting of the citizens of Aberdeen.

Question. Aberdeen is itself a small place, is it not?

Answer. About three or four thousand people.

Question. Was that meeting attended by citizens outside of the town to any considerable extent?

Answer. It was not at all, that I recollect of.

Question. Did the meeting embrace many democrats?

Answer. Some of both parties, mostly conservative.

Question. What was the character of the resolutions adopted, if you remember it?

Answer. I do not remember the character, though it was in opposition to this organization, which was then depredating over the county, or over parts of the county.

Question. Did the members of that meeting pledge themselves in those resolutions to use their personal influence to put a stop to these outrages?

Answer. They did.

Question. Have they acted in conformity with the resolutions since, so far as your information extends?

Answer. I know nothing to the contrary.

Question. One more question. You have enumerated several cases of murder, and, with the exception of the case which the Federal court has taken cognizance of, do you know of any punishment inflicted, or any indictment found, or any arrest made of the perpetrators of those outrages?

Answer. Quite a number were arrested and carried to Oxford in the spring. Since that time no indictments have been found, for the grand jury of the United States court has not been in session since.

Question. Has any action been taken by your State courts?

Answer. No action at all that I know of.

By Mr. BLAIR:

Question. It has not been in session since?

Answer. Yes, sir; we have had one district court.

Question. And grand jury?

Answer. And one grand jury since.

Question. One State court?

Answer. Yes, sir; the district court for Monroe County. It was in session six weeks. If any action was taken by the grand jury then, I have no knowledge of it.

By the CHAIRMAN:

Question. Then, so far as your information extends, the only action that has been taken to discover the authors of these outrages, and bring them to justice, has been in the Federal court?

Answer. Yes, sir.

By Mr. RICE:

Question. Were these murders you have spoken of notorious and well understood in the community as having taken place?

Answer. Understood through the entire county.

Question. Did your county paper publish the fact?

Answer. I do not know that it did in all cases.

Question. There is no controversy about the fact that these men were killed by disguised men in the community there?

Answer. I do not see how any man can keep from knowing the whole fact. It has been generally discussed around Aberdeen, where I live.

Question. Is there any general belief to the contrary?

Answer. None that I have any knowledge of.

By Mr. BLAIR:

Question. You say these cases were all taken before the grand jury at Oxford?

Answer. Some of them. The only indictments found have been before the grand jury at Oxford.

Question. How many indictments were found, and for what causes?

Answer. I am not able to state the number, but for the killing of Aleck Page and Dupree, I think.

Question. Are those the only ones?

Answer. The only ones I have any knowledge of.

Question. Then the other case was actually taken out of your hands, and you not even allowed to make a preliminary trial, by the United States officers?

Answer. Yes, sir; that is, the killing of Jack Dupree.

Question. No; the killing of the last one you spoke of, the prisoner, Dock Hendricks?

Answer. Yes, sir; I mixed the names.

Question. How, then, can the State courts take and cognizance of these cases when the United States absolutely step in and take the prisoner out of the hands of the State courts and out of the hands of the State officers?

Answer. This is the only case of the kind that has ever happened in the county.

Question. That has happened, however?

Answer. Yes, sir.

Question. There, where a prisoner was in the hands of the officer of the State courts, and when a day had been set by an officer of the State to make a preliminary examination, the United States court steps in and takes him out of their hands?

Answer. Yes, sir.

Question. You delivered him?

Answer. The sheriff delivered him. The prisoners were in the sheriff's hands.

Question. What right had the sheriff to deliver him when he was there committed by your order?

Answer. I do not pretend to know the right.

Question. You only know that the State was ousted of its jurisdiction by the action of the United States court?

Answer. Yes, sir; the prisoners were taken.

Question. And by the taking of the prisoners out of the hands of the State courts?

Answer. The investigation would have been made before me, but that they were taken under a writ issued from the United States commissioner at Corinth, I think, which deprived me of the investigation I would have made.

Question. You then are not to blame for not making that investigation and enforcing the laws of the State as far as was in your power?

Answer. I think not, for I would have done just what the law required of me.

Question. And you believe that the other courts and officers of the State would do their duty also.

Answer. I know nothing to the contrary.

Question. But the courts of the United States have stepped in and taken the prisoner, who was committed by your warrant, out of the hands of the sheriff and ousted your jurisdiction?

Answer. In one case only.

Question. Had you any other case before you?

Answer. No other case.

Question. If you had had a dozen would they not have done the same thing?

Answer. Likely they would.

Question. You say that indictments have been found in the cases of Jack Dupree and Aleck Page?

Answer. Yes, sir; I think that indictments were found by the grand jury of the United States court at Oxford in the spring.

Question. This man Hernberger, you say, was also killed?

Answer. It was so reported to me.

Question. You were not in the State at the time?

Answer. I think it was about the time that I returned from Texas, and the matter was spoken of very freely at or about the time I returned from Texas.

Question. Now, then, here are the cases of Dupree and Page and of Dock Hendricks, or of the parties charged with the killing of these men, you know have been taken charge of by the authorities of the United States court?

Answer. Yes, sir.

Question. There remain the cases of Hernberger and Abe Wamble.

Answer. If any indictments have been found they have not been executed.

Question. Do you know whether they have been found or not?

Answer. I do not.

Question. Was any investigation had in those cases?

Answer. None that I know of.

Question. None by the State courts?

Answer. None by the State courts that I have ever heard of.

Question. Any by the United States courts?

Answer. If so I have no knowledge of it. If any indictments have been found by the United States court they have not been executed.

Question. In the case of Hutchinson, of Lee County, you could not issue your writ, because it was not in your county?

Answer. It was outside of my jurisdiction.

Question. Do you know whether any inquest or other legal proceedings have been taken in that case?

Answer. I think not. I do not know that the body has ever been found. It has not been so reported.

Question. Do you not think that people, without going into an organization, would try to conceal their crimes?

Answer. I do.

Question. Do you not think that the relatives and friends of people charged with crime would have the same solicitude in regard to them whether they were or were not in an organization?

Answer. The same.

Question. The relatives and friends of a man charged with the commission of crime?

Answer. Separately?

Question. Yes.

Answer. I think likely that in the other case there would be more surroundings, more influence brought to bear.

Question. But his relatives and friends would have the same motives to protect and defend him?

Answer. They would certainly have the same so far as the individual was concerned.

Question. And if they were on the juries they would be likely to act just the same way as they would under other circumstances?

Answer. Much the same.

Question. Is it at all singular that relatives and friends of men charged with crime take some interest in them?

Answer. I think not.

Question. You say the citizens of Aberdeen held a meeting and expressed their reprobation of these crimes?

Answer. Yes, sir.

Question. That the meeting was composed principally of conservatives?

Answer. Conservative whites and some colored men; good citizens.

Question. They expressed their opposition to all lawlessness?

Answer. They did.

Question. And pledged themselves to——

Answer. To use their influence against it.

Question. Do you believe that those people were sincere?

Answer. I do.

Question. Do you think that the great body of the citizens of Monroe County are opposed to these irregularities, this lawlessness?

Answer. I cannot say that the great body of the citizens are opposed to it. There are many good citizens that I know to be opposed to it.

Question. Do you think the others are in favor of it?

Answer. They will not express any opposition to it, if they are not in favor of it.

Question. Do you believe that men who are themselves deprived of all control in a government which they helped to make, deprived of all share in its honors and emoluments, are as prompt to come forward and protect the government, and enforce its laws, as they would be if they had a share in the government?

Answer. Some of them may be.

Question. As a general thing, men who are deprived of all share in the government are not so prompt to enforce its laws and assert its power?

Answer. I know of nothing to the contrary.

Question. Do you not think it is human nature for a man situated in that way to lose his interest in public affairs?

Answer. Natural enough; I think that they would not have the same feeling in the matter that they would if they enjoyed all the rights and privileges of other citizens.

Question. In that sense then, by imposing disabilities upon the ablest and best citizens of the State, the energy of the State for the enforcement of its laws is paralyzed?

Answer. I do not think so, altogether.

Question. To a certain extent it is, by the withdrawal of such men from public life and public interest, or interest in public affairs?

Answer. So far as my knowledge goes, the hostility to the government does not arise from that class of men altogether.

Question. I am not talking about hostility to the government.

Answer. What was the question?

Question. The question was, whether men who are deprived of all control in the government are not apt to lose interest in the enforcement of its laws, to a certain extent?

Answer. I think they would, to some extent.

Question. And if that class of people should be the ablest, most experienced, and most influential citizens of the State, and if they should lose their interest in public affairs by reason of their being under disabilities, it would, to a certain extent, paralyze the operations of the law and the enforcement of the law?

Answer. I do not think it would interfere with the enforcement of the law materially.

By the CHAIRMAN:

Question. Do you know of anybody in Monroe County who has no share in the government at this time?

Answer. Yes, sir; there are some men laboring under disabilities.

Question. Are they protected by the laws equally with all other persons?

Answer. They are.

Question. Do they not vote in common with their fellow-citizens?

Answer. I think they have been voting in county and State elections.

Question. Is there any law at present disabling any citizen from voting, that you are aware of, unless he has been convicted of crime?

Answer. No, sir; none that I am aware of, for State and county officers. I do not know how it is about national offices.

Question. Do you know of any persons in Monroe County who are deprived of the privilege of holding office, except rebels, who voluntarily went into the rebellion after having once taken an oath to support the Constitution of the United States, and then violated it?

Answer. I do not.

Question. Do you regard that class of citizens who held office before the war, who had taken upon themselves an obligation to support the Constitution of the United States, and who afterward broke that oath and entered into the rebellion, as your best citizens?

Answer. I do not think they are our best citizens. They are, however, good citizens.

Question. Do you think there is material enough in that community to fill the offices without resorting to these men who have once been tried and found faithless?

Answer. I do.

Question. I will ask your opinion as to the extent of this organization, whatever its name or purposes, in Monroe County, the manifestations of which you have given in the cases which you have specified, where men have been taken out at night and murdered by disguised men?

Answer. I have no means of knowing the extent of the organization in the county.

Question. Have you any information whether the outrages you have described, and other outrages of which you have heard, have been committed by the same body of men, or by different gangs of men?

Answer. I think there are two bodies in the county that have operated separately, but they may all belong to the same organization.

Question. So far, I understand you to say, all attempts to penetrate the secrets of that organization and discover its membership have failed?

Answer. Except before the United States court.

By Mr. BLAIR:

Question. You undertook to say just now that men under disabilities had the equal protection of the laws of the country. How do you reconcile that statement with your other statement?

Answer. The equal protection of the laws; I think they enjoy the very same protection under the laws.

Question. Are they protected in the right to be preferred to office?

Answer. They are not.

Question. Has not every other citizen the protection in that right?

Answer. Aside from that thing alone, I think they enjoy the very same protection.

Question. Is not that a right which is taken away from them, and in which they are not protected by the law?

Answer. Naturally enough, it is taken away if they cannot enjoy it.

Question. If they cannot enjoy it, it is taken away; and therefore they are not protected in it?

Answer. They are not protected in that one thing.

Question. Then they are not equally protected with other citizens who have that right and are protected in it?

Answer. In that one thing.

By the CHAIRMAN:

Question. That right is taken away in every case where a man is convicted of crime, and disfranchised by the sentence of a court, is it not?

Answer. It is.

By Mr. BLAIR:

Question. Have they been convicted of crime and sentenced by a court?

Answer. Not that I know of.

COLUMBUS, MISSISSIPPI, *November* 13, 1871.

Captain GEORGE W. YATES sworn and examined.

By the CHAIRMAN:

Question. Please state your name, rank, and where you are at present stationed.

Answer. George W. Yates; captain of the Seventh Cavalry, United States Army. I am stationed at Meridian, Mississippi, at present.

Question. How long have you been in the State of Mississippi?

Answer. Nearly four months, sir; it will be four months on the 23d day of this month.

Question. What opportunities or means have you had of informing yourself of the condition of different parts of Mississippi as to peace and order, and the execution of the laws?

Answer. Well, sir, my opportunities have been limited. I know nothing as to whether the laws are properly executed except from hearsay and the opinion which I have formed myself.

Question. Have there been disturbances of the peace occasioned by men banded together which have been reported to you, or have otherwise come to your knowledge? You may furnish the committee with a statement of the cases and their particulars, as far as you are able to.

Answer. There have been one or two cases of Ku-Kluxism reported to me. In one instance a woman who lived twenty miles from Meridian, or thereabouts, came in and stated she was unable to get the civil authorities to do her justice; that the week before, or some days before, at night, an armed band had visited her house; had called for arms; had gone into the door and killed her husband. She recognized one of the party whose name was Stillwell. He was afterward arraigned before the civil authorities and tried, and proved an *alibi* and was cleared, I believe. I took some interest in the case, and questioned the woman closely. She came to me twice.

Question. Was she brought before the State or United States authorities?

Answer. She was brought before the county or city authorities. I asked her how she recognized this man who she said was in disguise. She said he had a clump-foot, and one man about her place had traced that trail in the direction of where this man Stillwell lived.

Question. Has anything further been done with the case?

Answer. I don't know, sir; I think not. I took some little interest in the case and inquired. I believe they told me that the man having proved an *alibi* the case was dropped. I spoke to the justice of the peace before whom the case was tried, and I think he told me the case was over with.

Question. In what county was that?

Answer. In Lauderdale.

Question. Did she inform you how many men were engaged in this outrage?

Answer. No, sir; she did not.

Question. Did she say they were all disguised?

Answer. I don't think she mentioned the number; I am rather positive that she said this man Stillwell was disguised, but that was the only trace which pointed toward development. I inquired particularly about him.

Question. Did they kill her husband in the house, or take him out?

Answer. They killed him in the house. She said they came for arms, and he did not have anything but an old gun that had not been in use for some time. They made him bring it out, and while in the act of bringing it out he was shot.

Question. Did she say what offense they charged against her husband?

Answer. No, sir; he was a negro. I know she came in and complained that the civil authorities did not seem to do her justice. I made inquiries in the case, (I was then in temporary command of the post,) and found there had been no inquest over the remains of her husband until several days after he had been killed. Then I found that the civil authorities were on the track, and I paid no further attention to it.

Question. What is the next case?

Answer. The next case was of a negro man living a few miles from Meridian—say within seven miles. A band of some parties visited his house at night and shot him, and set the house on fire and burned him up and two children. I went out with the sheriff to look after that matter, and the woman gave her version of the affair. She said the party came there, several people; that they called for arms, and finally killed her husband and told her to go to bed. They called for number one and told number one to set the house on fire. Subsequently, however, suspicion pointed to a colored man who lived in the immediate vicinity. He had been heard to say that he intended to Ku-Klux this old darkey. He was arrested on suspicion. The case, I think, has not been tried as yet. The woman seems very positive that the man who did the deed was a bald-headed man, and a white man. She went on to repeat what he had said; for instance, he was particular to repeat twice over every expression; he would say to her, "Get into that bed, get into that bed;" so, for instance, in calling for number one, he would say, "Number one, number one, put the house on fire, put the house on fire." This showed to my mind that there was some organization there.

Question. Was there anything done by the civil authorities in this case?

Answer. This negro man who was arrested on suspicion was brought to Meridian, and I think he was bailed, and the case has not been tried as yet. I think nothing further has been done than this arrest.

By Mr. BLAIR:

Question. What was this bald-headed man's name?

Answer. I don't know; she did not recognize him.

By the CHAIRMAN:

Question. How many men were concerned in this?

Answer. She said about half a dozen; but she seemed positive it was a white man that did the shooting.

Question. Did she say whether the men were disguised or not?

Answer. No, sir; she did not say; I do not think they were disguised; she made no mention of that at all; but I was inclined to believe myself that this fellow was killed by a negro, and from her story I was induced to believe that there had been an organization there, from the fact of this man repeating his expressions over and over again; calling for "number one, number one," &c. I heard this woman give the same testimony on three different occasions, once under oath, at the coroner's inquest.

Question. Were these statements all consistent with each other?

Answer. Yes, sir; they agreed perfectly. She, in the first place, made a statement to me, and then, in my presence, she made a statement to the sheriff again, and afterward to the coroner, under oath. Her testimony was precisely the same in each case.

Question. Have you known or heard of any other cases of violence committed by two or more men banded together, and in the night-time?

Answer. Well, sir, I was out in Winston County with the marshal; I just came in from there day before yesterday. We stopped at Governor Powers's place, or the place Governor Powers formerly owned.

By Mr. BLAIR:

Question. In Winston County, Mississippi?

Answer. Yes, sir; and the negroes told us there that in July last an armed band had approached the house for the purpose of attacking a man whose name I think was Powell; I will not be positive, but at any rate he was left in charge by Governor Powers to look after his plantation. They made a raid upon the house and the darkey fired upon them and killed one of their number whose name was Evans. They took him down to Dr. Kirk's store, a few miles distant, and he died there; that was merely hearsay.

By the CHAIRMAN:

Question. Did you understand that these men were disguised?

Answer. Yes, sir; so the darkey said.

By Mr. BLAIR:

Question. That was in Kemper County?

Answer. I believe, by the way, it is in Kemper County.

By the CHAIRMAN:

Question. Governor Powers himself testified before the committee in relation to that case; did you assist in making any arrest in Winston County?

Answer. I went there with a party of soldiers for the purpose of assisting the marshal, aiding him to serve the writs, but the parties had all abandoned their homes.

Question. The men named in the writs had left?

Answer. Yes, sir; all of them.

Question. Were those men charged with Ku-Klux outrages?

Answer. Yes, sir; and murder.

Question. How many of them had fled?

Answer. I knew of six, having seen their names in the marshal's hands, having been with him, and being unable to find them when we got into the country; there were more, but I did not know them.

By Mr. RICE:

Question. Was it reported that they had left the county?

Answer. Yes, sir.

By the CHAIRMAN:

Question. Have you heard of other outrages committed upon colored men that you have not enumerated?

Answer. I heard of one other case; I have heard, in fact, of several cases, but I cannot call them to mind now. I know of one other case that happened in Alabama. I took an interest in the matter, and wrote a communication in regard to it.

Question. What case was that?

Answer. There were two men who hired a plantation, or a portion of a plantation, from a doctor living in Gainesville, Alabama. I have forgotten his name; but I think his name was something like the name of the place; that it was Gaines, or something like it.

Question. Was that Dr. Choutteau?

Answer. No, sir; they had hired this place—I am not certain whether it was on shares or not. At all events, the rent for this land was due in December, and this man visited them some time in July last and told them that he wanted them to leave the place. They refused to do so. He took them both—they were brothers and negro men—across this river down here, the Tombigbee, and had them whipped, and confiscated their cotton, amounting to some five bales, and also some twenty-five bushels of corn, as they reckoned it. I wrote a letter to General Terry about it—there was no United States commissioner at Meridian, and I wrote a letter regarding the matter. It was returned, saying that the matter should be referred to the United States commissioner. There was a commissioner at Demopolis. I wrote to the commissioner, or sent this letter, and he forwarded to General Terry and asked to have the man sent down there before him to make affidavit; but they never went. I saw one of them in Meridian a few days ago and asked him if he had been down to see the commissioner at Demopolis. He said he was afraid to go. They had been living in Meridian ever since the occurrence had happened, since they were run away from their homes.

Question. Are these all the cases that occur to you now?

Answer. Yes, sir.

Question. Does the white population evince an earnest disposition, generally, to aid in stopping these outrages and assist the officers in discovering the perpetrators?

Answer. Well, there is a certain class of people in the country who consider these outrages very disastrous to the interests of the country, and who, I have no doubt, would be very glad to see them put down, but they do not seem to make any effort. I have often spoken to men of the country who thought it was as great a wrong as I did.

Question. Do you find a disposition anywhere to deny the existence of these organizations and the outrages that are imputed to them?

Answer. A disposition to deny them?

Question. Yes, sir; do you find that disposition?

Answer. I don't think I have heard any denial, any point-blank denial, except through the press—through the Mercury and Gazette there. I don't think the people generally believe there is such an organization; at least I have heard some of them say they did not believe there was such an organization.

Question. What is your opinion of the existence of an organization in this State of men with signs and passwords, by which they recognize each other, and formed for any of the following purposes: To drive from the country objectionable persons, or to harass or molest persons odious for any cause, or to punish negroes suspected of theft or other crimes, or to influence negroes in voting or abstaining from voting, or to promote the success of the conservative or democratic party and enable it to obtain the political control of the State and the offices?

Answer. Well, sir, I think that there is an organization of armed men in the country, who have signs and passwords, and modes of recognizing each other, and who maraud about the country for the purpose of driving away northern people, intimidating negroes, and doing damage generally. I think there is a class of people who evade the law, who have very little at stake themselves and very little to gain.

Question. The committee will be glad, Captain Yates, to have you give them any evidence upon which you have founded these opinions.

Answer. Well, sir, there is a class of men in the city of Meridian who are known as desperate characters; men who frequent bar-rooms—drinking men, who, upon a slight provocation, are in the habit of drawing their weapons, and intimidating citizens; these men have the reputation of being desperadoes, and in all public gatherings they seem to have a crowd about them who are influenced by them. They are men who have very little interest at stake; they are men of very little respectability or standing, still they wield this power among the citizens.

Question. Is it your opinion that this organization is recruited, or made up, of this class of men whom you have described?

Answer. I have no doubt at all that the majority come from that class. They told me up here in Winston County, in this Evans's case, that every time the old man, the leader of one of these Ku-Klux bands, who is sixty years of age, got on a drunk he would blow his horn, and the boys about the country would come in and join him, and during their orgie they would go around the country intimidating the negroes.

Question. This old man Evans you speak of lives in Winston County?

Answer. I think he lives in Winston County.

By Mr. BLAIR:

Question. Kemper County, is it not?

Answer. Governor Powers's place is in Kemper, but he lives just beyond the line, in Winston County, I think.

By the CHAIRMAN:

Question. You have heard, I suppose, from time to time, of a good many negroes being whipped by these disguised men at night, after being taken from their houses?

Answer. I have heard of but few cases. I have heard other people speak of a number of cases where men have been whipped by disguised parties, taken out from home at night.

Question. I am not speaking of cases within your personal knowledge, but where you have received this information from others?

Answer. Yes; I have heard of a number of cases.

Question. Have you known of any cases where any one implicated, as a member of these disguised bands, has been brought to justice, and punished in the State courts, for any of these outrages?

Answer. No, sir; there has been no State court in session since I have been here; I have only been here four months.

By Mr. BLAIR:

Question. You say Stillwell, who was arrested on a charge of killing a man twenty miles from Meridian, was tried in a preliminary trial and discharged?

Answer. Yes, sir; he proved an *alibi*, and was discharged.

Question. He proved that he was not there at the time the murder was committed?

Answer. Yes, sir.

Question. Who did he prove that by?

Answer. He proved it by I do not know how many witnesses, but by a satisfactory number of witnesses.

Question. This negro who was killed seven miles from Meridian, was shot in his house, and his house burnt, and he himself burnt up in it?

Answer. Yes, sir; after he was killed; and they burnt his two children also; his wife raised the board floor and crawled out and got away.

Question. You say suspicion pointed to a colored man who had threatened to Ku-Klux this old man?

Answer. Yes, sir; he had made threats the day before; he had been in town drinking and had gone to a white man and told him that this old fellow was in the habit of interfering with his hogs, I believe, and he intended to Ku-Klux him. The evidence was pretty conclusive against him, having made this threat, and coming home late at night, and his own story was very much questioned, and it was believed that he was the cause of the fellow's death, by me as well as the rest, until this women testified. She made a statement to the sheriff and swore to it before the marshal, in which she mentioned the expression used by the party that came there; that they were calling, "Number one," "number one set the house on fire," "set the house on fire," &c.

Question. How many were there?

Answer. She said about six.

Question. In disguise?

Answer. I don't know about that; I do not think she said they were disguised.

Question. She did not say?

Answer. She said that a man who did the shooting was a white man; she seemed to be positive about that. I questioned her pretty closely as to whether it might not be a man in disguise, with cotton on his head. She said he had a white beard, and she said he had a bald head and his hat off; that he had a long beard, and that she recognized the head, as I have mentioned. She said one man had a bad cough, and coughed incessantly. If I had gone to the place before the negroes commenced assembling there from curiosity to look at the premises burnt up, I could undoubtedly have traced the people who came there the night before, because it was presumed that they came on horseback. We saw indications of horses close to the house, but the negroes came from all the neighborhood about, assembling from curiosity, and trampled the whole country over so that it was impossible to find the trail. The country was very sandy, so that a horse would have made a pretty deep trail, and we would have been able to track them, but the negroes had ridden all over the country the next day before we got there, and had obliterated the trails that might have been found.

Question. In reference to this Gainesville matter, you say a man came to you from Gainesville, or a couple of them?

Answer. Two brothers, negroes, who lived in Meridian, who worked there, had been driven out of Gainesville, I think they said, in July, and they made the statement that this doctor had driven them away from the place; that they had entered into a contract with him to hire this land and pay him in December; that the man seemed to have got tired of his bargain, and ordered them away and took them out and whipped one of them and confiscated their crop, consisting of five bales of cotton and twenty-five bushels of corn, and there was also a wagon and pair of horses.

Question. They declined to make any affidavit?

Answer. They were afraid to go, yes. I wrote this communication, and it was referred back to me. They came up every day or two in order to see about it. I told them what I had done. Finally, when I got the answer from the commissioner at Demopolis, I told them they must go there and make affidavit where they stated to me their property was, and he would take some action; but they were afraid to go.

Question. They pretended that they were afraid?

Answer. Yes, sir; they pretended that they were afraid to go, or said so.

Question. Did it never occur to you that that was made up out of whole cloth, inasmuch as they failed to follow it up when they had the protection of the Government?

Answer. Well, they might have exaggerated this report, but I believed there was a great deal of truth in it. I believe that firmly now, because I talked with them both separately, and they told the same story. They told me afterwards that they had been told by other darkies that they had better let that thing drop, and they were very much intimidated. One fellow had had a good walloping, and was afraid that he might get another one.

Question. This committee has been in the county of Sumter, within a short distance of Gainesville, and examined witnesses from that town itself, and thoroughly sifted everything that happened there, and a great many things that did not, and there was no whisper of any such thing as this.

The CHAIRMAN. I have no idea that we got one-tenth of the evidence concerning outrages in that community.

By Mr. BLAIR:

Question. Considered together with what came under your observation, and in the light of this testimony, I want you to say whether you do not think that was made out of whole cloth?

Answer. Well, general, these men came to me for advice. I knew that the case came under the Ku-Klux law, but not having a commissioner there, I thought I would refer the matter to General Terry—this fracas having occurred in Alabama, outside of Mississippi; so I sat down after they told me what had happened, and wrote it out and referred it to him. After I had put the business in such train that it was easy to proceed, they seemed afraid to undertake further prosecution; and I really believe that there was a great deal of truth in it; I formed that opinion myself.

Question. Now, since you have ascertained that this committee was in that county, staid there a week and examined a number of witnesses from the neighborhood of Gainesville, and there was not a whimper about this transaction, not a word said about it, what do you think?

Answer. Well, this was a negro family, and it may have been that they were afraid to come out and tell what had happened.

By Mr. RICE:

Question. Did they leave there immediately after it occurred?

Answer. Yes, sir; they left there immediately, as soon as he could walk. One of these men said he was whipped so that he could not move for a week, and as soon as he could travel he left. I believe the law has been badly administered in this country. I think if the good people would exercise their influence, co-operating with the officers and control these fellows, this Ku-Klux Klan could be done away with in a great measure. As an illustration, in this Stillwell affair, they never held an inquest until the fellow had laid in his house four or five days; they were almost afraid to go. The sheriff came to me and said, "I have to go up in this county, and it is a pretty desperate county, and I want a big detail—twenty men and an officer." This was to go only a distance of twenty miles, when there was really scarce any danger at all. I could have gone there with two or three men. But the disposition here is to sympathize with these people, and the officers are afraid of this sympathy; there is too much of it manifested. In my opinion they do not exercise a proper control over the people; they are afraid.

By Mr. BLAIR:

Question. It is your opinion that the officers are inefficient?

Answer. I do most decidedly think so.

Question. That they are too fond of calling upon the troops to do the work they are paid to do?

Answer. Well, they seem to be afraid; they call on troops, to be sure, but they seem to be afraid to run the risk themselves.

Question. They want to hold the offices and do not want to perform the duties?

Answer. They do not want to exercise any control, or to run into any kind of danger.

By the CHAIRMAN:

Question. Does not their want of efficiency in the execution of the laws arise in a measure from an indisposition on the part of the whites to aid them in the performance of their duties; to the disposition to prevent them from executing their duties?

Answer. I think there is that disposition; I do not think they are firm enough in the execution of their duties; I do not think they take a stand sufficiently positive; they seem to be very easily intimidated; the sentiment is against the exercise of the powers of the law, in a measure, among these lawless fellows, and I do not think they take a sufficiently decided stand; they are almost afraid.

Question. In order to make officers efficient in the discharge of their duties, must there not be a sustaining public sentiment?

Answer. Yes, sir; I think so.

Question. Were there a sustaining public sentiment, would it be possible to bring these offenders to justice in the State courts—to convict and punish them? Suppose, for example, that there were Ku-Klux upon the juries, or men upon the juries who sympathized with this organization, would there not be a practical difficulty in executing the laws under such circumstances?

Answer. Undoubtedly public sentiment would be against the proper execution of the laws.

COLUMBUS, MISSISSIPPI, *November* 13, 1871.

JOSHUA HAIRSTON (colored) sworn and examined.

By the CHAIRMAN:

Question. Do you live in this county?

Answer. I do.

Question. How long have you lived there?

Answer. Fifteen years, sir.

Question. In what part of the county do you live?

Answer. I live south from here, down in the prairie.

Question. Have you been shot at by any men?

Answer. I have, sir.

Question. When did that occur?

Answer. I think it was on the 10th of this month, last year, the 10th or 15th; I forget the exact time.

Question. Under what circumstances?

Answer. I couldn't tell you; I don't know the circumstances I was shot at for.

Question. Were you upon the highway?

Answer. I was in my own house, abed and asleep, when they came to my house on a Thursday night, about 9 o'clock. They came to my door. I was living in a double cabin on a place I had rented there, and some of my hands were in an adjoining room to me. I was in the habit of not sleeping very sound. I heard them knock at the other cabin-door. I heard the woman in the next room to me say, "Josh isn't in here; he is in the other room." By this time my wife waked me up, and said there was some person calling me. I knew the man very well.

Question. You know the man who shot at you?

Answer. I knew the man very well, no quicker than I heard his voice. It hadn't been more than four hours since I had been talking with him. I saw him just about an hour by sun. It was 9 o'clock then. I told her it was nobody but Bill, and finally he said, "Come out to the door." I did'nt come directly to the door. I was always in the habit, when I went out, of taking my pistol in my hand. That night I had it in my pocket, but I hadn't taken it out, and she had moved my coat, and I did't get it for five or ten minutes. I didn't find my coat; and he called again for me to come out. He told me to come out. I asked him, then, before I opened, what he wanted; he said, "Josh, come out, I want to see you on some very particular business." I asked him again to tell me. He said, "No, come out here, I want to see you on something important;" and he turned his horse's head a little round, as I opened the crack of the door about as wide as my hand. He said, "Come out, come out here and show me the way to Crawfordsville." He was then in two miles of Crawfordsville, which is two miles from there right to my house. I then told him, "I won't do it, sir." As I said that, he raised up, and deliberately descended the pistol right into my face, and the pistol didn't go off; the cap busted; and as the cap busted I slammed the door; and he said, "Damn you, I'll have you, anyhow," and shot the latch off the door with a double-barrel shot gun.

By Mr. BLAIR:

Question. Did you see the pistol?

Answer. Yes, sir; I saw it; heard the crack; it wasn't further from my face than from here to that door—five yards. He might have been a little further, but I'll say that far, to be sure.

By the CHAIRMAN:

Question. Do you know who he was?
Answer. Yes, sir; I know him as well as I know any face in this place, or as I know my own in the glass.
Question. Did he have any disguise on?
Answer. No, sir; nothing but plain clothes, just as I talked to him alf an hour before sun.
Question. Have you any hesitation about giving his name?
Answer. None in the world.
Question. What was it?
Answer. Mr. William Moore, a colored man.
Question. Was any other person with him?
Answer. There was another man, but I didn't know him. He was either a white man or a very bright mulatto. But there was two with them I don't know. There was two more I didn't see. When I come to the end of it I'll tell you.
Question. Make it brief.
Answer. When he shot he said, "Damn your soul, I'll have you," and he shot a double-barrel shot-gun angling into my door; but it struck the side of the wall, before it came in the house. The next shot took the latch off, and went up in the ceiling of my house, into the roof. They went immediately round to the corner, and shot into the house at the stove, right at the corner.
Question. The next shot was at the corner of the house?
Answer. Yes, sir; at the corner. One came in at the door, and one in at the corner. Directly again they shot another right in over my bed. My wife was in it, but I was out. He came as quick as he could to the back door behind, and he says, "Boys, let's re-enforce and come and get him, anyhow, by God, or if we don't get him, we'll never get him."
Question. Did they re-enforce?
Answer. They didn't come into the house; they staid round there in the conversation for half an hour, as we're here now; and in the yard were my hands, a man named Lewis Hairston and Prelace Samuel. They were known to be there by the gentlemen, and I don't know but every one on the plantation saw them before they attacked me, and knew in their own conversation that there were Ku-Klux on the place. There was a partition carried up in the houses, the way they generally carry up darkies' houses. There was a partition between mine and the other house. It seemed they were going to get into my room anyhow. I climbed over the partition into the other fellow's house, and got his gun. His wife said, "I told my husband to come in here, but he would go out——"
Question. Did you examine the tracks of the horses the next morning?
Answer. Yes, sir.
Question. How many do you suppose there were in the party?
Answer. It was a very dry time to trace the horses. The ground was very hard. The prairie land isn't like this land here. I know I saw two on horses. The others told me there was five. I heard the voices of three, but I couldn't get them all.
Question. When was that?
Answer. On the 10th of this month, a year ago, if I am not mistaken.

By Mr. RICE:

Question. Did the boys on the place say these men were disguised?
Answer. Two of the men said they had on some kind of striped pants, and clothes with some kind of stripe up and down them; but I didn't see that man at all.

By the CHAIRMAN:

Question. Do you know, or have you heard, of any other colored men in that part of the country being Ku-Kluxed?
Answer. On that very same night, at Major Hairston's, there was a raid on a colored man, but I couldn't remember his name.
Question. What did they do?
Answer. They took him out and whipped him pretty badly. I don't know who did it. I saw him afterward. He was pretty badly beat up.
Question. Do you know of any other cases?
Answer. On the Monday night before they come to my house, there was a fellow killed over at Mr. Malone's plantation.
Question. Dick Malone?
Answer. Yes, sir.
Question. We have heard of that case, and you need not go into it.
Answer. Then I won't go into it.

By Mr. BLAIR:

Question. Did you say this case on George Hairston's place was on the same night on which you were shot at?

Answer. Yes, sir; the same night they were after me.

Question. Did you see this fellow, Bill Moore?

Answer. I saw him and talked with him four or five minutes before he attempted to shoot at all.

Question. You have no doubt about his identity?

Answer. I know him. He has a very peculiar dress-hat he always wore. It was a kind of black hat. It had got tolerably dirty, and it had a wide band round it. They wore that in the war. I looked at it while he talked with me. I knew him as well as any face in Columbus.

Question. He was not disguised?

Answer. Not at all. On the day we had him up on trial he was under bond of $2,000, and he was sent by the magistrate, or by the constable, to hunt a man to go on his bond, and in the time he was coming from where the trial was down to the depot the constable let him tear that band off of his hat and throw it away; and then held him under custody for two days, I think, in order that he might get bond—until the next day for trial; and then they had fixed up so much false witness on the next trial that they put me into costs $50 for having him up.

Question. Before whom was that trial?

Answer. Before Major Whitfield.

Question. Major Henry B. Whitfield?

Answer. Yes, sir.

Question. He gives the impression in his testimony that that was a white man who visited you?

Answer. Well, sir, I did not say there was not a white man there; but I say the man I talked with was not. As to who, and how many there were, I can't say. I know I saw two, and talked with one.

Question. His case was tried before Major Whitfield?

Answer. Yes, sir.

Question. In that trial you testified that this negro was the man who first shot at you?

Answer. I'll take a dead oath on it, if I am to be hung about it, that I know the man as well as I know Mr. Whitfield. I talked with him four minutes before he attempted to shoot. Then it run on; I wouldn't have had him taken up, but for his threats afterward.

Question. He does not state in his testimony that the case was tried before him at all, but says it was the general understanding in the country that this man was whipped or severely beaten. You were not beaten at all?

Answer. I have never been struck at all, except in fights with colored people, and not in fifteen years by any man at all.

Mr. BLAIR. I read the testimony of Henry B. Whitfield, page 423, in regard to a case that was tried before him, which is the case of which this witness is speaking, and which Major Whitfield does not say was tried before him, but attempts to put this appearance on the case. "It occurred in the fall, before the case I have just mentioned. The man whipped was a freedman, by the name of Hairston, on Major George Hairston's place. The general understanding in the country at the time was that this man was whipped or pretty severely beaten."

Mr. RICE. That is a case of which the witness has spoken. The witness has mentioned a man whipped on George Hairston's place.

WITNESS. I mean a man named Thompson, two miles from Crawfordsville. This man Hairston, I suppose, was ten or twelve miles from Mr. Whitfield's. I don't know whether that case was tried before any one.

By the CHAIRMAN:

Question. Was he severely beaten?

Answer. I was told he was pretty badly beat; he was not whipped himself, but beat with clubs. I don't say they whipped him; his head was clubbed.

By Mr. BLAIR:

Question. Was that the same night you were shot at?

Answer. Yes, sir.

Question. Was it by the same people?

Answer. I couldn't tell. It was seven miles from where I was. I saw him on his recovery. He was getting well, and I saw some pretty bad scars on his head at that time; and it was some three weeks before I saw him.

Question. Was that in Lowndes County?

Answer. Yes, sir; a little way from the Noxubee line. I suppose it was not more than half a mile from the Noxubee line. The man I rented my land from is Joseph J.

Thompson. He went to Lewis Hairston the next morning, the youngest man, and told him to go ahead and finish picking out the cotton, that nobody was going to interrupt him. That was Lewis Hairston. A man I had rented land from told him to go on and pick out the cotton; nobody would interrupt him.

By the CHAIRMAN:

Question. Are you on the grand jury here?

Answer. Yes, sir; I remained on the grand jury until Saturday night.

Question. How far do you live from here?

Answer. Twenty-five miles from here, going by the way of Crawfordsville and the railroad.

By Mr. BLAIR:

Question. Whitfield discharged this man that you identified?

Answer. He did.

Question. Notwithstanding you swore positively to his identity?

Answer. He discharged him in this way I told you. The first day of the trial, I think, it was decided. He then referred the case over to Thursday, in order to give him a chance to get him a lawyer; so it was said by the people down there; I don't know what his mind was in getting him a lawyer. I was so fearful they were going to turn him loose that I was advised I had better get me a lawyer, and I wrote up here for George Evans and Arnold, both lawyers, to come down. I come to get Buck Humphries, a lawyer here. I got him, and carried him down there, and knocked around there, and fooled with it, and finally I had to pay him $50 for nothing—for going there just to turn this man loose.

Question. You gave your evidence there just exactly as you have given it here to-day, identifying this man, Moore?

Answer. I did it clearer, I think, than I have given it here to-day, because I could remember of the white man. His hat was there in court to show, and known to Mr. Whitfield; and he knew that in ten minutes he tore the band off his hat, when he was out of his presence.

Question. Notwithstanding that, he discharged this man?

Answer. Yes, sir; and he and Mr. Humphries had some pretty sharp words about it.

By the CHAIRMAN:

Question. Did Mr. Moore give any evidence?

Answer. On the first day of the trial he hadn't a witness.

Question. Did he on the second trial?

Answer. On the second trial he had three.

Question. What did they prove?

Answer. They proved that he staid in their house from sundown to sunrise.

Question. The witnesses proved that he could not have shot at you?

Answer. They swore he was in their house, when I know directly that they swore to a lie, because when I talk to a man I know him.

Question. Moore proved by three witnesses that he could not have been there that night?

Answer. It was a gotten-up thing, that he was not there, to get him out of the law.

Question. At all events three witnesses swore that he was at home?

Answer. Yes, sir; of course they did. They swore that he was at home, but it always made a question to me where was the three witnesses on the first trial.

Question. He made an application, I suppose, to have his trial held over until he could get his witnesses and lawyer?

Answer. No, sir; not his witnesses, but to get his lawyer.

Question. Did his lawyer make an application to have a postponement?

Answer. He didn't have any lawyer then. Everything was got out on the first trial.

Question. How did the case come to be continued?

Answer. It was continued to get him out of it, just like every other case that has been brought up before the little law offices in this whole country. The man that has the biggest pile of money gets out.

By Mr. RICE:

Question. Did he have more than you?

Answer. No, sir; but his other Ku-Klux friends aided him.

By the CHAIRMAN:

Question. His Ku-Klux friends?

Answer. The people round there got him out.

By Mr. RICE:

Question. You think they belong to the Ku-Klux?

Answer. He does, or he wouldn't been there that night.

By the CHAIRMAN:

Question. Do you think there are Ku-Klux there?

Answer. There are many outrages round there in the night. I don't know who they are by.

Question. Are they by disguised men?

Answer. I couldn't say anything about disguises. They come directly out as men with guns and pistols and hunt men out at night and shoot them.

Question. Do you vote a republican ticket?

Answer. I do; and never expect to be anything else but a radical.

Question. How was Moore in politics?

Answer. I don't know what he was; I know he voted the other day; I don't think he has been anything much heretofore. He has been sort of leaning round toward the democratic party before, but now he votes radical.

Question. Heretofore he has been a democrat?

Answer. Here was the direct point: on the day Moore had his first trial he was to go to jail or give a two thousand dollar bond, but he and two of them had combined, and a young man appeared as a lawyer that never studied law in his life; and I objected, and it brought up a contradiction, and he said he should discharge him and get him a lawyer.

By Mr. BLAIR:

Question. You had had a quarrel with Moore before that?

Answer. Yes, sir; six weeks before that I had a fight with him and shot him, and was tried here and was cleared by paying $130 to a lawyer.

Question. You think that is the reason he attacked you?

Answer. I think that is one reason. The next reason is, I think, I was attacked by the farmers on my place to get my crop. As to my own people—of course I couldn't give it on oath—but I believe the people on the plantation was in the business that was going on; that is, the men I rented the land from—the Thompsons—they knew all about it. I sent to the old man—his house is close to Mr. Hairston's office—for his gun, and he sent word he wanted it himself, and I couldn't get it. The men were standing close by talking.

By the CHAIRMAN:

Question. Was this Thompson a white man?

Answer. Yes, sir.

Question. A good democrat?

Answer. Yes, sir; I suppose he is. There is another man down there in my neighborhood that has been shot at by Ku-Klux, and compromised for $150, and they never have paid him a bit of it.

Question. What is his name?

Answer. Mark Hairston.

Question. What did they do?

Answer. Shot at him, but didn't hit him. It was tried by the same Mr. Whitfield, and he was to see that the man got his money, but he has never got it. They compromised it, and it has never been brought to the grand jury.

By Mr. RICE:

Question. Who did that; white men?

Answer. They are very well-known men, I think. One of them was carried up the other day—Mr. Shields.

Question. Carried up to Oxford?

Answer. Yes, sir.

By Mr. BLAIR:

Question. You say it was compromised before?

Answer. It was in the way of being compromised; they fooled him by the way of paying $150 not to return it to the grand jury.

Question. Was that done in the presence of Mr. Whitfield?

Answer. Major Whitfield was the man promised to get his money.

By the CHAIRMAN:

Question. Did you hear him say that?

Answer. I was one of the grand jury, and heard him say it. It is no harm to tell that afterward.

By Mr. BLAIR:

Question. Whitfield deceived the man, and compromised this?

Answer. Yes, sir. He puts him off every time court comes up, until the grand jury is over; and here he has been knocked out of it, and it has been going on two years. He has the note.

By the CHAIRMAN:

Question. This note was given for the damages Mark Hairston had sustained?

Answer. They didn't injure him; they shot at him, and would have killed him if they could.

By Mr. BLAIR:

Question. It was simply compounding a felony?

Answer. I don't know what it was.

By Mr. RICE:

Question. I understand that Mr. Whitfield had nothing more to do with it than that Mr. Hairston gave him a note to collect?

Answer. No, sir. He was justice of the peace, and it was carried before him to be tried; and he tried these men, and put them on bail, and they gave bond. He had to appear before a grand jury, and return his bills; and he made the excuse for these gentlemen himself, that it had been compromised by promising to pay Hairston $150, and he said he would see that he got his money; and if they didn't pay him the money it would be brought up, and returned before the next grand jury. But it hasn't been done; and that is the way our country has been ruined up, kept back all the time.

COLUMBUS, MISSISSIPPI, *November* 13, 1871.

SANDERS FLINT (colored) sworn and examined.

By the CHAIRMAN:

Question. Where do you live?

Answer. Aberdeen.

Question. How long have you lived in Monroe County?

Answer. I came there in 1843, to Monroe.

Question. The committee have called you before them to inquire in reference to the murder of your two sons, Joseph and Willis Flint. We wish you to state the circumstances under which they were murdered.

Answer. Shall I tell you how the case started?

Question. Yes; tell all about it.

Answer. We went up there in the forks of the river and commenced——

Question. In the forks of what river?

Answer. The Tombigbee and Town Creek.

Question. At what time?

Answer. It was last Christmas a year ago. I don't remember the exact day of Christmas, but it was last Christmas a year ago. We staid there until the 13th day of November. No; that was the day he was killed. In October they got up a disputement about the crop, and the old man that was living there and my boys fell out about the crop, and they had a trial there, and put us all in jail.

Question. Who was that old man?

Answer. Brown Park.

Question. He fell out with your son about the division of the crop?

Answer. Yes, sir.

Question. Which son?

Answer. Joseph.

Question. You say Brown Park had your son put in jail?

Answer. Yes, sir; all three of us.

Question. You and your sons, Joseph and Willis?

Answer. Yes, sir.

Question. They put you in jail at Aberdeen?

Answer. At Athens.

Question. On what charge?

Answer. I forget what it was. Some kind of battery.

Question. Assault and battery?

Answer. Yes, sir; assault and battery.

Question. What took place then?

Answer. On the 13th day of October, at night, they took us out.

Question. Who took you out?

Answer. One of his sons, and the balance of the men. Do you want me to call the names of the men now?

Question. Were you taken out at night?

Answer. Yes, sir; taken out of jail.

By Mr. BLAIR:

Question. You say one of Brown Park's sons?

Answer. Yes, sir.

Question. And other men?

Answer. Yes, sir.

By the CHAIRMAN:

Question. How many men were concerned in taking you out?

Answer. Ten.

Question. What time in the night was this?

Answer. Well, sir, I don't know. I think it was about 12 o'clock, or a little after.

Question. Did these men who took you and your sons out have disguises on their faces or bodies?

Answer. They had some handkerchiefs tied on over their faces. They had no masks.

Question. Could you tell who the men were?

Answer. Yes, sir.

Question. Give us their names.

Answer. Robert Park, Samuel Young, Zackariah Westbrooks—we called him Zack—Williamson Westbrooks, and Bluford Westbrooks, and Purnell Smith. That makes six.

Question. Do you know any others?

Answer. There are two more I know—Click Marshall, and another one that they called Henry Hall; and there are two more that I can't think of exactly.

Question. How did you know them?

Answer. These men lived right by us, pretty near all of them, except Henry Hall; I never saw him before that night. The way I knew him was, we got into a mighty thick-settled neighborhood.

Question. Were they all young men?

Answer. Pretty near. Some few of them were married. The Westbrooks, I think, were married; and they all got to calling Henry Hall, and "Hall, Hall!" And one man came up behind him, and says, "Don't call that name; some men might be out, and detect him, and detect us all."

Question. Were those respectable young men that were engaged in this?

Answer. I think they were before they got into that.

Question. Did they stand well in that community before that—among the white people?

Answer. I never was acquainted with them but a little while. I went there Christmas, and that was in October that they took us out.

Question. Do you mean October of the next year?

Answer. Yes, sir. The next October; the same year, you may say. Christmas is the last month.

Question. Did you go there in October or Christmas?

Answer. In Christmas.

Question. Then it was the October of the next year? Does not October come before Christmas, in the year?

Answer. Yes, sir; that's so.

Question. Go on and tell the committee what those men did to you and your sons, after taking you out of jail; and, in the first place, how did they get you out of jail; did the jailer give them up the keys?

Answer. He said they took it from him.

Question. Did the jailer try to prevent them from taking you out?

Answer. He talked like he did when they first came up. He said he didn't know until they had come to the door; and when they come to the door, the first thing I heard or knew about it was—I was asleep, and the noise awakened me up—and I got up and peeped through the door, and they were all at the door where my youngest son was, and they called them, "Joe and Willis."

Question. Those are the names of your two sons?

Answer. The jailer asked what they wanted with them. They said, "We want them, and we're going to have them."

Question. What more did they say?

Answer. Then the jailer went to talking with them, and they all left like they were perfectly satisfied, and went down-stairs.

Question. With the jailer?

Answer. Yes, sir; back again. After a while they come up with the school-teacher that was there teaching school. He had been school-teacher in Aberdeen, and was teaching school there then.

Question. What was his name?

Answer. Mulhorn. That is what the jailer called him. He was a northern man.

Question. You say the jailer got the teacher?

Answer. He was living in the jail, and he came out at the noise, and came up-stairs with him. They told him to open the door. He had the key then; the jailer handed him the key, so he says, and he took the key.

Question. The jailer did not go up-stairs then?

Answer. No, sir; he didn't come up-stairs any more.

Question. He handed the key to the school-teacher?

Answer. Yes, sir; and the school-teacher come up-stairs with these men.

Question. What then?

Answer. Then they got the door open and took my youngest son out—that was Willis.

Question. Did they tell you what they wanted to do with him?

Answer. Not before they got us all out. They carried him down and put him under guard, and come back and took me and my oldest son, Joseph, out of jail. They put my oldest son on a mule, and me behind him. We rode on about two miles and a half, and they took out their bottles and gave us a dram apiece; and we rode on about six miles from Athens, and they stopped again, and one of them pulled out his watch and said it was about 2 o'clock, and going on 3 o'clock. And says he, "Do what you're going to do now, or daylight will catch us." He then pull out his bottle again and told us to take a dram for the last time, that they were going to kill us.

Question. Did your boys drink?

Answer. No, sir. Just as he pulled out the bottle, and one of them handed it to my oldest son, and he handed it across to me, the other that was guarding me snatched the bottle, and rode forward to hand it to the captain of the Klan, and that was the last I saw of that, for I jumped off and run away from them.

Question. Did you hear any firing after you left?

Answer. No, sir.

Question. What became of your two sons?

Answer. They were found in the Tombigbee bottom, at Cotton Gin; I reckon about half a mile from town.

Question. How far from where you made your escape?

Answer. Five miles.

Question. Was the river near this place where you made your escape?

Answer. No, sir; it was about three miles and a half off to the nearest place, I think.

Question. How long after this was it before your sons were found in the Bigbee River?

Answer. Eight days.

Question. The bodies had floated down the river?

Answer. They were not in the water at all; they just found them in the bottom, between the river and a lagoon.

Question. Did you examine the bodies to see whether they had been shot or hanged?

Answer. I did not at all; I never heard it until they were buried.

Question. Have you ever received any information as to how they came to their death?

Answer. Mr. Anderson, the sheriff's father, pursued them on that morning, and never stopped until they were found. He said they were shot; one of them, I think, in here, about his nose, [illustrating;] that his jaw-bone was broken, and the other ball went right in here, in the temple. They were shot pretty near the same place, both of them

Question. In the head?

Answer. Yes, sir.

Question. Did you identify their bodies by their clothing after they were killed?

Answer. Yes, sir; and there was one of them what you might know; the youngest one had a chain round his foot or ancle, and the other had a foot ruined with the rheumatic pains, and his toes grew under one another; and the colored boys in Cotton Gin, that were all raised with them, knew him by that.

Question. You have never seen your sons since?

Answer. No, sir.

Question. You do not doubt that they were killed that night?

Answer. Yes, sir; they were killed that night, because they said they were going to kill them.

Question. What has ever been done with those men who took you from the jail; have they been prosecuted?

Answer. They have taken them, and brought some of them up. There were five of them they had in custody; and while I was in Aberdeen, in prison, there was a fellow they called Smith, a brother of Colonel Smith, come in there to Aberdeen and took hold of me, and tried to drive me out of town to kill me, and the marshal happened to be close by, and they got him to know it, and he ran in there, and I got away from this man, and they took him and bound him over for five hundred dollars to the court; but he has never been tried; and Robert Park has never been tried; and Young has never been tried; I think he got away; he is gone to Texas.

Question. Who do you mean?

Answer. Robert Park and Young.

Question. Have both of them escaped?

Answer. Yes, sir.
Question. What has become of the Westbrooks?
Answer. They, I suppose, are all up there yet.
Question. Have they been taken up?
Answer. Yes, sir.
Question. In the State court or in the United States court?
Answer. In the State court.
Question. Have they ever been tried?
Answer. Yes, sir; they were tried there in the State court.
Question. Do you mean that indictments were found against them?
Answer. Yes, sir.
Question. Have they been tried and punished yet?
Answer. They never were punished at all. They cleared them—turned them out.
Question. What did they prove?
Answer. They proved that they were at home that night by some people that were up there, and the fact is the whole jury come out of that neighborhood that they were in.
Question. Out of the neighborhood where this murder was committed?
Answer. Yes, sir.
Question. What was done with Purnell Smith?
Answer. He was tried there in the court.
Question. Was he acquitted?
Answer. Yes, sir.
Question. What was done with Click Marshall?
Answer. He was acquitted.
Question. And Henry Hall?
Answer. He has never been seen.
Question. And these other two men whose names you could not give?
Answer. One of them was tried and acquitted, and the other was not. They all made their escape off to where nobody could get them.

By Mr. RICE:

Question. Who were they tried before?
Answer. Judge Meek.

By the CHAIRMAN:

Question. Did you swear on that trial that you knew these men?
Answer. Yes, sir. Two colored men were in the jail with me. After I swore to it they sent for these two colored men, and asked the man if he could point out any man that was in that crowd. They asked the men that were in prison to point out any man that was in the company that took me out of jail, and they came in and pointed out two of the men.
Question. Which ones?
Answer. Zack Westbrooks and his brother Blueford.
Question. He identified those two?
Answer. Yes, sir; the two prisoners came and identified them.
Question. And yet the jury acquitted these men?
Answer. Yes, sir.
Question. So that no one has been punished for the murder of your two sons?
Answer. No, sir; no one.
Question. All have been acquitted, or made their escape from the country?
Answer. All of them.

By Mr. RICE:

Question. Were they tried before a jury, or justice of the peace?
Answer. Before a jury.
Question. In the circuit court?
Answer. Yes, sir; they took away everything I made, I reckon; I had ten bales of cotton. All my corn and everything has been lying there. I have not got a cent for my year's work. Zack Westbrooks has a double-barrel shot-gun of mine, and I have tried to get them to get it, but none of them will go and get it.

By the CHAIRMAN:

Question. Who took possession of your cotton and other property?
Answer. After the old man, Brown Park, ran away, he come on to Aberdeen to court, and went back, and they looked for him back to my trial, and the first thing they knew he had run away to Texas.
Question. That is the father of Robert Park?
Answer. Yes, sir.
Question. He ran off to Texas?
Answer. Yes, sir; he left everything in the hands of his brother-in-law, Arch. Smith.

Question. Who took possession of your property when you were put in jail and your sons killed?

Answer. Arch. Smith the brother-in-law of Brown Park.

Question. Have you ever tried to recover it from them?

Answer. Yes, sir; I sent a lawyer up there after it immediately; and he went on up there, and I gave him an account of everything, and he come back, and when he come back he told me I would have to pay him $20 for what he had done, and he said he couldn't do anything. I called on him for my account that I gave him, and he has never made me no return of the account, or anything.

Question. Is that a lawyer living here?

Answer. He is living in Aberdeen.

Question Was this in Monroe County that you were living or at work at the time you were taken up and put in jail with your sons?

Answer. Yes, sir; three miles on the line between Lee and Monroe.

Question. Did you ever dare to come back to the neighborhood to live?

Answer. No, sir.

Question. You just left everything, and quitted the country?

Answer. Yes, sir; and come away.

Question. Do you know of any other colored people that have been whipped or killed?

Answer. There is a woman up there was whipped, or killed, and drowned. They put a sack over her head and drowned her, but I don't know who did it.

Question. What was her name?

Answer. Polly; I don't know who did it.

Question. Was she a colored woman?

Answer. Yes, sir.

Question. You say a sack was put over her head?

Answer. Yes, sir.

Question. What was done with her then?

Answer. Then threw her right in the river, at least they found her in the river with a sack tied over her head. The man that took her out told me last Wednesday.

Question. When did that occur?

Answer. It occurred the same year. I went up there on the night before. I don't know much about that no way.

Question Do you know of any colored people being whipped?

Answer. No, sir, I don't. I know of a fellow-servant of mine being killed. But I reckon you have all that. They got the two men.

Question. Who is that?

Answer. Dick Flint.

By Mr. RICE:

Question. Did you call him Dick Hendricks sometimes?

Answer. Yes, sir. It is the same man. He was sold to Hendricks.

By the CHAIRMAN:

Question. Tell us about that case.

Answer. I can't tell you only what I heard. He was killed up in the same neighborhood where I was run away from.

Question. You do not know anything about the killing?

Answer. No, sir.

Question. Where are you living now?

Answer. Living right in Aberdeen.

By Mr. RICE:

Question. Were you ever prosecuted for the assault and battery; did you ever have any trial for that?

Answer. No, sir. The men all run away and left me, and they acquitted me.

By Mr. BLAIR:

Question. What lawyer was that to whom you paid $20?

Answer. Mr. Mason Cummings. He told me the other day he was going to sue me for the money.

By the CHAIRMAN:

Question. Did you agree to pay him $20?

Answer. I didn't agree to pay him $20. I was to pay him $100 to go and get my crop; and when he come back he said he couldn't get it; and he charged me $20 for what he had done; and he wouldn't give up the account, and I wouldn't pay.

By Mr. BLAIR:

Question. Is he living there now?

Answer. Yes, sir; he is living a little piece the other side of Aberdeen. His office is in Aberdeen.

Question. Where is this Colonel Smith who tried to kill you afterward?

Answer. Jim Smith; he lives on Buttahatchee, up east of Aberdeen.

Question. That was not Purnell Smith?

Answer. No, sir; he is a brother of the one who helped to kill the boys.

COLUMBUS, MISSISSIPPI, *November* 13, 1871.

JOSEPH DAVIS (colored) sworn and examined.

By the CHAIRMAN:

Question. Where do you live?

Answer. At Aberdeen.

Question. How long have you lived in Monroe County?

Answer. Six or seven years; ever since and before the surrender.

Question. Were you in the war?

Answer. Yes, sir; I was in it a little.

Question. In the confederate service?

Answer. Yes, sir.

Question. Did you belong to a band in the Ku-Klux Klan?

Answer. Yes, sir.

Question. When did you join it?

Answer. I didn't join it at all; they came in and got me, and forced me to go with them.

Question. Who did that?

Answer. Jasper Webb, and Andrew Pope, and Whitfield Pope, and Tom Malone.

Question. What did they tell you they wanted you to do?

Answer. They told me they wanted me to go with them; and they asked me if I was in favor of Ku-Kluxing; I told them I was not; they said I was one of the strict radicals, and for that reason they were going to force me to go with them. Jasper Webb drew his knife on me at the same time, and told me I would have to go.

Question. How long ago was this?

Answer. It has been—I can't tell you exactly how long. It was along in the spring, about the time the spring first began to open.

Question. This last spring?

Answer. Yes, sir.

Question. Did they make you put on a disguise?

Answer. Yes, sir.

Question. Did you go out with them on horseback or on foot?

Answer. On horseback, or on a mule.

Question. How many of you were along?

Answer. Well, there was between sixty and seventy of them—or forty-odd of them, or fifty. There was between fifty and sixty, any way.

Question. Did you know them all?

Answer. No, sir; I didn't know them all.

Question. Where did you meet before you started out?

Answer. I didn't meet them; they come to my house and got me and the balance of that crowd to meet down to Billy Walton's. The principal of them met at Billy Walton's; some of them down below Billy Walton's.

Question. Was that in Monroe County?

Answer. Yes, sir.

Question. Where did you go from Walton's?

Answer. They went down to Bob Mays's.

Question. To where Jack Dupree lived?

Answer. Yes, sir.

Question. You went along with them?

Answer. Yes, sir.

Question. What time did they get to Bob Mays's?

Answer. I don't know exactly what time of night. I reckon it was between 9 and 10 o'clock.

Question. What did they do after they got there?

Answer. They got there, and they went to a fellow by the name of Henry Lewis. They went to his house, and called him out, and tried to get him out, and he wouldn't come out; and they left his house, and went to Dupree's house.

Question. What did they do there?

Answer. They called him to come out, and he didn't come out; but he got up and opened the door, and went back and got into bed; and then they came in and asked him to get up; and he didn't get right up out of bed, but he began to fight them; and they jumped on him, some five or six of them, and began to knock him with guns and sticks; and his wife was hollowing, and they drew their pistols on her, and told her if she hollowed, or said another word, they would blow her up, or they'd kill her, and then they taken him on out, and carried him down the road, down below Ross's Mill, somewhere in the swamp, and they whipped him; they whipped him until—well, they whipped him an hour or more, until he hollowed and went on so he could scarcely hollow; you could scarcely discern him hollow, so they said; and when they came back to where we were and the horses, they said they had cut his damned guts out.

Question. How many of them left the main body and went down to whip and kill him?

Answer. That night?

Question. Yes.

Answer. I don't know, sir, hardly how many left the horses and went down to where they whipped him.

Question. Did you stay with the horses?

Answer. Yes, sir.

Question. Did you hear them whipping him, and hear him hallooing?

Answer. Yes, sir. I could hear them beating him, and could hear him hollow.

Question. Was he a republican?

Answer. Yes, sir.

Question. What did they have against him?

Answer. Because he was a republican man. They said he was a republican man, and leading other men to be republican men—leading other parties to be republicans.

Question. Was he a leading man among the colored people?

Answer. He wasn't, to say a leading man particularly; but he had a right smart wit, and was a sort of teacher among them, and knowed more than the most of them, and told them what was right and wrong.

Question. Had he ever taught a colored school?

Answer. No, sir; I don't believe he had.

Question. What did they do after they got through with Dupree?

Answer. Well, after they got through with him, they all come back to their horses, and got on their horses and come home.

Question. What time in the night was it when you got home?

Answer. It was very nearly day.

Question. How far was this place where he was killed from where you lived?

Answer. I reckon it was a little over a mile; about a mile and a quarter.

Question. Did they swear you?

Answer. Yes, sir.

Question. Do you recollect what kind of an oath you took?

Answer. No, sir; not exactly. I can't exactly remember what they said to me; but I know they made me hold up my hand and swear I never would say anything about it, nor never tell anybody, nor know anything about it anyway.

Question. Who administered that oath to you?

Answer. Jasper Webb and Tom Malone.

Question. Where were you when they swore you?

Answer. I was not far from my house; just a piece from my house.

Question. Off from the road?

Answer. Yes, sir; they called me a piece from my house, and then did the talking down in the road.

Question. What did they threaten to do with you unless you went along with them?

Answer. They told me if I didn't go, that the Ku-Klux would come to see me, and they'd kill me if I didn't go with that band. They said the Ku-Klux would come to see me, and they'd kill me; and if I ever said anything about it, they said they would kill me.

Question. Was there any other colored man besides yourself on the trip?

Answer. Yes, sir.

Question. Who else?

Answer. Henry Hatch was along.

Question. Any other colored man?

Answer. Mike Forshee.

Question. Any other colored men besides Henry Hatch and Michael Forshee?

Answer. No, sir; not that was forced to come in. There was two more in it that went in it themselves.

Question. But those two men, Hatch and Forshee, were forced in it just like you?

Answer. Yes, sir.

Question. Do you know the two colored men that were not forced to go into it, that were along?

Answer. Burrill Willis and Jefferson Willis.

Question. Were they all mounted on horses?

Answer. Yes, sir; all of them.

Question. Had the horses any cover or disguises on?

Answer. Yes, sir, I think the horses were; I am not certain; but then the horses were pretty nearly all of one color, and I think by all of them being one color they were all dressed alike, and that made one color.

Question. How were the men disguised?

Answer. Some of them had on red, a red shroud on the body, like a coat, and some a white piece that came over the face, and some a black piece; and some had on a white shroud that came down over them like a coat.

Question. Were they all disguised?

Answer. Yes, sir, every one of them.

Question. Was that all that was done that night, whipping and killing Jack Dupree?

Answer. Yes, sir.

Question. Did you ever go out with them on another night?

Answer. Yes, sir.

Question. Go on and state it.

Answer. The next time they went out they went for Aleck Page, but they didn't catch him that night; he got away that night and run. They shot at him, though, some four or five shots; then, the next night, not very long after that, on a Wednesday night about the ninth of March, they came back after him again.

Question. After Aleck Page?

Answer. Yes, sir.

Question. Did they find him that night?

Answer. Yes, sir.

Question. Where did they find him?

Answer. They found him in his house, in bed.

Question. How many were along at that time?

Answer. Well, there was forty or thirty, or probably more than that.

Question. Were they all disguised that night?

Answer. Yes, sir; all of them were disguised.

Question. What did they do after they went to his house?

Answer. They went and called him, and told him to make up a light. He didn't seem to do it, and they gathered an axe and broke the door down and went in; and after they went in they called for a rope to tie him with, but they didn't have any rope, and Andrew Pope started under the bed and did, I think, cut a cord out of the bed to tie him with, and then there was a piece of rope hanging from the joist, hanging down in the house, and one of the men jerked it down; and whilst they all crowded round him, then they made me tie him. After they tied him they taken him out and put him up on a horse behind some one; I don't know who he got behind, but they put him up on the horse behind some one, and they taken him off.

Question. Where did they take him to?

Answer. I couldn't tell exactly where they carried him to. They carried him away off, a right smart piece in the woods.

Question. Do you know what they did with him there?

Answer. There they beat him and whipped him, and knocked him about right smart, and then they killed him.

Question. Did they shoot him or hang him?

Answer. They hung him.

Question. Did you see them do that?

Answer. I didn't see them hang him; but after they had hung him they sent one of the men down to the horses, where I was, for me to come up there, and I went up there, and the rope was round his neck, and he was there hanging at that time, and I know they hung him, for he was there hanging yet, at the time I got there.

Question. Was he dead at that time?

Answer. I don't think he was quite dead. After they let him down he seemed to move about a little, and one of them, I don't know who, struck him with a light-wood knot.

Question. A what?

Answer. A pine knot.

Question. What did they do after they had killed him?

Answer. They turned in, then, and buried him. They made us dig a hole, and buried him in it. There was several of them. I don't know who all dug the hole. They helped to dig it. Me and Henry helped to put him in the hole they dug, and to cover him up.

Question. Did they go home then?

Answer. Yes, sir; they talked round there right smart, and staid there a while, and talked round, and then they went home.

Question. What time did you get home that night?

Answer. I don't know hardly what time it was.

Question. How far was this place, where Page was hung, from where you lived?

Answer. From where he was to where I live was, I reckon, about three miles; and, I think, they must have went about a mile and a half or two miles, a mile and a half anyhow, from where I lived, right straight. It was pretty well north and east from where I lived.

Question. How late was it when you got home that night?

Answer. I don't know what time of night it was; it was a right smart while until day, but I couldn't tell what time of night it was.

Question. Was it day when you got home?

Answer. No, sir.

Question. Neither time?

Answer. No, sir.

Question. Did you ever go out again with them afterward; or any other company?

Answer. Yes, sir; the next time they went out they went after Rhett Willis and Simon Dunham.

Question. Was that Aleck Willis?

Answer. Yes, sir; they called him Rhett Willis.

Question. What did they do to them?

Answer. They got Rhett Willis, and took him out and whipped him. They whipped him ever so bad. They did Simon the same way.

Question. Did they tell them what they whipped them for?

Answer. Yes, sir. Simon was working for Bob Mays, and he and Bob Mays had fell out; and Bob Mays had got after him with his pistol to shoot him, and Simon went off; and while he was gone off, he thought he had better get him another place to live at, rather than to be there with a fuss; and because he left, that was what they whipped him for, to make him go back.

Question. What did they whip Dunham for?

Answer. That was the one. They whipped Dunham for leaving Bob Mays.

Question. What did they whip Willis for?

Answer. They whipped Willis for suing McNeice.

Question. Willis had sued McNeice to recover some money that was coming to him?

Answer. Yes, sir.

Question. What did they tell Willis and Dunham they would do to them if they ever told on them?

Answer. They didn't tell them, as I heard, that night, what they would do if they ever told on them; but they told them what they were whipping them for, and told them to tell all their friends in election day if they didn't vote the democratic ticket that they were going to do all of them just that same way.

Question. Do you know anything about the murder of Abram Wamble?

Answer. Yes, sir.

Question. Tell the committee what you know about that?

Answer. They went up, I don't know how far above Aberdeen it was; but they went up there, and went to his house, and called him out, and after they called him out, he came out. They didn't talk but very little to him. They took him out into the road, and didn't talk but very little to him before they shot him. They shot six or seven shots at him.

Question. Did they leave him lying in the road?

Answer. No, sir; they carried him outside the road.

Question. Did they bury him?

Answer. I don't know whether they buried him or not. I didn't go to where they were; after they buried him they were a right smart while coming back to the horses where I were. I don't know whether they buried him or not.

Question. How many were in the company that murdered Wamble?

Answer. Between fifty and sixty.

Question. Were they all disguised?

Answer. Yes, sir.

Answer. Was that the same night they whipped Dunham and Willis?

Answer. No, sir.

Question. Did they do any other mischief that night, except killing Wamble?

Answer. No, sir; they didn't do any other night.

Question. Do you know what they killed Wamble for?

Answer. No, sir; I dont know exactly what they killed him for. I never heard them say. I never heard what they wanted to kill him for.

Question. Did you ever go with them upon any other night?

Answer. No, sir.

Question. Those were all the times you went with them?

Answer. Yes, sir.

Question. Do you know what time it was when they killed Wamble?

Answer. No, sir; I couldn't tell what time it was.

Question. Was that the last time you were out?

Answer. Yes, sir.

Question. Was the same man always captain of the company?

Answer. I never did know which one was the captain, but Webb, and Tom Malone, and Whitfield Pope was the main men all the time, but they always give me the dressing and the taking them a bit. They were the very men I always knowed that did anything that I knowed of, or that I saw. They were the four leading men.

Question. Were they always along in every raid?

Answer. Yes, sir. I heard of two more being killed; that's Sandy Flint's two boys.

Question. You were not along at that time?

Answer. No, sir.

Question. Did you hear of any other colored men being whipped except them you have mentioned?

Answer. Yes, sir; I heard of some more, but I couldn't think of their names.

Question. What did you do with your disguise?

Answer. I given it to them; they taken it every time.

Question. Did the parents of Webb, Malone, and Whitfield Pope live there in that community?

Answer. In the neighborhood?

Question. Yes; in the neighborhood?

Answer. Yes; they lived there.

Question. Did these men pass for respectable young men?

Answer. No, sir. Whitfield, there nobody didn't like him. He has always been a torn-down man, him and Webb both; and there's nobody that ever went by Whitfield Pope's house that didn't 'preciate him no way.

Question. How was it with Malone?

Answer. I don't know. I never visited 'bout his house much.

Question. How is Andy Pope?

Answer. There didn't nobody visit about his house much.

Question. Were these married men?

Answer. Yes, sir.

Question. Did they own land?

Answer. Yes, sir.

By Mr. RICE:

Question. Planters?

Answer. Yes, sir.

By the CHAIRMAN:

Question. Did they raise cotton?

Answer. Yes, sir.

Question. Did they work any colored men on their plantation?

Answer. Yes, sir.

Question. How was it found out that you had been among them?

Answer. It wasn't found out at all; I told it.

Question. Who did you tell it to?

Answer. I told it to Mr. Wells.

Question. Colonel Wells, the district attorney?

Answer. Yes, sir.

Question. Had you been arrested—been taken?

Answer. Yes, sir.

Question. Who else was taken with you?

Answer. At that time?

Question. Yes.

Answer. There was Michael Forshee, and Henry Hatch, and Andy Crosby was taken from that place?

Question. From what place?

Answer. From Andy Crosby's place, where I was living at.

Question. They were arrested at the same time you were?

Answer. Yes, sir.

Question. Where were you taken to?

Answer. To Oxford. They came to Aberdeen on a Saturday night, and staid there Saturday and Sunday, and Monday went to Oxford.

Question. Was it at Oxford or at Aberdeen that you told Mr. Wells?

Answer. At Oxford.

Question. Where are Forshee and Hatch and Andy Crosby now?

Answer. Henry Hatch is in Aberdeen, and Mike Forshee and Andy Crosby are at the same place I am.

Question. Where?

Answer. At Andy Crosby's place.

Question. Are they under bond to appear at court?

Answer. Yes, sir.
Question. Who were you summoned before at Oxford?
Answer. Before Mr. Wells and all the jury that were there.

By Mr. RICE:

Question. Was it a grand jury?
Answer. Yes, sir.
Question. You were taken before a grand jury?
Answer. Yes, sir.

By the CHAIRMAN:

Question. Before you went with this crowd had you been a radical or democrat?
Answer. I had been a radical man from the very jump.
Question. How were these other colored men?
Answer. They were radicals too, the other two.
Question. The two that were forced in like you?
Answer. Yes, sir.
Question. How was it with the other two?
Answer. They were democrats; they had been democrats ever since they had been allowed to vote.
Question. Did you go with them for fear they would take your life if you did not go?
Answer. Yes, sir; they told me they would do it if I didn't go?
Question. Did you know anything against these colored men that were killed when you were along?
Answer. No, sir; not a thing.
Question. Did you know them all?
Answer. I knew Aleck Page. I did know Jack Dupree when I saw him; but I never was acquainted with him, and never had seen him but two or three times.
Question. Did they in each case come for you when they went upon these raids?
Answer. Yes, sir.
Question. They came by your house?
Answer. Yes, sir; they came after me.
Question. Would you know before hand when they were coming for you?
Answer. No, sir; I never knew. When they all broke up they never would say when they were going again, and I would never know until they came and called me.
Question. Did you ever find out where they held their meetings?
Answer. No, sir; that is something I never found out.
Question. Did they have any signs, grips, or passwords?
Answer. They did when they met anybody, or anything of that sort.
Question. Do you know what their signs were?
Answer. They would say something about "Shiloh," and all the foremost ones would understand it. I never did understand it; but they'd all understood it and know what to do.
Question. Did they have any whistles?
Answer. They had some kind of a whistle which went sort o' like a cane, or like blowing a quill. I don't know whether it was a quill or not.
Question. What did they use that whistle for?
Answer. That would be for all to come up, to crowd up together.
Question. Would any one take command of the company?
Answer. Some one would; but I don't know who it was, or which of them did.
Question. When you were out on these raids did you meet any persons on the road?
Answer. Yes, sir.
Question. What would you do when you met people on the road?
Answer. Sometimes we would meet one or two people and they'd ride right on by, aad nobody would speak or say nothing, but just keep straight forward; just the foremost ones that would see them would say, "Shiloh," and then they'd all hang their heads, or turn their heads, and nobody would say anything.
Question. When some one came they would say "Shiloh?"
Answer. Yes, sir; they'd always see them first.
Question. And then the men in the company would drop their heads?
Answer. Yes, sir.
Question. When you would ride by houses would not the dogs come out and bark at you?
Answer. Yes, sir; a great many times the dogs ran out and barked.
Question. Would not the inmates of the house get up and come out?
Answer. I don't know. Sometimes I suppose they did. I know we passed several houses where we could hear a lumbering about the house; and I allowed they got up to see what they could see; but nobody never would stop.
Question. Was your ride generally on moonlight nights or dark nights?
Answer. Sometimes it was moonlight nights and sometimes dark nights.

Question. Did you always get home before daylight?

Answer. Yes, sir; before it was good day; but only one night it was anywhere like near day.

Question. Do you know where they got their disguises.

Answer. No, sir.

Question. Or where they put them after they got through riding?

Answer. No, sir; I don't know where they put them, or where they got them; but I think they kept them in their houses.

Question. You knew but very few of the crowd?

Answer. No, sir; I didn't know but some six, or seven, or eight of them.

Question. You do not know where they came from?

Answer. No, sir. There was just such a number of them that I knew, and the rest I never did know.

Question. Did you ever go out with them when they were not covered with their disguises?

Answer. No, sir.

Question. They always had their disguises on?

Answer. Yes, sir.

Question. Did they always go on horseback?

Answer. Yes, sir; and they would always have on their disguises when they would start to go for anybody. Those that I knew, when they would come for me, wouldn't be disguised. They would call me out and fix up. They wouldn't be disguised. And when they met the whole company, and started for anybody, they would be fixed and disguised.

Question. You would see them put their disguises on.

Answer. Yes, sir.

Question. Where would they carry the disguises?

Answer. They would have them in their saddle-bags, or have them somewhere about them. I never could see where they kept them; it was dark.

Question. How many would come for you?

Answer. Three or four. Tom Malone and Jasper Webb and Andrew Pope and Whitfield Pope.

Question. Do you know what they killed Jack Dupree for?

Answer. They killed him for being a radical man. John Porter and Jasper Webb met him one day at the ferry; he was crossing the ferry going over to town, this last election before this. He was a sort of fore-light man among them, and one of the head men of the band or club that was going to Aberdeen to election.

Question. Is that the Loyal League?

Answer. Yes, sir. And as they were crossing the ferry, John Porter and Jasper Webb raised a fuss with them about going to vote, and all going to vote the republican ticket. And they had right smart words, and they sort o' fell out then, and they threatened him then, and threatened to kill him. And then some one of them wrote out an advertisement and published it in the paper, and stuck it up on the side of the road for no man to hire him in that county; but I suppose that he did get a home, and it went on a right smart while. He had been to Aberdeen this last spring—well, it was before the spring opened, directly after Christmas, I reckon, along in February or about the last of January, and Jasper Webb overtook him and Henry Lewis, and raised a fuss with him; he was drinking and sort of devilish, and he raised a fuss with Henry Lewis, and Henry Lewis galloped on away from him to not have a fuss, and he galloped up aside of him and would keep aside of him, and kept cursing him; and he started ahead once or twice and overtook us, and by that time Jack Dupree came up and Webb said to him that he wanted to get hold of him now; that he had had a few words with him once before, and that he was the very man he wanted to get hold of, and he just raised a fuss with Jack Dupree. And after he found there was too many along and he couldn't do anything, he galloped off and left the crowd and went on to Lushe Moore's and got Lushe Moore by the time the crowd came along there, and when we got there I heard Lushe Moore say, "By God, Jack Dupree is sure to go up if he is caught now." At that time Webb and Moore was standing there talking when we got there. In a few days, I reckon in two or three or four days, they went after this Jack Dupree and they caught him.

Question. Do you know what they killed Aleck Page for?

Answer. They killed him because he was a republican man, and would talk anywhere about republicanism, and because any time that they would meet him, or see him, or he would come to town with them, he would hold up for the republican party; and from him holding up for the republican party they would get into a fuss with him; they would raise a fuss with him; and they got to talking on the subject some time or other along last spring, and raised a fuss off of it—Tom Malone and Andrew Pope did; and for him holding up for the republican party they fell into a fuss, and they talked and went on right smart. He was talking to Andrew Pope, the man he was living with, and Tom Malone took it up and made an attempt to shoot him and kill him then; and

Andrew Pope at that time objected to his shooting him; and they fussed and went on all the way along home; and after they got home Aleck came up to Andrew Pope's house after some things Andrew Pope had got for him, and Tom Malone run out to shoot him, and Andrew Pope's wife hallooed and screamed so Andrew Pope kept him from shooting him; but he told him that night if he didn't shoot him that night, God damn him, in a few weeks he would get him and kill him, and that the Ku-Klux would come and see him; that no such a radical republican man as him could live in the country.

Question. Did I ask you what they killed Wamble for?

Answer. I never could learn what they killed him for. I never could discern no way what they killed him for.

By Mr. BLAIR:

Question. What was the color of the gowns they had on?

Answer. They had some red, and some black, and some white.

Question. What sort of a gown did you have on?

Answer. The one I had on was red.

Question. What did you have on your face?

Answer. Something black.

Question. Did you have any hat on?

Answer. No, sir; I didn't have no hat on at that time.

Question. You never had any hat on when you dressed up in disguise?

Answer. No, sir.

Question. Do you know Captain E. O. Sykes?

Answer. Yes, sir; I know him when I see him.

Question. Do you recollect meeting him in the main street of Aberdeen on Saturday, the 17th of June, the day when you were arrested?

Answer. No, sir.

Question. Do you recollect telling him that you knew nothing about the killing of Aleck Page "any more than a man in the grave?"

Answer. No, sir.

Question. Did you deny to him that you were a Ku-Klux?

Answer. No, sir.

Question. And say to him that you had been "Ku-Kluxing grass," mowing grass, that spring?

Answer. No, sir.

Question. Did you hear him speak to Henry Hatch about it?

Answer. No, sir; I never heard him say a word.

Question. Do you know Ann Forshee, the wife of Mike?

Answer. Yes, sir.

Question. Did you ever tell her that you were compelled to say that you were a Ku-Klux, in order to keep out of the penitentiary?

Answer. No, sir.

Question. You never told her that?

Answer. No, sir.

Question. You were at Mike Forshee's house at the time that you pretend that you were with this party killing Aleck Page?

The WITNESS. Was I at his house?

Mr. BLAIR. Yes.

The WITNESS. I don't understand you.

Question. You testified that you were present when Aleck Page was killed?

Answer. Yes, sir.

Question. At that very time were you not at Mike Forshee's house?

Answer. No, sir; I was not at his house.

Question. Were these men you have named, Jasper Webb, John Pope, Andrew Pope, and Whitfield Pope, the only men that were at your house at the time they called for you?

Answer. Yes, sir; them four men.

Question. And no others?

Answer. No, sir; not at my house; they didn't call for me, and they weren't the only men I knew in the party.

Question. Where was Tom Malone?

Answer. At what time?

Question. At that time?

Answer. The time they come for me?

Question. Yes.

Answer. He was one that came.

Question. It was Whitfield Pope, Tom Malone, and Andrew Pope. Who was the other?

Answer. Jasper Webb.

Question. Were those all?

Answer. Yes, sir.

Question. Did you not say that Johnny Ware was also with you?

Answer. Well, he did come once. He came the third time.

Question. He was not there when you went after Page?

Answer. Who?

Question. Ware?

Answer. Yes, sir; the time that they come and called for me to go after this Aleck Page, John Ware come.

Question. I thought you said only four were there?

Answer. There were only four with me regularly, that come regularly after me to get me on nights, and talked to me, and give me orders what to do, and quizzed me any. He never quizzed me any; them was the only ones that quizzed me any and talked to me any.

Question. Who buried Page?

Answer. I don't know who all they left to bnry him, but I was one, and Henry Hatch was one, and I don't know who the others were.

Question. Did you go afterwards and show the place where he was buried?

Answer. No, sir.

Question. Who did?

Answer. Jehu Wolf.

Question. Is he a negro?

Answer. He is a colored man.

Question. Who was along with him?

Answer. Jehu?

Question. Yes.

Answer. I don't know, sir; I didn't know him, if he was along I didn't know him.

Question. How could he know where the place was unless he was along?

Answer. Well, I don't know, sir; he maybe was along, but there was lots along I didn't know anything about. I didn't know half of them. I didn't say he wasn't along, but if he was he was like the rest; I didn't find him out. I didn't know half of them.

Question. How many colored men were there that you knew?

Answer. Mike Forshee, and Henry Hatch, besides myself, and Burrill Willis, and Jefferson Willis.

Question. That made five?

Answer. Yes, sir.

Question. And Jehu Wolf, if he was there, made six negroes?

Answer. I don't know whether he was there or not, if he was, I never found him out.

Question. Did you ever have any conversation with Colonel Huggins before you gave your testimony?

Answer. No, sir.

Question. You did not talk to him and tell him what you would prove before you went before a grand jury?

Answer. I did tell him that there was certain things that I knew, and certain things that I could tell about that party.

Question. When did you tell him that?

Answer. I told him that Sunday, I believe, at his house.

Question. That was before you were arrested?

Answer. That was Sunday. We went to Oxford Monday.

Question. The Sunday before the Monday when you went to Oxford; you were then under arrest?

Answer. Yes, sir; I wasn't under arrest, but I was there at his house. He sent for me to go to his house.

Question. When were you arrested; the next day or Saturday?

Answer. I wasn't arrested at all; they sent for me.

Question. How did they know you knew anything about this matter?

Answer. I don't know, sir; they sent for me and I come; I don't know how they knew it.

Question. What did they say when they sent there; what did Huggins say?

Answer. He didn't come after me; they sent a little boy after me, and he said for me to come there; that they wanted me to go to town; I asked him what for; he said they said "to witness something concerning the Ku-Klux," and I come.

Question. What did Huggins say to you when you went to his house?

Answer. He didn't say anything to me, that is he didn't say anything about asking me no questions, nor nothing of that sort. He talked some, but he didn't talk any concerning that.

Question. What did he say he sent for you for?

Answer. We all had to come there and stay, to go up to camp and stay, and he sent for us all to come and stay at his house; that we had orders from the colonel, Colonel

Rose, I think, or Major McCall, to go to Major Huggins's house and stay in the care of him until morning, and he sent for us all to come up there and stay; we did go to the camp at once, and then they sent for us to go to his house.

Question. Who went up to stay at Huggins's?

Answer. Me and Henry Hatch, and Mike Forshee, and Burrill Willis, and Jefferson Willis, and Jehu Wolf, and Fannie Page.

Question. That was the wife or widow of Aleck Page?

Answer. Yes, sir; that was killed.

Question. You all went up there that night and staid with Huggins?

Answer. Yes, sir; I don't think Fannie staid there that night; I think she come very soon next morning; but me and Jehu and Mike Forshe, did. He sent for us all to come there and stay that Sunday evening.

Question. What did he say to you when you were up there that night?

Answer. He didn't say anything, only just told us we had to stay there in his care until morning.

Question. Did he ask you any questions about what you would testify to?

Answer. No, sir; he never asked me no questions.

Question. Did he tell you that if you would come out and testify that you had been Ku-Kluxing you could get off?

Answer. No, sir; he never hinted such a thing as that to me; he never did.

Question. Did he know at the time that you had been with these Ku-Klux?

Answer. I don't know, sir, whether he did or not; I don't think he did; he may have known it, but I don't know as he did.

Question. How came you to be called as a witness; who told them what you knew?

Answer. I told what I knew about it.

Question. Whom did you tell?

Answer. I told Captain Wells.

Question. You did not tell him until after this time?

Answer. Which time?

Question. After you went up to Oxford.

Answer. No; I didn't tell him, but I told Colonel Huggins of it before I left his house; I talked with him, and told him concerning it, but he didn't ask me no questions. I was just simply talking to him when he sent for us that Sunday evening to come up there. We were sitting on the door-steps, and from one to another talking; not talking anything concerning that; and one of the boys, Rhett Willis, I think it was, asked him what was I arrested for—me and Mike and Henry. He said for witnessing concerning the Ku-Klux; and then I told him that I would tell all I knew about the Ku-Klux; I would tell it. He never asked me to tell nothing, nor anything of that sort.

Question. How did anybody know that you knew anything about it?

Answer. I didn't suppose anybody knew it until—well, I told it, or talked it to several of the boys, after we got into town, and to them coming on to town.

Question. That was after you were sent for?

Answer. Yes, sir.

Question. You had never talked to anybody before that?

Answer. No, sir; never.

Question. You never had told anybody that you had been out with the Ku-Klux before?

Answer. No, sir; not before that time.

Question. How did anybody know you had been out?

Answer. I don't know how they knew it; but I had never told anybody before that time.

Question. Had Henry Hatch ever told anybody?

Answer. Not as I know of; he said he never did tell, because they made us take our oath we never would chop it, or have any word to say about it. They told us if we did, just as sure as we were born, they would kill us; at the same time Jasper Webb drew his knife and put it to my throat and said he would cut my throat if I ever said anything about it, and I never said anything about it before that day.

Question. Did Hatch testify before the grand jury at the time you did?

Answer. Yes, sir.

Question. Did Mike Forshee testify at the same time?

Answer, No, sir.

Question. What has become of him? Did not he go up with you?

Answer. Yes, sir; he went up with us.

Question. Did he give any testimony?

Answer. No, sir; I think money kept him from giving any, or telling what he knew. When we were going up on the train Jasper Webb come to me and told me if I didn't tell nothing I knew about it, he would pay my way back home, and him and Andy Crosby would furnish me money when we got back home, and give me anything I wanted, and they'd do anything in the world for me, if I would only tell nothing about it; and he gave me a dollar at that time, and begged me to say nothing at all about it, nor nothing no way; and John Porter gave Mike Forshee a dollar, and told me for him not to say a word about nothing he knowed, and Mike being chicken-hearted some way another, and he paying him, kept him from telling what he knew about it. That's the reason he didn't give in no testimony.

Question. Did you say John Porter gave him a dollar?

Answer. Yes, sir; I saw him hand it to him out of his hand.

Question. Who was with you when Jasper gave you a dollar?

Answer. Well, one of the soldiers was sitting there, and three or four more of the boys; well, the whole car-full. It was on the car he gave me this dollar, and all that was on the cars saw him give me the dollar, and several of them asked me afterward what he gave me the dollar for, and I told them.

Question. Who asked you?

Answer. Mike and Henry asked me what did he give it to me for, and besides, some one of the Willis boys; I don't know which one now; some of them asked me, and some other people that were on there, that were just going somewhere, but not for that business; they asked me, and I told them, and what he gave it to me for.

Question. Which of the Willis boys?

Answer. I don't remember which.

Question. Was it Burrill Willis?

Answer. No, sir; his name is Henry Allen; I think it was him that asked me what did Webb give me the dollar for, if I am not mistaken; I am not really certain. I don't remember for certain which of the boys asked me, but several of them, I know, at that time asked me what he gave me the dollar for, and I told them he gave me the dollar and told me not to say nothing about what I knew, and said what he would do for me at that time. He said when we got up to Oxford we would be taken out of doors, and have no money, and he would furnish me money to come home; and he would give me money, and do anything for me after he got back home—anything I called on him for.

Question. Was Jasper Webb going up at the same time?

Answer. Yes, sir.

Question. Was he under arrest?

Answer. Yes, sir.

Question. Who was in jail with you?

Answer. Me and Henry was in together.

Question. In the same room?

Answer. Yes, sir.

Question. Anybody else in the room?

Answer. Me and Henry and Mike Forshee was in there for a few minutes together.

Question. You mean Henry Hatch?

Answer. Yes, sir.

Question. Was there nobody else in that room?

Answer. I don't remember. I don't think there were. I don't think there was in fact anybody except me and Henry Hatch and Mike; and me and Mike and Henry didn't stay in there together but just a few minutes. Me and Henry was in a room to ourselves.

Question. How long did you stay in the room?

Answer. Me and Henry?

Question. Yes.

Answer. We went there in the evening, and I think we staid in there all that night and until the next morning. I did; Henry staid in there a day or two.

Question. Did you ever have any quarrel with Aleck Page?

Answer. No, sir.

Question. You never had any words with him?

Answer. No, sir; I never had but a few words with him, and I didn't have any cross words then.

Question. What was that about?

Answer. Well, my sister-in-law and my wife said he came to my house one day that I wasn't there, and talked some very important talk; they said he talked some right smart vulgar talk that wasn't necessary, and I met him one night—no, I didn't meet him, but we had been to church one night—and on the way back from church I asked him did he say them words I heard he did. He said he didn't say them. I told him if he didn't say them, of course I couldn't say anything to him; but I told him if he said them words I wanted him to explain what right he had to speak such words as that; but he declared he didn't say the words; and I told him if he didn't say the words, of course I couldn't think hard of him, or say anything to him, and I never had no cross words with him.

Question. At the time you speak of, when you were sitting on Huggins's steps, you told for the first time about this thing?

Answer. That was the first time I had told anybody about it. That was the first time I said anything to him in his presence.

Question. What did you say; did you tell all about it then?

Answer. No, sir; I didn't tell him nothing about it; only I told him I knew some of the parties, and I could tell something about it; and he didn't ask me to tell him about it, nor I didn't tell him about it.

Question. He did not ask you what you knew?

Answer. No, sir.

Question. Did you know at that time what you had been arrested for?

Answer. No, sir; I didn't know what they had arrested me for. All the word I had ever got was, they wanted us to go to town; they said for witnessing something concerning the Ku-Klux; but didn't say what for, or anything about it. That is what the boy told me that came after me.

Question. You say Jefferson Willis and Burrill Willis were democrats?

Answer. Yes, sir.

Question. And went into it of their own accord?

Answer. Yes, sir.

Question. How do you know they went into it of their own accord?

Answer. I know they did from what I heard them say. Jeff. Willis was one of the big men; he was one of the big officers among them. He was the one that worked the horses, and the one that whipped them; he called himself "the Texas Bull," and did tell it.

Question. Jefferson did?

Answer. Yes, sir; and did tell it to some certain one, to somebody. Anyhow, the colored people got hold of it, that he told it to somebody. He told it, I think, at Billy Walton's store. If I mistake not, he asked Mr. Gay one day did he think he had a bull could whip him. Mr. Gay told him he didn't know; if he would come in the day-time, he didn't know but he had one could whip him; but if he come at night, he didn't know that he had, and called him "the Texas Bull" that whipped Simon and Rhett Willis.

Question. Who is Mr. Gay?

Answer. I don't know his given name, any more than Mr. Gay. He said he was the Texas Bull. Jefferson asked Mr. Gay did he think he had a bull at his house could whip him, and Mr. Gay told him he didn't know as he had if he would come at night; but if he would come by day, he didn't know but he had one could whip him. Then Jefferson was seen at night—some persons saw him. I never did exactly understand who saw him, but some people saw him not far from where he lived, on the night Dupree was killed. They saw him with his shroud on, coming through the field, just at daylight. He didn't have time to get home before, and was just coming across people's fields to get to his home.

Question. On the night that Jack Dupree was killed?

Answer. Yes, sir.

Question. You do not know who saw him?

Answer. No, sir; I don't remember who it was saw him, but I know I heard them all talking about it. A good many were talking about it, that they saw him.

Question. Do you know Mike Young?

Answer. No, sir.

Question. Did you ever hear of him?

Answer. I think I heard of such a name as Mike Young, but I don't know him. I don't know anything about it. I am not acquainted with him.

Question. How many times did you go out with them?

Answer. Five; I went out with them five times.

Question. The first time was where?

Answer. To Dupree's.

Question. The second time to Page's?

Answer. Yes, sir.

Question. Whom did you go to see the third time?

Answer. Page again.

Question. And the fourth time?

Answer. Rhett Willis and Simon Dunn.

Question. Whom the fifth time?

Answer. This Wamble man.

Question. Were those the only times you were out?

Answer. Yes, sir.

Question. How many times did you go out after the Aleck Page affair?

Answer. I only went twice with them after him. They went one time; the party went at him, I think, the three times, but I only went with them twice. One time I think they went after him, and I think his wife said he wasn't at home, and the next time they went I was with them, and he was there; he saw them and heard them, and he went out under the floor, and got away, and broke and run, and they shot at him several times.

COLUMBUS, MISSISSIPPI, *November* 13, 1871.

A. P. HUGGINS recalled.

[For the testimony previously given by this witness, see page 265.]

By the CHAIRMAN:

Question. You were examined at Washington before the general committee last summer, I believe, Colonel Huggins?

Answer. Yes, sir.

Question. There are certain facts which have transpired since your testimony was given about which I desire to interrogate you. Do you know Sarah A. Allan, a schoolmistress from Illinois, who came down to Monroe County for the purpose of teaching a colored school?

Answer. I do, very well.

Question. I neglected, when she was on the stand, to examine her in relation to a single matter. Do you know whether she could procure board in any white family in the neighborhood where she was teaching school?

Answer. I know that she could not. I went with her when she went to Cotton Gin, her place of teaching, and went with her all over town, to nearly all the houses, for it is a small place, but found it impossible to secure any place in a white family.

Question. What was the objection to her being received?

Answer. Simply because she taught a colored school, they could not take her.

Question. Was the prejudice such that they would not take a teacher of a colored school?

Answer. Yes, sir.

Question. You have heard of a visit which the Ku-Klux made to her?

Answer. Yes, sir. I was the county superintendent of schools at the time. I was in Washington at the time they visited her, but knew of it very well afterward.

Question. Do you know that she discontinued her school in consequence of her fears?

Answer. Yes, sir; she only taught six weeks out of four months which she was to teach.

Question. So far as she was permitted to teach, had she given satisfaction?

Answer. Entire satisfaction to all parties.

Question. Was she well qualified?

Answer. She was a very finely educated person.

Question. Was she a lady of unexceptionable character?

Answer. Perfectly; as good as any woman could have. She was sent by the American Missionary Society. A Christian lady and good woman. I knew her very well.

Question. Certain persons in Monroe County were arrested on process, either from the Federal court or United States commissioner, charged with being implicated in these outrages, and taken to Oxford, but afterward returned home on bail, I believe. Is that the case?

Answer. Yes, sir.

Question. State if you know anything about the ovation that was tendered to them upon their return, of citizens of Aberdeen.

Answer. A large number of persons met them at the depot. The train got in about 8 or 9 o'clock in the evening. There was shouting, and firing of cannon, and general rejoicing; it was heard at some houses very distant—over half a mile from the depot; the shouting and rejoicing were heard there. They also tried to get the band that belongs to the town, but the band refused to go out, thinking they might get into difficulty. The crowd tried to get the band to come out and receive them on that occasion.

Question. Can you account for the sympathy manifested for these men?

Answer. Yes, sir; a majority of those that were arrested were young men of culture and standing in the community, and were members of society—the first class of society there, and the sympathy was very great for them; and they had done nothing but, as they said, "whipped a Yankee and killed a few niggers." That was all their crime, and there was a general sympathy of the people.

By Mr. BLAIR:

Question. Did they say that?

Answer. Yes, sir.

Question. Who said it?

Answer. These parties.

Question. What party said it?

Answer. Well, sir, their papers said it.

Question. Which paper?

Answer. Some paper. I could not mention the name of the paper; it was in the southern part of this State. One of them said it—said they made a great hue and cry about whipping a Yankee and killing a few negroes; and I heard it remarked on the cars going up to Oxford with the prisoners that they were making a great ado about whipping a Yankee and killing a few negroes, and so on.

Question. You cannot remember anybody who said that?

Answer. I would not have known the parties' names; I heard the remarks made as I was traveling with the men on the cars, and read it in one of the papers of the State.

Question. You cannot remember the name of the paper?

Answer. No, sir; I do not remember the name of the paper.

Question. The remark did not strike you as singular then; you did not observe the name of the paper?

Answer. Well, the remarks were made so generally, senator, through the papers at the time, that it was of no great moment, but I think it was the Kosciusko paper that I saw it in; it was accounted a very trivial thing through the State, in public opinion; as I traveled through the State, back and forth, with the prisoners, it seemed to be a very small thing; one lady of one town remarked, as she was riding up on the cars, and I was sitting behind her, that she had heard that there was a great crowd of them who were arrested, and she supposed her sweetheart was in the crowd, and, if it was so, she would get herself ready, and was going on to Oxford. That was the general expression I heard on the cars; there was a feeling of sympathy, and the idea that nothing had occurred more than could have been expected, and that it was approved in the community.

Question. You are not prepared, now, to state the name of any person who made such a remark?

Answer. No, sir; I do not know the names of the parties. I was traveling, and they were remarks made mostly as I was on the train taking the prisoners; I was deputy marshal, and took them on. It created a great excitement wherever we stopped and changed cars; we changed cars at two different places, and the remarks were very common.

By the CHAIRMAN:

Question. In your testimony before the committee, at Washington, did you testify in relation to the murder of Doc Hendricks?

Answer. No, sir; Doc Hendricks was murdered about the 9th of last month.

Question. That occurred since you were before the committee?

Answer. Yes, sir; I was before the committee in July.

Question. You may state what you know or what you have been informed by reliable persons in regard to that murder.

Answer. A murder was committed in the neighborhood where Doc Hendricks was killed, on the night previous to his murder.

Question. Who was murdered previously?

Answer. A white man by the name of Garrett. They found the man alive a short time after he was shot; he stated that he did not know who killed him, and could call no names; he did not know who killed him. There were several colored men arrested the next day, on proper writ, and it seemed to fall on this Doc Hendricks, that he was the man, and by intimidation, and threatening, &c., by the crowd, as persons present told me, he made some concession, I think, and did say he killed him, and that night he was taken by three men to be taken to Aberdeen, to go to the jail. The next morning persons came on to town, and found me, and told me that Doc Hendricks was found dead between the place where the murder of Garrett was committed and Aberdeen. I had the coroner to go at once to the place. I have seen the coroner, and know his decision, and the decision of the jury; it was, that he was hung.

Question. You say that Hendricks was hung?

Answer. Yes, sir; he was hung to a sapling; his body was in that position when it was found. Colonel Rose also went up, and the sheriff, to make the arrest of the parties; they were at the place. You have had their testimony, or that of Colonel Rose. I have also seen the parties. I arrested them under the enforcement act, and took them before a commissioner.

Question. The persons who constituted the guard?

Answer. Yes, sir; and also the men who went up to go on their bond. They all acknowledged that these three men had this man in charge, but stated that a crowd of masked men came and took him away from them and killed him.

Question. How large a crowd did they say?

Answer. Twenty-five or thirty men was the statement.

Question. Could they identify any of the men?

Answer. No, sir; they did not know any of them at all.

Question. Did they explain the circumstances, where they were at the time the rescue was made?

Answer. Yes, sir; they told all about the circumstances, and were very free to talk.

Question. Did they point out the very locality?

Answer. They were willing to. I did not go to make the arrests.

Question. Do you know whether their account was verified afterward by an inspection of the ground?

Answer. Yes, sir; the location, the position, was verified.

Question. Were the horses' tracks as many as twenty-five or thirty?

Answer. Colonel Rose and the sheriff both informed me there were but very few horses' tracks; that there could not have been more than ten. The five men rode up there afterward that looked for the body—the five men that came on to Aberdeen and told me of the murder. Colonel Rose is satisfied that there could not have been more than ten men, in his estimation, on the horses on the ground.

Question. Have any other men, except those constituting the crowd, been arrested for the murder of Hendricks?

Answer. No, sir; no other parties; no one can identify any; no one knows any of them. Some fifty went to the house to take this Hendricks; they went to his house to take him away from there; but there were only three men that the justice gave them over into the hands of.

Question. Were the fifty men who went to the justice's office at that time white persons living in the community?

Answer. Yes, sir.

Question. There was no trouble in identifying them and knowing who they were?

Answer. No, sir; no trouble in that.

By Mr. RICE:

Question. Were the two men who took Hendricks, and the three men of the guard, a part of those fifty men?

Answer. Yes, sir; they composed a part of them.

By the CHAIRMAN:

Question. Had they been deputized?

Answer. One of them was deputized properly by the justice. They stated that they made no resistance; that they saw it was useless to try to defend the man, as such a crowd came to take him away.

Question. How long after night did they say it was?

Answer. It was about 10 o'clock, I think.

Question. How far had they proceeded from the justice's office toward Aberdeen?

Answer. Not over two miles, or a mile and a half.

Question. Then they had left the justice's office after night?

Answer. They left the justice's office and went to the house of the man detailed to take charge of him. It was two miles from the house of Mr. Legronne, the deputy sheriff that had him in charge. It was two miles, or a mile and a half, from the house. I think the trial was some three miles above that. They had taken him there to the house and got supper, and then gone on to Aberdeen.

Question. When they left the justice's office, was it about night?

Answer. O, no, sir; it was not night when they left the justice's office; my understanding is, it was in the day-time that they left the justice's office; and they went on to Mr. Legronne's, the deputy sheriff, and staid there until after night, about 8 o'clock, I think, and then went on about a mile and a half, and were interrupted, they said.

Question. If they had gone directly from the office of the magistrate to the jail, could they have reached it before night?

Answer. No, sir; I think not. It is some sixteen miles from Aberdeen; the jail is seven miles beyond there, but the calaboose is there.

Question. Are those men under recognizance to appear at court?

Answer. Yes, sir; fifteen hundred dollars each. They waived trial, and were willing to give bond.

Question. Has an indictment been found against them, or are they on recognizance from a warrant issued by the commissioner?

Answer. By the commissioner; that is all. There is no indictment.

Question. Do you know anything of the murder of Tobe Hutchinson?

Answer. Tobe Hutchinson was taken from his house. Yes, sir; I know with reference to it. He was taken out a week ago Friday night, by masked men, and has not been heard of since. It is supposed that he was killed.

Question. On Friday night?

Answer. Friday night a week ago.

Question. Did you understand under what circumstances he was taken from his house?

Answer. No, sir; not very thoroughly. Persons came to me on election day and told me; I was very busy and did not take much notice.

Question. Did you understand that it was done by a body of masked men?

Answer. Yes, sir; several masked men came and took him from his house. We will go and make search as soon as we can.

Question. Did you understand what his offense was?

Answer. No, sir.

Question. Was he a colored man?

Answer. Yes, sir.

Question. What is the general supposition; that he is alive or dead?

Answer. The supposition is that he is dead. He lived in an out-of-the-way country; the colored men are afraid to search. I tried to get them to go and search. They said they would not; they dare not.

Question. Why?

Answer. They are afraid that if they go and search they will be attacked themselves in searching. I could not encourage them to even try to find him. It is a very bad portion of our country.

Question. Did both those cases occur in Monroe County?

Answer. Tobe Hutchinson lives about a quarter of a mile from the county line, in Lee County.

Question. Where did Hendricks live?

Answer. In Monroe County.

Question. Do you know of any church-burning since you gave your testimony?

Answer. The colored church at Tupelo, the Methodist Episcopal church there, was burned about the 9th of last month—I think about the same day that Doc. Hendricks was killed. And they have undertaken to drive out Miss Davis, the postmistress at Tupelo, by every conceivable means—by threats, calling upon her, &c.

Question. What is her full name?

Answer. Miss Anna Davis. She is the postmistress at Tupelo, and this church was built mostly by her; she got up the subscription.

Question. You may state what indignities she has been subjected to, if you know or have been informed.

Answer. Well, sir, during the past year there is hardly any indignity that you can mention that Miss Davis has not been subjected to. They have been in her house—and I have heard her tell the story herself—they have come to her window at night and tried to come in; she has kept them out only by her pistol. She has received numbers of letters of the most insulting character. Persons came into the post-office and tried to drive her into the back room while she was in the post-office, telling her she should not deliver the mail; and statements to the effect that she was common with the negroes, and everything of that sort.

Question. Is she a northern woman?

Answer. Yes, sir. She has been a subject of general persecution in the community. She has taught a colored school there. I suppose there is no lady in the State, that I know of, who has been persecuted as Miss Davis has.

Question. Is she a respectable lady?

Answer. She is a respectable lady; a good Christian woman. She is a sister of the presiding elder of the Methodist Episcopal Church of the northern district of Mississippi. This church I speak of was built partly by her; she got subscriptions among her friends; and on the 9th of October the church was burned, at the same time that they were trying to drive her from the town.

Question. Tupelo is in what county?

Answer. In Lee County; it is the county-seat.

By Mr. BLAIR:

Question. Burned on the 9th of September?

Answer. The 9th of October; the 9th of last month, or about that time.

By the CHAIRMAN:

Question. Has anything ever transpired as to how this church was burned, or by whom?

Answer. There was the elder, and also Miss Davis, told me that they were willing to give the names of witnesses whenever the witnesses could be protected; but they were afraid to give any testimony under existing circumstances, and that they could not do it and return there; that if they pointed out these men, they would return and commit the same depredations over again. There were one or two arrests made there. A man named Freeman was arrested and taken on to Corinth, and released on a slight bond; whereupon he returned, and went to Miss Davis's house the very night he returned, and to other houses, and made his threats, and frightened the witnesses so that they will not give any testimony. They both told me that—the elder and his lady—they would not give any testimony in the case before any commissioner until they knew they could be protected by troops. They did not feel it safe to do so.

Question. You say Miss Davis, the postmistress, is a northern woman?

Answer. Yes, sir.

Question. Is that fact, coupled with the other facts that she has taught a colored school, and taken an interest in the education of the colored people, and is the postmistress, the cause of this persecution?

Answer. That is all. I can state that as a fact, that that is all that Miss Davis has done. I know her well.

Question. Are those the causes of her persecution?

Answer. Yes, sir; those simply; her interest in the church, to build it up, and in the schools; and then, when she went into the post-office, there was a great opposition to her; they said she should never deliver any mail.

Question. What was the ground of the opposition?

Answer. That she had been a colored teacher, and came there a northern woman, leading the freedmen.

Question. I will ask you to state what, if anything, you know of an attempt to burn the assessor's office in the third district of this State, at Okolona?

Answer. There were five Ku-Klux arrested about the 18th of October in Chickasaw County, and taken to Okolona, and Colonel Shattuck, the assessor, had them taken to his house for safe-keeping. The deputy marshal took them there, and that night his office was set on fire.

By Mr. BLAIR:

Question. Did you say five Ku-Klux were arrested in Chickasaw County and taken to Okolona?

Answer. Yes, sir; to stay all night waiting for the train, and they were taken to the residence of Colonel Shattuck, the assessor; and that night this office was set on fire, and quite a hole burned in it; but persons saw it and put it out before it destroyed the office.

By the CHAIRMAN:

Question. Is the office in his house?

Answer. No, sir; the office is up town, not more than one hundred and fifty or two hundred and fifty yards away from his residence.

Question. Has it ever been discovered who set it on fire?

Answer. No, sir. All the Government property that belongs to the assessor's office was in the office at the time.

Question. Have you been acting as deputy marshal this fall and making any arrests?

Answer. Yes, sir; I have made a good many arrests.

Question. Have you met with any interruption or obstruction in Oktibbeha County?

Answer. Yes, sir.

Question. What was the character of the interruption?

Answer. I went there on the 16th of September with some twenty-four warrants to serve, and made some arrests in the morning. On the 17th, as I was leaving town, the sheriff of the county came to me, the special deputy marshal, with a warrant to arrest me and the soldiers, I had as Ku-Klux; that we had gone into the country and gone into the town, and by trying to make arrests of these men, for whom we held warrants, that we had violated the enforcement act, and he insisted upon my surrendering with all the troops, prisoners, and all.

Question. You had gone, I understand, in company with troops, for the purpose of serving these warrants that you held as deputy marshal?

Answer. Yes, sir.

Question. Did you exhibit your warrants whenever you made arrests?

Answer. Yes, sir; certainly.

Question. Was your character as deputy marshal publicly known in the place?

Answer. Yes, sir; very well known.

Question. And you had made some arrests and was about leaving town on the 17th of October?

Answer. Yes, sir.

Answer. Yes, sir.

Question. Go on, and tell the particulars of the attempt of the sheriff to arrest you and those who had gone with you in making those arrests.

Answer. He came and read a warrant to me, and asked me if I would surrender myself. I told him that I could not, and then he asked me if I would surrender the troops; I told him that we had prisoners, and that I was on duty for the Government, and that I would not submit to an insult of that kind; that it was merely a farce. The deputy himself told me that he was very much of my mind; that it was simply a farce; he had been in the town all the time, and he said he should not insist upon it.

Question. The deputy marshal?

Answer. The deputy marshal; he was sheriff of the county; he told me he would do as I said in reference to it; I told him I certainly should not surrender under these circumstances; I would not give up United States troops with arms and under arms, but said I would take them to town to their command, and that the commanding officer might do as he pleased; and we got on our horses and left with our prisoners; and they gathered up fifty to a hundred men in town to come after us, and threatened, and got their shot-guns, and rode round there considerably, but they didn't come. The deputy marshal, however, sent me word that they were coming, and to look out; but we went back to West Point and staid that night, and at West Point the marshal came on again, and insisted that I should surrender, and also the troops, which I still refused to do; and went on to camp next day, and there received instructions to go back and arrest the men that were making this disturbance if they made any more or attempted anything further. The thing died out there. We never surrendered to the mob, and I went back and made still more arrests after that time.

Question. This deputy marshal you speak of was the sheriff of Oktibbeha County?

Answer. Yes, sir; the warrant was gotten out before a United States commissioner.

Question. What commissioner issued that warrant?

Answer. His name is Ellis.

Question. Do you know on what accusation it was issued?

Answer. Yes, sir; it was read to me—that I with the soldiers had conspired to take away the liberties and rights of Mrs. Ada Bell, whose husband we went to arrest; that we had conspired together for that purpose.

Question. You had a warrant for his arrest?

Answer. I had a warrant for the arrest of Mr. Bell, who had forfeited his bond once, and we had tried to get him several times. I went early in the morning to get him; we surrounded the house with soldiers.

Question. Is he considered a desperate man?

Answer. Yes, sir; one of the most desperate men in Oktibbeha County.

Question. This warrant was for his arrest?

Answer. Yes, sir.

By Mr. BLAIR:

Question. You say that this warrant recited that you had entered into a conspiracy to take away the liberties of whom?

Answer. Of Mrs. Ada Bell, the wife of the man I went to arrest.

By the CHAIRMAN:

Question. What had you done to Mrs. Bell?

Answer. Well, sir, the soldiers went into the house. One of the soldiers, the sergeant in charge, went into the room where one of the ladies was. The woman had her head covered up. He was searching the house at the time, and he went up to the bed, and says, "Hello! who is here?" The woman made a little scream, and put down the bed-clothes; he saw it was a lady, and walked out.

Question. Was it Mrs. Bell, or supposed to be her?

Answer. I don't know whether it was Mrs. Bell or not.

Question. Was Bell in the house then?

Answer. No, sir.

Question. Where did you find him?

Answer. He wasn't found at all.

Question. You did not arrest him?

Answer. Never have got him yet.

Question. Has he fled the country?

Answer. If he has not, he is lying in the swamps. We have been there several times to get him.

Question. Who made that affidavit upon which the warrant was issued by Ellis?

Answer. I don't know.

Question. Did you read the warrant to see that it had been issued on an affidavit?

Answer. No, sir; he simply read it to me; but there cannot be any question about its being properly gotten up, from the fact that Mr. Muldrow, the district attorney, and the commissioner, were the parties in the case.

Question. You refer to the warrants you held?

Answer. No, sir; that other one. These men all came to me, and told me it was a proper warrant, and they thought I ought to surrender. These were men I have confidence in, that they knew what they were doing, and I think that no improper warrant would be issued by Mr. Muldrow. I am satisfied that it was issued on some one's affidavit, but whose I don't know.

Question. Had the United States commissioner, Ellis, any son who was implicated in these Ku-Klux troubles?

Answer. I had a warrant for Gum Ellis—either his son or his nephew; I don't remember which.

Question. Did the commissioner know that fact?

Answer. Certainly; I had been in town all those two days while I was there. I was in town two days.

Question. Did you succeed in arresting Gum Ellis?

Answer. No, sir; he had left the town entirely.

Question. Since you testified at Washington, have the disturbances in that part of Mississippi, that you are acquainted with, abated any?

Answer. No, sir; not since the time that I gave testimony there. The election has rather increased the excitement. The election excitement has had a tendency to keep the people more or less disturbed, but since March there has been a great change for the better in our county.

By Mr. BLAIR:

Question. Were those parties who were arrested for the escape of Doc Hendricks arrested by the State authorities?

Answer. Yes, sir; by authority.

Question. Did you take them out of the hands of the State authorities?

Answer. The United States commissioner gave me a warrant to arrest them and bring them before him.

Question. Were they then in the custody of the officers of the State?

Answer. Yes, sir.

Question. By what right did you take them out of the custody of the officers of the State?

Answer. I received a warrant, as I stated to you, from the United States commissioner at Corinth, Mr. Mask, to bring them before him at once. I saw the marshal, and he sent me for the purpose of taking them away. Also the district attorney. I met them there at Corinth.

Question. You hold, then, that you have the right to take the prisoners out of the custody of officers of the State?

Answer. Yes, sir; I held the right that I was sent to do it; my superior officer sent me, and I went and did it. I think that I have the right to do it under the Ku-Klux law.

Question. And you did not feel yourself at liberty to surrender your own person into the hands of the authorities of the United States upon a proper warrant?

Answer. I did not feel that I had the right to surrender, under the circumstances, to a mere farce, the United States troops, with their arms in their hands and prisoners to guard; I did not think I could surrender them, and I have seen the Attorney General since, and he thinks quite with me, that I did right not to surrender.

By the CHAIRMAN:

Question. The attorney general of the State?

Answer. The Attorney General of the United States. He thinks so, under the circumstances, with prisoners to guard, &c.

By Mr. BLAIR:

Question. Then it is a matter within your discretion entirely whether you surrender yourself to the authority of the Government, when called upon to do so by a proper warrant, or not?

Answer. Well, sir, I took the responsibility of not doing so.

Question. And you call your resistance and refusal to submit to the law a resistance on the part of others to the authority of the United States, throwing obstruction in the way of process?

Answer. I call their attempts to stop me in my arresting the prisoners that I had warrants for in a proper way, and their interposing these obstructions, hindering me in the performance of my duties, as the constituted authority of the United States, civil and military united; I had soldiers with me.

Question. You think the military is an excuse for pretty much anything?

Answer. No, sir; I do not.

Question. Your objection was that you had the military there under arms, and they were not amenable to a proper warrant of a commissioner regularly appointed; that soldiers with their arms in their hands offered a sufficient excuse to you for refusing to surrender to an officer properly appointed by the Government of the United States, and under a warrant proper in all respects, and you refused?

Answer. I did, sir. I had the prisoners to guard, and I would not turn them loose. I took the responsibility; whatever that responsibility is I shall abide by it. I know it was simply a farce; that they were plotting for the purpose of obstructiong me from making arrests in Oktibbeha County. I was doing nothing more than is done every day in making arrests, searching houses.

Question. And you could put at defiance the authority of the Government of the United States with a dozen soldiers under your command?

Answer. I never have put at defiance the properly constituted authority of the United States. I never shall.

Question. I understood you to say this commissioner was regularly appointed?

Answer. When they conspired together with a mob to obstruct the United States authorities, I took the responsibility, leaving that to be judged of.

Question. You made yourself, then, the judge of whether that process should be executed or not?

Answer. I will state to you, Senator, that I went out to the railroad as soon as I could get there, and telegraphed for instructions as to what I should do, whether to surrender or not. As I stated to you, I was told by the Attorney General that he thought my course would be sustained under the circumstances.

By the CHAIRMAN:

Question. Did you telegraph to him for information?
Answer. I telegraphed to the district attorney.

By Mr. BLAIR:

Question. What did you say the soldiers took the liberty of doing with Mrs. Bell—stripping the clothes off of her when in bed?
Answer. No, sir; they went into the house, and went into the room where a person had the head covered, and the sergeant said, "Hello, who's here?" and the woman made a little scream, and took the clothes from her so that they could simply see the hair; didn't see the face; and he said, "Beg your pardon, madam," and left the room. There were two men there.
Question. Did he put his hands on the clothes?
Answer. No, sir; there were two witnesses to that fact that he didn't put his hand on the bed at all.
Question. Was the head covered up when he went up?
Answer. Yes, sir; she had the bed-clothes over her head.
Question. Was it covered up as he entered the room?
Answer. Yes, sir; when he went in the room it was covered up. He saw there was the body of a person in the bed, and he says, "Hello, who's here?" and when the clothes were thrown down sufficiently to show the head of hair, he left the room with an excuse.
Question. Did he throw them down?
Answer. No, sir; he didn't touch the bed at all.
Question. Who threw them down?
Answer. The person in the bed.
Question. How far?
Answer. Well, so that the head was seen, or the hair. I don't think he saw the face at all, from what was said.
Question. In what respect did Mrs. Ada Bell complain that her rights had been interfered with, as guaranteed by the enforcement bill?
Answer. I don't know, only that it was a conspiracy on our part to take away her rights and privileges under the enforcement act.
Question. Any specified right taken away?
Answer. No, sir; I don't there was.
Question. No allegation that there was?
Answer. I don't think there was any specified. I don't remember it, and I listened very attentively when the warrant was read to me.
Question. You were in the room yourself with the soldiers?
Answer. No, sir; I didn't go in that room at all.
Question. You permitted him to perambulate the house or rooms?
Answer. There were two others along; a guide pointed out the rooms, a recognizing man. There were two soldiers.
Question. You were not in the house?
Answer. No, sir; I was not in the house at all.
Question. What else was done in the house of which there was complaint?
Answer. Not a thing, I don't think; I know of nothing else. I think that that was all that the warrant said—that the charge was a conspiracy on the part of A. P. Huggins and fifteen persons, names unknown, (I remember that the soldiers' names were not known,) to take away the right of Ada Bell, to deprive Ada Bell of her rights, &c

By the CHAIRMAN:

Question. Was anything done beyond what was necessary to make a thorough search in that house for Bell, whom you were commissioned to arrest?
Answer. No, sir; not at all.

By Mr. BLAIR:

Question. What time was the house entered?
Answer. It was at least three-quarters of an hour after the sun was up; quite early in the morning.
Question. The woman was still in bed; had not risen from the bed?
Answer. No, sir; she was in bed.
Question. What was the name of the sergeant that entered her chamber?
Answer. That I do not know. He belonged to the Sixth Cavalry, Captain Sturgeon's company.

Question. Did you have the whole company with you?

Answer. We had fifteen.

Question. Who were the other persons that entered the room?

Answer. I don't know, general. I know the guide's name was McLachlan; the others, the soldiers, I did not know their names.

Question. The guide was not a soldier?

Answer. No, sir.

Question. Where does he live?

Answer. He formerly lived in Oktibbeha County. I do not know where he lives now. I do not think he is there.

Question. You do not know where he could be found?

Answer. No, sir.

Question. Where did you find him?

Answer. He was sent to me by the marshal to go as a guide. He came to Aberdeen before I left the town.

Question. Who is the marshal?

Answer. J. H. Pierce is the marshal of our district.

Question. You do not know where he could be found now?

Answer. I do not.

Question. Where did you leave him?

Answer. He went back to Aberdeen with me, and went from there for some place. I left him at Aberdeen. I think that sergeant's name was Smith—Sergeant Smith.

Question. That sergeant and the guide, and another soldier, you say, entered Mrs. Bell's chamber?

Answer. Yes, sir.

Question. Three of them?

Answer. Yes, sir.

Question. Is it Miss or Mrs. Anna Davis?

Answer. Miss, a young lady.

COLUMBUS, MISSISSIPPI, *November* 17, 1871.

A. P. HUGGINS recalled.

By Mr. RICE:

Question. It was stated here by Colonel Reynolds that you, as superintendent of the schools in Monroe County, had purchased furniture for two school-houses, a colored school-house and a white school-house, amounting to either five or six thousand dollars, or to six or seven thousand dollars, or that, at least, was what you had charged the school fund for that furniture. I wish you to make a statement of the amount furnished, of where you bought it, and what it cost.

Answer. The warrant issued for the school furniture, and which is all that comes out of the school fund in any way on the order issued by the board, amounted to a little over twenty-one hundred dollars for the whole county.

Question. That is the whole amount for the entire county?

Answer. Yes, sir; for the entire county, and the most of that goes into two schools at Aberdeen; and that includes also the black-boards, and globes, and stoves for all the school-houses in the county. Twenty-one hundred dollars is the whole.

Question. Where did you make the purchases?

Answer. In Saint Louis, although some of the things came from Chicago; but the Saint Louis firm furnished us everything.

Question. Did you charge the school fund anything more than it cost you delivered?

Answer. No, sir. The warrants were issued originally to the parties by the order of the board. Nothing was ever charged to the county.

Question. He said something about their being gotten somewhere up in Vermont. What is there about that?

Answer. Nothing in the world. We brought them all from Saint Louis.

Question. Have you never bought anything from Vermont of that character?

Answer. Nothing ever came from Vermont that I know of.

By the CHAIRMAN:

Question. Did you make a cent of personal profit out of these purchases?

Answer. No, sir; not a cent.

Question. Did any of your friends?

Answer. No, sir; not a thing.

COLUMBUS, MISSISSIPPI, *November* 13, 1871.

SAMUEL J. GHOLSON sworn and examined.

The CHAIRMAN. This witness having been called at the instance of the minority, the examination will be conducted by General Blair.

By Mr. BLAIR:

Question. Where do you reside, General Gholson?

Answer. I reside in Monroe County, Mississippi, in the town of Aberdeen.

Question. How long have you lived there?

Answer. I came to Mississippi as a citizen in March, 1830. I do not like to talk about things so far back.

Question. You have lived there ever since?

Answer. Yes, sir, in that county ever since March, 1830.

Question. Are you pretty well acquainted with the people?

Answer. Very well acquainted with the people of Northern Mississippi, as well as any one man is in the State, I have no doubt.

Question. We have had witnesses before us, general, among others, a colored man named Joe Davis, and several other colored men, who have testified to various outrages by what are called Ku-Klux in that county; the killing of various men; the first, I think, is Jack Dupree. What do you know about that, if anything?

Answer. I know nothing about it; I heard such a man was taken off of a plantation and had not been seen since.

Question. Whose plantation?

Answer. It belonged to a gentleman named Mays, or Jones & Mays, (I think that is the style of the farmers' plantation,) in Monroe County.

Question. It is not known, then, whether he is actually dead or alive?

Answer. No, sir; there have been sundry searches to find his dead body without success; Mr. Huggins, last June, collected one or two hundred negroes and searched the neighborhood very extensively, carrying some Federal soldiers with him, and alarming the women a good deal, to find Jack Dupree's body, and they could not find it; he was carried to where there was some withes and some logs, where they had run a cross-cut saw; he had been told that they whipped him to death there.

Question. He had been taken there by whom?

Answer. By some negroes; a large reward had been offered; at the same time some men were on trial at Pontotoc that had been arrested in that county.

Question. There is a negro man named Joe Davis who came before this committee and testified that he was present at Jack Dupree's house when he was attacked; that he was ordered to come out; that he (Davis) was present with a number of his own color—some five or six colored men—and some forty or fifty white men; "Dupree was ordered to open the door; he got up to open the door, and then went back to bed. They went in and had a struggle with him, and he was carried off; they carried him below Ross Mills; they whipped him there an hour, until he could scarcely halloo; said after they came back that they had cut his damned guts out;" he says also that the negro has never been seen since.

Answer. It was on the creek below Ross Mills that these withes were exhibited to Mr. Huggins by some negroes, where two or three great board-trees had been cut and sawed and split; as to anything else about it, I have no knowledge.

Question. Who were the negroes that showed him this?

Answer. I could not tell you here, but he had all the negroes in the neighborhood with him, to the number of two or three hundred.

Question. What negroes pretended to show him them?

Answer. That is what I cannot tell you at this time. I know there were so many with him it is impossible for me to identify any one of them that made the statement.

Question. Joe Davis himself was with him?

Answer. He was with him.

Question. You know that to be a fact?

Answer. Yes, sir; I know that from the statement of A., B., and C., who said they were along. I was not there.

Question. Was that before Joe Davis went to Oxford to testify?

Answer. It was after he went to Oxford, and before he returned. He went to Oxford and gave testimony before the grand jury, and came home and then went back to the trial, had on the *habeas corpus* of the men who were arrested—the case known as "The United States *vs.* Walton and others," that has been reported at some length; twenty-seven or eight, I think, were arrested under a warrant issued by Mr. Blackman, commissioner. They were taken to Oxford and retained four or five days, Blackman not making his appearance to try them. In the mean time the grand jury found bills against them. I had been in Oxford in attendance on the court, and was in the act of starting home, when I received a telegram from the defendants to remain there, that they had been arrested and wanted me as counsel there. I went back, and subsequently came home after the testimony.

Question. You were the counsel for them?

Answer. I was counsel for the defendants.

Question. In the *habeas corpus* case?

Answer. Yes, sir; am still counsel.

Question. Do you recollect the testimony introduced in that case?

Answer. Yes, sir; pretty well.

Question. Was it reported?

Answer. Yes, sir; it is very substantially reported in that book, [referring to a pamphlet produced by Mr. Blair, for which see appendix to the testimony of R. O. Reynolds,] I take it, or one just like it that I have. I should say a very accurate report of the testimony is to be found there.

Question. Is this a copy of that testimony?

Answer. Yes, sir. Joe swore in his testimony that the uniform was red and black; all the other witnesses swore that it was white. A man had been killed in Pontotoc, or was said to have been killed, and the uniform found on him was hung up at the Federal camp, stuffed, and a rope put around the neck—hung up representing a man. Joe was evidently swearing at that uniform; he swore that these men he went with had a red and black uniform.

By the CHAIRMAN:

Question. What did the other witnesses swear?

Answer. That it was white, except a binding, and around the holes which they said were made for the eyes and mouth, which was red.

By Mr. BLAIR:

Question. Was there any testimony, on that trial, to the effect that Joe Davis was not present?

Answer. There was.

Question. What testimony was that?

Answer. The testimony of some women—some colored women—and a man.

Question. Can you find that testimony in here and identify it, to make it a part of your testimony?

Answer. [Examining testimony of Ann Forshee, in pamphlet.] This does not seem to be what I thought it was; she swore that he was not there, and a colored blacksmith swore he was at his house the night Aleck Page was killed; staid at a house very close to his all night. Joe stated to Captain O. E. Sykes, as Captain Sykes has, since sworn, and Mr. Morgan, that he knew nothing about it, and never saw a Ku-Klux.

By the CHAIRMAN:

Question. Did you hear him make that statement?

Answer. I did not, sir; I heard them swear it in court.

By Mr. BLAIR:

Question. Here is the testimony of Captain O. E. Sykes and Ann Forshee. She says "The day that Aleck Page was killed, I and Mr. Pope went to town, (Aberdeen.) Joe Davis went off on Tuesday morning, and when we got back he was there." Does that mean at Aberdeen?

Answer. I suppose she means at home; that is, she went to town; not with Mr. Pope; it was with Mr. Crosby; that is a misstatement of names.

Question. The question asked is, "Did he say where he had been?" She answers, "He was at Mr. Kendrick's son-in-law's."

Answer. That gentleman lived between Mr. Crosby's, where she lived, and Aberdeen.

Question. Was that the day upon which Page was killed?

Answer. He was killed on the 29th of March; the day of the week, I think, was Wednesday, as they stated. The testimony showed that he was killed on the 29th of March, and that it was Wednesday.

Question. She proceeds, "I saw Joe yesterday was a week ago; he came to our house; I saw him on Sunday morning; I asked how they all was, and he said they all was in jail, and it was no use for us to go up here, (to Oxford,) for we would not be allowed to speak in court, as Mr. Huggins told him——

"District Attorney WELLS. Stop. Don't tell what Mr. Huggins told him.

"WITNESS. He said that if they would not say they were Ku-Klux, they would go to the penitentiary ninety-nine years, or get their necks broke."

Answer. That is what she swore that Joe Davis said.

Question. Captain O. E. Sykes, one of the counsel for the relators, was called, and testified as follows: "I know Joe Davis; I met him on Main street, in Aberdeen, on Saturday, the 17th of June, the day these parties were arrested. As I was going west I saw him on the street, in company with two niggers wearing the United States uniform. I considered they were a party under arrest, and I think asked L. J. Morgan about it. He said he thought they were in custody. I was attracted by Davis's appearance, as he was a large, stout man, and I called him to me, and asked him if he was one of the parties arrested and charged with being Ku-Klux or some other charge. I was surprised at a colored man being arrested for being a Ku-Klux. He said he was one of the number. He said he knew nothing more about the killing of Aleck Page than the man in the grave. He denied that he was a Ku-Klux, and said that he had been Ku-Kluxing grass all spring. I then asked Henry Hatch if he knew anything of the killing of Aleck Page, and he said he knew nothing about it. Above Aberville, near Holly Springs, I was in the car where the prisoners were, and went to get a drink of water. As I came back to my seat a negro caught me by the coat-tail. I turned, but did not know him. He said, 'I want you to tell Andy Pope not to talk too much.' I said, 'I don't know you. You must explain what you mean.' He replied, 'My name is Jehu Wolf, and if you tell Andy Pope not to talk so much, he will understand it.' I did not like the conversation, and thought the nigger was insolent when he said, 'Don't be afraid, I am on your side.' I said, 'What do you mean by saying you are on my side?' and he said, 'I mean the right side.' I said, 'Do you know anything about the death of Aleck Page?' and he said, 'No.' I asked, 'Do you know any parties connected with it?' and he said, 'No.'" Was that his testimony?

Answer. That was Captain Sykes's testimony on the *habeas corpus* case.

By the CHAIRMAN:

Question. How was this testimony taken upon the trial on the writ of *habeas corpus?*

Answer. It was taken down by a stenographer, who was sworn to take it down correctly; he read it over repeatedly when he was writing; he was stopped to read it off that we might compare.

Question. This pamphlet contains all the evidence given at that hearing?

Answer. If you mean all the evidence, it does, substantially; there are some mistakes in names.

Question. Were the prisoners discharged on that hearing?

Answer. Fifteen or sixteen were discharged on their own recognizances for $500; nine or ten were required to give $5,000 recognizances with securities, and two colored ones were discharged on a $1,000 recognizance of their own, and security.

Question. This was on the hearing before Judge Hill?

Answer. Yes, sir.

By Mr. BLAIR:

Question. What parties were discharged on their own recognizances; all the white men?

Answer. No, sir.

Question. How many of them?

Answer. Fifteen, as I recollect, sir.

Question. How many were held?

Answer. Eight.

Question. What were the names of those held?

Answer. Mr. Crosby, Malone, Ware, two of the Studdarts, Whitfield Pope, and Plummer Willis.

Question. Was Andrew held?

Answer. No, sir; he was never prosecuted; he was a witness for the United States.

By the CHAIRMAN:

Question. He turned State's evidence after his arrest?

Answer. He did not seem to know much; only that some disguised men came to his house; he never was arrested; I did not recognize him as a prisoner until I got there.

By Mr. BLAIR:

Question. Are those names you give the men who were held?

Answer. Yes, sir; on the five thousand dollar bond; the others were discharged on their own recognizances in the sum of $500, with notice that they need not attend the Federal court until November; the idea was that the others would be tried, and, if convicted, they then would try the balance; but if the eight against whom was the strongest testimony were discharged, as I understood, as their counsel, they would not molest the others at all.

Question. None of those men, then, were held against whom Joe Davis testified?

Answer. Yes, sir.

Question. Which one?

Answer. Willis and Malone were two Davis swore to as being there, and Whitfield Pope, and Johnny Ware.

Question. Were they discharged?

Answer. No, sir; Davis swore they were present at the killing of Page.

By the CHAIRMAN:

Question. Were all these four held?

Answer. Yes, sir; they were held in $5,000 bonds.

By Mr. BLAIR:

Question. Was Jasper Webb held?
Answer. Yes, sir.
Question. And Thomas Malone?
Answer. Yes, sir.
Question. Andrew Pope?
Answer. He was not held.
Question. Whitfield Pope?
Answer. Yes, sir; he was.
Question. Johnny Ware?
Answer. He was.
Question. Was Plummer Willis?
Answer. Yes, sir.
Question. Jeff Willis, colored?
Answer. He was required to give a thousand dollar bond.
Question. Mike Forshee, colored?
Answer. A thousand dollar bond.
Question. There were some other negroes implicated?
Answer. Yes, sir; they were discharged on the $500 recognizance.
Question. That is Jeff Willis?
Answer. Jeff Willis and another negro, sir—one I never knew.
Question. A Willis?
Answer. No, sir; not a Willis.
Question. Was it Jehu Wolf?
Answer. No, sir; he was a witness.

By the CHAIRMAN:

Question. Were those negroes required to give security?
Answer. The two required to give a thousand dollar bond were required to give security.

By Mr. BLAIR:

Question. Was there any other testimony except that of this negro?
Answer. Yes, sir.
Question. What else?
Answer. The testimony of Fanny Page, the wife of the man killed, and her daughter, Rosetta Page.
Question. Did she recognize anybody?
Answer. The wife said she recognized two.
Question. Who?
Answer. She said she recognized Webb and Malone.
Question. How did she recognize them; did she say?
Answer. By their voices, and by seeing one of them under his mask, when he stooped down. I do not remember which one she said she saw under his mask, or the piece that covered his face; the other, she said, she recognized by his voice. There was a great deal of testimony to show that she had said repeatedly, to white and black, that she did not know anybody, but she swore she did know these two.

By the CHAIRMAN:

Question. Did she say that she had made these statements under the influence of fear?
Answer. She denied that she had made them; she denied positively that she had made them.

By Mr. BLAIR:

Question. Who testified that she had made them?
Answer. Mr. Silas F. Kendricks, with whom she had lived, (he was sheriff for many years;) Mr. William J. Gordon, with whom she was living when subpœnaed as a witness, his wife; and I do not remember the name of the colored witness that stated the same thing.
Question. Was there any evidence introduced on the part of the persons held?
Answer. Yes, sir.
Question. What was the evidence?
Answer. The evidence was tending to prove an alibi; and it was proved very satisfactorily, I thought, for every one except Malone, who had only his wife. He is a poor man, and his family is a wife and small child; her testimony was as positive as it could be; she is a woman in bad health; the balance had what I thought was very abundant testimony. Willis, who was sworn to most positively, was proven by Mr.

Gordon, and Mr. Love, present deputy sheriff, to have been in Aberdeen the night of the killing. Mr. Love says he left him at 11 o'clock at night there, pretty drunk, at the office of Mr. Beckett. Mr. Gordon says at 11 o'clock, or half past 11, he came to the door of his store, heard him (Willis) talking, took him into his counting-room, pulled his coat and boots off, and locked him up asleep, and found him there next morning, still asleep; it was about thirteen miles from the place of the killing; the river was high, and was between the town and place of the killing; and I do not think it possible for Willis to have been there, because of that testimony of Mr. Gordon and Mr. Love, both being men of unquestioned veracity, one a democrat and one a republican.

By Mr. RICE:

Question. Was there any uncertainty as to whether that was the proper night?

Answer. No, sir; they were very positive that was the night, and that they heard of the killing next day, by persons coming into court; our circuit court was in session.

By Mr. BLAIR:

Question. This man Davis swore he was present at the murder of Dupree and of Page?

Answer. I never heard him examined in regard to Dupree at all.

Question. He swore before this committee that he was present at the killing of Page, Dupree, and Wamble, and the whipping of Simon Dunham and a negro named Willis?

Answer. The only examination of him I ever heard was on the trial for the killing of Page—the trial of the case of United States *vs.* Walton and others.

Question. Rett Willis, he called him, and Simon Dunham?

Answer. Yes, sir; I have heard of all those cases, but I myself know nothing about them. I can give what was said about them.

By the CHAIRMAN:

Question. Was there any doubt of the fact that Page had been killed?

Answer. No, sir.

Question. And killed by a body of men in disguise?

Answer. I do not think there was any doubt of the fact that he was killed, and killed by men in disguise.

By Mr. BLAIR:

Question. This negro says there were six negroes there and some twenty or thirty white men?

Answer. I do not know what number he gave at the court-house as being present; I recollect his stating at court that he was left with Henry Hatch, to hold horses, and afterward went to the house of Aleck Page, and tied him, and he was then carried off; but I do not think he stated, or I have no recollection of his stating, how many were present.

Question. He said here there were some thirty, forty, or fifty?

Answer. That is largely more that anybody stated it at that I examined. It was variously stated from twelve to twenty by the other witnesses.

Question. The evidence, you think, was very strong that the man was not there at the time?

Answer. I think so—convincing. I thought the testimony would satisfy anybody that he was not there at all. The reason I think the evidence was that he was carried off by disguised men and killed, Andrew Pope swears he was waked up about 12 o'clock by a noise at his door; that there were disguised men there; that they pinched him and punched him with a gun and told him then to stay in his house. The negro was missing and the body was found. That is the testimony that he was carried off by disguised men and killed. I do not believe myself that Joe Davis was there at all, or knows anything about it.

Question. What motive could he have had for saying he was there and present at all these Ku-Klux outrages?

Answer. I am not prepared to say, except that he was suspicioned of belonging, or charged with belonging, to a club or band of Ku-Klux himself, and charged that he had threatened the life of this negro that was killed.

Question. He denied in his testimony that he had had any quarrel with him?

Answer. Yes; he denied that positively.

Question. Was there any proof to show that he had quarreled with him?

Answer. No, sir; there was no proof on that trial to the contrary, but it can be proved. There was no proof on that trial to disprove his statement in regard to his threat.

Question. Is there any evidence to show by whom he was killed? You say there is evidence going to exonerate those charged with the killing.

Answer. There certainly is no evidence to show by whom he was killed. We adduced evidence to show that disguised men came from the direction of Alabama and were going in the direction of where this negro was living the night he was killed. As to who they were we have no information at all, nor was there any information to show who did kill him.

Question. Does that apply to Page or Dupree?

Answer. To Page; we have had no investigation of Dupree's case in the courts at all, sir.

Question. In the case of Wamble, has there been any investigation?

Answer. No, sir; his wife consulted me about it, and wanted me to prosecute some negroes whom she said had killed him; she said they had killed him because of his intercourse with their wives.

Question. What did she know about it?

Answer. I told her whenever she would adduce such evidence as I thought could convict them, I would prosecute them with a good deal of pleasure, and so did my nearest neighbor, who is a lawyer, Judge Houston—that we would not charge them for it if she would adduce such testimony as would convict them; she never returned to me even. I have not seen her since. She stated this, giving me the names of five negroes who had repeatedly threatened his life. He was a preacher. She said that it was on account of their wives, and that they intended to kill him, and she had no doubt they did kill him.

Question. Did she state the circumstances of his death?

Answer. Only that he was shot.

Question. Shot in his house?

Answer. Shot in the house, she said; by three men, is what she told me. Some white men in the neighborhood—Mr. Worden and others—were anxious they should be prosecuted, as it would be charged on the white men, and they were not guilty, and wanted the case prosecuted.

Question. He says they went to Abe Wamble's house, called him out, talked a little time to him, and shot him six or seven times outside of the door.

Answer. His wife said he was shot in the house by men standing outside of the door; she said that to me.

Question. This man says he was present?

Answer. I never heard that before.

Question. That he was holding the horses near this same party whom he alleges to have killed the others, or to have carried off Dupree and killed Page. They called him (Wamble) out of his house, talked a little while, and shot him six or seven times.

Answer. These men arrested for killing Page lived an average of twenty-five miles from where Wamble was killed, and at that time the Tombigbee River was high—so high it could only be passed by ferry-boats at some places. The river was between their residences and Wamble's, and it would have been easy to show where they crossed, if they did cross it.

The CHAIRMAN. He did not say the whole party were the same.

Mr. BLAIR. He said they were the same men, so far as he knew; that Andrew Pope was with them, and Whitefield Pope, Jasper Webb, Malone, and Johnny Ware; that those men were present on each night that they went out; he swears to them, and then he swears to Henry Hatch, and three other negroes, two of whom he says were democratic negroes.

The WITNESS. The two Willis negroes were democratic negroes, and so was Aleck Page; he had voted against the constitution and voted with us all the time, and was an open-mouthed, talking man.

Question. He says this Wamble was called out and shot six or seven times; and he said that the same men I have named to you were there; that he was present and held the horses, but he did not say he saw the shooting; he does not know whether they buried him; they were a smart while coming back to the horses where he was, after killing him; they did not do any other mischief that night. Now, you state that the distance between this place and where these parties lived was twenty-five miles?

Answer. The average distance from where he was killed to where Malone, Whitefield Pope, and Ware—who is a boy of nineteen, or possibly twenty—lived, was at least twenty-five miles. At that time the river was high between where they lived and where the negro was killed; they lived on the east side of the Bigbee, the negro lived on the west side; they lived in the sandy-land country, the negro in the black land or prairie land.

By the CHAIRMAN:

Question. Was there no bridge or ferry-boat to cross?

Answer. There is a ferry at Aberdeen and Cotton Gin, but it would have been easy to have proved their passage had they crossed a ferry; there were no bridges. It was a long ferriage at Cotton Gin; the low ground is what I mean; it was overflowed, and the boat would have had to run out a mile—a common flat-boat or ferry-boat.

By Mr. BLAIR:

Question. How do you know Page was a democrat?

Answer. I have heard him talk on the hustings repeatedly.

Question. Make speeches?

Answer. No, sir; we discussed our constitution very extensively; made speeches and had the negroes and white people together a great deal; and he was a noisy opponent of the constitution, asserting again and again he was a democrat; he said in the election of Governor Alcorn that he was a democrat; we all at Aberdeen recognized him as a democrat. Except when he was drinking he was a quiet man; when drunk he was said to be turbulent. He was recognized when a slave as a good negro.

Question. He (Davis) says they killed Dupree for being a republican man; that he was called the head man of the Loyal League; how is that?

Answer. I do not know anything about it. I understand them all to belong to the Loyal League; almost all the negroes in the country belong to Loyal Leagues; a great many have told me they belonged to them; I never knew whether he was president of a club or not; I have heard within the last week that he was president of a club when killed; I never heard it until recently.

Questin. He says they killed Aleck Page because he was a republican and held up for the republicans?

Answer. He was uniformly recognized as a democrat.

Question. He says they got to talking and raised a fuss; he was talking when Pope told him that he would kill him; that was on the road; Andrew Page's wife screamed and he did not shoot him that day, but told him "they would kill him, God damn him, before long;" this was said by Tom Malone. The witness testified that they raised a row with him because he was a republican, and threatened to kill him, and only failed to kill him because Andrew's wife screamed and prevented it?

Answer. That is something he did not testify to before the court; he gave no such testimony as that. I had a witness there to prove all about the difficulty on the road, and he did not testify anything about it, and consequently I did not introduce my witness; I had a witness there to prove all about that difficulty.

Question. The difficulty with Page and Malone?

Answer. Yes, sir.

Question. What was that difficulty about?

Answer. Page was drunk and abused them very much, and threw one of them out of the wagon, and talked to a lady improperly—very improperly; I should have shot him if I had been one of them—if it had been my wife or any other lady, as they told the story to me.

Question. He says that Jasper Webb gave him a dollar on the cars and told him not to say anything at the court?

Answer. That is something he did not testify to.

Question. He says Henry Allen saw it and asked him what he gave it to him for?

Answer. I do not know who Henry Allen is.

Question. He said a good many other parties saw it; that all the prisoners were standing around and saw it?

Answer. It is something I never heard of before; there was no testimony to that effect in court; I do not know any party named Henry Allen that was there; I went up with them, but saw nothing of that.

Question. He says that he also gave Forshee a dollar and that Forshee would not testify to anything?

Answer. Forshee was not along; he did not go up with us; he was in jail as a witness; he and the two Willis negroes were in jail as witnesses, having been brought up there before the grand jury. The money given to him, I expect, I and Colonel Reynolds gave; we gave some money to two negroes in jail; one of them I used to own and had fished with a good deal, and I regarded him as about as clever a man as any in the neighborhood when he was a slave, and have given him a drink—given him a little money frequently.

Question. He says Jeff Willis and Burrell Willis were democrats, and went into it of their own accord; the others, he says, were forced; that he and Hatch and Forshee were forced to go in?

Answer. We have always regarded Jeff Willis as a democrat; I do not know whether Burrell Willis is or not.

Question. He says that Jeff Willis was seen with his shroud on on the night of Dupree's killing?

Answer. We made no investigation about that, and I am not prepared to say anything about the Dupree killing at all.

Question. What is the best belief in regard to his killing; what was the alleged ground; why was he killed?

Answer. I never heard the reason given for it in my life; I was very loth to believe it had been so. I have heard it spoken of only to be reprobated—severely censured by the community. I never heard any reason or excuse for it.

By the CHAIRMAN:

Question. Of whose death do you speak?

Answer. Of Dupree's death. It was reprobated by the community universally.

By Mr. BLAIR:

Question. Do you know anything of the case that recently happened, in which a man, Kendrick, was taken from the hands of a deputy?

Answer. Yes, sir; I can give you the history of it, as detailed to me by a gentleman in the neigborhood and by the defendants themselves. I am counsel for them, employed by them to defend them, and I can also give you the statement of a very respectable gentleman as to the whole thing.

Question. Give the statement.

Answer. This man Kendrick had killed a hog belonging to an old gentleman named Garrett; had shot the hog and killed it between sundown and dark, and was carrying the hog along a path in the woods, going in the direction of his own house, when he met Mr. Garrett, the owner of the hog, hunting his horse, the old man having his bridle. His family consisted of himself and his daughter; his daughter is forty, perhaps, and he was over sixty.

Question. This Garrett?

Answer. Yes, sir. Upon meeting Garrett, the negro threw the hog down, and drew up his gun and shot Garrett instantly; Garrett fell; the negro ran off, and Garrett hallooed, and after hallooing a while, two men, hearing him, went to him; they found him very much exhausted; he bled a great deal; he had got so he could not halloo much when they reached there; they got him home, and he died almost immediately after getting into his house. They took the track of the man that seemed to have killed him, and tracked him up to Kendrick's house, where he was; took one of his shoes and fitted it into the tracks where he had been over soft ground, and it seemed to be the same shoe-track identically; the heels were freshly pulled off of his shoes; they had not been used since they were pulled off; the holes made by the pegs had not been filled up with dirt; he was arrested and taken before Squire Adonijah Elkins, and he appointed a Mr. Legronne an officer to superintend the court, and the inquest that was to be held over Garrett. He proceeded to act. Elkins, as justice of the peace, proceeded to try Hendricks. After this investigation he committed him to jail without bail, as guilty of murder. Mr. Legronne went to him then (he had been appointed an officer) and asked to be released, saying that it was a good way to town and he did not want to go. Elkins told him he was responsible and he must go—refused to release him; whereupon he summoned his brother, another Legronne, and Mr. Marshal to assist him; they went to one of the Legronnes' houses on the way to Aberdeen to get some supper or something to eat, (having had no dinner,) and started immediately to town. They had not got more than a mile or a mile and a half when they were met, as they stated, by a crowd of men who took the negro away from them and ordered them to take the road back or they would kill them. They asked to be permitted to go on to town and report; they were told that they had to go back exactly the way they came, or they would kill them, and they took the negro, and right there, from the testimony, killed them.

By Mr. RICE:

Question. Disguised men?

Answer. Not as the defendants told me; they said they were not disguised—that it was dark and they did not know them; did not recognize any of them. I asked if they were disguised and they said they were not disguised.

By Mr. BLAIR:

Question. Did this old man, Garrett, recognize Kendrick?

Answer. He did not identify him; he said he thought it was him, but he did not know whether it was—that he might do him injustice. I knew Garrett; he was a very conscientious, quiet, old man; he thought he might be mistaken, as it was getting pretty deep dusk and he would not state further than that.

Question. Was any one with Garrett?

Answer. No, sir; nor with Kendrick; they met in a wood, on the path, he carrying home a hog which was Garrett's hog; and immediately he threw down the hog and drew up his gun and shot him. Kendrick made this statement next day to the court, after he was convicted, that he had done it. The negroes present proposed to the white people that if they would give him to them, they would take him and kill him; they said it must not be done, for it would injure their reputation; they knew that he had killed old man Garrett.

Question. Did Kendrick make the confession that he had killed old man Garrett without intimidation?

Answer. So Captain Bennett, a very respectable old gentleman, and two or three other very worthy gentlemen told me—old gentlemen.

Question. That he voluntarily confessed?

Answer. Yes, sir; after Elkins committed him to jail he told them all about it; told them he had killed the hog, met Garrett, and thought Garrett was going to arrest him for killing the hog, and shot Garrett; and he expressed a great deal of regret at having done it. Captain Bennett is a man of my age, or older, and, with the three other old men, they said they had a little difficulty in keeping the negroes from killing this man for damaging their reputation; one or two cocked their pistols. The men composing the guard of the prisoner who was killed were arrested on a warrant issued by Captain Lee, mayor of Aberdeen; they were arrested by the sheriff, Mr. Anderson, and taken to Aberdeen. There were a great many negroes in town, and they manifested a good deal of disposition to use violence. I went up into the mayor's office, where they were. The father of one of them had come to town and employed me before they got there. I went into the mayor's office, where they were, and, after a little conversation, went out. The negroes were collecting up in groups, and showing a good deal of ill-feeling; one or more I heard swear they ought to be hung; and one swore, "Damn them, let's hang them." At that time he recognized me, and says, "Hush; there is the old devil that always saves them;" and with that they quit talking. I walked up to the group, but they stopped, and would not say another word. I went back, and Mr. Anderson suggested that we had better move them to the Yankee camp—the Federal camp; we call it the "Yankee camp." I thought it a good suggestion, and we started, two or three hundred negroes following, making angry demonstrations; they were a little boisterous, but we carried them to the camp. That was Saturday evening. Mr. Huggins took one of the negroes that had made the affidavit upon which Lee issued the warrant for murder, and went to Corinth with them; there the negro made an affidavit that brought the case completely within the Ku-Klux act, or the enforcement act, either; he swore there that the negro was killed by those three men disguised; and the commissioner there issued a warrant for them. That warrant Mr. Huggins took as a deputy marshal and brought back to Aberdeen, and took the men away from the sheriff's guard, and took them to Corinth, and put them in jail.

By the CHAIRMAN:

Question. Let me inquire why the negroes at Aberdeen manifested so much feeling against this guard; if, at the time of the preliminary trial before the squire, they wanted to kill this Kendrick for disgracing them?

Answer. It was a different set of men, and fifteen miles from that place. The men that wanted to kill him lived fifteen miles north of Aberdeen. Of these men in town no one of them had been at the trial; they were in town, and had, perhaps, a little liquor; they are apt to drink some when they come to town; all our black population do and become turbulent; and it was simply on the report or rumors they had heard. They did not offer any insult to me, except one man said, "There is the old devil that always saves them;" and I walked up to him, and he did not offer me any indignity or say anything I could take exception to; they stopped talking, but they got together in groups and talked, showing they were ill-disposed.

By Mr. BLAIR:

Question. The negroes present before the justice of the peace when Kendrick was committed heard the evidence?

Answer. Yes, sir, heard the trial.

Question. And heard his confession of his unprovoked murder of Garrett, and they were disposed to deal with him themselves?

Answer. Yes, sir; they told Captain Bennett and other old men, "If you white men will get out of the way we will dispose of him in a minute; he has injured our reputation and brings us into disrepute, and we will kill him." That was the statement made to me.

Question. Is it supposed that they did kill him or that any of them had anything to do with his killing?

Answer. All that I can tell you on that subject is this: Three gentlemen living on roads coming into the road that these men were on—the men in care of the negro were going right south from Camargo to Aberdeen on a direct road—the men that lived on two or three other roads said they saw crowds of men going in such a direction that they would meet this party about dark or a little after dark; and they were of opinion that they were white and black both.

By Mr. RICE:

Question. What did the three men who had them in charge say?

Answer. They said to me that they recognized nobody.

Question. Could they not tell whether they were white or colored?

Answer. I am not certain whether I asked them that; they said they did not know anybody and expressed regret that they did not; one showed marks on his hand where they had pulled the rope out of his hand, and it burned him pretty badly.

By Mr. BLAIR:

Question. The rope by which he held the negro?
Answer. Yes, sir, so he says.

By Mr. RICE:

Question. What time was the trial over?
Answer. Sundown.
Question. What time were they taken out of the hands of the crowd?
Answer. About 8 o'clock, or a little after; they had gone a mile and a half to Legronne's house, and got something to eat and started immediately, being afraid that if they kept him through the night he would be killed; and they started immediately to town.

By Mr. BLAIR:

Question. Were they alarmed by the threats of the negroes?
Answer. They seemed to be; they said they were; they said they expected him to be killed, but did not want him to be killed on their hands, and that was the reason that Legronne wanted to be released.
Question. What is the character of Legronne?
Answer. The two Legronnes are remarkable in this country for sobriety and morality; I never saw or heard of their taking a drink of liquor or having a difficulty with any man; I have known them well; their father is a German; he amassed a fortune and has quite an estate in land; they are men remarkable for staying at home and minding their own business.

By Mr. RICE:

Question. How about the other?
Answer. Mr. Marshall is the full average of men of the country, but not so sober; he does occasionally take a drink and frolic around like most southern young men; but nothing disrespectable; but he has not as much a character for morality; the Legronnes are exceptions to our general rule.

By Mr. BLAIR:

Question. Mr. Huggins has been before the committee this evening, and he states that a murder was committed in the neighborhood; a white man named Garrett was killed; he lived a few hours only; and stated that he did not know who killed him; several colored men were arrested; Doc. Hendricks—he called him Hendricks—was among the number; he made some confession, and was taken to be carried to Aberdeen, and was hung to a sapling. You state distinctly that this old man said he believed it was Hendricks or Kendrick killed him?
Answer. Yes, sir; Mr. Garrett stated that, but would not say it was him; but his opinion was it was Hendricks had killed him.
Question. And Hendricks subsequently made a full and free confession?
Answer. So Captain Bennett said—that he freely confessed, after the adjournment of the court, that he had killed him, and stated why.
Question. Did he make his crime so clear that the negroes there present were irritated, and wanted to kill him?
Answer. Captain Bennett and two or three of the old men, not the young men, present stated that distinctly to me more than once—that the negroes insisted that they should be allowed to kill him, and stated that he had injured them as a race and ought to be killed.
Question. Mr. Huggins says sixty or seventy men rode up there and asked that this man might be placed in their charge, to be carried to jail.
Answer. I never heard of that, if there was such a thing.

By Mr. RICE:

Question. He said sixty or seventy originally arrested him.
Answer. It may be so, but nothing of that kind has been stated in my presence.

By Mr. BLAIR:

Question. He said fifty men went to the trial of Hendricks, but he was delivered to those three men as a guard.
Answer. He was just turned over to one of them, who summoned the other two. That is the way they stated it to me.
Question. He stated "fifty men went to the trial of Hendricks, and they asked that Hendricks might be delivered to them, to be conveyed to prison."
Answer. If so, I never heard of it.

Question. "But he was delivered to the three men named."
Answer. I have stated as to that.

By the CHAIRMAN:

Question. This preliminary trial was largely attended?
Answer. I understood there were fifty or sixty men, black and white, at it; they lived in the neighborhood—maybe sixty or seventy.

By Mr. BLAIR:

Question. Did you hear anything of a man named Hutchinson, that was killed?
Answer. No, sir.
Question. Killed in Lee County?
Answer. No, sir.
Question. "Tobe Hutchinson, taken from his house a week ago last Friday?"
Answer. I have not heard of it. I was at court in Lee County all last week.
Question. "It was election day. They were masked. He was a colored man. The supposition is that he is dead. The colored men are afraid to search for his body, for fear of an attack. Every portion of our country up there"——
Answer. I was in Lee County all last week at the circuit court, and heard nothing of it in the world.
Question. Were you at Tupelo?
Answer. Yes, sir; all the week; left last Friday night, after church.
Question. "The colored church at Tupelo was burned the same day Hendricks was killed."
Answer. The church was burned two or three weeks ago, in the night.
Question. He says, "Miss Davis, postmistress, has been insulted and every indignity offered to her; they came to her window and tried to get in; kept out only by her pistol; she is a subject of general persecution. She is a respectable lady, a Christian, and a sister of the presiding elder of that district. The church was burned on the 9th of October. The elder and Miss Davis said they could give names of witnesses, but were afraid, because Freeman was bonded out upon some bail, and went back and insulted her again; was taken up upon her affidavit. She refuses to give testimony unless she can be protected. The causes of this: she kept a colored school; that she is the postmistress of the town, and that she is from the North. For these reasons she is the subject of persecution."
Answer. As I understood it, Freeman gave the colored people the ground upon which the church was built. The church was burned down some time in October. Miss Davis is postmistress. She is rather a good-looking woman, and is universally understood to be one of very easy virtue. Her reputation in that way is very bad. As to her veracity I have never heard that talked about. I could not say anything about whether I would or would not believe her, but I know her reputation in the other branch is very bad.
Question. Is she the subject of these persecutions and insults there in that community?
Answer. I never heard of it. I never heard of any one insulting her at all. I have been told again and again that the former sheriff of that county, Mr. Moore, pretty much abandoned his family and staid with her, until his neighbors threatened him with some punishment if he did not quit it.
Question. Did this man Freeman insult her?
Answer. I never heard of his insulting her. Some week or two after the church was burned, the sheriff arrested Freeman without any affidavits having been made or having any warrant. He arrested Freeman Saturday evening. He had been sick. He went up to his house and arrested him out in the yard, and put him under guard—summoned six men to guard him. They guarded him until Monday. Monday evening, when one of the guard was with him, three men named High, between whom and Freeman there had been a quarrel and a prosecution in the courts, made an attack on Freeman. Hallooing to Thomasson, one of the guard, to get out of the way, they commenced shooting at Freeman. They shot three times with shot-guns, hitting him in the leg and shooting several balls into the arm and hand. He fell, and when he got up, (he fell a second time,) they commenced shooting at him with pistols. They shot four or five pistol-shots at him. Whether it was the pistol-ball that hit him in the leg or not, I do not know; it caused the fall. His clothes was greatly cut on one side or the other, showing the passage of a load of buck-shot, that cut his coat, vest, and pantaloons very much, but did not draw blood anywhere except along the knee or leg—the upper part of the bone just below the knee. He got into a house. Some men collected up and stopped the shooting. He has been confined to his house since that time, with the doctors attending him. Two weeks ago or a little more, for some purpose or other, a United States officer, with about seventeen men, came to Tupelo, and about that time the marshal came down and said he had a warrant to arrest him, and put him under arrest. This officer with his men camped in his yard, and had him in charge until last

Thursday or Friday. On Thursday or Friday the lieutenant showed him an order from his superior officer ordering him to report somewhere else, and he left Freeman in his house unable to get away from it yet.

Question. When was he shot?

Answer. Two weeks ago to-day.

Question. When did he return from Oxford?

Answer. He has not been there.

Question. Never been there?

Answer. No, sir.

Question. Was he arrested on complaint of Miss Davis?

Answer. I do not know; he was first arrested by the sheriff; I have been counsel for him and his father these many years; his father was as clever a man as Almighty God ever made, and this Freeman is as good a man as ever lived when he does not have liquor. The sheriff arrested him first, and stated to me when I went up that he had no warrant and there had been no affidavit; he took him before Mr. Clayton, the United States commissioner, who certified that there was no warrant or affidavit, and he discharged him. Subsequently, the marshal came down and said he had a warrant, which he did not exhibit. Who made the affidavit upon which it was issued, I have no knowledge, and the marshal did not seem to know.

Question. What did this fight between him and the other parties grow out of?

Answer. No one knows; but it is the supposition that it has grown out of an old feud between the High family and the Freeman family, that have long been fighting. Two years ago Freeman shot one of the Highs and broke the thigh, laming him for life; it has been a war amongst them—fighting men on both sides, to some extent.

Question. Did you hear anything of the burning of Shattuck's office at Okolona?

Answer. Yes, sir.

Question. What do you know about that?

Answer. The day before the office was said to be set on fire, McCoy, who was formerly a United States officer, and who seems to be a deputy marshal now, went to the neighborhood of Buena Vista, in Chickasaw County, and arrested five or six men, under the enforcement act, he said. He carried them to Shattuck's office and kept them through the night. The next morning I came up on the train going to Corinth, and the statement made by the prisoners and others was that they attempted to burn the prisoners up in Shattuck's office. I never thought of anything else until I was told a day or two ago it was an effort of an incendiary to burn the office. The understanding they had was that it was an attempt to burn the men in the office.

By the CHAIRMAN:

Question. Were they in the office?

Answer. They were locked up in the office.

Question. Were they not confined in the house of Shattuck?

Answer. I can only give you the statement of the men; they said they were in the office.

By Mr. BLAIR:

Question. Did you see the men and the officer in charge also?

Answer. Yes, sir.

Question. They said they were in the office?

Answer. Yes, sir; in the office, and the office was set on fire.

Question. Did they say it was set on fire from the outside?

Answer. I did not ask; but they all thought it was an effort by the negroes to burn the defendants up; whether set on fire from the outside or the inside I did not inquire.

Question. Mr. Huggins says he acted as a deputy marshal in making the arrests in Oktibbeha County; that he had twenty-four warrants, and made several arrests out there; that the sheriff of that county came to arrest him, and demanded his surrender under the enforcement act, on the 17th of September. He read to him a warrant which had been issued by a United States commissioner in proper form, and demanded his surrender. All of which Huggins refused to do.

Answer. I can only tell you what I have been told; I know about the efforts to arrest these.

Question. The commissioner was Ellis; what did you hear about it?

Answer. That Huggins went to Bell's house with some soldiers to arrest him; Bell is the sheriff; that he was told Bell was not at home; that he and the soldiers went into the house and insulted the ladies in their bed-rooms, and examined their clothing to see whether they were men; for which, I think, Mr. Bell acted very shabbily that he did not kill him; in his place, I would hunt him up like I would a wolf.

Question. He states that he went into the room of Mrs. Bell, and found her head and everything covered?

Answer. Yes, sir; and then he removed the cover.

Question. He denies that he removed the cover from her?

Answer. Well, that is the statement of the ladies, and he should not deny it if she was a relation of mine. He would leave the world very quick.

By the CHAIRMAN:

Question. Who should?

Answer. Huggins should; I would kill him if he was the last man.

By Mr. RICE:

Question. If what he said was so, you would not; if this story was not so, he ought to deny it?

Answer. But if my wife had said so, he should not deny it.

Question. Even if it was not so?

Answer. No, sir; even if it was not so; that is part of our southern faith—if the wife says anything, we say it is so.

By the CHAIRMAN:

Question. You kill the man without hearing him?

Answer. Yes, sir, without hearing him.

Question. That is the common law of Mississippi?

Answer. Yes, sir; that is the common law of the South.

By Mr. BLAIR:

Question. There is no doubt these parties invaded this lady's room?

Answer. Well, sir, that is a place nobody that pretends to be a gentleman would have gone, in our opinion, in this country.

By Mr. CHAIRMAN:

Question. What sort of man was this Bell?

Answer. A very clever gentleman—the sheriff of the county; and, as I understood, the warrant Huggins refused to obey was a warrant issued by a justice of the peace to arrest him for an assault and battery.

Question. No, the warrant was issued by United States Commissioner Ellis.

Answer. Well, that may be all true. I do not know any such commissioner as Ellis.

Question. Under the Ku-Klux law for depriving this woman of her rights?

Answer. It would have been a very foolish thing on the part of Ellis. I do not know any such commissioner; but I do not know the commissioners in some counties, though I know a great many.

By Mr. BLAIR:

Question. Do you know anything about a man named McLachlan, who acted as guide for this man Huggins in his search?

Answer. No, sir; I do not know anything about him; I have just heard of such a man.

By the CHAIRMAN:

Question. Are you the counsel for Bell?

Answer. No, sir.

By Mr. BLAIR:

Question. He (Huggins) says the people of Aberdeen, after the prisoners were discharged, turned out *en masse* and hailed them with rejoicings on their return?

Answer. I did not go home with them. I remained at court defending some from Noxubee and Winston Counties, whose investigation or hearing was to come off after those from Aberdeen; consequently I can say nothing on that subject.

Question. He says further that the people did not consider the killing of three negroes and the whipping of a Yankee as anything out of the way; they did not think that was sufficient cause to arrest a southern man and carry him before a court; that that was a common expression, and he quoted some newspaper; he was not very distinct about the newspaper; but some newspaper, which he could not name—some Kosciusko paper?

Answer. I do not know that I ever saw the paper published in Kosciusko.

Question. Did you ever hear such an expression?

Answer. I never did. I have heard the killing of the negro universally reprobated. I know there is a good deal of prejudice against Mr. Huggins, and it had its origin in the belief that he was one of a number that had brought about dissensions between the white people and the negro. At the conclusion of the war there was a very good state of feeling between the white people and the negroes of this country universally. The constitution of 1868 would not have been voted down if the negro had not voted against it, because it disfranchised—to use their expression—"disfranchised old master." I judge from the negroes I owned; I had owned a good many; I heard them repeatedly say to me and others that they would not have voted against the constitution if it had allowed me to vote and hold an office; that they would not vote for any constitution that did not give old master a fair chance. Until the men from the Western and Northern States who intended to make politics a trade came to Mississippi, there never were two races of people agreeing better than we agreed with the negro. From that time they have got up dissensions amongst them, and ill feeling to some extent, but it is entirely owing, I think I can safely state, to such men as Mr. Huggins, who have brought it about to get office.

Question. Did you regard as true the statement that he made, that the people of your town hailed the return of those persons charged with being KuKlux with joy, because they did not regard the killing of three negroes and the whipping a Yankee as anything of consequence?

Answer. I know that is not so, as well as I can know anything; I cannot state it though, as positive knowledge.

Question. He says the expression was universal.

Answer. I know that the people in the town, at the time I was at home, before I returned with the prisoners, universally regretted that it was done and condemned the act. I know I heard a great deal of regret that Huggins was whipped; not because there was any good feeling for him, perhaps; but because of the effect it would have upon the country. I cannot say there was any good feeling for him, but I heard a great deal of disapprobation and regret at his having been whipped, and the reason given for it, a thousand times. The people at Aberdeen had been telegraphed as to the bail that those men were required to give; and they had been requested to notify their friends and have them all present, so that the men who had been away from home and under guard for three weeks could get on home that night; and they, to some extent, had prepared to give the bail, I understood; but I was not present, and I do not know what occurred. Mr. Reynolds can tell all about it when he comes up.

[At 6.15 p. m., pending the further examination of Samuel J. Gholson, the committee adjourned until to-morrow, at 9 a. m.]

COLUMBUS, MISSISSIPPI, *November* 14, 1871.

SAMUEL J. GHOLSON recalled.

By Mr. BLAIR:

Question. In respect to this tax for the schools, the school directors, including the superintendent of public schools, were called upon by the law to make an assessment?

Answer. To make up estimates for an assessment.

Question. The board of supervisors either adopted or rejected these estimates, and if they adopted them, ordered the tax to be collected?

Answer. It was the duty of the school commissioners to make estimates, and of the board of supervisors to adopt the estimates and make the assessment and order the collection, under the law of Mississippi.

Question. In the case of your county, was this estimate made?

Answer. Estimates were submitted by Mr. Huggins, as chairman of the board, without being put in form, without giving items; the gross amount was submitted to the court and rejected.

Question. What was the amount of his estimate.

Answer. Sixty-one thousand one hundred and eighty dollars, as I recollect it, for that county. It was submitted, and again a second time rejected. After that, four gentlemen and myself sought an interview with Mr. Huggins and Parson Ebert, a Methodist preacher that was connected with Bishop, and they met at my office—Mr. Howard, an old gentleman, a member of the Presbyterian Church, and Mr. Word, Clopton, a member of the Methodist Church, and Word and Houston and myself were there, and we had a long talk with them about it, we insisting that the estimate was too high; that it was an amount of tax the people could not pay, and that it would get up difficulties and break down the system. We were all in favor of the system of free schools. I have been an advocate of it all my life—from the time I was first a member of the legislature in 1836. The conversation was a long one—sometimes in good humor, and sometimes a little excited. Under the constitution of the State, Judge Houston and myself gave it as our opinion that they were bound to run the schools four months, and that that was as long as the pecuniary ability of the people would enable them to pay them; and we offered to guarantee that there should be no excitement if they should run the school for that time, at present, and not to be too extravagant in building. We also recommended that they should rescind the contract that they had made with myself and others on behalf of the Masonic fraternity, by which we had sold them a house and lot at $6,000. We offered to take the house and lot back; and we complained that they had furnished that school, which was a high school for colored people, very extravagantly—I reckon more extravagantly than any school I had ever seen. They declined to rescind that contract, and insisted upon carrying out the estimates they had made, and, as we predicted to them, that was what got up the excitement. The court, after the estimates were properly made, never agreed—no three of them. Two were colored, and three white men. No three of them ever agreed about it afterwards, and no assessment was made or tax collected for that purpose in that county.

Question. Notwithstanding the fact that no assessment was ever made or tax collected, did Huggins and the directors go on buying school-houses, one of them, as you say, costing $6,000, and employing school teachers all over the county?

Answer. He bought that house and rented a large brick building in town that had been built by the Baptist Church, and furnished that, too, as we thought, very extravagantly. Made contracts for building about twenty houses, and employing teachers at from fifty to one hundred and fifty dollars a month to teach schools through the country, without any assessment having been made or any tax collected. They had under their control, however, some funds belonging to what is known as the Chickasaw school fund. That was independent of the tax. That was a fund that the State owed the Chickasaw school fund—the interest on that fund.

Question. As to that amount of money coming from the Chickasaw fund, could they divert it to the buying and building of houses? Had they authority under the law to divert that fund?

Answer. That is a legal question. I think not, but it is strictly a legal question. I think that belonged to the different townships in the Chickasaw Nation proper; to each township.

Question. Is that the generally accepted view of the case—that it belongs to the different townships.

Answer. Yes, sir; amongst the board. I can explain how that fund originated.

Question. I would like you to do so.

Answer. By the terms of the Chickasaw treaty the Government recognized the right of soil in the Chickasaw Indians, and they refused to allow any of this reservation of the sixteenth sections which was guaranteed by the articles of session under which Mississippi was admitted into the Union originally. All the lands lying in the Chickasaw Nation were disposed of according to the treaty for the benefit of the Indians. By a special subsequent act of Congress the State of Mississippi appointed a commissioner, or three commissioners, to locate their lands equal in amount to the number of acres for sixteenth sections in the Chickasaw Nation. The land was located and sold, and the money went into the State treasury, and it is what is called the Chickasaw Fund.

Question. Then it stands strictly in lieu of the sixteenth sections which belong to the township?

Answer. Yes, sir; strictly in lieu of the sixteenth sections, and they belonged to each township.

Question. This man Huggins, and Ebert and his board, without any assessment having been made, after his estimates had been twice rejected, and without any collection of taxes, nevertheless went forward with his business of employing teachers, and building, renting, and furnishing school-houses?

Answer. Yes, sir, he did.

Question. Had they authority to do so?

Answer. No, sir; no legal authority that any of us knows of. I never could find any reason for it, except the mere exercise of power.

By Mr. RICE:

Question. Have they not a right to hereafter assess for these things?

Answer. I suppose so; there is an assessment on the county now to pay the previous indebtedness; it is being collected now; it has just commenced in the last few days.

By Mr. BLAIR:

Question. He speaks of a difficulty of some negroes here with old man Flint and his two sons. I wish you would give a statement of the whole of that affair, from beginning to end.

Answer. Well, sir, I have known Sanders Flint since he was quite young. He was raised by a Creek Indian who had married a Chickasaw woman. He was a man fifty-five years old, perhaps—I reckon he is that old; a very stout man. He was employed last year with his two sons by a man named Brown Park. Park and his sons furnished the land and the stock, and Flint and his boys were to work with Parks's sons, and get a third of the crop. When they went to divide, Flint contended that he was entitled to a third, and each one of his sons to a third, which constituted the whole crop. That got up a difficulty about the division. Flint struck old man Park with a hoe and a rail, and he, or one of his sons, stabbed one of Parks's sons so that they thought they had killed him. The other son ran off and got some other hands—other negroes on the place—and as they came up one of the Flints remarked that they had killed Charley, and had better get away; and they left and run off. After being out awhile, I do not know how long, they were arrested and taken before a justice of the peace, and in default of bail, in the sum of five hundred dollars, for an assault with intent to kill young Park, they were committed to jail. After they had been in jail two or three weeks, perhaps, twelve men, as the jailer swore, went to the jail in the night with shawls on, wrapped around their necks, and handkerchiefs tied over their faces; they went to the house of the jailer and told the jailer they wanted to put a man in jail and went with him to the jail; they forced him to open the door, and they took Flint and his two sons out of jail and started off with them. The old man made his escape in some way; the other two were found dead. Ten men were indicted for that in the State court, and five of them tried—three men by the name of Westbrook, a man by the name of Smith, and a man by the name of Marshall—they were tried before Judge B. B. Boone, a man, I think, of as much integrity as as anybody—what we would call a moderate republican, with a republican sheriff and circuit court—all three of them men of integrity. Boone has had that reputation, I believe, thoughout his life—a native of Chickasaw, raised in Mississippi. I defended the men that were indicted. They refused to give me a copy of the indictment showing the names of the defendants, except the four that were first arrested. After they were arrested and under guard, I learned, how I do not know, that Marshall was also indicted. I wrote a note to his father immediately that I understood one of his sons was indicted, and to bring his sons both up to town next morning, and we would ascertain which one it was. He was an old friend of mine. He came in next morning very promptly, with both of his sons, just as the court met, and I stated to the court and district attorney that I understood one of the Mr. Marshalls was in the indictment; that there were both of them—all three of them and whichever it was he was ready for trial. He stated which one it was, and he took his seat with the other defendants, and we then proceeded to try the case; and, after investigating all the testimony the State and defendants had, the case was submitted to the jury without argument, and they were acquitted, after an absence of ten or fifteen minutes. Each man of the first four certainly proved conclusively where he was through the entire night that the men were taken out of jail. Mr. Marshall's proof was not as conclusive, because he was engaged with a train of wagons hauling lumber from a planing-mill to the town of Okolona, and he could only prove where he was until half an hour after night, on the night they were taken out of jail, and where he was at day-break next morning, except by his wife, who stated that he had been at home that night; and it was about 17 or 18 miles from where he was at half after 8 o'clock to where the negroes were taken out of jail. Upon that proof they were acquitted. One of Parks's sons, and five other men said to have been engaged in it, left next morning after the court, and have not been back.

Question. This affair was purely a personal matter?

Answer. Purely a personal matter, as universally understood.

Question. Growing out of the difficulty?

Answer. Growing out of the difficulty about the crop. The colored people proposed to employ a counsel to prosecute. Huston and Reynolds offered to prosecute, and General Davis offered to prosecute, but each demanded that his fee should be paid or secured. The Governor was telegraphed by the colored people—Billy Ames particularly, one of our members of the legislature—to employ counsel, and he declined to do so. There was nobody prosecuted, except the district attorney, on the part of the State. Myself and my partner defended them.

Question. Is the district attorney a man of ability?

Answer. He is a young man of very respectable attainments; but a young man, an appointee of the present governor.

Question. "On the 1st of February" Mr. Huggins says (page 269) "a party of our men went about five miles north of Aberdeen, and took Alfred Whitfield, a colored man, and whipped him until he would say that he would vote the democratic ticket."

Answer. I had a talk with Albert or Alfred Whitfield—I cannot say which name it was; he is the same man—in company with Judge Meek, not long ago, on that subject. He says some men came to his house hunting somebody, and demanded he should open the door. He did not do it until they were about to break the door down, when he did open the door, and they struck him with a switch, six or eight licks, over his coat—that is what he told me—because he did not open the door; for no other purpose.

Question. Huggins says he was very severely beaten?

Answer. That is the man's statement to me—that they struck him six or eight licks over his coat because he did not open the door. Nothing was said to him about voting or anything else.

Question. "On the 3d of February an old freedman, whose name I do not now remember, was beaten by the same parties, and in about the same way. He was not made to promise to vote the democratic ticket. He lives near the Lee County line, in the northern part of the county." (Page 269.)

Answer. I never heard of it.

Question. What did Alfred Whitfield say in regard to the men being disguised?

Answer. My understanding was that they were disguised. I do not know that I asked him. I had the understanding that they were disguised. I have been taking a great deal of interest to try and stop this thing, is the reason I have been talking so much with everybody in connection with it. I am an old man, and have been here a long time, and have been trying to use any influence I might have, if there was any such organization in the country, to break it up, and I have talked with the negroes and white people on all occasions.

Question. "In the case of Albert Whitfield," this man Huggins says, "I heard it from the white people in the neighborhood, and I saw the back of Albert Whitfield myself."

Answer. Well, sir, I did not see his back. I only talked with him, and that not a great while ago, because I did not hear of it until I saw a publication, in a newspaper, of Mr. Huggins's testimony. I did not believe it was so, and that was the reason I talked with the negro. Judge Meek is a near neighbor of his, and he and I had a talk with the negro.

Question. Did Judge Meek say he had heard of it before?

Answer. Meek had the paper in his hand, and read it over to the negro, as it was published; and he said, "Alf, you know it is not so;" and he said it was not so—that he was struck six or eight licks over his coat. Meek is a republican himself, but, I understand, does not like Mr. Huggins; and he says, "He has got us into a heap of trouble."

Question. In the case of Jack Dupree, you have already spoken of that?

Answer. Yes, sir. I do not know anything of it, except I heard he was taken off by men, and has not been heard of since. I know the plantation on which he was said to have lived.

Question. Do you know anything about the whipping of Huggins?

Answer. Nothing, only what I heard Mr. Ross say, at whose house it occurred.

Question. What did Ross say about it?

Answer. Mr. Ross came to my office the second or third day afterward, (an old particular friend of mine,) and told me that some disguised men came to his house and demanded Mr. Huggins, and after some parley they took him and carried him away from the house three or four hundred yards, and required Ross to go along with them to see what was done. The men said they lived in Mobile. He went along, insisting that they should not kill him, telling them as a reason why they should not kill him that he had come to his house, and if he was killed he would have to account for him. They promised that they would not kill him. They told Mr. Huggins that he was getting the country into a great deal of trouble; he was imposing an enormous tax upon them for school purposes that they could not pay; that they had not the ability to pay; that he was hiring teachers at exorbitant prices; and that it was a swindling machine generally; that if he would go out of the country within ten days he should not be molested in any way; that he refused to go, and refused to promise to go; that they took his coat off, and asked him to change his opinion; he told them he would not do it; that some one of the men brought a strap, that he took to be a stirrup-leather, and the man, or men, struck him about twenty-five licks. He said they required him (Ross) to count. They struck him lightly at first twenty-five licks, and asked him what his opinion was. He told them he was still of the same opinion. He said another man, or other men, took the strap then and struck a little harder, until he was struck twenty-five licks more; and he was again asked what his opinion was. He said he had not changed his opinion. He said then a stouter man, who looked to be a very big man, took the strap and struck him harder twelve or fifteen licks, when Mr. Huggins told them if they would stop, he would go away and not molest the country any further. He said they gave him his clothes, then his coat, and told him they would send his pistol and knife they had taken from him to him; and carried Mr. Huggins back to his house, (Ross's house,) and the men disappeared, and he saw no more of them. They left his pistol and knife with his miller—he has a mill on the creek—and told the miller to give it to a man named Loughridge, a beat constable, and tell him to carry it to Mr. Huggins; that they did not want to rob him of his property. Loughridge brought the pistol and the knife to my office a day or two afterwards, and seemed to be a good deal excited himself.

Question. Did Mr. Ross make a statement—a written statement—under oath?

Answer. No, sir; not that I know of. He just made a statement over to me at my office.

Question. Huggins said he recognized two parties, John S. Roberts and John Porter?

Answer. I asked Mr. Ross if he knew any of them; I told him "I would really be glad to know." He said he looked at them closely, but he said he was excited—it was not worth while for any man, under the circumstances, to say that he was not excited—that he looked at them as carefully as he could; that he thought he knew everybody in the neighborhood, having lived there a number of years. He is a man who does right smart trading; he has a mill, and he was one of the committee to look after sundry things during the war. He said that he did not recognize any one of them, and did not think any man could. That was his language to me.

Question. Do you know Roberts?

Answer. Very well, ever since he was a child, and knew his father and mother well; they were near neighbors of mine when I lived on my plantation; my plantation and Robert's father's plantation were close together; when I was judge I lived on my plantation a good deal.

Question. Huggins says (page 274) "I knew the man (Roberts) pretty well, and I would have recognized him if he had not been marked in any way; but he has a large red scar, or mark, on his neck which runs up into his face, a red place which, I suppose, he has had from birth."

Answer. I never noticed it on him; it may be there.

Question. Is it such a mark that a man would see it at night—in a bright moonlight night?

Answer. I certainly think there is no such mark on him; but if there is, a man would not recognize it at such a time; I have no recollection of such a mark.

Question. You have been a neighbor, and have known him better than Mr. Huggins?

Answer. I have known him ever since he sucked his mother; I have been in the habit of seeing him every month or so ever since; I have known him ever since his birth. His father was an intimate friend of mine before either of us was married. If there is any such scar on him I do not know it. I cannot say it is not there.

Question. He did not state how he recognized Porter, but stated that he had recognized him?

Answer. Porter is a small man about thirty-five years old. Roberts is not more than twenty-three or four.

Question. "On the 11th of March, (page 277,) that was Saturday night, Aleck Stewart was whipped in the same neighborhood;" that is the neighborhood where Huggins had been whipped.

Answer. I know nothing of it, sir.

Question. "He had sued a white man the fall before. I have seen him, and heard his testimony before the court. He states that they told him that night that it was because he had sued Mr. McNeice." Joe Davis says that Simon Dunham was whipped for suing McNeice?

Answer. I never heard of either of them being whipped; I do not know anything about it at all.

Question. Who is McNeice?

Answer. He is a very poor man that lives in the neighborhood that Willis and Roberts live in, and the neighborhood, I suppose, these negroes lived in—Stewart and Dunham. I know where McNeice lives; he is a very poor man, and has asthma and phthisis, and is seldom out of his house.

Question. Does he employ any negroes?

Answer. Not that I know of; he is too poor; he did not even have a plow-horse, and I know his neighbors have had to support him, because I have had to contribute something in that way myself. He did not employ anybody.

Question. Suppose they had sued him, could they have made anything out of him?

Answer. No, sir; he has nothing but some children; his wife has been dead some years; he has nothing; he did not own a horse; I know he did not very well. He was one arrested and carried to court last June; I know myself and some others bought some provisions to feed his family on until he could get back; he had nothing for them to live on. I know his neighbors had to provide for his children when he was taken away from home; he has nothing at all but an apology of a bed or two, or something of the sort—one of the poorest men in the country. I cannot say, of course, that he did not employ a freedman, but I know he owns no land and no stock.

Question. He goes on and says: "His offense was suing Mr. McNeice; they did not want him to do it. At that time there were about fifty or sixty Ku-Klux present. The freedmen about there had made up their minds that they would watch for the Ku-Klux and fire into them if they saw any more. It was a distressing state of affairs; the killing of Dupree, the interruption of myself, and the breaking up of their schools had had a very demoralizing effect upon the freedmen. There were some seven or eight of them who took their guns, and knowing they were riding, followed them up and placed themselves in position. As they where whipping Stewart, the colored men fired into them, and one of them was probably killed; he died very mysteriously afterward, but I could not swear that he was killed; it was the opinion of the neighborhood that that was the way he came to his death."

Answer. Yes, sir, the man that died in that way was a man named Beckett, son of Dr. Beckett, a very respectable old gentleman; he died, as his physician, Dr. Tindall, stated, with the heart disease. He had eaten supper rather hearty, and was standing before the fire, and was taken with one of his spells, as they called it, and died in a very few minutes. It was charged, or reported, that Mr. Ford was shot at the same time. Mr. Ford was shot, with his own pistol, at Walton's store, in the presence of several men in sight, and amongst them Dr. Dowdell, who swore to it in the Federal court. He is a justice of the peace, and was there holding court. He said he had his pistol out, and letting down the click fired and hurt himself in the hand pretty badly; he saw it done and gave the date. The other man they said was wounded was Willis, who skinned his foot with a new pair of boots and was lame. I never saw his foot; I did not examine it, but I know as well about Beckett's as about any neighbor's death, and examined Ford's hand and examined Squire Dowdell about it.

Question. All this testimony you say was taken at Oxford?

Answer. Yes, sir.

Question. These men were all arrested?

Answer. Beckett was not arrested, because he was dead, but the other two were—Willis and Ford. Squire Dowdell was taken there as justice of the peace holding court, to prove how Ford was shot.

Question. What were Dowdell's politics?

Answer. Republican; an appointee of the present governor.

By the CHAIRMAN:

Question. What charge were Willis and Ford arrested on?

Answer. This same charge—for the murder of Aleck Page and the carrying off of Jack Dupree, as we suppose; we know about the murder of Page and we understand the charge—they have not been arraigned on the charge of killing Dupree——

By Mr. BLAIR:

Question. The fact being that Dupree's body has never been found?

Answer. No, sir; it has not.

Question. It is not known whether he is dead or alive?

Answer. No, sir; but still there is a bill of indictment for killing him.

By the CHAIRMAN:

Question. Is there any doubt about his death?

Answer. I do not think there is any doubt about it, if you want my opinion. Still it cannot be proven. I think he is dead; that is my opinion.

By Mr. BLAIR:

Question. The *corpus delicti* is essential?

Answer. It is essential, but it could not be proven.

Question. "A freedman named Alfred Skinner was attacked there by a band of disguised men," Huggins says?

Answer. I never heard of him.

Question. "He defended himself in his house, and they filled his house with shot. Persons who were sent there to investigate the matter have testified to the fact that there were shot there in the house, plenty of them."

Answer. I never heard of it, sir.

Question. "He fired on them," (from the house,) "and they did not get him. In the same neighborhood Joe Atkins was taken out by the same band; he was told that he was a radical, and made to hug a sapling—to take hold around the sapling and hug it while they whipped him severely; they beat him very badly; I have seen him myself and talked with him; he left the neighborhood, as also did Alfred Skinner, and came to Aberdeen?"

Answer. I never heard of him. I know a negro named Abner Atkins but, never heard of Joe Atkins; and never heard of any negro or white man named Atkins being whipped or molested.

Question. "On the same night that Aleck Stewart was whipped they also whipped a colored man who had been in the Federal Army during the war. He had left the place he was living on without the consent of the planter, and had hired himself out at another place. He was whipped and told that was what he was whipped for—leaving his place without the consent of his employer?"

Answer. I know nothing of it, sir. I heard of an old colored man being whipped in that neighborhood, who had testified in court. His name was Santee Butler. He was said to have been whipped by negroes because he testified in court against a negro named Burrill Hutchinson, who was tried for killing a white man named Reuben Crow. On the first trial there was a mixed jury, and it was a hung jury. Up to the time the jury reported they thought they might agree; but one of the jurors got very sick. The physician reported that if they detained the jury that juror might die, and the jury were discharged, and this old man, Santee Butler, who had been in jail and heard the confession of the defendant, Burrill Hutchinson, was examined as a witness. He was whipped I heard—I do not know it myself—by negroes for testifying against Burrill Hutchinson. Unless that is the case alluded to there, I never heard of it; he is an old man; he looked like he might be sixty-five years old.

Question You have already testified in regard to Aleck Page?

Answer. Yes, sir.

Question. Here is a point in the testimony of this man Huggins to which I wish to call your attention, (page 278:) "Joe Davis swears that he was the first man who took hold of him (Page) and pulled him out from under the bed; and that he was with him when he was killed." Did Davis give any such testimony?

Answer. Davis's testimony was that when he went to the house Aleck Page was standing out in the floor before the fire, and that he was told to tie him; that he took a piece of rope that was hanging up in the house somewhere and tied his arms with it; that somebody got a piece of the bed-cord with which he tied his hands; he was then taken out of the house and carried off.

Question. Huggins repeats this statement?

Answer. Well, that is what he swore on the examination.

Question. On the very next page he says that Davis was "put ahead where there was any danger; that if any man had been shot that night by the negro who was killed, it would have been the man who pulled him out from the under the bed; Joe Davis was made to do that?"

Answer. I do not think anybody pulled him from under the bed; according to the testimony of his wife and daughter, they found him under the bed, and told him to come out, and he came out himself, and was standing up in the house when Davis came up and tied him. According to the testimony of Aunt Fanny and her daughter, she said they made him come out from under the bed.

Question. In the killing of this man Wamble—your attention has been called to that—he says that "he was shot seven times, his body was found, and a coroner's inquest held; his family and neighbors saw the men who murdered him; they testify that they were masked men who did the murder"—from fifty to sixty men; is that the man you speak of as having employed you to defend him, or the man whose wife sought to employ you to prosecute some negroes for his death?

Answer. Yes, sir; his wife stated to me that she had no doubt he was killed by three negroes who had threatened to kill him, previously, in consequence of his intimacy with their wives.

Question. What was Fanny Page's testimony in regard to the killing of Wamble?

Answer. I never heard her give any testimony in regard to that at all; Mr. Huggins has had several interviews with her; he may have heard her say something; she never gave any testimony in court when I was present, in connection with Wamble, at all.

Question. "Tom Hornberger was taken from his house, at night, by between thirty and forty men, it was supposed, and killed; he was fairly filled with shot; that was about the 1st of April." Do you recollect that case?

Answer. I do not remember anything about that name; if I know it, it is by some other name. I think I have a memorandum of the names I recollect; [examining paper;] yes, sir; I have the name of Tom Hornberger or Durham, killed in February; the name I knew him by was Durham; he was reported to have been killed when he was disguised as a Ku-Klux himself; I know nothing of it at all, only the report.

Question. "On the 4th of April a man by the name of Peter—something—I have not his last name—was whipped, with his neck under a rail, until he would say that he was a democrat; that was in some other neighborhood."

Answer. I have never heard of it, sir.

Question. "About this time two of the members of the school board, who had voted for the estimate for a tax for school purposes, were notified by the Ku-Klux leaders to leave the board, and they did so; they were given them so long a time to go off, and told that they would be dealt with if they did not go."

Answer. I recollect seeing a publication from a colored man, that was either a member of the school board or a member of the police court—that is the old name; the supervisors' court is the present name of the court—in which he denied having said that he had ever been threatened. I do not know anything about whether anybody resigned or not.

Question. He said Mr. Eberts resigned and Mr. McCoy did not.

Answer. I recollect Doctor Eberts resigned; he proposed to go to Meridian to teach a female school there, but he has not left; he is still in Aberdeen; he did propose to go to Meridian to superintend a female school there.

Question. "About that time all the teachers on the east side of the Tombigbee River were called upon, and notified to close their schools, and all the schools were closed; there was not a school taught out on the east side of the river."

Answer. The schools were closed; I recollect hearing Mr. Boyd, who was teacher of one of them, and young Mr. Eberts, who was teacher of another one, say they had been notified to close their schools. I heard several other teachers say they had quit because there was no fund provided to pay them. The tax had not been levied. The schools were all closed. It was my understanding that they closed not until the end of four months. At the end of four months they were all closed. I heard these two teachers say they were notified to close their schools—Mr. Boyd and Mr. Eberts.

Question. "Several school-houses were burned—that of Miss Ward, near the city of Okolona." Do you recollect that?

Answer. I recollect hearing of the burning of a school-house; but that was not the name.

Question. Miss Anna Dance?

Answer. That is one; she is a native of the county—daughter of Mr. Fitzgerald. I know several neighbors spoke of it. I heard of the burning of her school-house. They gave their opinion that it was burned because she was a southern woman. I did not hear of the burning of the other lady's house. There was a church burned on the east side of the river—a Presbyterian church burned. Miss Dance was on the west side. There was very general inquiry to ascertain who burned the church, but without success. There was no school taught in it. It was a Presbyterian church, built by subscriptions—by contributions in that neighborhood—a frame house.

Question. Do you know anything about the whipping of one McBride, a school-teacher?

Answer. I do not think we have any such teacher; no, sir, I do not remember anything about that whipping. That must be a Chickasaw man.

Question. Yes; it was in Chickasaw County.

Answer. I have been told about the whipping of a man named Eccles, which was in Chickasaw, whom I have known ever since he was a child. He was whipped for incest. He was a bad man. I bought his land, or the land he was interested in, to get him out of the neighborhood in which I lived, because I believed he had burned my gin a good many years ago. He was a notoriously bad man, and was whipped because he was charged with incest. He was certainly a very bad man, whether he was guilty of that charge or not.

Question. Speaking of the excitement created by these Ku-Klux outrages, Huggins says: "The excitement was the most intense I have ever seen under any circumstances. The demoralization among the colored people was perfect."

Answer. There was no excitement there, I am sure; I once lived there; my plantation is there now—a large place, though not more than half of it under cultivation. It has been cultivated by negroes I raised; except one negro, all the negroes on it are negroes that came back some two years ago, and they are at work on that place. I did not pay much attention to that; I furnished them the stock. I did not want to go to planting, and went at it to accommodate the negroes we had raised, at the instance of my wife; they were doing no good and starving, and she considered it our duty to furnish them a home if we could do so. I know the Ku-Klux created very little excitement in that neighborhood; there was some political excitement gotten up there occasionally. In 1866 the Freedmen's Bureau commenced its operations there, and that is the origin of the first difficulties between the white people and the colored ones that ever arose in that country; the negroes were satisfied and the white men were satisfied, and we were getting along remarkably well, until the arbitrary and unauthorized action, as we thought of the bureau, requiring persons to retain and feed negroes they had owned, got up the first difficulties that we ever had in the county. They have been kept up by professional politicians since, and not by any ill-feeling that exists between the southern man and the negro, or the negro to him. It has only been at times that there has been any evidence of it, and that has been about election times.

Question. "Not a democrat has been attacked in that county, not one."

Answer. Well, sir, these men Boyd and Eberts whose schools were stopped, were both democrats; a man by the name of McClendon, who was raised there, I understood was whipped because of his open, notorious illicit cohabitation with a colored woman; he was a democrat; a man by the name of Wilson, I understood, who was said to be too familiar with a woman in the neighborhood, was notified that he had to desist, or he would be visited again; he was also a democrat.

By the CHAIRMAN:

Question. What county are you speaking of now?

Answer. Speaking of Monroe.

By Mr. BLAIR:

Question. Speaking of the parties who were arrested and carried to Oxford, he says: "These men were arrested for murder and a true bill found against them in the United States court. But the people could not have done more for them if they had just returned from a campaign in the war. When they were released on bond and went home, they were received with shoutings, the firing of cannons, and every demonstration that could possibly be made by the people. They tried to get bands of music to welcome them, but they would not come."

Answer. They were arrested on a warrant issued by Mr. Blackman, as commissioner, for violation of the enforcement act; that is what they were arrested for. After that arrest, and before they were tried by Judge Blackman, a bill of indictment was found against them for the murder of Aleck Page, and on a hearing upon *habeas corpus*, they were ordered back home from Oxford, in custody, to give their recognizances before Chancellor Whitfield. What occurred upon their return home I do not know, as I did not go back with them.

Question. Coming back again to this tax, he was asked, (page 288:) "*Question.* The tax levied in your county is the full amount allowed by law?—"*Answer.* No, sir; our taxable property in the county was about $4,000,000. We asked for a little less, I think, than $30,000, less than three-fourths of one per cent.; the limit fixed by the law is one and a half per cent." What was their estimate; was it $30,000, or more?

Answer. Sixty-one thousand one hundred and eighty dollars, as I recollect it.

Question. Then this statement is a falsehood?

Answer. That statement must be the last estimate that they put in. The estimate was afterward reduced; the estimates were altered after the first one was made; to what extent I am not able to say.

Question. The first estimate was $61,000?

Answer. Yes, sir.

Question. And it was disallowed?

Answer. Yes, sir.

Question. And then this subsequent estimate was made?

Answer. Yes, sir.

Question. And that was disallowed?

Answer. Yes, sir; and then there was still another one; and there were no two of them exactly alike.

Question. He was asked if it was obligatory on the board to raise the amount. He says, "Yes, sir, if we are within the limits of the law."

Answer. Judge Houston and myself, as lawyers, upon our professional reputation, advised the board it was obligatory upon them to raise money enough to run the schools four months, under the constitution of Mississippi, and that the balance was discretionary. I think any gentleman who reads the constitution will come to that same conclusion; at least that was our opinion, upon our professional veracity and reputation, sir—the opinion we gave the board.

Question. The supervisors can judge what is necessary to run the schools four months?

Answer. Yes, sir.

Question. That discretion is left with them?

Answer. Yes, sir. We considered, however, that it was their duty to raise a fund by taxation sufficient to run the schools four months, and that the balance of the year was entirely discretionary, and they were to judge what that was. For instance, we complained that they were paying teachers too high; spending too much money on buildings.

Question. Do you recollect anything about the affair of Colonel Lamar at the court?

Answer. Yes, sir; I was present.

Question. Was he counsel in the case before the court at that time?

Answer. Of these defendants arrested at Monroe?

Question. Yes, sir.

Answer. He was not.

Question. These defendants were on trial?

Answer. Yes, sir.

Question. What was the occasion?

Answer. He came into court, and complained that a man named Wissler, that he said was a dangerous, bad man, had insulted him, and dogged him about the streets armed, and had said he was a "damned rebel," and ought to be in jail; and seemed to demand that the court should either commit Wissler to jail or recognize him.

Question. Put him under bond to keep the peace?

Answer. Put him under bond; Wissler was in the court and seemed to be restive, and got up and started toward Lamar; I do not think angrily; Lamar ordered him to sit down; he did not do so; Lamar caught a chair, and told him if he did not sit down he would make him sit down. The judge seemed to be a little excited, and got up and ordered "silence!" an order to which they paid very little attention; he ordered the marshal to keep order, and what went with Wissler just at that time I do not know, but somebody pulled the chair down that Lamar had in his hand. General Featherstone, I recollect, was in court, and ordered the men to sit down; several got up, when somebody said, "Sit down." I sat down myself; Colonel Reynolds, I recollect, said, pretty loudly, "You Monroe men keep your seats;" that was to the prisoners; they were all together on some benches, right outside of the bar; there was not room for so many of them inside of the bar and the lawyers too; they were on some benches immediately outside of the bar. It is a badly furnished court-room, with just a little railing around that separates the lawyers from the crowd, and inside of that railing we set the juries on chairs; the court-room has not been furnished because it is a rented room; there is no court-house at Oxford; they are building one now. Colonel Reynolds hallooed, "You Monroe men keep your seats." I recollect the first impulse I had was to get up and go to them; I thought in an instant, if I get up and anybody puts their hand on another here, in good or bad humor, they could not be restrained; these men were my old neighbors' sons. I sat still and no prisoner moved; but this man, A. J. Pope, who was a witness, was out of his place, and, I think, inside of the bar. Colonel Reynolds stated that he was not, but I think he was; Colonel Reynolds caught him and made him sit down. He seemed to be alarmed. About that time some soldiers came to the door. Lamar was still demanding his right to speak, notwithstanding the order of the judge for him to take his seat. The marshal came up to him and spoke; what he said I do not know. Lamar struck him—struck him a pretty hard lick on the side of the face, reeling him. I know he did not fall; he struck him a pretty hard lick with his fist; that increased the excitement. Lamar went on speaking, and told the court that the court could imprison him, and he would go to jail; that he regarded imprisonment as a more honorable position than the position that some persons occupied. At that, I noticed one young gentleman, that I took to be a student—I do not know; he was a fine-looking man, I suppose six feet high—I noticed him applaud; the district attorney ordered him to be arrested. He did not move. I looked at him, and dreaded it when I looked at the man, for I thought if they attempted to arrest him he intended to fight, from his general appearance, and that was what I did not want to see. He did not move—nobody attempted to arrest him. That was all the applauding I saw done. Just at that time a soldier came in with his gun at a "ready," and I thought probably would shoot, until I looked at the man's face; and when I looked at his face, I saw there was no danger; that he was cool and at himself; he came in with an officer of some grade with his gun, and maneuvered it around amongst us pretty extensively, but did not make any demonstration to fire, and I did not feel any apprehension that he would fire; he looked a cool, quiet man, that was not excited. Everybody got still, and the soldiers retired. We went on, then, with our case. Afterward, by order of Judge Hill, Colonel Lamar was stricken from the rolls, and after that a day or two, or three days, upon the motion of the district attorney, Colonel Wells, he was reinstated; it produced high excitement. That is about the transaction as I can repeat it.

Question. There is another witness, Edward E. Holman. (Page 349.)

Answer. Mr. Holman was a member of the grand jury.

Question. He gives an account: "One man concerned in that was Lawyer Sykes, from Aberdeen." He says that Lawyer Sikes, and certain others, were tampering with witnesses and with the jury. What was there in that matter?

Answer. Well, I do not know anything about any tampering with witnesses or jury. Mr. Sykes is a young gentleman living at Aberdeen, a member of the bar, a very promising one, we think. He was at the court.

Question. The witness says, "Yes, sir; that witness [Confederate Sam] was tampered with right there by Sykes, who also charged our jury as being a packed jury. Judge Hill made him take up his traps and leave; he would not allow him to practice in that court. He had been counsel for the Ku-Klux."

Answer. Well, sir, that is a deliberate falsehood.

Question. "*Question.* Do you mean to say that the Judge disbarred him?—*Answer.* Yes, sir; for tampering with a witness."

Answer. That is not so.

Question. "*Question.* Was his name stricken from the roll of attorneys?—*Answer.* Yes, sir; I suppose so; the result was that he could not go any further with those Ku-Klux cases; so he took up his baggage and left."

Answer. That is not so—not one word of it.

Question. Was he counsel for the prisoners?

Answer. Mr. Sykes?

Question. Yes, sir.

Answer. He was volunteer counsel for some of the young men with whom he associated. I understood that Captain Sykes tendered his services to them; he is quite a young man. I advised him to go to the trial; he is able to do it; I advised him to go and hear the trial as matter of information.

Question. What took place in regard to the witnesses, who appeared before the jury, and were kept in prison?

Answer. I can tell you about Confederate Sam, all I know. There was a young gentleman from my own town, named McCloskey, who was employed to defend two men named Huger, that Confederate Sam was brought there to testify against; Sam had been kept in jail for some days, and he complained to Mr. McCloskey that the jury was threatening him, and keeping him in jail until he would swear in a particular way, and that he could not swear it. I told Mr. McCloskey to bring it to the notice of the court; he seemed to be diffident. I told Judge Hill, in open court, that I understood that somebody, called Confederate Sam, complained of being illegally confined and threatened, to be made to swear in a particular way before the jury, and, if the fact was so, I held it to be the duty of the court to protect him. Confederate Sam was then brought into court, and was required to give security in the penalty of a thousand dollars for his appearance at the next term of the court to testify. I complained that that was exorbitant; it was too high; that he could not give the bail, and would result in imprisoning him until next court; the judge reduced the amount to five hundred dollars, and agreed to let him go to Corinth before a commissioner, where he said he could give the bail, and the officer was ordered to take him to Corinth, and if he gave the bail, to discharge him; if he did not, to commit him to jail; what become of him after that, I do not know. I had no connection with the case, and was merely aiding Mr. McCloskey, who was just commencing the practice. Mr. Sykes had nothing to do with Confederate Sam. He said nothing about him at all in court, not a word. Sykes was examined by the defendants in a *habeas corpus* case, out of place, for his accommodation, as he wanted to go home, and did go home about that time; he was examined as a witness. But he was never censured by the court or stricken from the rolls, or anything of the kind. The witness either knowingly mistated or was swearing what somebody else said; he made a false statement in regard to that.

Question. If you know any other matter or thing in reference to this subject, which you think of importance, you may state it without further question.

Answer. Well, sir, I do not know that I do. I think there was a committee, or an organization, or an agreement, in 1866, in Monroe County, when we had no officers to keep order in the country, from which, I think, has grown all these charges of Ku-Klux. I think there was an agreement with some men there—I do not know the fact, but that is my opinion—to keep order in the country. It was at a time when there was no law, no officers, and we were in fear all the time of trouble; but we had none. The county was very quiet until after such men as Mr. Huggins, who are professional politicians, as we understand them, stirred up the difficulties in the country.

Question. What do you consider the source of all your trouble was?

Answer. I think it had its origin with the Freedman's Bureau, and then with men who came there to get office. I think Mr. Huggins has done more to get up the troubles than anybody else has, and that his object was to get into office.

Question. He has succeeded pretty well?

Answer. Very well. Not only succeeded himself but put in his friends. I believe if the reconstruction acts had enfranchised everybody in the country, there never would have been any difference between the white men and the blacks in the State that would have attracted any attention. There was a great deal of sympathy between them. We came out of the war with great confidence in the negro, because he had been very faithful during the war. We did not regard his emancipation as his fault or of his seeking.

Question. It is thought to be singular, by some persons who are rather disposed to sneer at the complaints made by the people of this taxation for school purposes, that they should complain of the very pitiful sum of money to be paid by a community as large as that of Monroe County. Now, I would ask you what is and what has been since the war the condition of your people financially?

Answer. Well, sir, in that county we came out of the war utterly broken up. Almost all the men in the county had been in the army; we lost all our stock; the slaves were emancipated; on a great many plantations houses and fencing were burned; and we were out of provisions, and at least ninety-nine men out of a hundred in debt; having nothing left but our land. A demoralization that followed the Freedmen's Bureau left nobody disposed to work out; that followed the action of the Freedmen's Bureau in 1866; it rendered it as much as we could do to make a bare subsistence, and if we were burdened with anything to any extent beyond that, we could not do it; we had no means to do it; we had no money and we had no stock; our plantations were destroyed by want of fencing; the hogs and the cattle were being killed every day, charged to the freedmen, who were idle and had become completely demoralized; and the white people were no doubt badly demoralized, and engaged in it, perhaps. There seemed to be complete licentiousness in that country for some time.

Question. I have heard it estimated by one of the witnesses that at least seven-tenths of the entire property, including the slaves, as a matter of course, of the State of Mississippi, had been destroyed by the war.

Answer. I have always made it higher than that by one-tenth; I have always estimated that eight-tenths of the entire property, including the negro, of course, were destroyed by the war. I have thought of it and tried to make estimates. This is the only neighborhood in the State that was not completely destroyed by the war.

Question. This county?

Answer. This county and a little part of Noxubee, a small part of Oktibbeha; the Federal forces never reached here.

Question. Upon this meagre remainder of your property the taxation since the war has been in what proportion to what it was upon the entire property before the war?

Answer. At least sixteen times as high.

Question. Including the school-tax or excluding?

Answer. Excluding it. Without the school-tax, in my county, the tax is about sixteen times as high as before the war.

By Mr. RICE:

Question. And with it, how much?

Answer. I do not know now what the school-tax is, and I cannot say.

By Mr. BLAIR:

Question. Is this by reason of the overvaluation of the property that remains?

Answer. No, sir; I do not think it is by reason of an overvaluation.

Question. Over-assessment?

Answer. It is an over-assessment.

Question. In the assessment of the property, is it assessed at a much larger value than it would really bring in the market?

Answer. Until this year it was. There is no market value of land in my county now; everybody wants to sell, and there are no buyers. I cannot say what land is worth there.

Question. Property is not assessed at an overestimate then?

Answer. The owner assesses his own property. It is the increase in the percentage upon property. The estimate is made upon real estate, on the oath of the owner. He puts in the property at his own valuation, and if the assessor thinks, or the board of supervisors think, the property is undervalued, they have a right to increase it so as to equalize, as they call it, the tax.

Question. Do they not frequently do that? For instance, one witness came before us and testified that he had purchased land for 25 cents an acre at a sale, and that it had been assessed at $10 an acre.

Answer. I do not doubt that such cases as that have frequently occurred.

Question. That he offered to take 50 cents an acre.

Answer. At the forced sales it is frequently sold below its value, and I have heard of a number of instances where I thought the courts raised the price very exorbitantly—these supervisors' courts. I have known instances in which the courts reduced the price. There are one or two instances in my own county.

Question. Is there any confidence that when the tax is collected it will be applied to proper purposes?

Answer. There is no confidence in this State that it will be applied to proper purposes, because the belief is that very extravagant appropriations will be made of it, as we think have been made; we know it.

Question. Is there any confidence in the officials of the State that they will apply it, even extravagantly, to any purposes of the State?

Answer. I do not think anybody believes that Governor Alcorn would knowingly plunder the State.

Question. Can that be said of all the officials who have control of the finances?

Answer. As far as I have heard it expressed, that is not said.

Question. Not believed of any of the rest?

Answer. No, sir, not believed of any of the rest. We think Governor Alcorn could be bought, but not by money; his purchase would be by office, or something of that sort. He is a proud, ambitious man.

By the CHAIRMAN:

Question. What official position did you hold, General Gholson, before the war?

Answer. If you want them all, it is a long list. I commenced in August, 1833, and I was in office up to the commencement of the war; one office or another all my life; but at the commencement of the war I was in the secession convention, and was judge of the Federal court, the district court of the United States, for the State of Mississippi, for twenty-two years immediately preceding the war.

Question. District judge?

Answer. Yes, sir; I was a member of the secession convention. I am a secessionist *per se*.

Question. Had you resigned your position as district judge before you went into the secession convention?

Answer. No, sir; I did not resign until the State seceded; I then notified the President of the United States I could not hold the court any longer.

Question. What civil and what military positions did you hold during the war?

Answer. I went into the confederate army as a private; was first a captain, then a major general of State troops, and, at the conclusion of the war, was a brigadier general in the regular confederate army.

Question. You held no civil position during the war?

Answer. No, sir; no civil position; I was in the field all the time; I had no time to hold any.

Question. Since the war you have not been in the legislature of the State?

Answer. Yes, sir.

Question. Which branch?

Answer. The house. I was speaker of the house of representatives.

Question. During what year or years?

Answer. 1866–'67.

Question. While you were a member of the legislature, did you oppose the ratification of the fourteenth amendment of the Constitution of the United States, proposed by Congress?

Answer. I did, sir. I opposed the fourteenth; I did not oppose the thirteenth, but did the fourteenth.

Question. You voted and spoke against it?

Answer. I do not remember whether I spoke against it; I voted against it; I probably may have spoken; I do not think it was discussed in the legislature; I do not think there was a speech made.

Question. Have you ever seen and conversed with a person whom you knew or suspected to belong to a secret organization, which practiced deeds of violence, or whose purpose was to commit violence under any condition of circumstances?

Answer. Yes, I have seen some that I suspected of belonging to it, and have conversed with them. I have never met with one, however, but what denied that he belonged to such an organization; I have tried to find such an organization unsuccessfully.

Question. Have you known or been informed of the locality where any such organization exists?

Answer. I have not known; I have been informed that it existed in the eastern part of Monroe County, and in the eastern part of Pontotoc County, Mississippi.

Question. Have you known or been informed of the place or places where any such organization met?

Answer. No nearer than that—the eastern part of Monroe County, and eastern part of Pontotoc County. As for Pontotoc County, I had better say this as to the locality; I was also informed that it existed in the neighborhood of a place known as Poplar Springs, in Pontotoc County.

Question. Have you known or been informed who constitute the organization, or any one or more persons who are members of the same?

Answer. I have not. I have tried to find out who constituted it. I have seen a number of gentlemen recently from the neighborhood of Poplar Springs—old men—and have tried my best to find out somebody, if there was such an organization, that was connected with it.

Question. Have you known or been informed whether members of such an organization take an oath or obligation, or enter into an agreement with one another, to be enforced by penalties?

Answer. All that I know is, that such a rumor exists in regard to such an organization.

Question. That the organization is oath-bound?

Answer. That is the rumor.

Question. That it has its pass-words, signs, and signals?

Answer. I have understood that it had signals and signs.

Question. Have you known or been informed by what name any such organization is known, either to themselves or to others?

Answer. The only name I ever heard of was Ku-Klux. I have heard of it more as an organization in Tennessee than anywhere else. I heard it had a locality in Mississippi, and tried to find it, without success.

Question. Have you known or been informed of the purpose or object of this organization?

Answer. Well, sir, the information that I have of its object was that it was intended to protect the women and children in the country against the colored race and white men that came into the State for the purpose of aiding the colored race in lawlessness.

Question. Have you known or been informed of the grievances this organization was formed to redress?

Answer. First it was said that its object was to protect the country at the time we had no legal officers in the State, and when we were disfranchised and outlawed, as we considered, by the Federal Government.

Question. What subsequent grievances was it for?

Answer. That is all I ever heard of. That was its object, and that object continues with the continuation of that disfranchisement.

Question. Have you seen, and under what circumstances, the disguise or disguises worn or said to be worn by a person popularly known as a Ku-Klux, or known by any other name?

Answer. I never saw but one, and that one was said to have been taken off of a young man that was killed in the town of Pontotoc, some time this year—some time in May, I think.

Question. You may describe that disguise.

Answer. It was a red jacket or sack, and black pants, with something that covered the head connected with the sack, and a piece that came over the face.

Question. So as to completely protect from discovery the face and person?

Answer. If the piece that came over the face was well kept down, I should say it would completely protect from discovery.

Question. Have you known, or been informed in any single case, of where the materials for these disguises are obtained, or by whom made up?

Answer. I never was. I heard a man say that a letter or note was left on his gate directing him to make some garments in some particular way; to put them back there; that the price for making them would be left when they were taken away.

Question. Was he a tailor?

Answer. He was then a farmer, but had been a tailor.

Question. What was his name?

Answer. Meek.

Question. Where does he live?

Answer. In Monroe County.

Question. Are you informed whether he made up these disguises?

Answer. I am not. I do not know whether he made them up; he did not say; he said it was to make some garments in a particular way.

Question. Have you been informed whether the materials were left with him?

Answer. As I understood him, they were left on the gate-post, where he was directed to return them when he had made them up.

Question. You have not been informed whether he made them or not?

Answer. My understanding is, that he did not; but I do not know the facts.

Question. What is his full name?

Answer. I do not think I can give it. His father's name is John E. Meek, but one of the sons made the declaration in town that he had been notified to make up some garments of some kind; I do not know what they were. I did not believe at that time he was in earnest; I thought he was quizzing a crowd that were around there.

Question. Will you please describe the locality where he lives, so that he can be found?

Answer. You can find him very readily if you just send for Judge Meek, in Aberdeen.

Question. Do you know where he lives?

Answer. Yes, sir; three or four miles from town.

Question. Have you known or been informed of any person procuring a horse, saddle, or bridle, or weapon, to be used in any ride or raid, to give either notice or warning, or inflict a whipping or other outrage upon any person or persons?

Answer. I have not, sir.

Question. After any outrage upon a colored man, his house, property, or family, have you known or been informed who were concerned, or any person concerned?

Answer. I have not, sir, other than the information that I heard at court in regard to the killing of Aleck Page.

Question. Have you seen, known, or been informed of any evidence tending to connect any person with any such outrage as I have mentioned?

Answer. All the evidence I have ever heard was the evidence on the trial before Judge Hill, on the trial of the case of *habeas corpus*, and the evidence on the trial of the Lagronnes. All the clients I have ever been employed by have earnestly protested and sworn that they were not guilty, and never had any connection with any such organization.

Question. Have you ever, yourself, been a member of any secret, oath-bound, organization, outside of the Masonic fraternity?

Answer. No, sir.

Question. Have you ever been consulted or advised with, by persons whom you had good reason to believe were members of a Ku-Klux organization, as to their operations or movements?

Answer. I never have.

Question. Were you not consulted in the spring or summer of 1871, as to operations of the Ku-Klux in Monroe County, and did you not, in pursuance thereof, meet with such persons, whom you believed were members of the Ku-Klux organization, for the purpose of consultation?

Answer. I asked three or four gentlemen at Aberdeen, whose names I can give you if you want them, in the spring of this year, after the killing of this man Page, if I would be justified in meeting with such an organization if I could, and said that if there was such an organization in the county I believed I could find it, and I could probably break it up if it existed, and asked what effect meeting with such an organization would likely have. I told them I was not afraid of its effect on me. I was perfectly willing to go into it disguised, or without a disguise, if I could stop such outrages as it was said were being perpetrated. They advised me by all means to do so, if I could. I tried to put myself in communication with them, but I failed, if there was any such thing. I talked with sundry that I thought belonged to it, if anybody did, and they all denied belonging.

Question. You may give the names of the persons you conferred with.

Answer. Dr. John L. Tindall, Robert S. Adams, John Holliday, and William Vesser, the present treasurer of the State.

Question. Had you good reason to believe that those persons, or some of them, were members of that organization; or, if they were not members, that they could give you information as to who were members?

Answer. I had no reason or idea that either one of them was a member of it at all. They were respectable citizens, whose integrity nobody could doubt; and if I went into it, and was prosecuted for it, my object was simply to have these men as witnesses, to testify to the object that I had in view in going into it. I had no idea that either of them had ever seen a Ku-Klux, knowingly, in their lives. They are very reputable, honorable men; very quiet men.

Question. What, according to your information, is the extent of the organization in Monroe County; how many members does it comprise?

Answer. I do not believe there is any organization there.

Question. Do you believe no one ever was there?

Answer. I think that in 1866 there was a formation, or something that would probably be called a committee of vigilance, whose object was to protect the country.

Question. By what name were they known?

Answer. I do not know that I know any name for them.

Question. What were they popularly called?

Answer. I think they were popularly called Ku-Klux. I think they had an existence in 1866 and 1867, and possibly they have yet.

Question. How extensive do you think the association at any time was?

Answer. I think it was very limited. I do not think there were many members, because I think we would have found it out if there were.

Question. How large do you think the membership was?

Answer. It would be mere supposition. I do not think more than twenty-five or thirty men on the east side of the river. I understood it existed in the town of Aberdeen, but I never could find out.

Question. What was the character of that association, from the information you obtained?

Answer. The best men in the country.

Question. Young men, or middle-aged men, or old men?

Answer. Comprised, I understood, of middle-aged and young men.

Question. And not exceeding at any time twenty-five?

Answer. Twenty-five or thirty was as large as I had any opinion.

Question. What was your opinion formed from?

Answer. From what I heard of being done in the country, nothing else. I heard it said that I was a member of it myself. I heard it said that A, B, and C were members of it.

Question. You have expressed the opinion that that association embraced the best men in the country. Will you give the reasons for that opinion?

Answer. I believe it was an organization that existed simply to preserve law and order in the country, and that no other men would be connected with it but men of that sort.

Question. Did you suppose such men were engaged in whipping negroes and white men, and, if occasion required, murdering them?

Answer. I did not, and I do not believe they did it.

Question. What do you suppose they confined their demonstrations to?

Answer. Simply alarming the country a little, so as to prevent a great number of depredations that were being committed upon stock and crops.

Question. How alarming the country?

Answer. Scaring them, to prevent stealing.

Question. In what mode?

Answer. By showing themselves in disguise.

Question. By riding through the country at night in disguise?

Answer. Yes, sir.

Question. In those grotesque costumes that have been ascribed to the Ku-Klux?

Answer. I do not know how they have been described; but in some way to inspire terror.

Question. I mean with gowns or frocks and masks on, and horns on their heads, and whistles, and arms, and with horses disguised; is that the character of disguise you refer to?

Answer. I never heard of any horses being disguised, and the disguises on the men I regarded as a matter of taste, until this examination at Pontotoc. I never heard that they all dressed in white, except on one occasion; I heard a lady, Mrs. Moore, say some disguised men passed her house; that they were all disguised, and all dressed in white, and making every kind of noise—some hooting like owls, some howling like dogs, some screaming, and making every sort of noise.

Question. Do you suppose the best men of your country would array themselves in such grotesque habiliments and bark like dogs, and howl like wolves, trooping through the country scaring negroes?

Answer. I do not; and if such a thing existed, I do not think those men were in it. I speak of 1866 and 1867; more recently, I know nothing about it.

Question. But I understand you in 1866 and 1867 they rode through the country in disguise?

Answer. I never heard of their riding about in disguise then. I heard such an organization existed in 1866.

Question. How did it manifest itself then?

Answer. I do not know. I never heard of its making a demonstration, except I heard of negroes and white men being threatened for stealing.

Question. Threatened by these bands of men?

Answer. By men—threatened with letters; and that men occasionally went to a man's house and told him if he did not behave himself——

Question. In the daylight, or night?

Answer. In the night.

Question. In how large bodies?

Answer. I generally heard of them at ten to twenty.

Question. Disguised, or not?

Answer. Said to be disguised.

Question. In these grotesque disguises?

Answer. I never heard a disguise described. It was said to be a disguise. I heard a man named Wilson was one, and a man named Owens was one.

Question. That were visited?

Answer. Yes, sir.

Question. White men?

Answer. Yes, sir.

Question. Did you hear that black men were also visited?

Answer. Yes, sir.

Question. By those disguised men?

Answer. Yes, sir.

Question. I recur to the question. Do you suppose the most respectable men in Monroe County would be engaged in midnight enterprises of that kind—visiting cabins of negroes and giving them warning?

Answer. I think they would at that time, because the country was without law and alarmed for its safety.

Question. Why should they have gone disguised, if this were a lawful enterprise; why should they not have gone in daylight?

Answer. They were afraid of being arrested by Federal officers—Federal spies, in the country; afraid of being carried from their homes.

Question. They went disguised for fear of arrest by Federal officers?

Answer. Yes, sir.

Question. They did not stand in fear of home tribunals?

Answer. No, sir. We had none.

Question. In 1866 or 1867?

Answer. We had some in 1867; but for about two years we were, as we considered, without officers, law, or authority at all.

Question. What reason have you for supposing this organization ceased to exist in 1867 or 1868?

Answer. In 1867 we began to come to the conclusion, from legislation we had had, that we had some home tribunals we could rely on that would protect the country.

Question. Was that the reason you supposed them disbanded?

Answer. That was the reason.

Question. How do you know that was the reason?

Answer. I do not know that; that is my own reason, and that was the reason with myself and the reason given in conversation I heard in the community.

Question. Did you ever converse, during those years—1866 and 1867—with any of those first-class gentlemen in the country who had composed together for the purposes of law and order, and who rode thus at midnight?

Answer. If I did I did not know it. I tried to converse with them. I am not certain but I should have been one of them if I could have found them.

Question. You say you think you would have become a member?

Answer. I think likely I would.

Question. You think you would have engaged in this trooping exercise?

Answer. I do not know that I would, I ride so badly now with one hand, but think likely I would have become an honorary member; but I would not have ridden around at night.

Question. You think it was a laudable organization?

Answer. I think it was a laudable one, and got up for a proper purpose.

Question. And that they did not exceed proper limits?

Answer. I think not, at that time.

Question. During those years did you hear of any whippings being inflicted?

Answer. I do not believe I did, sir.

Question. Did you hear of any murders committed?

Answer. I heard of murder being committed, if you call shooting men murder; they were charged with murder. I did not hear of secret assassinations.

Question. Did you hear of any murders committed by these men banded together?

Answer. I did not.

Question. Did you hear of any act of violence committed during 1866 or 1867 by those disguised bands of men that rode through the country?

Answer. I think I did hear of some acts of violence.

Question. Will you please describe them?

Answer. I think I heard of men being whipped for hog-stealing and for killing cattle.

Question. Black men or white men?

Answer. Both.

Question. Taken out of their cabins at night and whipped?

Answer. And some horse-stealers; I know I heard of some horse-stealers being killed in what is now Lee County, then Pontotoc County. Several were shot in daylight on one occasion.

Question. Did you ever understand the principles of this organization—how they were officered?

Answer. I never did. I have heard that they have somebody called a "cyclops;" somebody they called the "giant;" somebody they called the "wizard;" but which was the greater one I do not know.

Question. You heard they had their whistles, too?

Answer. I never heard of the whistle until the last few days, from the testimony of somebody or something within the last ten days.

Question. Did you hear that they met in lodges?

Answer. I heard that they met at places; I supposed, of course, it was in houses; I always heard of it as an encampment—that they had certain camps.

Question. Where were those camps said to be located?

Answer. I never heard one located; that is what I tried to find out, but could not find out.

Question. Did you understand they met in the woods or in the open plain?

Answer. I always understood they met at some house, but generally a private place.

Question. Did you understand their meetings were always in the night-time?

Answer. No, sir.

Question. Did you understand that they met openly in daylight and consulted together?

Answer. I have understood that they met in daylight and consulted together, but then they were not disguised.

Question. Did you understand that they met under such circumstances that the purpose of their meeting could be known?

Answer. I did not, and I understood they kept the purpose of their meeting to themselves.

Question. Did you understand that anybody except the members was allowed to attend the meetings?

Answer. I understood that there was not; nobody but the members were allowed to attend.

Question. And you understood that they were oath-bound?

Answer. Yes, sir.

Question. Did you understand what were the terms of that obligation?

Answer. I did not.

Question. Have you ever read it?

Answer. No, sir; not that I know of.

Question. Have you ever seen it?

Answer. Not that I know of.

Question. Have you ever heard it repeated?

Answer. No, sir.

Question. Have you ever heard the substance of it stated?

Answer. No, sir; only it was an oath to keep secret and aid the order.

Question. Who have you heard state the substance of the oath?

Answer. I have heard that much stated by A, B, and C, and I have seen that much published in a Mississippi paper, in connection with Dr. Compton, now superintendent of the lunatic asylum.

Question. You cannot give the name of any person you have heard state the terms of the oath or obligation?

Answer. I cannot; if I have heard anybody state it I cannot locate who it was now.

Question. Did you understand from the oath that those initiated swore to stand by each other and defend the secrets of their order?

Answer. I did not.

Question. Did you understand that they obligated themselves to carry out a decree of the encampment, or lodge, or council, or Klan, or whatever name the organization was known by?

Answer. All that I ever understood of it was that there was a combination to do certain things; what they were I never knew; that they were under the control of the decree of a society, or Klan, or encampment, or whatever it should be called.

Question. Did you understand it was simply a local institution, or was a subordinate association connected with a larger one?

Answer. In Mississippi, so far as I could find out, I understood it to be strictly local, and that they never had any general organization in the State, and that an encampment in that neighborhood was independent of one in any other neighborhood.

Question. Did you understand one obligation of the oath was to oppose the designs of the radical party?

Answer. I did not.

Question. Did you understand one of the terms of the obligation or oath to be to promote the success of the democratic party?

Answer. I did not; I understood it was to promote the success of the white man.

Question. Promote the success of the white man against whom?

Answer. Of the white race.

Question. As against the black race?

Answer. I cannot say it was, but it was to promote the success of the white race; I take it for granted it was against the black race.

Question. Did you understand also that they discriminated against northern men?

Answer. I did not, sir.

Question. Or that it sought to expel or drive out northern men?

Answer. I did not; I understood this, that it was intended to discriminate against anybody that would stir up strife in the country, or make politics a trade, thereby intending to obtain office at the expense of the peace of society.

Question. You understood it was directed against what are commonly known as carpet-baggers?

Answer. I understood them to be included in that; I have the understanding that their business was to obtain office at the expense of the peace of society in this country.

Question. You say that was to be counteracted by this order?

Answer. I do not know, because I never could find out its workings; the Klan was understood to exist in Memphis; I tried to find out there what its workings were, but could not do it.

Question. Did you go there for that purpose?

Answer. No, sir; I have not been there but once since the war; I have been too busy making my bread. I came out of the war badly broken up, with some debts that have taken all the means I could raise.

Question. You have testified to certain outrages that have been committed upon colored men, such as whipping and assassination, within the last two or three years; have you any doubt that these were committed by a regular organization?

Answer. My opinion is, that at least half of them were committed by negroes themselves upon negroes and white men, and that some were committed by white men; and that those by the white men were committed by these organizations. I think some of them were committed by negroes.

Question. Does it not appear that when these lawless men ride at night they have a common purpose, that is, they know where they are going and what they are going to accomplish?

Answer. Yes, sir; I think they know where they are going.

Question. Could such a common purpose be formed except upon consultation, and would not that consultation necessarily bring all the men together at one place—some point agreed upon?

Answer. I think likely it would.

Question. Then, again, if the purpose were an unlawful one, such as, if accomplished, would subject to punishment those concerned, would there not necessarily follow an agreement among themselves to stand by each other and punish those betraying their secrets?

Answer. I should think so, of course, if an unlawful object was had in view.

Question. In thus protecting their secrets, would not the members, if called as witnesses, be strongly tempted to evade the truth, and would not that temptation be increased in just the proportion of the hazards they would incur in case they were known?

Answer. That is a natural conclusion from the premises you lay down.

Question. Would there not, then, be a double motive to prevaricate in court, first, to save themselves from the vengeance of associates, and next, to protect themselves from punishment for the outrages inflicted?

Answer. I think so, sir.

Question. Would not, in your opinion, this motive become overruling, if the offense committed in which they were implicated were punishable by death or imprisonment in the penitentiary?

Answer. I think it might result in men's refusing to testify; when it came to such circumstances I should refuse to testify. I judge other men by myself. The court might imprison me.

Question. Would not a similar motive operate on the parents, brothers, and sisters of the party charged with being a Ku-Klux, and in a less degree operate upon remoter friends and relations, rendering the truth difficult to be obtained?

Answer. I do not think so; I do not think the parents or relatives, if they knew the facts, would prevaricate or swear falsely. But I think that, under the circumstances, they are less likely to know; the father is less likely to know of his sons belonging to such an order than anybody else.

Question. How could the son be absent all night, put on a disguise, and bring that disguise home; how could he ride his horse away and return, with the horse fatigued in the morning, without the family knowing it?

Answer. As I have heard these things rumored, not knowing them, if there were three or four encampments in a county, and an outrage would be committed in this neighborhood, the men who committed it were never the men that lived in the neighborhood, but men from a distance, coming in to do it. That is the way I have heard.

Question. That would imply, from the terms of your proposition, that there were different organizations that had communication with one another?

Answer. That is the way I have heard it. Say there would be four encampments in this county; an encampment in the southeast corner of the county, that had decreed somebody was to be punished there, the men that would do it would, perhaps, live in another county, or in a remote part of that county. That is the way I have heard it reported that it was done.

Question. Do you believe that is the actual condition of things?

Answer. I do not, but that is what I have heard; because I do not believe in a united organization at all in the State. I believe it is neighborhood or spasmodic efforts of young men to do things they wanted to conceal that has no doubt brought about the outrages recently committed in this State of Mississippi; and that is the way I have heard it reported, that that was the way it was done.

Question. In your opinion, would not the presence of a Ku-Klux, or the relative or near friend of one upon a jury, render it impracticable to find an indictment, or in case of a trial upon an indictment, render a conviction impossible, or at least improbable?

Answer. I cannot say, because in the case of those men now that were charged with taking Sanders Flint out of jail, the indictment was found in our county very promptly. I know that a jury of intelligent gentlemen, who were questioned closely as to the forming or expressing of opinions and everything of that sort, tried them, and that the testimony was very weak against them; and Sanders Flint, who swore, was discredited by white men and black men, who swore they would not believe him upon his oath. He is the man who swore to the identity of the men. He swore that the way he recognized them was by their voices, and upon cross-examination swore he had never talked with one of the men but once, and with the others but two or three times.

Question. You have been counsel for all, or nearly all, the persons charged with being engaged in this Ku-Klux enterprise in Monroe County, have you not?

Answer. Yes, sir; all of them in Monroe County that I know of; all that have been charged in that county.

Question. Have you known of a single case where a person implicated in any of these midnight outrages by disguised men has been convicted and punished?

Answer. I have known of the trial of but the five men that were charged with taking Sanders Flint and his two sons out of jail in Monroe County.

Question. And they were all acquitted?

Answer. Yes, sir.

Question. They had no difficulty in proving *alibis*, I suppose?

Answer. Four of them certainly proved, as conclusively as it could be proved, where they were during the day and night it occurred.

Question. Yet there is no doubt at all but what Flint's two sons were murdered?

Answer. I think there is not a doubt about it.

Question. And murdered by Ku-Klux?

Answer. I do not think they were Ku-Klux; they did not have the disguise said to belong to Ku-Klux. They were described by the jailer, Mr. Gilliland, a very clever man, rather a timid man, fifty years old; he swore that they were tall men; had shawls wrapped around their necks and handkerchiefs over their faces.

Question. You do not believe they were Ku-Klux, simply because they did not wear the usual habiliments of Ku-Klux?

Answer. They did not have the general appearance of Ku-Klux.

Question. But they were disguised and banded together?

Answer. They evidently came to Athens, where the jail is located, seven miles from the court-house, at a place where the court-house was formerly located; the court-house is at Aberdeen and the jail at Athens. They came there, evidently, together.

Question. And with a common purpose?

Answer. Their object seemed to be what they carried out—to take the men out of jail.

Question. What number?

Answer. He swore to twelve.

Question. Twelve actually effected the rescue; does he say that comprised all?

Answer. He said he thought there were some more men that came into town on a road from a different direction. These men came from the road on the southeast—rode into town. He thought there were men on the road.

Question. Picketing the road?

Answer. He said he thought there were men there, from the noise and what he saw.

Question. Did he express any opinion as to the number of men?

Answer. No, sir.

Question. To follow out this train of inquiry I was pursuing, I will ask one or two further questions. Would not men wholly unconnected with the order, and not sympathizing with its crimes, be reluctant, in your opinion, from motives of safety and personal interest, to give information tending to implicate a member, from fear of drawing down the vengeance of the order, or some of its members?

Answer. I think not, from the fact that I have heard very open and very constant condemnation of it, and men saying so couldn't have been safe if such an order existed, for the best men in the country would feel afraid of the ill-feeling of some member of the order; therefore we were all interested in putting it down if it existed.

Question. Do you not think that the apprehension of drawing down the vengeance of this order would deter timid negroes from giving any such information as they possessed?

Answer. I think likely it would deter not only timid negroes but timid white men; I think so, sir; I think it is very natural that it would deter timid men.

Question. Suppose a public meeting were held about it; all friends of peace and order were invited; and a resolution to make war upon the organization and break it up were adopted; would not that step compel all men to take sides, and those who sympathized with it would therefore be watched?

Answer. Well, I have seen one meeting of the sort in Aberdeen, and I have seen at one political meeting I attended a resolution of that sort adopted very unanimously.

Question. When was that?

Answer. Within the last few months.

Question. Was that meeting held in view of and because of the various outrages which had been committed in Monroe County, and which the courts had failed to punish?

Answer. I do not think there was any idea of censuring the courts at the meeting which was held in Aberdeen; but it was a meeting to condemn, and give publicity to the opinion that such proceedings were condemned by the community.

Question. That very meeting, then, admitted the existence of these outrages?

Answer. We had heard of them until it induced the getting up of the meeting in Aberdeen.

Question. The evidence was sufficiently strong that those outrages existed and were numerous to justify the calling of the meeting?

Answer. I suppose that induced it; I do not think that there was any evidence at the meeting at all, but it acted on the presumption that the outrages had been committed, and outrages or acts violative of law and order had been committed which ought to be condemned.

Question. Did the members of that meeting pledge themselves to aid personally in putting down these outrages?

Answer. I do not think they did.

Question. What effect did that meeting and its resolutions have in putting a stop to them?

Answer. I do not think it had any.

Question. Have they been as numerous as they were before?

Answer. I think not; I have not heard of them since; the only one I have heard since is this one charged to have been committed at Camargo, in the killing of Hendricks.

Question. When was this meeting called and held?

Answer. Some two months ago.

Question. There must have been an extraordinary state of things up there which called for and got men of the county to assemble together and take steps to put a stop to these outrages?

Answer. I do not know; I did not feel, and do not think anybody felt, any apprehensions for themselves, but I think it was done with a view to induce the belief that a majority of the community—a large majority of the community—was in favor of law and order.

Question. Was it felt that those outrages were a stain upon the good name of your county?

Answer. It certainly was.

Question. Who initiated that movement?

Answer. I cannot tell; I do not remember.

Question. Were you present at that meeting?

Answer. I was.

Question. How numerously was it attended?

Answer. It consisted pretty much of the citizens of the town; a meeting of the citizens of the town.

Question. Was any notice given of the meeting in the papers?

Answer. Yes, sir; there were placards and posters. I do not remember whether it was published in the papers or not.

Question. What statements were made at that meeting as to the commission of these outrages and their extent?

Answer. I do not think I can tell.

Question. Were they commented upon—the various whippings and killings?

Answer. No, sir; I do not think they were. I do not think there was any speech commenting upon any particular transaction.

Question. This was not a Quaker meeting?

Answer. No, sir.

Question. Will you tell what occurred there?

Answer. Well, sir, it was talked about that various reports had gone out of outrages, and that we were in favor of sustaining the civil authority, and maintaining law and order in the country, and that we condemned all violations of law.

Question. Was it rumored that those reports were true or false that had gone out?

Answer. It seemed to be rumored that they were true.

Question. Did you believe they were true?

Answer. I believed these men were killed and whipped; I have no doubt of it at all; the only question was as to who did it. There was no individual pledge further than a resolution that we would sustain law and order in the country; that we were opposed to all violations of law.

Question. How did the resolutions say that you would support law and order and endeavor to put a stop to these acts of lawlessness and violence?

Answer. There certainly was no detail in the resolution of the sort.

Question. Were there no comments upon any particular cases of whipping and killing?

Answer. I think not; I have no recollection that there were.

Question. How long did the meeting consult together?

Answer. Not very long; say an hour.

Question. Were the resolutions prepared beforehand?

Answer. I think they were; I do not remember who introduced them.

Question. Were they published in your county paper?

Answer. They were ordered to be published; I cannot say; I am not much a reader of newspapers; I cannot say whether they were published or not; my recollection is they were published.

Question. Will you give the substance of the resolutions as adopted?

Answer. They were substantially as I have stated; we pledged ourselves to sustain the administration of law in the country; and that we were opposed to violence and lawlessness in every shape.

Question. Was any plan suggested of getting up a counter-organization, an anti-Ku-Klux association, for the purpose of putting a stop to these outrages?

Answer. Not that I recollect of; I am very confident that there was not.

Question. Did any one speak of the locality of this organization?

Answer. No, sir; the understanding we have had was that it was in the eastern part, and it was also said that it existed to some extent in the town of Aberdeen, and it has been said that they have been seen in Aberdeen; I have watched for them in town two or three nights, and could never find them; but could hear the next morning that they had been in town the night before; and I have had policemen on guard to watch for them; I had a policeman, by the name of Stevens, who said he had watched for them all night the night they were reported to have been in town, and did not see them; he could not find them.

Question. Without giving the name of the person or persons, have any of the persons charged with being implicated in these murders or whippings, whom you have defended, ever confessed to you their connection with these bands of disguised men?

Answer. They have all universally denied it, every one to me; I understand that one man that was charged admitted a knowledge of one outrage; but to me they have every one denied it; I think every one swore they were not guilty in the case of Aleck Page, in the application for *habeas corpus;* each one.

Question. One person confessed to you his knowledge?

Answer. No, sir; not to me; I have understood he did confess his knowledge to others; to me he denied it.

Question. Did you, in the character of their counsel and confidential adviser, seek to learn from them whether they were actually implicated?

Answer. I did; I told them if they were to tell me it would enable me to make their defense more successfully than otherwise; to tell me everything they knew in connection with it, and what they had done; they denied all knowledge of it, and told me they could prove where they were, and by whom they could prove it.

Question. How does it happen, when the fact is admitted that these whippings and murders have been committed, nobody can be found who is concerned?

Answer. I will tell you how I account for it. We expect to prove on the trial hereafter, as we partly proved on the trial before Judge Hill, that the men who did this are not residents of Mississippi.

Question. That they came from Alabama?

Answer. Yes, sir; we expect to prove by the ferryman that put them over that he did put over a band of disguised men across the Buttahatchie; and by men that they passed their houses that night going in the direction where Aleck Page was killed.

Question. How should men in Alabama know anything about Aleck Page.

Answer. I do not think that they knew anything about him.

Question. Would not that seem to imply most strongly that there was a bond of union or communication between these lawless associations?

Answer. It certainly would, either that, or that they had been notified by some person.

Question. If they had been notified by some person such parties of men could not be extemporized right upon the moment, could they?

Answer. I think not.

Question. That would seem to imply that there was a regular organization in Alabama, would it not?

Answer. Yes, sir; and they are notified by a kindred organization in Mississippi, which held their organization for a particular purpose, and that purpose was known to somebody in Mississippi, who gave them information.

Question. Organized for a particular purpose, they could not be organized for the purpose of whipping Aleck Page, whom they did not know?

Answer. Organized for a general but particular purpose, and notified by somebody.

Question. You have spoken of another county in Mississippi—Pontotoc.

Answer. Yes, sir.

Question. You may state what your knowledge or information is as to the existence of an organization for the purpose of violence in that county.

Answer. Well, sir, all the knowledge I have of it is, I was told some time ago that there was danger of several counties, bordering on the Alabama line, being put under martial law; that it was believed that there was an organization in the neighborhood of Poplar Springs, in the county of Pontotoc, that was lawless, and that if any man in the world could break it up I could do it, as a great many young men there had been in the army with me, and that I was well known to all the old men. I sought an interview with several old men. At first they seemed to think I suspected them of being Ku-Klux, and they were rather indignant at me. I told them what my object was straight along, and that if any such organization existed I wanted to find it out, and if they knew anybody that belonged to it to tell them I wanted an interview with them; that I would have that interview with them, and they might be disguised so I would not know them, or I would have it with them without disguise; that I was not afraid of being prosecuted, and if I was I would take the consequences; and that I was anxious to quiet the country. They assured me that, so far as they knew, there was no such organization at all; that the crowd that went to Pontotoc the time the man was killed were boys, for frolic and fun; that they carried with them horns of a peculiar make, and something they called dumb-bell; that, I understand, is a raw hide stretched over a hollow drum, with a string in it waxed over, and pulling it by the string, as the fingers slip over it, and it makes a shrieking noise. They carried that to Pontotoc to scare Mr. Flournoy and break up the paper he was editing; they went there, went to his office; had possession of the office; did nothing in the world, no harm, and were going off when they were fired on and a man killed.

Question. They went there just for fun and frolic?

Answer. Yes, sir; these old gentlemen said just for fun and frolic, and made considerable noise in town, and going to town.

Question. You could not get upon the track of any organization?

Answer. No, sir.

Question. Was that after the public meeting in Aberdeen?

Answer. Afterward.

Question. How long?

Answer. Two or three weeks. The gentleman who told me was Mr. Morphis, our member of Congress, who seemed desirous to quiet the country; and, while we were political opponents, we were particular personal friends, and had been in the army together.

Question. Was this public meeting called in Aberdeen after the public prints had informed you that steps were being taken by the Chief Magistrate for the suppression of the writ of *habeas corpus* in certain portions of South Carolina?

Answer. I think it was before that; it was before the suspension of the writ in certain portions of South Carolina.

Question. Was it not after General Grant had given the notice?

Answer. Yes, sir.

Question. Was it not because of the notice that this meeting was held?

Answer. No, sir.

Question. Was it not because you had apprehensions that the writ of *habeas corpus* might be suspended in that portion of Mississippi?

Answer. We certainly had apprehensions of that before, and have had apprehensions for a year, that the writ of *habeas corpus* would be suspended in portions of Mississippi.

Question. Because of the existence of these disturbances?

Answer. Yes, sir; because of the reported existence of them, and we did not believe until the meeting in June that there could be any election in the State this fall.

Question. You say "reported disturbances;" have you any doubt of the existence of those disturbances?

Answer. I have no doubt of the existence of them to some extent, but think them greatly magnified; I think many more are reported than ever existed; but to some extent, I do not doubt it at all; I do not doubt that a church was burned in Tupelo some time ago, by somebody, and I know who is charged with it, and I know the man has been arrested; it was a colored church.

Question. There has been a very explicit recognition, by the legislature of Mississippi, of the existence of this organization, and of its depredations, has there not?

Answer. Yes, sir.

Question. I refer now to the act approved July 21, 1870, entitled "An act to prevent and punish certain crimes."

Answer. Yes, sir.

Question. The first section forbids any person appearing in a mask or disguise. The second section is as follows:

"*Be it further enacted*, That if any person or persons, masked or in disguise, shall prowl or travel, or ride, or walk, or be in the country or towns, or in any public place in this State, to the disturbance of the peace or the terror or the alarming of the citizens of any portion of this State, on conviction thereof, he or they shall be fined not less than one hundred nor more than five hundred dollars, and imprisoned in the jail of the county wherein convicted, at the discretion of the court before which conviction is had."

I will ask you to state, inasmuch as you are familiar with the practice in your State courts, whether there has been any conviction under this law, to your knowledge?

Answer. I have known of no trial under that law at all, unless the trial of the men that took Sanders Flint and sons out of jail, and I think that occurred before the passage of the act. There was a trial and conviction of two or three negroes in Lee County some time in the last two or three years, for whipping somebody, in disguise, in that county; but it was, I think, some mad, drunken negroes engaged in it; very little attention was paid to it; they were convicted, and imprisoned twenty or thirty days. I think that was before the passage of that act; I have known no trial under the act at all; no prosecutions under the act.

Question. The third section reads as follows:

"*Be it further enacted*, That if any person or persons, disguised or in mask, by day or by night, shall enter or attempt or threaten to enter, or shall demand or seek entrance or admission into or upon the house or inclosure, or where any person or persons shall then be, in this State, such entrance, attempt, threat, or demand shall be deemed a felony, and such person or persons so offending shall, upon conviction, be punished by imprisonment in the penitentiary, not less than one year nor more than five years."

This section assumes, does it not, that that practice was sufficiently common in this State to cause an enactment of this law?

Answer. It does, sir.

Question. Have you known of any punishment inflicted under that section?

Answer. I have not known of anything under it, sir; I can tell you what I may state; some gentleman came to my office four or five months ago, and told me that certain men were threatening to whip a man that lived in my county for living with a black woman pretty openly and notoriously, and I told him to go and tell them—I do not propose to give you the names—I told him to go and tell them if they did molest him in any way, that I would prosecute them to the end of the law; that is something that I suppose you may be allowed to know that would come under that act. They said that they proposed to whip him for living notoriously with a black woman. I told him to go and tell them I said if they attempted it, I would prosecute them to the end of the law; I heard no more of it; it has never been done; the man that was threatened was at my office two or three days ago.

Question. This law has been in force now for nearly a year and a half; have you known of any conviction under this third section?

Answer. I have known of no convictions and no prosecutions under it.

Question. The fourth section is directed against what seems from the evidence before us to be a very common class of offenses in this State and in Alabama. I will read it:

"*Be it further enacted*, That if any person or persons so prowling, or traveling, riding, walking, or being in the country, towns, or in any public place in this State, masked or in disguise, shall assault or beat another, the person or persons so offending shall be deemed guilty of a felony, and, upon conviction, shall be imprisoned in the penitentiary not less than five years, nor more than ten years."

That would seem to include all cases of whipping of negroes and white men by persons masked or disguised?

Answer. Yes, sir.

Question. Have you known of any conviction under that section?

Answer. I have known of no prosecution under it, and the reason that is given for it is that the Federal court has jurisdiction of all that class of cases; there has been no prosecutions in the State court in the circuit I have practiced in, that is, in the counties of Monroe, Chickasaw, Itawamba, Lee, and Prentiss.

Question. That would not still prevent the prosecution in the State courts, before the Federal courts have taken jurisdiction?

Answer. I understand the courts to have concurrent jurisdiction: but it seems to be conceded that the Federal courts are taking charge of everything covered by that act.

Question. But this is since the passage of the Ku-Klux bill last April?

Answer. Under the enforcement act, Judge Hill decided that whenever there is a combination of two or more persons to deprive any other person of a right guaranteed by the laws of the United States, they are liable to prosecution in the Federal court.

Question. When were those prosecutions set on foot in the Federal court?

Answer. Within twelve months.

Question. Before that were there any prosecutions in the State courts?

Answer. None that I know of, except some negroes in Lee County who were prosecuted for Ku-Kluxing another negro; they were found guilty by a mixed jury, and sentenced to twenty or thirty days by the court.

Question. How does it happen there is no difficulty in finding negroes guilty, and punishing them, and yet not a single white man has been convicted under that law?

Answer. That is the only case of a prosecution under that law at all that I have known in that circuit; I do not know the practice in any other circuit, for I have been busy with that and the Federal court, being almost all my time in court, having more than I can attend to physically; I have had other counsel employed in a good many cases.

Question. You have heard of the whipping of Alexander Willis and Simon Dunham, have you not?

Answer. No, sir, not until I heard of it here; they are cases said to have occurred in my county, but I never heard of them. Simon Dunham, and somebody by the name of Stewart, also; I do not know any such men. I heard that they were whipped, and that the men were fired on, and that those men died mysteriously afterward; but I never heard of it until very recently.

Question. You spoke of the testimony taken upon the *habeas corpus* trial, before Judge Hill, in the case of persons implicated in the Aleck Page murder.

Answer. Yes, sir.

Question. Is that a full report, or simply a synopsis of the proof; I speak of the pamphlet.

Answer. That is a very full report of all the testimony adduced; the district attorney announced at the time that he had other testimony that he would not introduce before that court.

Question. You say all the proof, except what was excluded by the district attorney, is embraced in this pamphlet, without any abridgement?

Answer. Well, it is a very substantial report of it; there are some little things I recollect not put down.

Question. Is it an abridgement of the proof?

Answer. Not much. The testimony of no one witness seemed to me to be intentionally abridged.

Question. Is the testimony put down *in hæc verba* as the witness delivered it?

Answer. As near it, I think, as any man would write it down. I do not think it is exactly in the language of the witness sometimes, but there is little difference.

Question. A short-hand reporter or writer would take it down in the words of the witness, would he not?

Answer. I do not know anything about it; I know very little about the short-hand report. A gentleman, said to be a short-hand writer, named Philp, wrote it down, and occasionally during its progress he was stopped, and he would read a page from his notes; he would read it himself, and nobody else could that was present, and it seemed to be very well reported. I could discover a word now and then [omitted.]

By Mr. BLAIR:

Question. You have read it since?

Answer. Yes, sir.

Question. Is it correct?

Answer. Very correct; some names are changed sometimes, and dates sometimes changed; I think it is a very correct report.

By the CHAIRMAN:

Question. It cannot be a complete report because the questions are not put down.

Answer. No, sir; but the substance is.

Question. Do not the questions and answers run in together, so that it is impossible to get the full meaning of the witness without having both the question and answer?

Answer. Having heard it, I think the testimony is easier to be understood from reading that without the question. Mr. Walter conducted the examination on the part of the prosecution; he was the oldest lawyer for the prosecution, and very able; and I think it is very fully given.

Question. This does not purport to give the questions?

Answer. No, sir; some of the questions are there. You will notice some of the questions I asked the witness are taken down on the examination-in-chief on the part of the defense; in the cross-examination it just says, cross-examination, and only gives a question here and there; Mr. Philp does not seem to have written down the questions at all.

Question. What did I understand you to state to the committee, as your opinion of the motive of Joe Davis in admitting, against the truth, his presence at all these Ku-Klux outrages?

Answer. My opinion was that negroes killed Aleck Page, and that Joe Davis was the leader in that. I do not know whether I stated that; that that was my opinion, that he and other negroes killed him.

Question. I understood you to state in your examination-in-chief that the evidence was strong that Joe Davis was not at the killing of Page at all?

Answer. No, sir.

Question. Did you not state that?

Answer. Yes, sir; Joe Davis was not at the killing; there is certainly testimony to show that he was not there.

Question. Did you not in your general statement say that the evidence was strong that Davis was not at the killing of Page?

Answer. I reckon what I stated was this, that it could be made strong that he was not there; the evidence as before that court was not strong that he was not there.

Question. Now, I understand you to say that you think he was the leader of the party?

Answer. That is my own opinion, that he was the leader of the party that killed him; but there can be testimony adduced proving that he was not there.

Question. So both sides can be proved?

Answer. There can be testimony on both sides, unless witnesses have made false statements to me since the trial.

Question. Then they certainly would swear false if they swore he was not there?

Answer. The witnesses might be mistaken; they might have thought he was there, but he was disguised, so that they could not have known him with certainty; he says, himself, he was disguised in red and black disguise, and states who gave it to him. Colored witnesses have stated to me facts since the trial, from which a strong showing could be made that he was not there.

Question. Have you any doubt that he was present at the killing of Jack Dupree?

Answer. I have no knowledge of the Jack Dupree case in the world, except just a rumor that he was taken off; that has never been investigated in my presence; I have no knowledge of it, no chance of investigating it.

Question. Have you any doubt that Hornberger was killed by disguised men?

Answer. The statement was made to me that he—that is, Durham—was killed, I believe, when he was disguised himself.

Question. In a raid?

Answer. At somebody's house.

Question. Whose house?

Answer. I cannot tell. I do not know.

Question. Give the committee all the information you have upon that case.

Answer. That was about sixteen miles from Aberdeen, north, at a time when the waters were high and roads bad, and my information is limited about it. The report made to me was that Hornberger—I think that was the one I know under a different name, Simon Durham—he was reported to me as having been killed in disguise, as a Ku-Klux himself, at the house of somebody that fired on the party with shot-guns.

Question. Who was your informant?

Answer. I cannot tell you. That was just a report in town, talked about a good deal, that they went to somebody's house, and whoever was in the house fired—man or men—fired with shot-guns; the party ran off, and next morning he was found, with a number of shot in him, dead, with the disguise still on him.

Question. What was your information as to the number concerned in that raid?

Answer. Ten to twenty.

Question. All blacks, or part blacks and part whites?

Answer. Not known at all, because they were said to be disguised.

Question. What was the purpose of the raid, according to your information?

Answer. They were hunting somebody, but who I do not know, because I have no recollection now at whose house it was said to have occurred.

Question. Was an inquest held?

Answer. I do not think there was an inquest held over anybody that was killed, except Aleck Page, in the county.

Question. What is the reason of that?

Answer. I do not know. Our coroner is a colored man, who, I recollect, did not understand his business very well. He reported it that the first inquest he ever held was over Aleck Page; he swore so at court, that he got the sheriff, Mr. Love, to go with him to see that the business was done correctly—Fielding Bumpus, a right intelligent colored man.

Question. You do not remember the place this raiding party visited; the name of the man?

Answer. No, sir; it was in the neighborhood of a little place called Camargo, in the northwest corner of Monroe County.

Question. Is that the same part of the county that Abe Wamble was killed?

Answer. Yes, sir.

Question. About the same time?

Answer. Some month or two months afterward. Durham was reported to have been killed in January and Wamble was killed in May, I think very early in May; it might have been in April, but I think it was May.

Question. How large was the band said to have been that killed Wamble?

Answer. All the knowledge I have of that was from his wife; she said she was his wife; she said he was killed by three men, and that they were negroes.

Question. Is it not quite possible that her nerves had been disturbed by the killing of her husband, and she gave you a false account?

Answer. I do not think she knew enough about it to justify me in instituting a prosecution, and I did not do it as she wanted it done, and I offered to prosecute, and told her, before she made an affidavit, she must learn more about it, and come back and see me, and I would prosecute it for her without pay, and so did Judge Houston.

Question. Is it not possible that she gave a false account to save herself from a visit from the real perpetrators of the outrage upon her husband?

Answer. Such a thing is certainly possible. She had no reason to do it with me, because she seemed to think I would do her justice; I did not know her.

Question. Has any effort ever been made to discover who the murderers of Wamble were?

Answer. I have been told there was; I have made no effort myself.

Question. What effort did you understand had been made?

Answer. Some gentlemen in the neighborhood told me they would hunt up all the testimony, and that, if they got any testimony to justify the prosecution of anybody, they would report to me.

Question. Did anybody feel disposed to prosecute the men engaged in his murder?

Answer. I know a man named Sam Word, and a gentlemen by the name of Baker, who talked to me about it; seemed anxious to have a prosecution, and told me they would learn all the facts if they could.

Question. Do you think they were entirely sincere and earnest?

Answer. I do.

Question. Why should they have been, since his crime was so odious that even his own race wanted to kill him?

Answer. I think they wanted whoever did it to be justified or prosecuted for the outrages, to quiet things in the country.

Question. Do you think there was any sentiment in Monroe County that would have punished the men who killed Wamble?

Answer. I do.

Question. Do you think any jury impaneled in that county would have sent to the penitentiary a white man for killing him?

Answer. I do; his crime was considered a very atrocious one; I speak of the white men, not the black ones; for I have had no talk with them.

Question. Was Wamble's crime regarded as very odious?

Answer. It was if he was guilty.

Question. There was no doubt of his guilt?

Answer. I have never heard it discussed except by his wife; she said he was killed because of his intimacy with these men's wives; and that he was a preacher. Mr. Word said he was a preacher, and he had heard it said he was intimate with those women, but he did not know the fact.

Question. Wamble was not the man who killed Garrett?

Answer. No, sir; that was Hendricks.

Question. Was anybody ever prosecuted for the killing of Hendricks?

Answer. Yes, sir; three men were arrested; two Mr. Legronnes and Clifton Marshall were arrested for killing Hendricks, on an affidavit by two colored men, in which they charged that they had murdered him; and Captain Lee, mayor of Aberdeen, issued a warrant, and they were arrested by a guard of Federal soldiers, and brought to town; immediately Mr. Huggins started with one of the negroes who made the affidavit before Lee to Corinth, before Commissioner Mask, and made an affidavit that brought the case completely within the Ku-Klux act. Mask issued a warrant which Mr. Huggins brought down as a deputy marshal, and took the defendants—the two Legronnes and Marshall.

Question. I remember your statement in relation to that; but was anybody outside of his guard ever arrested on the charge of killing Hendricks?

Answer. No, sir; not that I ever heard of.

Question. Has any attempt been made to discover the murderers?

Answer. Not that I have heard of; I have been out of the county since that time; I went with those gentlemen to Corinth; there they were bailed.

Question. Did the community condemn the killing of Hendricks?

Answer. Everybody I heard speak of it regretted it, and condemned it; I heard nobody speak of it but white men.

Question. Do you think any white man could be punished by a jury in your county for the killing of Hendricks, or rescue from his guard and subsequent murder?

Answer. I do.

Question. Do you think any man could be sent to the penitentiary for that act?

Answer. I do, if it could be proved on him. I think he could be sent to the penitentiary or hung for it.

Question. Yet the guilt of Hendricks seems to have been generally conceded?

Answer. Yes, sir; in killing old man Garrett.

Question. And there was general condemnation of the act?

Answer. Yes, sir; very general.

Question. Yet your opinion is, that public sentiment there is so sound in favor of the execution of the laws, that if it could be ascertained who were concerned in his rescue and murder they could be punished—hung or sent to the penitentiary?

Answer. Yes, sir; that is my opinion of the white people.

Question. Did it ever occur to you that the guard were imprudent, in view of all the circumstances, in taking Hendricks by night to such a great distance; in the disturbed condition of the country; with the known existence of these bodies of disguised men prowling through the country—that they were imprudent under such circumstances in exposing their prisoner?

Answer. I thought of that, sir, a good deal, and talked with them about it, and was of opinion that they ran as little risk, or less risk, in taking him away and starting to jail with him as they did in staying where they were with him. My opinion was that there was some risk either way, and as much one way as the other; or that there was less risk in taking him to jail than in remaining where they were.

Question. You think, then, he would have been rescued and killed anyhow?

Answer. I think as likely, or more likely, than if they took him on the road; I think there was more prospect of eluding or avoiding men on the road than at Legronne's house.

Question. Do you not think there were enough law-abiding men in that community to protect Hendricks from those lawless men?

Answer. I think there were if they were notified, and believed there was danger of his being rescued; I do not think the law-abiding men expected any such thing.

Question. But it seems that the constable, or the gentleman who was deputized as constable, had apprehensions of that sort?

Answer. I will tell you what was stated to me on that subject. He says a Mr. Clark, who is a respectable gentleman, came to him and told him after the negro was condemned, "Get out of this; you will get into a scrape;" and he immediately applied to the justice of the peace to release him; he told him he was responsible, and if he could not take him to jail nobody could, and he would not release him.

Question. The men attending that trial, fifty or sixty, belonged to the neighborhood, and were respectable gentlemen?

Answer. They belonged to the neighborhood, and I regarded them as highly respectable gentlemen.

Question. Would there have been any practical difficulty in the constable summoning them as a *posse* to guard the prisoner to the jail?

Answer. I think any of them would have obeyed his summons.

Question. Where, then, was the necessity of the constable exposing himself, under the circumstances, to have his prisoner rescued?

Answer. I do not think he thought—the man thought—there was any danger.

Question. Why, then, should he have been so reluctant to accept the office if he wished the magistrate to release him?

Answer. He is a very peaceable man, that has been about courts or towns very little. I think his object was merely to get out of the trouble, and stay at home and attend to his own business. A remarkably quiet, moral man was Mr. Lergonne. From his youth up he has never been known to have a lawsuit or to be about a court, if he could possibly avoid it; and I think it is his first attendance upon a court in his life. I think his inexperience exposed him to the censure that is upon him.

Question. Did I understand you to say you never had heard of Tobe Hutchinson being taken from his house last Friday week, or Friday after, by a body of masked men?

Answer. I never heard of it; I was in Lee County all last week until Friday night; that is, from Wednesday to Friday night, and did not hear of it.

Question. It is quite possible you might not have heard it, although you were there?

Answer. Certainly it is. I went there to defend a capital case in which a *venire* of seventy-five men were summoned, but still I might not have heard of it.

Question. You spoke of a colored church burned at Tupelo?

Answer. Yes, sir.

Question. Did not that burning occur on the same day Hendricks was killed by this mob?

Answer. I do not know. I think it occurred before that. I am pretty confident it did.

Question. Did you hear that this church was burned by a body of disguised men?

Answer. No, sir. I heard it was burned by a man named Freeman, who is under arrest for it now, or said to be under arrest for it. He has been arrested by the marshal.

Question. Did you understand that this church had been built under the influence of Miss Davis, postmistress; that she had made great exertions to secure the building of the church?

Answer. I understood the church had been built; the ground had been given to the congregation by this man Freeman, who is charged with burning it; and that it was built by contributions made by the town, black and white.

Question. Did you understand that she had been influential in getting up these contributions?

Answer. I did. I understood she used her ability to get them up—one that did it; and I also understood that her brother-in-law—I think her brother-in-law—was the presiding elder of that branch of the Methodist Church. It belongs, I understood, to the Methodist Church North.

Question. Is he the brother or brother-in-law?

Answer. I do not know, but I understand he is a brother-in-law.

Question. She is a northern woman, is she?

Answer. So said.

Question. Is there any prejudice felt against her on that account?

Answer. There is some prejudice—I have——

Question. Please to confine your answer to my question.

Answer. I have heard a great deal of prejudice expressed against her, not on account of her being a northern women, but her habits.

Question. Is there any prejudice entertained against her because of her being a northern woman?

Answer. Not that I know or have heard.

Question. Is there any prejudice against northern people coming down to your country to live?

Answer. Certainly not, unless they belong to that class which we consider professional politicians; whenever a man shows himself he belongs to that class, we are all opposed to him—every one.

Question. Is there any prejudice entertained in your community against men on account of their political sentiments, where they come from the North?

Answer. No, sir.

Question. None, whatever?

Answer. No, sir; only as I tell you, whenever they show that their object is to stir up strife between the races, and to obtain office, there is prejudice against them by the white race immediately.

Question. Are they treated with the same cordiality, where they attend to their own business, that resident white citizens are; I mean men coming from the North with outspoken sentiments, who belong to the radical party; make no disguise of their opinions, but go about there upon legitimate business, farming, or enter into business in that town; are they treated upon equality with your resident white population?

Answer. If you mean by that that social equality, which is included in inviting them and their families to our houses, I think there is a difference; but as to being politely treated, and in business matters, and on the street, there is no difference. I do not think we as cordially invite a northern man to our houses as we would a southern man.

Question. How long has Miss Davis been postmistress of Tupelo?

Answer. Some twelve months; I think a little more than that.

Question. Have you ever heard she has been in receipt of letters of an insulting character?

Answer. I have not.

Question. Have you heard that she has been molested in her office?

Answer. No, sir.

Question. She has taught a colored school there?

Answer. I have heard she has.

Question. Has she discharged her duty satisfactorily as postmistress?

Answer. I have heard no complaint. I have not been there a great deal, but I have heard no complaint of her as postmistress.

Question. You say you have heard things against her reputation?

Answer. Yes, sir; as a virtuous woman.

Question. Do you know a single northern person, male or female, who has come down into this country and taken an interest in your political affairs, who has not suffered in charcter; who has not been maligned?

Answer. Well, sir, I do not know that I have heard them denounced for anything but their politics.

Question. Has not some fault been found with their personal character, invariably?

Answer. I think not.

Question. Give me an exception, if you please.

Answer. Well, sir, begin at home; I never heard anything against Mr. Huggins's personal character until he became odious by his mingling with politics, and trying to get up, what we thought, an exorbitant school fund.

Question. Have you not heard something against his personal character?

Answer. No, sir; I never heard him accused of dishonesty; I never heard of him as a revenue assessor, but what he discharged his duty faithfully; I never heard a charge of official dishonesty; and so of Colonel Wells. I have never heard of any man speaking maligningly or disrespectfully of him as a gentleman. I heard him make a speech at Corinth, in company with General Ames, which I think was calculated to stir up strife. I heard him state there that the black man was interested in opposing all the land-owners of the country. I told him of that afterward—that I thought he went too far; that it was calculated to get up and keep up ill-feeling, and ought not to be done.

Question. How is it with Colonel Barry, your Representative in Congress?

Answer. Morphis is the Representative from my district; Barry is from this district. I never heard him spoken of except as a polititian of a very violent character. I do not know Barry personally at all.

Question. What other people than those you have enumerated from the North, and who take an interest in political matters, are there in Monroe County?

Answer. From the North?

Question. Yes, sir.

Answer. I think Mr. Huggins is the only northern man in Monroe County that has taken an interest in politics—that is, that has shown a disposition to be an office-holder. There are not a great many northern men in Monroe County.

Question. He is the only one you can think of?

Answer. There are some others there, but they have not been politicians.

Question. Any northern ladies besides Miss Davis?

Answer. There is; Judge Colby lives not far from Aberdeen, with a family of daughters grown and a wife; but further than to express his own political sentiments, he has never mingled with politics in any way. We have some northern men that are traders in the country, but, except that, we know they are of politics of a particular character; they have done nothing more than vote their own ticket, or express their opinions, and they seem to be very liberally patronized in the way of trade.

Question. Is it not true that almost every holder of office, State or Federal, at this time, had had his personal character traduced; has been charged with corruption and crimes of various sorts?

Answer. Well, sir, I have never heard any charge of that sort against the officers of my own county.

Question. Are they northern men?

Answer. No, sir; they are what we call scalawags; they are southern men.

Question. Are your people more tolerant toward them than toward carpet-baggers?

Answer. I think not; I think they are pretty bitter toward them, making less allowance for them than carpet-baggers, whenever they are "to the manner born," and under some obligations to home. Our sheriff and tax assessor, I think, are republicans, but are native southern men. I have never heard any charge of dishonesty against them at all.

Question. Their personal character is not attacked?

Answer. Not attacked. Mr. Anderson, the sheriff, is a native of the county, and everybody agrees he is an honest, good officer. I opposed him with all the energy in me, and never assailed his personal character, and never heard anybody else do so, and so with the circuit clerk. Our chancery clerk is a northern man, who is universally charged with being very incompetent; the fact is certainly so; no other charge against him. It is certainly true that at this time the appointees to office through the State are inefficient men, and they had to be that to get them from that particular political party; they are incompetent, the body of them. Material was not here then to make the officers and confine appointments, as Governor Alcorn did, to his own party.

Question. You think the men competent to fill the offices are all disqualified by the fourteenth amendment?

Answer. I mean the men that belong to the republican party of this State, the white men. O, no, there are good men belonging to both parties, but they are moderate men. There are enough to fill the offices. We have a very good circuit judge; a good circuit judge in this district, and in the district above us, Judge Davis; Judge Bradford is very good; the district attorney heretofore, Mr. Pate, in Judge Bradford's district, has been very incompetent.

Question. You have spoken of an attempt to burn the assessor's office in Okolona, and said your information was that the negroes attempted to burn up the prisoners?

Answer. I do not know that they confined it to negroes, but the prisoners stated, and the officer in charge stated, in the cars next day, that their opinion was it was an effort on the part of somebody to burn up the prisoners with the office.

Question. That could not have been accomplished at all, could it; that is, the prisoners could have easily got out of the house even in case it was fired, could they not?

Answer. I should think that is so; I never saw the office.

Question. Does not that theory seem to you very improbable?

Answer. It does. I never saw the office myself; I understand it is a frame building.

Question. One story?

Answer. So I understand. My understanding was it was a frame building and easily burned; but still my idea was, a man could very easily have got out of it if there were doors and windows.

Question. So that if the purpose was to burn up the prisoners, it would have been a very absurd attempt?

Answer. Yes, sir; I think so. No importance was attached to it in the statements made on the train. Okolona has been regarded as a very lawless place, sir.

Question. You spoke of the squad of men that went to Mr. Bell's house to arrest him, and of their having insulted his wife. Is it your information that Bell had been arrested formerly, and had given a recognizance to appear at court, and had forfeited it?

Answer. That he had never been arrested at all; that is my information.

Question. Had he never given bail?

Answer. My information is that he had not. Some gentlemen were arrested from that county and brought to the last June term of the Federal court, that gave bail, and I understood at the same time that there was process for Mr. Bell, but he never was arrested.

Question. What was Bell charged with?

Answer. For a violation of the enforcement act.

Question. In what?

Answer. In an effort to make somebody that was keeping a store at Starkville, leave there, the county-seat; some Irishman that lived there keeping a store; I understand he was charged, amongst other things, with an effort to make him leave.

Question. Did he abscond and get out of the way of an arrest?

Answer. Not that I have heard charged; I do not know; I have not been in the county.

Question. How did it happen that he was away when the deputy marshal went there?

Answer. I do not know; he was sheriff of the county at that time.

Question. Have you never heard that he attempted to avoid process?

Answer. Only that he was not found when these other men were; that he was not at home when Mr. Huggins went there.

Question. Have you never heard him spoken of as a desperate man?

Answer. No, sir; I have a different opinion of him.

Question. Or a man of violence?

Answer. No, sir; but as a man of firmness, and not likely to get into broils.

Question. If Mr. Huggins had a warrant for his arrest from the Federal court or a commissioner of the United States, was it not proper for him to find him?

Answer. Yes, sir; certainly it was.

Question. If he suspected he was secreted, was it not proper for him to search the different rooms?

Answer. I do not think it was proper to go into a lady's bed-room.

Question. Would he have been justified as an officer if he had left that house without finding Bell, and Bell were in that house?

Answer. Certainly not, if Bell was in the house; but my idea of these things is that a lady would not have made a false representation to him; that he should have taken her word for it; or, if he had any doubt about it, he should have still remained there until he ascertained the fact, without going into it without notice, so she could get out and dress.

Question. Is it your information that he was in the house at all?

Answer. It is my information that he was in the house in command of the soldiers; that he ordered the soldiers into the room.

Question. He states that he was not in the house.

Answer. I do not pretend to know the facts myself.

Question. If he had found him in his wife's bed-room it would have been all right to have entered the room?

Answer. Yes, sir.

Question. But if he was not there it was all wrong?

Answer. No, sir; the wrong consisted in entering the room without giving the lady notice to prepare for his reception; going in there to find a lady undressed—I think that was a violation of gentlemanly conduct, due from all men to ladies.

Question. You say there is a very strong prejudice against Mr. Huggins in that community?

Answer. Yes, sir.

Question. Is it not because he is a Federal officer and has sought to do his duty?

Answer. It is not because he was a Federal officer, for there was no prejudice expressed against him as a Federal officer that I heard of.

Question. Is there not a general prejudice in that community against Federal officers?

Answer. There is not against Federal officers.

Question. Is there no prejudice against the assessors and collectors of internal revenue?

Answer. The only prejudice I ever heard expressed against any Federal officer was expressed against these men that, some year or more than a year ago, seized property. There was a man there, who is now in prison, as a Federal officer, whose name, maybe it was Ellis, maybe it was Feriss, who went around and seized a great deal of property for violating the internal-revenue act in the running of distilleries; I heard a good deal of prejudice expressed against him. I am not certain of his name. Colonel Wells can tell you very well what it is, sir. He came in and plead guilty to the charge of collecting revenue when he was not a revenue officer, and he was ordered to be imprisoned at the last term of the Federal court.

Question. Is there any prejudice against the marshal or deputy of the United States for serving process?

Answer. No, sir; there is not. These men, last June—one-third of them—came into town, when they were notified there were warrants against them, and surrendered themselves without the officer going to find them. He seemed to go over the river with reluctance, where they lived, and took some soldiers with him. Colonel Reynolds and others said if he would give them the names of the men he wanted to arrest, they would get them to come over without taking soldiers over to alarm the women and children; and he gave them the names, and the men came in and immediately surrendered themselves.

[At 1.55 the committee took a recess of one hour, for dinner.]

By the CHAIRMAN:

Question. You have spoken of Mr. Huggins, and expressed the opinion that his unpopularity among the people originated in his bringing about dissensions between the two races. What official positions has Mr. Huggins held?

Answer. The offices of deputy assessor and school commissioner; the chairman of the board of school commissioners.

Question. Has Huggins been acting as deputy marshal?

Answer. Very recently he has, sir.

Question. What has he done outside of those official positions to incur prejudice?
Answer. He is understood to have organized political clubs in the country very extensively.
Question. Do you know that fact to be true?
Answer. No, sir.
Question. What clubs do you refer to?
Answer. To what are called Loyal Leagues.
Question. What objection is there to the formation of the Loyal Leagues?
Answer. It is understood that they inculcate differences between the races.
Question. Have you seen their constitution?
Answer. Not to know it.
Question. Have you ever been present at their meetings?
Answer. No, sir.
Question. How do you know the purpose of the organization?
Answer. I do not profess to know. I know nothing of it beyond its actions.
Question. What else?
Answer. His extravagance in the school system; building school-houses and furnishing them.
Question. Has he ever made political speeches?
Answer. I have not known of his making a speech of any kind. I have heard of his making speeches to clubs, but I do not know it.
Question. How do you know, then, he ever sought to array the black race against the white?
Answer. I do not know it; I do not pretend that I know it. I have seen him at meetings, but never heard him make a political speech.
Question. What meetings have you seen him at?
Answer. At political meetings.
Question. Republican meetings?
Answer. Yes, sir.
Question. That was in order?
Answer. Yes, sir. I never saw him act disorderly.
Question. It is made the duty by the school-law for the board of school directors to make estimates?
Answer. Yes, sir.
Question. Of the expense necessary to operate the schools, is it not?
Answer. Yes, sir.
Question. You spoke of estimates made by Mr. Huggins, as president of the board. He did nothing in doing that but what the law required him to do?
Answer. I thought he did; I thought he did more than the law required?
Question. In what respect?
Answer. Making his estimates to run the schools for the entire year, when I did not think the condition of the country was such as to justify them in that expense.
Question. How do you know he made estimates to run them the entire year?
Answer. I saw him and talked with him, in the presence of other gentlemen, in regard to that. He and Parson Eberts had a long conversation with myself and Mr. Word and Mr. Clopton and Mr. Howard and Judge Houston.
Question. Had there been any common schools since the war, in your county, before he became a member of this board?
Answer. There had been no free schools.
Question. This was originating a system, then?
Answer. Yes, sir.
Question. Inaugurating it for the first time?
Answer. Yes, sir.
Question. How many common schools had you in the county at the time this estimate was prepared?
Answer. I do not know, sir, how many were in the county. I do not know how many school-houses were in the county at the close of the war, or at the time this estimate was prepared, nor do I know how many the estimates were made for. There are about twenty building under contracts Mr. Huggins made.
Question. Outside of Aberdeen, were there any school-houses in the county before?
Answer. Yes, sir.
Question. Built out of the old congressional township fund?
Answer. Built generally by the contributions of neighborhoods.
Question. You have no opinion of the number of school-houses?
Answer. No, sir.
Question. Were they generally log school-houses?
Answer. Yes, sir; generally.
Question. Were they pretty well decayed and run down?
Answer. Some were, and some were not.
Question. Had any been built since the war?

Answer. Some few had been; not many.

Question. You say his estimates embraced the building of twenty?

Answer. I do not know how many his estimates embraced the building of, but about twenty were built or under contract.

Question. In your judgment, was that a larger number than was required?

Answer. It was a larger number than was required, I thought, for the districts they were placed in; and he refused to allow the neighborhoods to build houses, and refused to receive good houses that were tendered him without expense.

Question. Perhaps the locality of the houses did not suit the district?

Answer. One instance I will give you: north of Aberdeen, about six miles, a neighborhood offered him a frame house that had been built for a church, and the use of it indefinitely for school purposes, the congregation reserving the right to hold monthly meetings in it on Saturdays and Sundays. He refused it, and had one built within about two hundred and fifty yards.

Question. What objection did he make to receiving it?

Answer. That he thought he would not have entire control of it as he wished.

Question. How many sub-districts is your county divided into?

Answer. I do not know now. I did know.

Question. What is the size of the county?

Answer. It is rather a large county.

Question. As large as Lowndes?

Answer. Yes, sir.

Question. This county contains six hundred square miles; is Monroe as large?

Answer. I think so.

Question. All good land?

Answer. Yes, sir; of average land of the State; perhaps above the average.

Question. Is it devoted principally to raising cotton?

Answer. It has been, principally, to raising cotton.

Question. What is the number of your population, according to the last census?

Answer. We vote about 5,000 voters.

Question. That would give you a population of about 30,000.

Answer. Twenty-five is what we count it at.

Question. Is it more or less populous than Lowndes?

Answer. Less populous; Lowndes votes a thousand more than we do.

Question. How are the two races divided?

Answer. The registry shows about 1,100 more colored; the majority is colored.

Question. What is the enumeration of your children between six and twenty-one?

Answer. I do not know it now. I did know it.

Question. Would it, in your opinion, amount to 7,000?

Answer. I do not think it does.

Question. The enumeration of this county is a little upward of 8,000.

Answer. I do not think ours would be over 5,000, but it is only guessing.

Question. Supposing, then, there were 5,000 children entitled, under your school law, to the privileges of a common-school education, how many school-houses would be required to educate them?

Answer I do not think the house ought to have more than fifty for common schools through the country—ordinary neighborhood school-houses; I do not think they ought to be built large enough to contain more than fifty; but I am very poorly qualified to judge of the number that ought to be in a school, sir.

Question. That would indicate that you would have difficulty in the school-houses to accommodate the children?

Answer. I think that fifty would be enough for the common neighborhood school-house. I know quite a number of gentlemen in the neighborhood offered to build school-houses, such as they were willing for their children to go to school in, to avoid the tax; and Mr. Huggins declined to receive them.

Question. If you are right in your opinion that fifty is as large a number as a school-house should contain, and you have 5,000 children entitled to a common-school education, it would indicate that you should have a hundred school-houses?

Answer. Yes, sir.

Question. In point of fact, have you twenty, outside of those that have been built under the direction of your school board, lately?

Answer. I think there are more than that, but I cannot state positively. I think so from my knowledge of the neighborhood, but do not know the fact.

Question. Will you please state the valuation, for taxable purposes, of all the property, real and personal, in Monroe County?

Answer. Well, sir, I cannot state it, because I have not looked at the assessments; I do not know the amount.

Question. Do you think it would amount to as much as five or six millions?

Answer. I should say four or five millions, but it would be merely a guess.

Question. What is the average value of cotton lands in your county, per acre?

Answer. At this time, I do not think I can state, from the fact that there is no demand; there is a great deal of land on the market, offered for sale.

Question. What is it held at?

Answer. I know of very few sales. On the east side of the river, in what we call the sandy land—poor land—there have been two or three recent sales at ten dollars per acre, which I think a fair price. On the west side of the river, where the land at the commencement of the war was valued at forty-eight dollars an acre, I cannot say there is any price at all. It seems to be all in the market, and nobody wants to buy.

Question. What do the holders hold it at?

Answer. I do not know that they have any asking price.

Question. Would $25 an acre be a fair value?

Answer. I think it would be rather a high value; I do not think it is estimated that high.

Question. Did you suffer any of the ravages of war in your county?

Answer. Yes, sir; on the west side of the river all the gin-houses that had mills attached to them were burned; a great many out-houses, and some dwelling-houses; a great deal of fencing burnt, and the stock was all carried off. We lost our entire farming stock, almost, from the west half of the county.

Question. Were your fences destroyed?

Answer. Almost all; there is no fencing now; no fencing has been done since the war, scarcely; we cannot get the laborers to make fences; that is more trouble than anything else.

Question. What number of slaves had you before the war?

Answer. I do not know.

Question. You spoke of the great reduction of values in your county, and expressed the opinion that the value now was not more than two-tenths, or one-fifth, of what it was before the war?

Answer. Yes, sir.

Question. What proportion did the valuation of your slaves bear to the valuation of your real estate and other property?

Answer. The real estate on the west side of the river was estimated at forty to seventy-five dollars an acre, for land; on the east side of the river, in ran from five to thirty dollars an acre, in the sandy land. The river divides the county pretty nearly equally; the east side is sandy land, the west side is black land. The slaves were estimated at various prices, sometimes five hundred dollars, and sometimes higher than that; take the average of a plantation and mules, the full value averaged $150.

Question. What was the total valuation of your property, real and personal, in Monroe County, before the war?

Answer. I do not know, without looking at the statistics. I have not looked at them to tell.

Question. Did it amount, in your opinion, to more than ten millions?

Answer. Yes, sir; I think it would have amounted to fifteen or twenty millions; but I am guessing, because I cannot give you the number of slaves that were in the county, or anything else.

Question. You think that the present valuation is about five millions?

Answer. Not more than that.

Question. That would indicate that only one-third of the property, real and personal, had been detroyed, instead of four-fifths, would it not?

Answer. Yes, sir; I value land myself now higher than most of my neighbors do.

Question. You think, then, you are quite accurate in saying that four-fifths of your property has been lost in consequence of the war?

Answer. That is my opinion of the State.

Question. How do you reconcile that with your other statement, that the present value is five millions?

Answer. I am giving the value of my county in that, and in the eight-tenths I was giving the State.

Question. I ask as to Monroe County.

Answer. I think that the value of property in Monroe County now is about one-third of the value before the war. I think we have lost about two-thirds by the war.

Question. How much of that two-thirds was embraced in your slave property?

Answer. I cannot give it.

Question. Do you think your slave property was equal to all your other property combined, before the war?

Answer. I think it was valued at more than all the other combined; a great deal.

Question. Did it, in your opinion, embrace two-thirds of the valuation?

Answer. If I judge for myself, I should say it was more than two-thirds; my own plantation had on it $100,000 worth of personal property, whilst the plantation itself was not worth more than $15,000, in my opinion.

Question. Then, if the entire valuation of your property was $15,000,000, before the war and your slaves amounted to two-thirds of that entire valuation, it would seem as if you have lost nothing except slaves, because your present valuation is five millions, I understand you?

Answer. Yes, sir; that is my valuation; other men value their lands less than I do; my neighbors do; I am a higher man; I estimate our lands higher than most men do. I know that from conversations with my neighbors.

Question. Leaving your county-seat, Aberdeen, out of the question, what is the rate of taxation in your county for all purposes, State, county, school, and other purposes?

Answer. About 4½ per cent.

Question. Please give us the figures by which you arrive at that conclusion.

Answer. I cannot give them to you unless I had an estimate from home. We have State tax and county tax and pauper tax, bridge tax, school tax, and railroad tax; but I cannot give you any figures there. I am the poorest man to give figures you ever saw, unless I have the papers.

Question. At what rate is your State tax fixed?

Answer. One-half of one per cent.

Question. At what rate is your county tax fixed?

Answer. One-half of one per cent.

Question. Pauper tax?

Answer. I cannot tell you that.

Question. What is the rate of taxation for the railroad bonds?

Answer. I do not know; I cannot give you the figures on any other tax.

Question. You cannot give the figures on the school tax or bridge tax?

Answer. No, sir.

Question. How do you know it is 4½ per cent.?

Answer. I have that from the sheriff, who told me the other day.

By Mr. RICE:

Question. Your school tax cannot exceed one per cent. under the constitution?

Answer. No, sir.

By the CHAIRMAN:

Question. Your sheriff is not under oath here, and consequently I cannot cross-examine him?

Answer. I do not know. I asked him for my tax the other day, and he told me to count it at 4½ per cent.

Question. What is your entire property, upon which you pay tax, valued at, for taxation?

Answer. I cannot tell you now; I am paying taxes on fourteen hundred acres of land.

Question. What did you give it in at?

Answer. At $7 per acre.

Question. What else did you give in?

Answer. A house and lot; there is the same State and county tax on property in town and country.

By Mr. RICE:

Question. But there is a special tax in addition?

Answer. Yes, sir; I pay tax on a house and lot at $6,000.

By the CHAIRMAN:

Question. What other property?

Answer. Twelve mules.

Question. How much are they valued at?

Answer. One hundred and fifty dollars apiece.

Question. That is $1,800. What else?

Answer. I do not remember now the value of the wagons and tools on the farm.

Question. Well, make an estimate.

Answer. Well, sir, I suppose $400; there are two wagons and some farm-tools.

Question. Does that embrace all of your property in Monroe County subject to taxation?

Answer. No, sir; there is some household furniture and silverware in the house subject to taxation.

Question. Did you give that to the assessor?

Answer. Yes, sir.

Question. What is the value of it?

Answer. I do not know that I can give it. I cannot give it to you now. There is a piano.

Question. Give an estimate of the whole.

Answer. Well, I suppose you might put it down at $2,000, including carriages.

Question. That embraces now everything.

Answer. I should think that would cover it; I do not remember all the prices now, and may not be giving it to you accurately.

Question. What is the amount of tax on your property this year?

Answer. I do not know what it is this year. I paid this year $700, but that includes the city tax; and that includes a special railroad tax, to build a branch road from the Mobile road to the city, which is very high.

Question. Does that $700 cover your entire tax for one year?

Answer. No, sir.

Question. What is left out?

Answer. It is now doubled for this year; we have two taxes this year

By M. RICE:

Question. But it is one regular yearly tax?

Answer. Yes, sir.

By the CHAIRMAN:

Question. That includes your municipal tax?

Answer. Yes, sir.

Question. How much?

Answer. I do not remember now; a little over $700 includes it all—municipal, railroad, and every other tax. Some brood-mares were also in that; I think, too, some hogs and cattle, and a watch my wife had.

Question. Now will you please state what per cent. that will be?

Answer. That property is my wife's property; I have got no property.

Question. That makes $20,000 in all, and the tax is $700?

Answer. There is no school-tax in that; when that comes on there will be that much added.

Question. Are you sure that $20,000 embraces the entire valuation of your property?

Answer. Well, I can give you a schedule.

[The witness makes the following memoranda, which he reads and hands to the chairman.]

1,400 acres of land, at $7 each	$9,800
1 house and lot	6,000
40 acres wood-land	400
1 carriage	400
Silverware, taxable	250
1 gold watch	100
Jewelry	100
12 mules, at $150 each	1,800
2 brood-mares	300
Wagons and farming tools	400
Lots in Aberdeen	500
Total	19,850

Question. What is the total valuation?

Answer. Nineteen thousand eight hundred and fifty dollars—[$20,050.]

Question. I understood you to say that the amount of tax actually levied by the board of supervisors was one-half less, or perhaps more than one-half less than the original amount estimated, which you state to be $61,800.

Answer. The supervisors levied no tax for last year; they have levied a tax at this time; what the amount of that is I do not know; I have not stated it.

Question. They levied none last year?

Answer. No, sir; none were collected.

Question. The estimates were reduced?

Answer. Yes, sir.

Question. One-half or more?

Answer. Yes, sir; I think more than one-half.

Question. If reduced one-half, what would be the rate of tax on five millions' worth of property, to produce this sum?

Answer. I do not know, sir; I never counted it up, I am not apt to do that. I do not know what the reduction was, but I have understood it was reduced more than one-half.

Question. In point of fact, it would amount to one-half of one per cent., would it not?

Answer. I think it is down now to about $23,000, but I would not pretend to state that accurately.

Question. Is that complained of as oppressive?

Answer. I have not heard it complained of at all at present; not within the last year, since it was understood that it had been reduced. The school-board had been changed a good deal; there is no colored man on it now; they are all citizens of the country that everybody seems to have confidence in, and I do not think there will be any complaint of their estimates.

Question. I was about inquiring of you what number of bales of cotton were purchased in your county last year?

Answer. I cannot tell you; almost anybody else can. I cannot.

Question. Would you think as high as 30,000 bales?

Answer. I dislike to give an opinion. I have paid no attention to cotton since the war, except a little on my place. I have some old servants who came back there almost in spite of me; they are working part of the farm; I have been in the courts.

Question. Cotton has produced a good price?

Answer. Yes, sir; a good price has stimulated greatly to produce it.

Question. You have received a higher price for it since the war?

Answer. Yes, sir; a good deal higher.

Question. And there was a heavy crop produced last year?

Answer. There was between fifty and sixty bales made at my plantation last year, that used to make a heap; it is made by a few old servants, and I have little interest in it.

Question. Where should be the difficulty with your people in raising their school-tax?

Answer. At the time this was done we were very illy able to pay anything; very much pressed to make a living.

Question. This was last year?

Answer. Yes, sir; the crop of the year before last had been very poor, and everybody was very hard pressed to live. The farmers of my county universally complained that since the war all that had money lost money in trying to run farms cultivated by free labor; the men that have worked themselves, the poor men on the east side of the river, where the old man and his children have gone to work, made some money, but all the plantations I know of, except one, that have been run by freedmen, have lost money. Mr. Troop is the exception; every other gentleman I have conversed with reports that they have lost money.

Question. What has been their loss has been somebody else's gain, I suppose?

Answer. It may be so; I do not know outside of my own neighborhood. I know that from conversation with those gentlemen, not from my own experience.

Question. There are two parties now to share the product of the soil; there was only one party before?

Answer. I know the colored man does not seem to have made more than his living; just made bread and moderate clothing; and I think the great body of them have been fairly dealt with.

Question. Your soil produces as well as ever?

Answer. It is not worked; anybody can tell the difference.

Question. Not as much raised per acre?

Answer. O, no, sir; they do not average a third as much; it is not plowed and planted and hoed; they will not hoe; they always commence planting too late; the negro thinks if he plants a crop it will make itself; he has not got over the idea that old master used to be very rich and enjoyed himself very much; they think they can do the same now they are free; they do not realize the fact that a man must himself work almost every day in the year; they are not vicious as a race.

Question. So they behave themselves generally?

Answer. Yes, sir; they are not vicious as a race; they are quiet and peaceable when let alone; when they get liquor they are almost all liable to drink it; they are a race much more sinned against than sinning.

Question. You have referred once or twice to the return of the prisoners from Oxford, and have said you were not in Aberdeen at the time of their return; have you not been informed that they were received by the citizens with great demonstrations of applause; that they were welcomed with music and with the firing of cannon, and great demonstrations of favor?

Answer. I have been informed that some youngster, with the disapprobation of the older men, fired a cannon, and that everybody was rejoiced that they had not been imprisoned.

Question. Did everybody believe they were innocent?

Answer. That they were wrongfully arrested, and were rejoiced that they had not been imprisoned.

Question. But everybody believed that somebody had been guilty of this murder?

Answer. Yes, sir; let me explain to you the feeling, and what got it up. When these men were arrested Mr. Huggins is reported to have stated again and again to them and others that they were certain to be imprisoned at Oxford, or somewhere else, until the December term of the court, and that they would not be allowed bail. They were all poor men and all planters but two, and the community were sympathizing with them and their families very much, and were certainly very much relieved and rejoiced when they were allowed to return, and willing to go their bail for whatever was required.

Question. If the public believed they were innocent, the public must have had some opinion about who were guilty, must they not?

Answer. I do not know, sir. I was not home when they came home. I know there are various opinions about who was guilty now. I was not at home when they were arrested first. I came home after about half of them had been arrested and the other half had been sent for, to the country, and came in themselves. I was telegraphed not to go home, and remained at Oxford to defend them, when they were brought there. I only came home Saturday and went back Monday.

Question. You have given Mr. Ross's statement of the outrage on Huggins. This statement was not made under oath to you?

Answer. No, sir; to me as his friend and neighbor.

Question. Do you know that the statement given by Mr. Huggins, in his testimony, is not strictly true?

Answer. I do not; I only give you what Mr. Ross said. He is a man I rely upon. I have no disposition to say Mr. Huggins has not stated the truth.

Question. I will get you, in this connection, to give a statement of all the murders and whippings and other outrages said to have been committed in Monroe County by persons in disguise.

Answer. Well, sir, I have got a little piece of paper here with them written down on it, all that I know of, or that I have heard of.

Question. You had made that memorandum in contemplation of being examined here?

Answer. I made it here yesterday.

Question. You had had access to the Mississippi testimony, had you not?

Answer. No, sir.

Question. Had never seen it before?

Answer. The only part of the Mississippi testimony I had ever seen was a publication of Mr. Huggins's testimony in regard to this man Whitfield. I had seen a statement as to Mr. Little's testimony given in Washington City, that Mr. Little came out in a card and denied was correct. He asked the suspension of the public opinion until his testimony would be officially published. I had seen that, and that is all I had seen. The first case I have here is Sanders Flint and his sons. They were taken out of jail.

Question. We have that already.

Answer. The next is Hornberger, or Durham, January or February, 1871; Jack Dupree, February, 1871; Alexander Page, March, 1871; Abram Wamble, May, 1871; and an old man that was said to have been whipped; Santee Butler, said to have been whipped by negroes for testifying in court against a negro named Barrett Hutchinson; and Mr. Huggins's whipping. Wilson was said to have been notified if he did not desist from an evil practice with a woman in his neighborhood he would be visited again. Mr. McClendon was whipped for living in notorious adultery with a colored woman. Dock Hendricks was the last case. He was taken from his guard and killed on the way to jail. There is another case that occurred there that I have not stated. That is on this paper here. That is the prosecution of a colored man named Henry Harrison for an attempted rape on a white woman. He was prosecuted in the circuit court by Judge Houston, and defended by a young gentleman and myself, and convicted and sent to the penitentiary. I knew him as a boy, and regarded him as a very good slave. He drank a good deal after he was free. I have no doubt he was guilty. I was appointed for him by the court, and made the best defense for him I could.

Question. What is the next case?

Answer. The only other case I have in that county is the breaking up by the notice and the stopping of the schools. These are all the whippings and killings that I know of.

Question. How long a period of time does that cover?

Answer. Sanders Flint's case occurred some time last year. These all occurred last year and this.

Question. This embraces all the cases that have come to your knowledge?

Answer. All that have come to my knowledge. You asked me about three cases about which I never knew anything.

Question. Did you ever hear of the whipping of Simon Dunham?

Answer. No, sir.

Question. Did you ever hear of the whipping of Alexander Willis?

Answer. No, sir. There is somebody I have heard talked here about named Stewart. I never heard of that. I heard of the whipping of this man Eccles, in Chickasaw, but you are speaking of Monroe County now.

Question. Have you ever heard of the whipping of Albert Murphy?

Answer. No, sir.

Question. Dick Holliday?

Answer. No, sir.

Question. Have you heard of the whipping of Ed. Murphy?

Answer. No, sir.

Question. Jim Hicks?

Answer. No, sir.

Question. Jim Verner?

Answer. No, sir; I will tell you of another I did hear, I have not stated, that occurred some time last year; William McMillan, said to have been whipped west of Aberdeen, in the black land, a colored man; an indictment was presented to the grand jury against a party, and Mr. Little was on the grand jury, and they failed to find an indictment; we concluded there was nothing of it; all his brothers-in-law were charged with the whipping—two men named Coleman; the indictment was prepared before the grand jury against men for whipping William McMillan, a colored man. On that grand jury Mr. Little, our senator, was, and no indictment was found, and then we came to the conclusion there was nothing of it.

Question. Have you heard frequent instances of these disguised men riding through Monroe County?

Answer. I do not know; I cannot say I have heard frequent instances, but I have heard of it several times, three or four; several nights I heard of it.

Question. Did you hear generally that mischief was committed?

Answer. No, I did not generally hear that mischief was committed; the first I ever heard of it, a negro man came to my office and told me they had been at his house; he thought they came up through the ground; he showed a good deal of superstition about it, and said they boiled negroes' heads and made soup.

Question. What did they do to him?

Answer. Nothing, except they asked him for something to eat, and he had nothing to give them, and they scared him by groaning about the place, and came up from the ground under the house.

Question. Have you heard of many instances where people have received what is called Ku-Klux letters?

Answer. I have heard of three or four.

Question. What was the purport of those letters?

Answer. I heard Parson Eberts say he had received one notifying him to desist from teaching his school. Three or four young gentlemen living in Aberdeen, natives of the county, brought one to me some three or four months ago, in which they were threatened, and asked me what I thought about it, and what they ought to do; I think there were five names in it, perhaps; Mr. Clopton was one, Mr. Bradford. There were five or six names in it. I advised them to pay no attention to it in the world; that they could not be in any danger; that it was somebody trying to get up a little fun at their expense, in my opinion.

Question. You think these Ku-Klux letters were all dictated in a spirit of fun?

Answer. I do not think they all were; I thought that was, from the character of the young men; they were very clever, genteel young men.

Question. Have you ever heard of people leaving the country in consequence of receiving these Ku-Klux notices?

Answer. I heard a lady of some name, I do not remember it, who was teaching school at Cotton-Gin, left in consequence of a notice she had to desist from teaching school; I do not remember her name; I understood she left.

Question. Is that the only instance you heard of?

Answer. The only instance I have heard of in my county. Parson Eberts talked of leaving, and several of us advised him not to do it; insisted that he should not.

Question. Have you heard of school-houses being burned in your county?

Answer. I have heard of two being burned and one church.

Question. In what period of time?

Answer. Within a year from this time.

Question. Were they colored schools?

Answer. I think one was a white one, and the other was a colored school; I am certain of it.

Question. Was the act supposed to have been induced by the opposition to the school-tax?

Answer. I supposed it to be induced by dissatisfaction in the neighborhood with the location of the school-houses. At the burning of the church there was a meeting of the neighborhood, and a great deal of pains taken to ferret it out, and it failed; it was a Presbyterian church on the east side. Some gin-houses were burned; some supposed to be the work of an incendiary and some we know were accidental.

Question. You have expressed an opinion that the taxes are sixteen times higher than they were before the war. I will ask you for the facts upon which you base that opinion.

Answer. On the value of the property.

Question. What was the rate per cent. of taxation for all purposes before the war; that is to say, upon $100 valuation of property, what was the amount of taxes for all purposes, before the war?

Answer. We had on real estate about one-tenth of one per cent.; we paid on negroes variously, sometimes according to their value, and sometimes so much a head. The tax on them varied according to the opinion of the various legislatures ; it was frequently changed.

Question. Generally how much was it per capita?

Answer. Generally about 75 cents apiece.

Question. On a negro valued at $1,000?

Answer. It covered them all, so much apiece.

Question. They were generally valued at $1,000?

Answer. For the last few years before the war they got up to about that. They did not reach that until very recently before the war. The price continued to go up. Sometimes I have known negroes taxed as much as a dollar and a half.

Question. What other property was taxed?

Answer. There was no other property taxed unless you add the amount of household property above a certain value, gold and silver watches.

Question. Were mules and horses?

Answer. Pleasure-horses were taxed, saddle-horses or buggy, or carriage-horses, but not a work-horse, only pleasure-horses.

Question. Is there more money raised for the care of the poor now than there was before the war?

Answer. The pauper list has increased; there is not more per head; the number of paupers has increased.

Question. Is there more raised now for defraying the expense of criminals than before the war?

Answer. The expense of the State government, including the judiciary, is greatly more.

Question. Is there more raised for the purpose of repairing the highways and bridges than before the war?

Answer. No, sir; highways and bridges are ordered—the highways, not the bridges—the highways are ordered to be kept up by the labor of persons from sixteen to fifty-five years of age, living in the district where the roads are. The bridges are let out as a general rule to builders, and the price of building them is greatly higher than before the war.

Question. Are the salaries of your county officers higher than before the war?

Answer. Greatly higher; an average of at least 100 per cent. higher.

Question. The cost of living is greatly increased, is it not?

Answer. The cost of provisions is not higher—meat and bread; but rents are higher.

Question. Is clothing higher?

Answer. No, sir; ready-made clothing is selling in the stores as cheap as ever. Domestics are about as cheap.

Question. Take the ordinary expenses of a family, are they not increased at least one-third beyond what they were before the war?

Answer. If you leave out the hire of servants—a thing we knew nothing about until since the war—they are not. The servants' hire is a new item to us, and the rents are higher about the towns. The idea of hiring servants is something that never entered my head until since the war. I am hiring a cook for myself and my wife at $120 a year, with fire, food, &c.

Question. Do your county officials receive a greater compensation for their services than is right and proper?

Answer. I think they do. I think the sheriff, and tax-assessor, and chancery clerk receive a higher salary than their services are worth.

Question. Have you any greater number of county officials now than you had before the war; has there been an increase in the number of county officers?

Answer. I think not. There is an increase in the school-board.

Question. I am leaving that out of the question at present.

Answer. If you leave that out, there has not been.

Question. Leaving the school system and its machinery of officers out of the question, has there been any increase in the number of your State officers?

Answer. There has been an increase in the number of circuit judges; they have increased one-half; the district attorneys in the same proportion.

Question. The number of litigants in the courts has been increased more than one-half, has it not?

Answer. Immediately following the war it was; and since then it is less than it ever was since I have known this State.

Question. Before the war the slaves were not parties in court?

Answer. Yes, sir; they were prosecuted in court. We occasionally had a suit of a man sued by a slave—suit for his freedom.

Question. But these cases were very rare in civil suits?

Answer. In civil suits the slave could not be a party.

Question. They are now all suitors?

Answer. Yes, sir.

Question. Do not the blacks exceed the whites?

Answer. I think there is about fifteen, may be as much as twenty thousand voters, more blacks than whites. I do not know the excess of blacks, women and children, over the whites.

Question. Since they are invested with all the civil rights of white men, and may be suitors in court like the whites, has there not been a corresponding increase of civil business in your courts?

Answer. For the last two years there has been a hundred per cent. fewer suits brought in Northern Mississippi than at any time for twenty years before.

Question. But at the time your judiciary was enlarged—at the time the number of your circuits was increased—was there not a demand for the increase by reason of accumulation of business on the dockets?

Answer. At the time the circuits were increased, in half the counties in the State there was a larger number of cases on the dockets than had ever before been on them, which was the result of suits brought immediately after the war, and not disposed of; and in some counties many of them are still on the docket. In my county, for instance, we have not got through a civil docket since the war, and in some other counties, not many, that same state of things exists.

Question. Was not this increase in the circuits demanded by the legal profession?

Answer. Not so far as I know. We were very much, in the circuits north of this, astonished at the number of circuits made. We did not think there was any necessity for it, and we charged directly that it was done to pay certain politicians.

By Mr. RICE:

Question. Your judges, as a general thing, are not politicians?

Answer. No, sir. The circuit judge of this circuit, Judge Orr, was a politician. Judge Boone was a member of the legislature. Bradford was not, and Davis never had been a politician.

Question. None of them had been very active in politics?

Answer. Orr had; Judge Davis had not; and Judge Bradford had not.

By the CHAIRMAN:

Question. You have expressed the opinion that there was no confidence felt in the community that the taxes collected would be applied to proper purposes. Are you prepared to lay your finger upon any corrupt appropriation of the taxes in Monroe County?

Answer. I have not been at the legislature since I was a member of it, and that statement I intended to apply to the State tax.

Question. Now, I am questioning about matters right about home, where you are presumed to be familiar. When we get into disbursements of the State funds, we will go down to Jackson and examine the officials there. I want to inquire whether there is any charge of the corrupt use of money raised by tax from the county of Monroe?

Answer. I have heard of none. No such charge has been made in the county of Monroe.

Question. Leaving out of the question the school-tax, wherein, then, has there been an excessive assessment and levy of taxes?

Answer. We think there is an excessive assessment and levy of the State tax beyond the interests of the country.

Question. I am speaking of your county taxes.

Answer. Our county tax is limited to one-half. We cannot go beyond the State tax with our county tax. We have only complained in our county of excessive prices paid for building bridges.

Question. At the close of the war your bridges were mostly rotten, down, or in bad repair?

Answer. They were in very bad order universally.

Question. It became necessary to rebuild many?

Answer. Yes, sir; almost the whole of them.

Question. You did not complain of the rebuilding of the bridges, but think they have been built at too high a figure?

Answer. No, sir; we did not complain of the rebuilding, but we think they are rebuilt at very extravagant prices.

Question. What has been the practice in your county of building these bridges—by private contracts, or are they let out upon public notice and given to the lowest bidder?

Answer. They are let upon public notice, so far as I know.

Question. Who, then, is to blame if the bridges have been contracted at too high a figure?

Answer. I blame the court of supervisors in not rejecting the bids when they are given in at high figures—so high that everybody knows it is more than they are worth.

Question. Why was there not some competition among the bidders?

Answer. I do not know.

Question. The bridges had to be built, and they took the best method of ascertaining who would build them at the lowest figure?

Answer. No, sir; I do not think that is the best way. I think the best way is to let them out, with a right reserved to reject all the bids, which the court would not do.

Question. You would have the bridges go unbuilt, unless some person would offer to build them at prices you thought were reasonable?

Answer. I would, sir.

By Mr. RICE:

Question. You seem to think that the troubles that have been brought on the State here, have been brought on through the republican politicians, mainly?

Answer. Yes, sir; mainly. I think they commenced it. We have had some natives who went with them and were just as culpable.

Question. At the close of the war, you say, all was friendly between the two races?

Answer. Yes, sir.

Question. Each was working by the side of the other satisfied?

Answer. Each was certainly satisfied with the other. The utmost confidence seemed to prevail.

Question. In 1866, I believe you say, the Freedmen's Bureau began to interfere a little?

Answer. It commenced in 1865. The military of the Freedmen's Bureau commenced in 1865, and in 1866 made itself very odious, and made a great deal of dissension between the races.

Question. Was there much dissension got up in 1865?

Answer. Very little; but some showed itself before the end of 1865. The first that occurred in my county was by an order of the Freedmen's Bureau that certain persons should keep on their places and feed negroes who had belonged to them and refused to do anything in the world. That was the first trouble.

Question. When was that?

Answer. In 1865; in the fall of that year.

Question. What was the condition that they were disposed to leave the negroes in had there been no congressional legislation; what rights?

Answer. I do not know that I can say. We recognized at the surrender that the negro was free. Whether the people had generally matured any opinion as to what disposition was to be made of him, beyond the fact that he was to be recognized as a free man, I cannot say.

Question. Did not the white people of the State first commence restricting the rights of the negroes before any steps were taken the other way to counteract that? Did they not do that by some legislation in 1865 and 1866?

Answer. In 1865 and 1866 the legislature prohibited the negroes buying land—1866 and 1867.

Question. They assessed them for poll-tax, and prescribed a penalty for non-payment of it different from what it was for white men?

Answer. No, sir. The penalties are the same upon all men for not paying taxes, if I recollect right.

Question. With a view of getting these acts before the committee, I will submit two or three acts to you. The act you speak of in regard to preventing them from buying land and voting is this, [submitting laws of Mississippi.]

Answer. Yes, sir; that is the act. Chapter 4, page 82, of the laws of Mississippi for 1865 and 1866: "An act to confer civil rights on freedmen, and for other purposes."

Mr. RICE. Without reading it, I would like to have it incorporated. It is not long. [See page 883.]

The WITNESS. That was repealed by the same legislature the next winter.

Question. Portions of it were repealed?

Answer. Yes, sir. That act was passed in 1866; the session met in 1865.

Question. Was there another, "An act to amend the vagrant laws of the State?"

Answer. Yes, sir.

Question. Section 7 provides "that if any freedman free negro, or mulatto shall fail or refuse to pay any tax levied according to the provisions of the 6th section of this act, it shall be *prima facie* evidence of vagrancy, and it shall be the duty of the sheriff to arrest such freedman, free negro, or mulatto, or such person refusing or neglecting to pay such tax, and proceed at once to hire for the shortest time such delinquent tax-payer to any one who will pay the said tax, with accruing costs, giving preference to the employer if there be one." Was not that a discrimination?

Answer. The vagrant act for white men was about as stringent, if I recollect. That act was passed.

By the CHAIRMAN:

Question. Was that a democratic legislature?

Answer. Yes, sir; it was a democratic legislature.

By Mr. RICE:

Question. I would like to have this act incorporated in our record. [See page 886.] There is "An act to punish certain offenses therein named, and for other purposes." As it is not well defined in the heading, will you see if that act was passed also?

Answer. Yes sir: "An act to punish certain offenses therein named, and for other purposes," approved November 29, 1865.

Question. This is what I had reference to when I asked you if the white people of the State did not commence first restricting the rights of the negroes before there were any acts on the part of the freedmen to assert them?

Answer. I was answering in regard to the acts of neighborhoods, of masters, and not in regard to the legislature.

By Mr. BLAIR:

Question. Who is this Dr. Compton of whom you spoke?

Answer. Dr. Compton, when I first knew him, was a member of the legislature from Holly Springs. He was regarded as a clever gentleman.

Question. What is he now?

Answer. He is superintendent of the lunatic asylum. He is charged to have been a high officer in the Ku-Klux organization; said to have some title that they called a "giant;" what his office was I never knew. I tried to find out but could not do it. He has changed his politics within the last two years or less. He was editing a paper which was a democratic paper, but he has since become a bitter republican.

Question. Said to have been a "giant?"

Answer. A "giant" in the Ku-Klux family; what the office meant I do not know. They are said to have had a "cyclops," a "giant," and "wizard;" the "wizard" being the great man—the sovereign.

By Mr. CHAIRMAN:

Question. Who says he was a head man in that organization?

Answer. The papers published it. I have seen it charged on him in a paper at Jackson; and he has been repeatedly asked to deny that he was a "giant" in the order, and I believe he has never done it. The paper at Holly Springs, where he formerly lived, makes it.

By Mr. BLAIR:

Question. Was it made publicly by Mr. Barksdale in a speech?

Answer. Yes, sir. He published that he would prove it if Compton dared deny it.

Question. He is a "giant" now among the republicans, is he not?

Answer. He seems to be. He was selected as the editor of the present paper known as "The Leader."

Question. The organ of the governor?

Answer. Yes, sir. There are two organs. Governor Alcorn has one called "The Leader" and one called the "Pilot," which is under the superintendence of and in the interest of the lieutenant governor.

The acts of the legislature of Mississippi, submited by Mr. Rice, and referred to in the testimony of Samuel J. Gholson, are as follows:

CHAPTER IV.

AN ACT to confer civil rights on freedmen, and for other purposes.

SECTION 1. *Be it enacted by the legislature of the State of Mississippi,* That all freedmen, free negroes, and mulattoes may sue and be sued, implead and be impleaded, in all the courts of law and equity of this State, and may acquire personal property and choses in action, by descent or purchase, and may dispose of the same, in the same manner, and to the same extent that white persons may: *Provided,* that the provisions of this section shall not be so construed as to allow any freedman, free negro, or mulatto to rent or lease any lands or tenements, except in incorporated towns or cities, in which places the corporate authorities shall control the same.

SEC. 2. *Be it further enacted,* That all freedmen, free negroes and mulattoes, may intermarry with each other in the same manner and under the same regulations that are provided by law for white persons: *Provided,* That the clerk of probate shall keep separate records of the same.

SEC. 3. *Be it further enacted,* That all freedmen, free negroes and mulattoes, who do now and have heretofore lived and cohabited together as husband and wife, shall be taken and held in law as legally married, and the issue shall be taken and held as legitimate for all purposes. That it shall not be lawful for any freedman, free negro, or mulatto, to intermarry with any white person, nor for any white person to intermarry with any freedman, free negro, or mulatto; and any person who shall so intermarry shall be deemed guilty of felony, and, on conviction thereof, shall be confined in the State penitentiary for life: and those shall be deemed freedmen, free negroes, and mulattoes who are of pure negro blood, and those descended from a negro to the third generation inclusive, though one ancestor of each generation may have been a white person.

SEC. 4. *Be it further enacted*, That in addition to cases in which freedmen, free negroes, and mulattoes are now by law competent witnesses, freedmen, free negroes, or mulattoes shall be competent in civil cases when a party or parties to the suit, either plaintiff or plaintiffs, defendant or defendants, also in cases where freedmen, free negroes, and mulattoe is or are either plaintiff or plaintiffs, defendant or defendants, and a white person or white persons is or are the opposing party or parties, plaintiff or plaintiffs, defendant or defendants. They shall also be competent witnisses in all criminal prosecutions where the crime charged is alleged to have been committed by a white person upon or against the person or property of a freedman, free negro, or mulatto: *Provided*, That in all cases said witnesses shall be examined in open court on the stand, except, however, they may be examined before the grand jury, and shall in all cases be subject to the rules and tests of the common law as to competency and credibility.

SEC. 5. *Be it further enacted*, That every freedman, free negro, and mulatto shall, on the second Monday of January, one thousand eight hundred and sixty-six, and annually thereafter, have a lawful home or employment, and shall have written evidence thereof, as follows, to wit: if living in any incorporated city, town, or village, a license from the mayor thereof; and if living outside of any incorporated city, town, or village, from the member of the board of police of his beat, authorizing him or her to do irregular and job work, or a written contract, as provided in section sixth of this act, which licenses may be revoked for cause, at any time, by the authority granting the same.

SEC. 6. *Be it further enacted*, That all contracts for labor made with freedmen, free negroes, and mulattoes, for a longer period than one month, shall be in writing and in duplicate, attested and read to said freedman, free negro, or mulatto, by a beat, city, or county officer, or two disinterested white persons of the county in which the labor is to be performed, of which each party shall have one: and said contracts shall be taken and held as entire contracts, and if the laborer shall quit the service of the employer before expiration of his term of service, without good cause, he shall forfeit his wages for that year, up to the time of quitting.

SEC. 7. *Be it further enacted*, That every civil officer shall and every person may arrest and carry back to his or her legal employer any freedman, free negro, or mulatto who shall have quit the service of his or her employer before the expiration of his or her term of service without good cause; and said officer and person shall be entitled to receive, for arresting and carrying back every deserting employé aforesaid, the sum of $5, and 10 cents per mile from the place of arrest to the place of delivery, and the same shall be paid by the employer, and held as a set-off for so much against the wages of said deserting employé: *Provided*, That said arrested party, after being so returned, may appeal to a justice of the peace, or member of the board of police of the county, who, on notice to the alleged employer, shall try summarily whether said appellant is legally employed by the alleged employer, and has good cause to quit said employer; either party shall have the right to appeal to the county court, pending which the alleged deserter shall be remanded to the alleged employer, or otherwise disposed of as shall be right and just, and the decision of the county court shall be final.

SEC. 8. *Be it further enacted*, That upon affidavit made by the employer of any freedman, free negro, or mulatto, or other credible person, before any justice of the peace or member of the board of police, that any freedman, free negro, or mulatto, legally employed by said employer, has illegally deserted said employment, such justice of the peace, or member of the board of police shall issue his warrant or warrants, returnable before himself, or other such officer, directed to any sheriff, constable, or special deputy, commanding him to arrest said deserter, and return him or her to said employer, and the like proceedings shall be had as provided in the preceding section; and it shall be lawful for any officer to whom such warrant shall be directed, to execute said warrant in any county of this State, and that said warrant may be transmitted without indorsement to any like officer of another county, to be executed and returned as aforesaid, and the said employer shall pay the cost of said warrants and arrest and return, which shall be set-off for so much against the wages of said deserter.

SEC. 9. *Be it further enacted*, That if any person shall persuade, or attempt to persuade, entice, or cause any freedman, free negro, or mulatto to desert from the legal employment of any person before the expiration of his or her term of service, or shall knowingly employ any such deserting freedman, free negro, or mulatto, or shall knowingly give or sell to any such deserting freedman, free negro, or mulatto any food, raiment, or other thing, he or she shall be guilty of a misdemeanor, and, upon conviction, shall be fined not less than twenty-five dollars and not more than two hundred dollars and the costs; and if said fine and costs shall not be immediately paid, the court shall sentence said convict to not exceeding two months' imprisonment in the county jail, and he or she shall moreover be liable to the party injured in damages: *Provided*, if any person shall or shall attempt to persuade, entice, or cause any freedman, free negro, or mulatto to desert from any legal employment of any person, with the view to employ said freedman, free negro, or mulatto, without the limits of this State, such person, on conviction, shall be fined not less than fifty dollars and not more than five hundred dollars and costs, and if said fine and costs shall not be immediately paid, the court shall sentence said convict to not exceeding six months' imprisonment in the county jail.

SEC. 10. *Be it further enacted*, That it shall be lawful for any freedman, free negro, or mulatto, to charge any white person, freedman, free negro, or mulatto, by affidavit, with any criminal offense against his or her person or property, and upon such affidavit the proper process shall be issued and executed as if said affidavit was made by a white person; and it shall be lawful for any freedman, free negro, or mulatto, in any action, suit, or controversy pending, or about to be instituted, in any court of law of equity of this State, to make all needful and lawful affidavits as shall be necessary for the institution, prosecution, or defense of such suit or controversy.

SEC. 11. *Be it further enacted*, That the penal laws of this State, in all cases not otherwise specially provided for, shall apply and extend to all freedmen, free negroes, and mulattoes.

SEC. 12. *Be it further enacted*, That this act shall take effect and be in force from and after its passage.

Approved November 25, 1865.

CHAPTER VI.

AN ACT to amend the vagrant laws of the State.

SECTION 1. *Be it enacted by the legislature of the State of Mississippi*, That all rogues and vagabonds, idle and dissipated persons, beggars, jugglers, or persons practicing unlawful games or plays, runaways, common drunkards, common night-walkers, pilferers, lewd, wanton, or lascivious persons, in speech or behavior, common railers and brawlers, persons who neglect their calling or employment, misspend what they earn, or do not provide for the support of themselves or their families, or dependents, and all other idle and disorderly persons, including all who neglect all lawful business, or habitually misspend their time by frequenting houses of ill-fame, gaming-houses, or tippling-shops, shall be deemed and considered vagrants under the provisions of this act, and, on conviction thereof, shall be fined not exceeding one hundred dollars, with all accruing costs, and be imprisoned at the discretion of the court not exceeding ten days.

SEC. 2. *Be it further enacted*, That all freedmen, free negroes, and mulattoes in this State over the age of eighteen years, found on the second Monday in January, 1866, or thereafter, with no lawful employment or business, or found unlawfully assembling themselves together, either in the day or night time, and all white persons so assembling with freedmen, free negroes, or mulattoes, or usually associating with freedmen, free negroes, or mulattoes on terms of equality, or living in adultery or fornication with a freedwoman, free negro, or mulatto, shall be deemed vagrants, and, on conviction thereof, shall be fined in the sum of not exceeding, in the case of a freedman, free negro, or mulato, fifty dollars, and a white man two hundred dollars, and imprisoned at the discretion of the court, the free negro not exceeding ten days, and the white man not exceeding six months.

SEC. 3. *Be it further enacted*, That all justices of the peace, mayors, and aldermen of incorporated towns and cities of the several counties in this State shall have jurisdiction to try all questions of vagrancy in their respective towns, counties, and cities, and it is hereby made their duty, whenever they shall ascertain that any person or persons, in their respective towns, counties, and cities, are violating any of the provisions of this act, to have said party or parties arrested and brought before them, and immediately investigate said charge, and, on conviction, punish said party or parties as provided for herein. And it is hereby made the duty of all sheriffs, constables, town constables, city marshals, and all like officers, to report to some officer having jurisdiction all violations of any of the provisions of this act; and it shall be the duty of the county courts to inquire if any officers have neglected any of the duties required by this act, and in case any officer shall fail or neglect any duty herein, it shall be the duty of the county court to fine said officer, upon conviction, not exceeding one hundred dollars, to be paid into the county treasury for county purposes.

SEC. 4. *Be it further enacted*, That keepers of gaming-houses, houses of prostitution, all prostitutes, public or private, and all persons who derive their chief support in employments that militate against good morals or against law, shall be deemed and held to be vagrants.

SEC. 5. *Be it further enacted,* That all fines and forfeitures collected under the provisions of this act shall be paid into the county treasury for general county purposes; and in case any freedman, free negro, or mulatto shall fail for five days after the imposition of any fine or forfeiture upon him or her for violation of any of the provisions of this act, to pay the same, that it shall be and, is hereby, made the duty of the sheriff of the proper county to hire out said freedman, free negro, or mulatto to any person who will, for the shortest period of service, pay said fine or forfeiture and all costs: *Provided,* a preference shall be given to the employer, if there be one, in which case the employer shall be entitled to deduct and retain the amount so paid from the wages of such freedman, free negro, or mulatto, then due or to become due; and in case such freedman, free negro, or mulatto cannot be hired out, he or she may be dealt with as a pauper.

SEC. 6. *Be it further enacted,* That the same duties and liabilities existing among the white persons of this State shall attach to freedmen, free negroes, and mulattoes, to support their indigent families, and all colored paupers; and that in order to secure a support for such indigent freedmen, free negroes, and mulattoes, it shall be lawful, and it is hereby made the duty of the boards of county police of each county in this State, to levy a poll or capitation tax on each and every freedman, free negro, or mulatto, between the ages of eighteen and sixty years, not to exceed the sum of one dollar annually to each person so taxed, which tax, when collected, shall be paid into the county treasurer's hands, and constitute a fund, to be called the freedmen's pauper fund, which shall be applied by the commissioners of the poor for the maintenance of the poor of the freedmen, free negroes, and mulattoes of this State, under such regulations as may be established by the boards of county police, in the respective counties of this State.

SEC. 7. *Be it further enacted,* That if any freedman, free negro, or mulatto shall fail or refuse to pay any tax levied according to the provisions of the sixth section of this act, it shall be *prima facie* evidence of vagrancy, and it shall be the duty of the sheriff to arrest such freedman, free negro, or mulatto, or such person refusing or neglecting to pay such tax, and proceed at once to hire, for the shortest time, such delinquent tax-payer to any one who will pay the said tax, with accruing costs, giving preference to the employer, if there be one.

SEC. 8. *Be it further enacted,* That any person feeling himself or herself aggrieved by the judgment of any justice of the peace, mayor, or alderman, in cases arising under this act, may, within five days, appeal to the next term of the county court of the proper county, upon giving bond and security in a sum not less than twenty-five nor more than one hundred and fifty dollars, conditioned to appear and prosecute said appeal, and abide by the judgment of the county court and said appeal shall be tried *de novo* in the county court, and the decision of said court shall be final.

SEC. 9. *Be it further enacted.* That this act shall be in force, and take effect from its passage.

Approved November 24, 1865.

CHAPTER XXIII.

AN ACT to punish certain offenses therein named, and for other purposes.

SECTION 1. *Be it enacted by the legislature of the State of Mississippi,* That no freedman, free negro, or mulatto not in the military service of the United States Government, and not licensed so to do by the board of police of his or her county, shall keep or carry fire-arms of any kind, or any ammunition, dirk, or bowie-knife, and, on conviction thereof in the county court, shall be punished by fine, not exceeding ten dollars, and pay the costs of such proceedings; and all such arms or ammunition shall be forfeited to the informer, and it shall be the duty of every civil and military officer to arrest any freedman, free negro, or mulatto found with any such arms or ammunition, and cause him or her to be committed for trial in default of bail.

SEC. 2. *Be it further enacted,* That any freedman, free negro, or mulatto committing riots, routes, affrays, trespasses, malicious mischief, cruel treatment to animals, seditious speeches, insulting gestures, language, or acts, or assaults on any person, disturbance of the peace, exercising the functions of a minister of the Gospel without a license from some regularly organized church, vending spirituous or intoxicating liquors, or committing any other misdemeanor, the punishment of which is not specifically provided for by law, shall, upon conviction thereof in the county court, be fined not less than ten dollars and not more than one hundred dollars, and be imprisoned, at the discretion of the court, not exceeding thirty days.

SEC. 3. *Be it further enacted,* That if any white person shall sell, lend, or give to any freedman, free negro, or mulatto any fire-arms, dirk, or bowie-knife, or ammunition, or any spirituous or intoxicating liquors, such person or persons so offending, upon conviction thereof in the county court of his or her county, shall be fined not exceeding fifty dollars, and may be imprisoned, at the discretion of the court, not exceeding thirty days: *Provided,* That any master, mistress, or employer of any freedman, free negro, or mulatto may give to any freedman, free negro, or mulatto, apprenticed to or employed by such master, mistress, or employer, spirituous or intoxicating liquors, but not in sufficient quantities to produce intoxication.

SEC. 4. *Be it further enacted,* That all the penal and criminal laws now in force in this State defining offenses and prescribing the mode of punishment for crimes and misdemeanors committed by slaves, free negroes, or mulattoes, be, and and the same are hereby, re-enacted, and declared to be in full force and effect against freedmen, free negroes, and mulattoes, except so far as the mode and manner of trial and punishment have been changed or altered by law.

SEC. 5. *Be it further enacted,* That if any freedman, free negro, or mulatto, convicted of any of the misdemeanors provided against in this act, shall fail or refuse, for the space of five days after conviction, to pay the fine and costs imposed, such person shall be hired out by the sheriff or other officer, at public outcry, to any white person who will pay said fine and all costs, and take such convict for the shortest time.

SEC. 6. *Be it further enacted,* That this act shall be in force and take effect from and after its passage.

Approved November 29, 1865.

COLUMBUS, MISSISSIPPI, *November* 14, 1871.

JOSEPH BECKWITH (colored) sworn and examined.

By the CHAIRMAN:

Question. Where do you live?

Answer. At Widow Winn's, right the other side of the Loaxapallila River.

Question. In this county?

Answer. Yes, sir.

Question. How long have you lived here?

Answer. I have been living here now going on three years.

Question. Where did you live before you came here?

Answer. I lived at Judge Beckwith's, down in Lowndes County.

Question. Have you ever been visited by the Ku-Klux?

Answer. Yes, sir.

Question. When was that?

Answer. It was in the last cotton-planting time; in the last of March or the first of April.

Question. This year?

Answer. Yes, sir; in the 1st of April, it was.

Question. You may give to the committee the circumstances.

Answer. They called at my house and woke me up, and told me that they wanted to know the way to Mr. Hill's bridge; if I would please to go and show them; that they had been lost and rambling all night, and could not find the way. I told them I would do it; and I went on with them out at the gate, and pointed them the way to go; and this man jumped down off of his horse and pointed his pistol in my face. Says he, "I have a little settlement with you." I then immediately looked up and saw how they were fixed off, and I got frightened, and broke and run. They took after me and caught me. I undertook to jump over the fence, and they caught me and brought me back to the gate, and slipped a rope around my neck. They said, "That shows, you run off, that you are not a straight man." As they went on they said, "We are men from a long ways; we come arguing with the stars and the moon; we are hunting for dead folk's treasure." I told them I didn't know anything about that. "O, you have got to tell a better tale than that." They went on, and said no more. The first tree they came to they hung me up, and when I found myself, I was scrambling on the ground getting up. There did not but one man talk then. He says, "This place won't do. He loves to climb too damned well." They carried me on down lower, and there they hung me up twice, and the last time, when I came to, they asked me, now could I tell them anything about this treasure. "We come from a long ways; we are in a hurry, and we want to know." Says I, "I don't know anything about it. I told you all that I know." He says, then, "Don't you recollect a yellow boy you had hired?" I said, "Yes." He said, "Them is the very ones as sent me to you." He said he was digging at a pine-tree with spades and shovels, and there he found a pot of money with an iron hoop around it, and I would not let him pull it out. I told him, "Yes, sir, he found a hoop there, but I never paid any attention to it; I was a fixing my garden, and the boys says to me, 'There is money here.'" I said, 'No, there is not.'" They said there was an old man there in that place that lived there before I went there, that had caved there, and there was graves there. I said, "There is nothing of that; put the post in." I never pulled the hoop up, or paid any more attention to it. He said, "That was what we were told," and he said, "The money is there, and we are arguing with the stars and moon that money is there, and you have got it." I said, "No, if I knew anything about it, I would tell you." He says, "You have got to tell a better tale than that." He says, "Go and show me that pine-tree, and them spades and shovels, and that will save your life." They kept the rope on my neck, and carried me back to my house and garden until I found the hole, and they made me dig down there. I said "Let me get a light, I can't find it." They said, "You can't have a light; we argue with the stars and moon that it is here, but you won't dig in the right place." I said, "It is here." He said, "O, you know a better tale than that; you are telling lies; we are men hunting for dead folks' treasure, and we are going to have it, or destroy the last one of you here." They went on back there and commenced tying the rope to hang me up, and one of them left me, and the other talked to the other men—there was three or four there with me; they said there was a large company down the road further; I didn't see but these four. They hung me up there, and they went and talked to this man and came back, and he said, "You go next morning and get that hoop and iron, and them things all—the pot of money, or whatever it is, and have it ready against we come again; we will come soon; you know not when we will come;" and I have been looking for them ever since, and staying there and making a crop, and I have been uneasy. I have worked and made a crop, and worked in uneasiness all the time.

Question. How many men were there in this body?

Answer. There were four in my presence, but they said there was a large company down lower. They said, "We are not all, and this is our business, and we are going to have this money."

Question. Did they have any disguises on?

Answer. Yes, sir; that is what frightened me when I first saw them. When they first come to our house I never looked up at them. Says he, "I suppose this is your place?" I says, "No; I am working for Widow Winn."

Question. Did they come there on horseback?

Answer. Yes, sir. They rode right up to my house.

Question Were they armed?

Answer. Yes, sir; they were armed.

Question. What kind of disguises did they have on?

Answer. They seemed to be dressed in white all over their heads, and just common clothes. These were white men that were handling me; but them on horses, I could not tell you what sort they were.

Question. What time in the night was this?

Answer. It was about between 11 and 12 o'clock—about 10 o'clock, because they had me out some time, and when I got back and went up to the widow's house, she looked up at the watch and says, "It is now 12 o'clock," and I suppose they had me out about two hours.

Question. Were you much hurt?

Answer. Yes, sir. I was suffering for three months so that I couldn't see at all hardly, and I did no work for two or three weeks. My eyes were bloodshot for three months.

Question. When they hung you did you lose your consciousness?

Answer. O, yes, sir; I never knew a thing. They hung me up. I never knew nothing. When I came to I was scrambling on the ground.

Question. Have you ever seen any Ku-Klux before or since?

Answer. Never before or since.

Question. Have they been through your neighborhood?

Answer. Not that I know of. I heard of them way off, but they never had passed me.

Question. And this yellow boy was the cause of their being there?

Answer. They told me so. I couldn't make them out, but I knew the boy.

By Mr. Blair:

Question. The yellow boy, you say, was working with you, and one day in working he struck this pot or hoop with his spade?

Answer. Yes, sir; where I was fixing the garden.

Question. Did he make any remark?

Answer. Yes, sir; he says to me, "Uncle Jo, there is money here." I says, "No, there is no such thing here; it is nothing but a cave or a grave; don't pay any attention to it." I never paid no attention to nothing that way, until these men came and attacked me.

Question. They told you this boy had informed them of his supposed discovery?

Answer. Yes, sir.

Question. Who did they think the money belonged to?

Answer. Belonged to Mr. Winn.

Question. Was it supposed that old Mr. Winn had buried some money somewhere?

Answer. Yes, sir; they supposed that he buried it and I found it, or that boy found it and I wouldn't let him have it.

Question. When was it supposed that old Mr. Winn buried money?

Answer. Before he died.

Question. During the war?

Answer. Yes, sir; that they could not find.

Question. Is that rumored pretty extensively among the people here, that old Mr. Winn had buried money somewhere?

Answer. Some says not. I suppose the people thought he had a heap of money, and they never could tell where it was.

Question. That was the idea?

Answer. Yes, sir; and I suppose they concluded from that boy's tale that I had found it; but I never knew any more about it than you did.

Question. You did not know any of those men who had hold of you?

Answer. No, sir; only the one talking.

Question. You only saw four?

Answer. Yes, sir; only four that I could make out; but they told me a large company was down below.

Question. How far is that from here?

Answer. About three miles from here.

Question. What made you think one of them was a white man?

Answer. I knowed him. I knowed by his feel that he was a white man. Both of them were.

Question. How did you know; their faces were covered up?

Answer. Their faces were covered up, but by the feeling from their hands, and from the appearance of them, I knew they were white men.

Question. How could you say that; you could not see them?

Answer. No, sir; only the way they were dressed.

Question. Were the hands covered up, too?

Answer. No, sir; the hands were not covered up, but they were dressed in white men's clothes, certain. From the feeling of the hands when they took hold of my hand I was certain they were white.

Question. That is the only way you could judge of them—by the feeling of the hands?

Answer. Yes, sir.

Question. Their object undoubtedly was to get the treasure?

Answer. Yes, sir; this treasure.

Question. They did not want to hurt you except to make you tell where the money was.

Answer. I suppose not; they could have destroyed me if they had been a-mind to, I suppose; but after they did not find the money they let me alone; but they said they intended to come back again, for it was there, and they meant to have it; they were sent for this business.

Question. You think all their maltreatment of you was to make you tell where the money was?

Answer. Yes, sir; nothing else at all.

Question. They punished you to make you tell?

Answer. Yes, sir; nothing else which I had done, nothing else; that is the reason I got up so willing to show them the way.

By the CHAIRMAN:

Question. Have they ever been back since?

Answer. No, sir.

Question. Did you leave there or stay?

Answer. When I got able to walk I went back to the house.

Question. But do you live at the same place?

Answer. Yes, sir.

By Mr. BLAIR:

Question. Are you watching for them every night?

Answer. Yes, sir; watching every night; the pine tree is there now, and the hoop.

COLUMBUS, MISSISSIPPI, *November* 14, 1871.

JAMES HICKS (colored) sworn and examined.

By the CHAIRMAN:

Question. State where you live.

Answer. I live in Lowndes County, six miles from here, up on the military road.

Question. Have you ever lived in or near Caledonia?

Answer. Yes, sir; I lived a mile the other side of there; it has been something near a year now, about a year.

Question. How came you to leave there?

Answer. On account of the Ku-Klux.

Question. What did they do to you?

Answer. Well, they came to my house, and, as it happened, I got out of the way that night, and they went in where my wife was; they never whipped her; they threatened to pull her out of the bed, but they did not do much to her that night, and then I moved from there.

Question. Where did you move to?

Answer. I moved down here on Mr. Tommy Gray's place who lives here in Columbus; it is six miles from here.

Question. Did you move away from there on account of fear of the Ku-Klux?

Answer. Yes, sir.

Question. You may state whether you were followed by the Ku-Klux and whipped down here.

Answer. Yes, sir; they followed me down here. I reckon it was three months or four months before they came down here; they followed me down here and whipped me.

Question. Give us the particulars.

Answer. I could not principally say that I knew any of them, hardly, but two; I thought I knew Mr. Darden and Mr. Burton. I lived with them; Mr. Darden was the man I lived with.

Question. Before you moved from Caledonia?

Answer. Yes, sir.

Question. How long ago was it that they whipped you?

Answer. I reckon it has been five months; it was in April—no, it was in March, somewhere about the 18th or 19th of March.

Question. Did they come to your house at night?

Answer. Yes, sir; it was between midnight and day—I reckon about 1 o'clock.

Question. How many men came?

Answer. There was about forty men, I reckon.

Question. Had they disguises on?

Answer. Yes, sir; all of them were disguised, I believe, but two, and the others, I didn't know them; I don't think I know them.

By Mr. BLAIR:

Question. All disguised but what?

Answer. One of them had something over his face, and the other didn't have nothing on, but I didn't know him at all, and all the others were disguised.

By the CHAIRMAN:

Question. Were you abed and asleep at the time they came?

Answer. Yes, sir.

Question. How did they get into the house?

Answer. Well, Edmund Gray, he was present, I suppose—he had rented the place from Mr. Gray, and I just merely went in as a hand, and they called him out and I was in another room. I didn't get up when they called him; I laid, and they came and knocked at my door, and it had a loft to it, and I went up into the loft and they came in to get lights and made him come up there and get me, and they carried me out and whipped me; and they made my wife open the door and they whipped my wife, too.

Question. How many whipped you?

Answer. Two whipped me.

Question. How many times were you struck?

Answer. I reckon they gave me one hundred and fifty lashes; maybe more; maybe two hundred.

Question. What did they whip you with?

Answer. They whipped me with a strap.

Question. Did they tell you what they were whipping you for?

Answer. They said that they understood I had talked some talk concerning some white woman that was not nice, they thought, but I have witnesses that night that they tried to make me own, and I said that I didn't say it; it was only got up, that chat was, and they wanted to run me off, the man I lived with did, on account of my crop, and that was why they got the Ku-Klux to get after me, and that night they tried to make me own it, and I told them I didn't say it; and at last one of them said he reckoned I didn't say it, and there was no use to try to beat me to make me own what I didn't say, and Edmund Gray was present there and heard them say that.

Question. Did they come to your house on horseback?

Answer. Yes, sir.

Question. Did you see their horses?

Answer. Yes, sir.

Question. Did their horses have anything over them?

Answer. Their horses were all disguised, too, but a mule; this gentleman was not disguised; he rode a mule and it was not disguised, but all the others were on horses.

Question. Were these men armed?

Answer. Yes, sir; all of them had pistols principally, and Edmund Gray says they had as much as twelve double-barrel shot-guns, but I didn't see but one; he had a better chance to see than I did; all that I saw had pistols, gathered around me; I didn't see but one gun.

Question. How long were you laid up by your whipping?

Answer. I was not laid up at all; that is, I came to town that next day. They summoned me to come to town. For two or three days I did not do much; it was wet weather; bad weather. I didn't have very much to do. If it had been anything like hard work or bad work I would not have been fit for labor under a week and a half, I reckon; but it was just knocking about like, and I knocked about. I was near about ready to move, and I just worked a little on my house. I reckon it was a week and a half before I got able for good service.

Question. Did you move from there?

Answer. Yes, sir; on Mr. Gray's other place, about half a mile from there. Both of them places was his. We were all in one house. I didn't move on account of that at that time, though. I was going to move, anyhow, then.

Question. Have you found out who whipped you?

Answer. No, sir; I don't know who it was at all that whipped me.

Question. Has anybody ever been taken up for it or prosecuted?

Answer. No, sir; not that I know of. We reported here before the grand jury before that. Mr. Farmer reported here, and I don't think there was anything done about it.

By Mr. BLAIR:

Question. You moved out of the neighborhood after they first came to your house?

Answer. Yes, sir.

Question. You had been working a crop there on this place?

Answer. Yes, sir.

Question. You moved off and left your crop?

Answer. I left a portion of it; but they broke me teetotally up. I left my things and they would not allow me to go back there, and I had to slip back and get my wife and children the best I could. They took everything I had, and all my wife had, and broke us teetotally up. I had to come away with nothing. I am not able to say that I have got anything yet. I made a very good crop this year, and will be able to come out right smart, but I have lost all my house furniture; every bit of it.

Question. You say they whipped you to get your crop?

Answer. That is what I think. We had a fuss, me and him did. He never rested satisfied after that any more, and he shot at me four times with a pistol.

Question. Where did you have a fuss with him?

Answer. I was out in the big road. I never done anything, though, but he shot at me four times.

Question. That was after you were whipped?

Answer. No, sir; that was before I moved; that was the man I lived with; that was before ever I moved away, or before the Ku-Klux interfered with me; that was the beginning of it.

Question. He shot at you in the road?

Answer. Yes, sir.

Question. When was that?

Answer. That was in August; this last-gone August was a year.

Question. What did he shoot at you for?

Answer. Well, the man that I was cropping with, he said, told him some tales that I should have said; and he said he misunderstood him, and he didn't know but what I might have said it. I had been for some light-wood, and came by his house, and he was cursing me, and I said something to him. I asked him what I had done to him. I recollect saying that; and he said I had done enough. And I told him, "Well, if everybody was to do right there would be no fuss." And he then come on out and said, "If I came down there and fussed with him he would shoot my brains out." And he came out of his house, then, on the road. I was passing by and I kept on, and he followed me a good piece off. The first time he shot and the last time he was tolerably close with the pistol, though he never hit me.

Question. What were you doing this time?

Answer. I didn't do nothing. I didn't have nothing; I had my axe, too, but then I didn't want to—I knew I wouldn't—I oughtn't to hit him; at least I felt like if I hit him I would not be doing right, or, at least, I should not be protected no way. I knew the majority of the white people would punish me in some way or other, and for that reason I never hit him. I didn't want no fuss if I could get round him, and so I never did anything to him.

Question. Who was there?

Answer. There was nobody present there, but there was another black man, too, who was passing and heard it. There was nobody present when that happened, nobody but him and me. My wife was at her house, and she heard the report of the pistol and came down to see, but it was over before she got there.

Question. Was this near his house?

Answer. Yes, sir. Well, I reckon it was about fifty yards from his house, or not that far, not more than thirty when we first began, but I kept on walking and he followed me, and I reckon when we stopped it was sixty yards from his house.

Question. Was there anybody at his house?

Answer. Nobody but him and his wife.

Question. Was she out there; did she see it?

Answer. She was in the house. I don't know whether she saw it or not. I can't tell that. It was in the night.

Question. Has he no children?

Answer. Yes, sir; some little children—small children.

Question. What is this man Darden's first name?

Answer. Bill Darden.

Question. They never said, then, that you were intimate with some white woman up there?

Answer. No, sir; they didn't say that, nohow. They said some chat I had talked about that; they didn't say I had done anything, but they said that it was some talk that I had talked about them; they never said anything like that; but none of that wasn't so, because they all knowed there, black and white, that I had a wife and I never went out, and nobody can say they ever knew me to leave my house. I don't so much as talk blackguard about black women, much less white women.

Question. That is what they told you they whipped you about?

Answer. Yes, sir.

Question. Now, if they wanted to get rid of you, to get you off of that place, they had already got rid of you, for you had quit there before they whipped you?

Answer. Yes, sir.

Question. Then that could not have been the reason.

Answer. I know I had quit there before they whipped me?

Question. They could not have whipped you, then, to make you quit, for you had already quit?

Answer. No; I didn't say that they whipped me about that, but I believe they only whipped me about me and that man's falling out. I heard them say he said he allowed to have revenge out of me; and it looks very reasonable, too, that when they tried to put some poison in some meal when I left up there. I have got a witness for that; the man is right here. I give him some meal I left; and it was locked up in their charge, and they put arsenic in it, and if they hadn't put in too much they would have killed me and him too. That was in his charge; his and the other man that was on the place, and from that it looks reasonable that it couldn't have been anything else. I never had no white woman; and it looks like it might be concerning that, or they wouldn't have tried to kill me.

Question. They poisoned your meal?

Answer. Yes, sir; the man is in the other room; that is the witness for that—Lewis Perkins; he weighed the meal and sent for the doctor, and the doctor said that that was what was in it; and his wife liked to have died; and it liked to have killed all of us, and it would have done it if they hadn't put in too much.

Question. It was too big a dose?

Answer. Yes, sir.

Question. What doctor was that?

Answer. Doctor Parren.

Question. Where does he live?

Answer. I could not tell you exactly that. Lewis Perkins sent after him; he knows more than I do. He lives, though, I think, about three miles from his house, sort of north. I think not more than three miles, though.

COLUMBUS, MISSISSIPPI, *November* 14, 1871.

EDMUND GRAY (colored) sworn and examined.

By the CHAIRMAN:

Question. Where do you live?

Answer. I live seven miles north, or northeast of here, on the military road.

Question. Were you present at the time James Hicks, the witness just examined, was whipped?

Answer. I was there, sir; I was on the premises I had rented; he was living with me.

Question. Tell the committee about how many men were there.

Answer. Well, I thought there was a hundred and fifty, but I was scared that night mighty bad. I had been asleep; I tried to count them, but I don't know as I counted them all straight.

Question. Were they all disguised?

Answer. Every one except the one that whipped Jim Hicks. He only had a sheet or something around him.

Question. Did they come mounted?

Answer. They had horses all dressed. They had on dough-faces, and something on top of their caps like mules' ears, and the horses all dressed in sheets. They took my yard fence down and set it all in the road, and when I went out they were all around my house at every window and door, and some one was saying, "God damn the door, cut it down." At that time I went up and they said, "Come out here." In my scare I went out, and they told me to go back and make up a light. I went back and several of them put in their heads and said who was I, and I said, "Edmund Gray." He said, "I don't want you, I want Jim Hicks." I says, "He is in the other room." He says, "Make a light and go there," and I went, and when I got there Jim had gone out and up in the loft, and they called him and he wouldn't come down, and the captain says, "God damn him, throw a dozen loads up there; and I says, "Gentlemen, please don't shoot here over my family, for my sake." They stopped and didn't shoot, and they said I should take a light and go up there, and I took a light and went up there, and I thought to screen Jim Hicks and made out I didn't see him. They said, "You have two good eyes, if you don't see him we will put you in his shoes." Then I said, "Jim, come down." He didn't come down, but slipped down to another room, and they heard him. They were about to cut down the corner of the house with axes, and then I assisted him to come down to keep them from cutting the house. They told me to come out and my little son and another old man I had there, and they told me to lock my door, to lock my wife up. I told them no, my family was not going out of the house at all. They put us under arrest, and had guns or pistols over us while they whipped Jim. I heard them ask Jim Hicks, didn't he, since he left Caledonia, raise some talk about some women. Jim says, "Gentlemen, I didn't do it; I didn't say it," and another one came up and stopped him, and said, "Let me whip him; you do not know how to whip him;" and he turned him over and began to pin him very tight; but Jim never did own it, and one of them says, "You had better hold up that, Lewis," and the school-teacher was over there and would hear it, and they would get out of the way, and they had better turn him loose. They came to me then and said, "We have not drank any water in thirty days. We come all the way from old Virginny, and want some water. We want two buckets." I went and brought them two or three buckets of water. They told me they had just risen from the dead, and one of them says, "Now, do you know any of us?" I says, "No, gentlemen, I don't know none of you." They asked me that question three or four times. I told them all the time I didn't know any of them. That is about all I know. Last Thursday—last gone Thursday, a week ago—this man Darden, which whipped Jim, has been here to Columbus; he stopped there where Jim was, with a jug of whisky, begging Jim to come up to Caledonia and make up this fuss. I happened to be in the corner of the fence and heard them talking, and Jim promised to go, but I said to Jim, "If you go, I will report you to Major Whitfield, and you shan't go," and he hasn't been there. That is about all I know about it.

Question. At what time was this?

Answer. Well, it was along in February, I believe; I have almost forgotten; I was not quite ready to plant; it was along the last of February, I think.

Question. Did you know any of the men?

Answer. I didn't know any of them at all; they were all uniformed, so that I did not know them, only Jim's wife and Jim. After they were done whipping him, and were standing in the road talking, he told me, "I knew the man that whipped me, and it was Darden and another man, too," and his wife says she would swear to them two men; that she saw them and knew them well. Well, that is all I know. I didn't know any of them. I was a stranger there, and they were strangers to me.

By Mr. BLAIR:

Question. You say that this man Darden you saw a week ago last Thursday?

Answer. Last Thursday, a week ago, he was talking to Jim Hicks.

Question. Where did you see him?

Answer. Between my house and Jim Hicks's, in the lane.

Question. What did he say?

Answer. He says, "Jim, they all have lied on me about that; I never made that fuss." Jim Hicks told him he was down on him. He says, "Jim, I did not make it. If you will come up there, the boys want to see you badly, and we will make the thing all right, and you be certain to come," and Jim partly promised to go, and I stopped then in the corner of the fence and waited until they were done talking, and he gave his jug of whisky to him and told him to drink, and he wanted him to be certain to come next Saturday evening. I told Jim not to go, and if he did go up to Caledonia to see Mr. Darden about this thing I would report him to Major Whitfield.

Question. What would you do that for?

Answer. I didn't think it was right for him to make it up.

Question. What had Major Whitfield to do about it?

Answer. I don't know. I thought he was justice of the peace, and could keep Jim Hicks from going there.

Question. You thought he had authority to keep Hicks from going there?

Answer. Yes, sir; I thought so. I didn't think it was right if they whipped him; going in a man's yard, and in this way. I would not do it for no man; not for my daddy, after he came in my yard and whipped me, and then go to and make it up, because I would think he would do me more harm, or something.

Question. You were for getting Major Whitfield to prevent him from going up?

Answer. Yes, sir; I told him I would report him to Major Whitfield.

Question. Has Major Whitfield any more control over the colored people than anybody else?

Answer. No, sir; he is only justice of the peace here, and no more than anybody else.

Question. What was your idea in reporting it to him?

Answer. I thought he was justice of the peace.

Question. Did you suppose he had a right to prevent Jim from going up to that part of the county, or any other?

Answer. Yes, sir; I thought maybe he would.

Question. You thought maybe he would have the power, did you?

Answer. Yes, sir.

COLUMBUS, MISSISSIPPI, *November* 14, 1871.

ELYMAS NELSON (colored) sworn and examined.

By the CHAIRMAN:

Question. What is your name?

Answer. 'Lymas Nelson.

Question. Where do you live?

Answer. On Dr. James Whitfield's plantation, the other side of Artesia, about three miles, as near as I can get at it.

Question. Were you present at a political meeting at Artesia at the time a white man named Lee was killed?

Answer. Yes, sir; I was there.

Question. Did you notice this white man before he was shot, and see what he was doing?

Answer. I looked at him, sir.

Question. Did you see him speak to the speaker on the stand?

Answer. Yes, sir.

Question. What did he say to him?

Answer. He asked Mr. Bliss, was he a white man or a nigger. Mr. Bliss didn't say anything to him; he kept on speaking to the people—the multitude.

Question. What happened then?

Answer. He was standing with his hand in his pocket—in his side-pocket—so, [illustrating;] he had his left hand on his chin, rubbing it up and down, so, [illustrating;] and he asked Mr. Bliss that; and some colored people, I don't know who they were, come round him and said, "This man was going to have a fuss here, and they didn't want no cross-questioning," and Levi Jones, or Bean, came to him and told him he desired peace, and this white man said he was not going to say any more; and as near as I could get at it, about a minute after he spoke that, Mr. Bliss was speaking, and so many people were round, I could just discern the fire from a pistol over some one's shoulders.

Question. Was that the first shot that was fired?

Answer. Yes, sir; the first shot.

Question. And you saw a pistol?

Answer. Yes, sir; I saw the fire from the pistol. I said it was a pistol because there was so many people around me I couldn't see nothing else but a pistol; and some person asked, "Who was that shot?" and I looked and saw the white man running, and the people running after him.

Question. When you speak of the white man, do you mean this man Lee, who was afterward killed?

Answer. Yes, sir.

Question. Was the pistol fired from the place where he stood?

Answer. Yes, sir; right from the place where he stood.

Question. Did you see the pistol distinctly?

Answer. I didn't see the pistol; I saw him break and run; I saw the fire from it.

Question. You saw the fire from the pistol?

Answer. Yes, sir.

Question. And saw him break and run?

Answer. Yes, sir; immediately after the fire he broke and run.

By Mr. BLAIR:

Question. You say you saw the fire from the pistol over some one's shoulders?

Answer. Yes, sir.

Question. Whose shoulders?

Answer. I don't know; there was so many people there, I didn't know them.

Question. On which side of him were you standing?

Answer. I was standing on the east side of him, between him and Major Lewis's horse; his horse was hitched to a Jersey wagon; I was standing on the west side of the horse, and the man was between the men and the ditch on the other side of me, and I was standing between them and the horse and the speakers and the wagon.

Question. You were standing between the speaker and that man?

Answer. Yes, sir; Mr. Lee.

Question. Did Mr. Lee stand nearer to the stores than you did?

Answer. Yes, sir.

Question. Did you see anybody speak to Lee after he had interrupted the speaker?

Answer. I saw—I could not say how many there were, but there was about a dozen; they came up around him, and some of them, I don't know who it was, said, "This man is going to do some damage here," and "If you don't stop him and take him up, he will do some damage;" and Levi Jones told them to have peace, and spoke to the people, and that man was standing close by; this man was standing close by him, and this man spoke and said he was not going to say no more, and just had his hands so, [illustrating,] and fired off right in the midst of them. I couldn't see nothing; it was dusk anyhow, and I couldn't see nothing but the smoke from the pistol; and immediately after he fired he broke and run.

Question. You did not see him fire?

Answer. No, sir; I didn't see him fire, but from the report of the pistol. I saw him run immediately as he fired. The people run at it, and some one said, "Who is that shot?" and them standing beside him said it was this white man; and there was but one white man at the time, and that was him, right in the midst. I saw the fire coming right from where he was standing. There was so many people around him I could not see him hardly, after he spoke to Mr. Bliss; I only could see his head.

Question. How far were you from him?

Answer. I couldn't exactly say how far I was; as near as I can get at it, I think I was between seven and eight steps from him.

Question. Did you hear what he said when he said he would not talk any more?

Answer. Yes, sir; I was looking right at him, as straight as I am looking at you.

Question. You heard him speak to Mr. Bliss?

Answer. Yes, sir.

Question. You never saw the pistol?

Answer. No, sir; I didn't see the pistol.

Question. Did anybody pursue him?

Answer. In what way?

Question. You say he ran?

Answer. Yes, sir; he run.

Question. Did anybody run after him?

Answer. Yes, sir; a whole parcel of people run after him; all of them were running and squandering about. It scared me so I staid right at the horse; I was afraid somebody would shoot me.

Question. Did you see who killed him?

Answer. No, sir.

Question. Somebody killed him?

Answer. Yes, sir; somebody was compelled to kill him, if he was killed; but I don't know who killed him.

Question. You could not see?

Answer. No, sir.

Question. You could not see anything after you heard that pistol fired?

Answer. I could not say who killed him; I heard the pistol, and he run first, and they run after him. I heard some say "Ketch him!" I don't know who they were.

Question. Did you hear any gun shot?

Answer. Yes, sir; I heard guns shot.

Question. Did you hear who shot the guns?

Answer. No, sir.

Question. You didn't see anything go off except the pistol?

Answer. No, sir; I didn't see a pistol, but only the fire from it.

Question. Did you see the fire from the guns?

Answer. No, sir; there was so many people between me and the guns, I couldn't see.

Question. Were there a good many between you and the pistol too.

Answer. Yes, sir; but not near as many between me and the pistol when it fired as there was between me and the guns when that man run; and some were on horses, and some on foot, and saying, "Ketch him."

Question. Did they follow him on horses?

Answer. Yes, sir; the horses closed up on him; he was not far from the store. I couldn't say exactly how far, but he was aiming to get to the store from the way he run, and they hallooed, "Ketch him," and I heard them shoot. I couldn't say who fired; there were so many between me and the man I couldn't see. There was lots of people between me and him had guns.

Question. What did Mr. Lewis say?

Answer. He told the people to go home and be quiet, and not to have no disturbance.

Question. When did he say that?

Answer. That was after this man shot. Mr. Bliss was speaking before he shot, and he was speaking. He told the people they had had a fine time to-day. I couldn't say all he said, but he said, "Go home and be quiet, and don't disturb no person—nobody you come by; democrat or what not—but let every man be persuaded in his own opinion." That is what Mr. Bliss said. He is the gentleman that was speaking when Mr. Lee came up and spoke to him.

Question. What else?

Answer. Sir, I don't know nothing else.

Question. Did he stop speaking when the man fired his pistol?

Answer. Yes, sir; he stopped then.

Question. Then you did not hear anything but "Ketch him?"

Answer. I didn't hear anything else. After Mr. Lewis spoke he said, "Go home, people, and be quiet."

Question. When did he say that?

Answer. That was after the people had shot.

Question. After the people had shot?

Answer. Yes, sir.

Question. After they killed Mr. Lee?

Answer. That was after Mr. Lee was shot. He told Mr. Bliss what to say to the people after he had set down—to advise them to go home in peace. That was before Mr. Lee was shot; and after Mr. Lee was shot, again he told Mr. Bliss to tell them to go home and be quiet; and they had no more speaking after that, and all left there immediately after that.

Question. You did not leave until after they had shot Lee?

Answer. No, sir; I didn't.

Question. Did you go anywhere near where Lee was shot?

Answer. No, sir.

Question. Did you know any men that ran after him?

Answer. No, sir; I did not recognize a single man.

Question. You did not recognize any of those on horseback, closing up on him?

Answer. No, sir; I didn't know any man on horseback; I didn't know many people then. I have not been in the county long, and it was a crowd, and there were people from Oktibbeha County, and all about there; and I didn't know the people from them beats. I only knew people about Artesia, and there was so many around. I didn't know them, to know any one certainly, except Levi Jones.

Question. You knew Levi Jones?

Answer. Yes, sir.

Question. Levi Jones was standing close by Lee?

Answer. Yes, sir; he was sitting on his horse, nearly in front of Major Lewis's horse and buggy, and I was standing between his horse and Mr. Lewis, and he was sitting on the horse.

Question. Did Levi run after this man?

Answer. No, sir; he didn't. He didn't run after him.

Question. You do not know a single man that went after him?

Answer. I couldn't say that, for the men were after him; but I don't know them.

Question. I ask if you knew any of those that were after him?

Answer. No, sir; I didn't.

Question. Did you see their guns fired?

Answer. I saw some men throw their guns on their shoulder. I didn't see them shoot them off, but I heard them. I didn't know who they were.

Question. How many of them fired?

Answer. I don't know how many there were.

Question. How many reports did you hear?

Answer. They shot pretty much at once. I couldn't tell, sir. I couldn't say how many there were.

Question. Were there four?

Answer. I don't know how many there were.

Question. Were there five?

Answer. I couldn't say how many there was, sir.

Question. Were there two?

Answer. I couldn't say. I don't know how many there was. I might say one thing, and be wrong.

Question. Several persons were standing between you and where the pistol was discharged?

Answer. Yes, sir; a good many of them.

Question. How many?

Answer. I couldn't say, sir.

Question. As many as a dozen?

Answer. Yes, sir; I reckon more'n that. I know there was, because most of them that was between me and that man were on foot.

Question. Were they packed up close together?

Answer. Yes, sir; standing close together.

Question. You could not see Mr. Lee at all?

Answer. I saw Mr. Lee before he shot, and when he spoke to Mr. Bliss; and after he spoke to Mr. Bliss and asked, "Was he a white man or a nigger?" the people closed up around him, and I couldn't see nothing more but his head, and when I saw him, when he spoke, he had his hand so, [illustrating,] and Levi said—and there is more people besides him said—Levi spoke to the people and said he didn't want no fuss. They were walking up around him and saying, "This man is here for a fuss, and if we don't take him up he will do some damage." I don't know who they were, but they were saying, "This man is going to do some damage;" and immediately Levi said he didn't want no fuss here; "People, we want quietness and peace." This gentleman, Mr. Lee, said, "I won't say no more," and he had his hand so, [illustrating.] I recollect the time I put my eyes on Mr. Bliss. He was speaking, and I saw the smoke of the pistol from where he stood.

Question. At the same time?

Answer. Yes, sir; in a few minutes after he spoke and said he wasn't going to have any more to say.

Question. Than you looked at Mr. Bliss?

Answer. Yes, sir; I looked up and back at the fire from the pistol.

Question. And you looked at Mr. Bliss at that same time?

Answer. Yes, sir; I looked up at that time and back at the fire from the pistol, and I couldn't see nothing else of the pistol—nothing else; and the people run round, and some one said, "What is the matter?" And they said, "This white man has shot;" and they hallooed, "Ketch him," and they run after him; and I didn't know they were doing anything but ketching him until I heard the reports of the guns.

Question. How could you see the fire of the pistol and Mr. Bliss at the same time?

Answer. I didn't see him and Mr. Bliss at the same time. I said I looked up at Mr. Bliss, and when I took my eyes off of Mr. Bliss, when he spoke, I looked back at the fire from the pistol. I didn't see the pistol, but saw the fire from it, and heard the report.

Question. Which direction did the fire from the pistol take?

Answer. It took the direction right toward Mr. Bliss. Mr. Bliss was standing eastward, and he stood the right side of him, and he fired, and the report of it was right toward him, as he was standing in that direction.

Question. Right toward Mr. Bliss?

Answer. Yes, sir.

By the CHAIRMAN:

Question. Stand up and show us yourself, just in the position of Mr. Lee at the time that he replied to Mr. Bliss and said that he would not say any more. Show how his two hands were at that time.

Answer. It was just so, [illustrating;] and he said, "I won't say no more."

Question. His left hand upon his chin and his right hand under the lapel of his coat?

Answer. Yes, sir; just so, [illustrating.]

COLUMBUS, MISSISSIPPI, *November* 14, 1871.

LEWIS PERKINS (colored) sworn and examined.

By the CHAIRMAN:

Question. What is your name?

Answer. My registered paper is Lewis Perkins; my father's title is Lewis Wills.

Question. Where do you live, Mr. Perkins?

Answer. I live seven and a quarter miles north from here, on the military road.

Question. State if a man by the name of Mr. Farmer, a school-teacher, boarded with you at the time he was teaching school.

Answer. Yes, sir.

Question. What, if anything, do you know about his being driven away and his school broken up?

Answer. Well, sir, I was taken very suddenly by, as well as I could state the amount, of forty men arriving to my house, asking at the door, "Where is that damned school-teacher?" My wife reported as being a little scared—I don't know—and in immediately she spoke to them, and says she, "Come out, Mr. Farmer, and answer for yourself." He walked to the door. "How are you, gentlemen?" And says he, "I understand, sir, you are here teaching niggers and boarding with a nigger." Says he, "I am boarding with old man Lewis Perkins, which, you all know, is a nice, quiet old gentleman." Says he, "I haven't been long in this country; I don't know old man Perkins; but," says he, "are you from Chicago, sir?" Well, I can't say, but I think he said, "I am from New York, sir." Says he, "All ways you are boarding with a nigger; why don't you board with your own color?" "Gentlemen," says he, "I endeavored to do so, and I had not the opportunity to do so." Says he, "How can you prove that?" Says he, "I can go over to Mr. Whiteside's"—about a half a mile from that place—"I went there and tried to take board with them." After that his reply was, says he, "Why is the reason that they didn't board you?" Says he, "Gentlemen, I don't know." "Who authorized you to come here to teach niggers?" Says he, "Mr. Bishop and Mr. Simons and other authorities." "Well, Mr. Bishop"—that was remarked to my wife—"he is as black inside as that old nigger woman is outside."

Question. Did they say that to him?

Answer. Yes, sir. "Mr. Eggerson is all about."

Question. You mean Mr. Eggleston?

Answer. Yes, sir.

Question. He is the assessor here?

Answer. Yes, sir; I don't know what he is; he is not far off. He says, "He is all about;" that is to say, he is without principle; and Mr. Bishop was as black as my wife inside.

Question. You mean he said that Mr. Bishop was as black inside as your wife outside?

Answer. Yes, sir. Then the remarks was, "Come here, captain." Two gentlemen rode around the house, and one says, "We'll hang him, anyhow." "No," he says; "lieutenant, come here." They rode around the house, and says he, "Sir, I give you ten days to get away from here, and if you don't be away from here in ten days I wouldn't give you anything for your head nor body." Well, gentlemen, I think, as far as the United States oath is, I have delivered all I know with truth.

Question. What hour in the night was this?

Answer. As near as I can make a calculation, I think it was about one.

Question. You think there were about forty men in the crowd?

Answer. O, there was forty men, sir.

Question. Did they have any disguises on?

Answer. The whole was covered, excepting one old colored man, that my wife concluded was a servant of my old regular master—an acquaintance ever since she was a child—forty years back; and he is dead; I believe the Almighty God took him out of the world as soon as he got through.

Question. There was one colored man along with the crowd?

Answer. Yes, sir.

Question. You knew him?

Answer. My wife knew him, and drew the facts; I didn't know. I knew that I had performed the school-house and a church, that I devoted to give the Methodist Episcopal Church the entitle under the southern discipline; and I knew there had been a large argument on both sides of this school-house, contrary to the true facts and the sweet moral power of the word. I just stepped out of the way.

Question. Did you notice whether they were armed?

Answer. If they were they were all under the uniform.

Question. You didn't see any pistols?

Answer. No, sir; I didn't.

Question. How long had Mr. Farmer been teaching the school there?

Answer. As well as I could barely make a guess, telling the truth—I am only guessing at this; I can't form it as an oath—I think about two months before he was troubled.

Question. Had he given satisfaction as a teacher?

Answer. O, beautiful; Columbus itself couldn't touch him; it was the beautifulest thing I ever see in that section of the country or anywhere else; Columbus couldn't touch him.

Question. Was he a well-behaved or good man?

Answer. I think as good as Almighty God ever made. I'll give you a striking reason for why. He only labored to teach his children, and whatever they did, if he found any of them turning a word, it would be dissatisfaction, and No. 1 and unity, and he whipped them. All got along harmless if nobody interfered with them; and he was making himself so careful that he wouldn't interfere with no contracts; nothing but the true course of learning the history of the Bible, which he was sent there for; that is as high as the proportion can reach it.

Question. Was he a northern school-teacher?

Answer. Yes, sir.

Question. Do you know that he had tried to procure board in white families? Had he told you so?

Answer. I can prove it to-morrow, in a minute.

Question. Did he quit teaching school after the Ku-Klux visited him?

Answer. He quit on those terms. My wife got so much satisfied that she wasn't willing for him to stay there under the circumstances; but Mr. Farmer—I went up to Mr. Presley's mill, and spoke to Mr. Presley for lumber to build him a house outside of the African tribe. When he came there, I says, "Mr. Farmer, I will not set down to table with you; not that I am not as good as you, but it's not the rule of our country. I'll give you a good meal till you get your house, and when you get your house up, I'll allow my wife to make your bed and cook your meals, but I can't set at meals with you." I can prove I went to Mr. Presley's for lumber; I can prove it by Mr. Simons out here; I spoke to him about it. He wrote to Mr. Simons to that effect—to get lumber, to get a house, to raise his principle on his own side, upright.

Question. Do you know of any other teachers of colored schools being whipped?

Answer. Well, I couldn't know of anything, gentlemen, that would give me satisfaction on an oath to talk about. I have heard of a great deal in the neighborhood; but then if you come to talk under oath what I heard of the facts I would repeat before you, I couldn't tell anything.

Question. This is the only case that has fallen within your personal knowledge?

Answer. Yes, sir.

Question. And you have heard of other cases of colored schools being broken up and teachers driven off?

Answer. Yes, sir.

Question! Do you know or have you heard of any colored people being whipped by the Ku-Klux?

Answer. There was a Mr. Hicks you had in before you, was whipped in a quarter of a mile or less distance of my place, which was a few minutes before Mr. Farmer was threatened to leave there.

Question. He was whipped the same night the Ku-Klux visited your place?

Answer. Yes, sir.

Question. Have you heard of any other people being whipped besides Mr. Hicks?

Answer. I have, of several, not far—that is, six, seven, or eight miles; but to give you any ground that you could persevere on—excepting I had taken it up before I was warned to be here—I couldn't do it to a satisfaction.

Question. How many cases of whipping have you heard of?

Answer. Well, sir, as near as I can get at it, in the neighborhood, I don't think, to tell you the honest truth, not less than ten or twelve.

Question. Did you understand that these men were whipped by disguised men—Ku-Klux?

Answer. As far as our neighborhood is, I have never heard of a whipping there yet but what it was disguised.

Question. By disguised men?

Answer. Yes, sir; six, seven, eight, from that to nine and ten square.

Question. Have you ever yourself seen disguised men ride around at night, except upon this one occasion to which you have testified?

Answer. I never have.

Question. Have you often heard of them?

Answer. I have often heard, because I have got old and I am always at home at night, and I don't have the opportunity, but I have a fellow-servant which lived about thirty year with me—they went to his house this season—by the name of Collery, formerly of Eskridge, which he attacked next day; they are gone and in the woods now. He says, "Master Sam, you were with that party last night;" he said, "Master Sam, is that the way you aim to make an honest boy of me?" But they are there now taking out his crop, but they don't know where he is.

Question. Did they run him off?

Answer. Yes, sir; they are gone.

COLUMBUS, MISSISSIPPI, *November* 14, 1871.

REUBEN O. REYNOLDS sworn and examined.

The CHAIRMAN. As this witness has been called at the instance of the minority, General Blair will please conduct his examination.

By Mr. BLAIR:

Question. Colonel, will you give your residence?

Answer. Aberdeen, Mississippi.

Question. What is your profession?

Answer. I am a lawyer by profession.

Question. How long have you resided in Monroe County?

Answer. About thirty-five years.

Question. Have there been any disturbances of the peace in your county within the last year or two?

Answer. Yes, sir.

Question. Of what character are they?

Answer. Well, sir, we have such as occur in any country. We have had men killed. We have had no riots, I believe, or anything of the sort. I speak, of course, not of my personal knowledge, but what I know from others.

Question. We have had a gentleman who testified pretty extensively in regard to your county—Mr. Huggins. Do you know him?

Answer. I do, sir.

Question. Mr. A. P. Huggins?

Answer. Yes, sir; I know him; Colonel A. P. Huggins.

Question. He says there has been great discontent and many disturbances growing out of the question of the establishment of free schools.

Answer. I know something in reference to it. I know that in 1871, according to my recollection, the free-school system was first inaugurated in the State of Mississippi, and Mr. Huggins made an application to the board of supervisors, under an un-itemized account of some $60,000, for a tax to be assessed and levied and collected. He made extravagant expenditures for school-buildings, and his contracts for school-houses were regarded by the people as extravagant, and the pay which he allowed to the teachers was extravagant. That is what produced dissension and trouble in the county. I will state in reference to that that I know the sentiments of the white people on that subject, and that the free-school system is a popular system in the State of Mississippi; that there is no opposition to it from the mass of the citizens in my county.

Question. Mr. Huggins states that he proposed to join the Baptist church up there, and offered himself as a member, upon a letter from the church in the North, and he was refused because he had been in the Federal Army. Do you know anything of that?

Answer. All I know in reference to that is, I heard it stated that when Mr. Huggins made application to the church some member of it, or some one who had been a member of the church, objected, on the ground that it might have been him who shot his finger off in the war; but it was regarded as a joke there. I heard it laughed about. I heard this man taunted on the streets with it. I know that in the churches in my town no man would be proscribed merely because he had been in the Federal Army. I know, sir, that in the very church in which this is reported to have occurred—the Baptist church—a Mr. Colby—his name is, if I mistake not, F. Colby—who was a citizen of Chicago during the war, and a Union man, and who, as far as I ever heard him say, lent all his influence and his aid to the Federal cause, has been received as a member in it, with his entire family. I know another thing, sir, that Mr. Woodmansee, who was a Federal officer—that Mr. Woodmansee's wife was received as a member in the Presbyterian church.

Question. Do you believe the statement?

Answer. I do not.

Question. Do you believe that anybody in Aberdeen would believe such a statement?

Answer. I do not.

Question. Do you recollect anything in reference to an affair in regard to old Sanders Flint, and the killing of his two sons, and, previous to that, the affair out of which it grew?

Answer. I remember to have heard that Brown Parke and his sons had a fight with Sanders Flint and his sons, about a division of the crop; that old man Parke, the father, was severely bruised and the sons stabbed. I think the old man was beaten and the old man's son was stabbed. I heard that Flint—Sanders Flint—and his sons, after this occurrence, proposed to the negroes in the neighborhood to gather together and divide out the crops, and take possession of them and drive out the white people. I heard that they were arrested and bound over—no; they were committed to jail in default of bail—and that Sanders Flint and his two sons were taken out of jail, and two of them reported as killed, and Sanders Flint as having made his escape. I know, further, that the men that Sanders Flint says he identified were tried by as impartial a jury, I think, as could be summoned in my county. They were not the wealthiest men in it, but they were certainly honorable men, as far as I know them personally. They were acquitted. I recollect to have heard a portion of the trial, but not a great deal of it.

Answer. Did Flint identify any of the parties on the trial?

Question. My recollection on that is this: Flint was asked the question by the attorney for the prosecution who were the parties. After stating what had occurred, he was asked who were the parties engaged in it, and he designated every single one of the defendants. On cross-examination he was asked the question how he identified Bluford Westbrook. He stated that he identified him by his voice. He was then asked the question how long he had known Westbrook or how often he had seen him. He stated several times. I do not remember now how often, but not more than half a dozen. He was asked how often he had talked with him, and my recollection is that he stated once or twice, and that was the only means of identification. I recollect that instance well, because I recollect that, although he identified the man, yet the reasons for the identification were insufficient or the grounds upon which he based his identification were insufficient. The testimony was not sufficient to authorize the conviction of a single man. I know, furthermore, in reference to this case, that that outrage created as much horror and disgust among the white men of the county as it did amongst the blacks, and there was a strong disposition to ferret out the offenders, whoever they might be. Counsel were willing to prosecute in the case, if they could have been fee-paid. They did not desire to volunteer.

Question. Mr. Huggins, after giving an account of this affair, says that the men were all dismissed; that they did not find them guilty of anything at all, and then the republicans and all the rest were asked to give something to pay the lawyer's fee for defending them?

Answer. That statement may be true, sir. I have no knowledge of it. It was so inconsistent with anything that could have possibly occurred in the matter that I do not think it at all probable.

Question. "On the 1st of February a party of armed men went about five miles north of Aberdeen, and took out Alfred Whitfield, a colored man, and whipped him until he would say that he would vote the democratic ticket, but I do not know how many lashes they gave him." Do you recollect anything about that?

Answer. I know nothing of it. I never heard of Alfred Whitfield's whipping. Does that state that it occurred on the 1st of February, 1871?

Mr. BLAIR. Yes, sir.

The WITNESS. I was thinking whether I might not have perhaps been absent from the county at that time. I was in the county at that time, and I never heard of it.

Question. "On the 3d of February an old freedman, whose name I do not now remember, was beaten by the same party, and in about the same way, but he was not made to promise to vote the democratic ticket. Question. Where does he live? Answer. He lives near the Lee County line, in the northern part of the county."

Answer. I never heard of it. Of course I do not know anything in reference to it. I had a conversation with General Gholson in reference to Alfred Whitfield. I think I heard General Gholson say in reference to that case that he knew Alfred Whitfield, and perhaps some one came to his house at night and demanded admittance, and because he refused it they struck him a blow or so; but on the 1st of February, 1871, there was no prospect for an election, as I understood it, and as it was understood by the people of the State at the time. During the year 1871 there was no law passed by our legislature which authorized an election. The election law was not passed until certainly as late as May, and, I believe, in June, 1871.

Question. There was no occasion then to go around electioneering in that way or any other?

Answer. No, sir; and it was not the general expectation of the people in the State that an election would be ordered in 1871. There was a contest between the governor and the legislature on that subject; the governor was in favor of the election and a majority of the legislature opposed to it.

Question. Did you hear anything about the murder or the taking out of a man named Jack Dupree, the president of one of the republican clubs in the county, near Ross's mill?

Answer. Yes, sir.

Question. State what you know about that.

Answer. I know that Jack Dupree is reported to have been taken from his home by a party of disguised men and that he has not since made his appearance in the county. I know, furthermore, as to one of the men who has been indicted—Mr. Robert Mays—in the Federal court, for the murder of Jack Dupree. On the night he was killed, two negroes, one named Robert Odoneal and Lock—I do not remember his first name—came to Mays and told him this band of disguised men were there, and Mays got up and ordered his horse, and put on his pistol, and, in company with these negroes, pursued them several miles—pursued them as long, I believe, as he or the negroes thought there was any necessity for it, and he has been indicted for the murder. I know William D. Walton, Plummer Willis, John Roberts, Dudley Hutchinson, William Butler, Barbour Quarles, who were also jointly indicted, were at the residence of William D. Walton at the time the party of disguised men passed there, at a social gathering; that the fact can be and will be testified to by both respectable white and colored citizens of the county.

Question. You say the body of this man Dupree has not been found?

Answer. That is my information, and I have it from Mr. James W. Walker, who went with Mr. Huggins and the negro, Joe Davis—Joe Davis telling Colonel Huggins, as I learned, that he could point out the place where Dupree could be found. They took this justice of the peace along to hold an inquest over the body when it was found, and the justice of the peace telegraphed me at Oxford that they had gone with Joe Davis, and made the search and could not find his body.

Question. Joe Davis testified before this committee that he was present when this man was killed; that he was cut open and disemboweled and his body thrown into McKinley's Creek. Will you state if there was any testimony taken in the courts at Oxford going to show that this testimony of Davis is unreliable in any way?

Answer. Except upon this principle: that where the witness swears falsely in one thing he is false in all. It is a legal maxim, "*Falsus in uno, falsus in omnibus.*" Joe Davis testified, in reference to the killing of Aleck Page, that he was there present with the Ku-Klux Klan. We proved, and can prove, in addition to the proof we made, by Ann Forsbee, a colored woman, that on the morning of the 29th of March—which was, if my recollection serves me right, the night he was killed—he went to the vicinity of Aberdeen, and went to a place known as Martin's Bluff. We proved that by her. We proved by Jerry Vance—or we will prove by Jerry Vance—that he left his house after dark for the purpose of going down to his wife. He has two wives—one at Crosby's and the other at the place of a man by the name of Noah. We proved by this wife who lives at Noah's that he remained with her during the night of the 29th of March. We will prove by Mr. Noah that he was there at 10 o'clock that night. We proved further, in reference to it, Joe Davis stated, when he was arrested, to Captain E. O. Sykes, in Aberdeen, that he did not know who was connected with the Ku-Klux organization in Monroe County—did not know a Ku-Klux, and had never seen one; that all he had been doing that summer was "Ku-Kluxing grass."

Question. What did he mean by that?

Answer. Working.

Question. Cutting grass?

Answer. Killing grass; that is what he means. That was his remark. We will prove further that after his return from Oxford, and after the arrest of these parties, he told this same woman, Ann Forsbee, that she would never see her husband, Mike Forsbee, again, unless he would testify, as he (Joe Davis) had done, that he was a Ku-Klux. "But," said Ann to him, "you know Mike is no Ku-Klux." Says Joe, "I am no Ku-Klux either, but I had to swear false in order to release myself."

By the CHAIRMAN:

Question. Who did he say that to?

Answer. To Ann Forsbee.

By Mr. BLAIR:

Question. That testimony, I presume, is in the case of Aleck Page?

Answer. Yes, sir.

Question. On the *habeas corpus*?

Answer. Yes, sir, on the trial of writ of *habeas corpus*, except the testimony of Noah and Vance. Jerry Vance is a colored man.

Question. Is that all the testimony in that case? [Submitting to the witness a pamphlet entitled "Full report of the great Ku-Klux trial in the United States district court at Oxford, Mississippi." See page 936.]

Answer. As far as I have examined, that is an accurate report, and I have examined it. That is an accurate report of everything that occurred on that trial, down to the argument of counsel. I see in the argument of counsel several things that did not occur.

Mr. BLAIR. I do not propose to use the argument of counsel in any way.

The WITNESS. That is the testimony as far as that is concerned.

Question. Have you read it over carefully?

Answer. I have examined it. I have examined the testimony and the arguments of the counsel with one exception.

Question. Were you employed in the case?

Answer. Yes, sir.

Question. As counsel for the defendants?

Answer. Yes, sir; I was retained for all of them, with the exception of one, I believe.

By the CHAIRMAN:

Question. Do you say this pamphlet is a report, word for word, of the testimony as delivered by the witnesses, or do you say that it is an abstract containing the substantial matters sworn to by them?

Answer. I state that it is word for word, taken down by a short-hand reporter employed by the Government of the United States.

Question. You are sure of that?

Answer. I would not state it was word for word; of course I could not do that; but it is as accurate as any report of a trial could be.

Question. How can it be a correct report when scarcely one question is contained in the pamphlet? Do you not know that the answer predicates largely on the nature of the question, and could not be accurately given without the question were taken with the answer?

Answer. I think that it could be.

Question. Are not the answer and question uniformly dovetailed in every examination of a witness?

Answer. They are to a certain extent.

Question. Then how can you say this is a report word for word when not a question is there?

Answer. I can ask you a question and you can answer it, and I can make a report of the question and answer that will represent it exactly.

Question. You will have to manufacture a new answer by making the question and answer in one statement.

Answer. Yes, sir.

Question. That is the work of the reporter?

Answer. Yes, sir.

Question. And not the work of the witness?

Answer. Yes, sir; but I will state in reference to that report that it is indorsed by the United States district attorney, Mr. Wells. It is regarded by him as accurate; that it has been submitted to him I have no doubt, and I know he regards it as accurate.

Question. Did you hear all the testimony contained in the pamphlet?

Answer. I did.

Question. Did you take notes yourself?

Answer. No, sir; I rarely ever take notes upon testimony; it is not my usual practice.

Question. Is your memory sufficiently retentive to carry the testimony without notes?

Answer. It is where I prepare the case myself; where I am drawn into a case, and for the first time brought in it during the investigation, and know nothing of it previously, I have to take notes to assist my memory.

Question. But you never can anticipate and know what the opposing witness will testify to?

Answer. But I can recollect that.

Question. Without taking notes?

Answer. I think so—the substance.

Question. So as to report it *verbatim*?

Answer. No, sir; I could not do that. If you understood me to say my memory was sufficient to make a report of the testimony I have misled you. I stated that I depended upon my memory; that I rarely took notes as an attorney upon a trial, simply from the fact that I rely upon my memory of the testimony to assist me during the progress of the trial.

Question. You say the report is not true so far the arguments are concerned?

Answer. I stated that I saw a statement in there that I do not recollect was made by the counsel at the time; I may have been absent from the court-room when it was delivered, but I imagine not.

Question. To whose argument have you reference?

Answer. To the argument of the district attorney.

Question. Colonel Wells?

Answer. Yes, sir.

Question. Are the other speeches accurately reported?

Answer. As far as I know, they are. There is no speech from myself reported, nor from Colonel Walter; I suppose they are our briefs alone that are published.

Question. These speeches were corrected by the lawyers before going into print, were they not?

Answer. Mine was not; I cannot answer for the others.

Question. Is this a *verbatim* report?

Answer. No, sir; my argument is reported; nothing else.

Question. Was that a written argument?

Answer. Yes, sir; I had my brief which I used on the trial of the cause; I handed it to the reporter, and that is an accurate report of that brief.

Question. There is no difficulty in copying a paper?

Answer. Of course. I will state an additional fact in reference to it that escaped me. When we filed the petition for the writ of *habeas corpus*, of course we did not know what would be the result of it. It was our purpose to have the testimony spread upon the record, and, if bail were refused, to apply for a writ of *certiorari*, and take the case to the supreme court, and that report should be the basis of that movement.

Question. Was not one motive for the publication of this testimony and arguments of counsel to raise a fund, by the sale of this pamphlet, to defray the expenses of the defense of these men?

Answer. No, sir; and as an evidence of that, one of the counsel, out of his own pocket, paid $200 for the publication; and more than that, this pamphlet was published at the joint instance of Colonel Dowd and the district attorney, Mr. Wells—published by the consent and approbation of all of us.

Question. Please explain, then, why a pamphlet of one hundred pages retails at one dollar and a half.

Answer. I cannot tell you, except this: I have information about it. I am the counsel who paid $200—advanced that much money—to publish it. I did not desire, as General Gholson did not desire, that it should be published. Colonel Dowd came to me and told me he had made a contract for the publication of it, and desired my check for $200, and I gave it to him, and I have not been reimbursed. I will state in reference to it, that if every pamphlet we have got were sold, it would not pay the expense of publication, and as to the fees of counsel in the case, if they were to publish a thousand, and sell them at a dollar and a half apiece, it would not pay my own fee in the case, much less that of the other counsel in it.

Question. What number of copies were struck off?

Answer. Three hundred were furnished to us.

Question. I am asking you how many in all were struck off?

Answer. I do not know.

Question. I suppose the ambition of counsel to have their arguments or briefs in print had something to do with the publication?

Answer. Yes, sir.

By Mr. BLAIR:

Question. Do you know anything in reference to the whipping given to Huggins?

Answer. I heard of it as an occurrence in the county. I recollect the time, or about the time, it occurred. I know the reason that was assigned for his being whipped.

Question. What was it?

Answer. It was because he was the superintendent of public education of the county, and was seeking to get from the board of supervisors the levy of a very onerous school-tax.

Question. He was at the house of a man named Ross?

Answer. George Ross.

Question. Have you ever heard Ross make a statement about it?

Answer. Yes, sir.

By the CHAIRMAN:

Question. Is Mr. Ross living?

Answer. Yes, sir.

By Mr. BLAIR:

Question. Huggins testified that he recognized two men, John T. Roberts and John Porter. Do you know either of them?

Answer. I know them both.

Question. He says: "I recognized Roberts; I knew the man pretty well, and would have recognized him if he had not been marked in any way; but he has a large red scar or mark on his neck, which runs up into his face—a red place, which, I suppose, he has had from birth." Do you recollect any such mark as that upon Roberts?

Answer. I have known Roberts from his infancy, and I have no recollection of any such mark. I do not say it is not there. Certainly if there had been anything about his face that made it very peculiar, I would have observed it. I have seen him repeatedly during the last few years. During the Oxford trials, I saw him there for a month, consecutively.

Question. Is there such a mark on him that could be seen at night, by moonlight?

Answer. I do not think there is, sir.

Question. You say you never observed such a mark as that?

Answer. No, sir; not by daylight.

Question. You have been familiar with him?

Answer. I have known him from his infancy.

Question. He does not state in his testimony how he recognized Porter. He said he knew him.

Answer. I will state, in reference to that, that Colonel Huggins told Dr. John L. Tindal, and Dr. Gus Evans, and Mr. George W. Pennington, recently elected by the republicans clerk of the circuit court, that he did not recognize any of the party who whipped him.

By the CHAIRMAN:

Question. How do you know he told that?

Answer. I have conversed with each of these gentlemen in reference to it.

Question. Why did they not go down and contradict him?

Answer. I cannot tell you.

By Mr. BLAIR:

Question. He states on page 276: "On the same night that I was interrupted, about five miles from me, on the other side of the Buttahatchie, and, of course, I suppose, by a different Klan, or a part of that Klan who could not get across the river, Mr. Farmer, teaching the colored school there, was whipped very severely, and they broke up his school entirely."

Answer. I have no information as to Mr. Farmer.

Question. "On the 11th of March—that was Saturday night—Aleck Stewart was whipped in the same neighborhood. *Question.* In the neighborhood where you were whipped?—*Answer.* Yes, sir." Do you know anything of that?

Answer. I never heard of it.

Question. His evidence was this: "He had sued a white man the fall before. I have seen him and heard his testimony before the court. He states that they told him that night that it was because he had sued Mr. Macniece." Do you know Macniece?

Answer. Yes, sir; I know two Macnieces east of the river.

Question. While whipping this man Stewart, he says they were fired upon by a club of black men, and that one of the men was killed, and another wounded in the hand, and another in the heel.

Answer. I heard of that. I heard that they charged that Mr. Beckett, who had died very suddenly across the river, was killed in a rencounter of that sort; that Mr. Ford was shot in the hand, and Mr. Plummer Willis in the heel. I investigated the circumstances of each of these occurrences. Beckett died suddenly from heart disease, as his father and his sister and his brother and Dr. Dudley Hutchinson will testify; Mr. Ford was shot accidentally in the hand by his own pistol, in the presence of Dr. Dowdell and several others; and Plummer was lame from wearing a new boot that had rubbed his heel.

Question. And this whole report grows out of that, does it?

Answer. Yes, sir. I heard that report at Oxford, that they charged that they had a rencounter, and that a man had been killed and another man wounded; that Mr. Ford's hand had been shot, and that Plummer Willis had been shot in the heel. I investigated it with the result I tell you.

Question. Was it said that Beckett had been shot?

Answer. Yes, sir. He died suddenly. It was believed that he was killed by them.

Question. Was it stated that it was at the time of whipping Stewart?

Answer. Yes, sir; at the time of whipping some one. I believe it was Stewart. That is my recollection.

Question. What did you hear of the whipping of Stewart?

Answer. I never heard that any such man was whipped at all.

Question. Joe Davis testified before us that Simon Dunham was whipped for suing Macnice?

Answer. I knew nothing of that. Of course I do not know what Joe Davis testified before this committee.

Question. That was Joe Davis's testimony before the committee. He testified to the whipping of Dunham, and alleged as the cause of it that he had sued Macnice. Do you know Macnice?

Answer. I know two men by the name of Macnice on the east side of the river.

Question. Are either of them men of substance?

Answer. One of them is; the other is not.

Question. Which one?

Answer. The one that lives in this neighborhood. The one that lives in the immediate neighborhood of Stewart, and where Dunham lives, I do not suppose he has anything on earth. I think he is almost the object of charity. He was arrested, I know, and carried to Oxford, and his expenses, and the expenses of his witnesses, had to be defrayed by the Government. The other man is a man of substance; a man of some means.

Question. Does he live in the same neighborhood?

Answer. He lives north of there.

Question. How far?

Answer. Eight miles.

Question. He was not the man who was carried to Oxford?

Answer. The man of means was not carried to Oxford.

Question. And the accusation then was not against him?

Answer. No, sir; against the other. A judgment against the one I suppose that has reference to would be entirely worthless.

Question. You do not suppose anybody would bring suit against him?

Answer. No, sir.

Question. You do not suppose he had any negroes in his employ?

Answer. I presume not, sir.

Question. Do you know anything of a man named Alfred Skinner, a freedman, attacked by a band of disguised men?

Answer. I never heard of any such occurrence in the county. I do not know Alfred Skinner.

Question. He says, (page 278:) "He defended himself in his house, and they filled his house with shot." Have you any recollection of any such occurrence?

Answer. No, sir.

Question. He says, "In the same neighborhood Joe Adkins was taken out by the same band. He was told that he was a radical, and made to hug a sapling. He left the neighborhood, as also did Alfred Skinner, and came to Aberdeen." Did you ever hear of any such man as that being whipped?

Answer. I have not, sir.

Question. "On the same night that Aleck Stewart was whipped, they also whipped a colored man who had been in the Federal Army during the war. He had left the place he was living on without the consent of the planter, and hired himself out at another place. He was whipped."

Answer. I heard of the whipping of Simon Dunham, and I presume that has reference to him. I know Simon. He may have been in the Federal Army, but such is not my recollection, nor is it my opinion. My recollection is that none of the colored men on the eastern side of the river were ever in the Federal Army. It was only the colored men on the western side of the river, and Simon Dunham lived on the eastern side of the river, where there never were any Federal troops, and unless he was enlisted after the close of the war he was not in the Federal Army, and I believe there were no enlistments made after the close of the war.

Question. Did you understand what he was whipped for, if whipped at all?

Answer. I did not.

Question. In the case of this man Aleck Page, you know nothing more than appears in this published pamphlet of testimony?

Answer. No, sir; I know nothing more than appears there in reference to it. I know this, however: I saw it stated in the testimony of some of the witnesses before this committee, as published in the papers, that Aleck Page was killed because he was a republican. I have known him ever since he came to Monroe County, and I have heard him boast repeatedly of having voted the democratic ticket. I saw it stated also that he was killed because he was a radical. That is not the reason of it. He was killed, as it was understood at the time, for an insult which he had offered to Mrs. Andrew Pope.

Question. I find in Huggins's testimony this statement, (page 278:) "Joe Davis swears that he was the first man to take hold of him and pulled him out from under the bed; that he was with him when he was killed?"

Answer. Yes, sir.

Question. Is that Joe Davis's testimony as given before the court at Oxford?

Answer. Let me recollect; no, sir. It differs in this respect: I do not think that at Oxford he stated that he pulled him from under the bed. I think further, in reference to that, that he did not state at Oxford that he killed him.

Question. Did he say he was present when he was killed?

Answer. No; he stated at Oxford that he was not present when he was killed. He came up when he was killed; they brought him up to assist in burying him.

Question. Huggins swears that "he was a republican, and that was all. He lived in the hills, rather in the poorer section of the county." He alleges that he was killed because he was a republican.

Answer. Well, sir, I can only state, because I do not know the reason why he was killed—I can only state what was reported at that time, and what was generally understood as the cause of his being killed, and that was, as I have previously stated, the insult to Mrs. Andrew Pope.

Question. Is there any foundation for the statement that he was a republican?

Answer. What he may have been at the time he was killed I do not know. Previous to that time, in the election which was held in in Mississippi 1869, he certainly voted the democratic ticket.

Question. And there was no election subsequently?

Answer. No election subsequent to that, nor any election ordered at the time he was killed; nor was there any law for an election in the State of Mississippi during 1871.

By the CHAIRMAN:

Question. Did you hear him say he had voted the democratic ticket in 1869?

Answer. Yes, sir.

Question. You say he told you so?

Answer. I heard him boast of it. I think he has told me so himself.

By Mr. BLAIR:

Question. Do you know about the killing of one Abraham Wamble, a colored preacher?

Answer. I heard of its occurrence. That was in April or May of 1871.

Question. "On the 20th day of May last he was shot seven times."

Answer. It was in May, sir; on the 19th, instead of the 20th, according to my recollection; at least the parties are indicted for killing him on the night of the 19th.

Question. "His family and neighbors saw the men who murdered him. They testified that they were masked men who did the murder." Joe Davis also states that he was there at the time he was killed, and that the same parties killed him that were indicted for killing Page.

Answer. In reference to that, Wamble lives between thirty and forty miles from where Joe Davis lives, and it was almost impossible, as there was a river to cross, for that body of men to have gone up there and to have perpetrated the deed, as it is alleged that they did, without leaving some better evidence than the testimony of Joe Davis.

Question. You say that from where Joe Davis lived it was thirty miles to where Wambold was killed?

Answer. Yes, sir.

Question. And the river Tombigbee between?

Answer. Yes, sir; intervening.

Question. Then they would have had to have ridden sixty miles in one night to have committed the murder and returned again?

Answer. Yes, sir, and cross the river twice, and the river was not fordable at that season of the year; and they would have had to have crossed at some ferry on the river. There was no bridge, and it was not fordable.

Question. Did you ever hear any reason given for the killing of this man?

Answer. His wife came to Aberdeen, and, as I learned, consulted with Judge Houston, who is my law partner, and General Gholson, for the purpose of employing them to prosecute certain negroes for killing him, alleging that they had killed him because of criminal intimacy with their wives.

Question. This man, Mr. Huggins, alleges that he was killed because he was a radical. Did you hear of the killing of a man named Tom Hornberger?

Answer. No, sir; I did not.

Question. It is Tom Durham or Tom Hornberger?

Answer. I think, perhaps, I heard something in reference to it, but my recollection of what I heard is so indistinct that I am not even certain that I know anything about it at all, and I would not have recalled it if you had not mentioned the fact of the other *alias*.

Question. "On the 4th of April a man by the name of Porter something—I have not his last name—was whipped, with his neck under a rail, until he would say that he was a democrat?" That is the statement of Huggins, on page 281.

Answer. I never heard of it. I never heard of any such occurrence.

Question. "About this time, two of the members of the school-board, who had voted for an estimate for a tax for school purposes, were notified by the Ku-Klux leaders to leave the board, and they did so." Do you recollect anything of that?

Answer. I do not, sir. I heard it said that Dr. Ebert, who was a member of the school-board, and who was also a teacher of one of the schools in Aberdeen—a teacher of the white school—received some anonymous communications signed "K.-K. K.," threatening him. Where they came from, I do not know.

Question. Mr. Huggins says, "About that time, all the teachers on the east side of the Tombigbee River were called upon and notified to close their schools, and all the schools were closed. There was not a school taught out on the east side of the river."

Answer. I will state, in reference to that, that from the last of May until the middle of July I was absent from the county of Monroe. My recollection is that I left home the 1st of June, and did not return until July. I was absent in another part of the State.

Question. Do you know anything about the burning of some school-houses?

Answer. I do not, sir.

Question. Of Mrs. Anna Dance, who was teaching a white school, and her school-house burned?

Answer. I know Mrs. Dance very well. I knew her when she was a young lady.

Question. Is she a native of this country?

Answer. She is a native of Mississippi or Virginia, one. She has been living in Mississippi, certainly, twenty years.

Question. Her school-house would not have been burned from any antipathy to her?

Answer. No, sir. Her father and herself are popular in the neighborhood. My own parents reside in the immediate vicinity of Mrs. Dance.

Question. Did you ever hear of a Mr. Hanstine teaching a colored school who was notified to quit?

Question. Did you ever hear of a man from Chickasaw County by the name of McBride who was said to have been whipped?

Answer. Yes, sir; I know him when I see him.

Question. What do you know of him?

Answer. I know that he is reported to have been brought to this country by the immigration association, which was formed in Chickasaw and in Monroe Counties, as a common laborer, and I know that he is regarded by everybody who knows him as utterly worthless and unreliable.

Question. He speaks of the great excitement that was created by the breaking up of these schools and the demoralization among the colored people.

Answer. I saw no evidence of any demoralization.

Question. He says they were alarmed.

Answer. It was not manifested in the county, either in their labor or any demonstrations that they made, which I know of.

Question. He said that of all the persons attacked in the county there was not a single democrat—not one.

Answer. Well, I recollect a man by the name of McKendon—a white man—who was whipped.

By the CHAIRMAN:

Question. By the Ku-Klux?

Answer. He was whipped by some disguised men because of his adulterous connection with some one, and a man by the name of Owen for treating his wife improperly—one Wilson.

Question. Was he whipped?

Answer. Yes, sir; whipped, I think, but I am not certain; and a man by the name of Swansy.

By Mr. BLAIR:

Question. Were all these men democrats?

Answer. Yes, sir.

Question. And Aleck Page also?

Answer. Yes, sir. What Aleck Page was at the time of his death I do not know.

Question. You know he had been a democrat?

Answer. I know he had boasted that he had voted the democratic ticket. I never saw him vote the democratic ticket.

Question. Was it known publicly?

Answer. Yes, sir.

Question. He says that these men who had been conveyed to Oxford, when they had been released upon bond and came home, were received with intense satisfaction and great demonstrations of enthusiasm, as if they had returned from the war conquerors.

Answer. When we left Oxford a good many parties who had been arrested failed to give bond there, and were ordered to give bond before Chancellor Whitfield, at Aberdeen. General Gholson was detained a day longer than I was, and I went in company with the men who had been released. Either at Grand Junction or Corinth, or perhaps at Oxford, I telegraphed to Colonel Sale, law partner of Mr. Dowd, and Judge Houston and Mr. Hooper, all of whom were retained in the case with myself, and were exceedingly anxious to get home that night, that these people had been kept from their crops and families, and to have Chancellor Whitfield ready to approve their bonds, and to have their securities present. When I got to the depot at our home there was a promiscuous crowd present, I suppose not exceeding one hundred and fifty, and there was the general congratulation of the meeting of friends, and there was some cheering, and some boys out with an old cannon that they had made out of an anvil, as I understood, and they fired it off. There was not a single speech made.

By the CHAIRMAN:

Question. Any music?

Answer. There was not a single strain; if my recollection serves me there was not. I was there. I met Judge Houston, my partner, and told him I would go home and get my supper, and gave him the memorandum in my possession, and went down, and a good many of the men gave bond that night.

Question. Were there any ladies present?

Answer. Not a single one, except of the families of the parties arrested, that I recollect of, and the majority of the crowd were colored people. They were as demonstrative as anybody else. Whatever manifestation there was there in the way of cheering was no manifestation to these men as Ku-Klux, but it was a manifestation to them as quiet, orderly citizens, who it was believed by the people had been arrested improperly.

By Mr. BLAIR:

Question. He says one family took the whole band of Ku-Klux home with them to dinner—page 297.

Answer. That is not true. These men were arrested the first time on Saturday. I saw them. Let me state why I know it is not true. I saw them that morning, I saw them about noon. They were under the charge of an officer, not kept in strict guard. I was retained Saturday evening. They were released by Major McCoy that night, and returned to Aberdeen Sunday evening and were sent out to the military camp, and we started Monday morning to Oxford. We got back on Thursday night or Friday night—on Thursday night, I think—and the men had left town before the next day at dinner-time. That is true of—well, the majority of them, I will not say all.

Question. He states, "They asked if they could have the privilege of taking them home to dine with them; one of the first families in town, the most wealthy."

By the CHAIRMAN:

Question. Were any of them invited out to dinner or supper, or whatever the meal might be?

Answer. Yes, sir; two of the men—one of them served under me during the war—he spent the night with me at my invitation, not because he had been to Oxford, but as he usually does when he comes to Aberdeen.

Question. I am speaking about the fact of whether these men were taken to the houses?

Answer. They were at the houses of a good many citizens.

Question. That is the main fact I wanted to get at.

Answer. They were at the houses of a good many citizens.

By Mr. BLAIR:

Question. Were you present at the scene which has been described which took place between Colonel Lamar and the court?

Answer. Yes, sir.

Question. Was Colonel Lamar counsel for these prisoners?

Answer. He was not, sir.

Question. Did you see during the progress of his speech that the prisoners jumped over the bar and rolled up their sleeves, and the students of the university cheered, as did the citizens, at the speech of Lamar?

Answer. The prisoners did not jump over the bar or roll up their sleeves. I do not believe a man of them even stood up. That was an exception to the balance of the crowd. Whether any of the students cheered or not I do not know. The only cheer I heard came from a man whom Colonel Wells will recollect; his name is Belcher, a clerk in a drug-store there in Oxford.

Question. What was the cause for Lamar's remarks?

Answer. I can give you a description or account of the matter. It was during the progress of this trial. Some proposition was submitted to the counsel for the defense, and we retired for consultation in an adjoining room that opened into the court-room. In the position I occupied my face was fronting Judge Hill, and I could see him distinctly. Just after we got out of the court-room Colonel Lamar arose and commenced to address the court, stating that a few days before Judge Hill had bound over the Oktibbeha prisoners to keep the peace, that he desired the court to bind over a man who was there as a witness before the court, because he had been threatening him, dogging him on the streets of Oxford, as he believed, for the purpose of provoking a disturbance. My recollection of his remarks is, "I ask your honor to protect me from the cowardly assassin." I could not see Colonel Lamar from the position I occupied. I only saw Judge Hill and this man Wissler sitting on the steps to the left. When Colonel Lamar made the remark "cowardly assassin," Wissler jumped up and threw his hand behind him, and then I saw Colonel Lamar's chair coming over, and I ran into the court-room, and as soon as I got in the court-room the whole scene was before me. Wissler ran out under the chair, and Judge Hill caught it and threw it off to the left. Mr. Pierce, the marshal, remarked to Colonel Lamar, "I arrest you, Colonel Lamar." Colonel Lamar drew back and, with an oath, struck him. It was then that Colonel Manning, Colonel Walton, and General Featherston interfered and caught hold of Colonel Lamar. Judge Hill ordered everybody to sit down. I went into the aisle and remarked, "You Monroe County men keep your seats," alluding to these prisoners. Pope, who was summoned as a witness, was out of his seat, I presume, and attempted to pass me. I caught him by the collar and threw him down into the seat. He was a witness. My attention was then directed to the Federal soldiers at the door and I heard the click of their guns. General Featherston had come out in the mean time in the left aisle until the men could obey the order of the court and sit down. I, as soon as I heard that, remarked, "General, let us not let these soldiers fire;" and we went up to them and saw there was no officer there, and told them there was no use in interfering. They brought their guns down from a "ready" to an "order." Everything was quiet; Colonel Lamar still on the floor. Judge Hill ordered him to sit down. He remarked that he would not do it; that he claimed his constitutional right as a citizen to be heard, and said something else, which was handsome, so far as the rights of a citizen were concerned. To that Mr. Belcher applauded, and I think he was the only man in the house who did. Colonel Wells jumped up immediately, and he remarked to the marshal, "Arrest that man." My recollection, of course, is not perfect, as all of us would see it differently. I will state in reference to that also, that Mr. Emery, the foreman of the grand jury, was present in court at the time it occurred, and he ran out, and as he was passing the drug-store he saw some negroes and told them there was a fight going on at the court-house; to get their arms and go on immediately. I charged Mr. Emery with it in the court-room in a private conversation we had in reference to it, because of an account which appeared in the Holly Springs paper, charging these prisoners with having made demonstrations against the court; and he admitted that he did it when I charged him with it.

By the CHAIRMAN:

Question. Was this man Wissler, toward whom Colonel Lamar made the hostile demonstrations, the same person who was within two weeks past brutally murdered in his own house at Macon?

Answer. I understand he is the same.

By Mr. BLAIR:

Question. The same man who brutally burned up a man with kerosene oil at Corinth?

Answer. Yes, sir; the same man.

Question. Here is the statement of a witness by the name of Edward E. Holman, to which I wish to draw your attention. He states, page 341, that Lawyer Sykes's name was stricken from the roll of attorneys by Judge Hill, for tampering with the witnesses.

Answer. There is not a word of truth in it. So far from, that permit me to say that there is not a more honorable man in his profession in the State than Mr. Sykes.

Question. Then the fact is that the statement is not true?

Answer. It is not true.

Question. Is there anything now that occurred before that court that gives the slightest color to that statement?

Answer. Not one single thing that occurred there during that time. I was at the Federal court a month, every day except two that Mr. Sykes was, and I think I took some recreation on Sunday and Monday, and Captain Sykes remained, but nothing occurred at that trial out of which that statement could possibly have been fabricated.

Question. Do you know anything about the killing of a negro named Doc. Hendricks?

Answer. That occurred recently. I know that Doc. Hendricks is said to have killed a man by the name of Garnett or Garnett—I forgot which, but I believe it was Garrett; that he was committed to jail by the magistrate, put into the charge of three men, and on his way to jail he was taken out of their custody and, I understood, hung.

Question. Do you know anything about Tobe Hutchinson, a negro? He was taken from his house a week ago last Friday, and supposed to be killed on election day, in Lee County.

Answer. I do not know. I was in Lee County at the county court. I left there on Saturday before election day.

Question. This was on election day.

Answer. I never heard of it.

Question. Did you hear anything of the burning of a colored church at Tupelo?

Answer. Yes, sir.

Question. On the day Doc. Hendricks was killed?

Answer. No, sir; I am not positive as to the time, but certainly a month ago. My recollection may be at fault in reference to it.

By the CHAIRMAN:

Question. You think it was burned a month ago?

Answer. Yes, sir; longer than a month ago.

By Mr. BLAIR:

Question. Who is supposed to have burned the church. Was anybody arrested for it?

Answer. Well, sir, in reference to that, there was a party who testified that a man by the name of Freemen burned it, but her testimony was discredited.

Question. Who testified to that?

Answer. Well, sir; I do not remember her name. She is a woman who is living there. I think her name is Davis.

Question. Is she the postmistress.

Answer. Yes, sir; she is the postmistress.

Question. What is her character; you say she was discredited?

Answer. I only know what is said of her, of course, by those who know her. I have no personal acquaintance with her myself. I never saw her but twice in my life. I went into the post-office week before last in Tupelo, and saw her passing along the street. She is reported to be a strumpet. I will state that, and she is reported further to be unworthy of belief. That is her character in the town of Tupelo. I have no personal knowledge of anything concerning her.

Question. Did you hear anything of the burning of the office of Shattuck, or the attempt to burn it, in Okolona?

Answer. Yes, sir; I saw an account of it in a northern paper. I called the attention of Judge Houston, my law partner, to it, who was in attendance on the chancery court at Okolona. I asked him whether it was so or not. He told me an attempt was made to burn the office of Mr. Shattuck, but that the fire was put out by Mr. J. Wess Buchanan. That is all I know in reference to it.

Question. You do not know whether there were any Ku-Klux arrested, and in the house at the time that this occurred?

Answer. There was not.

Question. Not in the office?

Answer. There was not at the time. I say there was not; at least, that is my information. I am told that Mr. Buchanan and a negro put the fire out, and that it was evidently the work of an incendary; and these parties happened to be passing and saw it, and put it out.

Question. Mr. Huggins connects this affair with the circumstance that five Ku-Klux had been arrested in Chickasaw County and taken to Okolona to the residence of Mr. Shattuck, and that night his office was set on fire, but it was put out.

Answer. That is true as far as concerns the arrest of some men in southern Chickasaw County about that time. Where they were taken to, I do not know.

By the CHAIRMAN:

Question. You never heard that these were put in the office, though?

Answer. I never did. I don't think that could be. The office is a very small one.

By Mr. BLAIR:

Question. Did you ever hear anything of an expedition made by this man Huggins into Oktibbeha to make arrests?

Answer. Yes, sir; I heard of his going there several times.

Question. Searching for Bell?

Answer. You allude to his conduct to Mrs. Bell—his reported conduct?

Mr. BLAIR. Yes.

The WITNESS. I heard of that. I heard that he went there in company with some soldiers to Mr. Bell's house to look for Mr. Bell; that he went to the bed-room of Mrs. Bell, according to my recollection, and was told that Mr. Bell was not there; that he insisted upon ascertaining what her sex was, and pulled down the bed-clothes, and made an *exposé*.

Question. Who did you hear that from?

Answer. I heard it from Mr. Houston—Judge Houston—and I heard Mr. Klopton speak of it. I think I heard Judge Reuben Davis speak of it. I heard General Gholson speak of it.

Question. Is it the impression that such an outrage as that was committed upon a lady in her bed-room and in her bed?

Answer. I will state in reference to it, that Huggins says the soldiers did it. The soldiers, however, I hear say he did it, and the impression is that an outrage of that sort was perpetrated.

By Mr. RICE:

Question. Who professes to have heard Mrs. Bell say anything about it; any of them?

Answer. No, sir.

By Mr. BLAIR:

Question. The soldiers say Huggins did it?

Answer. I never heard them say so.

Question. You say that they make that report?

Answer. Yes, sir.

Question. Do you know anything about a man named McLaughlin, who was his guide on that occasion?

Answer. Yes, sir; I know him.

Question. Formerly a resident of Oktibbeha?

Answer. I know him. He was formerly a resident of Aberdeen. He taught a school in Aberdeen in 1869 or 1870. In 1869, I think. He is an Irishman. I saw him at Oxford in June.

Question. Did you hear anything of him in connection with this affair?

Answer. I did not, sir.

[The hour of 6 o'clock and thirty minutes p. m. having arrived, the committee adjourned until 9 o'clock to-morrow.]

COLUMBUS, MISSISSIPPI, *November* 15, 1871.

REUBEN O. REYNOLDS recalled.

The WITNESS. I desire to make a statement in reference to the killing of Aleck Page, which I omitted yesterday; that is, that the colored coroner in my country, Phil Bumpus, after the body was found, held an inquest over it, for the purpose of discovering who the murderers were, in connection with the deputy sheriff of Monroe, Mr. Love; that he examined all the witnesses whom he supposed had any knowledge of it, and the jury returned a verdict of death by hanging by persons unknown. That the wife of Aleck Page stated to Mr. Kendrick that she did not know who killed her husband, but that she suspected or that she recognized several negroes who were concerned in it.

By the CHAIRMAN:

Question. Did you hear her make that statement?

Answer. No, sir; I heard Mr. Kendrick testify to that statement in substance.

Question. You heard Kendrick testify that Mrs. Page said that?

Answer. Yes, sir.

Question. Was Mrs. Page under oath at the time that Kendrick says she said that?

Answer. She was not.

Question. Are you a native of this State, Colonel Reynolds?

Answer. I am not, sir.

Question. Of what State are you a native?

Answer. I am a native of the State of Georgia.

Question. You were the counsel, I understand, for these parties who were implicated in the murder of Page?

Answer. I was, sir; and permit me to state in reference to that subject that I was regularly retained and feed. I was a volunteer counsel.

Question. Has any one charged you with being a volunteer counsel?

Answer. Yes, sir.

Question. Any one in this committee?

Answer. No, sir. I was charged in papers with being a volunteer counsel.

Question. I think you took occasion to inform the committee yesterday that your fees would amount to some fifteen hundred dollars for your services in their defense?

Answer. More than that.

Question. You were not misunderstood by the committee. You may state whether you furnished the minority with a brief of the points upon which you would be examined yesterday.

Answer. I did not, sir.

Question. Had you conferred with General Gholson before you testified yesterday in relation to the various matters about which you would probably be interrogated?

Answer. We had conversed together in reference to it, yes, sir.

Question. Upon most of the matters about which you were interrogated, or upon which you testified yesterday?

Answer. The most of them. That is my recollection, sir.

Question. You may state to the committee whether you took a part in the late civil war.

Answer. I did, sir.

Question. Were you in the confederate service?

Answer. Yes, sir.

Question. In what capacity?

Answer. I was at the close of the war colonel of the Eleventh Mississippi Regiment?

Question. Had you held any office before the war?

Answer. I had not. I never held any political office in my life, or any office connected with politics.

Question. Did you see the estimate which Mr. Huggins, as president of the board of school directors, submitted to the board of supervisors?

Answer. I did, sir.

Question. You read that estimate over carefully?

Answer. Yes, sir.

Question. You are prepared, then, to state the contents of it now, are you?

Answer. Yes, sir, as far as I can state the contents of any paper at this distance of time.

Question. You may state as briefly as you can the contents of that estimate.

Answer. In the first application which he made to the board of supervisors, he represented for school purposes—pay of teachers and building houses—there was, I will say, about fifty thousand dollars necessary.

Question. Did he estimate how many houses were necessary?

Answer. My recollection is that he did not.

Question. Did he estimate how many teachers would have to be employed?

Answer. My recollection is that he did not. My recollection is that that was about the substance of the requisition; I am to state to you the subject of his requisition, and not what occurred, or the reason why it was objected to?

The CHAIRMAN. Yes, sir.

The WITNESS. Am I to state why it was objected to?

The CHAIRMAN. No; I do not care about that; only the substance of his estimate.

The WITNESS. The next requisition I recollect to have seen went more into detail. It made a statement in reference to the purchase of furniture for the two schools in Aberdeen. They went more into detail as to the number of school-houses, and more into detail as to the number of teachers, and the amount paid to each. That is my recollection.

Question. There was still a third one?

Answer. There was still a third one, but my recollection is that I never saw that third one.

Question. Whether that was itemized or not you do not know?

Answer. I do not.

Question. How much was the last item?

Answer. Twenty odd thousand dollars.

Question. How much was the second item?

Answer. Reduced from the original fifty thousand to about thirty-five thousand dollars.

Question. Do you know the number of scholars, between the ages of six and twenty-one years, in Monroe County?

Answer. I do not, sir. I can give you a statement of the voting population in my county, and that is the only accurate account I can give you.

Question. What does the census show is the population, white and black, of that county?

Answer. I do not know.

Question. As much as twenty-five or thirty thousand?

Answer. My recollection is that it is about twenty-five thousand.

Question. That would give you about how many children probably between six and twenty-one years of age?

Answer. I should say about seven or eight thousand.

Question. To educate that number would require how many school-houses?

Answer. Two hundred.

Question. How many school-houses, in point of fact, had you before the common-school system recently adopted in your State outside of Aberdeen?

Answer. I should say fifty.

Question. Were they log school-houses?

Answer. No, sir, not exclusively log school-houses; some were.

Question. Were they mostly log school-houses?

Answer. They were not. They were rather frame buildings—the most I have in my mind's eye were. Of course, I cannot be accurate now in my estimate to state that there may be fifty. I may be twenty-five or fifty school-houses from the real number.

Question. You may be, then, twenty-five in excess of the actual number?

Answer. Yes, sir. I may be twenty-five in excess of the actual number, but that is my estimate.

Question. On the supposition that there were fifty, there still would be required one hundred and fifty more?

Answer. Yes, sir; one hundred and fifty more.

Question. Do you know the valuation of the property, real and personal, for taxable purposes, in Monroe County?

Answer. Yes, sir; about $4,000,000.

Question. Is the property assessed for purposes of taxation at less than its actual value; if so, what per cent. less?

Answer. Yes, sir; less than its actual value, and I should say 20 per cent. less. The average would be about 10 per cent. less, I suppose. Some property in the county is assessed to its full value, and a portion probably is not; but I suppose that, upon the whole assessment, it is 10 per cent. less than its real value.

Question. Then, according to that, the actual value of property, personal and real, in Monroe County, would be about four million and a half of dollars, according to your opinion?

Answer. Yes, sir.

Question. Did I understand you to say that Mr. Huggins, as president of the board of school directors, had made extravagant contracts for school-houses?

Answer. Yes, sir.

Question. Do you mean for the building of school-house and for the purchase of houses at extravagant prices?

Answer. For both. In the first place, the contracts which he had made for school-houses, and the amounts which he had agreed to pay contractors, were exorbitant. The school-houses were usually eighteen by twenty, or twenty by twenty, I am not certain which, and he had agreed to pay in the neighborhood of four hundred dollars each.

Question. For the building of such school-houses?

Answer. Yes, sir.

Question. Does that include the purchase of ground?

Answer. Yes, sir. It was estimated that $250 would be a sufficient remuneration for a contractor for the building of those houses.

Question. You are speaking now of the materials as well as the labor?

Answer. I am speaking of the amount that would be paid to a contractor to build those houses. The material, land, labor, and everything would not cost more than $250.

Question. You speak of frame school-houses?

Answer. Yes, sir.

Question. Painted and plastered?

Answer. Yes, sir.

Question. Your opinion is that a school-house of the dimensions named, including the requisite ground for the site, could be built for $250?

Answer. Yes, sir, but not plastered. My recollection on that subject is that there was no item of plastering in the contract between Mr. Huggins and his contractor.

Question. The house would have to be either plastered or sealed?

Answer. I do not think it was contemplated that either should be done. That is my recollection.

Question. You saw the contracts?

Answer. No, sir; I did not.

Question. Were they let on public advertisement to the lowest bidder?

Answer. Not that I know of.

Question. Do you know that it was not so?

Answer. My information is that it was not, though of that I am not positive. I will state my means of knowledge as to the cost of the school-houses. A number of mechanics and men who were experienced in that kind of work were examined, not before the board of supervisors, but a committee of citizens, as to what should be the cost of that school-house, and they varied, but the average of them, my recollection is, was $250 for such school-houses as they were erecting at that time in Monroe County. I know the fact that the contractors under Mr. Huggins sublet their contracts, and made as high as from one hundred to one hundred and fifty dollars by subletting them.

Question. Do you know that as a matter of fact?

Answer. I know it in two instances simply. I can recollect the instances.

Question. Do you know what dressed lumber is worth per hundred in the part of the country where these school-houses were to be built.

Answer. Dressed lumber is worth about $20 a thousand, according to my recollection. I can state better on that subject. I know something as to the price of undressed lumber. It is $15 a thousand—fifteen to seventeen.

Question. Have you ever taken the trouble to sit down and make an estimate of the quantity of material that would enter into a building of that size, and the prices that the material would cost, in order to figure out the result?

Answer. In 1870, in connection with my partner, we proposed to build some houses, similar to that, upon a place which we owned, and in that way; we proposed to build the houses 18 by 20 feet as tenement houses. I recollect what our estimate was as to the cost of them. We supposed we could build them for $225.

Question. I suppose the school-houses have to be a grade better than tenement houses?

Answer. They would not be better than the tenement houses we proposed to erect.

Question. These school-houses were to be painted, I suppose?

Answer. I think not.

Question. Are you sure of that fact?

Answer. I am not. I will state that those I have seen that have been erected have none of them been painted, but I have not seen every one in the county; in fact, I have seen but one or two.

Question. You have said the prices paid the teachers were extravagant. Please state how the prices ranged for the various grades of the schools.

Answer. I think $150 were paid for first-class teachers.

Question. For what portion of the year?

Answer. One hundred and fifty dollars a month.

Question. How long were the schools intended to run?

Answer. Four or five months; I forget which.

Question. Now, for inferior grades of teachers, what prices were to be paid?

Answer. Seventy-five dollars, and I believe they paid in some instances as low as fifty. I know they did.

Question. The highest sum, $150, was to be paid to the teachers of the highest grade of schools?

Answer. Yes, sir.

Question. Was your classification primary, intermediate, and high school?

Answer. I think there were but two. They had primary schools and graded schools as they were called. I will state in reference to that, that I know very little in reference to the system. Let me see what is my recollection about that. There were two classifications. There were two district schools in Aberdeen, and the other schools were primary schools.

Question. Did you have a superintendent for all the schools in the county?

Answer. Mr. Huggins was superintendent.

Question. The president of the board of directors acted as superintendent of all the schools?

Answer. Yes, sir.

Question. What is the ordinary price per month of board in that county?

Answer. In the country?

Question. Yes, sir; where a room and other conveniences were furnished and board?

Answer. Ten to fifteen dollars a month in the country.

Question. What is it in town here?

Answer. Fifteen to twenty.

Question. Were the teachers employed generally males or females, or divided?

Answer. There was a fair division; an equal division, as far as my recollection serves me.

Question. The females receiving the lower price, and the male teachers the higher price?

Answer. That is my recollection. I think in Aberdeen there was rather an excess of females; in fact, I know there was.

Question. What in your opinion would be a fair compensation for the teachers for the portions of the year they would be engaged in teaching the school of different grades in the county? The committee would be glad to have your opinion.

Answer. Well, sir, I would say that $75 a month would be ample compensation for the class of teachers that were usually employed in the free schools in that county. I speak of those in the higher grades. Seventy-five dollars for those of the higher grades.

Question. How much for the lowest grade?

Answer. I should suppose $30.

Question. After paying their board how much, would be left for their clothing and personal expenses at these rates?

Answer. About $10 a month for those of the lowest grade; but they were very inferior teachers.

Question. Were they selected from your native population generally?

Answer. No, sir; they were not. Some few were selected, and the instances I mention as having been inferior teachers were selected from the native population.

Question. Were any of the teachers employed from northern States?

Answer. Yes, sir. Of their character and of their capacity I have no information.

Question. You think it would pay a gentleman or lady to come from the North down to your section of country and engage in teaching school four or five months in the year at thirty or thirty-five, forty or fifty dollars a month?

Answer. If they could get other employment during the year, I think it would be a fair compensation.

Question. What do professional men—lawyers of your community—generally make per year in their profession?

Answer. Well, sir, that varies very much with a man's professional capacity.

Question. Well, average it.

Answer. I suppose fifteen hundred dollars would be an average of the professional men in my county.

Question. What would be the average of the compensation which your physicians receive?

Answer. You see I am taking all now. I speak of the average; those who do not make a living, and those who make much more than a living.

By Mr. RICE:

Question. Do you mean fifteen hundred dollars clear?

Answer. Let me see. I put the estimate too high. I intended to put it clear. I shall say a thousand dollars was as much as they make, clear of all expenses, taking the average. I suppose the physicians make clear about $750, taking the average.

By the CHAIRMAN:

Question. You mean after paying all family expenses?

Answer. Yes, sir, I take the average of what they make. I take those who make nothing and those who make a good deal. That is for their labor during the entire year.

Question. You spoke of the murder of Flint's two sons as creating as much horror among the whites as among the blacks?

Answer. Yes, sir.

Question. You also stated that the attorneys of Aberdeen were willing to attend to prosecuting the offenders, provided they had been feed?

Answer. Yes, sir.

Question. That is not unusual in any community where lawyers abound, is it, colonel?

Answer. I think not.

Question. You do not know any one who would be disposed to have taken it up without a fee for the good of the community?

Answer. No, sir; no man would volunteer in a criminal matter. No attorney would volunteer in a criminal case unless he had some private feelings on the matter—in a capital case.

Question. It was felt to be a very great outrage, was it?

Answer. It was; and there was a very great desire felt to ferret out the offenders, whoever they might be.

Question. Nothing has ever transpired in your community tending to show who were concerned in the matter, as I understand you?

Answer. Some men, who lived in the neighborhood of Parke, immediately after the occurrence left Mississippi, and are reported to have fled to Arkansas and Texas. They have certainly disappeared, or are reported to have disappeared, from that portion of the State.

Question. Are they believed to have been concerned in the murder of these men?

Answer. Yes, sir, they are.

Question. Will you give us their names?

Answer. I do not know their names.

Question. How many fled?

Answer. Five, I understood. Five or six. General Gholson can give you their names exactly.

Question. Did they belong to the Parke family?

Answer. Well, sir, I think not. They are friends of Mr. Parke.

Question. Living in that neighborhood?

Answer. Yes, sir.

Question. Young men?

Answer. Young men, I understood, principally.
Question. Respectable gentlemen?
Answer. Yes, sir.
Question. Stood fair in the community?
Answer. Yes, sir.
Question. Were they planters, or planters' sons?
Answer. Yes, sir; they were farmers; we have no planters now. We are all farmers. We ceased to be planters after the close of the war, and we have all become farmers.
Question. How came the war to interfere with the use of the terms?
Answer. It changed the system of labor.
Question. You still plant?
Answer. We still plant, but we do it in the sense in which you use the term farmer, up in Indiana; we work ourselves.
Question. Is that generally the case with the old planters, that they are turning in and working themselves?
Answer. No, sir; a great many of them are incapacitated from doing it by age, but most of the young men of the country are at work.
Question. And wherever planters and their sons have turned in to work their plantations you have not had any complaint of poverty or distress, have you?
Answer. We have no complaint of poverty or distress in our country. I have never heard but very little of it. We have had a great many men who have been croaking at their losses, and now are croaking at everything that occurs, and I believe they would croak if everything went just as they wanted it to. But the majority of our people are not complaining of poverty and distress.

By Mr. BLAIR:

Question. They are, notwithstanding all that, very much impoverished, are they not?
Answer. Very much, indeed, by the results of the war; and they regard the taxation as very heavy.

By the CHAIRMAN:

Question. What is the rate of taxation upon the valuation of property in your county, real and personal, massing the whole tax together, outside of your town tax. I do not want to include the municipal tax. I would be glad to know what, upon the valuation, is the rate per cent. of tax?
Answer. I made the estimate as to the amount which is to be collected in this county between this date and the 1st of December or 1st of January, I am uncertain which.
Question. Does that include the tax of a previous year?
Answer. No, sir.
Question. It is simply for one year?
Answer. No, sir. It is for half a year. We had paid the tax already this year, and the estimate as made is nearly 2⅔ per cent., according to my recollection. I think it is 2.66⅔ per cent., or about that.
Question. Does that not cover the entire year?
Answer. No, sir.
Question. Or part of next year?
Answer. No, sir. We had, this year, two taxes. One of them was to be collected by 1st day of June. That tax was to be 2 per cent.
Question. What was that tax for?
Answer. That was for State and county purposes. The tax which is to be collected for State and county purposes between now and the 1st of January, 1872, is 2⅔ per cent. Then we will have no taxes, unless there is some change in our law by the next legislature, until the 1st of December, 1872; that is, between the 1st of September and December, 1872.
Question. This tax then virtually covers two years?
Answer. No, sir. It happens that it was the provision of the law, made by the legislature which was in session, that we should pay the double tax this year.

By Mr. RICE:

Question. Is it not a change of time in the collection of the tax?
Answer. It is a change in the fiscal year, but that change did not take place until after the tax as provided for by the old law had to be collected: and the result was, that in making the change the tax had to be doubled.

By the CHAIRMAN:

Question. But ordinarily?
Answer. Ordinarily we pay but one tax per year.
Question. What is the sum of the taxes for all purposes in a single year in your county, leaving out municipal taxes?
Answer. About 2⅓ per cent.

Question. Did I understand you to state yesterday that Mr. Huggins was whipped because he was trying to obtain from the board of supervisors a levy for the amount of his estimate?

Answer. I said in reference to that subject that it was understood in the county that he was whipped on account of the onerous school-tax he was seeking to levy.

Question. You think that was the only cause?

Answer. I do, sir.

Question. That board comprised five men?

Answer. It did, sir.

Question. I refer to the board of school directors, of which he was president.

Answer. I am not certain whether it was composed of five or seven.

Question. Had he any more authority than any other member of the board?

Answer. None, sir.

Question. Why was this indignity visited upon him alone?

Answer. Because the board was completely under his influence. He was the moving spirit in it.

Question. Had his active services in behalf of the republican party nothing to do with that outrage?

Answer. None whatever.

Question. How do you know that?

Answer. I know, sir, that my people have no animosity against any man who is a republican for that cause.

Question. Now he either had or had not authority to make that estimate. Did your people punish him because he had exceeded his authority or because he had erred in point of judgment?

Answer. Well, it was because it was believed that the estimate which he sought to levy was a corrupt one, and that he was deriving the benefit of the purchases of furniture, which he was purchasing at one price while he was getting pay from the county at another.

Question. Had he purchased a single article of furniture before this estimate was made?

Answer. Yes, sir, and it had been received at Aberdeen.

Question. Before any estimate was made or order by the board of supervisors?

Answer. Yes, sir.

Question. What authority had he, until the levy was made, to make a purchase?

Answer. None; we thought not, but still the purchases had been made and the furniture received.

Question. For the school-houses?

Answer. Yes, sir, made in Burlington; Vermont, and I heard a statement read from a Burlington paper, that he bought the property for so much and charged the county at double as much. I do not know whether it was true or false.

Question. Was it a democratic paper in Burlington, Vermont?

Answer. I do not know.

Question. Can you give its name?

Answer. I cannot.

Question. How did a Burlington paper ever find its way to your neighborhood?

Answer. I can't tell.

Question. Who received it?

Answer. I heard it read by a gentleman named Barry.

Question. Was he a northern man?

Answer. He was not, sir.

Question. That is all you know about the corruption imputed to Mr. Huggins in the purchase of furniture?

Answer. Yes, sir; that is all I know about it.

Question. Do you know the price at which he put it in his charges?

Answer. Not the exact sum. The furniture for each school-room, according to my recollection, was between thirty-five hundred and four thousand dollars.

Question. For all the schools?

Answer. No, sir; for two school-rooms. The estimate of furniture was between seven and eight thousand dollars.

Question. Two school-rooms only?

Answer. Yes, sir.

Question. Where were these two school-rooms?

Answer. At Aberdeen.

Question. Where did you see that charge?

Answer. In his return to the board of supervisors of the county.

Question. Between seven and eight thousand dollars for furniture for two school-rooms?

Answer. Yes, sir; that is my recollection.

Question. Is that on file among the records of that board?

Answer. I do not know, sir; it may not have been seven to eight, it may have been five to six thousand; it may have been twenty-five hundred to three thousand dollars. It was either between twenty-five hundred and three thousand or between thirty-five hundred and four thousand, I am uncertain which; but my recollection is that it was between thirty-five hundred and four thousand each.

Question. What kind of schools were those?

Answer. They were called graded schools under the school law.

Question. What branches were taught in them?

Answer. I do not know of my own knowledge.

Question. Was it one of these schools that a teacher was engaged at the rate of $150 per month?

Answer. Yes, sir.

Question. Were the higher English branches and the classics taught in that school?

Answer. My recollection is that they were.

Question. Music and painting also?

Answer. I do not know whether painting was or not; I understood that they taught music.

Question. Vocal and instrumental?

Answer. Vocal; I do not think they taught them instrumental.

Question. Were pupils prepared for admission to colleges in that school?

Answer. Not that I know of, sir.

By Mr. BLAIR:

Question. One of these was a colored school, and the other a white school?

Answer. Yes, sir.

By Mr. RICE:

Question. Does that furniture include all the seats?

Answer. It included the seats.

Question. And the desks?

Answer. Desks, geographical charts, astronomical charts, and anatomical charts; they had all.

By the CHAIRMAN:

Question. Philosophical apparatus?

Answer. No, sir; no apparatus, I believe.

Question. Globes?

Answer. Yes, sir.

Question. What else?

Answer. I stated that it embraced the seats, the desks, the black-boards, geographical charts, astronomical and anatomical charts. I never was in the school-room in my life, neither one of them.

By Mr. RICE:

Question. How many rooms were there, do you know?

Answer. I do not remember; I think there were three in the white school. The colored school was a very large building; I think perhaps there were four rooms in it.

Question. And a teacher for each room?

Answer. I do not know, sir; I can recollect the number of teachers in the white school by making a little estimate. Dr. Eberts, Mrs. Dow, Mr. Barnett, Mrs. Boss, and Miss Chapin were the five teachers, my recollection is, in the white school. I do not know who were in the other school.

By the CHAIRMAN:

Question. When you speak of the furniture for a single school, you mean all the different rooms for these five teachers?

Answer. Yes, sir; for the white school and the colored school in Aberdeen. I do not think there was any estimate for furniture in any of the other schools at all.

Question. Did you understand that a portion of the members of the school-board were required to resign by the public?

Answer. I did not, sir.

Question. You spoke of two members of the school-board being required to resign?

Answer. I do not think I so stated; I may have stated in reference to that; I do not remember that I did—that two did resign; whether they were required to resign by the people or not, I do not know.

Question. Did you not say something about their receiving a Ku-Klux notice?

Answer. I stated that I understood that Dr. Eberts had received a notice signed "K. K. K." about the time of his resignation.

Question. Did you understand that he resigned in consequence of that notification, and his apprehension that he was in danger unless he resigned?

Answer. I did not, sir; I understand he was told that there was no danger of any violence to him in the matter.

Question. Who told him that?

Answer. Dr. Tindall.

Question. You heard him tell him that?

Answer. No, sir; I did not. I never had but very few words of conversation with Dr. Eberts in my life, though he has been a minister in my place and had charge of the Methodist church; I know him personally.

Question. Do you not know a large number of teachers received notices from Ku-Klux to discontinue their schools?

Answer. I heard they received notifications to discontinue their schools.

Question. Did you not hear that the Ku-Klux rode to their dwellings at night, and called them out, and required them to resign their positions?

Answer. I did hear so in some cases.

Question. Did you not hear so in as many as half a dozen cases?

Answer. I think perhaps I did.

Question. What did you say of McBride, of Chickasaw County—that he had been Ku-Kluxed?

Answer. I do not think I stated that.

Question. You stated something about his being brought there by an immigration society?

Answer. I was asked did I know McBride, and I stated that I was informed that he was brought to Mississippi, by the immigration society, to Okolona. I was asked the question what I knew of him, and I stated that, from what I had heard others say and what I knew myself of him—I had seen the man—that he was a very worthless and trifling man.

Question. I understood you to say that, and now I wish you to state whether you heard that he had been whipped?

Answer. I did, sir.

Question. Did you understand that he had been whipped by a band of disguised men?

Answer. I did, sir.

Question. Did you understand the offense for which he was whipped; the specific offense?

Answer. No, sir; I did not.

Question. Where was he brought from; where did he come from?

Answer. He came from Chicago; he is an Irishman, and an unnaturalized citizen, as I have heard.

Question. What was he brought there by the immigration society for?

Answer. As a laborer.

Question. Did you hear of any other cases of whipping in Chickasaw besides that of McBride?

Answer. I heard of the case of Eckles.

Question. Was he whipped by a band of disguised men?

Answer. I understood that he was.

Question. Is that the only other case that you recall?

Answer. In Chickasaw County?

The CHAIRMAN. Yes.

The WITNESS. I think it is, judge. I might recall more; if some specific case were mentioned, I might recollect it.

Question. The cases of McLendon, Owen, Wilson, and Swanzy, that you mentioned yesterday evening, as men whipped, occurred in Monroe County, I believe?

Answer. Yes, sir. I will state in that connection, sir, that Eckles is a southern man, and the cause of his whipping, as I understood it, was some improper conduct as a citizen. I was trying to think what it was; it was on account of his being supposed to be guilty of the crime of incest.

Question. Supposed by the men who committed the violence upon him?

Answer. That is what was reported.

Question. That is a crime, I believe, that is punished by law?

Answer. Yes, sir.

Question. If it exists?

Answer. Yes, sir; of course.

Question. I suppose the same evidence that would satisfy the tribunal of Judge Lynch would satisfy one of your civil courts?

Answer. I do not know what would satisfy Judge Lynch. I never belonged to a lynching party in my life; but the testimony that would satisfy one of our courts would be such that it would be certain beyond a reasonable doubt. Whether the same testimony would be necessary before Judge Lynch or not, I do not know.

Question. You would not think that any man ought to be whipped or killed for an offense unless he was guilty beyond a reasonable doubt, even by lynchers?

Answer. No; by nobody. I recognize the supremacy of law in everything.

Question. Some of those whom you testified about yesterday, I believe, were cases where they were killed, and yet were never guilty nor suspected of being guilty of any offense. There is the case of Dupree, for example, who was never charged with any offense.

Answer. I never heard him charged with any offense at all. I heard Mr. May say, in reference to him, that he was the best laborer that he had upon his place. I heard him say he was a boisterous, high-tempered man, but that he was an especial favorite of his.

Question. It was a case, then, of obvious mistake on the part of the lynchers, if their vocation was to punish crime?

Answer. I do not know what it was. I do not know what was the reason that prompted it.

By Mr. BLAIR:

Question. That case has never been judicially examined?

Answer. Never.

By the CHAIRMAN:

Question. You speak about judicial examinations. I will inquire whether you have known a single case in your county, or in any of the adjoining counties, where any of the men charged with being connected with these midnight outrages, have ever been convicted and punished?

Answer. I speak, of course, of outrages committed by bands of men in disguise. I do not know of an instance, sir, excepting the case of Flint—but you ask for a conviction; I do not know of an instance.

Question. You spoke of the burning of the colored church at Tupelo; who testified that Freeman burned that church?

Answer. I understood that the postmistress there testified to that fact.

Question. You did not hear her testimony?

Answer. I did not. I understood that she testified that Freeman did it.

Question. You say that the testimony was discredited?

Answer. Yes, sir.

Question. Has public opinion settled down to this day upon the party or parties who burned that church?

Answer. Not that I know of, sir.

Question. It remains a mystery?

Answer. Yes, sir.

Question. You spoke of Miss Davis, and her bad character for truth and veracity, and for chastity?

Answer. As was represented to me by others.

Question. I will ask you to state who impeached her character for chastity, and for truth and veracity?

Answer. I understood that investigation was had by the grand jury of Lee County in this matter, and that she testified as to the fact of the burning, and counter-testimony was introduced before that grand jury, assailing her in the manner that I have mentioned.

Question. Did you get that information from a member of the grand jury?

Answer. I did not, sir.

Question. Did you get it from witnesses who testified before the grand jury?

Answer. I did not, sir.

Question. Did you get it from the prosecuting attorney?

Answer. I did not, sir.

Question. Who could know what she testified before the grand jury, except the law officers and the jurors themselves?

Answer. Well, sir, I can tell you who I got it from.

The CHAIRMAN. Please answer my question first.

The WITNESS. What was the question?

The CHAIRMAN. The question is this: Who could know what she testified before a grand jury except the prosecuting attorney, who always has admission to the grand jury room, or members of the grand jury themselves, and the witnesses?

Answer. No one; unless it would get out, as questions of that kind always do, by the imprudent remarks of members of the grand jury, or by witnesses themselves stating to outsiders what they had testified.

Question. Would you credit the statement of a grand juror as to what was sworn before the grand jury, after that grand juror had himself taken an oath to preserve the secrets of the grand jury room, and violated it by so telling you?

Answer. I would. Many a man would make an imprudent remark.

Question. Violate his oath, and still you would credit his statement not under oath?

Answer. A man might make an imprudent speech, and inferences might be drawn as to what the testimony was given before him there, without intending to violate his oath.

By Mr. RICE:

Question. Do grand juries in this State take impeaching testimony, calling witnesses before them for that purpose?

Answer. It is not usual, sir.

Question. There is no custom or law authorizing it?

Answer. No, sir.

By the CHAIRMAN:

Question. And yet you heard that she was impeached before the grand jury before which she appeared as a witness?

Answer. Yes, sir.

Question. And that, you say, is contrary to all rule?

Answer. It is, sir.

Question. Did you understand who were her accusers before the grand jury?

Answer. I did not.

Question. You understood that upon that occasion her character was discredited for truth and veracity, and for chastity?

Answer. Yes, sir.

Question. Did you understand that it was discredited by men who were interested in saving Ku-Klux from prosecution?

Answer. I did not. I know Freeman's position in Lee County. He is exceedingly unpopular with the citizens, and the citizens would be very glad to get rid of him.

Question. Do you understand that these rumors of her want of good character proceeded from Freeman?

Answer. No, sir.

Question. That he started them?

Answer. I do not know, sir. It was from citizens who testified before the grand jury. Freeman was not in a condition, I understood, to be brought before the grand jury. He is suffering from some wounds he received in a personal rencounter there with the Highs.

Question. If you know anything against the personal character of Miss Davis, state it.

Answer. Not of my own personal knowledge. I do not know one single suspicion against her character.

Question. Are you acquainted with her?

Answer. I saw her twice.

Question. Is her demeanor that of a lady?

Answer. I saw her at the post-office and walking along the streets, and saw nothing improper in her conduct.

Question. Does she discharge her duties with fidelity and propriety?

Answer. As far as I know she does. I have had but one single experience in the matter.

Question. Do you know that anybody talked against her except men who were extremely prejudiced against northern men and northern women?

Answer. You ask me the question if I know if men talk against her who are prejudiced against northern men and northern women. I do not know of any man in my State who has any prejudice against northern men and northern women. I state it frankly. I do not hold that any such prejudice exists.

Question. I think you said she had been the teacher of a colored school?

Answer. Not that I know of.

Question. Some other witness has stated that fact. Is there any prejudice felt against teachers of colored schools?

Answer. There is not.

Question. Has there been any such prejudice?

Answer. There has been this; the teachers of some of the colored schools have sought to inculcate doctrines in the minds of their pupils which many of us think are likely to produce discord and dissension among our people—the two races.

Question. What ideas have you known teachers of colored schools to inculcate in the minds of their pupils prejudicial to the interests of society?

Answer. I have one hired at my house now who communicates this fact to me, that she was taught in the colored school at Aberdeen that a war between the two races was inevitable, and that when that war came they must kill from the cradle up. I considered it as a mere—well, as I considered, I did not suppose she represented the thing properly. I suppose she was telling it simply for my gratification.

Question. Do you believe that any teacher of a colored school, male or female, there inculcated any such doctrines?

Answer. Yes, sir; I do.

Question. Name the teacher or teachers.

Answer. I believe that all the teachers, or a majority of the teachers connected with the colored schools at Aberdeen inculcated such doctrines.

Question. Do you know that fact?

Answer. I believe it.

Question. State the knowledge on which you ground such belief.

Answer. In the first place, the community believes it. In the next place, this pupil told me so.

Question. But you say you did not put any credit in her statement.

Answer. I have no doubt she exaggerated it, because I can hardly think it is human to do a thing of that sort, but evidently the doctrine inculcated in that school to these pupils was to array the black man against the white man—especially to prejudice him against the southern white man.

Question. You do not believe that Mrs. Dance ever taught such doctrines?

Answer. She taught a white school.

Question. You have known some southern gentlemen and southern ladies to teach colored schools, have you not?

Answer. Yes, sir.

Question. You do not think they ever inculcated such doctrines?

Answer. I do not believe they do.

Question. Teachers are selected indifferently from North and South?

Answer. They are.

Question. As the charge preferred is a very serious one, the committee will be obliged to you if you will give the evidence upon which this charge is made against the teachers of colored schools. We do not want any mere beliefs, but we want facts.

Answer. Well, sir, it is believed——

Mr. BLAIR. I think this is a very strange statement from the chairman, when we have been taking beliefs and surmises of so many.

The CHAIRMAN. Every belief must rest upon knowledge and information. It is of no value unless it is that kind of belief which is based upon information. If you have any knowledge or information relative to such teachings, the committee want it.

The WITNESS. I have the exaggerated statement, as I called it, the communication which I have stated, from one of the pupils of the school, which statement I regard as exaggerated. And then I have heard it mentioned with regret by the very best citizens of the town, who seemed to have similar information.

Question. Will you specify the precise character of the information which the best men of the town had?

Answer. It was from conversation with pupils of the school as to what occurred in the school-room.

Question. What did the pupils tell these people?

Answer. They stated that they were taught that a conflict between the two races was inevitable, and that when that conflict came, they must be prepared to exterminate the white race.

By Mr. RICE:

Question. Did intelligent teachers teach that doctrine?

Answer. Yes, sir.

Question. That the colored people should exterminate the white race?

Answer. Yes, sir; in our immediate section.

By the CHAIRMAN:

Question. You believe that such doctrines have been taught in your colored schools, do you?

Answer. Yes, sir, I do; and I believe where they are not taught in our colored schools it is an exception to the rule, rather than otherwise.

Question. Yet I understood you to say that there is no objection in the community to colored schools?

Answer. None, sir, to a proper system of colored schools.

Question. Then you qualify the statement made yesterday?

Answer. No, I do not qualify it at all. There is no opposition to colored schools.

Question. It is that there should not be colored schools if your people believe that such doctrines are inculcated among the colored children?

Answer. Judge, they may object to the teachings, or to the doctrines as taught by the teachers, without objecting to the system of schools itself. That is a distinction which I desire to draw.

Question. Was that the reason why the teachers last spring were so generally notified to discontinue their schools?

Answer. I do not know about that.

Question. We understand from other quarters that the sole cause for the Ku-Klux visitations was the oppressiveness of the school-tax. Is that your opinion?

Answer. My opinion is that it was a combination of both.

Question. You spoke of the attempted service of a warrant by Colonel Huggins, as special deputy marshal, accompanied by certain soldiers, upon Mr. Bell; was this in Aberdeen?

Answer. No, sir; it was in Oktibbeha County.

Question. Were you present at that time?

Answer. I was not.

Question. You know nothing of the facts, of your own knowledge?

Answer. I do not. Oktibbeha County is forty miles from my place of residence. I never was in the county in my life, I believe.

Question. Do you know this Mr. Bell?

Answer. I do not.

Question. Is he reported to be a man of violence—a desperate man?

Answer. I do not know him.

Question. You never heard of his character?

Answer. No, sir. I know several Bells in Oktibbeha County, by reputation. I think there is a large family of them.

Question. But this particular Bell?

Answer. I do not know him at all.

Question. This one that Mr. Huggins had the warrant for?

Answer. I do not know him at all.

Question. Have you ever heard that he is a desperate man?

Answer. I never did, because I do not know which man is referred to.

Question. Do you know whether the warrant which was got out for Mr. Huggins and his party was based upon any affidavit that was made?

Answer. I did not know that any had been issued for the arrest of Mr. Huggins and his party.

Question. Mr. Huggins states positively that he did not enter the house of Mr. Bell at all at the time the search was being made in the house for his arrest. In the absence of any positive information upon the subject, you would not discredit the statement of Colonel Huggins, would you?

Answer. I would prefer not to express my opinion upon that subject to you unless the committee desire me to do so.

Question. Did you ever get your information from any person that was present upon the occasion, that Colonel Huggins entered the room of Mrs. Bell?

Answer. I did not. I will state in addition that it was the mere rumor which I stated in my testimony yesterday, and the parties from whom I heard it heard it from mere circulating rumor.

Question. Have you ever seen or had a conversation with a person whom you knew or suspected of belonging to a secret organization which practiced deeds of violence, or whose purpose was to commit violence under any conditions or circumstances?

Answer. I never have in my life.

Question. Have you known or been informed of the locality where any such organization exists?

Answer. I have not.

Question. Have you heard that there was such an organization in Monroe County?

Answer. Yes, sir.

Question. Have you heard that there was such an organization in Pontotoc County?

Answer. Yes, sir.

Question. Have you heard that there was such an organization in any other county in Mississippi?

Answer. None that I know of, sir.

Question. Have you heard that there was such an organization in this county?

Answer. I have not, sir.

Question. Have you heard of repeated instances in different counties, other than those you have named, of the riding at night of bands of disguised men?

Answer. I have heard of some instances, but whether they could be called repeated instances or not I think is questionable.

Question. Do you know, or have you been informed, who constitute the band or association, or any one or more persons who were members of the same in your own county of Monroe?

Answer. I have not, sir.

Question. Have you no information whatever as to the persons who composed that band?

Answer. I have not, sir. I want to state in reference to that, by your permission, that I heard that there was a Ku-Klux organization upon the eastern side of the river. I live upon the western side, at Aberdeen. It was reported that a raid would be made upon our town about the time of the Meridian riot. A number of citizens met together for the purpose of devising ways and means to prevent it, and we called to our aid and into our councils a number of colored men in the town, and talked over the matter freely. From the evidence which we had, we became convinced that the negroes in the town had no knowledge of what was going on outside, but that some movement of a serious character was contemplated. Some one suggested that we had better get the assistance of the white men upon the eastern side of the river to repel any attack of that sort that might be made, and suggested this Ku-Klux organization. In connection with General Gholson and myself, the meeting suggested that we try to communicate with them. I endeavored in every way to find out some man there who belonged to that organization, and, sir, I will state that I think my search was a pretty vigilant one, made in a confidential way, and I could not find that there was any such organization in existence there, but that I heard of the very rumor which I told you in my examination—that there was such an organization in existence.

Question. Did you not hear of a great many outrages, particularly upon colored men, inflicted by men in disguise soon after that Meridian riot, in various parts of the country?

Answer. Well, about the time of the Meridian riot, I heard of some outrages that were inflicted upon colored men in the State. I do not know that they were numerous.

Question. Have you known or been informed whether the members of this organization take an oath or obligation, or enter into an agreement with one another to be enforced by penalties?

Answer. I have heard that through the public prints of the country.

Question. You have no other information upon the subject?

Answer. I have not, sir.

Question. Have you known or been informed by what name any such organization is known to themselves or others?

Answer. I have not been informed by what name the organization is known to themselves. I understand from the papers and from rumors that it is known as Ku-Klux.

Question. Have you known or been informed of the purpose or object of this organization?

Answer. I have not, sir.

Question. Have you known or been informed of the particular grievances this organization was formed to redress?

Answer. I have not, sir.

Question. Do you know, in point of fact, what grievances they generally do aid to correct or punish?

Answer. Well, sir, they seem to correct—to be a sort of vigilance committee to correct the morals of the country as they understand them. I do not think, so far as I have heard, or as far as my recollection extends in the State, that it is aimed at political effects or that it is political in its character.

Question. If they aimed to correct the morals of the country, and are operating in the interests of justice, it would seem to follow that the organization must be composed of very high-toned, moral gentlemen. Is it your understanding that it is so composed?

Answer. It is not my understanding, nor is it my understanding that they are operaing in the interests of justice.

Question. Is it your understanding that they are operating in the interests of good morals?

Answer. No, sir because good morals do not prompt the correcting of one evil by another evil.

Question. Have you ever seen, and, if so, under what circumstances, the disguises worn or said to be worn by these Ku-Klux?

Answer. I never saw one in my life, sir.

Question. Have you known or been informed of any single case where the material for the disguise was obtained, or by whom it was made up?

Answer. I have not, sir, in a single instance.

Question. Have you known or been informed of any person procuring a horse, saddle, bridle, or weapon to be used in any ride or raid, either to give notice or warning, or inflict a whipping or other outrage upon any person or person?

Answer. I have not, sir.

Question. Have you known or been informed of the raising of funds for the purpose of sustaining any organization of this character?

Answer. I have not, sir.

Question. I will ask you to give to the committee a list of the outrages which you have reason to believe, from reliable information, have been committed by disguised men upon citizens or inhabitants of Monroe County. You may make it very brief, giving the names and character of the persons.

Answer. Aleck Page, Jack Dupree, Abraham Wamble, Simon Dunham, Owen, McClenden, Wilson, Swanzy, Mr. Huggins. In what time do you ask?

The CHAIRMAN. At any time within two years past.

The WITNESS. Then Doc Hendricks. I think that is all, sir.

By Mr. BLAIR:

Question. Five of these were democrats—Owens, Swanzy, McClenden, Page, and Wilson?

Answer. Yes, sir; five of them.

By the CHAIRMAN:

Question. Do you know anything as to the signs or passwords of this order?

Answer. I do not.

Question. Has any one ever approached you and desired you to become a member of the organization?

Answer. No, sir, never.

Question. You never have seen a member of it, knowing he was a member?

Answer. I never have.

Question. You say you have made earnest efforts to discover whether any such organization exists in your county, and its membership?

Answer. Yes, sir; I have.

Question. Have you any idea of the extent of its membership in your county?

Answer. I do not believe any such organization exists in my county.

Question. Do you not believe that any of these bands that commit these outrages have originated in your county?

Answer. I have reason to believe, as far as that is concerned, that perhaps some of these outrages originated up in the northeastern portion of my county, composed partly of citizens of Alabama and partly citizens of Monroe. I think it was but a small neighborhood organization. I think it is the same organization which was in existence there in 1865 and 1866; and I can state that they were known as "Dow Blair's Regulators." You may take down the name. I give it as my opinion. I recollect in 1865 and 1866, just after the close of the war, there were a great many outrages perpetrated there upon citizens, a good many horses were stolen, and these men took it into their heads to commence regulating that matter. I recollect an instance, which I did not state, where they were indicted for whipping a white man, and I believe some of them were convicted for it. Of that I am not now positive. If General Gholson were here I could refresh his memory, but I believe that these outrages were perpetrated by that same band.

Question. All that you have mentioned?

Answer. Yes, sir.

Question. All the outrages?

Answer. No, sir; I will not state that, but I believe some of them were. Now, I am giving you my opinion—my theories. My impression in reference to the Wambold matter is that he was killed by a parcel of negroes. I believe Jack Dupree was killed by the men I tell you of.

Question. From the northeast part of Monroe County?

Answer. Yes, sir.

Question. Whom do you believe Aleck Page was killed by?

Answer. Well, sir, that is a matter of doubt. Two negroes confessed that they did it. I believe both their confessions were false.

Question. But the evidence was that twenty, or thirty, or forty were concerned?

Answer. I believe that the men that did that came from that neighborhood or from Alabama. We traced them over the ferry across the Buttahatchie, which, for a portion of the way, is about the dividing-line between Alabama and Mississippi, down to Hal Tucker's, twenty-five or thirty of them. Let me refresh my memory a moment; [referring to the pamphlet containing the Ku-Klux trials at Oxford.] I do not find it.

Question. What motive should the people of Alabama have to visit Monroe County and visit Page?

Answer. I cannot imagine.

Question. Is it your theory that they did come from across the line?

Answer. That is my theory.

Question. Then I should be glad if you could offer some explanation of the theory to the committee.

Answer. A witness by the name of Hal Tucker testifies that they crossed the ferry—a ferry across the Buttahatchie River; that they came from the direction of Alabama the night Aleck Page was murdered; that they returned in the same way, and went in the same direction.

Question. Page had never lived in Alabama?

Answer. Yes, sir, he had, I believe; but I do not think he had lived in that part. I think he lived south of that. He lived, though, in the adjoining county in Alabama to Monroe, but he had been in Mississippi a number of years.

Question. If it be true that the men who killed Page came from Alabama, would it not imply that there was an organization in Monroe County in correspondence with a similar organization in Alabama?

Answer. Alabama is almost in the neighborhood of where Page was killed. It is not very far to the Alabama line—twelve or fourteen miles.

Question. It is further than any knowledge of Page would extend, probably. He was an humble negro, of no prominence?

Answer. Yes, sir; no prominence at all.

Question. Would it not imply that there was some correspondence or understanding between the organization in Alabama and a similar organization in Mississippi?

Answer. I think not. I do not think it necessarily follows, at all.

Question. How do you account for it, then?

Answer. I will tell you. I suppose these men, whether they came from Alabama or Mississippi—and they could have come from eastern Mississippi—heard that Page had offered this insult to Mrs. Pope, and they thought it was such a one as demanded their interference, and that they came there to visit upon him the treatment which he received.

Question. Why should it not be left to the community in which the outrage had been offered to redress it?

Answer. I do not know in reference to that.

Question. Is not your theory defective upon that point?

Answer. I think not. Some neighbor there might have made the statement to these men in that neighborhood in which they lived.

Question. Had this lady any friends in that neighborhood in Alabama from which you suppose these men to have come?

Answer. Not that I know of. I do not know her family.

Question. Are these gentlemen represented to go round upon Quixotic enterprises of that sort, to redress social evils outside of the limits of their own State?

Answer. I did not state that they came from Alabama, mark you. I stated that they came from that direction. They may have come from eastern Monroe County, Mississippi; but certainly they did not come from the immediate neighborhood where he was killed.

Question. But on the supposition that they came from the State of Alabama, I repeat the question whether it does not follow, almost as a necessary inference, that they must have acted upon information given by some person or persons from within the State of Mississippi with whom they were in correspondence?

Answer. Or from personal knowledge which they may have had of the transaction themselves. I state that it does follow, as a necessary inference, if they came from the State of Alabama, that they acted either from information or from personal knowledge.

Question. They seemed, in coming to that neighborhood, to have come upon a common purpose; that they knew where they were going and what they were going to accomplish, did they not, obviously?

Answer. I do not know about that. I do not know that they knew what they were going to do, or what they were going to accomplish. I do not know in reference to that.

Question. Did they not ride in a body right to the house where Page lived, and take him out and hang him? Does not all that show that the members of that band had a common purpose and went to execute it?

Answer. I do not know that they rode in a body to the house.

Question. Is not that your information?

Answer. Yes, sir; they went there in a body.

Question. Could such common purpose be formed, except upon consultation, and would not that consultation necessarily bring all the men together at one place?

Answer. Of course; there could not exist a common purpose among separate men without previous concert.

Question. Then, again, if the purposes were an unlawful one, such as the whipping or killing of Page and such as, if accomplished, would subject to punishment those concerned, do you not think it would naturally follow that the men who entered upon that enterprise had entered into some kind of agreement, or had taken an oath to stand by each other and punish those who betrayed their secrets?

Answer. Yes, sir. If I went out at night to kill a man or whip another, in company with four or five men, I would have it understood that the thing should be kept secret, especially if I went in disguise; because going in that way is an evidence that the party desire to go under false colors, and I would require everybody who was a confederate with me to agree to keep it a secret, and of course require him to do it with every solemn pledge I could possibly invoke.

Question. Then you think the men who thus assembled upon Page's premises must have entered into an agreement or taken an obligation of that kind, do you?

Answer. I do, sir.

Question. They would likely have met, then, in some lodge or some secret place and entered into this agreement?

Answer. Yes, sir; they would, of course. It would not have been a secret agreement if any publicity had been given to it. Whatever was necessary to be done to make the agreement a secret they would do, of course.

Question. That would show that there was an organization either for this specific purpose or for a general purpose, would it not?

Answer. It would show this, that there was an organization for that specific purpose;

but merely because I kill you is no evidence that I have solemnly resolved to kill every member of this committee.

Question. But is it probable that thirty or forty men would have banded together for the purpose of killing a negro, whom the majority knew nothing about, living from fifteen to twenty miles from where they did, and against whom they had no personal grievance—is it likely, I say, that they would have come together for the specific purpose of killing him alone?

Answer. I think it is.

Question. Is that the way that people in this part of the country act?

Answer. I understand, at least it is my opinion, that if any man has committed a crime which, in the opinion of others, should render him subject to lynch-law, it is not only reasonable, but probable, that those men, who favored lynching him, should assemble together simply for the specific purpose of taking his life, and, after they had consummated the purpose of their agreement, then disband and have no organization.

Question. And you think it probable that such an organization might start up ten, fifteen, or twenty miles from the locality where the outrage was committed?

Answer. I think so.

Question. You think that natural and probable?

Answer. No, sir; I do not think it the most reasonable supposition. I think it most reasonable, if I and my neighbors determined to correct a private wrong in our own immediate neighborhood, that we ourselves should do it; but if we desired to evade the law to get some one else to do it. One neighbors can go and have the combination formed elsewhere and get it done in that way.

Question. Is it likely that a combination could be formed among strangers, who were wholly unacquainted with the persons to be slaughtered, such as you describe?

Answer. I think so.

Question. You think there are such elements now in the community that you could easily get a body of twenty men to go twenty miles to slaughter a man in cold blood, against whom they had no cause of offense?

Answer. I do not think so; but I think this, that in your State of Indiana, if a man from a certain neighborhood were to go and represent that an offense had been committed—for example, that a rape had been committed upon a woman by a man, and that he thought it demanded lynching—the neighborhood to whom he made the communication, if they were disposed in that way, as some of your people have in Indiana, would go down and render the assistance.

The CHAIRMAN. I think you are misinformed, sir, as to the condition of public morals and public opinion in Indiana. It has been a favorite topic with General Blair and some other gentlemen.

The WITNESS. I had no intention to reflect upon your people at all. I simply take my estimate of your people from the newspaper reports in reference to them, and I do not take a single democratic newspaper, except the semi-weekly Clarion. I read the New York Herald.

Question. So all efforts have failed, in the community in which you live, to penetrate the secrets of this organization?

Answer. Yes, sir.

Question. Although it has existed for the last five or six years, in your estimation?

Answer. Yes, sir.

Question. In the northwestern part of your county?

Answer. Yes, sir; it has.

Question. And not a single member has been brought to justice for any of its misdeeds?

Answer. No, sir; and not a single member has been brought to justice by the recent arrests made in the Federal courts.

Question. They all proved *alibis.*

Answer. They did; and in addition to that fact, in the most solemn manner possible these men deny ever having had any connection with any Ku-Klux organization, or any other organization which was illegal in its purposes.

Question. Has it not been so in every trial you have heard, where the attempt has been made to bring to justice the lawless men who have inflicted these outrages, that they have been able to prove an *alibi.*

Answer. In these cases we would not have attempted to prove an *alibi*, but have rested; we might have attempted that, but we would, in addition to that, have broken down the testimony of the prosecution by contradictions; but under the peculiar phase which this case presented in the Federal court, the common-law rule obtained—and it is the State rule now, under the recent decisions—that an indictment is *prima facie* evidence of guilt, and all the United States were required to do was to read their indictment, and it threw all the onus of proof upon us; and when we were charged with the commission of these offenses, there could be no justification. The only alternative left us was to prove an *alibi;* and in a case of that kind, as a legal proposition, the only evidence you can offer to rebut the charge is an *alibi.*

Question. And this is the defense that has uniformly prevailed in all these prosecutions?

Answer. Yes, sir, and the only one that can be made, as known to the law; and I put it to you as a question—I beg your pardon; I have no right to interrogate.

Question. Yet it is very evident, Colonel, that somebody has killed and whipped these men?

Answer. Yes, sir; it is.

Question. And yet your civil authorities are utterly baffled in the attempt to discover them?

Answer. Yes, sir; and so are the Federal authorities.

Question. And the courts are utterly paralyzed in all their efforts to stop these outrages?

Answer. I do not think that. I do not think they are paralyzed. Every single case of this kind has been investigated, I have no doubt, by the grand jury of Monroe County.

Question. One question further and I am done. Have you any doubt that any man, who was base enough to engage in an organization of this character, which contemplated the committing of murder, would commit perjury in a court of justice?

Answer. O, yes, sir. I think a man might, under the influence of passion and the excitement of the moment, commit murder; but yet, when called upon to swear as to what was the fact in reference to it, he would not perjure himself. And I do not believe this: I do not believe that these men would tell their counsel, in that confidence which exists between client and attorney, that they were innocent if they were guilty.

Question. I am not speaking only of the twenty-seven or twenty-eight men you were concerned in defending. I am not speaking of their innocence or guilt. The question put to you is, do you believe that any one of the forty or fifty concerned in the murder of Dupree or Page would go into a court of justice and state the truth?

Answer. Yes, sir; I believe it is possible. In any connection with the transaction?

The CHAIRMAN. Yes, sir.

The WITNESS. That they would go into a court of justice and swear that they did it?

The CHAIRMAN. Yes, sir.

The WITNESS. No, sir; I do not.

Question. Do you believe they would inform on men of that party who did it—would answer any question which would tend to criminate themselves?

Answer. Of course not. You could not make them answer any question which would tend to criminate themselves. They are sheltered by the Constitution of the United States in that matter, I believe, as in reference to every offense where a man is concerned in it. If you ask him in a court whether he was concerned or not, he would simply close his mouth and say, "I will not criminate myself."

Question. Would not that draw suspicion upon him?

Answer. The rule of law is that it should not.

Question. Would it not, in fact?

Answer. It would with me.

Question. Would it not with the community?

Answer. Yes, sir.

Question. Do you not believe that the men concerned in the murder of Page would go into a court of justice, and, with uplifted hand, swear they knew nothing about it?

Answer. No, sir, I do not; because I do not see what necessity there should be, if they were charged with it, of making that affidavit in a court of justice.

By Mr. RICE:

Question. I will ask one question. Suppose a man belonging to this Klan was interested to prove affirmatively an *alibi*. Do you think that his interest in protecting the Klan would be such that he would swear correctly in regard to the matter?

Answer. Well, sir, I know nothing about the Klan; but I do not believe that a man, where he knew another was guilty of a crime, would deliberately go into a court of justice and swear that the man was not there, and perjure himself. I believe there are some men that will do it.

Question. I will ask you in regard to another matter. You spoke of the instructions that were given by teachers of colored schools to their pupils. Is there any complaint about any evil instruction being given by the teachers of white schools to their pupils?

Answer. None, sir.

Question. Is what is known as the Ku-Klux law pretty generally condemned in this country?

Answer. It is condemned for this reason: that it is regarded as unconstitutional, but not because it attempts to put down disorders in the South, save this: that this is a matter of State policy, with which the General Government has no right, under the Constitution, to interfere. That is the condemnation which is visited upon it; that it is an interference of Congress in the domestic affairs of the State.

Question. The condemnation does not arise out of any fear that it will punish any who are engaged in these outrages?

Answer. No, sir; because I tell you I know the sentiment of my people in reference to the commission of these outrages, and they are against it, and are anxious for them to be put down.

By Mr. BLAIR:

Question. Now, in reference to the statement made by this man Joe Davis and Henry Hatch: if these men were so very anxious to keep their own secret, put on disguise and prowl around, is it probable that they would go to Joe Davis and Henry Hatch, two negroes well known as radicals, and, as they declare it, opposed to the Ku-Klux organization, and, without any disguise on at all, take them along as witnesses of their crime? Is that one of the probabilities?

Answer. I think not, sir. I think this in reference to that: if their purpose was the murder of colored men, I do not see any reason why they should go out of their own race to complete their organization. I do not see why they should trust a secret of that kind, and that solemnity and importance, to a member of the race they are charged with warring upon. It is like going into the camp of the enemy to get friends.

Question. In reference to the composition of this grand jury that made these indictments: how was it composed?

The WITNESS. Which grand jury?

Mr. BLAIR. The grand jury that found these indictments.

Answer. It was summoned by the marshal of the northern district.

Question. He just summoned whom he pleased?

Answer. Yes, sir; no, the judge of the district designates the county or counties from which the grand jury is to come, and they are summoned by the marshal or deputy marshal.

Question. He has the right to summon any person he pleases?

Answer. Yes, sir.

Question. In point of fact, did he summon any democrats on that jury?

Answer. There may have been two or three, or perhaps four, on the grand jury.

Question. And the balance of them were what?

Answer. They were regarded as republicans. I will state, in reference to that, that the indictment was not found until the second or third week of court, and if my recollection, or if my information is correct, there was not a single democrat upon the grand jury at that time.

Question. At the time bills were found?

Answer. Yes, sir.

Question. Now in reference to the summoning of the petit jurors. Has he the same right to summon whom he pleases?

Answer. Yes, sir.

Question. To go and pick out the jury?

Answer. The court simply directs from what county they shall come. That has been so always. That is the law of 1789—the old judiciary act. I believe it has been in force ever since, only this: that both the petit jury and the grand jury were required, either under the enforcement act or the Ku-Klux bill, to take a special oath, which is there put down; I forget what it is, but they swear that they have not been members of any political organization, or been in sympathy with it.

By the CHAIRMAN:

Question. Of a political organization?

Answer. Of the Ku-Klux organization, I mean.

By Mr. BLAIR:

Question. These men are charged with committing these crimes for political purposes, and, in fact, they are to be tried before those who are their political enemies?

Answer. Yes, sir; that is the fact of it.

By the CHAIRMAN:

Question. Is it a political offense, Ku-Kluxing the negroes; do you call that a political offense?

Answer. No, sir.

Question. That is what they were charged with in the Page case.

Answer. He asked me the question, if the men were charged with committing offenses against men on account of their politics, and are they not to be tried by their political enemies; and I stated that, in fact, they would. When we went to Oxford, as attorney of these men, we had no doubt of their innocence; and if it had been before a jury in a northern State we would not have hesitated to have put ourselves upon our plea of not guilty, and after we closed our testimony to have never argued the case at all; but the position of affairs at Oxford was such, the juries were of such a composition, that we were afraid they would be biased against our clients, and for that reason we sued out this writ of *habeas corpus*.

Question. You have the right of challenge, have you not, in the federal court?

Answer. Yes, sir.

Question. Have you any knowledge that the members of the petit or traverse jury are not proper good men?

Answer. They were mostly republicans.

Question. Were they men of good character?

Answer. Well, sir, I do not think so. I will say they were not.

Question. You knew them?

Answer. I knew many of them; some of them I did not know. There were some negroes on the jury, some colored men on the jury who were exceedingly clever, good citizens. One of them I had known always, and I did not think there was a man upon the jury, either white or black, who was his social equal or his equal in integrity. When I leave this out now——

Question. The colored man?

Answer. When I leave out a few of them, there were some of these who were exceedingly bitter and vindictive in their feelings. The most of the grand jury and petit jury were not men of good reputation and character in the country.

Question. Not of good reputation and character with the democrats, you mean?

Answer. No, sir.

Question. Or in the community in which they live?

Answer. In the community in which they live. Perhaps I will except from that remark Colonel Emery, who was the foreman of the grand jury. His reputation among the republicans is good; not among the democrats.

Question. Would it not be hard to get up a jury composed of republicans exclusively, in this State, that would be acceptable to democrats?

Answer. No, sir; I can go and take colored men in my county and try these men before them, and I would as leave risk them as to risk myself.

Question. You would sooner trust colored republicans than white?

Answer. Yes, sir; I mean white southern republicans; I make no reflection upon you. And there are some southern republicans who are as good men as there are in the country; and as an evidence of my feeling in that matter, I am upon the bond of republicans in my county.

By Mr. RICE:

Question. You were giving a theory, a while ago, that it is scarcely possible that the Ku-Klux should seek the aid of Joe Davis and Hatch to kill negroes; I ask if this may not be a plausible theory on the subject: that the four or five white men in the neighborhood that got Davis and Hatch to go to the meeting of the Ku-Klux—the balance being in disguise—may not have done so for the purpose of making these men guides, and putting them ahead, the balance of them keeping at a distance, so that they could not be identified by Davis or Hatch, and could not be identified by the parties they were to visit; that these four or five men of the neighborhood should fall back and not accompany the crowd, but leave the guidance of the party, so far as concerned the going to the place of the victim, to the colored men who were impressed. Is not that a plausible theory?

Answer. No, sir; it is not. No man who has ever seen Henry Hatch would ever trust him with a secret. He has not been before the committee.

Question. Would he be intrusted with any secret in that case? These men were at another place and can prove an *alibi* for that time.

Answer. If these white men were shrewd enough to get up a thing of the sort you state, they would know that Joe Davis and Hatch would believe that these men of the neighborhood, whom they recognized, were with them all the time, and were co-conspirators, whether with them or not.

Question. But these four or five men of the neighborhood we will suppose have gone away from the party, and they can thus turn around, when brought into court, and prove an *alibi* truthfully?

Answer. Suppose they do; suppose Joe Davis swears, or men of integrity swear, they started with the party, and they then go back. They are then equally as guilty as the men who themselves perpetrated the deed. But nobody would intrust a secret to Henry Hatch after conversing with him five minutes. He is little removed from an idiot, and I do not think he is a much stouter man than I am. If they wanted muscle they might have taken Joe Davis, if they had not plenty of muscle of their own.

Question. Hatch would do to hold their horses very well?

Answer. I do not think so.

By Mr. BLAIR:

Question. Are they driven to such necessity, fifty or sixty men, as to be obliged to carry these two men along with them to hold their horses?

Answer. I do not think so.

By the CHAIRMAN:

Question. Is not this a plausible theory: since so much has been said in the public press and otherwise, in relation to the Ku-Klux organization, would it not be an obvious policy with men who were going upon a raid, such as that against Page, to press into the service colored men for the purpose of creating the impression that these raids upon men of color were made by men of their own race?

Answer. I think not, sir; because if the colored men kept the secret it would never be known that any colored men were in it.

Question. But if found out, it would be known that colored people were mixed up in the raid?

Answer. I do not see how; because if I understand the disguises as represented by these witnesses to be worn by these men, it is impossible to tell them or to identify a single one of them. You could not do it. No man could go into a court of justice and tell me he recognized a man disguised that way, and make me believe it. I should place no confidence in his testimony.

Question. If these bands who commit these raids are composed of democrats, would there not be a strong motive to press into the service black republicans, for the purpose of showing that their organization was not of a political character, or that there was no political significance in the outrage committed?

Answer. I think not. To show you that it is not of a political character—if it was, every man in whom these men have any confidence in the community would know of their existence and their political purpose. Now, if they were southern soldiers, I do not believe there is a southern soldier in my county who, if there was an organization of that sort, would not intrust me with the secret; or if it was done for democratic purposes—not that I am a hot-headed democrat—I am not; I am conservative in my politics, but I more or less mingle or mix in a private way in politics in my county—and if there was an organization of that sort, of confederate soldiers, the democrats—General Gholson or myself—would know of it.

Question. Do you think there is a democrat who lives and breathes, who is mixed up in these outrages, who, let him be ever so friendly to you or General Gholson, would tell you he was privy to the murder of Page, Dupree, and others?

Answer. Yes, sir; if he knew the secret would be lodged in my breast. I would not let him tell me unless he told it in a confidential relation, and then if you ask me the question "Did he tell you?" I would say, "Gentlemen, I am his attorney. That is my secret."

Question. Would you receive any such secret in any other capacity than as an attorney?

Answer. No, sir; I would not. But I would receive the secret of the existence of an organization of that kind not as an attorney, but as one concerning which I would not, of course, perjure myself to keep. I do not suppose anybody who knows me would suspect any such thing for a moment. I would not perjure myself to keep the secret if called upon to testify before a court or this committee. If I had any knowledge of the existence of such an organization, I would tell you, and let the consequences fall where they might; but if a professional secret, that is protected by law, be asked, I would not communicate it; and when the question is asked if I know anything professionally which would injure this man, I would answer at once, "Gentlemen, I decline to answer that question."

By Mr. BLAIR:

Question. In reference to this question of *alibis*, the members of our committee have been very fond of sneering at the fact that that defense is frequently set up. Now, if a man was not there when the crime was committed, that is the natural and only defense?

Answer. It is. Where a man is charged with a crime of that kind there can be no justification in the law. There are but two defenses which can arise. One of them is that he was incapacitated in some physical way from committing the offense; the other that he was not present at the locality where the offense was committed. You may take it up, and look at it, and everything resolves itself into that. Suppose you were charged with my assassination—or rather, suppose that I am charged with your assassination—I beg pardon for making the illustration in the wrong way—and am indicted for it, and brought before the Federal court, where the indictment is made *prima facie* evidence of the fact; you see that to prove my innocence it must be by proving that I was not there; or if the proof should show that you were struck in a particular direction, or a particular place, or with a particular weapon, that I was physically incapacitated from striking in that way or using such a weapon. These are the only two defenses that can arise in such a case.

By the CHAIRMAN:

Question. The actual criminals always attempt to prove the *alibi*?

Answer. No, sir.

Question. Is it not a favorite defense with all criminals?

Answer. No, sir; because the law-books lay down that where the defendant attempts to prove an *alibi* and fails, it is a presumption of guilt, and, therefore, no lawyer will attempt anything of the sort unless he knows he can prove it to a dead certainty. Mr. Burrill, in his work on Circumstantial Evidence, states that where an *alibi* is proven it is the very strongest proof of innocence; but where an *alibi* is attempted and the party fails, I think it is a presumption of guilt; and a lawyer who had any skill in his profession would not attempt to prove an *alibi* unless he knew he could not be contradicted.

COLUMBUS, MISSISSIPPI, *November* 15, 1871.

The CHAIRMAN. Before proceeding further, we might as well dispose of the offer to introduce in evidence this pamphlet report of the hearing in Oxford, Mississippi, in June and July last, of the case *ex parte* Walton *et al.*, entitled "Full report of the great Ku-Klux trial in the United States district court at Oxford, Mississippi."

W. D. Walton, and nineteen others presented an application to Judge Hill, of the district court of United States for the northern district of Mississippi, praying a writ of *habeas corpus* against the marshal of the district, who held them in custody. They were a part of twenty-seven or twenty-eight men indicted in that court for going in disguise on the premises of Alexander Page, a colored man, corruptly banded together, as it is alleged, assaulting him, and finally killing him by hanging.

There was a trial had before the judge upon the *habeas corpus*, when forty or fifty witnesses were examined. Their testimony, including the application, indictment, &c., covers sixty-one pages of this pamphlet. The writ was dismissed, after a hearing of several days, and the relators discharged upon entering into recognizances, a part without bail, the others upon giving sureties.

Page was killed on the 29th of March, 1871, by a body of disguised men, who visited his house in the night-time. There is no question or doubt whatever of these two facts, viz: the killing, and that the deed was committed by men in disguise. This committee is not charged with the duty of discovering the men who committed the outrage.

The minority seek to introduce in evidence the testimony given upon the hearing before Judge Hill. The only office that would subserve would be, not to contradict any evidence as to the main facts, but simply to create doubts as to whether the right men had been accused.

If all is granted which this testimony conduces to establish, viz: that the persons then accused were innocent, it is not apparent how Congress or the country is interested in that fact.

I do not discover that the office of this proof, if allowed to go into our record, will be any other than to tend to show that the men there implicated were not guilty as charged in the indictment. I do not think this committee is interested in that question of fact. There seems to be no dispute whatever that Page was killed by a body of disguised men. We are charged simply with the duty of inquiring whether the laws are executed, and whether there is safety for life, person, and property in the late insurrectionary States. If the testimony given upon this hearing may go into our record, I do not see why the history of every similar trial upon a charge of outrage may not, upon the same principles, be admitted in evidence. This would swell the bulk of the record we are making in a degree that cannot be easily measured. In this single case it would add very many pages.

Greatly as I am desirous of accommodating General Blair, I am constrained to differ with him in his opinion that this evidence would subserve any useful purpose.

Mr. BLAIR. Upon the rule laid down by the chairman, it is manifiest that we should strike out about nine-tenths of the evidence we have already taken. A large part of it is in regard to drunken brawls, negro fights, personal altercations, and such violence as exists everywhere, and in all countries, and is certainly not pertinent to the inquiry which Congress sent us here to make. Upon the statement of the chairman, most of this evidence now offered is pertinent, as showing that this deed was done by armed men, or, as he says, an armed band of disguised men.

The CHAIRMAN. That has been already established by other evidence. There seems to be no dispute about the main facts.

Mr. BLAIR. Whether established or not, this is evidence upon the very subject which Congress sent us here to examine, as defined in the language quoted by the chairman; it is as pertinent as any evidence that has been taken; it is better than the hearsay the committee has already taken upon that point. To exclude the evidence of witnesses who testify to what they profess to know and to have seen, after admitting the hearsay of Huggins and others upon the same subject, seems to me a most extraordinary course.

The CHAIRMAN. I do not think Congress sent us down here to gather up pamphlet accounts of criminal trials that have taken place in the South, and substitute them for the testimony of witnesses——

Mr. BLAIR. Who do not pretend to know or to have seen the thing of which they speak. The merest hearsay has been given, and one witness made an effort to give this very testimony.

The CHAIRMAN. I suppose you will agree with me that there is no doubt as to the main facts—that Page was killed, and that it was done by a body of disguised men?

Mr. BLAIR. I do not desire that the chairman shall put any statement into my mouth. I say that Huggins, in his testimony, purports to give that evidence, and gives it not as it really was; yet we have taken Huggins's testimony and spread it upon the record, and now the original evidence, which he purported to give by hearsay, is refused.

This sub-committee has departed entirely from the precedents set by the chairman of the general committee, Senator Scott, when acting as chairman of the sub-committee in South Carolina, where every paper offered was allowed to go upon the record, and where the idea of objecting on account of volume or expense was not suggested; and now, after the enormous quantity of trash we have taken, and which has been taken by the general committee, this objection seems to me out of place.

Our record is already loaded with attempted descriptions of the very original testimony I now offer. Witnesses were called all the way from Mississippi to Washington to tell, through 30 or 40 pages, about this transaction; and now I offer the actual evidence which was given, and it is refused. Of course, I shall appeal to the general committee.

The CHAIRMAN. This decision is, of course, subject to the decision of the general committee. If I am wrong, the error can be easily corrected and this pamphlet can be made a part of the evidence.

If there was the least doubt of the fact that Page was killed, and killed in the night-time, and that it was done by a body of disguised men; or if this testimony tended to create a doubt as to the main facts, of course it would be admissible. Assume that all the men charged here were innocent, what has that to do with the main fact that such a killing took place?

Mr. BLAIR. It tends to show that it was a made-up job among the negroes, who actually killed Page, to charge it upon the white people.

The CHAIRMAN. It would make no difference at all whether it was done by white or black men——

Mr. BLAIR. A great difference.

The CHAIRMAN. Because they are equally subject to the law. There is nothing in this testimony, so far as I have examined it, that tends to show that negroes committed the deed.

At all events, the decision of the majority is that the pamphlet is excluded. I am sure I shall be happy to be corrected by the general committee if I am wrong.

[The action of the general committee is shown by the following extract from the journal of the committee, page 620:

"JOINT SELECT COMMITTEE,
"*Washington, D. C., December* 21, 1871.

"The Joint Select Committee met pursuant to the call of the chairman. Present, the chairman, (Mr. Scott,) Messrs. Bayard, Blair, Cox, Poland, Pool, Pratt, Rice, Stevenson, Van Trump, and Waddell.

* * * * * *

"Mr. PRATT, chairman of the sub-committee appointed to take testimony in the States of Tennessee, Alabama, and Mississippi, presented a report from which it appeared that during the investigation Mr. Blair had filed exceptions to the ruling of the chairman in relation to the admission of certain testimony and the exclusion of other testimony, as follows:

"3d. At Columbus, Mississippi, on November 4, 1871, Samuel J. Gholson, R. O. Reynolds, and other witnesses testified to the correctness of a printed report of the Ku-Klux trial at Oxford, Mississippi, (United State *vs.* Walton *et al.*) Mr. Blair offered in evidence, except that part containing the argument of counsel. It was excluded. Mr. Blair excepted, and appealed to the general committee.

"On the question, 'Will the joint committee sustain the ruling of the chairman of the sub-committee, (Mr. Pratt,) in excluding the report of said trial?' it was determined in the negative.

"*Ordered*, That said report, exclusive of the argument of counsel, be incorporated in the testimony."]

The document referred to above is as follows:

FULL REPORT OF THE GREAT KU-KLUX TRIAL.

The first important trial in the United States under the enforcement act, familiarly known as the Ku-Klux act, was commenced in the United States district court for the northern district of Mississippi, on Tuesday, the 28th day of June, 1871, before the Hon. Robert A. Hill, judge of said court, at Oxford, Mississippi.

The defendants were arrested on an indictment found by the grand jury at the June term of said court, under the sixth and seventh sections of the enforcement act, and appeared in court on a petition for a writ of *habeas corpus.*

THE COUNSEL.

The following were the counsel engaged in the case :

For the United States.—G. Wiley Wells, United States district attorney, northern district ; E. P. Jacobson, United States district attorney, southern district ; H. C. Blackman, H. W. Walter, Van H. Manning, and G. P. M. Turner.

For the relators.—W. F. Dowd, S. J. Gholson, R. O. Reynolds, R. E. Houston, J. D. McCluskey, and E. O. Sykes.

Official stenographer.—David M. Philip.

THE PETITION.

The following was the petition submitted to the court by counsel for the defendants:

To the Hon. Robert A. Hill, judge of the district court of the United States, with circuit court powers for the northern district of Mississippi.

The petition of William D. Walton, Barbour Quarles, John C. Porter, J. P. Willis, Jacob L. Loughridge, Andrew J. Crosby, William M. Butler, Andrew J. Pope, Henry McNeice, Thomas Malone, Robert L. Mays, James A. Roberts, John S. Roberts, Jasper Webb, James Neeland, Thomas J. Ford, James D. Hutchinson, Jefferson Willis, Burrill Willis, and Michael Forshee, respectfully showeth unto your honor—

That your petitioners are citizens of the county of Monroe, State of Mississippi, and of the United States of America, and of the northern district of Mississippi, and have never been heretofore charged with, or guilty of, a violation of the laws; that they are now engaged in farming, and the time, labor, and attention of your petitioners on their farms and in their business is absolute necessary to the support of themselves and families.

That on the 17th of June, A. D. 1871, they were arrested by one A. P. Huggins and others, the said Huggins claiming to act as special deputy United States marshal for the northern district of Mississippi, and by virtue of a warrant isssued by one H. C. Blackman, United States commissioner, alleging that your petitioners had violated the sixth and seventh sections of the act of Congress of May 31, A. D. 1870, were brought under arrest by said Huggins to Oxford, in said northern district, on the 19th instant. That they were so held in custody, and are now held in custody, by virtue of said warrant. That they cannot attach a copy of said warrant. That the affidavit upon which said warrant was issued, if any such affidavit was made, has not been seen by your petitioners or by their counsel. That the said Blackman, commissioner as aforesaid, has not been at the place designated in the warrant for the hearing of the charges preferred. They are informed by their counsel, and so state the fact to be, that no affidavit was made upon which to issue said warrant; and they are illegally and unlawfully held in custody.

You petitioners further state that on the 21st of June, 1871, the grand jury for the district court of the United States for the northern district of Mississippi returned into said district court an indictment against your petitioners, a copy of which is hereto attached, as Exhibit A, and made a part of this petition. That on the same day *capias* was issued to J. H. Pierce, marshal of the northern district, directing him to take the bodies of your petitioners, and hold the same in custody to answer said indictment. A copy of said *capias* is hereto attached, as Exhibit B, and made a part of this petition. That your petitioners are now held in custody by virtue of said *capias*, and are thereby imprisoned and deprived of their liberty unlawfully and illegally, and in violation of the Constitution and laws of the United States.

Your petitioners solemnly avow and state that they are not guilty as charged in said bill of indictment. That they did not on the 29th of March, A. D. 1871, or at any other time, go upon the premises of Alexander Page in disguise, nor were they present at the time of his alleged murder, nor did they aid, abet, assist, or counsel the same, nor were they interested or concerned in the same, either directly or indirectly, or in any manner whatsoever. That each and every fact in the bill of indictment stated touching their criminality is untrue in substance and every particular.

Your petitioners charge and state that the witnesses upon whose testimony the said bill of indictment was found, if they swore to the facts stated in the bill of indictment, perjured themselves. That before the investigation by the grand jury, said witnesses were threatened, tampered with, and suborned to swear against your petitioners, as your petitioners are informed and so state the fact to be. That one of the counsel of your petitioners applied to the district attorney of the northern district of Mississippi for a list of the witnesses upon whose testimony the bill of indictment was found. This legal and reasonable request was refused. The object of your counsel in making the application was to ascertain the names of the witnesses, and to show in this petition that they could not reasonably have had any knowledge of the facts testified to by them; and that on an inquiry before the coroner, they or a part thereof testified freely and voluntarily that they had no knowledge of the murder of Alexander Page, or the perpetrators of the same.

Your petitioners further state that the said Alexander Page, in the indictment alleged to have been murdered, was at the time of his death, and for several years previous thereto, a resident citizen of the county of Monroe, State of Mississippi, United States of America, and of said northern district of Mississippi.

Your petitioners further state that they are advised that the district court of the United States has no jurisdiction of crimes stated in said bill of indictment, because your petitioners and the said Alexander Page, at the time of the alleged murder, were citizens of Monroe County and State of Mississippi, and for all trespasses upon persons or property, as between citizens of the State, the courts of the State alone have jurisdiction.

Because further, said indictment does not allege any violation of the laws and Constitution of the United States, or charge any offense in violation of the laws and Constitution of the United States, and that an acquittal or conviction under said indictment would not be a bar to a subsequent prosecution under the laws of Mississippi.

Your petitioners therefore pay for a writ of *habeas corpus* commanding the marshal of the northern district of Mississippi to have the bodies of your petitioners before your honor at such time and place as your honor may designate, and that proper process may issue for all necessary witnesses, and that your petitioners may be discharged or bailed, as to your honor may seem just and equitable, under all the facts and circumstances in the case. And, as in duty bound, your petitioners will ever pray, &c.

W. D. WALTON.
B. QUARLES.
J. P. WILLIS.
his
BURRILL + WILLIS.
mark.
his
JEFF. + WILLIS.
mark.
J. S. ROBERTS.
ROBERT L. MAYS.
THOMAS MALONE.
W. M. BUTLER.
A. J. CROSBY.
J. D. HUTCHINSON.
his
HENRY + MCNEICE.
mark.
THOMAS J. FORD.
J. C. PORTER.
JASPER WEBB.
JAS. M. NEELAND.
A. J. POPE.
J. L. LOUGHRIDGE.
JAMES A. ROBERTS.
his
M. + FORSHEE.
mark.

THE AFFIDAVIT.

UNITED STATES OF AMERICA, *Northern District of Mississippi:*

This day personally appeared before me, George R. Hill, clerk of the district court of the United States for the northern district of Mississippi, the said petitioners, whose names were subscribed to said petition in my presence, who, being duly sworn, did depose and say that the facts stated in the foregoing petition, as of their own knowledge, are true, and those stated on the information of others they believe to be true.

his
JEFF. + WILLIS.
mark.
his
BURRILL + WILLIS.
mark.
his
MICHAEL + FORSHEE.
mark.
THOS. J. FORD.
B. QUARLES,
JAMES M. NEELAND.
JAMES A. ROBERTS.
W. M. BUTLER.
JASPER WEBB.
W. D. WALTON.
J. D. HUTCHINSON.
J. P. WILLIS.
A. J. POPE.
J. S. ROBERTS.
J. C. PORTER.
ROBT. L. MAYS.
J. L. LOUGHRIDGE.
A. J. CROSBY.
his
HENRY + MCNEICE.
mark.
THOS. MALONE.

Sworn to and subscribed before me the 22d day of June, 1871.

R. G. HILL, *Clerk.*

Exhibit A.

THE INDICTMENT.

United States of America, northern district of the State of Mississippi, district court, June term, 1871.

The grand jurors of the United States of America, elected, empaneled, sworn, and charged to inquire in and for the northern district of Mississippi at the June term, 1871, of the district court of the United States of America, for the district aforesaid, in the name and by the authority of the United States of America, upon their oaths do present and find: That Benjamin Lumpkin, Thomas Malone, Andrew J. Crosby, Jasper Webb, Whitfield Pope, Clinton Ross, John Porter, Stephen Crosby, David Studdith, John Studdith, Samuel Studdith, William D. Walton, Robert Mays, Barbour Quarles, William Butler, Jacob Loughridge, J. Plummer Willis, Dudley Hutchinson, James Neeland, John Roberts, Addison J. Roberts, Thomas J. Ford, John Ware, George E. Howell, Henry McNeice, Michael Forshee, Jefferson Willis, and Burrill Willis, of the northern district aforesaid, on the twenty-ninth day of March, in the year of our Lord eighteen hundred and seventy-one, in the northern district aforesaid, and within the jurisdiction of this court, did, among themselves, unlawfully, wickedly, and corruptly, band together, and did then and there, with force of arms, go in disguise on the premises of one Alexander Page, who was then and there a citizen of the United States of America aforesaid, and who was a man of color, and who at one time had been a slave in said United States of America, but was then and there a freedman by the Constitution of the said United States of America, entitled to the protection of his life, liberty, and property, with intent then and there to injure, oppress, threaten, and intimidate him, the said Alexander Page, and with intent then and there to hinder and prevent him, the said Alexander Page, in the protection of his life and liberty so secured to him by the said Constitution of the United States of America, and upon him, the said Alexander Page, freedman as aforesaid, and with the intent aforesaid, then and there make an assault, and him, the said Alexander Page, then and there did beat, wound, and ill-treat, and thereby then and there did hinder him, the said Alexander Page, in the protection of his life and liberty so secured to him by the Constitution aforesaid. And the grand jurors, upon their oaths as aforesaid, do further present and find: That the said Benjamin Lumpkin, Thomas Malone, Andrew J. Crosby, Jasper Webb, Whitfield Pope, Clinton Ross, John Porter, Stephen Crosby, David Studdith, John Studith, Samuel Studdith, William D. Walton, Robert Mays, Barbour Quarles, William Butler, Jacob Loughridge, J. Plummer Willis, Dudley Hutchinson, James Neeland, John Roberts, Addison J. Roberts, Thomas J. Ford, John Ware, George E. Howell, Henry McNeice, Michael Forshee, Jefferson Willis, and Burrill Willis, in the district aforesaid, on the twenty-ninth day of March, in the year of our Lord eighteen hundred and seventy-one, and whilst they were then and there so beating, wounding, and ill-treating him, the said Alexander Page, freedman as aforesaid, and while he was then and there entitled to the protection of his life and liberty aforesaid, and in the peace of God and of the United States of America, then and there being, as aforesaid, willfully, feloniously, and of their malice aforethought, in and upon him, the said Alexander Page, did make an assault, and with a rope about the neck of the said Alexander Page, then and there feloniously, willfully, and of their malice aforethought, they did put, fasten, and bind, and with the said rope about the neck of the said Alexander Page, freedman as aforesaid, so by them put, fastened, and bound him, the said Alexander Page, freedman as aforesaid, then and there feloniously, willfully, and of their malice aforethought, did choke and strangle, of which said choking and strangling the said Alexander Page then and there instantly died. And so the jurors aforesaid do say that the said Benjamin Lumpkin, Thomas Malone, Andrew J. Crosby, Jasper Webb, Whitfield Pope, Clinton Ross, John Porter, Stephen Crosby, David Studdith, John Studdith, Samuel Studdith, William D. Walton, Robert Mays, Barbour Quarles, William Butler, Jacob Loughridge, J. Plummer Willis, Dudley Hutchinson, James Neeland, John Roberts, Addison J. Roberts, Thomas J. Ford, John Ware, George E. Howell, Henry McNeice, Michael Forshee, Jefferson Willis, and Burrill Willis, in manner and form aforesaid, the said Alexander Page, freedman aforesaid, feloniously, willfully, and of their malice aforethought, did kill and murder, contrary to the provisions of the Constitution of the United States of America aforesaid, and against the peace and dignity of the United States of America.

2d. And the grand jurors, upon their oaths, do further present and find that the said Benjamin Lumpkins, Thomas Malone, Andrew J. Crosby, Jasper Webb, Whitfield Pope, Clinton Ross, John Porter, Steven Crosby, David Studdith, John Studdith, Samuel Studdith, William D. Walton, Robert Mays, Barbour Quarles, William Butler, Jacob Loughridge, J. Plummer Willis, Dudley Hutchinson, John Neeland, John Roberts, Addison J. Roberts, Thomas J. Ford, John Ware, George E. Howell, Henry McNeice, Michael Forshee, Jefferson Willis, and Burris Willis, of the northern district aforesaid, on the twenty-ninth day of March, in the year of our Lord eighteen hundred and seventy-one, in the northern district aforesaid, and within the jurisdiction of said court, with force and arms, did among themselves unlawfully, wickedly, and corruptly, band and conspire, and agree together, and did then and there go in disguise on the premises of one Alexander Page, in the peace of God and the United States of America, then and there being, and who was then and there a citizen of the United States of America, and who was then and there a man of color, and who had at one time prior thereto been a slave in the said State of Mississippi, and in the United States of America, and who was then and there a freedman, and who was then and there, by the laws of the United States of America, entitled to the benefit of personal security, with intent then and there to injure, oppress, threaten, and intimidate him, the said Alexander Page, and with intent then and there to hinder and prevent him, the said Alexander Page, in the enjoyment of personal security, so secured to him by the laws of the United States aforesaid, and upon him, the said Alexander Page, freedman aforesaid, and with the intent aforesaid, then and there did make an assault, and him, the said Alexander Page, did then and there beat, wound, and ill-treat, and thereby then and there did hinder and prevent him, the said Alexander Page, freedman as aforesaid, in the enjoyment of his right of personal security, so secured to him by the laws of the United States of America. And the grand jurors aforesaid do further present and find that Benjamin Lumpkin, Thomas Malone, Andrew J. Crosby, Jasper Webb, Whitfield Pope, Clinton Ross, John Porter, Stephen Crosby, David Studdith, John Studdith, Samuel Studdith, William D. Walton, Robert Mays, Barbour Quarles, William Butler, Jacob Loughridge, J. Plumber Willis, Dudley Hutchinson, James Neeland, John Roberts, Addison J. Roberts, Thomas J. Ford, John Ware, George E. Howell, Henry McNeice, Michael Forshee, Jefferson Willis, and Burrill Willis, in the district aforesaid, on the twenty-ninth day of March, in the year of our Lord eighteen hundred and seventy-one, and whilst they were then so beating, wounding, and ill-treating him, the said Alexander Page, freedman as aforesaid, and whilst he was then and there in the enjoyment of the right of personal security aforesaid, and in the peace of God and of the United States of America, then there being as aforesaid, feloniously, unlawfully, and of their malice aforethought, and in and upon the said Alexander Page did make an assault, and that the said Benjamin Lumpkin, Thomas Malone, Andrew J. Crosby, Jasper Webb, Whitfield Pope, Clinton Ross, John Porter, Stephen Crosby, David Studdith, John Studdith, Samuel Studdith, William D. Walton, Robert Mays, Barbour Quarles, William Butler, Jacob Loughridge, J. Plummer Willis, Dudley Hutchinson, James Neeland, John Roberts, Addison J. Roberts, Thomas J. Ford, John Ware, George E. Howell, Henry McNeice, Michael Forshee, Jefferson Willis, and Burrill Willis, of the northern district aforesaid, on the twenty-ninth day of March, in the year of our Lord eighteen hundred and seventy-one, in the northern district aforesaid, with a rope about the neck of the said Alexander Page, then and there feloniously, willfully, and of their malice aforethought, did put, fasten, and bind; and the said Benjamin Lumpkin, Thomas Malone, Andrew J. Crosby, Jasper Webb, Whitfield Pope, Clinton Ross, John Porter, Stephen Crosby, David Studdith, John Studdith, Samuel Studdith, William D. Walton, Robert Mays, Barbour Quarles, William Butler, Jacob Loughridge, J. Plummer Willis, and Burrill Willis, with the said rope about the neck of the said Alexander Page, freedman as aforesaid, put, fastened, and bound the said Alexander Page, freedman as aforesaid, then and there feloniously, willfully, and with their malice aforesaid, did choke and strangle, of which choking and strangling the said Alexander Page then and there instantly died. And the jurors aforesaid upon their oaths aforesaid, do say that the said Benjamin Lumpkin, Thomas Malone, Andrew J. Crosby, Jasper Webb, Whitfield Pope, Clinton Ross, John Porter, Stephen Crosby, David Studdith, John Studdith, Samuel Studdith, William D. Walton, Robert Mays, Barbour Quarles, William Butler, Jacob Loughridge, J. Plummer Willis, Dudley Hutchinson, James Neeland, John Roberts, Addison J. Roberts, Thomas J. Ford, John Ware, George B. Howell, Henry McNeice, Michael Forshee, Jefferson Willis, and Burrill Willis, in manner and form aforesaid, the said Alexander Page, freedman aforesaid, feloniously, willfully, and of their malice aforethought, did kill and murder, against the form of the statute in such case made and provided, and against the peace and dignity of the United States of America.

G. WILEY WELLS,
United States District Attorney, Northern District Mississippi.

THE CERTIFICATE.

UNITED STATES OF AMERICA, *Northern District of Mississippi:*

I, George R. Hill, clerk of the district court of the United States for said district, do certify that the foregoing is a true copy of an indictment returned into said court by the grand jury on the 21st day of June, A. D. 1871, that being a day of the June term of said court.

Given under my hand and seal of said court, at Oxford, the 28th day of June, A. D. 1871.

G. R. HILL, *Clerk.*

Exhibit B.

THE CAPIAS.

The President of the United States of America to the marshal of the northern district of Mississippi, greeting.

You are hereby commanded that you take Barbour Quarles, John C. Porter, J. P. Willis, Jacob L. Loughridge, Andrew J. Crosby, William M. Butler, Henry McNeice, Thos. Malone, Robert L. Mays, Jas. A. Roberts, John S. Roberts, Jasper Webb, James Neeland, Thos. J. Ford, James D. Hutchinson, Jefferson Willis, Burrell Willis, and Michael Forshee, if they shall be found in your district, and them safely keep, so that you may have them before the district court of the United States of America for northern district of Mississippi, to be held at the town of Oxford in said district, before the judge of the said court now in session, to answer unto the said United States upon a bill of indictment against them by the grand jury of the said district, lately found, for violation of the sixth and seventh sections of the enforcement act, and have then and there this writ.

Witness the Honorable Robert A. Hill, judge of the district court of the United States for the northern district of Mississippi, at Oxford, the first Monday of June, A. D. 1871, and ninety-fifth year of the Independence of the United States.

Issued the 21st day of June, 1871.

G. R. HILL, *Clerk.*

Come to hand date of issue.

J. H. PIERCE,
United States Marshal.

Executed personally by arresting the within-named Barbour Quarles, John C. Porter, J. P. Willis, Jacob L. Loughridge, Andrew J. Crosby, William M. Butler, Henry McNeice, Thomas Malone, Robert L. Mays, James A. Roberts, John S. Roberts, Jasper Webb, James Neeland, Thos. J. Ford, J. D. Hutchinson, Jefferson Willis, Burrell Willis, and Michael Forshee, and now hold them in custody.

J. H. PIERCE,
United States Marshal.

JUNE 22, 1871.

THE WRIT OF HABEAS CORPUS.

The President of the United States of America to the marshal of the northern district of Mississippi, greeting.

You are hereby commanded that you have the bodies of William D. Walton, Barbour Quarles, John C. Porter, J. P. Willis, Jacob L. Loughridge, Andrew J. Crosby, William M. Butler, Henry McNeice, Thomas Malone, Robert L. Mays, James A. Roberts, John S. Roberts, Jasper Webb, James Neeland, Thomas J. Ford, James D. Hutchinson, Jefferson Willis, Burrell Willis, and Michael Forshee, now under your custody, as it is said, and who are alleged to be "imprisoned and deprived of their liberty unlawfully and illegally, and in violation of the Constitution and laws of the United States," before the district court of the United States for the northern district of Mississippi, at the court-house in the town of Oxford, in said northern district of Mississippi, on the 22d day of June, A. D. 1871, at 3 o'clock p. m., to be dealt with according to law, and have you then and there this writ, with a return thereon of your doings in the premises.

Witness the Honorable Robert A. Hill, judge of the district court of the United States for the northern district of Mississippi, at Oxford, in said district, this 22d day of June, in the year of our Lord one thousand eight hundred and seventy-one.

G. R. HILL, *Clerk.*

THE MARSHAL'S RETURN.

I herewith return this writ into open court, and bring also into court the body of each of the within-named prisoners. They are in my custody as marshal of the United States of America by virtue of a *capias* issued from the district court of said United States, sitting for the northern district of the State of Mississippi, at Oxford. Said *capias* issued from said court on an indictment filed and found therein against said prisoners for murder, and are by me held under said *capias.*

J. H. PIERCE,
United States Marshal for said District.

JUNE 22, 1871.

THE RELATORS' TRAVERSE.

U. S. DISTRICT COURT,
Northern District of Mississippi:

Ex parte Walton et al.

WRIT OF HABEAS CORPUS.

And the said petitioners and prisoners, W. D. Walton *et al.*, come into open court and traverse the return made by the marshal in this case, who holds them as prisoners, and say that there is no valid or lawful indictment, or *capias* as stated in said return, but that said prisoners are held in custody without authority of law, and they are not guilty in manner and form as charged in said paper called an indictment.

REYNOLDS,
GHOLSON,
DOWD,
HOUSTON,
AND OTHERS,
Attorneys for Prisoners.

THE REPLICATION.

And the said United States, by the district attorney, moves to strike out the traverse of the defendants, because it is double, and both denies the truth of the return, and alleges facts to show that the detention is in contravention of the Constitution and laws of the United States.

G. WILEY WELLS,
United States Attorney, Northern District Mississippi.

The court ruled that testimony be heard in the case on the part of the relators.
The court then adjourned till half-past 8 o'clock on Wednesday morning.

SECOND DAY.

The court met at half-past 8 o'clock this (Wednesday) morning, Judge R. A. Hill presiding.

THE WITNESSES.

The witnesses on both sides in attendance were brought into court, sworn, and placed under the rule.

District Attorney Wells intimated to the court that in addition to the witnesses for the United States sworn and placed under the rule, he might call others, who were at that time beyond the jurisdiction of the court. The moment, however, that the witnesses in question arrived, he would give information of the fact, in order that they might be sworn and placed under the rule.

General Gholson, on behalf of the relators, said he had no objection to make.

The court suggested to counsel that, when exceptions were taken, it would greatly facilitate business if counsel would be brief in their arguments, as he felt he was quite competent to decide any question that might come up in the case without the arguments being unnecessarily long.

THE TESTIMONY FOR RELATORS.

The testimony on the part of the relators (the defense) was then proceeded with as follows:

Testimony of A. J. Pope.

Andrew J. Pope was the first witness called, and, on being examined by General Gholson, testified as follows:

Alex. Page was killed on a Wednesday night in March, as I have told you before in conversation, general. He was taken away from my place, I think it was on the 29th, but I don't exactly know the time. I think it was on the night of the 29th of March, 1871, when a disguised party came to my house. It was not exactly 1 o'clock; the clock struck 1 as they went out of my yard. When the clock struck 1 it was then the morning of the 30th. I had been asleep, but the noise of the party coming into my yard woke me up. This was in Monroe County, State of Mississippi. I know Mr. Hudson Butler and Mr. Wm. Ware. They live about one mile from my place. Mr. Jasper Webb also lives about a mile from me; Sam Stoddard about half a mile or a little over. I call my place seven miles from Aberdeen. I don't know exactly how far I am from Hutchinson's. It is about six or seven miles. Barbour Quarles is about the same distance; W. D. Walton about six miles; Addison Roberts I call fourteen miles off. I don't know about Jeff Willis, colored. Jacob Lochart's is in the neighborhood of Mr. Walton's, five or six miles off. Mr. Porter's is about five miles. I cannot tell about J. P. Williams's, as I never traveled down that road enough to know exactly.

Cross-examination:

Cross-examined by Mr. BLACKMAN: I know that it was on Wednesday night that the disguised party came into my yard. I was awakened up by them. I recollect the day of the week, because it was the night that Alex. Page was taken off my plantation. He lived about 125 yards from my house. I never saw him alive again. I did not see him until the inquest was held. I cannot tell whether it was two, three, or four days after he was taken away that the inquest was held. I don't know where he was killed. He was missing off my plantation. I fix the day he was taken away from the evidence given at the inquest. I cannot tell the date of the inquest. My attention was called to the fact that it was the 29th, because the next morning Alex. Page was missing. I will tell you how it was. We have service in our neighborhood every second Sunday, and this was after the second Sunday in March. I cannot tell the day of the week the month came in. I only know what they told me. By the time the inquest was held it was three or four days afterward. I can't tell the day of the week it was held. My wife knows. I fix the date from what the people told me. I don't know anything about the date. I know the darky went off on a Wednesday night. When I called him in the morning he was missing. My black folks came and told me he was missing. His being missed directed my attention to the day, because I lost his labor. I don't know that the party that came into my yard was looking for him. We were ditching the day before Alex. was taken away, but we did nothing the day after, as we were all so flustered. We commenced ditching on Monday or Tuesday. If it was Monday that we commenced, then we had worked three days. I can't remember whether we worked two or three days ditching. I am confident we worked two. We might have commenced on Monday and worked three. I don't know the day of the month we commenced. They tell me my memory is not very good. I will let people judge of that, for I cannot judge it myself. If I am not bothered I can state a fact, but if I am disturbed then it is different. The disguised men came about 1 o'clock. They remained ten or fifteen minutes. They did not come into the house. I talked with them five minutes. It was dark. The moon was not shining. It was a starlight night. The party had on white-looking garbs. There were eight or a dozen of them. They came making a fuss round my yard. I jumped up, when I heard them, and opened the door, but the door slipped out of my hand. They said they wanted to give me some advice. They did not give me any. They gave me a pinching and a gentle pounding. Some one pinched me with a gun. I don't recollect telling any one that I knew who pinched me. I never told that David Stoddard and Tom Malone pinched me.

General GHOLSON. I object.

District Attorney WELLS. We are laying a foundation for a contradiction.

The COURT. In that case the question is competent.

WITNESS. I never told any one. It was a fact that I was pounded and pinched. The party were on foot. I did not see any horses. I saw a double-barreled shot-gun, but I did not see any other arms of any kind. I never had any conversation with Jehu Wolf about this. There was a great talk among the colored people about Alex. being misssing, but I did not speak. I live a quarter section from the road. My own land is between my house and the road. It was a starlight night, and if there were any horses I did not see them. I was excited. I was not frightened when they came into my yard. I may have talked to them five or ten minutes. They simply said they wanted to give me advice. They said they would take me off and whip me, but they did not do it. They made no demonstration to do it. I went to the palings. I was ordered to come out, but I did not want to go. I went. My wife and children were there, but there was no one else but them. My wife started for my shoes, and they told her not to be scared. They then released my family and me. My family was frightened. That is all I know about it. I did not recognize any one from their faces. I will kiss the Bible on that. I cannot tell if the disguise would alter the height of a man. I came here to speak the truth. The party were dressed in something white. I did not see any trimming. The gowns came down to the ground. Their heads seemed to be wrapped up like. I cannot tell whether it was a hat or cap or wrapped up in a table-cloth. I only saw the white arrangement. I was excited some. I did not make any search for Alex. after I heard he was missing. He was in the habit of being at his work in the morning. He was always faithful at his work. They said he had the habit of running round at night. I did not make a search that morning. I sent my black fellow Jehu into my wheat-field. Alex. never was missing before. I made no effort to find him, although this was the first time he was missing. I did not go off the plantation. I did not hear a pounding down at Alex.'s door the night before he was missed. I went down to Fanny's cabin. I heard the circumstances from her. That was about sun-up. She told me the circumstances under which Alex. was taken away. She told me about the persons disguised.

Colonel REYNOLDS. Do not tell what she told you.

WITNESS. She stated the circumstances under which he was taken away; yet I made no effort to find him. I had plenty of work to do, but owing to the confusion they were all scared. On account of the confusion I made no effort to find Alex. I did not know what to think of it. I did not know anything about it, The clock struck 1 as the party left my yard. I did not know they had been at Alex.'s before that. I did not sleep for a long time after they left, on account of getting this pounding. Alex. lived about 120 or 125 steps from my house. I heard no pounding or calling at the door of his house. I don't know where the party went after they left my house. I don't know whether they were at Alex.'s before they were at my house.

Mr. REYNOLDS. We will recall the witness. Put him again under the rule.

Testimony of Mrs. Lucinda Cook.

Mrs. Lucinda Cook was next called.

General GHOLSON. Your honor, we propose to prove an *alibi* by this witness in regard to the defendant Henry McNeice.

On being examined by General Gholson, the witness testified as follows:

I live down ten miles from Aberdeen; I live beside the defendant, Henry McNeice, he is my brother. On the 29th of March last I was with him; I was sitting up with him; he was very sick; he was frequently sick; I could not tell all the nights I have sat up with him. He has not been able to do half an hour's work for a long time. He has three girls and one son; his son is here; I cannot tell how old he is; his eldest daughter is fifteen; the son is older, and the other two girls younger. I recollect being with him; I sat up with him; he was very bad. His wife died five years since. I recollect it was the 29th of March I sat up with him; I can recollect he kept his bed one week; he was very bad; I live alongside of him, and that is the reason I know so much about him. I know A. I. Pope; I don't know how far he lives from my brother. My brother has not been able to do a day's work for a long time. In March last his health was bad, and I was compelled to sit up with him. I don't precisely know the time when I first heard that Page was killed; I recollect the news came about the "nigger" being killed.

Cross-examination:

Cross-examined by Colonel MANNING: I am sister to McNeice, the defendant. I sat up with him on the night of the 29th of March. I was there the next day, when I heard that Alex. Page was killed; I don't remember who told me; I don't remember the time it was; I did not pay strict attention; I did not fix the date at all in my mind. My brother was sick all through March; I don't remember the exact night; he was sick several nights in succession. I know I was at my brother's when I heard of Alex.'s death; I did not pay attention how the news came. My brother's health has been bad all the time; he stays always at home, and he was unhealthy when his wife died; he chokes up as if it was his last breath; he has consumption, phthisic, or something else; I have seen him turn black in the face; he does nothing, and has been able to do only a very little work, and his little children do what little things is to do; he has been attended by Dr. Hutchinson. I never was a good hand to keep dates, and I can't remember the exact date. I know when he was bad his children came for me to go and sit up with him.

To General GHOLSON. He had bad spells in March which lasted a week; he had bad spells very often for a week or two; he chokes. When I heard of the death of Page, it was the day after I had sat up with my brother. I recollect sitting up with my brother during the latter part of March. I know I heard of the death the next day; I did not pay any attention as to who brought the news.

To Colonel MANNING. He was often sick and had choking spells; he had them before the war; I don't know it is asthma that ails him; he smothers and chokes when he lies down and he must sit up again; he looks as if it were his last breath, and that every breath would be his last. I don't know how I got the news of Page's death; I paid no attention about it.

Testimony of Powhatan McNeice.

Powhatan McNeice, a lad of fifteen, was next called and examined by General Gholson. In answer to certain questions by the court, he showed that he understood the nature of an oath, and was accepted as a witness.

He testified as follows: The defendant McNeice is my father. About last March my father was at home. He was sick. He was very low, and my sister and I had to sit up with him. I sat up with him some two or three times. I heard of the killing of Page last Sunday morning was a week ago. My father has been very bad, and was unable to attend to his family. My father does not stay away from home at nights. It was some Saturday night. I think it was in April when he was away from home. I sleep in the same room as my father. We have only one room. We sleep all together in the same room. He has not been able to work much. He has bad spells very often, especially if he has been out at night, or gets wet—smothering, wheezing at the same time. Billy Walton's store is half a mile from our house. He was worse at night and better by day. He was never absent from the house in March or April. I think he was absent in May, on a Saturday. I don't know how I recollect it was a Saturday night. I remember it was a Saturday night. There were two beds in our room. Father and I slept together. I sleep sound. I don't keep awake all night. He may have gone out and been away and I not know it. I sleep pretty hard sometimes. I sleep tolerably good. If he was absent at any time it was unbeknown to me. He may have got up and gone out, but I don't think he did. He went out on the Saturday, when the sun was high, and came home next day. I heard of Page's death a week ago last Saturday. I never heard about it in March. Mr. Jasper Webb told me about it. He was telling my father about it. He said Page was killed. I don't think my father was away a single day in April or March, except in the fields. We got to bed generally about bed-time—8 or 9 o'clock. I was there in the day-time. I never heard the circumstances of the death of Page till Saturday week. I have heard that Mr. Pope's plantation is ten or twelve miles from where we live. That is all I know about it. Nobody came but Dr. Hutchinson, as he did not need much doctoring, as it does not do him much good. He was worse in March, and up to the 1st of April. About the 1st of March he was badly bed-ridden, but I am not certain he was bad a week before. When not badly bed-ridden, he was up and about the fields now and then. He had bad spells three days apart, sometimes. They made him weak. My sister and I sat up with him, and when he was very bad my aunt came and sat up with him. She sat up two or three times with him. One time, I am certain, was last March. I don't think she sat up with him last month. She did not sit up with him from the 20th to the 30th of March.

The witness was not cross-examined.

Testimony of Lafayette Willis.

Lafayette Willis was the next witness called.

Colonel Reynolds said he wished to examine the witness in regard to the defendant, Henry McNeice.

Witness testified as follows: I am acquainted with Henry McNeice. I have known him for ten or fifteen years. He has been living on my land for two years. He has got the asthma. He is afraid to go out at night. I am very fond of hunting, and go out a good deal at night. He went out with me one night, and he was laid up in consequence. I wanted him to go again, but he was afraid to go, saying it would hurt his health. He was often complaining of his breath. He suffered worst when the weather changed, in spring and winter. He did better in warm weather. His children did the work about the place. I furnished him with a plow. He had a horse when he came there. I kept him in stock; and as I had cotton to haul, and other things to do, I told him when I got my hauling and my other work done I would furnish him with a horse. I know where Andrew's church is. It is about eight miles from where I live. I have always considered McNeice a quiet, inoffensive man, of an innocent, harmless character. I know his character among his neighbors. I never heard anything against him. I know him to be a good man, or I would not keep him on my place. I have known him familiarly for fourteen or fifteen years. I never knew anything of him, except his being an orderly, harmless, innocent man.

The witness was not cross-examined.

Testimony of John Kuykendall.

John Kuykendall was the next witness called, and on being examined by General Gholson testified as follows:

I am acquainted with Barbour Quarles. I staid with him in the latter part of March. He slept with me. I don't know exactly about the time of the month it was. I don't remember the night Mr. Wooten was there. Quarles and I slept in the same bed. We went to bed between 9 and 10 o'clock. We lay down. He left the lamp lighted, and lay and read in bed. I went next morning to Walton's and staid till about 12 o'clock, and then went to Wilson's. I don't know the exact time I heard of the death of Alexander Page. I saw some parties coming from Aberdeen. The report was running there. I met several squads of persons on the road. I met Mr. West, and he named the report. He told me of the death of Alexander Page. That is the reason I make it out that he was killed the night before, when I was at Quarles's. I am confident I staid there the night before. It was about the last of March. My business was attending a horse, passing round the country. Quarles's was one of the places I stopped with the horse. My arrangement was to stay all night with the horse. Quarles is a single man. John Wooten stays there, and a woman named Anna Jordan. She stays twenty steps from the house. She don't sleep in the same house with Quarles. There is a man named Tate working on the land. I have told you all that stay about the house. I have been in business. I don't think Quarles could have got out of bed that night without my knowing it. When he got up to blow his horn in the morning, about daylight, he awoke me. I went out with him. Wooten did not sleep in the same room with us. I went from Quarles's to Wilson's. I mean Jack Wilson. It is in the direction of west by north.

Cross-examination:

Cross-examined by Mr. BLACKMAN: I went in the evening to Quarles's. We went to bed between 9 and 10 o'clock and lay lay there till 11 o'clock. Walton's store was one of the standing places for my horse; there was no other place near Quarles's; he was keeping bachelor's hall; it is a good place to keep a horse. I went two miles away from the former place. I had bills printed when I went out first. Walton's store was one of the places mentioned on the bills. I have not got one of these bills; I have some at home; they were printed in Aberdeen, at Jonas's; I don't know the name of his newspaper.

Colonel REYNOLDS. The Examiner.

WITNESS. Quarles got up at daylight to blow his horn to wake up his hands. There was no niggers on the place. They were white hands. I got breakfast there. After I had been at Walton's store, and when I was going to Wilson's, I heard of this death. I was in the opposite direction when I heard it after I passed Quarles's place. I never measured the road; it was about three miles, I think. I met one fellow, then a squad; all had been at Aberdeen; I don't recollect who they were except West; I asked him what is the news; his name is James West. I was going down for some medicine It was along in the evening when I heard it. I don't know about the hour. I don't know how far I rode after I heard it. I stopped at Jack Wilson's. I am no judge of distances. I don't know when I got to Wilson's that night; I cannot fix any exact time; it was in the evening, the latter part of the day; I don't know as I can fix the time. I did not take any dinner there; I did not take any dinner at all. I fed my horse there. I was waiting for my customers there for them to come in. West did not tell me about the body being found; he had heard it from somebody. He came from Aberdeen. I don't know how many parties told me about the killing; I don't know any of the other parties; I heard it from other parties. I told General Gholson about it. I met West some miles from Aberdeen. I don't know how far it is from Quarles's to Aberdeen. I made trips with my stud-horse every eight or nine days. West told me Page was killed the night before.

Mr. BLACKMAN. What did he say?

General Gholson objected to the question.

The court ruled that the details could not be given of what was said.

Mr. Blackman said that if West said it was done *the* night before they could fix the *alibi*, but if he said *some* night before, it could not be done.

Mr. Turner said it all turned on the fact whether he used the article "a" or "the."

The court ruled that the question was not competent.

WITNESS. The meaning of what I said was, that we don't use grammar like you, but we just explain a thing by thus or so, [waving his hand.] We don't follow a fellow through to a "t," but just understand what is meant without grammar. I did not take it, from what he said, that it was more than the night before. I did not converse long with West. I don't remember that he talked about anything else. I know I was going for some medicine. We talked about five minutes. It might have been a quarter of an hour. I don't recollect how long I talked to the squad of men. I have lived about twenty-seven years in Monroe County. I have lived there nearly all my life. I used often to pass from Athens to Columbus, and that is the reason I don't know the other road so well. I have in my time been farming, merchandising, and running a stud-horse, and attending on him.

To General GHOLSON. I know the Buttahatchie. I traded at Columbus at one time. When I left Walton's I went to Wilson's that day, where I staid all night. General Gholson's place is west of south of it, close to a blacksmith's shop. I took my horse where there was the most custom. I generally told the people when I would be back again that way. I did not conform to the arrangement in my bill, as Sunday came in and I had to alter it.

To Mr. BLACKMAN. From General Gholson's place to Walton's is about four miles. I don't know the distance to Wilson's. It must be four or six miles. It was dark when I got to Wilson's that night.

Testimony of John Wooten.

John Wooten was next called, examined by General GHOLSON, and testified as follows:

I know the defendant Quarles. I have lived at his house for nearly five months. I keep the keys of the stable and have charge of the stock. I do all that myself. Quarles does not interfere. He has nothing to do with them. I remember Kuykendall. He is sitting there in court. He was at Mr. Quarles's on Tuesday or Wednesday in the latter part of March. There is a very severe dog in the yard, and he is so troublesome that nobody can pass him except the folks, and he even growls at them. He grumbles at me even, and nobody can pass him except he makes a noise. We breakfast tolerably early. Kuykendall was in the habit of leaving with his horse at six o'clock in the morning. From Quarles's to Walton's is two and a half miles, and from Walton's to General Gholson's is five miles. I don't know how far it is to Jack Wilson's. I was at Quarles's in March. Our rooms were not ten feet apart, and Quarles could not get up and go out without me knowing. He did not have anything to ride round with in the spring, as his mare had a colt and the mules were all at work. He doesn't give his stock to any of his hands to ride out on Sunday, and I can't get a horse to go and see my mother. I had the keys of the stable in March. I examined the stable. There were no marks on it, and no new tracks.

Cross-examination:

Cross-examined by Colonel MANNING: I keep the keys in my pocket, with my hand upon them by night or by day, asleep or awake. I keep them in my pocket. I have not my hand on them all the time. I don't put my pants under my pillow. I put them on a chair. I don't sleep sound. I am satisfied no one could get the keys out of my pants without me knowing it. I am pretty certain nobody did get the keys. I think it was Tuesday that Kuykendall was there in March. He came every ninth day. I don't know exactly what three times nine amounts to. Kuykendall was carrying round a horse. When he was there it was along about the middle of March. I saw no fresh tracks in front of the stable when I looked for them. The door was locked and the keys in my pocket. Quarles sometimes snores when he is sleeping and sometimes not. I know he never went out there at night.

To General GHOLSON: It was Tuesday or Wednesday that I saw Kuykendall at Quarles's. It was the last of the month.

To Colonel MANNING: I told you it was about the middle of the month.

To General GHOLSON: I can't either read or write.

To Colonel MANNING: I don't know anything about dates.

The court took a recess till 3 o'clock in the afternoon.

AFTERNOON SESSION.

Testimony of James Moore.

James Moore was the next witness called, and, on being examined by General Gholson, testified as follows:

I have known Mr. Quarles, the defendant, fifteen or twenty years. I know his general character, and know him to be a law-abiding citizen. I never knew him to be in a difficulty. He is considered to be a law-abiding citizen. I never knew him connected with lawsuits or trials. His place is eight or nine miles from A. J. Pope's. I don't know exactly where McNiece lives. I was born where I am now living—that is about thirty-five years ago. I don't recollect where I was on the 29th of March. I don't know that I know the day when Alexander Page was killed. I heard about it the next day that it occurred the night before. I was at the mill, about three miles from where it occurred, in the direction of Aberdeen. I think I carried down the report to Aberdeen myself. I reported it when I got there. It was told the day after it occurred. I remember meeting General Gholson. I left the mill before the 12 o'clock bell rang, and was in Aberdeen an hour after.

Cross-examination:

Cross-examined by Mr. TURNER: I heard of the killing between 10 and 11 o'clock. I think my partner, Mr. J. H. Anderson, told me at the mill. He was formerly sheriff of Monroe County. I went to the mill after breakfast. I heard the Ku-Klux had taken Page from Pope's and killed him. That was between 10 and 11 o'clock.

Testimony of W. E. Love.

W. E. Love was the next witness called, and, on being examined by General Gholson, testified as follows:

I am acquainted with the defendant Quarles. I have known him eight years. I am acquainted with his general character. He is an orderly, quiet, law-abiding citizen. I have never heard of his being engaged in any broils. I am a native of Monroe County. He is looked upon as a gentleman and a very clever man by his neighbors; all speak well of him. I was a deputy sheriff for some time, and have always heard him spoken of as a law-abiding citizen. He never had a case brought against him in the courts. He is considered a gentleman in his neighborhood. I think I heard of the killing of Alexander Page the day after it was said to have occurred.

Cross-examination:

Cross-examined by Mr. BLACKMAN: The news came by some of his neighbors. It was supposed he was killed, but we had no means of knowing how he was killed. I heard it next morning. It was the general talk about the streets. I think I heard it between 10 and 11 o'clock in Aberdeen. I don't remember whom I first heard mention it.

Testimony of Miss Elizabeth Webb.

Elizabeth Webb was next called and examined by General Gholson. She testified as follows:

I am the sister of the defendant, Jasper Webb. On the fourth Sunday in March I was at home. My father was taken sick that day. I would have gone to the preaching if my father had not been sick. My sister, Mrs. Bassham, and my sister Mary, sat up with father on Monday. She also sat up with him on Tuesday. I was there on both occasions. My brother Jasper came to the house before supper on Wednesday. I saw him during the night. I was up that night. Jasper left after breakfast the next morning. He sat up two nights. He came the next evening before supper. I don't remember whether it was that day or the next that I heard Alexander Page was killed. It was said to be Wednesday. James Bassham was there. My father is better. I don't think there was anybody else but those I have mentioned and myself there. The fourth Sunday in March was the regular preaching-day in the Presbyterian church in that neighborhood.

Cross-examination:

Cross-examined by Mr. TURNER: There is preaching there the fourth Sunday of the month. Father was taken sick that day. Defendant came there on Wednesday. I know my sister stopped up two nights with me. Both staid up on Monday. They were there on Tuesday. They staid three nights before my brother came. My sisters were there Sunday, Monday, and Tuesday. The defendant was there in the day-time but did not stay. It was after my father had taken sick that I heard about the killing. I heard of the coroner's inquest. I did not set up three nights all the time. I staid in father's room when he was sick. I saw that my brother never left the room. I don't think I ever lay down at all. We had no physician. My father got paralyzed and could not walk. I don't think my brother went to sleep. If he did I did not know it. He was there two straight nights. Father took sick on Sunday. My sister came back on Friday. I knew my brother was there because my sister was with him. I knew all the time he was there that night. I have nothing more to fix the time but what I have said. I have told that we had no physician, for he did not want one.

Testimony of James Bassham.

James Bassham was next called, and, on being examined by General Gholson, testified as follows:

I know the defendant, Jasper Webb. I remember the time I was sitting up with him with old Mr. Webb. It was Wednesday, 29th of March. There was no one else there except the family. My grandfather, old Mr. Webb, is about ninety years of age. I reckon he can get about with crutches. I think he was paralyzed. At the time of his sickness he lost the use of himself. He has got more use of himself than he had. My grandfather lives about three and a half miles from A. J. Pope's. I heard the next day about the killing of Alexander Page. I was then at home. I live about one and three-quarter miles from Pope. I heard it in the evening. My little sister and brother told me. They heard it from the school children at Murphy's. From Jasper's house to Pope's is one and a half miles. I staid all night at my grandfather's. I saw Webb there all night of Wednesday. He did not leave there, because we staid in the same room together. After my work was done for the day Jasper and I went to grandfather's.

Cross-examination:

Cross-examined by Colonel MANNING: I am a grandson of old Mr. Webb. I don't live with him. I live half a mile from him. I was at his house on the 29th of March. The "occurrence" occurred that night. It made an impression on my mind when I heard it. I heard next day that the Ku-Klux went there and killed this "nigger." I consulted an almanac that day. I did so to fix the date. It was a custom when any strange thing occurred to consult the almanac, to see what day it was for lucky and unlucky days. I don't remember when grandfather was taken sick. It was some days before that Wednesday when I went to see my grandfather. I and my uncle Jasper went together. I live with my mother. We sat up with him in grandfather's room. We staid in the same room. My mother had gone to see my grandfather before that. I don't know a boy called Alexander Stuart. I know Jack McDupre. I did not consult the almanac in his case. I consulted the almanac on the 30th. I heard about the killing from my little sister and brother. That was about three-quarters of a mile from Pope's place. I heard about the inquest some time after. I did not look at the almanac about that. The reason why is that an inquest is no unusual occurrence.

Testimony of General Gholson.

General Gholson, of counsel for the relators, was next examined by Colonel Reynolds, and testified as follows:

I know the general reputation of Jasper Webb. It is good for morality. He belongs to the Cumberland Presbyterian Church, and upholds the principles of the church, and is a quiet, sober man.

Testimony of Colonel W. F. Dowd.

Colonel W. F. Dowd, of counsel for the relators, was next called, and testified as follows:

I know Jasper Webb. I know his general reputation among his neighbors for morality, sobriety, and quietude. It is good.

Cross-examination:

Cross-examined by District Attorney WELLS: I am not a member of the Cumberland Presbyterian Church. I am half Baptist and half Presbyterian, but my better-half is a Presbyterian.

Testimony of Colonel R. O. Reynolds.

Colonel R. O. Reynolds, of counsel for the relators, was next called, and testified as follows:

I know Jasper Webb. His reputation for purity, morality, and quietude, is good among his neighbors. I don't know if he is a member of a church or not.

Testimony of Mrs. Sarah E. Malone.

Sarah E. Malone, wife of the defendant, Thomas Malone, was next called.

District Attorney Wells objected to a wife testifying in favor of her husband.

The court overruled the objection on the ground that it was in conformity with State practice.

Witness then testified as follows: I am the wife of the defendant, Thomas Malone. I was sick on the 29th of March, and I recollect where he was that night and day; he was at home; my recollection is good about it. I had disease of the heart, and I have been compelled to have him always with me at night during my sickness. He never left home that night. If he has to go away on business he always gets some lady to stay with me from the neighborhood. I have four children, the oldest of whom is eleven years of age. I heard of Alexander Page being taken; I heard it next evening; my husband had been to town, and when he came back he told me about it. From our house to Pope's is about a mile.

Cross-examination:

Cross-examined by Mr. TURNER. I have heart disease periodically. I know it was the 29th of March. I had been sick for several days. I am never well. If you will come and see how ill I am I can tell you how often I am attacked periodically. These attacks don't have any effect on my mind. During that periodical attack I had been taking medicine since Christmas. My husband went for the medicine on the 30th of March; I remember the 29th was Wednesday. My husband has never been absent from home since Christmas. He is not afraid to leave me in the day-time; it is at night it is most dangerous. I remember he went to town for medicine on the 30th of March, and that enables me to fix the date. My attention was first called to the fact that I was sick on the 29th, because my husband went for the medicine on the 30th. I examined the druggist's bill, because I wanted to settle it, and it was dated the 30th. I had the paper to look at. I want a man to understand what I say, and if you (Mr. Turner) can't understand what I say after telling you so often, I want the court to appoint somebody who can.

The court directed the witness to answer the questions of counsel.

Witness resumed: I told you I looked at the bill and saw it was the 30th; I looked at it since. It is my business whether I have any other papers since that time in my possession; I have some papers at home dated the 22d of March. I have no papers of medicine purchased since that time, but I had one before the one I spoke of.

That was not paid for at the time the other was; it is not paid for yet, I think. Mr. Malone purchased the medicine. I don't remember when he went down to pay the bill. He purchased the medicine from Eckford on the 30th of March.

Testimony of Silas F. Kendrick.

Silas F. Kendrick was the next witness called, and testified as follows:

I am acquainted with the defendant Malone, and have known him twelve or thirteen years; I know his general character for honesty, sobriety, and morality; it is good; he is a law-abiding citizen as far as I know him; I have always respected him; I have sold him goods, and all his neighbors give him a good character.

Testimony of Henry Alexander.

Henry Alexander was next called, and testified as follows:

I have been acquainted with the defendant Malone eleven or twelve years; he lived with me sixteen months; he is an honorable, law-abiding citizen.

Testimony of James Moore.

James Moore was next called, and testified as follows:

I have known Malone eight or ten years; he is looked upon by his neighbors as an honorable, law-abiding citizen.

Testimony of John Willis.

John Willis was next called, and testified as follows:

I have known Malone a long time; his character is good so far as I am aware, and I never heard anything to the contrary.

Testimony of Miss Mary Mays.

Miss Mary Mays was next called, and testified as follows:

I am sister of R. L. Mays, the defendant. I live with my brother, and was living there in the latter part of March. I was sick through March and April. My brother was sick nearly all through March; he was down seven days at a time. At that time I was up and compelled to wait on him from the 26th to 27th of March. For four or five days after, I was very sick; my brother could not leave the house in consequence of that sickness since the 7th of March until he was brought down here. I heard a "nigger" had been killed, but I never heard of Page till we were summoned to come here. I have been living with my brother four years, ever since he has been farming. I have been very much afflicted. My brother and sister, with the servants assisting, have been my nurses.

Cross-examination:

Cross-examined by Mr. BLACKMAN: I do say my brother was at home since 7th of March. He attended on me till he was brought here. He would return to his room late at night; and I don't believe he ever went out. I don't believe he had access to the yard. He sometimes kept his room till breakfast time, and I would not see him till then. I have been afflicted with neuralgia, which prevented me from sleeping; so that if he had gone out I would have heard him. The rooms are ordinary-sized rooms. He could go from his room into the yard. He could have stepped out in his stocking feet; but I don't think there even was any chance of his being out without me knowing it. We were ill both together once. I don't think he did ever go out in his stocking feet. He could have done it. In going into the yard from his own room he would require to come toward our room. Our rooms don't adjoin. There is a distinction between them. It is two houses built together, but not touching each other. He might have got a natural night's rest occasionally while I was sick. There are separate walls to the rooms. There are windows looking into the yard, but I don't think they were raised while I was sick.

Re-examined:

I was sick on the 26th of March, and my brother attended on me.

Re-cross-examination:

What fixes the date in my mind is the fact that I remember the 1st of April well. We had a good deal of company at the house at the time. I was then sick. My brother, from a distance, was there. He came on Thursday, and left Sunday. They planted corn, but as it rained they had to stop work. I was sick then, and they were waiting night and day on me.

Testimony of Miss Kate Mays.

Miss Kate Mays was next called, and testified as follows:

I live with my brother and sister. Including myself, we include all the family. In the latter part of March and beginning of April I was at home. I recollect that my brother was suffering severely with toothache. My sister was very sick at that time. I was sitting up with her and my brother, and I minded her through that sickness from the 26th of March till April. My brother was then at home from the beginning of March till April 10. The servant, Millie Locke, was all I had with me. My sister had a serious spell between the 26th or 27th of March till April. She suffered as much as I ever saw anybody suffer. She had to be lifted up and down like a child. I have a distinct recollection of all this.

Cross-examination:

Cross-examined by Mr. BLACKMAN: We had a physician visiting her at that time. Our brother came on the 27th or 28th of March, I don't know which, but it was during a paroxysm of my sister's sickness. When I wanted him I had only to call him. I am confident he visited the room every hour from 29th March to 10th of April. He had to have his medicine. He was not absent three hours from me any one night. If it was necessary to have him up all night, then he would stay up. I can't fix the date better than through the sickness. It is nothing unusual for my sister to have such attacks of sickness. She had them since last fall. Dr. Hutchison attended her.

To General GHOLSON. My brother was never away more than an hour at a time. He often slept on a pallet in my sister's room.

To Mr. BLACKMAN. I frequently raised the windows of the rooms during the latter part of March.

Testimony of Millie Locke.

Millie Locke (colored) was the next witness called, and testified as follows:

I know Mr. Mays, the defendant. I live at Bob Mays. I am the cook. During last March his sister was sick with neuralgia; she was very sick. He, besides looking after other things, had to sit up with his sister. I left him at the house every night when I came away. I left between 8 and 9 o'clock. I would see him in the morning when I went back. From his house to my house is only a short distance, and to get out of his house to get to the gate you must pass my house. It is about a hundred yards from his house to my house.

Cross-examination:

Cross-examined by Colonel WALTER: I have been living three years with Mr. Mays. It was rainy weather in March. On the 29th of March I was cooking at Mr. Mays. They were all sick. There was nobody else there but Bob and his sisters on the 30th of March or 1st of April. I heard Alexander Page was killed. It was about a week after he was killed that I heard it. I heard it among the black folks at church. I don't sleep very sound, and I don't think any person could go through the gate without me hearing them, unless I was asleep. I often saw Bob at daylight. He slept in my young mistress's room. Sometimes he was in bed in his own room, and sometimes up and dressed. I was there several times when Miss Mays was so bad that there would be a fire in the room. They never had the windows raised that I know of. I staid a week when she was very bad. Sometimes during that time he would lie down for a while, or he would sit up all night. When he was ready to go to bed he would go to his own room. We had company. I cannot read or write. I don't know what month this is or what day this is. Bob's brother did not come there while she was sick. He was there before she was taken sick.

To General GHOLSON. I don't think Miss Mays was sick before I heard Page was killed.

The court then adjourned till half-past 8 on Thursday morning.

THIRD DAY.

The court met this morning at half-past 8 o'clock, Hon. R. A. Hill, United States district judge, presiding.

The counsel for the United States and the relators were all present.

Testimony of Robert Odennal.

Robert Odennal (colored) was the first witness called on the part of the relators. On being examined by General Gholson, he testified as follows:

I live at Mays's and Jones's place, Monroe County. I am acquainted with Mr. Mays, and have known him since he was a small boy. I was at the place in March and April.

Robert Mays has not been in good health for six months. I was living in a house across the creek; it was a log-house. Last March I was over at Mr. Mays's house one evening and got forty pounds of meat; I staid there till 9 o'clock, when I takes my meat and left. At that time Miss Nancy Mays was very sick. Next morning I heard that Alexander Page was killed, and my wife told me that I was not to go over to the house-lot after night any more. That was Wednesday, and it was the next day, at 12 o'clock, news came down the road that Page had been killed. They said it had occurred the night before. My wife said that man was at the church on Sunday, and now look at the arrangement. Miss Nancy was confined to her bed when I got the meat, and I opened the door and asked her how she was. To get out of Mays's house to the road there is a gate seventy-five or one hundred yards from the house, and the other, which is half a mile away, is called the back gate. They both lead to the road. Millie Locke was cook at Mays's.

Cross-examination:

Cross-examined by Colonel WALTER: I was not raised by Mays; we were neighbors; we have been living near each other, and I have known him from a boy; we were good friends; he is a very respectable gentleman. I have been living there two years, and my cabin is three-quarters of a mile from the house. Millie was cook, and there were three men on the place and four women, and nine men on the other place. It shocked me very much to hear of Page's death; all were shocked. Millie's husband walked out into the field, and at 12 o'clock next day I heard of the death of Page. I got the meat from Bob Mays himself; we got it out of the smoke-house; we got the key, opened the door and went in; Bob weighed the meat and I held it up. It was about the 19th or 20th day of the month. Every month has thirty or thirty-one days. It was toward the last of the month. I am not a church member, but I was at church the Sunday before I got the meat. Bob Mays has a brother; his name is Thomas; he was there about the time I got the meat; I think he came there a day or two afterward. I don't know whether there were any company at the place at the time. Some colored women were helping to nurse Miss Nancy; some went over every night. The death of Page made us fearful to walk about at night. I don't think there was much rain that week. I recollect the 1st of April. I think it was the 19th or 20th of March that I got the meat. I don't know where Page lived. I don't know Pope's place. I know it was Wednesday night when I got the meat. I did not put it down in a book. I have got meat there before two or three times since Christmas; I got it three times, including the one time I have told you of. When I got it, it was put down in a day-book, and then at the end of the month it was put in the big book and in my book. I do not have my book here. I cannot read or write. I remember the date in my head. They sent for me to come here. They told me I was to state when Page's death was. I told them I could remember it as it was the day after I got the meat that I heard about it. Mays had the toothache, but he went out and weighed the meat. I don't remember whether it was moonlight. I lived three quarters of a mile from Mays's. I don't know whether he staid at his house that night. Two of the neighbors, Levi and Andy, went up to the mill—Mr. Ross's mill—the day after I got the meat, and they heard about Page. I heard it about 12 o'clock in the day. They did not say whether the body had been found. They said he was took off, but they did not say how he had been killed. They said they took him out on Wednesday night. I never heard that these men who took Page away on Wednesday night had been there before to take him off. The affair created a great sensation; we were all talking about it; I mean the colored people. This is the latter part of June. I don't know the day of the month. I came here with the other witnesses on Monday. I talked about the meat and told them about it, and said I got it the day before Page's death. They did not ask me about the meat till to-day. General Gholson asked me about it.

To General GHOLSON. I always respect Mr. Mays very much. He is kind to the black people.

To Colonel WALTER. I am not in favor of Ku-Klux. I don't want to have anything to do with it. Any one that wants to do with it can go along.

Testimony of Dr. Doudle.

Dr. A. A. Doudle was next called. On being examined by Colonel Reynolds, he testified as follows:

I hold the position of justice of the peace in Monroe County, and know Mr. R. L. Mays. I know him to be a gentleman of good reputation for peacefulness and orderly conduct. He has had a case or two before me. His reputation as a law-abiding citizen is equal to any one in the country; and I know nothing to the contrary.

Testimony of James Moore.

James Moore was recalled, and testified:

I have known the defendant Mays eight years. I know his general reputation for peaceful, orderly conduct. He is a law-abiding citizen.

Testimony of E. O. Sykes.

O. E. Sykes, of counsel for the defense, was next called, and testified:

I have known the defendant Mays for a great number of years. Our relations are of an intimate character. I know his general reputation, in Monroe County, as a man of peace and a law-abiding citizen. It is good.

Testimony of Robert E. Houston.

Robert E. Houston, of counsel for the defense, testified also to the reputation of Mr. Mays as a law-abiding citizen.

Testimony of Mrs. Lucy Crosby.

Mrs. Lucy Crosby was next called, and testified:

I am the wife of the defendant, A. J. Crosby. He has not been out of the house at night since January. His mother died in January. I recollect about his staying at home at nights very distinctly. No white persons stay at my house. My family is small. He never leaves home unless compelled by business. He stays at home very close. We stay in the same room and sleep in the same bed every night. He could not leave the bed or the room without me knowing it. I am timid, and he does not want to leave me alone long.

Cross-examined by Colonel MANNING. I know A. J. Pope's place. It is between five and six miles from our place. I remember hearing of Alex. Page's death. I heard it about Sunday after he was killed. It was done on the 29th of last March. He was missing, I think it was on a Wednesday. I know it was wet at the time, for we could not plow, and we went to Aberdeen, which is eight miles from my house. We got home before night.

To General GHOLSON. My husband staid at home on that Wednesday, the 29th of March. I know it from the fact that my little girl was restless, and I had to get up and get her some water. My husband was then in bed, and it was about midnight.

General Gholson testified to the general reputation of the defendant Crosby, which he said was very good among his neighbors for peaceful and orderly conduct. He is a law-abiding citizen.

Colonel Dowd corroborated General Gholson's testimony.

Frank C. Rickett and James Moore also corroborated the testimony of General Gholson.

Testimony of Ann Forshee.

Ann Forshee (colored) was next called, and testified:

I am the wife of Michael Forshee, (colored,) defendant. I recollect when we went to Aberdeen, last March, with my sister-in-law and a fellow named Hy Hatch. I know Mr. Andy Crosby. That is the man. He is a defendant. Mike was making a fence for the wheat-patch. When I came from Aberdeen he was still at the same place. I never heard of the killing of Page until Sunday. They said it was done on Wednesday night, the day I went down town. I am certain that Mike was at home that Wednesday night. I saw him through the night.

Cross-examined by Colonel WALTER. I am the wife of the prisoner. I went to town, (Aberdeen;) he did not go. I don't sleep soundly. I got home before supper; we had supper and my husband laid down. That was on Wednesday. On Sunday I heard of Page's death. I wake up every night through the night, sometimes at midnight; I do it every Thursday, Friday, Saturday, and Sunday; I did not get up that night; I waked once, and I think it was at midnight; I then awoke about daylight; I heard the chickens crow. I did not hear about the killing till Sunday. I did not hear about the body being taken up until a week or two after. A man named Tony Ward, who lives where Smith used to live, told me about Page being killed, but nothing about the body being taken up. I have never been at the Pope place. I know I went to Aberdeen on Wednesday. I did not go on Saturday. It was in March; I recollect it was about the 28th or 29th of March. I don't know what year this is. This is June or July, I don't know which. I don't know how many days there are in the month of April. April comes after March. July comes before March. Christmas comes in December. I don't know whether there are ten or fifteen months in a year. I don't know which month comes first. I don't know whether 19 or 29 comes first. I heard Tony Ward say the killing took place on the 28th or 29th of the month. He did not say it was Wednesday. He said it was the 29th of March.

Testimony of William Lansford.

William Lansford was next called, and testified as follows:

I live at Lafayette Willis's place, Monroe County. I know Jeff Willis, colored, one of the defendants; I live about ten yards from his house. From the middle of March till the 1st of April we were down on the river Tombeckbee; the water was so high that no man could get out; we went there in February; I recollect distinctly of Jeff being there all that time, and could not get out. My house is about ten yards from his. We worked together to make a crop. My wife was there, so was Jeff's wife; that was all except some children. The ground was overflowed, and came up close to our cabins from the sloughs; it was within a hundred yards at first, but it came up to within fifteen yards; we were entirely surrounded by water, and had no boat or skiff and could not get out.

Cross-examined by Mr. TURNER. The water was up last March, and was up till about the 1st of April; I don't know when it fell.

To General GHOLSON. I heard of Page's death after the water fell. I heard the killing happened on a Wednesday. The water was then up, but it was down when I heard it. We could not get out at that time.

To Mr. TURNER. It was last March when the water was up; it commenced to rise on Sunday. I don't know if April came in on a Sunday. Uncle Morg Hatch told me about Page being killed; I met him on the Aberdeen road on a Sunday. This was over three days after the river commenced to fall; it was on a Sunday. I don't know when the water commenced to rise; it was up on Sunday. It rained on Wednesday. I was living on the Tombeckbee when the river rose.

Testimony of Lizzie Willis.

Lizzie Willis (colored) was the next witness. She testified:

I live down the river, on Fayette Willis's plantation. Jeff Willis is my husband. The water was up the last week in March and the 1st of April; we could not get out; we had no boat or skiff, and Jeff could not swim; it was half a mile to the river, but the sloughs were all round our stoop; they had a skiff, but it was washed away when the river rose; the water stood up a considerable time. I heard of the killing some time in March. The water was up at the time. He had been killed three or four days before we heard it. Bill Lansford, his wife, and some children were with us when the water was up, and we were surrounded. It is about a mile to Pope's slough; we could not get there.

Testimony of Lafayette Willis.

Lafayette Willis was next called, and testified:

I know Jeff Willis. He has lived all his life with me. He belonged to my father. He is about a month older than I am, and has been with me since January, 1846. He was living on the river bottom in March of this year—between the river and the sloughs. He has been looking after my stock. I have always found him honest, and would trust with thousands. He came occasionally out of the bottom in March. I sometimes went down to the edge of the bottom to see how they were getting along. When the water rose, he and those with him could not get out. I wanted him to take my stock down there and look after it.

Cross-examined by Mr. BLACKMAN: I have been down at the bottom twice. I was down there in March, and told him to come out and report to me. I don't think I was down there five times. I saw him two or three times.

General Gholson testified to the peaceful and orderly conduct of Jeff Willis, whom he had known for many years. He had ever observed that Jeff was a law-abiding citizen, and always very timid.

Testimony of General Gholso

General Gholson was again placed on the stand, and testified as follows:

I have been a resident of Monroe County since 1830. Our court was in session in the middle of March and in April. The river was quite high at that time, and there was great difficulty in getting to such places as Okolona and Mobile. I went over to my plantation because I was going to Okolona. The water was up for some time.

Testimony of Jane Willis.

Jane Willis (colored) was the next witness called, and testified:

I am the wife of Burrill Willis, (colored,) and was living, last February, March, and April, at Henry Alexander's. I was there when I heard of Alex. Page being killed. At that time Miss Jane Roberts (Mrs. Alexander) came there. Burrill staid at Fayette Willis's, and was in the habit of coming to see me on Wednesdays and Saturdays. He came at nights. I recollect he came down there on Wednesday night with my daughter Rena. They came there between 8 and 9 o'clock. They staid all night, and went home next morning. I heard about Alex. Page being killed the next day, from some black folks. They said the Ku-Klux had been riding round; and I said if Rena had only thought the Ku-Klux were about, she would not have come to see me, if I had been a-dying. She was afraid of the Ku-Klux. Burrill never missed a week without coming to see me. He always came Wednesdays and Saturdays. He could not have got out of the room where we were sleeping that Wednesday night, without me knowing it. I had the toothache very bad, and Rena, who was in the same bed with Burrill and me, got up and got me some water. The black folks out in the fields, who told me about the killing, said the Ku-Klux had been riding out the night before, and had killed a nigger, after carrying him off. I told them that it was not my husband, for he had slept with me that night. Burrill was in bed with me, and when Rena got up to fetch the water he was asleep at the time, in the back of the bed.

Cross-examined by Mr. JACOBSON: I live two and a half miles from Jeff Willis. I live with Massa Willis.

To General GHOLSON: I was cooking at Henry Alexander's, which is five or six miles from Fayette Willis's place.

Cross-examination continued: I lived near the road, at Mr. Alexander's. Jeff Willis lives about a mile and a half from the road. When the black people told me a nigger had been killed, I said it was not my husband, for he had been at my house the night before. I mean the night the nigger was carried off. He has been in the habit of coming to see me every Wednesday and Saturday night since Christmas. He did it until I went home. I have a child at home besides Rena. She is about sixteen. My husband brought Rena down directly after Christmas. She came down herself to meeting. I can't write good, and did not make a memorandum of her visit. I did not write down the date when my husband came on that Wednesday night. I know it was not Saturday, for he got the clothes to be washed on Wednesday, to bring them back on Saturday night. He did so at that time. I told Rena where to get the clothes, and she got them out. I always got up and got them out for Burrill, but I was too sick that night. I make no memorandums, as you call them. I had no thinking about that Wednesday night. It was after that I heard about the killing. Nobody has ever asked me if I recollect that date. They told me the Ku-Klux always rode on Friday, and when they told me what had happened I said, "Why, it was not Friday night, and folks told me the Ku-Klux only ride on Friday night;" and they said, "That ain't nothing. They killed a man last night." I cannot tell the day of the month they did it. It was last March, or the first of April. I think it was the last week in March. It was either the last week in March or the first in April, but I think it was the last in March. They said it was twenty miles away where the Ku-Klux killed the man. I said it was not my husband, Burrill, who lived six miles away from where I lived. I had been to see him. Rena came with him and went back with him. She was working in the fields with him. He left me about daybreak.

Testimony of Rena Willis.

Rena Willis (colored) was next called, and testified:

Jane Willis is my mother; she was living at Henry Alexander's in January, February, and March of this year; I went down with my stepfather to see her last March; I staid all night; I staid in the room with ma; my stepfather was in bed and staid there all night; my stepfather went home with me in the morning. Burrill Willis is my stepfather—I mean the defendant, who is sitting there. From Lafayette Willis's house to Mr. Alexander's house is about six miles. My stepfather carried back some clothes to get washed. We came on Wednesday night and left again on Thursday morning. Ma was sick, and I got up through the night and got her some water; she was complaining of neuralgia; I was up once through the night; my stepfather was there then; that was about midnight.

Cross-examined by Colonel WALTER: My stepfather and I rode down on the same mule and came back the same way; he was a strong mule then; he was used for plowing; I don't think he could have been rode for any distance that night. On the next evening I heard of Alex. Page being taken off and killed; a man came over to our yard and told us about it; he lives near the road. I think it was in March. I can read, but I cannot write very good. I don't know where Mr. Pope's place is. I live with my stepfather; I went back with him on the same mule.

Testimony of Henry Alexander.

Henry Alexander was next called, and testified:

I know the defendant, Burrill Willis, and have known him a good many years—ever since I was a small boy. My wife was sick during March. Burrill's wife was cooking for me. He was in the habit of coming to my house on Wednesday and Saturday nights to see his wife. I did not particularly notice that he was there on the night of the last Wednesday in March. I recollect hearing of Alex. Page's death; Dr. Slater, who was attending on my wife, told me about it about the 1st of April; he said it occurred the Wednesday before. I think Burrill Willis was at my place that Wednesday night, to the best of my recollection; his wife's daughter came with him, I understood.

Cross-examined by Colonel MANNING: I think it was about the 1st of April that I heard about Page being killed. I never heard about the inquest. It was Burrill's custom to come and see his wife on Wednesdays and Saturdays. I think he was there on that Wednesday night I speak of. My wife was sick at the time, and was sick eight or ten days. He was there several times while my wife was sick. I don't think I can be in error in saying that Burrill was there on that Wednesday I spoke of. I thought my wife was going to die several days. That fixed the date in my mind. I don't know that I saw Rena there, although I have seen her there frequently, and also her sister. Burrill generally rode a mule when he came to my house.

General Gholson testified that Burrill was an industrious, law-abiding, orderly man, with as good a character as anybody in the county.

Henry Alexander corroborated General Gholson's testimony.

Colonel Reynolds also corroborated the testimony in regard to character.

Testimony of Mrs. Mary E. Neeland.

Mrs. Mary E. Neeland was the next witness called. She testified as follows:

I am the wife of the defendant, James Neeland. I have never been examined in a court of justice before. From the middle of March till the middle of April my husband was at home sick; he was taken sick about the middle of March, and continued sick two or three weeks; the bigger part of the time he was confined to his room, and part of the time only able to go out into the yard; during the last week in March he was worse; all that time he was not from home a single night. I have two little children—one a little girl about eight years of age, the other a little boy about four years old. We live on the widow Willis's land. I don't know A. J. Pope's place. About three days after it was done I heard of the death of Alex. Page; the news came through a nigger; I think he said it was done on Wednesday night; I think I heard it on Saturday. My husband was at home very sick about that time, and was not able to be out. The boys were working on the road, to the best of my opinion, and commenced work on Wednesday and finished Thursday, at the time this is said to have occurred. I was at home all that week, and so was my husband. I staid in the same room with him every night. There are five or six rooms in the house. I recollect about the commencement of the cotton-planting; it commenced on the 7th of April. On the day it commenced widow Willis came over to our house, and was taken sick soon after she came there; she now lives in Aberdeen; she came there on a visit and was sick.

Cross-examined by Mr. TURNER: My husband was taken sick in the middle of the month of March, and became worse. He was sick two or three weeks. He was bad about the last of March. He had taken sick about the 15th or 16th of March, and required all of my attention. All that time he had no physician, but had taken medicine. He was sick the last week in March. He was taken very sick when he was first taken down.

To General GHOLSON: Johnny Boyd attended to the stock while my husband was sick.

Testimony of John Boyd.

John Boyd was the next witness called, and testified as follows:

I never was a witness in a court before. I know the defendant, Neeland. I lived with him from the middle of March till last April. He was sick at that time, and was confined to bed most of the time. I was there at the house at the time, living and sleeping in the same room. I attended to the stock when he was sick. In the last week in March he was not able to be up. He was about the house all the time, I am certain of that. When we commenced planting cotton Mrs. Willis came over to our place, and she got very sick. She was there, at the house, about the middle of April, for a week. I first heard of the killing of Alex. Page about the 1st of April. I heard it was done about the 29th of March. Mr. Parkett told me about it. He is one of the men who works on the place. From Mr. Alexander's to Mr. Pope's is five or six miles, I think. Parkett said that the Ku-Klux had taken away Alex. Page, and he was killed; and I supposed he meant they killed him. Mr. Neeland was at home when the nigger Page was killed. He was down sick at the time.

Cross-examined by District Attorney WELLS: I have been with Mr. Neeland since Christmas. I cannot tell how many months I have been to work for him. I don't know as I can count up the months. I suppose Christmas is in January. I am familiar with the months, and think I would give Christmas to January. I have a pretty good memory, and think I have been with Mr. Neeland about five months, but I cannot tell exactly. Previous to his being sick I don't know how long I had been there. The sickness was in the last of March, and I know this because we commenced cotton-planting on the 7th of April, and we planted corn in the first week in March. He was not sick when we commenced planting corn, but he was sick soon afterward. He was sick two or three weeks, and it was nothing unusual for him to be taken sick. There was nobody there but me and my brother, but we could not plant because Mr. Neeland was sick. He is troubled with sickness all the time. When we were planting corn he was down there dropping truck. He was not confined to bed except this last March sickness. He dropped some corn the first week in March. Mr. and Mrs. Neeland, my brother, my sister, myself, and Mr. Parkett, all live there. Mr. Parkett lives a short distance off; the rest live in the house. I never saw the Ku-Klux riding about. I don't know what you call the Ku-Klux. If ever I have seen any of them I did not know it. What Mr. Parkett said was that they rode about the country, but I don't know nothing about the arrangement. Parkett said that the Ku-Klux rode about; but I don't know where, or whether they had days or nights for riding. That is all I know about the riding of the Ku-Klux. I live five or six miles from the place where Page was taken out and killed. In the beginning of March Mr. Neeland was helping me to plant corn. He was sometimes able to work a little in the field, but he had to give up work when he was taken down sick about the last of March. Dr. Salter attended him that sickness. I don't know how often he came. I know him when I see him. I never took charge of his horse. I saw him there during Mr. Neeland's sickness, but I cannot say how often. I will say that he has been there once, but I cannot say as to twice. He called to see Mr. Neeland and the baby between the middle of March and the first of April, when Mr. Neeland was down with his sickness.

To General GHOLSON: I suppose Mr. Neeland is ruptured. I don't know whether that will not allow him to work.

Testimony of S. F. Kendrick.

S. F. Kendrick was next called, and testified:

I have known defendant, Neeland, twenty-five years. I have held the offices of sheriff, justice of the peace, and been a member of the legislature. His general character is that he is peaceful, orderly, and a law-abiding man.

James Moore and Lafayette Willis corroborated the testimony as to character.

The court then adjourned till 3 p. m.

AFTERNOON SESSION.

The court met at 3 p. m., pursuant to adjournment.

Testimony of Mrs. M. A. Bronson.

Mrs. Mary A. Bronson was the next witness called. She testified as follows:

I am the sister of the defendant, J. C. Porter. We live together. My brother is a widower. In the last week in March I was at his home. I recollect that something occurred about this time which fixes the time in my memory. My brother had hired a gentleman to do ditching. He was to commence about the 27th or 29th of March. My brother was to go to Columbus on business, and be there by the 29th. He did not go, however, as one of his children, four years old, was very sick on the 28th; and my brother was at home on the 29th attending to the child. On the 29th of March we were sitting up with the child. My brother was sleeping in my room, and could not have left the room without my knowing it. He staid there all night. I knew of his intention to go away, but he did not go. I heard of the death of Alex. Page from some of our freedmen who had gone to Ross's mill. On the next day they told it in the evening after they came back. It is a quarter or half a mile to the mill. It is from seven to eight miles from my brother's house to A. J. Pope's place. The freedmen said they did not know who killed Page. My brother's wife died four years this fall. He has three children, aged twelve, eight, and four.

Cross-examined by Colonel WALTON: There was no physician called, and none of the neighbors came to the house while the child was sick. There were some freedmen working in the yard. They are not here. I am certain about the day—the 29th—and the sickness. The child could not have been taken sick the week before the man came to do the ditching. He came the next day, on the 30th. My brother was to have gone to Columbus on the 29th. The child was not dangerous, but he would not leave it. The freedmen said Alex. Page was taken off or killed. My brother did not go that week to Columbus. He went some time after. He was at home all night on the 29th. We sat up all night on the 29th with the child. It was sick three or four days. The nearest neighbor is a mile away. No one was there except my brother and myself. There was no physician. I do not know whether it was raining or not that night. I don't know whether it was moonlight or dark. I helped to nurse the child, and gave it medicine. I did not rest much that night. While I was resting my brother was up with the child. Croup was what was the matter with the child. My brother staid in my room the whole night with the baby. It was very sick with croup, and required the attention of both of us. I made no memorandum about the day the ditcher was to be there. He was a white laborer, and his name was Edwards. I did not hear his given name. He is not now down in that part of the country, and we have not seen him for some time. He was English. I don't know where he is. He remained three or four weeks.

To General GHOLSON. Baby was four months old when its mother died; it was petted very much.

General GHOLSON. The ditcher's name is Thomas Edward, and he is said to be in Marshall County.

General Gholson testified that the defendant Neeland was one of the best of citizens.

Lafayette Willis, James Moore, and A. O. Lowe corroborated the testimony as to character.

Testimony of Mrs. Rachel Hutchinson.

Mrs. Rachel Hutchinson was next called, and testified as follows:

I have never been examined in a court before. That is my son, John D. Hutchinson; he is one of the defendants. I know where my son was on the 28th, 29th, and 30th of March. He is a practicing physician, and on the 28th he had a very bad case; it was the case of a lady that needed all his attention. On the 29th he had several cases to attend to, and he was riding all day and all night. As my daughter was going over to her sister's, he thought I should be left at home all alone. I had, however, some company when he came home, and he was with me all night and slept in the same room with me. Since the death of my husband he has always done so. When he has to leave me at night to attend to a case he returns as soon as possible, as he never likes to leave me long alone. The presbytery of the Presbyterian church was to meet at Aberdeen on the 30th of March, and my daughter wished to go to Aberdeen to attend the meeting, and she went over to see her sister, Mrs. Walton, on Wednesday evening, to see whether she could accompany her to Aberdeen on the following day. My son, who had an important case to attend to professionally, thought I would not have company, as my daughter was absent, but company came in. This was on the night of the 29th. The presbytery was to commence on the 30th, (Thursday,) and my son went there on the 31st with his sister, but he did not remain. He returned to Aberdeen on the 2d of April, and came back on the following Sunday. As I have said, he came home on the night of Wednesday, the 29th, and found I had company. He slept in my room that night. He could not have left the room without my hearing him. There is a brick pavement outside, and it is impossible for any one to walk across it without me hearing them, as I don't sleep sound. I have often heard persons come for my son late at night, and I have frequently to wake him up. I seldom sleep sound.

Cross-examination:

Cross-examined by Colonel MANNING; I don't know Mr. Andrew Pope's place. I live eleven miles from Aberdeen. On the night of the 29th of March my son took supper with me, and then went to bed. He went to Aberdeen on Friday, and also on Sunday, when he brought back his sister. My son told me of the death of Alex. Page when he came back from Aberdeen. He is a practicing physician. I cannot tell where he was on the 11th of March. I don't know where he was on the 20th of April. I don't think he could have left my room without my hearing him, as I must have heard his footstep on the brick pavement. Besides, he had to go through two doors, to get outside, and I think I would even have heard any one without shoes walking about. I don't know where my son was on the night of the 10th of February.

Testimony of John Willis.

John Willis was the next witness. On being examined, he testified as follows:

I am acquainted with the defendant, Dr. Hutchinson. I recollect the 29th of March; it rained a good deal that day. My wife went over to Mrs. Hutchinson's. She is Mrs. Hutchinson's daughter. The reason I remember the date was that they were talking about the presbytery meeting at Aberbeen the next day. The defendent was talking of going to the presbytery if his mother, who was sick, was better. He went to Aberdeen with his sister, to the presbytery. He returned, and went back on Sunday, and came home, bringing his sister with him. I stopped at Mrs. Hutchinson's all night on the night of the 29th of March. The defendant, Dr. Hutchinson, was in the house all that night, and slept in the same room with me.

The witness was not cross-examined.

Testimony of James Moore.

James Moore was next examined, and testified as follows:

I have known Dr. Hutchinson about twenty years. I consider him a peaceful, law-abiding man. His general character is good. I don't know that he is a member of the church.

Testimony of Lafayette Willis.

Lafayette Willis testified as follows:

The father of Dr. Hutchinson was long a most respected member of the Presbyterian Church. I never knew the doctor to take even a drink of whisky. He is a deacon of the church, and is held up as a pattern by mothers to their sons. He is very attentive to his mother, and the whole family are affectionate and greatly attached to each other.

Testimony of General Gholson.

General S. J. Gholson testified as follows:

I knew the defendant Hutchinson's father. He was a practicing physician—an orderly, peaceful man, like his son. The defendant, Dr. Hutchinson, was one of my soldiers, and he was ever of a very peaceful disposition, and was seldom known even to partake in the camp frolics. His attachment to his mother is a striking feature in his character.

Testimony of Mrs. W. D. Walton.

Mrs. W. D. Walton was next called, and on being examined by Colonel REYNOLDS, she testified as follows:

I am the wife of W. D. Walton, one of the defendants now present. On the night of the 29th of March he was at home all night. We retired late. Mollie Willis and Miss Jennie Hutchinson were paying me a visit, and we sat up late. It must have been between one and two o'clock before we retired. The presbytery was to meet the next day, at Aberdeen. My sister, Miss Hutchinson, wanted me to go to the Presbytery, but I could not go. She went to Aberdeen on Friday, to attend the presbytery. My husband has not been away a single night from me since the beginning of the year 1871. He has not been from home all that time. Of course I slept in the same room with him that night. Yes, yes, he was in bed with me. (Laughter.) I have a family —a little baby one year old. Of course I slept in the same bed with my husband that night. The baby was in the cradle in front of the bed. I was lying in front of the bed, to be near baby, and my husband, Mr. Walton, was lying on the far side of the bed, and if he had wanted to get out of bed he would have been obliged to crawl over me. He did not crawl over me, or go out that night. I know that. (Laughter.)

Cross examined by Mr. TURNER—Of course my baby is pretty. You did not expect I would say anything but that it was real pretty. (Laughter.) My husband has only been absent one night in a whole year up till the time he was arrested. This was about three weeks before he was arrested. He is a merchant in a small way. He don't do much trade. He has no custom except negro trade. He has often been at the store late at night.

Mr. TURNER. You can stand aside, madam.

The witness, who was really handsome and most elegantly attired, made the court and counsel a most profound courtesy, tapped her husband on the head with her fan as she passed out of court, saying, in a cheerful, good-humored, laughing tone, "Good-by, Billy," and left the court amid a round of applause.

Testimony of Miss Jennie Hutchinson.

Miss Jennie Hutchinson was the next witness. She testified as follows:

On the 29th of March I was at the house of Mr. Walton, one of the defendants, who is my brother-in-law. Mollie Willis was with me, and we took supper there and remained all night. We staid up late. I don't exactly know the hour we retired. Mr. Walton was not absent during the night. I went over to see if my sister, Mrs. Walton, would go with me to Aberdeen to attend the presbytery; but she could not go.

The witness was not cross-examined.

Testimony of Miss Mollie Willis.

Miss Mollie Willis was the next witness. She testified as follows:

I recollect where I was on the 29th of March last. I was at Billy Walton's. I got there about four o'clock in the afternoon and remained there all night. Mr. Walton was at supper with us, and we sat up till late at night, playing at some games in which he participated. I remember the circumstance and the time, because the presbytery met in Aberdeen next day.

The witness was not cross-examined.

Testimony of Colonel R. O. Reynolds.

Colonel R. O. Reynolds, counsel for the defense, testified as follows:

The defendant Walton and I were boys together. I know his character is good;

and he would no more commit the crime with which he is charged than his honor the judge on the bench.

Testimony of General S. J. Gholson.

General S. J. Gholson testified as follows:

I know the defendant Walton. He is a peaceful, law-abiding citizen, and an exemplary young man.

Testimony of Captain R. E. Houston.

Captain R. E. Houston, of counsel for the defense, testified as follows:

I have known the defendant Walton since 1860, and intimately since 1866. I know his general character. It is unexceptional.

Testimony of Colonel Dowd.

Colonel W. F. Dowd testified as follows:

I have known the defendant Walton from boyhood. He is a moral, peaceable, quiet young man. He was elected deputy probate clerk by the people for Monroe County.

Testimony of Mrs. Mattie Anderson.

Mrs. Mattie Anderson was the next witness called. She testified as follows:

I am the daughter of Thomas J. Ford. On the night of the 29th of March I was at my father's house. I live there. He was at home at supper-time. J. A. Loughridge and William Butler were at our house that night. I was up late that night. The defendant Butler was calling upon the young ladies of the house. I have a young unmarried sister. Loughridge often comes to our house to spend the night. The reason I remember the date so well is because the presbytery was to meet in Aberdeen the next day, and I had an idea of going there myself. I suppose it was between one and two o'clock when we retired. Father retired early. I went into father's bedroom and slept there. I always do so when he is unwell. He was unwell that night. None of them were absent over half an hour during the night. I retired late. Father is not in the habit of staying away from home at night. I don't think there is a man who stays more at home.

Cross-examination:

Cross-examined by Colonel WALTON: I did not attend the meeting of the presbytery, because father was sick. I suppose it was between one and two o'clock when we retired on the night or the 29th, but I did not look at the time-piece. I remember it was very late. My sisters sat up also late. I heard of the death of Alex. Page perhaps a week after it happened. I think Mr. Dowd spoke about it. I don't know the distance from Pope's place to our house. It is, I should think, nine or ten miles. Butler remained that night at our house, and was at breakfast next morning. He is unmarried. I remained up until all retired. They could not have left the house without me knowing it.

To Colonel Reynolds: I assist my mother in the household affairs. My father is about sixty-five years of age. I was in the parlor the greater part of the time the night I refer to. Mr. Loughridge was at our house all night, and was there at breakfast in the morning.

To Colonel Walton: We all thought of going to the presbytery on the morning of the 30th of March. I did not go.

Testimony of Miss Florence Ford.

Miss Florence Ford was the next witness called. She testified as follows:

I am a daughter of the defendant, Thomas J. Ford. I recollect where I was on the night of March 29, 1871. I was at home. Mr. Loughridge, my brother-in-law, and Mr. William Butler were at our house. Mr. Butler was visiting my sister and myself. This was no unusual thing. They were all there at supper and remained all night. I went over a short time to call on Mrs. H. Alexander, who was formerly Imogene Roberts. She is a friend of our family. It would be twelve, one, or two o'clock before we retired that night. Mr. Loughridge and Mr. Butler were there next morning. The reason I recollect the date is that I expected to go to the presbytery at Aberdeen on the 30th of the month.

To Colonel Walton: I expected to go, but did not go as father was ill.

Testimony of General Gholson.

General Gholson testified as follows:

Mr. Thomas J. Ford, one of the defendants, came to Monroe County in 1835. I got intimately acquainted with him. He has ever borne an excellent character, and is a law-abiding citizen. He was a whig, while I was a democrat, but he always voted for me for all that. (Laughter.) I have known the defendant, Loughridge, since he was a child, and knew his grandfather and his father. He is a peaceful, quiet, orderly, law-abiding young man. I have known the defendant, Butler, seven years. He is an exemplary, quiet young man.

Colonel REYNOLDS. Do you know, General Gholson, that Mr. Butler is opposed to all kinds of secret societies like the Ku-Klux or the Masons?

District Attorney WELLS. Is the Ku-Klux a secret society?

Colonel REYNOLDS. You say it is.

District Attorney WELLS. I don't think I have said so.

General GHOLSON. I have heard he is opposed to secret societies. He is a quiet young man. Mr. Ford is sixty-four years of age. He is three years older than I am.

Testimony of Colonel Dowd.

Colonel W. F. Dowd testified as follows:

I have known the defendant, Ford, twenty-five years. He has ever been a quiet, orderly, law-abiding citizen. In regard to Loughridge, I may say he is considered an exemplary young man. I have not known Butler so long as I have known the others. He has always maintained a good character, and I never knew of him having suits against persons in court, or being engaged in any personal difficulty.

Testimony of Lafayette Willis.

Lafayette Willis was again called, and testified as follows:

I raised the defendant Butler from the time he was a child; he is a young man of very good character. I know Loughridge and Ford; they are law-abiding citizens. Ford is a near neighbor of mine; he has not been in good health lately, and has frequently had the use of my little carriage, as he was too feeble to ride far on horseback. The general health of Butler is good, but he is subject to chills and fever. It is bad for the chills to go out at night. They generally come on at night, and we have been advising him not to go out at night.

Testimony of General Gholson.

General Gholson testified as follows:

It is seven or eight miles from Ford's to Page's house.

Testimony of W. J. Gordon.

W. J. Gordon was the next witness called. He testified as follows:

I reside in Aberdeen, and I know the defendant J. P. Willis. I know where he was on the 29th of March. That night he staid in the store of which I have charge in Aberdeen; it is a hardware store. I found him on the street under the influence of liquor somewhere about eleven o'clock that night, and I took him into the back room of the store and locked him in; he was there the next morning when I returned. He bought some goods before he left, which I charged to him, and the charge is entered on the books on the 30th. I write up my books almost every night without exception. While I was in the store writing, for I do all the correspondence, I heard loud talking on the street. I went out; saw it was Mr. Willis under the influence of liquor, so I got him to come into the store, took him into the back room, where he lay down on the bed and went to sleep. I locked the door and went home, and when I returned the next morning he was still there. I am certain it was the 29th that I locked him in the store, as the entry on my books shows that the goods were bought that day. He could have got out at the window of the room, but it is rather high. Page's house is on the opposite side of the river and distant ten miles away. Owing to the high water at the time it was almost impossible for the ferrymen to cross at night. The ferrymen both live on the opposite side of the river from my store. It was eleven or half past eleven o'clock that night when I left Willis in my store.

Cross-examination:

Cross-examined by Mr. MANNING: The entry in my books shows that the goods were purchased on the 30th. I generally write up my books every night. I have a memorandum-book. I have sometimes postponed posting my books, but it is my custom generally to do it every night. When my business is pressing I may put it off till morning. I do a great portion of my writing at night. The purchase was made by Willis before I went to dinner; at least that is my impression. He told me he was going home. I have no recollection of the presbytery meeting on that day. It was about 11 o'clock at night on the 29th when I stepped out and brought in Willis into my store. After he lay down on the bed I removed his coat and boots, and he fell asleep. I saw him in the evening. He had been drinking. I always write up my books at night unless I have some pressing business. Business was not particularly brisk in the latter part of March, although it is generally our busy time. Mr. Shields is in the store at times, and acts as salesman. I am the book-keeper. When I heard Willis talking in the streets I did not recognize who was with him. I don't think it was raining, or that the moon was shining. I had no watch, but my impression is that it was eleven or half past eleven. Willis was not insensible when I brought him in, but he was pretty tight. The Methodists are better customers than the Presbyterians. (Laughter.)

To Colonel REYNOLDS. When the river is high business is always particularly dull. When I make a sale I enter it, and if it is to a regular customer I post the goods to his account; but if there is only one sale I keep a memorandum of it and enter it as cash when it is paid.

Testimony of Charles H. Eckford.

Charles H. Eckford was the next witness called. He testified as follows:

I live in Aberdeen and keep a prescription drug store. I know the defendant Willis. I saw him in Aberdeen, to the best of my belief, on the 29th of March. I could not positively swear that it was the 30th or the 29th. I have never known him to fail to come to my store when he comes to town. I think he was there the night of the party at Mr. John Holiday's. I don't know where he staid all night. The party was on the 30th.

Cross-examination:

Cross-examined by Colonel WALTER: The party was on the night before the 1st of April, because we staid there till morning, and a number of April-fool games were played. I saw him the day before the party, which was on the last day of March. The party was on the night of the day I saw him.

To Colonel REYNOLDS. I don't know how many days are in March. The party was on the night of the 31st, the night before April 1st, to my best belief.

Testimony of W. E. Love.

W. E. Love was recalled, and testified as follows:

I know the defendant, J. Plummer Willis. On the day or night of the 29th of March I saw him. I had been riding out on that day. I got back to town about dark. I live a mile out of town and had to go through the town to get home. I met Willis, and as I had not seen him in town for some time I staid with him till about 11 o'clock and then went home. I left him in Mr. Beckett's office. That was on the night of the 29th of March. No one could get across the river at that time, as it was very high. Pope's farm is on the opposite side of the river. The ferryman will cross at night when the river is down, but not when it is high. Willis had been drinking that night.

Cross-examination:

Cross-examined by Judge BLACKMAN: Willis and I were together several hours. I remember that next morning between 10 and 12 o'clock I heard of Alex. Page's death. It is eight miles from Aberdeen to Mr. A. J. Pope's place. I don't remember who told me of Page's death; it was a general rumor all through the town of Aberdeen; I heard he had been killed or taken off from home and had not been seen since; I don't suppose anybody knew he was killed, but only that he had been taken off. I got home about half past 11 o'clock on the night of the 29th. I was riding, and left town about 11 o'clock or a little after. I don't remember what kind of a night it was, or whether it was raining or the moon shining. I don't remember about the moon or what quarter it was then in. I am a deputy sheriff, but I took no action when I heard of Page's death. I suppose it was six or eight days after that that I heard that a negro named Jehu Wolf had found the body of Page. The coroner took me; he was afraid to go over to where the body was said to have been found, and I agreed to go with him.

Colonel DOWD. I wish to know whether the asking of the question about the officers not taking action is intended to show that they did but do their duty.

Colonel WALTER. It is to fix the date more particularly.

Colonel DOWD. Then I have no objection how often you ask it. The officers have done their duty.

The COURT. This is not the time to try the officers of the county.

WITNESS. It was the first time I had heard of the finding of the body. The river is between A. J. Pope's place and Aberdeen. I recollect the meeting of the presbytery about that time, but do not know whether it was before or after this affair.

Testimony of General Gholson.

General Gholson testified that he had known the defendant Willis from a child. He was an honorable, peaceful, law-abiding man.

Testimony of Colonel Dowd.

Colonel Dowd testified as follows:

I have known the defendant Willis several years. His character is very good, and he is considered a peaceful citizen.

Testimony of Colonel Reynolds.

Colonel Reynolds testified as follows:

I have known Willis a long time; he is a superior man, and has as good a reputation as any man in Monroe County.

Testimony of Henry Alexander.

Henry Alexander was next called, and testified as follows:

I am acquainted with defendant John Roberts, who is my brother-in-law. On the nights of the 28th, 29th, and 30th of March he staid at my house. His sister was very sick at the time. He sat up all night with her, went away in the morning, and rode back in the evening. His sister was sick for two weeks from the 28th. I am impressed with the fact that he was there on the 29th from the fact that my wife, his sister, had a child, and came very near dying. During the time he was there he was up and in through the room all night. It is eight miles from my place to A. J. Pope's place, and fourteen miles to General Gholson's place. On the evening of the 29th Mr. Roberts came to my house before sundown and staid all night. Dr. Salter was in attendance on my wife. He came there on Thursday, and told me about Page's affair as having occurred the night before. Roberts was at my house all the night before. Claude Taylor (colored) made the fires and cleaned up the rooms.

Cross-examination:

Cross-examined by Colonel MANNING: My wife did not get so bad till the 28th, when she became very ill, but not so bad as she afterward was. She grew worse, and the doctor was called and came on the 28th. Defendant Roberts was at my house on the night of the 29th; he staid up part of the night, I reckon till about 12 or 1 o'clock. There were several persons there sitting up. He was in the room from time to time during the night. He slept in another room. There was nothing that called my attention to show he went to bed at 12 o'clock, but I believe he did retire at that time. I don't recollect what kind of a night it was, and I don't think it was raining. I cannot tell whether it rained on the night of the 30th. I was in the other room where Mr. Roberts slept as much as I was in my wife's room. After he went to bed I saw no more of him that night until daylight, about 4 o'clock in the morning. It is fifteen miles from my place to General Gholson's place. It was a day or two before the 28th that my wife commenced complaining. Mr. Roberts was there on 30th. I did not sleep with him. We sat up half the night. That was the case on the 29th. He lives at my house, and has been living with me a year ago since last fall. He is generally at home except when business calls him off. I cannot tell where he was on Febouary 10. He was at my house on the 11th of March. My brother, James Alexander, was there at the time; he staid with him. I was there the greater portion of the time. I am not able to state where he was on the 20th of April.

Testimony of James Alexander.

James Alexander was next called. He testified as follows:

I am acquainted with the defendant Roberts; he is my brother-in-law. On the 28th, 29th, and 30th of March he was at my brother's house. My brother's wife was sick; she is Roberts's sister. On the night of the 29th he was there at my brother's; he slept with me part of the night; we were up till about two o'clock, and then retired; we slept in the same bed; he was there in bed when I awoke at daylight. My brother's wife's child died, and the mother came near dying. Dr. Salter was attending on her. Two or three days after the 29th we heard about Page being carried off; Dr. Salter told us; he came there on Wednesday, staid till Thursday, went home, came back that evening, and staid all night; he was there two or three nights, as my brother's wife was very ill; he told us the killing or taking off took place on Wednesday night; that was the night I slept in the same bed with the defendant Roberts.

Cross-examination:

Cross-examined by Mr. TURNER: I fix the time because it was the time I heard about the killing of Page. We sat up three, four, or five nights; I sat up two or three nights myself; there was more company. We first heard of Page's death two or three days after it occurred. I recollect it from the fact that my sister-in-law was sick at the time. I heard it on Friday. On Tuesday night Roberts was at my brother's house. He was there all day Wednesday and Wednesday night; he did not leave the place on Thursday.

Testimony of Clark Taylor.

Clark Taylor (colored) was next called, and testified as follows:

I live at Henry Alexander's, and knew John Roberts. During the last week in March I was at home. On Wednesday night I saw him there. Mr. Alexander's wife was sick —she was very sick. I was making the fires, and being called to resuscitate the fire in Mrs. Alexander's room, I went in there, and Mr. Roberts was sitting in his sister's room. Dr. Salter was attending on Mrs. Alexander. A few days after that Wednesday night I heard that Alex. Page had been killed. They said it had been done on the 9th of March. I don't know what day of the week it was that Mrs. Alexander was taken sick, nor do I know how long she was sick. They sat up with her for a week.

Cross-examination:

Cross-examined by Colonel WALTER: I say that I think it was about the 9th of March that they told me Alex. Page was killed. I was fire-maker in the room where Mr. Roberts's sister was sick. Every time I went in I found him there. I was called in every night. I did not stop up all night. I do not recollect Roberts's riding out at night. I don't know that he rode out that Wednesday night. If he had he would have called me to catch his horse for him if I had been about the house. I would have put the horse up.

Testimony of Lafayette Willis.

Lafayette Willis was recalled and testified as follows:

I am acquainted with the defendants, John and Addison Roberts. They have the character of being quiet, peaceable men, and are reckoned among our best citizens. Addison Roberts stays at home so close that I have not seen him out in twelve months, and have not met him over three times in that time.

Testimony of James Moore.

James Moore was recalled, and testified as follows:

I am acquainted with John and Addison Roberts. Their general character is good. They are law-abiding citizens, and I never heard of either of them having a difficulty in my life.

General Gholson said A. A. Dowden would corroborate the testimony of Mr. Moore. He was not called.

Testimony of Mrs. Julia Roberts.

Mrs. Julia Roberts was next called. She testified as follows:

I am the wife of the defendant, Addison Roberts. I recollect where he was during the last week in March. He was at home all the week. My recollection is distinct on this point. I know he was at home every night, and on the 28th and on the 29th. We heard that his sister, Mrs. Alexander, was quite sick on the 28th. I have three children. They are all small. He was at home all that week, and slept in the same room and in the same bed with me. If he had attempted to get up and go out, I would have known it. I heard of Page's death three or four days after it occurred. A negro told it, but did not say how it was done.

Cross-examination:

Cross-examined by Colonel WALTER: I don't know Mr. Pope's place. I am certain it was the 29th that Mrs. Alexander was sick. She was sick several days. It was the 28th my husband was away. It was the first night of Mrs. Alexander's sickness. He could not have left the bed or the room without my knowing it. I am such a coward that the slightest movement wakes me. I am certain he was at home on the night of the 29th. I retired about nine o'clock that night. That is our usual hour for retiring. I heard three or four days afterward that the dead body of Page had been found. A negro boy told it.

Testimony of Jackson Roberts.

Jackson Roberts (colored) was the next witness. He testified as follows:

I live on Mr. Addison Roberts's place. I live in the house and work on the farm. I have made fires since the last week in March. I remember the 29th of March, and know that Mr. Roberts was at home on the Wednesday and Thursday of that week. I don't recollect any nights he was away. I make the fires. They were in bed always in the morning when I went in to make the fires.

Cross-examination:

Cross-examined by Colonel WALTER.—I know the time he was at Aberdeen. Other times he was at home. I made the fires in the morning at daylight and in the evening at 9 o'clock. When I made the fires in the morning I always found Roberts in bed with his wife.

The court then adjourned till half-past 8 o'clock on Friday morning.

FOURTH DAY.

The court met at half-past 8 o'clock this morning, pursuant to adjournment. Judge Hill presiding.

Testimony of Henry Tucker.

Henry Tucker (colored) was the first witness called this morning. He testified as follows:

I live in Monroe County, about four miles from Athens. I was at home on the 29th of March. It was my birth-day, and my wife was sick. I live near the forks of the road that leads to Hamilton, Fayette County, Alabama. I have seen men in disguise pass my house at night. As it was my birth-day on the 29th, I asked my mother to dinner, but she did not get there in time. My brother-in-law was there and wanted to go home, but I wanted him to stay, and he staid. I have seen disguised men come down the road near my house as if they were coming from Alabama. Some come down that night, but I don't know whether they took the direction of Pope's place. It was about 10 o'clock at night and time for me to go to bed. It is my belief it was the 29th. The men were in white all over. I was in the road about forty yards from them, and saw they were all in white, riding on horses. I had seen them before, and they did not scare me. As they passed, two of them got down from their horses and got my gourd to get water. They always came in the same direction. I don't know whether they took to the right or left after leaving my house. I live near the Alabama line. I have understood that Mr. Pope's place is four miles distant, but I never was there.

Cross-examination:

Cross-examined by Colonel WALTER: I was born in Monroe County, and have lived there forty-five years. I have lived in my present neighborhood since the war. It is four miles from Athens. A good deal of people are always going to Alabama.

To Colonel REYNOLDS: I did not see the men in white return that night.

To Colonel WALTER: I think they passed my house about 10 o'clock at night. They were going at a walk. I don't think there was more than ten or twelve of them. I think the moon gave a little light that night, at least for a part of the night; I am not, however, certain about that. I was about forty steps from them when they passed me. They could be seen some distance away. I noticed they took the left-hand road about fifty yards after passing my house. John Warner was at my house that night; he lives about six miles from where I live. He knew nothing about me going out and seeing the men in white pass. I don't recollect who I told this to. I was not excited when I saw them, because I had seen them several times before, and they couldn't scare me. I don't think I mentioned it to any one. I had neighbors stopping with me Saturday was a week ago, but I never said to them what I had seen. I did not tell my wife. I told Mr. Jones about it. I don't know whether he is a defendant, nor do I know his reasons for asking me about it. I said something about it when I heard Page had been killed. I did not know Page. I never was at Page's place; it was some miles from my house. When I saw the men in disguise pass it was on Wednesday night. On Friday I heard about Page's affair, and that he had been killed. I told what I had seen, and was asked if they were Ku-Klux. I said I did not know, as they passed and went on. I was not uneasy when they passed, as I had seen them several times before. I could not help feeling curious, but they did not scare me to death. They rode up to my gate and two of them got my gourd to get water. This was about the 1st of February or last of March. I heard two days after that Page was killed. I don't recollect telling anybody. It is dangerous to talk about them. I cannot tell how often I had seen them pass. I recollect now that two days after I saw the Ku-Klux pass I heard of Alex. Page's death. That was on Friday. His wife asked me when the men had passed, and I told her. She told me they had been at her house. I live within four miles of Pope's place. There were four colored people lived on that road. I have been at church since I saw the men in white pass my house. I have neighbors who live half a mile, three-quarters, and a mile and a half from my place. I have never visited them once in my life; if I did I don't recollect that I told about the Ku-Klux passing my house till last Saturday week. I thought very little about it. I was told by a colored man on the Sunday after that he had see the Ku-Klux. I don't recollect whether he told me he saw them passing his house. He had heard Page was killed. Isaac Morgan was the man. I don't recollect that any other body said they had seen them. I feel bad that I did not tell it before I did. From my house to Jones's house is about a mile and a half or two miles. He is not here. I did not hear them speak as they passed. They were going south toward Hamilton. The nearest white man to me on the road lives fifty or sixty yards off it. A colored man has a place between him and me. I never heard him speak about Page or Ku-Klux. Mr. Murray Walton is the white man's name. The next white man is named Jones. I belonged to old John Tucker, Governor Tucker's father, before the war. I am forty-six years of age next birthday; that is the age they told me I am, and that it was in the Bible. I was forty-five last 29th of March.

I am satisfied that what I saw was on the 29th. I did not go into the house for my mother when the Ku-Klux passed; she would have liked to have seen them. I was in the field when I heard the sound of horses' feet. My mother, my brother, and my wife were all in the house when they passed, and when I went into the house I did not say anything about the Ku-Klux I had seen that I recollect. I don't recollect saying anything about it till after I heard Page was killed. I can't say whether I said anything about the Ku-Klux to my wife. I don't know whether they rode horses or mules, as the gowns came down so far. The Ku-Klux came back that night. I heard that Alex. Page had been found blindfolded and with his throat cut. God only knows where these Ku-Klux came from, for I don't know. Anybody living beside me may be a Ku-Klux, but I don't know it.

To Colonel REYNOLDS: I spoke to L. J. Morgan about this thing. I did not talk much about it, as I think that too much talking does harm; and I attend to my own business.

To Colonel WALTER: I don't know what people say about my talking, and don't care what they say.

Testimony of Colonel Dowd.

Colonel Dowd testified that he had known the witness for about twenty years, and that he was a truthful, honest man.

Colonel Walter wanted to know if they needed to prove the character of their own witness.

Colonel DOWD. I acknowledge that it is not strictly legal to do so, but we wish it all to go to Washington.

Testimony of General Gholson.

General Gholson was next examined, and stated that the defendants on an average lived about eight miles from Pope's place. Tucker, he said, lived nine miles from the Alabama line. The general reputation of Fayetteville is——

District Attorney WELLS, (interrupting.) We are not trying the reputation of Fayetteville.

General GHOLSON. The general opinion is that they are lawless up near the line in Alabama.

Colonel WALTER. We are not trying a county in Alabama, and the citizens of Fayetteville are not on trial here.

Colonel Dowd said the question was not one of character but of circumstances, and the defense wanted to prove that a band of disguised men passed Tucker's house, going in the direction of Page's house, on the night he was killed.

Colonel WALTER. I contend the inquiry is not in order.

The court ruled that they could not lead testimony in regard to the reputation of a community. That the disguised men came from the direction they did was merely a circumstance in the case.

General Gholson informed the court that the relators had closed their testimony in chief.

The court took a recess till 3 o'clock.

AFTERNOON SESSION.

At 3 o'clock in the afternoon the court resumed, Judge Hill presiding.

Motion to strike out testimony.

Mr. Blackman rose and said that after consultation the counsel for the Government had concluded to submit the following motion, and were prepared to argue it at present if the counsel for the relators so desired. The motion was as follows:

In the district court of the United States for the northern district of Mississippi.

THE UNITED STATES
vs. } On habeas corpus.
W. D. WALTON *et al.*

And now comes the United States by its attorney and moves the court to exclude from its consideration and strike out all evidence offered tending or intended to prove an *alibi*, for the reason that the court cannot, under the law upon *habeas corpus*, inquire into the main issue, or consider evidence intended to show any other fact, on this hearing, than the single question as to whether the relators are detained in contravention of the Constitution and laws of the United States.

G. WILEY WELLS,
United States Attorney, Northern District.

Colonel DOWD. We wish to urge that this question has already been settled, as the records of the court will show. Every point of this kind was raised at the inception of the case, which will be seen by reference to the records.

Colonel Walter said his motion at the inception of the case was in reference to the double traverse, but the motion introduced by District Attorney Wells had never been before the court.

Colonel DOWD. We (the counsel for the defense) have no disposition to argue the motion at present. Let it come up in the main argument.

The COURT. Let the motion be filed.

TESTIMONY FOR THE UNITED STATES.

Testimony of Felix Bumpus.

Felix Bumpus (colored) was the first witness called on behalf of the Government. On being examined by District Attorney Wells, he testified as follows:

I reside in Aberdeen, Mississippi. I am coroner of Monroe County. In April I took up or exhumed the body of Alex. Page, who was killed. On the 6th of April I was notified that a body had been found dead, and on the 7th I prepared to make an examination. I went to Mr. Andrew J. Pope's place and inquired for Jehu Wolf, who had found the body, and we went to the place where the body was found. After "grabbling" the earth for eight or ten inches we came upon the body. It was buried in a wood about four or five miles from Mr. Pope's place. The body was that of Alex. Page. We found the arms pinioned with a rope and a rope round the neck. We lifted the body partially out of the grave and we examined it as well as we could. The deputy sheriff summoned a jury, and I examined the witnesses. We found that the name of the party dead was Alex. Page; that his hands were tied with rope, and also his arms. There was a rope round the neck, but we saw no wounds on the body. I did not examine his head. We did not take the body fully out of the grave. We put it back as we found it. It was buried in the woods on a hill-side, with the head down the hill toward the east. I noticed a log near the place, about ten feet from the foot of the grave. This was about four or five miles from Mr. Pope's place. That was the place I was told on which Page had been living. We found horses' tracks about fifty yards from the grave. The grave was close to an old field. There were some leaves on the top of the grave, which was smoothed level with the ground. The rope round his neck seemed to be as thick as my finger. I think his hands were tied with the same kind of rope. The body was not decomposed. Death had only taken place a short time, as the body was not offensive. A colored man named Jehu Wolf took us to the place. I found him at Mr. A. J. Pope's. He lives there. I made my return of the facts to the circuit court clerk at Aberdeen, and it was filed there. The neck of the deceased seemed to be bloody. The blood came from his nose. I had no physician there. I found no more rope there than what I have told you about. The verdict was that "Alex. Page came to his death by hanging." This was in Monroe County, in this State.

Cross-examination:

Cross-examined by Colonel REYNOLDS: I went to Mr. Pope's before I found the body Jehu Wolf pointed out where the body was buried. This was about four or five miles from Pope's, in a northeasterly direction. I have seen Jehu Wolf since. I believe he has been summoned here as a witness for the United States. Jehu Wolf and Andrew J. Pope were both witnesses before me. I briefly made inquiry of Alex. Page's wife.

Testimony of Jehu Wolf.

Jehu Wolf (colored) was the next witness called. On being examined by district attorney Wells he testified as follows:

I live with Mr. Pope, in Monroe County, in this State. I remember the night Alex. Page was taken away. It was the last Wednesday night in March. I was in bed that night before he was taken away. Between ten and eleven o'clock that night three persons came to my door and waked me up by shouting out, "Hey, old man; get up." My wife waked me up, for she heard them first. There was nobody in the house but my wife and children. I got up and went to the door, and I heard a great knocking at Alex. Page's house, which was near my house. As soon as the knocking commenced the men in front of my house began to talk to me. The man who stood at the door shouted to me, "Don't you come out here." I said, "I am compelled to come out;" and he said, "Do it in the house." The door came back in a way that made a little crack, and I could see a man standing right in front of the door, which was shut. This man called out, "What kind of a man is Alex. Page?" I told him he was a very clever kind of a man, and very friendly. He then said, "Is he not sometimes saucy?" I said, "I don't know. He is a very clever man." I heard this man's voice right plain. It was David Stoddard.

General GHOLSON. He is not on trial.

WITNESS. I heard his voice quite plain when be asked me what kind of a man Page was. I told him not to come in and scare my wife; and he called out, "O, no Patsy, don't be scared." I catched his voice. He said, "What was you and Alex. Page doing to-day?" I said, "I went off to get my shoe mended." The man at the side of the house then began to talk. I did not see him, but I heard his voice quite plain. He gave the other man some signals in case I would catch his voice, and he began to talk thick, like "Ah, ah, ah." I catched David Stoddard's voice, for they talked right smart a while. They talked until the noise ceased at Alex. Page's house. They called out to me, "Jehu, take care. Jehu, you work hard; attend to your business and you're all right." They then went away. I heard the party all move off. They came past my house. I heard them move out. I did not go after them when they went away. I went out at daylight, and went first up to Mr. A. J. Pope's. I said to him, "Do you know that they came last night and took away Alex. Page?" He said, "Well, damn their souls, they came and punched me, and abused me and punched me with a shot-gun." He then said the mules have got out of the yard. It had been raining a little, and after I got out at the gate to look for the mules I found tracks. I followed them up. We met Ashbury Butler. Mr. Pope, who was with me, spoke to Butler. Mr. Pope had to go to Aberdeen, and he told me to go and look at the wheat. I went and looked at the wheat, and then went back to get my breakfast. I then started out again, and walked for about four miles. I found that the tracks were still on the road. They then took down a field and changed to the right. I came to a fence, and began to get scared. I was scared a while. I was standing where people could see me. I saw the tracks of horses in the field. I saw where persons stepped in the horses' tracks, as the horses had gone first. I thought I would go back home. About one hundred and fifty yards as I came back I thought I saw tracks in the broom-sage. There was a big log up from there, and I went to the log and I looked to the right, and stood there a while and looked about, and then I saw some blood. And I said, "That is human blood." I again got scared, and I looked down again, and about two feet from the blood I saw a little red dirt; and I stopped right there, as I was all of a scare. There was some leaves on the ground, and the dirt was red. I got down on my knees and began "scrabbling" the dirt first this way, then that way, and when I had "scrabbled" away a good deal of the dirt my hand got in the dead man's whiskers; and the dead man said, "Aah," or something like a groan; and I started up an' ran, and did not stop till I was about a mile from the place.

General GHOLSON: Did the corpse groan?

WITNESS. Yes, it did sir; and I took and put right back home as fast as I could. (Laughter.) I told my wife first about it. I told Andrew Pope also. I told him I had found the body of Alex. Page. My wife told Alex.'s wife and her daughter. I did not go back to the grave next day. I went back with Mr. Love, Felix Bumpus, Mr. Pope, and Mr. Taylor. It was a week after, I think. They went out to see if it was Alex. Page. We saw the head and part of the body. They did not take it clear out of the grave. We saw the head and the face. I recognized it was Alex. Page's face. It had on his every-day clothes. There was a rope round his neck; it had broke his neck; it looked black. Some person was trying to raise up the body. There was a rope round his neck. The piece of rope came off when the man put his hand under it and felt his neck. The rope was about the size of my finger. Aunt Fanny Page said they got it out of her bed.

Colonel REYNOLDS. Don't say what she said.

WITNESS. I did not see any other rope round the body but the one round his neck, There was no person in my house the night the men came there but my wife and child. My wife waked me up. She heard the voice first. The next day was the last Thursday in March. That was the day I found the grave.

Cross-examination:

Cross-examined by Colonel REYNOLDS: I lived last year with A. J. Pope. I was at John Pope's the year before, and was at Dr. Brower's before that. The men I spoke about came there on Wednesday night. It was the last Wednesday in March. The first thing I heard that night was a person shouting, "Hey, old man, what you doing in there?" They staid at my house fifteen or twenty minutes. My wife woke me up; she pinched me and I woke; first thing I knew was my wife pinching me; then I heard, "Hey, old man, what you doing in there?" I live in a small log-house; it had only one door and no window; it was chinked. When I went to the door the man was standing right in front of the door with his foot on the step. I was at the door and peeped out at a crack. The door was shut. The crack was where the door shuts. I peeped out at the right side. There was a man right close to the door. The door was about the center of the house. The other man was at the end of the house; I could hear him but I could not see him. I heard a signal given not to talk. I did not see the man standing at the corner of the house, but I heard him talking. I recognized the voice of the man in front of the door. It was David Stoddard; I knew his voice. Some one said, "A-ah, O-oh, that is not the way to talk." The man at the side of the house talked in a disguised voice. The man at the door gave the other man the signal. They gave signals backward and forward in a broken voice. In the morning I went up to Pope's house and told him what had been done. He told me to go and see the wheat, and after I came back he told me to go and look for Alex. and the mule. It is about three miles to the wheat-field. I got back between seven and eight o'clock. I got my breakfast and went and nailed up Aunt Fanny's door. About ten o'clock I was told to go and look for Alex. Page and the mule. I told my wife they had taken Alex. off. I heard Alex. as they passed my house. I went out for Alex. and the mule until I came to the wood, as I told before, and I "grappled" for him with my hand and struck among his whiskers. When I struck him he made a noise, or groaned. I ran off whenever he made the noise. When I heard the noise I was so badly scared I did not take time to put back the earth. I saw some blood there. I did not say at the examination that he raised hisself and gave a groan; I just simply heard him groan; I think I heard him groan, he did groan; at least there was a noise; I will swear there was a noise made; I stated this before the coroner's inquest. I saw blood on the ground.

Colonel REYNOLDS. Did you not say at the coroner's inquest, "I caught hold of his head and he throwed back his head and made a strange noise?"

WITNESS. No, sir. O, no, sir.

Colonel REYNOLDS. Did you not say at the inquest, "I then pulled the leaves over him?"

WITNESS. No, sir.

Colonel REYNOLDS. Did you not say that you ran off and went home?

WITNESS. Yes, sir.

Colonel REYNOLDS. Did you not say at the inquest, "I told them not to say anything about this, (meaning the finding of the body,) and that I expected to leave in the morning."

WITNESS. Yes, sir.

Colonel REYNOLDS. Then you say that you did not tell the coroner that when you found Alex., and touched him, he "throwed back his head and made a strange noise?"

WITNESS. I did not say he throwed back his head. I said he made a strange noise. I saw blood on the leaves over the grave. I don't know as I said I pulled the leaves and dirt over the grave before I ran off. I cannot recollect now. I know he did not throw up his head. There was a noise made. I recollect Monday morning, the 19th of June. I came to Oxford that day, but I don't recollect seeing you or General Gholson between Aberdeen and Aberdeen Junction on the train.

Colonel REYNOLDS. Did you not tell General Gholson on the train that you did not recognize a single man who was at Alex. Pages that night?

WITNESS. No, sir.

Colonel REYNOLDS. As we came along on the train, and after we got on the main track of the Mobile and Ohio Railroad, in presence of Captain McClusky and Captain Houston, did you not, in answer to a question, say "you did not know a single man that night?"

WITNESS. No, sir. We did have no such talk. I did not tell you that, for I knew two of them.

Colonel REYNOLDS. Did you not tell Captain Houston that you did not recognize a single white man that night, and to come into the car and you would tell him all about it?

WITNESS. I did not.

Colonel REYNOLDS. Did you not tell him about Abbeville, or between that and Holly Springs. "I am on your side. Tell Andy Pope not to talk so much?"

WITNESS. No, sir.

To District Attorney WELLS. They did not pester me. One gentleman did. I knew two who were there that night.

Colonel DOWD objected. He said the question in regard to the pestering of the witness was leading.

District Attorney WELLS. I will modify the question. Witness, had you any conversation with any one on the train?

WITNESS. I had a conversation with Captain Sykes. He asked me if I knew any persons who were at Page's that night, and I told him I knew two of them. He wanted me to tell him who they were; but I told him, "No, sir; I cannot tell you now." I was in the car for colored people. Aunt Fanny was with me most the time. I had only one conversation with Captain Sykes. I did not see these gentlemen frequently in the colored car. Me and Aunt Fanny sat together nearly all the time.

District Attorney WELLS. Do you remember having a conversation with Colonel Reynolds at the drug store at the corner of the square in Oxford last Tuesday morning?

WITNESS. I recollect I had a conversation with him at the drug store. He asked me if I knew any of the men that were at Alex. Page's that night, and I told him I knew two of them. He asked me some more questions, and I said, "No; I will not tell you about it." I do not remember having a conversation with Captain Houston on the Mobile and Ohio Railroad. I had no conversation with Captain McClusky. When I was standing on the outside of the car Wash. Willis told me to go inside, or I might fall off. I never told any gentleman to come inside the car. I did not have any conversation with any one except Captain Sykes. That is Captain Houston, (pointing to Captain Sykes.) Here is Colonel Reynolds, and that is General Gholson. I knew Stoddard's voice. I did not recognize the name of the other man, but I knew his voice. There were three men at my house. One of them was Whitfield Pope. General Gholson might have come in the same car with me from Aberdeen to Aberdeen Junction, but I would not like to swear he did or did not. I do swear I had no conversation with him.

Testimony of Fanny Page.

Fanny Page (colored) was next called and examined by District Attorney Wells. She testified as follows:

I live in Aberdeen, at Bill Gordon's. My husband is not alive. I have been living at Mr. Gordon's since he was killed. His name was Alex. Page. When he was killed we were living at Mr. Andrew Pope's, over the river. I don't know where my husband is now. I saw him on the last Wednesday in March. He did not go off and leave me. Some men came that night, took him off, and killed him. They came all round the house. My old man was in bed, and the men took axes, broke the doors down and smashed them in. They were dressed in long gowns. Their faces were covered with a piece of cloth with holes for the eyes, the mouth, and the nose, with red all round the holes. They could see out at the holes. The cloth came down over their faces. As they walked about it would fly up. They tried to keep it down; but it would fly up and show their faces. The house was full of them. I was in bed, and they came to me and said, "Where is the old man?" I said I believe he has gone somewhere—to some of the neighbors' houses. They made up a light on the hearth and commenced looking about for the old man. They found him under my bed, and made him come out and put on his clothes. They cut the bed-cord from my bed and they tied my husband's hands and arms and blindfolded him. They took him out, and took him away after they had blindfolded him with a handkerchief. They covered his face with it. I was sitting up in my bed while the party were in the house. I recognized some of them—Joe Davis, (colored,) Henry Hatch, (colored,) Mike Forshee, (colored,) Ben Lumpkin, (colored,) Mr. Andrew Crosby, Jasper Webb, Tom Malone, David Studdart, John Studdart, and Whitfield Pope. I saw others there, but these were all I recognized. I saw their faces. I recognized that night, by seeing their faces, Tom Malone, Jasper Webb, Andy Crosby, Dave and John Studdart, and Whitfield Pope. I am certain they were there that night. I knew them by their faces and their walk. It was cloudy that night and had been raining some. The moon was shining, but not much. They made up a light in the house, so that I could see them plainly when the cloth flew up on their faces. Some of them threw it up. I lived at Whitfield Pope's, and I knew him well. They made a big light in the house. They were in there a right smart while before they found the old man. There was a fire nearly out on the hearth, and they made up a fire for themselves, and you could see all round the house. After they had tied my husband they told me and my daughter to work hard and take care how we talked to the white people, or they would do something to us. My daughter was sitting up in her bed at the time. The gowns came down clear to their feet. Some had shorter gowns, and I could see that they wore pants and boots or shoes. In the party were four colored men whom I recogized. Their names were Joe Davis, Mike Forshee, Henry Hatch, and Ben Lumpkin. I have not seen my husband, dead or alive, since he was taken away. I did not go to the place where he was buried. I was told he was buried four miles from where I lived. I was told he was dead. It had been raining that evening, and the moon was shining. It was light enough for us to see what was going on, and to see the men were dressed up in white. When they left I looked after them, and I saw them go up the road. They had my old man with them. When they came across the field I did not hear the sound of the horses. I could not give a guess how many were in the party. There might have been fifteen or twenty.

Cross-examination:

Cross-examined by Colonel DOWD: I was married to Alex. Page just before the surrender, at Peter Dawkins's, near Aberdeen. I was at Whitfield Pope's last year. We lived at Bill Gholson's after the surrender. Then we lived at Sheriff Kendrick's. The third year at Mr. Fitzpatrick's. The fourth year at Dr. Robertson's. The fifth year at Whitfield Pope's, and this year at Andy Pope's. I went to Andy Pope's directly after Christmas. My house is a good large house. I reckon it was twenty feet square. There was a light on the hearth when the men came in, and they made up a light with some pine. There was coals in the fire, but there was no light until they made one. There were two doors to the house, one on each side. It was a single log-cabin. My daughter, Rosetta, was in bed when they came in. I had two beds. She occupied one and the old man and me the other. Rosetta is my daughter by my first husband. I did not see the moon when they took my husband away. We never heard them until they were round the house. The old man waked up first. We did not open the door. We said nothing. They had two axes, and burst in the doors with them. They burst in both doors. I did not do anything, but sat up in bed. My bed was in the northeast corner. They came in at both doors. The chimney is next to sunrise. They knocked down both doors at once. I did not go and see Jehu Wolf the next morning. I did not go anywhere. My daughter and Jehu's wife said the next morning they would go and look for the old man. Andy Pope sent Jehu to look for him. Jehu found him. I was in bed two days sick. I heard late in the evening that Jehu had found his body. I did not go up to the grave, and was not at the coroner's examination. We went to bed early that night.

To District Attorney WELLS. They had been there for my husband before. I think it was two or three weeks before. They did not get him, as he ran away, and they shot at him. I never got up that night. I never went out.

To Colonel DOWD. I did not go up to the inquest. I first knew Tom Malone when I lived at Whitfield Pope's last year. I worked in the field at Whitfield Pope's. His house was not far from my house; it was about a hundred yards. Alex. and I both worked in the field. I saw Mr. Malone at Andy Pope's. He came right often to Whitfield Pope's last year; I reckon he came more than four or five times; they visited one another; they were brothers-in-law; I have been close to him. I have been at Mrs. Malone's house. The road that goes up to Pope's house is near my house. I was certain it was him. I never saw him before last year that I know of. I was never at Mr. Pope's house when Mr. Malone was there. I always worked out in the field. I have seen Malone since I went to Andy Pope's several times. My husband was killed last March. I cannot tell the number of months in a year. I did not say it was the 29th; I said it was the last Wednesday in March. I never saw Malone except at the two places I have told you. I never saw him nowhere else. I recognized Malone in the house that night by his voice. The masks came down to their breasts, and they had horns or tassels on their heads. They had gowns with sleeves. The masks all came down round their necks. I could not see their faces when they first came in. I sat up in bed when they came in, and lay down before they went away. The bed was as high as this table. Rosetta's bed was on the other side of mine. She got up in bed and some of the men talked to her. As they were hunting round for the old man their masks would fly up and show their faces. I don't know who made up the light. I knew Joe Davis; I lived close to him last year, not quite half a mile away; I saw him nearly every Sunday as I went by to church all through the year; I never saw him go to church; that was the way I came to recognize him first in the house. Sometimes I went to church and sometimes staid at home on Sunday. I have seen Joe Davis at Andy Middleton's, and we picked cotton together at Sheriff Kendrick's. I know his voice and his face well; I know it was him I saw in the house. I knew Henry Hatch at Sheriff Kendrick's. I don't know who got under the bed to get the old man out. He never answered them when they called to him to come out. I was on the bed when they went under it to fetch him out. I don't know who stooped down; I could not see their faces when they stooped down. When they broke in the door the moon shone in. I got acquainted with Henry Hatch at Sheriff Kendrick's; he worked there; I was working there the same year. That was the same year I worked for Whitfield Pope. I plowed there two months, and then went back to Mr. Pope's to get our crop. I knew his voice and saw his face. I knew Mike Forshee; I saw him at our house and also at the church; I saw him a heap of times last year when he came to church on Sunday, and when I went backward and forward; he was not a member of the church at all; he came to my house one Sunday last year; I was never at his house. The first I knew of Jasper Webb was when I saw him last year at Andy Middleton's, a black man living on his place. I went over there to visit Middleton. It was Sunday, but I don't remember what Sunday it was. We were working a crop at home. I saw him several times, but that was the first time I saw him to know him. He staid talking to Andy. I don't know what his business with Andy was. Andy's house was a right large house, about forty or fifty feet square. It was larger than my house. It was a log-house with two beds in it. I was not close to Mr. Webb, but I saw him well enough. He was in the house about half an hour. They were on one side of the house and I was on the other. I have seen him riding up to Whitfield Pope's. I did not see him after I went to Andy Pope's to live. He was no relation of the Popes. He was not there often. He came there week-days and might have been there once a month. I worked in the field and did not see him once a month. I don't think I saw him every two months. I must have seen him once in three or four months. I never saw him from the time I got to Andy Pope's till I saw him at my house that night. I have never seen him except at the times I have mentioned. I was never in the same room with him except at Middleton's and in my own house. I spoke to him once going along the road. I saw his face in my house and recognized his voice. I first saw Andy Crosby at Whitfield Pope's. I also saw him going along the road. When we were going to church the people said it was him. He came by Mr. Willis's, but I don't know where he was going. I never saw him on a week-day. I saw him two Sundays, but never saw him except these two times. I would not know Mr. Crosby now among all these folks. That is Mr. Crosby, (pointing to defendant McNeice.) The men made up a large light in my house and staid I don't know how long. The old man made no resistance. They made him come out from under the bed and put on his clothes. Rosetta and I staid in our beds. I am certain I saw Mike Forshee. He is a ginger-colored fellow. I never picked cotton with him. They tied my husband with the bed-cord. They tied his hands across in front and then tied his arms. They took a piece of rope that was hanging up away with them. Henry Hatch is a ginger-cake colored nigger. I did not follow the men that took off my old man. I got up as they were going away and looked after them. They were going to the gate, which is about one hundred yards from my house. They went up to Pope's house. I saw his door open and he came out in his drawers. I knew him by his voice. I don't know whether any of the white men I saw in the house tied my husband, for I did not know who did it. He was close to the hearth when they tied him. Ben Lumpkin's face was to him at the time.

The court adjourned till Saturday morning at half past 8 o'clock.

FIFTH DAY.

The court met this (Saturday) morning, pursuant to adjournment, Judge Hill, presiding.

Fanny Page was again placed on the witness-stand, and testified as follows, (Colonel Reynolds conducting the examination:)

I was at Andy Pope's two months after my husband was taken away. I then went to Aberdeen, to Bill Gordon's. When I was at Mr. Pope's I had three axes. They were all out of doors. I was cooking at Mrs. Gordon's about the 7th of June. I did not tell Mr. Gordon that I did not know any man who took my husband away. I remember Mr. Gordon helping me to cord up my bed. He told me the cord was too short; and I told him that the cord was cut by the men when they took my husband off, and that was the reason it was so short. He did not ask me whether I knew any of the men. I remember the night I went up to Huggins's house. I saw the coroner, Felix Bumpus, there. A black man came to me to go to Mr. Huggins's. The white folks had not gone to bed when I came back. I left my little child behind me. Mr. Gordon did not ask, the next morning, what I had told. Mr. Gordon asked me if I had been sent for. I did not say that I could tell the negroes that were in the house that night, but that I did not know the white men. I told Mr. Gordon I had been sent for. I had a conversation with Sheriff Kendrick at Mr. Pope's. I went over after my husband was killed, and told him I did not want to stay there now, and wanted to go away. I did not tell him that I did not know who took my husband away, as he did not ask me the question. I said I wanted to go away, as they had come and taken off my husband and killed him, and he was now dead. I remember when Felix Bumpus, the coroner, came to my gate, and when I told him my husband was killed. That was all we said. He did not tell me to go before the jury. I did not tell him that I did not know who took away my husband. I saw "Button" Love in the lane the day the inquest met. I did not speak to him at all, and did not tell him I did not know who took off my husband and killed him. I did not see him after I came to Aberdeen, about the 7th of June. I know Mike Forshee. I have seen him several times. That is him over there.

District Attorney WELLS. When you were told to point out Crosby yesterday two of the defendants rose, one behind the other; which did you mean was Crosby?

WITNESS. I told you at first I could not tell him among so many people.

District Attorney WELLS. You were asked about the gowns these men wore. Explain about them and the masks.

WITNESS. They had on long white gowns and masks coming down over their faces, with kind of caps with tassels on the head. They covered all round the head. When they stooped down under the bed I could not see their faces. I don't know whether the dresses made the men look high or low, tall or short.

District Attorney WELLS. Why did you not make mention of all this at the time?

Colonel Dowd objected to the question.

The court overruled the objection.

WITNESS. I never said no such words to Mr. Gordon, that I did not know who the men were. I never told Sheriff Kendrick what has been said—that I said I did not want to speak about this thing till the proper time. I went down, after my husband was taken away, to Sheriff Kendrick's, but he did not ask me who it was took off my husband. I had a conversation with Felix Bumpus, but I did not say who it was. I think there were more than ten persons came into the house that night. I did not recognize any more than those I have spoken about. While I lived at Whitfield Pope's I saw Malone there. He said to me, "How d'ye?" when he was passing me. All they said to me when they went out was, "Work hard, and mind how you talk to the white folks; and stay here."

TESTIMONY OF JOE DAVIS.

Joe Davis (colored) was next examined by District Attorney Wells, and testified as follows:

I live at Mr. Andrew Crosby's, in Monroe County, in this State.

District Attorney WELLS. Now, have you ever been in company at night with parties in disguise?

WITNESS. Yes, sir. They had red gowns, and some had black and some had white concerns on their faces. The first time I was out with them was last March. They came to my house once or twice, or maybe three times, to get me to go out with them. I don't know exactly the time it was the first time they passed by. When they came for me it was in March. They called me out, and asked me if I was in favor of the Ku-Klux. I said I was not. They took me along with them, and I went to Alex. Page's with the band. I was there twice. The last time I was there was the 29th of March, on a Wednesday. They went after him and took him out. Among those who were there was Henry Hatch, (colored,) Jasper Webb, Thomas Malone, Andy Pope, Whitfield Pope, Johnny Ware, J. Plummer Willis, Jeff Willis, (colored,) Mike Forshee, (colored.) These were all that I knew in the band. There were more beside them. There was fifty or sixty there. I went there on a horse. It was one of Andy Pope's horses. When I went out with them Webb, Malone, or Johnny Ware always gave me a horse. I don't know who gave me the disguise. It was red and black. I had a face-mask and a red and black cap. We stopped the horses before we got close to Page's, and I was left to hold the horses. They went to the house, and a young man came back to where I was standing and told me to go up into the house. I told them I did not want to go, but they told me I must go, and I went. They kindled up a fire on the hearth. Alex. Page was there at the bed when I went into the house. There was a piece of rope hanging up in the house, and they told me to take it and tie his hands with it. I said, "No," but they ordered me to do it. Page got up, and I tied his hands in front and then tied his arms. Andy Pope cut the bed cord and put the rope round Alex.'s neck and led him out. Then I saw one of them take a handkerchief and put it over his head and face, so as to blindfold him. They then brought him out of the house. I went back to the horses, and we all got on our horses and went down the road toward Athens, traveling east. I never lived up in that neighborhood. It was a sort of moon shining that night. I don't know exactly how long they traveled with him. They went toward Athens for two or three miles, and then carried him out into the woods. They halted and told me to secure the horses, and took Page further into the woods. They whipped him. I could hear them whipping him. I heard him making a great noise. They then came back and told me to go up into the woods, and I went and saw Alex. Page lying dead on the ground, with a rope around his neck and his hands tied. I don't know what they did with him, as I did not see him till they had done killing him. They took me and another black fellow to look after the horses. I did not hear any pistols or guns fired off. I don't know whether Page was shot or hung, but I should say he was hung. They staid long enough around there to dig a grave. I heard them say they had killed him after they came back to the horses. They called me and Henry Hatch to go up to the grave, and we took hold of him and put him in the grave. There was a good many took hold of him beside us. We then raked the dirt on him and then raked leaves on it. It was dark, and I don't know how deep the grave was. There was a big log close by the grave. After we had buried the body we got on our horses and every one "put out" for home. I wore a disguise. Johnny Ware, Tom Malone, and Jasper Webb gave it to me. I heard Alex. Page ask the men to let him pray before they killed him, but they would not allow him to do it. After they took him into the woods he said he wanted to see his wife, but they told him never to mind his wife now. He again asked them to let him pray, but they would not allow him. That is Jasper Webb, that is Tom Malone, that is J. Plummer Willis, that is Mike Forshee, that is Jeff Willis, [pointing to several of the defendants.] I don't see Johnny Ware among these men.

Cross-examination:

Cross-examined by Colonel REYNOLDS: All those I have just pointed out were there that night. When once I know a man I know him. I am from Lauderdale County. I came to Monroe five or six years ago. I have lived with Crosby all this year. I don't know if any one would have known me. I don't know that any one could tell who I was with my mask on, as it completely covered my face, and came down to my breast. The gown I had on came down to my knees. I don't think I would have known Crosby if he had not spoken. I do not know that I would know his voice. Any one who wore that disguise could not be told except by his voice. Sometimes I could not see their faces, but I would know them by their voices. That was the only way I could tell who they were. They could not tell it was me unless I let them see my face. That is for certain; although they might think they knew me if I did not raise up my disguise. They would not know a man unless he talked. I could not tell them unless they gave me a sign to let me know who they were. I did not want to hurt Alex. Page, as we were good friends. Once before, when a knife was drawn on him, I went up and saved his life when no one would go and try to do it. The horses were left about a hundred yards from the house. I was out another time with them, but I don't recollect the month, nor the day of the month, nor the day of the week. When they went up to the house and got in, some of them came back and told me to go up and tie Page. Henry Hatch was with me, holding the horses. I don't know how many was up there. I did not take any account of them, but there may have been fifteen or twenty. Mike Forshee was with me down at the horses before they came for me to go to the house. He was not in the house when I got there. Andy Pope got the cord out of the bed to tie Page. He was not in bed when I got there. I never saw him in bed. I did not see him in his drawers. When the party came to Page's they went pass Jehu Wolf's house. I was disguised like the others. I did not know they had killed Page until they called me up to put him in his grave. I never told Jehu Wolf where he was buried. I don't know that Jehu Wolf helped to put the body in the grave. I know that Henry Hatch and I put him in the grave. They did not take off his wet clothes. I don't know who all helped, but I know Henry Hatch and I put him in. They had all on long gowns. I did not see any hatchets or axes. I rode behind the party. I was the hindmost. They came for me to go out with them. They never taught me any Ku-Klux signs. They never taught me anything. They never showed me to put out my arm or to raise my leg for a signal. All through the day before we went out that night I was in the field plowing the corn-patch. I had had supper, and they came for me between 10 and 11 o'clock. Tom Malone, Whitfield Pope, and Johnny Ware came for me. They called me out, and asked me if I was in favor of the Ku-Klux. I said, "No;" and then they said I belonged to the radical party, and to go slow. They had no disguise on then at that time. I don't know where they kept their disguises. I went off with them, and went two miles before I put on my disguise. I went out north from my house along the road to Alex. Page's house. The whole party met on the road and stopped and put on their disguises. Jasper Webb, Johnny Ware, Whitfield Pope, Andy Pope, Mike Forshee were all that went up with me that night. Jasper Webb, Whitfield Pope, and Johnny Ware left my house with me. I don't know how deep the grave was. I helped to cover up the body. A short helve-hoe was all I had to work with, and to fill in the dirt. It was ten or fifteen minutes before I went back to the horses. I left before the filling in of the grave was finished. I did not see what the others were doing when we were putting him in the grave. He did not move, but looked as if he was dead. I did not go back to the grave. I don't know what was done to the grave after I left. I did what I was ordered to do. I did not see any blood. The moon was shining, but the light was not good. I did not see Page's face. I knew it was him, for did I not help to tie him and go along with him? I know it was him. I did not look for blood. It was dark. I saw no blood on the ground. I heard them say it was Alex. Page. I stooped right over and lifted him into the grave. I looked toward his head. I saw a rope round his neck. It was about half a yard long. We went along the road and then went into the woods, where they dug the grave. I don't know that we went through a sage-field. If I had gone through it I would have known it. I don't know where the sage-field was. I don't know Captain Sykes. I have seen him several times, but I never saw him among the Ku-Klux. I saw him in Aberdeen on the Main street, opposite the Commercial Hotel. He did not ask me if I knew who killed Alex. Page, or if I had ever seen a Ku-Klux. No, sir. I did not say to him that I did not know any more about the killing of Alex. Page than the man in his grave.

Colonel REYNOLDS. Did you not tell certain parties in front of the drug-store in the town of Oxford that you had to tell lies to get clear, and to swear to lies?

WITNESS. No, sir.

Colonel REYNOLDS. Did you not tell Mike Forshee, in the presence of Mike Young, in the jail in Oxford, this week or the last, that Mike had better swear lies, as you had sworn and got clear?

WITNESS. No, sir.

Colonel REYNOLDS. Did you not tell Mike Forshee, in presence of Mike Young, that if he swore he was a Ku-Klux he would get clear?

WITNESS. No, sir. I was brought here with the rest of the prisoners. I was at home last Sunday. I saw Ann Forshee. I saw her at my house about 11 o'clock in the day. I did not say in her presence that unless Mike did as I had done he would never get home.

Colonel REYNOLDS. Did you not tell Jeff Willis and Burrill Willis, in the jail in Oxford, that unless they all swore they were Ku-Klux they would never get home?

WITNESS. I never spoke to them anything of the kind. I never went into the part of the jail where they were. Page and I never had a "fuss." He spoke a few important words to my wife at one time. I asked him about it, and he said if he had said it it was all right. He spoke some blackguard words to my wife and her sister. I did not have a "fuss" with him about it. When I was summoned to come here I was arrested by a man. I don't know that he said if I swore against the others I would be released. I don't think I was brought up into a room. I was carried into the jury room. Where it is I don't know. I was never in this room before. I don't know that a white man had a conversation with me. Mr. Huggins had no conversation with me. He has never talked to me about the case. He spoke to me about all they had arrested, and spoke about Roberts and such men being arrested for being Ku-Klux. I never told Huggins what I could swear to. I have never talked to any white man about it since I came to town. I have never told anybody what I would swear to. Wash Willis was not in the jail with me. I believe he was in jail one night. Wash Willis did not tell me to swear I was a Ku-Klux and I would get home. We did not talk about anything but a chaw of tobacco and getting something to eat. They told me I was a radical when they came for me that night. I did not see a Loyal-League signal given me by Ezra Larkin, or Isaiah Reynolds. I don't know what you mean when you put your finger to your throat and draw it round.

District Attorney Wells objected, and wished to know if counsel wanted to investigate Loyal League signs.

Colonel Reynolds withdrew the question, and asked the witness: Have you been offered $800 by any one, if you find the body of Jack Dupre?

WITNESS. No, sir.

District Attorney Wells objected, although the question had been already answered.

Colonel Reynolds withdrew the question and answer.

WITNESS. Henry Hatch, Wash. Willis, Mike Young, and myself were all in the same room in jail. Triplet was there one night. He was with Henry and I alone.

The court took a recess until 3 o'clock, afternoon.

AFTERNOON SESSION.

The court resumed at 3 o'clock afternoon.

Witness resumed: The day of the week I was "out" the second time was Saturday. When I first saw Alex. Page that night he was out of bed, and standing on the floor. When Whitfield Pope and the others came for me they inquired if I was in favor of the Ku-Klux, and I said, no. They then said I was a radical, and they wanted me to go with them. I asked them where they were going, and they told me they wanted me to take care of the horses. That was all they said. They told me after that if I reported what I had seen they would hang me as they had done that man. The grave was full when I went away. I helped to put the leaves over it. I helped to rake the leaves. If I went through a sage-field I don't remember it. Ann Forshee came to my house last Sunday. My wife was there, and we had a conversation in presence of my wife and Henry Hatch's wife. She was only there part of the time. She came in just before Ann went out. I don't know Mike Young. There was no one in the jail but black people. I have been "out" three or four times. There was no particular place of meeting. The biggest part met at Walton's store. They met there twice to my knowing. I did not have a conversation with Jasper Webb in Aberdeen just before coming here. He spoke to me on the train, and said to me, "I suppose you don't know enough to make a tell out of this. You be on the watch, and don't tell anything, or know nothing, and don't let them pick anything out of you."

District Attorney WELLS. Witness, were any threats made?

Colonel DOWD. Stop, witness; I object.

District Attorney Wells contended he had the right to ask the question.

The court ruled he might do so on the re-examination.

WITNESS. I cannot tell the day of the month it was the first time I was "out" with the Ku-Klux. I don't know exactly what month it was. I know what month this is. I believe it was in February that I was first "out" with them. I don't know whether it was the first, last, or middle of the month. The next time was shortly after the murder of Jack Dupree. I don't know the difference of time between the first and second times. It may have been a week. The third time I don't know what I was doing that day. I was plowing the day before. The fourth time I don't know when it was. It was something like a week or two from the first time. It may have been two weeks, or maybe three or four weeks. It was right smart of time between the times. There was about a week between the fourth and fifth times. I was not out six times. I don't know as I was out five times. There was a third time and a fourth time. I could not tell all about it. I said I did not know if I was out four or five times. I was out once after Alex. Page's affair. It was not long ago. I think it was about the first of June or last of May, or somewhere along in June. I don't know the day of the month. I was at Walton's store, I believe, in February. I met a good many of the Ku-Klux at the store, and some were down the road. The second time was a week or ten days after. I know it was in that month. It was two or three weeks after, or a little less. When they came and told me that they wanted me to go and take care of the horses on the night we went to Alexander Page's, there was some talk of the "clubs" coming in on them. That was what was said. I mean by that

that the colored people were coming in on them, but they did not come. I mean that the "niggers" would club together to take any one away from the Ku-Klux. The Ku-Klux knew that when the niggers knew that they were going to take out a man out to whip him or kill him they would club together to prevent them. The colored people would go together to prevent the Ku-Klux taking that man away. I did not say I belonged to a club.

General Gholson informed the court that Captain Houston, one of the counsel for the defense, was anxious to leave that day for home, and before he left the relators wished to call him to give testimony in rebuttal.

The court stated that, with the consent of counsel on the side of the Government, the testimony could be taken at the present stage of the proceedings.

District Attorney Wells said he had no objection to offer.

Testimony in rebuttal of Captain R. E. Houston.

Captain R. E. Houston being sworn testified in rebuttal as follows:

I had a conversation at Boonville with Jehu Wolf, one of the witnesses for the Government in this case, as we were coming upon the train from Aberdeen. I had got off at Boonville for the purpose of seeing Captain Surratt, and while on the platform a colored man called to me, "Is that you, Massa Bob?" I replied it was, and he said to me, "I am Jehu Wolf; I am going to Oxford as a witness, but I don't know anything about any white man being connected with the killing of Alex. Page. Tell Andy Pope that he talks too much. Come into the car and I will tell you all about it." I did go into the car, as we thought Huggins was tampering with the witnesses. Wolf made the remarks I have stated in the presence of General Gholson and Colonel Reynolds. I went up to where Mr. Huggins was sitting, so as to prevent him talking to the witnesses. That witness Wolf was on the stand this morning.

Cross-examination:

Cross-examined by Mr. Blackman: It was about half past 12 o'clock in the day the circumstances I have related took place. I had not been riding in the same car with the witness Wolf. I had stepped off the train to see Captain Surratt when the witness called me, by saying, "That you, Massa Bob?" and I replied, "It is." General Gholson, Colonel Reynolds, and Captain Surratt were with me at the time. The witness Wolf said, "I did not know a white man in the matter of Page's killing. It was niggers done it. Tell Mr. Andy Pope he is talking too much." I never saw Whitfield Pope till yesterday.

The court then adjourned till half past 8 o'clock on Monday morning.

SIXTH DAY.

The court met this (Monday) morning, at half past 8 o'clock, pursuant to adjournment, Judge Hill presiding.

Testimony of Rosetta Dawkins.

Rosetta Dawkins (colored) was the first witness called on behalf of the Government this morning. On being examined by District Attorney Wells she testified as follows:

I am the step-daughter of Alex. Page, who was killed.

Colonel Dowd, on the part of the defense, wished the witness examined by the court as to whether she was aware of the nature of an oath.

The court made the necessary examination and declared the witness competent.

Witness. I live in Mississippi. I don't know what county I live in, but I live four miles above Aberdeen, My mother's name is Fanny Page, and my stepfather's name was Alex. Page. The last time I saw him was on a Wednesday night. I don't know what month it was, but I was living at the time at A. J. Pope's place, at the other side of the river. I was at the house where my mother and stepfather lived. My stepfather was taken off one night. I saw him alive that night; I have never seen him since, alive or dead. I saw the men take him off, but I could not tell how many were in the house. They broke the doors down and came in; they had axes. There were two doors to the house, and they broke them both down and came in. My stepfather was not in bed when they came in. The first I heard them say was, "Open the door." We kept quiet in the house when they said this.

District Attorney Wells. Did they come into the house?

Colonel Reynolds objected, as the question was leading.

The court stated that in order to save time the witness could state what was done that night.

District Attorney Wells. All I wish is that the witness shall explain explicitly what took place that night.

WITNESS. They came into the house and commenced looking for my stepfather, and asked where he was. I did not know where he was until I saw some one coming with a gun and getting him to come out from under the bed. Then they took him, blindfolded him, tied him, and took him out. The house was crowded full that night. It was a sort of cloudy night. I could see, for I sat up in bed when the men came in. After they got hold of him they tied him, blindfolded him, and took him out. Before taking him away they cut the bed-cord of mother's bed. They made up a light with some pine they found in the house; they made it up in the fire-place. They kindled a fire in the fire-place. I knew two of the men who were there—Mr. Thomas Malone and Ben Lumpkin, (colored.) That is Mr. Malone, over there. Ben Lumpkin is not here in the room. The persons who came into the house were dressed in long white gowns; some had jackets and pants. They had something on their heads and faces, with holes for their mouths, eyes, and noses. Some had tassels or horns on their heads; some had black faces, like false faces; some had on pieces of cloth over their faces, which would fly up and you could see their faces. In the morning after I went to look for my stepfather, but could not find him. When they caught hold of him in the house he fell upon his knees, but they made him get up and put on his clothes. He started to talk to them, but they made him get up. I saw a good many of their faces, but knew only two of the persons in the house.

District Attorney WELLS. Look round the room and see if there are any persons in the room that you saw that night.

WITNESS. I think I see one, (pointing to Addison Roberts, one of the defendants.) There is another, I think, (pointing to Mr. Carter, a citizen of Oxford, a spectator.) I don't think I know any more.

Colonel DOWD. Mr. Carter is not charged in the indictment.

District Attorney WELLS. I admit that Mr. Carter was in Oxford on the 29th of March.

WITNESS. The parties remained about the house about an hour. My stepfather's hands were tied at the wrists, and he was blindfolded.

Cross-examination:

Cross-examined by Colonel DOWD: I left my home near Aberdeen the day before yesterday. I live with Robert Inge, four miles from Aberdeen. I left there on Friday to go to Aberdeen with a black fellow named Edmond Duncan, who came for me. He told me he wanted me to go down where my mother was. I never had any talk with any white man about this affair. I never talked to anybody about it. I did not talk to this black man about it. I lived first with William Gholson, and then I lived with Sheriff Kendrick; next I lived with Mr. Kirkpatrick; then with Dr. Robertson, and last year with Whitfield Pope, and this year with Mr. Peter Douten. At Mr. Whitfield Pope's I worked on the farm with my mother; and stepfather had a crop there. Mr. Malone lived about a mile from Mr. Whitfield Pope's. Malone used to come backward and forward there. It was very late when the men were at my stepfather's house. We had been asleep, and were awoke by "hollering" outside. It was about one hundred and fifty yards from our house to Mr. Pope's house. I staid at my mother's; I did not stay at the white folks' house. I have seen Mr. Malone riding up to Mr. Pope's house. He would speak to me in the yard. I only said "How d'ye" to Mr. Malone when I saw him in the yard. I have seen him passing by, but I never had any words with him except "How d'ye." I never had any cross words with him. Malone was dressed like the rest of them. It was white all around, and reached from their heads to their feet. They had something on their faces which some of them threw up as they were working around. They were all around my bed. I never said anything. I knew Mr. Malone. He was near my bed, and the cloth over his face flew up, and I knew him by his face. When they stooped down it would fly up. They tried to keep it down around the neck when they went to do anything, but it would fly up when they let it go. I don't know who poked the gun at my stepfather, to bring him out from under the bed. They told him to come out. They could see all around the house. I did not cut the bed-cord. I don't know who did that. They called for a rope, and I told them I had no rope. They tied his hands with the rope. They cut off enough of the bed-cord to tie him, and one of them took out a handkerchief and blindfolded him. They made him sit down near to the fire-place, about three feet from it, and made him put his shoes and coat on, but no hat. The chimney is toward sunrise. My mother's bed was in the northeast corner of the room, and my bed in the southwest corner. They brought him clean across and came between the beds, where there was a bright light, and one of them took a handkerchief out and blindfolded him. Next morning Patsy, Jehu's wife, and I followed the horses' tracks two or three miles, and then we came back when we could not get any trace of him. There was a good many horses' tracks, and they tore up the road mightily. There had been rain. We went as far as West's house, and then turned back. We saw the tracks go on. We thought it was about three miles from home. Jehu and Mr. Pope started before us. They came back and told us to go and search. Jehu went a little piece up the road, and came back and told us to go and look for him. I don't know who built up the fire. Two or three were around the bed with gowns on till the man tied him. I don't know who got the ropes. They just took him away. They were in the house about a quarter of an hour or more. I am twenty-one years of age. I am married. I could not tell who tied him.

Mr. McCluskey, one of the counsel for the defense, stood up at the request of Colonel Dowd.

Colonel Dowd. Witness, is that the man?

District Attorney Wells. I object to this method of identification.

The court sustained the objection.

Witness. I never sat down to talk with Mr. Malone. He was never sparking me. [Laughter.] He never went down to my house with me or came down to see me. He never said nothing wrong to me. When the men were in the house I was sitting up in bed and had my child in my arms. Malone came close to the bed and said to me, "Do you know any one in this crowd?" I told him "No." He said "I had better not know any of them, and not to speak about white folks, but to go to work or it would not be good for me." I saw a heap of faces that I did not know.

Colonel Dowd. Look round the room and see if you see any persons you saw there that night.

Witness. I see Mr. Malone over there, and I think I saw that other man, (pointing to Addison Roberts, a defendant,) but I don't know his name. I never saw the two men I pointed out before or since. I have seen Mr. Malone before. There was a heap of faces I had never seen. I never told anybody about this affair until I came here this morning. I left Aberdeen on Saturday morning. I came here by myself. I staid first at Corinth. I don't know the name of the people I staid with there. A man gave me money in Aberdeen. They said it was the sheriff. Mr. Huggins gave me the money. He said $9.50 would fetch me here. Huggins sent for me, and I came down to the town to his office, and he handed me the money. Huggins sent word by Edmond Duncan, and he came to Aberdeen with me. I never said anything to Edmond about this. I had no more money than what Mr. Huggins gave me. He gave me a $5 bill, and the other bill was a $6 bill. He only gave me two bills. On Sunday morning I was at Corinth. I saw the train coming, and went and bought my ticket. They told me where to get off and where to change cars. I saw my mother when she got her breakfast this morning. She told me not to be scared in the court, and not to tell a story, but to tell all I knew. She asked me if they sent for me, and I said yes. She told me to tell all I knew, and not to tell more than I knew. She did not tell me she had experience about telling more than she knew. I did not tell her what I knew.

To District Attorney Wells. Duncan came for me on Friday night, and I went back to Aberdeen with him. I don't know what time we got there. The money was given to me on Friday night. I am not acquainted with Mr. Huggins. I rode up to the door of his office, and they told me who he was. I only knew where his office was when they told me. A man came out and gave me money. He was a tall man. He came to the door and handed me the money. He told me I had to take the train. I don't know the color of his whiskers. It was night at the time. Edmond told me he was Mr. Huggins. They said the man who gave me the money was the sheriff. I cannot count money. I have got to get somebody to tell me. He told me it was $9.50, and it would take me here.

District Attorney Wells. It appears to me, your honor, that the counsel for the defense are endeavoring to asperse the character of Colonel Huggins, and make him out the prosecutor in this case. Owing to the course pursued by the defense, I wish to be sworn in order that I may make a statement under oath.

Testimony of District Attorney Wells.

District Attorney G. W. Wells was then sworn, and testified as follows:

I know, of my own knowledge, that Huggins was here in Oxford on Friday night, and could not have been in Aberdeen that night. I know that the witness was sent for, by telegraph to the sheriff of Monroe County, who sent her here.

Testimony of United States Marshal Peirce.

Captain J. H. Peirce, United States marshal, testified:

I telegraphed to Mr. Anderson, sheriff of Monroe County, to send the witness, Dawkins, here, and he did so.

Testimony of Henry Hatch.

Henry Hatch, (colored,) on being examined by Colonel Walter, testified as follows:

I remember where I was the night Alex. Page was killed. I was with them that killed him. At that time I was living with Andrew Crosby. They came to my house and got me. It was pretty late in the night when they came for me. I went to Alex. Page's house. When we got there we went in and took Alex. out

We fetched him out and tied him, and then took him off into the woods. I cannot tell how far we went. I was not there exactly when Alex. was killed. It was a cloudy, dingy night. The moon was shining a little. When I could see, I could discover a man striking him with a stick. This was in the woods. Alex. was standing at the time this man was striking him. I saw him afterward, when he was killed. He was dead. I touched him. I helped to bury him. Joe Davis helped me to bury him. I helped to cover him up. There were four men helped to cover him up. The grave was covered with leaves and dirt. They all came away after the grave was covered. I could not tell how many was there. I was in Alex.'s house. I don't know how many were in the house. There was a good many. I don't think there was twenty. There was about seventy-five men that I saw altogether in the party. I knew some of those men. I knew Plummer Willis, Andy Crosby, John Porter, Andy Pope, Whitfield Pope, Tom Malone, Stephen Crosby, and Billy Walton.

Colonel WALTER. Point out Andy Crosby.

WITNESS. I don't konw anybody else in the room.

He then pointed out W. F. Tabor, who lives three miles south of the mouth of Tippo, State of Mississippi, and H. C. Harris, a citizen of Oxford, who were among the spectators.

Colonel WALTER. Did you call out the name of the first man you recognized?

WITNESS. I called "Tom Malone."

Colonel WALTER. Did you call it first or did somebody else call it for you?

WITNESS. Some one said that is Tom Malone.

Cross-examination:

Cross-examined by General GHOLSON: I did not know that man, (Tabor.) Some one said he was Tom Malone. His features are like Tom Malone's.

Colonel WALTER. I will now ask the prisoners to stand up.

Colonel REYNOLDS. I contend that the other side have had the opportunity of making a full test for identification.

The COURT. The test has been sufficiently made.

WITNESS. On the night Alex. was killed, I cannot tell who called me first. I think my wife waked me up when Andy and Whitfield Pope came after me. They asked me if I was in favor of the Ku-Klux, and I told them I was not. They cautioned me, and told me to follow them, and put me on a horse behind one of them. They had white clothes with them, which they gave to me. I don't know who gave them to me. The clothes were plumb white, with a false face, which came down over my face. The clothes came down to my ankles. In the false face there was holes for the mouth, the eyes, and the nose. It came down to my breast. I went among the first that went into Page's. I was in the house with Whitfield Pope, Andy Pope, Andrew Crosby, John Porter, and Stephen Crosby. They made up a light. I don't know who made it up. Alex. Page was under the bed, and they fetched him out and took him out doors and tied him. They tied him with a rope round his wrists and round his arms. I came out with two men. I did not see all they done in the house. I saw Alex. Page after he was brought out. They carried him to where the horses were. There was more than one or five did this, but not ten. I was behind some one on horseback. I saw there Whitfield Pope, Andy Pope, and Joe Davis. I saw Whitfield and Andy Pope at the grave. I saw their faces. I saw Aunt Fanny and her daughter in the house. There was a big log near the grave. I never went to the grave afterwards. I don't know where they got the rope from to tie his hands.

Cross-examination:

Cross-examined by Colonel REYNOLDS: I saw Joe Davis there there that night; I am certain I saw him; I went home with Joe; he was dressed in white, and had red round his eyes and mouth; he had on a piece of white cloth that came over his face and down to the middle of his breast. I went to Alex. Page's house with the crowd. I was behind. I was not there at the time they killed him; I was back about a hundred yards from them. There were some trees on the rise of the ground; it was like a grove—tolerably thick. The moon was shining bright when we were there. It was tolerable late in the night when we left home. We went straight to Alex.'s house. I saw them strike Alex. with a stick. I did not dig his grave—I simply helped to cover him up. Joe Davis did not dig his grave, but he helped to put him in his grave. There was no light in the house when we went in there. I went in with the crowd. I did not stay to hold the horses. Joe Davis tied Alex. outside the house. Joe was there. I don't know that Joe was sent for from the horses to tie him. I know Crosby; I live with him. Crosby did not come for me that night; A. Pope and Whitfield Pope came for me. I never saw that gentleman (Captain Sykes) before; I did not see him in the cars coming here. I recollect the Saturday I was brought to Aberdeen. I know Eckford & Dortch's drug-store. I know Main street. I don't recollect Captain Sykes asking me whether I knew anything about the Ku-Klux. I did not tell him that I did not know anything about the killing of Alex. Page. I know General Gholson and I know you, Colonel Reynolds.

Colonel REYNOLDS. Do you recollect that between Aberdeen and the junction, on the train coming here, you were asked what you knew about the killing of Alex. Page and the whipping of Huggins, and did you not tell us that you knew nothing about the Ku-Klux, and knew no man, black or white, who had been engaged in the killing of Page or whipping of Huggins?

The WITNESS. I did not.

District Attorney WELLS. I object, as no name is given.

Colonel REYNOLDS. Did we not tell you, if you wanted to tell us anything, to tell the truth; and did you not say you knew nothing about Alex. Page or Jack Dupree's deaths, or the Ku-Klux?

The WITNESS. I did not. I don't recollect having seen you on the train. I don't recollect Huggins and Wash Willis whispering together. The last time I saw General Gholson was in Aberdeen, until I saw him here. The last time I saw you (Colonel Reynolds) was in Aberdeen. I never saw Captain Sykes before, that I know of. I did not belong to Dr. Hatch before the war. I belonged to old man Hatch, who lives on the Cotton Gin road, in Monroe County.

To Colonel WALTER. I saw a good many persons on the cars as I was coming from Aberdeen to the junction. I don't know the Mobile and Ohio Railroad. There was a right smart lot of people from the junction to Corinth on the train. I had very little to say to any person on the train. That gentleman is Dr. McClusky that used to be. He and a northern man and I all had a drink of water together. I held the horses near the grave while the killing was going on, and then went and helped to bury the body.

District Attorney WELLS. Your honor, we will close here on behalf of the United States.

REBUTTING TESTIMONY.

Testimony of Colonel R. O. Reynolds.

Colonel R. O. Reynolds, one of the counsel for the relators, was called, and testified as follows:

I had a conversation on the train, between Aberdeen and the junction, about two weeks ago. I went into the nigger-car for the purpose of smoking, and there found Dr. Hutchinson, (one of the defendants,) General Gholson, and Father Blankque, (a Catholic priest.) I was sitting near Henry Hatch, and was talking to him. I recollect I cautioned him, and said, "Hatch, if you don't want to answer my questions, don't do it; but whatever you tell me, tell me the truth;" and he said he would tell me all he knew. I then asked, "Do you know anything about the killing of Alex. Page or Jack Dupree, or the Ku-Klux?" He said, "I don't know anything about it, and I never saw a Ku-Klux in my life." That is about the substance of what took place. I also asked Jehu Wolf, on the train, where he lived, and he said at Andy Pope's. I asked him what he knew about the killing of Alex. Page, and he said he did not know nothing about it, or any one, white or black, connected with it. While I was talking to this witness, Huggins came and whispered to Wash Willis, and every one was quiet immediately, as Wash Willis went to all the witnesses and spoke to them. I saw three negroes—Isaiah Reynolds and Satis Larkin, and a third one, whose name I do not know—call Joe Davis by name and give him a secret signal by passing the finger round the front of the throat, from ear to ear.

Colonel Walter said it would require to be proved that Joe heard his name called and saw the sign before they could accept the testimony.

Colonel REYNOLDS. Joe was nearer to them than I was, and I heard them call him.

The COURT. It is of no importance.

Cross-examination:

Cross-examined by Colonel WALTER: Dr. Dudley Hutchinson, General Gholson, and the Catholic priest were all present when this conversation took place. The cars were making the usual noise.

Testimony of Captain E. O. Sykes.

Captain E. O. Sykes, one of the counsel for the relators, was called, and testified as follows:

I know Joe Davis; I met him on Main street, in Aberdeen, on Saturday, the 17th of June—the day these parties were arrested. As I was going west, I saw him on the street, in company with two niggers, wearing the United States uniform. I considered they were a party under arrest, and I think I asked L. J. Morgan about it. He said he thought they were in custody. I was attracted by Davis's appearance, as he was a large, stout man, and I called him to me, and asked him if he was one of the parties arrested and charged with being Ku-Klux, or some other charge. I was surprised at a colored man being arrested for being a Ku-Klux. He said he was one of the number.

He said he knew nothing about the killing of Alex. Page than the man in the grave. He denied that he was a Ku-Klux, and said he had been Ku-Kluxing grass all spring. I then asked Henry Hatch if he knew anything of the killing of Alex. Page, and he said he knew nothing about it. Above Aberville, near Holly Springs, I was in the car where the prisoners were, and went to get a drink of water. As I came back to my seat, a negro caught me by the coat-tail. I turned, but did not know him. He said, "I want you to tell Andy Pope not to talk too much." I said, "I don't know you; you must explain what you mean." He replied, "My name is Jehu Wolf, and if you tell Andy Pope not to talk so much, he will understand." I did not like the conversation, and thought the nigger was insolent, when he said, "Don't be afraid; I am on your side." I said, "What do you mean by saying you are on my side?" and he said, "I mean the right side." I said, "Do you know anything about the death of Alex. Page, and he said, "No." I asked, "Do you know any parties connected with it?" and he said, "No."

Cross-examination:

Cross-examined by Colonel WALTER: The cars were moving rapidly all this time, and with the usual noise. The first I saw of Davis was in Aberdeen. He said he was to report at the court-house at 1 o'clock, and so had been informed by Major McCoy, who was the officer in charge of the squad. It was then about 11 o'clock. That was on Saturday, and we left for Oxford on Monday. A good many persons were not arrested by the guard or marshals. Major McCoy wrote notes to the parties that he had warrants for their arrest, and to come in and save further trouble, and they came. William Butler, J. D. Hutchinson, and J. L. Loughridge, and others received notes of that character from Major McCoy. Some of the notes were written in my presence in Colonel Reynolds's back-room. Some of the parties, after reporting, were allowed to return home and get their clothes before being brought to Oxford.

Testimony of Hubert C. Harris.

Hubert C. Harris was called, and testified as follows:

I was pointed out in court by the witness Hatch as being the defendant Porter. I have never been in Monroe County in my life.

Testimony of W. F. Tabor.

W. F. Tabor was called, and testified as follows:

I reside twelve miles from Oxford. I was at home on the 29th of March. I was pointed out by the witness Hatch as Tom Malone to-day.

Testimony of B. F. Hall.

B. F. Hall was called, and testified as follows:

I was sitting in front of Mr. Tabor in the court-room, and I understood the darky Hatch to call his name Tom Malone.

Cross-examination:

Cross-examined by Colonel WALTER: I think some one sitting near said, "Let him alone."

Testimony of S. J. Gholson.

General S. J. Gholson was recalled, and testified as follows:

I heard a conversation on the cars between Aberdeen and Aberdeen Junction, as we were coming to Oxford. I went into the black-car and asked a Catholic priest to go with me. I know Henry Hatch, and I asked him what he was going to do at Oxford. He said he never saw a Ku-Klux, and knew nothing about the death of Alex. Page. I heard the conversation between Colonel Reynolds and Hatch. The car was noisy. I recollect the conversation with Jehu Wolf, word for word. He said it was "onpossible" to recognize any of the men that took off Alex. Page. I heard you (Colonel Reynolds) tell them, if they told anything, to tell the truth, and I thought I had neglected to caution them. I remember when at Boonville, when I was standing with Captain Surratt, Wolf called out to Captain Houston, "That you, Massa Bob?" and on being told that he was Captain Houston—in reply to certain questions—said, "I don't know any of the Ku-Klux that carried off Alex. Page, and did not know any white man connected with it." He asked Captain Houston to come inside the car, but I don't know whether he went in or not.

Testimony of Felix Bumpus.

Felix Bumpus (colored) was recalled, and testified as follows:

I am the coroner of Monroe County. I am a republican.

(District Attorney Wells objected to the introduction of politics. The court sustained the objection.)

WITNESS. I held the inquest on the body of Alex. Page on the 7th of April. I had a conversation with Page's wife after the inquest in front of her house. Andy Pope and Mr. Love came down with me, and I rode up to Mrs. Page's gate. I asked her if she was Alex. Page's wife. She said she was. I asked her if she had lost her husband, and she said she had. I asked her if she knew any of the men who carried him off, and she said "No." She said she could not tell the number of the men who came into the house and took him off. She said the house was full and a good many out of doors. The grave of Page was leveled with the ground. There was some few leaves on it. We could not tell it had been scooped, as there had been a good deal of rain. I examined Jehu Wolf. That memorandum is his testimony taken at the time. I did not examine the head of deceased.

Wolf's testimony.

Colonel Reynolds read the following as Jehu Wolf's testimony as taken at the coroner's inquest:

"*Jehu Wolf's testimony.*

"The next day, in the morning on Thursday, in search of a mule, I found the mule's tracks in the mouth of the lane, and tracked her within three hundred yards of the body of Alex. Page. I then found the horse-tracks, which led within two hundred yards of the said body. I then saw the broom-sage smashed down within twenty steps of the said body, in an old field. I then started around the foot of the hill below the field. I then saw blood on the ground in front of me and went to the spot and raked away some leaves, and found the body of Alex. Page. I then caught hold of his head, and he throwed back his head and made a strange noise. I then pulled the leaves over him again and ran off and went back home. I told my wife I had found Alex. with his throat cut, when she asked me if I had found him. I then told Mr. Pope, upon his asking me if I had found Alex., and I told him not to say anything about it, and that I expected to leave in the morning."

(WITNESS resumed.) Wolf swore that he did not know any one that was there.

Cross-examination:

Cross-examined by Colonel MANNING: The statement just read was taken down by Mr. Love at the place. I asked the questions, and he put down the evidence. Mr. Love was the acting sheriff. I don't know Mr. Love's handwriting, but what has been read I believe were the words spoken by Jehu Wolf at the inquest. Jehu did not sign the paper. It was written in pencil and written at the grave. I don't know whether it was read over to Jehu in my presence. It was not read to me. I asked the questions, and I supposed Mr. Love put down the answers. Mr. George Pennington, circuit court clerk, showed me this paper. I left Aberdeen on Saturday. I went to his office to inquire the date of the inquest, and he showed me this paper, which was on file. I did not read it. I can read writing. I looked at the date of the paper and then left. Mr. West, Mr. Taylor, Mr. Love, Jehu Wolf, and others whose names I don't remember were present at the inquest. Andy Pope and Jehu Wolf was examined as witnesses. I asked Aunt Fanny Page how many came to the cabin the night Alex. was taken away, and she told me she did not know. I was through my official duties by that time. The verdict had been rendered, and I did not call to examine her as a witness. She was not sworn. I went up to Andy Pope's and then went to Jehu's before the inquest. I was within one hundred yards of Aunt Fanny's house at that time. I knew Alex.'s wife, and knew he had been taken away from his house, but I was not certain of finding the body. That was the reason I did not call Aunt Fanny to go with us. Jehu had told me he had found the body; but as it was my first inquest I did not know very well what to do. I may have asked her more questions, but I am positive she said she did not know any of the persons. It was a casual conversation. After I got home I may have told it to several parties. I don't know to whom I told it first. I told it to Mr. Pennington and the sheriff, and may have told it to several colored people. I was asked why I did not make arrests, and I told them because I did not get sufficient information. I asked Aunt Fanny who were in the house, and she said they were all disguised. I asked her if she recognized any of the parties, and she said she did not. When Jehu said he was going to leave the country, he was asked, "Why?" and he said "that, as he had found the body of Alex., perhaps they would kill him for reporting it." I can read this paper, but it would be painful to my eyes to do so. If that is not down about Jehu leaving the country, in his testimony, it should be down. Jehu was excited. I was right smart excited myself. Aunt Fanny did not appear as if she wanted to talk to me. She looked cool and sad, as if she had trouble on her heart and mind. She did not say she did not want to tell. She appeared as if she did not want to talk to me. I observed horses' tracks in the old field. It had been raining and the tracks were not plain. And I don't know whether the grave had been disturbed. The tracks were about one hundred or two hundred yards from the grave. There was a log close to the grave.

To Colonel DOWD. I reported to the sheriff and the circuit clerk that I could not find the names of the parties who carried off Alex. Page and killed him.

Colonel DOWD. If you had found them would you have arrested them?

(District Attorney WELLS objected. The witness cannot tell you what he would have done.

The court sustained the objection.)

The WITNESS. I went out of my way to see Aunt Fanny. I did not know she was Page's wife when I went out to the grave.

The court took a recess till 3 o'clock afternoon.

AFTERNOON SESSION.

The court met at 3 o'clock, Judge Hill presiding.

Testimony of Silas F. Kendrick.

Silas F. Kendrick was then examined and testified:

I reside in Monroe County, about a mile and a quarter from Pope's. I know Fanny Page, and have known her three and a half years. I had a conversation with her within a week after the death of her husband. It was on a Saturday. She came to my place during the week and told me of her husband having been taken from her home and murdered. She had been living with me the year before, and she was to come to me on the 25th or 28th of last March, but she did not come. She came at the time I have said. She came down to me in the field, and as she seemed sad, I said, "Aunt Fanny, what is the matter?" and she said, "Massa Silas, I am not very well; I am sick, and have not slept for a night or two." I saw there was something wrong, and I asked her, and then she told me that Alex. had been killed. That was the first I had heard of it. She said they came and carried him off. She said they knocked at both doors and came in and asked for a light. I think she said she got up, and said, "I will get a light with some pine." She told Alex. not to run, and they turned down her bed, cut the cord, and tied Alex. with it. She said she was certain they had killed him. I told her to go to bed; that he would come back, and they had perhaps only carried him off. She said she was certain they had killed him, and said, "If you will never tell I will tell you who told me." She said that it was Jehu Wolf, who was living on Pope's place, who had told her Alex. was killed. He had tracked the horses and found the body. I asked her if she had recognized any of the persons who came into the house and took Alex. away, and she said, "La, no, you never see such things as they had on their heads; you could not tell whether they were women or men, and could not recognize anybody." She wanted to come to my house, and said she was under no obligations to Mr. Pope. It was late on Saturday evening, and I told her I could not go up that evening for her little stock and things, and to go home that evening and come back, and I would go for her things the next morning. That is the substance of the conversation. I never asked the color of the dresses the men wore.

Cross-examination:

Cross-examined by District Attorney WELLS: My farm does not join Pope's. Part of two farms divide our places. The road when it gets to my place stops. I live nearer Aberdeen than Pope does. He sometimes travels the road that passes my house. It is not the regular road. I live a mile and a half from Pope's. I had not heard of Alex. Page being carried off and killed till Fanny told me. She told me it took place on Wednesday. There are no colored people on my place except two bound children. I have seven children. My eldest daughter is seventeen, and I have a boy of thirteen. They don't attend school. I have been acquainted with Fanny for three years. She promised to work for me, but did not come at the time she promised. I was plowing when she came to me in the field, and she appeared to be dejected. She said she had not slept the last night. She was cast down and dejected, and I asked her what was the matter, as I saw something in her appearance that made me think there was something wrong. I asked her if she had been sick, and she said, "No, Massa Silas, but I did not sleep." She then told me that Alex. was killed. I asked her how she knew, and said it is not so, and she said, "It is so." She then said, "If you will not tell I will tell you who did it. Jehu Wolf tracked the horses and found the body of Alex." She enjoined secrecy on me and appeared to think somebody would hurt Jehu. If she said any more, I do not know it.

Testimony of W. J. Gordon.

W. J. Gordon, on being examined, testified as follows:

I know Fanny Page, the wife of Alexander Page. She came to my house on the 7th of June. I had a conversation with her the night she came there. I was cording up her bed, and the bed-cord was too short, when she told me it was cut for the purpose of tying Alexander the night he was taken away and killed. I asked her, "Did you know anybody who was there that night?" and she said, "I could not recognize them, they were dressed up so. I thought I knew some of the niggers." That was all she said about them. I remember her leaving my house and going to Huggins's. She left her child behind her, and next morning I asked her where she had gone, and she said. "To see Mr. Huggins and Felix Bumpus, to give in my testimony." I said, "Did you tell them all who was there?" and she said, "They said I must tell all, I think it was."

Cross-examination:

Cross-examined by Colonel WALTER: She came to my house on the 7th of June, and staid there till she came to this place. It was on the 7th or 8th of June. The night afterwards I was helping to cord up her bed. She appeared dejected, and she told me she felt bad. I recollect the cord was short, and she said it had been cut to tie her husband's hands before he was killed. She said they were all so disguised she could not recognize them, but she thought she knew some of the niggers. When she came back from seeing Mr. Huggins and Felix Bumpus, I asked her if she had told them all who were there, and she said, "No;" but they told her she must come up and state those she thought was there. This occurred a week after. I have not seen her until I saw her the other day.

Ann Forshee.

Ann Forshee, (colored,) on being examined, testified as follows:

I am the wife of Mike Forshee, one of the defendants. The day that Alex. Page was killed, I and Mr. Pope went to town, (Aberdeen.) Joe Davis went off on Tuesday morning, and when he got back he was there.

Colonel WALTER. Did he say where he had been?

WITNESS. He was at Mr. Kendrick's son-in-law's. I saw Joe yesterday was a week ago. He came to our house. I saw him on Sunday morning. I asked him how they all was, and he said they all was in jail, and it was no use for us to go up here, (to Oxford,) for we would not be allowed to speak in court, as Mr. Huggins told him——

District Attorney WELLS. Stop. Don't tell what Mr. Huggins told him.

WITNESS. He said that if they would not say they were Ku-Klux, they would go to the penitentiary ninety-nine years, or get their necks broke.

Cross-examination:

Cross-examined by Mr. TURNER: I went to town on Wednesday, and got back on Wednesday evening. Joe Davis left on Tuesday morning. He did not come back that night. He came home with us on Wednesday night. He said he was going to town when we came back. He was at Mr. Kendrick's son-in-law's place. On Sunday morning a conversation took place at Joe's place. He asked me was I going up here, as it was no use, as I would not be allowed to swear in court. They were all confined in jail, he said, on the broad of their backs. His wife, his sister-in-law, and Henry Hatch's wife were all there, and he said that Mike and the others must swear they were Ku-Klux if they wanted to get out. He said he had been talking to Mike about it, and Mike had said he had never been a Ku-Klux, and he was not going to swear to a lie. Mike said he never had been one, and would not tell a lie. Joe said they knew he was, and that he had been persuaded by the white folks. He said if they would only swear false they would get off, and if it had not been for that we would never have seen his face again. He said they never would get out no way except they came up and swore they were Ku-Klux. He said they were confined in jail on the broad of their backs, two and two. He said if they did not come up and swear, it would be penitentiary for ninety-nine years, or they would be hung. I asked him if he swore he was one, and he said if he had not done so we would never have seen his face any more. I believe that is all. He tried to get Mike to turn. He said Mike said he never had been one, and was not going to swear what was not so. I went away, and my business was such I could not get back after dinner. I did not see Joe again. I have had no conversation with him since they came for me that day.

To General GHOLSON. That was after you left going to Mr. Ford's from Mr. Crosby's.

District Attorney WELLS. There are two witnesses, your honor, on the way who will testify as to this conversation at Joe Davis's house. They will be here to-morrow.

The COURT. We cannot wait on witnesses now. They ought to be in attendance.

General GHOLSON. We may send for some more on our side.

District Attorney WELLS. The case for the prosecution is closed, and I would here remark to your honor that the Government has other witnesses of equal importance to those examined, whom I do not intend to introduce upon this examination, as it is not final.

Colonel DOWD. The counsel for the relators have agreed to close their entire argument in five hours, if such an arrangement is agreeable to the other side—to take up only five hours each.

The COURT. If the witnesses the district attorney referred to come to-night they can be heard to-morrow.

District Attorney Wells said he had no objection to make the arrangement proposed, to limit the argument to five hours on each side.

The court then adjourned till half-past 8 o'clock on Tuesday morning.

SEVENTH DAY.

The court met at half-past 8 o'clock this (Tuesday) morning, pursuant to adjournment, Judge Hill presiding.

THE ARGUMENT.

Colonel Dowd, of the counsel for the relators, informed the court that they were now prepared to proceed with the argument.

A MOTION.

District Attorney Wells said: We have a motion previously entered at the close of the testimony for the relators, "to strike out all evidence offered tending or intended to prove an *alibi*, for the reason that the court cannot, under the law upon *habeas corpus*, inquire into the main issue, or consider evidence intended to show any other fact on this hearing than the single question as to whether the relators are detained in contravention of the Constitution and laws of the United States." We wish the court to dispose of that motion before the argument on the main question is proceeded with. In arguing the motion we will keep within the five hours proposed by counsel on the other side, and include it in the time specified.

Colonel Dowd. The motion made by the district attorney has already been disposed of, and if it is insisted on I will enter a preliminary motion for the discharge of the defendants. We have the opening and the closing of the argument, and this move seems to me to be made to deprive us of the closing argument.

District Attorney Wells. I agree with Colonel Dowd that he has the right to make the motion he has just stated. We can also argue that motion. We wish our motion argued separately and independent.

Mr. Blackman contended that the motion made by the district attorney was well taken under the statute of 1867.

RULING OF THE COURT.

The Court. I will settle this question without argument. The question is simply this: "Are the relators legally held?" And if it is proved that they are illegally held, then they will be discharged. His honor quoted Marshall and Copeland in support of his opinion, and overruled the motion to strike out the testimony.

Mr. Turner, of counsel for the Government. Let the opinion of the court go on the record.

Mr. Blackman. I desire that the motion should appear on the record, to show that it was overruled by the court.

The Court. I have no objection to that.

The arguments of R. O. Reynolds, esq., for the relators, H. W. Walter, esq., for the United States, and G. Wiley Wells, esq., district attorney for the United States, followed, and court adjourned.

EIGHTH DAY.

The court met at 8.30 this (Wednesday) morning, pursuant to adjournment, Judge Hill presiding.

W. F. Dowd, esq., for the relators, delivered the closing argument.

DECISION OF JUDGE HILL.

Judge Hill then delivered the following decision in the case:

Thomas Malone et al., ex parte.

This is a proceeding by writ of *habeas corpus*, had upon the application of the relators, who in their petition allege that they are restrained of their personal liberty contrary to the Constitution and laws of the United States. The proceeding is had under the act of Congress, approved in the year 1857; and, as required by that act, the causes of detention are shown, which are that they are held in custody by J. H. Pierce, marshal of this district, by virtue of a *capias* issued by the clerk of this court, founded upon an indictment returned into court by the grand jury.

The relators take no objection to the form of either, but insist that the said indictment and proceedings are void, for the reason that the offense charged is not an offense against the Constitution or laws of the United States, but against the laws of the State of Mississippi, and that this court has no jurisdiction to hold them in custody therefor; and that if this court had such jurisdiction, that they are not guilty of the charge against them; and that if not entitled to be discharged entirely for the first ground stated, that they are entitled to be discharged upon bail.

The indictment charges that the relators, in the county of Monroe, on the 29th day of March last, and within this district, did unlawfully band and conspire together and go in disguise upon the premises of one Alexander Page, who was then and there a citizen of the United States, and was then and there entitled to the protection of life and liberty under the Constitution and laws of the United States, with intent then and there to injure, oppress, threaten, and intimidate him, the said Alexander Page, and with intent then and there to hinder and prevent him, the said Alexander Page, in the protection of his life and liberty, so secured to him by the Constitution and laws of the United States; and that the said Alexander Page the said relators (the defendants in said indictment) did kill and murder, contrary to the statutes of the United States, &c. This is the substance of the offense charged.

The question presented is one of most vital importance to the people of the State and of the nation, for the laws of Congress in Mississippi are the same in every State, in this particular, throughout the entire Union.

The exact line of demarkation between the jurisdiction of the State and Federal courts is one about which there has been much controversy; and at no period has this been more so than now, since, as a result of the attempted severance of the Union, so many of the old landmarks have been obliterated, and much of the former order renewed.

Unless where the jurisdiction is concurrent, the assumption of jurisdiction by the one belonging to the other is illegal and void; yea, more, would be an invasion of the rights of those against whom they are brought to bear, and no judge can be too careful in examining the ground and ascertaining where his jurisdiction stops. I sincerely regret that the circumstances are such as to afford me so little time to investigate the momentous question presented; and were this the final trial involving the life or liberty of the relators, would feel it my duty to take longer time to consider the question, but as neither are now necessarily involved, will proceed to state the conclusions to which I have arrived within the time allotted me, reserving the right upon the trial, should one be had before me, to correct any errors into which, upon more mature deliberation, I shall find I have fallen.

It has been urged by relators' counsel, with a zeal and ability seldom equaled, that as both the relators and the deceased were both residents and citizens of the State, that neither the amendments to the Constitution, nor the act of Congress approved May 31st, 1870, for the violation of which the indictment is preferred, have any application to the offense charged; that the indictment charges the crime of murder, and nothing else, and of which the State courts alone have jurisdiction.

It is conceded by relators' counsel that Congress has the power, by appropriate legislation, to secure to the *citizens* of the United States the rights conferred by the Constitution and laws of the United States, but he denies that life and personal liberty are among those rights; and this is the main question in this controversy. Is this so, or not? and, if so, does the 6th section of the act of 1870 provide a punishment for those who deprive, or attempt to deprive, the citizen of them?

Before the adoption of the fourteenth amendment, the Constitution of the United States was silent on the subject, or at least gave no more than a silent recognition of them; their protection was left to the Constitution and laws of the State, the Federal Government being prohibited from restricting them.

But, as a result of the war, four millions of people who had before enjoyed no rights recognized by the Constitution of any State, or of the United States, were made free, and most of whom remained where they had been held as slaves, and where their sudden emancipation created against them, as such, a deep prejudice by the white race with whom, and among whom, they had formerly resided as slaves. Again, many who had formerly resided in the loyal States, and had aided and succeeded in the establishment of the authority of the United States over those who had persistently endeavored, for four long years, to throw it off, and between whom it was natural that more or less animosity should exist, Congress felt bound to protect those whom they had, by their arms, made free, and those who had risked their lives in saving the Union from disruption, and to give and secure to them, in any portion of the Union, equal rights and protection under the law; and, to secure this end, the fourteenth amendment was adopted, thus placing the restriction upon the States, and by making all the classes mentioned citizens of the United States and of the State in which they resided, without distinction of race, color, or previous condition of servitude, and giving equal protection to all; giving protection to those rights which, before, they were prohibited from taking away. The fourth article of the amendment provides against unnecessary seizure, &c.; I take it to mean the seizure of the person, as well as things; and the fifth amendment provides against the deprivation of life or liberty, without due process of law. Had this change in the organic law omitted, either by positive provision or by necessary implication, these inestimable rights and immunities, it would have been an omission of those, without which all others sink into insignificance. I am, therefore, inclined to the opinion that these rights are intended to be secured and protected, as a result of this change in the fundamental law, as amended. To secure these rights it was necessary that power should be given to Congress to make such legislation as might be thought necessary to secure the end intended, and that that legislation should be had. The next inquiry is, what was the purpose and intention of the provisions of the 6th and 7th sections of the act referred to, and upon which the indictment referred to is founded. The 6th section of the act, among other things, provides that "if two or more persons shall band or conspire together, or go in disguise upon the public highway, or upon the premises of another, with intent to injure, oppress, threaten, or intimidate any *citizen*, with intent to prevent or hinder his free exercise and enjoyment of any right or privilege granted or secured to him by the Constitution or laws of the United States," such person shall be deemed guilty of felony, and, upon conviction, shall be punished, &c.

To constitute the offense there must have been a banding together, or conspiracy, between two or more persons, or two or more persons must have gone, in disguise, upon the public highway, or upon the premises of another, with intent to deprive some citizen of the United States (the fact that a man is a citizen of a State renders him the no less a citizen of the United States) some right or privilege secured under the Constitution or laws of the United States. The indictment, in this case, does charge that the relators did band and conspire together, and did go on the premises of said Alexander Page, with the intent to deprive and hinder him, the said Alexander Page, who was then and there a citizen of the United States, of his life and liberty, so secured to him by the Constitution and laws of the United States; and does contain a sufficient charge, under the sixth section of this act, provided the rights mentioned are among those so secured, and which I hold is the case.

Much greater difficulty will be found in the proper application of the seventh section, which provides "that if, in the act of violating any of the provisions of the fifth and sixth sections, any other felony, crime, or misdemeanor shall be committed, the offender, on conviction of the violations of said sections, shall be punished for the same, with such punishments as are attached to said felonies, crimes, and misdemeanors by the laws of the State in which the offense may be committed."

This section creates no offense, the offense is created by the former sections, and only increases the punishment to be inflicted for the offense charged. It does not propose to oust the State court of its jurisdiction to prosecute and punish the offender for the offense against the laws of the State, but recognizes such right. The statement in the indictment that the parties charged killed and murdered Alexander Page, was perhaps necessary, as charging facts which, upon conviction for the offense charged under the sixth section, as an aggravation of the offense and an increase of the punishment. I entertain very serious doubts whether or not the punishment provided in the seventh section can be imposed where it extends to life or limb, or whether such was the intention of the law-makers. I am strongly inclined to the opinion that it cannot and was not so intended; nor is it necessary to consider, at this time, whether any portion of it can be applied in any case.

Having come to my present conclusion, that the indictment does charge an offense under the sixth section of the act, and one for which the party may be prosecuted, and, if found guilty, punished by fine and imprisonment, I must decline to discharge the relators from the prosecution.

The first question being settled, the last will be considered; that is, are the relators or any of them entitled to bail? The authority to bail persons charged with the commission of criminal offenses against the United States will be found in Conkling's Treatise, p. 579.

The Constitution, in the eighth article of amendments, provides that excessive bail shall not be required. The statute above referred to makes all cases bailable before the officers authorized to take bail except in capital cases, in which one of the courts of the United States, or one of the judges thereof, alone can take bail, it being a discretionary right in such court or judge, having due regard to the circumstances, testimony, and usages of law.

The object of the law is not to punish offenders until after conviction. The object of commitment is simply to secure the attendance of the accused at the trial. If this can be done by taking his recognizance in a sufficient amount, with sufficient sureties, it is more humane to the accused, and attains all that the law requires. In this State prisons have been found a poor security in favor either of the State or Government or the accused. The inducement to forfeit the recognizance in the United States courts is much less than in the State courts; for the reason that the process reaches to every part of the Union, and the chances for ultimate escape are very few.

There having been a bill of indictment returned into court, I do not deem that I have a right to discharge any of the relators for the want of evidence heard upon the question of bail, as it is not known to me, and cannot be known, what testimony was before the grand jury. The district attorney might have declined introducing any testimony, and I cannot know what testimony he may have reserved for the trial. It is otherwise before the finding of the indictment; there the *onus* is upon the Government, and unless a *prima facie* case is made out the accused will be discharged.

The relators not shown by the proof of the Government to have been connected with the commission of the offense will be discharged upon their own recognizance, in the sum of five hundred dollars each, conditioned for their appearance; and that, in the mean time, they will keep the peace towards all the citizens of the United States; if they are peaceable, quiet citizens—which it is claimed, and which I hope they are—they will not object to this last condition; and if they are not, such a condition can do them no harm, and may do good.

The white men who are relators, who have been implicated by the proof of the Government, will each enter into recognizance in the sum of five thousand dollars; and will also give recognizance, in a like sum, with two or more good and sufficient sureties, conditioned for the appearance of the defendants; and that, in the mean time, they will keep the peace towards all the citizens of the United States, the security of which is the main purpose of this law.

ORDER OF COURT.

Judge Hill then made the following order, admitting the relators to bail:

THOS. MALONE, *et al.*, *ex parte.* } *Writ of habeas corpus.*

This day the argument of this cause was resumed and concluded, and the court being sufficiently advised as to the questions in the premises, and being satisfied that the relators are properly held in custody of the marshal by virtue of a *capias* issued from this court upon an indictment found and returned by the grand jury for an offense of which this court has jurisdiction, it is ordered and adjudged by the court that the writ herein be dismissed. But, it appearing to the court that said relators are entitled to be discharged from custody upon their entering in recognizance as follows, to-wit: J. C. Porter, J. S. Roberts, J. A. A. Roberts, J. L. Loughridge, W. M. Butler, Robert L. Mays, J. D. Hutchinson, W. D. Walton, J. M. Neeland, Thomas J. Ford, Burrill Willis, Barbour Quarles, G. W. Howell, Samuel Studdart, Clinton Ross, Benjamin Lumpkins, each in the sum of five hundred dollars, conditioned that they will appear and answer said indictments when notified so to do by the district attorney, and that in the mean time they keep the peace toward all the citizens of the United States. And that J. P. Willis, Thomas Malone, Jasper Webb, John Ware, A. J. Crosby, Whitfield Pope, David Studdard, and John Studdard, shall each give their recognizance in the sum of five thousand dollars, and that they also procure the recognizance of one or more good and sufficient sureties in the sum of five thousand dollars, conditioned that they will make their appearance before this court on the second Monday of the next term thereof, and from day to day of said term, and from term to term answer said indictment, and that, in the mean time, they keep the peace toward all the citizens of the United States. And that Jefferson Willis and Michael Forshee each enter into a recognizance in the sum of one thousand dollars, with one or more sureties in the like sum, but to be void on like conditions, and that such of said relators as are not prepared to give the recognizance with sureties at the present term be conveyed to Aberdeen, Mississippi, by the marshal, and that said recognizances be taken before Chancellor Whitfield, as special commissioner of this court, and that said cause be continued until the second Monday of the next term of this court.

The court then adjourned.

COLUMBUS, MISSISSIPPI, *November* 15, 1871.

HOMER C. POWERS sworn and examined.

By the CHAIRMAN:

Question. Please state your residence and official position?

Answer. Starkville, Mississippi; I am sheriff of Oktibbeha County.

Question. Starkville is the county-seat of Oktibbeha County, I believe?

Answer. Yes, sir.

Question. How long have you resided in that county?

Answer. I have not made it my permanent home until I came there in September, 1860, with my family.

Question. Have you lived there since that time?

Answer. Yes, sir.

Question. What business had you engaged in when you first came to that county?

Answer. I was planting corn and cotton.

Question. When were you elected sheriff?

Answer. I was appointed sheriff by General Gillem, in April, 1868.

Question. Have you been holding the office since that time?

Answer. Yes, sir.

Question. The committee desire to be informed of the condition of your county as to peace and good order, and to learn whether any disturbances have occurred, and whether the rights of person or property have been invaded by men banded together. You may proceed, without further inquiry, to give the committee all the information in your possession upon this subject.

Answer. Well, sir, from the time I came into the county and during the time I was sheriff, from 1868 until the spring of 1871, we had what I call a very peaceable county; there was nothing occurred in the nature of violent measures in the county. In the spring of 1871, I think it was in April last, there were rumors through the county that there was a band of disguised men traveling around at nights in different neighborhoods. The first that I ever heard of it, that called my attention to it, was a circumstance that occurred about three miles south of Starkville.

Question. What was that?

Answer. There was a negro by the name of Daniel Oyster came in one morning and reported that a band of men came to his cabin the night before.

Question. What did you say his name was?

Answer. He called his name Daniel Oyster or Rogers. I am not now certain which the people called him. He has been called by both names.

Question. Proceed with the statement that he made to you.

Answer. He said they came and asked for some other person—I have forgotten the name of the negro—and that he did not tell them where he was; I do not remember whether he knew or what was the reason, but he did not tell them, at least. They then caught hold of him and whipped him on his back.

Question. Did he tell you how large the body of men was?

Answer. I do not remember what he told me about it; I can only give my impression about it; I do not remember the number.

Question. Did he say they were disguised?

Answer. Yes, sir; he said they were disguised and had sheets on them; he said they had some kind of blankets thrown over their horses.

Question. Did they allege any offense against him for which they whipped him?

Answer. No, sir; I think not. The man that employs him is one of the best citizens of our county; it was supposed afterward that they had made a mistake and got the wrong man, because this old fellow, Daniel, was considered a very faithful negro—a good negro; he is one that bears a good character. It was always supposed, in what talk I heard on the street, when people were speaking about it the next morning, that it was very bad that such a thing should occur; it was the first that had occurred, and it seemed to excite every person, and it was the general supposition, as I recollect, that they had got a different man from the one they were hunting for.

Question. Are those all the particulars you remember of this case?

Answer. Yes, sir.

Question. Go on to the next.

Answer. The old fellow was there; wanted to know what he could do about it. I told him if he could identify any of the men they could be arrested; but, of course, if he could not tell who they were, I could not do anything about it, and there the matter dropped.

Question. No one was ever discovered?

Answer. No, sir; not that I know of. I do not know but that that case may have been before the United States courts. I do not know positively whether it was or not. There may have been some developments made there that I do not know anything about. There was never anything discovered about it at home.

Question. What is the next case that occurs to you?

Answer. These all follow in quick succession; there were just a few nights between. Rumors came in in the morning; there were rumors of parties riding at night within six miles south of where this occurred; this is the rumor at what is called the lower rice plantation; it is a large plantation; there were one or two, I do not remember which; that was the rumor given. That never was reported to me at all, but it was talked of everywhere over the country. I do not remember whether I heard the name of the man whipped, but I heard that a man was whipped, one or more, and that the band which was riding that night was very large; I recollect that part of it.

Question. What did they do with this man?

Answer. They whipped a man down there; I do not know how bad; that was just the rumor through the country. These things were beginning to attract the attention of the people, who were wondering where it was going to lead to; it was something new in the county.

Question. Was it represented that these men were disguised?

Answer. Yes, sir; they were disguised with sheets on; something of the kind thrown over the horses.

Question. These are all the particulars you know in relation to that transaction?

Answer. Yes, sir.

Question. Was it a matter of general understanding that the colored man was whipped by them?

Answer. Yes, sir; that was the public rumor. These men never came and reported that case.

Question. What is the next case?

Answer. About the same time—I do not remember whether it was before or after—a negro man came from Cedar Bluff, a precinct rather in the northern portion of the county. He came into my office one morning, and asked if it was any harm for a lot of men to come to his door at night and try to break it open when he had locked it, if he had a gun in there for him to shoot and kill one of them; he asked if the law would have done anything to him in such a case. I told him the law would protect a man if he killed another in self-defense, when he thought his life was in danger; that if his life was in actual danger, and he killed a man in self-defense, the law would not punish him for it.

Question. What did he tell you was the occasion of his asking you this?

Answer. He said the night before a body of men—not very large, but about six, he thought; and, he thought, boys or young men—came to his house. I asked him particularly about it, because I thought maybe we could get hold of it. It was in a pretty good neighborhood, and I asked everybody about it.

Question. What did he say they did?

Answer. He said they demanded admittance into his house; he got against the door to keep them out; they shoved the door; they had superior strength and pushed him, with the door, back, so that they got in the house. He said his wife was lying on the bed. They claimed that they were hunting some other man, too.

Question. What did they do to him?

Answer. They struck him. He had a scar on his face, somewhere, I do not remember where it was; but they struck him with some kind of club or stick, or, it may be, the butt of a pistol; I do not remember about that. He had quite a scuffle with one of them; he slipped under his arm and ran out of the door, and they shot some pistols. From what he said I do not think they shot to kill, because they could have killed him there. That is my impression. As he ran away they shot several shots with pistols.

Question. Did they do any mischief in his house?

Answer. They searched under the bed, I believe, and around, but I do not remember about it. They went, then, to another cabin right near there, in the same neighborhood—I do not know whose it was; I just recollect the general outlines of the story—and they shot into another cabin and wounded a colored boy about fifteen or sixteen years old.

Question. Do you recollect whose cabin it was?

Answer. No, sir. I do not think he was wounded very seriously, from the fact that I heard he was doing well in a few days, and that is the last I ever heard of it.

Question. Well, go on.

Answer. There is a small place up there, called Tampico, about five miles from Cedar Bluff. There was a freedmen's school there. That school-house was burned. It was burned early in the night. About 3 o'clock the next morning—the same morning on which this other cabin was shot into—about 3 o'clock, there were a couple of young men, white men, riding along that road up there—this is just the story, the history of the events that occurred up there, as I heard it within a day or two—there was some man, supposed to be a negro, that shot one of these men as they were riding along at 3 o'clock that morning. I got this from the physician that went up from Starkville to attend the wounded man.

Question. This negro shot one of the two white men?

Answer. Yes, sir, at 3 o'clock, and killed him; the man died.

Question. Do you know the name of the white man who was killed?

Answer. I can think of it in a moment; I do not remember it just now.

By Mr. RICE:

Question. Was he in disguise?

Answer. That we never knew.

By Mr. BLAIR:

Question. Was it ever stated that he was in disguise?

Answer. No, sir; it was never stated, that I know of. This was the explanation, or the neighborhood explanation, as to how his death came about—that is the reason the suspicion centered on a negro named John Plair, or Muse: The white people up there said the reason they suspected John Plair was because this man was shot, receiving two wounds—one from a shot-gun barrel, and one from a rifle barrel; and John Plair was known to have such a gun in his possession; so it was said.

By the CHAIRMAN:

Question. Was he taken up?

Answer. They said that John Plair was heard to say that these men had been riding around and shooting at colored people and frightening them long enough, and it was time they commenced to do something; that he told it when he got home to his wife. I do not know how they heard that or anything about it, but that was the public story, that he said to his wife that he had killed one damned Ku-Klux.

Question. Was any inquest held over the body of the white man?

Answer. No, sir; I do not think there was. He did not die immediately; he was taken and attended upon by the physicians for a day or two or more, and he died finally. The people heard of this and suspicion centered upon John Plair next day, and they went to his cabin, to arrest him—I think it was to his cabin; it was to the place where he was. He told them he would not be arrested unless they got a warrant. There was a justice of the peace living up in that part of the county. They went to him and got out a warrant; he made a special deputy of a young man up there in that neighborhood to execute the process. This young man came down then and served the warrant on John Plair, and started in company with a guard to Starkville with him. The rumor of this thing reached Starkville about this time and it was exaggerated very much. I heard that there were about four or five negroes, or ten maybe, in a cabin up there, or in a house, and that one had killed a white man and refused to surrender, and that the white people of the whole country were flocking there. My wife was very sick at the time, and I sent two deputies up there to make whatever arrests were necessary and to allay the excitement; but it turned out there was very little of it when they got up there. There are two large swamps between Starkville and Tampico; when this occurred they had got through the second swamp.

By Mr. RICE:

Question. With the prisoner?

Answer. No, sir. My two deputies were going up. I am telling you now what they said when they got back. When they got through that second swamp, at some place above the second swamp—I do not know how far—they met this John Plair, in company with that special deputy, and several others acting as a guard. They said they found that he was in custody, and they found out the general history of the thing, and how it was running, and thinking he would have a fair trial, and that where anything has occurred in a neighborhood in which the witnesses were a good way from the place where the trial is to be, it was best to look after the witnesses, my deputy took a list of the witnesses necessary, as he thought, and he took subpœnas along, and thought it would be a good opportunity, as a company were collected at Tampico, to find them, so he went on up to Tampico to get the witnesses. I do not know how long they staid there, but not a great while; but they met some of the men, and everything seemed quiet; everybody was going home; they turned around to come back to town. When they got to the north end of a certain swamp there, which is a very large and dark one, at the time of day when it was just getting dark, and was then a little after dusk, as they were coming toward town at quite a distance from where what I am going to relate occurred, they said all at once the whole woods seemed to be full of shots of guns, a great many being fired at one time. They couldn't form an idea how many; it was after dark, and it came up so sudden, the guns and pistols flashing, and there was a general tumult of running horses through the woods, so that they could not get any correct idea of how many there were or where it came from. The party then came on toward home just as fast as their horses could bring them, toward Starkville. I was waiting for them. I asked what occurred. They told me this story about meeting John Plair, and about going to the town, and so on, till they got nearly to where he was, when they heard the crowd ahead of them, and heard the firing suddenly, and saw horses running in different directions. The man said he came on just as fast as he could. He didn't know what had become of John Plair; he didn't know whether he was killed or what. This was about 10 o'clock. He couldn't give me any further information. The next morning the justice of the peace at Starkville had me to summon a jury of inquest; and I went with that jury to the place where this body was supposed to be, as we knew he had been killed; at least everybody supposed that, although we didn't find it out from any person that had seen him.

By the CHAIRMAN:

Question. Go on with your statement.

Answer. We went and found that John Plair had got with his guard down to a little turn in the swamp, where there is a sort of angle in the road; there it is a very thick bushy place, extending out in the direction from which he was going, and there he must have been shot at about that spot. He had then turned and run up a creek. He ran about twenty or thirty rods, maybe twenty rods, before he fell, bleeding all the way. We found his body lying there.

Question. Was he dead?

Answer. Yes, sir; he was lying on his face, with his hat in his hand, showing that he had been running. He had fallen down on his face, and had not been moved. There were twenty-three bullet-holes in him. There was one bullet-hole that went in one side, right at his temple here, and you could feel the ball right in there, on the opposite side of the head, showing that some one had been close to him. We probed the wound; it reached nearly through his head from temple to temple.

Question. Did you converse with the members of the guard or with the deputy constable?

Answer. I did; I met him on the road that morning. He came right to Starkville, and showed me his papers, and wanted to know how to make out the return. I told him to make out the return in accordance with the facts.

Question. What account did he give?

Answer. He said he was coming along with the guard, deputy and all, and John Plair was walking.

Question. How many were there in the crowd?

Answer. I don't remember the number—three or four.

Question. Were they all mounted except John Plair?

Answer. Yes, sir; and Plair they kept in front. He said that when they came to this place, or about where we found the body—I recollect there was a little angle in the road there, and a wet place, a crossing-place—and they turned the angle there, he said that when he got there, all at once the firing commenced, perfectly deafening, and the negro commenced to run. He said that was the last he saw of him. I don't remember whether he followed him or not, but I got that impression some way.

Question. Did he see any of these men of the attacking party?

Answer. It was very dark in there; this was after night, and in a swamp besides. He said there seemed to be a great many men and horses, and all at once there was a shot fired in advance, a single shot, and then general firing; that this negro commenced to run, and they commenced following and shooting as fast as they could. I think he told me he tried to keep out of the way. They followed shooting, until about the time the negro dropped, and then another shot was given in the air, and everybody dispersed as quick as they came. I don't think he followed up to see where the negro lay.

Question. Did the party turn back or keep on their way to Starkville—the guard?

Answer. The guard came on to Starkville next morning. I don't know where they went that night. I met them next morning coming to Starkville; I met them as they were coming up. As I was going back, he showed me this paper, and wanted to know how to make his return to the justice's court.

Question. Did the deputy tell you whether these men were disguised or not?

Answer. No, sir; no person told me whether they were disguised.

Question. Did you question them in regard to that?

Answer. I don't know, but the impression was it was so dark they couldn't tell. I may have asked; I likely did, because that was the time we heard so much about disguised men in the county; it was about this same time, this same week, or same fortnight. I think likely I questioned them, but I can't remember. I remember that no person knew whether they were disguised or not.

Question. Could he form any opinion as to the number of men that made this assault?

Answer. No, sir. I think there was a very large number.

Question. All mounted?

Answer. Yes, sir; that was the impression of every person I questioned; that there were a great many men there.

Question. Did you converse with any one of the crowd besides the deputy?

Answer. No, sir.

Question. Were you acquainted with them?

Answer. No, sir; that is off in a part of the country in these swamps that we at Starkville didn't have much to do with.

By Mr. RICE:

Question. Did he explain how it was that, in the dark, they could shoot so many shots at the negro and not hit the guard?

Answer. I asked him that; he said the negro was kept in front a certain distance. I thought of that, and asked him that, and he said that must have been the reason; that they must have been very close to distinguish, because nobody else was hurt in the whole crowd.

By the CHAIRMAN:

Question. Were these men, who were guarding the prisoner, examined before the jury of inquest?

Answer. No, sir; there was no examination made of any witnesses.

Question. Has there ever been any inquiry into the matter since?

Answer. I think that matter was up before the grand jury at the next term of the court. I think so, from the witnesses that were summoned from the neighborhood where it occurred, but there never was any bill found or any public exposition made of it; that is my impression.

Question. Is it the supposition that the white man that was killed by Plair was one of the gang that had been concerned in visiting the negro cabins?

Answer. I don't know that. I don't know whether he was or not.

Question. I ask whether it was the supposition or rumor.

Answer. The general rumor was—that was the only rumor I heard about it—that that was the excuse for suspecting Plair; that Plair had said that these men were disguised, and that these disguised men had run around long enough imposing on black people and shooting them and whipping them, and he was going to play at that himself a little.

Question. Did Plair live in the neighborhood where the negro cabins had been visited?

Answer. Yes, sir; these negroes all belonged to one settlement up there; it is sparsely settled, so far as negroes are concerned. The other part of the county is thickly settled with negroes, but that part is largely white, except right there.

Question. Did you ever receive any information as to who burned the freedmen's school?

Answer. No, sir; I did not. Some of the citizens up there went right to work and built it up again in a very few days.

Question. Was it supposed that these white men riding along the road, one of whom was shot by Plair, had been concerned in the burning of the freedmen's school-house?

Answer. I don't know whether it was supposed or not. It was supposed that that was what started the whole excitement, on account of its having occurred early in in the evening, and the next morning these other things occurred.

Question. You may go on with the cases you were giving of outrages.

Answer. Only a very few evenings after this occurred, there was a negro named Mingo Rogers, who lives, or did live, about three miles west of Starkville, came to my house after night and told me that the night before a body of disguised men, about six in number, had come to his house. He said it was a body of disguised men with sheets over their horses, came to his front-door, or door, and I supposed in was the front-door, and forced it open, and called for another negro named Jesse Higgins; that Jesse Higgins jumped out through a hole in the wall, or through a window, one of these little loop-holes that they have in their cabins, and got away; that he did the same thing and got away too. He laid off there in some bushes near by, where he could hear something going on, and he had an idea of what occurred. He said they were threatening his wife, and trying to make her tell where Jesse Higgins was. They seemed to be more after Jesse Higgins, from his story, than they were after him.

Question. Did they do any mischief in the house?

Answer. Nothing more than threatening his wife—and generally perhaps; I have forgotten what he did say; I remember that they were trying to force her to tell; he could hear them trying to get her to tell where this Jesse Higgins was. He came and told me that he had laid out all that night, and this night up to the present time, and had got tired of it, and wanted to know what he could do to make him safe in his home; I asked him if he couldn't form some opinion as to who these men were, or tell some way in which they could be identified and brought before a justice of the peace. I told him I thought we could put a stop to it if we could get at them, and identify any of the parties; he said he couldn't. I told him I didn't know what he could do, but told him to watch, and try to get close to them and identify them; he finally agreed to take that advice, and was going to try to secrete himself close enough on the next night, so that the next time they came he could tell them.

Question. Did the party return the next night?

Answer. No; I think he kept hearing things that kept him very much frightened, because he came back next night after this with his little bundle of clothes wrapped up, ready to go away. Whether they came twice or not I don't know; I don't really remember whether they visited his house twice or not. He came there with a little bundle of clothes, and told me he had made up his mind that he couldn't live in that way—losing his sleep; and he wanted me to take a few personal effects which he had—some cows and hogs, and a mule that he had in part paid for. He wanted me to see the owner of the mule, and effect some trade to get part of his money back, and to send it to him; he said he would write to me where he went, and to send his family to him with it.

Question. Did he leave?

Answer. Yes, sir; he left.

Question. Did he leave the county?

Answer. Yes, sir; I say he left the county; I suppose he did; it is generally understood that he did; he has never been there again.

Question. What became of Jesse Higgins; did he leave the county too?

Answer. Yes, sir; he left the county. I know the employer. I saw the man on whose place they lived, about the stock, and made some inquiries about what they had there and what could be done with it. The reason I say they left—though I have no positive information about that—is, I remember he lamented it very much, and said it would break him up in his crop, and he regretted very much that they had left. He sent back, or got some person else to—the property was tangled up so I couldn't do anything with it—and he got his affairs settled up by some one of his own color; I don't know anything more about that.

Question. Do any other cases of outrage occur to you?

Answer. There is this McLachlan case occurred in our county, in between these times while this was going on; I have forgotten just when it was. This negro, Rogers, was the last case I know of.

Question. What was the McLachlan case?

Answer. McLachlan was a Scotchman. He came there about eighteen months before, I think. It was last spring when this occurred. He had been living there about eighteen months, according to my recollection. He came there, and said he was sent there by the Methodist Church North, to preach to the colored people there—what they called the Methodist Church North there; they had established it separate from the other Methodist Church that they had in town.

Question. Was it a colored or white church?

Answer. Colored; the members were colored. He went to teaching a colored school and preaching to them sometimes. After he had been there about six months he received an anonymous letter, handed at the post-office, and brought it to my office and showed it to me. It was a warning to him to leave the county in so many days.

Question. How was it signed?

Answer. I don't remember; the word anonymous may have been there; or else not signed at all.

Question. It warned him to leave?

Answer. Yes, sir.

Question. Did it specify the reasons for that?

Answer. I don't think it did. It may have referred in some way to his living with negroes, or something else, but I don't remember. He seemed very much alarmed about it. I showed it to Colonel Muldrow, who is a very influential citizen there. This was long before any violence had occurred in our county that I ever heard of. I told McLachlan at the time that I thought it was a joke by some school-boy, or something of the sort, because I had never heard of such a thing before. Colonel Muldrow siad, to satisfy McLachlan, he would call a meeting of the citizens, and we did call a meeting of the citizens, and had a large meeting in the court-house. Colonel Muldrow, or myself, read the letter to the meeting. There was a resolution introduced indorsing McLachlan's course as a teacher of colored pupils and colored people, and saying that they denounced any attempt that would be made, or denounced all such anonymous communications, and any attempt to drive him away. It was opposed a little, a very light opposition in that meeting, and passed the meeting. That gave him a sense of security then, and he went on teaching his school and preaching, as he had been doing.

Question. Was he molested afterward?

Answer. He went on preaching and teaching until last winter, some time, I think, toward spring. There was what they called a freedman's exchange-store started there, composed of about a hundred stockholders of from $5 to $20 each. They employed McLachlan to be their agent to take charge of that store for them—this was about the time that the free schools came into operation in our State—and McLachlan quit teaching his private school, and didn't apply for a position in the free school, but recommended another man, and another man taught that free school, composed of about the same scholars, the same patrons that had been patronizing his school, but he still preached to the negroes on Sundays, and had this store; they had put up quite a church there by this time, and he was preaching in that church about the time this other event occurred that I have just related, which was all in about two or three weeks. One night this event occurred; the citizens were called up at midnight, or late in the night—I don't remember what time it was—with the alarm that a lot of freedmen, with arms, had gathered at this McLachlan's store, and they were afraid the town would be set on fire, or the citizens attacked, or something done. That was the rumor that went out. I wasn't waked that night; my wife was sick; some men came to my house to waken me, but they knew my wife was sick; my sleeping-room was some distance from the door, and they, knowing she was sick, didn't try to get me awake, and went away. These men, all the white men in the town, or as many as they could get out that night, got their guns and went up toward this store. After they got up to the store pretty soon there was a small crowd of freedmen—I don't know how many, whether small or large—came out of the store, and got on their mules and went away. A good many of these men that were called out to guard the town, as they supposed, took it for granted that these freedmen were going out in the country to raise more, and it created quite an excitement, and they staid up all night, but nothing occurred. It afterward turned out that these freedmen had been in the habit of collecting there more or less. It was just about the time the Ku-Klux excitement was highest, and there were some of them come in with guns on their shoulders when they were riding their mules in that night. It was a certain Tuesday night; I remember that, because that was the version given afterward; that was the night that the meeting of the stockholders took place, and there were a hundred of them, and if they all got together it would be a pretty large crowd; but I don't think they ever got a hundred of them together in that store.

Question. The stockholders were all colored men?

Answer. Yes, sir.

Question. Was this the night of their meeting?

Answer. Yes, sir; and I think that was what it started from, and the fact that some few of these men brought guns. The reason they gave for bringing the guns was that the roads were not safe after night; excitement was running pretty high there at the time—higher than I have seen it before or since.

Question. Did these freedmen at that store commit any violence or depredations?

Answer. No, sir; I never heard that charged. The way it occurred was, some one saw them coming there with guns, and there was quite an unusual crowd, and there being an excitement then, they watched them very closely, but they never stopped to think, but supposed that something would happen, and at once waked up the citizens. They turned out to protect the town, but nothing was done except to watch.

Question. No violence was committed?

Answer. No, sir; by neither side. The citizens waited until morning; in the morning there was some swearing down around the stores, like a crowd of men will do, but nothing was done until morning. When McLachlan opened his store, he knew about this excitement. He opened the store, he said, for his usual business; and there were some men standing there with guns. This was the guard that had been up all night. They told him they believed there was a lot of armed men in his house, and they demanded the right to go in and search for them and for arms; they believed he had arms secreted there. He told them they couldn't search his house—that they had no law for it. They went and got some kind of a writ from a justice of the peace, or the mayor that was then, with an affidavit of several men; several names were signed to an affidavit; I have seen the paper—it was shown in court afterward at Holly Springs; it was very irregular, and the affidavits irregular—still it purported to be an affidavit. They brought it to him and told him, "We have a paper to serve on you, to arrest you;" and they did arrest him, and went into the store and searched it, and found five guns, three of them broken Army guns, kind of relics of army times that were put for sale in the store, I believe three of them, and two shot-guns loaded. They also found two revolvers loaded. They took them and carried them over to the mayor's office, and they took him with them. When they got there, the mayor asked them what charges they had to prefer against this man McLachlan; they made some statement, I don't know what it was, but the mayor told them there was not sufficient ground for a case, and McLachlan was at liberty. He went back to his store; that all occurred in a few minutes. I came up town about 8 or 9 o'clock, at my usual time, and found they had proceeded thus far when I came up. There was considerable excitement; I could see that something more than usual was going on, and inquired the cause, and learned what I have told you. I went and asked McLachlan what was the occasion of it and how it happened that he had created such a suspicion, and he told me it was the meeting of the stockholders, and told me what I have told you. He complained to me, and said there was a good deal of excitement and that they got up a great deal of prejudice, and they had taken his arms, and it was pretty hard. I told him if they had released him, of course he should have his arms, and to send for them. He sent over and got them, but I saw that his having these arms in this exciting time, taking them back before the crowd, was not advisable. I heard the remark made, "He is just preparing," or something like that, and it seemed to excite the crowd. I therefore went up and told Mr. McLachlan to let me take these three guns—I was trying to allay the excitement. I told him I didn't want to take away his means of self-defense; I said, "This case is so unusual—I don't pretend to know anything about it—but here is an excitement caused by your making an unusual display of arms. Let me take three of these guns—those that are not loaded; they can't do any good anyhow. I will not take from you the means of self-defense. I have no right to. I don't do it as an officer, but I advise you to let me have those three guns, and take them away, in order to show to these foolish boys that you don't propose to have a stack of arms here, and I am sure it will have a good effect." It happened to strike me that it would have a good effect; he let me have the three guns, and I took them over to my office and locked them up. The rumors kept coming in on both sides that the negroes were getting excited in the country, and the white people were excited, and we thought Starkville would be in danger that night. I never saw anything to give cause to that rumor, and don't know where it started, but it was the fact that such rumors did come in all the time. I called together some of the citizens there in my office, and asked them what they thought had better be done; there seemed to be such an excitement, I wanted to see how we could get things back to the old order again It was advised that I should summon about twenty of the most moderate and best men to stand as a guard that night. The rumors had gone out to the country, so that we expected a large crowd of men in, and if they came there we feared there was some danger of excitement, and then there was in reality danger without them. Our object was to station guards on the outposts of the town, and whenever anybody came up to tell them that the town could take care of itself, and that there was no occasion for them. We did so. I summoned about twenty men and placed them around the town at different public avenues leading into town on the outskirts. At midnight, or about half-past 12 o'clock, I went to my house—my wife was very sick at this time—and I never saw anything more quiet. Two or three men came in from different places where they had been posted, and said large crowds of men had come up from different directions, and they halted them. The men on guard were white men, and they asked if there was any danger there. The guard told them no, Starkville could take care of itself fully, and that we only wanted the people to go home, so they turned back, both sides; that is, both of these parties. Everything seemed quiet, and I went down home. McLachlan's store is situated in this way; there is a little alley between his store and the court-house which was never used for buggies or wagons; there is a deep gully in it, a washed place, and I didn't put any guard there. I didn't think of McLachlan's store that night, any more than the rest of the town; I was just trying to keep these people out, and didn't think particularly about his store, but as it turned out it would have been well if I had put a guard there. I heard that about 1 o'clock there was some men came in—I didn't take my clothes off; my wife was sick, and I was sitting there—some men came to me and told me they believed McLachlan's store was broken into. Things were getting quiet; the guards would go to their houses once in a while, but they had heard a big noise. We all ran up there, and when I got there I found his front door had a panel broken out of it, but they hadn't succeeded in breaking it clear open. It was quite a large hole in the panel of the door. I called to him; he wouldn't come out until he heard my voice. There was quite a number of the crowd there then. He didn't come out until he heard my voice, and then he came to the door, and I told him to open it and let me in. I asked him what had occurred; what had made this. He said that a lot of men had come up on this side of the alley, marching in regular file or regular order, and had come around to his front door and demanded admittance. He told them they could not come in. They told him if he didn't let them in they would break the door open and kill him. He said they should not come in. They then took some heavy thing, timber or something, and broke down the door; and that was the noise that we heard down there. It happened that one of the guard was nearly opposite to an old livery-stable at this time. When these men came up he said there were about twelve men, he thought, who came with guns. This guard was a merchant named Hogan, an old citizen. He said that they came up and demanded admittance. I don't know as he told them anything, or what he did tell them, but the sum of the story was that, not getting admittance, they commenced breaking in the door; that McLachlan hollered murder; that he, being alone, was paralyzed, and didn't do a thing. The rest of the guard, being away off at different places, didn't make any effort at the moment, but the guard, in different places, hearing the noise, came, one or two of them first, in advance of any of the rest. Two men came up in front of the court-house, and when they got that far these men all turned and went off in regular order. They cocked their guns and told them to halt. They asked them something; I have forgotten what they did say, but some words passed. They didn't come any nearer to those two, but at the same time came this tramping on the sidewalk, and these men went back the same way they came from, and called to him as they passed him, "We'll get you to-morrow night, sure. All hell can't save you to-morrow night," or something like that. That kept up the excitement, and we staid up until morning watching that house. The next morning a great many citizens of the town went to McLachlan and told him that they didn't see any way to put a stop to this thing; that it was directed to him; that he hadn't anything at stake except his fixtures there, and they advised him to go away, as they could not guard him always, and they thought he had better leave the county. He said he would go if he was promised safe-conduct out of the county. They came to me and told me that McLachlan had concluded to go. I went to see him about it. I told him I wouldn't advise anybody to leave the county; he must be his own adviser; that I thought it a pretty hard thing for a man to have to leave a place where he wanted to stay; but if he wanted to go I would do the best I could to give him safe protection; would summon as many men as was necessary to take him to the railroad, or, if he thought it was dangerous, to take him down by a new road. There were three different points on the railroad he could reach; they were not far from each other. I supposed he would go with us. We were to start about 4 o'clock, giving us time to get to the railroad before dark. At that time I went up for him, but he had gone; he had become frightened. There was a great deal of stir on the streets about who were going with him. Nobody knew who were summoned. The freedmen were carrying rumors, and it so excited him that he didn't wait, but slipped out of his back door and went off through this alley and got away himself. He went out on a large plantation, where there were a good many freedmen, and got horses there, and two or three went with him and conducted him to the next station on the railroad above West Point. He never came back until he came to identify some parties with the United States marshal.

Question. What became of his goods?

Answer. He left the key with me, and I called a meeting of the stockholders. They knew where he was gone. I told them I wanted them to take a vote as to whom I should leave the keys with, and they left them with one of the most intelligent freedmen there, who was also one of the largest stockholders, and he has been conducting it since. His name is Tom Woody.

Question. Was it said that the ten or twelve men who attacked the store on that night by this side passage-way were disguised?

Answer. Yes, sir; McLachlan said they were disguised. He saw them by the aid of a side window. He had both rooms locked of his main store, and the front door was locked. He was back in the inner room, and expected to make a desperate struggle; but there was a window or some kind of an opening—I don't remember just how—I think there must be a window there; I recollect of hearing that in evidence; they had that up at Holly Springs when I was sent for there before the commissioner's court; that he looked out through that side of the house; I don't know what he looked through.

Question. Was he able to identify any of the men?

Answer. I understood not; I know he said not there; but I think afterward he said he could up there at Holly Springs; but what he told me there at the time was under great excitement and fear, and I don't know but that McLachlan then thought I was one of those who were conspiring against him. I think from the way it turned out afterward that he thought I was as much after him as the rest; he thought I should have placed a special guard around his store, and because I didn't, he thought there was something wrong. My impression is that McLachlan is not a man very well posted in the ways of the world.

Question. Was he a man of good personal character?

Answer. So far as I have heard, he was. I never heard anything said against his character.

Question. Does that finish the list of disturbances in your county?

Answer. Yes, sir; as far as I can recollect them; that is all that made any impression on me.

Question. State whether this outbreak in your peaceable county occurred about the time of the Meridian riot, or soon after that.

Answer. I came from Meridian two days after that riot occurred, and it was not very long after that; I don't know how soon it was, but it wasn't long.

Question. Did you hear of similar outbreaks in other counties about the same time?

Answer. I never heard anything very definitely that I could state. I recollect hearing rumors about freedmen's schools being burned in Winston County along about that spring-time, but I don't know anything about it myself. It was all we could do to look after our home affairs in that excitement.

Question. How long did this period of excitement continue in your county after the first outbreak?

Answer. I think all these I have related occurred in the space of four weeks.

Question. Have any of the men concerned in the deeds of violence you have narrated ever been punished?

Answer. Not that I know of. A great many have been arrested since and put under bond in our county?

Question. On process from the State or United States court?

Answer. The United States court.

Question. For all of these outrages or some particular ones?

Answer. I can't tell you. I assisted the United States marshal there in making quite a number of arrests. The first arrests made came from McLachlan's case. He went to the United States authorities up at Oxford or Holly Springs. He brought the case before the United States commissioner, and the *capias* read at the time I saw it for violation of the enforcement act.

Question. You do not know to the commission of what particular acts those arrests related?

Answer. No, sir. I think the first set of arrests made were on account of the McLachlan case; in fact I knew it, because I went to the examination trial before the commissioner, when seven or eight were bound over.

Question. Were they citizens of that town?

Answer. Yes, sir, mostly; they are all citizens of the county, and mostly of the town; some of them of the town.

Question. Have any arrests been made on account of the murder of this prisoner?

Answer. I do not know that there have been or not. I have no way of knowing. There have been arrests made there since the McLachlan arrests; quite a number have been made since the grand jury adjourned. A great many witnesses went up from our county to the grand jury at Oxford, and arrests were made under bills found there but what cases I can't tell.

Question. Have you any knowledge or information of the existence of a regular organized band in your county that is committing these outrages?

Answer. No, sir; nothing of my own knowledge. All the knowledge I have is drawn from what I have told here.

Question. Is it your information and belief that these deeds of violence were committed by the same band of men or by different bands of men?

Answer. I have no way of telling; I can't form an opinion of it even; these things occurred in rapid succession. It was all done under excitement. I have heard a great many of the best men in the county talk about it, and there is no settled opinion about it. I have no way of forming an opinion more than any other citizen. It never came before me officially, or in the form of any information or complaint that would lead to detection. I never could tell whether it was never done for fear of going before court, or why. I thought sometimes they ought to have some idea of who it was, but I never could get them to say.

Question. Do you think there was any apprehension felt by citizens that if they went before the court and complained they might be subjected to Ku-Klux outrages themselves?

Answer. I used to think of that when I was questioning them, and I used to question them with a view of that; I used to say let us come and try and see what we can do, and all that.

Question. Was there any opposition to colored schools up there?

Answer. Not much; there has never been in our county. The school system has worked very well in our county.

Question. Do you know of any other school having been interrupted except the one you have referred to?

Answer. No, sir; I do not know of any other one; I think there has been but one?

Question. Have you heard of any other teachers being warned or notified to leave?

Answer. No, sir; not in that county.

By Mr. BLAIR:

Question. McLacklan told you he didn't recognize any of this party?

Answer. Yes, sir; that was my understanding at the time. The reason I recollect so well is this: We were trying to get at it to stop it in some way. We had very good judicial officers, justices of the peace and all that, and the district attorney of this district lives right there, and I thought if I could identify one or two of these men and arrest them it would stop the whole of it. I was very anxious to get at them, and I asked McLachlan, and he told me he didn't know any one of them, but I always reconciled that with what he said elsewhere by the fact that he was afraid to tell; he was very much excited and alarmed. He called "murder" that night so loud that they heard him nearly all over town. It was the next morning when I asked him whether he knew these parties or not.

Question. He said they were disguised?

Answer. Yes, sir; he said so in court; he swore to it at Holly Springs.

Question. Did you hear him say he recognized them afterward?

Answer. Yes, sir; he said in court that he recognized one or two of them; I think that is it; that is what I remember about it—that he said he recognized them.

Question. Did he state who they were?

Answer. Yes, sir; I believe he did, he mentioned those men who were sitting right in court. McLachlan was telling the history of it, and they asked him who were among these men, were any of the parties then present connected with it, and he mentioned the names of two that were sitting there as he was telling this thing in court. That is my recollection of his testimony.

Question. Had these men been arrested?

Answer. Yes, sir.

Question. They were then under arrest?

Answer. Yes, sir; they were then going through a course of examination under arrest.

Question. What was done with the men?

Answer. The were placed under bond to appear in the United States court; one of them has run off and forfeited his bond.

Question. Who was he?

Answer. J. J. Bell; I can't say that he has forfeited his bond; but that is the public rumor; he has gone away, he is not seen there. His family have moved home to his wife's father's, and he has broken up housekeeping and is supposed to be gone.

By the CHAIRMAN:

Question. Is that the Bell that Colonel Huggins attempted to arrest?

Answer. Yes, sir; he has run off. They were going to arrest him under other charges.

Question. What kind of a man was he?

Answer. A pretty wild boy, a reckless young fellow; he was always considered so by everybody; by his own people; his own family. I never knew personally anything about him, except that public rumor gave him that name. What I heard of him around town was that he was wild—what you would call a wild boy.

By Mr. BLAIR:

Question. He was put under bond for that and then sought to be arrested for some other offense.

Answer. He was taken before the United States commissioner's court or before the United States court and put under one bond, and then the grand jury met and found bills, and the United States marshal came down to make arrests under those bills. This was under that process that this last attempt was made.

Question. Do you know for what the second attempt to arrest him was made?

Answer. No, sir; they had two or three papers for him; I saw the papers myself; I do not know that I saw the inside of them, but I think I did; I think it was for violation of the enforcement act. These capiases were written in such general terms that I could not tell, by reading them, the specific offense. I saw one of the last ones; it said violation of the enforcement act, but didn't say in what particular.

Question. They went to his house to arrest him?

Answer. Yes, sir.

Question. Did they know he was gone before they went to his house?

Answer. I suppose not; they just came in, and went to his house first; they had not stopped at any other place. He was not gone then; he was in town. It was early in the morning; he always came up town pretty early, to get a drink, and he was standing on the side-walk when they went by; they didn't know him, it seemed, but went right on to his house, a short distance further, and put a guard around the house, and two or three of them rushed into the house, but he was not there. In the mean time, Bell had heard of their coming to his house, and he slipped around and got his horse, and took over the hills and got away.

Question. What did they do at his house?

Answer. Searched the rooms all through his house. I was not down there with them, I can only tell what they told me when they came back.

Question. Tell it.

Answer. Colonel Huggins said he sent the sergeant in with one or two men,who went from one room to another, and they found Mrs. Bell in her night-clothes; she told them, "Search my room; he is not here," but they paid no attention to her, and went on into another room; the sergeant said the minute he went to enter that room, somebody in bed covered up the head; he supposed that he had got his man, and went to pull off the cover, when the woman screamed with all her might; he said, "Excuse me, I thought you were a man," and turned around and went out of the room. I am now telling you what the sergeant told me when he came away.

Question. He said he tried to pull the clothes off of her?

Answer. He said he saw some person covering the head up rapidly, or in a hurried manner, and he rushed up. He supposed he had the man he was after, and ran up and pulled the clothes down far enough to see her head, and saw it was a woman; she screamed, and he said, "Pardon me." Now I remember, by the way, her father told me the same story, and he said that was what she had told him. I know the thing was talked about in town, and a report got out the same day about that, and he said, "Isn't this a perfect outrage," and I said, "Certainly, it is;" and I went on and spoke of it and he told me that.

Question. What was that that you spoke of?

Answer. I spoke of the rumor. It was alleged that they had pulled the clothes off of her, and I said, "I don't think any human being would do that;" and I told the people I would inquire; and then I went and asked Colonel Huggins, and he said that he didn't go in the room; that the sergeant went in; and I went to the sergeant and told him to tell me what had occurred, and this was his story: After this thing had blown over the girls had left town pretty quickly. I didn't know who this girl was, but her father came into my office one morning; that is, the father of Mrs. Bell. The name of that young lady was Caston. I said to him, Mrs. Bell's father and the father-in-law of Mr. J. J. Bell, what I have told you. The excitement had subsided then, and I asked him about it. He said they came in without ever showing any writ, but rushed right into the house. I said, "Joiner, what did they do then?" He said, "They rushed into the house; my daughter, Mrs. Bell, got up and told them, 'You can search my room;' that she came out in her night-clothes, but they went from that room into Miss Caston's room, where she was sleeping; that she commenced screaming as soon as the man put his hands on her bed-clothes." I said, "Joiner"—we called him Joiner—"did they pull the clothes down, or how far; did they expose her person out of deviltry, or in a wanton manner?" He says, "She never said so." I asked him very particularly about it, and he made that reply. I questioned him very carefully, because the question had been raised there, and I wanted to satisfy myself at least.

Question. Did he say she had told him anything about it?

Answer. I do not know whether it was her story or his own daughter's.

Question. You say the lady was named Caston, and was a visitor of Mrs. Bell?

Answer. Mrs. Bell is the daughter of Joiner. I said, "Tell me what the ladies said about it." There was no way of getting their story until I saw him, from the fact that they went away pretty soon, and then I wouldn't have gone to them anyhow to ask them about such a matter. That was the first chance I had to learn the other side of the rumor.

Question. Was some writ sued out against those parties?

Answer. Against Huggins?

Question. Yes, sir.

Answer. Yes, sir; there was.

Question. What was it?

Answer. The United States commissioner there, named Ellis, happened to come to town about the time the story got out. These men came in Friday morning, and staid all day Friday and Saturday night, until Sunday morning, and this story kept getting larger and larger. They finally got it out that these men had searched the beds so closely, and scrutinized the woman so closely, that they found blood on her chemise. The story kept getting worse and worse, and the United States commissioner, Mr. Ellis, living up in a remote part of the county, happening to come to town, some lawyers thought they could make a case out of that, and Nash, a young lawyer, came to me and said, "You are deputized as deputy United States marshal by this court, Ellis's court, to arrest Huggins and all his men." It was an unusual proceeding, and I knew I had to proceed cautiously. I told him I would read it to Colonel Huggins, and see whether I could arrest him or not, but he had a force there. I went and read it to him, but he said he could not be detained from performing his duty as an officer; that he knew the law, and that he had never heard of such a thing as that. He said he didn't propose to be detained there unless he found that there was some law about it that he did not know of then; that he couldn't be arrested in the discharge of his duty as an officer; that he had a bundle of papers there to execute, and didn't propose to be stopped as long as we chose to keep him to make an examination there. I told him I would take his reply, and he said that, if they would show him any law by which it became his duty, he would stop. I went back and gave his reply to the attorneys. They said, "We will look up the law, then." That was Sunday morning.

By the CHAIRMAN:

Question. Who were these attorneys?

Answer. A man named Nash was the principal attorney.

By Mr. BLAIR:

Question. What was the affidavit?

Answer. It was nothing about taking down clothes, but it was as to intimidating and frightening women—mentioning the names.

By Mr. RICE:

Question. Who made it?

Answer. I don't remember; it was some man in the town.

Question. It was not one of these women?

Answer. No, sir.

By Mr. BLAIR:

Question. You do not know by whom the affidavit was made?

Answer. No, sir. I think the writ read, "Whereas affidavit has been made." I do not think it said who by, but I am not certain.

Question. You never saw the affidavit?

Answer. I don't think I did see the affidavit; I saw the writ—it was put in my hands.

Question. Did the writ recite the affidavit or its purport?

Answer. Yes, sir; it said something about it; that the affidavit had been made. These writs, I suppose, all read the usual way; I don't remember how this writ did read. I remember it was a writ issued from the United States commissioner to me to execute upon Colonel Huggins and his men—his posse of soldiers there; I don't remember the wording of the writ.

Question. So Huggins refused to surrender to the writ?

Answer. Yes, sir; he told me, "If they find any law to satisfy, I will be here an hour or so." His men were putting up their saddles and he was going back to West Point.

Question. He wanted to argue the jurisdiction with the United States commissioner?

Answer. Yes, sir; he didn't want to be stopped, he said, on that duty. I went back and told them what he had said, and they said they would look up the law. There was a

United States law book, in pamphlet form, of acts of Congress in reference to this enforcement act, and they were looking for that particular volume, and it was in the chancery clerk's office, and he was gone with the key, and Huggins got tired of waiting, and said he would go anyhow.

Question. He required that the law should be produced as well as the writ?

Answer. Yes, sir; and he went off. As soon as it was known that he had gone with his men, they demanded that I should take that paper and serve it anyhow. There was the place where I wanted the law, too. I told them I would serve it, as long as I thought there would be no harm done, but I certainly wouldn't summon a wild lot of young fellows to run against these men; that I knew Huggins had told these men not to be arrested, so I said I was not going into anything of the kind. I wouldn't have done it for anything.

Question. You would have arrested him if he had submitted to the arrest?

Answer. I would.

Question. You would have taken him before the commissioner?

Answer. Yes, sir.

Question. It was simply because he put you at defiance, and had the guns to do it, that you did not arrest him?

Answer. He didn't put me at defiance. I went to him and left it to him. I said, "I have promised to read this writ to you." I said that just so long as it was a formal matter that was concerned I would go through all that part, but I wouldn't do any more. They told me, after Huggins had gone, "We want you to take that writ and execute it anyhow." I said, "I will not do it; if you want me to execute the writ after my own style, the way I told you and the way I agreed to, I will do it in my own way; appoint another United States deputy marshal, if you want him to take it." They found the new law by this time. I said, "I will take that new law to Huggins and read it to him and his men;" but they didn't want to take it in that way, and so I handed the writ back to them. Then they summoned a posse—I don't know that they summoned a posse, but they went through all the form of summoning a posse, and the word went out that they were going to follow the soldiers and take them; and the streets were lined with horses in a few minutes, and the people were getting their arms ready. Finally the commissioner spoke to me—the commissioner had not talked to me about this, only the attorney. The commissioner said he didn't like to see things going that far. I told him, "These men can be arrested easily enough, because they belong to a certain command, and they are only going to their command to Aberdeen. I don't know what is to become of Huggins, because he is a private citizen, but these soldiers can be found at any time; I don't know anything about the law points, but I don't want to have any difficulty." The United States commissioner told those boys then not to go, and he gave me back the writ and told me to serve it as I saw fit. Then I took the law and the writ, and went down to West Point in my buggy, and got there just after they did, as they were putting up their horses. I told Colonel Huggins that I had come over to read him that law and show him the writ. I didn't know but he would feel like going back to have an investigation; these charges were standing there, and they were talking a good deal about it, that he might go back and clear it up. He said it was simply a thing to keep him from making other arrests. I took some citizens along to identify the soldiers. I asked him if I might call up the soldiers and read the writ to them; he said, "Yes," and I spoke to them, and the sergeant said, "You must think I am a damned fool. I shan't stop for anything of this kind. You must think I am a damned fool, to take soldiers around and listen to every one who chooses to stop me in this way. I am going back to my colonel, and I will surrender whenever he tells me to, and not before." We found we were barking up the wrong tree, and we left.

[The following was subsequently received and ordered to be appended to the testimony of H. C. Powers:

Hon. D. D. PRATT, *Chairman Committee :*

In my hurry to close my testimony before dinner, I neglected to make a full statement in regard to the attempt to arrest Colonel Huggins and the soldiers with him; and I wish to add the following: After my attempt to read the warrant to the soldiers, Colonel Huggins came to me and said he should return the soldiers to their command, and the commanding officer might take his own course in regard to surrendering them, and if they were surrendered he would return with them, and if they were not surrendered he would return himself, and asked me to meet him at West Point, as he did not wish to go to Starkville by himself. The next day I went to West Point to meet him, but he and the soldiers arrived there before I did, and had proceeded on their way to Starkville by a different route from the one I came. Huggins and the soldiers returned to Starkville and remained there for several days, and no one asked for their arrest or prosecution.

H. C. POWERS.]

COLUMBUS, MISSISSIPPI, *November* 15, 1871.

OSCAR C. BROTHERS sworn and examined.

The CHAIRMAN. As this witness is called at the instance of the minority, his examination will be conducted by General Blair.

By Mr. BLAIR:

Question. Doctor, will you give your residence and profession?
Answer. Physician; Artesia, Mississippi.
Question. State, Dr. Brothers, if you were present at the time of the meeting in Artesia, when young Lee was killed?
Answer. I was, sir.
Question. What position did you occupy in the crowd?
The WITNESS. Do you want a plain, succinct statement of all the facts?
Mr. BLAIR. Give us a statement of all the facts in regard to the killing of Lee, so far as they came under your observation.
The WITNESS. Well, sir, on Saturday morning, as I was at Artesia, at my office, I understood there was to be a radical meeting at Prairie Hill, which is about five or six miles distant from Artesia. No one spoke of expecting the crowd to come to Artesia; none of us apprehended anything of that kind. They apprehended nothing, really. In the afternoon my attention was called by the sound of a drum and fife and considerable yelling of voices coming up the railroad. They turned across from the railroad in the direction of Smith's, north of Artesia, marched across into the grove, then down what is known as the Robinson road, passing Artesia—it was a party numbering, I suppose, six or seven or eight hundred—down to the culvert. I noticed that a freedman, Levi Jones, was mounted at the head of the column. They were, or seemed to be, divided off into columns, each having its commander; at least, men riding with swords. There seemed to be one company armed with guns. Mr. Lewis was in about the center of the crowd in a buggy. Mr. Bliss, I think, was in a carriage. They turned around and came back, nearly in front of the station-house, on the commons, where the buggy and carriage halted, and immediately the crowd surrounded them, and speaking began—by whom, I do not know. One of my friends suggested that we get on our horses and ride up and hear what they had to say. We did so. We rode in among the cavalry, or among the mounted men with guns. I will not pretend to say they were cavalry or what they were. I suppose we were about twenty paces from the speaker. After having been there about three minutes I saw smoke emanating from a gun. I either saw, or imagined I saw, about this much of the barrel, [illustrating.]
Question. About a foot?
Answer. Yes, sir; about a foot. The first impression that struck me was that one of the freedmen had become tired of cheering and had shot off his gun as a matter of applause.
Question. Did you hear the sound at the same time?
Answer. O, yes, sir; I heard the sound distinctly, of course, and I am satisfied that it was the sound of a gun. I am satisfied of that in my own mind by what I saw. It was the sound of a gun, and it was a gun that I saw. It seemed to be within three or four feet of the buggy in which the speaker was. Then there seemed to be a dead silence of from three to five seconds, when I heard the yell of "White man, kill him, kill him, kill him," by a considerable number of voices. Immediately thereafter the crowd went rather west. The crowd seemed to shove—not the whole crowd, but the crowd from the buggy out west—seemed to move in that direction of one accord, accompanied with a firing or discharge of six or seven guns or pistols, or something—six or seven fire-arms. As soon as that was over some of the party hollered, "Boys, to your wagons, and get your guns." I saw some parties coming to a two-horse wagon, or mule wagon—I do not know which—and take out three or four guns. I rode up to the wagon, when a negro took out a carpet sack of what I supposed to be pistols—in fact I saw the impression of them. I remarked to him, "For God's sake, don't take those pistols out of there. The white men of Artesia have got nothing to do with this difficulty, and let it stop." His answer was, "I'll be damned if I am not going to take them in the crowd," and went off with them. I then rode near Mr. Perkins's store, when I saw my servant and told him to hold my horse, and dismounted and went to the dead body. Accompanying me, or just behind me, was Mr. Pearce, and, I think, Dr. Zuber; he came up about the same time. I found there Mr. Lewis and Mr. Bliss, and Squire Elmore, who is a magistrate under Governor Alcorn's appointment. I said to Mr. Lewis, "Can't you disperse this crowd? We feel alarmed. Already one innocent man has been killed from an accidental discharge of a gun in the hands of one of your own men"—meaning——

By the CHAIRMAN:

Question. Did what?
Answer. One innocent man had been killed from an accidental discharge of a gun in

the hands of one of your own men, meaning, of course, that that was the prime [cause,] not that that shooting of the first gun had killed him. Thereupon I said, "If you don't do it I will take the matter into my own hands and telegraph to West Point and Columbus," and I think I added Meridian, "and get men to disperse them, or protect ourselves." I don't know which I said, but one or the other. Mr. Lewis said, "Yes, yes, I can disperse them," and he did something or said something which was, at the time, inexplicable to me, and the crowd dispersed as if by magic. That ended it. Gentlemen, that is all.

By Mr. BLAIR:

Question. Did you see——

The WITNESS. While we are there, let it come in, if you please: neither of these gentlemen at that time claimed that they were shot at, or that they were in any danger, in my hearing.

Question. Had you seen Lewis before the discharge of this first gun?

Answer. No, sir. I did not see Mr. Lewis. He was, perhaps, in the carriage, but I did not see him. I noticed only the man that was speaking, and I was noticing the speaker, to listen and hear what he said. My object in going up there was to hear the tenor of his speech, and find out if he was endeavoring to get the freedmen to act in a conciliatory manner to the white people, or if it was an incendiary speech or one that would inflame their minds against us.

Question. Had you seen Lee?

Answer. I had not.

Question. Did you hear Lee make any remarks?

Answer. I did not. I heard no remarks from him.

Question. When did you first see Lee?

Answer. After he had been shot.

Question. You did not see him previous to that?

Answer. No, sir. I had never seen him before in my life, that I know of.

Question. Was there more than one discharge of a gun or pistol, prior to the outcries of "White man, kill him?"

Answer. No, sir; only one. That was this one I saw the smoke emanating from, as I thought. I am satisfied as well as I am of anything.

Question. Did you tell Mr. Lewis, when you met him at the dead body of this man Lee, that you saw the smoke and flame of the discharge coming from the pistol in the hands of Lee?

Answer. I did not, sir.

Question. He testified before this committee that you made that remark to him, connected with a remark that you did not think he intended to fire at any one, or to kill any one, or do any damage?

Answer. Well, if you have got only that witness, as it comes to a matter of truth between Mr. Lewis and myself, I will say that this is the first time and the last time I ever spoke to the gentleman in my life, that I remember. Squire Elmore was there, and I would like you to have him here to state what I said, for he can say whether I said it, and prove it on me.

Question. State whether you said it or not?

Answer. I did not, most assuredly. I said, as near as I can remember, what I have told you.

Question. You did not make the other statement?

Answer. I did not.

Question. You had not seen the man Lee, at all?

Answer. Never, until he was dead.

Question. Was any pistol discovered near his body?

Answer. None, sir, that I saw or heard of that afternoon, or that night. I heard the next morning that he had a pistol; there was no such report that night that I heard of. Well, there was one freedman who testified to that fact, that he had a pistol, and he was turned over to the magistrate for perjury. It was proven that what he told was not so—that he did not have a pistol—by other freedmen and white men who were near.

Question. Were you present at the coroner's inquest?

Answer. I was. I was one of the witnesses.

Question. What was the name of the freedman who testified that Lee had a pistol?

Answer. Wiley Stewart. He lives with Mr. J. W. Cannon and Mr. W. A. Crump.

Question. What was the testimony of the other witnesses as to the fact of his having a pistol?

Answer. Well, it was to the effect that it was seen proper by the magistrate to throw this man's evidence out. They just asked to have him committed for perjury or something. I do not know anything about law, but I know that——

By the CHAIRMAN:

Question. Who asked that?

Answer. I do not know, sir. Some party asked if that could not be done after his evidence was contradicted to such a very great extent, and the magistrate told him to step aside, and put him in charge, I think, of Stanton Cromwell.

By Mr. BLAIR:

Question. Was any pistol found on the ground?

Answer. None that I had ever seen or known of.

Question. Near the body?

Answer. None, sir.

Question. Who first got to the body after the man was killed?

Answer. If I mistake not, Squire Elmore says he got to the body the first man after he was killed.

Question. Did he see any pistol on him?

Answer. He says not.

Question. Or near him?

Answer. He says not.

Question. Did any of the negroes go up to the body after the man was killed?

Answer. There were none when I was there; I do not know whether they did or not. When I went there they seemed, as is customary with their race, to have a sort of instinct to get away from a corpse, and they were back ten or fifteen steps, perhaps. They seemed to have fallen back from it, and it was left there, and only these gentlemen around it, that I spoke of, that I know of.

Question. When the negroes fired upon the man they were very close to him?

Answer. They must have been right in contact with him. The gun that killed him was so close that it burned his coat and his shirt, and burned the skin of his flesh; even in so near contact that the very wadding went into the man's body.

Question. How many wounds had he upon him?

Answer. He had one saber wound, perhaps, that would have produced concussion of the brain and killed him, and that was all except a slight saber wound on his shoulder. He had a saber wound on the head that might have produced concussion of the brain, or been followed by inflammation of the brain, and killed him, or he could have recovered from that, and another slight saber wound on the shoulder.

Question. And the gun-shot wound?

Answer. Yes, sir.

Question. Was the saber wound on the head easily discernable as he lay upon the ground; could a man see it without looking closely to the head?

Answer. Well, I hardly know what you mean by that.

Question. Could you observe the saber wound he received upon his head?

Answer. Yes, sir; I do not know that I would have done it, that the gash would have been so large that I could have noticed it, but for the blood that had escaped, because it was rather back.

Question. Back of the head?

Answer. Yes, sir. It was evidently struck as the party was going from him—struck from behind on the top; and this wound on the shoulder seemed to have been struck from a distance so great that just the point of the saber cut it in that way, [illustrating]—not with the blade in this way, [illustrating,] but just the point.

Question. Did you see the man when he was shot down—when he fell?

Answer. No, sir; I could not see anything at all for the crowd—not any particular individual; the whole mass were just as thick as they could possibly stand, and the whole mass just shoved that way with the cry of "Kill him, kill him," and the discharge of that gun.

Question. Were you on a horse?

Answer. Yes, sir; on a tall horse.

Question. Could you see over the head and see the man running?

Answer. No, sir; I did not see that at all; I never saw him until I saw him lying there.

Question. Did the first gun discharged sound in the direction that the man Lee was standing?

Answer. Yes, sir; it was on the west side of the wagon.

Question. Were you on the east side of the wagon?

Answer. Yes, sir; rather north of east; I was about where that bookcase stands in the northeast corner of this room, and that gentleman in the middle of the room was the wagon where the speakers were, and the gun seemed to have been fired off in about the same proportion as that southwest corner of the room, [illustrating,] and the killing then was done some fifteen feet from that.

The CHAIRMAN. Perhaps you could make a little diagram which would illustrate the positions better than your description.

The WITNESS. Yes, sir.

[The witness made the following diagram:]

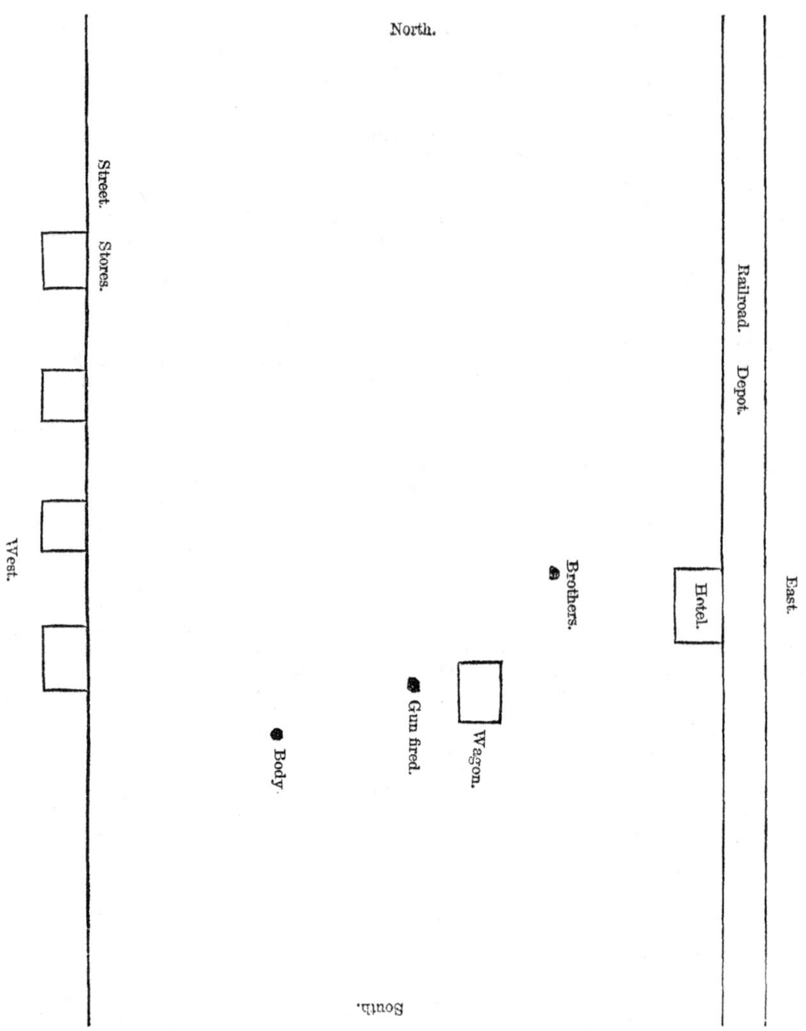

By Mr. BLAIR:

Question. Who went there with you?

Answer. Doctor Zuber and Mr. Pearce and Jimmy Cook, a lad about nineteen years old, and Jimmy Randall, a lad about the same age.

Question. All went up to the body?

Answer. No, sir; we rode up to hear the speakers. We noticed the gun when it fired and were a part of the audience.

Question. Have you conversed with all these gentlemen since about this circumstance?

Answer. O, we have talked it over. They had some of these gentlemen before the coroner's jury.

Question. Did all these gentlemen you have named and who were there with you agree in the fact that it was a gun that was fired?

Answer. All who were before the coroner's jury swore that it was a gun, and, to the best of their knowledge, they saw the gun or the smoke of the gun.

Question. How many persons swore that?

Answer. There was Mr. Pearce and Doctor Zuber and these other young men; it was proved so satisfactory at the coroner's inquest that they did not think it necessary to call them. They were living out some mile and a half or two miles from the town.

Question. Have you seen these other two young men since?

Answer. No, sir; I do not think I have.

Question. Did you talk with them after this occurrence?

Answer. No, sir.

Question. You three testified—you, Pearce, and Zuber—that it was a gun and you saw it?

Answer. Yes, sir; that is my understanding of their testimony.

Question. You are very clear in your recollection about this matter?

Answer. I am, indeed, sir.

Question. Do you know a negro boy by the name of Lymus Nelson, who lives at James Whitfield's plantation, beyond Artesia?

Answer. No, sir; I may even have practiced physic upon him and not know him by name.

Question. He was here before the committee the other day and testified that he heard the discharge and saw the fire from what he said was a pistol over somebody's shoulder in the very place which was occupied by this Lee, or where Lee was standing?

Answer. Well, I can't say that these gentlemen's or my eyes were superior to others, but I tell you that I swear most positively, to the best of my knowledge and belief, that that smoke did come out of the gun; that it was a gun; and, moreover, I believe honestly that it was done as a matter of applause. That was the first impression that struck me, and from what I can find out, I do honestly believe that the gun was fired as a matter of applause. Further, to corroborate that, I understand that during the speaking at Prairie Hill a similar discharge, perhaps the same gun or some other, was fired off. A gun was fired off from in the crowd, which was an accidental discharge. We knew nothing of the parties coming there. Nobody expected the crowd to come there that afternoon.

Question. You say that Lewis, at your instance, dispersed the crowd by giving some command that you did not understand?

Answer. I say he did something or said something, and I suppose that was the cause of it, whereupon the crowd dispersed, as if by magic. I never saw men disperse more quietly and easily, and, in fact, I never saw men go away as quietly.

Question. Did you hear what he said, or see what he did?

Answer. No, sir; but Squire Elmore testified before the coroner's jury that he waived his hand either this way or that way, [illustrating,] held it aloft, and in either a semicircle, or laterally, in that way.

Question. At that signal the crowd dispersed?

Answer. Yes, sir.

Question. Did it make the impression that he had complete control of the crowd?

Answer. He had the most complete control, as much as any man ever had over a parcel of beings. No man ever had more control over others. You can see it there to-day.

Question. You think if he had designed he could have exercised the same control before the man was killed?

Answer. I cannot say that with an infuriated lot of freedmen, who had perhaps been drinking, he could have done it in so short a time; but if he had had time, he could have done it. But just as that gun was fired, if these negroes had all believed that Lewis or Bliss were shot at, I do not think any word of his would have prevented them from killing him. I do not think it would have taken effect so soon; but in the time that a man could control anything he could control them. If a man could control an army in that length of time, he could control his men that soon.

Question. As soon as he got them to understand what he wished?

Answer. Yes, sir; what he desired or what he wished, just that soon they would have acted or not acted.

Question. Did you see him do anything after the gun fired, and when the negroes were pursuing Lee?

Answer. No, sir; I did not see him until then. Senator Pratt, if there is a contradiction in regard to what I said about the dead body, I will be very much pleased if you would have Squire Elmore brought here. He is an appointee of Governor Alcorn, and looked upon as coalescing with that party.

Question. Was Elmore before the grand jury?

Answer. Yes, sir; he was before the grand jury.

Question. You were before the grand jury?

Answer. Yes, sir; you will find all our evidence before them.

Question. Were these other parties that you spoke of also?

Answer. I think, perhaps, they were all before the grand jury, and maybe some, perhaps, that I do not mention. Maybe W. H. Randall was there. Although he is my brother-in-law, and living with me, I have never asked him or talked with him, so far as I remember now. I do not remember whether he was close to me at the time.

By the CHAIRMAN:

Question. Do I understand you that Mr. Bliss was in one buggy and Lewis in another, or both in the same?

Answer. That is my impression; that one was in one, and one in the other; two persons in one, and one in the other.

Question. How did these two buggies stand in relation to each other when the crowd came to a halt; were they standing side by side, or how far apart were they?

Answer. I could not say anything positive in reference to how far apart they were, or how they were standing. I did not notice that.

Question. You feel very positive that there were two buggies there?

Answer. A carriage and a buggy—two vehicles.

Question. One was in one, and the other in the other.

Answer. No, sir; I am not positive how they were when they passed along. I am not positive as to that; nor am I positive that Mr. Bliss was in a buggy or carriage?

Question. Was there two distinct vehicles?

Answer. Yes, sir; I think so. That is my impression.

Question. At the time the speaking was going on did each one remain in his own vehicle?

Answer. I do not remember that, Mr. Pratt.

Question. Or were they both in the same vehicle?

Answer. I do not know. I did not see Mr. Lewis at the time, for I was listening to Mr. Bliss talking. I only saw them when they passed.

Question. Bliss was speaking at the time?

Answer. Yes, sir.

Question. Did you notice whether any white man was with him in his vehicle?

Answer. I did not, sir.

Question. Did you see Mr. Rose there?

Answer. I do not know him, sir. I never saw him.

Question. Did you see any other white man in the neighborhood of the vehicle except the speaker, Mr. Bliss?

Answer. I did not notice any other at all. I did not notice any other white man. My attention was called to this party speaking, and I watched him closely, and listened attentively.

Question. You are not able, then, to state the position of the other vehicle which conveyed Lewis?

Answer. No, sir; I am not.

Question. You saw it in the procession, but after the crowd came to a halt you did not notice it further?

Answer. No, sir; I did not notice it further.

Question. You noticed only the one in which Mr. Bliss was speaking?

Answer. Yes, sir.

Question. That was drawn by a single horse or mule?

Answer. I declare I did not notice that. There was the wagon from which the guns were taken. I did not notice whether they were mules or horses. The scene was as I have told you.

Question. You stood between the hotel and the vehicle Bliss was speaking from.

Answer. Yes, sir; a little north of that.

Question. And about how far from the vehicle was your horse standing?

Answer. About twenty paces, I reckon.

Question. You could easily look over the whole crowd as you were mounted that way?

Answer. No, sir; you could look over and beyond the crowd, but it would be very difficult to tell who was in the crowd, because they were so thick.

Question. But from your position you were above the crowd, so that you could take in at a glance the whole crowd before you?

Answer. Yes, sir; except that to my right and left; because, if you understand, I was in among the mounted men or freedmen. I rode up right among the freedmen.

Question. Was there an unobstructed view between you and the speaker?

Answer. Unobstructed far enough for the vision to pass.

Question. I mean were there any horsemen intervening between you and the speaker?

Answer. Yes, sir; horsemen were ahead of me, but I could see. For instance, if there is a space between these two gentlemen a foot and a half wide I could see a speaker ten or fifteen feet beyond them.

Question. The vehicle was between you and the place where the gun was fired, as I understand you?

Answer. Yes, sir; I saw the wagon here and the guns fired here, [illustrating by the diagram.]

Question. Then the wagon was between you and the place where the gun was fired?

Answer. Yes, sir; rather between us. The wagon was rather to the south.

Question. I take your diagram and ask if you, posted as you are represented there, and a gun having been fired off on the opposite side of the wagon in which the speaker stood, would not that wagon and speaker be right in the line of vision between you and the point where the gun was fired?

Answer. As I told you, so far as the diagram is concerned, I can state that it was not quite in line. Here I was, as this shows, and here was the man firing the gun, [illustrating by the diagram.]

Question. You were about twenty paces from where the wagon was?

Answer. Yes, sir.

Question. How far was it from where the gun was fired?

Answer. I suppose about four feet beyond that; three or four feet from the speaker the gun was fired.

Question. You think the man that held the gun then was within four feet of the speaker?

Answer. Yes, sir.

Question. That must have been right close up against the vehicle?

Answer. Yes, sir; I thought so.

Question. Were you looking at the speaker at the time you heard the discharge of the gun?

Answer. Yes, sir; I was looking at the speaker, as if I would look at that gentleman over there.

Question. If you were looking at the speaker were you not looking toward the spot where the gun was fired?

Answer. Yes, sir; with the vision I could take the range of both.

Question. Would there be some deflection?

Answer. Some little deflection, but not sufficient but what a man could see. The eye can change its position very rapidly. I might be looking at this point, and the gun shoot over there, and I would see it. I would see the smoke before the sound even at that distance, and yet my eyes could be thrown up quick enough to see it all.

Question. At the distance of twenty or twenty-two paces do you think you would see the smoke before you would hear the report?

Answer. If there would be any difference at all—yes, I say that in a distance of one hundred yards there would be a difference, but the difference is very slight. If I look at General Blair's head over here, and there is a gun fired off there, I can see the smoke because it is unusual, and the report would be combined. I would see it at the same time. My vision and attention were attracted to it so soon that before the gun was withdrawn I could see it, as I thought.

Question. Tell the committee what the speaker was saying at the time the gun was fired?

Answer. Well, really, I never have thought about what he was saying from the very moment he spoke. Let me recollect; I will see if I can think of it. [Pausing.] I do not know that I can recall anything he said, except I observed that so far as I heard there was nothing that was calculated to arouse any feelings of animosity between the whites and the blacks. I heard nothing of that. I was listening for that.

Question. He was speaking properly and temperately?

Answer. Yes, sir; I can say that for him.

Question. But you do not know the subject he was discussing?

Answer. No, sir, I do not. I can't tell you.

Question. How long did you listen to him?

Answer. Three or five minutes, I suppose.

Question. Can you not recall what he said during that time?

Answer. No, sir; because we pay so little attention to those things. If he had said anything inflammatory I should have noticed it.

Question. Were you talking with any person after you rode up there?

Answer. No, sir; I do not know that we exchanged any words at all while there.

Question. These friends you mention were standing beside you?

Answer. Yes, sir; in rather close proximity.

Question. Any of them mounted?

Answer. Yes, sir; Dr. Zuber and Mr. Pearce were mounted.

Question. Were they on each side of you?

Answer. I do not remember but they were. We just rode in.

Question. Did you arm yourself before you rode in.

Answer. No, sir. I never carried a pistol in my life. I am no more afraid of those negroes out there than nothing, although the report was circulated all around there that they were to kill me; that I am the man they went there to kill.

Question. I suppose from what you stated that the crowd was bent on mischief?

Answer. I did not know they were coming until they came there armed and marching. It would arouse any man that had a family at a place like Artesia, with fifteen or twenty-five of them to one of us.

Question. Did you not take the precaution, when going among the crowd that you thought were making dangerous demonstrations, to protect yourself?

The WITNESS. With those people there?

The CHAIRMAN. Yes.

The WITNESS. Why, sir, I am no more afraid of them than I am of you. I have been raised right there with them. If one man had said, "Dr. Brothers; kill him," I know I would have been killed in a twinkling if possible, but it would have required somebody to have put them on—something more than a negro to kill me. I have been practicing physic for them ever since 1865, and working and practicing among them extensively.

Question. You think, if Lewis had said "Kill Dr. Brothers," it would have been enough?

Answer. I just know they would have killed me—five hundred guns; and to-day if he would give the word they would do it. If he had the same crowd that he had that day and said, "Boys, kill him," it would be enough.

Question. Do you think they would kill any man in the community?

Answer. Yes, any man in the community, and you if they did not know you. If he had said, "Kill Senator Pratt," and they did not know you, they would have killed you that day.

Question. He must be almost omnipotent among the freedmen?

Answer. If you lived here you would know it.

Question. He was candidate for sheriff at that time?

Answer. Yes, sir. They believe everything in the world that a man who allies himself with them tells them, and they believe nothing another tells them.

Question. Is Lewis a northern or a southern man?

Answer. A Northern man. Whereas they would not ask him for a chew of tobacco, or to borrow a horse, but ask me, they would still obey him in anything he told them.

Question. Is Mr. Lewis a man of good personal habits and deportment?

Answer. I do not know anything about him. I never spoke to him to that time. I never saw him under the influence of liquor.

Question. How came you to know he had such an all-powerful sway over the negroes?

Answer. I could just tell that from the negroes; I could tell it from my negroes and other negroes talking about Mr. Lewis, and "How are you going to vote; are you going to vote like Mr. Lewis and Mr. Whitfield says?"

Question. Do you think Mr. Whitfield has the same influence that Mr. Lewis has over them?

Answer. I do not think that at the time he exerted such an influence, from the fact that he was not a candidate. If he had been a candidate for the same office he would have exerted the same influence; but he was a candidate for an office that they were not taught to look upon as of so much importance.

Question. You never heard of Mr. Lewis or Mr. Whitfield counseling these men to kill this man or that man, did you?

Answer. No, sir.

Question. You never heard of any violence inflicted under the dictation of either of these men, did you?

Answer. No, sir, none.

Question. What makes you say that the negroes are so completely under the domination and control of Mr. Lewis that they would violate the laws of God and the laws of the country at the bare suggestion of a wish from Mr. Lewis?

Answer. Well, I have gathered that about the same way you would gather it. If your children were going to school you would soon find out if the teacher had very great influence over the children, and yet you might not ask them how many times they had been whipped. They tell me they do whatever Lewis says do, in the way of voting, and everything of that kind. I do not say that he could take one man and make him do it, nor perhaps ten; but if he gets up eight hundred or a thousand, marching with drum and fife, and goes to Prairie Hill, and speaks to them, and marches five miles past houses, whooping and yelling, and excited, even without whisky, that would excite them very much; it even excitedme. I cannot see a crowd passing here whooping and yelling, with double barreled shot-guns, without it excites me at once.

Question. How excite you?

Answer. I do not know that I can express the excitement.

Question. Do you mean that it would excite you so that you would be under a sort of mesmeric influence of the speaker, so that you would kill anybody at his beck?

Answer. Not at all.

Question. What makes you think other men would be influenced differently from yourself?

Answer. Because it did it; there was an accidental discharge of a gun, and they did kill a man there, and that is why I think they would do it; they did do it.

Question. I repeat the question whether any person on horseback or mules were between you and the vehicle in which the speaker was standing?

Answer. I think there were; but not sufficient to obstruct my vision.

Question. How many do you now think were on horseback between you and the vehicle?

Answer. I did not notice anything of that.

Question. Do you think a dozen?

Answer. I can't tell you anything about that.

Question. They were mounted and afoot indiscriminately through there between you and the vehicle?

Answer. Yes, sir; I might say they were.

Question. All colored men, no white men?

Answer. Yes, sir; there were these two white men and these two lads.

Question. Were the white men mounted between you and the speaker's stand?

Answer. They were there; I do not know whether they were ahead of me or behind.

Question. Were they mounted?

Answer. Yes, sir; Dr. Zuber and Mr. Pearce were.

Question. Were they between you and the vehicle, on each side of you?

Answer. I declare, Senator, I don't understand your object with me; are you endeavoring to confuse me or to have me tell the plain fact?

The CHAIRMAN. I want the truth.

The WITNESS. You want to know how it was. Here might have been a cavalryman, and here one, and here one, [illustrating] and I might have been here. Say I was here, and Mr. Pearce there, and Dr. Zuber over there——

Question. You have no idea how many men were between the position you occupied on your horse and this vehicle in which the speaker was?

Answer. Not a sufficient number to obstruct my vision.

Question. That is not an answer. I want the number that you suppose were there on horseback?

Answer. I do not know; I could not suppose.

Question. Do you think there were as many as a dozen?

Answer. I do not know, sir.

Question. Now if they were mounted on horses or mules, were not their heads as high as yours?

Answer. The most I noticed were mounted on horses.

Question. Did you have to change your position at any time in order to get a full view of the speaker?

Answer. No, sir; everything was very quiet; you never saw men more attentive in your life.

Question. Was there any moving about in the crowd?

Answer. I did not discover any.

Question. They were all still?

Answer. They seemed very attentive; as attentive an audience as you ever saw on a commons in your life.

Question. You didn't see Mr. Lee until you saw his dead body?

Answer. No, sir.

Question. You spoke of having seen the smoke and fire emanate from the barrel of the gun?

Answer. Yes, sir.

Question. What was the direction of the smoke and fire from the wagon? Was it southwest or west?

Answer. West.

Question. Was it right west?

Answer. Nearly due west from the wagon.

Question. And you were a little north of east?

Answer. Yes, sir.

Question. Now, how many paces, or rather how many feet, in your opinion, were you from the place where you saw the fire and the smoke?

Answer. I was, I suppose, about twenty paces, and the fire was within three or four feet of the buggy—say within four feet of the buggy. That was, the discharge of the gun.

Question. Did you notice the direction of it, as to whether it was perpendicular or whether it was in a sloping direction?

Answer. It was above an angle of forty-five degrees; just about that. [Illustrating.] In other words, very nearly the position of a gun in the position in which a gun should stand if a man were to hold it in this way, [illustrating,] and you might pull the trigger of it, as I have very often done shooting a gun myself.

Question. Was that fire and smoke in the direction of the speaker?

Answer. It issued up but not in the direction of the speaker.

Question. You have already said it was not perpendicular?

Answer. Yes.

Question. But at an angle of more than forty-five degrees inclining?

Answer. Yes, sir; at an angle upward of more than forty-five degrees. If you take a gun and hold it down it will stand in just about that position. [Illustrating.] That is about forty-five degrees, is it not? Well, that is the angle that it was when it was fired.

Question. The angle you indicate is about sixty degrees.

Answer. Yes, sir; it was about that.

Question. So that the direction of the fire and smoke, as it issued from this barrel, was toward the buggy where the speaker was?

Answer. Yes, sir. Or here was the buggy, and that inclination would be in that way. If it was any inclination at all it was a little toward the speaker, which goes to corroborate my theory, which I believe in yet, that this man had got tired and hoarse with shouting and put that gun down and shot it.

Question. That is barely speculative or imaginary on your part?

Answer. Yes, sir; wholly so.

Question. You did not see the man that held the gun or see him pull the trigger?

Answer. No, sir; of course not.

Question. You did not see him at all?

Answer. I hope you will not take this down to have me swear to it. It is speculation.

Question. Are you sure you saw the upper part of the barrel?

Answer. Yes, sir.

Question. About one foot of it?

Answer. Yes, sir.

Question. Could you tell whether it was a rifle or musket?

Answer. I think it was a musket. I could not tell a musket from a single-barreled shot-gun.

Question. Did your vision rest upon it after you saw the fire and the smoke?

Answer. No, sir. Immediately after that my vision was attracted to the cry, "White man; kill him; kill him!" My vision was carried to these parties, and that smoke came just like it would out of a crowd—up. There was no clear, distinct smoke further than that.

Question. Did you see any other gun in the neighborhood of this discharge?

Answer. Yes, sir; there were several other guns.

Question. How were they holding them; on their shoulders?

Answer. Some of them had their guns on their shoulders; and I could see more in the neighborhood—if you call the neighborhood right close about him—around him had guns.

Question. I limit my question to the spot where you saw the smoke and fire.

Answer. No, sir; I saw no gun elevated there.

Question. Did you notice any other guns there?

Answer. No, sir; I did not see any there. I do not say whether they were there or not. My attention was not called to that.

Question. If Lee was the only white man in the crowd or in that part of the crowd, how did it happen that you, mounted on horseback and having a clear view of the speaker's stand and of the spot from whence this discharge came, did not see the white man?

Answer. Because it would be an impossibility to have seen unless he had been that much taller than the negroes that he was surrounded by.

Question. Among the black faces would not his white face be distinct?

Answer. If some man had called my attention to that white man I might have seen him; but with my attention attracted to the speaker I would not have noticed a man standing there.

Question. Did you see a man running about that moment?

Answer. Yes, sir; I saw a great many men running.

Question. Did you see any single man run off?

Answer. No, sir.

Question. Did you see the general rush?

Answer. Yes, sir; they all went right forward.

Question. If the white man commenced running first you did not see that fact?

Answer. I did not, sir. I never saw the white man until he was dead.

Question. How far was the body, as you saw it afterward, from the wagon in which the speaker stood?

Answer. I suppose some fifteen—I tell you that is guessing; it will be a guess, now. If you want a guess——

Question. I want your best opinion.

Answer. I can't tell you anything, because my position where I was standing in relation to the wagon was such that, at the time that my attention was called to it, I could not tell, for when the body was there the wagon was gone; when I looked at the body I did not look at the wagon. In fact, I did not know where the dead man was until I went around there; and then I could not have noticed where the wagon was at the time that I was standing in my first position, because all were gone when I did look and notice them, but I would judge, Senator, that it was maybe twenty or twenty-five feet.

Question. From the place where the wagon had stood?

Answer. Yes, sir.

Question. When did you leave the position you were occupying on horseback after the gun fired?

Answer. After the volley of guns and the cry of "Boys, to your wagons, and get your guns." Then I left. These parties came and took three or four guns out of this wagon and the boy took the pistols, and I made that remark and then I rode on up nearly to Mr. Perkins, and I saw my servant and said, "John, take my horse."

Question. How long a space elapsed from the time you heard the first gun until you saw the body?

Answer. Well, I do not know how time flies under such excitement. It would be a very, very rough estimate if I were to make one. It was not a long time; that I can say. I do not know that I can say more than that. I would not like to.

Question. In what direction had the shot entered Lee's body? You say there were two saber cuts, and that he was shot once in the body?

Answer. Yes, sir.

Question. Please state the direction of that shot or bullet.

Answer. It was done with shot—with squirrel-shot. It was just about there; [illustrating;] just above the point of the hip-bone; I do not remember which one, though. I did not notice the wound there until I got over to the house. It entered just above the hip—either the right or left hip—ranging inward and downward.

Question. During the time you were sitting on the horse, did you hear any interruption of the speaker?

Answer. Not a thing. I understood there was an interruption, but I never discovered the slightest myself.

Question. What have you heard was the nature of the interruption?

Answer. I have understood by some freedmen out there that—no; I never understood it from them, either—but I understood from some parties at Crawfordsville that Mr. Lewis said the man hollered and asked Mr. Bliss if he was a white man or a negro, and that he remarked to him, if he wanted to come and join the Native Sons of the South, to come and do it and get blessed. I saw that in a letter, I think.

Question. A letter of Mr. Lewis?

Answer. Yes, sir; or heard of it. I don't know which.

Question. Was there not testimony given on the coroner's inquest that Lee had interrupted the speaker by asking him if he was a white man or a negro?

Answer. None that I know of; unless Wiley Stewart gave it.

Question. What is your impression?

Answer. I do not have any impression about it, unless he could have done that, from the fact that he testified to this other thing—that the party had a pistol.

Question. Were a great many witnesses examined on that inquest?

Answer. Yes, sir.

Question. You think not more than one testified to that interruption?

Answer. I do not remember more than one.

Question. Do you recollect that that one did?

Answer. No, sir; I do not remember that even this one did.

Question. Was it contradicted by any one? How many swore that nothing was said or that there was no interruption?

Answer. I swore I heard none, and Mr. Pearce and Dr. Zuber swore that they had heard none, I think.

Question. Was the speaker's voice directed toward you at the time he was speaking and when you rode up there?

Answer. No, sir; he was looking a little southwest, I think.

Question. Was he looking in the direction where the gun was fired?

Answer. No, sir; the gun was west, and he was looking southwest. He could have taken, perhaps, a view of it.

Question. Then, from the position you occupied, you could not see the speaker's face?

Answer. I could see his side-face; see his gestures.

Question. You could hear him distinctly?

Answer. Yes, sir; very well. I heard him. I only noticed this fact. I went up there to hear what sort of a speech he was going to make. I notice, and can testify to the fact, that he did not make what is considered an inflammatory speech.

Question. You heard the sentences as they dropped from his mouth?

Answer. Yes, sir.

Question. Was there any applause from the freedmen?

Answer. Yes, sir; I heard one round of applause, and not very heavy at that.

Question. Just a shout?

Answer. Yes, sir.

Question. No words of approval except that shout?

Answer. I do not remember any.

Question. "That's the right talk," or something of the sort?

Answer. No, sir; I do not remember any. Just a yell, like freedmen would yell—"Hugh, hugh." They don't yell like white folks anyhow.

Question. If you were where you describe yourself as being, is it possible that a person, looking into the face of the speaker, could have uttered these words, "Are you a white man or a negro," and been heard by the speaker and not heard by you?

Answer. Yes, sir; it is very possible.

Question. Did you notice that the speaker came to a halt at any time in the flow of his sentences?

Answer. No, sir; I did not notice that.

Question. Do you think it would have attracted your attention if he had. If any one had asked him a question clearly, and he had paused a moment and answered it, do you think your attention was directed to him enough to have noticed that fact?

Answer. Yes, sir; I think I should have noticed anything of the sort, unless it had been done in a very mild manner. If there had been any aggravating tone I would have noticed it.

Question. Is not this the case, that you, going there in rather an excited manner, seeing, as you say, an unusually large crowd, coming unexpectedly with guns, and drums, and muskets, and being, as you say, influenced by the presence of this crowd, surrounded at the moment by seven or eight hundred men——

Answer. Yes, sir.

Question. I say is it not quite possible that your attention was not fixed closely all the time on what the speaker was saying?

Answer. No, sir; my attention was fixed on the speaker, because I had nothing in the world to go up there for but to ascertain from the nature of his remarks as to whether it would be inflammatory or not.

Question. Was your attention so fixed that you would not notice anything going on to the right or left, or rear of you?

Answer. Anything unusual and loud enough to have attracted my attention would have been noticed, I think, if it was in close proximity to where I was looking, and had not been behind me.

Question. You think you had been sitting there about five minutes before you saw this?

Answer. Yes, sir; three to five minutes.

Question. At least five minutes?

Answer. No, sir; three to five minutes.

Question. Time passes very insensibly on such occasions?

Answer. Yes, sir; you do not notice it.

Question. How long was this before sundown?

Answer. I can't tell that; it was late in the afternoon.

Question. The sun had not gone down?

Answer. No, sir; I do not think it had.

Question. Who said, "Boys, to your wagons and get your guns?"

Answer. I do not know, sir.

Question. Who said, "White man; kill him?"

Answer. I do not know, sir; a great number of voices said, "Kill him, kill him."

Question. You spoke of a negro taking out a carpet-sack, of what you supposed to be pistols. Did you see him take them out?

Answer. No, sir.

Question. Do you know it was a bag of pistols?

Answer. That was my impression. I said, "For God sake don't take those pistols out in this crowd; the men of Artesia have nothing to do with this thing." He said, "I'll be damned if I don't take them out." That made me think——

Question. Was this after the firing was over?

Answer. Yes, sir.

Question. How long did the firing continue?

Answer. I suppose it continued a second and a half, or two seconds, may be; just about the time you could discharge and hear the different discharges, even making a supposition that there were six or seven guns.

Question. You say you went to Perkins's store. Is that the first store on the diagram?

Answer. Bryan's is the first store. I did not go to any. Mr. Perkins's is the one I rode nearest to.

Question. That is the second one?

Answer. Yes, sir.

Question. When you arrived where the body was lying, you found Lewis and Bliss, and Squire Elmore, the justice of the peace, there?

Answer. Yes, sir.

Question. Did you mean, when you said to Lewis that you would telegraph for men, that you would telegraph for troops?

Answer. I just meant if the men did not disperse and quit the killing, we would just telegraph for anybody in the world who would help us.

Question. Did you tell him who you were going to telegraph for?

Answer. No, sir; I did not think about anything but self-protection then.

Question. Was he, at the time, standing by the dead body?

Answer. Yes, sir; near it.

Question. When you asked him if he could not disperse the crowd?

Answer. Yes, sir.

Question. He was not then in a vehicle, or above the crowd, but right in the midst of them?

Answer. No. The crowd I spoke of was the crowd around the dead body. The others were off some distance from them—the negroes.

Question. The whole six or seven hundred were still on the ground?

Answer. Some of them had got on their horses and gone. The train moved out by that time—about the time of this hollering, "Boys, to your wagons and get your guns." I suppose this man belonged to that train, and after they crossed the railroad, north of where this was, a considerable number of these mounted men went up there, and I heard the discharge of several pistols up there; and I afterward heard that several of them just shot off their pistols, as a matter of amusement, in going on.

Question. What did Mr. Lewis say to the crowd, when he told you he would disperse them?

Answer. I do not know that he—I say he did, or said something; I do not know what he could have done; and I went on to say if there were any signs——

Question. I heard what you testified to. My question is, whether he said anything to the crowd, and, if so, what he said.

Answer. No, sir; I did not hear him say anything at all; but there was something done.

Question. But did he make any remark to the crowd?

Answer. I do not know, sir. There was something done to disperse the crowd.

Question. I want to know what was done. Did he or Bliss make any remark to the crowd?

Answer. Not that I am aware of.

Question. Do you know that he did not?

Answer. No, sir.

Question. Then he may have told the crowd to disperse?

Answer. He may have done it.

Question. You say that neither of these men—Lewis or Bliss—claimed that they were shot at, or in any danger, to your knowledge. Did you question them upon that point?

Answer. No, sir.

Question. Did you have any conversation with Bliss or Lewis upon that point, at that time, or at any time?

Answer. No, sir; but I understood from Mr. Pearce that he ask Mr. Bliss if he thought the man shot at him, and he said no. That is a gentleman from Illinois, who moved down here year before last.

Question. You have no personal knowledge on that subject at all?

Answer. Only that it would have been very natural, when I made the remark, "We feel alarmed," for one of them to say, if they thought they were in danger, "I think we are the men in danger."

Question. What did you say to have drawn out such a reply?

Answer. "We feel alarmed. Can't you disperse this crowd?" I think if I had been shot at I would have said, "You are not the men to be alarmed. I want protection myself. I am the man that needs protection."

Question. That is the only reason?

Answer. And the fact that he would have said so anyhow. It would have been perfectly natural for you, Senator, to have said so, then.

Question. But I understood that you were an entire stranger to him, and never had seen him before.

Answer. I never had met him. I never knew the man until that evening.

Question. Why should he have gone into an explanation to you, a stranger?

Answer. Because here was Squire Elmore he knew very well, and he would have remarked it to him.

Question. It is a question of taste whether he would have done so or not, is it not?

Answer. I should think he would have made the remark if he had thought he had been shot at. It is very natural.

Question. You are speaking now of Mr. Lewis or Mr. Bliss?

Answer. I am speaking of both of them. If either of them had been shot at they would have said, "I am the man that has been shot at, or is in danger."

Question. Was any question asked them on that subject?
Answer. I understood that Mr. Pearce did.
Question. Did you hear it?
Answer. No, sir. I did not, only what Mr. Pearce told me since.
Question. What was the name of the freedman, who testified to Lee having a pistol?
Answer. Wiley Stewart.
Question. He swore that he saw Lee have a pistol?
Answer. Yes, sir, I think he did. That is my understanding.
Question. Swore that he saw the pistol go off; the smoke and the fire?
Answer. I do not remember whether he went into that, or whether he explained it so particular; but my impression is that he swore that this man Lee had a pistol.
Question. Did you make search that evening to discover whether any pistol had been dropped by Lee or anybody?
Answer. On the ground?
Question. Yes, sir.
Answer. No, sir; only right around the body, within a short compass.
Question. Lee must have run some twenty feet or more before he fell?
Answer. I did not see how far. I do not know where he was before.
Question. Suppose Lee was standing near where that gun was fired?
Answer. Yes, sir; then he would have had to go some distance.
Question. How far?
Answer. My guess was twenty-five feet, but I do not know that I came within ten feet of it.
Question. If he held a pistol, and was running for his life, is it not quite possible that he would have dropped the pistol in running, if he thought the object of the crowd was to assassinate him for discharging the pistol? Is it not very natural that he would have thrown it or dropped it as he ran?
Answer. If he had had a pistol, I should think he would have dropped it.
Question. Now, there were hundreds of people right around there, around the track that he took in running?
Answer. There were a great many persons.
Question. If he had dropped the pistol in running, it was very easy for the negroes to have picked it up, and you know nothing about it?
Answer. Yes, sir; that was very easy.
Question. And this Stewart did swear positively that he saw him have a pistol, and discharge it?
Answer. But yet it was in so great conflict with the other testimony that he was turned over to the magistrate for perjury.
Question. Has he been bound over on that charge? Has anybody made an affidavit charging him with perjury?
Answer. I think not. He is about home. I do not reckon anything has ever been done with him. I told some parties myself; in fact, this man came and told me—Wiley Stewart did—came and told me over in Mr. Lee's office that he would come over here before the grand jury, and testify anything that I wanted him to testify. Says I, "Wiley, did I ever advise you to tell a lie? Has not my advice, on the other hand, always been to tell the truth?" He says, "Doctor Brothers, I will tell the truth. I was so badly scared that night you all had me there, I didn't know what I did say. I didn't know what I was talking about."
Question. Was that the night of the killing?
Answer. Yes, sir, at the inquest.
Question. The inquest was held the same night?
Answer. Yes, sir, and upon that I asked some of the parties, or I told Squire Elmore, I think, "Don't say anything more about it, for Wiley tells me he was so badly frightened he didn't know what he said, and there is no use in putting the boy in jail—using any force against him."
Question. Was that the same night that he gave his evidence?
Answer. No; that was several days afterward he told me was so badly frightened.
Question. Was he held in custody that night by the magistrate?
Answer. No, sir, but he was turned over in custody.
Question. How long did he remain turned over in custody?
Answer. I do not know.
Question. Was he kept in custody that night?
Answer. I do not know whether he was or not. I left him, and did not see him until I saw him over in Columbus.
Question. And nobody has made an affidavit charging him with perjury?
Answer. No, sir. I think they all agreed to let it pass off. He is a good boy, a faithful, honest-working fellow, and he told me he was so badly frightened—he says, "Doctor, I'll declare to God I didn't know what I was saying."
Question. Where did he say he was standing at the time this pistol was fired off?
Answer. He said he was standing right at the man. At one time he said he was three

feet off. He said, "I was standing right by him, and the man fired it when I was right by him;" and again he said, "I was three feet off." There was a contradiction of testimony such as you, perhaps, never heard.

Question. He never in his contradictions, which you speak of, said that he was more than three feet off?

Answer. No, sir. I do not know about the distance, but in other points he contradicted himself.

Question. On what other points did he contradict himself?

Answer. I do not remember. If his testimony was taken down, you could see. I do not know whether it was taken down or not.

Question. Who called him as a witness; the State?

Answer. Yes, sir.

Question. There was only one side?

Answer. Yes, sir, only one side.

Question. The magistrate called him as a witness, because of his personal knowledge of the facts, as he stood near Lee?

Answer. Yes, sir.

Question. And he swore that he stood within three feet of Lee, and saw him draw the pistol and fire it?

Answer. He said he saw him when he shot, and then said he did not see him, but saw the smoke. He said every way. He said he did, and said he didn't.

Question. Did he say Lee fired in the direction of the speaker?

Answer. That is what he said, and then said he was running, and even went to say, and swore to it—they questioned him time and again—that Lee, when he began to run, continued to run and shoot his pistol three or four times. He was asked why he did not hit somebody, and he said he did not know, but he knew that, and then he said he did not shoot at all.

Question. What motive had he to swear falsely? He was taken up right on the heels of the killing, was he not; examined the same evening after this occurred?

Answer. Yes, sir; some hour or two, or couple of hours, perhaps. I cannot tell his motive.

Question. There has been some effort to make some political capital out of this affair at Artesia, has there not?

Answer. None that I know of, sir. There has been this: that we—I have felt that I would be very glad to have what we here term the Ku-Klux committee come down here and investigate that case, for I thought surely that was one we would not be censured for, at any rate; if we had been censured for any crime at all, that we would not be censured for that, at any rate.

By Mr. RICE:

Question. You say several guns were fired immediately after the first gun that you saw?

Answer. Yes, sir; after this cry of "White man; kill him; kill him."

Question. How do you account for no one being hit in the crowd, if so many guns were fired?

Answer. I cannot tell, sir. I cannot account for it.

Question. Did you hear all the evidence before the coroner's jury?

Answer. I think I heard most of it.

Question. Was there any given there showing that either Lewis or Bliss had anything to do with bringing on this shooting?

Answer. None, except the fact that they were the great centers of attraction.

Question. Did not the evidence show that the shooting arose out of the firing of this first gun?

Answer. Clearly, it did.

Question. And not anything before that?

Answer. Yes, sir. That gun might have been fired on purpose, but my idea was it was an applause.

Question. How could anybody have anticipated that Lee would have been there, so as to make any arrangement in advance for the firing of that gun?

Answer. That could not have been done at all, unless the crowd mistook Lee for me. We were about the same sized men, and it was whispered all around the country that they were there to kill me. They passed by me. Mrs. Cole said she heard one of the freedmen say, "We have killed the wrong man," or "You have killed the wrong man."

Question. You were in the crowd of freedmen?

Answer. No, sir. I was over here among the mounted men.

Question. Were they freedmen?

Answer. Yes, sir.

Question. You were in plain view of them?

Answer. Yes, sir. But it was not as easy to kill me—to get rid of me—as if I had been down in the crowd and mixed up, for, probably, some one would have known me, and they could not have got rid of me as easily as they did of this man, unless I had been in his situation.

Question. Was it more difficult to have shot a man where you were than in the midst of that dense crowd?

Answer. It would have required deliberate aim to have shot me without shooting anybody else. It would have depended on the man that shot. It would have been certain that somebody would have been right at him to have taken the man.

Question. Who did you contemplate telegraphing to for assistance?

Answer. I did not contemplate anybody—just anybody. Some of them went on to make remarks: "By God! if the white people are not satisfied"—so they told us that evening—"By God! if they are not satisfied, we will kill them all and burn up the place."

Question. You heard these remarks?

Answer. No, sir; I heard that they were said; but these remarks were not to me.

Question. What caused you to say that?

Answer. I did not know what a whole parcel of maddened freedmen would do. One man had been killed. I was satisfied that he was killed innocently. I did not know but I would be killed next. I would have been willing to fight with anybody.

Question. You were not alarmed?

Answer. I was alarmed, but not enough alarmed to run. I told Lewis so. I used the word "we." I said, "We are alarmed." If you had been there you would have been alarmed, too, in that same condition. I tell you it was rather squally. It was the squalliest times I have ever gone through.

Question. Was the attention of the crowd directed to anybody but Lee?

The WITNESS. In what way?

Mr. RICE. At the time they moved?

Answer. No, sir; they did not seem attracted to any one but the party they were moving to at the time. I didn't know upon whom they were moving, or who they contemplated killing.

Question. You had no one in your mind that you were going to dispatch to at Columbus or Aberdeen?

Answer. No, sir. If they got into a fight I would telegraph to Columbus. Before the crowd did leave I believe I did instigate a dispatch, and telegraph here that already one innocent man had been killed, and perhaps we would need assistance; but after the crowd quieted off I went back and telegraphed not to come; that we did not want anybody. A man went over to the depot, who was an acquaintance of his, and wrote out a telegraph and sent to Meridian for men to come up to assist.

Question. Who did you telegraph to?

Answer. I do not know whether I signed my name or not; I think not. I take the censure if there is any. I think I instigated the dispatch.

Question. You do not know whom it was to?

Answer. No, sir.

By the CHAIRMAN:

Question. Was there any demonstration of violence made against any person after Lee was killed?

Answer. None that I know of.

Question. The crowd peaceably dispersed and went home?

Answer. O, yes, sir. Everything was quiet, and very soon not a rioter was there. It quieted down so soon that this dispatch was not necessary. On that we telegraphed to these gentlemen over here that everything was quiet, and there was no danger.

By Mr. BLAIR:

Question. Was the gun that was first fired—that you saw fired—in the midst of the crowd of negroes?

Answer. It was, as I thought, within three or four feet of the wagon.

Question. Were there many negroes around it?

Answer. Yes, sir.

Question. How far around did the negroes extend?

Answer. Fifteen to twenty feet around; twenty feet at least.

Question. This gun was fired off in the middle of the crowd?

Answer. This gun was fired off close to the carriage in the middle of the crowd.

Question. Were they packed up pretty closely near the place where the gun went off?

Answer. Yes, sir; pretty close.

Question. As close as men ordinarily get in public meetings?

Answer. Yes, sir; where they are interested to get close to the speaker.

Question. Did you hear from anybody afterward where this man Lee was standing at the time? Was it on the outskirts of the crowd?

Answer. I do not know, general. I haven't heard any one say. I cannot say for certain.

Question. You do not know yourself?
Answer. No, sir.

By Mr. RICE:

Question. Was this colored man Stewart immediately ordered into custody upon his giving his testimony?
Answer. After he gave it I think he was.

By the CHAIRMAN:

Question. Are you the chief of an order known as the Native Sons of the South?
Answer. No, sir; I am not.
Question. Do you belong to the organization?
Answer. I do.
Question. Are you just a private in it, or an officer?
Answer. I do not know whether I am a private or not. I am no officer in it at all.
Question. How long have you belonged to the organization?
Answer. Well, about—I have just been considered a "Native Son of the South," and have worn a "Native Son of the South" cap. I have never taken any oath at all, or anything of the sort. I just consider myself a "Native Son of the South" to this effect: "Boys we want to get together now; we want to put down these men who come here—carpet-baggers; we want you to unite with us; we want to allow you all your privileges and are in favor of everything you want, and will grant you everything; but we want to put men in office that we know; men who are honest, and identified with us in interest and feeling. Now come, let us work together. We are willing to divide the offices with you, and everything. Let us meet together and nominate our ticket;" and we did meet together, had "Native Son of the South" on the head, and put two negroes on for representatives, and two white men.
Question. When did you join the order?
Answer. I never joined it. There has been no joining. I have been considered one—to meet with them.
Question. Have they a constitution?
Answer. Not that I know of.
Question. How do you know what their principles are unless there is a constitution?
Answer. Those are the declared principles.
Question. Where are they declared; in what instrument?
Answer. O, I do not know the instrument. I saw it declared in an instrument drawn up.
Question. How declared?
Answer. Just an instrument in writing; "We hereby declare our principles to be so and so."
Question. You signed it?
Answer. No, sir; I never did.
Question. Who did?
Answer. I do not know whether anybody signed it. I never saw any man do it.
Question. Where did you see that paper?
Answer. I never read one of them. I saw a paper said to be that. I never read it.
Question. Where did you see it?
Answer. At Artesia.
Question. In what room or building?
Answer. Well, the building was not occupied by anybody except as a store-house for corn.
Question. Who were present at the time you saw the paper?
Answer. Squire Gum, Walsh Lowry, a freedman, Silas Crumm, and several others.
Question. Did you meet there by accident or by arrangement?
Answer. O, we just met there. We appointed to meet there. For instance, we gave one big barbecue, and we appointed men to go around and solicit contributions.
Question. For what?
Answer. For a barbecue—a neighborhood barbecue.
Question. Did you meet in that room to give a barbecue?
Answer. Yes, sir.
Question. That was the time you saw this writing?
Answer. No, sir; I did not see any writing at all that I remember.
Question. You have spoken of a writing containing this agreement. When and where did you see it?
Answer. I saw it at that point—in that room.
Question. Did you see anybody sign it?
Answer. No, sir; no signature is ever required to it.
Question. Who drew it up?
Answer. I do not know who drew it up.
Question. Was it read over to all of you?

Answer. No, sir. You are getting at something that I reckon is not what you are after. It was just—nothing to sign; just as I told you. We go on saying, "Boys, we want to get rid of carpet-baggers; put native men in office; men whom we know and trust, and men from whom you rent your land. We want to protect you in your privileges of voting, in the privilege of holding property, and in all your rights, and to keep up the schools and everything; only we want you to unite with us." It was meant for nothing in the world except not to have the name of the democratic party there.

Question. That is a very nice piece of composition; who got it up?

Answer. I do not know who got it up. Really I am honest in that. I do not.

Question. What was it there for?

Answer. It was there just as a writing to explain what we proposed to do; nothing in the world but holding conventions to explain what we proposed to do; trying to get men to vote with us just as all people do; as you would do.

Question. That is the constitution of the Native Sons of the South?

Answer. No, sir; no constitution.

Question. What do you call it, an agreement?

Answer. No, sir; we do not call it anything at all. We call it a written declaration of what we would do.

Question. Was it your declaration of principles?

Answer. Yes, sir.

Question. Every man who joined that order consented to that platform of principles?

Answer. Yes, sir, I suppose so; if anybody joined it. I do not know that anybody joined it. I never did.

Question. Are you in the habit of wearing the badge?

Answer. Yes, sir; I have worn the cap.

Question. What is the uniform of the Native Sons?

Answer. None, except a cap.

Question. A glazed cap?

Answer. Yes, sir; with "Native Son of the South." I have two or three of them over home now.

Question. When was it that this uniform was adopted?

Answer. It never was adopted as I know of.

Question. How did you all agree to wear that kind of a cap?

Answer. I told you I just went into the meeting with these men. I was considered, without ever going in or joining, or anything of the sort, a Native Son of the South, because I was a native son of the South.

Question. Where did the caps come from; they did not fall from the clouds?

Answer. No, sir; I reckon they were made.

Question. Who sent for them?

Answer. I do not know?

Question. Did you buy yours?

Answer. No, sir.

Question. Where did you get it?

Answer. In Columbus here.

Question. Who from?

Answer. I just went around in a drug-store here and got it.

Question. Did the drug-store man keep them for sale?

Answer. No, sir.

Question. Did he give this to you?

Answer. No, sir; I just took it.

Question. Did you ask him for the privilege?

Answer. No, sir.

Question. You took it without any leave?

Answer. Yes, sir.

Question. Who was the man who kept the store—the druggist?

Answer. Senator, don't; don't ask me about a little trivial thing; don't. If you want to have fun out of me don't make me tell such a thing.

The CHAIRMAN. I never was more serious in my life. I want to learn about the Native Sons of the South.

The WITNESS. I am a Native Son of the South. They are men who were born and reared here, and are identified with us. They proposed to band together as a political organization, as democrats or republicans would do, and nominate candidates and vote for them, and elect them if they could.

Question. Do you let radicals in?

Answer. Would we? We would let in anybody that would vote with us.

Question. Let scalawags in?

Answer. Yes, sir, if they would turn.

Question. Do what?

Answer. If they would get to be what we do not consider a scalawag. Of course they would have to.

Question. They would have to subscribe to this platform of principles.
Answer. Yes, sir.

By Mr. RICE:

Question. Would you let carpet-baggers in?
Answer. No; because they were not native sons of the South. You all understand what it was; we wanted to vote the freedmen; we were honest in it.

By the CHAIRMAN:

Question. You let the colored men in?
Answer. O, yes, sir; of course.
Question. You all stood on a platform of equality in the lodge—the members of that order?
Answer. Yes, sir. One man had the same voice as another. We were here in open conference, or whatever you call it. We met in the court-house.
Question. I understand your demonstrations are rather public. I have seen your caps, and want to know where these caps came from, and how you came to find out that this particular cap was at the drug-store in Columbus?
Answer. I just saw them there, and went around and took one.
Question. You did not know they were there before you saw them?
Answer. No, sir.
Question. Were there any left after you got yours?
Answer. I believe there were some left.
Question. How large a package?
Answer. But few of them.
Question. Who handed it to you?
Answer. Nobody.
Question. How did you find out about it?
Answer. I just saw it. It was lying up on the side of the house, on the base-shelf.

By Mr. RICE:

Question. Did you take more than one?
Answer. No, sir; I thought that was enough.
Question. I thought you said you had two or three of them.
Answer. I have a brother-in-law. I got one for him at home; and this body-servant of mine, I got one for him; he is entitled to one.

By the CHAIRMAN:

Question. Your Native Sons of the South get together once in a while and talk over their matters?
The WITNESS. Political matters?
The CHAIRMAN. No; other matters or affairs of their society.
The WITNESS. O, yes.
Question. Where do they meet?
Answer. We have not met since the election. There is no object now.
Question. Before the election where did you meet?
Answer. In my store-house; in a house I have rented that belongs to another party. I rented it to another party and they keep it as a grocery, and I go and take the crowd, without anybody's consent, in there.
Question. You always know when you are going to meet together?
Answer. We know. I would go down and say to six or eight men, "Boys, let's go and fix up and see if we can't have a barbecue," or "Who will favor it?" This was done just before the election.
Question. There are no secrets among you are there?
Answer. I do not know whether there are or not. I never took any oath. They never gave any to me. I did not get up the organization at all.
Question. Did anybody ever tell you he took an oath?
Answer. No, sir. I reckon they did though.
Question. You reckon they did take an oath?
Answer. Yes, sir.
Question. But no one ever told you so?
Answer. No, sir.
Question. What makes you suppose so?
Answer. I suppose that in getting up an organization of that sort they would.

By Mr. RICE:

Question. Did you ever administer an oath?
Answer. No, sir.

By the CHAIRMAN:

Question. Did you never hear it administered?

Answer. Yes, sir.

Question. Will you repeat that oath?

Answer. "I do solemnly and sincerely promise and swear that"—well, I do not know how I can do that. I suppose if I have promised these men not to tell—but I did not tell them I would not.

Question. But you have never sworn you would not tell it?

Answer. But, if they saw proper to let me in there without that, ought I to do it? That is coming to honesty; and if it comes to that, I would go anywhere in the world—to Oxford, or anywhere. You see I can't do that. If it is wrong I would like to know. If it is not wrong I will tell you. All the negroes and men know it; all the freedmen that belong to it know it. I will tell you them and you can send for them. I am willing to make that much public.

The CHAIRMAN. I do not want to press you, if you think it would be an unwarrantable breach of confidence.

The WITNESS. I think every man would feel as I do; I think every man would assume it would be blazoned to the world—written in letters as big as the world. But I do not know that I have the right to tell it. I can tell you men who can tell you. I think every man in it is willing to let eveything that is done in it be as light as day.

The CHAIRMAN. If you state to the committee that you have scruples about stating the oath I will not press it.

The WITNESS. My scruples are to this effect: that, whereas I would be willing to have everything done by the Native Sons of the South known to the whole world, I do not know whether my friends would like me to state it.

Question. I will not press you further on that. I wish to ask you one further question. Certain men have been arrested for the murder of this man Lee, or at least charged with a riot if not with the murder?

Answer. Yes, sir.

Question. Some are in jail, are they not?

Answer. I do not know. I have understood so.

Question. Have some been discharged upon bail?

Answer. I do not know.

Question. Have some been released entirely who were originally arrested?

Answer. I understand so. I know this because some were taken over there.

Question. Did you ever tell any of these persons arrested that if they would be released you could procure their release if they would join the Native Sons of the South?

Answer. No, sir, because we never had a meeting of the Native Sons of the South since that happened.

Question. But have you ever given any encouragement to them in any way?

Answer. No, sir.

Question. In that way?

Answer. No, sir.

Question. Have you ever sought to proselyte men to become members of that society?

Answer. No, sir.

Question. Never asked anybody to join it?

Answer. No, sir.

Question. Never recommended it to anybody?

Answer. I may have spoken of it as a good thing, and said that it was. The objects of it, so far as I understood, were quite as good, and the same thing as the republican party, with the exception that we preferred men here to hold our offices who were natives. That is all the difference.

Question. Your organization, I suppose, embraced none but democrats and conservatives?

Answer. O, yes, it does. It is the republican party divested of the element we call carpet-baggers.

Question. So that it is comprehensive enough to embrace the whole native community?

Answer. Yes, sir.

Question. Of all shades of political opinion?

Answer. Yes, sir.

Question. It is a general combination against carpet-baggers?

Answer. No, it is not, only this. I would not like to be understood by you gentlemen so.

Question. One further question. You have said, I believe, that you were a "Native Son." Were you in the army during the war?

Answer. Yes, sir.

Question. What was your rank in the confederate army?

Answer. I was a surgeon.

By Mr. RICE:

Question. Was the coroner's jury all composed of members of this order of which you spoke in the Lee case?

Answer. There was not any member of that order that I know of.
Question. On the jury?
Answer. No, sir.

COLUMBUS, MISSISSIPPI, *November* 15, 1871.

RUFUS B. STONE sworn and examined.

By the CHAIRMAN:

Question. Where do you reside?
Answer. At Aberdeen, Mississippi.
Question. How long have you lived there?
Answer. I have lived at Aberdeen two or three months.
Question. Where did you live before?
Answer. At Okolona, Chickasaw County, Mississippi. I have lived there two or three years. I have been nearly three years in the State.
Question. What has been your occupation?
Answer. I have been in the internal-revenue service as chief clerk in the assessor's office, and assistant assessor of internal revenue of the first division, third district.
Question. State what knowledge or information you have as to the burning of any school-houses either in Monroe or Chickasaw or any other counties.
Answer. Well, in the county of Chickasaw I remember there were a good number—several burned down, but I do not remember the number. I knew the circumstances of perhaps half a dozen; one at Prairie Mound, one at Palo Alto. That at Palo Alto was burned within the last month. In the county of Monroe there were twenty-six school-houses burned.
Question. Twenty-six burned in Monroe County?
Answer. Yes, sir.
Question. Within what space of time?
Answer. Well, from the 1st of February, I presume, until the 1st of June, perhaps. I do remember exactly the dates. It was during that period; during the spring of 1871.
Question. Do you know of any other county than Chickasaw and Monroe in which any school-houses have been burned?
Answer. Yes, sir, in the county of Lee, a school-house in Tupelo, the county-seat, where the colored school was taught by Miss Davis, was burned about a month ago, I think, or six weeks ago.
Question. Speaking of Miss Davis, are you personally acquainted with her?
Answer. Yes, sir.
Question. How long have you known her?
Answer. Ever since I have been in the State—the last two or three years.
Question. It has been charged by certain parties here that she was not a women of good character for virtue or for truth and veracity. You may state what her character is.
Answer. Her character is excellent so far as I know. I do not think there are any grounds at all for any such statement as that. She has the reputation among all—everybody in fact that I know with whom she is acquainted—of being a lady of excellent character.
Question. Is her character good for chastity?
Answer. I think it is.
Question. Is it good for truth and veracity?
Answer. I think it is.
Question. You may state whether certain parties up in that neighborhood are very bitter against her.
Answer. Yes, sir; they are.
Question. Do you know out of what that bitterness grows?
Answer. From the fact that she is teaching, and has been teaching, a colored school there, and that she is the only person there, male or female, who advocates republican principles; she is the support of the republican party in that county—the nucleus around which the colored people gather.
Question. She is also postmistress, is she not?
Answer. Yes, sir.
Question. You have spoken of one school-house in Lee County, at Tupelo, burned. Do you know of any other school-houses than those you have mentioned as having been burned?
Answer. I do not know that I think of any now.
Question. I will ask you to state what you know, if anything, of any teachers of schools in Monroe County having been threatened or warned to leave or having received Ku-Klux letters.

Answer. I know that all the teachers east of the Tombigbee River, which runs through the middle of the county, or near it, were warned to leave the county and leave their schools, and threatened in case they should not leave. Several teachers I know came to Okolona from their several schools in the county, Okolona being within a few miles of the county line. Mr. Richardson was one; he taught in the northern part of the county; Mr. Gessner and Miss Allan. There were other teachers there. Those teachers came there as a place of refuge. Other teachers sought refuge in Aberdeen. Mr. Waterbury and, in fact, all the teachers of colored schools in the county were warned to leave, and did leave their schools, and their schools were broken up, except the one at Aberdeen—the Union school.

Question. What, if anything, do you know of a Ku-Klux visit paid Miss Allan, the lady you have already spoken of?

Answer. She was visited by a band of masked men at night. It was about 2 o'clock at night. They rapped at the door and demanded entrance, and finally—she had retired, of course—she struck a light and let them in, and, I think, some half a dozen came in the room.

Mr. BLAIR. She gave an account of that herself.

The CHAIRMAN. I will not press you for the particulars of that, inasmuch as she has testified of that herself. Do you know personally anything of the whipping that was administered by disguised men to Colonel Huggins?

Answer. I of course only know what I have heard—not personally.

Question. What is your information as to the cause of that whipping—what the crowd of disguised men said they were whipping him for?

Answer. Well, I think that the cause was double perhaps; that is, that it had reference to the fact that he was county superintendent, and that he was a leader in the radical party of the county—the so-called radical party—the republican party of the county; that they were opposed to the free-school system, and were indignant because taxes were levied upon them to support colored schools in the county.

Question. When you speak of "them," whom do you refer to as the persons opposed to the establishment of commonschools?

Answer. I referred then directly to the party administering the whipping.

Question. What has been, or was at the time the schools were inaugurated, the position of the white residents of the county generally in reference to the school system?

Answer. I think that they were opposed to it. That was the prevailing sentiment.

Question. Have they become more reconciled to it since?

Answer. I do not think they have.

Question. What is the feeling in that community in relation to colored schools?

Answer. They are opposed to their support by the people of the county by taxation. That is the prevailing sentiment; of course, there are exceptions.

Question. Are you acquainted with General Gholson and with Colonel Reynolds, both of them attorneys and counselors at law in Aberdeen?

Answer. Just a passing acquaintance; I am not intimately acquainted with either of them that is, personally; of course, I know them by reputation.

Question. What are understood to be their sentiments in relation to the administration of the Government and in reference to the measures of Congress generally and in relation to the South?

Answer. I do not know that their views have changed materially from those that they held during the war, in which they supported the confederate government. In fact I know it is said that General Gholson, when elected speaker of the house of representatives of this State, in 1865, when he raised and unfurled the United States flag, as was customary at the opening of the session, in making his remarks stated that it was not from any respect for the Government, or for that emblem, or the Government which he represented, that he performed that ceremony, but because he was compelled to by the custom.

Question. You have understood that he made that remark?

Answer. That is currently reported.

By Mr. BLAIR:

Question. Who told you that he made that remark?

Answer. A good many people. I have heard it remarked by a good many people. Colonel Shattuck was one. He is the assessor of internal revenue for this district. I think he is the first man who ever mentioned it to me, as he was living in the State before I was. Since then I have heard it spoken of by a great many people.

Question. Did Shattuck say he heard it?

Answer. I think not. I think he was not in the legislature. I think that no man acquainted with the public history of the State during that time will doubt it though, because it was a well-known fact.

Question. How do you know it to be a fact? Did you ever hear a man who heard him say that repeat it as coming from him?

Answer. I do not know. I never thought to question it, because it was generally admitted to be true.

Question. By whom?

Answer. By public men generally; intelligent men, acquainted with affairs.

Question. Give us the names of some of the public men who admitted it to be true or stated it to be true.

Answer. I do not remember the names, because I never thought to remember them, but I have heard it mentioned on several occasions.

By the CHAIRMAN:

Question. What is their attitude and feeling toward northern men who come into Mississippi and settle, so far as you have observed?

Answer. I think that it is one of direct opposition. They are not friendly to northern men. I would say that especially in respect to General Gholson. I am not so well acquainted with Colonel Reynolds. I would not say that in reference to him.

Question. Are they generally the counsel selected by men who are charged with being Ku-Klux?

Answer. Yes, sir; I think thay are. General Gholson's services have been sought and he has volunteered them on every occasion, I think, when there was any necessity for it. I know that a few days ago, when parties were arrested in Aberdeen and taken to Corinth, he called on them twice. There were two different parties arrested under the enforcement act.

Question. Is it your understanding that they are not cordial or friendly disposed toward men from the North who have come down into this part of Mississippi and settled?

Answer. Yes, sir.

Question. What, if anything, do know of the persecution of one Emmons?

Answer. He was living in Chickasaw County, about six or eight miles from Okolona, teaching a colored school. He came from Chicago with the intention of locating at Meridian in some mercantile pursuit, but met with some losses on the way and stopped at Okolona and engaged to teach a colored school there. After he had been there a week or two he was waited on by two or three different committees of the citizens living in the neighborhood and requested to leave, and, refusing to leave, in a few days they sent him a written notice signed by Ku-Klux, the organization, chief of the Ku-Klux Klan, or something of the kind. They sent him several such communications by hand and by leaving them at his house, and afterward they came to his house and came into his yard. They came to his house at night, and he had a guard of colored men in and about the house; as soon as they learned it they beat a retreat, of course, and run away. Well, he was persecuted in that way for some time; in fact, the feeling was one of intense bitterness toward him throughout the whole community. I remember on one occasion, when it was necessary for him to go to the county-seat, Houston, to procure some school-books, a party of desperadoes there came upon him, and dragged him into a store and knocked him and brandished a knife over his head and threatened him, and told him they would kill him unless he left the county, but he finally escaped from them by dodging out of the back door of the store and got away without being hurt.

Question. Did you learn this from him?

Answer. Yes, sir; he came in one day with a bullet-hole through his hat, which, he said, was fired on the way from Houston to his home or to the school-house. He was so persecuted finally that he thought it best to leave, and did move to another portion of the county, where, I think, he still lives.

Question. Do you know one Woodmansee?

Answer. No, sir; I am not personally acquainted with him; I know him by sight.

Question. What have you known or heard of the efforts made against him in the late canvass?

Answer. I have not heard of any efforts against him in the canvass, but I have heard of his making threats in the late canvass.

Question. Was he a candidate for nomination?

Answer. I do not know that he was; I do not think he was.

Question. Was he a speaker during the recent canvass?

Answer. Yes, sir.

Question. A democratic speaker?

Answer. Yes, sir; he canvassed the county.

Question. Did you hear him make any speeches?

Answer. No, sir.

Question. Have you been informed of the tenor of any of the speeches he made?

Answer. Yes, sir.

Question. What threats have you understood he made?

Answer. It was made the 4th of November, I think—just three or four days before the election. A meeting was held on the plantation of Mr. Samuel Patterson, in the edge of Chickasaw or Monroe County, near the county line—I am not certain in which county, but it was while he was making a canvass in Chickasaw County. There was in attendance, of course, a large assemblage of colored men, and he told them this—the language he used, as I learned it from ten or a dozen different colored men who came into the office at Aberdeen, was substantially like this: "I dare you to vote the republican ticket. If the radical ticket carries the county of Chickasaw at the election there will be Ku-Klux at every bush, and I will be one of them." He says, "You need not think you can vote the radical ticket without my knowing it, for I shall be at the box at Buena Vista and Egypt and Okolona, and I shall know every man who does it and mark the colored men as they come up and vote the radical ticket, and if the radical ticket carries the election in Chickasaw the bullets will fly to the hearts of the colored men who take part with them or vote the radical ticket." That was the language substantially.

Question. You say that was told you by several colored men who said they had heard the speech?

Answer. Yes, sir.

Question. Who is this Woodmansee that makes such bloody declarations?

Answer. He is a physician living at Houston; he formerly lived at Monroe.

Question. That is the way the speech was reported to you?

Answer. Yes, sir; I would not undertake to report it in that way if it had not been reported to me by so many different parties who I knew had not been together or conspired.

Question. Do you say the man was sober?

Answer. Yes, sir; he made speeches in other portions of the county afterward and before of similar tenor.

Question. As you are informed?

Answer. Yes, sir.

Question. He was advocating the democratic ticket?

Answer. Yes, sir; he spoke on that occasion with the candidate for the State senate, the democratic candidate at that place.

Question. What, if anything, do you know of the shooting at Gardner?

Answer. There was nothing masked or perhaps of a Ku-Klux nature about that, except Gardner was known to be a republican, and he is carrying on the plantation of Captain Shattuck, who was candidate for chancery clerk on the republican ticket in Chickasaw County; and I just got a letter a few days ago from one of the senators from the twenty-fourth, or Chickasaw district, stating that, as Gardner was riding from Palo Alto out of town, a man stepped out of the door of a house and fired a lot of buckshot out of a double-barreled gun. None of them hit him, but they fell around him. There was no provocation further than his well-known political opinions.

Question. What if anything do you know of the whipping of Aleck Willis? Have you heard of that?

Answer. Yes, sir.

Question. I will not ask you to go into details in these cases, because the committee have heard of that before. Have you heard of the murder of Jack Dupree?

Answer. Yes, sir;

Question. Have you heard of the murder of Aleck Page?

Answer. Yes, sir.

Question. And of Tom Hornberger?

Answer. Yes, sir.

Question. You may state to the committee what you know about the murder of Hornberger—what information you have on this subject.

Answer. It is very limited. It does not go much beyond the fact that he was taken out and murdered by a body of masked men. He lived about five or six miles of Okolona, in Monroe County.

Question. Have you heard also of the murder of Abram Wamble?

Answer. Yes, sir.

Question. Have you heard also of the murder of Dock Hendricks?

Answer. Yes, sir.

Question. Were those murders all in Monroe County or in the edge of Lee?

Answer. Yes, sir; those were in Monroe County on the edge of Lee.

Question. What do you know of the firing of the office of Colonel Shattuck, assessor of internal revenue?

Answer. It occurred in this way: The deputy United States marshal came into the county to make some arrests under the enforcement act, and did make some arrests. Five or six persons he arrested at Buena Vista and that neighborhood, the center of the county, and returned with them to Okolona, which is on the railroad, and lodged them in a dwelling-house which was then vacant and which belonged to Colonel Shattuck, the assessor. Feeling was very much excited over these arrests during the day, and a good many people gathered in from the country, so that, in the opinion of Colonel Shattuck, and the deputy marshal, and his assessors, and others, it was thought probable an assault might be made to rescue the prisoners, and an additional guard was placed there. In fact, Colonel Shattuck himself and the assistant deputy marshal and two or three other men slept in the house where the prisoners were, and in the night—perhaps not later than 10 o'clock; I am not sure of the time—the assessor's office was set on fire under the porch, the evident object being to draw out the guard, and McCoy especially, for the purpose, as it was thought, of killing McCoy and releasing the prisoners, as McCoy had become very obnoxious to a certain class of people from the fact that he was very efficient in making arrests under the enforcement act.

Question. Did you see the marks of the fire afterward on the building?

Answer. No, sir; I have not been at the place.

Question. This is your information on the subject?

Answer. Yes, sir; I was informed to that effect by Colonel Shattuck himself and by the clerk in the office and several other parties and McCoy.

Question. The testimony of General Gholson is that he was informed that the prisoners were confined in Colonel Shattuck's, the assessor's, office?

Answer. No, sir; that is not so.

By Mr. BLAIR:

Question. You say that is not his information?

Answer. No, sir; I referred to the fact; that is not the fact.

Question. What do you know about the fact; you have not been there?

Answer. I suppose Colonel Shattuck would know the fact as well as any one else, as he not only had charge of the office, but was on guard over the prisoners, and the prisoners were, he says, lodged in his dwelling-house.

Question. And he knew also that it was the evident design to set fire to one house in which the prisoners were not, so as to kill certain men and release the prisoners?

Answer. Yes, sir.

Question. The evident design?

Answer. I think so. I do not know what other object they could have. They certainly were not maliciously disposed toward Colonel Shattuck; in fact, he is quite popular in the county and with people at Okolona, and is respected by all classes.

Question. How many school-houses did you say were burned in Monroe?

Answer. Twenty-six. I am informed by the county superintendent. I do not know personally the number.

Question. Who is the county superintendent?

Answer. Colonel Allen P. Huggins.

Question. Are you not mistaken about that?

Answer. No, sir; I am not mistaken as to my information.

Question. Colonel Huggins said nothing about twenty-six school-houses being burned here on his oath a day or two ago, and he was very prompt to state about all that were burned too.

Answer. I do not know anything about that. I am very positive that that is the information he has given me. Personally I know of quite a number of them being burned.

Question. Which ones?

Answer. The one near Okolona especially, within two miles or two miles and a half, near the plantation of Captain J. W. Noe; it was not on his plantation, but in the neighborhood.

Question. What others do you know?

Answer. There were others in five or six miles of Okolona, east in the county.

Question. Colonel Huggins, when he was here, testified to the burning of three only. That was all he knew about them. When did he give you this information?

Answer. Only a few days ago.

Question. Before he came down here.

Answer. No, sir; since. I think he mentioned the fact that he did not think to speak of it when he was before the committee. He did not think to speak of it when he was on this subject of burning the school-houses.

Question. How many do you know of your own knowledge?

Answer. In the county of Monroe?

Question. Yes.

Answer. I could not say, because there was—at the time I never supposed, perhaps, the public attention would be called so directly to it, and did not make a note of it, either in mind or any other way; but I know I heard of them occasionally, now and then, schools being burned, and I should think perhaps ten or a dozen in all.

Question. Between these periods of time you spoke of?

Answer. Yes, sir.

Question. Between February and June?

Answer. Yes, sir.

Question. You were not at that time living in Monroe?

Answer. I was living at Okolona, within two miles of the county line.

Question. Who told you the reason for whipping Huggins?

Answer. I do not know that anybody in particular told me. I think I have heard

Colonel Shattuck mention what was said to him, from which I drew that inference, as well as from the sentiment of the county and of the people, the well-known opposition to the free-school system and the bitter opposition to the republican party and republicans generally, especially northern men, and particularly on the eastern side of the river, east of the river Tombigbee.

Question. Speaking of General Gholson and Mr. Reynolds, you say you do not know that their views have changed since the war?

Answer. Yes sir; that is, with reference to the Government and the "lost cause."

Question. What do you know about their views; you say you are not intimate with them?"

Answer. No, sir; I do not know from any other source than general report and from the fact that I did mention his conduct in performing the ceremony of raising the flag at the opening of the legislature, and I know the fact that General Gholson has been considered the head and front of the democratic party in Monroe County, and perhaps in the State. My information or opinion in reference to him is formed partly from the fact that it is the general understanding that he is at the head of, or was at the head of, the Ku-Klux organization in the county.

Question. That is the general understanding, is it?

Answer. I think so. I have heard so. I have heard it mentioned by several men.

Question. Mention what parties among whom that is the general understanding?

Answer. Well, among members of the republican party, certainly, in that county and vicinity.

Question. That he is recognized as the head of the democratic party in the county, and of the most bitter——

Answer. One of the most bitter toward northern men, northern institutions and republican principles, and the General Government that there is in the State. There is no question about that.

Question. He is recognized in that way among republicans?

Answer. Yes, sir.

Question. I suppose you do not associate enough among the democrats to know what their sentiments are on the subject?

Answer. The sentiment in the country rather bars me from much social privileges with the people, but then, business has brought me in contact with them more or less every day, and, living with them, I know something of their feelings and opinions and belief.

Question. Did you ever hear General Gholson express the opinions you attribute to him?

Answer. I never had the satisfaction of hearing him make a speech or say anything in public.

Question. Then you do not purport to give anything you have ever heard him say?

Answer. No, sir; nothing at all.

Question. You only give the gossip of the people you associate with?

Answer. I would rather object to the term gossip.

Question. You have not even been in company with General Gholson?

Answer. Not very often; only occasionally on the car or in the street, or somewhere. I am not personally acquainted with him.

Question. He is considered a man of character, is he not?

Answer. So far as I know.

Question. You say he is looked up to in the community?

Answer. Certainly he is; he is a very popular man with a class.

Question. He is a man who has held high position among his fellow-citizens?

Answer. Yes, sir; I understand he has been in office for the last thirty or forty years, most of the time. I do not know; that is what I understand.

Question. And you say he is regarded as the head of the Ku-Klux there?

Answer. Yes, sir.

Question. Have you heard of any raids that he has been out on?

Answer. No, sir. The people that go out on raids are very careful not to let their identity be known, so far as my observation extends.

Question. It seems that the gentleman has not been able to keep his secret from you about his being at the head of the Ku-Klux, though?

Answer. Well, that is his misfortune.

Question. It must be a very great misfortune to him?

Answer. I think it is; he is known so generally, as I derive my information from the common opinion of the community. I think it is a misfortune for any one to be known by such a character.

Question. And you pretend to say there is any such common opinion in that county?

Answer. Yes, sir; I think there is.

Question. Can you name any respectable man that ever told you anything of the sort?

Answer. I know, as I said before, that people of the opposite party recognized him as such; members of the republican party in that county, and in Chickasaw, where I have lived.

Question. Can you give the name of any respectable man who ever told you so?

Answer. I do not know that there is any; that I ever heard any man who does know that he is so and so, because it would be presumed that it is beyond the means of their attaining very readily as to who is at the head of the band, or who was the originator of it, but I have heard it stated by responsible and reliable men that he was considered so, and that in their opinion he was, or had a hand in originating it, and was at the head of the organization in the county and vicinity.

Question. Who were those men?

The WITNESS. Is it necessary for me to name them; is it required?

Mr. BLAIR. I have asked you the question—you can name them or not.

The WITNESS. They are prominent members of the republican party in the counties of Monroe and Chickasaw.

Mr. BLAIR. That is not giving us their names.

The WITNESS. Is it required?

Mr. BLAIR. I have asked you for their names.

Mr. RICE. If you have any reason why you do not want to mention them, you can state it.

The WITNESS. I should prefer not to mention names. If you urge it, however, I will state the names of the prominent members of the republican party in those two counties.

Mr. BLAIR. Who told you so?

The WITNESS. From whom I derived the information.

Mr. BLAIR. Who gave you this information?

The WITNESS. Yes. I would not, unless it was absolutely required and unavoidable, state the name of any man who gave me any such information in regard to anybody, but I would simply state that fact, that it is a common opinion among those people—among the leaders of the republican party, to say no further. If not of the people generally, it certainly is of the leaders of the republican party.

Mr. BLAIR. You do not feel inclined to give their names?

The WITNESS. No, sir; I would not want to do that. I would, if it be any satisfaction, give the names of the prominent men of the party in those two counties, and simply state that that is the belief and opinion which is held among such men.

Mr. BLAIR. The question I asked you was who told you that?

Mr. RICE. I think he ought to be excused from stating, as he requests.

The CHAIRMAN. If the disclosure of their names would bring those gentlemen into trouble with a gentleman of the prominence of General Gholson in the county, I do not think the witness should be required to give their names. He can exercise his opinion, however.

The WITNESS. I should prefer not to, unless the circumstances required.

The CHAIRMAN. I wish to express my opinion of this qualification—if the disclosure would bring them into trouble, or expose them to persecution.

The WITNESS. I have no doubt but if these men were brought before the committee they would confirm the statement I have made themselves.

Mr. BLAIR. It is a great pity we are deprived of their evidence.

The WITNESS. In fact, if the question should be pressed, I do not know that I could state any individual, perhaps I could, who had told me on any certain, particular occasion, that such was the fact, but yet I know that all these people, or a good many of them, have expressed the opinion that such was the fact, and have expressed it to me.

By Mr. BLAIR:

Question. You say General Gholson volunteered to defend the Ku-Klux prisoners?

Answer. So I am informed.

Question. He states that he did not; that he was employed, and a fee given him.

Answer. That alters my opinion, then; but it does not change the fact that that was my information. It probably was not so, and he probably did not volunteer, but that was, the information I had, and I think it was the deputy marshal told me so.

Question. I just wanted to find out the state of your opinion.

Answer. Yes; it was nothing further than that. I would not lay any particular stress upon that, because I do not know it myself. My information probably was not reliable, and could not be, under the circumstances, but that was the understanding which I had, and other parties had.

Question. Who was it fired at Gardner, at he went through Palo Alto?

Answer. I do not know the name, although the person is named and he perhaps is arrested by this time; at any rate the matter was referred at once to the civil authorities. Gardner had gone to Okolona at the time I received the information, to present the matter to the sheriff there, I presume.

Question. Did Gardner tell you about it?

Answer. No, sir; Senator Abbott wrote me the letter containing the information.

Question. Where does he live?

Answer. He lives at Palo Alto, in about a mile of the place upon which Gardner lives.

By the CHAIRMAN:

Question. Was Gardner a republican?

Answer. Yes, sir.

Question. Was he obnoxious on account of his political sentiments in that community?

Answer. I do not know that he was. He was a northern man, and the man who owned the plantation which he was conducting was a republican, and, more than that, was a candidate on the republican ticket for chancery clerk of the county.

Question. Who was the man who fired upon him?

Answer. I do not remember the name; in fact, the name was not given to me, but the fact stated that the man was known.

By Mr. BLAIR:

Question. Did you hear the speech of this Woodmansee?

Answer. No, sir; I did not.

Question. Did you ever hear him speak?

Answer. I do not think I ever heard him make any public speech. I did not say anything about one case that I think you have no testimony about—Tobe Hutchinson.

By the CHAIRMAN:

Question. State what you know about that.

Answer. He was taken, I am informed, out of his house at night, by a band of masked men, and nothing was heard from him for a long time afterward; but within the last three or four days his body has been found lying on the edge of the river, with his throat cut. He was taken out about the 3d of November, I think.

Question. Of this present month?

Answer. Yes, sir; and some three or four colored men came to Aberdeen to get assistance in finding the body. They stated the fact there that they were afraid to go out to hunt for the body. The colored people there, his friends and relatives, were afraid to make any search whatever for the body. He was living on the edge of Lee County, in the fork of the river, the Bigbee Fork, as it is called, where Old Town Creek and the Talipanila unite to form the Tombigbee River. He was the only colored hand, I think, on the plantation, and the information we have on that subject is that he was taken out by the masked men who came on the plantation, and told his employer to bring out Hutchinson. This white man told colored men of it, and they told of it at Aberdeen. They said that he refused to bring him out, and threatened them if they did not go away; but they came in and took him out, and carried him away.

Question. Tobe Hutchinson was a colored man?

Answer. Yes, sir.

Question. Do you know what his offense was, or what they charged him with?

Answer. No, sir.

Question. Did you understand how numerous this body of disguised men was?

Answer. I think I heard it stated that there were about ten or a dozen of them, not a large body; that is my impression.

Question. He was killed the night of the 3d of November?

Answer. Yes, sir; as near as I remember.

Question. And his body has been discovered only within three or four days?

Answer. Yes, sir; they were afraid, as they stated, to go and hunt for the body, and no one else went to hunt, and they came to Aberdeen for assistance. They thought they could get troops to go help hunt the body, but the authorities did not then give them any assistance; but by some means they accidentally came upon the body the other day.

Question. Is there any other case in your mind about which you have not been questioned?

Answer. Yes, sir.

By Mr. BLAIR:

Question. Whose place was this?

Answer. I have forgotten the man's name. It is just my impression that the name was Marshall, but I am not sure about it, and I cannot give it as testimony. There were a good many cases of whipping, and quite a number of murders, which happened during that space of time, and which I took no notice of, and in fact have no remembrance of the names now, and the details of the facts, but there was a good deal of riding by masked men, and whipping and murder in Chickasaw, as well as in Monroe, especially up the line of the railroad, in Chickasaw, back of the Loctanoochee Creek, which divides the county. Beyond the creek the contour of the country is different. It is a hilly country, and the population is of a different class. There was a great deal of whipping and murdering and riding of masked men in that neighborhood, and school-houses burned; in fact it has been considered a lawless portion of the county and of the country.

By the CHAIRMAN:

Question. How long a period of time have outrages of that character that you have described been going on?

Answer. They were especially prevalent during the spring of 1871, but more or less it has been going on ever since the spring of 1869.

Question. Have the perpetrators of these outrages you have described committed by men in disguise been detected in any cases you know of?

Answer. Not in any instances I know of.

Question. There have been some arrrests, I understand, and cases now pending in the United States court?

Answer. Yes, sir.

Question. But none have been convicted as yet?

Answer. No, sir.

Question. You may state what has been the effect of these outrages upon the colored people as to alarming them.

Answer. It has terrified them. Well, at that time, during the spring of 1871, the terror was universal throughout those two counties of Monroe and Chickasaw; it was a perfect reign of terror. The people, white and black both, slept with their arms close by them, in a good many instance. In fact the leading men among the colored population, and especially those known as prominent republicans and leaders, were obliged, or thought they were obliged, to leave their houses at night and sleep elsewhere; and some of them were guarded; as for one instance I know, in the case of several men in Chickasaw, they were guarded by fifty men or a hundred or one hundred and twenty-five men every night for a long time.

Question. Do you know of any outrages of this kind that you have described having been committed by disguised men upon democrats?

Answer. No, sir; I do not. There is one case I would like to mention.

Question. What case is that?

Answer. Which occurred at the time—in fact, about a year ago last July. There was nothing masked about it; it was done in broad, open daylight. It was the murder of Drury Bailey. He was a colored man, a merchant there, a member of the leading colored mercantile house in Okolona, and very prominent in the town and county as a leader among the colored people; of pronounced republican opinions, a very firm, decided man, an intelligent man. He was very obnoxious to those white people who belonged to the democratic party, because, by his efforts in great part in the county, the republican ticket was elected in 1869, some time during the summer. He had been threatened very frequently since the election. He was obliged to sleep out of his house, and, in fact, attacked on several occasions, with intent to kill, I should think. Weights were thrown at him, and he was clubbed, &c., until one day in the summer—I think it was in July—he was walking from his store to his house, about sundown, with his wife by his side, on his arm, and, in the main street of Okolona, just as he reached a corner where he was to turn to go to his house not far distant, a man stepped out from a corner and came up to him and drew his pistol and shot him, and instantly he fell dead. No arrest was made. The colored people gathered in a large body and surrounded the house where he was supposed to be—the house where he sought refuge from the colored people; but they were unable to take him. He got a horse and escaped over to Alabama, and there he was at the last accounts I heard from him. It was a case which excited a good deal of feeling there in the vicinity and county, because Drury Bailey was recognized as the leader of the colored people there.

By Mr. BLAIR:

Question. What was the name of the man that you say killed Drury Bailey?

Answer. Turner.

Question. What was his first name?

Answer. I am not positive, but I think it was Isaac. I would not say that, positively. His name was Turner.

Question. Was he recognized at the time?

Answer. O, yes, sir.

Question. Has there been any effort to get him returned from Alabama?

Answer. None that I know, only an effort of this nature, by a detective which Governor Alcorn sent out: I think he made some investigations, and tried to learn his whereabouts. I think, in fact, he did learn where he was. I think it was pretty well known where he was in Alabama. But he was unable to get the co-operation of the civil authorities to such an extent as to make the arrest.

Question. Did he ever get a paper from the governor of this State demanding the arrest?

Answer. Who ever get it?

Question. Did he ever get a requisition?

The WITNESS. The sheriff?

Mr. BLAIR. Yes.

Answer. I do not know; not that I know of; I do not remember it; he may have done so; if he has it slipped my mind, or I do not know anything about it.

Question. Where in Alabama did you understand the man was?

Answer. Near the line; I have forgotten the place now; I did know it at one time.

Question. Who gave you this information as to his whereabouts?

Answer. Well, it came to impress itself on my mind, now, from the investigation of the detective. He learned definitely where he was; in fact, as I remember, he did make an attempt to take him at one time, but he got away from him, over in Alabama. At any rate, he has a brother still living there in Okolona, or still had some months ago, who knew his whereabouts and, I suppose, communicated it to his friends, so that it was known there where he was.

Question. Turner's brother?

Answer. Yes, sir; that is my impression. He has a brother there, and he received letters from him, it was said. I am not personally acquainted with his brother, any more than a passing acquaintance.

Question. What was Turner's occupation?

Answer. I do not know if he had any. He was in, perhaps, a drinking-saloon there for a time. He was not a permanent resident of the place. He had a brother there, and was staying there for some time. It was said he had killed a man in Alabama, and came there to escape; that he ran away and came there.

Question. Did you ever see him yourself?

Answer. O, yes, sir.

Question. Had he ever had any quarrel with Bailey?

Answer. None that I know of; but when he did the shooting he stated that he was a damned radical, or something of that sort.

By the CHAIRMAN:

Question. I was about asking you if this Turner was a democrat?

Answer. O, yes, sir; that is, I do not know anything to the contrary; I would not say; I do not think he ever voted while he was there at Okolona. His brother is a democrat, and his friends; and, from the fact that he made that remark when shooting him, it left no doubt on my mind that he was a democrat.

The following communication was subsequently received from the foregoing witness:

"UNITED STATES INTERNAL REVENUE,
"ASSESSOR'S OFFICE, THIRD DISTRICT MISSISSIPPI,
"*Okolona, December* 25, 1871.

"SIR: In the testimony recently rendered before your honorable committee, at Columbus, Mississippi, I stated that I was informed, by the superintendent of education for Monroe County, that twenty-six school-houses were burned in that county during the winter of 1871. While still confident that such was my information, I am, upon consultation with Colonel Huggins, equally sure that it was his intention to represent only that 'twenty-six schools were *broken up*.' Is it not possible that my testimony may be accordingly corrected? I would especially desire that, if nothing more, this item may be altogether *stricken out*, leaving with reference to this matter only my statement that I had *personal knowledge* of ten or twelve school-houses having been burned in the counties of Monroe and Chickasaw.

"I have the honor to be, very respectfully, your obedient servant,
"R. B. STONE.

"Hon. D. D. PRATT, U. S. Senate,
"*Chairman Congressional Investigating Committee for Mississippi, Washington, D. C.*"

COLUMBUS, MISSISSIPPI, *November* 15, 1871.

E. RAYMOND BLISS sworn and examined.

By the CHAIRMAN:

Question. Where do you live?

Answer. I have lived three miles west of Artesia, in this county—Lowndes County.

Question. State to the committee whether you were a speaker upon the occasion of what is known as the Artesia riot, at the time a man by the name of Lee was killed.

Answer. I was, sir.

Question. Without going into the details of that affair, which have been gone over fully by several witnesses, you may come right to the point of what you were saying at the time you were interrupted, if you were interrupted at all, by this man Lee?

Answer. Well, sir, I could not remember the exact language that I made use of at the time he asked me the question which he did. I could repeat the language which I used at the time he fired the shot.

By Mr. BLAIR:

Question. At the time he what?

Answer. At the time the shot was fired, if you want me to give that language.

By the CHAIRMAN:

Question. What was the nature of his interruption?

Answer. He asked me, said he, "Are you a white man?" Those were the words he used. He asked it in a very insulting manner.

Question. Did you make any response to that inquiry?

Answer. No, sir.

Question. Did you check your speech for a moment?

Answer. No, sir; I do not think I did. I simply turned to look at the man to see who it was, and then turned and kept right on as though nothing had occurrred.

Question. Had you noticed him before in the crowd?

Answer. No, sir; I did not know he was there.

Question. Had you ever seen him before?

Answer. No, sir.

Question. After this interruption did you go on with your speech?

Answer. Yes, sir; as though nothing had happened, up to the time the shot was fired.

Question. Did you see that shot fired?

Answer. I saw the smoke from the pistol.

Question. Did you see a pistol?

Answer. No, sir, I did not see the pistol.

Question. How do you know the smoke proceeded from a pistol?

Answer. I could tell from the report that it was a pistol-shot. It was not more than ten feet from me when it was fired, and I turned instantly, and saw the smoke, and could tell it was a pistol, and not any other weapon.

Question. Did he stand on your left or right?

Answer. On my left.

Question. Did the smoke proceed from where he was standing?

Answer. Yes, sir, directly; just where the smoke was, I saw his back as he started and ran.

Question. Immediately afterward?

Answer. Immediately.

Question. Before there had been any movement in the crowd?

Answer. Yes, sir; the freedmen did not move then. It seems to me about five seconds after the smoke before there was any movement; then he turned to run.

Question. You say he was right where you saw the smoke?

Answer. Yes, sir, I state that positively; it was just as I could see.

Question. State what followed.

Answer. As he ran, what I saw was, he ran to the left, and turned to the right just at the outskirts of the crowd, and I stood in the buggy and looked over their heads, and from the direction he was I saw the flash of two pistol-shots, and then immediately behind him there were some five or six shots fired, and some one said the man had been killed.

Question. You say you heard two pistol-shots?

Answer. I not only heard, but saw them.

Question. Saw them after the first pistol-shot when he was near the stand?

Answer. Yes, sir; that was when he was near the outskirts of the crowd.

Question. Did you see the pistol-shot smoke where he was?

Answer. Yes, sir; just about where he was then, and where he was when he fell—where I found him when I went out.

Question. Were you in the buggy all this time?

Answer. Yes, sir.

Question. Where was Mr. Lewis; in the same buggy?

Answer. Yes, sir; he was sitting at my right when the shot was fired, and when the crowd ran after the man he rose and stood beside me, and halloed to them to come back.

Question. Had he sat beside you all the time you were speaking?

Answer. Yes, sir.

Question. Did you and Lewis ride together in this buggy, or in different buggies?

Answer. He rode in the buggy, and I on horseback, until we got there. I got off and we both took seat in the buggy.

Question. Dr. Brothers swears you and he rode in different carriages on the ground?

Answer. I rode on horseback.

Question. The doctor is mistaken?

Answer. He is mistaken if he says I rode in a vehicle.

Question. He states that he did not see Lewis sitting in the buggy with you when speaking.

Answer. He was sitting there, but I do not think Dr. Brothers—he might not have noticed him. I saw Dr. Brothers when he rode up on his horse. I do not suppose he had been there scarcely a minute when this thing took place—not much longer than that.

Question. You saw him when he rode up?

Answer. Yes, sir.

Question. Were there any horsemen between him and the stand where you were speaking?

Answer. Yes, sir; I think there were. There were a good many freedmen on horses and mules, and they were in front, and, I presume, some between him and the buggy.

Question. From his position and the intervening horsemen between him and the stand, and between him and Lee, do you think he was in a position to have seen distinctly what occurred at the time the pistol was fired?

Answer. No sir; I do not. I do not think he saw the man at all there. He could not from the position he was in, considering the fact also that it was just at dusk.

Question. He states that, though he did not see the white man, or Lee, or any white man, he saw the firing and the smoke before he heard the report, and that he saw it emanate, or proceed, from the barrel of a gun; that he saw about a foot of the barrel.

Answer. Well, I can state here what Dr. Brothers said on the ground, over this man's dead body.

Question. We want that.

Answer. When Major Lewis and myself got down from the buggy and went over to look at this man to see if we knew him, Dr. Brothers and a gentleman named Pierce came up at the same time, and Brothers said to Lewis, "I do not think that that man fiered that shot purposely. I saw the smoke from his pistol, but think he did it accidentally." Those are the words Dr. Brothers used over that man's body, and this man Pierce assented to it, and said the same, while I said that I thought at first that it proceeded from a musket, from the fact that there stood near this man a colored man with a gun, with the butt of it on the ground. But, as I stated, the moment I turned and saw the smoke just as it left the pistol—as you know how smoke does when it ascends in a sort of inverted cone—the smoke was higher than the muzzle of the man's gun and could not have come from it, and a little to the left. Those are the words Brothers used there. What he says since I do not know, but he said that over that man's body.

Question. When you saw the discharge from the pistol in what direction was it pointed?

Answer. The smoke, when I saw it, was ascending. I could not tell in what direction it may have been fired.

Question. You did not hear the whistling of the bullet?

Answer. No, sir; though a freedman in the buggy said he did at that time, though I have understood since that he denies it.

Question. What do you know, if anything, or what information have you of a pistol being picked up on the ground in the road or track which this man Lee took when he turned and fled?

Answer. I simply have heard that a freedman had found a pistol there—a freedman living in Oktibbeha County; but who he was I do not know. I did hear his name, but I have forgotten.

Question. Were you present at the coroner's inquest?

Answer. No, sir.

Question. You did not hear the evidence given?

Answer. No, sir; not at all.

Question. Have you heard that a colored man named Stewart, on that occasion, testified that he saw Lee fire the pistol?

Answer. Yes, sir; I believe I heard that. I have heard a great many freedmen say they saw the man when he drew his pistol. At least twenty of them say they saw the man coming in, holding his hand under his coat after he asked the question, and when I paid no attention to him that he held his hand under his coat, and that they saw him when he drew his pistol.

Question. Did you notice whether there were any saber-cuts on his person?

Answer. No, sir; I do not think there were, for this reason: when I stood in the buggy I saw a man strike with a stick, and I presume he struck this man. Several were standing around and I could not see where he struck, but, from the manner, I have no doubt he struck some man.

Question. There was a wound on his head?

Answer. I do not know; he was lying on his back when I saw him, and there was no mark of violence on his person. He had evidently had a clean shirt on, and it was as spotless as my own now. Some of the papers said they tramped on him, but that was false. His clothes were clean.

Question. There was no insult offered to his dead body?

Answer. No, sir; not a particle.

Question. You did not examine his head to see if there was any wound there?

Answer. No, sir; I did not.

By Mr. BLAIR:

Question. You say there was a man standing right by him with a gun in his hand?

Answer. Yes, sir; perhaps three or four feet from him, and perhaps three or four feet between him and the man killed.

By the CHAIRMAN:

Question. How near to your buggy, where you spoke, did this man Lee stand?

Answer. I suppose about ten feet; I cannot say exactly.

Question. How far from you did this Dr. Brothers sit upon his horse?

Answer. Well, he came in at the extreme right of the crowd. It was, at least, I should think, forty or fifty yards from the buggy, and this man was killed nearly the same distance the other side. Dr. Brothers was nearly one hundred yards from where the man was killed.

By Mr. BLAIR:

Question. Was Lee standing on the outskirts of the crowd?

Answer. At what time, general?

Question. At the time he interrupted you?

Answer. No, sir; he was standing within a very few feet of the buggy—ten feet, or less.

Question. Did he remain standing in that position?

Answer. Yes, sir; he remained there until I saw him start and run. He may have moved around a little, but not very much. I did not notice that he did.

Question. Was he surrounded by the negroes when you understood him to interrupt you?

Answer. Yes, sir; the negroes were quite a large crowd; he was, of course, at the inside of the crowd. I do not think there were many between him and the buggy, though. There may have been a few.

Question. There were a great many outside of him—beyond him?

Answer. Yes, sir; the crowd was mostly outside of him; we were right in the center of the crowd.

Question. Where was he when shot; was he outside of the crowd?

Answer. Yes sir; just about the outskirts of the crowd; he had just about reached the outside of the crowd.

Question. How did he make his way through this crowd?

Answer. Well, as I saw him run, he sort of threw up his hands, dodged right through and the whole crowd seemed to surge back and forth, and at first the negroes did not all of them seem to understand—those farthest back—what the matter was, and in the general movement he got out.

Question. You did not see any pistol in his hand?

Answer. No, sir; I did not see any pistol.

Question. At any time?

Answer. No, sir; I can only say from what I did see, I should say and as near as I think anybody could say, he did have one.

Question. How could you say that without seeing it?

Answer. I could see the effects of the pistol, and his general conduct. Putting the whole thing together, in my own mind, I am perfectly satisfied the man had a pistol.

Question. From his manner?

Answer. Yes, sir; from the fact I saw the smoke just at the same instant that he turned and ran, and I should say he certainly had a pistol, which he fired. I could not see any other solution to the question.

Question. What was the name of the freedman you heard found the pistol?

Answer. I do not remember his name. It was at the time we were in custody, and there was considerable excitement, and I have forgotten. I had forgotten almost the entire fact, though I had heard it, until it was brought to my mind just now.

Question. You did not hear it that evening?

Answer. No, sir.

Question. Did you go to his body immediately after he fell?

Answer. It was perhaps two or three minutes; I stood in the buggy to see if there was to be any further demonstration. I did not know but the man had friends there and there would be a general riot; that they would take it up; so I staid in the buggy to see what further effect it would have, and when I saw it was quieted down a little I went over to where he was.

Question. You did not hear at that time of any man having a pistol?

Answer. No, sir; but I heard next morning that he had gone into a store there and bought some cartridges.

Question. What store?

Answer. I think it was Mr. Cole's—Bryan & Cole's. They both—Mr. Bryan and Cole—deny that he did. I asked them both.

Question. You heard that he had gone in there to get ammunition, and they deny it?

Answer. Yes, sir; I heard it, and when I came up Monday morning I stopped and asked Mr. Bryan and Cole both, and they said he did not; that they did not keep cartridges in their store.

Question. You say you saw two pistol-shots while he was running?

Answer. Yes, sir.

Question. Then a shot from a gun?

Answer. No, sir; I could not say anything about a gun. There were five or six shots, I should say, all almost instantaneously. I could not tell what they were. I paid no particular attention at the time.

Question. You said they were pistol-shots; do you mean they were pistol-shots?

Answer. I say the first two shots were pistol-shots.

Question. Who fired them?

Answer. I could not say positively. I said they came from the direction in which this man was running, and I judge he was the man who fired them; and it was not until after those two shots were fired in the direction, as I saw by the smoke, of those pursuing the man, that those other shots were fired that killed him. I had no idea that the freedmen intended to kill the man when they started after him.

Question. You say you did not see him fire; you only heard the sound of the pistol?

Answer. The first shot?

Question. Yes.

Answer. I heard the sound and saw the smoke.

Question. And the second report?

Answer. The second shot I saw the smoke, and saw the flash, and heard the report.

Question. Then you must have seen who shot if you saw the flash?

Answer. No, sir; the crowd there were at least forty or fifty yards away, and the crowd was in commotion at the time, and I could not see who shot. I only saw in the direction of the crowd the motion, which way the man was going. It was from that direction the shots were fired, and it was from the other direction, as I distinctly say, that they were returned.

Question. Was it possible for him to have fired at that crowd of pursuers without hitting them?

Answer. Yes, sir; he evidently fired over his shoulder as he ran, I think it probable at least, and he shot naturally too high, as he naturally would, running and shooting over his shoulder.

Question. If he had fired over his shoulder you certainly could have seen it, because that would have raised his hand?

Answer. I do not think it would have raised it much; it would have been about the same as if he had put it up to his eye.

Question. No; if he had raised it above his shoulder, he would have raised it high enough to miss his shoulder, and far enough from his head for you to have seen it?

Answer. If a man threw his pistol on his shoulder, and he naturally rested on the shoulder, there would not be the least danger of his hitting himself, shooting over his shoulder; and besides, it is a very common way, sometimes, of firing pistols.

Question. I should think it was a very uncommon way of firing a pistol. I never heard of such a performance before in my life. You were looking directly toward him at that time?

Answer. At the time the shot was fired?

Question. Yes, sir.

Answer. No, sir.

By Mr. RICE:

Question. When the two shots were fired?

Answer. Yes, sir; I was then trying to see what I could of him.

By Mr. BLAIR:

Question. You were standing in a buggy?

Answer. Yes, sir.

Question. That would raise you above his pursuers?

Answer. Yes, sir; some considerably.

Question. If he had elevated his hand above his shoulder to fire, you could not have failed to see it?

Answer. Yes, if there was a man between him and me, because I looked down upon them; at the distance they were, the difference in position would not have made much difference from what it would have been if I had been on the same level with them.

Question. What! not if his pursuers were a few feet from him, it would not have made a difference?

Answer. But I am speaking of the crowd between me and the man killed, who could have hid him from my sight, as they did, for I could not distinguish the man as he ran out almost in a straight line, bearing a little to the right; when he made the turn I lost sight of him completely in the general movement of the crowd, and could only tell about the direction where he was.

Question. Then you did not see the pistol that was fired?

Answer. No, sir.

Question. You did not see in whose hands it was?

Answer. No, sir. I only saw the flash of the pistol in the direction about where he was when he was shot.

Question. Would it have been possible for him to have shot back in the direction of that crowd, without hitting some one?

Answer. I think it was just exactly as probable that he shot twice at them and missed, as that they shot five or six times at him and hit no one else but him, and he only once. There was just as much of a crowd where he was as where they were.

Question. But he was outside of the crowd at the time when the firing took place?

Answer. Just at the outskirts of it, and the crowd were below him, just as they were before; he had not got to the further limits of the crowd north, but was at the west, on the west.

Question. Still he was on the outside of the crowd on the west?

Answer. Yes, he was, about; but when I saw them they seemed to be all about him, and had headed him off evidently, for the man I saw raise the stick and strike was standing north of him evidently, from the direction in which he struck, if he struck at him, as I suppose he did. That is the reason I say it seems to me as improbable that they could have shot and missed, as for him to have shot and missed.

Question. Could you distinguish the sound of the shots?

Answer. I could not; when the five or six shots were fired I could not tell what they were particularly; though, of course, if there is only one or two, I can very easily detect the difference between a pistol and gun shot; but I could not when so many were fired, and taking into consideration the excitement at the same time. Of course, my mind was not led to that, and I did not suspect even when the shots were being fired—I had no idea that anybody was going to be killed. I did not think of it until some one came and told me the man had been killed.

Question. Then you say you did not distinguish or discriminate between any of the sounds or shots?

Answer. No, sir; not after the first two shots fired. The first two shots were pistol-shots, but the others were fired almost instantaneously, and it was impossible to tell what they were.

Question. What made you think they were pistol-shots?

Answer. Simply my own judgment in the matter. I have heard pistol and gun shots so often that when they are fired within a few rods of me I can very easily tell which is a pistol-shot and which a gun-shot.

Question. Would it not depend a good deal on the charge—a small charge in a gun would sound like a pistol?

Answer. Yes, sir; it might, something, but there would be a little difference in the sound of a gun and a pistol, even with the same charge in both of them.

Question. But all pistols do not sound alike, either?

Answer. No, sir; I do not suppose they do.

Question. The explosion of the powder produces the sound; it is the quantity of powder that increases the sound, is it not, whether a gun or pistol?

Answer. Yes, sir; and taking into consideration the length of the barrel would make the difference.

Question. That does not add to the sound, does it?

Answer. I think so. I think I can tell the difference between a gun-shot and a pistol-shot, with the same charge of powder in them—that is to say, take the same number of grains, and put them in a shot-gun or musket, and I can tell the difference between it and the firing of a pistol.

By Mr. Rice:

Question. And can tell it from both, if fired from a rifle?

Answer. Yes, sir; it makes a different sound from any of the others.

By Mr. Blair:

Question. What would be the difference?

Answer. The sound of the rifle is much sharper than the musket, and the sound of the musket heavier than the shot-gun.

Question. Does not the sharp sound of the rifle come from the ball as well as the powder?

Answer. I was going to say, the difference comes from the way they are ordinarily loaded. Of course, you might load these different weapons so as to deceive me, but not after loading them in the ordinary way.

Question. You could easily tell the sound of a rifle, because the resistance of the bullet in a rifle gives it a sharper sound?

Answer. Yes, sir.

By Mr. RICE:

Question. The longer that resistance the greater the difference between it and a short barrel?

Answer. That is what I think. When it comes to the air sooner it would make a different sound from the one that is retained longer; though I do not know that I could explain the philosophy of the thing.

By Mr. BLAIR:

Question. This pistol he had, then, was evidently a repeating pistol, was it?

Answer. Yes, sir; I should say he had a revolver, if he had any pistol at all.

Question. And that he fired three distinct shots?

Answer. Yes, sir.

By the CHAIRMAN:

Question. Dr. Brothers states that when he reached the body of Lee he found Lewis, yourself, and Squire Elmore, a justice of the peace of Governor Alcorn's appointment, already there.

Answer. Yes, sir.

Question. He says that he made this remark to Lewis: "Cannot you disperse this crowd? We feel alarmed; already one innocent man has been killed from an accidental discharge in the hands of one of your men." Did you hear that set speech made by the doctor?

Answer. No, sir; he never made any such set speech; I deny it emphatically. The speech Dr. Brothers made about dispersing the crowd was made after Lewis and myself started to go home; and when we started to go home—Dr. Brothers had up to that time talked very nice and peaceably about this thing; I do not know whether he thought he would get himself hurt or not; he is not a man of any very great nerve—when we started to go he would not let us go without saying something a little mean, and then he said to us if we did not disperse this crowd he would telegraph for somebody to make them go. That is all.

Question. Did he say one innocent man had been killed by an accidental discharge in the hands of one of your own men?

Answer. No, sir; he did not say that.

By Mr. BLAIR:

Question. He did not say that either?

Answer. Dr. Brothers is a man who would do all he could against a man behind his back, but not a man who would face any man on anything. Dr. Brothers would not tell me anything of that kind. He will try to make use of law, and anything of that kind, but he dares not face anybody on it and make a personal issue of it.

The CHAIRMAN. Dr. Brothers testified, speaking of the time when he went to the dead body, "I said to Mr. Lewis, 'Can't you disperse this crowd. We feel alarmed; already one innocent man has been killed from an accidental discharge of a gun in the hands of one of your own men.'"

The WITNESS. He never made any speech about an innocent man being killed. He said what I have stated.

Question. He says he remarked to Lewis if he did not do that he would take the matter into his own hands and telegraph, and get men; and that Lewis replied, "Yes, yes, I can disperse them," and that he did or said something inexplicable, that he waved his hand, and that the crowd dispersed as if by magic. He laid great stress upon the mysterious motion, the effect of which was the instant dispersion of the crowd. Now, if there was any magic used upon that occasion, or any mysterious gesture that that crowd recognized and obeyed, I wish you to describe it to this committee.

Answer. I am sure I never saw any such gesture as that at all. All the gesture that I heard, or saw, or know anything of was this: instead of my going home where I lived, or both of us, he got into his buggy and said, "Boys, let us go home," and about a hundred freedmen staid there, and said they would not go home until we did; that they feared a further row; and when we went they all went too.

Question. He expressed the opinion that Mr. Lewis had such absolute control over the crowd that they would have killed any man at his instance?

Answer. I do not believe any such thing.

COLUMBUS, MISSISSIPPI, *November* 16, 1871.

WILLIAM W. HUMPHRIES, JR., sworn and examined.

The CHAIRMAN. As this witness is called by the minority, General Blair may examine him.

By Mr. BLAIR:

Question. Please state your name, residence, and occupation.

Answer. William W. Humphries, jr.; Columbus, Mississippi; I am a lawyer by profession.

Question. How long have you resided here?

Answer. I was born here, sir, and have resided here since that time, a period of thirty-one years.

Question. The principal object of inquiry which the committee have in view is the general condition of the country; the maintenance of law and order, and whether there are any disturbances; particularly whether there are any of what are called Ku-Klux outrages. I wish you to state fully all of that description that have come within your knowledge or observation.

Answer. I was informed, gentlemen, on Monday that I would be called as a witness before this committee. Since that time I have run back over a number of what I might term alleged violations of the law, and have refreshed my mind and made a memorandum of those that I remember. [Producing a memorandum paper.] I will state just here that some matters to which I allude have come under my personal observation. There are others in which my information came to me from the fact that I was engaged in the cases, either prosecuting or defending. Others I know upon information received from other persons.

Question. Well, sir, that is legitimate here if it comes to you in such a way that you believe it.

Answer. In regard to Ku-Kluxing and Ku-Klux, I never saw but one person whom I supposed came properly under that head or denomination, and to that I attached but little importance. I saw a party arrested in the town of Columbus, some months since, disguised with a mask and other fancy disguise. He was arrested here by the chief of police, Captain Donnelly, and brought into a place known as Kane's saloon, or Merchants' Exchange. He was unmasked, his disguise taken from him, and he proved to be a negro of the town. He was carried either to the jail or calaboose, I do not remember which. The chief of police called upon me and desired me to prosecute the case, with a view to receiving the reward which the governor had offered for the arrest and identification of a Ku-Klux. I advised him that I would not prosecute the case, as it was simply a negro in disguise, and it would be best to pass it by.

Question. He had not done anything?

Answer. O, no, sir; I suppose it was merely an attempt to frighten; it was more for mischief or deviltry, or something of the sort, than anything else; at least that was my opinion and my impression, and for that reason I gave the officer this advice, which was acted upon.

The next violation of law to which I call the attention of the committee is the case of a man by the name of Bridges, a constable in Noxubee County, who is said to have made an arrest of a party in Noxubee who afterward made his escape. That party was charged with having stolen a mule from a gentleman named Moore.

By the CHAIRMAN:

Question. We have had very full particulars of that case. Unless General Blair desires it, you need not go over it.

Answer. I will pass from it, then.

By Mr. BLAIR:

Question. I do not care for it, except to ask one question. Some witnesses before us, especially Mr. Whitfield, have brought that thing up, and I want to know if the witness knows Mr. Whitfield's knowledge of it, and can tell whether he knew the real state of the facts when he gave the description of it.

Answer. I have read Mr. Whitfield's testimony in an article or pamphlet form, or rather in a book of four or five hundred pages, in which I have found his version of it. It does not accord with the facts in that case. There is an entirely different state of facts in truth.

Question. You need not go into the particulars of it.

Answer. I will state this in connection with that matter. It has undergone a thorough judicial examination in this court-house before Judge Orr, the judge of this judicial district. I was present and heard the witnesses examined. Shall I go on?

Question. Yes, sir.

Answer. The next case is that of Seaton and Reynolds. This I regard as a violation of law, but if a case of the kind is ever justifiable, I think that was the case. I think the action taken by the parties, whoever they may have been, was entirely justifiable, and I will now state the facts. A gentleman by the name of Tyler, who is an exceedingly clever man, a northern man by birth, moved to Columbus for the purpose of living here, and settled himself here. These men, of whom I spoke, attempted to commit a robbery upon Mr. Tyler. The proof was positive—I may say clear and plain—certainly as to one of them, if not as to both. They were tried and, upon a mere technicality, acquitted. The community were very indignant. These parties were mere adventurers, not known to the community, and the community were indignant that this attempt had been made, more especially from the fact that Mr. Tyler was a northern man. He was a good citizen. He was liked in the community, and the community felt that any attempt upon him would be a reflection upon them. I believe it was in the night that these parties were taken out and whipped. I presume, without knowing it, that that is the fact. It seemed to be the general impression of the community that they were whipped from the fact that they had made this attempt to commit a robbery, and to perhaps take life, and that they had been discharged and escaped punishment, upon a technicality, by an ignorant jury.

By the CHAIRMAN:

Question. Were they whipped by men in disguise?

Answer. Really I do not know; I can only state what I have heard on that point. I have heard that the men were disguised. The grand jury investigated the case, but they were unable to ascertain who the parties were. The wife of the prisoner, who was present, indentified the district attorney as one, but it was known that the district attorney was not present, and that was treated laughingly. Everybody knew that he was not there. She stated that she thought he was the men, but she herself became satisfied subsequently that she was mistaken.

The next is the case of a negro man by the name of James Hicks. Now, this I am stating upon information. The committee will understand in regard to many of these matters, that I now state them upon information, which I believe to be true, and I will give the names of the parties informing me if desired. James Hicks, a negro, was whipped for stating that he had had sexual intercourse with a lady in Caledonia, or that he could have intercourse with her, language that was disrespectful and insulting. This happened, I think, some time in February last. The circuit court was at that time in session, and perhaps the next morning after the whipping a number of us heard of it. In the mean time Judge Orr had given his grand jury a special charge to investigate the case. Witnesses were going before a grand jury and a party of us were standing outside of the court-house discussing the matter, and I got the information which I gave you from gentlemen and witnesses who made these statements. About the time we were discussing this matter a young gentleman, named Farmer, who was a school-teacher, teaching at a short distance from Columbus walked up into the crowd. I saw him as he walked up, and after the gentleman who was then talking got through, I jocularly remarked to the crowd that I had been informed that Farmer was visited on the same night, and that they had intended to whip him, but for some reason had postponed his flogging until that night. I remained in the crowd a few minutes, and then went over to my office, which is directly in front of the court-house, and was followed there by Mr. Farmer. He came into my office, and desired to know of me if I was in earnest in saying that he woald be whipped that night. I replied that the remark had been jocularly made; that I knew nothing about it. Whereupon he said, "They do me very great injustice, sir. I did not indorse the statement of that negro, nor did I say I had sexual intercourse, or that the negro had sexual intercourse, with the lady, and in makiag this charge they do me injustice." That was in substance the conversation I had with him.

By Mr. BLAIR:

Question. I see that Mr. Huggins, of Aberdeen, page 277, makes the same statement about this man Farmer that is made by Whitfield—that he was taken out and very severely whipped and driven away from his school.

Answer. If Mr. Farmer was ever whipped I never heard of it. It may be true, but I never heard that he was whipped. I heard that he was threatened. He told me so himself, and stated to me the reasons why he was threatened, but said that they were not true.

Question. That he was supposed to have indorsed the statement of this negro?

Answer. Yes, sir; or words to that effect. Now, I cannot undertake to quote the exact language, but I state substantially to you what he said.

Question. He said that they had paid him a visit about that, but had not whipped him?

Answer. Yes, sir; they paid him a visit, and threatened him, and charged him with having indorsed that statement, or made a similar statement that the negro Hicks had made, in regard to this lady living in Caledonia.

Question. Go on with your statement now.

Answer. The next case I know of is the case of Mason, a negro man killed on Hulbert's plantation, near Columbus. The facts in that case were simply these: This boy Mason and a negro man named Andy Hulbert had had a quarrel upon the place in regard to some matter, which resulted in rather a severe fight between them. While they were fighting Mr. Hulbert had them parted. He ordered them to desist and had them parted. They separated from each other with threats. Either that night, or maybe one or two nights after that, I do not remember the exact time, this man was killed. The next day an accusation was lodged against this boy Andy Hulbert. One negro there, I believe, also accused Mr. Cal Hulbert, the owner of the place. I was one of the attorneys in that case. The case was tried before R. C. Harrison, a negro justice of the peace in the town of Columbus. The main facts brought out were these, that a party had come—some said two or three, some as high as a half a dozen, or seven or eight—the testimony was conflicting on that point—had come to his house, and shot him, by firing into the door, or into the house in some way; I have forgotten the testimony as to that; there was a conflict of testimony. The ground of the charge was that they had quarreled and threatened each other, and, at the time of the killing, Andy was missing from his house, and did not come up until some time afterward. One negro accused Cal Hulbert, and a number of negroes testified that as soon as the shot was fired they repaired to his house, a few hundred yards distant, and found him undressed, in bed, and asleep. Upon this statement of facts the case against him was dismissed. Andy, however, was tried, and the facts brought out. I defended him. My opinion at the time was that there were circumstances strongly pointing to him. He had had a difficulty with the man; they had parted with threats; he was absent from his house at the time of the killing, which was between 12 o'clock and daylight. Circumstances pointed to him as one of the guilty parties, but there was not sufficient testimony to convict him, and the result was that he was discharged.

By the CHAIRMAN:

Question. When did this occur?

Answer. I can tell you exactly by reference to my books.

Question. The exact date is not material; in what year was it?

Answer. It was either the latter part of last year or the early part of this. My memory in regard to dates is bad, and where I can furnish a date accurately, if desired, I would prefer to do that.

By Mr. BLAIR:

Question. Did Mr. Whitfield give an account of this difficulty in his testimony?

Answer. He did, sir; and he misrepresents the state of facts. Mr. Whitfield called at my office, and I gave to him a full history of this case. I notice in his examination before your committee he states that there was no coroner's inquest, nor any investigation of the case, and the records of this court, of the court before which he was tried, which are now in this court-house, will show that there was an investigation, a public investigation, in the town of Columbus, before the magistrate, Harrison, as I have stated.

Question. He was made aware of the fact?

Answer. He called at my office and inquired of me in regard to the case. I stated all the facts that I have related to you. It was a public matter, sir. It was known in the community at the time the man had been killed. The parties were charged with it, and they were tried before a court of justice. The matter was investigated, and at the time, I suppose, nearly every citizen, at least a great many of the citizens, must have known a case of that importance, where a party was killed right in the vicinity of the town, the prisoner brought here, and arraigned and tried before a justice's court.

Question. State the next case.

Answer. A man by the name of Hairston, near Crawfordsville, a negro, was visited at his house one night. I think that was in December last; by referring to my books I could ascertain, for I was an attorney in the case, and I could give you accurate information as to the date. His house was surrounded by a party of men, fired into, and an attempt made to kill this man. That, however, did not succeed. As soon as Hairston, the negro, could get off he left, and came to Columbus, stated his case to me, and requested me to prosecute the parties, which I consented to do, and accordingly repaired to Crawfordsville for that purpose. The party charged with this offense was a negro, named Moore, living in the town of Crawfordsville, who was identified by Hairston, himself, and by his wife, as one of the parties firing. They also recognized another man, who was either a mulatto or a white man, but which they could not determine. Who the other parties were they did not know. Moore, the negro, whom Hairston recognized, was arraigned and tried before Henry B. Whitfield, then a justice of the peace. The case was tried before him, and he discharged the prisoner.

Question. He omits the mention of that in his arraignment of the people of this county. He probably did not want to implicate a negro in a transaction of that kind.

Answer. I do not know in regard to that, but I did not observe any mention made of it in his testimony before your committee.

Question. He speaks of a Hairston, a freedman, who was whipped on Major George Hairston's place?

Answer. That, I presume, was a different case. This man was not whipped. By the bye, he was a member of the grand jury at the present term of the court, and is now in town.

Question. He has been before the committee, and gave the same statement that you do.

Answer. Whitfield was the presiding magistrate in the case.

Question. And must have known it?

Answer. Of course, he knew it, as he presided in the case. Another case, which I conceived to be a violation of the law, in which there was no doubt of the fact, a very flagrant, outrageous violation of the law, was the case of an old negro, named Joe Beckwith, who lives out here upon Colonel Wynn's old place. Colonel Wynn is now dead. I believe that the wife of his son, who is also dead, is now living there. It was rumored in the community that Colonel Wynn had buried some gold there during the war. This old negro, in digging on one occasion, struck some sort of iron box, or something of the kind, I cannot state just what it was, but somehow the impression got out in the neighborhood that this old negro knew where the gold was, and, either that night, or two or three nights afterward, a party of men went there and hung him. He did not die from the effects of it, but the old man was severely injured. It was an unjustifiable violation of the law. Major E. G. Eggleston, the father of the lady living on the place—his daughter had married the son of Colonel Wynn—talked with me about the matter. He was exceedingly anxious to ascertain the party and bring them to justice. I put myself to some trouble in order to do the same thing, and the community generally were anxious to ascertain who the parties were. Their object, no doubt, was robbery, and they had acted badly and ought to have been punished, and would have been severely punished, I presume, if their names could have been ascertained.

Question. The old negro could not give you any information as to the names?

Answer. He did not know. He was an honest, good old negro, I have been informed, a good, clever old man.

Question. The statement of the old man before the committee was that he and a yellow boy were digging, and the yellow boy struck this iron, and he suspected that the yellow boy communicated the fact.

Answer. Yes, sir; I remember now to have heard that statement also in connection with the matter, but old man Joe was the fellow that was hung and received all the mistreatment, which was very severe. I think I heard from Major Eggleston that he was confined to his bed for some time.

Question. What became of that yellow boy?

Answer. I heard at the time and have heard since, but my recollection does not serve me at this time, and I cannot tell.

Question. Proceed with your statement.

Answer. The next is in regard to the case of Major Doss, at Macon. Mrs. Brantley was on trial for being accessory to the murder of her husband. I was in Macon prosecuting the case at the time this disturbance occurred. Doss, it seems, was related to the lady in some way, and during the progress of the trial came into the court-house drunk and behaved himself in a very disorderly manner, and treated the court, which consisted merely of magistrates and was not a circuit court, with great contempt. By order of the court he was arrested by the sheriff, McHenry, and Colonel Baskerville. McHenry is the sheriff of the county. They arrested him.

Question. We have had a pretty full statement of that case.

Answer. I will pass from that, then, and make no further mention of it. A most flagrant outrage and violation of law was in the killing of old man McDaniel. He was a white man who lived some twelve or fifteen miles from Columbus. He left Columbus one evening and started for his home, got half a mile from town, and was murdered by some negroes. A negro named Charley was convicted of having killed him.

By the CHAIRMAN:

Question. What was that negro's name?

Answer. Charley Humphries. He was hung for it, and upon his gallows, just before he was hung, he made a full confession, in which he gave the names of Tom Barry and others who had assisted him, Tom Barry being present at the time. The object, I presume, was robbery. Thomas McGaughey was a white man living upon my father's plantation, and was beaten and severely whipped by the negroes on the plantation.

By Mr. BLAIR:

Question. What was his offense, colonel?

Answer. He gave them some order that they differed about, and they got into a quarrel and concluded that they would flog him, and double-teamed, and did so.

By the CHAIRMAN:

Question. Was that done at night, by men in disguise?

Answer. No, sir; in broad open daylight; they had no disguise on.

By Mr. BLAIR:

Question. That does not look like those negroes were under much intimidation?

Answer. Not a particle; no more than you are. On the contrary, I consider them about as daring as anybody. And as further evidence of the fact, I witnessed on the streets of Columbus a negro, named Solomon Shaw, pull out his repeater and fire four or five times at a young gentleman named Fernandez Pope, here, in broad daylight. Another case of that sort occurred some four or five months ago. It was the case of a negro drawing his knife and chasing his employer and his brother out of the field; to use his own language, he made them "whoop for the landing." That was his expression in his statement of the facts. I might mention still another case, of George Triplet, who got mad with the manager of General Harris's plantation, took a club and beat him half to death. The manager's name was Winston. I saw him in town a few days ago, and on his head was a terrible gash. The negro had beat him senseless. The negro is in town now.

By the CHAIRMAN:

Question. What was done with the negro?

Answer. He was put in jail for two months. The judge sentenced him, under the law, to four months, but gave him the privilege of working on the streets for two months, and then be discharged. I defended that case. I will say, in vindication of Judge Orr, that the facts did not fully come out. Mr. Winston was sick and did not come here, and I put in a plea of guilty, and succeeded in reducing the punishment.

Question. What was done with the negroes who whipped Thomas McGaughey?

Answer. They were put in jail for a few weeks, and the case was finally disposed of in some way, I have forgotten how.

Question. What was done with Sol. Shaw, who pulled out his repeater and fired in at Pope in broad daylight?

Answer. My impression is—in fact I know it, because I was in the case—that he was tried before the magistrate and, I think, gave bond to appear at the circuit court. Whether the case has been disposed of I do not know. It may have been. I do not know, but by reference to the records I can tell you if you desire to know. Just there permit me to state what I omitted to say in connection with the case of Solomon Shaw, that Pope also fired at him.

Question. What was done with the four or five men who made this attack upon the white men in the field and ran them off—the case you mentioned after Shaw?

Answer. There was only one negro engaged in that; one negro ran two white men off. The case was tried and the jury acquitted the party on the ground that one of the white men had a pistol in his pocket, and if he was such an infamous coward as to allow that, he ought to have been killed. So one or two of the jury stated to me; that when a white man would permit a negro to run him out of his own field with a bowie-knife, and the fact was developed that the white man was at that time armed with a pistol, they had no sympathy with him, and the negro had been in jail for three or four months, and I think it was the sense of the jury that he was rather a plucky fellow, while the other was rather a coward, and the negro had done about right. I was district attorney *pro tempore* at the time, in the absence of the regular district attorney.

By Mr. BLAIR:

Question. These instances do not seem to show that the negroes are in a state of terror and intimidation?

Answer. So far from it, I will mention some much a head of those I have alluded to.

By the CHAIRMAN:

Question. They show likewise that the law deals very promptly with them when they are guilty of offenses. If they are disguised there does not seem to be much difficulty in finding them out.

Answer. Old man Hughes, a white man, lived out on Billup's place. He was shot in his bed by a negro. My information is, that one of the negroes did the shooting, but that several negroes were engaged in concocting the plan.

Question. Were they disguised?

Answer. I was not informed that they were. I presume not, sir; but he did not say that it was done at night. It was an assassination. Now this case is stated upon information. I do not think I saw them at all. Some one gave me the information as to who shot the man.

Question. Was he killed?

Answer. No, sir; he was wounded, simply. The Artesia murder, I suppose, you have heard fully in regard to.

Question. Yes, sir.

Answer. Melton Odeneal, a gentleman living in the county, was fired upon and shot at by a negro, whose name he gave me to be Mace Cox.

Question. Was this in the day-time or in the night?

Answer. In the day-time. He was passing along the road, and a negro shot him from the woods.

By Mr. BLAIR:

Question. What was done with the negro?

Answer. Nothing, Mr. Odeneal says, and, I presume, he had reason to believe it. He was satisfied that Mace Cox was the party. I do not know that the proof was positive or plain.

Question. Were any arrests made?

Answer. I am not aware of the fact that an arrest was made, and I am not prepared to say that there was none. These facts were communicated to me by Mr. Odeneal himself. Dick Lamp, a white man, was very severely denounced and cursed upon the streets of Columbus two or three weeks ago, sir.

Question. What was done with the negro?

Answer. Nothing; no attention was paid to it. George Young, a democratic negro, went out to Artesia to make a speech. When he got there it was late in the evening. He was taken out by thirty or forty negroes, and for his democracy they gave him two or three hundred lashes. I saw him afterward, and examined him four or five days ago. Since the election, a negro man was shot by another negro in this county, I believe it was at Artesia, for having voted the democratic ticket.

Question. What was his name?

Answer. I have forgotten his name, but I can give you the name of the party who witnessed the transaction.

Question. Shot for making a speech?

Answer. No, sir; for voting the democratic ticket. I can furnish you witnesses to the transaction, if desired.

Question. Was he killed?

Answer. No, sir; not killed. I saw Frank Blake, who was another democrat, knocked beaten, and cuffed for being a democrat. He was offering some motion, I heard, in a republican meeting.

Question. Was he a negro?

Answer. He was, and a democrat. The facts, I understand to be, were: There was a meeting in the court-house. Blake came in and made some motion, or said something, I do not know what—I was not there. They began to beat him. He ran from the court-house. They pursued him through the town, kicking and cuffing him. He finally made his way to Blair's drug-store, where the sheriff was at the time, and the sheriff and a *posse*, with drawn pistols, had to keep them off.

Question. This was a republican meeting?

Answer. Yes, sir.

Question. And he got up and offered some motion?

Answer. Yes, sir; what it was I do not remember. I only know he was severely beaten, and pursued by a large crowd through the streets, and it was with the utmost difficulty that the sheriff and citizens could save his life. James B. Bell was sheriff at the time. I saw him with his pistol drawn, surrounded by citizens trying to keep them back. Blake, in the mean time, had gone into David Blair's drug-store, upon Market and Main streets, one hundred and fifty or two hundred yards from the court-house.

On this subject of intimidation, a neighbor named Bowler was guilty of some violation of law—I have forgotten what—let me see; perhaps he had been charged with a riot—I think that was it; and a *capias* was issued. I think that was the offense he was charged with. At all events, a *capias* had been issued. Samuel Kline was then sheriff, and went with a *posse* to arrest him. He said, by God, he would not be arrested, and turned with his pistol and fired five or six times. The sheriff had two gentlemen with him—two or three. They finally succeeded in shooting him.

Question. They shot Bowler and arrested him?

Answer. Yes, sir; they finally shot him.

Question. Did they arrest him alive or dead?

Answer. Alive, sir. He recovered, and is now somewhere, but where I do not know. He was indicted, but nothing was ever done with him. He gave bond and left the country.

Mr. A. H. Hargrove, a gentleman going to his plantation, was fired upon four miles from town, at Nail's bridge, on the Macon road.

By the CHAIRMAN:

Question. Was this in the day-time?

Answer. Yes, sir. Well, it was late in the evening, I think, if my memory serves me aright.

Question. Was he fired on by a single individual or a party?

Answer. One, sir; a negro, I was informed, shot at him. It was an attempt, I imagine, to assassinate. It was not an open matter. It was done in the woods. How the conclusion was arrived at that it was a negro I am not informed or advised, for my information is not that Mr. Hargrove saw the party who did the firing; hence, I cannot state how they arrived at that conclusion, but in some way satisfactorily to himself and to his friends. By seeing him, I perhaps could answer that question.

A negro in town by the name of Mormon voted the democratic ticket. I have not conversed with him, but I was informed on yesterday by a party of gentlemen that he had been waited on and threatened with a severe whipping for his action.

There are two policemen in the town of Columbus, Wylie Johnson and Moses Randall, who informed me on yesterday that they had been discharged from the city police for having voted for a democrat in the beat election, and perhaps for sheriff. Whether this be true or not I do not know. I give you my means of information. I do not know that it is necessary to mention it; but as you have told me to mention all the cases that I recollect or know of, I state it.

I might mention the case of the arrest of Jerry Dowsing, the sheriff of this county, and his *posse*, who were taken up to Oxford in this Artesia matter, charged, I believe, with violating the enforcement act in some way. I have here, in connection with that matter, if it is desired that the committee should see them, some papers which I would submit.

By Mr. BLAIR:

Question. What are they?

Answer. The first is a paper from Judge J. A. Orr, judge of the seventh judicial circuit, which is a letter of instructions to this officer.

Question. Will you read that?

Answer. It is as follows:

"COLUMBUS, MISSISSIPPI, *November* 7, 1871.

"After the death of Hugh Lee at Artesia, on the 21st of October, there was exhibited to me the verdict of the jury of inquest, giving the names of six persons as guilty of the murder of said Lee. The justice of the peace, acting coroner, and the sheriff were present. Colonel H. L. Muldrow, district attorney, and myself were applied to for instruction. On a comparison of the two statutes touching the case, my instructions, after consultation with the district attorney, to the sheriff was, to make the arrest of the parties charged by the jury of inquest, and that it was not necessary for the issuance of a warrant for that purpose. (See chapter crimes and misdemeanors, title, arrest, rev. code of 1857.) This section authorizes an officer to make arrest of any person committing a felony without warrant, and the verdict of the jury was a sufficient basis on which the officer could in good faith act under the belief that a felony had been committed.

"As to other arrests by Sheriff Dowsing, I can say that I pointed out to him the statute above referred to, and advised him that it was competent for him to arrest any other person who had been guilty of a felony without warrant.

"J. A. ORR,

"*Judge Seventh Judicial District, Mississippi.*"

By the CHAIRMAN:

Question. That was a case where the verdict rendered on a coroner's inquest was by a jury of twelve?

Answer. Yes, sir; I will read that verdict.

Question. Before you read it I will ask whether there is any law in Mississippi authorizing a coroner's jury of twelve men?

Answer. I will refer you to the statute.

Question. I supposed that you were familiar with the statute.

Answer. My opinion is that twelve was improper; but I can refer you to the statute.

Question. If not allowed by a statute, what value at all has a verdict by such a jury?

Answer. I will state that that is a legal question, and I would not like to swear to any legal opinion. I will refer you to the statute itself. I have it in my office, or it can be obtained in the next room.

Question. I simply ask your opinion; if you are not prepared to give it, you may go on.

Answer. I will simply state this in relation to my opinion. I do not remember the phraseology of the statute, and without referring to the statute I, of course, would not like to express an opinion, although my impression is that, according to the phraseology of the statute, twelve was not the proper number to constitute that jury.

By Mr. BLAIR:

Question. But, as Judge Orr says, it was sufficient to serve as a basis for the action of the sheriff?

Answer. Why, sir, it is not necessary, under the laws in this State, for a party to have a warrant at all to arrest a man who commits a felony. It is not necessary. That question I can answer.

By the CHAIRMAN:

Question. Under that view of the law, is this anything more than the expression of an opinion by twelve men not under oath? Has it any further legality?

Answer. I have not read the paper. That paper was handed to me to be presented to this committee by a friend, Mr. Dowsing.

By Mr. RICE:

Question. I would like to hear it read.

Answer. It is as follows:

"STATE OF MISSISSIPPI, *Lowndes County:*

"The undersigned, composing a jury of inquest, summoned over the dead body of Hugh Lee, at Artesia, in said county, on the 21st day of October, A. D. 1871, render, as our verdict, that the said Hugh Lee came to his death at the hands of a band of armed rioters, in said county and State, on the 21st day of October, 1871; that said band of rioters was composed of Levi Jones, (*alias* Levi Bean,) Ben. Bonnor, Andrew Moore, —— Rose, and divers others persons, whose names are unknown to the jury; and that H. W. Lewis and E. R. Bliss were present then and there, exercising control over said band of armed rioters aforesaid, are guilty of the murder of the said Hugh Lee.

"J. T. HARRISON.	SQUIRE GUMM, his x mark.
"T. B. FRANKLIN.	CANADA LALE, his x mark.
"W. L. ELLIS.	WATT SPRAGGINS, his x mark.
"O. C. BROTHERS.	GILFORD PETTY, his x mark.
"J. M. BARRON.	JORDAN RICE, his x mark.
"W. H. PERKINS.	THORNTON SMITH.

"STATE OF MISSISSIPPI, *Lowndes County:*

"I, John W. Elmore, a justice of the peace in and for beat No. 4, in said county and State, do hereby certify that the above is the verdict of the jury of inquest over the body of Hugh Lee, held at Artesia, in said county, on the 21st day of October, A. D. 1871.

"Given under my hand and seal this the 21st day of October, A. D. 1871.

[SEAL.] "J. W. ELMORE,
Justice of the Peace."

By the CHAIRMAN:

Question. Will you look over these names and state to the committee whether every one of them are not democrats?

Answer. I find J. T. Harrison here first. He is a democrat. T. B. Franklin, second. He is a democrat. W. L. Ellis. I do not know the man or his politics. The next name I cannot read. J. M. Barron is the fourth. I never heard of him. W. H. Perkins. I do not know his politics; my impression is that he is neither a democrat nor a republican, but somewhat upon the fence and upon the conservative order. Squire Gumm. He is the biggest radical, I reckon, in the county of Lowndes, and is a negro. I know him well. He is an influential, leading, radical negro of the county, and lives at Artesia. Canada Lale. He is a negro. I do not know his politics. I know the polities of the negroes generally, but what his are I cannot tell. Watt Spraggins I do not know. I presume he is a negro. He signs by his mark. So with Gilford Petty and Jordan Rice. They all sign their marks, and I presume they are negroes. I do not know them or their politics. As a general thing, the negroes in this country—I may safely say ninety-nine out of a hundred—belong to the republican party. The next name is Thornton Smith. He is a negro, and I believe I could state that I know his politics to be republican. After reading this paper, I think the majority of them are members of the republican party, or what we term here the radical party.

By Mr. BLAIR:

Question. They were all under oath, were they not?

Answer. Yes, sir. J. W. Elmore, I think, is a radical justice of the peace, but I do not think that had anything to do with it; whether democrats or radicals, I think they were honest in the discharge of their duty.

Question. Do you think they were honest in implicating —— Rose as one of the rioters?

Answer. I should dislike to believe otherwise, in the absence of any proof, that citizens, in the sworn discharge of their duty, would be influenced by a motive of that kind, whilst it is possible that a man who was a democrat might be base enough to try to implicate a republican. When a verdict of a jury of that sort was before me, of a majority of republicans, I think they would not be influenced by such a motive. I cannot think so.

Question. Did you ever receive any information that either Bliss or Lewis aided or abetted the colored people in this riot?

Answer. Will you repeat that question?

Question. Did you ever receive any reliable information that either Lewis or Bliss aided or abetted in that riot?

Answer. I have heard, sir, a number of conflicting reports in regard to that matter. I have heard that Mr. Lewis and Mr. Bliss were speaking at Artesia. I have heard that they had been speaking at Prairie Hill, from which place they had brought these parties. I have heard persons speak very harshly of them, and I have heard others speak kindly of them. There has been a conflict of opinion.

Question. My question is whether you have any reliable information that they aided or abetted in that riot?

Answer. I will state, sir, that a gentleman, in whom I have every confidence, told me they did. Among them I could mention several, but I don't believe, sir—the question you propounded is rather unusual. I will state that I am connected with this prosecution, and I do not care to prejudice any man's case by stating what I believe about it.

Question. You need not spare their feelings or mine.

Answer. It is not at all on that ground, understand me; as a matter of public justice, I state to you this: I have heard a number of reliable parties state that they believed that Mr. Lewis and Mr. Bliss both were, if not legally yet morally, guilty and responsible for the action of those negroes. I have heard them state facts in connection therewith which, if true—and which I have no doubt they believe to be true—would implicate those men. I have heard other parties, that were equally credible, state that they thought they had nothing to do with it, and were not apprised of it.

By Mr. RICE:

Question. Have you heard Dr. Brothers's story?

Answer. Yes, sir; I have heard him speak of it.

Question. Which way was he?

Answer. I heard Dr. Brothers make a statement of this sort: that he had been informed that Lewis had made some statement——

Question. But as to their being implicated?

Answer. I think Dr. Brothers is of opinion that they are implicated. From the tenor of his conversation and general remarks, without stating whether they were guilty or innocent, I inferred that they were decidedly guilty and implicated. I have heard his statement. I have heard him discuss this matter, but these facts, or rather this matter that I have just talked of, are only upon information. I will state nothing to you upon information that I do not believe to be reliable, and when I hear conflicting statements I can only give you those statements, for it is impossible for me to discriminate or determine which is correct.

By Mr. BLAIR:

Question. What is the other paper you have, colonel?

Answer. Here is a paper signed by W. E. Gibbs, (foreman of the grand jury,) J. F. Galloway, C. B. Canfield, Joshua Harriston, Elzy Richards, A. M. Green, A. Stewart, Thomas Seale, Robert Gleed, H. C. Long, J. T. Harrison, jr., M. Witherspoon, J. H. Brazier, G. M. Barksdale, and Samuel Kline. It is attested by the seal of the court. I have not read it. It was handed to me with the papers I mentioned a while ago, and I am not apprised of the nature of the paper.

By the CHAIRMAN:

Question. Who handed it to you?

Answer. Colonel Gibbs, I think, sir.

The CHAIRMAN. [After examining the paper exhibited.] I don't see the value of that paper.

Mr. BLAIR. It is only confirmatory.

The CHAIRMAN. Do you desire it incorporated in the record?

Mr. BLAIR. I do not care anything about it. I do not insist.

The WITNESS. I desire just here to correct a mistake which I made a few moments ago. I think, in giving you the name of the party who is supposed to have fired at Odeneal as Mace Cox, Jim Sherman should have been given instead of Mace Cox. Mace Cox is a negro who was killed down in the vicinity of Moore's Bluff. A young man by the name of Goldsby has been indicted for his murder and has fled the country. I think the governor has offered a reward for him, but I am not certain about that. I think the cause of that difficulty was something in relation to a negro woman. Both professed to have some claims to her regard and they differed, and I think it was an assassination.

By the CHAIRMAN:

Question. Were they both colored?

Answer. No, sir; one was a white man and the other a negro man.

By Mr. RICE:

Question. Which is the white man?

Answer. The white man is the one indicted for the murder. A member of the grand jury tells me it was upon the evidence of his sister and other parties. I presume that the case would be made out as they were knowing of the facts, if rumor can be relied on, which you gentlemen understand how much importance to attach to. The grand jury, at all events, found a bill of indictment.

By Mr. BLAIR:

Question. Have you stated all the cases within your knowledge or information?

Answer. No, sir; I have not. There is a class or character of cases that, if I would attempt to tell you about them, would take too much time here. I could not give the time to it, and I am sure the time of you gentlemen is too important to listen to them. It is in regard to the stealing that is going on in the country. The amount of stealing that is going on in the country is alarming. It is perfectly startling. All the hogs in the country are being killed and stolen; cattle are being stolen and killed up, and I might almost say that the country is without stock. My father, at the close of the war, had, I think, about five hundred hogs. I do not think he has forty now. Well, it is almost impossible to break it up. The negroes, as a general thing, commit these depredations; in fact, in almost every instance; but if they do not steal property to the amount of $25 it is only petty larceny, and you cannot send them to the penitentiary, under the statute. It is therefore difficult to break it up, though the state of things, to some extent, is improving. The reason we cannot break it up is they do not care anything about being sent to jail. They care nothing about locking them up in jail and feeding them a month, and it seems to be regarded by them almost as a pleasant recreation, judging from the way they take it. When they go to jail they are made heroes of by their friends. It puts them under no social disadvantage, and they do not care for it. As an evidence of how the stock of the country is being destroyed, whilst I am not familiar with statistics, I can say that prior to the war in this country we raised all our meat; some meat being brought here, it is true, but a very small amount, comparatively. At present I have no doubt the importations of meat would astonish you gentlemen, in comparison with what it was before. Well, the stealing of the cotton too is a source of very great annoyance to the planter. The negroes steal their corn also. That you gentlemen may properly appreciate that matter, I would suggest that you look at the records of this court, which are in one of the adjoining rooms. I cannot state exactly, for I have not counted the cases, but I think you will find that not less than fifteen hundred have been indicted for stealing in this way.

By Mr. RICE:

Question. Have you any remedy to suggest?

Answer. Yes, sir. I do not know what it will do, but, in my judgment, I think it will be a remedy. It is diminishing now to some extent; crime of all character is diminishing. I will read to you the report of our grand jury upon that point in a few minutes—this grand jury and also the grand jury of February—but the remedy I would suggest has, to a certain extent, already been applied, and that is a system of education to enlighten and inform these people and make them better people. It is by the diffusion of knowledge among them. I think that will, to some extent, cure them, by informing them. It may seem strange to you when I tell you of this open-handed stealing. You have no such thing in your country; but you will reflect that they were suddenly turned loose on society immediately after the war, perfectly unbridled, no restraint placed upon them, bare of money, with little moral perception; you will see how they can fall into vice and crime. Sometimes you find excellent negroes. I know a number as high-toned and honorable as white men; I know a number of such, but I speak of the class. They are improving, and I think the longer they mix with men and act upon their own responsibility, and the more knowledge they get, the better they will become. I think it has sometimes happened that some violations of law that I have alluded to have arisen from this stealing. This, however, is opinion; I do not state it as a fact; but in my judgment sometimes communities and people have felt outraged. I have not a doubt that some of the offenses I have alluded to—I speak of the general class, and not of any particular cases that I have mentioned—have sometimes happened in that way.

By the CHAIRMAN:

Question. Do you refer to what are called Ku-Klux outrages as having originated from that grievance?

Answer. No, sir. I know of no Ku-Klux outrages in this country. I know of none, sir. I am not a member of any such organization, and know of no operations.

Question. Never heard of any?

Answer. Yes, sir. I made no such statement. I have heard of them. The case of Jim Hicks I heard of as a Ku-Klux outrage, the negro whipped for stating that he had had sexual intercourse with a white lady, or making insulting remarks about this lady. The case of the negro killed at Caledonia, on Hulbert's plantation, was called a Ku-Klux outrage; the negroes who attacked and fired into Josh Hairston's house, and this case of Frank Young. All these operations, I think, would come under that general head.

Question. I misunderstood, then, the drift of your statement when you said you knew of no Ku-Klux outrages in this country.

Answer. Will you repeat that?

Question. I misunderstood, I suppose, the drift of what you meant to say when you said you knew of no Ku-Klux outrages in this country.

Answer. I do not mean to say that I know of no violations of law. I regard all these cases as violations of law; but if violations of law are, under any circumstances, justifiable, and the people are authorized to redress personal grievances or private wrong, these cases are sometimes justifiable; for example, the case of Jim Hicks; in my opinion he ought to have been whipped. If you or I had made that statement, in all likelihood we would have been shot; but he, being a negro, was chastised, and, so far as my reading extends, the laws of the country and the moral sentiment and tone of the people are that, for certain offenses and outrages against domestic happiness and private circles, where a party takes the law in his own hands and even kills a man, he is justifiable. In my last statement I meant to be understood as saying that this class of cases may be denominated, generally, Ku-Klux matters. Some I do not indorse; others I do. There are some where I have no acquaintance with the facts that led to the whipping or shooting, and know nothing about them. Our criminal law, however, at this time is vigorously enforced, I think. We have upon the bench of this district, I think, at this time, one of the best circuit judges I ever saw; that is, he is a man who understands his profession as a rational science. He is a fine officer upon the bench.

Question. How is your judiciary generally?

Answer. I have heard the judiciary by some complimented; by others it is not so well thought of. There are many fine judges in the State, I imagine, but on that subject I cannot give you information to which I would attach any importance, from the fact that I have not been before those judges, and can only form an opinion when I see a judge presiding.

By Mr. BLAIR:

Question. You know what the reputation of them generally is?

Answer. Well, sir, in reputation it is a fair judiciary—a very good judiciary, sir. I have heard no complaint against the judiciary; that is, generally; in particular instances there may be objection to it.

Question. In reference to the difficulty of dealing with these matters, it has been alleged to rest entirely with the juries. Are not your grand juries composed by your board of supervisors?

Answer. Why, most undoubtedly, sir.

Question. The boards of supervisors throughout the State were radicals?

Answer. Yes, sir, generally; they are so here; that is my information—that they are generally.

Question. Were they not appointed throughout the State?

Answer. Yes, sir; they were appointed under the present administration; recently they have been elected; since the last board of supervisors were appointed—that is, that appointed the last grand jury—recently the boards have been elected throughout the State at the late election.

Question. Prior to that they were all appointed by Governor Alcorn?

Answer. O, yes, sir; they were Alcorn appointees.

Question. And they have the selection of your grand juries entirely?

Answer. Yes, sir.

Question. It has been alleged that these outrages committed on the negroes were for political effect and to control and intimidate them; have you any belief as to that?

Answer. Why, general, that is simply a ridiculous farce; it is a shameful sham, sir. The idea of intimidation! I speak now of Lowndes County. There are about four thousand negro voters in this county. Talk about intimidating them! The whites are intimidated. I will give you an instance; it has occurred in this place.

Question. What is the number of white voters in the county?

Answer. About fifteen hundred. Why, sir, they march publicly in the streets with drums and fifes, and banners flying, yelling and whooping and hallooing, deliver speeches in the court-house, denounce white men bitterly, and denounce the democratic party. They are open, vindictive, and bitter. I can name numbers of cases where in speeches white men in the county have been denounced by them. They are as open in their meetings and as vindictive in denunciation as democrats; both parties do it. I do not state that it is confined to them. The sheriff was sent out to arrest these prisoners. I mention this to illustrate whether there is any intimidation among the negroes. When he brought these prisoners into town the negroes swarmed upon the streets and threatened to burn and tear down the jail. The people were alarmed lest there should be a riot. Judge Orr came to town; a detail was made from the military companies here. Captain Vaughn and Captain Holmes, one a white man and the other a negro, were detailed to preserve the peace. All the town was alarmed. Judge Orr was sent for a mile from town, at night, to come and try to quell this matter. Captain Donnelly, the jailer, stated to me that it was really exciting to see the manner and feeling that were manifested. They made threats and declared that they would take them out. Some threatened they would burn the town. No, sir; I do not think any sane man would undertake to state that the negroes of Lowndes County, in voting, were intimidated, or that they have not a full opportunity to exercise freedom of the ballot. This, however, I will state: that the negroes are intimidated whenever they desire to vote the democratic ticket. It is not that they are afraid to vote the republican ticket.

Question. Do you think that a great many more negroes would vote the democratic ticket if no intimidation was employed against them?

Answer. I have not a doubt of it, sir. No, sir; as you are upon that point, in regard to intimidation and the enforcement of the law, I will say that I have taken some pains to look into that matter and to consult with different parties to see if their opinions accorded with mine, and I will read you a little instrument here from a number of gentlemen upon that point. [Producing a paper.]

The CHAIRMAN. Will you let me see that paper before you read it?

Answer. Yes, sir. In the town of Columbus I have heard negroes speak in the public street in very bitter and denunciatory style. I have heard that in the court-house.

The CHAIRMAN. Who drew up this paper?

Answer. It was drawn up by a gentleman named Matthews, sir.

By Mr. RICE:

Question. Is Matthews a republican?

Answer. No, sir.

By the CHAIRMAN:

Question. Gotten up on yesterday?

Answer. Yes, sir.

Question. For the purpose of being presented to this committee?

Answer. It was, sir; for that purpose.

Question. Do you know whether all these persons signing this paper vote the republican ticket at this time or not?

Answer. I have reason to believe that they do. I have never doubted it. I know many of them are prominent and leading republicans, who have been elected to office as republicans. H. C. Powers, sheriff of Oktibbeha County, who signed on yesterday, and Josiah Stallings, of this county, the circuit clerk, whose majority, I think, was perhaps, three thousand, are prominent republicans. Mr. Hendricks is the deputy sheriff of Mr. Lewis, recently elected sheriff. Mr. Dowsing was sheriff of this county, appointed by Alcorn, and was a candidate in the late election for sheriff.

Question. This paper purports to be signed by citizens of the State of Mississippi and of Lowndes County. It is known to this committee that one of them, Mr. H. C. Powers, who was a witness here, is a citizen of Oktibbeha County.

Answer. He so states—that he is a citizen of Oktibbeha County.

Question. These gentleman undertake to speak for the whole State, as I understand them in his paper. They certify to a certain condition of things within the borders of the entire State.

Answer. I will say why it was that I presented that paper to these gentlemen for signature: I represented to each one of them I had been summoned to come before your committee, and expected to be interrogated touching these matters and things which are therein set forth, and I conversed with members of the democratic party and with members of the republican party. I desired, so far as I could, to ascertain and know, to be informed and advised, as to the opinions and sentiments of the people, without respect to party. I had been advised that I would not only be called upon to state facts that I might myself know, but information which I had and which I believed to be reliable. Hence I went to these parties and obtained that paper. The object I had in view was stated to the gentlemen who signed that paper.

Question. There are certain statements here that I should myself desire to examine these parties upon as to the truth of these statements and as to their means of information.

Answer. Do not understand me, Senator, as desiring to present that paper. I have no disposition as to that matter at all; I merely exhibit it to show you upon what I have based the opinions I have expressed in regard to the matter set forth there.

The CHAIRMAN. I think these gentlemen had better be here in person.

Mr. BLAIR. I desire to have this paper incorporated. It is the expression of the sentiments of a certain class of citizens upon this point. It has been held competent for witnesses to testify as to other peoples' statements and opinions. I cannot see why this statement by men of their own opinions should not be admitted. Oral declarations of men at a distance have been proven, and there is much less ground for excluding written declarations like this, upon which there can be no mistake.

The CHAIRMAN. I will take the opinion of the committee upon the admissibility of this paper.

The question being, shall the above-mentioned paper be admitted in evidence—

The ayes and noes were taken, and resulted as follows:

AYE—Mr. Blair.

NOES—Mr. Rice and the Chairman.

So the paper was rejected.

By Mr. BLAIR:

Question. In reference to these school matters; does that paper speak on that subject?

Answer. Yes, sir. I can state substantially what is said about the schools; and that paper, I think, reflects the general sentiment and opinion of the community as to schools.

Question. What is the general opinion of the democratic party in reference to the system of free schools?

Answer. I think as a party they are not opposed to a system of free schools; so far from it in this county, upon the general principle that the diffusion of knowledge and education among these people will make them better citizens, that if we can infuse into them some moral sense or perception of what is right—in other words, teach them, educate them—I think our people are of the opinion that it will tend in a great measure to break up crime, as petty larceny and crime of that character. In other words, it will elevate them in the scale of being and make them better people. We are opposed, however, to a loose, open-handed system of taxation. As you are aware, sir, the people here are impoverished. I think at least seven-tenths of the property of this State was destroyed by the results of the war. We were in a terrible condition at that time—in a most deplorable condition; many people were in debt; many were broken up completely. Those who had something left were so crippled that their condition was really distressing. Yet I believe that even those people are willing to be taxed, provided that taxation be commensurate will their ability to pay. I have talked on this subject with a great many leading democrats and republicans, all of whom were property-holders. Now and then you find a man who is opposed to it, but an extremist, a hot-headed fellow, who is as full of secession as he was *ante bellum*, or during the war. Such men are fanatics. You find not only republican but democratic fanatics, and these, as I presume, you have in all communities.

Question. The objection, then, to the schools, as I understand you, was to the heavy taxation in the impoverished condition of the people?

Answer. That, sir, is the only objection I have ever heard urged.

Question. What are the taxes now for other purposes; are they as heavy as can well be borne upon the remnant of property that has been left to the people of the State.

Answer. I wish very much, sir, that I had a paper setting forth the taxes and expenditures in this State prior to the war, and subsequently, taking the sessions of the different legislatures. I have not that paper with me, but it would be startling; it would be surprising—very surprising. In answer to that question I will state that our taxes are very much larger; I think four or five or six times as great. And not only that, but in considering this question of taxation, it is to be remembered that taxes formerly were small, and we were what we might term a rich and prosperous people. Now, about seven-tenths of the property has been destroyed. I say seven-tenths; it may not be quite so much, and may be more. I merely make the general approximation the general statement. The tax is only upon three-tenths of the amount of property that was formerly paid out, and the tax has to be multiplied by five or four.

By the CHAIRMAN:

Question. General Gholson says sixteen times greater than before the war.

Answer. He may be correct; I do not know.

By Mr. BLAIR:

Question. That is, comparing the difference in property and the difference in taxes?

Answer. I make the estimate in that way: the tax being four or five times as much, and that upon only three-tenths as much property. You can figure what the ratio is. In giving you these figures I desire to say it is not the result of any statistics I have in my mind at this time. It is a general estimate, about which I may be in error on one side or the other. I cannot undertake to be accurate.

Question. You say you have seen a statement which purports to give the amount of taxes for the different legislatures before the war and since?

Answer. Yes, sir.

Question. What is your recollection of that statement?

Answer. That it is many times larger. I can refer you to that statement or tell you where you can obtain it. I would not undertake to report that paper without having it before me. There was so much of it, but the statement is perfectly startling. If the committee desire I can tell them where it is or procure it. I saw the statement published, and it can be obtained. Our taxes are much larger, heavier, and more burdensome. Why, if you would come here when the taxes are being collected, it would startle you, gentlemen, to see the number of tracts of land sold by the sheriff as forfeited.

By Mr. RICE:

Question. Are the disbursements greater than under the democratic legislature in the war in 1865-1866?

Answer. The war was not in 1865-1866.

Question. Are the disbursements greater now than then?

Answer. I cannot tell you. I only can say that the disbursements since the war have been very great, and much larger than at any time prior to the war. Take, for example, the expenses of the public printing and the expenses of the legislature, or for the officers of the State, which have been multiplied in every department. I think I am safe—yes, I know I am safe—in saying that the expenditures are much larger, far larger than they were before.

By Mr. BLAIR:

Question. You stated that large quantities of land were sold for taxes?

Answer. Yes, sir; large quantities. Now, when we sell lands for taxes in this State the law authorizes the party to redeem his lands in two years by paying a very large per cent. besides paying all fees incidental to delinquents' sale and publication, and to redeem in two years, but he pays only about 30 or 35 per cent. There is a regular per centum added, and interest added, and expenses, and all which would amount altogether to 30 or 35 per cent., with two years for redemption; and if it is not redeemed in that time the party purchasing, by filing his bill, can obtain a title absolute. Not only that, but what will be still more surprising to you, we have a system of leasing our lands in this State which began a great many years ago. These deeds or releases are dated, generally, in 1821, when the lands were leased for ninety-nine years renewable. They were sixteenth-section lands. Take for example lands in and about Columbus. They were leased for nominal sums. I own a lot down in town here upon which the lease is ten or eleven dollars, payable annually. I pay that every year, but if I do not pay it the lease is forfeited, and anybody who buys get an absolute title. Sometimes the lease will amount to 30 cents on a lot, sometimes five or ten dollars. There are cases here recently where the parties have actually not paid their leases, but have permitted them to pass unpaid.

Question. Town lots?

Answer. Yes, sir. I have heard of a few cases where they have passed by. I am not prepared to say that it has been from an absolute inability to pay. I take it that the parties would not have permitted their leases to have been forfeited if able to pay. It may have been neglect, but in regard to the taxes it is notorious that our people have been oppressed, and that their lands have been sold, and they have been subjected to enormous expenses.

By the CHAIRMAN:

Question. What is the sum total of taxes in any year that has been paid by this county?

Answer. I cannot tell you.

Question. Does it amount to a hundred thousand dollars?

Answer. Senator, I would have stated that in the first instance if I had known that you desired that information; I can obtain it in a few minutes; it is in the court-house.

Question. When you spoke of taxes being excessive, I supposed you had all these data in your mind, or the facts upon which you predicated the opinion.

Answer. If you mean the exact figures or record before me, I have not such data. I speak from general information just I have set forth to you. I have the general information—knowledge of these general facts. I have seen these statements published in the papers, and have discussed them with private individuals. I am not prepared with the figures and amounts now, but I could obtain them for you very quickly if they are desired. All the records of this county are in this court-house, and you can see them very soon if you wish to inquire further in regard to the county taxes and assessments.

By Mr. BLAIR:

Question. Is it not very much more difficult for a poor man to pay even a small tax than for a wealthy man to pay a large one?

Answer. It is so in all communities.

By Mr. RICE:

Question. Then it is hardest on the negroes?

Answer. So far as the negroes are concerned, you will find that they pay little or no tax. I particularly invite your attention, if you desire information on that point, to the record which is here at hand and easily obtained.

By Mr. BLAIR:

Question. There is a certain amount of property exempt from taxation?

Answer. No, sir. I think all property is taxable.

Question. Is not $250 exempt under the law?

Answer. No, sir. I think everything is liable for taxes.

By Mr. RICE:

Question. In Alabama I think $300 is exempt.

Answer. I do not wish to enter into a legal discussion with you gentlemen on this point unless you desire it.

By Mr. BLAIR:

Question. Of course not.

Answer. But I will state my view on that point, or what I think the statute states, if you wish to know.

Question. I simply asked the question, whether any property was exempt?

Answer. I do not understand the statute of this State to exempt any property, except from execution. For example, we have our homestead exemption. If I get a judgment against a man for a thousand or ten thousand dollars, the law says that when the execution is issued the sheriff shall not levy upon his homestead, or cow, calf, mule, or wagon, and a certain amount of meat. That is the homestead exemption law of this State, but I do not understand that to apply to taxes. Hence you will find that every man, if possible, will rake and scrape enough together if he can get the money to pay the taxes upon his homestead, and such exempted property as may be assessed to him.

Question. There are several gentlemen who have testified before this committee, among others Mr. Whitfield, Mr. Gleed, and Colonel Eggleston, as to these outrages here. I want now particularly to call your attention to the witness Henry B. Whitfield, and ask you what is his character, what is his standing, what is his general reputation for truth and veracity?

Answer. In regard to that, General Blair, I would make this statement. While, of course, I would not decline to answer your question, but will cheerfully do so if it is insisted upon, I would say that on yesterday Mr. Whitfield called at my office and requested me not to discuss his character, or to make any statement about it to this committee. He did so, I presume, from motives of delicacy, and I said to him that I would not do so unless called upon by the committee. If you desire any information, however, upon that point, as a matter of duty I will tell you what I know.

Question. Well, sir, I understand, generally, that his character is bad, and he has given his testimony in a way to defame this whole people here, and I desire to know from you what his character is.

Answer. I stated to Mr. Whitfield that if I gave any testimony before this committee as to him, I would inform him what I said in the committee-room, and with that view I have made a memorandum upon this piece of paper, [producing a paper,] in order that I may give him the information, that he may vindicate himself if the committee desire that he should so.

The witness reads as follows:

In dealing with his character it is difficult to assign, speaking of Henry B. Whitfield, his leading vice. It might be deemed invidious to make comparisons, and to give pre-eminence to one over other rival qualities and gifts, where all have high claims of distinction; but his reputation for lying and obtaining money under false pretenses, perhaps, is higher than for anything else; and in thus assigning pre-eminence to these traits of his character, I do it without the least disposition to derogate from other brilliant characteristics belonging to the same general category. Now, some men are liars from instinct, some from vanity, some from a sort of necessity, others are enticed away by the beguilements of pleasure, or seduced by evil example and education. Whitfield belongs to a higher class of the fine arts in this department of *belles-lettres*. He is a natural liar, just as some horses are natural pacers, and some dogs are natural setters; he never labors a lie; he lies with a relish, with a coming appetite growing with what it feeds upon. He applies his art to the practical purposes of life. His lying is encyclopedical; it is what German criticism calls many-sided. It embraces all subjects without distinction or partiality; it was equally good upon all, "From grave to gay, from lively to severe." He occasionally adopts a fact to start with; but, like a Sheffield razor, and the crude ore, the workmanship, polish, and value are all his own. A Thibet shawl could as well be credited to the insensate goat that grew the wool, as the author of a fact Whitfield honored with his skill could claim to be the inventor of his story. In a word, he is an enlarged edition of Ovid Bolus, as described by Joe Baldwin in the Flush times of Alabama and Mississippi, endowed perhaps with less honor and more rascality.

In making this statement as to the general reputation and general character of Henry B. Whitfield, I desire to state upon what I base that statement. In the first instance, gentlemen of the jury, Henry B. Whitfield was indicted in the State of Alabama charged with having obtained from Governor Winston of that State a large amount of money under false pretenses. As evidence of that fact I herewith hand you [producing a paper] a transcript of a bill of indictment against Henry B. Whitfield returned by the grand jury to the city court of Mobile at the general term, 1868, of said court, in which the bill of indictment is set forth; the transcript is certified to as correct by the clerk of that court under the seal of the city court of Mobile. I hand you the copy. I have been informed that he left that State; that the governor offered a reward for him—whether the reward was offered or not I do not know myself—but this I do know, that the governor of Alabama made a requisition on the governor of Mississippi for Mr. Whitfield. I have before me Governor Alcorn's reasons for not delivering Mr. Whitfield in response to that requisition to the governor of Alabama, which paper I now hand you, [producing a paper.] I will state to the committee that Mr. Whitfield is advised of this. I informed him of this bill of indictment and urged him to go to Mobile to answer it. He has not done so. I will now show you some of the facts upon which this bill of indictment was based that you may understand——

The CHAIRMAN. I do not suppose it will be necessary to go into the details of those matters.

The WITNESS. Only for this reason: I have stated that this man was a man of bad character, and in the habit of obtaining money under false pretenses. It is always unpleasant to be called upon to make a statement in regard to a party of that character, and I do so only in the discharge of my duty as a witness here. Having made the statement, I do not wish that it shall rest upon my bare assertion. I have papers, writings, here signed by Henry B. Whitfield, which I think in a great measure tend to establish and sustain the charges contained in that bill of indictment. Here is also the trust deed by ——

The CHAIRMAN. My opinion is that where the witness has made a statement of the fact that a party has been indicted in a court and produced a copy of the record here, it is sufficient for the purposes of our inquiry without incumbering the record with the indictment itself.

The WITNESS. Senator, I will submit this to your committee. You have called upon me to answer a question of a delicate nature and character ——

The CHAIRMAN. I do not choose to argue the matter with you; you are a witness. I state simply to the committee my opinion is against the introduction into our record of a copy of the bill of indictment, though I have no objection to a witness stating that such a thing occurred and the offense for which this party was indicted, but I think that that is all that the committee needs.

Mr. BLAIR. I consider the record evidence the best evidence, and think we are entitled to have it.

Mr. RICE. In proving general reputation, the statement made by the witness is sufficient, and you need not press it by proving particular acts, unless it is brought out by cross-examination.

Mr. BLAIR. We are not in this committee tied up by any of the rules of evidence. They are departed from every day. The committee seem to take great pleasure in going into matters which would not be considered for a single moment in a court of law. This man, Whitfield's, evidence has been delivered, and is relied upon. We have the right now to show that he is a man who cannot be believed upon anything, by the oral testimony of this witness, by the still better evidence of the indictment itself, and the demand of the government of the State for his delivery to the courts of Alabama, and the refusal of the governor of Mississippi upon a technical ground, and then the actual paper for the execution of which he was indicted.

The CHAIRMAN. If the fact that he was indicted should become a matter of controversy, doubtless that evidence would be proper, but when the witness has stated the fact that he was indicted; that a requisition was made upon the governor of Mississippi for his rendition to the authorities of Alabama, I imagine that that is all that is essential, until those facts are brought into question.

Mr. BLAIR. Then I understand the committee excludes this evidence from the record?

The CHAIRMAN. It is excluded, unless there should be testimony to controvert the fact that he was indicted for obtaining money under false pretenses, and that a requisition was made.

Mr. BLAIR. I desire to reserve the question for the general committee upon this point, including the response of Governor Alcorn to the requisition of the governor of Alabama.

[The action of the general committee upon the exception taken by Mr. Blair is shown in the following extract from the journal of the committee, p. 620:

"JOINT SELECT COMMITTEE,
"*Washington, D. C., December* 21, 1871.

"The joint select committee met pursuant to the call of the chairman.

"Present: The chairman, (Mr. Scott,) Messrs. Bayard, Blair, Cox, Poland, Pool, Pratt, Rice, Stevenson, Van Trump, and Waddell.

* * * * * * *

"Mr. Pratt, chairman of the sub-committee appointed to take testimony in the States of Tennessee, Alabama, and Mississippi, presented a report from which it appeared that during the investigation Mr. Blair had filed exceptions to the ruling of the chairman in relation to the admission of certain testimony and the exclusion of other testimony, as follows:

* * * * * * *

"4th. At Columbus, Mississippi, on November 16, 1871, W. H. Humphries was called by the minority, and testified to the bad character of Henry B. Whitfield, a witness called by the majority, and exhibited a copy of an indictment against Whitfield. Mr. Blair offered it in evidence. It was excluded. Mr. Blair excepted, and appealed to the general committee.

"On the question, 'Will the joint committee sustain the ruling of the chairman of the sub-committee (Mr. Pratt) in excluding the said copy of an indictment?' the yeas and nays were required, and were as follows:

"YEAS—Messrs. Poland, Pool, Pratt, Rice, Stevenson, and Scott, (chairman)—6.

"NAYS—Messrs. Bayard, Blair, Cox, Van Trump, and Waddell—5.

"So the question was determined in the affirmative."]

By Mr. BLAIR:

Question. The paper which you now offer [the witness having produced a paper] is, as I understand, a deed of trust?

Answer. It is a paper signed by Mr. Whitfield himself; it is a trust deed.

Question. Upon what?

Answer. Upon certain property which he agreed to ship to Winston & Co., of Mobile, and that he did not ship, and in which he makes the false pretenses alleged in that bill of indictment.

Question. As I understand you, he had obtained money from Governor Winston?

Answer. Yes, sir; about $4,000.

Question. Upon what pretense?

Answer. Upon false pretenses, as alleged in the bill of indictment.

Question. What were those pretenses?

Answer. I will state those pretenses as I am informed and have reason to believe, and am sustained by the instrument in my possession, signed by himself.

The CHAIRMAN. I understand that the whole purpose of this evidence is to discredit the testimony which Mr. Whitfield has given before the committee at Washington.

Mr. BLAIR. That is the object of it, sir.

The CHAIRMAN. On the question of character you are confined in this examination to general evidence. I do not understand that the general committee has ever made any other ruling or order upon that point. The injustice of any other course is very apparent. Mr. Whitfield is not before the committee for the purpose of cross-examining this witness, or giving evidence as to the particular facts upon which the indictment at Mobile was founded. If he were upon trial and had an opportunity to explain these matters, the impropriety would not be so great.

Mr. BLAIR. The community he has assailed and defamed were not before this committee to defend themselves. I desire to appeal from this ruling to the general committee.

The CHAIRMAN. It is your privilege.

Mr. BLAIR. For the purpose of doing that I ask the witness to state the character of the instrument which is now before this sub-committee.

The CHAIRMAN. That is ruled out.

Mr. BLAIR. The instrument is ruled out, but I want our record to note the instrument itself that I now offer to prove and put in evidence.

The CHAIRMAN. The record will note the fact that such evidence was offered. You can make any indorsement on the paper for the purpose of identification that you desire, and it can be laid before the general committee, but neither this paper nor the contents of it can be given in evidence here.

The WITNESS. I cannot part with this paper. It is very valuable, not only in the court of Mobile, but it represents dollars and cents. It has been intrusted to me. It is not my property, and I cannot part with it.

By the CHAIRMAN:

Question. I speak of the deed of trust.

Answer. Yes, sir; this is the deed of trust itself. You may take a copy of it, or I can state generally its contents, but unless I am required to do so—and I have no idea that this committee would take property from me that does not belong to me—I cannot part with it. I have no objection to a copy being taken, or to submitting it to you for perusal.

By Mr. BLAIR:

Question. You can intrust it to our clerk for the purpose of having a copy made?

Answer. I have no objection to that. Shall I proceed?

Question. Yes, sir.

Answer. The next matter in connection with this subject is in relation to two paper writings, both signed by Henry B. Whitfield, by which he obtained money under false pretenses from Frank M. Shepherd, of this county, to the amount of $1,600.

The CHAIRMAN. That paper is ruled out for the same reasons as the former.

By Mr. BLAIR:

Question. Do you require these papers?

Answer. Well, sir, this is a promissory note for $1,600. It is of no account, and I presume Mr. Shepherd would not care anything about it. The committee can have that paper, but I cannot state it without explanation. You will not understand it, for the facts will not appear. You place me in a delicate and false position, unless you allow me to explain these matters.

The CHAIRMAN. The committee have decided that you cannot enter into specific facts on this subject.

Mr. BLAIR. The witness can make the explanation, I suppose; and if the facts and the papers are ruled out, his statement in regard to that will be ruled out also; but if these papers go before the general committee and are admitted, they ought to be admitted with his explanation.

The CHAIRMAN. He may identify the papers in any manner he sees proper, that they may become evidence in case the general committee shall see proper to receive them; but if the papers are excluded, I could not, of course, allow the witness to go on and give the contents of the papers, and thus, indirectly, place them on the record.

Mr. BLAIR. I do not propose to do that, because that part of his evidence would be stricken out with the exclusion of the papers, except the fact that he has offered to produce such papers. The witness says the papers will not explain themselves, and I desire that he may make the explanation, which, of course, will fall with the papers if they are not received by the general committee.

Mr. RICE. I understand the principle on which the paper is excluded is that we cannot go into specific facts.

Mr. BLAIR. But suppose the general committee takes a different view from that taken by a majority of the sub-committee here, then we should not be able to procure from the witness, as he would not be before the general committee, this statement, which he thinks is necessary, in explanation of that paper. I want, now, to get his explanation, which he thinks necessary to accompany these papers; and, as a matter of course, if the general committee, at Washington, should agree with the majority of the sub-committee here, that explanation would go with the papers and be stricken from our record; but, if received, the paper and the explanation would go together. I think I am entitled to that.

The CHAIRMAN. I do not know, of course, what the character of the explanation offered is, but if to enlarge or diminish the contents of a written paper, of course, by well-settled principles, it cannot be received.

The WITNESS. Senator Pratt, may I be permitted to address you a moment upon one or two points that you have suggested, in justice to myself?

The CHAIRMAN. I would prefer that you would confine yourself to responses to questions asked you.

The WITNESS. You misunderstand me. It is not to insist upon any line different from you gentlemen, but to inform you that I am placed in a ridiculous position; for you are not doing me justice in requiring me to answer questions and produce papers which are unintelligible in themselves, and will, therefore, make me appear in that light.

The CHAIRMAN. You are not required to produce a single paper. The decision of the majority of the committee is that you shall be confined to a general statement of the character of Mr. Whitfield.

The WITNESS. Then why do you take these papers away from me and propose to incorporate them in your record?

The CHAIRMAN. We do not take them away from you. The decision is that the papers do not go into the record. You are at liberty to retain these papers in your possession.

The WITNESS. I have no choice about the matter. I simply ask to not be required to answer questions unless I may give an explanation, and, if it be consistent with your rules, shall do so in future.

Mr. BLAIR. I make the distinct proposition, and ask the decision of this committee upon it, that the witness make such explanation to accompany these papers as he sees proper, to be received or not with the papers.

The CHAIRMAN. If the general committee shall think these papers admissible in evidence you will have the right, of course, to call Mr. Humphries before the committee as a witness to make such explanations as may be deemed necessary, but the papers themselves being excluded I cannot conceive the value of any explanation respecting those papers.

Mr. BLAIR. I will now ask the witness as to the character of Major Eggleston.

The WITNESS. In connection with that matter I will state that so far as General Eggleston is concerned, I know nothing of my own knowledge derogatory to his character as a gentleman, or to his standing as a citizen and a good man, but I have heard many things derogatory to the general character of General Eggleston in the community. Among them I heard recently of this charge of a forgery—I do not know that the committee is conversant with it—in which he and Major Henry B. Whitfield were engaged. I have reason to believe, and in fact I have been informed that a bill of indictment was found against General Eggleston at this term of the circuit court by the grand jury for forgery. The bill of indictment, if I am correct, and I think there is no doubt about it, is in the next room, the circuit clerk's room, and I will go for it if the committee desire it. Mr. Whitfield was connected in that bill and came very nearly being elected, as the lawyers term it, to a bill. The grand jury is composed of fifteen. The law requires twelve to find a bill, and I am informed that General Eggleston was indicted for forgery, by members of the grand jury.

Question. What is the political character of that grand jury?

Answer. I have the names here; it is republican; the republican element predominated there very largely, I think. I will tell you in a moment. I will count them in a moment and give you more definite information. As to this indictment for forgery I have not seen it, but it is in Josiah Stalling's room, if I am correct, which adjoins this, and I will get it if it is there and you desire it. I presume there is no doubt about it. The names of the grand jury are as follows: W. E. Gibbs, democrat; J. F. Galloway, radical; C. B. Canfield, I think he is a democrat; Joshua Hairston, radical; Elzy Richards, radical; A. M. Green, democrat; A. Stewart, radical; Thomas Seale, radical; Robert Gleed, radical and a member elect of the Senate from this district; H. C. Long, democrat; J. T. Harrison, jr., democrat; M. Witherspoon—if he is the Witherspoon I am thinking of, he is also a radical; J. H. Brazier, democrat; G. M. Barksdale, I do not know him or his politics; I do not know which of the Barksdales it is. Samuel Kline is a radical and ex-sheriff. He has been an old sheriff here since the war, and is a radical. The majority of this grand jury are members of the republican party, but it takes twelve to find a bill. Now, in regard to Whitfield's connection with that I do not understand the bill was found against him. He lacked, some one said, one vote, or maybe two, of being elected. I understand, or have been informed, as to how the forgery——

By the CHAIRMAN:

Question. How did you become informed of the secrets of the grand-jury room?

Answer. I heard it on the street and went to the circuit clerk on yesterday and asked him to let me see the bill of indictment. I told him why it was——

Question. I speak of what was done in the grand-jury room. You say that Mr. Whitfield came within so many votes of being elected. How did you learn that?

Answer. I do not remember. I heard it on the street.

Question. Did you hear it from a member of the grand jury?

Answer. I do not remember that I did. I conceive that there would have been no impropriety in the statement. The object of the grand jury keeping their proceedings secret is this: that when they find a bill of indictment the party may not be advised of it, lest he will get out of the way before being arrested. Hence the policy of the law is to not let him know it until the *capias* is served. But it is impossible to keep many things which occur before the grand jury from becoming public, because the witnesses are summoned into the grand-jury room.

Question. Are not your grand juries charged by the judge when impaneled never to disclose the secrets of a grand-jury room, unless regularly called upon to do it in a court of justice?

Answer. I am not aware that such an oath is administered by the judge. I will show you a copy of the oath, if you desire to see it, and it will speak for itself. A revised code is, perhaps, on the table over there. I see there is a law library in this room.

By Mr. BLAIR:

Question. Gleed has also been before this committee?

Answer. So far as Gleed is concerned, I know nothing in regard to Gleed of my own personal knowledge. I can make a general statement in reference to him. It is simply to this effect: I heard a party, who was a democrat, and a prominent democrat, and I will say an extreme democrat, charge Gleed publicly with having been bribed by Mr. Dass with $500 to act for him in the late election, and that he had taken Dass's $500, and would not give it back, though he had deserted Dass, and did not stand by him. The same party charged that during Gleed's membership in the State senate he had received bribes there, and that he had witnesses, and would produce them, if called for. Whether these facts are proved or not, I do not know. I heard the charge made, and an offer to produce the witnesses, and I heard a gentleman who was referred to as one of the witnesses say he could substantiate the facts. The names of these parties I can give you. I do not speak of my own knowledge. So far as Gleed is concerned, I know nothing of any bad conduct on his part myself. I will say that Mr. Abram Murdock, president of the Mobile and Ohio Railroad, told me that when he was in Jackson, with Mr. Van Hook, a brother of George W. Van Hook, the present chancery clerk of this county, that Gleed came into a banking-house, or possibly an insurance establishment, where he had money on hand, with two $500 bills, which he wanted changed. He stated at the time that bribery and corruption was going on in Jackson, and he was a little surprised that a man who was engaged in no business, who did not receive his pay in money, but in State warrants, should come with bills of that amount. He did not say that he came by them by bribery, or how, but simply stated that a good deal of that was going on. At the conclusion of the war, Gleed, I think, was a common laboring man here, a poor man of course.

Question. He had been a slave?

Answer. Yes, sir; he had little or no property. He was a teamster, probably with two or three animals. Finally he built himself a nice little house—by the way, we passed it the other day in driving, you will remember, general.

Mr. BLAIR. Yes.

The WITNESS. It is a neat cottage-house that may have cost $1,500 or $2,500. I should make that general estimate; such a house as a gentleman or a merchant with a good stock of goods on hand and doing a fine business might have. He is also dealing in real estate, and is the owner of considerable land in the county, I hear. I sold him some land as trustee—a lot belonging to Iverson Lewis. I was a trustee for that and other lands. Now, I merely mentioned that when the war closed a few years ago he was a poor man, while he is now a man of considerable means; he has been engaged in politics most of the time. You gentlemen know better whether that is very lucrative than myself; I do not know how it pays.

By the CHAIRMAN:

Question. What is his general character?

Answer. These charges I have made are specific.

Question. I ask for his general character?

Answer. I will answer your question if you will permit me to do it in my own way. Among his people he is highly thought of. They look upon him almost as a demi-god. The white people, I think, dislike him very much, and in justice to Mr. Gleed I would state that he is the leader of his party, and it may be that their dislike to him arises from the fact that he is a prominent man, and they regard him as vindictive and bitter, and many of them regard him as a man dangerous to the peace and good order of society. I make that statement in justice to him. I never knew him to be guilty of a dishonorable act in my life.

Question. Is his character for truth and veracity good?

Answer. I have only heard it questioned in the manner I speak of. Now, the parties that made this statement remarked that he was an infamous man, and a scoundrel, and a liar.

Question. I am speaking of his general character for truth and veracity?

Answer. I know nothing to the contrary except that I have stated. I say that among his own people I believe his character is high; they look upon him as a demi-god almost.

By Mr. BLAIR:

Question. Do his own people set any value at all upon good character as to truth and veracity; are those elements of good character with them?

Answer. There are some who do; there are some good black people, honest and truthful. I do not think, however, there are very many; as a general thing they do not. Let a negro go to jail for stealing, and he will come out and be generally as well received as before; they make nothing of it. The records of this court will speak in thunder-tones upon that point—in fact I might say the records of the courts all over the State.

By the CHAIRMAN:

Question. Before passing from this subject I would like to know what is the general character for truth and veracity of General Eggleston?

Answer. I have known General Eggleston as a man, and he has always struck me as being a good citizen, and a gentleman in his behavior and deportment. I never heard any man, friend or foe, charge him with being a liar. I don't think I ever heard that charge brought against him.

Question. Would you believe him under oath?

Answer. I would most undoubtedly; I should believe General Eggleston. But when you call upon me to make this statement, you require me to state what I have heard, and I make this statement in regard to this bill of indictment.

Question. I did not ask you in relation to that. I now ask you whether you would believe Gleed under oath?

Answer. Yes, sir; I would believe Gleed under oath. I will answer that I would believe Gleed under oath, but I will make this qualification: I would believe him, unless it was in regard to some matter where his zeal and fanaticism might betray him into an error that he, perhaps, would not be guilty of in speaking of matters that he could talk about without being influenced by feeling, or passion, or excitement. I think that he would be a man that, under circumstances of that sort, could not be relied upon, sir; that is my individual opinion.

By Mr. BLAIR:

Question. There is a statement made by this witness, Henry B. Whitfield, in reference to Joe Beckwith, (page 424,) which just strikes my eye:

"We undertook to investigate that case through the police, and we were pretty well satisfied as to who the parties were and where they came from; but the evidence was not sufficient to insure their conviction, although the presumption was so great as to amount almost to a moral certainty. The man who wanted them prosecuted was not willing, upon the strength of the evidence as it stood, to make an affidavit against the parties."

Do you know about that?

Answer. I presume he alludes to Major Eggleston. I know he was engaged to prosecute them; he talked to me about it, and would have prosecuted if he had had any reasonable ground to prosecute. I know the sentiment of the community was to prosecute them. They were anxious to prosecute them, but could not discover them.

Question. Is it the fact that you were pretty well satisfied as to who the parties were and where they came from?

Answer. No, sir; I do not believe it. I do not believe that anybody was satisfied. I investigated, or looked into the matter myself, and I never heard it charged to any individual. If any party was ever suspected I am not aware of it.

Question. Who were engaged in the investigation?

Answer. I was spoken to by Major Eggleston myself. I was not employed by him. I do much of his business, and I presume I would have been employed if any prosecution had been set on foot. He mentioned it in my office one day. I felt an interest in knowing. It was an outrage that should have been punished, and severely punished.

Question. Before the conclusion of your evidence I want you to state to the committee what you consider the present condition of affairs here, and whether you think there is an improvement.

Answer. Our grand jury express their opinion in these words, which I adopt as my own: "The grand jury are pleased to report (so far as brought to their knowledge) that crime of all classes in Lowndes County have greatly diminished." I hand you a copy of their report. [The witness produces the report of the grand jury, which will be found at the end of his testimony.] I think, sir, that the peace and good order of society is improving very much. The most complaint is petty larceny; this constant, eternal stealing. There are by far fewer assaults and batteries, few murders, and crime of that character has greatly diminished. This country is returning to a basis of peace, and I hope will return to one of prosperity before a great while.

Question. Is there any other matter or thing in reference to the general condition of the country that you desire to state?

Answer. I have no disposition, general, to make a statement in regard to any specific matter. If there is anything you desire to ask about I will answer.

Question. I ask if there is any other matter or thing in reference to the general condition of the country that you desire to state?

Answer. Not the slightest that I desire to state. Is it permissible to speak of any other matter I desire to say?

Question. Yes, sir.

Answer. I have in my possession proofs of, I reckon, any number of individual acts of felony and lying on the part of Major Whitfield, which I can produce and sustain before this committee, if you desire to have them; individual acts, which, in justice to myself, having made this statement concerning him, I will present if the committee desire to hear them.

By the CHAIRMAN:

Question. What part did you take in the late war?

Answer. I was in the war, sir, most of the time; first I was an adjutant on the staff of Major General Earl Van Dorn, in the early part of the war, when he was the major general in the State of Mississippi. Subsequent to that time I was on the staff of General Clark, in the capacity of an aid. I then organized a company in the town of Columbus, and was elected its captain. Subsequent to that time, when the company disbanded, I was elected lieutenant of a company, and was captain of the company at the close of the war.

Question. Have you related all the instances of outrage that have come to your knowledge?

Answer. No, sir; a great many I have not related, from the fact that they did not occur to me. I presume you might ask me in regard to matters that you have before you that have escaped my memory; there may be some.

Question. When did you make the memorandum from which you have testified to-day?

Answer. I have been making it for two or three days; noting down these cases as they occurred to me.

Question. At whose request?

Answer. Nobody's. I made it for myself.

Question. With the purpose of coming before this committee?

Answer. No, sir. I did not request to come before this committee. I was summoned here by your sergeant-at-arms.

Question. Did you commence the memorandum before or after you were summoned?

Answer. After I was summoned; I should say after I was notified.

Question. Before or after you were summoned?

Answer. Since I was summoned. I was summoned on Monday, I think.

The SERGEANT-AT-ARMS, (Mr. McGuire.) Monday afternoon.

The WITNESS. Yes, sir; in fact I was summoned before that. On Sunday afternoon I was told by General Blair that he desired me as a witness.

By the CHAIRMAN:

Question. You minuted down there all the instances of the outrages committed of which you have any knowledge or information?

Answer. I did not say so, sir; on the contrary, I distinctly stated that I had minuted down such as I remembered and all that I did remember. There may be others that I have not mentioned.

Question. If there are any others, please state them,

Answer. I have stated all that I remember at this time—no, I have not either. I can state others. I have heard about the whipping of Huggins up here in Monroe County, and I have heard about a negro by the name of Nettles; about some negroes killed in Monroe County, and a number of cases I have heard about that are not in this county. I have heard of them generally. I do not know what the facts are.

Question. Have you given all the instances of which you have any knowledge or information in this county.

Answer. No, sir; I remember some cases now that I have not mentioned, in regard to some teachers. In looking over Mr. Whitfield's testimony, all of which I have read, there are a number of cases I have not mentioned. I knew nothing of the facts. The cases I have alluded to in my testimony were cases which I became acquainted with, because I was counsel in some of these cases, and other matters I had heard and been informed of and knew all about, while still other matters I did not know about.

Question. When did you first see Mr. Whitfield's testimony?

Answer. I suppose it was probably a month ago.

Question. Did you see it in a volume of printed testimony taken by the committee appointed under a joint resolution of Congress?

Answer. It was a printed volume, and I presume it was the volume you allude to.

Question. Where did you obtain that volume.

Answer. I will state my information upon that point.

Question. State the fact; you know where you got it.

Answer. I shall state nothing else than fact, either from my own knowledge or information.

Question. I ask you directly where you obtained that volume?

Answer. I have no hesitation in answering your question, and will do it in my own way. The volume was handed to me by a gentleman of the name of Pope, who lives in the town of Columbus; that was some three or four days ago. My information is that it was sent to a gentleman named Lyon, who is one of the chancellors of this State, and was said to have been sent to him by some member of your committee.

Question. I understood you to say that you had seen the testimony of Mr. Whitfield a month ago?

Answer. I did. I saw another volume. I have seen two volumes of this testimony. A month ago I saw one at the office of Colonel Beverly Matthews, in Columbus. He read over to me Mr. Whitfield's testimony in his office.

Question. Where did he get it?

Answer. I do not know.

Question. Did he inform you?

Answer. He did not.

Question. You have no knowledge of where he received his copy?

Answer. No, sir; no further than this: subsequent to that time I understood it was from a gentleman named Landrum. Where he had obtained it I know nothing. The volume I alluded to as having read three or four days ago I understood belonged to Mr. Lyon; some of you gentlemen of this committee perhaps had sent it to him. Chancellor Lyon I allude to.

By Mr. BLAIR:

Question. Who is Chancellor Lyon?

Answer. One of the judges of the State appointed by Governor Alcorn.

Question. A republican?

Answer. He is regarded as a radical.

Question. Who did you understand sent it to him?

Answer. Somebody stated that it was Senator Pratt; whether you, Mr. Chairman, are the gentleman or not I do not know.

The CHAIRMAN. He stated falsely; I never sent a copy to anybody. I have never parted with the volume which was intrusted to me.

The WITNESS. I do not allege that you sent it at all. I do not know whence it came.

By the CHAIRMAN:

Question. Do you know Joseph F. Galloway, a teacher in this county?

Answer. I do not know that I ever saw him.

Question. Did you ever hear that he was called upon by disguised men in the night-time and warned to discontinue his school, and threatened with woe if they had to come upon him again?

Answer. I think that Mr. Whitfield, in his testimony, makes that statement. I read it.

Question. Is that the only knowledge that you have on that subject?

Answer. No, sir; I have heard the matter discussed right here in this town.

Question. I simply ask you whether you have heard whether that school was broken up?

Answer. Yes, sir; that he received some letter or communication.

Question. Did you ever hear that Ely Tapley, a school-teacher, was also visited by the Ku-Klux and ordered to stop teaching?

Answer. I do not know Ely Tapley. I do not remember to have heard of that case. I do not remember the name, nor do I know the party.

Question. Did you ever hear that a body of disguised men called upon Squire Webb and ordered him to stop teaching school?

Answer. I do not remember to have heard anything about Squire Webb, unless it is in the testimony of Whitfield.

Question. Did you ever hear that they called on a man named Minter and ordered him not to send his children to any common school?

Answer. Minter, from Caledonia; is that connected with the Kennon matter?

Question. I do not know what matter it is connected with.

Answer. If it has any reference to that matter I have heard of it.

Question. Did you ever hear that they called on a Miss Booth and Mr. Myers, teachers, and ordered them to desist from teaching school?

Answer. I do not remember anything about that case, sir. If you desire to get accurate information as to what I have heard, if you will furnish me with a list I will tell you, or with a copy of Mr. Whitfield's testimony, which I have read; some of those cases I have seen there, but I do not remember their names; the parties are strangers to me.

Question. Did you ever hear of a man of the name of Jerry Conn, and their telling him that he must quit drinking?

The WITNESS. Where does he live?

The CHAIRMAN. I do not know in what part of the county.

Answer. I do not remember the names. If you will acquaint me with the facts I might remember the case, especially the cases in Whitfield's testimony. I have read all of that, but I am not acquainted with the parties, or I do not know them, unless you identify the cases particularly. I may state that I have not heard of a case, when I have.

Question. Did you ever hear of their killing a man by the name of Brown, who was teacher of a colored school, and warning him not to teach?

Answer. Never. I do not remember to have heard of such a case. I will state in that connection that I have heard of a number of these cases where they have called upon parties; whether they were disguised or how, or who they were, I do not know, but I have heard of a number of cases, and I repeat, I will not attempt to identify the names, for I do not remember them.

Question. Did you ever hear of men disguised visiting the house of Albert Handy, in this county, and entering his house?

The WITNESS. Where does Albert Handy live, and what were the facts connected with that matter?

The CHAIRMAN. They were looking for the deacon of the church, a man named Stewart, who had made his escape; did you ever hear of the circumstance?

The WITNESS. Was that in Monroe or Lowndes County?

The CHAIRMAN. In Lowndes County.

Answer. I may have it confounded with another. I heard of a case in Monroe County where a negro preacher had been whipped who was charged with having sexual intercourse with the sistern, as the negroes term it. I cannot undertake to state, but if you will furnish me with the *data* I request, I can tell you all of these matters, Mr. Pratt.

Question. Did you ever hear of the whipping of a colored man named George Irion?

The WITNESS. In what part of the county?

The CHAIRMAN. I cannot tell you.

The WITNESS. Was it on the Malone plantation—no, that negro was perhaps killed on the Malone plantation. I remember that on the Noxubee line a negro was whipped, but I think that was on Major Hairston's plantation. I do not remember the case you allude to.

Question. Did you ever hear of the whipping by disguised men of a colored man named Ed Murphy, at Hutchinson's plantation?

Answer. I do not remember it.

Question. Did you ever hear of a case of Robert Wells, a colored man, who was badly whipped?

The WITNESS. When did that occur?

The CHAIRMAN. That occurred last winter some time.

Answer. I do not remember that case.

Question. Did you ever hear of the whipping of a colored man named Joe Turner, who worked with John Stevenson?

Answer. Yes, sir; I have heard of the whipping of Joe Turner, but the facts and circumstances connected with it I do not remember. I think I saw Joe Turner; I am not certain, but seems to me I have seen him in town within the last week; I think I know the negro, and, if I am not mistaken, he is in the county at this time.

Question. Did you hear that he was whipped by men in disguise?

Answer. I do not remember the particular case. In some of the cases I have no doubt that I have heard of them, though I cannot identify them, and in some of these cases the parties who flogged them, I was informed at the time, were in disguise.

Question. Did you ever hear of the murder of Page by men in disguise?

Answer. Yes, sir; I do not know how it was done; my impression is that they were in disguise; I have been informed so; the name is familiar.

Question. It created considerable talk in this country?

The WITNESS. That was in Monroe County, was it not?

Question. Did you ever hear of the murder of Dupree?

The WITNESS. Was that in Noxubee?

Mr. BLAIR. That was in Monroe.

Answer. I have no doubt that I have heard of the cases to which you allude, and that if I could get the facts and circumstances before me, the general rumor, I would be able to identify the parties. I think it likely I have heard of the cases to which you make reference.

By the CHAIRMAN:

Question. Did you ever hear of the case of Joe Beckwith?

Answer. I think I remember about the facts in that case. He was an old man living out on the Wynne place.

Question. Is that the case you speak of where he was hung?

Answer. Yes, sir; that is the case; a very outrageous case, too.

Question. You spoke, I believe, of the case of James Hicks?

Answer. Yes, sir; I alluded to that.

Question. Did you ever hear of the case of Mr. Farmer, a school-teacher?

Answer. Yes, sir; I heard it from his own lips.

Question. Did you have that case in your memorandum?

Answer. Yes, sir; I mentioned it.

Question. Have you heard of the case of the sons of Sanders Flint, of Monroe County?

Answer. I do not remember the case, sir; it may be that I heard of it.

Question. You heard of the case of Mr. Leake, a school-teacher on this side of the river, and of masked men coming to his house and warning him to discontinue his school?

Answer. Yes, sir; I heard Mr. Leake's version of the matter, and Mr. Whitfield's version of it. I do not know anything of the facts relative to it, however.

Question. Did you understand that he was visited by men in disguise.

Answer. I read Mr. Whitfield's statement.

Question. Is that the only knowledge you have on that subject?

Answer. I do not remember; I may have heard others speak on the subject; I remember to have heard something in connection with it.

Question. Did you ever hear of the case of Mr. Philips, who went to Crawford last spring to teach a colored school, and was accosted by ten or twelve men who threatened him and told him he must stop teaching; that they had no use for his sort?

Answer. I do not remember the case, sir.

Question. You have furnished the committee from your memorandum a good many cases of outrages. Will you state, generally, whether these outrages were inflicted by men in disguise and in the night-time?

Answer. I have been informed, sir, that some of them were at night and by parties in disguise; some of them were in the day-time, sir. In mentioning the different cases alluded to by myself, I think I stated in each case where the parties were disguised and the time and place and the manner in which it was done.

Question. In the case of Hairston, did you understand that the men who made the assault upon him and his house were disguised?

Answer. I did not state that from information; I stated that I was an attorney in the case and representing the man himself; I stated the facts as they were delivered on the trial of the case before me, sir; I heard the witnesses; it was at Crawfordsville.

Question. Did you understand that the parties were disguised?

Answer. I do not remember whether they were disguised or not; my impression is that they were disguised, and the thing that induced me to believe that such was the testimony is, that a number of witnesses, five or six, saw the party when they came and did not know who they were, and it is the fact, if my memory is correct, that possibly the horses and men were both disguised. Now, this man Moore was recognized by his voice, and not only by Josh Hairston, but by his wife and another party. They stated that they took one to be a mulatto or negro, which would seem to indicate that he was not disguised, but I will not be positive in regard to it.

Question. I understood you to say that you had never seen but one person with his disguise or mask on.

Answer. Only one; and, really, I attach no special importance to that, sir.

Question. You have heard of bands of disguised men in this county prowling through the country in the night-time?

Answer. Yes, sir.

Question. Frequently?

Answer. No, sir; very seldom.

Question. How many cases altogether and ranging over what period of time?

Answer. I think I have heard of bands of disguised men in the county upon four or five, or maybe seven or eight cases—possibly it might be ten; I cannot say; I do not know; I cannot tell you about that.

Question. What time did they first make their appearance in this county?

Answer. Well, sir, it may have been as far back as two or three years ago; I really do not know.

Question. Two or three years?

Answer. It may be. Yes; I presume within that time. It may be that I have heard of it twelve or fifteen times.

Question. With the exception of the case in town that you have mentioned, have you ever heard of any of the members of these organizations having been detected?

Answer. Let me understand the purport of your question again, if you please.

Question. The question is whether, with the exception of the negro in this town, you have ever known or been informed of the detection of any member of these disguised bands of men?

Answer. I understand you. I have heard of a number of indictments being found in the Federal courts against parties living in Monroe County, and perhaps other parties—who are the parties I do not know—for violation of the enforcement act and for killing parties in disguise. In regard to this negro, however, I stated the fact that I did not think he designed to do any harm. I think it was more a matter of deviltry than anything else, and so advised the chief of the police.

Question. Have any indictments been found against these parties until the present year?

Answer. The parties I allude to—I never knew any indictment to be found in this court against a man for being a Ku-Klux. I have known many indictments against parties for violation of law—white men for striking or whipping negroes, and I have known many indictments against negroes for striking white men. I have known indictments for murder to be found against white men for assassinating a negro. I allude particularly to the case of young Goldsby, charged with assassination. I do not know whether it was in disguise or not. He is indicted for it, or murder.

Question. Have you known of any arrests being made or punishments being inflicted upon any persons concerned in these midnight outrages committed by bands of men in disguise, with the exception of the indictments which you say have been found in the Federal courts?

Answer. No, sir; I do not remember further than the cases I have stated where parties have been arrested and tried. I have mentioned a number of cases beyond these cases. I have known none others; none occur to me at this time.

Question. With the exception of the case you have mentioned in town, have you ever seen and conversed with a person whom you knew or suspected to belong to a secret organization which practiced deeds of violence, or whose purpose was to commit violence under any condition or circumstances?

Answer. I know of no such organization, and have talked with no person that I had reason to believe was a member of it.

Question. Have you known, or been informed, of the locality where any such organization exists?

Answer. I have not, sir.

Question. Have you known, or been informed, of the place or places where any such organization met?

Answer. I know nothing about that, sir. I have not.

Question. My question is whether you know, or have been informed, on that subject?

Answer. I answer the question without mental reservation or self-evasion, fully and unreservedly.

Question. My question is whether you have any information of that kind?

Answer. I have none, sir.

Question. The question is double. It addresses itself to your knowledge and information?

Answer. I reply in both senses, without any disposition to evade it.

Question. Have you known, or been informed, who constitute the bands, associations, or combinations who commit these acts, or any one of the persons who are members of the same?

Answer. I neither know nor have been informed.

Question. Do you know, or have you been informed, whether the members of this Ku-Klux organization take an oath or obligation of secrecy to mutually aid each other in evading legal penalties for the commission of crime?

Answer. I neither know, nor have I been informed, of any such organization.

Question Do you know the name by which such organization is known to the members or others?

Answer. Neither, sir.

Question. Have you known, or been informed, of the purpose or object of such organization?

Answer. No, sir.

Question. Have you known, or been informed, of the grievances such organization was formed to redress?

Answer. No, sir; yet I do know of secret organizations, but none of any such character. Here is "the Native Sons of the South."

Question. Tell us all you know about them.

Answer. Well, it is a silly, ridiculous, fool thing, sir; the object, spirit, and intent of the organization was to induce the negroes of the county to act with the white people, to win them from the carpet-baggers, to influence them; in other words it was a political maneuver. Those are the objects, and the only objects.

Question. When was that order started?

Answer. I think, sir, it originated in this county—that is my information—some months back. I do not know how long. There was a printed pamphlet. I have seen it repeatedly.

Question. Are you a member of the order?

Answer. I have never joined it regularly. My connection with it amounts simply to this: I was requested by a party of gentlemen to organize a number of negroes into the order, which I undertook. I began, but became so thoroughly disgusted with the foolery of it that I retired and reported back to these gentlemen.

Question. Have you ever seen its constitution?

Answer. Yes, sir; repeatedly.

Question. Do the members on initiation take an oath?

Answer. Yes, sir.

Question. Will you please to repeat that oath.

Answer. I will not, for I do not know it. I could give you the substance of it. The oath is ridiculous and foolish. They first swear that they will never divulge the fact that they are members of the order, or even know who are, and then go on and swear that they will support men who live in the South, "Native Sons of the South;" that they will advocate an economical administration of the Government; that they will, so far as in their power by legal means, protect the rights of white men and black men without distinction of race or color. There is a good deal of it. They swear not to disclose the fact that they are members, which is a very foolish, silly thing, for as soon as they get through with the oath a badge is pinned on the waistcoat, and they wear a cap with the words upon it, "Native Sons of the South," which is a contradiction direct to their oath. There is a good deal of nonsense in the initiation and ritual. For example, in initiating there is a rather bombastic, sophomoric strain gone through.

Question. Who got it up?

Answer. My information is that a gentleman named Landrum and three or four others.

Question. How large is its membership?

Answer. I have heard it numbered 400 or 500 in the county, but I do not believe it. I state that from the fact that if they had that many members they did not vote the ticket.

Question. Was its object political?

Answer. Yes, sir; so far as I am informed, and, in fact, I think I know all about it.

Question. It was to elect the native sons of the South?

Answer. It was simply a political movement, designed to get the negro to act with the white people of the country, and to oppose carpet-baggers. It is a silly, ridiculous thing. If you desire it, I suppose I can get you the pamphlet.

Question. Does it contain the oath?

Answer. Yes, sir; the constitution, by-laws, and oath.

Question. Pass-words?

Answer. Yes, sir; signs, oath, and everything.

Question. When was that pamphlet published?

Answer. I really do not know. It was handed to me by a party named Cannon, a few weeks since.

Question. In its organization and for some time it was a secret affair?

Answer. I never knew it to be a secret affair. It was open and notorious.

Question. Why were members sworn to secrecy?

Answer. I remarked just now that that was a ridiculous farce; that they were sworn to secrecy, and not to tell that they were members, and then they went right out with a badge and cap proclaiming them "Native Sons of the South."

Question. You spoke of the disguises worn by these men who have inflicted murders, and warned school-teachers, &c.

Answer. In presenting your question do not state that I said thus and so; do not place words in my mouth; I do not presume you do it intentionally.

Question. Have you not repeatedly referred to offenses committed by men in disguise?

Answer. I have; but I claim the right to use my own language in answering questions.

Question. Go on, then, and describe the character of the disguise worn by these men.

Answer. I have heard, sometimes, that they had masks and that there was an extra large coat, or may be a shirt, around them; I have heard only general statements.

Question. Did you hear that their horses were disguised?

Answer. Yes, sir; perhaps by sheets or quilts.

Question. Did you hear that the men who rode in these parties had horns on their heads?

Answer. I do not remember to have heard such a statement—yes, I do; I think probably twelve or eighteen months ago I heard such a statement, but recently I have not.

Question. Now, having referred to the disguise, I recur to the question I was about putting to you. Have you known, or been informed in any single case, of where the material for such disguises was obtained, or by whom made up?

Answer. Never in any single case.

Question. Have you known, or been informed, of any person procuring a horse, saddle, bridle, or weapon, to be used in any raid, or ride, either to give notice or warning, or inflict whipping, or other outrage upon any person or persons?

Answer. Never, sir.

Question. In any outrage committed upon a colored man or his family, have you known or been informed of any person concerned therein?

Answer. Not further than I have mentioned in my examination-in-chief.

Question. Have you seen, or been informed, of any evidence tending to connect any person with these disguised bands of men who had committed these outrages?

Answer. In regard to the cases at Crawford, I presume, and have heard, that there is evidence connecting them with it, but the nature of it I do not know, and have not seen further than the testimony before your committee. I have read that.

Question. You have thought, I dare say, a good deal on the subject of these outrages committed by men in disguise, in the night-time?

Answer. Yes, sir; I frequently thought on the subject.

Question. And in common with other men have deplored these outrages, and sought to learn the cause, have you not?

Answer. In connection with good citizens, I condemn any violation of law. I have not made it my business to go out and inquire, or look up these cases, as I am a practicing lawyer, and it does not become any man in my profession to hunt up testimony, or cases, or busy himself in that way.

Question. The latter part of my question is, whether you have sought to learn the origin or cause of this organization?

Answer. I do not know of the organization you allude to. I know of no such organizations. I would be glad to know the origin and history of all such, and would take great pleasure in exposing them if I did know.

Question. When these men ride at night does it not appear that they have a common purpose; that is, that they know where they are going and what they are going to accomplish?

Answer. I know nothing about their riding at night, or where they go, or how they come. I should suppose if a party was armed and riding and organized that they would not be foolish enough to start out without knowing where they were going and having some common purpose to accomplish.

Question. Could such a common purpose be formed without consultation, and would it not necessarily bring all together at one place?

Answer. That is axiomatic and self-evident, that where men gather together there must be some concert of action.

Question. Then, again, if the purpose were an unlawful one, such as if accomplished would subject to punishment those concerned, would not there naturally follow an agreement among themselves to stand by each other and punish those who betray their secrets?

Answer. About that I cannot tell. It is simply inferential, however. Your questions are all argument; they are a chain; in general I agree with you that any such organization existing for common purposes and aims does act by preconcert, but that they would have oaths, I cannot say, though I think where men band together to commit crime they would always do so. If two men come together to perpetrate an assassination, it seems to me that they would not disclose the fact, and they would make a promise to keep it secret, and that very secrecy I should take as the reason why the law could not ferret out and bring these men to justice—the secrecy which they observed.

Question. In thus protecting their own secrets, would not the members if called as witnesses be strongly tempted to evade the truth, and would not that temptation be increased in just the proportion of the risks they would incur in case the truth were known?

Answer. It would be a very great temptation, I should think, sir; where a bad man commits a crime in connection with another party, if he is called upon to testify against his accomplice, I should think the fact that he was *particeps criminis* would induce him to swear falsely. He would probably commit perjury.

Question. Would there not then be a double motive to prevaricate in court; first, to save themselves from the vengeance of their associates, and next to protect themselves from punishment for the outrages inflicted?

Answer. No, sir; I would answer that in this way: I do not believe that one, two, or a dozen men committing crime would have any greater fear whatever, for a man who commits a crime is generally timid. I do not think there would be fear incurred as to the fact being known. I do not think they would fear vengeance. I think they might seek the law as a protection. The law will protect a man who becomes State's evidence, and I think that would be an inducement for a man to make a statement of the whole of the fact, in order to clear himself and secure the clemency of the law extended to him. I do not think there would be a double motive to secrecy. The single motive of which you speak, I think, would exist in a very eminent degree; a party would not tell on the other parties, because they might turn in and tell upon him. But there is another motive that might induce him to tell, that in the event he was discovered, and became State's evidence, he would not be prosecuted but protected. There are two motives, one to keep it secret, and the other to disclose the crime. As far as the practice in our State courts of all the district attorneys and the judges is concerned, where the State has been unable to make out a case against a party indicted for violation of law, if any party, however guilty, will come forward and make a statement to the court of the facts, the district attorney will enter what we term a *nol. pros.* as to him.

Question. Has there been any earnest effort on the part of men in this community to put a stop to these midnight outrages?

Answer. I think there has been an earnest effort. I base that opinion on repeated conversations which I have had with the judge of our district.

Question. What efforts have been made; what have been the efforts made on the part of your people?

Answer. The effort to which I allude is the charge of the judge at every term to the grand jury, directing them to use every means in their power to bring witnesses before them—to investigate cases of this character, to ferret them out.

Question. He is required by the Ku-Klux law to give that charge?

Answer. Yes, sir; and I believe the grand juries have carried into effect this charge, as far as they could, and, in many instances, they have brought parties to justice by bills of indictment. Sometimes they have been convicted, sometimes acquitted—that is, for infractions of the law; sometimes for whipping negroes.

Question. I am not speaking of ordinary infractions of the law.

Answer. I mean the general class of cases that I alluded to in my examination-in-chief. I take this case of Goldsby, who was charged with assassination——

Question. Will you please confine your answers to my question?

Answer. If I have not done so, pardon me; I did not intend to do otherwise.

Question. I do not suppose that you intended to do it; but I was speaking of a particular class of crimes—crimes committed by men banded together and disguised, and in the night-time—such as visiting the houses of people; warning teachers to desist from teaching schools; and whipping negroes at night; such as taking men out and hanging or shooting them.

Answer. I understand you.

Question. What I desire to inquire is, what concerted or combined movement has been made in this community, at any time, to put a stop to these outrages?

Answer. I understand your question and will answer it in this way: that all good people in our community denounce such conduct in severe and bitter terms. They have opposed it, and, whenever they could in any way bring a party to justice, they would take great pleasure in doing it. I am satisfied they would act with concert and unity if they knew where to begin. I know of no concerted action of the people, by coming together or trying to rise, *en masse*, to bring offenders to justice. It was out of their power; but, as I said, the general sentiment of the good people here is against that thing. They have denounced it, and, in that way, they have made an effort to break this thing up, and, to a great extent, it has been successful. As evidence of the fact, I refer to the records of the court and the report of the grand jury, which states that crime is diminishing. A year or two ago these things were more frequent. That is the way it has been brought about by the denunciation of the people.

Question. The testimony before the committee is, that these outrages were never so frequent or flagrant as during this present year.

Answer. Do you suppose I care anything about the testimony before your committee? I am not to be influenced in my testimony by such statements of fact as I understand to have been made here. I give my testimony as I believe it, and I am not influenced by what other witnesses have told you. You ask me questions, and I answer them as I understand them; and I refer to the records of the court and the grand juries who made these reports.

Question. Do you apply this statement to this county, or the adjoining counties, when you say these outrages are on the decrease?

Answer. I can only say that my knowledge and acquaintance is particularly confined to what transpired in my own county. I have been informed that similar reports have been made in other counties, by grand juries—that law is being restored. I speak for Lowndes County, and refer to the record, which I can produce, to establish the fact that crime is on the decrease. The records of this court will establish that crime of all character is largely on the decrease. That record is in this court-house.

Question. Is it not within your information that there have been, within the past year, at least a dozen whippings and killings, by men banded together and in disguise, in this and in the adjoining county of Monroe?

Answer. I have stated as fully as I can on that subject in my testimony-in-chief and in reply to many questions which you have asked me to-day. I again refer you to the record—I cannot state the number. I have heard of different cases that I have cited. There are other cases which I have not cited, and which I, perhaps, may have heard of at some time. I have stated the circumstances of these whippings as communicated to me. In other words, I have stated as fully and as much in detail as I have knowledge of and am capable of stating. I have attempted to state them to you fully.

Question. Have you ever attempted, yourself, to discover who were implicated in any of these outrages by disguised men?

Answer. Yes, sir; I have made some of the most earnest efforts to make a discovery of that sort that I ever made in my life, in my professional capacity, and I will state what cases they were, if you desire to know.

Question. It is not necessary. Is it your information that these bands, who have committed, in Lowndes County, the outrages to which you have referred, have originated in this county, or have they come from some adjoining county or State?

Answer. I have repeatedly stated to you that I have no information as to those points—who they are or where they come from. I have told you that I know nothing about them.

Question. Would there, in your opinion, be any practical difficulty in following up these bands, after one of their midnight raids, and discovering where they came from?

Answer. That question is not a matter of testimony. It addresses itself to the common sense of a man. I will tell you what I think about it, if you think it is worth anything to you.

Question. Do you know, or have you——

Answer. Let me answer. There would be great practical difficulty, if a band would come of, suppose, twenty men, disguised and organized, into this community, and commit an outrage at midnight upon some citizen. You know perfectly well it would be difficult to follow them; the citizens are all asleep; nobody knows anything about it. When they come into your county nobody is expecting them; they do what they desire; before the people are alarmed or the officers are notified they are gone.

Question. Would there be any difficulty in following their tracks when daylight came?

Answer. I do not know; I cannot state. I have never attempted to follow their tracks. You know as much about that as I can state; it is only a matter of opinion.

Question. Is it your information that your people have followed these horses' tracks, in any instance, and endeavored to discover who the parties in the band were.

Answer. I think not only the people but the officers of the law have attempted to make, and have actually made, discoveries, and parties have been prosecuted. I have been engaged in those prosecutions. Sometimes the parties got out of the way.

Question. Why do you express the opinion that no Ku-Klux organization exists or has existed in Lowndes County, in the face of the fact that so many outrages have been committed by bands of disguised men?

Answer. I will tell you, sir. I have lived in this county all my life; I know the people well. I believe that I would know if any organization of that character—any Ku-Klux organization—existed. I believe I would have been advised of it or would have heard of it.

Question. Do you believe that the members would have told you?

Answer. Yes, sir; I believe that in the organization of it I would have been consulted. I believe the members would have told me. I know the people of this county, and I do not believe that such an organization exists. Another branch of that question struck me when you propounded it; will you repeat it?

Question. I asked why you expressed the opinion that no Ku-Klux organization exists or has existed in Lowndes County, in the face of the fact that so many outrages have been committed by bands of disguised men?

Answer. In regard to the fact that outrages have been committed, those outrages are before you; they are simple facts about which I have testified. I think, in many instances, the causes leading to these whippings were private matters. For example, in some neighborhoods I think parties have been whipped for stealing, robbery, plunder, and in other cases negroes have been whipped for insulting white women. In other cases white men have been whipped; in one case a party for sleeping with his aunt; in another case a negro preacher for having sexual intercourse—or being charged with it—with members of his congregation. In a great many, and I believe the majority, of the cases, the whippings have been inflicted by individuals for matters that they thought the law could not reach. Take, for example, these cases of insulting language; there is a common sentiment, I believe, all over the country which justifies a man in taking the law into his own hands in such cases.

Question. Do you believe these outrages you have detailed, where committed by disguised men banded together, were all committed by the same band or were they by different bands?

Answer. I do not know of any band committing them at all. I suppose different parties in different neighborhoods have committed them. Sometimes I believe a negro has been whipped by four or five men in the neighborhood, who thought he was getting to be too big a man on account of his politics, and in another case for stealing.

Question. Suppose forty or forty-five or fifty men were banded together for the commission of an outrage, such as killing a negro; is it your opinion that that organization sprang up with the necessity of that occasion, or was it a regular organization, which exercised its jurisdiction over all similar grievances?

Answer. I do not believe there is any regular organization. I have never thought so. I do not believe now that there is any regular organization. There may be, although I am not advised of it. I think in many cases private parties have redressed private wrongs.

Question. Do you think the Ku-Klux organization has existed in Mississippi?

Answer. I think so; I think it likely.

Question. Have you any knowledge of it?

Answer. No, sir; I never saw a member of it.

Question. Were you ever approached by any person to become a member?

Answer. Not that I am aware of. What do you mean by approach; asking me to join it?

Question. Yes, sir; certainly.

Answer. I never was.

Question. Do you know what the obligation taken by members of that order is?

Answer. I have seen some publications in the papers, time and again, that you have seen, I suppose. Where there has been so much smoke there may have been some fire.

Question. Is that the only knowledge you have—that derived from newspapers?

Answer. No, sir; I have heard hundreds of individuals discussing these matters. I remember that Gleed, a colored senator, received a notice signed in some singular way—blood and thunder, perhaps, or some fool thing—apparently emanating from a Ku-Klux, or something of the sort, giving him a warning.

Question. Were you ever present when an oath or obligation was given to a person in reference to being a member of a secret organization?

Answer. Many and many a time. I am a Mason and an Odd-Fellow, but I do not propose to give you the oaths we take there.

Question. Outside of those organizations, have you ever been present upon any occasion when an oath was administered in a secret organization?

Answer. I have, in the Native Sons of the South. I have seen the oaths administered there and I have seen the oath administered in other political societies.

Question. What other political societies?

Answer. Democratic clubs, sir, and a society known, I believe, as "Seventy-six;" that is my recollection.

Question. What was that society organized for?

Answer. Purely a political matter, in the interest of the democratic party.

Question. When was that?

Answer. I do not know how long it has been. I have been a member of it, and am now a member of it.

Question. Was it secret?

Answer. It was secret to this extent: Their candidates were nominated in the society by the members of the society; they had their committees and all their wire working.

Question. Did they take an oath?

Answer. Yes, sir.

Question. What was the oath. Repeat it.

Answer. I cannot repeat it.

Question. Give the substance of it.

Answer. It was that they would insist upon a rigid economical administration of the Government, and they would do all they could to protect the interests of the democratic party; that they would endeavor to restore constitutional liberty and bring about peace and order. That was the general substance; in other words, it was a purely political organization.

Question. Did it have its signs and pass-words?

Answer. Yes, sir; I think there were several signs—I know there were. I could give them to you. I presume it would make no difference.

Question. It had its officers?

Answer. It had a president of the club and a secretary.

Question. By what name was he known?

Answer. As the governor, and there was a secretary and treasurer; but in regard to these matters, I can give you a copy of the constitution. I never entered into anything that I feared to tell. I do not suppose there is any objection in the world to giving it to you.

Question. Is there any other secret organization that you have entered other than you have named?

Answer. Yes, sir; I have been a member of two or three similar political organizations in the last four or five years, with similar objects.

Question. State their names.

Answer. One was called the "Union Club," then the "Seventy-six," and then these "Native Sons."

Question. Those are all you recollect?

Answer. Yes, sir.

Question. Were they all oath-bound?

Answer. No, sir; I do not think the Union Club was. I do not think we took an oath there; I do not remember if we did; but in all these matters in reference to this society that I spoke of a while ago and its constitution—I could get it for you.

Question. What are your feelings toward Mr. Whitfield, the witness concerning whom you have spoken; are they kindly or otherwise?

Answer. Mr. Whitfield and I are upon pleasant relations. I do not dislike Mr. Whitfield as a man.

Question. Are your personal relations good?

Answer. Let me finish my answer there. Major Whitfield is connected with me by family ties. My law-partner is a relative of Major Whitfield and Major Whitfield married a cousin of mine. I meet him and am friendly with him on the street and everywhere. He was in my office yesterday, and requested me not to read to you that bill of indictment, nor to mention these matters. I promised not to do so unless examined upon them, and it became my duty to state fully in regard to him. I moreover told him that I would state to him what I had said to this committee; that he might select three friends, and I would select three, and they might select a dozen, and if they said, after learning what I had said of him here, that I had done him any injustice, I would then come before this committee and make all amends. I believe that, in what I have said of him, I reflect the sentiments of his own brother, Major George Whitfield. That gentleman became very much incensed at being taken for Henry Whitfield, at Artesia, where he was introduced to General Stafford as Major Henry Whitfield.

Question. Did Major Whitfield and your father run at the same time on the conservative or Dent ticket?

Answer. No, sir.

Question. Did you?

Answer. My father did not. I was a candidate at the same time with Major Whitfield, on the same ticket; we were both on the same platform. At this time, however, we are not. Mr. Whitfield is a member of the republican party.

Question. Did you support him at that time?

Answer. I did, sir.

Question. Did you advocate his election?

Answer. No, sir; I advocated my own; and I advocated the success of the general ticket.

Question. He was thought worthy in 1869 to represent the principles of that party?

Answer. At that election there was no general convention. Some twelve or fifteen gentlemen made out that ticket. It was then difficult to get anybody to run——

Question. Was he supported by that party?

Answer. Let me get through.

Question. I want to bring this examination to a close.

Answer. I hope you will.

Question. If you will just confine yourself to answering my questions, we will get through sooner.

Answer. I shall not be dictated to by you, sir, as to how I shall be examined or how I shall answer questions.

Question. I wish to bring your examination to a close, and will do so very soon if you confine yourself to answering my question.

Answer. When I am under oath I shall not answer to suit the convenience of the committee. I am under oath, and I shall answer questions in my own way. If you do not wish me to answer them I shall take great pleasure in retiring.

Question. You have been on the stand for nearly four hours, and there are many other witnesses waiting to be examined, and, therefore, I desire to have your statements as briefly given as possible.

Answer. Senator Pratt, I am not here at my own instance; it is not of my own seeking.

Question. My question was whether Henry B. Whitfield was, in 1869, supported by the conservative or Dent party.

Answer. I understand your question; I understood it then and I understand it now.

Question. Will you please to answer it?

Answer. I will answer it, with your permission, in my own way. It was difficult at that time to induce any man to run on that ticket, as it is difficult now, because it requires a sacrifice on his part. It was with the utmost difficulty that candidates were obtained. When we run we know we will be defeated by overwhelming majorities. Major Whitfield and myself and others were placed there as a *dernier ressort.*

Question. Was he supported by that party?

Answer. I suppose he received the general white vote of the county.

Question. Did he get as large a vote as you did?

Answer. I do not remember; the vote was about the same. I do not think there were probably twenty votes difference.

Question. Were his antecedents at that time as well known as now?

Answer. They were not.

Question. Did you know them at that time?

Answer. I did not; nothing like as well as I do now. All I have alluded to and fifty other matters, which, with your permission, I will now present to you, were not known then. On the contrary, his antecedents were remarkably little known; but case after case and case after case came to light, with which I can furnish you the facts. I have them right here. I can bring the witnesses before you.

COLUMBUS, MISSISSIPPI, *November* 17, 1871.

WILLIAM W. HUMPHRIES recalled.

Mr. BLAIR. Captain Humphries, a statement has been made before this committee, involving a charge that you had, in a case pending in the chancery court in this city, abstracted a deposition from the files of the court and substituted another in its place. The committee have thought it but just that you should have an opportunity of replying to that statement.

The WITNESS. The facts, gentlemen, in connection with that matter are very brief. A gentleman by the name of William S. Smith, living in Columbus, had employed D. R. Dashiel, a lawyer residing here, to file a bill of divorce. Dashiel was appointed a general insurance agent for several States, and retired from the practice of the law, and a young man named Wood, about twenty-one years of age, went into his office with general directions to wind up his business. After Dashiel retired I was employed to take charge of this case, which has been pending about two years. Wood, thinking that he had charge of the case also, which was a misapprehension on his part, (he was not employed,) proceeded to take some deposition. Smith heard of it and came to my office, and remarked to me, "Wood is in the office, taking the deposition of a man named Johns in my case." I went in and arrested the proceeding at once, at the instance of Mr. Smith. He stated that Mr. Wood had not been employed by him; that he was but a young man, and the case was too important. I took the deposition *de novo;* it had not been sworn to, nor had it been filed among the papers in the case. Chancellor Lyon, subsequent to that time, directed his clerk—I am too fast; he wrote out a statement himself and directed his clerk to file it, which his clerk at first declined. He called on him a second time to do it; he still declined. He finally peremptorily ordered him to do it, and he did file a statement of that sort. As soon as I heard of it, I called the attention of the members of the bar to the fact. They investigated it, and ignored and treated the matter as false. I will state to the gentlemen of the committee just here that I have in my pocket the statement of the chancery clerk in regard to that matter, which I will ask you to have read in your hearing; also, the statement of Mr. Wood, the other gentleman, with the permission of the committee.

The CHAIRMAN. That is right, sir.

The WITNESS. I would be glad to read the statement of the chancery clerk.

Question. Is that statement sworn to?

Answer. I do not remember. It was given to me at the time. I understood, when I heard of this matter, that there was a reflection on me, and, while I cared nothing about the individual opinion of the party himself, I felt it due to myself to invite the investigation of the bar to the matter, and for that reason I requested the clerk to make a statement, in order that this matter might have a professional investigation.

Question. I simply inquired whether that statement was sworn to.

Answer. I will examine, sir. [Examining the paper.] It is not sworn to, but the clerk is here, and every word and line of the paper is in his handwriting. Not one word was suggested or written by me. It is all in his handwriting. This is the clerk of Chancellor Lyon's court. I will read it:

"According to the special request of W. W. Humphries, jr., I make the following statement in writing in regard to a certain affidavit, sworn to and subscribed by me on the 12th day of May, 1871, and filed by Early Hendrick, clerk of the chancery court of Lowndes County:"

Permit me to say here, by way of parenthesis, that Harris Baldwin was the deputy clerk.

"On the same day, in the case of William S. Smith *vs.* Mollie Smith, No. 228, at the October term of said court, (1870,) this case was first presented to the court in which I was deputy clerk. The chancellor of said court, Theodoric C. Lyon, being aware that S. J. Johns, whose deposition had previously been taken in said cause, had deposed in the case, and that said deposition did not appear in the record of the same, inquired of the undersigned as to the existence and whereabouts of said deposition, when I made the statements in substance contained in said deposition. It was then that I was requested to make a deposition or affidavit of the facts as contained in said deposition by said Lyon. This I did not do. At the January term, 1871, I was requested to make the affidavit as above stated, but, upon my expressing some reluctance in doing so, I was required so to do by said Lyon. The affidavit was written some time in January last, but was not sworn to or filed until the 12th day of May, 1871, when the same was sworn to by affiant, and filed by Early Hendrick, the clerk of said court, as of the 9th day of February, 1871. The said affidavit was made in accordance with a written memorandum furnished by said Lyon of the facts he wished deposed to in said deposition. S. J. Johns was caused to come before Mr. J. M. Wood, who, I then understood and believed, was counsel in the case, associated as such with Thomas R. Dashiel. The affidavit above referred to contains a statement to the effect that the 'deposition thus taken was filed, as he believes, among the papers in said cause.' This belief was founded upon the official habit of filing each affidavit as soon as the testimony is closed. The act of filing the deposition I do not recollect, and, after a statement from Captain Humphries, think the deposition was not filed. I understand from Mr. Smith that the reason why a second deposition of Johns was taken in the case was because neither complainant or his attorneys were present when the first one was taken. These facts I know to be true.

"HARRIS BALDWIN."

Here is a statement also from Mr. Wood.

Question. When was this statement by the chancery clerk prepared and handed to you?

Answer. When the facts were all fresh.

Question. At what date?

Answer. About the 19th of May, 1871, sir.

Here is Mr. Wood's statement. I will read it:

"COLUMBUS, MISSISSIPPI, *May* 19, 1871.

"I was requested by Captain T. R. Dashiel, who was the solicitor of William S. Smith in the filing of a certain bill of divorce in the chancery court of Lowndes County, filed March 25, 1868, No. 220, in which William S. Smith was plaintiff and Mollie Smith was defendant—said Dashiel being about to leave, requested me to take certain depositions therein on or about the —— day of ——— 187—. Stephen J. Johns was caused to come before Harris Baldwin, commissioner, at my office, for the purpose of having his deposition in said cause taken, which we proceeded to do. About the time the same had been completed William S. Smith, the complainant in said cause, and W. W. Humphries, attorney, of the firm of Humphries & Sykes, came into my office. Captain Humphries, seeing what Johns had stated, objected to the filing of that deposition, from the fact that there were other matters of which he was aware and about which he had not testified. Said paper or deposition was not filed or placed among the papers in said cause. Some time subsequently said Baldwin called upon me and said that the first deposition of Johns had not been filed and was not among the papers. He desired the same and inquired where it was. Captain Humphries, who informed me that said paper or deposition was in his possession, stated that he did not intend to file said paper or make it a part of the record in said cause.

"J. M. WOOD."

That deposition referred to there I have in my possession, and have it subject to the inspection of this committee, if desired. In addition to that fact, William S. Smith, the plaintiff in this case, was also present, who knew and states that the party had not sworn to it; that it was never filed nor made a part of the record in the case.

By the CHAIRMAN:

Question. What is your practice in taking depositions? Do you swear the witness to testify the truth, the whole truth, and nothing but the truth, before commencing the deposition?

Answer. Yes, sir; but he does not sign it until after it is written. It cannot be made a part of the record until it is signed and marked "filed" by the clerk.

Question. He is not sworn afterward?

Answer. No, sir; he is first sworn to state the truth, the whole truth, and nothing but the truth, but the paper is in the power of the attorney until it is subscribed by the witness and marked "filed" by the clerk. Our habit is, and always has been, when we take testimony which is reduced to writing, after the witness has completed the delivery of his testimony, to hand it back, in order that he may read it over, or it is read to him before he signs it, in order that he may know that what he therein states is as he desired to state it.

Question. Was the adverse party present at the time this deposition was taken?

Answer. No, sir; the party was insane.

Question. Was the guardian *ad litem*?

Answer. No, sir; the party was insane; that was the ground of the bill of divorce; that she had been insane at the time of the marriage; that a deception was used.

Question. Neither the defendant, nor the defendant's attorney, nor the guardian *ad litem* were present?

Answer. No, sir; nor, under the statute, is it necessary, provided notice be given; at the time this deposition was taken, I did not know that the party had been summoned to appear there; it was done by Mr. Wood, under a mistaken view, thinking he was in the case. He having been directed by Mr. Dashiel, who had retired from practice to wind up his business, he was not aware that Mr. Smith had employed Humphries & Sykes.

Question. Had notice been served to take the deposition of Johns?

Answer. It must have been served. I say so from this fact: that he would not have appeared before a commissioner unless the notice had been served in due form, but; as I said, I knew nothing of his appearance. Smith came to my office and informed me that young Wood was taking a deposition without authority, and that he was too young to be intrusted with so important a case.

Question. I was not inquiring whether the witness was notified to attend, but whether a notice of the intention of the plaintiff to take the deposition of the witness had been served on the guardian *ad litem?*

Answer. Really I cannot tell you, but the records will show that fact. I cannot tell, as I had not had anything to do with the notice to this witness. I did not attend to the notice.

By Mr. BLAIR:

Question. Was there any feeling between you and Chancellor Lyon which might have induced him to make the statement he did in this matter?

Answer. Well, in regard to that matter I can only state this: I have repeatedly, both publicly and privately, denounced Chancellor Lyon as a coward, a deserter, and as a scoundrel, from the fact that he was cashiered during the war by a general court-martial, which was ratified at Richmond; and among many charges were those, I think, of cowardice and attempting to induce his men to desert. I had been active in opposing his appointment as chancellor, and many members of the bar in the district, and almost all our community, opposed it, on the ground of his incompetence and the fact that we did not deem him morally qualified to conduct the duties of this office. I had also denounced him for bribery and corruption in his office, and he is aware of the fact that I had been preparing articles of impeachment against him to submit to the legislature. He is aware of the fact that I have in my possession certificates to the effect that since he has been upon the bench he has received a bribe to decide a case in a certain way; that he received a bribe, and not only prepared the bill himself, but made his clerk write it out and then corrected it; that he went to the defendant in the case and offered her a hundred dollars to sign an answer which he had prepared, which money was paid to the defendant. He subsequently made the complainant in the bill, which was in a case of divorce, swear that there was no collusion in the matter, and the complainant was the man who paid the defendant $100. I have all these papers in my possession, signed and certified to. I have the certificate of the chancery clerk that Mr. Lyon did prepare this bill and that he did conduct the case, and that he was chancellor at the time; in other words, the papers are here in this envelope, subject to your inspection, showing where he has received the bribe, and conducted this case, [exhibiting papers,] and he is aware of the fact that I am preparing articles of impeachment to present to the coming legislature. I have forbidden this man to speak to me months ago. I do not allow him to speak to me. I have a letter in my possession which I wrote to him, forbidding him to speak to me, renouncing all social intercourse whatever, which was handed to him by Mr. F. M. Lee, of Columbus, a gentleman of high social standing and moral worth, known to the entire community.

Question. The only matter I wanted to elicit was whether there was a personal quarrel between you?

Answer. Well, gentlemen, so far as that is concerned I can say I have no special enmity against Theodoric Lyon. I have stated these facts. Of course I have no respect for the man.

Question. He has knowledge of the matter which you have stated?

Answer. Why, sir, I have communicated there facts to him; he knows them. He knows that I propose to present these articles of impeachment. He is aware of these facts; he has known this for months. All the papers to which I have alluded are in those envelopes before me.

Question. The committee do not care about going into them. I wanted to know whether there was any controversy between you.

Answer. He knows, in addition, that I have denounced him for practicing law and receiving notes for collection and other matters which are positively forbidden by the statutory provisions of our State. The statute makes it a crime and misdemeanor, and says that any party guilty of that sort shall be impeached.

By the CHAIRMAN:

Question. If I understand this paper of Harris Baldwin, which is not sworn to, it is a recantation of certain statements of fact made by him in this affidavit on file to which Chancellor Lyon referred?

Answer. All I know in regard to that is this, Senator: When I was informed that he had had a paper placed on the files of his court reflecting upon myself, I immediately applied to the clerk for information. I desired him to make me a statement of the facts, that I might call the attention of our bar to it. I know nothing about any conversation had with the clerk further than the clerk stated to me and as set forth in the paper.

Question. You never have seen the affidavit of Harris Baldwin?

Answer. Yes, sir.

Question. Does this statement contradict the statement of facts made by him in that affidavit?

Answer. It has been so long since I looked at that paper that I really cannot tell you. I cannot go into the *minutia*, but he states in that paper that Lyon requested him to file a statement of which he furnished a written memorandum; that he refused to do so, and when required to do so he did at last file it. That paper sets forth the facts of the case.

Question. That affidavit was by Baldwin himself?

Answer. That is my impression; it was prepared by Mr. Lyon, but made by Mr. Baldwin.

Question. Do you know what is stated in that affidavit?

Answer. I think substantially he may have stated that Johns was called before him to testify; that he had taken his testimony, and that in the second deposition the statements made by Johns were different from those made in the first, and that I had destroyed or not permitted the first deposition to be filed.

Question. Did he state in that first affidavit that he had filed that deposition?

Answer. I would not undertake to state about the contents of the paper from my memory. I will go and get it if you desire it. It is in the court-house. I can get it very quickly, and the contents of the instrument, perhaps, would be more satisfactory than I can now state it from memory. I have forgotten really what he set forth. This may to some extent contradict it.

Question. I omitted to ask you a question the other day, when you were before the committee. You then produced a paper, from which you read a philippic, if you will pardon the term, against Major Whitfield, of this place, denouncing him as a common liar, &c. That paper has gone into the evidence. What I desire to inquire of you is this: When did you prepare that paper?

Answer. I prepared that paper after I was subpœnaed to come before this committee. It was written two or three days before it was presented here. You will observe, in the conclusion of this paper, I state that Major Whitfield reminds me of Ovid Bolus, as described in the Flush Times of Alabama and Mississippi, by Joe Baldwin, the author of that book. My ideas are taken from Baldwin's description of Bolus. I think I prepared it two or three days before I came here, but I had read that paper before a number of citizens, among others, Rev. Mr. Cottrell, the Methodist pastor, David P. Blair, Dr. Larscomb, and a number of gentlemen in town, and asking if they thought what I stated was substantially true, and if it was his reputation and character in the community. They stated that they did think so.

Question. Did you read it to Mr. Matthews, an attorney in this place?

Answer. Beverly Matthews?

Question. Yes, sir.

Answer. I think likely I did. I read it to quite a number.

Question. Did you read it to James T. Harrison, an attorney of this city?

Answer. I think likely I did. I do not remember now, but I read it to quite a number of citizens. I stated to his brother, Major George Whitfield, and the husband of his niece, the contents of the paper, and what I have stated, and requested them to go and state to Major Whitfield that I had given such testimony, and if his brother-in-law, Mr. John Sykes, or Captain Turner Sykes, who married his niece, with a committee of gentlemen would state that I had done him injustice, I would take pleasure in coming before this committee and modifying my testimony.

By Mr. RICE:

Question. Did you know at the time you prepared this paper that you were going to be called to swear to his character?

Answer. I did suppose that I would, and prepared it with an especial view, because Major Whitfield had come to my office several days before I came before this committee, and earnestly begged me not to say anything about the bill of indictment or this Kansas matter, where he had obtained money under false pretenses, and not to produce papers in connection with a number of transactions.

Question. Did you go to him with that paper before you were sworn?

Answer. Yes, sir; I went to him with a paper that I introduced the other day, and requested him to sign it. He told me, in the presence of Dr. Matthews, Colonel Henry Pope, and David P. Blair, and several other gentlemen, that he would sign that paper, but it was not sufficiently strong, and he would prepare another and give it to me. I saw him afterward. He told me he had written a paper which was stronger and better, and he would bring it to me the next morning.

By the CHAIRMAN:

Question. Had you prepared this article which you afterward gave in evidence concerning Major Whitfield's character at the time you approached Major Whitfield with that paper which you asked him to sign?

Answer. Do you mean the article prepared to be signed by republicans?

Question. Yes, sir.

Answer. I did not prepare that at all.

Question. Had you prepared this article in relation to Major Whitfield's character, which you have given in evidence before this committee, before you presented that paper, which you have just mentioned, for his signature?

Answer. I had prepared that article, and I will state now that one of the objects I had in view was to get his name to that paper.

Question. You did not show him this article?

Answer. It was my belief that Major Whitfield would sign it, and he did promise to sign it, and he evaded it. He did promise it in the presence of the gentlemen I have mentioned, or to write a stronger paper. The only objection he made was to one or two expressions which he did not exactly approve, and he said he would write a stronger paper and take it around and get the republicans to sign it.

Question. Did you call upon him afterward?

Answer. I did, and he told me that he had prepared that paper, and that it was at the mayor's office; but he was busy in a matter in which he was engaged then, and would bring it to my office the next morning, which he did not do. I would thank you, gentlemen, to give me the written memorandum which I gave you the other day, of what I said about him. I told his brother what I had said, and that I had referred to him when denouncing Major Whitfield.

Question. That was a very elaborate article, and evidently required considerable labor for its preparation?

Answer. I am not entitled to the credit of that article. The expressions there have considerable force and, I think, some beauty. Much of it is borrowed. The original is Joe Baldwin's delineation of Ovid Bolus, who was a member of our bar in the early history of this State. He describes Ovid Bolus in his book. Whitfield reminds me more of him than any other man I ever saw, and in delineating his character that was fresh in my mind. Having promised him that I would state to him what I told you, I felt it was proper he should know it, from the fact that you have here a sort of inquisitorial investigation, and a party cannot come in here and hear the testimony given. You sit with closed doors. It is not like an examination in a public court-room, and a party attacked has no chance.

The CHAIRMAN. The outsiders seem to know what is going on here as well as we do.

The WITNESS. That frequently happens where gentlemen hear it, but it is not generally known in the community. A few special friends of your own, or of General Blair, may become acquainted with those matters, but as a general thing it is not known.

Report of the grand jury referred to by William W. Humphries.

To Hon. J. A. ORR, *judge, &c.:*

The grand jurors of the county of Lowndes, at the October term of the circuit court of said county, beg leave to respectfully report that they have been diligently engaged in the discharge of the various duties imposed upon them by law, and they respectfully plead as an excuse for their lengthy session the importance of one case, the investigation of which alone has consumed fifteen days, by reason of the number of witnesses examined, and the difficulty of having those witnesses from this and adjoining counties brought before them promptly.

The grand jury are pleased to report (so far as brought to their knowledge) that crime of all classes in Lowndes County have greatly diminished.

They have carefully inspected the county jail, find it well kept, and its sanitary regulations as good as the jailer can adopt, the number of its inmates considered. We found a considerable number in jail, who are serving out short terms of imprisonment for petty larceny and other grades of misdemeanors, at a heavy cost to tax-payers of our State and county—a burden, which, we think, might be greatly, if not entirely remedied by the adoption of suggestions contained in our *memorial* to the State legislature, respectfully submitted through your honor, and which accompanies this report.

The grand jury would report that, in their opinion, the county jail is insecure, if we may except the dungeon. We find the outer walls of the building very much warped, thereby susceptible of being easily broken through. We would state, however, that we saw inside improvements being made by mechanics, which, when completed, will add greatly to its security in retaining prisoners, though we are of opinion that the cost of above-mentioned improvements would be more economically expended if applied to a new and more substantial building than the present jail.

The public roads are generally in a passable condition, though needing considerable work and repairs.

We deem it incumbent on us to acknowledge the efficient and valuable services of Colonel Muldrow, district attorney, and hereby tender to him our thanks for the same.

W. E. GIBBS.	ROBT. GLEED.
J. F. GALLOWAY.	H. C. LONG.
C. B. CANFIELD.	J. T. HARRISON, JR.
JOSHUA HAIRSTON.	M. WITHERSPOON.
ELZY RICHARDS.	J. H. BRAZIER.
A. M. GREEN.	G. M. BARKSDALE.
A. STEWART.	SAM'L KLINE.
THOS. SEALE.	

COLUMBUS, MISSISSIPPI, *November* 16, 1871.

JOHN McCOY sworn and examined.

By the CHAIRMAN:

Question. State your residence and occupation?

Answer. I reside at Corinth, Mississippi; deputy United States marshal.

Question. How long have you been serving as deputy marshal?

Answer. About two months.

Question. In what counties in Northern Mississippi are you acquainted with the condition of society as to peace and good order?

Answer. I am acquainted in Lowndes, Monroe, Lee, Chickasaw, Tippah, Alcorn, and Tishemingo.

Question. Have you been engaged in making arrests under indictments found by the Federal courts?

Answer. Yes, sir; I have been engaged constantly for two months.

Question. Have you been resisted?

Answer. I was at one time, sir, at Okolona.

Question. Give us the circumstances attending that?

Answer. I had some prisoners there under indictments found by the grand jury. I brought them to Okolona to the hotel, and while I was there, shortly after noon on the 22d of October, there was a party of men came up there with pistols, and were very boisterous around the house, and threatend to take the prisoners from me—around the hotel I should say—and I stepped out on the porch, and asked them who they were looking for; they said they were looking for the deputy marshal. I told them I was the man. I asked them what they wanted; they said they wanted the prisoners. I told them the first man that laid hands on me, or attempted to resist me, I would put eighteen buckshot through him. They went off then, and I saw that if I remained there—at least that was my honest opinion—that if I remained at the hotel, they would take the prisoners from me. I moved them to Colonel Shattuck's private residence. He is United States assessor for that district. It was generally understood that I was to go off on the night train, but before the time came I was apprised that a band would be at the depot to resist me, and take the prisoners from me, and I declined going until next morning. That night they found out that I had foiled them in their undertaking, and they went to Colonel Shattuck's office and set it on fire, with the intention, in my opinion, of drawing Colonel Shattuck and his brother, who were assisting me in guarding the prisoners, from me, and then wresting the prisoners from me.

Question. You may go on now and state any outrages perpetrated by disguised bands of men that have come to your knowledge in any of the counties you have named.

Mr. RICE. I suggest that he exclude this county and Monroe from his testimony; it will not be necessary to go over them any more.

The CHAIRMAN. Very well; leaving out Lowndes and Monroe Counties.

Answer. In Tishemingo County, on the 30th of September, a band of disguised men went to the house of a widow woman, Mrs. Hunnicut, and they demanded entrance. It was refused them, and they fired through the door, and shot the widow Hunnicut's daughter and her son, and inflicted a very serious wound on the daughter, which she will never recover from.

Question. Did you understand how numerous that band was?

Answer. There were about fourteen of them.

Question. When was this?

Answer. This was the 30th of September last. Shortly after that I went——

By Mr. BLAIR:

Question. You say fired on the house?

Answer. Yes, sir; fired through the door.

Question. And wounded whom?

Answer. Wounded John Hunnicut and Catharine Hunnicut.

By Mr. RICE:

Question. Two children?

Answer. Yes, sir; they were grown. Shortly after that I went to the county there, in company with District Attorney Wells and Marshal Pierce, and I captured the lieutenant of the band. He at once came out and made all the acknowledgments. He stated that he belonged to the band; that he was the lieutenant of the band; that he was there at Hunnicut's at the time the shooting was done, and knew the party that did it, and gave the names of several other persons, whom I arrested—all told, seven, I believe. I believe, in my statement, I said six, but afterward I arrested another one, which made it seven—Marlow, the last one.

By the CHAIRMAN:

Question. Did he tell you anything about the organization of which he was an officer?

Answer. Yes, sir; here is the sworn statement, or a copy of it—[producing a paper]—the questions of the district attorney, and his answers, which I will read, with your permission.

[The witness read as follows:

"*Question.* When were you sworn into the Ku-Klux Klan?

"*Answer.* I was sworn into the Ku-Klux Organization Klan by Captain Jack Voal and Joe McDonald in McNary County term in 1869.

"*Question.* What were their objects at that time?

"*Answer.* Their objects were to keep down the radicals and negroes.

"*Question.* State as much as you know as to the oath you have taken?

"*Answer.* Well, you will solemnly swear before God and man that you will support the Ku-Klux Klan in all its transactions outside of civil law, and pass no by-words to any outsider. So help you God.

"*Question.* What were the by-words?

"*Answer.* In time a man should get into trouble and wanted assistance they were Blucher, Avalanche, or Star.

"*Question.* Did you at any time go on raids with that Klan?

"*Answer.* Yes; the first raid was taken there was twenty-five of us; we went to Sam Meeks's and found before arriving there that Sam Meeks was not at home; we found him about four miles from there, at John Meeks. Sam Meeks was a colored man. The Klan shot at him five times. There was a musket shot at him, loaded with an ounce ball and eighteen buck-shot. I do not remember all who shot at him, but George Marlow shot at him with a musket containing eighteen buck-shot and an ounce ball. I never saw the negro afterwards, but heard that he was shot.

"*Question.* Did you have any officers to your organization?

"*Answer.* Yes; Captain Joe Hicks was captain; but in case of his absence I acted, being lieutenant of the band."]

Question. Has he made any statement in addition to what is written down there?

Answer. No, sir; no particular statement.

Question. Is he under recognizance to appear at court now?

Answer. No, sir; he is under arrest and in confinement.

Question. Is there any other case that came to your knowledge in that county?

Answer. There are divers cases, but not to my knowledge.

Question. Have you heard of other cases?

Answer. O, yes, sir; of many cases.

Question. What was their general character; were they whippings or killings?

Answer. They were whippings and killings both.

Question. You may pass on to other counties; take Lee next; that is adjoining.

Answer. Well, sir; I do not know anything in particular about Lee County; the condition of affairs is very bad there now—very bad. A few nights ago a deputy United States marshal went there to make an arrest, and a party of citizens at Tupelo turned out and resisted him.

Question. Did you understand how large a party?

Answer. There were about fifteen of them.

Question. This was in Tupelo?

Answer. Yes, sir; near Tupelo.

Question. Is that the place where a Miss Davis is postmistress?

Answer. Yes, sir.

Question. Are you acquainted with that lady, by character?

Answer. I know her by character.

Question. Have you heard her frequently spoken of?

Answer. Yes, sir; frequently.

Question. What is her general character for chastity and for truth and veracity?

Answer. Well, I do not suppose any one around there has a better character than Miss Davis; I don't know of any one; I have never heard her spoken disrespectfully of in my life. Everybody speaks highly of her in Tupelo.

Question. Do you know of any burning of churches or school-houses in that county?

Answer. Yes, sir; there was a church or school-house burned in Tupelo, I believe about a month ago. I don't remember the exact time.

Question. What was the arrest made in Lee County by the deputy marshal, of which you spoke, where he met with resistance?

Answer. It was made for the murder of a colored man.

Question. Do you recollect the name of the colored man?

Answer. I do not; the warrant has never been in my hands, and I don't remember his name.

Question. You say you heard of numerous cases of whipping and killing in that county of Lee?

Answer. Yes, sir, various cases, but I do not remember any of them. They are so frequent here that unless it comes right near around me, I do not pay much attention to them.

Question. You may go on and speak of the other counties you enumerated?

Answer. Well, in all the counties I have mentioned there have been whippings and murders committed almost weekly for the last nine months, but I do not know any of the parties. I have heard, I think, but I do not know any of the parties, of my own knowledge.

Question. Were you ever present at the capture of any of the Ku-Klux?

Answer. Yes, sir; I captured seven in Tishemingo County.

Question. You may state the time and circumstances?

Answer. I do not remember the exact time; it was about the 15th of October of this year; I arrested seven in that county; I got their costumes—all of their costumes; and three of them made acknowledgments of being members of the Klan.

Question. Where did you find their costumes?

Answer. At their houses. They acknowledged to have worn them; they belonged to the band; three of them acknowledged that that was the oath.

Question. The oath you have already read?

Answer. Yes, sir.

Question. On what charge were they arrested—for whipping or killing, or what was the nature of their offense?

Answer. It was for both, I believe; they were arrested for both—attempting murder and whipping.

Question. Where are these disguises?

Answer. Colonel Wells has them. I can have them before the committee in a few minutes.

Question. They are here in town?

Answer. Yes, sir.

Question. Are there any other facts within your knowledge about which I have not interrogated you?

Answer. None particularly, I believe, sir, outside of Monroe County.

By Mr. BLAIR:

Question. How long have you lived in Mississippi?

Answer. I have been here since the 30th of March last.

Question. Where did you come from?

Answer. Kentucky.

Question. Were you never here before?

Answer. Yes, sir; I was in the State nearly two years on staff duty with General Carlin. I was here as an officer of the Army, and served nearly two years on General Carlin's staff.

Question. In what part of the country were you?

Answer. At Vicksburgh.

Question. Then your entire acquaintance with this part of the country dates from last March?

Answer. Yes, sir.

Question. You are not, then, so familiar with the counties you have mentioned by any long residence?

Answer. No, sir.

Question. Your familiarity with the country comes entirely from different official duties you have been called upon to perform?

Answer. Yes, sir.

Question. In visiting, casually, these several counties in your district?

Answer. Yes, sir.

Question. How often have you been in Lee County?

Answer. I have been there four times, I believe.

Question. How long did you remain at any one time?

Answer. I was not there longer than one day at any one time.

Question. Which county do you reside in?

Answer. I reside in Alcorn County.

Question. That is the county in which Corinth is situated.

Answer. Yes, sir.

Question. How often have you been in Tishemingo?

Answer. I suppose a dozen times.

Question. You have gone only when you were sent upon official matters as deputy marshal?

Answer. Yes, sir.

Question. How long did you remain?

Answer. I remained once in the county a week.

Question. On the other occasions?

Answer. I would not remain more than a day.

Question. Never remained more than a day except on one occasion?

Answer. No, sir; except on one occasion.

Question. How many visits have you made to Chickasaw?

Answer. Two.

Question. How long have you remained?

Answer. One time I was two days in Chickasaw. I was in Okalona; one time I was there one day, the next time two days.

Question. How often have you been in this county?

Answer. Twice; I was at Caledonia once, and once here.

Question. How long did you remain here?

Answer. I remained here four days.

Question. Did you, in your visits to these different counties, when you remained so brief a time, become well acquainted with the people and the condition of the county as to peace and order?

Answer. I think I did; I got pretty well acquainted.

Question. In passing through a county, and remaining there one day, you became possessed of the entire facts in reference to its condition?

Answer. Yes, sir; I could understand the condition of affairs in half a day.

Question. You were satisfied you knew all about it?

Answer. I was satisfied of its condition of affairs in half a day. I was compelled to be, not in all of the counties, but in some of them—most of them.

Question. You say that it was in Okolona, I believe, you had prisoners under indictment?

Answer. Yes, sir.

Question. At the hotel a party of men, with pistols, threatened to take the prisoners?

Answer. Yes, sir.

Question. And you threatened them with buck-shot?

Answer. Yes, sir.

Question. You say the prisoners were taken from the hotel?

Answer. I took the prisoners from the hotel to Colonel Shattuck's private residence.

Question. These same parties went and burned Shuttuck's office, did they?

Answer. I am not positive that they did it; but some parties did.

Question. You stated that they burned Shattuck's office because they wanted to draw the attention of your guard away from the house, so they might attack the house?

Answer. That is my honest opinion.

Question. What do you found that on?

Answer. I found that on the condition of affairs there. Everybody seemed to be angry because we had those prisoners there, and I heard of a good deal of talk next morning around there about Colonel Shattuck having the prisoners at his house, cursing him.

Question. Now, it is a mere conjecture of your own; you have no evidence whatever to found that opinion on?

Answer. Well, I do not know; I think I have.

Question. What evidence have you?

Answer. The general conduct of the people.

Question. What was the general conduct of the people that led you to suppose that they did, with this purpose in their hearts, set fire to a house?

Answer. Because they went to the depot that night to take the prisoners from me, and after that this thing occurred.

Question. You believe, and have reason to believe, that these same men did actually, and with this purpose, set fire to Shattuck's office?

Answer. These same men, or some others like them did, I am satisfied.

Question. You did not see anybody set fire to it?

Answer. No, sir.

Question. You never saw anybody that saw them set fire to it?

Answer. No, sir; but I saw the man who put it out.

Question. Did he have anything to do with setting it on fire?

Answer. I do not know; I suppose not. He was a colored man.

Question. What did he say; that he saw who set it on fire?

Answer. No, sir; he did not say who set it on fire.

Question. You did not see anybody set fire to it?

Answer. No, sir.

Question. And you do not know who did set fire to it?

Answer. I did not see it set on fire, or anybody that did.

Question. And you have no testimony tending to implicate any one?

Answer. No particular one at all; but it certainly was set on fire by some one, because it was set on fire in such a place it could not have caught fire, no fire being in that building the evening before, for I was there myself.

Question. And you have just drawn the conclusion in your own mind that it was done with that purpose?

Answer. Yes, sir.

Question. Without any further knowledge on that subject?

Answer. Yes, sir; that is my conclusion, exactly.

Question. And from no other premises; it is nothing but a conjecture? You say there was a party of men in Tishemingo County set fire, on the 30th of September, to Widow Hunnicut's house?

Answer. No, sir; I did not say set fire. They fired into the house.

Question. Do you know what purpose they went there for?

Answer. No, sir; I do not.

Question. Did you ever hear any one state any reason for this?

Answer. Yes, sir; I have heard John Hunnicut state that they had served a notice on him, and they called there to whip him and he resisted them, or did not exactly resist them, but held the doors. That is his statement.

Question. What did they serve a notice on him for?

Answer. Well, they stated in their notice the belief that he was a little too intimate with his mother.

Question. That was the alleged cause?

Answer. Yes, sir; that was the alleged cause of the notice being served, I believe.

Question. That he was guilty of incest with his mother?

Answer. Yes, sir.

Question. You stated that you had captured the lieutenant of the band who committed this outrage—who fired into this house; what did he allege was the reason for that movement?

Answer. He said they just went there for fun.

Question. Just fired at people for fun—shot at them?

Answer. Yes, sir; that is what he says.

Question. Is that the only reason he gave?

Answer. The only reason in the world; he said they went there for fun, and some of the boys got mad, and fired into the house because they would not let them have entrance.

Question. Did you have any conversation with him as to this notice, and the reason alleged in that notice for going there?

Answer. No particular conversation with him, I believe. I had with some of the members of the band.

Question. You had with some of the others?

Answer. Yes, sir.

Question. What did they allege?

Answer. They alleged that the reason for going there was that they wanted to whip young Hunnicut for being too intimate with his mother.

Question. You state that the same party went in search of Sam. Meeks, and found him at John Meeks's, his brother?

Answer. That is a different party; that was some time ago that occurred.

Question. When did that occur?

Answer. That was at Meeks's; that occurred in 1869; that was the first ride he took; it was in 1869. They went to Sam. Meeks's house, or near there, and found, before arriving there, that Sam. Meeks was not at home; they found him about four miles from there, at John Meeks's; that is this man's statement.

Question. You say they fired on Sam. Meeks and shot him with buck-shot?

Answer. Yes, sir; that is the statement.

Question. That some of the party said it was Sam. Marlow that shot him?

Answer. Yes, sir; Thomas Marlow that shot at him.

Question. What was given as the reason for going and firing upon Meeks?

Answer. There was no particular reason given to me, sir.

Question. You do not understand that they alleged any motive whatever?

Answer. No, sir; none at all.

Question. You have only been once in Lee County, did you say?

Answer. I have been four times in Lee County.

Question. Never remained there more than one day?

Answer. No, sir.

Question. Did you get thoroughly acquainted with the character of everybody in that time?

Answer. Not everybody. I got pretty well acquainted with the condition of affairs there, though.

Question. You do not suppose you are as well acquainted with the characters of everybody there as people who have resided there for many years?

Answer. O, no, sir.

Question. Not as well acquainted, perhaps, with Miss Davis as many who are resident there?

Answer. O, no, certainly not. I have always heard her spoken of as being a very nice lady by every one.

Question. What colored men were those men you had in charge, arrested for killing?

Answer. In Lee County?

Question. Yes.

Answer. I do not remember the name of the colored man. I remember the name of the man I arrested. One of the parties was Freeman; he was one man.

Question. On the charge of killing a colored man?

Answer. On the charge of murder, and also burning a school-house.

Question. You do not remember the name of the man he murdered?

Answer. No, sir.

Question. Do you not know that that was an affray in which the man was badly shot?

Answer. No, sir; I was not apprised of that at all. My understanding is that Mr. Freeman was shot over another difficulty—for shooting the father of a couple of young men there.

Question. Shot in what?

Answer. He was shot for shooting the father of two young men in town there. I do not remember their names.

By Mr. RICE:

Question. High?

Answer. That is the name.

By Mr. BLAIR:

Question. What were the circumstances of the killing of this colored man, for whose murder you say he was arrested?

Answer. I do not know the circumstances connected with it at all.

Question. You became conversant with everything in the county, except the particular business you went about?

Answer. No, sir. I do not pretend to say I became conversant with everything in the county, with every particular case, but I became sufficiently conversant to know there was a band of Ku-Klux prowling through the county constantly, and whipping people at will. I got my information from the best men in the county.

Question. You say you captured in Tishemingo County, on the 11th of October, seven Ku-Klux?

Answer. Yes, sir.

Question. With their costumes?

Answer. Yes, sir.

Question. Three of whom made acknowledgments to you?

Answer. Yes, sir.

Question. What were the names of these parties who made acknowledgments to you?

Answer. John Whittaker, two of the Reynolds boys. I do not remember their names now.

Question. Where do they live in Tishemingo?

Answer. About four miles north of Burnsville.

Question. What did they acknowledge?

Answer. They acknowledged to have been members of the band, and to have been at Hunnicut's when that firing was done, and to have been at various other places on other occasions, on several raids. They did not enumerate them all to me.

Question. What particular ones did they enumerate to you?

Answer. I believe the Hunnicut difficulty was the only particular raid they did enumerate to me.

By the CHAIRMAN:

Question. For the purpose of informing yourself of the condition of the community, who did you generally put yourself in communication with when you went to a county to serve warrants?

Answer. I would put myself in communication with the assessor, or collector, or men who I knew were friends to the Government.

Question. Your information of the general condition of the country in that particular county would be derived from this source?

Answer. Yes, sir.

Question. Is it your information and belief that in all those counties the Ku-Klux have been in the habit of riding out in disguise and inflicting outrages upon colored people?

Answer. Yes, sir.

Question. In all the counties you have mentioned?

Answer. Yes, sir; every one of them,

Question. What is your information as to these disturbances having been particularly numerous during last spring, soon after the Meridian riot?

Answer. I do not understand that question exactly.

Question. I wanted to learn from you whether these outrages of which you spoke occurred more particularly last spring, soon after the riot at Meridian?

Answer. Yes, sir; they were much more frequent last spring than they have been here recently. Last spring there seemed to be a general outbreak everywhere all over the country, or all over the State, I should say. There was scarcely a night in Monroe County that they did not ride. I know that of my own knowledge.

Question. What is the character of this Freeman you spoke of, about in Tupelo?

Answer. He is a desperate character.

Question. Do you know the character of this man Bell, for whom Colonel Huggins had a warrant, but who made his escape?

Answer. No, sir; I do not.

COLUMBUS, MISSISSIPPI, *November* 16, 1871.

WILLIAM B. KOLB sworn and examined.

By the CHAIRMAN:

Question. State your place of residence and occupation?

Answer. I am a citizen of this county—Lowndes County; I am a mechanic by profession, though I taught school a portion of the present year—four months—a public school.

Question. You may state whether you were interrupted or molested at any time when you were teaching school?

Answer. Yes, sir; I was.

Question. When, and under what circumstances?

Answer. It was some time in April; either the first or second Saturday in April; I am not certain.

Question. Under what circumstances?

Answer. About between 11 and 12 o'clock at night some person hailed at my gate. I was sleeping. My wife told me some person had hailed. I got up and went to the door, and saw some person there in disguise. He spoke in a foreign tone, and asked if Mr. Kolb was at home. I told him he was. He said, "Step here Mr. Kolb, I have a note for you." I walked out to the gate. He was standing in front. I felt a little mischievous. I wanted to see who it was, and I stood back, as if I was afraid, and he rode up and reached over the gate, and, as he reached over, I walked up to him. My face was within about two feet of his face. He was masked and disguised from toe to crown. As I took the note he turned away, and we had no more talk. He rode off about one hundred and fifty yards, where he joined a company of between thirty and forty, I suppose. After they had stood there for some time—I remained watching them—they rode on, rather by my house, or in front of it, passed about eighty yards, and turned to the right, and took the pathway, and all rode off in double file, all disguised.

Question. Were their horsemen disguised?

Answer. Yes, sir; I do not know that they all were; most of them were. The man who came to the gate was riding a mule. It was covered. I supposed that night it was a mule, and next morning noticed mule-tracks.

Question. What was the note?

Answer. The note was about this: "Mr. W. B. KOLB: You are hereby notified to discontinue your public school immediately, or woe will be your leather." Appended was: "You are at liberty to teach a private school, or school by private subscription." I think that was about the note, *verbatim*.

Question. How was it signed?

Answer. "K. K. K."

Question. Had it any insignia or device on it; any pictures?

Answer. No, sir; it was a piece of account-paper, I think, written on. I think nothing more to it, anyway—rather rudely folded up.

Question. Were you ever visited subsequenty to that?

Answer. No, sir; I never was.

Question. Did you ever receive any letters after that?

Answer. No, sir.

Question. Were any messages sent to you?

Answer. No, sir; none.

Question. Did you discontinue your school?

Answer. Yes, sir; I did for a while. I intended going on, but some of my neighbors and our director, Mr. Johnson, told me he thought probably it would be better to suspend, if it would meet the approbation of the patrons, for a short time, until things quieted down. I went to the school with a view of going on, and called the patrons together, and told them I would hold them responsible for the payment of the school in the event that I did not get pay—public pay; and they asked me to suspend one month. I did so. At the end of that time I was sick, and could not resume my school until two months. I taught out my school according to the contract.

Question. How long had you been teaching that school when visited?

Answer. Nine weeks.

Question. Have you any knowledge or information who were in this body?

Answer. No, sir; I knew no person. I could not identify any person.

Question. Are you informed whether they visited any other teachers about that time?

Answer. Yes, sir; they visited all the teachers in that vicinity on the Wednesday night before.

Question. How many teachers did you understand they visited?

Answer. There was A. L. Myers, Ruffin Webb, Mrs. Martha Kennon, and Mr. J. F. Galloway were visited about that time. I do not know whether on that same night or not. I was informed this. I do not know this to be so; but that was my information. They were visited on Wednesday night, and I on Saturday night. I suppose one of the main reasons was my school was some five miles from home, and I did not go home regularly; it is too far to pass.

Question. So they must have been out riding two distinct nights, Saturday night and Wednesday night, visiting teachers?

Answer. Yes, sir; I suppose so. They were at my house Saturday night.

Question. Did you hear of any other place being visited the same night they visited you?

Answer. Well, I understood they were at Mr. Campbell's, a neighbor of mine. I didn't hear of any other.

Question. Have you heard of any negroes being whipped by disguised men in the county?

Answer. I have. About that time a negro man was whipped in the eastern portion of this county named Jim Hicks—a short time prior to that, perhaps two or three weeks.

Question. The committee have heard the particulars of his whipping, and you need not repeat them. Have you heard of any other cases?

Answer. There was a boy named Frank—I will not be certain about it; I do not remember by what name he goes—at Dr. Thomas's, was whipped by them; at least they were there.

Question. Did you understand the offense for which he was whipped?

Answer. No, sir; I did not learn.

Question. Are there any other facts within your knowledge that you have not been questioned about?

Answer. I cannot call to mind anything of the kind. There were two other places I heard of them visiting. Nothing done. They merely made calls and made inquiry.

Question. On what night?

Answer. I could not say what night. A gentleman called on me yesterday, old Mr. Ager, and said they called at his house about that time. He said they called there and made some little inquiry. I do not remember what now, but not of much importance, and rode off. That was about daybreak. It was about that time—I think, if I recollect right, it was Wednesday night—they went to see the school-teachers. There was only a small squad of them there. There was another gentleman I forgot—Mr. W. A. Stevenson, the ex-supervisor of this county.

Question. Did you understand they visited his house?

Answer. Yes, sir; he told me so.

Question. What did they do?

Answer. They did nothing. On yesterday he stated—we were talking about it—he said they did not say anything much, only told him what he must do. He did not tell me what that was.

Question. Did these various ridings through the country, by disguised men at night, create any alarm among the people?

Answer. Yes, sir; it terrified the people pretty considerable, and intimidated them a great deal.

Question. Did it have the effect of stopping the public-schools in a measure?

Answer. That was the main cause. There were some of them stopped only for a short time. The most of them resumed their schools. The patrons agreed to become responsible, and they went on.

By Mr. BLAIR;

Question. They did not threaten you in any way?

Answer. Nothing more than the statement in the note. The man turned away as soon as I took hold of the note, and turned his head from me. I could see the mouth and eyes and nose very plainly. It was bright moonlight; but I could not identify him.

Question. He offered you no indignity?

Answer. None at all. He treated me very politely, under the circumstances.

Question. What was the objection to the schools?

Answer. My opinion is that they had no objection to the schools, but to the system. I think that school-tax—breaking it up was their design. I am satisfied of it.

Question. Their object was to stop the onerous tax of that county?

Answer. Yes, sir; that was their motive, I think.

By the CHAIRMAN:

Question. They are in favor of public-schools, I understand, but against taxation to support them?

Answer. Well, sir, I could not say what their notions are. The nature of the organization is such that I do not know anything about them.

By Mr. BLAIR:

Question. After you got well, you continued your school?

Answer. Yes, sir; I continued my school, and closed as the contract required.

Question. You suspended one or two months?

Answer. Yes, sir. I do not remember the time I suspended, probably more than a month. The health of my family was bad.

Question. You named a number of teachers in your vicinity who were visited in like manner. Did they have similar treatment?

Answer. No, sir; they called upon them in person. There was one reason why they did not come to my house, a matter of some delicacy. My wife was in a condition when she ought not to have been frightened, and they staid away on that account, I think.

Question. Was the notice similar to the one they gave you?

Answer. I was informed that they told others that they came to notify them that if they went on with their schools they would do their work for nothing; that they had better hold their patrons responsible, as they intended stopping the payment of the school tax.

Question. That was rather a friendly act, than otherwise, to advise them to look to somebody else?

Answer. It was a kindness to the teachers that was rather assumed, though.

Question. They did not want them to work for nothing?

Answer. Yes, sir.

Question. You say Jim Hicks was whipped?

Answer. Yes, sir.

Question. What for?

Answer. I understood it was for some insult.

Question. Was it for boasting of intimacy with some white woman?

Answer. No, sir; for insults to some old citizens. He cropped with Dr. Robinson, of Caledonia, and the old doctor is a very straight man, and he could not get him to a settlement. He kept the account, I suppose, correctly, and Hicks was not satisfied with it, and talked very unkindly to him, and I suppose they got hold of it.

Question. Do you know Hicks?

Answer. Yes, sir.

Question. What sort of a negro is he?

Answer. Well, his status or his disposition?

Question. His character.

Answer. I think he is, from what I learn, (he never treated me amiss,) but he is rather overbearing and insulting when he is not pleased. He has had three or four difficulties in the last three or four years with white men. He has never treated me amiss.

Question. Did you know Darden?

Answer. Yes, sir.

Question. Did you ever hear that Darden had shot at Hicks three or four times?

Answer. Yes, sir.

Question. What for?

Answer. A difficulty about the crop. He was cropping with Darden.

Question. Give the particulars of the difficulty.

Answer. I suppose I heard the pistol fired. I was helping to build a mill at some distance from it, probably half a mile, or three-quarters of a mile, or a mile. Darden has a very shrill voice, and is tolerably profane. I heard him one night. I stepped out and I heard his voice, and a pistol fired, and at an interval of about a minute another, and about a quarter of a minute, until he fired again, and then the noise or talking ceased for a minute or two, and then they commenced again and that ceased.

Question. Did you have any conversation with Darden about it afterward?

Answer. Yes, sir.

Question. What did he say?

Answer. He told me that Hicks had threatened him; he had threatened him that day. I think he had told Burton, a white man working there, that he intended taking his ax and knocking him in the head; and about the time he was retiring Hicks did come in the yard with his ax. He said he had his clothes off, and Hicks came in the yard and called him to the gate; the gate is very close to the door of his dwelling. He stepped to the door and ordered him away, and he would not go, and there was a disagreeable conversation started, and he went out with his pistol. He said he did not intend to hit him at all. He said he shot to scare, but he wanted to make him believe he would hit him, and to get him away; that he thought he would hurt him if he did not get him away.

Question. He supposed he had come there for that purpose?

Answer. Yes, sir.

Question. He had been notified of that?

Answer. Yes, sir; he told Burton, and Burton told Darden. He and Burton had had some words in the field, and Burton had come to the house and told what Hicks had said; and when he came that night he thought he was going to make his threat good; that Burton's statement was correct, and Hicks was going to kill him.

Question. Do you know Burton?

Answer. Yes, sir.

Question. Did you ever have any conversation with him about it?

Answer. No, sir.

Question. You say a boy named Frank was whipped?

Answer. Yes, sir; I believe his name was Cockerham. I think that was his name. Anyhow, he was working for Dr. Thomas, Thomas & Kidd, at their mill.

Question. What did they go there to whip him for?

Answer. I do not know; probably some little theft, it strikes me; taking some book, or something of that kind—some little petty theft.

Question. You say you are not certain whether they whipped him or not?

Answer. No, sir. They frightened him considerably, I suppose. I am not certain whether they whipped him or not, and I am not certain what the theft was.

Question. Were those parties in disguise?

Answer. I understood so.

Question. You say they visited Stevenson?

Answer. Yes, sir.

Question. Did they do anything to him?

Answer. Nothing.

Question. Was he keeping school?

Answer. No, sir.

Question. What was he doing?

Answer. He was a member of the board of supervisors of district No. 1, and he stated to me yesterday—I asked him what they said—he said, "They told me what I must do;" and he said no more about it. Soon after the school tax was rescinded, and I suppose that that was what they told him he had to do.

Question. Rescind the school tax?

Answer. Yes, sir.

COLUMBUS, MISSISSIPPI, *November* 8, 1871.

EDWARD CARTER (colored) sworn and examined.

By the CHAIRMAN:

Question. Where do you live?

Answer. I am staying close to Mr. Brown's plantation; teaching school up there; about eleven miles.

Question. In this county?

Answer. No, sir; half of the plantation is in this county, and the other half in Sanford, Alabama.

Question. Where did you come here from?

Answer. From Tuscaloosa, Alabama.

Question. When did you leave there?

Answer. On the 11th of September.

Question. How came you to leave there and come here?

Answer. I was run away from there by a procession of men that came there on the 8th, disguised; running off me and my family.

Question. On the 8th of September?

Answer. Yes, sir.

Question. Did they come to your house in the night-time?

Answer. They came about 7 o'clock, I reckon.

Question. At night?

Answer. Yes, sir.

Question. How many were there?

Answer. I can't tell how many. They hitched their horses in the bushes, and some came to the house.

Question. How were they disguised?

Answer. They had handkerchiefs on their faces; the one that came that I saw had his jaws bound. He came to the gate and hailed, like he had business, and had the gate open, and ordered me to come out and march up the hill; I objected. He held a pistol in his hand. I backed down and run to the house, about thirty steps, and when I run off he fired the pistol at me; it missed me as I ran, and it went through the entry, and struck the table in the entry; the bullet struck it, and went to the back yard, and hit the fence. I ran off two or three hundred yards, and stopped, to go back. They fired a pistol again, and I went off to the man I rented of, J. W. Mayfield, to get some protection—about a mile off. He told me to stay away that night, and I staid an hour or two, and went back again, and they knocked around right smart, and cut up, and at the time they cut up, my daughter was in the lot, milking the cows, and my little boy, nine years old next December; she had a light in the lot and was milking, and two of them came in there, before she knew anybody was in the lot, and in scuffling their hats fell off, and one was John Cook, that used to be in Mississippi, here, and the other Diller Suddith. He was raised about two miles and a half from me. She went to holler, and John Cook put a leather girth on her neck, to prevent her hollering, and they carried her about a quarter or a half a mile from the house, and they ravished her.

Question. These two men did?

Answer. Yes, sir.

By Mr. BLAIR:

Question. John Clark, and who?

Answer. Diller Suddith.

By the CHAIRMAN:

Question. How many men did you say came there with Cook and Suddith?

Answer. I couldn't tell how many.

Question. How many do you think?

Answer. I can't tell. I went out next day where they hitched the horses, and they were a long train, and all about the woods, and beside the road, and the whole woods was tramped up—nearly an acre of ground.

Question. What did they charge you with?

Answer. There was no charge against me. I never could learn, and I have inquired of the neighbors what report they made, and I learned they run me off to get what I had.

Question. How long did you stay there after that night?

Answer. I laid out Saturday night and Sunday night, and Monday night I went down to the landlord's house I rented land from, to see what I could learn from him, and talked to him. Two of these men came with a double-barreled gun, and I got mighty uneasy; I didn't know what they meant by it. They told him they wanted to go driving next day; he said he didn't know what they meant.

By Mr. BLAIR:

Question. Was that Mayfield?

Answer. Yes, sir.

Question. What was his first name?

Answer. James W. Mayfield.

Question. Does he live at Tuscaloosa?

Answer. Yes, sir; at Gizzardville. He told me he didn't consider me safe then there at night, and it was best to stay out of the way awhile, anyhow, till things got somewhat quiet, and his wife said, "John Cook was here cussing, and John Cook said this rape case, he acknowledged he had done that, and that he intended to do it again, and would do what he pleased with all of them, but 'lowed to kill the mother first." That was my wife, that he allowed to kill her first, and that he would do it to all of them; and I thought it was the safest plan to go away.

By the CHAIRMAN:

Question. Did you ever prosecute either Cook or Diller Suddith?
Answer. No, sir.
Question. Why?
Answer. I had no protection there at all; they threatened to kill me, because I told in the neighborhood what they had done; we had no friends. Since I have left, they have taken everything I had, and sold it, and I have nothing to go upon—crop and all.
Question. Did you bring your family here?
Answer. I have two children here, and two up there now with their grandfather.

By Mr. BLAIR:

Question. Did you hear Mrs. Mayfield say John Cook admitted that he had ravished your daughter?
Answer. She told my wife so, and I was not five steps from her when she told it.
Question. You heard it?
Answer. Yes, sir.
Question. Where was that; at your house?
Answer. That was down at her house, out in the yard.
Question. What sort of people are these Mayfields?
Answer. Some people have right smart charges against them, but he always seemed a very clever sort of man to me and those around him.
Question. Does he own a large plantation?
Answer. Not very large, not where he lives, but he has got a good deal of land—two or three plantations.
Question. An educated man?
Answer. A very good education.
Question. Is he a planter, or professional man?
Answer. Well, he is a planter.
Question. Who is John Cook?
Answer. He is a son of old Silas Cook, who used to live out here not far from Columbus, here. He formerly lived here, but now he lives forty odd miles from here.
Question. What does Cook do?
Answer. Well, he is making a small crop this year.
Question. John Cook?
Answer. Yes, sir.
Question. Close by where you lived?
Answer. About three miles from me.
Question. Who is Diller Suddith?
Answer. He lives about two and a half miles from me, just close neighbor of John Cook.
Question. What does he do?
Answer. He farms with his daddy, though I don't think he is up there now. Him and Jim Suddith passed through here on the 4th of last month—October. They took the cars here.
Question. Where did they go?
Answer. I don't know where they went to; whether they stopped in the State or not. They aimed to stop in the State, before they got into such big fusses up there, but since that I don't know where they went to, or whether they stopped or not.

By the CHAIRMAN:

Question. Did you hear of any other colored people being disturbed in that part of the country?
Answer. Not right where I was, but a man is down here I am well acquainted with that run from Fayette County, Alabama, in March.
Question. Did you hear much about the Ku-Klux riding in Tuscaloosa County?
Answer. I could hear right smart of it, but not from good authority to make a report of it myself. We could hear a good deal of it. Furthermore, about my case; there was two men of my acquaintance who told me they knew nearly the whole party.

COLUMBUS, MISSISSIPPI, *November* 16, 1871.

HENRY CLARK sworn and examined.

By the CHAIRMAN:

Question. What is your occupation?

Answer. I am employed at present, and have been for some time, by Colonel Wells. I have been employed by Colonel Wells as a detective for this northern district for some time, with headquarters in Oxford.

Question. State if you have made special efforts to discover the organization and locality of what is known as the Ku-Klux Klan?

Answer. Yes, sir; I have made that my business entirely.

Question. You may go on and detail to the committee now what success has attended your efforts?

Answer. Well, sir, I was stationed last summer in Tippah County, near the county-seat of that county. I went in there with a view of getting what information I could in regard to the organization. While there I was notified several times to move from that locality, by the way of a notice stuck up in front of my residence, with a rope about four feet long, I should think, with a hangman's knot fastened at one end of it, in which I was told that, if I did not leave at such a time, I would find myself hanging at the end of it. I did not respect their order, and remained three some six weeks after they had notified me to leave. I made a reply to the note, and informing them with my pencil, as I found it stuck on a tree in front of my house—I replied, in case any of them got tired of living, they could come around and see me, and I would do the best I could for them; and I remained on until about the first of October in that locality; then I had some chance of joining or the promise of joining the organization; that is, they insisted I should join them, after they found out I was attending to my own business, and did not appear to be meddling with any of them; and I since have had the captain of the organization of that department arrested, and four of his company, and they are now in bonds.

Question. Did you join the organization?

Answer. No, sir; I was down with congestion of the brain about that time, and was not able to be out.

Question. What discoveries did you make in reference to the nature and objects of the organization?

Answer. I have seen from twenty-five to forty in uniform at one time there in that locality.

Question. Under what circumstances?

Answer. Well, sir, I have seen when they have been going to the houses of different parties for the purpose of whipping, beating, and intimidating. I know of one Mr. Mask there; they came to his house and took him out and hit him thirty-nine licks. They had no particular charge against him, only they wanted to get into possession of a tract of land he was at that time living on, and notified him if he did not leave at such a time, by a Sunday night—this was Thursday—they would either whip him or hang him. They did not wait for Sunday night, but came on Saturday night and took him out, with his brother Bogan Mask, and hit Silas Mask thirty-nine licks, being so many licks apiece for each one accompanying the party; and his brother stood by and saw every lick hit. The captain of this party—I suppose you require their names?

By Mr. RICE:

Question. Give us their names.

Answer. The captain of this party is Harris Taylor. He was well known in Tippah County. He was captain of the organization; that is, of one department of the organization, but there is another department known there as the "Woods organization," that is, the "Woods company." I do not know how the man spells his first name, but they call him A. Woods. He is captain of another organization there. I have been investigating some cases in that county, and no longer than day before yesterday a lady came to me and swore out a warrant, now in my possession, which you can read, which involves positively three, and proposes to involve nine others who were accompanying these three who committed the outrage.

By the CHAIRMAN:

Question. Did she state the fact to you?

Answer. Yes, sir; I know the facts and the time they occurred. I am conversant with the whole.

Question. Without referring to this paper you may go on and state your information in relation to it.

Answer. My information is this. Her name is Sykes—widow Sykes. Her husband died not long since. She had a very valuable tract of land, which was located in the midst, as you might say, of this company of Harris Taylor's. They wanted to come in possession, the company did, of this tract of land, or to get a chance to rent it, or buy it cheap. She would neither sell nor rent; and to get possession of this land, they notified her to leave against such a time, and if she did not leave they threatened to hang her. They came to her house and had another interview. She did not leave, and they came to her house, and at that time her daughters—she has four daughters—one of them was lying very low, and they brought a rope, and before she was aware they had surrounded the house, and came close to the bed where the daughter was lying, and proposed to take the mother out and hang her if she disobeyed their orders. The doctor who attended the daughter says that it was the cause of the daughter losing her mind. She was scared at their appearance. She has never been in her right mind since. He says that is the cause of her losing her mind. They went away promising her, if she would leave by October first, they would not molest her, but if she did not they would take both her and her daughters out and hang them. They started back to this lady's house, as she did not leave by the first of October, with a rope, and with their switches or whips, and were met on the way by a close neighbor of Mrs. Sykes, named Miller, and he persuaded them not to go there on account of her children all lying very low, but they went on and called out one of the daughters who was then well. They called her out to the road, and her little brother of ten years and her sister crying and begging for her. They had her there and displayed the rope and switches in front of the house; but they cried and begged and hallooed, until they were afraid it would rouse the neighbors, and they told her if they did not leave immediately they would use the rope the next time they went; and Mrs. Sykes was compelled, under those circumstances, to leave the country, and left that county entirely, leaving her property all there, and moved out in the vicinity of Corinth to get protection. She is a lady of good character. Her character and the character of her family can be substantiated by the best and most reliable citizens of Tippah County, both her character and the character of her family. I know many parties of that section of the country who have been whipped. They came to my house along in the early part of the season, and took out, within three hundred yards of my house, a colored man belonging to Judge Green. They laid him over a flour barrel, tied his hands and feet on the under side of the flour barrel, and hit him one hundred and fifty licks, from which he could not get out of his bed for several days.

By Mr. BLAIR:

Question. At your house?

Answer. No, sir; in front of my house, about three hundred yards, in a negro cabin on Judge Green's plantation, which adjoins mine. They took him out and whipped him until he was not able to get out of his bed for several days; because they sent to my house for medicines several different times. On the same night they went——

Question. What was the name of that man?

Answer. Tillman Green, sir. He belonged to Judge Green before the war. They went the same night about a quarter of a mile north of Tillman Green's, and there they took out a colored man named Armisted Boyd. He belonged to a Mr. Boyd before the war, who is now a representative from that county. They took him out and hit him seventy-five licks with switches, which kept him confined to the house two or three days; and his clothing, after they had licked him—he was then working for a man named Yancey, a resident of Tippah County for thirty-five years, and came to Mr. Yancey the following day—he laid out in the woods that night—and his clothes were all stuck to the flesh, so that Mr. Yancey and myself had to go to work and dress his wounds, where they had cut him and drew his blood. His clothes had stuck to him. They told him if he ever told any one in that neighborhood they would kill him, and he never told any one except us, except the man who was employed by Mr. Yancey. They then came out another time, about three miles further, to a man named Albert Thomas, a colored man who belonged formerly to a man named Thomas—P. R. Thomas—and took him out and hit him, I think, a hundred licks. The trouble they had with him was because he would not agree to crop with the party that they wanted him to. There was one of the organization wanted him to come and crop with him, and he would not agree to it, and they took him out and hit him about one hundred licks. There is another man in that immediate neighborhood, named—it is right hard to remember names, especially these colored people—Joseph Brooks, a colored man in very good standing. I think he is elected justice of the peace of the county. They took him out last spring and licked him; I do not remember how many licks they gave him; at any rate they notified him that if he sounded the name of Ku-Klux again, death would be his penalty; and I sold him a plantation, only about a month and a half ago, in Tippah County there, a small place—160 acres.

By the CHAIRMAN:

Question. Did all these outrages you have mentioned occur in the same county?

Answer. Yes, sir; in the immediate neighborhood of seven miles.

Question. In what period of time?

Answer. Within the last six months. I know of a great many other outrages of that nature, but I cannot remember the names of the parties. I never made a minute of it. I did not know I would ever be called on for their names; they were in that county; and I know a great many that have occurred outside of that county.

Question. You may proceed to speak of any outrages of a kindred character outside of that county.

Answer. Well, sir, I am conversant with this affair that occurred here last summer, at Pontotoc, wherein was Mr. Flournoy.

Question. Was he the editor of the newspaper "Equal Rights?"

Answer. Yes, sir. I know one party arrested not long since by the name of Harden. He was arrested and gave bonds. I know a number of parties in that; Dillard was one. I know his folks well. He is a man of very poor character. He always did bear a very poor character. I have known them by reputation for the last ten or eleven years—ten years ago in particular. I used to ride all through that country, all in below Columbus. I was at that time a scout in this department. I served as a scout in this department during the whole war, and below here some distance I was captured—or rather west of here, near New Albany, in Union County, by Dillard's brother-in-law, during the war. They took me to Andersonville, and I remained there six or eight months. They have always had an antipathy to me since that, and I have met their family since. At the time this Dillard was killed at Pontotoc, by Judge Pollard, he was put into an ox-cart and sent into the country where his family lived. When they took him out there his wife would not come near the body at all, or have anything to do with it, and his own relatives refused to have anything to do with burying his body. A few of the neighbors turned out and buried the body, and but very few at that. Now, there is a man in Pontotoc, or has been within the last ten days, by the name of Pitts, who is circulating a contribution paper, or subscription paper, to raise funds to build a monument over this man Dillard; he is raising funds to build a monument over this man Dillard, who was known to be one of the most desperate characters who has ever inhabited that section of the country. I have known him by reputation for ten years, and his family. He never has borne any character whatever, and his own friends, when he was returned to them, would not have anything to do with his remains. Now he is circulating this paper and getting funds to erect a monument, when he was only a midnight assassin, and was killed with the garb on him, as has been sworn to.

By Mr. RICE:

Question. Are those who pay this of the same sort?

Answer. It would look so. I know there was about sixty names on this subscription list, of which I know the greater portion of the men, which I propose to work up hereafter. This man Dillard—his relatives undertook to assassinate me not long since, on account of their knowing that I was, as they termed it, a Yankee, and had been connected with the United States forces since the commencement of the war at Corinth, and through this department at Memphis, Corinth, and Nashville. I have been threatened a great many times this summer by different parties there, but they never have hurt me.

By the CHAIRMAN:

Question. Have you been informed of any other outrages than those you have mentioned?

Answer. Yes, sir; there are a great many different outrages in different parts of the department, but I cannot call some of them to my memory; I have not got their names; I did not make a memorandum of their names. When they telegraphed for me I was not at home, or I could have got a memorandum of all the names. I know they whipped a man up near Rienzi, in Alcorn County, last spring; I do not remember his name now; I talked with him shortly afterward. I know of some twelve or fifteen cases that occurred within a limit of seven or eight miles of Ripley, in Tippah County, Mississippi. They notified me a great many times last summer that if I did not leave they should do so and so, but I paid no attention to it, and was well armed; I never went around much after dark; they never interrupted me.

Question. Have you ever informed yourself of the strength of that organization?

Answer. I have, in reference to Tippah County. In that county the organization, I think, safely speaking, is about seventy-five; there are three companies in that county that I know of.

Question. Do you know by what name they are known among themselves?

Answer. You mean to say what their pass-words are?

Question. No; what is the name of the order?

Answer. They go by their captain's name, each company; Captain Taylor's is one company, Woods's is another; the other company I never got the captain's name; he lives on the Hatchie River, adjoining Alcorn County.

Question. Did you ever learn the oath?

Answer. I have learned some portion of it, but as to remembering it, I do not.

Question. You have seen their disguises?

Answer. Yes, sir; quite often—in fact, I accompanied the United States marshal in the capture of some of their disguises; I have some of their photographs. After we captured them we went to a photograph establishment and had them photographed with their disguises on, three of them. I have not got them with me.

Question. Have you informed yourself of the objects of this organization?

Answer. Yes, sir—that is, I have conversed with them a great deal, and with those who have turned States' evidence, and those who have not. The object of this organization is to allow no man who was not in the confederate army, or who did not vote the democratic ticket, to allow no one who does not vote the democratic ticket, to hold any position whatever in the Southern States. They last spring intimidated most of the people in that neighborhood, the poorer class of people, that were not better informed, that if they voted otherwise than that, that they would lick the last one of them. They went upon one plantation where there are seventy hands employed, and took the hands out and drew them up in line, and made that statement to them, that if they heard of their voting any other ticket than the democratic ticket, they would lick the last one of them.

Question. Do you know of an organization called the "Robertson Family?"

Answer. Yes, sir; I am quite familiar with an organization of that description.

Question. How large are its numbers?

Answer. I suppose twelve to fifteen hundred, at the last interview I had with any of the parties. I am quite intimate with some of the members——

Question. Have you any intimation of the purposes?

Answer. Yes, sir. That organization was organized only a short time ago, with the intention of carrying the present or last election.

Question. Where was it organized?

Answer. The headquarters of that organization is in Pontotoc.

Question. How far does it extend beyond that county?

Answer. Yes, sir; it extends up into Monroe County, and into the edge of Tippah County.

By Mr. BLAIR:

Question. Where did it originate?

Answer. It originated in Pontotoc; so I have been informed by members of the organization. If I mistake not—I do not know whether I have it here—but I have the names of the leaders and a synopsis of their oath.

By the CHAIRMAN:

Question. Is it a secret organization like the Ku-Klux Klan?

Answer. Yes, sir; it is a secret organization, and the oath of that organization is precisely the same oath as the first Ku-Klux or South Carolina oath—the oath of the Ku-Klux of South Carolina. I have not seen the oath myself; that is the statement made to me by one of the organization—who I know to be one of the organization of the "Robertson Family."

Question. Do they ride, like the Ku-Klux, at night?

Answer. Not that I know of; they have their regular meetings, Thursdays and Saturday nights, as far as I have heard. I can give you information as to the man who is the leader or head man of it. [Consulting a paper.]

Question. Do they have their pass-words and signs?

Answer. Yes, sir; I know their pass-words, but do not know their grips; I have never been able to get advanced that far into the business. The present sheriff of Pontotoc County, now elected, is the leader of that organization. He is the head man of that organization to the best of my knowledge.

Question. You say it is a political organization?

Answer. I could not answer as to that, sir. Their objects have been to carry the elections. That I understand to be the object of the organization. I do not say that it is a political organization. No man is allowed to join the organization unless he proposes to vote the democratic ticket. They propose to break up the trade of every merchant in the county who does not join that organization. They propose to break his trade up. Some merchants have told me, in Pontotoc, that they dared not keep out of the organization; they had to join the organization or else give up trade entirely; they had a small stock, and were compelled to abide by the customs of the country. If they did not join the organization they could not get trade. They are sworn not to trade with any man unless he belongs to the organization. The whole upper part of the county belongs to that organization; and of course a man cannot give up his trade. There is another organization in this county that is similar to that, but under another title.

Question. What is this organization here?

Answer. This is known as the "Native Sons," I believe. I have one of their badges; it is not here. They have an organization numbering some eight hundred; so the leader of the organization told me about a week ago.

By Mr. RICE:

Question. What is his political character? Who is the leader?

Answer. Dr. Landrum, I believe, is the leader of that organization.

By the CHAIRMAN:

Question. Have you any information tending to connect any particular persons, in this county, with any of these secret organizations—leading men?

Answer. Yes, sir; I know a number of the leading men in this county who are connected with this organization known as the "Native Sons." As I have had some of them under arrest on other charges, they acknowledged to me they were the men who drew up the platform and by-laws of this organization.

Question. Have you any information tending to show that any of the leading men in this or Monroe County are or have been connected in the past with the Ku-Klux organization?

Answer. I do not know that I have, sir; I know the parties who drew this platform up for the Native Sons, who got up the by-laws.

Question. Have you the platform with you?

Answer. No, sir; I have not. I did have a copy of it, but it is in Oxford, sir, in the United States marshal's office there. Dr. J. H. Cannon is one of the parties who arranged the platform, one of the head men; in fact, I went down there a week ago last Sunday, with the deputy United States marshal, to arrest both him and Dr. Bonsall and some other parties there; and in his store we found a whole box of glazed caps. On the piece here in front was printed in gilt letters, "Native Sons." I took the doctor in charge, and took them to Oxford, Mississippi, and rode with him, and he explained to me on the road what the intentions were, what the organization was got up for, and how many there was in the organization at the present time. He said the organization at that time numbered seven or eight hundred in this county; and that the organization was got up to carry the election; he said if he had not been arrested at that time, him and Dr. Bonsall, and one or two others we did arrest in this county, that there would have been no difficulty in carrying the election; he said they had the right to have a secret organization of that nature, as well as the republicans did to have a secret organization, known as the Loyal League, which used to exist here.

Question. Did you learn their manner of carrying that election?

Answer. No, sir; not further than that they simply, according to their oath, were compelled to vote one ticket; the members were compelled to vote alike in any election; they were not to split in any particular.

Question. You understood that was one part of their obligation?

Answer. Yes, sir; some of those parties were candidates—one in particular was a candidate.

Question. Did you ever hear whether Dr. Brothers was a member of that order—Dr. Brothers, of Artesia?

Answer. I never learned positively; I heard he was, but I do not know positively.

Question. Did you ever learn whether a lawyer in this city, named Humphries, was a member?

Answer. I understood he was—a week ago last Sunday—that he was a member, but through parties here in town, and I know nothing definite of it myself.

Question. Are you informed whether any of the lawyers of Aberdeen are members of it?

Answer. No, sir; I am not. In the northern district I am more familiar than I am here at the present time; I know this whole section of the country though; I have rode through it ten years ago when the Army was through on this Columbus & Charleston railroad, and the headquarters was at Nashville; I was a scout for the Army here for a number of years.

By Mr. BLAIR:

Question. Were Dr. Cannon and Dr. Bonsall arrested because they were members of this organization?

Answer. No, sir; for violating the enforcement act, passed May 31, 1870.

Question. What was the alleged violation?

Answer. Well, sir, arresting men without a *capias*, without warrant; they are now under bonds of fifteen hundred dollars each to appear at the United States court at Oxford.

Question. Did you ever see the affidavit on which they were arrested?

Answer. Yes, sir.

Question. What did it set forth?

Answer. Merely what I have stated—violation of the enforcement act, passed May 31, 1870, arresting men without any warrant, depriving them of rights and liberties.

Question. Who were the men—it must have sta ed—who were arrested without a warrant?

Answer. Mr. Miller is one of them—an overseer on Mr. Lewis's plantation.

Question. Who else?

Answer. Mr. Rose, a mail agent on the Mobile and Ohio Railroad.

Question. Any others?

Answer. Some others, but I do not remember their names, sir.

Question. Who issued that warrant?

Answer. I forget, sir, which commissioner, but I think the commissioner at Corinth; I will not be positive; it was by a United States commissioner; my impression is, by the commissioner at Corinth.

Question. Who made the affidavit?

Answer. Mr. Rose was one of the parties who made the affidavit.

Question. The affidavit was simply to the effect that he and others were arrested without a *capias?*

Answer. Yes, sir.

Question. And alleged that that was in violation of the act of Congress?

Answer. Yes, sir; the deputy sheriff of this county came to arrest Mr. Miller, and did not show him the *capias*, and he refused to go with him on this ground; he afterward summoned a *posse* of twelve men to go and make the arrest; the *posse* summoned supposed the deputy sheriff had the proper papers, of course, and went and made the arrest by force.

Question. Was any other ground alleged in this affidavit as a violation of the enforcement act?

Answer. I do not know, sir; I am not familiar with that case. I know nothing further than that I accompanied the United States marshal in making the arrest; I simply saw the affidavit, and did not look over it closely.

Question. The "Robertson Family" is an organization kindred to the one you call 'the Native Sons of the South?"

Answer. I suppose it is, sir.

Question. Of the same character?

Answer. Not exactly the same character; their oath is not exactly the same; I have seen the oath of the Native Sons, and have had facilities; I can see it at any time, and get a copy of the by-laws and regulations of the Native Sons, because one of the parties who belonged to it, one of the head men, is very intimate with me, and told me he would at any time furnish me a copy of it; I asked him for it as a favor; he said he would.

Question. They do not, therefore, make much of a secret of it?

Answer. It is considerable of a secret; they do not propose to allow any one in unless they join the organization.

Question. One of the principal men offered you one?

Answer. I had one of the principal men in custody at that time, and I have known him for several years, and he told me he had drawn up the platform, and that he intended to send a copy of it to Governor Alcorn, and he said it was nothing of a serious nature, merely a secret organization to carry the coming election; that was some time ago that he proposed to send it to Governor Alcorn.

Question. He did not care much for secrecy, did he?

Answer. I do not know about that.

Question. The committee has been offered several copies of it here.

Answer. I do not know whether he considers it a secret or not.

Question. He could not have considered it a secret, if he had proffered to send it to Governor Alcorn?

Answer. I do not think it is probable the committee has been offered a copy of the by-laws and regulations of the "Robertson Family."

Question. No; I think this is the first word of the "Robertson family."

Answer. I think you will find other evidence to substantiate that.

Question. I was asking you a question at the time about another matter.

Answer. I do not know as to the secrecy of these Native Sons, any more than I have in my possession one of their caps, and one of their badges, in which there is a badge, perhaps the size of a Mexican dollar, with a looking-glass on the one side, and a breastpin on the other, stamped "Native Sons."

Question. You had no difficulty in obtaining its secrets yourself?

Answer. Not much to get into possession of what little information I have in regard to that organization.

Question. How did you ingratiate yourself with them to become one?

Answer. Because I have been an acquaintance of one of that organization for over twelve years.

Question. Then they are in the habit of telling their secrets to their acquaintances?

Answer. I do not say they ever gave me any of their vows or conditions, any further than I have seen a portion of their oath, but I saw it when they were not aware of it. I was in the office of one of the head men of the organization, and was running over his papers, and happened to see it.

Question. He left it lying around loose, did he?

Answer. It was in his private office.

Question. He left it lying around in his private office so you could see it?

Answer. I do not know that he did it for that purpose. I did not put it in that shape.

Question. But it was there to be seen by any person in his private office?

Answer. Yes, sir. I do not suppose any one was permitted, as a general thing, in his private office at that time; I had assisted in making his arrest, or was deputized by the United States marshal to make his arrest.

Question. That put you on very intimate footing with him, I suppose; did you make any profession of any kind to gain his confidence?

Answer. No, sir.

Question. He knew you were one of the deputies of the marshal?

Answer. Yes, sir.

Question. He did not take very particular pains to keep this matter from you?

Answer. He had no chance; it was on Sunday when I made the arrest; he was not in the house at the time.

Question. Were you authorized to search his papers?

Answer. No, sir; but his papers were lying there on the desk; he told me, though, that he would give me a copy at any time I called on him of the by-laws and regulations of the organization, because he and I had talked considerably on that subject—the nature of the organization, and what it was for; he said to me that they had as good a right to have it as republicans.

Question. Then, in fact, he made no secrecy of it?

Answer. He made no secrecy to me, but told me about seven hundred belonged to the organization, that were sworn in.

Question. He had told you pretty much all the particulars you have given to the committee, without reservation?

Answer. No, sir; I cannot say he told me all.

Question. Who was that person?

Answer. He is a man living in Crawford, sir, in this State.

Question. What is his name?

Answer. Dr. Cannon.

Question. He lives in Crawford, in this county?

Answer. Yes, sir.

Question. How did you get into the secrets of the "Robertson Family?"

Answer. I got into their secrets through the aid of some friends I have, living in this county and Monroe County.

Question. Were they members of the organization?

Answer. No, sir; they were not members of the organization, but had intimate friends who were.

Question. Did you make any profession to obtain the secrets; profess yourself friendly to the objects, &c.?

Answer. Well, sir, this question I will be compelled to withhold at the present time, sir, in the situation—anything like that.

Question. You do not propose to give it to the committee?

Answer. I propose to give my information, as far as I have any, in reference to that matter; as there are some things which have not come to light yet, but in a short time will be brought to light, I will give as far as I know positively.

Question. This is not a question of the information that is to be brought to light; it is simply the manner and the means you used to obtain the information we want to know.

Answer. But would it not involve other parties who wish to keep their names silent? That is the question. If I promise a man to keep his name silent in a thing of that kind, to let me into a secret organization or the character of it, have I the right to divulge his name? I ask the committee is that proper?

Question. I understand the parties who gave you this information were not members of the "Robertson Family?"

Answer. They were not, but had intimate friends who were. I have conversed with persons who say they belong to the "Robertson Family," and belong to it from the simple fact that if they do not belong to it it breaks up their trade entirely. They are merchants, who depend on their trade for a livelihood; and if they had not joined the "Robertson Family" their trade would have been cut off entirely, as they told me; that is, the organization had sworn to trade with none other but those who belong to the organization.

Question. With members of the "Robertson Family?"

Answer. Yes, sir.

Question. They choose to do their business with members, or with people who are their friends?

Answer. Yes, sir.

Question. Who unite with them in their votes?

Answer. Yes, sir.

Question. Well, do you not do your own business with people you prefer to do it with?

Answer. I do it wherever I can trade the cheapest; I have no special friends in regard to anything of that kind.

Question. But nobody can constrain you to do business with one person or another?

Answer. No, sir; but where a whole county, or portions of a county, especially the voting population of a county, are sworn to trade with a party, and there is a party that do not belong to their organization, they can very easily break him up in business. I am that conversant with this country and community.

By Mr. RICE:

Question. Freeze him out?

Answer. Yes, sir; where a merchant has small capital or a limited profession, they would very soon.

By Mr. BLAIR:

Question. Is that illegal? Does it subject a man to penalties for the violation of the enforcement act, to take an oath that he will not trade with anybody in particular?

Answer. I am not an attorney; I am not posted on the United States laws on that subject.

Question. That is all you know about the "Robertson Family;" that they are pledged to trade with certain people and not with others?

Answer. All I know about it is what I have stated to the committee. I think there will be other witnesses before the committee who will substantiate these facts.

Question. You never saw the oath of the South Carolina Ku-Klux, did you?

Answer. I have seen a portion of it, sir.

Question. What is it?

Answer. I do not remember, sir, at the present time. I know some of it; I saw a copy of a portion of it at one time.

Question. You say the present sheriff of Pontotoc is the head of the "Robertson Family?"

Answer. That is my understanding, sir.

Question. What is his name?

Answer. Saddler is the present sheriff—the elected sheriff of Pontotoc County.

Question. Elected at the recent election?

Answer. Yes, sir. It is my opinion that he is connected with another organization, from what information I can get.

Question. What organization is that?

Answer. Known as the Ku-Klux Klan.

Question. What information have you about that? That is exactly what we are looking for.

Answer. Well, sir, I have this information from parties who have met him face to face in disguise.

Question. Who are the parties?

Answer. Well, sir, Judge Pollard is one.

Question. Where does Judge Pollard live?

Answer. I think Judge Pollard lives in Okolona; perhaps he may live in Pontotoc. I think his present residence is in Okolona.

Question. Did Judge Pollard have his disguise on at the same time?

Answer. No, sir; I did not state that. I stated that he had met this man when he was in disguise.

Question. How did he know him?

Answer. That, sir, I am not able to answer. Judge Pollard, no doubt, will answer that when he is brought before the committee.

Question. How do you know the judge knew him?

Answer. From what the judge informed me.

Question. What did he tell you?

Answer. He told me he knew this man Saddler; that he was persuaded he knew him; that he led the organization that made the attempt to assassinate Mr. Flournoy, when Dillard was killed. Mr. Saddler's father came up and testified to knowing one or two of the mules wounded in this Ku-Klux raid into Pontotoc. Several horses and mules were wounded. This man came into Pontotoc in two or three days, where Judge Pollard had this stock in his possession, and he swore to his property. Judge Pollard made him swear to it before he would let him depart, and Judge Pollard will turn over to this committee his oath or affidavit, that the property that was raided by the Ku-Klux that night was his property.

Question. The fact that the stock belonged to Saddler is proof positive?

Answer. No, sir; I did not pretend to say that. There is other proof; I tell you I have been informed; I do not propose to swear that this man led that Ku-Klux organization at all, but I have been informed so by the most reliable citizens in this country.

Question. That is just what we want to get at, what the most reliable citizens say and know.

Answer. I think Judge Pollard and some others will say it.

Question. Judge Pollard, then, told you the facts you are now stating?

Answer. Yes, sir; and it is the opinion of some others who spoke to me on that subject.

Question. What others?

Answer. Sir, I do not remember their names.

Question. How do you know they are such reliable men then?

Answer. I am speaking of Judge Pollard on this particular question.

Question. He is but one citizen, not the most of the citizens in the county; he is but one.

Answer. There are others, I think, will corroborate the statement, sir, that are summoned to appear.

Question. Do you know any others?

Answer. That have made such statements as that?

Question. Yes.

Answer. Yes. I know of some others.

Question. Who are they?

Answer. But prefer to keep their names secret, as they are all right in the midst of this organization; their property all lies there, and at any moment that their names are divulged, their property would be burned up entirely; so they have stated to me; that they dare not come out and express themselves in regard to this thing, on account of their property being burned up as already threatened; men as reliable as any in the northern district of Mississippi; I could give their names, but I would prefer their not being used.

Question. Just now you stated you did not remember their names?

Answer. I do not remember some of their names.

Question. Now you give another excuse for not giving their names.

Answer. I do not remember some of their names; but as to your speaking of their being only one reliable citizen—I could name them, but this gentleman, and not only him but one other who is a man of property and good standing, and lives right in their midst, did ask me as a favor never to mention their names in the matter; they told me who they were satisfied in their minds was the leader of the organization, and if put upon their oath, undoubtedly they could substantiate it. One of them is an editor of a paper, a man worth considerable property. I know that there is such an organization exists, because I have seen then in disguise at different times.

Question. The Robertson Family?

Answer. No, sir; not the Robertson Family; I was speaking of the Ku-Klux Klan; I have seen them in disguise several times.

Question. Where?

Answer. In Tippah County.

Question. Was that when you were trying to become a member of it?

Answer. Previous to that, sir.

Question. Why did they not take you in?

Answer. Because I was taken sick at that time with congestion of the brain, and removed from that place.

Question. You have not been back there since?

Answer. Not to make it my permanent home; I have been in there several times on business; I believe twice with the United States marshal.

Question. That is not a good way to become a member, to go with a United States marshal, is it?

Answer. But at the time I was there I did not go in with the United States marshal to become a member; that was previous.

Question. Did I understand you to say you went in there with a view of working yourself into the organization?

Answer. No, sir; I did not state that, I believe; I did not wish to.

Question. What did you say?

Answer. I said I had the promise of joining the organization: that they insisted upon my joining it, after I had been there some time; that I was conversant with some of the members and I could be a member; and they would send my name in at the very next meeting; but I was taken sick when the next meeting came; it was Saturday night; I was taken down with congestion of the brain, and Dr. Carter and Dr. Murray of that section waited on me; and I was sick for some time.

Question. It was your object and intention to join them in order to bring them to justice?

Answer. That was my object, exactly.

Question. You proposed to take the oath with that view?

Answer. I proposed to join the organization with a view of ferreting the thing out as close as I could.

Question. You proposed to take the oath, which they usually demanded, with that view?

Answer. I did not propose to take the oath if I could otherwise avoid it.

Question. But you intended to do it of you had to?

Answer. No, sir; I did not say what I intended to do.

Question. Did not the members joining have to do it? Could they join without taking it?

Answer. I do not know as they could, but they could very easily get the names of the members without taking it, because it is not to be supposed that there are none others attend to their meetings without being parties to the organization; and my knowing the organization, as I do, in Tippah, Alcorn, Monroe, and this county, in case my name passed in favorably, of course all I would have to do would have been to have gone up and taken the oath and become a member; and in going there I could easily have become knowing to all the names of these persons; that is, I know many of them personally.

Question. Then you proposed not to take the oath?

Answer. I did not propose to do it if I could otherwise avoid it, sir.

Question. You considered, I suppose, that the end justified the means; that if you had to swear with the intention of exposing them, you could do so rightfully?

Answer. I should not have done it without consulting the district attorney.

Question. I understood that you were already in consultation with the district attorney and that that was your business.

Answer. But I should not have taken the oath without consulting further with the district attorney.

Question. Would you have called him into the meeting?

Answer. No, sir; I should not have been very likely to have done so; I could have applied to his office in Oxford, as I was in his employment.

Question. You have given some examples of these outrages: Joseph Brooks, a colored man?

Answer. Yes, sir.

Question. They threatened him with whipping?

Answer. Yes, sir; not only threatened but whipped him.

Question. What for?

Answer. I do not know, sir, the reason why they whipped him.

Question. Albert Thomas—they whipped him because he would not agree to crop with them?

Answer. Yes, sir; that is the reason they attributed the night they came there and whipped him; he is a colored man who used to belong to one of the supervisors now of that county—R. R. Thomas.

Question. Armisted Boyd—what did they whip him for?

Answer. I do not remember the entire charge they had against him.

Question. What was any part of the charge they had against him.

Answer. I believe they charged him, in his own words, for not working as they wanted him to work on the plantation where he was then engaged.

Question. He did not do enough work?

Answer. No, sir; he did not work as they wanted him to; he was working for an old man named Yancey, a resident for thirty-odd years; Mr. Yancey moved him then up close to his dwelling-house, and told him he would protect him.

Question. You have told that before, but what was it they whipped him for?

Answer. I am not able to state as to the exact facts, what their intention was, because I do not know their intentions in whipping him, entirely.

Question. What was alleged; what did the boy say about it; what did they tell the boy they whipped him for?

Answer. They told the boy they whipped him on account of his not working better, as I understood it.

Question. Tillman Green—he was whipped over a barrel; what was it for?

Answer. Well, sir, Tillman Green obtained a plantation of Judge Green, and had raised a very poor crop, I think, that season, a very poor crop of cotton and corn, the plantation having been used some twenty-five years, as near as I can tell, and the ground pretty well worn out. He was not able to pay all his indebtedness from it, and they told him it was on account of his being negligent in working the crop that he had not paid it, and when they came there they remarked to him when they whipped him—so Green told me—"Now, God damn you, if you do not work better next season, you will find yourself hanging to one of these trees in front of your house." They took him out and tied him over a barrel and gave him a hundred and fifty.

Question. That is what Green told you?

Answer. That is what Tillman Green himself told me, the man that was licked.

Question. Did you ever hear Judge Green say anything about it?

Answer. Yes, sir; not in particular about that case, but he told me that as he was going from Buena Vista across to where I was stationed, "I heard the Ku-Klux inquire about Till"—he called him Till—"How is Till getting along." He said, "As Till lived in front of my house, some of the men were inquiring about him, over in the Saddler neighborhood, and they wanted to know how he was working this season. That was not long ago;" he said "I expect their intention was to call on him again;" that is what Judge Green told me.

Question. The widow Sykes, you say, was molested in order to get possession of her land?

Answer. Yes, sir.

Question. Did they calculate to have any title to the land in any way?

Answer. No, sir; but they wanted her to leave, so they could either rent or buy. Their motive was, from what Mrs. Sykes tells me, to intimidate her; to get her to leave, so she would have to sell her land; to make it disagreeable for her to live there, and she, a widow, would be compelled to either leave or sell it. I have her affidavit in my pocket in reference to it.

Question. Let us see that affidavit.

Answer. Yes, sir, [producing it;] but I do not think it has any tendency in reference to the land. It was sworn out before the United States commissioner.

By the CHAIRMAN:

Question. While the general is examining that paper, I will ask you a question or two. Has the activity of this Ku-Klux order been checked by the late proceedings in the United States courts?

Answer. I think it has to a great extent.

Question. What is your information as to whether there are distinct, different bands in the same county, or does one county comprise a single organization?

Answer. These are different bands, but all of the same tendency.

By Mr. RICE:

Question. Under a common head?

Answer. Yes, sir, under the one; there are different companies; they are organized like a regiment, as you might say, all companies.

By the CHAIRMAN:

Question. There is a connection between the different bands?

Answer. Yes, sir; different companies.

Question. Do you understand that they have a connection with other bands in other counties?

Answer. As to that I cannot answer.

Question. Do you understand whether there is any superior lodge or council for the entire State?

Answer. For the entire State I do not; but for the county I do.

By Mr. BLAIR:

Question. The fact as to the cause of their molesting Mrs. Sykes is not contained in her affidavit?

Answer. No, sir.

Question. But you say it was imparted to you by her?

Answer. Yes, sir, and to the United States commissioner at the same time.

Question. She made a statement which was for the purpose of getting her property?

Answer. Yes, sir; to get possession of her property.

Question. Did she make any other statement in reference to it?

Answer. She made several statements, but I do not know that I could remember all of them. In fact, one of these parties who came to her house, this man James Strickland, who is a brother of the Strickland who was in the senate this last term; she had partially raised him—had, in fact, nursed him since he was a small child at school; he had been very familiar at her house. Mr. Strickland, the father of this James Strickland, being a widower when this boy was quite young, she had partially raised him, she said, in taking care of the family.

Question. That was not one of the reasons why he wanted to drive her off the place?

Answer. No, sir.

Question. I am asking after that.

Answer. I give you all I know about that—her statement; she has made several statements to me that I do not remember, that is, spoken in such a way I did not; I suppose it would be of advantage to me to state, because I do not know the exact remark she made about it; but I know her language all had a tendency to show me they wanted to get possession of her property, in some way or shape; either wanted to run her off, or so she would either be compelled to sell at reduced rates or rent.

Question. They never told her that was their object?

Answer. They have tried to purchase her property—members of this organization—so she tells me.

Question. One of these parties she names?

Answer. Yes, sir; not one of the parties she names in the affidavit here, but one of the parties who I proposed to incriminate in the organization, sir; there were nine others came to her house with those three she has sworn to, but her daughter being absent from the district at present, her mother says she will swear to others in the organization; there were twelve in the organization that came to her house; only three of them she swears to.

Question. That she recognized?

Answer. That she recognized and knows; and why she knows them is because they have been raised up in one sense on adjoining plantations to her all their lives, and went to school with her own children.

Question. Why did they give you the threat about the rope, if you went there professing to be a friend anxious to join their organization?

Answer. I went there attending to my own affairs; that is, I did not let my business be known. I settled in the immediate neighborhood and staid at home, any further than going out to Ripley to the post-office; and I got acquainted with some of the neighbors; they considered I was a "God damned Yankee," and did not know what my business was in there, if you wish the term; that I was a "God damned Yankee," and they believed I was sent in there for some purpose, they did not know positively; I have a copy of the notice which was left at the tree in front of my house, that if I did not get away in such a length of time, that I would find myself hanging to the end of the rope. I think my wife has the rope now in her possession.

Question. You stated on your direct examination that you went there for the purpose of finding them out.

Answer. I said that, sir; but I attended to my own affairs.

Question. You went there on purpose to get informed in regard to the Ku-Klux?

Answer. Yes, sir.

Question. That was your business there?

Answer. Yes, sir.

Question. If you went there for that purpose, I suppose you conducted yourself in such a way as to gain the confidence of the Ku-Klux?

Answer. That was my intention, to the best of my ability.

Question. Was it to be expected that under such circumstances they would threaten you with a rope and immediately offer to admit you to membership?

Answer. Until they found I had nothing to do; if any man, I do not care who, going to that country is a stranger, without he uses the same phrases as the community at large, they condemn him as being a Yankee, and until they have a test that he is not a Yankee, they hold him and consider him as such; they consider him a Yankee until fully satisfied that he is not. Persons born and raised in the Northern States have a different way of expressing themselves; they have a different speech, in fact, than the parties born and raised in the Southern States; especially those who are living back from railroads.

Question. You went in there for the purpose of uniting with this organization as a matter of course?

Answer. I went in with the purpose of trying to ferret out this organization, and understand who the leader of it was, and get all the information possible in regard to it.

Question. Then you took steps at once to ingratiate yourself with those people?

Answer. At a certain degree, I did.

Question. You offered to join them and sought membership?

Answer. I had offers of joining them, sir.

Question. Would they offer to take you in as a member, and at the same time threaten you with a rope?

Answer. This was some time afterward.

Question. You had managed in the mean time to gain their confidence?

Answer. Yes, sir.

Question. Did you tell them you were a northern man?

Answer. No, sir.

Question. What did you tell them?

Answer. I was not asked as to that question; they asked me if I was a Yankee, and I told them I was not; I am a native of Missouri, and do not consider myself under that title—as a Yankee.

Question. You do not?

Answer. No, sir.

Question. What part of Missouri were you born in?

Answer. I was born in Saint Louis.

Question. When did you leave Saint Louis?

Answer. Well, sir, I left Saint Louis sixteen years ago last April; I have been in the northern service, in different branches, ever since.

Question. What branch of the public service?

Answer. I was with a surveying party, that organized shortly after I left Saint Louis, through into New Mexico.

Question. What surveying party?

Answer. The first party that I was with was the Government surveying party into New Mexico; and after the war came on I joined the Army, and after being with the Army some little time I was appointed a scout, and was a scout in this department at the time I was captured; I was captured at New Albany, or near there, in Union County, in this State, on General Smith's cavalry raid; he resides within a short distance of Chicago; I was on that cavalry raid with the expectation of joining General Sherman at West Point; he was coming through Meridian to make a junction in that vicinity; we were driven back, and after crossing the Tallahatchie River to New Albany, I was sent out to reconnoiter, and was captured and taken to Andersonville, and remained there during the summer, and from that went to Charleston, South Carolina, and there I made my escape over on to what was called Bull's Island, and was recaptured again by the coast scouts, and put on Sullivan's Island, and kept under fire thirty days, and then taken to Florence, and kept there until I became helpless, and was paroled and sent around on the United States flag-ship to Annapolis, Maryland. I was paroled at Florence. I joined immediately again then. My time was out six months at that time. I tried to get my back installment, but could not get it; I joined immediately my command, and General John Wilson started through Eastport, Mississippi, on his raid.

Question. What party of surveyors did you go on?

Answer. Well, sir, Mr. Morris was head man of the party of surveyors I was on.

Question. Was it a Government party?

Answer. That was my understanding, sir.

Question. Was Mr. Morris in the military service of the Government?

Answer. I do not know whether he was or not; I was quite young at the time I joined them; went independent; we lived independent in the train, and I assisted in surveying through on that road; from there I went to Fort Arbuckle and in the Comanche Nation, and from that down to Los Vegas and Fort Union and Santa Fé, and afterward left the party there, and down to Yula to the silver mines; they were then mined by the French; I went through there as a herder of stock with a man from New Mexico; I do not remember his name now; I have it at home; after returning I joined Albert G. Brackett's regiment, an officer of the regular Army, who had served thirty-two years in the regular Army; his nephew and myself joined together in the same company.

By the CHAIRMAN:

Question. Colonel Albert G. Brackett?

Answer. Yes, sir. I am very intimately acquainted with him and his two brothers—Dr. Brackett and Lawyer Brackett, recently of Chicago; and whenever I go up there in that section I always make it my home with Mr. Brackett's family in Chicago; I have not seen him since about 1865; I came with Albert G. Brackett and his regiment through the southern part of Missouri and Arkansas, in that Cotton Plant fight, to Helena, and remained there until along in the spring, when we were removed to this department, our regiment being a cavalry regiment, and joined General Hatch's brigade; I accompanied General Grierson on a portion of his raid through Mississippi; I served, I suppose, altogether, between three and four years along on this line of the Memphis and Charleston Railroad, both north and south; I do not know that there is a trail within a hundred miles of that road, either way, I am not conversant with; I rode over all of it during the war and since the surrender; I have been perfectly conversant with this locality.

By Mr. BLAIR:

Question. You say these parties in Tippah County whipped a man named Mask?

Answer. Yes, sir.

Question. They wanted possession of the land he was living on?

Answer. The land which his father owned; he was living on it; his father had moved away; they wanted to get possession of it.

Question. Had they any title to it in any way?

Answer. None whatever. Their intimidating Mr. Mask excited Mr. Mask's father to go down there, and to have to sell the property at reduced rates, which he did, and moved to Alcorn County; he is living five miles from Corinth at present, on a stream called Tuscumbia.

Question. Are both the Masks living there?

Answer. Yes, sir; they are all living there at the present time; because it was disagreeable for them to live in Tippah County, where they formerly resided; they are parties who have lived there for twenty-eight years; Mr. Mask told me since he had moved to that section of the country he was one of the pretty early settlers of that locality; I think it was twenty-eight years, or near that.

Question. How near did you live to where Mask lived?

Answer. Where Mask was whipped?

Question. Yes, sir.

Answer. Some seven miles.

Question. Were you living there at the time he was whipped?

Answer. No, sir; I came in immediately after.

Question. You had conversation with him about it?

Answer. Yes, sir; several of them; and also with parties who were implicated in whipping him, that he has since sworn to; in fact I will tell a little conversation between one of the parties. This Mask has since sworn to a man named Cartwright, who is under bonds. He and myself were going to town, or rather he overtook me going to Ripley, five or six miles; when we got about half way we met Mask on the road, and this fellow acknowledged to me, and commenced to tell me; in the first place he commenced to tell me how the Ku-Klux had scourged this fellow a short time before; how he had licked him and beat him; he said he was a "damned rascal." "He is a damned rascal"—in that way he said it; he says, "We made it mighty hot for him a short time ago;" and he says, "He has moved off, and now this Mask had to move away his family. They gave him orders, after they licked him, if he did not move away in a certain number of hours they would hang him, and at the same time notified his brother if he did not see that Silas Mask did move away that they would hang him, and of course this man moved away on to Judge Thompson's plantation"—now probate judge, I believe, of that county, if I am not mistaken.

Question. What did he say; he "made it hot for him?"

Answer. They did not give any reason to him, any more than Cartright said to me, "He is a damned rascal, and we made it very hot for him," and went on and stated some of the circumstances at that time, when we rode to town; the way the conversation came up, Cartwright and I were riding together and met this man Mask coming out from town.

Question. He did not tell you in what his "damned rascality" consisted?

Answer. No, sir.

Question. You did not inquire?

Answer. No, sir; I did not inquire into it at all. I know immediately after they whipped Mask, Mask had these parties arrested which he has now got arrested through the United States court; he had them arrested through the civil authorities of Ripley, and they paid their lawyer a hundred and ten dollars; and Mask being a poor man he could not pay his lawyer as much money; the firm consisted of Faulkner & Thompson; this Mask has employed Thompson, I understand, and then they turned around and employed lawyer Faulkner, a partner in the firm, and gave him a hundred and ten dollars, and Mask, not having any money to give, gave his lawyer no more than his work during the season. Judge Thompson moved him right on his plantation to secure his lawyer's fee. They went on with the trial before the justice of the peace, Squire Owen; the trial never did have any decision, but released this party of Ku-Klux immediately after the examination, and he never would permit this man Mask's witnesses all to be sworn; his principal witnesses were not sworn; I can testify to that myself; they called upon this justice of the peace, in Ripley, the other day, after these men were arrested by the United States authorities; they called upon this justice to state that this case had been decided; he told them he would not, because this man Mask never had justice. The case was tried before him, and never any decision made of it. This is this justice of the peace's statement, in Ripley. He will state so before the United States court; it was before him the preliminary examination was held.

Question. In the case of none of these parties whose names you have given, not one of them, was there any political cause assigned for the maltreatment of any man or person whose name you have given, and for whom you have attempted to assign a reason for their being punished. You have assigned causes, and in no single instance has that cause been assigned?

Answer. For those whipped, no, sir; I do not know that I have assigned any other cause, or any cause of a political nature.

By the CHAIRMAN:

Question. What is the character of the men comprising this Klan, so far as you have become acquainted with the membership?

Answer. Well, sir, as far as I have become acquainted with this organization, they are men who are ignorant, very ignorant, as a general thing; and men, too, with very limited capital; I have never known of a wealthy man belonging to the organization, unless he was a man who joined it in order to defeat the party.

Question. Have they any backers, or sympathizers, or friends among the influential class of the community?

Answer. I think they have, sir, to some extent. I have known men who have sympathized with the Ku-Klux Klan, who have been in very good circumstances; but I have known other instances where they have told me they were afraid to do anything else except to sympathize with the cause; if they did, they did it at the risk of their lives. I say this, that there is no man that dare go into Tippah County and get upon a box and make a republican speech, and condemn the Ku-Klux Klan; if he can get out of that county without a body-guard, I am willing to let my life go as a forfeit; not only in that county, but some others—get up and make a speech and condemn that organization.

By Mr. BLAIR:

Question. You say you were raised in Saint Louis?

Answer. I was born in Missouri.

Question. Do your friends live there now?

Answer. I have some acquaintances living in Missouri. I have no relatives living in Saint Louis.

Question. What acquaintances have you there now?

Answer. I have a number of acquaintances in Saint Louis; Mr. Burt, living in Saint Louis.

Question. What is his first name?

Answer. Mr. George Burt, of Saint Louis, is a friend of mine.

Question. What does he do?

Answer. He is keeping a wholesale house—or was the last I knew of him. I have very little intercourse with him. My mother now resides in Adrian, Michigan.

Question. He keeps a wholesale what?

Answer. A wholesale grocery, at the last I knew of him. I knew Mr. Perkins, sir, of Memphis; he was prosecuting attorney in the United States court; I have known him for several years; and C. C. Cameron, of Arkansas, who was a member of the senate there.

Question. I am inquiring about Saint Louis.

Answer. I have but very few acquaintances there; I have been away from Saint Louis a long time, ever since the commencement of the war; before that I was there.

Question. Do you know anybody else there in Saint Louis?

Answer. Yes; I could think of others; W. W. Judy, of Saint Louis.

Question. What does he do?

Answer. He keeps a game store opposite the post-office, on Third street—right across from the post-office on Third street.

Question. Who else do you know there?

Answer. Well, I could speak of a great many parties there I know, but they are parties who are not perhaps leaders; I am speaking of those who are wealthy and able. A great many of my old acquaintances have left Saint Louis since I was acquainted with that section of the country; I have not been there to stay any since long some time before the war. I have different parties who I am acquainted with in different States—men of standing—that I could give you; men of good standing in different States that I could give you reference to—Judge Bond of New York.

COLUMBUS, MISSISSIPPI, *November* 16, 1871.

AUSTIN POLLARD sworn and examined.

By the CHAIRMAN:

Question. State your place of residence and official position.

Answer. Austin Pollard; my residence is Okolona, Chickasaw County, Mississippi. My official position is chancellor of the seventh judicial district of Mississippi.

Question. What counties does that district comprise?

Answer. The counties of Chickasaw, Octibbeha, Pontotoc, and Union.

Question. How long have you lived in Chickasaw County?

Answer. I have lived there since the 20th day of August, 1866; I might explain further that I was born in Greene County, Alabama. My father moved, as I understand, to Aberdeen, in Monroe County, when I was about six months old, in 1836. I never lived anywhere except in the State of Mississippi that I know of, except during the time my father resided in Alabama.

Question. Do you know of any acts of violence which have been committed in any of the counties in your district, by bodies of men in disguise, and in the night-time, or have you been informed of any such acts of violence?

Answer. I do know of acts of violence committed in one of the counties comprised in my district, the county of Pontotoc.

Question. You may state to the committee any instances.

Answer. I do not remember their date, but I think it was the night of the 12th of May last. I had been on a hunting excursion, or hunting with some firiends of mine; and afterward we met in the jail of the county of Pontotoc, at the court-house in the town of Pontotoc; I was there in company with W. R. Todd, deputy sheriff of Pontotoc county; B. F. Duke, a citizen of the town of Pontotoc; really I forget the names of the other men, but there were four of us, playing a game of euchre, and John L. Gorman, a citizen and resident of the town of Pontotoc, who was present during the game of euchre, who had gone out, came back, and told us, "Gentlemen, they are here;" and I asked him, "Who are here?" He said, "The Ku-Klux are here." I asked him—the question was asked, I will not say I asked him—"Where are they?" "They are in the court-house yard." I told him to go and show them to me; he said, "Yes, I can." We all of us dispersed; I went to a drug-store, Bolton's drug-store, and I found in the drug-store a young man named Bradford, a son of Judge Bradford, I do not remember his given name; I asked him if he had any weapons; he told me that he had a pistol. I told him to give it to me quick. He gave me the pistol, and told me, "I will go with you." I told him no, I did not want him; but I was going out on the street. We went then to C. D. & J. B. Fontain's office, a lawyer's office; there we met Charles D. Fontain, jr., the chancery clerk then; he met me at the door, and gave me a double-barreled shot-gun. I then delivered my pistol over to the same young man who gave it to me. We went in the rear of Fontain's office, in the town of Pontotoc. After arriving in the rear of what I understand to be—I do not know the names of the places there in town, and I will refresh my memory by a memorandum. [Examining a printed leaf, which will be found at the end of his testimony.] I do not see it. I do not refresh my memory by this memorandum; but it was in the rear of what used to be an old wood-shop in the town. It is almost directly west of Fontain's office. Upon arriving there, in company with Deputy Sheriff W. R. Todd, Mr. Gorman came to me and asked me if I had not better send for Colonel Flournoy; and I asked the question where I was to send for him; the answer was, "They are after him." I told him, "Certainly; send and bring him here to me immediately." Mr. Gorman and another man, whose name I do not now remember—I know him almost as well as I know myself—went off, and they, with Flournoy, came back. After they came back there was some little consultation between us as to what we should do. Some of the parties wanted us to fire upon them immediately, because we saw them coming from the direction that we understood they were at. I told them no; not to fire at them; that I did not want any blood shed, but I wanted law and order to prevail. Some of the crowd—I do not know who—suggested to me that, as I was chancellor of the district, I should go and demand their surrender. I told them, "Very well, gentlemen; I will demand it, gentlemen, myself." Soon afterward I saw them; I saw a party of disguised men—about, I think, not less than ten nor more than twenty, with horses, also disguised; I stepped out from the corner of the house where I was, and asked this question, "Gentlemen, if your mission is one of peace and pleasantry, you will not be molested; if, on the other hand, you are for bloodshed, in the name and by virtue of the laws of the State of Mississippi, I demand that you surrender." Instantly, almost, a pistol-shot was fired from the crowd of men I saw in disguise; very soon afterward, I might say instantly, another pistol-shot was fired, and I heard a voice from another street commanding them to "Halt," and then another pistol was fired from the Ku-Klux band, as I believe, and then the firing became general upon both sides, and the young men who were with me fired, and I think there were about thirty shots fired in all on both sides. We patrolled the streets of Pontotoc that night, and I heard no more disturbances or confusion of any kind until about a quarter to four in the morning, a gentleman directed my attention to the fact that there was a man lying there dead. I went to him and felt of his pulse, and did then believe he was dead. Colonel Charles D. Fontain, our lawyer, went, and he pronounced that he was not dead but was breathing; and then I went myself and called Dr. Charles Waller, a physician, and asked him to come and examine; I got no reply from him, and I went back to the man again and found out that Colonel Fontain was right, that the man was breathing. I then called upon Mr. Johnny Brooks to assist me to take the mask off of his face so that he could breathe. John Brooks is a citizen of Pontotoc now. With my knife and my assistance he took his mask off of his face. We took the man into the jail of Pontotoc County—the same room I was in, mentioned in the first part of my examination; he remained until about sunrise, or a little after, when he died. Colonel Flournoy came over before he did die, and there was some conversation going on between the parties in the room; Colonel Flournoy said, "I know what you came for; you came to kill Flournoy and his men; the fellow said, "Yes, sir."

Question. Now, who was that man that was killed?

Answer. Well, sir, I do not know his name; I never saw him before. He gave his name as George F. Dillard. I have understood since it was Richard Dillard. I understood he gave the name of his brother, who was killed at the battle of Shiloh.

Question. What, if anything, do you know of a subsequent——

Answer. I want to volunteer—write it down in that way—after that occurrence, I remained in the town of Pontotoc until my term of court ought to be held in Union County. That was Friday, May 12. I ought to have held the court the next Monday week. I remained in Pontotoc until the next Saturday week. The thing occurred

Friday night, and the next morning was Saturday. Saturday week afterward was the time I remained there, when they had a public meeting—a public meeting was held, and I found a large concourse of citizens, and this paper [producing the paper given at the end of his testimony] was being circulated that morning.

Question. Please to read it.

Answer. I will read it and hand it to you. [The witness read the paper aloud.] The gentleman who published that I know. His name is Dr. Porter. He told me he had a small press for advertising his business; and the fact that some of the paper is small caps, and some coarser print than others, is because it was all he had. On the Saturday I told you of, he got up in a public meeting and said he knew that was false.

Question. What was false?

Answer. That paper just read; and that he only published it to conciliate what he conceived to be a rowdy set; and said he was sorry that he had published it. I saw him destroy a large number of copies of it, and he begged me not to show the paper again. I told him I would do it, for it was a libel, and that I knew it, and I was responsible to him personally for it. He told me he was sorry he had published anything of the kind.

Question. What was the object of this public meeting you spoke of?

Answer. It was called for the purpose of, or it was called a law and order meeting, called by Colonel Fontain and Jefferson Wilson and o hers. The object, as I understood, was to frown down, by a public meeting, any efforts at Ku-Kluxism or any other secret political organization.

Question. Have you had any Ku-Kluxism in that county since that time?

Answer. Not to my knowledge, sir.

Question. Have you had any information of any Ku-Klux outrages in this county since that time?

Answer. The only information I have was derived from the sheriff of the county, who told me there was a man taking a subscription list for the purpose of raising a fund to erect a monument over this man Dillard who was killed.

Question. Did you understand how much was raised?

Answer. I did not, sir. I will say further, before the committee, as to that, the man who was killed, I took his mask off of him, including the mask over his face, a pair of pants made out of black calico, and what we called in the army a blouse. We took them off of him. They were all of them black; and the blouse had white ribbons of some kind—very common. His pants had a white ribbon here, and they were over a brown jeans suit. I examined his pocket-book to see what he had, with a view of giving it to his family. I found in it his registration papers—nothing else. No receipts or papers of any kind.

Question. What aged man was he?

Answer. As far as I could judge, I do not know what his age was. He was about twenty-five or twenty-eight years of age.

By Mr. RICE:

Question. What name was in the registration papers?

Answer. Richard Dillard.

By the CHAIRMAN:

Question. Had there been any Ku-Klux demonstrations in that county before that?

Answer. None that I know of or had heard of either.

Question. Do you say you never have heard of any Ku-Klux demonstrations, except this one, in that county?

Answer. Before that time I did not. I do not know of any, nor have I heard of any, before that time.

Question. Since that time have you heard of any?

Answer. Yes, sir.

Question. You may state the particulars of such as you have heard.

Answer. I have understood that I could not hold the chancery court of Union County; that a meeting had been held in the camp of the Ku-Klux, and that if I attempted to hold the court I would "go up."

Question. How did that information come to you?

Answer. I got it from Colonel Flournoy.

Question. Did he tell you what his information was?

Answer. He told me he understood he and I both would go together; that he was to be assassinated any how, and that if I attempted to hold court in that county that I would go up.

Question. Did he tell you the source of his information?

Answer. He did not.

Question. Have you held court there since?

Answer. No, sir; I have missed two courts in that county on account of these threats.

Question. Have you reason to believe that you would be in danger if you held court in that county?

Answer. I do really believe I will be in danger if I hold the courts in that county now.

Question. Why do you apprehend danger at this time?

Answer. Because I have information that they have made a threat that all these men connected with "the Pontotoc affair," to use an expression, one of whom I am, would be assassinated.

Question. Is it your understanding that this band of men that came into Pontotoc came from Union County?

Answer. No, sir.

Question. Where is it your information that they came from?

Answer. They came from Cherry Creek and Poplar Springs, in Pontotoc County, on the way from Pontotoc to New Albany.

Question. Have you ever been able to ascertain who were in that company that night?

Answer. No, sir; not directly.

Question. How do you infer that they came from these two localities that you speak of?

Answer. From the fact that two men were arrested who lived in that neighborhood, and I visited a negro man who came from the plantation of a man named Saddler, and he told me he had information that they were from that neighborhood.

Question. Why do you suppose the people of Union County felt interested in this matter?

Answer. I do not think that the people of Union County are directly interested against my holding court; on the contrary, I believe they would be anxious for me to hold it; but on my route from Pontotoc to Union County I believe I would be in danger.

Question. Have you heard of Ku-Klux disturbances in any other part of your district?

Answer. Yes, sir.

Question. You may state the particulars?

Answer. I do not remember the date exactly; but it was just prior to this time of holding my court in Oktibbeha County, on the first Monday in April. During the April term of court there at Starkville there was a disturbance. I was on the street late at night. I found a good many freedmen there. They were busy doing something, I did not know what. Next morning a man by the name of McLachlan was arrested and brought before the mayor. I went up, of course. I talked with the freedmen. I did not talk with McLachlan at all. I advised them that they ought to go to their plantations and go to work; that they were not interested in this political question at all; that that did not affect them. A fellow, a freedman whose name I do not know—I never asked him—told me that he had been asked by McLachlan to protect him. I asked him what he wanted to do that for. He told me that he did not know. I said, "You go home and go to work, and as long as this McLachlan behaves himself and does right he will be protected by the officials of the country." Soon afterward the crowd at the mayor's office dispersed. I heard nothing more about it until the next morning. On the next day I understood that McLachlan's house had been forced; that they had broken the doors down. As soon as I found that was the fact I went to his house and asked him what was the matter. He told me the Ku-Klux had been there that night. I asked him if he was afaid of them. He told me no, he was not; and I asked him what threats they had made. He said they told him he had to leave that town. I told him I understood the same thing, and I advised him to leave; but, says I, "If you have not money enough to leave, I have money in my pocket, and I will give it to you, and leave now until the excitement is all over; you can come back after that." He told me he would do so.

Question. He left, did he?

Answer. You ask me now from my own knowledge. I do not know. I am satisfied he left, because I met him at Muldon Station, at Aberdeen junction, on the railroad. Next morning I left myself.

Question. Was this the Scotchman who had been teaching a colored school?

Answer. He was a Methodist preacher, who taught a colored school. He had a store in the town of Starkville.

Question. We have had the details of his case.

Answer. I do not know anything of the particulars. I understood he was one of the stockholders of a store there, and was preaching to the negroes.

Question. Have you heard of any other disturbances or outrages?

Answer. I have heard of some in Monroe.

Question. We have had testimony as to Monroe County. I mean as to your circuit or district.

Answer. Well, a man named John Conkerton told me he had been arrested by a band of disguised men. He lives at Pikeville, or rather near Egypt, in Chickasaw County. He was taken out, in his drawers, on the turnpike, on the Soctanoochee Bottom; that he made his escape from the parties and went back to his house and got his double-barreled shot-gun and shot at them. He found afterwards three dead horses in the bottom. He told me he knew who the parties were, and upon inquiring from him he declined to give the names.

Question. How many did he say were in the party?

Answer. I do not remember.

Question. Did he say they were disguised?

Answer. Yes, sir.

Question. Did you learn from him whether they were armed?

Answer. Yes, sir; he told me they were armed.

Question. Have you heard of any cases of colored men being taken out and whipped by disguised men?

Answer. No, sir; I have not.

Question. Then this embraces all the cases of which you have information?

Answer. I have this information—I do not know whether it is reliable or not, nor do I believe it is reliable—I am working a plantation myself in Chickasaw County. I have understood that my plantation is to be visited by that same Klan Conkerton is connected with, and I have written them a notice that I would be there when they came, if they let me know the day.

Question. Do you know what the object of this disguised party that visited Pontotoc at the time you mentioned in the first part of your statement was?

Answer. No, sir; I do not know, of my own knowledge, what their object was. I do know that this man Gorman, of whom I spoke, told me he had himself expected them to come some time, he did not know when, and he had to go to the office to protect it. Gorman was a printer at Flournoy's office. That was his excuse for leaving us; he said he wanted to go and protect the office. We had hardly missed him when he came came, back and told us, "They are here."

Question. He had received previous information that they were coming there?

Answer. That was my impression. I do not know that he had.

By Mr. BLAIR:

Question. Did Gorman ever tell you that he had received any notice?

Answer. No; he told me—he did not tell me specially anything; he spoke to the crowd; he says, "I have got to go to Flournoy's office. We have understood that they are coming here to destroy the office." We asked him the question, who were. He said, "The Ku-Klux."

Question. Did they go to the office?

Answer. Not that I know of, sir. I only know what Gorman told me.

Question. Do you not know that they did not go to the office; that they left immediately after your firing upon them?

Answer. The only time I ever saw them was when we fired upon them. They were close to the office then. Gorman told me they were at the court-house when he came back again.

Question. You do not know what was their intention, except from what Gorman said?

Answer. No, sir; I do not.

Question. He never told you what was the expression upon the occasion?

Answer. Nothing more than I have said.

Question. You said you were present in the jail when this man Dillard died?

Answer. I did not say so.

Question. I understood you to say so.

Answer. You misunderstood me.

Question. You were not with him when he died?

Answer. I did not see him when he died. I saw him a few moments before he did die.

Question. Well, when he was *in articulo mortis?*

Answer. Yes, sir.

Question. You heard him respond to what Flournoy said?

Answer. Yes, sir. He was not then in what we call *articulo mortis.* You know that is a legal question—in the article of death. He was then, of course, suffering from his wounds. He was wounded frequently in his back; all his wounds were from the back. In response to inquiries from me, he told me that he did not know who took him there; he had no idea how he got there; that they forced him to go. I asked him, "Do you know who brought you here." He said, "No, sir, I do not." Says I, "Do you undertake to say now, dying as you are, that you have come here to kick up this fuss in this town without knowing why or wherefore you came?" He said, "Yes, sir." After he told me that I sent a man, Mr. Lyon, of Pontotoc, to his mother to tell her he was there, and if she wanted to do anything for him, to come as soon as she could; and I went to the man, dying as he was, and told him, "If you want to send a private message to your friends or relatives or anybody, deliver it to me and I will not breathe it to a human being." He says, "I have nothing in the world to deliver." After that he (Flournoy) came in and told him, "I understand what you came here for; that you came after Flournoy, and wanted to kill him;" and he said, "Yes, sir."

Question. After saying repeatedly before that that he did not know what he came for?

Answer. Yes, sir; he said he did not know anybody connected with it; and I will state, further, that I understood from Mr. Lyon, whom I sent after his mother, that she told him that she could not come; that she was sick, and that she knew he was going that night and begged him not to go.

Question. Are you certain that he understood what Flournoy said?

Answer. Yes, sir.

Question. And his response was clear?

Answer. Just as clear as anybody's response was. He said, "Yes, sir," every time, and whenever I asked him, "Do you know who was there with you," he said, "No, sir." There was no connected conversation in any part of his dying declarations at all. He did not make any narrative at all; it was simply in response to questions. I asked, "Do you know who was here with you?" "No, sir." "Who brought you here?" "I do not know, sir." Just short answers in that way.

Question. What did Flournoy say?

Answer. My recollection is that he said, "I understand what you came here for; you came after Flournoy, did you not?" He said, "Yes, sir."

Question. Was that all that Flournoy said?

Answer. No, I will not say that.

Question. I mean to which he responded?

Answer. There was a great deal of conversation after that, and I do not remember any part of it.

Question. But I want to know the exact words he used to which the dying man responded.

Answer. My recollection is just as I have said. "I know what you have come here for; you have come after Flournoy; is not that so?" I do not remember whether he said that, but I recollect that was the point to which his mind was directed, and the fellow said, "Yes, sir."

Question. Was anything said to imply that he was to kill Flournoy?

Answer. No, sir; I do not remember that he said anything further than I have said, "You came after Flournoy."

Question. There was nothing to imply that he came to do Flournoy any damage or damages, or kill him?

Answer. That is a mere matter of opinion of my own.

Question. I want to know what the man said, or what was said to him to which he replied?

Answer. My recollection is he said, "I understand what you came here for. I know all about it. You came here after Flournoy, did you not?" and he said, "Yes, sir."

By the CHAIRMAN:

Question. Is he the same Colonel Flournoy that testified before the committee at Washington?

Answer. I suppose, so, sir—Robert W. Flournoy, of Pontotoc.

By Mr. BLAIR:

Question. You say that this Pontotoc band proposed to prevent you from holding the court in Union; that you have that information?

Answer. Yes, sir.

Question. That you had it from Flournoy?

Answer. Yes, sir.

Question. And you say that you never asked Flournoy what was his source of information?

Answer. I did not, sir.

Question. Did you not have curiosity enough to know how he came into possession of it?

Answer. By way of explanation I will say this: I had previously written to the clerk of that court to know whether there was any necessity for my attending court. I told him in view of the excitement of the election, unless there was some important case pending, some case involving some rights, I would not go there. He wrote to me there were only three cases; that the parties who wanted hearing were anxious to get divorced. I wrote to him afterward and ascertained that they had no testimony in the case at all, and the statute—now changing the rule in reference to chancery cases—requires that the testimony of parties, whether in interest or not, shall be in writing.

I found that there was no testimony of that sort, and, of course, I did not care anything about the threats.

Question. Then, I understand, it was not on account of the threats?

Answer. No, sir.

Question. But because there was no important business, that you did not hold your court?

Answer. Yes, sir; the two things combined, you might say.

Question. When you wrote you had it in your mind not to go unless there was important business?

Answer. Yes, sir.

Question. That was before you got this information?

Answer. Yes, sir; long before.

Question. When the reply was returned that there was no important business—the only business pending was not ready for adjudication—that alone was the reason for your not going?

Answer. Yes, sir.

Question. And you say you did not lay any stress upon those threats?

Answer. No, sir; I say now, if the threats were reiterated again, and I knew it was important for the public service, that I would go there and hold a court independently of them.

Question. I ask the question, because from your first statement the impression might have been given that you declined to hold the court on account of those threats, whereas, I understand, you declined to hold it on account of the fact that there was no important business pending and ready?

Answer. I did not decline to hold court on account of threats; and I am chancellor now, and expect to hold the next term of my court independently of threats.

Question. You did not think enough before of the threats to ask who made them, or the source of his information?

Answer. I did not ask the question.

Question. If it had been a matter of any great interest, if you had felt that there was really any danger, would you not have made diligent inquiry as to the quarter from which it was coming?

Answer. If I had thought it was necessary to the public interest for me to hold the court, I would have found out the man's name and shot his head off if I could.

Question. How many times did John Conkerton shoot to kill three horses?

Answer. I never saw him shoot at all; nor have I any information that he shot at all.

Question. I understood you to say that John Conkerton, of Chickasaw, shot?

Answer. O, John Conkerton; I did understand that he shot once at a crowd. He told me they were drinking out of a bottle of whisky, and he shot at the crowd.

Question. He killed three horses at one shot?

Answer. He told me he found three horses in Soctanoochee Bottom, the creek that runs through my plantation and down by Pikeville.

Question. He only fired one shot and killed three horses?

Answer. I cannot tell you that. He stated he found three horses in the bottom.

Question. Did he intend you to infer that he killed them all?

Answer. No, sir; he told me he shot at the crowd and he wounded somebody; and he told me he knew who the man was he had wounded; and that there were three horses found in the bottom.

Question. Three horses found in the bottom?

Answer. Yes, sir; one was a gray horse.

Question. The horses were not killed?

Answer. They were dead then.

Question. All killed?

Answer. So he told me. I asked him the question, "Did you kill those horses?" Says he, "I do not know. I shot at the crowd; and I understand that there is a doctor now attending to these men—some of them that I wounded. I do not know that those horses that I found killed in the bottom were all killed at the time, but I know some of them were."

Question. How many times did he shoot?

Answer. I do not remember that he told me. He told me he shot.

Question. Did you understand that he had shot once?

Answer. No, sir; I do not remember whether he shot once or twice.

By Mr. RICE:

Question. What did he shoot with?

Answer. He told me he had a double-barreled shot-gun and shot at the parties. They were on the turnpike, and he was in his drawers and without his stockings. They had taken him out of his house.

By Mr. BLAIR:

Question. He killed three horses; and how many men were wounded?

Answer. He told me he did not know how many horses he had killed.

Question. Three horses he found dead?

Answer. He saw three horses dead. He did not know how many men. He told me he understood one was wounded and was attended by the physician.

Question. He knew one was wounded?

Answer. He said he understood one was wounded. He gave me the name.

Question. Do you recollect the name?

Answer. Yes, sir.

Question. What was it?

Answer. Wesley Pulliam.

Question. I understood you to say two or three were wounded?

Answer. He told me he thought he wounded two or three.

Question. He did not give you but one name?

Answer. Only one; that one.

Question. Did you inquire in the neighborhood to find out whether this Pulliam was actually wounded?

Answer. I did not; being a conservator of the peace, I, of course, did not put myself to any trouble to get any more information than he voluntarily gave me.

Question. Why not? I should suppose that it was your duty to follow it up.

Answer. Therein you and I differ.

Question. It was in part of your district, and it was part of your duty to follow it up.

Answer. Your name is General Frank Blair and my name is Pollard, and you and I differ as far as the legal proposition is concerned. If it is necessary I will argue it with you. If you come and give me information against anybody for violating the laws, I will issue my warrant. I do not care what party or clique you belong to; and I never absent myself for any violation of law.

Question. You did not issue any process against Pulliam, did you?

Answer. No, sir; I did not do it upon affidavit; and I asked him the question directly, "Will you hold up your hand and swear to it?" He says, "I do not know that this is a fact, but I believe it is so."

Question. You did not take enough interest in the matter to make any further inquiry?

Answer. In what matter?

Question. In the matter of the shooting of this man.

Answer. I did not, sir, because parties interested declined to do anything before me.

Question. He expressed his conviction that it was so, though; but declined to make the affidavit?

Answer. Yes, sir.

Question. And there the matter was allowed to rest?

Answer. In the Pontotoc affair I was appealed to not to do anything. I told them, "I do not shirk any responsibility. I intend to prosecute every man to conviction who had any part in this Pontotoc affair, and I am not afraid of them. The only trouble is, it may be that I cannot go home at night. I know I can do it in the day-time; and I expect to go home in day-time."

Question. You were anxious to prosecute in Pontotoc?

Answer. I was anxious to prosecute the Pontotoc affair, as I was every violation of the law, and I appealed to this man Conkerton to hold up his hand and swear it there in the swamp as he was. He told me he did not know certain about it.

Question. Then you did not believe him—you did not believe his story?

Answer. I say this, that I did not believe that he was satisfied that Pulliam was one of the men, but did believe that he was taken out. He told me he would swear that—in his drawers, out of his bed—but he did not know anybody connected with it, except he suspected that was the man. I told him if he had any reason to suspect or believe that this other man was the man, that this man Pulliam had anything to do with it, just to swear so, and I would arrest him. He told me he did not know; it was a mere suspicion of his own, and he had no testimony against him; and told me further that he had overheard meetings of what we understand, or I understand, to be Ku-Kluxes; and that they changed this afterwards in the same neighborhood—changed their name afterwards to "Jack Robinson;" and that they were sworn to protect each other—each one. They went into the Robinson——

Question. They went into the Robinson family then, did they?

Answer. That is what he told me.

Question. Did he know any of the parties he overheard?

Answer. He told me he did know, but would not tell what their names were.

By the CHAIRMAN:

Question. Was this Conkerton a colored man or a white man?

Answer. He is a white man; a foreigner. I do not know whether he is an Irishman or a German. I believe he is a German, though.

By Mr. BLAIR:

Question. Is Dr. Porter the author of the paper you read?

Answer. He told me he was.

Question. What sort of a man is Dr. Porter?

Answer. He is a dentist, residing in Pontotoc or near Pontotoc. I do not know whether he lives in town or not. He has also a nursery at his house.

Question. Did he purport to give the true state of the case in regard to this masquerade?

Answer. If I remember right he said that he knew what he had published was not true, and that he only published it to conciliate what he considered to be a state of marauders, and that he was sorry he had done what he had. He also stated in the public meeting held that Saturday after—Friday was the 12th, Saturday the 20th of May—that he was willing that Colonel Charles D. Fontaine, W. W. Leland, a citizen of Pontotoc, and Richard Bolton, should sign a retraction of that article.

Question. He was willing that they should do it?

Answer. Yes, sir.

Question. Do it for him?

Answer. For him—write the article and he would sign it. I asked all of them to send me a copy of it. I do not know whether he ever signed a retraction or not; but I never have received a copy of it.

Question. Who composed this meeting in favor of law and order?

Answer. It was presided over by Charles D. Fontaine. Charles B. Mitchell was secretary; and it was composed of citizens of Pontotoc County, except myself. I did not reside in Pontotoc, but was present, so far as I know or believe.

Question. Was it attended generally?

Answer. It was not a large meeting.

Question. Who composed the meeting?

Answer. It was composed mostly of the citizens of the town—Pontotoc.

Question. The best people in the town; those among the best citizens?

Answer. Yes, sir.

Question. There was a general attendance among all of those?

Answer. Yes, sir.

Question. Without regard to party?

Answer. Without regard to party.

Question. Of what politics is Fontaine?

Answer. I believe he co-operated with the democratic party. He is dead now.

Question. What was the politics of the gentleman who was secretary?

Answer. He is the district attorney now elected. He is a democrat.

Question. Was the meeting composed largely of democrats?

Answer. It was composed of both parties. I did not notice the difference. Colonel Fontaine was, at my suggestion, appointed chairman of the committee, because I knew him to be a personal friend of my own.

Question. Did the meeting pass resolutions?

Answer. Yes, sir.

Question. Denouncing this Ku-Klux business?

Answer. My recollection of the character of the resolutions is that they were such as I wanted adopted. They are published in the Clarion, I believe, over the signature of Fontaine and Mitchell. I do not remember the wording of it.

Question. Were they denunciatory of this lawlessness generally?

Answer. Yes, sir; they were.

Question. Did they purport to give any account of this affair?

Answer. I told you I did not want to testify about anything I do not know. I do not remember now. I recollect being at the meeting, and I recollect what was done, as far as I can remember, but I do not so far as the giving an account of what was done, and the reasons for doing it. I cannot say. I only know this: I was satisfied as an officer with the resolutions.

Question. Did they make any allusion to what had transpired?

Answer. My remembrance is that they denounced it, and called upon all good citizens of the country to oppose it; further than that, Colonel Bolton got up with a copy of the paper I have presented to the committee in his hand, and called the attention of the meeting to that document. As soon as he did so, Colonel Leland told him not to make any speech upon it, until he heard from the other document. Directly afterward Dr. Porter got up, and stated what I have told you a while ago; that he knew when he wrote it that it was a falsehood, and he had only written it to conciliate what he considered a lawless crowd. He thought he was an unimportant individual in that community; that he wrote that paper for the purpose of conciliating those men; and he knew he had done what was wrong, and was sorry for it. He offered Colonel Fontaine, Mr. Leland, and Colonel Bolton to write a retraction.

The printed, leaves presented and referred to by the foregoing witness, A. Pollard, page 1103, are as follows:

THE PONTOTOC TIMES.

PUBLISHED IN PONTOTOC MISS.

BY DR. H H PORTER. FREE. VOL. 1, NO. 1.

LOCAL.

As the incidents of the past week have been of the most exciting and interesting character, and there being no paper published here which is generally red by the white people; I propose publishing a brief account of what transpired on last Friday night the 12th Inst.

It is with feelings of the most profound regret, sadness, and shame, that we record the doings of that unhappy night! It was about eleven oclock a company of masked serenaders made its appearance on the square, with horns, bells, tin pans; — In fact, all sorts of things that would make a racket; with which they were amuseing themselves and all whom they could attract.

From a consciousness of theirown deserts. it appears that some persons imagined them to be "sure enough KUKLUX" and right after themselves. Accordingly; a company of men, 10 or 12, that had been keeping late hours over on the east side of the square, (This needs no explanation;) were paraded armed with double-barrel shotguns, loaded with buekshot and ambushed in Ren. Grant's wood shop. As the company approached, starting out. (It is a little amusing. Mr. F- still will not belieVe but that they were kuklux, and right after himself.) Poor pitiful wretch! It is said "The wicked flee wen no man pursue" these, — spare us the word "drunken" madcaps. who would have been most likely to havc been into a caper of the same kind had it been presented to themselves, discharged a rakeing fire of upwards of 20 guns at short distauce; killing one of the boys. [Richard Dillard.] dead and wounding many horses, several of which were collected up and returned io their proper owners. The precise amount of the damage is not yet ascertained; but from accounts, must be very great. This much for late hours, whisky, and bad company. Young: men Take warning!

The boys who did this thing, are repenting in sack-cloth and ashes and we most sincerely ask and hope their forgiveness. Oh that money could compensate! But Alas! But as for old Floury; It appears he still thinks he's been "killing Injuns." Strange to tell, not a rad came to old Floury's beckon; And as for darkies; It is stated on good authority; that had the town been raked with a fine-tooth eomb, not a hair of one could have been found. They promise however, to do better next time, and as a token of their fidelity it is stated, stand picket of nights while their worshIpful sleep.

Government troops have been sent for who arrived Tuesday night, but learning the true nature of the case, have either gone off or resting from the fatigue of their hurried march hither. The thing appears to have been seized upon, by some disturber of the peace, for a stratagem to get an army quartered on us for some imaginary purpose: But failure accounts for strain of vulgar abuses which "EQUAL RIGHTS" pours forth on the defenseless head of Gov. ALCORN. The whole thing; together with the raid on the Governor calls to memory an anecdote of the late war, recnily related by a friend. It is this. One night while the armies were quartered near ATLANTA, Ga. a terrible rattle of musketry and roar of cannon commenced up near by. All was to arms; and in breathless suspense awaiting the expected charge. The battle raged with terrible fury till the dawn of day when it abated and ceased. Next morning Gen. FEATHERSTON pressed all the ink in camps to darken the light'ning bugs' sterns to keep his men from shooting.

That these boys meant no harm is evident from various circumstances.

If they meant harm they would have been sly, done their work and off. Moreover; tbey were not armed as men for mischief; besides; They have been parading frequently, of late, and never offered harm or offense to any one; and the very scamps that shot need not hesitate to have gone out and shook hands with them; And yet, could fire, from ambuscade, into what they knew to be a company of friends; Because they could do it under cover of LAW. Bravo!

Now my colored friends; A word to you. YOU ARE DELUDED BY A SET OF MEN WHOSE INFAMOUS ANTECEDENTS AND MORALS WERE OF SUCH CHARACTER THAT THE WHITE PEOPLE SCORNED TO GIVE THEM OFFICE. THEY THOUGHT THE WHITE FOKS WERE DISFRANCHISED; AND THEY WOULD BE FIRST TO WHEEDLE IN WITH YOU FOR OFFICE: BUT DONT YOU SEE WHAT FOOLS THEY HAVE MADE OF THEMSELVES? IF It HADN't BEEN FOR tHESE. YOU WERE SO PROUD OF YOUR FREEDOM AS NEVER to HAVE tHOUGHT OF RIVALING The VHITF MAN,

Now; Just come right away Say to' them, Bega! You is fooled us. We sees now if we lib among de white folks we mus lub one anuder, or aluz hab de Deb'l and de white folks aluz be too much f'h darkiz. You and dese-yer yanky jis tries to set us gins de whit folx an dat sets dem Gins us til da almos ready to be Killin us lihe DoGs redy. I iZ Gwine quit dis Foolishness and Jine de white foax.

Do this, and my word for it, you need not fear kuklux any more but as long as you expect to be lords of the land, loiter about in idleness, do nothing and have nothing, and depend on the white men to furnish you meat and bread, pay the taxes to educate your children, while you hold back, and do all you can agaigst them: you may expect discontent and resistance to manifest its—self, and a failure at last.

COLUMBUS, MISSISSIPPI, *November* 17, 1872.

LEWIS WALBURG sworn and examined.

By the CHAIRMAN:

Question. State your name, residence, and occupation.

Answer. Residence, Columbus, Mississippi. I am captain of police.

Question. How long have you lived in this county?

Answer. Since 1859.

Question. Are you acquainted with Mr. H. B. Whitfield, who testified before the committee at Washington, and who lives in this place?

Answer. I am, sir.

Question. How long have you been acquainted with him?

Answer. About eleven years.

Question. Are you acquainted with his general moral character?

Answer. I am, sir.

Question. Are you acquainted with his character for truth and veracity in this community?

Answer. I am, sir.

Question. You may state whether his general moral character is good?

Answer. It is, sir. I have been doing business with him now from 1865. I went out to his place on the 16th of June, and staid there with him until 1868, a little over three years, and had business with him every day, and found him a truthful, straightforward, honest man.

Question. How is his character in this community for truth and veracity?

Answer. Good, I think, sir, good.

Question. Would you believe him under oath?

Answer. I should, sir, believe his word.

Question. Are you acquainted with W. W. Humphries, jr., esq., an attorney of this city, who testified before this committee on yesterday?

Answer. I am.

Question. How long have you known him?

Answer. I have personally known him several years—not as long as I have Major Whitfield.

Question. Are you acquainted with his character and standing in this community?

Answer. Yes, sir.

Question. You may state what his character is?

Answer. He stands right fair here. He stands well here in the community.

Question. How is his private character?

Answer. Very good, sir; I never heard a word said against him by anybody. Do you want me to make one little explanation here?

Question. Yes, sir.

Answer. He and Major Whitfield had a case. He had a case before the mayor a short time ago, and the decision the mayor made went adverse to him and against him, and it caused some hard feeling between the two at the time.

Question. Do you know that his feelings are unkind toward Major Whitfield?

Answer. I cannot state it positively, only that this affair made hard words at the mayor's office. I have been with the major ever since he was mayor of the city of Columbus here. I have seen him almost every day, and seen him try almost every case before him, and I think he has dealt fair and square with everybody.

By Mr. BLAIR:

Question. Major Whitfield is the mayor of the city?

Answer. Yes, sir, ever since May.

Question. You received your appointment from him as chief of police?

Answer. No, sir; I received it from the board of aldermen.

Question. Is he one of the board?

Answer. He is president of the board. We make it a rule to promote the old policeman. I was the oldest at the time I was appointed.

Question. Did you ever hear of an indictment against Major Whitfield, found in the courts of Mobile, for swindling Governor Winston out of $4,000?

Answer. No, sir; I did not. I never heard of that.

Question. You never heard that such an indictment was found, and a requisition made on the governor of Mississippi for the surrender of Major Whitfield?

Answer. I heard a short time ago, in such a roundabout way that I could not rely on it, that there was a requisition made on the governor, but I do not know what for. I did not hear any of the particulars.

Question. You did not hear that it was for swindling Governor Winston out of $4,000?

Answer. No, sir; I did not. I heard that in such a roundabout way I could not put any reliance in it.

Question. You heard a good deal of it, though?

Answer. No, sir; I heard it mentioned only one time.

Question. Did you hear that Major Whitfield had swindled his brother by giving him a mortgage on land that was already mortgaged?

Answer. I heard George Whitfield had a claim against him.

Question. Did you hear out of what it grew?

Answer. No, sir; I did not. I know George very intimately—as well as I do the major. He told me that the major owed him money; that he had lost a good deal of money by the major; but he never told me how; he didn't tell me that. He only told me he had lost a great deal by him.

Question. Did he not tell you he had lost the money by his obtaining the money on false pretenses?

Answer. No, sir; he did not give me any of the particulars, and I did not like to inquire into a family matter.

Question. Did his brother George seem to have any hard feeling about it?

Answer. He didn't like it.

Question. What did he say?

Answer. I cannot remember the words, because he was in his business office.

Question. Did he not express the opinion to you that his brother had behaved rascally toward him?

Answer. Not in those words.

Question. But the opinion?

Answer. No; he just said the major swindled him, or owed him eight or ten thousand—he did not say "swindled," he said "owed," him eight or ten thousand dollars. I don't know the exact amount.

Question. Did he not give you to understand he had done it in some unfair way?

Answer. No, sir; I don't think he did. He asked me some question about division of property—if I knew anything about it—and I told him what I knew. That is all he asked.

Question. What property?

Answer. The mill property—the plantation out there.

Question. What question did he ask you about it?

Answer. He asked me if I knew how it was divided. I told him I did. I was present at the time it was divided. Do you wish me to explain how I told him?

Question. Yes.

Answer. I told him that the major said he would take for his and his wife's share the place where the mill was on, and the upper portion of the place toward Oktibbeha, that lay in Oktibbeha, and the balance they drew straws for—the other children did. It was a mill property. They thought dividing the mill, it would make them come out about even—the difference in the value of the land.

Question. Did he not say to you then that that was intended to avoid a deed of trust which was put on record in this county, and that the selection of the portion which lay in Oktibbeha left it outside of the deed of trust?

Answer. No, sir. He asked me if I would make that statement in court, if called as a witness. I told him I would. He told me to see Captain Sykes, Columbus, and tell him that I told him I would do it.

Question. You say his character is fair?

Answer. Yes, sir.

Question. Who did you ever hear say he had a fair character?

Answer. A good many of them.

Question. Give us the names of some of the respectable people in town who say he has a fair character.

Answer. Some of them will be here in a short time. Morton—Colonel Morton—he lives here in town.

Question. Give us some more of them.

Answer. Chancellor Lyon, or Judge Lyon. I think if you call on any of the ministers here—Mr. Carson, the Baptist minister, or Mr. Stainbock.

Question. Who else did you ever hear speak of him who gave him a high character?

Answer. I can mention other parties around here: J. Van Hook, judge of the probate court, or used to be; he is not now; also our present sheriff, Major Lewis.

Question. Is that all?

Answer. No; do you want more names?

Question. Yes, I want the names of all you have heard give him a good character.

Answer. Before he went to this committee in Washington I don't think there was a fairer standing man in town. After that, they all got down on him.

Question. All got down on him after that?

Answer. A good many did; some did.

Question. What did they say about him?

Answer. That his evidence was not fair and just.

Question. Did they say anything else?

Answer. They gave him a pretty good cursing.

Question. Did they say pretty generally that he was a swindler?

Answer. He took the bankrupt law in 1868, and the men he owed money to said so.

Question. He owes a good deal of money around?

Answer. Yes, sir. Like a good many others in this country, he was unfortunate in business, and had to take the benefit of the bankrupt law; and the men he owes money to do not like him.

Question. Are these all the men you have heard give him a good character?

Answer. As a fair-dealing mayor, I can refer to almost every man in town.

Question. I am not speaking of him as mayor, but his general character.

Answer. Call in Mr. Sykes.

Question. John Sykes, jr.?

Answer. John, right here at the corner.

Question. The old gentleman?

Answer. No, sir.

Question. The young lawyer?

Answer. No, sir; a farmer and planter, who lives up by the church here on the corner; John Sykes.

Question. Who else?

Answer. You can call in—let me think; I want to get some real hard old democrats now; I want to bring both parties now. Bring in George Frazee—I know he thinks he is a good man.

Question. You have heard him speak highly of him?

Answer. Yes, sir, I have; Dr. John W. Spillman.

Question. Go on.

Answer. You might bring in Colonel Gibbs; I have heard him speak well of him.

Question. What is the colonel's first name?

Answer. I do not remember his first name. Everybody in town knows him. There is only one man named Gibbs in town. These are democrats, now you have got some of both kinds.

Question. Go on.

Answer. I would just to call—just mention men in town as I pick them up—call in Dave Blair.

Question. You have heard him speak highly of him?

Answer. I have heard him speak well of him, not highly. I have never heard him say a word against him.

Question. Go on.

Mr. RICE. You had better give him some darkies now, so as to show all classes.

The WITNESS. I want to give both kinds. I can name a whole lot of darkies to you. Do you want them too? I try to mix them. You have some of both parties. I can call the colored people now.

By Mr. BLAIR:

Question. Go on, and name any respectable people who think and speak well of him.

Answer. Thaddeus James, a colored man; Robert Gleed—and I will call in a white man, William S. White, the jailor.

COLUMBUS, MISSISSIPPI, *November* 17, 1871.

JOHN MORTON sworn and examined.

By the CHAIRMAN:

Question. State your place of residence and occupation.

Answer. I reside at this place.

Question. What is your occupation?

Answer. I was a planter—was; I have not got much now.
Question. How long have you lived in this county?
Answer. I have lived here for thirty-one years, sir.
Question. Lived in Columbus during that time?
Answer. Yes, sir.
Question. Are you acquainted with Major H. B. Whitfield, a citizen of this town, who gave evidence before the committee at Washington?
Answer. Yes, sir; I am acquainted with Henry B. Whitfield.
Question. How long have you known him?
Answer. Well, I have known him since a child, sir.
Question. You may state what is and has been his character and standing in this community.
Answer. Well, sir, up to since the surrender Henry Whitfield's character has been as good as that of any young man ever raised in this county or this town, to my knowledge. After the surrender he went to building a factory, and I suppose he, for an error of judgment or something, got involved in his pecuniary matters, and persons who had dealings with him complained of him not complying with them. I think that was entirely want of judgment. I believe he would have done right if he had had the means to have done it, but he was like a great many other men—he was too sanguine in his business, and could not comply with his promises.
Question. Are you acquainted with his character for truth and veracity?
Answer. Well, sir, I have been always of opinion that he was as truthful a man as lived in the community.
Question. Would you believe him under oath?
Answer. Yes, sir; I think I would.
Question. Are you acquainted with W. W. Humphries, jr., esq., an attorney of this city?
Answer. Yes, sir.
Question. You may state his character and standing in this community as a man.
Answer. So far as I know, his character has been very good. There have been some rumors about him, and about Henry, too. Since Henry changed his politics there has been a good deal said about him; and there is something said about Humphries's morals that I am not cognizant of, and I do not know of it myself.
Question. I am asking as to his general character—whether his private character is good.
Answer. Well, as far as I know, it is good, sir.
Question. Is he a bitter man in his feelings?
Answer. I think he is rather so, sir.
Question. You think where he has a prejudice against a man he would be unjust toward him?
Answer. I do not know, sir. I am not well enough acquainted with him to answer that question. He is pretty arbitrary, I think, and pretty dictatorial in his manner.
Question. You think he is inclined to be vindictive?
Answer. I think so. In a case, a lawsuit, I had, I sued a man for a debt, and he was employed against me, and he rather insinuated some things to me that gave me a prejudice against him, because we had been friendly up to that time. He was a young man, and I rather an old man, and I am inclined to be kind to all young men who are raised about the place, and thought it was rather unwarranted in him.

By Mr. BLAIR:

Question. You state that Henry Whitfield got into business and failed?
Answer. Yes, sir.
Question. Did you ever hear that he gave a mortgage or lien to Governor Winston for $4,000 upon his crop and the products of his factory, and ship these products to Saint Louis, and failed to ship any portion to Governor Winston in Mobile, under his contract, upon which he had received money, and that he was indicted in the courts of Mobile for obtaining money under false pretenses, and requisition made upon the governor of this State for him under that indictment?
Answer. No, sir; I never heard that. I never heard it; that is the first intimation I have ever had of that thing.
Question. Did you ever hear that he obtained money from his own brother upon false pretenses, and swindled him out of it?
Answer. I know he had a difficulty with his brothers, or that his brothers did with him, rather, and one of them had a lawsuit with him, and that was partly about his getting goods under—well, without their knowledge or consent, or without their sanction, I think. I heard he ordered a carriage for his wife—may be I am mistaken; George Whitfield's wife, perhaps; Henry was going to New York, and he was a partner in the firm of Whitfield, Billips & Co., of Mobile. He went to New York, and George Whitfield's wife gave him a letter with an order in it, and it was not opened, I heard, until he got to New York. When he got to New York, she ordered a good many

things, among the rest a fine carriage, and shipped it to Mobile. George would not receive it, and threw it back on his brother's hands, and he was thrown out of the firm from the fact of his buying it without his brother's sanction and order. That is what I heard.

Question. You did not hear that he obtained a large amount of money from his brother, and pretended to give him a mortgage for it upon property already mortgaged?

Answer. No, sir; I did not hear that. I think I have heard that he did give a mortgage on property already mortgaged, but do not know who it was to. I heard those rumors about down here.

Question. You do not know whether it was his brother or not?

Answer. No, sir; I do not know whether it was his brother or not.

Question. You never heard of his swindling Governor Winston?

Answer. No, sir; that is the first intimation I ever had of that.

Question. And never heard of the requisition made on the governor of this State for him?

Answer. No, sir; I never did.

Question. You say that he is a man of fair standing in this town?

Answer. He always has been. There has been a great deal of talk about him since he joined the republican or radical party, and people have been down on him a good deal. I do not know what his conduct has been. From what I have heard—I have no proof of it; he has been my friend and a relative of my wife—I do not indorse his conduct in whatever he may have done that is wrong.

Question. You think, then, that this denunciation of him is well-founded?

Answer. I do not know about that. I never have seen his testimony. I do not know what that is. I heard he testified up here, in this case, to Mrs. Kenron's being an old lady. That is not so, because she is not exceeding forty-five years old, and the young man Kenron is not her son, but is a step-son. I understood he testified about the old woman and her one-armed son. I have never seen the testimony, though, and I can only speak of what I heard. I do not interfere with politics; I have nothing to do with them only to vote. As to these other cases that have been cited to you—the rumors about the violence and killing of people, and whipping of them—there were some of them in different counties, I do not know anything about, only from general rumor, and do not know about them except that; not the times or dates.

Question. I am not referring to what is said in relation to his testimony before this committee, but his character in this community.

Answer. Well, his character in this community, as far as I have known, up to within the last year or so, has been as good as any man's in it. He did, as I told you, disappoint people in his pecuniary matters about his factory; I understood that there was a good deal of complaint about him—a good many censured him; and some, too, did not censure him; they believed his purposes were good—that he would have done it if he could.

Question. Did you not hear he was censured for making false statements about his property, and obtaining money and credit in that way?

Answer. I have heard that.

Question. Was not that a universal complaint?

Answer. It was pretty general with those whom he had ——

Question. That he had made false statements upon which he obtained credits and money?

Answer. Well, I do not know whether I could say that he had made particularly false statements, but he had made some statements he had not complied with. I do not know much about his creditors. I know one or two men I have heard talk about it.

Question. If you knew the fact to be, that he had obtained a credit of $4,000 from Governor Winston, upon the agreement to ship to Governor Winston his cotton, and materials, or rather the products of his manufactory, and that instead of complying with that contract he had deliberately sent that cotton and the products of his manufactory to Saint Louis, and obtained money upon them, what would you say about his character?

Answer. I would not think that was right.

Question. Would you not consider that swindling?

Answer. I would consider it deceiving General Anthony Winston—Governor Winston.

Question. Could there be any other name for it than swindling, if a man, having made a deliberate contract and obtained money upon it, should falsely and fraudulently sell the product to others to get their money?

Answer. It would be very wrong; I will say that—it would be mighty wrong.

Question. Would you say that a man who would do such a thing as that was a credible man; that he was a man of good character?

Answer. From that circumstance I would not think he was credible in that. I do not think he ought to have done it, and if he did it he did wrong; but I do not know that he did it, for I never heard of it until I heard it from you. Possibly there are some things about him I have never heard, for, knowing the relation in which he stands to my family, it is not made public to me. Henry is a good, kind-hearted man; there never was a better boy raised about here, and his great objection is he cannot say no to anybody, and he stood fair here up to the time he joined the republican party.

By the CHAIRMAN:

Question. Who have been down on him since he joined the republican party—the democrats or republicans?

Answer. Mostly the democrats, I reckon. The conservatives, a great many of them, done that, because they run him here as a candidate for the legislature, and did all they could to have him on the democratic ticket, and when he failed to get elected he turned and joined the republican party.

Question. Was he not generally and warmly supported by the conservative party here at the time he ran for the legislature?

Answer. Yes, sir; I think so.

Question. And nothing was said against him then?

Answer. Not that I know of. I do not remember of hearing anything said against him then.

Question. When a man becomes unfortunate, and is compelled to take the benefit of the bankrupt-law, it is no unusual thing for his creditors to urge complaints?

Answer. No, sir; that is so. I hear them abusing and cursing a great many men here on that account.

Question. A great many men here have been compelled to take the benefit of that law?

Answer. Yes, sir; and some of them are driving good carriages and horses.

Question. Their estates do not pay much to creditors?

Answer. No, sir. I denounce anything of the kind. If a man is not broke, he ought not to do it. I know men who, it is said, borrowed large amounts, and never paid a dollar of it, and never shipped their cotton that way, and they are now conservative men; but I do not think any the better of him for that.

By Mr. RICE:

Question. At that time Henry Whitfield was badly broke?

Answer. Yes, sir; badly broke.

By Mr. BLAIR:

Question. Getting pay for cotton twice, then, is not considered honest?

Answer. No, sir. I do not consider it honest in any man to do that.

By the CHAIRMAN:

Question. You do not know anything about the facts in that case?

Answer. No, sir; I do not know anything about the facts.

COLUMBUS, MISSISSIPPI, *November* 17, 1871.

THEODORIC L. LYON sworn and examined.

By the CHAIRMAN:

Question. Please to state your residence and official position.

Answer. Columbus, Mississippi; chancellor of the fifth district of Mississippi.

Question. How long have you lived in Columbus?

Answer. With the exception of seven years this has been my home since 1841.

Question. Please to state to the committee whether you are acquainted with Major Henry B. Whitfield, the gentleman who testified before the committee at Washington.

Answer. I am acquainted with Major Henry B. Whitfield.

Question. How long, and how intimately have you known him?

Answer. Well, sir, I have known him since my boyhood. I have been associated with him during the last ten years intimately. Shall I explain the nature of that association?

Question. You may.

Answer. Well, sir, Major Whitfield and I were together in raising a company for the confederate service in 1862. We were associated in that company together in the same tent—the same mess. We were associated more or less during the war—off and on through the whole war from that time. I have been intimate in his family. I have been frequently in his house. His wife was a particular and special friend of my family. That was one bond of intimacy between us. Since the war we have lived together here in the same town, or at least for the most part. He was at his place in the country, some few miles off, but here every few days, and I have seen him continually from that time to this. I have had business transactions with him. I have lent him money, and have lost money by him—two or three thousand dollars; I think about $2,800 I lost by him. Before my promotion to the bench I was his attorney in many matters, and the attorney of his wife in her matters of separate property.

Question. What is his character and standing in this community for truth and veracity?

Answer. Well, sir, there are many men in this community at the present time who would not place implicit reliance upon the statements of Major Whitfield, perhaps with some reason, or with at least the appearance of reason. Will you allow me to state there or to further explain that, Senator Pratt?

Question. Yes, sir.

Answer. I was just going on to say that formerly, that is to say, before Major Whitfield's financial disasters, no man in this community stood higher than he in every possible way. He stood well, ahead, in fact, in his church. He stood ahead in this community. I think he stood, probably, in the estimation of this community and in the public approbation and kindly feeling, before any other man in it. In 1866–'67 and 1868, Major Whitfield became involved through a factory that he established near here, and such was the implicit confidence which the people had in him, of all kinds and classes, that he was enabled to borrow money in every direction upon his own name. He failed in his factory; failed utterly; he was utterly ruined. I speak as his attorney when I say that he was ruined even to the extent of the gold watch which his father presented to him and which has his name inscribed in it, which passed through my hands to pay his debts. He involved himself; he involved his friends; he involved his family, and would have beggared his wife had it not been for the interposition of her friends; he would have beggared his wife and children. He made no effort, to the best of my knowledge as his attorney and her attorney, to save one dollar from his creditors in any possible way. The result of the disappointment felt in him by his numerous creditors, the aggregate of his indebtedness to whom amounted to forty or fifty thousand dollars, possibly more; I speak without positive knowledge; and which was generally diffused over the country, for everybody and anybody would lend to him; men, women, and children would have lent him, for there never was a man who had such a hold on the feelings of this community as Henry B. Whitfield, in the days of his prosperity gone by—the result of the disappointment conseqent on his financial disaster naturally changed the feelings of the people against him to a considerable extent. He was accused in many quarters of having made and broken promises, of having betrayed his friends, and many things were said by persons who lost by him to his discredit and disparagement. Am I too particular and minute, Senator?

Question. Not at all?

Answer. If I am allowed to I will explain just here. I think it positively necessary, in order to do justice to Major Whitfield, to show the causes of the present feelings against him in the minds of some.

Question. You are quite correct in giving the explanation.

Answer. From a most intimate knowledge of Major Whitfield during this time, and repeated conversations with him concerning his business matters and embarrassments, and from my intimate knowledge of his character and nature, I have never been able to bring myself to the conclusion that his intentions were dishonest, but I have felt that in many cases great injustice, and probably in all cases some injustice, was done him. So thorough was my conviction of this that I never so much as uttered one word of complaint against him myself for the losses I sustained by him, though I thought the circumstances might have justified it, but for the belief which I had, and which I have already expressed. I will say that Major Whitfield is a peculiar man in some respects. In the first place he is a most sanguine man. He believes, and implicitly believes, what he wants to believe. Hence in many cases he would be led to make promises and say things, honestly hoping and believing that they would be realized, when in fact common reason and common sense would show that they could not be realized. Then, again, he is one of the kindest men I ever met, the most so I think of any men I have ever seen; he is the most uniformly and universally obliging. He cannot refuse a negro anything. Men of high or low degree are all just alike with him in their petitions before him, and have been so since he was a boy; everybody that wanted to use his buggy and horses, all and anything he had men would borrow of him and use; anything that any man wanted of him he did not hesitate to ask of Major Whitfield; he was as kind to the negroes in the days of slavery as he is now. He was a teacher in the Sabbath-school, where he taught them to read and write. He was regarded as universal property in anything he had; he could not say "no" to any man; to this day he cannot say no—scarce to his enemies. This sentiment I believe to be one reason of his having been betrayed so often into promises, or rather another and second cause of his having been led into promises which he could not redeem, which common sense and cool calculation would have shown him he could not redeem in the operations of his factory. In the operations of his factory and business—his finances—he became almost, if not quite, a monomaniac during the days when the crisis was on him. I heard his book-keeper, William H. Perkins, of Artesia, speak of it, and I heard his family physician, Doctor A. A. Lyon, who was resident in his family at this time, and I heard his brother-in-law, John H. Sykes, who lost money by him and was bitter against him at that time, express doubts as to his positive sanity upon many matters, particularly during those months—I may say during 1867 or 1868. I do not remember the exact dates. I could illustrate the state of his mind by a little instance which I remember myself, which probably it is not necessary to put down at length, showing the utter singularity, to say the least of it, of his conclusions in reference to many things. He was almost crazy upon the subject of continuing his factory. He thought it was going to succeed; thought to borrow this much here and that cotton there, or get rid of his advances from Saint Louis merchants and per cents on sales and manufactures. He had just one idea in everything, that he could get through. He was going day and night; he seemed the most energetic man I ever saw, moving property over the country; leaving no stone unturned to raise money and obtain cotton, begging it, I may say; going on more after the style of Goodyear than any one else, in the time when he was pushing his India-rubber scheme. It is said by his biographer that he was insane at one time, filled with the idea of his India-rubber manufacture. Major Whitfield's wife, when he was taking everything she had and using up all her property, said she believed he would give the blood in his veins to keep the factory from stopping. This much of his history will sufficiently explain my knowledge and understanding of his character.

Question. Taking into consideration all the expressions of opinion which you have heard in respect to Major Whitfield in this community, what is the general result?

Answer. Let me first add further to this one other cause of the present distrust of him. Another cause is the hue and cry raised against him because of his recent political connection, and his testimony given before the Ku-Klux committee at Washington City, which testimony I have never read. That would complete the list of causes which explain the present state of public opinion against him. It must be admitted, sir, that public opinion is against him in this community very decidedly.

Question. When you speak of public opinion do you speak of that which proceeds from the democratic part of the community?

Answer. When I speak of public opinion I refer to the opinions of those who ordinarily make public opinion in the community; that is, to the controlling minds of the community, and they, for the most part in this community, are members of the democratic party.

Question. Since his pecuniary misfortunes has he been a candidate for public office upon the conservative ticket?

Answer. Yes, sir; he was a candidate for office at the time of the Dent movement in this State; he was then a candidate for the legislature.

Question. Was that subsequent to his bankruptcy?

Answer. It was.

Question. State whether he received a democratic nomination; and, if so, for what office?

Answer. He received the nomination for the legislature, I think.

Question. Was he generally supported by that party?

Answer. Yes, sir, I think he was.

Question. Did he run on the same ticket with W. W. Humphries?

Answer. I have had nothing to do with politics myself, especially since my promotion to the bench in this last year and a half, and cannot give you the best testimony on such subjects.

Question. I was asking you if he ran upon the same ticket with W. W. Humphries?

Answer. Yes, sir; and went about over the country, my understanding is, with Humphries, hail-fellow well met, speaking together, making divers appointments, &c.

Question. Was anything urged against his moral character and fitness at that time?

Answer. Not that I remember. I do not now recollect to have heard anything of the sort urged against him then generally. I may have heard some remark against him from some creditor who had thought himself injured.

Question. Anything more than is urged in similar cases when a man is compelled to take the benefit of the bankrupt law and divide his assets among his creditors?

Answer. I have heard more said in his case than I would expect to be said ordinarily.

By Mr. Rice:

Question. Did you then when he was a candidate?

Answer. O, no, sir; not then, but I have heard at all times more from the peculiar relation he bore to this community. He was the most universally popular and loved man in all this county by men, women, and children, negroes, everybody.

By the Chairman:

Question. I understand you to say that you were his attorney in his application for a discharge?

Answer. I was not in that. I was counsel for him in bankruptcy matters. I was counsel for him in a dozen or more cases.

Question. Is it your belief that he honestly surrendered all his property to his creditors?

Answer. It is my belief that his creditors got everything he had. I have heard since that a vessel at the factory ought to have been turned over, as it was not under mortgage. The personal property was exceptionable; but I will say this: I was counsel for no man that went into bankruptcy that I thought so utterly surrendered everything as Henry B. Whitfield. He has nothing, as far as I am capable of judging. He has nothing left in the wide world. He mortgaged, pledged, and promised, and used every effort to obtain money, and at the time of his great trials in business, of which I have spoken, he used almost undue influences to get his wife to part with the little she had to feed his children.

Question. In order to satisfy his creditors?

Answer. Yes, sir; he sold his fine house, when, under the laws of this State, he could have kept it from his creditors, and he sold almost the entire furniture in it, or at least the best furniture in it, and surrendered as completely as I ever knew a debtor to do.

Question. Was it a pretty general thing for business men in this community to take the benefit of the bankrupt-law?

Answer. Yes, sir; pretty generally; at least, so generally that it is not used very often here as a stigma on a man's character; that is not generally so referred to.

Question. From your knowledge of Major Whitfield—your intimate acquaintance with him and his business transactions—would you believe him under oath?

Answer. Why, sir, in any ordinary matter—in any matter, whether his interests were involved or not, I would believe him under oath. I have never been able to divest myself of the belief that he is a good man, a Christian man, though it takes some charity to believe that on the facts presented.

Question: State whether it brought down a good deal of unpleasant comment upon Major Whitfield when he joined the radical party?

Answer. Yes, sir; it did certainly. I may say that I have not agreed with Major Whitfield at all times in his opinions. I have not been an intimate counselor with him in his politics. I have heard him express himself time and again, and I have differed at times with his political views. I do not know exactly; I have not followed him as closely in his politics as otherwise, and my testimony would not be so full as to that point as what might be stated by others; but I think I can say that he did bring a good deal of unpleasant comment upon himself by joining the radical party. At the time he ran, of which you spoke, I thought Major Whitfield ought not to have run on the democratic ticket. However, that is a thing which it is not necessary for me to explain. I will say this, that my personal friendship at all times led me to support Henry Whitfield.

Question. State whether he is a man of good habits.

Answer. He is a man of good habits. I never have seen him drunk, nor heard him swear an oath.

Question. Is he a man of general propriety in his conduct?

Answer. Yes, sir; altogether so; a most peaceable man in the community; a man that is law-abiding in all things, as far as I know. Nothing has ever been said against his character that I know save at the time of his bankruptcy, in consequence of his bankruptcy, and because of his connection with the radical party or with politics; for something was said against his coming out on the Dent ticket. He was regarded as a moderate man, a conservative man, or, as we called it, a Union man; and his coming out and affiliating with Humphries, and others like him, always known as extremists and "Malignants," as we called them, or "Red-Tongues," as they are sometimes called, was regarded as a bad movement. He was, therefore, regarded unfavorably by some when he went into the Dent movement. When he joined the radical party the condemnation was very general, almost universal. I have never heard him condemned for anything but those things, but for no immoral act or anything of the kind.

Question. You spoke a moment since of W. W. Humphries, jr., an attorney of this city, as having run upon the same ticket with Major Whitfield, and their canvassing the county together, I believe. How long have you been acquainted with Mr. Humphries?

Answer. May I just say here, and have it entered upon the records, that I probably am not a good witness in the case of Mr. Humphries; that while I believe I am dispassionate in most opinions, and make my utmost endeavor to cultivate a spirit of that kind, especially in my present position, and upon general principles, yet my estimation of Captain Humphries and my feelings toward him are really such that I do not know whether I could do the man justice—do Captain Humphries justice. I do not wish to speak disrespectfully of him.

Question. Has he been a practicing attorney in your court?

Answer. He has, sir; and I would be glad not to be compelled to give any testimony concerning him. Allow me to say, in the way of parenthesis, that the relations between Captain Humphries's family and my family have been good in all times. His father and my father, his mother and my mother, and his uncle were friends. My father was pastor of the Presbyterian Church, and a professor in the university at Oxford. I have never had any trouble with members of his family, but I will say that unpleasant matters have arisen between Captain Humphries and myself, and I should regret to give any testimony concerning him, especially if I had to give it against him, for the reasons I have stated; first, as I might give it in such a way as not to do full justice to him and to myself; and second, the relations between his family and mine. I feel friendly to his father and his uncle, but I do not speak to Captain Humphries.

Question. I would be glad to know if any charges have been brought to your knowledge as chancellor, in connection with his conduct as an attorney in your court. If there are any facts in that regard lying within your knowledge, the committee would be glad to be informed of them.

Answer. No formal charges have been brought against him, to my knowledge.

Question. Has he retired from practice in your court?

Answer. He has, sir.

Question. Under what circumstances and for what reasons?

Answer. He has never told me his reasons, nor has there been any communication on the subject between us; however, I am under oath to tell the whole truth if I am pressed. I see I shall be compelled to state some things I would gladly avoid mentioning, for the reasons I have stated to the committee, but, which, if they, in their best judgment, insist upon, of course I must answer. Yet, I would be glad not to be pressed upon this subject, gentlemen, for the reasons I have stated, unless you feel it your duty to urge the question.

Question. He has appeared before this committee as a witness, and I think it proper that the committee should be informed of his standing and reputation in this community as a man of character and a man of truth and veracity. He made serious charges against another witness, and the committee desire to learn how far his statements are to be credited. To that end we desire to know his position and standing in this community as an attorney and as a man.

Answer. I will state, gentlemen, at the outset, that my testimony may not be taken for more than it is worth; that I really feel that I may not be able to do Captain Humphries justice. I am not afraid to express my opinions on any subject before any body of men; but the circumstances that exist in this present case between him and myself and his and mine are peculiar.

By Mr. BLAIR:

Question. The question asked you is a very distinct one: What is his character in the community?

Answer. Well, sir, if a man despises another one, or dislikes him greatly—I do not wish to argue with the committee—but if a man dislikes another exceedingly, it is a question whether his opinion of that man's standing in the community is the best evidence. I will answer any question the committee desire me to. I do not want to be contumacious or to show any sort of disrespect by the objections I am making. I understand the necessities imposed upon you in your investigation to inquire into the standing of witnesses.

By the CHAIRMAN:

Question. If you know the general moral character and standing of W. W. Humphries in the community, the committee would be glad to have the benefit of that information.

Answer. Well, sir, I will say first, that apart from matters that have come to my knowledge since I have been upon the chancery bench, and through his being a practitioner in my court, I have very little knowledge of things that are to Captain Humphries's discredit.

Question. What charges have been brought to your knowledge as chancellor?

Answer. I was about to complete my statement. I have heard a great deal said against Captain Humphries in the community.

Question. Of what character?

Answer. Tending to his prejudice, to his discredit in almost every way. The truth is, in many instances—in all instances, I may say—I know nothing about him. I have had no business transactions with Mr. Humphries in my life, or very few—none that have brought any of these facts to my knowledge.

Question. Is his reputation that of being a moral man?

Answer. His reputation is not that of being a moral man.

Question. What charges have been brought to your knowledge as chancellor connected with his conduct as an attorney?

Answer. No formal charges have been brought, as I said before, but an affidavit is on file in the chancery court which will explain itself and which covers part of that in which I have considered him derelict in his duties as an attorney in that court under his oath.

Question. Could you state the substance of that affidavit?

Answer. Yes, sir. That affidavit, I will say, was filed by the clerk, or by the deputy clerk, and charges him with having taken from the court, or received from the court, a deposition in a certain cause pending wherein he was counsel for the complainant.

Question. And withholding it?

Answer. And with having never returned it. I believe the affidavit charges the offense more strongly and more clearly than I stated. I believe that affidavit, according to the best of my recollection, further charges him with having substituted in its stead another deposition of different import.

Question. Is Captain Humphries regarded as a vindictive man in his feelings?

Answer. I should say he is regarded as an exceedingly vindictive man in his feelings, and yet a man of certain kindliness of nature. There is no man would do more against another than he, if moved. He is an implacable man. I know him well.

Question. If his feelings were vindictive toward a man, do you think he would be capable of doing him justice?

Answer. I do not, sir.

By Mr. Blair:

Question. You state that Major Whitfield was greatly embarrassed by his business transactions?

Answer. He was, sir.

Question. Do you know anything of a transaction of his in which he contracted with Governor Winston, of Mobile, Alabama, to send his cotton and the products of his factory to Governor Winston, as a commission merchant in Mobile, and received advances amounting to $4,000 from Governor Winston, giving a deed of trust upon the property, which he signed and subsequently refused to acknowledge, and that he sent the product of his factory and his cotton to St. Louis to another commission merchant, receiving money for it?

Answer. I do not, sir. He never acquainted me with that transaction, if any such took place.

Question. Did you hear that he was indicted in the city court of Mobile for obtaining money from Governor Winston on false pretenses, arising out of this transaction, and that there was a requisition on the governor of this State—Mississippi—for him?

Answer. I never heard that he was indicted until the last day or two, upon any charge, and I did not hear then upon what charge. I heard it was for some transaction with Governor Winston. I have heard his wife speak in days gone by, years since, about some trouble he had with Governor Winston, but I never heard anything about the requisition made upon Governor Alcorn until since I was in the court-house. I heard it mentioned at the door.

Question. By whom?

Answer. I was trying to think; it was not at the door either, it was by Major Whitfield himself, who called by my house, in going down, he said, to see Mr. Cason, the Baptist minister. He said something about it, if I could remember his exact words. He said very little about it, but remarked something of a requisition which had been made or was charged to have been made, I am not sure which. I was in a hurry and was writing a little piece at the time. He came, he said, to notify me to be here promptly at 9 o'clock, and he said something about a requisition having been made, or that it was charged as having been made, upon Governor Alcorn for him. I never heard of it until half an hour ago, and it was at my own house, not in the office, as I thought at first.

Question. Is such a transaction as I have described consistent with a fair and honorable character?

Answer. I think not.

Question. If you had known the facts to be as I state, it would it have changed your opinion?

Answer. If I had known them to be absolutely so, and this transaction had not taken place at the time to which I have referred, that is, the time of his great trouble about his manufactory, when his wife said he did not use to sleep, but lay rolling all night long, and when I believed he was scarcely responsible for his acts—on that ground I forgave him for his injury to me, and if such a thing as you have mentioned took place—if that transaction had been entered into under any circumstances but those—I should think it inconsistent with honesty of purpose.

Question. Do you think any man entering into a deliberate contract to do certain acts for which he received money; that is, to send certain products fabricated by the very money thus obtained, and failing to do so, but sending these products to other parties and obtaining money again for their sale to those parties—that those acts are consistent with a high character?

Answer. I should think that such a man, with a knowing and understanding mind, was an unprincipled man and a scoundrel.

Question. And a swindler?

Answer. Yes, sir; and a swindler. That is my opinion, sir.

Question. Suppose the person who should bring this evidence to your knowledge should produce, in the first place, Whitfield's deed of trust, signed by himself, and his acknowledgment that he had received $4,000 from Governor Winston, and positively prove his contract to send and deliver these goods to Governor Winston, and then should produce the proof that, so far from complying with a written contract, he had deliberately forwarded the goods to Saint Louis and obtained money upon them, no matter what may have been your opinion of the person producing this testimony, if he likewise produced the formal indictment from the court of Mobile, certified to properly, and the requisition upon the governor of Mississippi for this man, and the governor's response giving technical reasons for declining to deliver this man up, would you not consider that ample testimony of the transaction?

Answer. To prove the facts I should consider that ample testimony. It would not affect the nature of the facts that they were made known by a man that was not wholly reliable or was greatly prejudiced against the party. That would be my judgment, at least.

Question. Did you ever hear of a transaction of Major Henry B. Whitfield with his brother George Whitfield?

Answer. Yes, sir; I know all about it.

Question. What is the character of it?

Answer. Well, sir, I have talked with Major Whitfield about that, and with his wife and with his brother, and have been counsel for Mrs. Whitfield in the matter, in conjunction with Judge Orr. I regard that transaction as one that reflects no credit upon Major Whitfield, as I have told him and his wife and his brother, but I have looked upon it, and his brother, I think, looks upon it in the same light as myself—for I have conversed with him upon the subject—as one of the results of the dreadful straits to which he was brought at the time of his bankruptcy, and the peculiar state of mind he was in at that time, and for some time subsequent thereto. It was a transaction the equity merits and justice of which I never approved, and I said so. I am not responsible for it as his legal adviser. I must say, since I have mentioned the fact, that I was counsel, in conjunction with Judge Orr, in ascertaining Mrs. Whitfield's rights against Major Whitfield, or her case against his claim, based upon that transaction, and I was not responsible myself as her attorney for the effort made to defeat, as I regarded, the just and equitable claim of Major Whitfield by taking advantage of a legal technicality. My advice was against it. Judge Orr was the chief counsel in the matter.

Question. I want you to give us a history of that transaction.

Answer. I will, as well as I can recollect, but there have been so many transactions in which Major Whitfield has been engaged——

Question. Of a similar character?

Answer. Not exactly, but which have required, justice compels me to say, charity, and the charitable judgment; that is, similar transactions about that time, all about that time; but I never heard one word of reproach, gentlemen, it must be said to Major Whitfield's credit, until these troubles, and since then in reference to his political relations.

Question. What are the facts in that matter?

Answer. The facts are, as I understand them, that his brother George Whitfield lent him money upon the promise that he would secure him with an undivided interest that he possessed in the estate of his father-in-law, Colonel Alexander Young; I think it was a one-fifth interest; that he did give his brother a trust-deed or mortgage, and that afterward the land was divided by the probate court of this county upon due and legal notice. I must say, first, that the greater part of this land lay in Lowndes County, but a little of it was over the border, in Oktibbeha County; and about the time he was going utterly to pieces, and when he had sold his wife's house in town and everything he had, and moved to the country, he had a partition; I think that he got the partition decreed by the probate court here, upon due and legal notice. I do not know whether he had it done or not. I never talked with Major Whitfield much about this subject. I have talked more with his wife about it; I was her counsel. To state it as strongly as it can be against him, he had his fifth part thrown over in Oktibbeha County. In the mean time there were serious complaints made by his wife's friends, her sisters and relatives, at the disposition which Major Whitfield was making of her property, and Major Whitfield was drawn into decided trouble with her family, her brothers and her sister, Mrs. John H. Sykes, and her husband; and he made a deed to his wife of this land that lay in Oktibbeha County, it having been set apart by the probate court as his part of the estate, an undivided one-fifth which he had given to secure the money he had borrowed from his brother, Major George Whitfield. He then had the deed that he gave his wife recorded in Oktibbeha County, and his wife took the ground in her desperation, for it was a matter of desperation in those times, so much so, that I might state a little matter which ought not to go on the record, but which would explain the reason why Mrs. Whitfield favored this thing in justice to her; Mrs. Whitfield, I will say, in her desperation, claimed her right to this land against Major George Whitfield, upon the ground that he might as well lose as for her to be ruined, utterly; and that her debt against her husband for property converted was to be considered equal, if not before his; that was the ground she took, and I never could dispossess her mind thoroughly of the morality of that idea; she is a most honorable woman, and of an honorable family. If I am allowed, right here, in my own defense, I will say that I am an intimate personal friend of Mrs. Whitfield; a friend of her brothers and sisters, and was of her father and mother. Her father, in his lifetime, and her mother, in her lifetime, were dear friends of my father and mother, and I have been her friend, and have served her without money or price on many occasions, and Henry B. Whitfield, for her sake, and the sake of her family. That accounts for my having been, under all circumstances, probably to some extent a charitable viewer of things which, in other persons, I might not have judged so charitably.

Question. I understand this transaction of Major Whitfield with his brother is reduced down to this proposition: that he borrowed money from his brother upon the credit of a mortgage executed by him, which mortgage was put on record in this county; that the subsequent division of the property threw that portion which came to Major Whitfield into Oktibbeha County; that he either procured this division or the division was accidentally made in that way, and he took advantage of that fact to deed the property to his wife, and thus defeated the prior mortgage given to his brother, upon the credit of which he had raised money?

Answer. That is all correct, as I understand it, with this exception, and I know the fact, or at least my recollection is, that his undivided interest in this property was deeded to Mrs. Whitfield before the partition.

Question. After it was already mortgaged?

Answer. Yes, sir; I think so. I know so.

Question. Subsequent to the mortgage to his brother?

Answer. Yes, sir; but Major Whitfield was of that hopeful sort that he would have believed that he could have delivered that property honestly at the time. I cannot believe, and never have believed, that his intentions were dishonest. I explain much that he has done in that way, that he was of that hopeful, enthusiastic sort, believing what he wanted, and believing unreasonable things sometimes.

Question. Did he hope and believe it when he deliberately recorded the deed to his wife in Oktibbeha County, after the division of the estate; do you think he was sanguine and hopeful then?

Answer. No, sir; I do not believe he did at that time.

Question. You think he then deliberately intended to destroy the interests his brother had in that property?

Answer. Yes, sir; and preferred his wife, as he used to state it, to his brother.

By Mr. RICE:

Question. Did he owe her money?

Answer. Yes, sir; all that came from her father's estate he swallowed up.

By Mr. BLAIR:

Question. Would his brother have allowed him money upon any such mortgage, if he had presumed that any such conflict would have come up between him and his wife?

Answer. I presume not; but his brother told me the other day that he has lent him money since this transaction, and that, under the circumstances, he did not judge him harshly.

Question. Is not that an additional reason why Henry B. Whitfield should not have swindled the man who had that kind feeling toward him?

Answer. If it was swindling, sir, in ordinary human judgment I should say it was an additional reason.

Question. You think it is necessary in this transaction to produce the impression that this man was not of sound mind, in order to protect him from the inevitable inference that he was a swindler?

Answer. Yes, sir; I think that is the ground; for many persons have discussed these things, and that is the ground I have taken with many persons, that he was not in perfectly sound mind in reference to his financial matters in those days, through the continual strain and stress upon him day and night, circulating round and round, round and round, in the idea of keeping the factory going and preserving himself from ruin—keeping himself from swamping. He lost his good name and all. That was the idea of his family physician; that was the idea of his book-keeper in reference to him, one of the best men in our county now, Mr. William H. Perkins, a merchant of Artesia, and his brother-in-law, John H. Sykes, who judges him very harshly, who says he cannot love a brother if he lost money by him. That was the opinion he expressed to me at that time, that he then had doubts in his mind on this subject. I can illustrate this by one little thing which I now remember hearing Major Whitfield say, to show the utter infatuation of the man. He was reading the New York Herald, in which there was a call for a meeting of factory men from the whole United States. At this time Major Whitfield's factory had closed; mortgages were covering his property in every direction—for he would mortgage everything, and has done it since, and gone into bankruptcy, mortgaging even his wife's property, and his children's property, so that she had to refuse to recognize the mortgage—had to take that issue. He did that here as I am credibly informed by his wife——

Question. How far——

The WITNESS. Let me finish this matter. He was reading that paper and saw this call for the convention. He just threw down the paper, and sprang up, exclaiming, "I am going there," stamping his foot; "I will attend that convention certainly; I must go." We all knew—his wife knew—that at that time Major Whitfield had sent over a bushel of wheat by a negro, and gave him half of it to raise a dollar to buy some actual necessaries; that I had sold his father's present to him, the watch which I have mentioned. My brother was present, and was perfectly acquainted with the circumstances. Major Whitfield looked around a little and said, "I will go if I can beg or borrow the money or steal it." That was his expression. Nobody said anything. I am free to say right there that I am compelled to have some such interpretation in order to lead me to the opinion that Henry B. Whitfield is at heart not a dishonest man. I do not come before this committee in anybody's interest.

By the CHAIRMAN:

Question. Notwithstanding all these doubtful transactions which you have detailed, occurring when he was deeply embarrassed and struggling to relieve himself, do you still believe that Major Whltfield is a man of honest purposes?

Answer. I do believe that Major Whitfield is a man of honest purpose.

By Mr. BLAIR:

Question. What do you believe was his purpose when he made a contract with Governor Winston, of Alabama, and received $4,000 of the governor's money upon it, engaging his cotton to him and the product of his factory, which contract he deliberately violated, and sent the product elsewhere after he received the money?

Answer. I think his purpose was to get Governor Winston's money.

Question. Without giving him any consideration for it?

Answer. I do not say that. I think he hoped and expected at the time he made that promise to give him a consideration. He served me in pretty nearly the same way in my matter, in regard to some money. I will tell that if you desire.

Question. Go on.

Answer. He gave me a crop of corn—I do not want to go into my own personal matters, but if it is necessary to do justice to Major Whitfield, I will proceed.

Question. He gave you a crop?

Answer. Yes, sir; as part of the payment of my claim against him. I had just lent him freely part of this money of which I speak—a thousand dollars at one time; I had not much to lend, and I lent him $500 at another time, in those days when he was borrowing from everybody. He was beginning then to be embarrassed, but I thought it was a time for me to show my friendship for him and his family. He was trying to bolster up his credit, and I believed him honest, and hoped he would get through. A note was put in my hand to collect, and I made an arrangement to collect or settle it, and he to refund the note to me, $712; that was the sum of his indebtedness to me then, if I recollect. I have his note also for $1,825—those two things, $1,825 and $712. I will add that I have never collected a dollor for legal services in all this time, but he set apart this crop of corn for me. He told me, "I am being pressed; I will do all I can for you." I answered, "Henry, just make provision for me as well as you can; anything you can honestly do for me, do it." He set apart for me a crop of corn. I never saw the crop; he told me it was mine; it was worth, I think, about seventeen or eighteen hundred dollars; it did not cover the whole of my claim, but went that far. I never asked him for any mortgages or security. He afterward sold that crop of corn which he had set apart.

Question. Did he give you the shucks?

Answer. No, sir; I never got the shucks, or even the cobs. He made me a present afterward of something that cost him $75, and I credited that on the back of one of the notes without his knowing it. That was all I ever got in payment of them, but I do not judge him harshly for these things with my knowledge of him and his circumstances at that time, and I have never said one unkind word to him about it.

Question. You are an intimate friend of him and his family?

Answer. I am a very intimate friend of his family, particularly his wife.

Question. You are disposed, as you say yourself, to judge him with the greatest charity?

Answer. Yes, sir; I am disposed to say everything for him that I can say.

Question. As a matter of course, these transactions are judged by the community, who are not his intimate friends, and who have not that kind feeling and bias toward him, differently. What is the judgment of the community on these transactions?

Answer. Well, sir, most persons would not trust Henry Whitfield with money at this time in this community; some persons would. I have lent him money since, showing my faith in him, and he has paid me. I lent him money without note or security, and he paid it as he promised. His brother, George Whitfield, told me he had lent him money since these transactions, and that he had no ill-will or ill-feeling toward him, and he is now disposed, I understand to make some arrangement by which his wife can secure some of that Oktibbeha land—to make out a piece of woodland that remained of her father's property.

Question. Do you not think that men who were not allied to Henry B. Whitfield as closely in blood as George Whitfield, or in friendship as yourself, would not look as charitably upon these transactions?

Answer. I think so.

Question. And that the community at large would place no reliance upon or faith in him?

Answer. I cannot say that they would place no reliance upon him or faith in him, but I will say that the faith of the community is greatly shaken in Major Whitfield through these transactions; they have been brought into general discussion, and the community is prejudged against him because of his political relations more lately than before.

Question. Does Major Whitfield, when he goes into anything as he did in this factory, go in with the same credulity and activity that he did in that matter?

Answer. Well, sir, Major Whitfield goes into a thing zealously, energetically, confidently, and hopefully, whatever it may be, equal to any man that, I think, I ever knew, if not beyond—I scarce know how to phrase the remainder of the sentence—I think I never knew a man who had these characteristics in more overwhelming development in his nature.

Question. Has he gone into politics in the same way?

Answer. Yes, sir; just in the same way. I have not been with him in politics, as I have said, and I do not know what he has done there so well, but I understand that he has gone into politics in the same way.

Question. He believes everything on his side?

Answer. I think he is positive. I have never talked much with Major Whitfield on politics, or in reference to his political views, but from what little I have heard from him, I have come to the conclusion that he has got to be zealously, sincerely, and enthusiastically a republican and a radical.

Question. And blindly?

Answer. No, sir; I will not say blindly, but I will say enthusiastically and honestly.

Question. You think he is inclined to believe all——

Answer. I will add and radically. I do not want to record him there as being so extreme as to affect his sincerity or belief. I do not think he means any evil.

Question. You think he is inclined to believe everything said on his side?

Answer. Not everything; but he is inclined to believe what is said on his side. It is consistent with his character. I see the point and drift of the examination. It is true that he is inclined to believe everything that is said on his side, and has a way of believing what he wants to believe as much as any man I ever saw. That is a principle in human nature, however, that in greater or less degree is universal, and has been seen by every observer of human nature from the days of Aristotle to our own; for Aristotle, or was it Pythagoras, said, "Men believe what they want to believe, and find that which they look for?" I think Major Whitfield is one of that class.

Question. You think he would give testimony here in that spirit?

Answer. He would be biased somewhat, but he would not testify anything before this committee that he did not believe.

Question. But you think it is very easy for him to believe what is on his side?

Answer. That is the necessary conclusion from what I have said, but I will add that in the recital of facts I have never known any man whom I believed more accurate than Major Whitfield. His memory is remarkable. You can read over to him a document, and he will repeat the document—not in sum and substance, as most men would under such circumstances, but repeat it almost *verbatim et literatim*. He can go through it by word. He can remember names and dates and places with marvelous accuracy. I have heard this observation made concerning him.

Question. Do you think he would believe as firmly in anything that would give political capital to his party and aid his own political prospects as he did in his being able to pay Governor Winston's claim, after he had sold the cotton and the products of his factory to somebody else, which he had promised to Governor Winston?

Answer. I think he would. He would believe as firmly in the one as in the other.

Question. You think he could reconcile himself to believe any such facts in the same manner?

Answer. Let me qualify that; if he was in the same state of mind that he was then.

Question. You say he has been covered with a great deal of obloquy by reason of his political conduct?

Answer. He has, sir; insomuch that it has taken very considerable moral courage for his friends to stand by him and recognize their friendship for him. That must be admitted, not so much so now, I think, as some time past. The country has got into such a state that the people are feeling more liberal, more just in judgment. I believe much injustice was done to Major Whitfield in their judgment on his testimony, though I have never read it.

Question. Did he deny that it was an accurate report which was shown here?

Answer. Yes, sir. He told me that there was this error in the report—that is, in the newspaper report: he said that he was reported as having testified to things from his personal knowledge which, in fact, he testified to as hearsay.

Question. You have seen a copy of that report?

Answer. I did of the newspaper report, but not of the other or official report.

Question. You have had the other?

Answer. Well, sir, I never read it.

Question. Did you have a pamphlet copy of it in your possession?

Answer. No, sir.

Question. You say you do not think yourself capable of doing justice to Mr. Humphries?

Answer. I am afraid I would not, and hence my disinclination to testify in regard to him.

Question. On account of some personal reason?

Answer. Personal matters. I do not speak to him when I meet him, nor he to me; nor have we since that affair occurred in the chancery court; nor has he attended the sittings of my court.

Question. If what you have stated in reference to a certain affidavit, about the withdrawal of a paper and the substitution of another, is correct; and if such an affidavit is on file in your court, is it not your duty to take notice of it judicially?

Answer. Well, sir, it may be my duty to take notice of it judicially.

Question. Have you ever done that?

Answer. The matter has not been disposed of finally. I have ordered it to be put on record. This occurred only last April, or, probably, May, and I have not regarded the matter as fully settled or determined, and have been much troubled in my mind to know exactly what I ought to do in the matter.

Question. Who filed that affidavit?

Answer. The deputy clerk.

Question. That was for the purpose of bringing it to your attention?

Answer. No, sir. I ordered it done; that was the grievance.

Question. You ordered it?

Answer. I ordered it done. The clerk stated to me the fact that Captain Humphries had taken this deposition from the court under his oath as an attorney, and that he had not returned it, and that, when called upon for it, he had denied all knowledge of it. He stated that circumstances had come to his knowledge from other testimony that led him to believe that Captain Humphries had taken the deposition with the intention of suppressing it; that another deposition had been filed in its place in Captain Humphries' own handwriting, which deposition was of different import from the former deposition. I asked him particularly if he was positive as to the truth of these facts. He made them known to me as I was holding court, sitting on the bench at the time, whispering them over the desk. He said that they were so. I commanded him then to reduce them to such form as would admit of their being put upon the record; to write them out and swear to them before the clerk of the court. I spoke of the matter to no one, being pained and amazed, not amazed exactly, either, but deeply pained and deeply troubled for various reasons—my personal friendliness with Captain Humphries, my friendship for his family and his family for mine, and the trouble which I believed would be consequent upon the whole matter, and which was afterward consequent upon the matter, by the knowledge of Captain Humphries character. I spoke to no one, however, but waited to see whether he would make use of the forgery or the deposition alleged to be forged. I waited for probably several months, from one term of court to the other. I do not willingly, I will say parenthetically, state these facts. I have kept them from the town as well as I was able, and have used them only for my own protection, but upon the trial I watched with care for this affidavit, this deposition. Captain Humphries rose and read the bill; it was a bill for divorce, in which no counsel were upon the other side. Divorce was claimed upon the ground of insanity, it being alleged that the woman was insane. She was living out of the State, and had no friend or counsel to represent her. In reading the bill Captain Humphries read what is a necessary allegation under our statute, which was to the effect that the woman was insane at the time of marriage. The original bill alleged before and after the marriage. I had called attention at a former term, when they tried to press the case through the court to a decision, to the fact that the bill needed amendment in that particular, and when Captain Humphries read it I was watching carefully the whole matter, and had it in my mind without speaking of it for months, as I have remarked. Possibly I may have spoken of it to my brother or father, or a member of the bar, but not publicly; but when Captain Humphries read the bill, he read clearly and distinctly the material allegation, which was, that she was insane before, and at the time thereof, and since that time; and I made a memorandum of it upon my desk, thinking the bill had been amended without leave of court. The operation of an amendment would have been to continue it one term, and the man Captain Humphries represented was said to be engaged to be married to another woman, and was exceedingly anxious to get the thing through in great haste, and, as he expressed it, he was nearly crazy on the subject, and I presumed that the leave had not been asked, because it would have operated as a continuance. As I said, I made a memorandum of this when read, and heard it through to the end, or rather I made no comment, but allowed the case to go on. Captain Humphries rose, and began to read the depositions in the case, of which perhaps a dozen were there, a large pile of papers, when he dropped them in a minute, and said, "Mr. Baldwin, do you read the depositions;" nobody was in court, probably not another attorney but himself; Mr. Baldwin was the deputy clerk of the commissioner. He said, "Read these depositions," and Mr. Baldwin rose, and read through all the depositions, but did not read the deposition which was said to have been forged, that of S. J. Johns, who was a relative of the woman, and whose testimony was considered very important, and whose old testimony, as given in the first deposition, the clerk told me was adverse to the complainant, or to the decree for divorce—a man, however, of no high standing. I was carefully and painfully waiting to see if that deposition would be read. Captain Humphries rose when the others were finished, and with a marvelous degree of assurance remarked, there was another paper the clerk had not read, a deposition of S. J. Johns, and began and read through a deposition which was favorable to the complainant. He then spoke for an hour or two in the case, read his authorities, and pressed me for a decree. He rose with the decree in his hand, and pressed me to make the decree without further consideration. He urged it, and pressed and pressed. He is a most pertinacious man in his manner before a court. He is generally known for that. I affected to be in doubt whether I would sign a decree or not. He was then holding the decree in his hand. I really wanted to get my hands on the papers. I leaned on my hand a little while, as though I was about to sign the decree, and at last remarked, "Hand me the decree, hand me the papers;" doubling them up in that way, [illustrating,] Captain Humphries at once strapped all the papers together, and handed them to me. As soon as I had them in my hand, I remarked, "I will take the case under advisement." Without saying a word, Captain Humphries took up his hat and left the court-room. Before I left my seat, however, I opened the bill and looked to see if it had been interpolated without leave of court, but it was not; but the allegation, which I regarded as essential, to wit, that the party was insane at the time, &c., was not in the bill, and had been interpolated by Captain Humphries in reading the bill. I had made a memorandum to that effect on a little piece of paper. I then looked at the deposition of S. J. Johns, and saw it was in the handwriting of Captain Humphries, which I knew well, and which was very different from the handwriting of the commissioner, whose duty it was to take all depositions, of course. It appeared to be signed by S. J. Johns in his own hand, and it was marked "file" by the clerk of the court. I thought it possible—barely possible—that the thing might have occurred through Captain Humphries ignorance of chancery practice, though it was hardly to be believed. The decree that he had tried to get me to sign was written out, and it is now on file; it was written in the same hand and with the same colored ink with this deposition of S. J. Johns, a very peculiar ink—a yellow-reddish, faded ink. I have ordered it to be kept carefully by the clerk, and it is to be found there in his office. It showed that they had been prepared out of the same inkstand, with this reddish-brown ink. I, however, will say that on the hearing or before the hearing of the case, I found the clerk had not filed this affidavit I had told him to file. Captain Humphries has the character of being a fighting man, a bullying man; he has been in repeated difficulties, and has the character of being very overbearing. I have known him, however, from childhood; we lived near one another and never had a difficulty; I knew him and he knew me, and we had always been friendly enough. I found that the clerk had not filed that deposition or affidavit as I had ordered. I told him to put his statement to me in writing at once, and file it. He put it in writing and showed it to me. He had put this paper with the papers, but had not filed it yet. He is a young man, however, and Captain Humphries had been to him talking with him, I understand; in fact, Captain Humphries told me on the street a few days before that he had spoken to Baldwin, and that Baldwin had disclaimed any intention to file it. I remarked to him that I was responsible. He is responsible for having told me the facts, for I did not know anything about them, but I am responsible for the filing of the deposition, presuming it was filed when the case came on. It was not filed, and I ordered the clerk to file it in my presence, which he there did. That was the difficulty I had in getting the affidavit filed. They took an appeal upon the case. It was decided adversely to Captain Humphries, and they, or his partner, took an appeal upon the case. He, however, had nothing to do with the case at the last term of the court, when it came on to be heard. He was not present when it was argued. They have never prosecuted the appeal, and the papers rest now, I presume, in the chancery office, and can be inspected by this committee. I will say that out of that grew a personal trouble between Captain Humphries and myself, just as I anticipated and expected; that I carried arms upon my person to protect myself from him; that I received two notes from him which were offensive, one of them very offensive; but that he never spoke to me on the subject, and, indeed, no word has ever passed between us from the time he closed that case to the present hour. I am willing in the matter to allow every charitable construction, and to believe that Captain Humphries did not fully appreciate the enormity of the offense he was committing. Under our statute, the mutilation of the public records is a crime punishable by imprisonment in the penitentiary, and forgery is punishable in the same way. I am willing to add that Captain Humphries may not have fully known he was committing the offense. He may possibly have thought that an attorney had a right to write a deposition; but the disappearance of the other which is not in the record and cannot be found, rather rebuts that belief, I must say.

Question. There has been no adjudication of this matter; it is simply an affidavit alleging the belief of the clerk, Baldwin?

Answer. He just alleges it as a fact in the affidavit that Captain Humphries did do thus and so. The clerk told me, however, I will add, general, that one Wood, an attorney, a young man who first appeared in this divorce case, now no longer here, and whose testimony cannot be had without great difficulty, as he has moved to Louisville, Kentucky, who was first engaged in this case—this, however, is mere hearsay; however, I will go on and state that this young man Wood told him that Captain Humphries had been to him to get him to abstract this first deposition taken, which was adverse to the divorce, or to the complainant, and that he had quit the case because of it, and that Humphries had been retained, with a fee of $200, because of the dissatisfaction on the part of Smith, the party applying for the divorce, with what he had done; that Humphries had asked him to withdraw this deposition, to get it out, and that he quit the case because of that. Baldwin told me that, I may add, at the time, I think, that he told me that Humphries had taken the deposition. I think it was all stated in the same connection, but I am not sure of that.

Question. Did he see Humphries take the deposition?

Answer. I do not know, sir. I do not know anything further relative to the abstraction and its suppression than I have stated, and that is altogether upon the hearsay of others.

Question. You know what he told you?

Answer. Yes, sir.

Question. That is what I am asking for. Did he tell you that he saw him take the deposition?

Answer. He told me that he had taken it. I think he said that he had delivered it to him, and that upon his calling for it Humphries said he had not it, and pretended to have no knowledge of it. These transactions referred to did not, of course, occur at one time, but happened in the course of several months, from the first to the last.

Question. The deposition of Johns that was on file was signed by Johns?

Answer. Yes, sir; taken regularly before the commissioner, Harris Baldwin, and Harris Baldwin says it was marked "filed." That is the universal practice, without exception; instantly upon closing a deposition it is marked "filed."

Question. Was this second deposition so marked?

Answer. Yes, sir, it was marked filed. Harley Hendrick, the clerk of the court, who is an intemperate man, told me that he was called over to Captain Humprhies's office and asked to sign the papers there and did it.

Question. Was Johns there?

Answer. I am not sure whether Johns was present or not. I may add that I went into Captain Humphries's office on one occasion, and found him and Johns and Smith all sitting together, and Humphries writing at the desk. I was on friendly terms with him and went in to get a book. My appearance seemed to create some confusion among them, which I noticed, but at the time I had no knowledge of this affair, and I only recalled it afterward; but what they were doing then may have had no connection whatever with this affair.

Question. You have no reason to believe that the second deposition was not signed by Johns?

Answer. No, sir; I have no reason to believe so. I know nothing about it. I have never been able to see Johns on the subject. I may say that I was told that Johns remarked there was something squally in the matter; that is, in the application for the divorce, and the case made out—that there was injustice done.

Question. Whom did he remark that to?

Answer. I do not remember now. That had no reference to this deposition, however, but referred to the merits of the original bill, and I then appointed Johns guardian *ad litem* for this insane person, the defendant. I never could get Johns to file any answer. He left the place and went off. His appointment at the time was strongly opposed by Captain Humphries, but he never filed any answer. He left the place, and I have never spoken to him since his leaving. I notified him the day after he had been appointed. Passing him on the street I remarked, "You have been appointed guardian *ad litem* in that case, and the court will expect you to be full and explicit and just in your statement." He wagged his head, and rolled his eyes, and made the impression rather that there were some very dark things in that case. I did not stop to seek or learn anything from him, as the case had not then been heard.

Question. Did he make it appear by rolling his eyes and wagging his head that there was something dark?

Answer. He turned his head to one side; it was his usual manner. You may strike out the expression "rolled his eyes." It was rather the impression on my mind that I was attempting to convey than a literal description of the facts.

Question. What did he say?

Answer. I do not remember. It was more his manner that I marked. He promised to file a faithful answer, but he did not then and never did. It is the only case I have met in my practice where I could not get a guardian *ad litem* to answer. The oldest attorney in the court said he had never heard of a case in which a guardian *ad litem* could not be made to answer before. I may add that I do not know anything against the honesty and integrity of purpose of this man Johns in this matter.

Question. Nevertheless, you have insinuated a good deal?

Answer. Whatever I have intimated, I do not know anything beyond what I have stated. My insinuations, as you call them, are based upon my solemn convictions from what I have stated. I do not know anything more except, possibly, the general character of Johns, and I am not sure that I am acquainted with that.

Question. Is his general character bad?

Answer. Yes, sir; Johns's general character is not good. I do not know that I am fully sure of that.

Question. Is it a proper thing for a chancellor to appoint a man whose character is bad a guardian *ad litem*.

Answer. It would not be, but it is proper to appoint the nearest of kin to represent a party, and for that reason alone I appointed Johns. The woman had been married and had come from a different State, a different place, and none here knew much about her, and I could not find any one who I thought was more suitable than a man who was related to her. I think he was her uncle or her cousin. His name was suggested to me as a proper person, as one who would know her and would attend to her interests.

Question. Do you mean to insinuate in that way that he was a party to improper practices?

Answer. No, sir; I think Johns, who is a laboring man, a mechanic, would be very ignorant of legal procedure, and in that way might have been made guilty of things which were irregular without any intention to prevent justice.

Question. It is not your purpose, then, to create an impression that he did anything wrong or improper in this matter?

Answer. It is not my desire to create any impression that would do injustice to Johns in any way; and, as I have said, I do not know that he has intentionally done anything wrong in the case. I have my own beliefs about it, but you have the full grounds of those beliefs, and you can judge as to how much credit they are entitled to. As far as I now remember and know, I have stated those grounds fully. Johns has left the county, or left this place, and I do not know where he is.

Question. The full grounds you stated were that he rolled his eyes a little.

Answer. Yes, sir; considerably. He is a man who has a significant way of talking. He is a man who—if I am pressed upon that—I may state, would, from his manner of speech, his actions and looks, impress you as much as by his words. He has a sort of significance in his ways, does not talk much or say much, but shakes his head over a thing; and you can form, perhaps, some conception of the manner of the man and the impression made upon my mind by my allusion to his rolling his eyes.

Question. You think there was deep design about it?

Answer. Yes, sir; some deep design. From what Johns said to me on the street I believe there was some deep design.

Question. What did he say?

Answer. I desire to change that; not from what he said, but from the impression conveyed by his manner; and his words, such as they were, aided to create that impression. I do not recollect them distinctly now. It was a matter to which, at the time, I did not attach that importance which after circumstances have given it, and which you can well see would be a sufficient explanation for my not being more accurate in my statement of his words.

Question. You formed the opinion then and there that there was some dark design?

Answer. I formed the opinion then and there that this divorce was sought upon improper and unjust grounds.

Question. Was it not your duty then to appoint some other person guardian *ad litem?*

Answer. I am possibly misapprehended right there. There was no impression on my mind that Johns was working in conjunction with anybody else against the interest of the defendant, but that the complainant was the party who was operating against her interests, and hence I was the more impressed with the fact at the time that he was the proper man for the place, that he knew the facts.

Question. Did he make any signs by which you understood the complainant to be designated?

Answer. Well, sir, the complainant's name was mentioned. I gave the information to him that he had been appointed. He may have received his notification regularly from the clerk, but, in passing him on the street, I remarked it to him, and then this little conversation passed, these few words, and the impression was made upon my mind, as I have before indicated, but not that he was in any conspiracy.

By Mr. RICE:

Question. But that he knew all about it?

Answer. That he knew certain facts which might establish the fact that there was a conspiracy to get a divorce unlawfully and unjustly.

By Mr. BLAIR:

Question. He made signs to signify that?

Answer. In words and signs together he made that impression; in his manner he made that impression on my mind; I passed it without giving it any great consideration at the time; at least I did not give it that consideration which I have since given it, and which after circumstances made me attach to it. I do not remember that I have referred to the fact before in any presence. I have talked very little about it as a matter of judicial propriety.

Question. Subsequent occurrences enabled you to interpret these signs better than you could at the moment?

Answer. Subsequent circumstances made me attach more importance to them than I did at the moment.

Question. You have no memory of any words used?

Answer. None at all that I now recollect—words to the effect that wrong was intended to the woman, that was all—was intended against her, and sought to be carried out by the complainant Smith, the husband. He made no allusion to Captain Humphries; he said nothing that directly referred to Captain Humphries in one way or another, and I could have believed what I thought he sought to impress upon me without implicating Captain Humphries in any way at all, for he might have been imposed upon by his own client in the matter. You see this was prior to these after occurrences which I have narrated, these things running over a period of nine or ten months. This case first came up at the July term, and was not settled until the April or May term of the following year. The decree was not given until April or May of the following year.

COLUMBUS, MISSISSIPPI, *November* 17, 1871.

JEREMIAH H. CASON sworn and examined.

By the CHAIRMAN:

Question. Where do you reside?

Answer. In Columbus, Mississippi.

Question. What is your occupation?

Answer. I am a minister of the Gospel. I am the pastor of the Baptist Church in this place.

Question. How long have you been acquainted with Major H. B. Whitfield, a citizen of this place?

Answer. I made his acquaintance in 1859.

Question. Have you been acquainted with him from that time to this?

Answer. Yes, sir, I have.

Question. Do you know what is his general character and standing in this community as a man of veracity or otherwise, or rather are you acquainted with his general character and standing in the community?

Answer. I suppose I am acquainted with it. Yes, sir; I will answer that affirmatively. I am acquainted with his general character.

Question. You may state what his character is for truth and veracity in this community.

Answer. I would rather just state my own convictions than to state for the community, if it would be admissible.

Question. You may state both.

Answer. I know—I would rather that was not written down—I want to say I know there is quite a variety of opinion about it; and, as there are two sides to the question, it would perhaps be not best to state it as a whole.

By Mr. BLAIR:

Question. State the facts.

Answer. My confidence in him was unshaken until the time he closed up his factory. I do not remember what time it was; it has been two or three years ago. At that time I heard a number of persons complaining of his treating them badly in financial transactions, and that shook my confidence in him at that time. I do not know how many persons, but a number of persons complained that he had obtained cotton from them under promise to return it, and failed to do so, when he ought to have known that he was not able to. I then heard nothing more against him until since his report before this Ku-Klux committee at Washington, but I have heard his report criticised until my confidence is shaken again in him.

By the CHAIRMAN:

Question. Who is that report criticised by; what political party?

Answer. Well, sir, the people generally have criticised his report. I have not associated with any persons of the radical party. That has been a small party. I do not know that I have heard the opinion of a single man of that party, but the citizens, I think, generally, were displeased with his report.

Question. Displeased because of what?

Answer. Well, sir, it was accused of being false; that he made statements that were thought to be false.

Question. False in the whole, or false in some particulars?

Answer. False in some particulars. He may have made some correct statements.

Question. Was that opinion of the community based upon a newspaper account of the evidence which he had given at Washington?

Answer. There was a newspaper account of that evidence, and there was a pamphlet, I understood the report of the committee, that has been in the community in pamphlet or book form. I have not seen it in book-form. I have heard there was such a thing.

Question. There were particular facts in that statement that he made at Washington, then, that were commented upon as untrue?

Answer. Yes, sir.

Question. Do you recollect what particular statements, attributed to him in that newspaper account, were criticised as untrue?

Answer. I have heard the statement that the Ku-Klux would not have disturbed men if they had been democrats, criticised generally. I have heard a good many persons speak of that.

Question. Did these persons who criticised this report deny the existence of Ku-Klux outrages in the community?

Answer. I suppose they did, sir.

Question. Was the criticism to the effect that it was untrue that there was such an organization here that had committed the outrages that he had described?

Answer. Yes, sir.

Question. From your own knowledge of Major Whitfield, from your long acquaintance with him, would you believe him under oath?

Answer. I would believe him if his business transactions were settled up, and if his report in the Ku-Klux matter were set straight; but these matters have shaken my confidence in him. Aside from them, I know nothing against him.

Question. Do you know that any statement he made in reference to these Ku-Klux outrages were untrue?

Answer. Of my personal knowledge I do not, though I have never examined that report carefully, and only have the general rumor of what he stated. Now, I have understood that he stated that radicals were not safe in this community, in this county, in their persons. I do not know that he stated it. I have heard that he stated it. I have a personal knowledge that that statement is not true. I know they are safe, for I have met them at all places, all parts of the city, in my duties as a minister, in the night and in the day-time, and I have met them in every part of the county unattended, and I know they are safe in their persons here, and have been ever since I have been in the city.

Question. Have you been informed that there have been outrages committed by disguised men, upon the persons of radicals, in any part of the county?

Answer. I have not, sir.

Question. Have you no information as to any negroes being whipped?

Answer. I have no information as to any negroes being whipped in the county. I may have heard of such a thing, but I have no information of it; and if I have heard of it, I do not remember it at this time. To the best of my knowledge I will say that I do not know of any negroes having been whipped in the county by any Ku-Klux or any disguised men.

Question. Have you any information of any persons being killed by disguised men in the county of Lowndes?

Answer. No, sir; I do not remember a single instance of a man being killed. If you will state some fact I may have my memory aroused, but I do not remember any person killed now, and I have been here three years.

Question. Have you any information of men in disguise having visited school-teachers and broken up their schools?

Answer. Well, now, I have heard—I know nothing of the matter, except what was stated in Whitfield's report before the committee on his testimony about schools. I was not aware of it until that time, and I never heard that question canvassed, and I do not know. I have no opinion on that subject. I saw that statement in Whitfield's report, in the newspaper account of it, and I have never heard that discussed.

Question. Your associations in this community, I take it, have not brought you in contact extensively with the colored people?

Answer. I have preached for the colored people frequently. I lecture the children in their Sabbath-school; I was at their Sabbath-school last Sabbath, and my relation with them has been very pleasant.

Question. Have you no information from the negroes of any Ku-Klux outrages having been inflicted upon them?

Answer. No, sir; none at all.

By Mr. BLAIR:

Question. You say your confidence in Whitfield was shaken at the time that he closed his factory?

Answer. Yes, sir.

Question. Did you ever happen to hear in regard to Major Whitfield obtaining money upon a contract with Governor Winston, of Alabama, to ship to Governor Winston the product of his factory, of his cotton crop, and upon which contract he obtained $4,000 from Governor Winston, of Mobile, Alabama, and then, in violation of this contract, shipped the product of his factory elsewhere, and obtained money for it?

Answer. That fact has not been brought to my knowledge. I heard that he had obtained money under false pretenses in the city of Mobile, and that an indictment was found against him in the court there, but the names of the parties I had not heard.

Question. You had heard, also, of his obtaining money from his brother?

Answer. Yes, sir; I have heard of that case.

Question. And giving his brother a deed of trust upon an interest in certain property, which property, it was afterward found upon a division, was in Oktibbeha County; that he immediately deeded it to his wife, and put the deed upon record, and thus defrauded his brother?

Answer. Yes, sir; I have heard that.

Question. You heard of his obtaining cotton from various persons?

Answer. Yes, sir; there is a member of our church, a widow, Mrs. Askew, makes a complaint of that sort.

Question. What does she say?

Answer. She says he bought out fourteen bales of her cotton, promising to return it in a few days; and he did not return it, and made her various promises to pay it at once without paying, she says; and told her a great many falsehoods about paying it, and she never could get anything from him.

Question. Do you know of his entering into a great many transactions of that character?

Answer. I have heard of a great many.

Question. Did you hear that he got ——

Answer. I will state that I heard of them, perhaps, because I was the pastor of his church, and persons made complaint to me, and a good many persons wanted me to put him upon his trial before our church; but he was away a good deal of his time, and I did not like to see proceedings instituted against a man absent, and since his political career commenced, I did not wish to have him tried, because I was afraid that his trial would have a political bearing; but we had agreed among ourselves not to have him put upon his trial, until after his election, and after his election we intended to have his conduct investigated by a committee of the church. I will state that Major Whitfield is willing, professes to be willing, for that investigation, and it will take place.

Question. You heard of a great many transactions similar to that of the Widow Askew?

Answer. Yes, sir.

Question. Did you hear of his obtaining cotton in that way from negroes?

Answer. I did not, sir. My attention has not been called to cases of that sort.

Question. Did you not hear that he had, in running his factory and supplying it with cotton, obtained, under various devices and promises, from the freedmen their little cotton?

Answer. My attention has not been called to those facts in regard to the freedmen.

Question. But it has to many other instances.

Answer. Yes, sir.

Question. You say your confidence in him was shaken?

Answer. Yes, sir. Truthful people made complaints that made an impression on my mind; but I had looked upon him as a very good man before.

Question. This talk was universal through the community, was it not?

Answer. Pretty general, sir.

Question. Known to pretty much the whole community?

Answer. Yes, sir.

Question. And great astonishment expressed?

Answer. Yes, sir; great astonishment.

Question. And the opinion of the community in regard to those transactions, and in regard to his testimony before the Ku-Klux committee had been canvassed extensively?

Answer. Yes, sir; I have heard a good deal about it.

Question. What is the opinion of the community as to his truth and veracity—the intelligent community?

Answer. (After a pause.) I must answer that question upon the expression I have of the community?

Question. Yes, sir.

Answer. I will say that the opinion of the community is decidedly unfavorable to him as a man of truth and veracity. I want it understood that, so far as I know, this opinion is based on his financial transactions, and this report before the committee. I want that understood. So far as I know, these have given the coloring to his reputation. Aside from those things no man stands higher than he did.

Question. Or was made a matter of more universal comment?

Answer. Yes, sir; for he was the leader of our Sabbath-school. He used to lecture in the church, and was a prominent man. He went to all our associations and conventions, and stood very high.

Question. The fact that he stood thus high—that he stood so fair before the community—would make it more difficult to shake the confidence of the people in him?

Answer. Yes, sir.

Question. If he had been a man of ordinary character, or of no positive character one way or the other, and such transactions had been reported and believed about him in the community, there would be no difficulty in stamping him, or much less difficulty in stamping him than a man who had formerly borne so high a character?

Answer. There would be less difficulty in locating a man of equivocal character than there would Major Whitfield.

Question. In other words, did he not have the benefit of a very high character and high connections in the country?

Answer. Yes, sir; high family relations; no man stood higher.

Question. It required an accumulation of evidence to break down the strong position he previously held?

Answer. Yes, sir; it certainly did; there is no doubt about that.

Question. Yet you say it is your opinion that the confidence of the community was actually shaken?

Answer. Actually shaken, sir; that is my candid opinion; I cannot help it; I firmly believe it, sir.

By Mr. RICE:

Question. About what time did his factory close?

Answer. I have a little flush of headache to-day, and my mind does not act just as readily as it will at other times.

Question. Was it before or after the legislature of 1869?

Answer. His factory closed before I came to this place—three years ago.

Question. He has run for the legislature since then on the democratic ticket, has he not?

Answer. Yes, sir.

Question. And been supported by the democratic community here?

Answer. Yes, sir; for the legislature.

Question. The next blur in regard to his character arose out of this evidence given in Washington, did it?

Answer. Yes, sir; the next attack that I heard upon him as a man of truth and veracity grew out of this. I have stated that.

By the CHAIRMAN:

Question. Was a good deal of prejudice created against Major Whitfield by the fact of his joining the republican party?

Answer. Yes, sir.

COLUMBUS, MISSISSIPPI, *November* 17, 1871.

EDWARD CROSBY (colored) sworn and examined.

By the CHAIRMAN:

Question. Where do you live?

Answer. Right near Aberdeen—ten miles east of Aberdeen.

Question. State whether you were ever visited by the Ku-Klux; and, if so, under what circumstances.

Answer. I have been visited by them. They came to my house, and came into my house. I went out to get my little child a drink of water and saw them coming. My wife asked me what they were. I said I reckoned they were what we called Ku-Klux. It looked like there were thirty-odd of them, and I didn't know but what they might interfere with me, and I just stepped aside, out in the yard to the smoke-house. They came up there, and three of them got down and came in the house and called for me, and she told them I had gone over to Mr. Crosby's. They asked her if I didn't have right smart business there, and she said she didn't know; that I had gone over there to see my sister, she reckoned. She didn't know but they might want something to do to me, and interfere with me, and they knocked around a while and off they went.

Question. Was this in the night-time?

Answer. Yes, sir.

Question. Were they disguised?

Answer. Yes, sir.

Question. Had you been attempting to get up a free-school in your neighborhood?

Answer. Yes, sir.

Question. Colored school?

Answer. Yes, sir.

Question. Do you know whether their visit to you had reference to this effort?

Answer. No, sir; I don't know only this: I had spoken for a school, and I had heard a little chat of that, and I didn't know but what they heard it, and that was the thing they were after.

Question. Were their horses disguised?

Answer. Yes, sir.

Question. What time in the night was this?

Answer. I don't know; along in the fore part of the night, as near as I can get at it.

Question. Did you know any of the men?

Answer. No, sir; I didn't get close enough to know them. I could have known them, I expect, if I was close up, but I was afraid to venture.

Question. Did they ever come back?

Answer. No, sir.

Question. What do you know as to the whipping of Green T. Roberts?

Answer. Only from hearsay. He told me himself. They didn't whip him. They took him out and punched him and knocked him about right smart, but didn't whip him.

Question. Was he a colored man?

Answer. He was a white man—a neighbor of mine.

Question. Who took him out?

Answer. The Ku-Klux.

Question. Did he tell you they came after night for him?

Answer. Yes, sir, after night. I was there only a few days after that.

Question. How many did he tell you?

Answer. He didn't tell me how many there were. He didn't know himself; but I understood there were seventy-odd. They visited Mr. Dowdell, also, the same night.

Question. Were these men also disguised; both themselves and their horses?

Answer. Yes, sir.

Question. What, if anything, do you know of any colored men being afraid to vote the republican ticket and voting the democratic ticket at the election this month, in order to save their property, and to save themselves from being outraged?

Answer. Well, sir, the day of the election there was, I reckon, thirty or forty; I didn't count them, but between that amount; they spoke of voting the radical ticket. It was my intention to go for the purpose. I had went around and saw several colored friends on that business, and the morning of the election I went there very soon. I knew some of the party would come in and maybe they would prevent us from voting as we wanted to. I called for the republican tickets and they said there was none on the ground. I knocked around amongst them, and I called a fellow named Mr. Dowdell, and asked if there would be any there; he said he didn't know; he asked me how I was going to vote; I told him my opinion, but I was cramped for fear. They said if we didn't act as they wanted they would drop us at once. There is only a few of us, living amongst them like lost sheep where we can do the best; and they were voting and they stood back and got the colored population and pushed them in front and let them vote first, and told them there was no republican tickets on the ground. I didn't see but three after I voted. Shortly after I voted, Mr. James Wilson came with some, and a portion of the colored people had done voting. I met Mr. Henderson; I was going on to the other box at the Baptist church. He asked if there were any colored voters there; I told him there was thirty or forty, and there was no republican tickets there. Mr. Wilson had some in his pocket, but I didn't see them. I saw that I was beat at my own game, and I had got on my horse and dropped out.

Question. Who told you that unless the colored people voted the democratic ticket it would be worse for them?

Answer. Several in the neighborhood. Mr. Crosby said as long as I voted as he voted I could stay where I was, but he says, "Whenever Ned votes my rights away from me I cast him down."

Question. Was he a democrat?

Answer. A dead-out democrat.

Question. Did you hear any other white men make the same declaration?

Answer. Not particular; I only heard them talking through each other about the colored population. I heard Mr. Jerome Lamb—he lived nigh Athens—tell a fellow named Aleck that lived on his place, he spoke to him and asked him if he was going to vote as he did; Aleck told him he was—he did this in fear, mind you—and Aleck went and voted, and after he voted he said, "Aleck, come to me;" says he, "Now, Aleck, you have voted?" Aleck says, "Yes, sir;" he said, "Well, now, Aleck, you built some very nice houses. Now, I want you to wind your business up right carefully. I am done with you; off of my land."

Question. Had Aleck voted the republican ticket?

Answer. Yes, sir.

Question. Did all the colored men except these three vote the democratic ticket that day?

Answer. Up at Grub Springs all voted the democratic ticket. There was no republican ticket given to the colored people at all.

Question. Did they vote the democratic ticket from fear that they would be thrown out of employment or injured?

Answer. That was their intention. You see pretty nigh every one of them was the same way I was, but there was none there; and then they were all living on white people's land, and were pretty fearful. The Ku-Klux had been ranging around through them, and they were all a little fearful.

Question. Do you think they were all radical in sentiment, and would have been glad to have voted the radical ticket if uninfluenced?

Answer. They would. They had a little distinction up amongst themselves—the white and colored people. One of them said, "Ned, put in a republican ticket." Well, there was none on the ground, and I remarked, "If there is any radical tickets on the ground I will take one of them, and I will not take a democratic ticket, and I will fold them up and drop that in the box, and they will never tell the difference," and it got out that I had voted the radical ticket, and some were very harsh about it.

Question. Would the colored people of your county vote the radical ticket if left alone?

Answer. Well, sir, I suppose they would have done it.

By Mr. BLAIR:

Question. Whose land were you living on, Ned?

Answer. Mr. Crosby's.

Question. You say Mr. Crosby asked you to vote the democratic ticket?

Answer. He asked me would I do it, and I told him I would. He told my neighbor right there if Ned would vote the democratic ticket Ned could stay where he was, but whenever Ned voted against him Ned was off.

Question. You told him you were going to vote the democratic ticket?

Answer. Yes, sir; for fear; but my intention was the whole time to vote the radical ticket.

Question. Mr. Crosby never tell you so?

Answer. He never told me so, but he said it right there, and he came in the field where I was picking cotton, and said, "You propose to be a great democrat, but I have found out what you are." I says, "Master, I am a democrat." He says, "I will find out. Go ahead, sir; I will find out."

Question. So he did not believe you exactly?

Answer. He didn't believe me exactly. The reason I told him this was for fear. All of our colored population since the Ku-Klux have been visiting about, have all been in fear of trouble. There has been nights I didn't sleep more than an hour, and if there had been a stick cracked very light, I would have sprung up in the bed.

Question. He never told you must leave his land?

Answer. No, sir; not to me. I only heard it from a particular friend of his in the neighborhood.

Question. How do you know but what the neighbor told a story?

Answer. He is a man of truth, and he is there. I went down the next night or so after that to get some vinegar, and I was talking about moving off, and that they didn't treat me right, and he told me what Mr. Crosby had said.

Question. Did you talk to him about moving?

Answer. No, sir; to another neighbor. He wanted to buy some land.

Question. Did this man who told you this want you to come to him?

Answer. No, sir; he didn't have land sufficient for me. He did not have more than enough for himself.

Question. Did he talk to you about going to another place?

Answer. No, sir.

Question. When you went there for the vinegar and talked about going somewhere else, did he encourage you to go?

Answer. No, sir; not at all; only I told him what I wanted to do; that I didn't think I was getting my rights.

Question. When you went in to vote, you say you did not find any republican tickets?

Answer. There was none there until after I had voted, and then only three.

Question. Whose fault was that?

Answer. They told us there would be none on the ground—us colored people.

Question. Whose fault was that?

Answer. There it is now. I don't know whose fault it was. Mr. Anderson said he had sent some there.

Question. By whom?

Answer. By Mr. Wilson, I think. I would not be certain if Mr. James Wilson had them in his pocket. I didn't see them until I got on my horse.

Question. If they did not bring any republican tickets there, it was their own fault?

Answer. Mr. Anderson brought some, but it was too late.

Question. But it was no fault of the democrats that the republican tickets were not there. It was none of their business to bring them?

Answer. It was not their fault, but they said there would be none on the ground, and pushed the colored population right in to vote.

Question. The colored people were so anxious to vote that they would vote any ticket rather than not vote at all?

Answer. The men came with the ones on the place, riding their horses and mules, and they gave back to them and put them right in foremost.

Question. That was giving away to them?

Answer. It was in one sense, but giving them no chance to choose their tickets.

Question. That was not the fault of the democrats that the republicans did not bring them tickets to vote, but the democrats stood back and gave them a privilege of voting?

Answer. They just wrote their tickets out and gave them the tickets to vote.

Question. They gave them their horses to come to the election?

Answer. Yes, sir; I came with them.

Question. You have not complained of that?

Answer. Yes, sir; I have.

Question. What, the lending of the horses?

Answer. No, sir; but if they would have given them a fair showing after they got on the ground to choose their tickets and vote as they got ready, they would have all voted the republican ticket, no doubt of it, because I had went around and saw them; but they interfered. You see they lived on the land, and just as they voted the republican ticket they were all done. We all understood that. We went in rotation pretty well.

Question. Who is Mr. Anderson?

Answer. Mr. Hop Anderson.

Question. Is he the sheriff of the county?

Answer. No, sir; but his son is.

Question. He brought the tickets out?

Answer. Yes, sir. He is outside of the door there now.

Question. Did he bring the tickets to this poll?

Answer. Yes, sir; and Mr. James Wilson, but the colored people had got through voting.

Question. They did not wait for the tickets?

Answer. No, sir; they told them there would be none on the ground.

Question. What did those people who visited your house say to you; they just asked where you were?

Answer. Yes, sir; they just asked where I was.

Question. They did not make any threats?

Answer. None at all.

Question. They probably just wanted to see you?

Answer. I expect they did.

Question. Anxious to shake hands with you?

Answer. I had rather not that they shake hands with me.

Question. It seems that they were more friendly than you were?

Answer. I didn't care about meeting them at all. I know a man that is a friend would not come in disguise. I took them to be men, as well as I knew. I took them to be men.

Question. You did not know any of them?

Answer. No, sir; none at all.

Question. Who is Mr. Green T. Roberts?

Answer. He is a man that lives up there in the country with us—a white gentleman.

Question. What are his politics?

Answer. Democratic.

Question. You say they knocked him about right smartly?

Answer. Yes, sir.

Question. On account of politics?

Answer. No, sir.

Question. What for?

Answer. He is a man that stays at home and attends to his own business. His wife is dead, and he took a woman there to take care of his children, and some of them got miffed up at it, and I heard talk that the paper-faces were going to visit him; and sure enough, one night they came. Some call them Ku-Klux and some paper-faces.

Question. It was thought that he was visited for taking this woman there?

Answer. Yes, sir.

Question. Who is Mr. Dowdell?

Answer. He is a doctor living right there, close in the settlement.

Question. They visited him that night?

Answer. Yes, sir; the night they visited Mr. Roberts they visited him.

Question. What for?

Answer. I don't know what it was for. I am not able to tell.

Question. Did you hear anything about it?

Answer. I heard different speeches about it. I didn't hear what it was about at all.

Question. What were his politics?

Answer. I don't know. He voted the democratic ticket, but I don't know what his intentions had been. He had been accused of being a republican, but I don't know what his politics was.

Question. You say he voted the democratic ticket?

Answer. Yes, sir; he voted the democratic ticket.

Question. You went to Mr. Dowdell and asked him for tickets?

Answer. I didn't go to him. I went and asked him as a friend how he was going to vote. I didn't care about coming out before too many people on election day.

Question. You voted the radical ticket?

Answer. No, sir; I didn't.

Question. Did you vote at all?

Answer. I voted the democratic ticket.

Question. What did you do that for?

Answer. There were republican tickets on the ground, but not until I had voted. Then I saw three.

Question. Who was Mr. James Harson?

Answer. James Wilson, you mean?

Question. Is he a republican?

Answer. Yes, sir.

Question. Was he there?

Answer. Yes, sir.

Question. Did he vote the republican ticket?

Answer. Yes, sir; they say he did. He said so himself this morning.

Question. What do you mean by saying Mr. Crosby said if you voted his ticket it was all right, but if not he would cast you down? You did not mean that he threatened to whip you?

Answer. I didn't mean that.

Question. But that he would employ other men?

Answer. He might employ other men, or something or other might happen, I don't know what. All of us live a little in doubt. We didn't know hardly what to be at times.

Question. Do you know that Mr. Jerome Lamb asked Aleck if he was going to vote as he did?

Answer. Yes, sir.

Question. How do you know?

Answer. I was right there.

Question. You heard Aleck say he was?

Answer. Yes, sir.

Question. And you know he made him leave his land?

Answer. I don't know that he left. I don't know whether he has got his crop gathered yet.

Question. Then he has not left yet?

Answer. Not as I know of.

Question. Do you know how Aleck voted?

Answer. He voted a republican ticket. That is what they told me. He went up to the box and put—I didn't see him put it in, but he went up to the box, and came back then; and Mr. Lamb told him to come back to him after he voted.

Question. What place is this at which you vote?

Answer. Grubb Springs.

COLUMBUS, MISSISSIPPI, *November* 17, 1871.

JOHN H. ANDERSON sworn and examined.

By the CHAIRMAN:

Question. Please state your residence and occupation.

Answer. I reside east of Aberdeen about six miles, in Monroe County, and I am a farmer by occupation.

Question. The committee have called you to learn what information you have in relation to the existence of the Ku-Klux Klan in your part of the country, or of men banded together and masked, riding and prowling through the country in the night-time. You may give what information you have upon that subject.

Answer. Well, sir, I am fully satisfied that there has been an organized band or bands in the county of Monroe for the last year until recently. I do not think there has been any riding there very recently, but previous to that they were riding about twice a week—once or twice a week.

By Mr. RICE:

Question. Previous to what time?

Answer. Previous to the arrest of these men alleged to be Ku-Klux.

By the CHAIRMAN:

Question. You speak of arrests made under process from the Federal court?

Answer. Yes, sir; previous to that.

Question. This put a stop to this riding?

Answer. Yes, sir; they have ceased since that. There has been none since that that I know of.

Question. Have you ever seen these bands themselves?

Answer. Yes, sir. I have seen them on two occasions.

Question. You may state the circumstances.

Answer. Well, the first I saw was the night that Mr. Huggins was whipped.

Question. How large was that number?

Answer. Those that I saw that night were, I think, ten in number.

Question. Did they ride past your farm?

Answer. No, sir. I was some six miles east of my farm, on the old Hamilton road.

Question. Did you meet them?

Answer. No, sir. I didn't meet them. I was near the road and saw them pass.

Question. Were they disguised?

Answer. Yes, sir, and riding quite fast. It was a little after dark, but quite early in the evening.

Question. How far from the place where Mr. Huggins was staying?

Answer. About five miles, and they were going in that direction.

Question. In the direction of where he was whipped?

Answer. Yes, sir. I had learned that evening that the Ku-Klux would ride that night, and that they expected to have some trouble near Ross's mill, where the whipping occurred, but there was no name mentioned.

Question. Upon what other occasion did you see them riding?

Answer. It was after that. I was out in the same section of country, and I heard something that I thought was wild geese, and I stopped my horse. I had been out over the Buttahatchie. I am deputy sheriff—my son is the sheriff—I was out over there attending to some business, and was going home. It was some 10 or 11 o'clock, and I heard something similar, as I thought, to wild geese. I stopped my horse and listened. They were nearly a quarter of a mile from me, and I heard the horses' feet. I listened then, and I heard various noises, and I was satisfied that it was the Ku-Klux; and I rode outside of the road and hitched my horse, and got back close to the road, behind a tree, and they passed me within about ten steps. They made all manner of noises conceivable, nearly.

Question. How large a troop was riding at that time?

Answer. I should think about forty, according to the best calculation I could make.

Question. Were they and their horses disguised?

Answer. Yes, sir; they and their horses were disguised?

Question. Did you hear of any mischief committed that night?

Answer. I did not.

Question. Do you know where they went to?

Answer. I do not.

Question. How late in the evening was this?

Answer. I could not tell exactly, but I think between 10 and 11 o'clock at night.

Question. You have heard of various other ridings beside those which you have seen?

Answer. A great many; a great many. I was deputy sheriff, as I remarked. The Ku-Klux took three negroes out of jail. I was the deputy, and my son was jailer. I followed them, and held the inquest over two of the negroes that they killed.

Question. You refer to the Flints?

Answer. Yes, sir; the Flints. I was the officer who summoned the jury, and the justice of the peace, and held the inquest on them.

Question. Have you heard of numerous whippings inflicted by these Ku-Klux upon negroes?

Answer. O, yes, sir. A negro was taken one night not two miles from me, and killed. That was Aleck Page.

Question. I speak particularly now of whippings. Have you heard of many instances of the kind?

Answer. Repeated, sir; repeated, sir. There was one living not more than two and a half miles off—Santee Butler—that was whipped by them.

Question. State the particulars of that case.

Answer. They whipped him. I never knew the particulars. I think the offense alleged against him was that he was too intimate with some white woman there; that was the alleged offense.

Question. Was he severely whipped?

Answer. He told me he was. I don't know. I didn't see it, but he told me they whipped him very badly. He told me so himself.

Question. Do you recollect any other case of whipping?

Answer. They got after a negro named Andy Burnes, in the same neighborhood, and he came to my house about daylight. They shot at him, and it went through his pantaloons, just across his knee, but he got away from them. There were several in the neighborhood of the Willis's. They whipped one of the Willis negroes.

Question. Do you refer to Aleck Willis?

Answer. I do not know what his other name is; he is one of the Willis boys. They whipped Simon Dunham, and, I think, they whipped three down there, sir. They have killed about nine negroes in our county and one white man, in about twelve months.

Question. The Ku-Klux did?

Answer. Disguised men did. I think they called themselves now, from the best information I could get, "Seventy-six."

Question. Have you any information as to how extensive this organization is in Monroe County?

Answer. Well, sir, it has been pretty extensive.

Question. How large is it represented to be?

Answer. Well, sir, I expect, from the best information I can get, that it is all of three hundred strong.

Question. Have you made it your study to learn as much as you could in relation to this organization and its objects?

Answer. In some degree I have, because they have threatened to lift me out of my boots, as it is termed. I have learned that from several sources. I was solicited by one of the Ku-Klux, as I supposed then and suppose now, to join them. I gave him some very sound advice on the subject that displeased them, and they threatened that if I didn't mind, they would lift me out of my boots.

Question. Did he tell you anything about the objects of the organization when he was soliciting you to join it?

Answer. Well, he said they were disposed to keep the negro in his right position, and they knew I was in sentiment a Ku-Klux. He said he was not a Ku-Klux, but he could find the Ku-Klux if I would go and join them with him.

Question. Did he give you any information about the men who belonged to the organization?

Answer. O, no; he denied being a Ku-Klux, but told me what I say—that he knew I was a Ku-Klux in sentiment; that all white men were Ku-Klux in sentiment; and he could find the Ku-Klux if I meant to join them.

Question. Was he a man of respectability?

Answer. Yes, sir; a respectable man; a clever man.

Question. A man of property?

Answer. No, sir; rather a poor man; a middle-aged man.

Question. A man of family?

Answer. Yes, sir; he has grown children.

Question. What is your information as to the character of the men who compose this Klan or order?

Answer. Well, sir, my own opinion from every information I have got is this: There is a road that, immediately after you cross the Tombigbee, runs almost northeast. The river divides the two divisions; then from the road the river is about half-way between the two, and that section of country thereabouts is what they call the old Hamilton road to the upper end of the county, and to the right of that country the people with a few exceptions—say of old men—belong, in my opinion, to the Ku-Klux Klan, or the "Seventy-six," as they call themselves.

By Mr. BLAIR:

Question. That is east of the river?

Answer. East of the Tombigbee river and east of the Buttahatchie River, adjoining the Alabama line.

By the CHAIRMAN:

Question. Are they men of property?

Answer. Some of them are right good livers; but as a general thing it is rather a poor country. I think the object, I am clearly of opinion—have I the right to give that?

The CHAIRMAN. Yes, sir.

The WITNESS. From all the information I have, I am clearly of opinion that the object was to intimidate the negro, and either vote him or keep him from voting, for I had heard it bragged of that they intended either to vote him or keep him from voting, and not only him, but the white man that saw proper to vote and act for himself; and, more than that, I do not believe that any white man that saw proper to vote the republican ticket would have been permitted to live on the east side of the Tombigbee River if there hadn't been a stop put to them; that is my honest conviction.

Question. Was there any concerted, earnest movement made by the leading men of Monroe County to put a stop to these outrages?

Answer. None that I know of. I solicited a relation of Judge Gholson, knowing that they all claimed to be democrats over there, and believing that General Gholson had more influence than any other man in the county of Monroe with them; I sent a relation to him, to request of him his assistance in helping us to put a stop to it, but he professed utter ignorance, and if he ever did anything, I never knew it.

Question. Is it your opinion that if General Gholson were to take the stump and canvass the county, denouncing these outrages and striving earnestly to break up this organization, he could do it?

Answer. I do, sir.

Question. Do you believe that the democratic party in that county could break it up?

Answer. I believe the leaders of the democratic party could. I have advised with the leaders myself there. Some of the best men on our side of the river told them of the evil results, and asked them, as a favor to the country and to the citizens, to assist in putting a stop to it.

Question. What answers would they give?

Answer. Some would answer in this way; that they didn't know who to approach, or how to begin to put that down. Some of the old men, the good citizens, would say that they didn't know how to commence; that they were willing, but didn't know how to start. I never said anything to General Gholson personally, but James Moore, his relative, did, as he told me. He had requested the judge to assist him.

Question. Is General Gholson supposed to look with favor or approbation upon the practices of the Ku-Klux Klan?

Answer. I will not do the judge injustice. I would not do that knowingly; but there are a great many in the county, sir, think that the judge could have put it down long ago if he had seen proper to do so.

Question. Has he ever been known to denounce these outrages, or make any earnest effort to stop them?

Answer. I never heard of it.

Question. What, in your opinion, would be the effect of a severe resolution of censure, adopted by a democratic convention in the county, denouncing these outrages; what would be its effect in putting a stop to them?

Answer. I believe in the first place that the Ku-Klux are all democrats. I do not say that all democrats are Ku-Klux, but I believe that all Ku-Klux are democrats, and I believe they could stop it if they wanted to do it.

Mr. BLAIR. Judge Gholson has been before this committee, Mr. Anderson, and he has testified that he has used all his influence to stop it.

The WITNESS. In what way, general?

Mr. BLAIR. That is his testimony; that he had used his influence in every way that he could.

The WITNESS. I have been in the county a good while and at every public meeting, and I have never heard, from any source, that Judge Gholson made any public demonstration to stop it. He may have given some advice recently, but if he has I have never heard of it.

Question, (By Mr. BLAIR.) I did not ask you if you had ever heard it, but he has given that testimony under oath.

Answer. Well, I suppose he knows whether he has or not. I have no right to question what advice he gave. I never heard of it. I never heard of any public demonstration by him.

Question. Do you believe he would make such a statement under oath unless it was true?

Answer. I believe he may have given some advice; I never heard of his making a public demonstration.

Question. Do you believe Judge Gholson would state, under oath, that he had given his influence, and all his influence, to stop it, if it were not true? Do you believe that he would state things that were not so?

Answer. I don't reckon the general would state anything but what is correct about it; but I never have known him to do anything of that kind.

Question. His reputation for truth and veracity is unquestioned?

Answer. Yes, sir; I never heard it questioned as far as that is concerned; but I am fully satisfied that the general has never made any public demonstration, or I certainly would have heard of it.

Question. General Gholson is under disabilities, is he not?

Answer. Yes, sir.

Question. A great many of your leading men are?

Answer. I am myself, sir. I was sheriff at the time of the war.

Question. And you are now acting as deputy sheriff?

Answer. Yes, sir. My son is sheriff. He was appointed by Governor Alcorn and elected the other day.

Question. What is your son's name?

Answer. Stephen C. Anderson.

Question. Do you know whether he was subpœnaed to come here yesterday?

Answer. I heard this young gentleman [the sergeant-at-arms] say he telegraphed him. I left Aberdeen—I was in Aberdeen day before yesterday, and he knew nothing of it then. He knew I was coming here, but he didn't know anything about a subpœna for himself. They telegraphed him yesterday evening, perhaps.

Question. Does he live in the town of Aberdeen?

Answer. Yes, sir. His office is at the court-house; but he may have been off on business.

Question. Would it be possible for him to come here to-day?

Answer. He will be here to-night, I expect, on the train.

Question. What time to-night?

Answer. The train comes in some time to-night, between nine and ten o'clock, I think.

By Mr. RICE:

Question. It comes to Artesia at nine o'clock and thirty minutes, and reaches here about 11 or 12 o'clock, does it not?

Answer. Yes, sir. He will be down on the train to-night, I reckon, sir.

By the CHAIRMAN:

Question. You are well acquainted, of course, with Colonel Reynolds?

Answer. Yes, sir.

Question. Is he a man of influence and position in your county?

Answer. Quite so, sir; very much of a gentleman. He is in every point of view.

Question. Prominent in the democratic party?

Answer. Yes, sir.

Question. A man who exercises considerable influence over the minds of the people of your county?

Answer. The people have a great deal of confidence in Colonel Reynolds. He stands as fair as anybody.

Question. Have you known him to come out and take any public position against these outrages, making an earnest effort to put a stop to it?

Answer. I never heard of it.

Question. Have you heard of any denunciation by him against this Ku-Klux organization.

Answer. Not a particle.

Question. Do you think if he were to take a position of that kind, and endeavor to break up this organization and bring it into bad odor in that community, his efforts would be successful?

Answer. I think they would be; he would have a great deal of influence in the party. He stands as fair as anybody. I am fully satisfied that if Gholson, and Sales, and Reynolds, and the prominent democrats of the county were to use their influence, they could have quieted it long since.

By Mr. BLAIR:

Question. You say you believe all the Ku-Klux are democrats?

Answer. I do, sir; but I do not say that all democrats are Ku-Klux. Understand that, general, but I believe that all the Ku-Klux are democrats. Off in that region of country over there where they have been raiding and tearing up the country so, the last one of them voted the democratic ticket, and they denounced every man that didn't chime in with them. That is the reason, I say, that I honestly believe that if there had not been a stop put to it, a man that did not belong to the democratic party, or did not vote the democratic ticket, would not have been permitted to live there. Doctor Dowdell told me he wanted to vote the republican ticket, but, he said, "I live here among the Ku-Klux, and I am afraid, and I voted the democratic ticket." The Ku-Klux had him twice; he told me so himself. I don't know what for. He was one of Alcorn's appointees. He said he was actually afraid of his life, and afraid to vote the republican ticket.

Question. Did you not vote it?

Answer. No, sir; I voted the radical ticket, and I voted an open ticket, and told them I did, and I wanted them to know I was twenty-one years old, and voted that independent of any one.

Question. Have you been molested on account of your voting?

Answer. No, sir.

Question. No Ku-Klux have visited you?

Answer. No, sir.

Question. They never terrified you?

Answer. No, sir. I have been threatened by them, and many a night have I listened for them, many a night.

Question. Who threatened you?

Answer. Well, I have understood it from various sources that this Ku-Klux gang were coming. This very man that asked me to join it told me.

Question. Who is he?

Answer. I can't think of his name now. I will think of it directly. He solicited me to join it the month after Christmas, and I told him no, I would not. I was a peace officer, and didn't believe in it no how. The day my son and myself hung a negro, by virtue of law, at Athens, he came to me, and told me some ten or twelve of the boys, as he called them, had visited him in reference to what had passed between him and me on the Ku-Klux business, and to know what I said about the Ku-Klux. He said he told them I had not said anything but what a gentleman had a right to say; that I had given some good advice of what would be the evil results if they did not quit it. They had understood I had cursed them and abused them, and said a great deal about them and him which I didn't say. He told me they had come to see him in reference to it, and he had told them that I had not said anything more than a gentleman had a right to do, and he said they left then, satisfied. I understood from various sources that they had threatened me. There is no doubt about that at all.

Question. What other source did you hear it from?

Answer. He didn't tell me that they threatened me; he told me they came to see him. Well, I heard it from a freedman in the first place, that heard some of them talking what they intended if I didn't mind; that I was talking a little too much. And I heard it from a particular friend of mine. I do not know that I am bound to give his name. I am satisfied that he was a Ku-Klux. He told me not a month ago that if it had not been for him and some other of my friends, they would have molested me; but he did not say in what way.

Question. But they never have molested you?

Answer. No, sir; they never have; but it seems as if they had a tolerably strong desire, too; and if it had not been for some influential men in their party, they would have done it. It was Nathan Pulham that asked me to join the Ku-Klux. He just remarked this; he asked if I didn't want to join the Ku-Klux. I told him no. He remarked that he was satisfied I was a Ku-Klux in principle, and, says he, "I am no Ku-Klux, but," says he, "I can find them if you will go and join them." I told him no, I didn't want to join them. It was him that told me afterward, after the conversation between him and me in reference to the Ku-Klux Klan, that eight or ten had come to see him, and that they had misunderstood what I had stated to him, and came to see him in reference to it.

Question. I understood you to say you were a republican?

Answer. I am. I have always been a Henry Clay whig—born and raised in East Tennessee, Hawkins County—but have voted the republican ticket recently.

Question. Did he suppose a Henry Clay whig and a republican would join the Ku-Klux?

Answer. I do not know what he supposed.

Question. Did he know you were a Henry Clay whig and a republican?

Answer. Yes, sir; he knew I was a republican, because everybody knew that.

Question. He supposed you were made out of the right material to make a Ku-Klux, did he?

Answer. I do not know what he supposed. He just remarked to me that he knew I was a Ku-Klux in principle.

Question. His idea, then, does not conform with yours?

Answer. He was mistaken in the man; entirely mistaken.

Question. He was not mistaken about your being a Henry Clay whig and a radical?

Answer. No, sir; I am no radical; I am a republican. There is a good deal of difference between a radical and a republican.

Mr. BLAIR. Not much.

The WITNESS. Right smart. One is extreme, while the other is not extreme. A man could be a republican and not be a radical.

Question. He knew your position?

Answer. Yes, sir.

Question. When he invited you to join?

Answer. He knew I had been a whig, because I had been a whig ever since I had been in Monroe County, and always in a minority; yet I was elected sheriff when there was four hundred and fifty political majority against me.

Question. He knew you were a republican?

Answer. I suppose he did. I never kept it a secret.

Question. These things were pretty well known in regard to who was a republican? There were not many of them among the white men?

Answer. Not many of them east of the Bigby River. There were a few, but not many. They were very odious, and denounced in the bitterest terms.

Question. Therefore, it was more than likely that he knew your position?

Answer. I have no doubt he did.

Question. Yet, knowing your position as an old line whig and a republican, he invited you to join the Ku-Klux, saying he knew you were a Ku-Klux in principle?

Answer. He told me so, but I told him he was mistaken.

Question. It shows that he had a different idea about the composition of the Ku-Klux from what you have—that they are all democrats?

Answer. I do not know of any one of my own knowledge that is, or that I think is a Ku-Klux, but what I believe is a democrat.

Question. It seems he had a different opinion about that?

Answer. Well, I do not know what his opinion was; he did not express it on that point.

Question. Did he not manifest his opinion to you?

Answer. He said he knew I was a Ku-Klux in principle. I told him he didn't know any such thing.

Question. You think he knew more about the Ku-Klux than you did?

Answer. I was satisfied he was a Ku-Klux at the time I was talking to him, and ever since.

Question. If he did know about them, and was a Ku-Klux, and he made that estimate of the material, do you not think that, in all probability, you are mistaken as to the kind of material in the Ku-Klux order?

Answer. No, sir; I do not think I am. I am just as well satisfied of that as that I am alive.

Question. Do you not believe that he knows more about them than you do?

Answer. Of course I do. He was a Ku-Klux, I believe.

Question. He probably knows more of the material in the Ku-Klux order than you do?

Answer. Of course he does.

Question. He did not consider that you, as a republican, and an old-line Clay whig, would be out of place in the order?

Answer. Well, he invited me to join it, but I told him he was mistaken in the man.

Question. It seems that he was mistaken in the man, but not probably mistaken in the general material of which the order is made up?

Answer. I do not know that he reflected upon that. I cannot say as to that. I can't tell you what his views were on that subject.

Question. If this organization had been composed entirely of democrats, and was to favor the objects of the democrats, would he have approached a republican, and have invited him to come into it? Would it not have been inconsistent?

Answer. I do not know what view he took of it. I do not know what his motives were. I cannot tell.

Question. The question I ask you is very plain.

Answer. I will answer it if I know how.

Question. If it had been composed entirely of democrats, and its objects had been to advance the democratic cause in any way, would he have approached a man he knew to be a republican?

Answer. I can't tell whether he would or not. He would have the right to do so, if he saw proper. He may have supposed that public opinion might drive me in there with the democratic party. Politics was not so high then as they have been since. I do not know what he conceived, sir.

Question. I am not asking you whether you knew what he conceived exactly.

Answer. I could not tell you his motives.

Question. I am asking you whether, in the nature of things, he would have approached you, knowing you to be a republican, and ask you to join an organization, the object of which was to put down the republicans. Is that a natural thing?

Answer. He might have gone out of his line of business. I can't tell what he thought about it, because I don't know what his object was. He approached me.

Question. I did not ask what he thought about it, but whether it was a natural thing for him to do under such circumstances, to approach a republican, and ask him to unite with a democratic organization for democratic objects.

Answer. Well, in electioneering I have always endeavored to get as many votes on my side as I could get. I have been a candidate several times, and I reckon he put it up in that way—that he would like to get as many republicans in there as he could get. I don't know what his object was.

Question. What was the name of the white man who was killed?

Answer. His name was Trailer. He was the first man, I think, that was killed in the county. It was, perhaps, in September or October, twelve months. Trailer was the first man killed in the county by disguised men, I believe.

Question. Where did he live?

Answer. In the northeast corner of the county—rather east of Smithville.

Question. What did he do?

Answer. It was alleged—and I suppose it was so—they killed him away from home, at rather a lewd place—they said he was too intimate with a woman living in the country, and the disguised men rode up there, as I learned from his neighbors, to see him, and it was the opinion of everybody that they did not intend to kill him at that time; but he was very obstreperous; perhaps he had been drinking a little. They asked him to open the door; he would not permit it. They broke it down, and as they came in he struck one of them, and hurt him pretty badly, and they shot him and killed him.

Question. You have heard of the killing of Garrett?

Answer. Yes, sir; that was done recently. I knew Mr. Garrett very well. He lived at Camargo; he was a very clever gentleman; as clever an old man as in Monroe County.

Question. He was killed by a negro named Hendricks?

Answer. Yes, sir. I knew the negro very well that killed him.

By the CHAIRMAN:

Question. Was that the same Hendricks afterward killed by the Ku-Klux?

Answer. Yes, sir.

By Mr. BLAIR:

Question. You say these Flints were taken out of jail and killed?

Answer. Yes, sir. Three were taken out, and two killed. One got away.

Question. They were in jail for what offense?

Answer. They were in jail for having a difficulty with Brown Parke and his two sons. That was alleged. They were indicted, tried, and committed to jail for assault and battery with intent to kill. They were in jail, and chained in jail.

Question. They had assaulted Brown Parke and one of his sons?

Answer. Two of them. Three of the Flints, the old man and his two boys. They took them out of jail. They were all chained.

Question. Did the Flints inflict any injury upon Parke?

Answer. Yes, sir, one of them was cut a good deal. Parke's second son was pretty badly cut.

Question. Was the old man struck a blow?

Answer. I don't know whether they hit him or not; probably they did. I know they had a right smart fight.

Question. What was it about?

Answer. Something about the division of the crop, or gathering of the crop.

Question. What did they claim?

Answer. That Mr. Parke was cheating them, and not making a fair division, and a fuss arose. They claimed that each was to have one-third. I didn't hear what they claimed. I understood that was what the fuss arose about.

Question. The crop was cultivated on shares, and Parke agreed to give the Flints a third of the crop?

Answer. Yes, sir.

Question. Flint and each of his sons claimed that they were entitled to a third each?

Answer. I do not know that; I could not tell about that; but I know it originated about the crop.

Question. Santee Butler was whipped for intimacy with some white woman?

Answer. That was alleged.

Question. Andy Burns; how about him?

Answer. Andy Burns had two white women living in the yard. I know that of my own knowledge. I was there, and saw them living in the yard. They got after Andy and shot at him—shot him across the knee, but didn't hurt him. He came to my house next morning very early. He left there, and the white women left there, and went off, and were living in some house belonging to old Santee Butler, and I presume that Santee was playing the same game that Andy was, and they took him up and whipped him very severely.

Question. These affairs both grew out of women?

Answer. Yes, sir; Santee and Andy.

Question. What was this Willis whipped for?

Answer. I don't know.

Question. What was Simon Dunham whipped for?

Answer. I don't know. That is below me some six or eight miles. I don't know what that was about. I did hear, but I can't say it is so. It is the rumor. It seems that the Ku-Klux had their headquarters at a Presbyterian church not far from Ross's mill; they met there, and put on disguises at nights. They met at headquarters, and somebody burned it up, and they supposed this boy Dunham had some hand in it. That was the supposition as to the ground upon which they whipped him.

By the CHAIRMAN:

Question. Have you ever heard of the whipping of Aleck Wilson by the Ku-Klux, and that they were fired into, and twenty-two or three of them threw off their uniforms and were discovered?

Answer. I have heard this: that they whipped the boy, and while they were whipping him, or about the time they ceased whipping him, they were fired into. I never heard any more than that.

By Mr. BLAIR:

Question. That was Henry Wilson?

Answer. It was one of the Willis boys. They call him Rhett Willis for short. I do not know what his name is, but they call him Rhett Willis. It may be a nickname.

Question. What did they whip him for?

Answer. I understood it was because he sued an old man there. They alleged it while they were whipping him, I understood. Rhett told me so himself. He lived about a mile and a half from me. He told me that an old man named McNiece would not pay him at the end of the year, and he sued McNiece for his proportionable part of the cotton, and they whipped him because he saw proper to sue old McNiece.

By the CHAIRMAN:

Question. This McNiece owned a plantation there?

Answer. Yes, sir; about a mile and a half from me.

By Mr. BLAIR:

Question. In all these cases you have not alleged a single case that looked to politics?

Answer. That may be. I am stating the facts as they exist as far as I know.

Question. Yet you pretend to draw the inference that all this is done for political purposes?

Answer. I think so.

Question. But in none of these whippings and shootings that you have named have you shown any political cause for it whatever.

Answer. It may be; but, at the same time, there are a great many circumstances outside of that, general, and you ask me for my opinion; I only give it for what it is worth. My honest opinion is, that the Ku-Klux organization in the county was formed for political effect. They either intended to drive the negro from the polls or vote him. I have heard that on divers of occasions, that they either intended to vote him or that they did not intend that he should vote at all.

Question. You know of no act of theirs that looks to that?

Answer. Well, I don't know that I could say, for I have never heard any of them say positively that they intended to do that. I have heard several of them in my travels say that they would vote the negro the next time.

Question. Were they Ku-Klux?

Answer. They were democrats.

Question. Did you know they were Ku-Klux?

Answer. No, sir; I could not say that they were.

Question. Do you know that they had anything to do with the Ku-Klux?

Answer. I do not know that they had. They sympathized with them, though. You can't find a democrat in the county—they were mad from one end of the county to the other, and just boiled all over when the Ku-Klux were arrested. They just boiled all over from one end of the county to the other. My son helped to arrest them, and they vilified him, and told more lies on him than ever you heard of—than ever you did hear of on top of the globe, because he saw proper to help arrest them.

By the CHAIRMAN:

Question. When a republican renders himself obnoxious to the democrats of Monroe County by reason of his prominence, earnestness, and energy, have they a fashion of raising lies on him, and blackening his private character?

Answer. Well, I could not say, but I know this much about it—I have learned this much about it—that myself and my son, and the circuit clerk, were denounced publicly at Aberdeen. They called us scalawags, and they said they hated the scalawags a good deal worse than they did the carpet-baggers, because they saw proper to turn against the country, as they termed it. I know they are very bitter, and denounce us from one end of the county to the other.

By Mr. BLAIR:

Question. But they were anxious for you to join the Ku-Klux?

Answer. This gentleman I told you of was, sir, but he was mistaken in his man, general.

Question. But that was the estimate he formed of a republican?

Answer. I do not know what estimate he formed.

COLUMBUS, MISSISSIPPI, *November* 17, 1871.

JAMES T. WILSON, Sr., sworn and examined.

By the CHAIRMAN:

Question. Please to state your residence and occupation.

Answer. I live in Monroe county; I am a farmer.

Question. How long have you lived there?

Answer. All my life. I was fifty years old last June. I was born and raised in that county.

Question. Have you ever been visited by the Ku-Klux?

Answer. Well, sir, I have been visited there twice by them, sir.

Question. State everything, the circumstances.

Answer. Well, sir, one night—I was not there at home; I can only state what my wife stated; I do not suppose you will take that.

Question. State in brief what she stated.

Answer. I will state it as short as I can. I was at Aberdeen on some business, and did not get home until 11 o'clock at night. There was a company rode up there, I reckon about 10 o'clock in the night, some time about that, as she stated.

Question. Were they disguised?

Answer. Yes, sir; they had on white wrappers; and they hallooed, "Halloo, come out. We hurt nobody." She had just laid down. She got up in her underclothes, and stepped to the piazza. It is a double house. They said, "Madam, did you ever see anything like this before?" She says, "Sir, I don't see that." Says he, "Madam, you had better put on your specs." He talked in an Irish brogue, or thick. She told him she didn't know she could see any better in the dark with specs than without. They asked where I was. She said at Aberdeen. They asked would I be at home that night. She said she didn't know, but likely I might; that I was on business, and sometimes

I staid at my brother's near Aberdeen, and sometimes with John H. Hendricks; he was on the road coming home. He said, "He is like a great many other men in our county; he has a great deal of business to attend to after night." She did not know; when I had business I generally went and attended to that business; whether night or day-time, didn't make any difference. Says he, "We are around notifying that kind of men. You tell Mr. Wilson for the future to stay at home of a night." She told him she would do so. He said, and to "give Mr. Wilson their best compliments, if you please." A gentleman and lady put up and staid all night at my house. I can't think of his name now; he lives up the Sipsey, though.

Question. No matter about the name.

Answer. That is all they did that night.

Question. How many did she say there were in the crowd?

Answer. She could not count them; they were scattered around, outside of the palings, on their horses; they never came inside of the yard on that night.

Question. State the second visit.

Answer. The next time they came back there one night about 8 o'clock in the night. I was sitting by the fireside, and the first thing I knew fifteen or twenty were in the yard.

Question. Disguised men?

Answer. Yes, sir; all dressed in uniform, with faces covered and white wrappers on. He asked me if I would come to the door, a couple of steps in the piazza, and asked me if I would walk up to the negro cabins and settle a difficulty. I said, "Of course, gentlemen, I am not afraid of any of that sort. If you will hold on I will walk with you." I got up and got my pistol and stuck it in my bosom. I was in my shirt sleeves. It was a very bright moonshiny night; the moon was very bright. I walked with them to a negro house. They went in there in search of an old negro woman that had been living at my house ever since the surrender. She was not at home that night. One of them stepped up to me and looked me in the face, sticking his face into mine rather. He says, "Did you ever see anything like this before; did you ever see me before?" I said very probably, if he had that off of his face, I had seen him a thousand times. He asked me where she was. I told him she was at my son's; had gone over there to a log-rolling, to help cook the dinner for the hands; I reckon so; I don't know anything to the contrary. They went over there and rode up to my son's and got down in the yard and asked him out, and asked him if he didn't want to join their sort. He told them he didn't want to join any of their sort. He said, "If you please, keep your damned mouth shut for the future;" and they asked for the old negro woman, and found her in the negro cabin there, and took her out, and made him stand by and count the licks, and they whipped her with a leather strap or paddle two or three feet long, fastened on a stick like this ruler. [Illustrating.] It is at my house. They put thirty-nine on her. I examined her back next morning. It was Sabbath morning. I told her she was not cut any. She was bruised right smartly. I asked her if she knew any of the party. She said she couldn't swear to any of the party. I said "Old lady, you are not killed; you keep your mouth shut about any of the party. You know how things are in this country, and if you don't the next thing you will be killed. Now, keep your mouth shut, and don't you say a word to a living human in the neighborhood. If you do you may be gone up. I don't know—I can't tell anything about this matter now—I don't know what will be the issue here." There was nothing more said. I asked her the morning I started here, for she is still in my house, if she could identify any of this party. She said she could not with safety.

Question. Did she know what she was beaten for?

Answer. Yes, sir; they told her. I could state it if you thought it was necessary, but it would take me some time to tell it.

Question. Do you know or have you been informed of any other whippings or outrages committed by this band?

Answer. No, sir; I do not know anything of my own knowledge. I have heard of a good deal. I saw one man that had been killed. They said that party killed him.

Question. Who was that?

Answer. I found him in the woods myself. I saw him, but he was found before I knew were he was. He was found, and an inquest was held over him about two miles from where I live. I had a little son and a little negro boy living there, and sent them to an old field to drive up some sheep, and they saw some buzzards flying about, and got scared at the sight of the dead man. They never saw anybody dead before.

Question. What is the name of the negro who was killed?

Answer. Aleck Page.

Question. The committee have inquired into his killing. You need not dwell upon that. How long have these raids of the Ku-Klux been going on?

Answer. The first I was informed of the matter, the first I ever heard of such a thing, was last fall, in October, say a year ago. I went to a camp-meeting with my wife and was attending there, near Athens, the county-seat of Monroe County. The preacher in charge was John Gregory. He lived in Smithville, Monroe County. He rode the circuit there. He stated to me that there was a "terrible occurrence" up in our country the other night. Says I, "O, what was that?" Says he, "There was a white man killed up there the other night, and a very clever man. He was in the army with me in my company. I knew him very well." "Who was it?" said I. Said he, "It was a fellow named Trailer." "What was he killed for?" said I. "I cannot tell," says he. "There has been nobody pursued the parties; and I suppose he was at a sort of loose house where there were some women, and they went in on him and ordered him out. He being a very stout man, refused to come. They punched him with a gun, and he jerked one of the guns out of their hands and hauled away, and knocked one of them on the head so he lay limber, and another one shot him through and killed him." That was the statement of the man.

Question. Did anybody find out who killed him?

Answer. I asked. "No, they can't make no discovery," says he. Says I, "That's awkward; you can't find out who did the killing." He says, "I have been told it is a party called the Ku-Klux party." Says I, "I thought we had no Ku-Klux in our country. What sort of party is Ku-Klux?" That was the first knowledge I had of any such thing.

Question. And that was two years ago, last fall?

Answer. Yes, sir: last September a year ago.

By Mr. RICE:

Question. Was it one or two years ago?

Answer. Two years ago this September was the first I ever heard of it. They said they came from Alabama. They gave Alabama the name of it.

By Mr. BLAIR:

Question. What was this old woman whipped for?

Answer. Well, I will tell you. I can state it if you have time to listen. I will do it in as short a time and manner as I can. One of her young mistresses and another woman was in the settlement living there. There was a woman that this party—the Ku-Klux party—had ordered off. I suppose she was in the family-way. She was a sort of loose woman.

Question. Who was this woman, her young mistress?

Answer. This woman was ordered off, I say, and a short time after that she died. She was in the family-way, and from the scare she died; but she had had the chills and the dropsy, and everything else pretty near. She was diseased and died very suddenly, and it was stated her daughter dragged her over the house; and this old negro woman told those two women that her daughter did drag her over the house. She was buried, and the doctors took her up to examine her; there had been no inquest held; and this old negro woman told these two young women that this woman's daughter dragged her over the house, as I said. I reckon the old woman didn't tell that right. Her daughter did not make that statement. I reckon they said this. The old negro woman was at the burying-ground when they took this woman up, and these two women were there, and they said that she had said this. I said I didn't believe her daughter dragged her over the house. They said, "the old woman says it." I said, "I will call her then;" and I called her and I asked her, and then she said, "I never said it;" and then the white woman said, "You did say it;" and she said, "I didn't say it;" and then one of the white women jumped at a walking-cane I had to strike her with it. I was squatting down at the grave-yard, leaning on a walking-cane and she aimed to jerk the stick out of my hand to strike the woman, but I would not allow the lady to have the stick to strike her. There was a justice of the peace there, and I thought that was no place for such a fuss. After that time this party that I spoke of aimed to whip this woman, for they said she had disputed two white ladies' word and called them a liar; but she didn't call them a liar, but disputed what they said. Now that is what they whipped her for precisely. I only told her, after she got the whipping, it would learn her hereafter to hold her tongue, and not talk too much; that she had no business to say one thing and then say another; and I told her that was the way people got into these difficulties, and I cautioned her for the future not to talk any more about things.

COLUMBUS, MISSISSIPPI, *November* 17, 1871.

G. WILEY WELLS sworn and examined.

By the CHAIRMAN:

Question. Colonel, please state your residence and official position.

Answer. I reside in Holly Springs, Marshall County, Mississippi. I am the United

States district attorney for the northern district of Mississippi, embracing thirty-three counties—one-half of the State.

Question. How long have you held that position?

Answer. For about two years.

Question. During that time have you become well acquainted with the sentiments and feelings of the people of Northern Mississippi?

Answer. Yes, sir; I am very conversant with the feelings and sentiments of the people of that portion of the State?

Question. What is the feeling between the native-born citizens of the South and northern men who have come into the State and settled?

Answer. Well, sir, there are two classes of people in the State who are native-born, and the feelings that emanate from these two classes are distinct. There is one class that feels a bitter hatred to northern people, while there is another class, but a smaller portion, who are the most respectable element, who seem to desire harmony, and who treat northern men with a degree of respect and kindness that the others are not willing to accord to them.

Question. You may state whether there is or is not much bitterness and hostility exhibited by the democrats of Northern Mississippi toward the republicans of this State.

Answer. Well, sir; a northern man who comes here and is willing to affiliate with them and remain a silent looker-on in political affairs, will receive very courteous treatment and kindness, but a person who attempts to exercise freedom of thought, who entertains and expresses his political convictions, labors under the operation of an ostracism in society, and he is placed under a ban. If he is a democrat, a man will be received to a certain extent in society although he is a northern man; but if he is a republican, the feeling is different. I do not know that I can express it exactly, but it is something like this: "You have no right here; you are a stranger here; you have no interests here; therefore you have no right to assert your political convictions." The feeling is very hostile in some localities. Now, in Marshall County the feeling is not as hostile as in other counties, and perhaps also in De Soto; but take all this tier of counties, Winston, Noxubee, Latour, Lowndes, Monroe, Alcorn, Tishemingo, and Tippah, and it is very violent. In fact, in several of these counties it is impossible for a northern man to live. Tippah, I mention particularly, and Tishemingo.

Question. Leaving out the black element here, how is the society of Northern Mississippi classified or divided?

Answer. Well, sir, it is divided, as I said before, into two classes; the respectable element living mostly in the towns and villages, as in Columbus, Holly Springs, and such towns; for example, the members of the bar or ministers of the gospel, and that class of citizens, who will accord to you a passing recognition on the street, will treat you kindly; while in the interior of the counties, away from these villages, and away from railroads, the most bitter, hostile feeling prevails against republicans. These are the two classes I spoke of before, and these are their sentiments. I am speaking now from my personal experience among them.

Question. I suppose that your professional duties have brought you pretty extensively into contact with this organization known as the Ku-Klux Klan?

Answer. Yes, sir.

Question. I understand that several bills of indictment against men suspected of belonging to that organization have been found in the Federal court. I will ask you to state to the committee the result of your investigation, as to the existence of this organization, its objects, and purposes.

Answer. I commenced the prosecutions in the United States court about the 15th day of May, 1871. I have been engaged constantly, traveling or otherwise, prosecuting my duties day and night, away from my home much of the time since that date up to this period. In fact, I have not been at home to exceed three weeks since these prosecutions have commenced. I have now under indictment between two and three hundred persons. I have under bond for appearance at court perhaps thirty-five to fifty.

By Mr. Blair:

Question. You say you have three hundred indicted?

Answer. Yes, sir; embraced in about thirty or forty indictments.

Question. And between fifty and sixty have given bond?

Answer. Between thirty-five and fifty, or in that neighborhood. I have investigated the matter pretty thoroughly, I believe. I have striven to ascertain the aims and objects of this organization, because it became a settled fact soon after I began these prosecutions, that there was an extensive organization which had its surroundings and ramifications over a large portion of my district. It seemed to be under one management, or, at least, its different parts were co-operating together. In some instances I found this organization in one county performing certain deeds of violence in another county, while the organization where these deeds were executed would return and reciprocate by committing similar acts in the county of the organization first mentioned. I found also that they had specific objects, for this reason; the persons who were maltreated by them, whipped, shot, &c., were of a particular class, mostly blacks; in fact, nearly all were blacks; and, when they were not blacks, they were republicans, who were white men; some few native-born, others northern men. The aim and objects I have also ascertained from parties who have turned State's evidence, and I have the most positive and conclusive proof that, the purposes of the organization were to carry the elections by terrorizing and keeping away from the polls the blacks, and by obliging them to vote the democratic ticket. It seemed to be supported to a great extent by the democratic party, for the reason that, up to the time I commenced these prosecutions, no man had received a more flattering recognition from members of the democratic party than myself, by way of friendship, and in my intercourse with the bar, and from members of the press; but the instant I commenced these prosecutions it was heralded throughout this district, and the most violent and slanderous attacks upon me were begun, no reason being assigned, except that I was prosecuting innocent persons. The howl became incessant, and these people, who had been my friends before, called upon me and cautioned me that perhaps I was using the powers conferred by Congress for partisan purposes, and said I was liked very well as a gentleman, and they had formed an attachment for me, but they added that they were sorry to think I was led off into this vile operation which was but a scheme of certain politicians to punish innocent men for the purpose of obtaining evidence there was such an organization, and declaring that they did not believe there was such an organization at all. For some time I had my doubts, when I first commenced these investigations, as to whether the organization was a complete and systematic arrangement, but I became convinced of that by two reasons: first, the dresses worn by these men were everywhere similar, and the pass-words and signs were nearly everywhere quite the same. The *modus operandi* in each county was very similar, and the plans and operations of all seemed to be in accordance with each other. For instance, if a man was driven by the Ku-Klux from one county to another, the Ku-Klux party there would drive him off, and he seemed to be made a particular object of persecution by them everywhere. I therefore concluded there must be means of communication where there was such manifest co-operation. After I had received the confessions of some of the men engaged in these Ku-Klux outrages, who gave me full statement of the objects and operations of the Klan, their declarations confirmed my belief, which was before based on the reasons I have given, that it was a well-formed system, devised for a particular object, and that object expressed in their oaths. One party I captured, by the name of Whittaker, who is in Oxford now, made a confession to me, in which he divulged the oaths, signs, grips, and pass-words, and gave me a history of the organization; stated the length of time he had been connected with it; the number of operations in which they have been engaged; stated the number of men they had whipped; and gave the names of men that had been killed by them. He revealed, also, the names of the men by whom he had been sworn into this organization. He had become a lieutenant in the Ku-Klux organization. Now, this Ku-Klux Klan started in from the lower end of my district. It was in Winston County, and then it extended up to the Tennessee line to Tishemingo and Alcorn Counties, taking in all this whole tier of counties, and sweeping over the district. It had run as far as the Tennessee line toward the north, in this State, and westward to the Mississippi River, when the first Ku-Klux parties were brought to trial. We commenced a vigorous prosecution, sparing no time nor means in bringing these parties to justice. After discovering them, we had about two hundred of them indicted in the court. This seemed to strike terror into the organization, and then it lulled. After the court adjourned things were quieted down for several weeks, We were making some arrests. They lulled down to such a degree that the same terrorism did not exist in the district which had prevailed previous to the commencement of that court. The papers were teeming with articles concerning the Ku-Klux bill passed by Congress, and that seemed to have had the effect to suppress them for the time being, until that law came to be discussed among certain lawyers here, by whom it was thought to be a very defective act, and they expressed the opinion that it would be a hard and difficult matter to punish any person under either the enforcement act or Ku-Klux bill as passed by Congress. I do not know that I have a copy of it, but in one of the papers, either the Prentiss Recorder or Iuka Gazette, an article was published by a man named Dr. Davis, of Iuka, in one of these papers, in which that fact was made known, and it stated to them that so far as punishment in the United States court was concerned, the authorities would find their hands full, as the laws would not reach these cases, and parties need have no fears except from the State authorities; that the State was expected to take care of itself; that the United States had no business to interfere; that the United States and its authorities were exceeding their jurisdiction, and would find that these prosecutions would have to be abandoned. About that period the organization seemed to spring into existence again, and the authorities were being overpowered in different portions of the district. Reports were coming in to me asking for assistance; negroes were coming into Holly Springs, imploring me to protect them, and I started out in my district again, and caused the arrest of large numbers. During one of these periods when I was in the district with Marshal Pierce and Deputy McCoy, we captured a band of six men that belonged to a Klan which existed in Tishemingo County. We also captured their uniforms complete. These uniforms I have here now in this room, and can exhibit them to the committee. I have also a photograph which I had taken of these parties in their uniforms after they had surrendered.

By the CHAIRMAN:

Question. Will you produce that photograph at this point of your examination?

Answer. This is the photograph that was taken at Corinth. [The witness produced a photograph representing three men in disguise, and filed it with his testimony.]

Question. Was that photograph taken from the parties who were arrested?

Answer. Two of the figues here represented are those of the parties arrested. One figure is that of another person who put on the disguise for the purpose of being taken in this picture, so that the disguise might be exhibited. One of these was the party who turned State's evidence. The other confessed to having worn the disguise and he was in jail.

By Mr. RICE:

Question. And the third is a negro?

Answer. No, sir; the third is Lieutenant McCoy, deputy United States marshal, wearing the disguise for that purpose.

By the CHAIRMAN:

Question. Please state the outrages which have fallen within your knowledge and information.

Answer. In reference to these outrages I have presented I can give them to you, taking them along as they came, though a little irregularly perhaps. One of the cases investigated was that of John W. Avery, of Winston County, a native of this State, who was engaged in teaching school. His school-house was burned. The Ku-Klux waited upon him, and informed him that the free-school system could not be put in force in this State, and that no man should teach in that county, under this school system, as the Ku-Klux Klan had received orders from general headquarters to demolish the school-houses, and drive out the teachers; that they had waited upon him as a friend, to advise him to immediately leave the county; that while they were his friends, they were under a sworn oath in the Klan to do whatever was commanded, and as they had received orders these would have to be executed.

Question. Did he discontinue his school?

Answer. He discontinued the school. The school-house was burned. He then commenced at another house known as the "Black house," I think; then they destroyed that house.

Question. In what county was that?

Answer. In Winston County. At the same time they waited upon one of the trustees—the board of trustees, as they are called—and demanded of him some scrip that had been placed in his hands, as a school-fund, by the State. They took from that party, whose name is Eaves, the scrip, built a bonfire, and burned all of the scrip they had for school purposes in that county. I may remark that, according to his testimony, and that of Mr. Murff, and some others whose sworn statements were taken, nearly or quite all the schools were discontinued in that county on account of this terrorism, and a large number of the school-houses were burned or destroyed. They stated that it was a scheme gotten up by the radicals of the State to educate the negroes so that they might be more than equal with the whites; that they might become superior to the whites, and then terrorize and rule over the whites, and they declared that they would not permit it. About the same time Solomon Triplett, a colored man, was killed.

The CHAIRMAN. You need not enter into the particulars of the case of Triplett, as the committee has taken full evidence in regard to it.

The WITNESS. Did you have the case of Johnson Kitt, killed?

Question. Will you name the case?

Answer. Solomon Triplett was killed about the same time that this party I have mentioned was driven out. You have the particulars of that case. Johnson Kitt was killed in Winston County. Has the evidence shown you the object in the killing of Triplett?

Question. You may state what the object was.

Answer. The evidence in my possession shows the reason Solomon Triplett was killed. I mean now, evidence that is conclusive and positive upon that point. It was that he had been raised at a Mrs. Triplett's; had exercised the right of suffrage at the election before; that Mr. Triplett informed him that it would be impossible for him to remain on his farm and vote as he did; that Sol told him he was willing to leave; that he went to a man, an old justice of the peace, whose name I do not remember—a relative of Triplett—and asked to be protected; this old man told him he had done only what was right; that he did not believe in the negroes voting, but he had a right to vote, and might come on his place and live; he then moved from Triplett's place to this man's, and in about three or four weeks afterward he was shot sitting by his wife in his house. A colored man, who was lying within ten feet of them, saw the Klan coming to the house, and recognized of that company Mr. John Q. Triplett, who has now run out of the country, two McElhaney boys, and a Mr. Eaves.

By Mr. BLAIR:

Question. Who was that colored man?

Answer. That man is William Coleman. The others have been arrested, and they are under bonds of ten thousand dollars. Mr. Triplett is under bond now. I will also mention, though a little out of order here, in connection with this man Avery, spoken of before, they asked him to join the organization, and told him they would protect him; that he would do well by so doing, and gave him reasons why he ought to join the organization. They stated at the time that all he would have to do would be to take the material for disguises to Helen Avery, a sister-in-law of his father—one of his brothers was indicted in this very matter—and Mrs. Eaves, the wife of Buck Eaves, and have them made in such disguises as they were in the habit of wearing. He was told that Buck Eaves was lieutenant of the company. Now, to return to the evidence in regard to Triplett; I think that man was William Coleman, though I am not positive, and cannot now find the memorandum.

By the CHAIRMAN:

Question. What is your information as to Johnson Kitt?

Answer. That he was killed. I have no particular information about that.

Question. Pass on to the next case.

Answer. I come next to Mr. Alexander W. Murff, minister of the gospel, residing in Winston County. He was appointed by the Methodist conference, which held its sessions at Water Valley, Mississippi, as the designated pastor for that particular parish or location. He was also appointed about the same time school-director. He was following his business as a minister of the gospel, and also performing the duties of school-director, when the Klan waited upon him and informed him that he must resign that position; that no man could be allowed to hold any position from the radicals of this State, or with the intention of putting in operation so infamous a system as the free-school system. He still held out until gentlemen of known character and respectability—the names of the parties I do not know—waited upon him and told him it would not be safe to hold the position as school-director any longer. Influenced by this intimidation, and the threats which were made against him, he resigned the position. That was about March, 1871.

By Mr. BLAIR:

Question. Who was that man?

Answer. His full name was Alexander W. Murff. He was a Methodist minister.

By the CHAIRMAN:

Question. Will you give the next case?

Answer. The next one is that of Peter Atkins, a colored man in Monroe County. The Ku-Klux visited his house several times. He made his escape upon one occasion, and while they were there they stated that they intended to kill him on sight. The party that visited him there was dressed in white. They came back the next night; he had made his escape when they first visited his house, and they then whipped his step-father, Joe Atkins, and my information is that the Ku-Klux were riding there every Saturday night, and had been for at least three months prior to the meeting of the June term of my court, and a perfect state of terror prevailed in that section of the county. I found, on visiting that county and examining witnesses, that the effect of their operations was that a state of terror prevailed to such an extent that it was almost impossible, unless they were assured of protection in every way, to induce them to state even the most trivial circumstance in regard to the Ku-Klux. They had been so completely impregnated with the belief that these persons lived in the moon; they had been so frightened by the exhibition of skeleton arms, and by the shaking of bones, and by an arrangement or contrivance by which these men would throw a gallon of water into their mouths, that these things had induced the belief among the negroes that they were spirits of those slain at Shiloh, and that they knew every act that people performed. It was, therefore, almost impossible to extract testimony from any of them. They could only be induced to make any statement after assurances of protection, and that the Ku-Klux should not know anything about it. The Ku-Klux gave this man, Atkins, two hundred lashes, under which he suffered so severely that he was not able to get out of his bed for three days. He lives nineteen miles from Aberdeen. The same night that they got after Atkins they whipped Alfred Connell and Huke Siss; and they also shot Henry Hanson. A white man who had raised this Atkins, by the name of Bluke Atkins, told Peter Atkins that if he did not remain with him on his farm he would have him Ku-Kluxed, and shortly after that he was Ku-Kluxed. The next case is that of Joe Turner, of Lowndes County, near Caledonia, who was whipped in the most shocking manner by the Ku-Klux, who were dressed in white gowns. Some of them had gowns on that were bound in red. They made him lie down in the road, and stripped him. His back and arms were cut up very badly. These parties who had been whipped exhibited their backs to me in many instances, or, where they came into the grand jury room, I had them stripped, and then examined their persons.

The CHAIRMAN. You need not pause upon that case, as we have taken testimony in relation to it.

The WITNESS. The next case is a party of Ku-Klux who went to John Campbell's store, which is five miles and a half west of Corinth, in the month of June, and robbed him. They also whipped a white man, named E. J. Stubblefield, four miles from Corinth. The Ku-Klux came to his house in a large party; declared that he was a damned radical; and that was the reason why he was whipped. He lives four miles from Corinth. He had voted for Alcorn. They whipped him very hard, and ordered him to leave by the next morning. They made him lie upon a stump while he was whipped. He described the position—holding his hands down on either side while four men whipped him. They had been to his house once before and broken open his doors, but he was away. They went to his nephew's the same night—Stubblefield is quite an old man—and attempted to whip him. He started to run; they struck him over the head with a pistol—fired at him; but he made his escape. I refer now to the nephew.

By Mr. BLAIR:

Question. What was the nephew's name; was it Stubblefield?

Answer. I cannot tell you that. He simply made the statement in regard to his nephew. I never had the nephew before me. I expect to have him at the coming term of court. This Klan recognize each other by throwing their hands in this shape, [illustrating,] by the ear, giving taps with the right hand upon the lobe or point or outside of the ear. In this same Klan I have evidence showing another motion, which is, passing the hand over the ear, with a movement of the forefinger from the bottom to the top, over the ear, behind the ear. This gang have pantaloons and bodies made in red and yellow. This same party went into Purdy, Tennessee, and broke open the jail there, and let the prisoners out. One was a Ku-Klux who had been committed for murder. These facts you can find out more fully by subpœnaing witnesses from about Corinth. This is the same Klan that did it. The clothes that are described as being worn by this Klan are of the same character as those I have in my possession. They were in Tishemingo County and in the adjoining county.

By the CHAIRMAN:

Question. Will you pass to the next case?

Answer. On the 9th of March last, A. P. Huggins, United States assistant assessor of internal revenue and school superintendent, was whipped. I believe you have the details of that case.

The CHAIRMAN. Yes, sir; you need not dwell upon it.

The WITNESS. On the 12th of May, 1871, a raid was made by the Ku-Klux into Pontotoc, for the purpose of breaking up a republican paper published by Flournoy. You have inqnired into that, I believe?

The CHAIRMAN. Yes, sir; we have some evidence in regard to that.

The WITNESS. One of the partners was killed; four are indicted who were in it. I have positive evidence of their having ridden about and whipped and killed other parties in that county.

By the CHAIRMAN:

Question. Give the next case.

Answer. On the 18th of March, 1871, a large gang of Ku-Klux, in Noxubee County, whipped the wife of Frazier Duncan and otherwise abused her in the most disgraceful manner. There were counted to be sixty in this gang. They drove Frazier off. This gang was dressed in white. They had long white gowns; some of them were trimmed with red; they beat the woman nearly to death; they struck her with guns several blows, for the reason that she would not tell where her husband was. He had made his escape just before they came to the house, and was lying out in the woods. In March a band of disguised men killed a freedman near Corinth by the name of Turner. He was shot through the head. The evidence is that he was a good man, but a very positive negro; that at the election he had resisted the orders of certain democratic office-seekers; they were called conservatives then, I believe; it was at the Dent election in 1869. He had carried a large number to the poll and caused them by certain language to vote as they chose, saying that he would protect them. It is supposed that that was the reason he was killed, although no reason is assigned, except that a Mr. Harrison, who resides at Corinth, and who is indicted as accessory to the murder, said, upon a coroner's inquest which was held upon the body, that the party had killed the wrong negro; that there was a mistake; that they were intending to kill another man.

Question. What county is Corinth in?

Answer. Alcorn County. About this same time or soon after, a colored school-teacher, who had come, I think, from some Northern State, or from Kentucky, was thrown into a well after being taken from his house. His name I cannot now give you. The facts you can obtain there from Mayor Mask, or any of the officials in Corinth. About two weeks afterward another party—I think his name was Williams, I am not positive of that, but these facts can also be obtained from Mayor Mask and others in Corinth—was taken out and tied to a gate-post, and shot and killed. Soon after this, a party of disguised men went armed to the jail at Rienzi, Tishemingo County, and broke open the jail-doors, and took out a man just committed by a magistrate for stealing an over-coat out of a hotel, and who was said to be a northern man, and shot him. They also took out two negroes, and one of the negroes they hung. The other negro got down and made a terrible prayer, and they returned him back in his cell after whipping him. These facts were given to me by the circuit clerk, who was on the ground and saw the operation. This band of disguised men said to him, "Do you recognize any of the horses or men here?" He told them he did not. They told him that if he did, and it was ever reported, that they would know that it came from him; that he would be summarily dealt with. The next case I have is that of Alexander Hughes, of Noxubee County.

Question. Was he whipped or killed?

Answer. He was whipped, and they hung him also. They took him out about a quarter of a mile, made him get down on his knees, and put a rope around his neck.

The CHAIRMAN. We do not care for the details of that case, as we have testimony concerning it.

The WITNESS. The next case is that of a man named E. C. Echols, who lives in Chickasaw County, near Sparta. The circumstances are these; Mr. Echols is a native of Mississippi. He had been boarding a man named McBride, who had been teaching a colored school in the vicinity. A band of disguised men waited on him on the 29th of April, composed of from nine to fifteen men; they broke open his door, came into his house, and, as he sprang out of bed, he asked what was wanted. His wife and babe were in the bed; the party fired at him, and the ball grazed him and passed into the wall. At the time he was before me, the evidence of the scar made by the ball was apparent. The point where the ball lodged was so near his wife, that it was almost a miracle that she escaped being killed. He sprang out of bed and demanded what they wanted. They exclaimed, "O, God damn you, we are after you; we've got you now; we'll fix you; we'll give you hell; we have come to kill you." He asked them again what they wanted of him; what he had done. When they came in the house he said he thought some one was in distress, but as soon as he got up and the party made this declaration, they took him from the house a short distance from the door, and after binding him commenced to lash him. He says he received in the neighborhood of two hundred lashes. He thought for a time that he should faint and drop down from the lashing, it was so severe; the blood trickled down to his heels. At the time I saw him his back was like a piece of pounded beefsteak; his arms, too, were raw. His wife ran out, and they seized her and beat her; the marks were upon her arms and upon her neck where they had beaten her. A young lady, a sister-in-law, Almira Wyndham, a sister of Mr. Echols's wife, attempted to go out of the house, and was met by one of these young men whom she recognized. She was thrown back over a trunk, and was laid up for some time from the effects of the shock. Nearly all the parties were recognized in this instance, and I have had them indicted. Upon sending the United States marshal alone to make the arrest, they had an arrangement, as they had heard that these witnesses had gone up and testified, whereby they communicated the fact to these parties. The marshal chased a man who was flying some eight miles. He arrived at the house just far enough behind to see the party he wanted jump on a fresh horse and escape. He went down to Sparta, and every one of these men in that region had fled. Soon after that he sent down a deputy named Jones, with a few soldiers; he left the soldiers a short distance off. One man came up to him and said, "God damn you, what do you want? I am Roeback; you are an officer; do you think you can take me out?" He said, "I came here to perform my duty," and the man replied, "You can't take me. There's not enough Yankees to take me." Thinking that he had not sufficient force, he came back to Oxford. Deputy McCoy and Marshal Pierce, with a small band of soldiers, left from this place in Chickasaw and started up in the interior, and just as they got into town, the word had been conveyed, evidently, that the Yankees were coming. Roeback jumped on his horse and left. McCoy emptied his revolver at him, pursued him, brought him down, and brought him to Corinth under arrest. A short time after this they waited upon McBride, a young man who had been boarding at Echols's house, and whipped him.

Mr. BLAIR. He has been before the committee.

The WITNESS. I think he was in Washington as a witness before you. The next case is a party of disguised men whipped and hung Betsey Lucas in Noxubee County. I think this was some time in March. They took her out in her night-gown, and even removed that article of covering, and whipped her in the most shameful manner, at the same time putting a line or strap around her neck, and swung it over the limb of a tree and drew her up, stopping her breath until she was nearly dead. I will remark here that McBride was whipped May 4, 1871. He had been teaching a colored school, and also a Sunday-school there. This same party that I spoke of in Noxubee, as whipping Betsey Lucas, on the same night whipped Eliza Hinton, a colored woman.

Mr. BLAIR. All these cases have been testified to before the committee.

The WITNESS. I am merely noticing the parties in the cases in which indictments have been found. Some of the parties are under indictment, and as high as thirty were in one band. The next case is a band of disguised men who drove Mingo Rogers off. He lived in Oktibbeha County. He is now in Holly Springs. On the same night they also whipped Jesse Higgins twice. This was a most outrageous case—this of Higgins. They not only whipped him, but threw him on the ground, and stamped him. They whipped him about ten lashes apiece, and there were ten or fifteen in the band. They then made him get up and made him bunt his head against a tree, and at each time that he would bunt it they would lash him from behind to bunt harder. They told this negro Rogers that they they would kill him, as he was engaged with a man named McLachlan in a co-operation store. McLachlan was a northern Methodist minister, and settled there, and was driven out of the country. Have you taken the evidence in his case?

Mr. BLAIR. Yes, sir; both of them.

The WITNESS. Rogers left a large crop there. He would not go back again afterward, because prominent men had told him it would not be safe, and I think advised him to stay away. The next case is on the 6th of April, 1871, near Corinth, Alcorn County. A party of disguised men, dressed in black and white gowns, with high peaked hats, whipped and beat in a shameful manner Andy Graham. The testimony of the section boss, an Irishman who had charge of him, shows that Andy was engaged on section fifty-three on the Mobile and Ohio Railroad.

By the CHAIRMAN:

Question. A colored man?

Answer. Yes, sir; but he can read and write, and was regarded as a leader among colored men—a very formidable republican. He had organized a club, and was very active in politics. They took him out one night as he came home—he was returning on a hand-car, with a band of other colored men—they tied his feet to the iron bar on one side of the road, and strapped his hands to the other bar. It was about time for the 9 o'clock train to pass. They told him that they understood that he intended, if the radicals would stand by him, to break up the Ku-Klux; and they said that they came from three thousand miles away in the moon; that they were the spirits of the men killed at Shiloh. They left him for some time. Then they commenced to beat him with hickory sticks about the size of my small finger. The switches with which he was whipped were, some of them, lying on the ground, and some of them were obtained by men whom I sent for them. Merely to confirm the testimony of these men, I sent an individual there, who found the switches. Some of them were twisted together, and bound at the butt and top. I saw this man's back, and, with the exception of one other man, whose case I have mentioned before, it was lacerated as bad as anything I ever saw in my life. There were places on his back in which I could lay the forefinger, and also around his neck, and on his face, and over his body. The man carries the scars of this whipping to-day. They went to this man's house, and also to the houses of other colored men who were employed on this same section, and took all the arms they could find in their houses, and a quantity of money, and destroyed a large amount of clothing in the houses.

Question. How large were these sticks?

Answer. They were poles about eight or nine feet long, of sticks or withes, about as large as my small finger. After they had whipped this man Graham, they untied him, and commenced whipping John Glenn, another colored man, right at the same place and time. All of the men there had their hands tied, but they did not strip these men I have just mentioned. After this Graham went to town to the sheriff, whose name is Haynie—and who I believe to be a member of the Ku-Klux—the sheriff of Alcorn County, a man whose brother is now indicted in the district court as the captain of one of these bands, and made complaint to him, exhibiting his back, his wounds, and asking what he could do, and if the sheriff could protect him. The sheriff turned him off, and told him all he had to do was to keep quiet, and not make any fuss about it, and they would probably not visit him again. He then went to Mayor Mask, who immediately issued a warrant for the parties described by Graham as being the ones who had been whipping him, and arrested them; and upon the examination the evidence was conclusive and full. They were bound over in the sum of $1,000. They immediately went back to this man Graham, took him out again, and whipped him a second time, saying to him, "Yes, God damn you; you have been out to report us. We will teach you how to report us; we know that you did. You said that the men who whipped you lived in this county. Didn't we tell you that we lived in the moon?" After they had beat him this time, he came over to Holly Springs, and came to me, and told his story. I drew up an affidavit upon it, and the warrant was issued by the United States commissioner, H. C. Blackman, and the parties were arrested. They are all under bonds of $2,000 now for their appearance at the December term of court. They also said to this man at the time they whipped him that they had understood that the negroes had pistols, and it was against the law for negroes to carry pistols, and therefore they took them away. This same party, at the same time, whipped three other colored men, whose names are Manuel Lawrence, Green Williams, and Edmund Glenn; that was the same night. Then they came back after they were arrested and whipped them again; and they have driven them away. They have since got a place below, on the Mobile and Ohio Railroad.

The Ku-Klux also visited the section boss, and told him they would take him out and hang him if he did not discharge these negroes and take them off; that he could get plenty of white men to do the work. He refused to do it, and finally Mayor Mask sent up a protection of two other men to work with him on the road, and they are staying there with him at work. One of the means of identification of these men was that one of the party accused was discovered in Corinth with the identical pistol they had taken away on this night from Glenn. As near as the witnesses could estimate it, they each got two hundred lashes. That was the estimate I made from the number of men whom they said were there, and the number of lashes given by each. It amounted to two hundred lashes in the aggregate. I must say that I never saw a more outrageous lashing than these men received.

On the 8th of March, in Alcorn County, a party of disguised men whipped George Maybray, and a freedmen who lived in his house by the name of Harry. Now, the facts of this case are these: George Maybray was an industrious colored man, and had bought a piece of property or land from a man named Haynie—a brother of this sheriff whom I have mentioned—and this same party, Haynie, was accused of being the captain of a band. He purchased it just after the war closed. He was to have a deed upon his payment for the land. He cleared the land, fenced it, and made the entire payment in full, and then asked for his deed. He was refused, and went to Sheriff Haynie, and asked him to assist him in getting a deed, saying that he had made the full payment. I may mention also that he had built a log-house and he had a crop of cotton on the land as well as sweet potatoes, goober peas or peanuts, and some stock. This man Haynie told him that he was willing to give him the same price for the land, as it then stood, that he had originally given for it. This the man refused to take, stating that he had bought it for a home, and wanted to buy more land instead of selling what he had. Haynie then told him that he must understand that negroes could not own any property there, and that the first thing he would know would be that he would be Ku-Kluxed for his impudence. The man made three or four demands upon Haynie for the deed, and each time was refused. At last, on the 8th of March, these disguised men came and visited him, and among them he recognized Haynie as one, and has positive evidence to prove it. They whipped him and attempted to kill him, but he escaped in the woods, they shooting at him as he ran. On the 15th of April another party or the same party visited him; he thinks they were the same men, but is not certain. They were ten in number. They came to his house, took him out, and whipped him very badly. The first time he was lashed considerably, but the last time he was whipped in a manner like this other man whom I have mentioned—very badly. I saw his back and body. He was also beaten over the shoulders with a gun and badly lamed in his left arm, and was driven off; he is now living in the village of Corinth, and picking around in the best way he can to get a living. Every one there who knows him speaks in the highest terms of him as being an honest, upright, thrifty negro.

In Winston County, on the 10th of May, a band of disguised men whipped Nancy Edmonds, and obliged her to go back to a place she had lived and go to work. That was the cause then stated—that she had left Mr. Triplett's and had no business to go running about the country. They whipped her most unmercifully and sent her back.

Now, the next case I shall speak of is in connection with the previous person I spoke of as being whipped in Alcorn County, and only a part of whose name was known—Turner, I think.

Question. He was shot through the head because he would not vote the conservative ticket?

Answer. Yes, sir; he voted a band of men, and voted them or asserted his rights. This is the statement of one of the parties who was induced to seek this party and bring him over; that is, this Turner, and bring him over to the house of a certain citizen named Harrison, and also a Mr. Lee, who is a prominent republican in that county, and a native of the State. He is a prominent man, and is said to be a very brave man. This negro lived on his place. This man, Willis Harrison, I spoke of as being indicted for this murder, asked Samuel Stovall, a colored man, what chance there was to get this man to his house from over there, pointing toward Mr. Lee's house. He said he was mad with Mr. Lee, and wanted to get a chance at him; that if he ever came across him he would kill him, and wanted him to get that man Nero to come over there; that he was the one they wanted to kill. He was a very faithful man at Mr. Lee's house. He said if he would get Nero over there he would pay him. The man answered that he would go over and see. The man's statement is, "The first time I told him Mr. Harrison wanted to see him, and asked him if he would come over to my house to-night. He didn't come; said he would come over before long. The second time, I asked him to come over a week after Harrison said he should not stay at Lee's; he would say he should not. I heard Harrison say the wrong negro was killed when Turner was killed; that it was Nero that he was after; that he would pay him off if he could get Nero over to my house. I told Harrison what he said when I came up. He asked what Nero said. I had been living with Mr. Harrison about a month. I was picking cotton when he told me to get him to come to my house. I was picking cotton when Turner was killed. My house is a quarter of a mile from Harrison's. I saw them coming back from Turner's house, after he was killed the same night." Now, the party referred to there as coming back from this house is the band of disguised men.

On the 7th of November, 1870, in Noxubee County, a band of disguised men killed a colored man named Dick Malone.

The CHAIRMAN. Of that we have the full particulars, and you need not dwell upon it.

The WITNESS. William Coleman, who had been a party whipped, and who had been before the grand jury, was sent home by me for the purpose of procuring certain evidence which was said to be in the county. Upon his arrival in Macon, Mississippi, he was arrested, as he stepped off the cars, by the city marshal, who accosted him by saying, "Yes, damn you, you have been to Oxford. Didn't Whistler take you there?" He said he had been to Corinth. The marshal said, "You are a damned liar. You have no business walking around here until morning," and he took his carpet-sack from him and also searched his pockets. In the search he found a letter I had sent by him to a party in Noxubee County, which was to be carried privately, and was to get certain parties whom I wanted for evidence. The letter was abstracted from Coleman's valise, and I know not yet what has become of it. As soon as he got out of jail he returned to Oxford. This same William Coleman was knocked down and whipped on the 20th day of April. A large party of men visited him; they were in disguise.

The CHAIRMAN. We have the details of his case.

The WITNESS. Also, about the same time, a preacher by the name of Nathan Cannon was whipped; have you evidence of that?

The CHAIRMAN. Yes, sir.

The WITNESS. You have, I suppose, the evidence of the murder of Alexander Page, complete?

The CHAIRMAN. Yes, sir.

The WITNESS. The facts are given in a publication of the *habeas corpus* case.

Mr. BLAIR. They will not take the evidence here.

The WITNESS. It is considered pretty good evidence down here, as the parties all attempted to prove an *alibi*. Singularly enough, it happened that all these parties indicted had some member of their families who were sick on the particular night of the murder, in a region of country fifteen miles in circumference.

Mr. BLAIR. I object to that. The committee has not admitted it here.

The WITNESS. Albert May was whipped in Noxubee County, about April. Jane Hotcher was whipped in Noxubee about the same time, or a short time after. Now, in Noxubee County a large number of men, who had been summoned regularly and appeared before the grand jury at Oxford, were run off out of the county, and I have never heard from them. I have done everything I could to obtain information in regard to them, but it is impossible to find where they are. Certain men there had them in their custody at a certain time after they were subpœnaed, and perhaps at the next court I may be able to develop some of the facts in regard to those things. A large number of men were kept from coming before the grand jury by threats of being killed or whipped, and when men were brought there upon attachments, they made the statement that the reason they did not come was because they were afraid their lives would be taken. Some of the men have been indicted in the court for intimidation. Some are under arrest and bound over for appearance.

Isaiah Lewis was killed in Noxubee County in the latter part of May. One of the jury of inquest was implicated by the evidence. The evidence went to show that the jury of inquest had men upon it belonging to the Ku-Klux organization itself. They reported a verdict that he was killed by unknown hands.

Rhett Willis was whipped in Monroe County.

The CHAIRMAN. We have the evidence in regard to that.

The WITNESS. Also Simon Duncan.

The CHAIRMAN. We have that case, too.

The WITNESS. Also in Tippah County, about the 1st of January, Willis Mask was whipped, and some time in February Thurman Green was whipped by men in disguise.

Armistead Boyd was whipped some time after that; running along, I do not know the exact date, but in February or March, Joseph Brooks, colored, was whipped.

Albert Thomas, colored, was whipped.

Mrs. Jane Sykes was whipped.

Charles Boyd also. Those cases were in Tippah County.

Now, there is in Chickasaw County a young colored man named Early Bresle. I have had the parties arrested and bound over for appearance before the grand jury; they outraged him, firing at him, but did not whip him, though they attempted. He made his escape out of the window; they firing at him as he escaped. Soon after he saw a prominent farmer, who had been trying to influence him in regard to political matters, returning home from the direction of this house from which Bresle had escaped, and he identified the horse which he was on as one of the horses which was standing by the house when he left. Bresle was then lying in the woods, and I think he was wounded slightly in the shoulder; I have forgotten the particular circumstances.

I have mentioned this band in Alcorn County—I am giving my evidence a little disconnected, but there has been so much of this thing that I can only try to get it in the best shape I can. This band in Tishemingo County had for their pass-word "Blucher," or "Avalanche," or "Star." That is the hailing sign. The answer to that or to either of these words is, "Who comes there?" The reply, "You know who." The response, "I know what?" Then upon coming together they extend their hands, for recognizing, in this manner, [illustrating,] extending the thumb on a straight line upon the hand of the other party, and rubbing the forefinger twice across the wrist in that manner. In wishing to recognize a party in the day-time, it is done by taking hold of the lappel of the coat, with the thumb of the hand extended to the front partly, and in the air. The party recognizing the one, responds by placing the closed or shut hand on the right hip, with the thumb extended straight out into the air. The other stroke of recognition is by a stroke of the whiskers once or twice. If the party recognizes the sign he returns it by placing his thumbs in the waistband of his pants, with the hand closed except that the forefingers are extended in that shape, [illustrating.] These signs are very similar in a number of counties—in fact are all similar. The oaths used by them in two counties are about the same. I have the oath at home, at Holly Springs, and thought I had it with me when I came down, but I find that it is not among my papers. I cannot give it literally, but substantially it is, "You do solemnly swear, in the presence of Almighty God and before this assembly of witnesses, that you will do the acts commanded of you by the commander of this Ku-Klux Klan, outside of the civil law, so help you God." That is about the substance and point. There is some other verbiage in it. The question to the candidate, when initiated, is, "What are the objects of the Ku-Klux Klan?" Answer: "It is to suppress the negro and keep him in the position where he belongs, and to see that the democratic party controls this country." The party who made the confession of these facts, which I have stated, was sworn in by Captain Jack Veal, a noted democratic politician in Tennessee, and a man who is said to have done more in political matters in this end of Tennessee than any other one man. This party was sworn in at a democratic barbacue, where as many as over a hundred and fifty persons were united to the organization. This party stated to me that in Tennessee and in Mississippi, throughout Alcorn, and Tishemingo Counties, and McNairy County, Tennessee, they had killed three colored men and one white man, and had whipped seventeen persons. He said that he had desired to get out of the organization for some time, but that the other members were so closely watched for fear that they might reveal some facts connected with the organization that he had been afraid that his life would be taken, and had been waiting to move to Arkansas in order to get out of the order. This is the same band to which this man belonged, of whom I have just spoken, and a photograph of whom I have furnished. The party who made the revelations is one of those pictured in the photograph.

On the 30th of September of this year, they called upon a family named Honeycutt, and shot through the door, shooting a woman—a young lady—in the arm and also in the side, and probably disabling her for life. They also shot away nearly half of the thumb of John Honeycutt, the wound extending down to the wrist. I investigated that matter as well as I could. The case, as nearly as I could get at it, was this: This man has given me no reason except that they had been asked to come over by a certain man who is the nominee for constable, or something of the sort, of Tishemingo. He stated that he asked them to go there; that man's name is Marlow. He was running for the position of constable or sheriff. During the war John Honeycutt was conscripted into the confederate army. His brother, at that time, was in the Union Army. The family were accused of having Union proclivities, and also accused of having furnished information to General Grant's army of certain movements of the confederate troops. Soon after John Honeycutt was conscripted, he deserted from the confederate army. Since that time, the old lady tells me, they have had no peace in that country. This man Marlow has offered to buy her land at a very low price several times. She is possessed of considerable property. She says they offered to buy her land at a very reduced price, much less than it was worth, and told her it was better for her to sell and go out of the country than remain and be harrassed by the Ku-Klux. It was said she had quite a sum of gold in the house—fifteen hundred or two thousand dollars; this is wrong. She did not say that it was fifteen hundred, but said it was estimated by them at about fifteen hundred, and they supposed it was that amount. The probability was that this Klan visited her house to rob her, and she believes that the real cause of her being persecuted was on account of her son's desertion from the confederate army, and the accusation against them of having given information to the Union Army.

The Ku-Klux also drove off from Tishemingo County Mr. Newman. They first whipped him and then drove him away from his family. He is now living in Arkansas, at some point I do not know where. His wife has sold the property there, and has left. What the object of that whipping was I have not been able to ascertain.

By the CHAIRMAN:

Question. Was he a colored man?

Answer. No, sir; he was a white man; a blacksmith. He ran away from the country while the war was going on—running up to Tennessee, and was engaged as a scout. I ascertained simply these facts.

M. Richardson, near Rienzi, a white man, was whipped on the 1st day of April, 1871, by persons in disguise. They beat him most unmercifully. He is a republican, or at least is accused of it. These are about all the cases of parties indicted and under arrest that I have, the cases for which indictments have been found, and for which parties have been placed under arrest; but there has been other cases reported where parties were not recognized, and no action has been taken by the authorities.

Question. So far as your knowledge and information extend, how is this organization divided as to working members, and those who plan the deeds of violence?

Answer. My observation and investigation have brought me to this conclusion: I think the organization is divided into two classes. There is the working or executing class who ride, who do the raiding, and whipping, and shooting. Another class is composed of respectable citizens, who point the finger of scorn at some certain person or designate a man, and influence these parties to commit these deeds of violence. That class is composed of a respectable portion of the community. While in some instances they are the raiding members to a certain extent, the respectable members of society being brought into these operations themselves, yet I do not believe that the working members in this organization constitute the most respectable portion of society. Take, for instance, Corinth, and the members of the bar, all very prominent—I do not refer to them as being in this class at all in Corinth, for I do not believe that they are—but were they to point the finger of scorn at me, and habitually remark that I ought to be driven from the country, that would be communicated to the captain of the organization at some point, and soon they would visit me to whip or outrage me in some manner. This element of society, spoken of by me, is in perfect sympathy with the organization, for you never hear one word of censure or opposition. If such an expression is ever used it is done in private. I have talked with the citizens, and would say to men, "Gentlemen, you are influential men and lead society. I believe that if your voices were raised in condemnation of these wrongs you could suppress them at once. If you will try you can soon do it. Call a meeting of the citizens and say this thing shall not be continued." But I have never yet been able to get such a meeting called as that, and I classify this Ku-Klux organization as being divided into two classes; one, those who are composed of the most respectable portions of the community, and whose influence and expressions give direction and countenance to the acts of others, while the other class is composed of bad men, capable of doing anything, who do the work.

Question. What evidence have you, if any, of sympathy being exhibited by the men, women, and children of the community where these organizations practice their deeds of violence?

Answer. Well, sir; first, hostility is shown toward officers in my position; also toward those making arrests or trying to ferret out these parties. Secondly, by the manner in which they conceal all evidence and traces of the Ku-Klux having ridden or of their residing in the country. They universally declare "there have been no Ku-Klux in this country; we have not seen such a thing," when in fact we traced their depredations from one point to another, and when the strongest evidence shows that they have been riding for weeks and months right in that community. Not only that, but if you will take the little children at the houses and talk to them alone, they will reveal the fact. They will say, "We have often seen the Ku-Klux and we were not

Electrotype furnished by Harpers' Weekly, (Vol. XVI, p. 73.)

FROM A PHOTOGRAPH SUBMITTED BY HON. G. WILEY WELLS, OF DISGUISES EXHIBITED TO THE COMMITTEE.

scared;" and they will say they were not scared because their parents told them not to be frightened; but if you ask the parents, they will assure you that there are no Ku-Klux in the county, and that no depredations have been committed, unless it may be that they have heard that such a man has been whipped, but did not believe it. Next, the exultation they exhibit over certain depredations. For instance, when Colonel Huggins was whipped, the whole community declared, and showed by their behavior, that they thought when he had been whipped he had received just treatment. In other cases they say, "The damned niggers ought to be whipped." You receive no aid in prosecuting them, and no sympathy; but the man who is endeavoring to ferret them out is violently assailed by the public generally. The women, who have made the garments in which these men go disguised, will deny having ever made the garments. In one case I found, from a boy of fourteen years, that he was at the house and saw the very young lady who had given this denial making these garments. Portions of those very disguises I have here in my satchel now.

Question. What is your opinion, from the consideration you have given to this subject, as to the composition of the bands who inflict these deeds of violence? Are they generally young or middle-aged men?

Answer. Generally, they are young men. In one or two cases I have found amongst them older men—say forty-five years of age. Occasionally they are married men, but they are, principally, unmarried men. These bands are made up of a class of men, generally, ranging from eighteen to thirty-five years of age.

Question. Do you think it possible that they could be members of a band of that kind, riding weekly or semi-weekly, without the other members of the family knowing the fact?

Answer. No, sir; it is utterly impossible For example, at the time of the Pontotoc raid, I examined Mr. Saddler, whose son was accused of being in that raid. The evidence showed that a mule belonging to Mr. Saddler was shot at Pontotoc and captured and put in the livery-stable there. His saddle was on the mule. His son, Tom Saddler, has just been eelcted sheriff of the county—the democratic candidate. His father testified that the son was away from home that night; that he felt uneasy about him, as the band had been very frequently past his house, but he did not know whether they were Ku-Klux or not; he never had heard of any outrages, and did not know their objects, but was afraid Tom might be out riding and commit some devilment. But the next morning he came home and the mule was gone; that he felt uneasy about it when he heard of the trouble at Pontotoc, and therefore told Tom he had better take up his things and go to Texas; but he did not think Tom was in the raid. Now I have the proofs that Tom Saddler was the captain of this organization; that he was the main man—the leader. I also proved that old man Saddler said Flournoy ought to be killed, and his press ought to be broken up, and the whole damned tribe of radicals driven out of the State.

Question. You have examined a good many of the disguises worn by the Ku-Klux. Are they skillfully made up? Apparently fabricated by tailors, or by the female members of the families to which these men belong?

Answer. There is considerable art displayed in making them. Some of them show a good deal of skill. Whether the ingenuity belongs to the tailor or the family, I do not know; but I believe they are principally made in the families. I have some disguises here which I can exhibit to you, that you may see them and thus be better able to judge of the facts. I think they are made by the women who are members of the same families to which the men belong who use them.

Question. Do these bands generally go on horseback?

Answer. Only in two instances have I found that they have gone on foot. Generally they are on horseback.

Question. If the communities in which these men live, and where they hold their meetings, were earnestly endeavoring to penetrate the secrets of this organization, to find out the men who belong to it, would there be, in your opinion, any practical difficulty in ascertaining where these masks are bought, where the materials of these disguises are purchased, and who made them; where the horses were obtained for the raids; where the arms were procured, &c.?

Answer. Not in the least. They could not exist in concealment one hour if the state of facts you mentioned existed—that is, if they were earnestly endeavoring to find them out.

Question. These men uniformly ride in the night-time and are not seen in the day-time with their disguises?

Answer. No, sir; they are never seen except at night. I can exhibit to you the disguises I have mentioned. [The witness here produced and exhibited several suits of fantastically decorated disguises.] There is one of the uniforms which was captured, which I left with Senator Warner, which has a whistle attached. The whistle is made with a small piece of cane, with a shot inside of it, which vibrates and makes a shrill, piercing sound. [A negro man was here called into the room, and a disguise put on him.] This disguise is decorated with white pieces sewed on it in patterns representing the moon and stars, hearts, crosses, &c., in different parts of the body. Here are various face-disguises—one red, two of them are white, with holes cut in them for the eyes and mouth. This one, which is a terrible-looking one, is an officer's disguise, and has a flap over the mouth so contrived that upon his blowing it makes a vibrating noise.

Question. What is the character of defense pursued in the prosecutions that you have caused to be instituted against the members of this order?

Answer. Universally an *alibi*. In not a single case has there been any other defense set up. I might remark here that one of the statements communicated to me by this party, who was a member, and also Mr. Avery, in Winston County, was this: "If you or any other man were to come up and swear identifying me, I would produce plenty of witnesses to prove that you could not be believed under oath. Then, also, I could prove that I was at a certain place at that particular time." I have evidence in my possession where a man named Hooker turned State's evidence in this case of Stubblefield, in which he makes exactly the same statement—that at a certain house in that county they could prove that a large number of them were present that night with others, at a point far distant from the point where they were, in fact, making that raid. The defense consists, universally, in an *alibi*, and an attempt to break down the prosecuting witnesses.

Question. Where a person has been whipped, killed, or otherwise outraged by these bands, what is the course pursued by the friends of this order as to traducing the character of the deceased, or the person whipped or otherwise outraged, and contriving some plausible pretext for the outrage?

Answer. That is indulged in in every case that I have investigated. It makes no difference who the person was or what his character, or whether the party—woman or man—has been whipped, shot, or hung, they at once commence to assert and circulate charges; and they seem to have a method whereby they impregnate the community with the belief that the person so whipped or outraged was guilty of crimes, was a terrible enemy to society, and that, in fact, it was a justice to society that the party was killed or whipped; that it ought to have been done. That seems to be their general practice. You may go into one county and hear of a murder committed, and pass to another neighborhood or district where you would suppose it was not known, and speak of it there, and you will immediately hear the same excuse offered for the murder as in the place where it was committed, as in Winston County. I found that in several instances, when I did not suppose that the murder was known at all, as I had only just found out that the man was killed, by means of detectives who were working it up, upon speaking of it to other gentlemen, they at once said that it was really a benefit to society that such a party was killed.

Question. What is the course pursued towards the witnesses who appear in these prosecutions on behalf of the Government?

Answer. Invariably they are denounced; and these men will bring witnesses to court—respectable parties—who will swear that these men cannot be believed under oath, accusing them of getting up these cases in order to obtain the rewards. I scarcely know a single man who has been brought as a witness in the cases which have been brought to my attention, whether native-born to this country or a northern man—whether a negro or a white man—but he has been universally pronounced both a liar and a scoundrel, and all the charges possible brought up against him. In some instances, they have gone so far as to indict such men upon frivolous pretexts in the counties where these parties have come from.

Question. You alluded, a while ago, to a man named Wissler, who was killed some few days since in Macon, Noxubee County. Will you please state to the committee any fact within your knowledge or information which tends to show that the men connected with this organization perpetrated or incited that assassination, and all facts connected with his case?

Answer. I am very glad that the committee will allow me to make the statement, because there has been so much said in regard to that case that is wholly untrue, and so much parade made through the newspapers, that I would like to have the matter set right publicly. Mr. Wissler came to Oxford as a witness upon certain Ku-Klux trials that were then pending, and while he was there a difficulty arose somewhat after this manner, so Wissler told me: He was standing on the street talking with a colored man, when a drunken man came up and assaulted him with something, saying, "You damned son of a bitch," or language to that effect, when Wissler immediately turned around and struck him, but instantly discovering that he was drunk he turned and left him. Soon after he met General Lamar on the steps of the court-house as he was coming up, and accosted him. General Lamar soon after came into the court-room, and as Wissler was walking out of the court-room, he said to the judge, "I want this man that is leaving arrested." Whistler immediately turned around and came back, facing General Lamar, about four feet from him, when General Lamar says, "May it please your honor, I was standing below here just now, when I saw this beast, this wretch—for I know no other name to apply to him—knock down a poor inebriate, who had just come up to him and accosted him in a genteel manner. He soon after met me on the steps and accosted me in words like these, 'What time does the court meet?' By his language I judged that he was a foreigner, and I passed him by, for I do not speak to such men." Wissler was, by this time, sitting on the steps leading to the judge's seat. After he made this declaration he says, "I started to ride away on my horse, when I heard one of the men in the company ask, 'Who is that?' to which Wisstler replied, 'That is General Lamar, the damned——' and the rest was lost to me as I went away. Now, sir, as some of the most respectable citizens in this community are placed under arrest here for a violation of the peace, I ask your honor to put this wretch under a bond that he shall keep the peace."

Question. To whom was this language addressed?

Answer. To Judge Hill; it was while we were trying the Ku-Klux prisoners from Monroe County at the Oxford Court. Mr. Wissler rose and, General Lamar afterward said, stepped toward him. I was not looking at him at the moment. I saw him rise and turn about half around, as if to face the judge, and say something in his defense. I myself was waiting and watching for an opportunity to say to General Lamar if this man had violated any of his rights he should send him to the mayor's court, and not bring him there. Before I could say that, Whistler rose and turned. As he turned around Lamar jerked up a chair and started toward him. Whistler rushed back to the judge, as if for protection. The judge started up, and, with his hands extended, cried, "General Lamar!" and stood crying, "General Lamar! General Lamar! General Lamar!" while General Lamar was advancing toward him with a heavy wooden-bottom chair raised, approaching the rostrum. I started across to take hold of Lamar to quiet him. I knew him to be a very nervous man, and we were warm friends. Before I got to him the marshal, who was unarmed and back of me, stepped toward him. At that instant General Lamar dropped the chair. Before I could say a word he hauled off and struck the marshal a powerful blow, breaking a small bone at the cap of the eye. When Marshal Pierce was knocked down the scene was one of perfect excitement. The Ku-Klux prisoners jumped over into the bar, from the prisoners' box where they were guarded, stripped up their sleeves, crying, "Go for them, God damn 'em; go for 'em." A scene of utter confusion followed. Some of the lawyers—General Featherstone and Colonel Manning—took General Lamar out into a side-room. I begged them to take him away, as there would be trouble if they did not. General Lamar came back into the court-room, and said, "Sir, this has been, perhaps, somewhat disgraceful"—I will repeat his language as nearly as I can, and it was impressed on my mind because of the excitement of the occasion and my friendship for him and my consciousness that we were in such a disgraceful scene. He said, "This has, perhaps, been a disgraceful affair on my part here in this court, but I want it understood here distinctly, now and forever, that while you are here shackling the freedom of these people, you, sitting upon that bench, with your minions, cannot for one moment suppress my voice when it is raised in behalf of liberty and justice. Sir, before I will close my mouth, or have it closed by your hirelings, I will allow the dust of Oxford to drink my blood. You may send me to jail, you may fine me if you will, but understand, you and all the rest, that you cannot for one moment shackle the freedom of this body of mine nor stifle my voice." The students and some other men, who were in the back part of the court-room, commenced cheering and applauding and slapping their hands. The judge said, "Arrest those men." I thought it time, as the marshal was confused and scarce able to make out what he was doing, and that it was my duty to speak out. There were two soldiers in the court-house. I said to the soldiers, "Bring these men in the bar." General Lamar walked up to me and said to me, "Sit down." I told him, "No, sir; I am an officer and I shall try to keep order." And I told him, "Sir, you must not put your hands upon me." At that moment a number of young men who had rushed out when the occurrence commenced were returning, some of them with pistols drawn, others with pistols buckled upon them. They came into the court-room. I stepped out of the bar and told the soldiers again to arrest them. They stood mute and did not do a thing. The foreman of the grand jury, B. B. Emery, had run out, at the commencement of the excitement, to the camp of Lieutenant De Rodo, and got six men with carbines, who came up into the court-room while everything was in a state of confusion. Instantly the crowd dispersed, everything was quiet, and the judge adjourned the court. It is due, since this affair has been brought up, to state that Colonel Reynolds and Colonel Dowd, counsel for the prisoners, from the first, did their utmost to keep the prisoners in their places, and also to suppress the disturbance. The next morning after the court had been adjourned, the judge went to the court-room. He was sick, and said he was exhausted and did not feel like holding court, and entered an order, which reads something like this: "Whereas a most disgraceful scene has occurred in the United States court, in which J. Q. C. Lamar was the actor, and while he has made ample apology to myself, personally, for the outrage committed, yet, as I am the representative of a great Government, and the dignity of the court should be preserved, it is deemed proper and necessary that his name should be stricken from the list of attorneys." General Lamar was disbarred from practice two weeks. He apologized to the marshal for what he had done; said he was very sorry; and he also apologized in open court to the judge. After he had been disbarred two weeks, I moved his re-admission, and he was admitted to practice. This man Whistler, who had been the cause of all this, started away immediately. He had already been designated to perform certain duties in serving writs for arrests down below here. Seeing the general feeling that prevailed of excitement among the democratic members of the bar, who declared that Whistler was a miserable wretch, Marshal Pierce concluded that it would be best to send him down with some men who had been ordered to go back and give bond. I had never met the man before; in fact, had never seen him until this occurrence. It was determined to have him sent down with another party to make arrests, and, in company with Mr. Lewis, he was made deputy marshal for the occasion. He left Oxford to go to Winston County, or Macon, taking certain prisoners to give bond before the United States commissioner. When he got as far as Corinth he telegraphed to me that he was arrested, but in a few days I received notice that he had been released from arrest and had gone on. He came back from Macon, and when he got to Oxford he informed me that an accident had occurred while at Corinth, at the table, in which a man had been burned, and that they had arrested him for it, but that upon investigation he had been acquitted; that they also accused him of having robbed the man of $600. He started to return to his home, and when he arrived at Corinth, on his return, he was arrested again, whereupon he immediately telegraphed to me. I telegraphed to the Department of Justice at Washington and received a notification from them to go there and defend him. I immediately went to Corinth, where I investigated the whole matter thoroughly, and had all the evidence reduced to writing. The record is now in the possession of Squire Dodson, of Corinth, a justice of the peace. I found that they had had an examination. I learned from Squire Dodson, the presiding justice at the first trial, that they had had an examination there of his case upon a charge of an assault with a burning-lamp, with intent to kill and murder; that they went into an examination, two of the best lawyers of Corinth being employed to prosecute Wissler. He engaged one lawyer to take his case. They called all the witnesses who were at the table at the time the accident occurred, and also swore this man Shipley, the man who was burned, before he died. Upon all the testimony these lawyers stated that there was no evidence which would support the charge, and they dropped it and gave up the case, and Whistler was dismissed; but when he came back he was arrested a second time. A warrant was sworn out charging him with manslaughter.

Question. How long was this subsequent to his discharge?

Answer. About five days. He had gone down to Winston, and, in the mean time, the man, Shipley, had died. After Shipley's death Wissler was re-arrested, and that was the time I went to Corinth. I found that they had gone to Rienzi, a distance of twelve or fourteen miles, in order to procure a justice of the peace to come there to sit at the trial. At first they had intended to take him there, to Rienzi. I objected to this stranger coming there and trying the case, when there were two or three justices in the town of standing and honor, well acquainted with the law, and insisted that they should at least admit one of the justices of the peace there to sit on the case. I found a terrible state of excitement existing in Corinth. Violent epithets were used by certain men in regard to United States officials. One man named McMullan seemed to instigate the whole scheme, working up the points and denouncing Wissler and the United States officials generally. After making an arrangement that we might call an associate justice, we chose Squire Dodson and went to trial. The facts shown by the testimony were simply as follows, and the evidence will bear me out in my statement: Whistler was stopping at the Mallett House with the prisoners whom he had in custody when he was interrupted by a man named Shipley, a tobacco-drummer from Kentucky—a man, by the way, for whom I had an affidavit upon which a warrant had been issued for his arrest, for carrying on an illicit tobacco trade for manufacturers in Kentucky. He accosted him with, "Who are you?" This was addressed generally to the crowd, some six or seven prisoners being present. One of the prisoners answered, "We are prisoners with this man here, charged with Ku-Kluxing." Shipley says, "Why in hell don't you go away then? I would like to see myself conducted about by one man, and as many as there are of you." Whistler remarked, "You must not interrupt me in the discharge of my duty or interfere with these men. If you do, I shall take you in out of the cold." Directly afterward he left and went across the room and returning said to them, "I'll be damned if I would be led around by such a damned deputy marshal as that." Whistler spoke to him again not to interfere. He said, "I was only in fun. Now come out and take a drink with me, to assure me that it's all right." Whistler said, "I don't know, sir; I don't know anything about that; but I want you to keep away from these men." Whistler started out of his hotel, and got only a short distance when he was overtaken by Shipley, who says, "God damn you, you must drink with me, to show me that this thing is settled." Whistler answered, "I have no objection," and they went into Mr. Hill's drinking-saloon, a short distance from the Scruggs House, and the evidence of the bar-keeper is that Wissler took, as a drink, a sherry-cobbler and the other man straight whisky. In reaching in his pocket for the money, Shipley not finding the money readily, Whistler put his hand in his pocket and handed out the change for the drinks, when Shipley drew it out and said, "No, sir; I always have enough to treat my friends and a dollar or two left for others; but I will take another drink with you as you are so anxious to pay for it." After a few words similar to this, Whistler says, "Very well, what will you have?" and he took a cigar and this man took whisky. This man Shipley then insisted on going to a fair that was going on at Corinth. Whistler said, "No, I have prisoners along and can't go." (It was a kind of festival that was going on in Corinth.) After he asked him to go the fair, Whistler says, "I have been here now longer than I ought to, and I must go back to my prisoners." Shipley says, "By God, you must go." Whistler says, "No, I can't." Then the bar-keeper remarked, "It is a colored fair." Shipley says, "Then I don't go." Whistler, mean time, had started to go and was just leaving for the Scruggs House when Shipley was informed that the festival was a colored fair. This man Shipley came along with him. Directly he (Whistler) found that his pistol was gone, and started back, saying, "I must go and get my pistol." As he turned around Shipley says, "No, I just took it out of your pocket for fun." They then went on in company to the Scrugg's House. When they got into the Scruggs House they walked down to the bar. Shipley remained in the bar-room. Whistler went into the dining-room and sat down, and after a few moments Shipley came in and took a seat beside him. A number of prisoners, the chambermaid—whose name I do not remember now —the steward of the hotel, and a stranger were sitting at the same table. After Whistler sat down, it seems for some reason that he concluded his supper sooner than the others. The evidence is that he got up before Shipley did and started to the door and turned back and came to the table and put his hand on Shipley's shoulder and said something which no one distinguished, but seemingly friendly, when he said, "I haven't got it." One of the prisoners on the other side of the table says, "I heard it drop on the floor," meaning the pistol; whether he used the word pistol or not I do not know. Whistler pulled back the chair and stooped down to find it. Shipley says, "Take the lamp." Whistler then took the lamp, looked down on the floor, found his pistol, rose, and was attempting to put the lamp on the table. One of the witnesses, Julia Burns, the chambermaid, testified that when he had got the lamp so that the pedestal was at about the height of the table it was moving backward and forward, and moved so once or twice very near or directly over the person of Shipley; that then it exploded with a loud noise.

Question. The lamp or chimney?

Answer. The lamp and chimney. It was oscillating—that was her word; that the lamp exploded with a loud noise, and everything was in flames, and she ran. Mr. Norville, the steward of the hotel, testified that when the lamp was at about the same height it moved to the right once, and to the left, and then fell to the floor, and everything was in flames. To the best of his judgment and belief the lamp separated at the joint between the pedestal and globe. It was united by a brass band and plaster of Paris. He testified that the lamp had frequently been out of repair; that it had been repaired by the clerk; that he believed it out of repair at this time; that he thought the oscillation was caused by this looseness of the joint, and he stated that the pedestal of the lamp remained in his hands while the globe fell to the floor. The colored boy, who stood immediately behind him, testified that the lamp was raised up perpendicularly; that the flames shot up out of the chimney; that he had got it to the height of the table when it seemed to fall over to the left, and he raised up his left hand to catch it, and it turned to the right and fell to the floor. These are the three witnesses who noticed it at the time, and that is their testimony almost *verbatim*. After the flames broke out Shipley started and ran to the door, one or two hundred yards, through the bar-room, and out to the stoop, where he jumped into a trough, which is used by passengers for washing. Immediately a crowd of thirty-five or fifty persons surrounded him; he was covered up with water and his clothes were taken off. The lamp could not have burst. The evidence was that his pants were consumed, from the bottom of the pants and drawers, up to the waist-band; that two inches of one pocket was entirely burned off and six inches of the other was entirely consumed, while his shirt-bosom was not burned nor his waist-coat. This crowd surrounded him, and, soon after, Shipley says, "Take care of those pants." They gathered them up and put them under his head. This was after they had been thrown off on the walk below, and at that time it was testified that there was, probably, a hundred and twenty-five men on the step, and more were coming. They took him out then and moved him to a room in the hotel. In the morning he sent for the clerk, Pope Scruggs, and said, "I would like to get my pocket-book; I was told that you had it." Scruggs said, "This is a mistake;" and then remarked, "It must be lost somewhere;" and Mr. Scruggs went out and, soon after, a man named Mullet went in. Mullet testified that he said to this man who was dying, "I believe that man turned the lamp over on you, intending to rob you and burn you up." From that moment—the first moment that the thought was entertained—this became an established fact, and it spread over the entire town that that was the fact. In support of that they brought in a witness to prove that Mr. Whistler had been in the barber-shop the next morning, where he had taken out a roll of bills as large as his arm; that the barber judged there was five hundred and fifty or six hundred dollars in it, but it would not vary more than $50 in the amount, one way or the other I asked him the denomination of the bills; he could not tell, only that there were a great many $20 notes. Mr. Lewis is neither a republican nor a carpet-bagger, but resides here. He is a man of very high character. He was in the barber-shop at the time, and stood beside Whistler when he was counting the money. He said that it amounted to one hundred and sixty odd dollars, which was just the amount of money, less the amount expended in transporting the prisoners to Corinth, furnished him by the United States marshal when he left Oxford. This witness was there and saw the entire amount counted over. They introduced evidence of the dying declarations of this man that he believed that Whistler had burned him for the purpose of robbing him, and that he had lost his life for this reason. The justices disagreeed in reference to the case. One held that Whistler ought to be committed and his bond fixed at $2,000. The other thought he ought to be discharged, as there was no evidence to hold him. I immediately sued on a writ of *habeas corpus*, and took it before Judge Davis, the circuit judge of the ninth judicial district, at Holly Springs, Marshall County; and Judge Davis informed me that the public prejudice was so strong, in consequence of what had been said, and also from there having been a number of articles published in the paper, wherein, among other things, this man Whistler was nicknamed "Coal-Oil Charley;" and the democratic paper, the Appeal, published in Memphis, having taken it up and endeavored to bring this man into disrepute, dragging his wife into the scene, &c.—articles appearing in regard to her virtue and in regard to this man's mother and his father and, indeed, the whole family—that he would be obliged to go to Alcorn County and hear the case. I begged him to remain and hear the evidence, as taken down by Major Wofford, the editor of the Corinth News, who was a perfect gentleman, the editor of a democratic paper published there, and who had taken the evidence by order of the court. I had asked them there to select some man for the purpose, and I asked Major Wofford to do it, and he did so. I told the judge that the evidence had been taken down by Major Wofford; that both the members of the court had certified to the correctness of his record of the evidence. By this means he would be outside of the influence of the excitement which prevailed in Corinth, and could hear and adjudicate the matter where he was better than by going to Alcorn County. The judge said, "No; I must go there. I have to reside here, and public prejudice is so strong that it would hardly answer for me to take that course." I told him very well; it was impossible for me to go. He went and, I understand, called the witnesses and went through the case *de novo*; and when he had gotten through the case he held Whistler to bail in the sum of $5,000. All this I forwarded to the Attorney General's Office. Whistler was placed in jail. I then went to Jackson and drew up a petition asking a writ of error, and the judges informed me that they were willing to issue the necessary writ; and, about that time, I saw Governor Powers, who told me he was willing to go up there and bail him out. I told him, if that was the case, I would rather take that course than to have this writ of error taken out. He then went up and bailed Whistler out, on a bond of $5,000, and Whistler returned home. During the time he was in jail he was deprived of his letters. I was not allowed to write to him as an attorney, under cover or seal, but my letters were opened and were taken out and hawked about the streets of Corinth. One of the telegrams which I had sent to him was published in the Memphis Appeal, and one of my letters was retained in the office of a lawyer in Corinth—at least, it was there, as I am credibly informed; one was copied by the sheriff and sent to Judge Davis, because I remarked something in it in regard to Judge Davis's course. No persons were allowed to visit him while confined in his cell, and while he was there a man named McMullin went into his cell, drew a revolver, and said to him, "Now, God damn you, Wells is gone, and you have got no friends, and this is the thing will finish you. It will make no difference to you whether you remain here or get away, God damn you. There's a hole for you in this country, and you have got to get into it," and words of that character. This is a statement as put in writing by Whistler, before his death. Whistler asked for protection. I went to Judge Davis and told him this man was being threatened in jail, and it was not safe for him to remain there. I asked him to change Whistler from Alcorn County to Marshall, where he would be safe. Judge Davis said, "Unless the citizens of Alcorn County are willing to swear that it is unsafe for him to remain, I do not want to put the State to the expense of removing him to Marshall County." After this conversation with Judge Davis, in reference to his safety, Whistler received a note, in writing, from some party, telling him, "When you get out of jail you will want to travel North, not South; go the other way." Soon after he came out of jail he was assassinated, being shot through the window. I have been investigating that case since I have been here in Columbus, within a few days, and have information that is quite conclusive to me and will be positive, I think, that Whistler was murdered by the Triplett organization.

By Mr. RICE :

Question. In Winston County?

Answer. Yes, sir. Triplett was the brother-in-law of this man Whistler. Whistler possessed the evidence of Triplett being the prime mover in and the controlling gentleman in the organization. There is also a chain of facts which I will show from other evidence that I have now. These men have never ceased to persecute Whistler from the time that he was before the grand jury at Oxford. The evidence will show that two men shot him through the window; that they were at the window when he was shot. One of them is a prominent citizen in Noxubee County. I would rather not give any further information on the subject, as I do not think it would be prudent to disclose the names at present, as the parties are not yet arrested, although I have already drawn the papers, and shall soon have them under arrest. These are the reasons why I believe that the assassination of Whistler was procured by this band of outlaws.

By the CHAIRMAN:

Question. You have alluded in your testimony to Mr. Huggins, of Aberdeen, and the fact of his being whipped by a band of disguised men. Some attempt has been made before this committee to throw discredit upon the statements of Colonel Huggins and his character. Please to state if you are well acquainted with Mr. Huggins.

Answer. Yes, sir; I have been acquainted with him ever since I came into the State—two years ago.

Question. Is he a man of good habits and character or not?

Answer. He is a man of excellent habits, of good character; a man whom I have always understood to be above reproach. The only thing I know that has been said against him is simply that these men in Monroe County have attempted to disgrace him or bring reproach upon him on account of his political affiliation with the republican party.

Question. Is that a common thing toward republican office-holders, both State and Federal?

Answer. Yes, sir; it is universally so, with hardly an exception.

Question. Do you know Miss Davis, who is postmistress at, I think, Tupelo?

Answer. Yes, sir.

Question. Are you acquainted with her?

Answer. I am not personally acquainted with her. I knew her by reputation and by having met her. I have had considerable correspondence with her in an official capacity, and know her by reputation.

Question. Certain legal gentlemen of Aberdeen, who have been witnesses before this committee, have stated that her character for chastity was bad. One witness went so far as to say that she had the character of being a strumpet. Please to state what her character is among those who are well acquainted with her.

Answer. Among those with whom I associate, and who are well acquainted with Miss Davis, and have known her since she has been in the State, her character is above reproach. I never heard it intimated that she was anything but a virtuous woman; a Christian lady, doing a good work there—educating the colored children, trying to bring them up to the standard of morality and intelligence which should prevail in a Christian community.

Question. Is she a northern woman?

Answer. Yes, sir. She is a sister-in-law of the presiding elder in the Northern Methodist Church in this conference—Rev. Mr. McDonald.

Question. State what persecutions she has been subjected to.

Answer. There was a man named Freeman, said to be a desperado, a man without character and devoid of principle, a drunken reprobate and ruffian, who went to her house one night about midnight, opened the shutter of the window in her room, and was about entering, when she met him at the window with a drawn pistol, and defended herself and her chastity by driving this man off. The wife of this man, Mrs. Freeman, so I have been informed, waited upon Miss Davis the next day, and besought her with tears not to make this public, saying, that if she had any more grievances to come to her with them; and for a time Miss Davis and Mrs. Freeman were quite intimate, and consulted together in regard to Freeman's conduct. Soon after this, Freeman attacked a colored girl, a pupil of Miss Davis—Miss Davis was teaching a school, and had taken special pains to teach this girl her duty, and a proper regard for virtue and chastity—Freeman, at 10 or 11 o'clock, at night, (I think on Sunday,) met her at the house where her friends were, with a pistol, made her get into a buggy, drove her through the town, and there, against her will, had carnal knowledge of her—ravished her; and from his outrageous conduct the girl was confined to her bed for weeks. He was indicted for it, but ran away after he was indicted. He is one of the most notorious characters in Northern Mississippi, as a desperado. I hardly know a man who gives him any other character, except it be General Gholson. On the cars the other evening we were speaking of him, and I mentioned his burning down the church there. General Gholson then told me he was of a very good family, was a very brave man; but when in drink he would do anything, and said, "I called to see him the other day and he was badly wounded." He is the only man I ever heard speak of Freeman with any degree of respect whatever.

Question. What are the circumstances of the burning of that church?

Answer. This man Freeman had declared on the street, in the presence of his friends and in the hearing of a certain colored man, and the postmistress, I believe, that no damned radical church should stand one hour in that community; that the damned church should be burned. About five or six days after that, when service was out one night, Miss Davis was coming from church, and, it being a moonlight night, she saw two men skulking around back of the church. She separated herself from those with her, and went alone to a hill overlooking the place, and there saw this man whom she knew to be Freeman, for she had met him frequently—indeed, he had just passed her going there as he went to the church—she saw him strike the matches, go around the corner of the church out of her sight, and in five minutes the church was in flames, which destroyed it.

Question. What are the sentiments of this Ku-Klux Klan and their sympathizers and friends toward the system of common schools, and particularly so far as they relate to the education of colored children?

Answer. The uniform feeling and sentiment of those people, of the sympathizers of the Ku-Klux is, that this common-school system is not to be put into operation; that the colored folks ought to be able to take care of their own children; that the people ought not to be taxed to educate them. Universally through the Klans and among their sympathizers the system meets with the most hearty opposition. I believe that in many counties many of their raids and whippings have been principally aimed at school-teachers and school-houses, to drive away the teachers and break up the schools.

Question. Have you any information that the school-houses, where these colored children are educated, have been burned?

Answer. Yes, sir; I have heard of such burnings in Winston, Noxubee, Pontotoc, Lowndes, Union, and Tishemingo, and Alcorn, and Tippah, and a number in Lafloor, and one in De Soto and La Fayette, and others in other counties. In some of these counties the entire school system has been broken up. They have driven off the teachers. Where the teachers have been whipped, they have been informed by prominent citizens that it was not safe for them to remain in the county.

Question. Have you heard of colored churches being burned?

Answer. Only one, at Tupelo. There was one burned in Winston County, but they were using it for a school at that time. It had been given up for use as a school-house.

By Mr. BLAIR:

Question. When were you summoned before this committee?

Answer. I received a dispatch, I think, on Friday.

Question. Last Friday?

Answer. Yes, sir; I think so.

Question. A week ago?

Answer. Yes, sir; before you left Macon, I think, I received the summons.

Question. That was before last Thursday?

Answer. Yes; it was before last Thursday.

Question. It was about eight or ten days ago?

Answer. It was last Thursday week, about eight or ten days ago.

Question. Have you been in consultation with the committee ever since?

Answer. No, sir; I have not been in consultation with them. I have visited them. I have met Senator Rice and Senator Pratt at the table at the hotel, and I have visited them. I do not know that I understand what you mean by having been in consultation.

Question. I want merely to know whether you have stated to the members of the committee what you could prove?

Answer. I have stated to them this: that society was in a terrible condition here and that they ought to stay longer than two weeks in order to get the facts of the situation here fully.

Mr. BLAIR. I have asked the witness these questions because in making any such examination as this, it was to be expected that if a member of the minority of the committee was sent down here to accompany the sub-committee, he was entitled to know if any fair examination of the condition of the country was proposed, when witnesses were to be called to testify as to transactions in distant parts of the State, in order that he might have subpœnas issued for witnesses from these districts, to attend and explain, or controvert, if possible, the testimony given by the witnesses called by the majority. Inasmuch as it has been known to the majority of the committee that this witness would be put on the stand from the time of their arrival in this place, and as I have had no intimation of the tenor of his testimony, I have not been able, of course, to call witnesses from the counties of Alcorn, Tishemingo, and other distant parts of the State, to explain the transactions to which he has testified here by hearsay, and all sorts of——

The WITNESS. It is not exactly hearsay, general, but sworn evidence of witnesses, which I have repeated.

Mr. BLAIR. The testimony of the prosecution, and one side of the case only, is all that has been attempted to be brought before the committee by this witness, and no opportunity is allowed me, by timely notification, to produce testimony explanatory or contradictory of that which has been given.

The CHAIRMAN. This witness has been in your sight every day since he arrived in town, and you might fairly have inferred from his official position and presumed knowledge that he would be called as a witness, and what would have been the general character of his testimony.

Mr. BLAIR. I did not know his official position, nor presumed knowledge, nor whether he lived here or where.

The CHAIRMAN. You knew he was the district attorney of the United States for this district.

Mr. BLAIR. I did not.

The WITNESS. I was introduced to you as district attorney. I do not know anything about how I was called.

Mr. BLAIR. In the calling of this witness, at this hour, when the determination of the committee had been arrived at to adjourn to-night, it is utterly impossible for me to call any witness to testify in answer to him, and in this the object of sending this committee down here has been defeated, so far as the ends of justice and truth are concerned. This is done, not only in the case of this witness, but in the whole body of witnesses introduced here to-day from a distance, and that course has been pursued at almost every place we have visited. I want to put that on the record as my statement.

The CHAIRMAN. Let there be put on the record of the committee, side by side with it, the statement that the minority has never ceased to grumble at the action of the majority from the time we first started out, although there has been every disposition on our part to accommodate the minority. Subpœnas for witnesses have never been refused save in one single case, after we had reached the State of Mississippi, when we were asked to subpœna witnesses from Tuscaloosa County, Alabama. The minority of the committee throughout this investigation have been allowed a fair share of the time in the examination of witnesses. Nearly, if not quite, one-half of the time of the committee, since it first started out, has been occupied by the minority in producing its testimony, and throughout this investigation there has been no disposition to deal unfairly with the rights of the minority.

Mr. BLAIR. I am willing that the testimony should show for itself. I deny the statement that I have had a fair share of the time of the committee, or any other courtesy extended to me to which I was entitled. I believe, if the ends of justice were had in view, that I was entitled to know when witnesses were to be called from any particular portion of the State, but I have never been allowed to know it; and in this case, although I have made complaint of similar cases heretofore, the same kind of treatment has been repeated.

The CHAIRMAN. In relation to this particular witness I will say, that he has, for nearly a week, sat at the same table with all the members of the committee at the hotel. I think the minority must have known his official position, and that the majority designed using him as a witness. It seems to me impossible that that should not have been inferred.

Mr. BLAIR. I will state again that I did not know the gentleman's official position. I knew his name, and that is all. I have no cross-examination to make of the witness.

COLUMBUS, MISSISSIPPI, *November* 17, 1871.

WILLIAM H. PERKINS sworn and examined.

The CHAIRMAN. As this witness is called at the instance of the minority, General Blair will please open the examination.

By Mr. BLAIR:

Question. Where do you reside?

Answer. At Artesia, thirteen miles west of this, in Lowndes County.

Question. Were you present in Artesia, and did you there witness the killing of a man named Lee by a negro crowd?

Answer. I was there, but did not witness it. It occurred within a hundred yards of my front door of my store, but I did not see the killing. I saw the crowd over Lee when he was down, after he had been shot and killed, but I did not see the occurrence.

Question. Were you present at the examination of the witnesses at the inquest?

Answer. I was on the coroner's jury.

Question. What facts were proven?

Answer. That the first shot fired was fired in the air, and was fired either from a rifle or a carbine. That was the uniform testimony; and that thereupon Mr. Lee started out of the crowd, fearing there would be a row, or something of the kind; that some one hallooed, "Who did that; who shot?" and somebody else replied, "White man," and then another voice says, "Kill him! kill him!" and they pursued him and struck him over the head. He fell down in the common there, and then he was shot in the back with a rifle or gun of some sort; he had a saber-wound also.

Question. Were the negroes who shot him identified?

Answer. Not that I know of. I saw several standing over him.

Question. How many witnesses testified as to the first discharge, or that the first gun was discharged into the air?

Answer. There were six or seven, sir.

Question. Name the witnesses.

Answer. Dr. O. C. Brothers, H. T. Pearce, J. H. Cook, Stanton Cromwell, Dr. D. J. Zuber. I cannot think of the other names just at this moment.

Question. You say there were six or seven?

Answer. I think there were seven.

Question. Did any one testify to this young man Lee firing a pistol?

Answer. No, sir; there was one colored man who testified that he fired a pistol, but he got so confused in his testimony that we did not regard it much. On being closely questioned, he got very much confused, and told two or three different tales about it.

Question. Did he contradict himself?

Answer. Yes, sir; very clearly. He first said he saw the pistol; saw Mr. Lee with the pistol; that the witness was sitting on his mule, close by. He said afterward that he did not see the pistol, but he saw the smoke. He got very much confused in his statement, so that we did not attach much importance to it.

Question. What was the evidence about his having a pistol at all?

Answer. There was none in the world that we could discover.

Question. Was there any pistol discovered on him after he fell?

Answer. No, sir; none in his possession; we asked that. Dr. Zuper and Dr. Brothers both examined him soon after he fell, and we asked them both if they saw any weapon about him, and they said "none."

Question. Who was the first person that came to the body?

Answer. That I do not know. I think Mr. Elmore. By the way, Mr. Elmore was another witness—John W. Elmore. I think he was one of the first persons who got to his dead body. He stated that he ran up there when they were standing over him and prevented them from shooting him again, and prevented any further violence. He was the magistrate of the beat, sir.

Question. Had any one then laid hands upon the man, or taken hold of him when Mr. Elmore got up to him?

Answer. No, sir; excepting a colored man who had caught him by his coat as he fell.

Question. Did Elmore say he saw any pistol upon him?

Answer. No, sir; he did not see any.

Question. Was any testimony taken as to his having had a pistol upon him before he went into the crowd?

Answer. We had nothing explicit upon that point further than what Mr. Boswell and Mr. F. M. Sanford, of Meridian, testified. They testified to his uniformly quiet, rather shrinking character; that he was never in the habit of carrying a pistol.

Question. Had they been with him that day?

Answer. Yes, sir; he came from Mr. Askew's house, where they were building. He was working for Mr. Sanford—one of his hands, as a carpenter. He left Mr. Askew's house about 1 o'clock, and came to the depot preparatory to going to his home at Enterprise, at night, by the train. This occurrence was at nearly sun-down; it was just before night, between 4 and 5 o'clock.

Question. Had Sanford and Boswell been with him that day?

Answer. Yes, sir. I do not know that Mr. Boswell had; he was working with Mr. Sanford. I do not think he had been with Mr. Boswell that day. Mr. Boswell is a railroad repairer, or carpenter, and he was not in Boswell's employ at the time; but Mr. Boswell testified to his good character while he was in his employ.

Question. What did Sanford say on the subject of his carrying weapons?

Answer. He said he was not in the habit of carrying them at all.

Question. Did he say as to his knowledge whether he had owned or possessed any weapon?

Answer. I am mistaken, if you understood me to say that Mr. Sanford was a witness before the coroner's jury. I did not mean that. This is private information I got at different times. He was not there until the next day. He was not a witness before the coroner's jury. Mr. Boswell was; I did not intend to say that Mr. Sanford was.

By the CHAIRMAN:

Question. I did not catch the first part of your statement, and I may be betrayed into asking you upon matters you have testified about. Were you on the jury of inquest?

Answer. Yes, sir.

Question. Were you foreman?

Answer. No, sir.

Question. Was any attorney present conducting the investigation?

Answer. Yes, sir.

Question. Who?

Answer. Mr. Meek. Two, Mr. Meek and Joe Lee.

Question. Were they both democrats?

Answer. Yes, sir.

Question. How long did this investigation last?

Answer. We were there from 9 o'clock until 12.

Question. How many witnesses were examined?

Answer. We examined some six or seven.

Question. How many colored witnesses?

Answer. Two of the seven.

Question. The remainder were white men?

Answer. Yes, sir; the jury was composed of six white men and six colored.

Question. Who empaneled the jury?

Answer. The magistrate is directed to do it.

Question. Is he clothed with the powers of a coroner by your law?

Answer. Really I do not know whether he is or not.

Question. Do you know whether he has any powers to hold an inquest of that kind?

Answer. I just take it for granted that he had from the fact that it was done in that way.

Question. The jury consisted of twelve instead of six?

Answer. Yes, sir; six colored men and six white men.

Question. Were the witnesses closely examined as to the character of the weapon from which the fire and smoke proceeded?

Answer. They were questioned pretty closely; yes, sir.

Question. How near did the witnesses stand to the place from which the gun or pistol was discharged?

Answer. Some of them were very close to it. Dr. Zuber for one was within half a dozen paces; Mr. Pearce was a little further off; Dr. Brothers further off still. Mr. Pearce was very positive about its being either a rifle or a carbine, and he stated to us that he saw considerable of the muzzle; that it was pointed in the air at an angle of about ninety degrees, or nearly perpendicular.

Question. In what direction did he say the barrel was pointed?

Answer. Nearly perpendicular.

Question. Inclining towards the stand where the speaker was?

Answer. I do not know as to that.

Question. Was he questioned as to the point, or were any of the witnesses, whether the barrel was inclined; if there was an inclination in the direction of the stand?

Answer. I do not remember of that question being asked. They mostly testified that it was perpendicular, or if anything a little inclined, but nearly perpendicular.

Question. The testimony showed that Mr. Bliss was speaking at the time?

Answer. Yes, sir.

Question. Standing in his buggy?

Answer. Yes, sir.

Question. He was in a position, therefore, to observe what transpired, better than any one else?

Answer. Yes, sir; I think so.

Question. Why was he not summoned before the jury?

Answer. Well, sir, he had gone away; both Mr. Bliss and Mr. Lewis had gone home, and we took such witnesses as we could get immediately at hand.

Question. Did not the witnesses who testified before you swear that there was a very great crowd at the time?

Answer. Yes, sir; we knew that; most of the jury knew that.

Question. Did the witnesses swear that they were looking at the speaker at the time the discharge took place?

Answer. Some of them were looking in the direction of the speaker, but as we can see two objects at once in that way, we did not question them particularly as to that—both points being within range of the eye.

Question. But they swore that upon the discharge of this gun or pistol, whatever the weapon was, that Lee turned and commenced running out of the crowd?

Answer. Yes, sir.

Question. Immediately upon its discharge?

Answer. Yes, sir.

Question. Did it appear why he turned and ran?

Answer. No, sir; the impression made upon my mind, and I think upon the minds of all the jurors, was that he was one of those timid sort of young men, and he was fearful that there would be a difficulty.

Question. Why should not the balance of the crowd have started at the report?

Answer. He was the only white man in the crowd about the wagon.

Question. I understood that Mr Pearce was standing within a few paces of him?

Answer. That is so.

Question. Why should not other white men, and, for that matter, colored men, have commenced running away at the same time that Lee did?

Answer. I do not know as to that.

Question. Was there any evidence tending to show what the cause was which made Lee turn and flee through the crowd the moment the discharge took place?

Answer. No, sir.

Question. But the fact was that he turned and commenced getting out of the crowd as fast as he could immediately upon the discharge of this weapon?

Answer. Yes, sir; that was the fact stated.

Question. Was there any testimony on the point whether Lee had interrupted the speaker?

Answer. There was not, sir.

Question. Was the question asked to any witness?

Answer. Let me think a moment. I believe there was a question asked.

Question. Did you hear it testified by any of the witnesses that Lee asked the speaker if he was a white man?

Answer. I believe that question was asked, sir; to the best of my recollection it was Stanton Cromwell, a colored man, who testified that Lee asked, or some one asked, whether he was a white man or a negro. That was Stanton Cromwell who testified that.

Question. Was that fact contradicted by any witnesses?

Answer. No other witness seemed to know anything about it that I remember.

Question. Was Cromwell standing near him?

Answer. Near the wagon where Bliss was speaking.

Question. In a position where he could have heard them if the words were spoken?

Answer. Yes, sir; I suppose so.

Question. Do you recollect the name of the colored man who swore that Lee fired a pistol?

Answer. Wiley Stewart.

Question. Was he one who testified before the coroner's jury.

Answer. Yes, sir.

Question. Is he a colored man of good character?

Answer. Well, he has always been very civil, and of good character, so far as I know. I never knew anything against him.

Question. He lives in that neighborhood?

Answer. Yes, sir.

Question. Until he gave that testimony you never heard his character for truth drawn in question?

Answer. No, sir; I never heard but very little said about him. He was a quiet, inoffensive sort of a colored man.

Question. He was not in any way implicated in this affair?

Answer. No, sir.

Question. He had no motive to tell an untruth that you could discover?

Answer. No, sir.

Question. You say that there was no evidence that Lee had a pistol, and that there was none found on him. Suppose the fact to have been that he, in point of fact, discharged the pistol, and commenced running out of the crowd, and was pursued, and dropped the pistol before he fell; then, of course, no pistol would have been found upon his person, and very naturally it would have been picked up by some of the crowd?

Answer. Yes, sir; I should think that might possibly have happened.

Question. If he had fired that pistol and was fleeing because of the gathering wrath of the crowd, would he not naturally have thrown the pistol away in running, trying to make his escape from the crowd?

Answer. Well, sir; I should think that that might be so. Mr. Elmore—if you will allow me to mention what he testified—not Mr. Elmore, but a young Mr. Alston, testified before the coroner's jury that he saw him very soon after he turned around to come out of the crowd—he was standing right in range to see him—coming toward him. He said that somebody grabbed at him, and struck at him, and they seemed to be turning on him, and he seized his hat in this manner, [illustrating,] and had his hands over his head with his hat off and in his hand, as if he was trying to protect his head, and running toward Mr. Alston, who was standing in the store door below mine.

Question. Was Lee understood to be a democrat?

Answer. I never heard of the man before that day. I have no idea whether he was a democrat or a republican.

Question. Have you heard since?

Answer. No, sir; I never have. I do not know what his political sentiments were.

Question. Was there a feeling of irritation on the part of the democrats about Artesia at the strong demonstration which the negroes were making upon that evening?

Answer. It was not so much a feeling of irritation as fear of the results. They came there—they evidently had been drinking during the day; they had guns, and we were very much afraid that something serious might happen, because they were so excited, so enthused, and knowing their character so well we were afraid something might happen.

Question. They had made no hostile demonstration up to this point?

Answer. No, sir.

Question. They were not given to acts of violence in their political assemblages?

Answer. No, sir; but when under the influence of liquor in a crowd, as in that case, we think them rather uncontrollable and dangerous.

Question. You do not mean to say that the whole crowd was under the influence of liquor?

Answer. No, sir; not the whole crowd; I knew a great many there who were not, and who do not drink habitually.

Question. Was that anything more than an ordinary political demonstration?

Answer. Yes, sir; it was, because they came there marching in a sort of regimental style, and carrying guns and various paraphernalia; they had badges on.

Question. Nobody had been threatened?

Answer. O, no, sir.

Question. They had a large meeting at Prairie Hill?

Answer. Yes, sir; about five miles from there, and the day passed off very quietly; speeches were made; and it was only in the afternoon that they proposed to march back by way of Artesia.

Question. Was that not because there had been a political meeting at Artesia a short time before?

Answer. That is what we heard.

Question. Did they not want to show their numerical strength there in Artesia?

Answer. I think that was it; indeed we were told. Levi Jones, who is the leading man, I believe, of the League club at Artesia, and a sort of influential man among the colored people, proposed to march back by way of Artesia to show the "Native Sons" that they were nowhere.

Question. Was there anything in that evidence tending to show that Bliss or Lewis who accompanied that crowd, one of whom was a candidate for sheriff, aided or abetted or counseled or encouraged in any manner this violence upon Lee?

Answer. No, sir.

By Mr. Rice:

Question. Or that they counseled any riotous proceeding whatever?

Answer. No, sir; there was no evidence of that kind produced there.

By the Chairman:

Question. Was there any evidence that Mr. Bliss or Mr. Lewis on that occasion addressed any inflammatory remarks to the negroes calculated to raise excitement or arouse their prejudice against the whites?

Answer. No, sir; no such evidence was introduced.

Question. Can you explain why these two men were implicated as aiders and abettors in that riot.

Answer. Simply upon the ground that the meeting was held at Prairie Hill, and we thought they ought to have advised them, under the circumstances—having drank freely of liquor, which was furnished bountifully, and having fire-arms—we thought they ought to have advised them to disperse there, instead of marching as a regiment or brigade, in the style they did, by this circuitous route, to make this display and come to Artesia, and believing, as we did, that they had this control over the crowd, they could have dispersed or rallied them or controlled them in any way they chose.

Question. Is it not within your knowledge that the democrats have taken up this matter and sought to make some capital out of it, claiming that Lee was a democrat, and that he was killed by the radical negroes because he was a democrat?

Answer. I am not aware of any effort to make capital out of it.

Question. Have you not seen such statements broadcast in the democratic papers?

Answer. I saw a statement in the Mobile Register, laying the blame on those who gathered such a crowd together and allowed them to have arms and to march about.

Question. Was not the charge that a democrat had been slaughtered by the radicals?

Answer. No, sir; I did not see that in that statement.

COLUMBUS, MISSISSIPPI, *November* 17, 1871.

JOSEPH N. BISHOP sworn and examined.

By the CHAIRMAN:

Question. Please to state your residence and official position.

Answer. Columbus, Mississippi; county superintendendent of education.

Question. Are you the same gentleman who issued a circular, dated in the month of June last, which has been before this committee?

Answer. Yes, sir.

Question. It is alleged by a Mr. Sykes, of this town, that you laid before the board of supervisors a very extravagant estimate, amounting, according to his statement, to $2,800, for the rent of two school-houses, and for a stove and for fire-wood in the sub-district where his plantation was; I do not remember any other items. He proceeded to say that one of the school-houses belonged to him, and that he charged no rent; and as to the other school-house, that the owner charged no rent, I believe, or a small sum. Please to state what the facts are.

Answer. The board of school-directors met; in the first place, the board was organized in December; and when the board was organized they could not tell exactly what would be the expense for running the schools of the county for the coming year. When the board met it was understood that each one of the members should ascertain about what it would cost in each of the supervisors' beats of the county for school-buildings and teachers, and bring it before the board at the next meeting, who would put it together and see how much it would be. We did not know the number of educable children in each beat, and it was the duty of the school directors to bring these numbers together. These estimates were brought in and put together; some of them were made by an approximation, according to the number of educable children in the beats. They were put together and found to amount to somewhere about $40,000, the whole approximate expense. The board saw that that was too much, and they cut this down, and asked the board of supervisors to levy a tax of about $21,000 for the whole county, taking the different beats together. This approximate estimate for the different beats amounted to about $40,000. I do not know what it was in that beat where Captain Sykes's property is, but I do not wish to dispute Captain Sykes's statement of whatever it was estimated at; but I state the facts of what we have expended there. We asked the board of supervisors to levy a tax of about $21,000. Several of the citizens are opposed to this school-system—I say opposed to this school-system, because I judge from their actions and from their words—their language. They got together and held a meeting, and said this tax was too much, and got hold of this paper which was prepared by the board of supervisors, it was said, and took the different beats, and said the expenses were so much, and that it was not necessary to have so much expense; and they discussed the expense of the various beats. In the mean time, while this was going on—this excitement here in the place—I was invited to come before the meeting of citizens here, to explain to them. I did so, the best I could, but there was a spirit there at the meeting to override, or they did not want to find out the true condition of the county, but they were mad, and bound to rescind the tax. The next day they came before the board of supervisors—I think they were in session at the same time—and by some influence of the lawyers and citizens they got the board to rescind the whole school-tax, and the result was we had no tax the last year for public schools.

Question. Mr. Sykes says the book containing that estimate has been spirited away, and he has not been able to find it out. Is there any foundation for that charge?

Answer. I never saw the book since it went into the hands of the committee.

Question. The committee of citizens obtained possession of it?

Answer. Yes, sir; I will swear to that, and I have not seen it since.

Question. Was he one of the committee?

Answer. Yes, sir.

Question. You may state briefly to the committee the condition of the county, as to school-houses outside of the city of Columbus, at the time this common-school system was inaugurated, in December last, in Lowndes County.

Answer. I will have to refer to my circular. There were no school-buildings in the county, except buildings that had been used for private schools at Crawfordville, Artesia, Mayhew, West Point, and Caledonia—points like that, where they had been keeping private schools for some time past; and through the county there were among the freedmen little buildings which they used for churches in some places, and perhaps a few buildings used for private schools, taught by private teachers.

Question. Was there any public-school building which had been built after the war from the school fund?

Answer. None that I know of outside of Columbus; none that I know of now.

Question. I see in your circular that you estimate that there should be forty-six school-houses, I think, in order to accommodate the number of educable children in the county.

Answer. I presume that is correct. It is somewhere about that number, I will say, without examining it.

Question. The private-school houses you speak of were not, of course, public property, but belonging to individuals?

Answer. Yes, sir.

Question. You had no right to use them without the consent of the owners of the property?

Answer. No, sir.

Question. Do you recollect what your estimate was as to the cost of school-houses to be built?

Answer. I cannot tell now. My memory would not serve me to tell the estimate for the county. As I said before, the estimate, in the first place, was a rough estimate, made out in order that we might ascertain somewhere about what the expense would be for the county.

Question. You treated this sub-district in which Captain Sykes's property was situated as you treated all other districts—made an estimate for what would be the cost for placing the necessary buildings there to educate the children?

Answer. The school-director of that beat did.

Question. Without knowing anything of the particular facts of that sub-district?

Answer. No, sir; nothing at all.

Question. It is charged that you made extravagant estimates for school-furniture, books, charts, globes, and things of that sort, for the purpose of furnishing these schools and making them ready for the reception of scholars. What are the facts?

Answer. For the whole county the furniture for the white schools cost $1,678.70; the colored schools none. I will state further, while I am stating about this, there are some charges for reading-charts for primary schools, &c., which would make the whole for the maps, reading-charts, geographical charts, globes, blackboards, &c., furnished to white schools, $805.90; maps, reading-charts, blackboards, &c., furnished colored schools, $300; making a total of $2,784.60.

Question. Were those the lowest estimates you could make of the furniture absolutely necessary for these school buildings?

Answer. Yes, sir.

By Mr. RICE:

Question. Those are actual purchases?

Answer. Yes, sir; this was purchased. Our school buildings at Crawfordsville, Artesia, Mayhew, West Point, and Caledonia, and New Hope were taught by first-class teachers. Our high schools are first-class schools. In these buildings, when we purchased them, or rented them, there were some of them had a few cheap wooden benches in them. I think one or two had some cheap pine desks that stood up high, but when the public school opened the number of pupils increased so that there were not seats or desks for them, and the school directors thought it was the cheapest to buy the furniture, when they did buy, that would be permanent. They needed it at once, and it was the quickest way we could get it, and we purchased it at that time.

By the CHAIRMAN:

Question. Did you purchase school furniture of the most approved pattern?

Answer. We purchased of the Western Publishing Company, at Saint Louis.

Question. At lower figures than it could have been manufactured here, in your opinion?

Answer. They could not manufacture that kind of furniture here. It was school furniture with cast legs and hard-wood tops; furniture they could not very well make here, I think.

Question. Did you purchase at reasonable prices?

Answer. Yes, sir; it is as cheap, if not cheaper, than they sell those articles anywhere North or West.

Question. It is alleged by Mr. Sykes that you contracted with teachers at extravagant rates—$50 to $150 per month. What are the facts?

Answer. There were five or six or seven teachers in these schools I speak of. They had been teachers of private schools at these places. They demanded $150 a month and board. They said there was public opinion against them; that is, on the part of a great many; they did not know how they would get their pay—whether they would get dollar for dollar. They knew it would be paid in school warrants, and they asked $150 a month. Another reason they brought in was that they were only hired for five months in the year; that was one objection. The board was compelled to hire teachers in the county for that price.

Question. For first-class schools?

Answer. Yes, sir; only six teachers in the county, and we had over sixty teachers in the county.

Question. Could you have obtained that degree of competency at any less price at that time?

Answer. We might have obtained by sending abroad, but I could not state. We could not get teachers at that time for less. They had taught here in the county. They were acquainted with the people that we believed would send to Aberdeen and these schools. I do not think that we could have got the teachers for any less. Those were their charges.

Question. What was the rate paid for suitable accommodations for a teacher in the country at that time?

Answer. Well, I cannot say. I do not know what board cost in the country then or what it is now. I should have to approximate only. I do not think I could answer that question and be sure I was near it. It would be owing to the place where he boarded.

Question. Answer from your general knowledge.

Answer. Well, board ranges from $20 to $30; that is the general price. Five or six teachers here in the city paid $30 last year.

Question. It is charged by Mr. Sykes that you purchased two or three buildings at extravagant prices. State the facts in relation to those purchases.

Mr. RICE. One at West Point and one at Crawfordsville are the two he spoke of.

Answer. There was a committee sent to those places to investigate and inquire into the facts, and the committee reported that the buildings could be bought cheaper than they could build them for, or than the cost of the buildings, and the principal of the school now at Crawfordsville has offered to bring the architect, or the gentleman who put up the building, who is here in the city, to prove that the building cost more than he sold it to us for.

By Mr. RICE:

Question. What did you give for it?

Answer. The building at Crawfordsville is a two-story building; we paid for that $5,000 in warrants; in payments not all in one year; and the one at West Point we bought for $6,000.

Question. With sufficient ground around it?

Answer. The one at West Point has five or six acres, and the one at Crawfordsville has three.

Question. Are they brick buildings or wood?

Answer. Both are wood. This one at Crawfordsville has several rooms in it; every room plastered, and it is a comfortable school-building.

Question. How many rooms are there in it?

Answer. As many as six or seven rooms, and one hall.

Question. A good school-building?

Answer. Very good.

Question. Worth the money?

Answer. Yes, sir; I am sure it could not be put up for the price.

Question. Do you think the other is worth the money paid for it?

Answer. I do candidly think so. I think both the buildings are.

Question. In regard to this furniture, did the county get it for just what you paid for it?

Answer. Just what we had to pay.

Question. The county was not charged any more than the furniture cost delivered here?

Answer. O, no, the same price; and another thing, the county has not paid for the furniture yet, you might say. The parties waited for three months or so, and then sent us orders to send the warrants. All the warrants were sold at a discount, and the warrants are not paid yet that I know of.

By the CHAIRMAN:

Question. I believe there were some imputations that you had or was suspected of having made some sort of speculation in your operations as president of the board of directors in purchasing school-houses and school furniture. State whether you made any personal profit as president of the board in any of these contracts.

Answer. Well, sir, I will state to the committee that I made no money out of it in any way. Furthermore, I have been before the grand jury of this county three times any way, I think four, with my books, and I demanded of them to summon the clerk of the board, and every school-director, and the attorney for the board, and any citizens of the county, I did not care whom, to examine my books, and ascertain if there had been a cent of money misapplied in any way.

Question. Was this done because of the hue and cry that certain parties had raised against your administration here as school superintendent?

Answer. Yes, sir; there was everything done to oppose me, and the public school system. I was attacked by the paper now published in this place. There were two or three charges in it which were directly false, as I can prove by twenty men. I went before the grand jury and made these statements. I stated that these things were false, and I hoped I was in a country where we had law and protection, I said, "These are incorrect statements, and I ask you to examine my books and subpœna witnesses here to examine them, and ascertain whether these reports are correct."

Question. In other words, you demanded an investigation, in order if there were anything in these charges it might be known, and the grand jury might take cognizance of them?

Answer. Yes, sir.

Question. Did they find any indictment against you?

Answer. No, sir; I went before them here last week, too.

By Mr. BLAIR:

Question. Where is that original estimate that you made?

Answer. I would like to say some more about Mr. Sykes's school-house down here. I want to say what we have expended there. I asked a man about the school-building yesterday, and he said it belonged to some colored people. I believe it is on Mr. Sykes's land. We hired a teacher to teach there four months, at $40 a month. Mr. Sykes spoke to me, and said the building was small; that it was not large enough to accommodate the people on his plantation, and he wanted to know if the board would do something to make the building larger. I acted upon his suggestion, and the board allowed a warrant of $50 to make the building larger, and make some seats for it. The order is there on the books, and never has been drawn to this day, and the building has never been repaired. The pay of the teacher, four months, at $40 a month, is every bit of money that has been expended on his plantation.

Question. What has become of that original estimate that you made?

Answer. I do not know. It was not left in my office.

Question. Where is the proper place for that estimate to be?

Answer. I do not know that either.

Question. You do not know?

Answer. I presume that the proper place would be with the secretary; the books and that estimate, and everything, went into the hands of this self-constituted committee here, and I have never seen it since. I do not know what has become of it. There was a committee self-constituted here last March, some time in the spring, and they got our books.

Question. Is there not a proper place for the books that belong to the school-board to be kept?

Answer. Yes, sir.

Question. Where?

Answer. The books that belong to my office are in my office; and the books that belong to the clerk's office are in the clerk's office.

Question. You do not know where that book is?

Answer. I never saw it since that committee had it.

By the CHAIRMAN:

Question. Was Mr. Sykes on that committee?

Answer. He was chairman of it.

By Mr. BLAIR:

Question. The book is not to be found now?

Answer. So I understand.

COLUMBUS, MISSISSIPPI, *November* 17, 1871.

BEVERLY MATTHEWS sworn and examined.

The CHAIRMAN. As this witness is called at the instance of the minority, I will request General Blair to open the examination.

By Mr. BLAIR:

Question. Will you please to state your residence and profession?

Answer. Columbus, Mississippi. I am a lawyer by profession.

Question. Do you know Major Henry B. Whitfield?

Answer. Yes, sir.

Question. What is his character for truth and veracity in this community?

Answer. I am reluctant to say anything on that subject. Mr. Whitfield and myself have been personal friends for fifteen or twenty years. I was the law-partner of his brother-in-law, Mr. Isham Harrison, now dead. The question you asked me implies the opinion of the community in regard to him, not my individual opinion?

Question. Yes, sir.

Answer. I am of the opinion that three-fourths of the intelligent property-holding people of this community would not believe him on oath.

Question. Are you pretty well acquainted with the opinion of the community?

Answer. I have heard his character spoken of very frequently in this immediate community, and in this county, and in the county of Noxubee, and in the county of Oktibbeha, and in the county of Pickens, Alabama. I have seen a certified copy of an indictment obtained in the city of Mobile, Alabama, before the grand jury of the city court, for obtaining $4,000 of money, either from John A. Winston, or the commission-house known as John A. Winston & Co. I have been consulted professionally, in this county, by parties from whom he obtained money under false pretenses. I have had republicans and democrats speak to me of similar transactions in adjoining counties. I have heard the members of the Baptist church, to which he belongs, speak of him, and my opinion is that they would not believe him on oath. I do not believe the members of the bar here would believe him on oath. I do not believe that the property-holding and intelligent masses, or the democratic party, with whom he was activel yand zealously associated about a year ago, would believe him on oath.

By the CHAIRMAN:

Question. Do you think they would have believed him on oath at the time he was their candidate and ran for the legislature?

Answer. When he connected himself, a little over a year ago, with what was called the Dent movement in this State, a good many of his transactions were not then known; if known at all, they were known to a very few. So far as I am personally concerned, many of them have come to my knowledge since that time. I did not know of the indictment against him in Mobile, for obtaining money from Governor Winston. I did not know of his getting money from old man Sheperd up here at West Point. I did not know of his getting money from a venerable old man who died a short time since, George H. Law, up here at Waverly, who consulted me, and I brought suit against Whitfield. I did not know of his getting $2,800 from Mr. James Sykes; of his getting a thousand dollars from John E. Styles. I did not know then of his getting money from the Askews, in the way of cotton and corn, and I did not know of his getting cotton and money from other people, which I have since learned.

Question. Have you taken pains to collect these items since?

Answer. They have been mentioned to me; I never sought any information against him. This matter of Sykes I did not know until a week since. When I was over at Oktibbeha court some time since, John S. Warley was speaking of him, and told me of an uncle of his, or of his wife's, who came down there from Ohio with a lot of mules, and told Mr. Warley he would sell them to any of our people Mr. Warley would recommend. He said he sold two mules for $400 to a gentleman named William Bell—I know the man, an elderly man—and that Bell executed a mortgage or trust deed upon his property; the notes were to mature in twelve months. About the time of the maturity of the paper, this same gentleman returned from Indiana with another lot of mules, and said to Mr. Warley, "I will dispose of these as I did the others, on your recommendation." He happened to meet Mr. Bell, and asked him if he was ready to take up his notes. He said he was, remarking, "I sold my crop of cotton a few days ago to Mr. Henry B. Whitfield, and he tells me has the money ready, and I will give you an order on him for the money, and you can go and collect it at your option." These gentlemen remarked: "We are going into that neighborhood with our lot of mules, and you can give us an order upon him to the amount of your indebtedness to us, and if he pays it we will surrender the security we have upon your notes." They went down in the neighborhood of Mr. Whitfield, and called upon him, and he stated that he had purchased Bell's cotton and owed him the money, but he did not have any funds there; that his funds were in Saint Louis, and, said Whitfield, "I wish you to give me twenty days on half of the indebtedness and thirty days on the balance, and I will make drafts on a Saint Louis house accordingly." They readily assented to that, and he made his paper. They held the paper until maturity came, and then sent it forward, when the pretended Saint Louis house answered that they had no acquaintance or business correspondence whatever with this man Whitfield.

Question. Do you know those facts?

Answer. I am only telling you what Mr. Warley told me.

Question. I did not call for these details.

Answer. You asked me the question if I had collected this information myself.

Question. I did not ask you to go on with further details of your information, but whether you had collected information.

Answer. I will stop there with the additional information that they answered that they had no business acquaintance with any such man as Mr. Whitfield, and finally Mr. Whitfield paid it in a certificate of bankruptcy.

Question. I have not called upon you for any of these items, but I cannot control your answers.

Answer. I beg pardon.

Question. What are your personal relations with Mr. Whitfield?

Answer. Very friendly, so far as I know.

Question. And your feelings are kindly toward him?

Answer. Very, very. No man in the community regrets more the general estimation in which he is now held.

Question. Do you recognize him as a friend on the street?

Answer. No, sir; I would not take any man as my friend who was under such serious charges.

Question. Are you upon speaking terms with him when you meet him?

Answer. Yes, sir.

Question. There has been nothing of an unfriendly character between you and him?

Answer. Not a single unkind word.

Question. No business transactions?

Answer. No, sir; I never had a business transaction with him directly in my life.

Question. Where did you see the copy of the indictment that you have spoken of?

Answer. I saw it in this town.

Question. Who procured that copy?

Answer. I do not know.

Question. Where did you see it?

Answer. I saw it in the hands of—I forget whether Mr. Abram S. Humphries or who.

Question. Is that the attorney Humphries here?

Answer. No, sir.

Question. His uncle?

Answer. Yes, sir. There was a requisition made upon Governor Alcorn for him, and he declined to give him up.

Question. I did not call for that information. The committee have had abundant information upon that point.

Answer. I was accounting for his presence here. I do not know of it of my own personal knowledge, except that I saw it in the hands of a gentleman whose name I have mentioned.

Question. I understood you to say that he had been upon the democratic and conservative ticket for the general assembly or legislature?

Answer. For the legislature.

Question. Was that in 1869 or 1870?

Answer. Eighteen hundred and sixty-eight.

Question. Was it on the Dent ticket?

Answer. Yes, sir.

Question. Was that in 1868 or 1869?

Answer. Perhaps it was in 1869. I remember I was in Washington in 1868 until July or August.

Question. Was not that after his failure in business, and after he had applied for a discharge under the bankrupt law?

The WITNESS. What, after?

The CHAIRMAN. His running for the legislature as a candidate on the same ticket with Mr. Humphries.

Answer. I cannot speak accurately as to the time of his discharge. He came and employed me to assist him to procure his discharge in bankruptcy. My recollection is, however—I admit that he did not file his petition for discharge until some time in December.

Question. Then, if he ran in 1869, it was long after he filed his application?

Answer. It depends upon the term of the court at which he commenced proceedings.

Question. If he filed it in 1868, and ran in the fall of 1869, several months intervened?

Answer. If he filed it in the fall of 1868, of course it antedated his candidacy for the legislature.

Question. The facts of his failure were, then, known at the time he was a candidate and supported by the conservative party?

Answer. Yes, sir; the facts of his insolvency were known; that is, that his petition was filed in the bankrupt court, or it might have been known. It very often happens that it is known.

By Mr. RICE:

Question. Do they not give notice to the creditors?

Answer. Of course the creditors know it, but it may not be generally known.

By the CHAIRMAN:

Question. Was not the fact generally known that he had failed in business?

Answer. O, yes, sir.

Question. Please state what effect this failure in business had upon his career as a candidate. Did he get his full party strength? Did he run neck and neck with Captain Humphries on the same ticket?

Answer. My impression is that there was no great difference in the votes for the different candidates. I cannot speak accurately about it, because I do not remember.

Question. Was it urged at that time that he was a man of no moral character or principle, and not to be believed under oath, and a man not of truth and veracity?

Answer. If it was so urged I have never heard it. I have stated in my preliminary examination that it was only within a few months that these facts came to my knowledge.

Question. Was this matter ever stirred up against him until he had been before the congressional committee at Washington, and until certain damaging testimony, showing the existence of a wide-spread Ku-Klux organization in this part of the country, and putting his finger upon a great many outrages committed by that order?

The WITNESS. Was this matter stirred up against him prior to the giving of his testimony at Washington?

The CHAIRMAN. That is what I asked you.

Answer. I suppose I heard fifty persons, business men in town, say prior to that, that they would not believe him on oath; that they had been defrauded by him.

Question. You have spoken, you say, of the opinion of three-fourths of the community; will you speak of the remaining fourth?

Answer. As to the whites connected with the republican party in this county, I do not know their opinion of him, nor do I know the opinion of the colored population.

Question. Do not the colored population constitute greatly the majority in this county?

Answer. Yes, sir; but I said the intelligent property-holding people. I presume the colored people of this county generally think very favorably of him; if they do not so think I am not aware of it.

Question. Do you not think they would all believe him under oath?

Answer. I have no doubt of it.

Question. Do you not believe they think his character for truth and veracity is good?

Answer. I have no doubt of it.

Question. Have they not elected him to office?

Answer. Yes, sir.

Question. What office is he holding at the present time?

Answer. The office of district attorney.

Question. Is there a very good feeling, Mr. Matthews, entertained by the democratic portion of this community toward that class of men termed—I will not so classify them—in the popular slang of the day, scalawags?

Answer. Well, sir, it depends on who they are and how they demean themselves. I know some parties in this State who are called scalawags; that is, people who are to the manor born, who have joined the republican party, between whom, and any gentleman in the country known as a democrat, or as holding no party affiliations, there is no difference made socially or otherwise.

Question. Does not the term *per se* imply dishonor?

Answer. Well, I cannot say that it does.

Question. Would not calling a man a scalawag in this community cast odium upon him?

Answer. It does in some sense—that odium is measured very much by his own conduct.

Question. Let his conduct, officially and personally, be characterized with entire propriety, does he not remain a scalawag in the mind of the democratic portion of the community?

Answer. I do not think so. There may be instances where the term scalawag as applied to a particular man would imply some dishonor. I have now in my mind gentlemen born and raised here, who have been engaged in business all their lives, and who have been office-holders under Governor Alcorn, to whom that term is applied, and I know that socially, and in all the intercourse possible, their standing is as good as before they accepted office.

Question. Has any effort been made to gather up testimony in order to break down the character of Major Whitfield as a witness before this congressional committee?

Answer. Not within my knowledge, sir.

Question. Have you any information that a copy of the indictment you spoke of was obtained for that purpose?

Answer. No, sir; I understand that an effort was made some time ago, and I myself was spoken to about the propriety or about the possibility of Governor Alcorn yielding to a requisition of the governor of Alabama, and I said that I did not think Governor Alcorn would give him up.

Question. I understand you to say, from your long acquaintance with Major Whitfield, you would not believe him under oath?

Answer. I did not say so, sir; I asked if I was to give my individual opinion or my idea of the general estimate in which he was held in the community.

Question. I misunderstood, then, the drift of your answer. I will ask you the question: from your acquaintance with Major Whitfield, testifying in a matter about which he has no personal interest, would you believe him under oath?

Answer. If I take the general opinion of him as my guide in making up my judgment of the value of his testimony, I am constrained to say I would not.

Question. Taking your knowledge of the man, drawn from your long acquaintance with him, would you believe him under oath?

Answer. I stated I never had a disagreeable word or discussion with him; that we had been friends. Our friendship has been unbroken for fifteen or twenty years. I have known him when he was pointed to by the elderly men of this community as a model man, as a zealous member of the Baptist Church, an active teacher of the Sabbath-school.

Question. You are not answering my question.

Answer. What is it?

Question. I have asked you, would you, from your own knowledge of the man, believe him under oath in a matter in which he had no personal interest?

Answer. I answer, if I received the public judgment of him as a criterion of the value I should put on his testimony, I would not.

Question. Do you receive that criterion?

Answer. I believe it to be true and just.

Question. Then you would not believe him?

Answer. I would not, acting on the basis of the public judgment, and not the result of my individual opinion.

Question. I have been asking you for the result of your individual opinion.

Answer. I say I have never had a disagreeable occurrence or word to pass between him and myself upon any subject-matter, except here, at the last term of the court—and that was only temporary—when it was reported to me that he was calling the laborers from my plantation to give testimony here without resorting to the legal means of getting them before the jury. I then went to him and asked him if it was true, and told him if it was, I should make it a personal matter with him; and he said it was not. Beyond that not a single disagreeable word or transaction has ever transpired between that gentleman and myself.

Question. Then I understand you to say that you would not believe him under oath?

Answer. No, sir, I would not.

By Mr. RICE:

Question. When did this public judgment against Major Whitfield commence manifesting itself in the community?

Answer. I suppose, from what I have heard within the last twelve months, and within the last six months particularly, that this has been going on all the time.

Question. When did it become widespread in the community, before or since he joined the radical party?

Answer. With a great many, before.

Question. You had heard it before?

Answer. I had not heard of these numbers of cases; I had heard of quite a number, but it has come to me from almost every direction, and from parties who say they have had transactions with him.

Question. When did you hear of this public condemnation, from which you formed the opinion that you would not believe him under oath; when did that manifest itself?

Answer. I suppose I may say it commenced last spring with me.

Question. These creditors that are so loud in their complaints now were all swindled, and knew they were swindled, as far back as 1868, when he failed?

Answer. A good many were. The creditors being swindled does not constitute the volume of testimony against him.

Question. You spoke of fifty or a hundred creditors prior to the 4th of August?

Answer. I did not say fifty or a hundred creditors prior to the 4th of August. I said this public opinion is a matter of a gradual growth; it is not confined to the opinion of gentlemen who have lost money by him. He was appointed to the office of justice of the peace out here by Governor Alcorn, and I have heard from negroes and white folks that he extorted money from them, exercising the powers of his office, selling property of the negroes which was exempt by law, and appropriating unlawful fees.

Question. When did you hear that?

Answer. Last summer and spring.

Question. Since he joined the radical party?

Answer. I do not know when he joined the radical party.

Question. You have heard that substantially since he joined the radical party?

Answer. I did not say so.

Question. Will you give me the date; twelve months?

Answer. A good deal has come to me since. My attention was called to his conduct at Artesia because my plantation is there, within two miles of that place, where he held his court; and I have been there and heard the neighbors, colored and white, talking about the unlawful and arbitrary exercise of his authority as justice of the peace—selling a negro woman's chickens and cows and pigs under execution when he knew they were exempt.

Question. The negroes all vote for him, though; do they not?

Answer. I do not know that they do or not.

COLUMBUS, MISSISSIPPI, *November* 17, 1871.

JAMES T. HARRISON sworn and examined.

The CHAIRMAN. As this witness has been summoned at the instance of the minority, General Blair will please conduct his examination.

By Mr. BLAIR:

Question. Please to state your residence and profession.

Answer. I am a resident of this town of Columbus, and have been since 1837. I am a lawyer by profession; I am now engaged in the practice of law; I am the senior member of the Columbus bar.

Question. State if you are acquainted with a gentleman by the name of Henry B. Whitfield.

Answer. I am, sir. I have known him from his early youth upward.

Question. Do you know his character and reputation for truth and veracity in the community?

Answer. Well, sir, so far as a lawyer is concerned, if it is upon what his reputation is for truth and veracity, I know this: I have known him from his youth upward, and I better give, I suppose, what I know about him. If the naked question is, what I believe, or if I am to state what is his general character for truth and veracity, I can say that I will answer any question that is desired; and if my individual opinion is required, I will state the fact; just as you prefer, but, of course, I would like you to ask the questions, and to know what I am to answer.

Question. What is the reputation and character of Henry B. Whitfield for truth and veracity in this community?

Answer. Well, sir, among the respectable and intelligent portion of this community, my opinion is that his reputation is very bad, and, in addition to that fact, I will state that that is my individual opinion.

Question. Would you believe him on his oath?

Answer. Well, sir, in a case where he was politically concerned, or his political interests were concerned, I would not do it.

Question. Do you base your opinion upon knowledge of any transaction of his?

Answer. Upon my own knowledge of individual transactions with him, and upon the testimony of witnesses upon whose faith and credit I have unbounded confidence, and upon his general course and conduct for the last twelve or eighteen months, and facts I know in addition to these. But I will add, however, if you please, that it mortifies me to have to make the admission, for he is connected with my family, so far as that is concerned.

By Mr. RICE:

Question. He has formerly been in very good standing in this community?

Answer. O, yes, sir. There was a time when he was considered a very fair man; a man of good character. He has been a member of the legal profession.

Question. How many years since his character became as notoriously bad as you speak of?

Answer. Well, sir, I did not use the expression that it has become notoriously bad.

Question. You said "very bad."

Answer. I do not think I used the words "very bad."

Question. That was my understanding.

Answer. O, well, that is your inference from what I stated, but not what I said, unless I am mistaken.

By the CHAIRMAN:

Question. "His character is very bad;" that is what I understood you to say.

Answer. You put it in the superlative—is very bad—and that is different.

Question. Your statement, if I took it down rightly, is, "Among the intelligent portion of this community his character is very bad, and that is my own opinion."

Answer. Yes, sir; that is what I stated.

By Mr. RICE:

Question. How long since this very bad character has been manifest in this community?

Answer. Well, sir, it is difficult to tell how long everything has become public, but it is within the last two or three years.

Question. What was his character in 1869, when he was a candidate for the legislature?

Answer. In 1869 his character, so far as I know, had not been generally developed, except as to a few cotton transactions, and his taking the benefit of the bankrupt law, and not paying his debts, and things of that sort. A good many tales were circulated without having much influence on public opinion, so far as that matter was concerned.

Question. What was his character then?

Answer. His character at that time, so far as I knew it, except these individual transactions that were known to some persons, was fair enough. I never heard of anything.

Question. He was nominated and voted for by the democrats of this county at that time?

Answer. Well, sir, I doubt that very much. What they call nominated and voted for, I do not know what they call it, so far as this country is concerned, the democrats or the republicans; they were disposed to take anything.

Question. Did he receive the——

Answer. Hold on until I explain that. I have been an old whig all my life, and I have never belonged to the democratic party, or the republican party, or any of these organizations, so far as that matter is concerned. I voted for him myself, if that is the point.

Question. I was not asking that. How did the white people generally in this county—the respectable white people—vote?

Answer. The respectable people were somewhat mixed up in what we called the "Dent movement."

Question. Did they generally vote for him?

Answer. They generally voted, my opinion is—I don't know how, except as to myself and others. I voted for him myself, and I think most of the people did, and he had been a secessionist and a democrat. He had been in the war. He had helped the whole thing and fought it through—not quite so much fight either; still, he was a secessionist and a democrat, and was voted for by the democrats; but I, being an old whig, voted for him too, and I suppose most of the old whigs voted for him too, but I cannot say certainly. I never have been tinkering much in politics.

Question. Has most of this bad character that has been given to him been given to him within the last six or twelve months—most of this talk about him?

Answer. Well, sir, if you want me to state my knowledge upon the subject, I can do it. I have heard him talked of.

Question. I ask as to this general bad character.

Answer. This general bad character has developed more and more for the last twelve months, or six months, or three months—well, within less than three months—for the last month.

Question. And the last ten days?

Answer. No, sir; it has culminated in the proofs that have been produced against him. The whole matter came out as a matter of testimony, and public opinion, where these things are known, has culminated against him; commencing and getting at one fact after another fact, it has thus developed.

Question. So far as financial matters are concerned, when he filed his petition in bankruptcy in the spring of 1868, his creditors knew then that they had lost their debts substantially, did they not?

Answer. I can say that I did, so far as I was concerned—what he owed me. I suppose the others did. I supposed it was a gone-up case, except I believed at the same time that he was able to pay, as far as that is concerned. I was asked to assist in fixing his property and his wife's property so as to fix it upon her, and I have never been paid by him or her. They are owing still. That is an individual instance only. Others are in the same way.

Question. Notice was given to his creditors as the law required?

Answer. I have no doubt about that. I did not file his individual application, but I was one of the counsel in the case. We filed an application for Baskerville, Whitfield & Co., whatever the name of the concern was, but he was one of them; he took the benefit of the bankrupt law in the ordinary way.

By the CHAIRMAN:

Question. How many citizens of this county took the benefit of the bankrupt law?

Answer. Really, sir, that is not a fact that is within my knowledge at all.

Question. Was it a very general thing?

Answer. No, sir; not a general thing at all.

Question. Were there a hundred cases, would you think?

Answer. O, yes; I reckon a hundred. Some of the merchants took it, of course. He was a merchant; he had been speculating in cotton.

Question. Many of the planters?

Answer. Not a great many, but some took it.

Question. Did the creditors realize anything of the debtors?

Answer. I regret to say that, as a general thing, they did not realize much. I am in that unfortunate position that I lost myself considerably in that way.

Question. Was it a remarkable thing in this community that he should apply for the bankrupt law?

Answer. No, sir. I never insinuated that it was any reflection upon him that he took the benefit of the bankrupt law.

Question. Is he a member of the Baptist Church?

Answer. He is a member, so far as I know and believe.

Question. Has he, since he took the benefit of the bankrupt law, been a delegate to the Baptist——

Answer. Permit me to remark, in addition to that matter, if the church is brought up, that he has removed from the country and belongs to the Baptist Church. His membership is in this town, and if I am to state on this subject, I will say that my own people are members of that church, and that he is in very bad odor in that church.

Question. I was about to ask if he has not been regularly up to this time the delegate from the Baptist church here to the State conventions, district associations, representing this church in these bodies generally?

Answer. I cannot state further than this, that he has not been residing in town. He has been living over in Artesia.

Question. Have you heard that he has been a delegate from his church to the district and State associations?

Answer. I do not know. I think it is very probable—very possible.

Question. He has been, since that time, elected district attorney?

Answer. He has been elected within a few weeks. He was the regular nominee of the republican convention of this county, and with these others he went through on the regular ticket straight out.

Question. He received the full republican vote?

Answer. I reckon pretty nearly. I do not know what the full republican vote is.

Question. He was elected by a large square majority?

Answer. O, yes, sir. In this district there are three colored votes to one white vote.

Question. He is very well thought of by the colored people?

Answer. I doubt that very much. Among a class he is.

Question. Is not his character good among the colored people generally?

Answer. Permit me to remark that, so far as that is concerned, I do not associate generally with the colored people, except those I know. As to his standing among the colored people, I know nothing about it, except that I see him associating with them, and they tell me that he is engaged in these secret Leagues with them, and that he is a great one among them; but I do not know anything of that myself, but I see him going among them.

Question. They constitute two-thirds, at least, of your community, do they not?

Answer. O, yes, fully two-thirds—what you mean is the community in this county of Lowndes?

The CHAIRMAN. Yes, sir; certainly.

The WITNESS. Of course you can add, so far as the registered votes are concerned, that my recollection is that the colored vote is about three and a half to one of the white vote in this county.

Question. So far as your information extends, did he not receive the full colored vote when he was a candidate for district attorney?

Answer. Well, no; not what you call the full colored vote. There are some of the colored votes that do not belong exactly to his party. I suppose he got the full colored vote of his county, but there are colored persons here, I suppose, that do not belong. I dabble very little in politics, but there are a number of them, I understand. The number I do not know. I suppose the great majority voted the other way.

Question. Looking to that portion of your community, in forming an estimate of what Major Whitfield's character for truth and veracity is, do you not believe that it is good?

Answer. Well, sir, my opinion is that three-fourths or nine-tenths of the colored population of this county have formed no idea on that subject at all, or they know him only as a mere political partisan.

Question. I understood you to say they believed in him, and voted for him?

Answer. They voted the ticket.

Question. Is he a favorite?

Answer. I did not state that.

Question. Do you think that he is?

Answer. I know this: that he has figured among them, and received the nomination for district attorney, and been elected; that he has been indorsed here by the press of his party, and has received the nomination and been elected upon the ticket; but that, so far as the colored population is concerned, the great majority of them, as I am informed and believe, belong either to what they call the Loyal Leagues or republican clubs, &c., whatever you may call them. I never belonged to a secret society in my life, and only know what I have heard of it; he has been the League nominee, and has been elected right square out on the fact of his being indorsed by the party.

Question. Is it your belief that he is respected and trusted by the colored people of this county?

Answer. I do not believe the great majority of the colored people know or care anything about him, except that he was the party nominee, and they voted the straight ticket. I do not think they know anything about him particularly.

Question. Did it excite the animosity of the conservative party when he became a radical?

Answer. On the contrary, sir, I think they parted with him as our Saviour did with Judas Iscariot. They considered that he had sold himself, and they were mortified that he should have been so lost. I know him——

Question. My question was whether there was any political animosity engendered by his joining the radical party?

Answer. None in the world, further than the idea that he had been a secessionist and a democrat, and had been in the war, and had done everything he possibly could for the democratic party; had been reared a democrat; his father was a democrat, and the whole concern of them, and he never went over until the eleventh hour, when they gave him the position of a justice of the peace in this county; and my deliberate judgment, as an individual, is that it is the opinion of nine-tenths of the intelligent portion of this community that he sold himself for office.

Question. Did the press—democratic press—denounce him in similar terms?

Answer. I do not know what the democratic press said. I suppose they spoke about him as the press generally does. I did not notice.

Question. As a Judas to his party?

Answer. I do not know whether they ever talked much about it.

Question. Did they ever talk about him in different terms from what they did when he was their candidate on the Dent ticket?

Answer. I do not remember much said or done about that canvass, except I know it was a magnificent failure. I took very little part in it.

Question. You speak now of the Dent movement?

Answer. I speak about what they call in this State the Dent movement. They supported it here, and Henry Whitfield and others were for putting in some old democrats and running Dent. I do not think it succeeded very well. I know he was in the movement, though. I remember I have heard him say so.

Question. The democratic press treated him cleverly then, did it not, eulogizing him in high terms?

Answer. Really, I do not think he was of sufficient importance for the democratic press to have noticed him very much. Here let me add now that, so far as he is concerned, he and I have been on kindly terms toward each other. He has been a member of the bar, and I am disposed to do him every justice I can. In addition to that fact his family has been connected with mine, and are Baptists all together. He has been with our folks there in that, and they are still identified. I want that put in my statement, that if there has been a man who has been a straight-out secessionist and democrat in this county, he and his whole generation are of that sort; his father before him, and all the way through; and if that party produced this present state of affairs, he has contributed to it as much as any man in this county, and he never deserted that party until the whole thing was over, and the Dent movement failed; but when they offered him an office, when the whole thing had played out, secession had played out, and the Dent movement played out, he wabbled and went over.

By Mr. RICE:

Question. It was time to wabble, was it not?

Answer. Unquestionably, for a man who would desert all his principles and become a traitor to his party—put that down, if you please—a traitor to his party, a traitor to his race, a traitor to his religion, a traitor to his family; and add to that, if you will call upon his church to testify, or call upon his own party to testify, or upon his own family to testify, or the records of his country to testify, they can draw their own inferences from these facts.

COLUMBUS, MISSISSIPPI, *November* 17, 1871.

WASHINGTON WILLIS (colored) sworn and examined.

By the CHAIRMAN:

Question. Where do you live?

Answer. Monroe County, near Aberdeen.

Question. Were you present at the time Alexander Willis was whipped by the Ku-Klux?

Answer. Yes, sir.

Question. Where were you posted at the time so as to know?

Answer. Well, sir, when I first heard them Saturday night we were at the meeting-house. When we first heard the reports we all went to the road, and I heard them coming up the road, and I just got over the fence and laid down in the corner of the fence until they passed me, and after they passed me I got in the road and followed on behind them to see where they were going, and they went up to Miss Lavinia Willis's place—Widow Willis's place—and they went to get this boy out, and I reckon they brung him in about fifty yards of the road and commenced whipping him.

Question. How many were there?

Answer. Well, sir, there was a good many. I can't tell you how many, but some particular ones I knew.

Question. About how many would you think?

Answer. Well, sir, it looked like there was about sixty-five or seventy of them.

Question. Were they all disguised?

Answer. Yes, sir.

Question. Did they come there on horseback?

Answer. Yes, sir; they were all on horseback.

Question. Were their horses all disguised?

Answer. Only six of the horses were disguised.

Question. Go on and state what occurred in reference to the whipping.

Answer. While they were whipping him some one commenced shooting at them, and then they run out of the clothes they had on—run out of the disguise.

Question. Who commenced shooting?

Answer. Some clubbing party commenced shooting at them while they were whipping this boy.

Question. Do you mean Loyal League, or what do you mean by club?

Answer. Yes, sir; the club we had. They commenced shooting at them, and they pulled off their clothes, and they said we must break ranks or we will be surrounded.

Question. How many were engaged in firing into the Ku-Klux gang?

Answer. There were three of them that night engaged at that.

Question. Did they hit any of them?

Answer. I don't know whether any of them were hit or not. I couldn't swear, but I know some of them that were in the company that night were dead by the next Saturday night.

Question. What did they do with their disguises?

Answer. Kept them with them. They took them off and kept them with them.

Question. What time was this?

Answer. It was in March. I don't know exactly what time. It was on a Saturday night.

Question. Last March?

Answer. Yes, sir.

Question. Did you know any of the men?

Answer. Yes, sir.

Question. Who were they?

Answer. I know Barbour Quarles, William Butler, Plummer Willis, John Willis, Pope Mayes, and Jonny Roberts.

Question. How did you know them?

Answer. When they commenced pulling off the clothes I was right by. They had to come right along by me, and when they came along I knew them just as good as I knew myself, because they all came together right along by me.

Question. Have any of these since been indicted in the courts for this?

Answer. Yes, sir; they have all been taken to Oxford.

Question. Were you a witness against them?

Answer. Yes, sir.

Question. Do you know what they whipped Willis for?

Answer. Yes, sir.

Question. What?

Answer. For suing a man by the name of McNiece.

Question. Is he a planter?

Answer. Yes, sir.

Question. Does he own a plantation near here?

Answer. Yes, sir; he lived up towards Athens, and this fellow worked up there with him a year. When he came away he wouldn't pay him, and he sued him for it, and that night they whipped him.

Question. Did they tell him that?

Answer. Yes, sir; they told him they would learn him how to sue a white man; but colored men were with them, one named Jefferson Willis.

Question. With whom?

Answer. With them men that night. One was named Jefferson Willis and the other Burril Willis.

Question. How came these colored men to be with the Ku-Klux?

Answer. I don't know.

Question. Were you ever asked to join the Ku-Klux?

Answer. Yes, sir, I was asked to join them.

Question. By whom?

Answer. By my young master.

Question. What is his name?

Answer. Barbour Quarles.

Question. Was it before that night or after that night?

Answer. It was before they ever rode the first time.

Question. What did he say to you?

Answer. He told me—he asked me—some one had killed a young heifer of mine, and taken my cotton, and he asked me didn't I want to join them and stop them; to whip them; to make them stop it. I told him him no, sir. I didn't know anything about it. I didn't care to join, because I didn't know who it was done it. It was done, and I didn't know who done it. He said I could find out. They had protection to whip all people that did such as that; protection to whip them to make them stop it.

Question. Did he tell you who he had protection from?

Answer. Yes, sir; he called several names he said they had for protection.

Question. Whom did he name?

Answer. Well, he named a man by the name of Mr. Blair, from Missouri, and a General Forrest, and a man by the name of Mr. Lynch, he said they had for protection.

Question. Did you join?

Answer. No, sir.

Question. Have you been back there since you gave evidence before the court at Oxford?

Answer. Yes, sir.

Question. To live?

Answer. No, sir; I have been living here all the time

Question. Are you afraid to go back there?

Answer. No, sir.

Question. Did these Ku-Klux create a good deal of alarm among the colored people while they were riding through the country?

Answer. Yes, sir, they did. I reckon some of them didn't stay in their houses for months.

Question. Have you heard of a good many whippings that have been administered to colored people?

Answer. No, sir; not since March. They whipped a right smart of them around there before March.

Question. But not much since?

Answer. No, sir; I haven't heard of any one whipped since.

COLUMBUS, MISSISSIPPI, *November* 17, 1871.

ABRAM S. HUMPHRIES sworn and examined.

The CHAIRMAN. As this witness is called at the instance of the minority, I will request General Blair to open the examination.

By Mr. BLAIR:

Question. Will you state your residence and b[illegible]

Answer. My residence is in this place—Columbus; my business is merchandising, banking, and planting. I am engaged in all these occupations, sir.

Question. What do you know in reference to a transaction in which a colored man or white man was visited by his neighbors in this county at night for imposing upon a colored man?

Answer. Well, incidentally, last week an old gentleman, who is an old acquaintance and friend of mine, came into the store and asked me if I would purchase his cotton. I told him if I liked the cotton and we could agree on the price I would buy it. He turned around and remarked there was a black man there had some that he would like me to buy also. He then stated, "I have just got him out of a difficulty, and brought him on to town with me, and brought his cotton with me," and went on then to relate the circumstances. Turning and pointing to the black man, he says, "This black man has been living in our neighborhood a good many years, and is a very excellent man; the neighbors all appreciate him as a good and industrious man. He has been living with a bad man—Nathan Arnold—for three years, and the products of his labor have been absorbed for the three years. It took about all he made to pay the claims Arnold brought up against him." The intimation was that Arnold made claims enough to cover the proceeds of his labor until this year. "The black man," he says, "has lost confidence in Arnold, and went to Mr. Keasler. He is a gentleman who lives a neighbor to Arnold. The black man went to Mr. Keasler and asked him to gin his cotton. Keasler owns a good deal of land in the neighborhood. He asked him to furnish him land for the next year; Keasler told him yes. The black man commenced hauling his cotton to Keasler's gin, and Arnold went down to the court-house at Carrollton and took out a judgment on his cotton and oxen and corn and everything he had, upon a note purporting to be $400. When the attachment was levied Mr. Keasler and others began to investigate it. They did not see how it was possible that the black man could owe Arnold anything, but there was his name on the note. They asked him how it happened that he had given Arnold any note. He said to Keasler he did not give him any note, but they said, "Here is your name." He says, "I will tell you how it happened: My son-in-law, who was working at another place, came to me and told me to get him ten bushels of corn. Mr. Arnold had the corn, and I asked him for it. He told me yes, he would do it, and to "just sign this order for the ten bushels of corn." And he says, "I supposed I was signing an order for ten bushels of corn, and Arnold had a note written for $400." Mr. Keasler says he mentioned this to the neighbors that were coming into his mill and gin, and that the sheriff had his cotton and the oxen and his property. That night, or the next night, some fifteen or twenty men went to Arnold's house—I do not remember whether disguised or openly—and told him he had committed a forgery on this black man, and if he did not go to the court-house the next day and dismiss the attachment and give up his cotton, oxen, and property, they would prosecute him, or they would come there in the course of a night or two and deal with him themselves. Arnold went and dismissed the attachment, and turned over to this black man his corn and oxen and cotton. It was a circumstance where two or three were present, and were perhaps in the company that visited Mr. Arnold. The black man seemed to be very grateful to these people. He spoke in high terms of the manner in which they had protected him in getting his oxen and cotton. That is all I know about that case. I think Mr. Keasler said that the men told him that they would not wait for the law, because the negro was not able to stand a lawsuit, and that they themselves would visit Arnold personally and inflict punishment upon him if he did not go and withdraw the attachment and deliver up the property.

DEPARTMENT OF THE INTERIOR,
Washington, D. C., December 19, 1871.

DEAR SIR: The Commissioner of Education, Hon. John Eaton, has forwarded to me a copy of your communication, requesting so much of the report of the "superintendent of schools in the State of Mississippi as relates to the destruction of school-houses, cruelty to children, &c., for that State."

The Commissioner of the Bureau of Education has also transmitted to me what purports to be extracts from official reports, relating to outrages committed upon school officers and teachers during the year, which I have the honor to inclose herewith, in answer to your note addressed to the Bureau of Education, above referred to.

I have the honor to be, very respectfully yours,

C. DELANO.

Hon. JOHN SCOTT,
United States Senate, Washington, D. C.

B.

DEPARTMENT OF EDUCATION, STATE OF MISSISSIPPI,
Jackson, December 2, 1871.

DEAR SIR: Inclosed please find extracts from official reports relating to outrages committed upon school officers and teachers during the year.

* * * * * *

Very respectfully,

H. R. PEASE,
Superintendent of Education.

Hon. JOHN EATON, Jr.,
Commissioner of Education, Washington, D. C.

C.

Accompanying extracts from official reports, relating to outrages committed upon school officers and teachers in Mississippi:

In the introduction and development of the new civil polity recently adopted in this State, no one feature or measure of which has been so difficult to adjust as the free public school system. The institution of slavery, with its long cherished caste discriminations, prejudices, passions, and concomitant educational theories, such as the Divine right of a certain class, based upon "blood and bullion," to monopolize mental development and all high intellectual culture; private educational enterprises, and family schools for the education of the "upper classes" or "first circles;" the rich not to be taxed to educate the poor; the masses not to be allowed more than the simplest elementary education—just enough to elevate them a degree above the brute—thus to render them more efficient as laborers under the direction and control of capital in the hands of the educated few, had taken deeper root and become more fully interwoven into the social and political system, probably, in this, than in any other of the late reconstructed States.

The introduction of the People's School was, as a natural sequence, regarded as an innovator not to be tolerated—a blow struck that would eventuate in the utter overthrow of all that remained of the peculiar social and political institutions of the southern American aristocracy. This was the prevailing sentiment among the wealthy and intelligent classes in every community. Opposition to the system of public schools was greatly augmented by a class of idle politicians and an unscrupulous partisan press, resulting, in many instances, in open hostility and violence toward school officers and teachers, burning school-houses and churches used for school purposes, and otherwise destroying property by lawless bands of incendiaries and mobs.

The following extracts from official reports of school officers and teachers will exhibit the character of hostility manifested in many portions of the State. J. Ebbert, principal of the Aberdeen Academy, Monroe County, reports: 'You are no doubt aware of the outrage committed upon Mr. A. P. Huggins, our county superintendent of education. I am constrained to make this communication in view of the sad condition of our schools. Mr. Huggins has left, and we do not know whether he will return or not. The board of school directors is disorganized, a large number of schools have been broken up, and others have received orders from the Ku-Klux to discontinue. Everything is in a demoralized condition, and our school system is bound to be broken up. Cannot something be done immediately to avert this calamity?" Colonel A. P. Huggins, referred to, was taken out of his bed by a band of Ku-Klux assassins and whipped in a most unmerciful manner, and ordered to leave the county on pain of death at the hands of the Klan.

The superintendent of Union County reports: "A band of disguised men, numbering fifteen, called upon Mr. Newson at midnight and ordered him to discontinue his school or suffer a fearful penalty." He was teaching a colored school, which he was compelled to close.

The superintendent of Chickasaw County reports: "I obtain the following facts: F. B. Emmens and Cornelius McBride, both teachers of colored schools, have been badly abused. The latter terribly whipped by a disguised party. Also that three houses have been burned. One of the three was a church tendered for the use of the colored people as a school-house. The other two houses were built by the colored people expressly for school purposes." The superintendent further adds: "I am unable to account for these outrages, unless it be opposition to colored schools, all the damage being to that class of schools. In several neighborhoods I have found it impossible to obtain teachers for the colored schools, so great is the fear of these disguised men."

The superintendent of Lowndes County reports: "To give you each and every case of unlawful disturbance against the free public schools of this county would swell my communication to an unexpected length. I can only briefly say that several of my teachers have been visited by a body of disguised men known as Ku-Klux. All the teachers were white and of southern birth, except Mr. Farmer, who was obliged to leave the county. Three teachers of colored schools were obliged to close their schools. Just after the command of the Ku-Klux that no more free schools should be taught, I visited a white school taught by a lady, and found only four pupils present. The children and their parents were so badly frightened that the school was all but broken up. I requested the lady to continue, which she did. The circumstances have been such that in nearly every case the teachers could do nothing but obey the command of the Ku-Klux and close school. One teacher is a southern gentleman and a Congregational minister. On one occasion he went several miles from home and preached to the colored people. The Ku-Klux called on him at midnight and told him he would not be allowed to preach any more, and also ordered him to close his school, taught on his own farm and in his own house. He disobeyed the order, and continued to do what he thought right. They visited him again, called him out, and said they did not propose to hurt him, but wanted to notify him that he could neither preach or teach any more, but added, perhaps he might when the election was over, and wanted him to promise that he would do neither. He answered them by saying, 'Whether I shall obey God or man, judge ye.' I have heard no further particulars. Several parties in the county, not teachers, have been violently treated by the Ku-Klux. Other information relating to the Klan and their intimidations in this county could be given, but at present I refrain from doing so."

From Holmes County the report comes "that the same spirit that elsewhere breaks out in the bloody acts of the masked assassin and the dark deeds of the midnight riders has only found vent here in decorating the colored school-houses with a composition of tar, paint, or lamp-black, insulting the lady teachers on the streets and through the post-office, and in inditing letters of advice or warning to the county superintendent, subscribing always the cabalistic K. K. K."

In Oktibbeha County one teacher was stoned, and one school-house burned, in which a colored school was being taught at the time.

In Warren County one teacher was threatened by letters from the K. K. K., and closed his school.

The superintendent of Choctaw County states that "late in the fall of 1870 two churches in that county were burned. Also a school-house in April and another in May were both burned by unknown parties and the schools broken up."

The superintendent of Winston County reports a terrible state of affairs in that county: "The burning of two churches used for schools and four school-houses;" also "that a band of disguised men visited the house of Mr. Fox and compelled him to stop teaching a free school. They then went to the house of a colored teacher, and failing to find him, they amused themselves by burning his trunk and other property, and carried away between twenty-five and thirty dollars in money. William Kennedy and J. L. Johnson, men of integrity and unimpeachable character, were warned by letter that unless they closed their schools they would be killed. Also the Rev. John Avery, warned in the same way, but continued to teach. His school-house was burned, and he again warned, but being a man of considerable nerve he obtained another house and again commenced his school. That house was burned two days after he began teaching. In every case of violence or house-burning the teachers were those chosen by the people themselves, and in no case did the property belong to the county, but in almost every instance to the colored citizens. The cause of these outrages is opposition to the free-school system, especially to that part of the law which gives the colored youth equal advantages with the white. The men who commit these acts of violence are stimulated and encouraged by designing politicians. At present there is not a colored school in operation in the county. There have been, by burning and otherwise, eleven public schools broken up in this county."

In Yalabusha County one school-house was burned.

In Lafayette County two school-houses burned and one teacher shot, the bullet passing through his mouth, severing his tongue.

In Noxubee County one church used for school purposes and one school-house have been burned. Two other schools have been entirely broken up by threatening the teachers with hanging unless they closed their schools. In Rankin County, one school-house burned. A colored teacher of Lauderdale County writes: "Isaac Radford was notified by a drop-letter to leave the place in a given time or forfeit his life. He and his family immediately moved away. Things are very unsettled here, and the colored people are making arrangements to leave unless the murderers and midnight riders can be ferreted out. If the United States Government does not take hold of the case the schools will be of no benefit to the colored people. Two churches and school-houses belonging to the freedmen were burned and the teachers obliged to leave.

The superintendent of Tippah County reports that "On or about the 3d of March, 1871, Mr. C. E. Dry, a white man engaged as a teacher in a colored school, was waited upon by several masked men and ordered to quit teaching and to leave the country.

The reason assigned by these men that the negroes must go to work. Another school-house burned in December, 1870."

Report from Wayne County: "On or about the 12th of March, a school-house was burned near Waynesborough."

A teacher in Chickasaw County reports that a body of masked men surrounded his house about midnight, and demanded that he come out or they would burn the house. He managed to get out of the house through a back window, when he was discovered, whereupon several shots were fired at him. The assassins pursued and caught him and beat him in a most brutal manner. His offense was teaching a colored school.

The superintendent of Lauderdale County reports that "On or about the 26th of March, 1871, a party of seven masked men waited upon John Riter, teacher, and ordered him to leave the county on penalty of death if he returned. They then proceeded to his school-house and burned it to the ground. Another teacher, by the name of V. G Grougert, was visited on the night of the 10th of March by a band of Ku-Klux, and taken from his bed, stripped of his clothing, and beaten with one hundred and fifty lashes, literally cutting the flesh on his back into shreds. He was ordered to leave the county in twenty-four hours, on pain of death. This teacher was a quiet, inoffensive man, never having meddled with politics. All the teachers, seven in number, engaged in teaching the negroes at Meridian, were driven away at the time of the riot. Four school-houses have been destroyed by fire, the work of Ku-Klux incendiaries.

www.ingramcontent.com/pod-product-compliance
Lightning Source LLC
LaVergne TN
LVHW021225110826
845150LV00002B/251

* 9 7 8 1 4 2 5 5 6 3 7 7 6 *